The Official

SCRABBLE

Crossword Game

Players

DICTIONARY

FIFTH EDITION

The Official SCRABBLE® Players

Crossword Game

Players

FIFTH EDITION

Merriam-Webster

Merriam-Webster, Incorporated

Springfield, Massachusetts

Library of Congress Cataloging-in-Publication Data

The official Scrabble players dictionary.—Fifth Edition.
    pages cm
ISBN 978-0-87779-421-9
1. Scrabble (Game)—Glossaries, vocabularies, etc. I. Merriam-Webster, Inc.
GV1507.S3O36 2014
793.734—dc23

2014010346

Made in the United States of America

4th Printing   R R Donnelley, Harrisonburg, VA   2015   September

P₃ REFACE

P₃ **REFACE** • This is the fifth edition of the enormously popular *The Official SCRABBLE Players Dictionary*, and it includes some 5,000 words not found in the previous edition. This edition includes the new qualified entries found in *Merriam-Webster's Collegiate® Dictionary, Eleventh Edition* and features expanded coverage of Canadian words not previously entered in *The Official SCRABBLE Players Dictionary*. This dictionary has been prepared especially for lovers of SCRABBLE crossword games and is endorsed by the North American SCRABBLE Players Association (NASPA) for recreational and school use.

It is important to remember that *The Official SCRABBLE Players Dictionary* was edited solely with this limited purpose in mind. It is not intended to serve as a general dictionary of English; thus, such important features of general dictionaries as definitions of multiple senses, pronunciation respellings, etymologies, and usage labels are omitted. It is also important to remember that this specialized dictionary contains words of up to eight letters and their inflections.

It is the intention of the makers of SCRABBLE crossword games that they be enjoyed by children and adults alike. With this consideration in mind, words likely to offend players of the game have been omitted from this edition. The words omitted are those that would qualify for a warning usage note on the basis of standards applied in other Merriam-Webster™ dictionaries.

The detailed organization and special features of the dictionary are explained in the Introduction which follows. It should be read with care by all who use the dictionary. Now that this new updated work is available, we are confident that it will afford satisfaction and enjoyment to SCRABBLE crossword game players everywhere.

We gratefully acknowledge the contributions of the members of the North American SCRABBLE Players Association, who, with Jim Pate as cochairman, culled and compiled all the SCRABBLE-qualified words from the latest standard dictionaries. Their painstaking efforts have been invaluable to the preparation of this edition. Their names are as follows: Timothy Bottorff, Ross Brown, James Cherry, John Chew, Chris Cree, Kurt Davies, Robert Gillis, Adam Henderson, Peter R. Huszagh, Dallas Johnson, Chris Lipe, Bob Lipton, George MacAulay, Anna Miransky, Paul Mulik, and Matthew Tunnicliffe.

James G. Lowe
General Editor

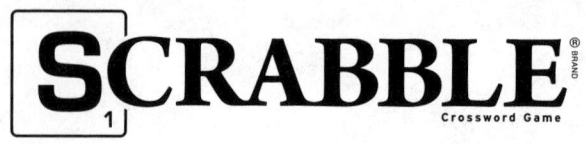

Every letter counts in SCRABBLE, the classic word game with the iconic gameboard.

And every word that counts is right here in *The Official SCRABBLE Players Dictionary* by Merriam-Webster. The SCRABBLE game has always been a case of "your word against mine," and when you go for a challenge, you want to be sure you're not going to be the player to lose their turn! The game of SCRABBLE might be seen by some as just a little friendly competition, but to win, you've got to choose your words and your spaces very carefully to get those high scores. Look for hooks, shuffle the tiles on your rack and use your letters well. May the best words win!

For more information on all things SCRABBLE, go to Hasbro.com/Scrabble.

The Official SCRABBLE Players Dictionary
has been endorsed by the North American
SCRABBLE Players Association (NASPA).

NASPA is a community of tournament, club and avid home players of the SCRABBLE Brand Crossword Game. We foster an atmosphere for people of all skill levels to play their favorite game, improve their abilities and above all, meet people who share a similar love of the game. For more information about our clubs, tournaments and other activities, please find us on Facebook or Twitter (@NASPA), or contact us at:

info@scrabbleplayers.org
www.scrabbleplayers.org

NTRODUCTION • **MAIN ENTRIES** • Main entries are listed in boldface type and are set flush with the left-hand margin of each column. Except for an occasional cross-reference (such as **UNDERLAIN** past participle of underlie), main entries contain from two to eight letters, since words within this range are considered to be most useful to SCRABBLE crossword game players. Words that are not permissible in SCRABBLE crossword games have not been included in this dictionary. Thus, proper names, words requiring hyphens or apostrophes, words considered foreign, and abbreviations have been omitted. Because dictionaries have different criteria for selecting entries, several American and Canadian standard dictionaries were consulted in preparing the list of main entries for this book. Obsolete, archaic, slang, and nonstandard words are included because they are permitted by the rules of the game. All variant forms of a main entry are shown at their own alphabetical places and defined in terms of the principal form. **Words that exceed eight letters in length and are not inflected forms of main entries in this dictionary should be looked up in a standard dictionary.** *Merriam-Webster's Collegiate® Dictionary, Eleventh Edition,* is recommended as a reference for longer words.

PARTS OF SPEECH • An italic label indicating a part of speech follows each main entry except cross-references, for which the label is given at the root word. The eight traditional parts of speech are indicated as follows:

n	noun
v	verb
adj	adjective
adv	adverb
pron	pronoun
prep	preposition
conj	conjunction
interj	interjection

When a word can be used as more than one part of speech, each part of speech is entered separately if the inflected forms are not spelled alike. For example, both the adjective *humble* and the verb *humble* are entered because the inflected forms vary.

HUMBLE   *adj* **-BLER, -BLEST** modest
HUMBLE   *v* **-BLED, -BLING, -BLES** to reduce the pride of

On the other hand, the verb *rage* is entered while the noun *rage* is not because the inflected form *rages* at the verb is spelled the same as the plural form of the noun. In a dictionary for SCRABBLE crossword game players, entry of the noun is therefore redundant. Homographs (words spelled alike) which may be used as the same part of speech are treated in the same way. For example, *lie* is entered as a verb twice because the inflected forms are spelled differently.

LIE	*v* **LAY, LAIN, LYING, LIES** to be or get into a horizontal position
LIE	*v* **LIED, LYING, LIES** to speak falsely

If both sets of inflected forms were spelled alike, only one *lie* would be entered in this dictionary. In this way the dictionary includes as many different spellings as possible yet avoids wasting space with repeated entry of words spelled in the same way. The SCRABBLE crossword game player, after all, needs only one entry to justify a play.

INFLECTED FORMS ●

Inflected forms include the past tense, past participle, present participle, and present tense third person singular of verbs, the plural of nouns, and the comparative and superlative of adjectives and adverbs. They are shown in boldface capital letters immediately following the part-of-speech label. Irregular inflected forms are listed as main entries when they fall four or more alphabetical places away from the root word (see **Cross-References** below). All inflected forms are allowable for play in SCRABBLE crossword games.

The principal parts of the majority of verbs are shown as **-ED, -ING, -S** (or **-ES** when applicable). This indicates that the past tense and past participle are formed simply by adding *-ed* to the entry word, that the present participle is formed simply by adding *-ing* to the entry word, and that the present third person singular is formed simply by adding *-s* (or *-es*) to the entry word.

SWARM	*v* **-ED, -ING, -S** to move in a large group

When inflection of an entry word involves any spelling change in addition to the suffixal ending (such as the dropping of a final *-e*, the doubling of a final consonant, or the changing of a final *-y* to *-i-*) or when the inflection is irregular, the inflected forms given indicate such changes.

MOVE	*v* **MOVED, MOVING, MOVES** to change from one position to another
DOT	*v* **DOTTED, DOTTING, DOTS** to cover with dots (tiny round marks)
CRY	*v* **CRIED, CRYING, CRIES** to weep
BREAK	*v* **BROKE, BROKEN, BREAKING, BREAKS** to reduce to fragments

For verbs of more than one syllable, either the last syllable or the last two syllables are shown to indicate spelling changes.

CANCEL	*v* **-CELED, -CELING, -CELS** or **-CELLED, -CELLING, -CELS** to annul

INDICATE   *v* **-CATED, -CATING, -CATES** to point out

The plurals of nouns are preceded by the abbreviation "pl." Most plurals are shown as **-S** (or **-ES** when applicable) to indicate that the plural is formed simply by adding the given suffix to the entry word.

PIZZA   *n* pl. **-S** an Italian open pie

When pluralizing a noun involves any spelling change in addition to the suffixal ending (such as the changing of a final -y to -i- or a final -f to -v-) or when the plural is irregular, the plural form shown indicates such change.

LEFTY   *n* pl. **-TIES** a left-handed person
CALF   *n* pl. **CALVES** or **CALFS** a young cow or bull
INDEX   *n* pl. **INDEXES** or **INDICES** a type of reference guide at the end of a book

In such cases involving polysyllabic nouns at least the last syllable is shown.

AVIARY   *n* pl. **-ARIES** a large enclosure for live birds

For the sake of clarity, two groups of nouns that are confusing to many, those ending in -o and those ending in -y, are always indicated in this dictionary by showing at least the last syllable, even though no spelling change is involved.

POLO   *n* pl. **-LOS** a game played on horseback
TURKEY   *n* pl. **-KEYS** a large American bird

Variant plurals are shown wherever they add another word permissible in SCRABBLE crossword games.

DODO   *n* pl. **-DOS** or **-DOES** an extinct flightless bird

Plurals which have the same form as the singular are shown only when they are the only plural for that entry. This is done to show that for the entry in question it is not permissible to add **-S** (or **-ES**) to the singular to create a plural.

SHEEP   *n* pl. **SHEEP** a ruminant mammal
MOOSE   *n* pl. **MOOSE** a ruminant mammal

Otherwise, they are omitted and only the plural with the inflection is shown.

HADDOCK   *n* pl. **-S** a food fish

The italic label *n/pl* is given to two kinds of nouns. One is the plural noun that has no singular form.

MORES   *n/pl* the customs of a particular group

The other is the plural noun of which the singular form contains more than eight letters and is not entered in this dictionary.

> **SENSORIA** *n/pl* the parts of the brain concerned with
> the reception and interpretation of
> sensory stimuli

Sensorium, the singular form, has nine letters and therefore is not entered.

The comparative and superlative forms of adjectives and adverbs are shown, when applicable, immediately following the part-of-speech label. Any spelling changes are indicated in the forms shown.

> **NEAR**   *adj* **NEARER, NEAREST** situated within a
>   short distance
> **FAR**   *adv* **FARTHER, FARTHEST** or
>   **FURTHER, FURTHEST** at or to a great
>   distance
> **GLUEY**   *adj* **GLUIER, GLUIEST** resembling glue

Not all adjectives or adverbs can be inflected, and only those inflected forms shown are acceptable. None of the adjectives and adverbs listed as run-on entries in this dictionary have inflected forms.

RUN-ON ENTRIES   ●   A main entry may be followed by one or

more derivatives in boldface type with a different part-of-speech label. These are run-on entries. Run-on entries are not defined since their meanings are readily derivable from the meaning of the root word.

> **PLAY**   *v* **-ED, -ING, -S,** to engage in amusement
>   or sport **PLAYABLE** *adj*
> **HAMULUS**   *n* pl. **-LI** a small hook **HAMULAR,**
>   **HAMULATE, HAMULOSE, HAMULOUS**
>   *adj*

No entry has been run on at another if it would fall alphabetically four or more places from the entry. **When you do not find a word at its own place, it is always wise to check several entries above and below to see if it is run on.**

CROSS-REFERENCES   ●   A cross-reference is a main entry that

is an inflected form of another word (such as the plural form of a noun, the past tense form of a verb, or the comparative form of an adjective). An inflected form is entered as a main entry if it undergoes a spelling change in addition to or instead of suffixation *and* if it falls alphabetically four or more places away from the root word.

For example, in the entries reproduced below, **SCARING** is a main entry because it involves a spelling change (the final *-e* of *scare* is dropped) besides the addition of the **-ING** ending and because it falls four or more places from the entry **SCARE**. On the other hand, *scares* is not a main entry because it involves no spelling change beyond the addition of the ending **-S**. **SCARIER** and **SCARIEST** are main entries because they involve a spelling change (the *-e-* is dropped and the final *-y* is changed to *-i-*) besides the addition of the **-ER, -EST** endings and they fall more four or more places from the entry **SCARY**.

SCARE	*v* **SCARED, SCARING, SCARES** to frighten

. . .

SCARIER	comparative of scarey and scary
SCARIEST	superlative of scarey and scary
SCARING	present participle of scare

. . .

SCARY	*adj* **SCARIER, SCARIEST** frightening

This policy is intended to make the word desired as easy to find as possible without wasting space. Nevertheless, many inflected forms will appear only at the main entry. **You should always look at several entries above and below the expected place if you do not find the desired word as a main entry.**

Cross-reference entries for present tense third person singular forms of verbs use the abbreviation "sing."

DEFINITIONS ● In most cases, only one very brief definition is given for each main entry since definitions do not play a significant role in the SCRABBLE crossword game. This definition serves only to orient the player in a general way to a single meaning of the word. It is not intended to have all the precision and detail of a definition in a good general dictionary.

When a word consisting of eight or fewer letters appears in a definition but is not an entry in this dictionary, it is glossed in parentheses. For example, at the entry for the verb *plank*, the noun "planks" is used in the definition and is glossed because the noun *plank* is not a separate entry.

PLANK	*v* **-ED, -ING, -S** to cover with planks (long, flat pieces of lumber)

A main entry that is a variant form of another entry is defined in terms of the most common form, which is entered and defined at its own alphabetical place.

PEROGI	*n* pl. **-ES** pierogi
PEROGIE	*n* pl. **-S** pierogi
PEROGY	*n* pl. **-GIES** pierogi

. . .

PIEROGI	*n* pl. **-ES** a small dumpling with a filling

SCRABBLE crossword game players in Canada will be pleased to learn that variant forms such as *honour*, *centre*, and *cheque*, which are often omitted from general dictionaries, have also been included in this book.

Many Canadian words have also been added to this edition, including *fricot, gatch, inukshuk, poutine, quinzhee, rodney,* and *steamie.*

LISTS OF UNDEFINED WORDS ● Two separate lists of undefined words appear below the entries that begin with RE- and with UN-. These words are not defined because they are self-explanatory: their meanings are simply the sum of a meaning of the prefix *re-* or *un-* and a meaning of the root word. All of their inflected forms are given, however.

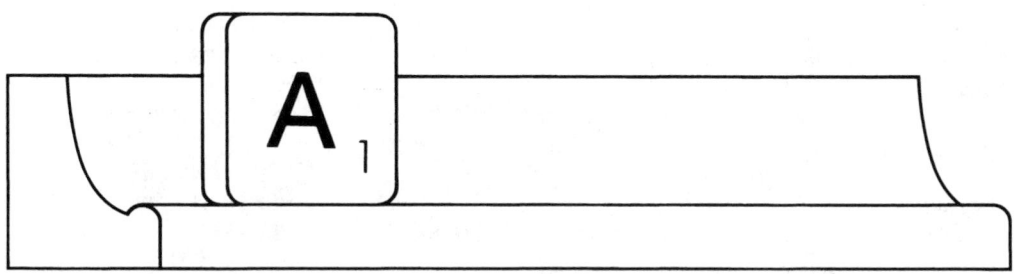

AA	*n* pl. **-S** rough, cindery lava	**ABATER**	*n* pl. **-S** one that abates
AAH	*v* **-ED, -ING, -S** to exclaim in amazement, joy, or surprise	**ABATIS**	*n* pl. **-TISES** a barrier made of felled trees
AAL	*n* pl. **-S** an East Indian shrub	**ABATOR**	*n* pl. **-S** one that unlawfully seizes an inheritance
AALII	*n* pl. **-S** a tropical tree	**ABATTIS**	*n* pl. **-TISES** abatis
AARDVARK	*n* pl. **-S** an African mammal	**ABATTOIR**	*n* pl. **-S** a slaughterhouse
AARDWOLF	*n* pl. **-WOLVES** an African mammal	**ABAXIAL**	*adj* situated away from the axis
AARGH	*interj* — used to express disgust	**ABAXILE**	*adj* abaxial
AARRGH	*interj* aargh	**ABAYA**	*n* pl. **-S** a long loose robe worn by Arab women
AARRGHH	*interj* aargh		
AASVOGEL	*n* pl. **-S** a vulture	**ABBA**	*n* pl. **-S** father — used as a title of honor
AB	*n* pl. **-S** an abdominal muscle		
ABA	*n* pl. **-S** a sleeveless garment worn by Arabs	**ABBACY**	*n* pl. **-CIES** the office of an abbot
		ABBATIAL	*adj* pertaining to an abbot
ABACA	*n* pl. **-S** a Philippine plant	**ABBE**	*n* pl. **-S** an abbot
ABACK	*adv* toward the back	**ABBESS**	*n* pl. **-ES** the female superior of a convent of nuns
ABACUS	*n* pl. **-CUSES** or **-CI** a calculating device	**ABBEY**	*n* pl. **-BEYS** a monastery or convent
ABAFT	*adv* toward the stern		
ABAKA	*n* pl. **-S** abaca	**ABBOT**	*n* pl. **-S** the superior of a monastery
ABALONE	*n* pl. **-S** an edible shellfish	**ABBOTCY**	*n* pl. **-CIES** abbacy
ABAMP	*n* pl. **-S** abampere	**ABDICATE**	*v* **-CATED, -CATING, -CATES** to give up formally
ABAMPERE	*n* pl. **-S** a unit of electric current		
ABANDON	*v* **-ED, -ING, -S** to leave or give up completely	**ABDOMEN**	*n* pl. **-MENS** or **-MINA** the body cavity containing the viscera
ABAPICAL	*adj* directed away from the apex	**ABDUCE**	*v* **-DUCED, -DUCING, -DUCES** to abduct
ABASE	*v* **ABASED, ABASING, ABASES** to lower in rank, prestige, or esteem **ABASEDLY** *adv*	**ABDUCENS**	*n* pl. **-CENTES** a cranial nerve
		ABDUCENT	*adj* serving to abduct
		ABDUCING	present participle of abduce
ABASER	*n* pl. **-S** one that abases	**ABDUCT**	*v* **-ED, -ING, -S** to draw away from the original position
ABASH	*v* **-ED, -ING, -ES** to make ashamed or embarrassed		
ABASIA	*n* pl. **-S** a defect in muscular coordination in walking	**ABDUCTEE**	*n* pl. **-S** one that has been abducted
ABASING	present participle of abase	**ABDUCTOR**	*n* pl. **-S** or **-ES** an abducent muscle
ABATE	*v* **ABATED, ABATING, ABATES** to reduce in degree or intensity **ABATABLE** *adj*	**ABEAM**	*adv* at right angles to the keel of a ship

ABED	*adv* in bed	**ABLAZE**	*adj* being on fire
ABEGGING	*adj* begging	**ABLE**	*adj* **ABLER, ABLEST** having sufficient power, skill, or resources
ABELE	*n* pl. **-S** a Eurasian tree		
ABELIA	*n* pl. **-S** an Asian or Mexican shrub	**ABLE**	*n* pl. **-S** a communications code word for the letter A
ABELIAN	*adj* being a commutative group in mathematics		
		ABLED	*adj* capable of unimpaired function
ABELMOSK	*n* pl. **-S** a tropical herb	**ABLEGATE**	*n* pl. **-S** a papal envoy
ABERRANT	*n* pl. **-S** a deviant	**ABLEISM**	*n* pl. **-S** prejudice or discrimination against disabled people
ABET	*v* **ABETTED, ABETTING, ABETS** to encourage and support		
		ABLEIST	*n* pl. **-S** one that practices ableism
ABETMENT	*n* pl. **-S** the act of abetting	**ABLER**	comparative of able
ABETTAL	*n* pl. **-S** abetment	**ABLEST**	superlative of able
ABETTED	past tense of abet	**ABLINGS**	*adv* ablins
ABETTER	*n* pl. **-S** abettor	**ABLINS**	*adv* perhaps
ABETTING	present participle of abet	**ABLOOM**	*adj* blooming
ABETTOR	*n* pl. **-S** one that abets	**ABLUENT**	*n* pl. **-S** a cleansing agent
ABEYANCE	*n* pl. **-S** temporary inactivity	**ABLUSH**	*adj* blushing
ABEYANCY	*n* pl. **-CIES** abeyance	**ABLUTED**	*adj* washed clean
ABEYANT	*adj* marked by abeyance	**ABLUTION**	*n* pl. **-S** a washing
ABFARAD	*n* pl. **-S** a unit of capacitance	**ABLY**	*adv* in an able manner
ABHENRY	*n* pl. **-RYS** or **-RIES** a unit of inductance	**ABMHO**	*n* pl. **-MHOS** a unit of electrical conductance
ABHOR	*v* **-HORRED, -HORRING, -HORS** to loathe	**ABNEGATE**	*v* **-GATED, -GATING, -GATES** to deny to oneself
ABHORRER	*n* pl. **-S** one that abhors	**ABNORMAL**	*n* pl. **-S** a mentally deficient person
ABIDANCE	*n* pl. **-S** the act of abiding	**ABOARD**	*adv* into, in, or on a ship, train, or airplane
ABIDE	*v* **ABIDED** or **ABODE, ABIDING, ABIDES** to accept without objection		
		ABODE	*v* **ABODED, ABODING, ABODES** to forebode
ABIDER	*n* pl. **-S** one that abides	**ABOHM**	*n* pl. **-S** a unit of electrical resistance
ABIGAIL	*n* pl. **-S** a lady's maid		
ABILITY	*n* pl. **-TIES** the quality of being able to do something	**ABOIDEAU**	*n* pl. **-DEAUS** or **-DEAUX** a type of dike
ABIOSIS	*n* pl. **-OSES** absence of life **ABIOTIC** *adj*	**ABOIL**	*adj* boiling
		ABOITEAU	*n* pl. **-TEAUS** or **-TEAUX** aboideau
ABJECT	*adj* sunk to a low condition **ABJECTLY** *adv*	**ABOLISH**	*v* **-ED, -ING, -ES** to do away with
ABJURE	*v* **-JURED, -JURING, -JURES** to renounce under oath	**ABOLLA**	*n* pl. **-LAE** a cloak worn in ancient Rome
		ABOMA	*n* pl. **-S** a South American snake
ABJURER	*n* pl. **-S** one that abjures	**ABOMASAL**	*adj* pertaining to the abomasum
ABLATE	*v* **-LATED, -LATING, -LATES** to remove by cutting	**ABOMASUM**	*n* pl. **-SA** the fourth stomach of a ruminant
ABLATION	*n* pl. **-S** surgical removal of a bodily part	**ABOMASUS**	*n* pl. **-MASI** abomasum
ABLATIVE	*n* pl. **-S** a grammatical case	**ABOON**	*adv* above
ABLATOR	*n* pl. **-S** one that ablates	**ABORAL**	*adj* situated away from the mouth **ABORALLY** *adv*
ABLAUT	*n* pl. **-S** a patterned change in root vowels of verb forms		
		ABORNING	*adv* while being born

ABORT *v* **-ED, -ING, -S** to bring forth a fetus prematurely

ABORTER *n* pl. **-S** one that aborts

ABORTION *n* pl. **-S** induced expulsion of a nonviable fetus

ABORTIVE *adj* failing to succeed

ABORTUS *n* pl. **-ES** an aborted fetus

ABOUGHT past tense of aby and abye

ABOULIA *n* pl. **-S** abulia **ABOULIC** *adj*

ABOUND *v* **-ED, -ING, -S** to have a large number or amount

ABOUT *adv* approximately

ABOVE *n* pl. **-S** something that is above (in a higher place)

ABRACHIA *n* pl. **-S** a lack of arms

ABRADANT *n* pl. **-S** an abrasive

ABRADE *v* **ABRADED, ABRADING, ABRADES** to wear away by friction

ABRADER *n* pl. **-S** a tool for abrading

ABRASION *n* pl. **-S** the act of abrading

ABRASIVE *n* pl. **-S** an abrading substance

ABREACT *v* **-ED, -ING, -S** to release repressed emotions by reliving the original traumatic experience

ABREAST *adv* side by side

ABRI *n* pl. **-S** a bomb shelter

ABRIDGE *v* **ABRIDGED, ABRIDGING, ABRIDGES** to reduce the length of

ABRIDGER *n* pl. **-S** one that abridges

ABROACH *adj* astir

ABROAD *adv* out of one's own country

ABROGATE *v* **-GATED, -GATING, -GATES** to abolish by authoritative action

ABROSIA *n* pl. **-S** a fasting from food

ABRUPT *adj* **-RUPTER, -RUPTEST** rudely brief **ABRUPTLY** *adv*

ABSCESS *v* **-ED, -ING, -ES** to form an abscess (a localized collection of pus surrounded by inflamed tissue)

ABSCISE *v* **-SCISED, -SCISING, -SCISES** to cut off

ABSCISIN *n* pl. **-S** a regulatory substance found in plants

ABSCISSA *n* pl. **-SAS** or **-SAE** a particular geometric coordinate

ABSCOND *v* **-ED, -ING, -S** to depart suddenly and secretly

ABSEIL *v* **-ED, -ING, -S** to rappel

ABSEILER *n* **-S** one that abseils

ABSENCE *n* pl. **-S** the state of being away

ABSENT *v* **-ED, -ING, -S** to take or keep away

ABSENTEE *n* pl. **-S** one that is not present

ABSENTER *n* pl. **-S** one that absents himself

ABSENTLY *adv* in an inattentive manner

ABSINTH *n* pl. **-S** absinthe

ABSINTHE *n* pl. **-S** a bitter liqueur

ABSOLUTE *adj* **-LUTER, -LUTEST** free from restriction

ABSOLUTE *n* pl. **-S** something that is absolute

ABSOLVE *v* **-SOLVED, -SOLVING, -SOLVES** to free from the consequences of an action

ABSOLVER *n* pl. **-S** one that absolves

ABSONANT *adj* unreasonable

ABSORB *v* **-ED, -ING, -S** to take up or in

ABSORBER *n* pl. **-S** one that absorbs

ABSTAIN *v* **-ED, -ING, -S** to refrain voluntarily

ABSTERGE *v* **-STERGED, -STERGING, -STERGES** to cleanse by wiping

ABSTRACT *adj* **-STRACTER, -STRACTEST** difficult to understand

ABSTRACT *v* **-ED, -ING, -S** to take away

ABSTRICT *v* **-ED, -ING, -S** to form by cutting off

ABSTRUSE *adj* **-STRUSER, -STRUSEST** difficult to understand

ABSURD *adj* **-SURDER, -SURDEST** ridiculously incongruous or unreasonable **ABSURDLY** *adv*

ABSURD *n* pl. **-S** the condition in which man exists in an irrational and meaningless universe

ABUBBLE *adj* bubbling

ABULIA *n* pl. **-S** loss of willpower **ABULIC** *adj*

ABUNDANT *adj* present in great quantity

ABUSE *v* **ABUSED, ABUSING, ABUSES** to use wrongly or improperly **ABUSABLE** *adj*

ABUSER *n* pl. **-S** one that abuses

ABUSIVE *adj* characterized by wrong or improper use

ABUT *v* **ABUTTED, ABUTTING, ABUTS** to touch along a border

ABUTILON *n* pl. **-S** a flowering plant

ABUTMENT *n* pl. **-S** something that abuts

ABUTTAL *n* pl. **-S** an abutment

ABUTTED	past tense of abut
ABUTTER	*n* pl. **-S** one that abuts
ABUTTING	present participle of abut
ABUZZ	*adj* buzzing
ABVOLT	*n* pl. **-S** a unit of electromotive force
ABWATT	*n* pl. **-S** a unit of power
ABY	*v* **ABOUGHT, ABYING, ABYS** to pay the penalty for
ABYE	*v* **ABOUGHT, ABYING, ABYES** to aby
ABYSM	*n* pl. **-S** an abyss
ABYSMAL	*adj* immeasurably deep
ABYSS	*n* pl. **-ES** a bottomless chasm **ABYSSAL** *adj*
ACACIA	*n* pl. **-S** a flowering tree or shrub
ACADEME	*n* pl. **-S** a place of instruction
ACADEMIA	*n* pl. **-S** scholastic life or environment
ACADEMIC	*n* pl. **-S** a college student or teacher
ACADEMY	*n* pl. **-MIES** a secondary school
ACAI	*n* pl. **-S** a purple berrylike fruit of a tropical palm
ACAJOU	*n* pl. **-S** a tropical tree
ACALEPH	*n* pl. **-LEPHS** or **-LEPHAE** a jellyfish
ACALEPHE	*n* pl. **-S** acaleph
ACANTHA	*n* pl. **-THAE** a sharp spiny part
ACANTHUS	*n* pl. **-THUSES** or **-THI** a prickly herb
ACAPNIA	*n* pl. **-S** a lack of carbon dioxide in blood and tissues
ACARBOSE	*n* pl. **-S** a drug for treating diabetes
ACARI	pl. of acarus
ACARID	*n* pl. **-S** a type of arachnid
ACARIDAN	*n* pl. **-S** acarid
ACARINE	*n* pl. **-S** acarid
ACAROID	*adj* resembling an acarid
ACARPOUS	*adj* not producing fruit
ACARUS	*n* pl. **-RI** a mite
ACAUDAL	*adj* having no tail
ACAUDATE	*adj* acaudal
ACAULINE	*adj* having no stem
ACAULOSE	*adj* acauline
ACAULOUS	*adj* acauline
ACCEDE	*v* **-CEDED, -CEDING, -CEDES** to consent
ACCEDER	*n* pl. **-S** one that accedes
ACCENT	*v* **-ED, -ING, -S** to pronounce with prominence
ACCENTOR	*n* pl. **-S** a songbird
ACCEPT	*v* **-ED, -ING, -S** to receive willingly
ACCEPTEE	*n* pl. **-S** one that is accepted
ACCEPTER	*n* pl. **-S** one that accepts
ACCEPTOR	*n* pl. **-S** accepter
ACCESS	*v* **-ED, -ING, -ES** to get at
ACCIDENT	*n* pl. **-S** an unexpected or unintentional occurrence
ACCIDIA	*n* pl. **-S** acedia
ACCIDIE	*n* pl. **-S** acedia
ACCLAIM	*v* **-ED, -ING, -S** to shout approval of
ACCOLADE	*v* **-LADED, -LADING, -LADES** to praise
ACCORD	*v* **-ED, -ING, -S** to bring into agreement
ACCORDER	*n* pl. **-S** one that accords
ACCOST	*v* **-ED, -ING, -S** to approach and speak to first
ACCOUNT	*v* **-ED, -ING, -S** to give an explanation
ACCOUTER	*v* **-ED, -ING, -S** to equip
ACCOUTRE	*v* **-TRED, -TRING, -TRES** to accouter
ACCREDIT	*v* **-ED, -ING, -S** to give official authorization to
ACCRETE	*v* **-CRETED, -CRETING, -CRETES** to grow together
ACCRUAL	*n* pl. **-S** the act of accruing
ACCRUE	*v* **-CRUED, -CRUING, -CRUES** to come as an increase or addition
ACCURACY	*n* pl. **-CIES** the quality of being accurate
ACCURATE	*adj* free from error
ACCURSED	*adj* damnable
ACCURST	*adj* accursed
ACCUSAL	*n* pl. **-S** the act of accusing
ACCUSANT	*n* pl. **-S** an accuser
ACCUSE	*v* **-CUSED, -CUSING, -CUSES** to make an assertion against
ACCUSER	*n* pl. **-S** one that accuses
ACCUSTOM	*v* **-ED, -ING, -S** to make familiar
ACE	*v* **ACED, ACING, ACES** to score a point against in a single stroke
ACEDIA	*n* pl. **-S** apathy
ACELDAMA	*n* pl. **-S** a place of bloodshed

ACENTRIC   *adj* having no center

ACEQUIA   *n* pl. **-S** an irrigation ditch or canal

ACERATE   *adj* acerose

ACERATED   *adj* acerose

ACERB   *adj* **ACERBER, ACERBEST** sour

ACERBATE   *v* **-BATED, -BATING, -BATES** to make sour

ACERBIC   *adj* acerb

ACERBITY   *n* pl. **-TIES** sourness

ACEROLA   *n* pl. **-S** a West Indian shrub

ACEROSE   *adj* needle-shaped

ACEROUS   *adj* acerose

ACERVATE   *adj* growing in compact clusters

ACERVULI   *n/pl* spore-producing organs of certain fungi

ACESCENT   *n* pl. **-S** something that is slightly sour

ACETA   pl. of acetum

ACETAL   *n* pl. **-S** a flammable liquid

ACETAMID   *n* pl. **-S** an amide of acetic acid

ACETATE   *n* pl. **-S** a salt of acetic acid **ACETATED** *adj*

ACETIC   *adj* pertaining to vinegar

ACETIFY   *v* **-FIED, -FYING, -FIES** to convert into vinegar

ACETIN   *n* pl. **-S** a chemical compound

ACETONE   *n* pl. **-S** a flammable liquid **ACETONIC** *adj*

ACETOSE   *adj* acetous

ACETOUS   *adj* tasting like vinegar

ACETOXYL   *n* pl. **-S** a univalent radical

ACETUM   *n* pl. **-TA** vinegar

ACETYL   *n* pl. **-S** a univalent radical **ACETYLIC** *adj*

ACHE   *v* **ACHED, ACHING, ACHES** to suffer a dull, continuous pain

ACHENE   *n* pl. **-S** a type of fruit **ACHENIAL** *adj*

ACHIER   comparative of achy

ACHIEST   superlative of achy

ACHIEVE   *v* **ACHIEVED, ACHIEVING, ACHIEVES** to carry out successfully

ACHIEVER   *n* pl. **-S** one that achieves

ACHILLEA   *n* pl. **-S** yarrow

ACHINESS   *n* pl. **-ES** the state of being achy

ACHING   present participle of ache

ACHINGLY   *adv* in an aching manner

ACHIOTE   *n* pl. **-S** a yellowish red dye

ACHIRAL   *adj* pertaining to a symmetrical molecule

ACHOLIA   *n* pl. **-S** a lack of bile

ACHOO   *interj* ahchoo

ACHROMAT   *n* pl. **-S** a type of lens

ACHROMIC   *adj* having no color

ACHY   *adj* **ACHIER, ACHIEST** aching

ACICULA   *n* pl. **-LAS** or **-LAE** a needlelike part or process **ACICULAR** *adj*

ACICULUM   *n* pl. **-LUMS** or **-LA** a bristlelike part

ACID   *n* pl. **-S** a type of chemical compound

ACIDEMIA   *n* pl. **-S** a condition of increased acidity of the blood

ACIDHEAD   *n* pl. **-S** one who uses LSD

ACIDIC   *adj* sour

ACIDIFY   *v* **-FIED, -FYING, -FIES** to convert into an acid

ACIDITY   *n* pl. **-TIES** sourness

ACIDLY   *adv* sourly

ACIDNESS   *n* pl. **-ES** acidity

ACIDOSIS   *n* pl. **-DOSES** an abnormal condition of the blood **ACIDOTIC** *adj*

ACIDURIA   *n* pl. **-S** a condition of having excessive amounts of acid in the urine

ACIDY   *adj* sour

ACIERATE   *v* **-ATED, -ATING, -ATES** to turn into steel

ACIFORM   *adj* needle-shaped

ACING   present participle of ace

ACINUS   *n* pl. **-NI** a small, saclike division of a gland **ACINAR, ACINIC, ACINOSE, ACINOUS** *adj*

ACKEE   *n* pl. **-S** akee

ACLINIC   *adj* having no inclination

ACME   *n* pl. **-S** the highest point **ACMATIC, ACMIC** *adj*

ACNE   *n* pl. **-S** a skin disease **ACNED** *adj*

ACNODE   *n* pl. **-S** an element of a mathematical set that is isolated from the other elements

ACOCK   *adj* cocked

ACOELOUS   *adj* lacking a true body cavity

ACOLD   *adj* cold

ACOLYTE   *n* pl. **-S** an assistant

ACONITE   *n* pl. **-S** a poisonous herb **ACONITIC** *adj*

ACONITUM   *n* pl. **-S** aconite

ACORN   *n* pl. **-S** the fruit of the oak tree **ACORNED** *adj*

ACOUSTIC   *n* pl. **-S** a hearing aid

ACQUAINT   *v* **-ED, -ING, -S** to cause to know

ACQUEST   *n* pl. **-S** something acquired

ACQUIRE   *v* **-QUIRED, -QUIRING, -QUIRES** to come into possession of

ACQUIREE   *n* pl. **-S** one that is acquired

ACQUIRER   *n* pl. **-S** one that acquires

ACQUIT   *v* **-QUITTED, -QUITTING, -QUITS** to free or clear from a charge of fault or crime

ACRASIA   *n* pl. **-S** a lack of self-control **ACRATIC** *adj*

ACRASIN   *n* pl. **-S** a substance secreted by the cells of a slime mold

ACRE   *n* pl. **-S** a unit of area

ACREAGE   *n* pl. **-S** area in acres

ACRED   *adj* owning many acres

ACRID   *adj* **-RIDER, -RIDEST** sharp and harsh to the taste or smell

ACRIDINE   *n* pl. **-S** a chemical compound

ACRIDITY   *n* pl. **-TIES** the state of being acrid

ACRIDLY   *adv* in an acrid manner

ACRIMONY   *n* pl. **-NIES** sharpness or bitterness of speech or temper

ACRO   *n* pl. **ACROS** a skiing event in which a skier performs acrobatic moves to music

ACROBAT   *n* pl. **-S** one skilled in feats of agility and balance

ACRODONT   *n* pl. **-S** an animal having rootless teeth

ACROGEN   *n* pl. **-S** a plant growing at the apex only

ACROLECT   *n* pl. **-S** a high form of a language

ACROLEIN   *n* pl. **-S** a flammable liquid

ACROLITH   *n* pl. **-S** a type of statue

ACROMION   *n* pl. **-MIA** the outward end of the shoulder blade **ACROMIAL** *adj*

ACRONIC   *adj* occurring at sunset

ACRONYM   *n* pl. **-S** a word formed from the initials of a compound term or series of words

ACROSOME   *n* pl. **-S** a thin sac at the head of a sperm

ACROSS   *prep* from one side of to the other

ACROSTIC   *n* pl. **-S** a poem in which certain letters taken in order form a word or phrase

ACROTISM   *n* pl. **-S** weakness of the pulse **ACROTIC** *adj*

ACRYLATE   *n* pl. **-S** an acrylic

ACRYLIC   *n* pl. **-S** a type of resin

ACT   *v* **-ED, -ING, -S** to do something

ACTA   *n/pl* recorded proceedings

ACTABLE   *adj* suitable for performance on the stage

ACTIN   *n* pl. **-S** a protein in muscle tissue

ACTINAL   *adj* having tentacles

ACTING   *n* pl. **-S** the occupation of an actor

ACTINIA   *n* pl. **-IAS** or **-IAE** a marine animal

ACTINIAN   *n* pl. **-S** actinia

ACTINIC   *adj* pertaining to actinism

ACTINIDE   *n* pl. **-S** any of a series of radioactive elements

ACTINISM   *n* pl. **-S** the property of radiant energy that effects chemical changes

ACTINIUM   *n* pl. **-S** a radioactive element

ACTINOID   *n* pl. **-S** an actinide

ACTINON   *n* pl. **-S** an isotope of radon

ACTION   *v* **-ED, -ING, -S** to bring a lawsuit against

ACTIONER   *n* pl. **-S** a film with exciting action

ACTIVATE   *v* **-VATED, -VATING, -VATES** to set in motion

ACTIVE   *n* pl. **-S** a participating member of an organization

ACTIVELY   *adv* with activity

ACTIVISM   *n* pl. **-S** a doctrine that emphasizes direct and decisive action

ACTIVIST   *n* pl. **-S** an advocate of activism

ACTIVITY   *n* pl. **-TIES** brisk action or movement

ACTIVIZE   *v* **-IZED, -IZING, -IZES** to activate

ACTOR   *n* pl. **-S** a theatrical performer **ACTORISH, ACTORLY** *adj*

ACTRESS   *n* pl. **-ES** a female actor **ACTRESSY** *adj*

ACTUAL   *adj* existing in fact **ACTUALLY** *adv*

ACTUARY   *n* pl. **-ARIES** a statistician who computes insurance risks and premiums

ACTUATE   *v* **-ATED, -ATING, -ATES** to set into action or motion

ACTUATOR   *n* pl. **-S** one that actuates

ACUATE   *adj* sharp

ACUITY   *n* pl. **-ITIES** sharpness

ACULEATE   *n* pl. **-S** a stinging insect

ACULEUS   *n* pl. **-LEI** a sharp-pointed part

ACUMEN   *n* pl. **-S** mental keenness

ACUTANCE   *n* pl. **-S** a measure of photographic clarity

ACUTE   *adj* **ACUTER, ACUTEST** marked by sharpness or severity **ACUTELY** *adv*

ACUTE   *n* pl. **-S** a type of accent mark

ACYCLIC   *adj* not cyclic

ACYL   *n* pl. **-S** a univalent radical

ACYLATE   *v* **-ATED, -ATING, -ATES** to introduce acyl into

ACYLOIN   *n* pl. **-S** a type of chemical compound

AD   *n* pl. **-S** an advertisement

ADAGE   *n* pl. **-S** a traditional saying expressing a common observation **ADAGIAL** *adj*

ADAGIO   *n* pl. **-GIOS** a musical composition or movement played in a slow tempo

ADAMANCE   *n* pl. **-S** adamancy

ADAMANCY   *n* pl. **-CIES** unyielding hardness

ADAMANT   *n* pl. **-S** an extremely hard substance

ADAMSITE   *n* pl. **-S** a lung-irritating gas

ADAPT   *v* **-ED, -ING, -S** to make suitable

ADAPTER   *n* pl. **-S** one that adapts

ADAPTION   *n* pl. **-S** the act of adapting **ADAPTIVE** *adj*

ADAPTOR   *n* pl. **-S** adapter

ADAXIAL   *adj* situated on the same side as

ADBOT   *n* pl. **-S** a specialized computer program

ADD   *v* **-ED, -ING, -S** to combine or join so as to bring about an increase **ADDABLE** *adj*

ADDAX   *n* pl. **-ES** a large antelope

ADDEDLY   *adv* additionally

ADDEND   *n* pl. **-S** a number to be added to another

ADDENDUM   *n* pl. **-DUMS** or **-DA** something added or to be added

ADDER   *n* pl. **-S** a venomous snake

ADDIBLE   *adj* capable of being added

ADDICT   *v* **-ED, -ING, -S** to devote or surrender to something habitually or compulsively

ADDITION   *n* pl. **-S** something added

ADDITIVE   *n* pl. **-S** a substance added to another to impart desirable qualities

ADDITORY   *adj* making an addition

ADDLE   *v* **-DLED, -DLING, -DLES** to confuse

ADDRESS   *v* **-DRESSED** or **-DREST, -DRESSING, -DRESSES** to speak to

ADDUCE   *v* **-DUCED, -DUCING, -DUCES** to bring forward as evidence

ADDUCENT   *adj* serving to adduct

ADDUCER   *n* pl. **-S** one that adduces

ADDUCING   present participle of adduce

ADDUCT   *v* **-ED, -ING, -S** to draw toward the main axis

ADDUCTOR   *n* pl. **-S** an adducent muscle

ADEEM   *v* **-ED, -ING, -S** to take away

ADELGID   *n* pl. **-S** a small insect

ADENINE   *n* pl. **-S** an alkaloid

ADENITIS   *n* pl. **-TISES** inflammation of a lymph node

ADENOID   *n* pl. **-S** an enlarged lymphoid growth behind the pharynx

ADENOMA   *n* pl. **-MAS** or **-MATA** a tumor of glandular origin

ADENOSIS   *n* pl. **-NOSES** abnormal growth of glandular tissue

ADENYL   *n* pl. **-S** a univalent radical

ADEPT   *adj* **ADEPTER, ADEPTEST** highly skilled **ADEPTLY** *adv*

ADEPT   *n* pl. **-S** an adept person

ADEQUACY   *n* pl. **-CIES** the state of being adequate

ADEQUATE   *adj* sufficient for a specific requirement

ADHERE   *v* **-HERED, -HERING, -HERES** to become or remain attached or close to something

ADHEREND   *n* pl. **-S** the surface to which an adhesive adheres

ADHERENT   *n* pl. **-S** a supporter

ADHERER   *n* pl. **-S** one that adheres

ADHERING   present participle of adhere

ADHESION   *n* pl. **-S** the act of adhering

ADHESIVE   *n* pl. **-S** a substance that causes adhesion

ADHIBIT   *v* **-ED, -ING, -S** to take or let in

ADIEU   *n* pl. **ADIEUS** or **ADIEUX** a farewell

ADIOS   *n* pl. **-OSES** goodbye

ADIPOSE   *n* pl. **-S** animal fat **ADIPIC** *adj*

ADIPOSIS   *n* pl. **-POSES** obesity

ADIPOUS   *adj* pertaining to adipose

ADIT   *n* pl. **-S** an entrance

ADJACENT   *adj* next to

ADJOIN   *v* **-ED, -ING, -S** to lie next to

ADJOINT   *n* pl. **-S** a type of mathematical matrix

ADJOURN   *v* **-ED, -ING, -S** to suspend until a later time

ADJUDGE   *v* **-JUDGED, -JUDGING, -JUDGES** to determine judicially

ADJUNCT   *n* pl. **-S** something attached in a subordinate position

ADJURE   *v* **-JURED, -JURING, -JURES** to command solemnly

ADJURER   *n* pl. **-S** one that adjures

ADJUROR   *n* pl. **-S** adjurer

ADJUST   *v* **-ED, -ING, -S** to bring to a more satisfactory state

ADJUSTER   *n* pl. **-S** one that adjusts

ADJUSTOR   *n* pl. **-S** adjuster

ADJUTANT   *n* pl. **-S** an assistant

ADJUVANT   *n* pl. **-S** an assistant

ADLAND   *n* pl. **-S** the world of advertising

ADMAN   *n* pl. **-MEN** a man employed in the advertising business

ADMASS   *n* pl. **-ES** mass-media advertising

ADMIN   *n* pl. **-S** an administration

ADMIRAL   *n* pl. **-S** a high-ranking naval officer

ADMIRE   *v* **-MIRED, -MIRING, -MIRES** to regard with wonder, pleasure, and approval

ADMIRER   *n* pl. **-S** one that admires

ADMIT   *v* **-MITTED, -MITTING, -MITS** to allow to enter

ADMITTEE   *n* pl. **-S** one that is admitted

ADMITTER   *n* pl. **-S** one that admits

ADMIX   *v* **-MIXED** or **-MIXT, -MIXING, -MIXES** to mix

ADMONISH   *v* **-ED, -ING, -ES** to reprove mildly or kindly

ADNATE   *adj* joined to another part or organ

ADNATION   *n* pl. **-S** the state of being adnate

ADNEXA   *n/pl* conjoined anatomical parts **ADNEXAL** *adj*

ADNOUN   *n* pl. **-S** an adjective when used as a noun

ADO   *n* pl. **ADOS** bustling excitement

ADOBE   *n* pl. **-S** an unburnt, sun-dried brick

ADOBO   *n* pl. **-BOS** a Philippine dish of fish or meat

ADONIS   *n* pl. **-ISES** a handsome young man

ADOPT   *v* **-ED, -ING, -S** to take into one's family by legal means

ADOPTEE   *n* pl. **-S** one that is adopted

ADOPTER   *n* pl. **-S** one that adopts

ADOPTION   *n* pl. **-S** the act of adopting **ADOPTIVE** *adj*

ADORABLE   *adj* worthy of being adored **ADORABLY** *adv*

ADORE   *v* **ADORED, ADORING, ADORES** to love deeply

ADORER   *n* pl. **-S** one that adores

ADORN   *v* **-ED, -ING, -S** to add something to for the purpose of making more attractive

ADORNER   *n* pl. **-S** one that adorns

ADOWN   *adv* downward

ADOZE   *adj* dozing

ADRENAL   *n* pl. **-S** an endocrine gland

ADRIFT   *adj* drifting

ADROIT   *adj* **ADROITER, ADROITEST** skillful **ADROITLY** *adv*

ADSCRIPT   *n* pl. **-S** a distinguishing symbol written after another character

ADSORB   *v* **-ED, -ING, -S** to gather on a surface in a condensed layer

ADSORBER   *n* pl. **-S** one that adsorbs

ADSUKI   *n* pl. **-S** adzuki

ADULARIA   *n* pl. **-S** a mineral

ADULATE   *v* **-LATED, -LATING, -LATES** to praise excessively

ADULATOR   *n* pl. **-S** one that adulates

ADULT   *n* pl. **-S** a fully developed individual

ADULTERY   *n* pl. **-TERIES** voluntary sexual intercourse between a married person and someone other than his or her spouse

ADULTLY   *adv* in a manner typical of an adult

ADUMBRAL   *adj* shadowy

ADUNC   *adj* bent inward

ADUNCATE   *adj* adunc

ADUNCOUS *adj* adunc

ADUST *adj* scorched

ADVANCE *v* **-VANCED, -VANCING, -VANCES** to move or cause to move ahead

ADVANCER *n* pl. **-S** one that advances

ADVECT *v* **-ED, -ING, -S** to convey or transport by the flow of a fluid

ADVENT *n* pl. **-S** arrival

ADVERB *n* pl. **-S** a word used to modify a verb, adjective, or other adverb

ADVERSE *adj* acting in opposition

ADVERT *v* **-ED, -ING, -S** to call attention

ADVICE *n* pl. **-S** recommendation regarding a decision or action

ADVISE *v* **-VISED, -VISING, -VISES** to give advice to

ADVISEE *n* pl. **-S** one that is advised

ADVISER *n* pl. **-S** one that advises

ADVISING present participle of advise

ADVISOR *n* pl. **-S** adviser

ADVISORY *n* pl. **-RIES** a report giving information

ADVOCAAT *n* pl. **-S** a liqueur consisting of brandy, sugar, and eggs

ADVOCACY *n* pl. **-CIES** the act of advocating

ADVOCATE *v* **-CATED, -CATING, -CATES** to speak in favor of

ADVOWSON *n* pl. **-S** the right of presenting a nominee to a vacant church office

ADWARE *n* pl. **-S** computer software that is provided free but has advertisements

ADWOMAN *n* pl. **-MEN** a woman employed in the advertising business

ADYNAMIA *n* pl. **-S** lack of physical strength **ADYNAMIC** *adj*

ADYTUM *n* pl. **-TA** an inner sanctuary in an ancient temple

ADZ *v* **-ED, -ING, -ES** to shape (wood) with an adz (a cutting tool)

ADZE *v* **ADZED, ADZING, ADZES** to adz

ADZUKI *n* pl. **-S** the edible seed of an Asian plant

AE *adj* one

AECIA pl. of aecium

AECIAL *adj* pertaining to an aecium

AECIDIAL *adj* pertaining to an aecium

AECIDIUM *n* pl. **-IA** an aecium

AECIUM *n* pl. **-IA** a spore-producing organ of certain fungi

AEDES *n* pl. **AEDES** any of a genus of mosquitoes

AEDILE *n* pl. **-S** a magistrate of ancient Rome

AEDINE *adj* pertaining to an aedes

AEGIS *n* pl. **-GISES** protection

AEGROTAT *n* pl **-S** a certificate excusing an ill student from an examination

AENEOUS *adj* having a greenish gold color

AENEUS *adj* aeneous

AEOLIAN *adj* eolian

AEON *n* pl. **-S** eon

AEONIAN *adj* eonian

AEONIC *adj* eonian

AEQUORIN *n* pl. **-S** a protein secreted by jellyfish

AERADIO *n* pl. **-DIOS** a Canadian radio service for pilots

AERATE *v* **-ATED, -ATING, -ATES** to supply with air

AERATION *n* pl. **-S** the act of aerating

AERATOR *n* pl. **-S** one that aerates

AERIAL *n* pl. **-S** an antenna

AERIALLY *adv* in a manner pertaining to the air

AERIE *n* pl. **-S** a bird's nest built high on a mountain or cliff **AERIED** *adj*

AERIER comparative of aery

AERIES pl. of aery

AERIEST superlative of aery

AERIFORM *adj* having the form of air

AERIFY *v* **-FIED, -FYING, -FIES** to aerate

AERILY *adv* in an aery manner

AERO *adj* pertaining to aircraft

AEROBAT *n* pl. **-S** one that performs feats in an aircraft

AEROBE *n* pl. **-S** an organism that requires oxygen to live **AEROBIC** *adj*

AEROBICS *n/pl* exercises for conditioning the heart and lungs by increasing oxygen consumption

AEROBIUM *n* pl. **-BIA** aerobe

AERODUCT *n* pl. **-S** a type of jet engine

AERODYNE *n* pl. **-S** an aircraft that is heavier than air

AEROFOIL *n* pl. **-S** airfoil

AEROGEL *n* pl. **-S** a highly porous solid

AEROGRAM *n* pl. **-S** an airmail letter

AEROLITE   *n* pl. **-S** a meteorite containing more stone than iron

AEROLITH   *n* pl. **-S** aerolite

AEROLOGY   *n* pl. **-GIES** the study of the atmosphere

AERONAUT   *n* pl. **-S** one who operates an airship

AERONOMY   *n* pl. **-MIES** the study of the upper atmosphere

AEROSAT   *n* pl. **-S** a satellite for use in air-traffic control

AEROSOL   *n* pl. **-S** a gaseous suspension of fine solid or liquid particles

AEROSTAT   *n* pl. **-S** an aircraft that is lighter than air

AERUGO   *n* pl. **-GOS** a green film that forms on copper

AERY   *adj* **AERIER, AERIEST** airy

AERY   *n* pl. **AERIES** aerie

AESTHETE   *n* pl. **-S** esthete

AESTIVAL   *adj* estival

AETATIS   *adj* of the age of

AETHER   *n* pl. **-S** the upper region of the atmosphere **AETHERIC** *adj*

AFAR   *n* pl. **-S** a great distance

AFEARD   *adj* afraid

AFEARED   *adj* afeard

AFEBRILE   *adj* having no fever

AFF   *adv* off

AFFABLE   *adj* easy to talk to **AFFABLY** *adv*

AFFAIR   *n* pl. **-S** anything done or to be done

AFFAIRE   *n* pl. **-S** a brief amorous relationship

AFFECT   *v* **-ED, -ING, -S** to give a false appearance of

AFFECTER   *n* pl. **-S** one that affects

AFFERENT   *n* pl. **-S** a nerve that conveys impulses toward a nerve center

AFFIANCE   *v* **-ANCED, -ANCING, -ANCES** to betroth

AFFIANT   *n* pl. **-S** one who makes a written declaration under oath

AFFICHE   *n* pl. **-S** a poster

AFFINAL   *adj* related by marriage

AFFINE   *n* pl. **-S** a relative by marriage

AFFINED   *adj* closely related

AFFINELY   *adv* in the manner of a type of mathematical mapping

AFFINITY   *n* pl. **-TIES** a natural attraction or inclination

AFFIRM   *v* **-ED, -ING, -S** to state positively

AFFIRMER   *n* pl. **-S** one that affirms

AFFIX   *v* **-ED, -ING, -ES** to attach

AFFIXAL   *adj* pertaining to a prefix or suffix

AFFIXER   *n* pl. **-S** one that affixes

AFFIXIAL   *adj* affixal

AFFLATUS   *n* pl. **-ES** a creative inspiration

AFFLICT   *v* **-ED, -ING, -S** to distress with mental or physical pain

AFFLUENT   *n* pl. **-S** a stream that flows into another

AFFLUX   *n* pl. **-ES** a flowing toward a point

AFFORD   *v* **-ED, -ING, -S** to have sufficient means for

AFFOREST   *v* **-ED, -ING, -S** to convert into forest

AFFRAY   *v* **-ED, -ING, -S** to frighten

AFFRAYER   *n* pl. **-S** one that affrays

AFFRIGHT   *v* **-ED, -ING, -S** to frighten

AFFRONT   *v* **-ED, -ING, -S** to insult openly

AFFUSION   *n* pl. **-S** an act of pouring a liquid on

AFGHAN   *n* pl. **-S** a woolen blanket or shawl

AFGHANI   *n* pl. **-S** a monetary unit of Afghanistan

AFIELD   *adv* in the field

AFIRE   *adj* being on fire

AFLAME   *adj* flaming

AFLOAT   *adj* floating

AFLUTTER   *adj* nervously excited

AFOOT   *adv* on foot

AFORE   *adv* before

AFOUL   *adj* entangled

AFRAID   *adj* filled with apprehension

AFREET   *n* pl. **-S** an evil spirit in Arabic mythology

AFRESH   *adv* anew

AFRIT   *n* pl. **-S** afreet

AFRO   *n* pl. **AFROS** a curly or frizzy hairstyle

AFT   *adv* toward the stern

AFTER   *prep* behind in place or order

AFTERS   *n/pl* dessert

AFTERTAX   *adj* remaining after payment of taxes

AFTMOST *adj* nearest the stern

AFTOSA *n* pl. **-S** a disease of hoofed mammals

AG *n* pl. **-S** agriculture

AGA *n* pl. **-S** a high-ranking Turkish military officer

AGAIN *adv* once more

AGAINST *prep* in opposition to

AGALLOCH *n* pl. **-S** the fragrant wood of a tropical tree

AGALWOOD *n* pl. **-S** agalloch

AGAMA *n* pl. **-S** a tropical lizard

AGAMETE *n* pl. **-S** an asexual reproductive cell

AGAMIC *adj* asexual

AGAMID *n* pl. **-S** an Old World lizard

AGAMOUS *adj* agamic

AGAPE *n* pl. **-PES** or **-PAE** or **-PAI** a communal meal of fellowship **AGAPEIC** *adj*

AGAR *n* pl. **-S** a viscous substance obtained from certain seaweeds

AGARIC *n* pl. **-S** any of a family of fungi

AGAROSE *n* pl. **-S** a sugar obtained from agar

AGATE *n* pl. **-S** a variety of quartz **AGATOID** *adj*

AGATIZE *v* **-IZED, -IZING, -IZES** to cause to resemble agate

AGAVE *n* pl. **-S** a tropical plant

AGAZE *adj* gazing

AGE *v* **AGED, AGING** or **AGEING, AGES** to grow old

AGEDLY *adv* in the manner of an old person

AGEDNESS *n* pl. **-ES** oldness

AGEE *adv* to one side

AGEING *n* pl. **-S** aging

AGEISM *n* pl. **-S** discrimination based on age

AGEIST *n* pl. **-S** an advocate of ageism

AGELESS *adj* never growing old

AGELONG *adj* lasting for a long time

AGEMATE *n* pl. **-S** a person of the same age as another

AGENCY *n* pl. **-CIES** an organization that does business for others

AGENDA *n* pl. **-S** a list of things to be done

AGENDUM *n* pl. **-S** an item on an agenda

AGENE *n* pl. **-S** a chemical compound used in bleaching flour

AGENESIA *n* pl. **-S** agenesis

AGENESIS *n* pl. **AGENESES** absence or imperfect development of a bodily part **AGENETIC** *adj*

AGENIZE *v* **-NIZED, -NIZING, -NIZES** to treat with agene

AGENT *v* **-ED, -ING, -S** to act as a representative for **AGENTIAL** *adj*

AGENTING *n* pl. **-S** the business or activities of an agent

AGENTIVE *n* pl. **-S** a word part that denotes the doer of an action

AGENTRY *n* pl. **-RIES** the office or duties of an agent

AGER *n* pl. **-S** one that ages

AGERATUM *n* pl. **-S** a flowering plant

AGGADA *n* pl. **-DAS** or **-DOT** or **-DOTH** haggadah

AGGADAH *n* pl. **-DAHS** or **-DOT** or **-DOTH** haggadah

AGGADIC *adj* haggadic

AGGER *n* pl. **-S** a mound of earth used as a fortification

AGGIE *n* pl. **-S** a type of playing marble

AGGRADE *v* **-GRADED, -GRADING, -GRADES** to fill with detrital material

AGGRESS *v* **-ED, -ING, -ES** to commit the first act of hostility

AGGRIEVE *v* **-GRIEVED, -GRIEVING, -GRIEVES** to distress

AGGRO *n* pl. **-GROS** a rivalry or grievance

AGHA *n* pl. **-S** aga

AGHAST *adj* shocked by something horrible

AGILE *adj* able to move quickly and easily **AGILELY** *adv*

AGILITY *n* pl. **-TIES** the quality of being agile

AGIN *prep* against

AGING *n* pl. **-S** the process of growing old

AGINNER *n* pl. **-S** one that is against change

AGIO *n* pl. **AGIOS** a premium paid for the exchange of one currency for another

AGIOTAGE *n* pl. **-S** the business of a broker

AGISM *n* pl. **-S** ageism

AGIST *v* **-ED, -ING, -S** to feed and take care of for a fee, as livestock

AGITA *n* pl. **-S** a feeling of agitation

AGITATE *v* **-TATED, -TATING, -TATES** to move with a violent, irregular action **AGITABLE** *adj*

AGITATO *adj* fast and stirring — used as a musical direction

AGITATOR *n* pl. **-S** one that agitates

AGITPROP *n* pl. **-S** pro-Communist propaganda

AGLARE *adj* glaring

AGLEAM *adj* gleaming

AGLEE *adv* agley

AGLET *n* pl. **-S** a metal sheath at the end of a lace

AGLEY *adv* awry

AGLIMMER *adj* glimmering

AGLITTER *adj* glittering

AGLOO *n* pl. **AGLOOS** an air hole through the ice made by a seal

AGLOW *adj* glowing

AGLU *n* pl. **-S** agloo

AGLY *adv* agley

AGLYCON *n* pl. **-S** a type of chemical compound

AGLYCONE *n* pl. **-S** aglycon

AGMA *n* pl. **-S** eng

AGMINATE *adj* clustered together

AGNAIL *n* pl. **-S** a piece of loose skin at the base of a fingernail

AGNATE *n* pl. **-S** a relative on the father's side **AGNATIC** *adj*

AGNATHAN *n* pl. **-S** one of a group of jawless vertebrates

AGNATION *n* pl. **-S** the relationship of agnates

AGNIZE *v* **-NIZED, -NIZING, -NIZES** to acknowledge

AGNOMEN *n* pl. **-MENS** or **-MINA** an additional name given to an ancient Roman

AGNOSIA *n* pl. **-S** loss of ability to recognize familiar objects

AGNOSTIC *n* pl. **-S** one who disclaims any knowledge of God

AGO *adv* in the past

AGOG *adv* in a state of eager curiosity

AGON *n* pl. **-S** or **-ES** the dramatic conflict between the main characters in a Greek play

AGONAL *adj* pertaining to agony

AGONE *adv* ago

AGONIC *adj* not forming an angle

AGONIES pl. of agony

AGONISE *v* **-NISED, -NISING, -NISES** to agonize

AGONISM *n* pl. **-S** a contest or struggle

AGONIST *n* pl. **-S** one that is engaged in a struggle

AGONIZE *v* **-NIZED, -NIZING, -NIZES** to suffer extreme pain

AGONY *n* pl. **-NIES** extreme pain

AGORA *n* pl. **-RAS** or **-RAE** a marketplace in ancient Greece

AGORA *n* pl. **AGOROT** or **AGOROTH** a monetary unit of Israel

AGOUTI *n* pl. **-S** or **-ES** a burrowing rodent

AGOUTY *n* pl. **-TIES** agouti

AGRAFE *n* pl. **-S** agraffe

AGRAFFE *n* pl. **-S** an ornamental clasp

AGRAPHA *n/pl* the sayings of Jesus not found in the Bible

AGRAPHIA *n* pl. **-S** a mental disorder marked by inability to write **AGRAPHIC** *adj*

AGRARIAN *n* pl. **-S** one who favors equal distribution of land

AGRAVIC *adj* pertaining to a condition of no gravitation

AGREE *v* **AGREED, AGREEING, AGREES** to have the same opinion

AGRESTAL *adj* growing wild

AGRESTIC *adj* rural

AGRIA *n* pl. **-S** severe pustular eruption

AGRIMONY *n* pl. **-NIES** a perennial herb

AGRO *n* pl. **AGROS** a student of agricultural science

AGROLOGY *n* pl. **-GIES** the science of soils in relation to crops

AGRONOMY *n* pl. **-MIES** the application of scientific principles to the cultivation of land

AGROUND *adv* on the ground

AGRYPNIA *n* pl. **-S** insomnia

AGUACATE *n* pl. **-S** an avocado

AGUE *n* pl. **-S** a malarial fever **AGUED** *adj* **AGUELIKE, AGUISH** *adj* **AGUISHLY** *adv*

AGUEWEED *n* pl. **-S** a flowering plant

AH *v* **-ED, -ING, -S** aah

AHA *interj* — used to express surprise, triumph, or derision

AHCHOO *interj* — used to represent the sound of a sneeze

AHEAD   *adv* at or to the front

AHEM   *interj* — used to attract attention

AHI   *n* pl. **-S** a marine food fish

AHIMSA   *n* pl. **-S** the Hindu principle of nonviolence

AHOLD   *n* pl. **-S** a hold or grasp of something

AHORSE   *adv* on a horse

AHOY   *interj* — used in hailing a ship or person

AHULL   *adj* abandoned and flooded, as a ship

AI   *n* pl. **-S** a three-toed sloth

AIBLINS   *adv* ablins

AID   *v* **-ED, -ING, -S** to help

AIDE   *n* pl. **-S** an assistant

AIDER   *n* pl. **-S** one that aids

AIDFUL   *adj* helpful

AIDLESS   *adj* helpless

AIDMAN   *n* pl. **-MEN** a corpsman

AIGLET   *n* pl. **-S** aglet

AIGRET   *n* pl. **-S** aigrette

AIGRETTE   *n* pl. **-S** a tuft of feathers worn as a head ornament

AIGUILLE   *n* pl. **-S** a sharp, pointed mountain peak

AIKIDO   *n* pl. **-DOS** a Japanese art of self-defense

AIL   *v* **-ED, -ING, -S** to cause pain or discomfort to

AILERON   *n* pl. **-S** a movable control surface on an airplane wing

AILMENT   *n* pl. **-S** a physical or mental disorder

AIM   *v* **-ED, -ING, -S** to direct toward a specified object or goal

AIMER   *n* pl. **-S** one that aims

AIMFUL   *adj* full of purpose **AIMFULLY** *adv*

AIMLESS   *adj* lacking direction or purpose

AIN   *n* pl. **-S** ayin

AINSELL   *n* pl. **-S** own self

AIOLI   *n* pl. **-S** garlic mayonnaise

AIR   *adv* **AIRER, AIREST** early

AIR   *v* **-ED, -ING, -S** to expose to the air (the mixture of gases that surrounds the earth)

AIRBAG   *n* pl. **-S** an inflatable safety device in an automobile

AIRBASE   *n* pl. **-S** a military base for aircraft

AIRBOAT   *n* pl. **-S** a boat used in swampy areas

AIRBORNE   *adj* flying

AIRBOUND   *adj* stopped up by air

AIRBRUSH   *v* **-ED, -ING, -ES** to apply in a fine spray by compressed air, as paint

AIRBURST   *n* pl. **-S** an explosion in the air

AIRBUS   *n* pl. **-BUSES** or **-BUSSES** a passenger airplane

AIRCHECK   *n* pl. **-S** a recording made from a radio broadcast

AIRCOACH   *n* pl. **-ES** the cheaper class of accommodations in commercial aircraft

AIRCRAFT   *n* pl. **AIRCRAFT** any machine or device capable of flying

AIRCREW   *n* pl. **-S** the crew of an aircraft

AIRDATE   *n* pl. **-S** the scheduled date of a broadcast

AIRDROME   *n* pl. **-S** an airport

AIRDROP   *v* **-DROPPED, -DROPPING, -DROPS** to drop from an aircraft

AIRER   *n* pl. **-S** a frame on which to dry clothes

AIRFARE   *n* pl. **-S** payment for travel by airplane

AIRFIELD   *n* pl. **-S** an airport

AIRFLOW   *n* pl. **-S** a flow of air

AIRFOIL   *n* pl. **-S** a part of an aircraft designed to provide lift or control

AIRFRAME   *n* pl. **-S** the framework and external covering of an airplane

AIRGLOW   *n* pl. **-S** a glow in the upper atmosphere

AIRHEAD   *n* pl. **-S** a stupid person

AIRHOLE   *n* pl. **-S** a hole to let air in or out

AIRIER   comparative of airy

AIRIEST   superlative of airy

AIRILY   *adv* in an airy manner

AIRINESS   *n* pl. **-ES** the state of being airy

AIRING   *n* pl. **-S** an exposure to the air

AIRLESS   *adj* having no air

AIRLIFT   *v* **-ED, -ING, -S** to transport by airplane

AIRLIKE   *adj* resembling air

AIRLINE   *n* pl. **-S** an air transportation system

AIRLINER   *n* pl. **-S** a large passenger aircraft

AIRLOCK   *n* pl. **-S** a blockage in a pipe caused by an air bubble

AIRMAIL   v **-ED, -ING, -S** to send mail by airplane

AIRMAN   n pl. **-MEN** an aviator

AIRN   n pl. **-S** iron (a mineral element)

AIRPARK   n pl. **-S** a small airport

AIRPLANE   n pl. **-S** a winged aircraft propelled by jet engines or propellers

AIRPLAY   n pl. **-PLAYS** the playing of a record on a radio program

AIRPORT   n pl. **-S** a tract of land maintained for the landing and takeoff of aircraft

AIRPOST   n pl. **-S** a system of conveying mail by airplane

AIRPOWER   n pl. **-S** the military strength of a nation's air force

AIRPROOF   v **-ED, -ING, -S** to make impermeable to air

AIRSCAPE   n pl. **-S** a view of the earth from an aircraft or a high position

AIRSCREW   n pl. **-S** an airplane propeller

AIRSHED   n pl. **-S** the air supply of a given region

AIRSHIP   n pl. **-S** a lighter-than-air aircraft having propulsion and steering systems

AIRSHOT   n pl. **-S** an aircheck

AIRSHOW   n pl. **-S** an exhibition of aircraft stunts

AIRSICK   adj nauseated from flying in an airplane

AIRSIDE   n pl. **-S** the side of an airport terminal facing the aircraft

AIRSOME   adj cold

AIRSPACE   n pl. **-S** the portion of the atmosphere above a particular land area

AIRSPEED   n pl. **-S** the speed of an aircraft with relation to the air

AIRSTRIP   n pl. **-S** a runway

AIRT   v **-ED, -ING, -S** to guide

AIRTH   v **-ED, -ING, -S** to airt

AIRTIGHT   adj not allowing air to escape or enter

AIRTIME   n pl. **-S** the time when a broadcast begins

AIRTRAM   n pl. **-S** an aerial cable car

AIRVAC   n pl. **-S** evacuation by air ambulance

AIRWARD   adv toward the sky

AIRWAVE   n pl. **-S** the medium of radio and television transmission

AIRWAY   n pl. **-WAYS** a passageway in which air circulates

AIRWISE   adj skillful in aviation

AIRWOMAN   n pl. **-WOMEN** a female aviator

AIRY   adj **AIRIER, AIRIEST** having the nature of air

AISLE   n pl. **-S** a passageway between sections of seats **AISLED** adj

AISLEWAY   n pl. **-WAYS** an aisle

AIT   n pl. **-S** a small island

AITCH   n pl. **-ES** the letter H

AIVER   n pl. **-S** a draft horse

AIYEE   interj — used to express great alarm

AJAR   adj partly open

AJEE   adv agee

AJI   n pl. **-S** a type of chili pepper

AJIVA   n pl. **-S** inanimate matter

AJOWAN   n pl. **-S** the fruit of an Egyptian plant

AJUGA   n pl. **-S** a flowering plant

AKEBIA   n pl. **-S** a climbing shrub

AKEE   n pl. **-S** a tropical tree

AKELA   n pl. **-S** a leader of a cub scout pack

AKENE   n pl. **-S** achene

AKIMBO   adj having hands on hips and elbows bent outward

AKIN   adj related by blood

AKINESIA   n pl. **-S** loss of muscle function **AKINETIC** adj

AKRASIA   n pl. **-S** acrasia **AKRATIC** adj

AKVAVIT   n pl. **-S** aquavit

AL   n pl. **-S** an East Indian tree

ALA   n pl. **ALAE** a wing or winglike part

ALACHLOR   n pl. **-S** an herbicide

ALACK   interj — used to express sorrow or regret

ALACRITY   n pl. **-TIES** cheerful promptness

ALAE   pl. of ala

ALAMEDA   n pl. **-S** a shaded walkway

ALAMO   n pl. **-MOS** a softwood tree

ALAMODE   n pl. **-S** a silk fabric

ALAN   n pl. **-S** a large hunting dog

ALAND   n pl. **-S** alan

ALANE	*adj* alone
ALANG	*adv* along
ALANIN	*n* pl. **-S** alanine
ALANINE	*n* pl. **-S** an amino acid
ALANT	*n* pl. **-S** alan
ALANYL	*n* pl. **-S** a univalent radical
ALAR	*adj* pertaining to wings
ALARM	*v* **-ED, -ING, -S** to frighten by a sudden revelation of possible injury
ALARMISM	*n* pl. **-S** the practice of alarming others needlessly
ALARMIST	*n* pl. **-S** one who alarms others needlessly
ALARUM	*v* **-ED, -ING, -S** to alarm
ALARY	*adj* alar
ALAS	*interj* — used to express sorrow or regret
ALASKA	*n* pl. **-S** a heavy fabric
ALASTOR	*n* pl. **-S** an avenging deity in Greek tragedy
ALATE	*n* pl. **-S** a winged insect
ALATED	*adj* having wings
ALATION	*n* pl. **-S** the state of having wings
ALB	*n* pl. **-S** a long-sleeved vestment
ALBA	*n* pl. **-S** the white substance of the brain
ALBACORE	*n* pl. **-S** a marine food fish
ALBATA	*n* pl. **-S** an alloy of copper, nickel, and zinc
ALBEDO	*n* pl. **-DOS** or **-DOES** the ratio of the light reflected by a planet to that received by it
ALBEIT	*conj* although
ALBICORE	*n* pl. **-S** albacore
ALBINAL	*adj* albinic
ALBINIC	*adj* pertaining to albinism
ALBINISM	*n* pl. **-S** the condition of being an albino
ALBINO	*n* pl. **-NOS** an organism lacking normal pigmentation
ALBITE	*n* pl. **-S** a mineral **ALBITIC** *adj*
ALBIZIA	*n* pl. **-S** a tropical tree
ALBIZZIA	*n* pl. **-S** albizia
ALBUM	*n* pl. **-S** a book for preserving photographs or stamps
ALBUMEN	*n* pl. **-S** the white of an egg
ALBUMIN	*n* pl. **-S** a simple protein
ALBUMOSE	*n* pl. **-S** a proteose
ALBURNUM	*n* pl. **-S** sapwood
ALCADE	*n* pl. **-S** alcalde
ALCAHEST	*n* pl. **-S** alkahest
ALCAIC	*n* pl. **-S** a type of verse form
ALCAIDE	*n* pl. **-S** the commander of a Spanish fortress
ALCALDE	*n* pl. **-S** the mayor of a Spanish town
ALCAYDE	*n* pl. **-S** alcaide
ALCAZAR	*n* pl. **-S** a Spanish fortress or palace
ALCHEMY	*n* pl. **-MIES** a medieval form of chemistry **ALCHEMIC** *adj*
ALCHYMY	*n* pl. **-MIES** alchemy
ALCID	*n* pl. **-S** a diving seabird
ALCIDINE	*adj* pertaining to a family of seabirds
ALCOHOL	*n* pl. **-S** a flammable liquid
ALCOOL	*n* pl. **-S** an alcoholic liquor
ALCOPOP	*n* pl. **-S** a flavored beverage containing 4-6 percent alcohol
ALCOVE	*n* pl. **-S** a recessed section of a room **ALCOVED** *adj*
ALDEHYDE	*n* pl. **-S** a type of chemical compound
ALDER	*n* pl. **-S** a shrub or small tree
ALDERFLY	*n* pl. **-FLIES** a winged insect
ALDERMAN	*n* pl. **-MEN** a member of a municipal legislative body
ALDICARB	*n* pl. **-S** a pesticide
ALDOL	*n* pl. **-S** a chemical compound
ALDOLASE	*n* pl. **-S** an enzyme
ALDOSE	*n* pl. **-S** a type of sugar
ALDRIN	*n* pl. **-S** an insecticide
ALE	*n* pl. **-S** an alcoholic beverage
ALEATORY	*adj* pertaining to luck
ALEC	*n* pl. **-S** a herring
ALEE	*adv* toward the side of a vessel sheltered from the wind
ALEF	*n* pl. **-S** aleph
ALEGAR	*n* pl. **-S** sour ale
ALEHOUSE	*n* pl. **-S** a tavern where ale is sold
ALEMBIC	*n* pl. **-S** an apparatus formerly used in distilling
ALENCON	*n* pl. **-S** a needlepoint lace
ALEPH	*n* pl. **-S** a Hebrew letter
ALERT	*adj* **ALERTER, ALERTEST** ready for sudden action **ALERTLY** *adv*

ALERT   *v* **-ED, -ING, -S** to warn

ALEURON   *n* pl. **-S** aleurone

ALEURONE   *n* pl. **-S** protein matter found in the seeds of certain plants

ALEVIN   *n* pl. **-S** a young fish

ALEWIFE   *n* pl. **-WIVES** a marine fish

ALEXIA   *n* pl. **-S** a cerebral disorder marked by the loss of the ability to read **ALEXIC** *adj*

ALEXIN   *n* pl. **-S** a substance in the blood that aids in the destruction of bacteria

ALEXINE   *n* pl. **-S** alexin

ALFA   *n* pl. **-S** a communications code word for the letter A

ALFAKI   *n* pl. **-S** alfaqui

ALFALFA   *n* pl. **-S** a plant cultivated for use as hay and forage

ALFAQUI   *n* pl. **-S** a teacher of Muslim law

ALFAQUIN   *n* pl. **-S** alfaqui

ALFORJA   *n* pl. **-S** a leather bag

ALFREDO   *adj* served with a white cheese sauce

ALFRESCO   *adv* outdoors

ALGA   *n* pl. **-GAS** or **-GAE** any of a group of primitive aquatic plants **ALGAL** *adj*

ALGAROBA   *n* pl. **-S** the mesquite

ALGEBRA   *n* pl. **-S** a branch of mathematics

ALGERINE   *n* pl. **-S** a woolen fabric

ALGICIDE   *n* pl. **-S** a substance used to kill algae

ALGID   *adj* cold

ALGIDITY   *n* pl. **-TIES** coldness

ALGIN   *n* pl. **-S** a viscous substance obtained from certain algae

ALGINATE   *n* pl. **-S** a chemical salt

ALGOID   *adj* resembling algae

ALGOLOGY   *n* pl. **-GIES** the study of algae

ALGOR   *n* pl. **-S** coldness

ALGORISM   *n* pl. **-S** the Arabic system of arithmetic notation

ALGUACIL   *n* pl. **-S** a constable in a Spanish-speaking country

ALGUAZIL   *n* pl. **-S** alguacil

ALGUM   *n* pl. **-S** almug

ALIAS   *v* **-ED, -ING, -ES** to assign an assumed name to

ALIASING   *n* pl. **-S** the appearance of distortions in computer graphics

ALIBI   *v* **-BIED, -BIING, -BIS** or **-BIES** to make excuses for oneself

ALIBLE   *adj* nourishing

ALIDAD   *n* pl. **-S** alidade

ALIDADE   *n* pl. **-S** a device used in angular measurement

ALIEN   *v* **-ED, -ING, -S** to transfer to another, as property

ALIENAGE   *n* pl. **-S** the state of being foreign

ALIENATE   *v* **-ATED, -ATING, -ATES** to make indifferent or unfriendly

ALIENEE   *n* pl. **-S** one to whom property is transferred

ALIENER   *n* pl. **-S** alienor

ALIENISM   *n* pl. **-S** alienage

ALIENIST   *n* pl. **-S** a physician who treats mental disorders

ALIENLY   *adv* in a foreign manner

ALIENOR   *n* pl. **-S** one that transfers property

ALIF   *n* pl. **-S** an Arabic letter

ALIFORM   *adj* shaped like a wing

ALIGHT   *v* **ALIGHTED** or **ALIT, ALIGHTING, ALIGHTS** to come down from something

ALIGN   *v* **-ED, -ING, -S** to arrange in a straight line

ALIGNER   *n* pl. **-S** one that aligns

ALIKE   *adj* having close resemblance

ALIMENT   *v* **-ED, -ING, -S** to nourish

ALIMONY   *n* pl. **-NIES** an allowance paid to a woman by her divorced husband

ALINE   *v* **ALINED, ALINING, ALINES** to align

ALINER   *n* pl. **-S** aligner

ALIPED   *n* pl. **-S** an animal having a membrane connecting the toes

ALIQUANT   *adj* not dividing evenly into another number

ALIQUOT   *n* pl. **-S** a number that divides evenly into another

ALIST   *adj* leaning to one side

ALIT   a past tense of alight

ALIUNDE   *adv* from a source extrinsic to the matter at hand

ALIVE   *adj* having life

ALIYA   *n* pl. **-S** aliyah

ALIYAH *n* pl. **-YAHS** or **-YOS** or **-YOT** or **-YOTH** the immigration of Jews to Israel

ALIZARIN *n* pl. **-S** a red dye

ALKAHEST *n* pl. **-S** the hypothetical universal solvent sought by alchemists

ALKALI *n* pl. **-LIS** or **-LIES** a type of chemical compound **ALKALIC** *adj*

ALKALIFY *v* **-FIED, -FYING, -FIES** to alkalize

ALKALIN *adj* alkaline

ALKALINE *adj* containing an alkali

ALKALISE *v* **-LISED, -LISING, -LISES** to alkalize

ALKALIZE *v* **-LIZED, -LIZING, -LIZES** to convert into an alkali

ALKALOID *n* pl. **-S** a type of chemical compound

ALKANE *n* pl. **-S** a type of chemical compound

ALKANET *n* pl. **-S** a European plant

ALKENE *n* pl. **-S** a type of chemical compound

ALKIE *n* pl. **-S** alky

ALKIES pl. of alky

ALKINE *n* pl. **-S** alkyne

ALKOXIDE *n* pl. **-S** a type of chemical salt

ALKOXY *adj* containing a univalent radical composed of alkyl united with oxygen

ALKY *n* pl. **-KIES** one who is habitually drunk

ALKYD *n* pl. **-S** a synthetic resin

ALKYL *n* pl. **-S** a univalent radical **ALKYLIC** *adj*

ALKYLATE *v* **-ATED, -ATING, -ATES** to combine with alkyl

ALKYNE *n* pl. **-S** a type of chemical compound

ALL *n* pl. **-S** everything that one has

ALLANITE *n* pl. **-S** a mineral

ALLAY *v* **-ED, -ING, -S** to reduce in intensity or severity

ALLAYER *n* pl. **-S** one that allays

ALLEE *n* pl. **-S** a tree-lined walkway

ALLEGE *v* **-LEGED, -LEGING, -LEGES** to assert without proof or before proving

ALLEGER *n* pl. **-S** one that alleges

ALLEGORY *n* pl. **-RIES** a story presenting a moral principle

ALLEGRO *n* pl. **-GROS** a musical passage played in rapid tempo

ALLELE *n* pl. **-S** any of several forms of a gene **ALLELIC** *adj*

ALLELISM *n* pl. **-S** the state of possessing alleles

ALLELUIA *n* pl. **-S** a song of praise to God

ALLERGEN *n* pl. **-S** a substance capable of inducing an allergy

ALLERGIC *adj* pertaining to allergy

ALLERGIN *n* pl. **-S** allergen

ALLERGY *n* pl. **-GIES** a state of hypersensitive reaction to certain things

ALLEY *n* pl. **-LEYS** a narrow passageway

ALLEYWAY *n* pl. **-WAYS** an alley

ALLHEAL *n* pl. **-S** a medicinal herb

ALLIABLE *adj* capable of being allied

ALLIAK *n* pl. **-S** an Inuit sledge

ALLIANCE *n* pl. **-S** an association formed to further the common interests of its members

ALLICIN *n* pl. **-S** a liquid compound

ALLIED past tense of ally

ALLIES present 3d person sing. of ally

ALLIUM *n* pl. **-S** a bulbous herb

ALLOBAR *n* pl. **-S** a change in barometric pressure

ALLOCATE *v* **-CATED, -CATING, -CATES** to set apart for a particular purpose

ALLOD *n* pl. **-S** allodium

ALLODIUM *n* pl. **-DIA** land held in absolute ownership **ALLODIAL** *adj*

ALLOGAMY *n* pl. **-MIES** fertilization of a flower by pollen from another

ALLONGE *n* pl. **-S** an addition to a document

ALLONYM *n* pl. **-S** the name of one person assumed by another

ALLOPATH *n* pl. **-S** one who treats diseases by producing effects incompatible with those of the disease

ALLOSAUR *n* pl. **-S** a large dinosaur

ALLOT *v* **-LOTTED, -LOTTING, -LOTS** to give as a share or portion

ALLOTTEE *n* pl. **-S** one to whom something is allotted

ALLOTTER *n* pl. **-S** one that allots

ALLOTYPE *n* pl. **-S** a type of antibody

ALLOTYPY *n* pl. **-TYPIES** the condition of being an allotype

ALLOVER	*n* pl. **-S** a fabric having a pattern extending over the entire surface
ALLOW	*v* **-ED, -ING, -S** to put no obstacle in the way of
ALLOXAN	*n* pl. **-S** a chemical compound
ALLOY	*v* **-ED, -ING, -S** to combine to form an alloy (a homogenous mixture of metals)
ALLSEED	*n* pl. **-S** a plant having many seeds
ALLSORTS	*n/pl* assorted small candies
ALLSPICE	*n* pl. **-S** a tropical tree
ALLUDE	*v* **-LUDED, -LUDING, -LUDES** to make an indirect reference
ALLURE	*v* **-LURED, -LURING, -LURES** to attract with something desirable
ALLURER	*n* pl. **-S** one that allures
ALLUSION	*n* pl. **-S** the act of alluding **ALLUSIVE** *adj*
ALLUVIA	a pl. of alluvium
ALLUVIAL	*n* pl. **-S** soil composed of alluvium
ALLUVION	*n* pl. **-S** alluvium
ALLUVIUM	*n* pl. **-VIUMS** or **-VIA** detrital material deposited by running water
ALLY	*v* **-LIED, -LYING, -LIES** to unite in a formal relationship
ALLYL	*n* pl. **-S** a univalent radical **ALLYLIC** *adj*
ALMA	*n* pl. **-S** almah
ALMAGEST	*n* pl. **-S** a medieval treatise on astrology or alchemy
ALMAH	*n* pl. **-S** an Egyptian girl who sings and dances professionally
ALMANAC	*n* pl. **-S** an annual publication containing general information
ALMANACK	*n* pl. **-S** almanac
ALME	*n* pl. **-S** almah
ALMEH	*n* pl. **-S** almah
ALMEMAR	*n* pl. **-S** a bema
ALMIGHTY	*adj* having absolute power over all
ALMNER	*n* pl. **-S** almoner
ALMOND	*n* pl. **-S** the edible nut of a small tree **ALMONDY** *adj*
ALMONER	*n* pl. **-S** one that distributes alms
ALMONRY	*n* pl. **-RIES** a place where alms are distributed
ALMOST	*adv* very nearly
ALMS	*n* pl. **ALMS** money or goods given to the poor
ALMSMAN	*n* pl. **-MEN** one who receives alms

ALMUCE	*n* pl. **-S** a hooded cape
ALMUD	*n* pl. **-S** a Spanish unit of capacity
ALMUDE	*n* pl. **-S** almud
ALMUG	*n* pl. **-S** a precious wood mentioned in the Bible
ALNICO	*n* pl. **-COS** an alloy containing aluminum, nickel, and cobalt
ALODIUM	*n* pl. **-DIA** allodium **ALODIAL** *adj*
ALOE	*n* pl. **-S** an African plant **ALOETIC** *adj*
ALOFT	*adv* in or into the air
ALOGICAL	*adj* being outside the bounds of that to which logic can apply
ALOHA	*n* pl. **-S** love — used as a greeting or farewell
ALOIN	*n* pl. **-S** a laxative
ALONE	*adj* apart from others
ALONG	*adv* onward
ALOOF	*adj* distant in interest or feeling **ALOOFLY** *adv*
ALOPECIA	*n* pl. **-S** baldness **ALOPECIC** *adj*
ALOUD	*adv* audibly
ALOW	*adv* in or to a lower position
ALP	*n* pl. **-S** a high mountain
ALPACA	*n* pl. **-S** a ruminant mammal
ALPHA	*n* pl. **-S** a Greek letter
ALPHABET	*v* **-ED, -ING, -S** to arrange in the customary order of the letters of a language
ALPHORN	*n* pl. **-S** a wooden horn used by Swiss herdsmen
ALPHOSIS	*n* pl. **-SISES** lack of skin pigmentation
ALPHYL	*n* pl. **-S** a univalent radical
ALPINE	*n* pl. **-S** a plant native to high mountain regions
ALPINELY	*adv* in a lofty manner
ALPINISM	*n* pl. **-S** mountain climbing
ALPINIST	*n* pl. **-S** a mountain climber
ALREADY	*adv* by this time
ALRIGHT	*adj* satisfactory
ALSIKE	*n* pl. **-S** a European clover
ALSO	*adv* in addition
ALT	*n* pl. **-S** a high-pitched musical note
ALTAR	*n* pl. **-S** a raised structure used in worship
ALTER	*v* **-ED, -ING, -S** to make different

ALTERANT	*n* pl. **-S** something that alters
ALTERER	*n* pl. **-S** one that alters
ALTERITY	*n* pl. **-TIES** the state of being other or different
ALTHAEA	*n* pl. **-S** althea
ALTHEA	*n* pl. **-S** a flowering plant
ALTHO	*conj* although
ALTHORN	*n* pl. **-S** a brass wind instrument
ALTHOUGH	*conj* despite the fact that
ALTITUDE	*n* pl. **-S** the vertical elevation of an object above a given level
ALTO	*n* pl. **-TOS** a low female singing voice
ALTOIST	*n* pl. **-S** one who plays the alto saxophone
ALTRUISM	*n* pl. **-S** selfless devotion to the welfare of others
ALTRUIST	*n* pl. **-S** one that practices altruism
ALUDEL	*n* pl. **-S** a pear-shaped vessel
ALULA	*n* pl. **-LAE** a tuft of feathers on the first digit of a bird's wing **ALULAR** *adj*
ALUM	*n* pl. **-S** a chemical compound
ALUMIN	*n* pl. **-S** alumina
ALUMINA	*n* pl. **-S** an oxide of aluminum
ALUMINE	*n* pl. **-S** alumina
ALUMINUM	*n* pl. **-S** a metallic element **ALUMINIC** *adj*
ALUMNA	*n* pl. **-NAE** a female graduate
ALUMNUS	*n* pl. **-NI** a male graduate
ALUMROOT	*n* pl. **-S** a flowering plant
ALUNITE	*n* pl. **-S** a mineral
ALVAR	*n* pl. **-S** an area of exposed limestone
ALVEOLAR	*n* pl. **-S** a sound produced with the tongue touching a place just behind the front teeth
ALVEOLUS	*n* pl. **-LI** a small anatomical cavity
ALVINE	*adj* pertaining to the abdomen and lower intestines
ALWAY	*adv* always
ALWAYS	*adv* at all times
ALYSSUM	*n* pl. **-S** a flowering plant
AM	present 1st person sing. of be
AMA	*n* pl. **-S** amah
AMADAVAT	*n* pl. **-S** an Asian songbird
AMADOU	*n* pl. **-S** a substance prepared from fungi for use as tinder

AMAH	*n* pl. **-S** an Oriental nurse
AMAIN	*adv* with full strength
AMALGAM	*n* pl. **-S** an alloy of mercury with another metal
AMANDINE	*adj* prepared with almonds
AMANITA	*n* pl. **-S** any of a genus of poisonous fungi
AMANITIN	*n* pl. **-S** a chemical compound
AMARANTH	*n* pl. **-S** a flowering plant
AMARELLE	*n* pl. **-S** a variety of sour cherry
AMARETTI	*n/pl* macaroons made with bitter almonds
AMARETTO	*n* pl. **-TOS** a kind of liqueur
AMARNA	*adj* pertaining to a certain historical period of ancient Egypt
AMARONE	*n* pl. **-S** a dry red wine
AMASS	*v* **-ED, -ING, -ES** to gather
AMASSER	*n* pl. **-S** one that amasses
AMATEUR	*n* pl. **-S** one that engages in an activity for pleasure
AMATIVE	*adj* amorous
AMATOL	*n* pl. **-S** a powerful explosive
AMATORY	*adj* pertaining to sexual love
AMAUTI	*n* pl. **-S** amautik
AMAUTIK	*n* pl. **-S** an Inuit woman's parka
AMAZE	*v* **AMAZED, AMAZING, AMAZES** to overwhelm with surprise or wonder **AMAZEDLY** *adv*
AMAZON	*n* pl. **-S** a tall, powerful woman
AMBAGE	*n* pl. **-S** a winding path
AMBARI	*n* pl. **-S** ambary
AMBARY	*n* pl. **-RIES** an East Indian plant
AMBEER	*n* pl. **-S** tobacco juice
AMBER	*n* pl. **-S** a fossil resin
AMBERINA	*n* pl. **-S** a type of glassware
AMBEROID	*n* pl. **-S** ambroid
AMBERY	*n* pl. **-BERIES** ambry
AMBIANCE	*n* pl. **-S** ambience
AMBIENCE	*n* pl. **-S** the character, mood, or atmosphere of a place or situation
AMBIENT	*n* pl. **-S** ambience
AMBIT	*n* pl. **-S** the external boundary of something
AMBITION	*v* **-ED, -ING, -S** to seek with eagerness
AMBIVERT	*n* pl. **-S** a person whose personality type is intermediate between introvert and extravert

AMBLE	*v* **-BLED, -BLING, -BLES** to saunter
AMBLER	*n* pl. **-S** one that ambles
AMBO	*n* pl. **AMBOS** or **AMBONES** a pulpit in an early Christian church
AMBOINA	*n* pl. **-S** amboyna
AMBOYNA	*n* pl. **-S** the mottled wood of an Indonesian tree
AMBRIES	pl. of ambry
AMBROID	*n* pl. **-S** a synthetic amber
AMBROSIA	*n* pl. **-S** the food of the Greek and Roman gods
AMBRY	*n* pl. **-BRIES** a recess in a church wall for sacred vessels
AMBSACE	*n* pl. **-S** bad luck
AMBULANT	*adj* ambulating
AMBULATE	*v* **-LATED, -LATING, -LATES** to move or walk about
AMBUSH	*v* **-ED, -ING, -ES** to attack from a concealed place
AMBUSHER	*n* pl. **-S** one that ambushes
AMEBA	*n* pl. **-BAS** or **-BAE** amoeba **AMEBAN, AMEBIC, AMEBOID** *adj*
AMEBEAN	*adj* alternately responding
AMEER	*n* pl. **-S** amir
AMEERATE	*n* pl. **-S** amirate
AMELCORN	*n* pl. **-S** a variety of wheat
AMEN	*n* pl. **-S** a word used at the end of a prayer to express agreement
AMENABLE	*adj* capable of being persuaded **AMENABLY** *adv*
AMEND	*v* **-ED, -ING, -S** to improve
AMENDER	*n* pl. **-S** one that amends
AMENITY	*n* pl. **-TIES** the quality of being pleasant or agreeable
AMENT	*n* pl. **-S** a mentally deficient person
AMENTIA	*n* pl. **-S** mental deficiency
AMENTUM	*n* pl. **-TA** ament
AMERCE	*v* **AMERCED, AMERCING, AMERCES** to punish by imposing an arbitrary fine
AMERCER	*n* pl. **-S** one that amerces
AMESACE	*n* pl. **-S** ambsace
AMETHYST	*n* pl. **-S** a variety of quartz
AMI	*n* pl. **-S** a friend
AMIA	*n* pl. **-S** a freshwater fish
AMIABLE	*adj* having a pleasant disposition **AMIABLY** *adv*
AMIANTUS	*n* pl. **-ES** a variety of asbestos
AMICABLE	*adj* friendly **AMICABLY** *adv*
AMICE	*n* pl. **-S** a vestment worn about the neck and shoulders
AMICUS	*n* pl. **AMICI** one not party to a lawsuit but permitted by the court to advise it
AMID	*n* pl. **-S** amide
AMIDASE	*n* pl. **-S** an enzyme
AMIDE	*n* pl. **-S** a type of chemical compound **AMIDIC** *adj*
AMIDIN	*n* pl. **-S** the soluble matter of starch
AMIDINE	*n* pl. **-S** a type of chemical compound
AMIDO	*adj* containing an amide united with an acid radical
AMIDOGEN	*n* pl. **-S** a univalent chemical radical
AMIDOL	*n* pl. **-S** a chemical compound
AMIDONE	*n* pl. **-S** a chemical compound
AMIDSHIP	*adv* toward the middle of a ship
AMIDST	*prep* in the midst of
AMIE	*n* pl. **-S** a female friend
AMIGA	*n* pl. **-S** a female friend
AMIGO	*n* pl. **-GOS** a friend
AMIN	*n* pl. **-S** amine
AMINE	*n* pl. **-S** a type of chemical compound **AMINIC** *adj*
AMINITY	*n* pl. **-TIES** the state of being an amine
AMINO	*n* pl. **-NOS** a chemical group present in amines
AMIR	*n* pl. **-S** a Muslim prince or governor
AMIRATE	*n* pl. **-S** the rank of an amir
AMISS	*adj* being out of proper order
AMITIES	pl. of amity
AMITOSIS	*n* pl. **-TOSES** a type of cell division **AMITOTIC** *adj*
AMITROLE	*n* pl. **-S** an herbicide
AMITY	*n* pl. **-TIES** friendship
AMMETER	*n* pl. **-S** an instrument for measuring amperage
AMMINE	*n* pl. **-S** a type of chemical compound
AMMINO	*adj* pertaining to an ammine
AMMO	*n* pl. **-MOS** ammunition
AMMOCETE	*n* pl. **-S** the larva of a lamprey

AMMOLITE *n* pl. **-S** the fossilized shell of an ammonite

AMMONAL *n* pl. **-S** a powerful explosive

AMMONIA *n* pl. **-S** a pungent gas

AMMONIAC *n* pl. **-S** a gum resin

AMMONIC *adj* pertaining to ammonia

AMMONIFY *v* **-FIED, -FYING, -FIES** to treat with ammonia

AMMONITE *n* pl. **-S** the coiled shell of an extinct mollusk

AMMONIUM *n* pl. **-S** a univalent chemical radical

AMMONO *adj* containing ammonia

AMMONOID *n* pl. **-S** ammonite

AMNESIA *n* pl. **-S** loss of memory

AMNESIAC *n* pl. **-S** one suffering from amnesia

AMNESIC *n* pl. **-S** amnesiac

AMNESTIC *adj* pertaining to amnesia

AMNESTY *v* **-TIED, -TYING, -TIES** to pardon

AMNIO *n* pl. **-NIOS** a surgical insertion of a needle into the uterus

AMNION *n* pl. **-NIONS** or **-NIA** a membranous sac enclosing an embryo **AMNIC, AMNIONIC, AMNIOTIC** *adj*

AMNIOTE *n* pl. **-S** a vertebrate that develops an amnion during the embryonic stage

AMOEBA *n* pl. **-BAS** or **-BAE** a unicellular microscopic organism **AMOEBAN, AMOEBIC, AMOEBOID** *adj*

AMOEBEAN *adj* amebean

AMOK *n* pl. **-S** a murderous frenzy

AMOLE *n* pl. **-S** a plant root used as a substitute for soap

AMONG *prep* in the midst of

AMONGST *prep* among

AMORAL *adj* lacking a sense of right and wrong **AMORALLY** *adv*

AMORETTO *n* pl. **-TOS** or **-TI** a cupid

AMORINO *n* pl. **-NI** an amoretto

AMORIST *n* pl. **-S** a lover

AMOROSO *n* pl. **-SOS** a type of wine

AMOROUS *adj* pertaining to love

AMORT *adj* being without life

AMORTISE *v* **-TISED, -TISING, -TISES** to amortize

AMORTIZE *v* **-TIZED, -TIZING, -TIZES** to liquidate gradually, as a debt

AMOSITE *n* pl. **-S** a type of asbestos

AMOTION *n* pl. **-S** the removal of a corporate officer from his office

AMOUNT *v* **-ED, -ING, -S** to combine to yield a sum

AMOUR *n* pl. **-S** a love affair

AMP *v* **-ED, -ING, -S** to amplify

AMPERAGE *n* pl. **-S** the strength of an electric current expressed in amperes

AMPERE *n* pl. **-S** a unit of electric current strength

AMPHIBIA *n/pl* organisms adapted for life both on land and in water

AMPHIOXI *n/pl* lancelets

AMPHIPOD *n* pl. **-S** a small crustacean

AMPHORA *n* pl. **-RAS** or **-RAE** a narrow-necked jar used in ancient Greece **AMPHORAL** *adj*

AMPLE *adj* **-PLER, -PLEST** abundant **AMPLY** *adv*

AMPLEXUS *n* pl. **-ES** the mating embrace of frogs

AMPLIFY *v* **-FIED, -FYING, -FIES** to make larger or more powerful

AMPOULE *n* pl. **-S** ampule

AMPUL *n* pl. **-S** ampule

AMPULE *n* pl. **-S** a small glass vial

AMPULLA *n* pl. **-LAE** a globular bottle used in ancient Rome **AMPULLAR** *adj*

AMPUTATE *v* **-TATED, -TATING, -TATES** to cut off by surgical means

AMPUTEE *n* pl. **-S** one that has had a limb amputated

AMREETA *n* pl. **-S** amrita

AMRIT *n* pl. **-S** amrita

AMRITA *n* pl. **-S** a beverage that bestows immortality in Hindu mythology

AMTRAC *n* pl. **-S** a military vehicle equipped to move on land and water

AMTRACK *n* pl. **-S** amtrac

AMTRAK *n* pl. **-S** amtrac

AMU *n* pl. **-S** a unit of mass

AMUCK *n* pl. **-S** amok

AMULET *n* pl. **-S** an object worn to protect against evil or injury

AMUSE *v* **AMUSED, AMUSING, AMUSES** to occupy pleasingly **AMUSABLE** *adj* **AMUSEDLY** *adv*

AMUSER *n* pl. **-S** one that amuses

AMUSIA *n* pl. **-S** the inability to recognize musical sounds

AMUSIVE *adj* amusing

AMYGDALA *n* pl. **-LAE** an almond-shaped anatomical part

AMYGDALE *n* pl. **-S** amygdule

AMYGDULE *n* pl. **-S** a small gas bubble in lava

AMYL *n* pl. **-S** a univalent radical

AMYLASE *n* pl. **-S** an enzyme

AMYLENE *n* pl. **-S** a flammable liquid

AMYLIC *adj* pertaining to amyl

AMYLOGEN *n* pl. **-S** amylose

AMYLOID *n* pl. **-S** a hard protein deposit resulting from degeneration of tissue

AMYLOSE *n* pl. **-S** the relatively soluble component of starch

AMYLUM *n* pl. **-S** starch (a solid carbohydrate)

AN *indefinite article* — used before words beginning with a vowel sound

ANA *n* pl. **-S** a collection of miscellaneous information about a particular subject

ANABAENA *n* pl. **-S** a freshwater alga

ANABAS *n* pl. **-ES** a freshwater fish

ANABASIS *n* pl. **-ASES** a military advance

ANABATIC *adj* pertaining to rising wind currents

ANABLEPS *n* pl. **-ES** a freshwater fish

ANABOLIC *adj* pertaining to a process by which food is built up into protoplasm

ANACONDA *n* pl. **-S** a large snake

ANADEM *n* pl. **-S** a wreath for the head

ANAEMIA *n* pl. **-S** anemia **ANAEMIC** *adj*

ANAEROBE *n* pl. **-S** an organism that does not require oxygen to live

ANAGLYPH *n* pl. **-S** a type of carved ornament

ANAGOGE *n* pl. **-S** a spiritual interpretation of words **ANAGOGIC** *adj*

ANAGOGY *n* pl. **-GIES** anagoge

ANAGRAM *v* **-GRAMMED, -GRAMMING, -GRAMS** to transpose the letters of a word or phrase to form a new one

ANAL *adj* pertaining to the anus

ANALCIME *n* pl. **-S** analcite

ANALCITE *n* pl. **-S** a mineral

ANALECTA *n/pl* analects

ANALECTS *n/pl* selections from a literary work or group of works

ANALEMMA *n* pl. **-MAS** or **-MATA** a type of graduated scale

ANALGIA *n* pl. **-S** inability to feel pain

ANALITY *n* pl. **-TIES** a type of psychological state

ANALLY *adv* at or through the anus

ANALOG *n* pl. **-S** analogue

ANALOGIC *adj* pertaining to an analogy

ANALOGUE *n* pl. **-S** something that bears an analogy to something else

ANALOGY *n* pl. **-GIES** resemblance in some respects between things otherwise unlike

ANALYSE *v* **-LYSED, -LYSING, -LYSES** to analyze

ANALYSER *n* pl. **-S** analyzer

ANALYSIS *n* pl. **-YSES** the separation of a whole into its parts

ANALYST *n* pl. **-S** one that analyzes

ANALYTE *n* pl. **-S** a substance being analyzed

ANALYTIC *adj* pertaining to analysis

ANALYZE *v* **-LYZED, -LYZING, -LYZES** to subject to analysis

ANALYZER *n* pl. **-S** one that analyzes

ANANDA *n* pl. **-S** extreme happiness

ANANKE *n* pl. **-S** a compelling necessity in ancient Greek religion

ANAPAEST *n* pl. **-S** anapest

ANAPEST *n* pl. **-S** a type of metrical foot

ANAPHASE *n* pl. **-S** a stage of mitosis

ANAPHOR *n* pl. **-S** a word or phrase that takes reference from a preceding word or phrase

ANAPHORA *n* pl. **-S** the repetition of a word or phrase at the beginning of several successive verses or sentences

ANARCH *n* pl. **-S** an advocate of anarchy

ANARCHY *n* pl. **-CHIES** absence of government **ANARCHIC** *adj*

ANASARCA *n* pl. **-S** a form of dropsy

ANATASE *n* pl. **-S** a mineral

ANATHEMA *n* pl. **-MAS** or **-MATA** a formal ecclesiastical ban or curse

ANATOMY *n* pl. **-MIES** the structure of an organism **ANATOMIC** *adj*

ANATOXIN *n* pl. **-S** a toxoid

ANATTO *n* pl. **-TOS** annatto

ANCESTOR *v* **-ED, -ING, -S** to be an ancestor (a person from whom one is descended) of

ANCESTRY *n* pl. **-TRIES** a line or body of ancestors

ANCHO *n* pl. **-CHOS** a chili pepper

ANCHOR *v* **-ED, -ING, -S** to secure by means of an anchor (a device for holding a floating vessel in place)

ANCHORET *n* pl. **-S** a recluse

ANCHOVY *n* pl. **-VIES** a small food fish

ANCHUSA *n* pl. **-S** a hairy-stemmed plant

ANCHUSIN *n* pl. **-S** a red dye

ANCIENT *adj* **-CIENTER, -CIENTEST** of or pertaining to time long past

ANCIENT *n* pl. **-S** one who lived in ancient times

ANCILLA *n* pl. **-LAS** or **-LAE** a helper

ANCON *n* pl. **-ES** the elbow **ANCONAL, ANCONEAL, ANCONOID** *adj*

ANCONE *n* pl. **-S** ancon

ANCRESS *n* pl. **-ES** a female recluse

AND *n* pl. **-S** an added condition or stipulation

ANDANTE *n* pl. **-S** a moderately slow musical passage

ANDESITE *n* pl. **-S** a volcanic rock

ANDESYTE *n* pl. **-S** andesite

ANDIRON *n* pl. **-S** a metal support for holding wood in a fireplace

ANDRO *n* pl. **-DROS** a steroid sex hormone

ANDROGEN *n* pl. **-S** a male sex hormone

ANDROID *n* pl. **-S** a synthetic man

ANE *n* pl. **-S** one

ANEAR *v* **-ED, -ING, -S** to approach

ANECDOTE *n* pl. **-DOTES** or **-DOTA** a brief story

ANECHOIC *adj* neither having nor producing echoes

ANELE *v* **ANELED, ANELING, ANELES** to anoint

ANEMIA *n* pl. **-S** a disorder of the blood **ANEMIC** *adj*

ANEMONE *n* pl. **-S** a flowering plant

ANEMOSIS *n* pl. **-MOSES** separation of rings of growth in timber due to wind

ANENST *prep* anent

ANENT *prep* in regard to

ANERGIA *n* pl. **-S** anergy

ANERGY *n* pl. **-GIES** lack of energy **ANERGIC** *adj*

ANEROID *n* pl. **-S** a type of barometer

ANESTRUS *n* pl. **-TRI** a period of sexual dormancy

ANETHOL *n* pl. **-S** anethole

ANETHOLE *n* pl. **-S** a chemical compound

ANEURIN *n* pl. **-S** thiamine

ANEURISM *n* pl. **-S** aneurysm

ANEURYSM *n* pl. **-S** an abnormal blood-filled dilation of a blood vessel

ANEW *adv* once more

ANGA *n* pl. **-S** any of the eight practices of yoga

ANGAKOK *n* pl. **-S** an Inuit medicine man

ANGARIA *n* pl. **-S** angary

ANGARY *n* pl. **-RIES** the right of a warring state to seize neutral property

ANGEL *v* **-ED, -ING, -S** to support financially

ANGELIC *adj* pertaining to an angel (a winged celestial being)

ANGELICA *n* pl. **-S** an aromatic herb

ANGELUS *n* pl. **-ES** a Roman Catholic prayer

ANGER *v* **-ED, -ING, -S** to make angry

ANGERLY *adv* in an angry manner

ANGINA *n* pl. **-S** a disease marked by spasmodic attacks of intense pain **ANGINAL, ANGINOSE, ANGINOUS** *adj*

ANGIOMA *n* pl. **-MAS** or **-MATA** a tumor composed of blood or lymph vessels

ANGLE *v* **-GLED, -GLING, -GLES** to fish with a hook and line

ANGLEPOD *n* pl. **-S** a flowering plant

ANGLER *n* pl. **-S** one that angles

ANGLICE *adv* in readily understood English

ANGLING *n* pl. **-S** the sport of fishing

ANGLO *n* pl. **-GLOS** a white North American of non-Hispanic or non-French descent

ANGORA *n* pl. **-S** the long, silky hair of a domestic goat

ANGRY *adj* **-GRIER, -GRIEST** feeling strong displeasure or hostility **ANGRILY** *adv*

ANGST *n* pl. **-S** a feeling of anxiety or dread

ANGSTROM *n* pl. **-S** a unit of length

ANGSTY *adj* **ANGSTIER, ANGSTIEST** feeling anxiety or dread

ANGUINE *adj* resembling a snake

ANGUISH *v* **-ED, -ING, -ES** to suffer extreme pain

ANGULAR *adj* having sharp corners

ANGULATE *v* **-LATED, -LATING, -LATES** to make angular

ANGULOSE *adj* angular

ANGULOUS *adj* angular

ANHEDRAL *n* pl. **-S** the downward inclination of an aircraft's wing

ANHINGA *n* pl. **-S** an aquatic bird

ANI *n* pl. **-S** a tropical American bird

ANIL *n* pl. **-S** a West Indian shrub

ANILE *adj* resembling an old woman

ANILIN *n* pl. **-S** aniline

ANILINE *n* pl. **-S** a chemical compound

ANILITY *n* pl. **-TIES** the state of being anile

ANIMA *n* pl. **-S** the soul

ANIMACY *n* pl. **-CIES** the state of being alive

ANIMAL *n* pl. **-S** a living organism typically capable of voluntary motion and sensation **ANIMALIC** *adj*

ANIMALLY *adv* physically

ANIMATE *v* **-MATED, -MATING, -MATES** to give life to

ANIMATER *n* pl. **-S** animator

ANIMATO *n* pl. **-TOS** or **-TI** a musical passage played in a lively manner

ANIMATOR *n* pl. **-S** one that animates

ANIME *n* pl. **-S** a resin obtained from a tropical tree

ANIMI *n* pl. **-S** anime

ANIMISM *n* pl. **-S** the belief that souls may exist apart from bodies

ANIMIST *n* pl. **-S** an adherent of animism

ANIMUS *n* pl. **-ES** a feeling of hostility

ANION *n* pl. **-S** a negatively charged ion **ANIONIC** *adj*

ANISE *n* pl. **-S** a North African plant

ANISEED *n* pl. **-S** the seed of the anise used as a flavoring

ANISETTE *n* pl. **-S** a liqueur flavored with aniseed

ANISIC *adj* pertaining to an anise

ANISOLE *n* pl. **-S** a chemical compound

ANKERITE *n* pl. **-S** a mineral

ANKH *n* pl. **-S** an Egyptian symbol of enduring life

ANKLE *v* **-KLED, -KLING, -KLES** to walk

ANKLET *n* pl. **-S** an ornament for the ankle

ANKUS *n* pl. **-ES** an elephant goad

ANKUSH *n* pl. **-ES** ankus

ANKYLOSE *v* **-LOSED, -LOSING, -LOSES** to unite or grow together, as the bones of a joint

ANLACE *n* pl. **-S** a medieval dagger

ANLAGE *n* pl. **-GES** or **-GEN** the initial cell structure from which an embryonic organ develops

ANLAS *n* pl. **-ES** anlace

ANNA *n* pl. **-S** a former coin of India and Pakistan

ANNAL *n* pl. **-S** a record of a single year

ANNALIST *n* pl. **-S** a historian

ANNATES *n/pl* the first year's revenue of a bishop paid to the pope

ANNATTO *n* pl. **-TOS** a yellowish-red dye

ANNEAL *v* **-ED, -ING, -S** to toughen

ANNEALER *n* pl. **-S** one that anneals

ANNELID *n* pl. **-S** any of a phylum of segmented worms

ANNEX *v* **-ED, -ING, -ES** to add or attach

ANNEXE *n* pl. **-S** something added or attached

ANNONA *n* pl. **-S** a tropical tree

ANNOTATE *v* **-TATED, -TATING, -TATES** to furnish with critical or explanatory notes

ANNOUNCE *v* **-NOUNCED, -NOUNCING, -NOUNCES** to make known publicly

ANNOY *v* **-ED, -ING, -S** to be troublesome to

ANNOYER *n* pl. **-S** one that annoys

ANNUAL *n* pl. **-S** a publication issued once a year

ANNUALLY *adv* once a year

ANNUITY *n* pl. **-TIES** an allowance or income paid at regular intervals

ANNUL *v* **-NULLED, -NULLING, -NULS** to make or declare void or invalid

ANNULAR *adj* shaped like a ring

ANNULATE *adj* composed of or furnished with rings

ANNULET *n* pl. **-S** a small ring

ANNULI   a pl. of annulus

ANNULLED   past tense of annul

ANNULLING   present participle of annul

ANNULUS   *n* pl. **-LUSES** or **-LI** a ring or ringlike part **ANNULOSE** *adj*

ANOA   *n* pl. **-S** a wild ox

ANODE   *n* pl. **-S** a positively charged electrode **ANODAL, ANODIC** *adj* **ANODALLY** *adv*

ANODISE   *v* **-ISED, -ISING, -ISES** to anodize

ANODISER   *n* pl. **-S** anodizer

ANODIZE   *v* **-IZED, -IZING, -IZES** to coat with a protective film by chemical means

ANODIZER   *n* pl. **-S** one that anodizes

ANODYNE   *n* pl. **-S** a medicine that relieves pain **ANODYNIC** *adj*

ANOINT   *v* **-ED, -ING, -S** to apply oil to as a sacred rite

ANOINTER   *n* pl. **-S** one that anoints

ANOLE   *n* pl. **-S** a tropical lizard

ANOLYTE   *n* pl. **-S** the part of an electricity-conducting solution nearest the anode

ANOMALY   *n* pl. **-LIES** a deviation from the common rule, type, or form

ANOMIE   *n* pl. **-S** a collapse of the social structures governing a given society **ANOMIC** *adj*

ANOMY   *n* pl. **-MIES** anomie

ANON   *adv* at another time

ANONYM   *n* pl. **-S** a false or assumed name

ANOOPSIA   *n* pl. **-S** a visual defect

ANOPIA   *n* pl. **-S** anoopsia

ANOPSIA   *n* pl. **-S** anoopsia

ANORAK   *n* pl. **-S** a parka

ANORETIC   *n* pl. **-S** anorexic

ANOREXIA   *n* pl. **-S** loss of appetite

ANOREXIC   *n* pl. **-S** one affected with anorexia

ANOREXY   *n* pl. **-OREXIES** anorexia

ANORTHIC   *adj* denoting a certain type of crystal system

ANOSMIA   *n* pl. **-S** loss of the sense of smell **ANOSMIC** *adj*

ANOTHER   *adj* one more

ANOVULAR   *adj* not involving ovulation

ANOXEMIA   *n* pl. **-S** a disorder of the blood **ANOXEMIC** *adj*

ANOXIA   *n* pl. **-S** absence of oxygen **ANOXIC** *adj*

ANSA   *n* pl. **-SAE** the projecting part of Saturn's rings

ANSATE   *adj* having a handle

ANSATED   *adj* ansate

ANSERINE   *n* pl. **-S** a chemical compound

ANSEROUS   *adj* silly

ANSWER   *v* **-ED, -ING, -S** to say, write, or act in return

ANSWERER   *n* pl. **-S** one that answers

ANT   *n* pl. **-S** a small insect

ANTA   *n* pl. **-TAS** or **-TAE** a pilaster formed at the termination of a wall

ANTACID   *n* pl. **-S** a substance that neutralizes acid

ANTALGIC   *n* pl. **-S** an anodyne

ANTBEAR   *n* pl. **-S** an aardvark

ANTE   *v* **ANTED** or **ANTEED, ANTEING, ANTES** to put a fixed stake into the pot before the cards are dealt in poker

ANTEATER   *n* pl. **-S** any of several mammals that feed on ants

ANTECEDE   *v* **-CEDED, -CEDING, -CEDES** to precede

ANTEDATE   *v* **-DATED, -DATING, -DATES** to be of an earlier date than

ANTEFIX   *n* pl. **-FIXES** or **-FIXAE** or **-FIXA** an upright ornament at the eaves of a tiled roof

ANTELOPE   *n* pl. **-S** a ruminant mammal

ANTENNA   *n* pl. **-NAS** or **-NAE** a metallic device for sending or receiving radio waves **ANTENNAL** *adj*

ANTEPAST   *n* pl. **-S** an appetizer

ANTERIOR   *adj* situated in or toward the front

ANTEROOM   *n* pl. **-S** a waiting room

ANTES   present 3d person sing. of ante

ANTETYPE   *n* pl. **-S** an earlier form

ANTEVERT   *v* **-ED, -ING, -S** to displace by tipping forward

ANTHELIA   *n/pl* halolike areas seen in the sky opposite the sun

ANTHELIX   *n* pl. **-LIXES** or **-LICES** the inner curved ridge on the cartilage of the external ear

ANTHEM   *v* **-ED, -ING, -S** to praise in a song

ANTHEMIA   *n/pl* decorative floral patterns used in Greek art

ANTHEMIC *adj* pertaining to an anthem (a song of praise)

ANTHER *n* pl. **-S** the pollen-bearing part of a stamen **ANTHERAL** *adj*

ANTHERID *n* pl. **-S** a male reproductive organ of certain plants

ANTHESIS *n* pl. **-THESES** the full bloom of a flower

ANTHILL *n* pl. **-S** a mound formed by ants in building their nest

ANTHODIA *n/pl* flower heads of certain plants

ANTHOID *adj* resembling a flower

ANTHRAX *n* pl. **-THRAXES** or **-THRACES** an infectious disease

ANTHRO *n* pl **-THROS** anthropology

ANTI *n* pl. **-S** one that is opposed

ANTIACNE *adj* effective against acne

ANTIAIR *adj* directed against attacking aircraft

ANTIAR *n* pl. **-S** an arrow poison

ANTIARIN *n* pl. **-S** antiar

ANTIATOM *n* pl. **-S** an atom comprised of antiparticles

ANTIBIAS *adj* opposed to bias

ANTIBODY *n* pl. **-BODIES** a body protein that produces immunity against certain microorganisms or toxins

ANTIBOSS *adj* opposed to bosses

ANTIBUG *adj* effective against bugs

ANTIC *v* **-TICKED, -TICKING, -TICS** to act in a clownish manner

ANTICAR *adj* opposed to cars

ANTICITY *adj* opposed to cities

ANTICK *v* **-ED, -ING, -S** to antic

ANTICLY *adv* in a clownish manner

ANTICOLD *adj* effective against the common cold

ANTICULT *n* pl. **-S** a group opposed to a cult

ANTIDORA *n/pl* holy breads

ANTIDOTE *v* **-DOTED, -DOTING, -DOTES** to counteract the effects of a poison with a remedy

ANTIDRUG *adj* opposed to illicit drugs

ANTIFAT *adj* preventing the formation of fat

ANTIFLU *adj* combating the flu

ANTIFOAM *adj* reducing or preventing foam

ANTIFOG *adj* preventing the buildup of moisture on a surface

ANTIFUR *adj* opposed to the wearing of animal furs

ANTIGANG *adj* opposed to gangs

ANTIGAY *adj* opposed to homosexuals

ANTIGEN *n* pl. **-S** a substance that stimulates the production of antibodies

ANTIGENE *n* pl. **-S** antigen

ANTIGUN *adj* opposed to guns

ANTIHERO *n* pl. **-ROES** a protagonist who is notably lacking in heroic qualities

ANTIJAM *adj* blocking interfering signals

ANTIKING *n* pl. **-S** a usurping king

ANTILEAK *adj* preventing leaks

ANTILEFT *adj* opposed to leftism

ANTILIFE *adj* opposed to life

ANTILOCK *adj* designed to prevent the wheels of a vehicle from locking

ANTILOG *n* pl. **-S** the number corresponding to a given logarithm

ANTILOGY *n* pl. **-GIES** a contradiction in terms or ideas

ANTIMALE *adj* opposed to men

ANTIMAN *adj* antimale

ANTIMASK *n* pl. **-S** a comic performance between the acts of a masque

ANTIMERE *n* pl. **-S** a part of an organism symmetrical with a part on the opposite side of the main axis

ANTIMINE *adj* effective against mines

ANTIMONY *n* pl. **-NIES** a metallic element

ANTING *n* pl. **-S** the deliberate placing, by certain birds, of living ants among the feathers

ANTINODE *n* pl. **-S** a region between adjacent nodes

ANTINOME *n* pl. **-S** one that is opposite to another

ANTINOMY *n* pl. **-MIES** a contradiction between two seemingly valid principles

ANTINUKE *n* pl. **-S** a person who opposes the use of nuclear power plants or nuclear weapons

ANTIPHON *n* pl. **-S** a psalm or hymn sung responsively

ANTIPILL *adj* opposing the use of contraceptive pills

ANTIPODE *n* pl. **-S** an exact opposite

ANTIPOLE *n* pl. **-S** the opposite pole

ANTIPOPE   *n* pl. **-S** one claiming to be pope in opposition to the one chosen by church law

ANTIPORN   *adj* opposed to pornography

ANTIPOT   *adj* opposing the use of pot (marijuana)

ANTIPYIC   *n* pl. **-S** a medicine that prevents the formation of pus

ANTIQUE   *v* **-TIQUED, -TIQUING, -TIQUES** to give an appearance of age to

ANTIQUER   *n* pl. **-S** one that antiques

ANTIRAPE   *adj* concerned with preventing rape

ANTIRED   *adj* opposed to communism

ANTIRIOT   *adj* designed to prevent or end riots

ANTIROCK   *adj* opposed to rock music

ANTIROLL   *adj* designed to reduce roll

ANTIRUST   *n* pl. **-S** something that prevents rust

ANTISAG   *adj* designed to prevent sagging

ANTISERA   *n/pl* serums that contain antibodies

ANTISEX   *adj* opposed to sexual activity

ANTISHIP   *adj* designed for use against ships

ANTISKID   *adj* designed to prevent skidding

ANTISLIP   *adj* designed to prevent slipping

ANTISMOG   *adj* designed to reduce pollutants that cause smog

ANTISMUT   *adj* opposed to pornography

ANTISNOB   *n* pl. **-S** one that is opposed to snobbery

ANTISPAM   *adj* designed to block spam (unsolicited email)

ANTISTAT   *n* pl. **-S** an agent for preventing the buildup of static electricity

ANTITANK   *adj* designed to combat tanks

ANTITAX   *adj* opposing taxes

ANTITYPE   *n* pl. **-S** an opposite type

ANTIWAR   *adj* opposing war

ANTIWEAR   *adj* designed to reduce the effects of long or hard use

ANTIWEED   *adj* concerned with the destruction of weeds

ANTLER   *n* pl. **-S** the horn of an animal of the deer family **ANTLERED** *adj*

ANTLIKE   *adj* resembling an ant

ANTLION   *n* pl. **-S** a predatory insect

ANTONYM   *n* pl. **-S** a word opposite in meaning to another

ANTONYMY   *n* pl. **-MIES** the state of being an antonym

ANTRA   a pl. of antrum

ANTRAL   *adj* pertaining to an antrum

ANTRE   *n* pl. **-S** a cave (a hollow place in the earth)

ANTRORSE   *adj* directed forward or upward

ANTRUM   *n* pl. **-TRUMS** or **-TRA** a cavity in a bone

ANTSY   *adj* **-SIER, -SIEST** fidgety

ANURA   *n/pl* frogs and toads

ANURAL   *adj* anurous

ANURAN   *n* pl. **-S** a frog or toad

ANURESIS   *n* pl. **-RESES** inability to urinate **ANURETIC** *adj*

ANURIA   *n* pl. **-S** absence of urine **ANURIC** *adj*

ANUROUS   *adj* having no tail

ANUS   *n* pl. **-ES** the excretory opening at the end of the alimentary canal

ANVIL   *v* **-VILED, -VILING, -VILS** or **-VILLED, -VILLING, -VILS** to shape on an anvil (a heavy iron block)

ANVILTOP   *n* pl. **-S** an anvil-shaped cloud mass

ANXIETY   *n* pl. **-ETIES** painful or apprehensive uneasiness of mind

ANXIOUS   *adj* full of anxiety

ANY   *adj* one, no matter which

ANYBODY   *n* pl. **-BODIES** a person of some importance

ANYHOW   *adv* in any way

ANYMORE   *adv* at the present time

ANYON   *n* pl. **-S** a subatomic particle

ANYONE   *pron* any person

ANYPLACE   *adv* in any place

ANYTHING   *n* pl. **-S** a thing of any kind

ANYTIME   *adv* at any time

ANYWAY   *adv* in any way

ANYWAYS   *adv* anyway

ANYWHERE   *n* pl. **-S** any place

ANYWISE   *adv* in any way

AORIST   *n* pl. **-S** a verb tense **AORISTIC** *adj*

AORTA   *n* pl. **-TAS** or **-TAE** a main artery **AORTAL, AORTIC** *adj*

AOUDAD   *n* pl. **-S** a wild sheep

APACE   *adv* swiftly

APACHE *n* pl. **-S** a Parisian gangster

APAGOGE *n* pl. **-S** establishment of a thesis by showing its contrary to be absurd **APAGOGIC** *adj*

APANAGE *n* pl. **-S** appanage

APAREJO *n* pl. **-JOS** a type of saddle

APART *adv* not together

APATETIC *adj* having coloration serving as natural camouflage

APATHY *n* pl. **-THIES** lack of emotion

APATITE *n* pl. **-S** a mineral

APE *v* **APED, APING, APES** to mimic

APEAK *adv* in a vertical position

APEEK *adv* apeak

APELIKE *adj* resembling an ape (a large, tailless primate)

APEMAN *n* pl. **-MEN** an extinct apelike primate

APER *n* pl. **-S** one that apes

APERCU *n* pl. **-S** a brief summary

APERIENT *n* pl. **-S** a mild laxative

APERITIF *n* pl. **-S** an alcoholic drink taken before a meal

APERTURE *n* pl. **-S** an opening

APERY *n* pl. **-ERIES** the act of aping

APETALY *n* pl. **-ALIES** the state of having no petals

APEX *n* pl. **APEXES** or **APICES** the highest point

APHAGIA *n* pl. **-S** inability to swallow

APHANITE *n* pl. **-S** an igneous rock

APHASIA *n* pl. **-S** loss of the ability to use words

APHASIAC *n* pl. **-S** one suffering from aphasia

APHASIC *n* pl. **-S** aphasiac

APHELION *n* pl. **-ELIONS** or **-ELIA** the point in a planetary orbit farthest from the sun **APHELIAN** *adj*

APHESIS *n* pl. **-ESES** the loss of an unstressed vowel from the beginning of a word **APHETIC** *adj*

APHID *n* pl. **-S** any of a family of small, soft-bodied insects

APHIDIAN *n* pl. **-S** an aphid

APHIS *n* pl. **APHIDES** an aphid

APHOLATE *n* pl. **-S** a chemical used to control houseflies

APHONIA *n* pl. **-S** loss of voice

APHONIC *n* pl. **-S** one affected with aphonia

APHONY *n* pl. **-NIES** aphonia

APHORISE *v* **-RISED, -RISING, -RISES** to aphorize

APHORISM *n* pl. **-S** a brief statement of a truth or principle

APHORIST *n* pl. **-S** one that aphorizes

APHORIZE *v* **-RIZED, -RIZING, -RIZES** to write or speak in aphorisms

APHOTIC *adj* lacking light

APHTHA *n* pl. **-THAE** a small blister in the mouth or stomach **APHTHOUS** *adj*

APHYLLY *n* pl. **-LIES** the state of being leafless

APIAN *adj* pertaining to bees

APIARIAN *n* pl. **-S** an apiarist

APIARIST *n* pl. **-S** a person who raises bees

APIARY *n* pl. **-ARIES** a place where bees are kept

APICAL *n* pl. **-S** a sound articulated with the apex (tip) of the tongue

APICALLY *adv* at or toward the apex

APICES a pl. of apex

APICULUS *n* pl. **-LI** a sharp point at the end of a leaf

APIECE *adv* for each one

APIMANIA *n* pl. **-S** an excessive interest in bees

APING present participle of ape

APIOLOGY *n* pl. **-GIES** the study of bees

APISH *adj* slavishly or foolishly imitative **APISHLY** *adv*

APLANAT *n* pl. **-S** a type of reflecting or refracting surface

APLASIA *n* pl. **-S** defective development of an organ or part

APLASTIC *adj* not plastic

APLENTY *adj* being in sufficient quantity

APLITE *n* pl. **-S** a fine-grained rock **APLITIC** *adj*

APLOMB *n* pl. **-S** self-confidence

APNEA *n* pl. **-S** temporary cessation of respiration **APNEAL, APNEIC** *adj*

APNOEA *n* pl. **-S** apnea **APNOEAL, APNOEIC** *adj*

APO *n* pl. **APOS** a type of protein

APOAPSIS *n* pl. **-APSIDES** or **-APSES** the high point in an orbit

APOCARP *n* pl. **-S** a fruit having separated carpels

APOCARPY   *n* pl. **-PIES** the state of being an apocarp

APOCOPE   *n* pl. **-S** an omission of the last sound of a word **APOCOPIC** *adj*

APOCRINE   *adj* pertaining to a type of gland

APOD   *n* pl. **-S** an apodal animal

APODAL   *adj* having no feet or footlike appendages

APODOSIS   *n* pl. **-OSES** the main clause of a conditional sentence

APODOUS   *adj* apodal

APOGAMY   *n* pl. **-MIES** a form of plant reproduction **APOGAMIC** *adj*

APOGEE   *n* pl. **-S** the point in the orbit of a body which is farthest from the earth **APOGEAL, APOGEAN, APOGEIC** *adj*

APOLLO   *n* pl. **-LOS** a handsome young man

APOLOG   *n* pl. **-S** apologue

APOLOGAL   *adj* pertaining to an apologue

APOLOGIA   *n* pl. **-GIAS** or **-GIAE** a formal justification or defense

APOLOGUE   *n* pl. **-S** an allegory

APOLOGY   *n* pl. **-GIES** an expression of regret for some error or offense

APOLUNE   *n* pl. **-S** the point in the orbit of a body which is farthest from the moon

APOMICT   *n* pl. **-S** an organism produced by apomixis

APOMIXIS   *n* pl. **-MIXES** a type of reproductive process

APOPHONY   *n* pl. **-NIES** ablaut

APOPHYGE   *n* pl. **-S** a concave curve in a column

APOPLEXY   *n* pl. **-PLEXIES** a sudden loss of sensation and muscular control

APORIA   *n* pl. **-S** an expression of doubt for rhetorical effect

APORT   *adv* on or toward the left side of a ship

APOSPORY   *n* pl. **-RIES** a type of reproduction without spore formation

APOSTACY   *n* pl. **-CIES** apostasy

APOSTASY   *n* pl. **-SIES** an abandonment of one's faith or principles

APOSTATE   *n* pl. **-S** one who commits apostasy

APOSTIL   *n* pl. **-S** a marginal note

APOSTLE   *n* pl. **-S** a disciple sent forth by Christ to preach the gospel

APOTHECE   *n* pl. **-S** a spore-producing organ of certain fungi

APOTHEGM   *n* pl. **-S** a maxim

APOTHEM   *n* pl. **-S** the perpendicular from the center to any side of a regular polygon

APP   *n* pl. **-S** a computer program for a major task

APPAL   *v* **-PALLED, -PALLING, -PALS** to appall

APPALL   *v* **-ED, -ING, -S** to fill with horror or dismay

APPANAGE   *n* pl. **-S** land or revenue granted to a member of a royal family

APPARAT   *n* pl. **-S** a political organization

APPAREL   *v* **-ELED, -ELING, -ELS** or **-ELLED, -ELLING, -ELS** to provide with outer garments

APPARENT   *adj* easily seen

APPEAL   *v* **-ED, -ING, -S** to make an earnest request

APPEALER   *n* pl. **-S** one that appeals

APPEAR   *v* **-ED, -ING, -S** to come into view

APPEASE   *v* **-PEASED, -PEASING, -PEASES** to bring to a state of peace or contentment

APPEASER   *n* pl. **-S** one that appeases

APPEL   *n* pl. **-S** a feint in fencing

APPELLEE   *n* pl. **-S** the defendant in a type of judicial proceeding

APPELLOR   *n* pl. **-S** a confessed criminal who accuses an accomplice

APPEND   *v* **-ED, -ING, -S** to add as a supplement

APPENDIX   *n* pl. **-DIXES** or **-DICES** a collection of supplementary material at the end of a book

APPESTAT   *n* pl. **-S** the mechanism in the central nervous system that regulates appetite

APPETENT   *adj* marked by strong desire

APPETITE   *n* pl. **-S** a desire for food or drink

APPLAUD   *v* **-ED, -ING, -S** to express approval by clapping the hands

APPLAUSE   *n* pl. **-S** the sound made by persons applauding

APPLE   *n* pl. **-S** an edible fruit

APPLET   *n* pl. **-S** a computer program for a simple task

APPLEY   *adj* **APPLIER, APPLIEST** resembling or suggestive of an apple

APPLIED past tense of apply

APPLIER n pl. **-S** one that applies

APPLIQUE v **-QUED, -QUEING, -QUES** to apply as a decoration to a larger surface

APPLY v **-PLIED, -PLYING, -PLIES** to bring into contact with something

APPOINT v **-ED, -ING, -S** to name or assign to a position or office

APPOSE v **-POSED, -POSING, -POSES** to place side by side

APPOSER n pl. **-S** one that apposes

APPOSITE adj relevant

APPRAISE v **-PRAISED, -PRAISING, -PRAISES** to set a value on

APPRESS v **-ED, -ING, -ES** to press close to something else

APPRISE v **-PRISED, -PRISING, -PRISES** to notify

APPRISER n pl. **-S** one that apprises

APPRIZE v **-PRIZED, -PRIZING, -PRIZES** to appraise

APPRIZER n pl. **-S** one that apprizes

APPROACH v **-ED, -ING, -ES** to come near or nearer to

APPROVAL n pl. **-S** the act of approving

APPROVE v **-PROVED, -PROVING, -PROVES** to regard favorably

APPROVER n pl. **-S** one that approves

APPULSE n pl. **-S** the approach of one moving body toward another

APRAXIA n pl. **-S** loss of the ability to perform coordinated movements **APRACTIC, APRAXIC** adj

APRES prep after

APRICOT n pl. **-S** an edible fruit

APRON v **-ED, -ING, -S** to provide with an apron (a garment worn to protect one's clothing)

APROPOS adj relevant

APROTIC adj being a type of solvent

APSE n pl. **-S** a domed, semicircular projection of a building **APSIDAL** adj

APSIS n pl. **-SIDES** an apse

APT adj **APTER, APTEST** suitable

APTERAL adj apterous

APTERIUM n pl. **-RIA** a bare area of skin between feathers

APTEROUS adj having no wings

APTERYX n pl. **-ES** the kiwi

APTITUDE n pl. **-S** an ability

APTLY adv in an apt manner

APTNESS n pl. **-ES** the quality of being apt

APYRASE n pl. **-S** an enzyme

APYRETIC adj having no fever

AQUA n pl. **AQUAS** or **AQUAE** water (a transparent, tasteless, odorless liquid)

AQUACADE n pl. **-S** a swimming and diving exhibition

AQUAFARM v **-ED, -ING, -S** to cultivate food fish

AQUAFIT n pl. **-S** an exercise class in water

AQUANAUT n pl. **-S** a scuba diver trained to live in underwater installations

AQUARIA a pl. of aquarium

AQUARIAL adj pertaining to an aquarium

AQUARIAN n pl. **-S** a member of the old sects that used water rather than wine in religious ceremonies

AQUARIST n pl. **-S** one who keeps an aquarium

AQUARIUM n pl. **-IUMS** or **-IA** a water-filled enclosure in which aquatic animals are kept

AQUATIC n pl. **-S** an organism living or growing in or near water

AQUATINT v **-ED, -ING, -S** to etch, using a certain process

AQUATONE n pl. **-S** a type of printing process

AQUAVIT n pl. **-S** a Scandinavian liquor

AQUEDUCT n pl. **-S** a water conduit

AQUEOUS adj pertaining to water

AQUIFER n pl. **-S** a water-bearing rock formation

AQUILINE adj curving like an eagle's beak

AQUIVER adj quivering

AR n pl. **-S** the letter R

ARABESK n pl. **-S** a design of intertwined floral figures

ARABIC adj derived from gum arabic

ARABICA n pl. **-S** an evergreen shrub that produces coffee beans

ARABIS n pl. **-ES** a mat-forming plant

ARABIZE v **-IZED, -IZING, -IZES** to cause to acquire Arabic customs

ARABLE n pl. **-S** land suitable for cultivation

ARACEOUS adj belonging to the arum family of plants

ARACHNID	*n* pl. **-S** any of a class of segmented invertebrate animals
ARAK	*n* pl. **-S** arrack
ARAME	*n* pl. **-S** an edible seaweed
ARAMID	*n* pl. **-S** a type of chemical compound
ARANEID	*n* pl. **-S** a spider
ARAPAIMA	*n* pl. **-S** a large food fish
ARAROBA	*n* pl. **-S** a Brazilian tree
ARB	*n* pl. **-S** a type of stock trader
ARBALEST	*n* pl. **-S** a type of crossbow
ARBALIST	*n* pl. **-S** arbalest
ARBELEST	*n* pl. **-S** arbalest
ARBITER	*n* pl. **-S** one chosen or appointed to judge a disputed issue **ARBITRAL** *adj*
ARBOR	*n* pl. **-ES** a tree when contrasted with a shrub
ARBOR	*n* pl. **-S** a shady garden shelter
ARBOREAL	*adj* living in trees
ARBORED	*adj* having trees
ARBORETA	*n/pl* places for the study and exhibition of trees
ARBORIST	*n* pl. **-S** a tree specialist
ARBORIZE	*v* **-IZED, -IZING, -IZES** to form many branches
ARBOROUS	*adj* pertaining to trees
ARBOUR	*n* pl. **-S** a shady garden shelter **ARBOURED** *adj*
ARBUSCLE	*n* pl. **-S** a dwarf tree
ARBUTE	*n* pl. **-S** an evergreen tree **ARBUTEAN** *adj*
ARBUTUS	*n* pl. **-ES** an evergreen tree
ARC	*v* **ARCED, ARCING, ARCS** or **ARCKED, ARCKING, ARCS** to move in a curved course
ARCADE	*v* **-CADED, -CADING, -CADES** to provide with an arcade (a series of arches)
ARCADIA	*n* pl. **-S** a region of simple pleasure and quiet
ARCADIAN	*n* pl. **-S** one who lives in an arcadia
ARCADING	*n* pl. **-S** an arcade
ARCANE	*adj* mysterious **ARCANELY** *adv*
ARCANUM	*n* pl. **-NUMS** or **-NA** a mystery
ARCATURE	*n* pl. **-S** a small arcade
ARCH	*v* **-ED, -ING, -ES** to bend like an arch (a curved structure spanning an opening)
ARCHAEA	*n/pl* a large group of microorganisms **ARCHAEAL** *adj*
ARCHAEAN	*n* pl. **-S** a microorganism of the archaea
ARCHAEON	*n* pl. **-CHAEA** archaean
ARCHAIC	*adj* pertaining to an earlier time
ARCHAISE	*v* **-ISED, -ISING, -ISES** to archaize
ARCHAISM	*n* pl. **-S** an archaic word, idiom, or expression
ARCHAIST	*n* pl. **-S** one that archaizes
ARCHAIZE	*v* **-IZED, -IZING, -IZES** to use archaisms
ARCHDUKE	*n* pl. **-S** an Austrian prince
ARCHER	*n* pl. **-S** one that shoots with a bow and arrow
ARCHERY	*n* pl. **-CHERIES** the sport of shooting with a bow and arrow
ARCHFOE	*n* pl. **-S** a principal foe
ARCHI	pl. of arco
ARCHIL	*n* pl. **-S** orchil
ARCHINE	*n* pl. **-S** a Russian unit of linear measure
ARCHING	*n* pl. **-S** a series of arches
ARCHIVE	*v* **-CHIVED, -CHIVING, -CHIVES** to file in an archive (a place where records are kept) **ARCHIVAL** *adj*
ARCHLY	*adv* slyly
ARCHNESS	*n* pl. **-ES** slyness
ARCHON	*n* pl. **-S** a magistrate of ancient Athens
ARCHWAY	*n* pl. **-WAYS** a passageway under an arch
ARCIFORM	*adj* having the form of an arch
ARCING	*n* pl. **-S** the curved form of an arc
ARCKED	a past tense of arc
ARCKING	a present participle of arc
ARCO	*n* pl, **ARCHI** a note or passage played with the bow of stringed instruments
ARCSINE	*n* pl. **-S** the inverse function to the sine
ARCTIC	*n* pl. **-S** a warm, waterproof overshoe
ARCUATE	*adj* curved like a bow
ARCUATED	*adj* arcuate
ARCUS	*n* pl. **-ES** an arch-shaped cloud
ARDEB	*n* pl. **-S** an Egyptian unit of capacity
ARDENCY	*n* pl. **-CIES** ardor

ARDENT *adj* characterized by intense emotion **ARDENTLY** *adv*

ARDOR *n* pl. **-S** intensity of emotion

ARDOUR *n* pl. **-S** ardor

ARDUOUS *adj* involving great labor or hardship

ARE *n* pl. **-S** a unit of surface measure

AREA *n* pl. **-S** a particular extent of space or surface **AREAL** *adj* **AREALLY** *adv*

AREA *n* pl. **AREAE** a section of the cerebral cortex having a specific function

AREAWAY *n* pl. **-WAYS** a sunken area leading to a basement entrance

ARECA *n* pl. **-S** a tropical tree

AREG *n/pl* areas of shifting desert sand dunes

AREIC *adj* pertaining to a region of the earth contributing little surface drainage

ARENA *n* pl. **-S** an enclosed area for contests

ARENE *n* pl. **-S** an aromatic compound

ARENITE *n* pl. **-S** rock made up chiefly of sand grains

ARENOSE *adj* sandy

ARENOUS *adj* arenose

AREOLA *n* pl. **-LAS** or **-LAE** a small space in a network of leaf veins **AREOLAR, AREOLATE** *adj*

AREOLE *n* pl. **-S** areola

AREOLOGY *n* pl. **-GIES** the study of the planet Mars

AREPA *n* pl. **-S** a cornmeal cake

ARETE *n* pl. **-S** a sharp mountain ridge

ARETHUSA *n* pl. **-S** a flowering plant

ARF *n* pl. **-S** a barking sound

ARGAL *n* pl. **-S** argol

ARGALA *n* pl. **-S** a type of stork

ARGALI *n* pl. **-S** a wild sheep

ARGENT *n* pl. **-S** silver **ARGENTAL, ARGENTIC** *adj*

ARGENTUM *n* pl. **-S** silver

ARGH *interj* aargh

ARGIL *n* pl. **-S** a white clay

ARGINASE *n* pl. **-S** an enzyme

ARGININE *n* pl. **-S** an amino acid

ARGLE *v* **-GLED, -GLING, -GLES** to argue

ARGOL *n* pl. **-S** a crust deposited in wine casks during aging

ARGON *n* pl. **-S** a gaseous element

ARGONAUT *n* pl. **-S** a marine mollusk

ARGOSY *n* pl. **-SIES** a large merchant ship

ARGOT *n* pl. **-S** a specialized vocabulary **ARGOTIC** *adj*

ARGUABLE *adj* capable of being argued about **ARGUABLY** *adv*

ARGUE *v* **-GUED, -GUING, -GUES** to present reasons for or against

ARGUER *n* pl. **-S** one that argues

ARGUFIER *n* pl. **-S** one that argufies

ARGUFY *v* **-FIED, -FYING, -FIES** to argue stubbornly

ARGUING present participle of argue

ARGUMENT *n* pl. **-S** a discussion involving differing points of view

ARGUS *n* pl. **-ES** an East Indian pheasant

ARGYLE *n* pl. **-S** a knitting pattern

ARGYLL *n* pl. **-S** argyle

ARHAT *n* pl. **-S** a Buddhist who has attained nirvana

ARIA *n* pl. **-S** an elaborate melody for a single voice

ARIARY *n* pl. **ARIARY** a monetary unit of Madagascar

ARID *adj* **-IDER, -IDEST** extremely dry **ARIDLY** *adv*

ARIDITY *n* pl. **-TIES** the state of being arid

ARIDNESS *n* pl. **-ES** aridity

ARIEL *n* pl. **-S** an African gazelle

ARIETTA *n* pl. **-S** a short aria

ARIETTE *n* pl. **-S** arietta

ARIGHT *adv* rightly; correctly

ARIL *n* pl. **-S** an outer covering of certain seeds **ARILED, ARILLATE, ARILLOID** *adj*

ARILLODE *n* pl. **-S** a type of aril

ARIOSE *adj* characterized by melody

ARIOSO *n* pl. **-SOS** or **-SI** a musical passage resembling an aria

ARISE *v* **AROSE, ARISEN, ARISING, ARISES** to get up

ARISTA *n* pl. **-TAS** or **-TAE** a bristlelike structure or appendage **ARISTATE** *adj*

ARISTO *n* pl. **-TOS** an aristocrat

ARK *n* pl. **-S** a large boat

ARKOSE   n pl. **-S** a type of sandstone **ARKOSIC** adj

ARLES   n/pl money paid to bind a bargain

ARM   v **-ED, -ING, -S** to supply with weapons

ARMADA   n pl. **-S** a fleet of warships

ARMAGNAC   n pl. **-S** a French brandy

ARMAMENT   n pl. **-S** a military force equipped for war

ARMATURE   v **-TURED, -TURING, -TURES** to furnish with armor

ARMBAND   n pl. **-S** a band worn around an arm (an upper appendage of the human body)

ARMCHAIR   n pl. **-S** a chair with armrests

ARMER   n pl. **-S** one that arms

ARMET   n pl. **-S** a medieval helmet

ARMFUL   n pl. **ARMFULS** or **ARMSFUL** as much as the arm can hold

ARMGUARD   n pl. **-S** a covering to protect the arm

ARMHOLE   n pl. **-S** an opening for the arm in a garment

ARMIES   pl. of army

ARMIGER   n pl. **-S** one who carries the armor of a knight

ARMIGERO   n pl. **-GEROS** armiger

ARMILLA   n pl. **-LAS** or **-LAE** a thin membrane around the stem of certain fungi

ARMING   n pl. **-S** the act of one that arms

ARMLESS   adj having no arms

ARMLET   n pl. **-S** an armband

ARMLIKE   adj resembling an arm

ARMLOAD   n pl. **-S** an armful

ARMLOCK   n pl. **-S** a hold in wrestling

ARMOIRE   n pl. **-S** a large, ornate cabinet

ARMONICA   n pl. **-S** a type of musical instrument

ARMOR   v **-ED, -ING, -S** to furnish with armor (a defensive covering)

ARMORER   n pl. **-S** one that makes or repairs armor

ARMORIAL   n pl. **-S** a treatise on heraldry

ARMORY   n pl. **-MORIES** a place where weapons are stored

ARMOUR   v **-ED, -ING, -S** to armor

ARMOURER   n pl. **-S** armorer

ARMOURY   n pl. **-MOURIES** armory

ARMPIT   n pl. **-S** the hollow under the arm at the shoulder

ARMREST   n pl. **-S** a support for the arm

ARMSFUL   a pl. of armful

ARMURE   n pl. **-S** a woven fabric

ARMY   n pl. **-MIES** a large body of men trained and armed for war

ARMYWORM   n pl. **-S** a destructive moth larva

ARNATTO   n pl. **-TOS** annatto

ARNICA   n pl. **-S** a perennial herb

ARNOTTO   n pl. **-TOS** a tropical tree

AROID   n pl. **-S** a flowering plant

AROINT   v **-ED, -ING, -S** to drive away

AROMA   n pl. **-S** a pleasant odor

AROMATIC   n pl. **-S** a fragrant plant or substance

AROSE   past tense of arise

AROUND   prep on all sides of

AROUSAL   n pl. **-S** the act of arousing

AROUSE   v **AROUSED, AROUSING, AROUSES** to stimulate

AROUSER   n pl. **-S** one that arouses

AROYNT   v **-ED, -ING, -S** to aroint

ARPEGGIO   n pl. **-GIOS** a technique of playing a musical chord

ARPEN   n pl. **-S** arpent

ARPENT   n pl. **-S** an old French unit of area

ARQUEBUS   n pl. **-ES** an early portable firearm

ARRACK   n pl. **-S** an Oriental liquor

ARRAIGN   v **-ED, -ING, -S** to call before a court of law to answer an indictment

ARRANGE   v **-RANGED, -RANGING, -RANGES** to put in definite or proper order

ARRANGER   n pl. **-S** one that arranges

ARRANT   adj outright **ARRANTLY** adv

ARRAS   n pl. **-ES** a tapestry **ARRASED** adj

ARRAY   v **-ED, -ING, -S** to place in proper or desired order

ARRAYAL   n pl. **-S** the act of arraying

ARRAYER   n pl. **-S** one that arrays

ARREAR   n pl. **-S** an unpaid and overdue debt

ARREST   v **-ED, -ING, -S** to seize and hold by legal authority

ARRESTEE   n pl. **-S** one that is arrested

ARRESTER   n pl. **-S** one that arrests

ARRESTOR	*n* pl. **-S** arrester
ARRHIZAL	*adj* rootless
ARRIBA	*interj* — used to express pleasure
ARRIS	*n* pl. **-RISES** a ridge formed by the meeting of two surfaces
ARRIVAL	*n* pl. **-S** the act of arriving
ARRIVE	*v* **-RIVED, -RIVING, -RIVES** to reach a destination
ARRIVER	*n* pl. **-S** one that arrives
ARROBA	*n* pl. **-S** a Spanish unit of weight
ARROGANT	*adj* overly convinced of one's own worth or importance
ARROGATE	*v* **-GATED, -GATING, -GATES** to claim or take without right
ARROW	*v* **-ED, -ING, -S** to indicate the proper position of with an arrow (a linear figure with a wedge-shaped end)
ARROWY	*adj* moving swiftly
ARROYO	*n* pl. **-ROYOS** a brook or creek
ARROZ	*n* pl. **ARROCES** or **ARROZES** rice
ARSENAL	*n* pl. **-S** a collection or supply of weapons
ARSENATE	*n* pl. **-S** a chemical salt
ARSENIC	*n* pl. **-S** a metallic element
ARSENIDE	*n* pl. **-S** an arsenic compound
ARSENITE	*n* pl. **-S** a chemical salt
ARSENO	*adj* containing a certain bivalent chemical radical
ARSENOUS	*adj* pertaining to arsenic
ARSES	pl. of arsis
ARSHIN	*n* pl. **-S** archine
ARSINE	*n* pl. **-S** a poisonous gas
ARSINO	*adj* containing a certain univalent chemical radical
ARSIS	*n* pl. **ARSES** the unaccented part of a musical measure
ARSON	*n* pl. **-S** the malicious or fraudulent burning of property **ARSONOUS** *adj*
ARSONIST	*n* pl. **-S** one that commits arson
ART	*n* pl. **-S** an esthetically pleasing and meaningful arrangement of elements
ARTAL	a pl. of rotl
ARTEFACT	*n* pl. **-S** artifact
ARTEL	*n* pl. **-S** a collective farm in Russia
ARTERIAL	*n* pl. **-S** a type of highway
ARTERY	*n* pl. **-TERIES** a vessel that carries blood away from the heart
ARTESIAN	*adj* pertaining to a type of well
ARTFUL	*adj* crafty **ARTFULLY** *adv*
ARTICLE	*v* **-CLED, -CLING, -CLES** to charge with specific offenses
ARTIER	comparative of arty
ARTIEST	superlative of arty
ARTIFACT	*n* pl. **-S** an object made by man
ARTIFICE	*n* pl. **-S** a clever stratagem
ARTIGI	*n* pl. **-S** atigi
ARTILY	*adv* in an arty manner
ARTINESS	*n* pl. **-ES** the quality of being arty
ARTISAN	*n* pl. **-S** a trained or skilled workman
ARTIST	*n* pl. **-S** one who practices one of the fine arts
ARTISTE	*n* pl. **-S** a skilled public performer
ARTISTIC	*adj* characteristic of art
ARTISTRY	*n* pl. **-RIES** artistic quality or workmanship
ARTLESS	*adj* lacking cunning or guile
ARTMAKER	*n* pl. **-S** one that produces art
ARTSIE	*n* pl. **-S** a student in an arts program
ARTSY	*adj* **-SIER, -SIEST** arty
ARTWORK	*n* pl. **-S** illustrative or decorative work in printed matter
ARTY	*adj* **ARTIER, ARTIEST** showily or pretentiously artistic
ARUGOLA	*n* pl. **-S** arugula
ARUGULA	*n* pl. **-S** a European annual herb
ARUM	*n* pl. **-S** a flowering plant
ARUSPEX	*n* pl. **-PICES** haruspex
ARVAL	*adj* pertaining to plowed land
ARVO	*n* pl. **-VOS** afternoon
ARYL	*n* pl. **-S** a univalent radical
ARYTHMIA	*n* pl. **-S** an irregularity in the rhythm of the heartbeat **ARYTHMIC** *adj*
AS	*adv* to the same degree
ASANA	*n* pl. **-S** a posture in yoga
ASARUM	*n* pl. **-S** a perennial herb
ASBESTOS	*n* pl. **-ES** a mineral **ASBESTIC** *adj*
ASBESTUS	*n* pl. **-ES** asbestos
ASCARED	*adj* afraid
ASCARID	*n* pl. **-S** a parasitic worm
ASCARIS	*n* pl. **-RISES** or **-RIDES** ascarid

ASCEND   *v* **-ED, -ING, -S** to go or move upward

ASCENDER   *n* pl. **-S** one that ascends

ASCENT   *n* pl. **-S** the act of ascending

ASCESIS   *n* pl. **-CESES** the conduct of an ascetic

ASCETIC   *n* pl. **-S** one who practices extreme self-denial for religious reasons

ASCI   pl. of ascus

ASCIDIAN   *n* pl. **-S** a small marine animal

ASCIDIUM   *n* pl. **-DIA** a flask-shaped plant appendage

ASCITES   *n* pl. **ASCITES** accumulation of serous fluid in the abdomen **ASCITIC** *adj*

ASCOCARP   *n* pl. **-S** a spore-producing organ of certain fungi

ASCON   *n* pl. **-S** a type of sponge **ASCONOID** *adj*

ASCORBIC   *adj* relieving scurvy

ASCOT   *n* pl. **-S** a broad neck scarf

ASCRIBE   *v* **-CRIBED, -CRIBING, -CRIBES** to attribute to a specified cause, source, or origin

ASCUS   *n* pl. **ASCI** a spore sac in certain fungi

ASDIC   *n* pl. **-S** sonar

ASEA   *adv* at sea

ASEISMIC   *adj* not subject to earthquakes

ASEPSIS   *n* pl. **-SEPSES** the condition of being aseptic

ASEPTIC   *adj* free from germs

ASEXUAL   *adj* occurring or performed without sexual action

ASH   *v* **-ED, -ING, -ES** to convert into ash (the residue of a substance that has been burned)

ASHAMED   *adj* feeling shame, guilt, or disgrace

ASHCAKE   *n* pl. **-S** a cornmeal cake

ASHCAN   *n* pl. **-S** a metal receptacle for garbage

ASHEN   *adj* consisting of ashes

ASHFALL   *n* pl. **-S** a deposit of volcanic ash

ASHIER   comparative of ashy

ASHIEST   superlative of ashy

ASHINE   *adj* shining

ASHINESS   *n* pl. **-ES** the condition of being ashy

ASHLAR   *v* **-ED, -ING, -S** to build with squared stones

ASHLER   *v* **-ED, -ING, -S** to ashlar

ASHLESS   *adj* having no ashes

ASHMAN   *n* pl. **-MEN** one who collects and removes ashes

ASHORE   *adv* toward or on the shore

ASHPAN   *n* pl. **-S** a tray under a grate to catch the ashes

ASHPLANT   *n* pl. **-S** a walking stick

ASHRAM   *n* pl. **-S** a secluded dwelling of a Hindu sage

ASHRAMA   *n* pl. **-S** a stage of life in Hinduism

ASHTANGA   *n* pl. **-S** a type of yoga

ASHTRAY   *n* pl. **-TRAYS** a receptacle for tobacco ashes

ASHY   *adj* **ASHIER, ASHIEST** covered with ashes

ASIDE   *n* pl. **-S** a comment by an actor intended to be heard by the audience but not the other actors

ASININE   *adj* obstinately stupid or silly

ASK   *v* **-ED, -ING, -S** to put a question to

ASKANCE   *adv* with a side glance

ASKANT   *adv* askance

ASKARI   *n* pl. **-S** a soldier or police officer of eastern Africa

ASKER   *n* pl. **-S** one that asks

ASKESIS   *n* pl. **ASKESES** ascesis

ASKEW   *adv* to one side

ASKING   *n* pl. **-S** the act of one who asks

ASKOS   *n* pl. **ASKOI** an oil jar used in ancient Greece

ASLANT   *adj* slanting

ASLEEP   *adj* sleeping

ASLOPE   *adj* sloping

ASLOSH   *adj* covered with water

ASOCIAL   *n* pl. **-S** one that avoids the company of others

ASP   *n* pl. **-S** a venomous snake

ASPARKLE   *adj* sparkling

ASPECT   *n* pl. **-S** appearance of something to the eye or mind

ASPEN   *n* pl. **-S** any of several poplars

ASPER   *n* pl. **-S** a Turkish money of account

ASPERATE   *v* **-ATED, -ATING, -ATES** to make uneven

ASPERGES   *n* pl. **ASPERGES** a Roman Catholic rite

ASPERITY _n_ pl. **-TIES** acrimony

ASPERSE _v_ **-PERSED, -PERSING, -PERSES** to spread false charges against

ASPERSER _n_ pl. **-S** one that asperses

ASPERSOR _n_ pl. **-S** asperser

ASPHALT _v_ **-ED, -ING, -S** to coat with asphalt (a substance used for paving and roofing)

ASPHERIC _adj_ varying slightly from an exactly spherical shape

ASPHODEL _n_ pl. **-S** a flowering plant

ASPHYXIA _n_ pl. **-S** unconsciousness caused by lack of oxygen

ASPHYXY _n_ pl. **-PHYXIES** asphyxia

ASPIC _n_ pl. **-S** the asp

ASPIRANT _n_ pl. **-S** one that aspires

ASPIRATA _n_ pl. **-TAE** a type of plosive

ASPIRATE _v_ **-RATED, -RATING, -RATES** to pronounce with an initial release of breath

ASPIRE _v_ **-PIRED, -PIRING, -PIRES** to have an earnest desire or ambition

ASPIRER _n_ pl. **-S** an aspirant

ASPIRIN _n_ pl. **-S** a pain reliever

ASPIRING present participle of aspire

ASPIS _n_ pl. **-PISES** aspic

ASPISH _adj_ resembling an asp

ASPRAWL _adj_ sprawling

ASQUINT _adv_ with a sidelong glance

ASRAMA _n_ pl. **-S** ashram

ASS _n_ pl. **-ES** a hoofed mammal

ASSAGAI _v_ **-GAIED, -GAIING, -GAIS** to pierce with a light spear

ASSAI _n_ pl. **-S** a tropical tree

ASSAIL _v_ **-ED, -ING, -S** to attack

ASSAILER _n_ pl. **-S** one that assails

ASSASSIN _n_ pl. **-S** a murderer

ASSAULT _v_ **-ED, -ING, -S** to attack

ASSAY _v_ **-ED, -ING, -S** to attempt

ASSAYER _n_ pl. **-S** one that assays

ASSEGAI _v_ **-GAIED, -GAIING, -GAIS** to assagai

ASSEMBLE _v_ **-BLED, -BLING, -BLES** to come or bring together

ASSEMBLY _n_ pl. **-BLIES** the act of assembling

ASSENT _v_ **-ED, -ING, -S** to express agreement

ASSENTER _n_ pl. **-S** one that assents

ASSENTOR _n_ pl. **-S** assenter

ASSERT _v_ **-ED, -ING, -S** to state positively

ASSERTER _n_ pl. **-S** one that asserts

ASSERTOR _n_ pl. **-S** asserter

ASSESS _v_ **-ED, -ING, -ES** to estimate the value of for taxation

ASSESSOR _n_ pl. **-S** one that assesses

ASSET _n_ pl. **-S** a useful quality or thing

ASSIGN _v_ **-ED, -ING, -S** to set apart for a particular purpose

ASSIGNAT _n_ pl. **-S** one of the notes issued as currency by the French revolutionary government

ASSIGNEE _n_ pl. **-S** one to whom property or right is legally transferred

ASSIGNER _n_ pl. **-S** one that assigns

ASSIGNOR _n_ pl. **-S** one who legally transfers property or right

ASSIST _v_ **-ED, -ING, -S** to give aid or support to

ASSISTER _n_ pl. **-S** one that assists

ASSISTOR _n_ pl. **-S** assister

ASSIZE _n_ pl. **-S** a session of a legislative or judicial body

ASSLIKE _adj_ resembling an ass

ASSOIL _v_ **-ED, -ING, -S** to pardon

ASSONANT _n_ pl. **-S** a word or syllable that resembles another in sound

ASSONATE _v_ **-NATED, -NATING, -NATES** to use a word or syllable that resembles another in sound

ASSORT _v_ **-ED, -ING, -S** to distribute into groups according to kind or class

ASSORTER _n_ pl. **-S** one that assorts

ASSUAGE _v_ **-SUAGED, -SUAGING, -SUAGES** to make less severe

ASSUAGER _n_ pl. **-S** one that assuages

ASSUME _v_ **-SUMED, -SUMING, -SUMES** to take on

ASSUMER _n_ pl. **-S** one that assumes

ASSURE _v_ **-SURED, -SURING, -SURES** to insure

ASSURED _n_ pl. **-S** an insured person

ASSURER _n_ pl. **-S** one that assures

ASSURING present participle of assure

ASSUROR _n_ pl. **-S** assurer

ASSWAGE _v_ **-SWAGED, -SWAGING, -SWAGES** to assuage

ASTANGA _n_ pl. **-S** ashtanga

ASTASIA   *n* pl. **-S** inability to stand resulting from muscular incoordination

ASTATIC   *adj* unstable

ASTATINE   *n* pl. **-S** a radioactive element

ASTER   *n* pl. **-S** a flowering plant

ASTERIA   *n* pl. **-S** a gemstone cut to exhibit asterism

ASTERISK   *v* **-ED, -ING, -S** to mark with an asterisk (a star-shaped printing mark)

ASTERISM   *n* pl. **-S** a property of certain minerals of showing a starlike luminous figure

ASTERN   *adv* at or toward the rear of a ship

ASTERNAL   *adj* not connected to the sternum

ASTEROID   *n* pl. **-S** a type of celestial body

ASTHANGA   *n* pl, **-S** ashtanga

ASTHENIA   *n* pl. **-S** lack of strength

ASTHENIC   *n* pl. **-S** a slender, lightly muscled person

ASTHENY   *n* pl. **-NIES** asthenia

ASTHMA   *n* pl. **-S** a respiratory disease

ASTIGMIA   *n* pl. **-S** a visual defect

ASTILBE   *n* pl. **-S** an Asian perennial

ASTIR   *adj* moving about

ASTOMOUS   *adj* having no stomata

ASTONISH   *v* **-ED, -ING, -ES** to fill with sudden wonder or surprise

ASTONY   *v* **-TONIED, -TONYING, -TONIES** to astonish

ASTOUND   *v* **-ED, -ING, -S** to amaze

ASTRAGAL   *n* pl. **-S** a convex molding

ASTRAL   *n* pl. **-S** a type of oil lamp

ASTRALLY   *adv* in a stellar manner

ASTRAY   *adv* off the right course

ASTRICT   *v* **-ED, -ING, -S** to restrict

ASTRIDE   *adv* with one leg on each side

ASTRINGE   *v* **-TRINGED, -TRINGING, -TRINGES** to bind or draw together

ASTUTE   *adj* shrewd **ASTUTELY** *adv*

ASTYLAR   *adj* having no columns

ASUNDER   *adv* into pieces

ASURA   *n* pl. **-S** a Hindu demon

ASWARM   *adj* swarming

ASWIM   *adj* swimming

ASWIRL   *adj* swirling

ASWOON   *adj* swooning

ASYLUM   *n* pl. **-LUMS** or **-LA** an institution for the care of the mentally ill

ASYNDETA   *n/pl* omissions of certain conjunctions

AT   *prep* in the position of

ATABAL   *n* pl. **-S** a type of drum

ATABRINE   *n* pl. **-S** a drug to treat malaria

ATACTIC   *adj* showing no regularity of structure

ATAGHAN   *n* pl. **-S** yataghan

ATALAYA   *n* pl. **-S** a watchtower

ATAMAN   *n* pl. **-S** a hetman

ATAMASCO   *n* pl. **-COS** a flowering plant

ATAP   *n* pl. **-S** the nipa palm tree

ATARAXIA   *n* pl. **-S** peace of mind

ATARAXIC   *n* pl. **-S** a tranquilizing drug

ATARAXY   *n* pl. **-RAXIES** ataraxia

ATAVIC   *adj* pertaining to a remote ancestor

ATAVISM   *n* pl. **-S** the reappearance of a genetic characteristic after several generations of absence

ATAVIST   *n* pl. **-S** an individual displaying atavism

ATAXIA   *n* pl. **-S** loss of muscular coordination

ATAXIC   *n* pl. **-S** one suffering from ataxia

ATAXY   *n* pl. **ATAXIES** ataxia

ATE   *n* pl. **-S** blind impulse or reckless ambition that drives one to ruin

ATECHNIC   *adj* lacking technical knowledge

ATELIC   *adj* pertaining to a type of verb form

ATELIER   *n* pl. **-S** a workshop or studio

ATEMOYA   *n* pl. **-S** a fruit of a hybrid tropical tree

ATENOLOL   *n* pl. **-S** a drug to treat hypertension

ATHANASY   *n* pl. **-SIES** immortality

ATHEISM   *n* pl. **-S** the belief that there is no God

ATHEIST   *n* pl. **-S** a believer in atheism

ATHELING   *n* pl. **-S** an Anglo-Saxon prince or nobleman

ATHENEUM   *n* pl. **-S** a literary institution

ATHEROMA   *n* pl. **-MAS** or **-MATA** a disease of the arteries

ATHETOID   *adj* affected with a type of nervous disorder

ATHIRST   *adj* having a strong desire

ATHLETE   *n* pl. **-S** one skilled in feats of physical strength and agility **ATHLETIC** *adj*

ATHODYD   *n* pl. **-S** a type of jet engine

ATHWART   *adv* from side to side

ATIGI   *n* pl. **-S** a type of Inuit parka

ATILT   *adj* being in a tilted position

ATINGLE   *adj* tingling

ATISHOO   *interj* ahchoo

ATLAS   *n* pl. **ATLASES** or **ATLANTES** a male figure used as a supporting column

ATLATL   *n* pl. **-S** a device for throwing a spear or dart

ATMA   *n* pl. **-S** atman

ATMAN   *n* pl. **-S** the individual soul in Hinduism

ATOLL   *n* pl. **-S** a coral island

ATOM   *n* pl. **-S** the smallest unit of an element **ATOMIC, ATOMICAL** *adj*

ATOMICS   *n/pl* the science dealing with atoms

ATOMIES   pl. of atomy

ATOMISE   *v* **-ISED, -ISING, -ISES** to atomize

ATOMISER   *n* pl. **-S** atomizer

ATOMISM   *n* pl. **-S** the theory that the universe is composed of simple, indivisible, minute particles

ATOMIST   *n* pl. **-S** an adherent of atomism

ATOMIZE   *v* **-IZED, -IZING, -IZES** to reduce to a fine spray

ATOMIZER   *n* pl. **-S** a device for atomizing liquids

ATOMY   *n* pl. **-MIES** a tiny particle

ATONAL   *adj* lacking tonality **ATONALLY** *adv*

ATONE   *v* **ATONED, ATONING, ATONES** to make amends or reparation **ATONABLE** *adj*

ATONER   *n* pl. **-S** one that atones

ATONIA   *n* pl. **-S** atony

ATONIC   *n* pl. **-S** an unaccented syllable or word

ATONING   present participle of atone

ATONY   *n* pl. **-NIES** muscular weakness

ATOP   *adj* being on or at the top

ATOPY   *n* pl. **-PIES** a type of allergy **ATOPIC** *adj*

ATRAZINE   *n* pl. **-S** an herbicide

ATREMBLE   *adj* trembling

ATRESIA   *n* pl. **-S** absence or closure of a natural bodily passage **ATRESIC, ATRETIC** *adj*

ATRIA   a pl. of atrium

ATRIAL   *adj* pertaining to an atrium

ATRIP   *adj* aweigh

ATRIUM   *n* pl. **ATRIUMS** or **ATRIA** the main room of an ancient Roman house

ATROCITY   *n* pl. **-TIES** a heinous act

ATROPHIA   *n* pl. **-S** a wasting away of the body or any of its parts **ATROPHIC** *adj*

ATROPHY   *v* **-PHIED, -PHYING, -PHIES** to waste away

ATROPIN   *n* pl. **-S** atropine

ATROPINE   *n* pl. **-S** a poisonous alkaloid

ATROPISM   *n* pl. **-S** atropine poisoning

ATT   *n* pl. **ATT** a monetary unit of Laos

ATTABOY   *n* pl. **-BOYS** an expression of encouragement or approval to a man or boy

ATTACH   *v* **-ED, -ING, -ES** to connect as an associated part

ATTACHE   *n* pl. **-S** a diplomatic official

ATTACHER   *n* pl. **-S** one that attaches

ATTACK   *v* **-ED, -ING, -S** to set upon violently

ATTACKER   *n* pl. **-S** one that attacks

ATTAGIRL   *interj* — used to express encouragement or approval to a woman or girl

ATTAIN   *v* **-ED, -ING, -S** to gain or achieve by mental or physical effort

ATTAINER   *n* pl. **-S** one that attains

ATTAINT   *v* **-ED, -ING, -S** to disgrace

ATTAR   *n* pl. **-S** a fragrant oil

ATTEMPER   *v* **-ED, -ING, -S** to modify the temperature of

ATTEMPT   *v* **-ED, -ING, -S** to make an effort to do or accomplish

ATTEND   *v* **-ED, -ING, -S** to be present at

ATTENDEE   *n* pl. **-S** an attender

ATTENDER   *n* pl. **-S** one that attends

ATTENT   *adj* heedful

ATTEST   *v* **-ED, -ING, -S** to affirm to be true or genuine

ATTESTER   *n* pl. **-S** one that attests

ATTESTOR   *n* pl. **-S** attester

ATTIC   *n* pl. **-S** a story or room directly below the roof of a house

ATTICISM — *n* pl. **-S** a concise and elegant expression

ATTICIST — *n* pl. **-S** one who uses atticisms

ATTICIZE — *v* **-CIZED, -CIZING, -CIZES** to use atticisms

ATTIRE — *v* **-TIRED, -TIRING, -TIRES** to clothe

ATTITUDE — *n* pl. **-S** a state of mind with regard to some matter

ATTORN — *v* **-ED, -ING, -S** to acknowledge a new owner as one's landlord

ATTORNEY — *n* pl. **-NEYS** a lawyer (a member of the legal profession)

ATTRACT — *v* **-ED, -ING, -S** to cause to approach or adhere

ATTRIT — *v* **-TRITTED, -TRITTING, -TRITS** to lose by attrition

ATTRITE — *v* **-TRITED, -TRITING, -TRITES** to attrit

ATTUNE — *v* **-TUNED, -TUNING, -TUNES** to bring into harmony

ATWAIN — *adv* in two

ATWEEN — *prep* between

ATWITTER — *adj* twittering

ATYPIC — *adj* atypical

ATYPICAL — *adj* not typical

AUBADE — *n* pl. **-S** a morning song

AUBERGE — *n* pl. **-S** an inn

AUBRETIA — *n* pl. **-S** aubrieta

AUBRIETA — *n* pl. **-S** a flowering plant

AUBURN — *n* pl. **-S** a reddish brown color

AUCTION — *v* **-ED, -ING, -S** to sell publicly to the highest bidder

AUCUBA — *n* pl. **-S** a shrub of the dogwood family

AUDACITY — *n* pl. **-TIES** boldness

AUDAD — *n* pl. **-S** aoudad

AUDIAL — *adj* aural

AUDIBLE — *v* **-BLED, -BLING, -BLES** to call a substitute play in football

AUDIBLY — *adv* in a way so as to be heard

AUDIENCE — *n* pl. **-S** a group of listeners or spectators

AUDIENT — *n* pl. **-S** one that hears

AUDILE — *n* pl. **-S** one whose mental imagery is chiefly auditory

AUDING — *n* pl. **-S** the process of hearing, recognizing, and interpreting a spoken language

AUDIO — *n* pl. **-DIOS** sound reception or transmission

AUDIT — *v* **-ED, -ING, -S** to examine with intent to verify

AUDITEE — *n* pl. **-S** one that is audited

AUDITION — *v* **-ED, -ING, -S** to give a trial performance

AUDITIVE — *n* pl. **-S** an auditory

AUDITOR — *n* pl. **-S** one that audits

AUDITORY — *n* pl. **-RIES** a group of listeners

AUGEND — *n* pl. **-S** a number to which another is to be added

AUGER — *n* pl. **-S** a tool for boring

AUGH — *interj* — used to express despair or frustration

AUGHT — *n* pl. **-S** a zero

AUGITE — *n* pl. **-S** a mineral **AUGITIC** *adj*

AUGMENT — *v* **-ED, -ING, -S** to increase

AUGUR — *v* **-ED, -ING, -S** to foretell from omens

AUGURAL — *adj* pertaining to augury

AUGURER — *n* pl. **-S** one that augurs

AUGURY — *n* pl. **-RIES** the practice of auguring

AUGUST — *adj* **-GUSTER, -GUSTEST** inspiring reverence or admiration **AUGUSTLY** *adv*

AUK — *n* pl. **-S** a diving seabird

AUKLET — *n* pl. **-S** a small auk

AULD — *adj* **AULDER, AULDEST** old

AULIC — *adj* pertaining to a royal court

AUMBRY — *n* pl. **-BRIES** ambry

AUNT — *n* pl. **-S** the sister of one's father or mother

AUNTHOOD — *n* pl. **-S** the state of being an aunt

AUNTIE — *n* pl. **-S** aunt

AUNTIES — pl. of aunty

AUNTLIKE — *adj* resembling an aunt

AUNTLY — *adj* **-LIER, -LIEST** of or suggesting an aunt

AUNTY — *n* pl. **AUNTIES** aunt

AURA — *n* pl. **-RAS** or **-RAE** an invisible emanation

AURAL — *adj* pertaining to the sense of hearing **AURALLY** *adv*

AURALITY — *n* pl. **-TIES** the quality of being aural

AURAR — pl. of eyrir

AURATE — *adj* having ears

AURATED *adj* aurate

AUREATE *adj* golden

AUREI pl. of aureus

AUREOLA *n* pl. **-LAS** or **-LAE** a halo

AUREOLE *v* **-OLED, -OLING, -OLES** to surround with a halo

AURES pl. of auris

AUREUS *n* pl. **-REI** a gold coin of ancient Rome

AURIC *adj* pertaining to gold

AURICLE *n* pl. **-S** an ear or ear-shaped part **AURICLED** *adj*

AURICULA *n* pl. **-LAS** or **-LAE** an auricle

AURIFORM *adj* ear-shaped

AURIS *n* pl. **AURES** the ear

AURIST *n* pl. **-S** a specialist in diseases of the ear

AUROCHS *n* pl. **-ES** an extinct European ox

AURORA *n* pl. **-RAS** or **-RAE** the rising light of the morning **AURORAL, AUROREAN** *adj*

AUROUS *adj* pertaining to gold

AURUM *n* pl. **-S** gold

AUSFORM *v* **-ED, -ING, -S** to subject steel to a strengthening process

AUSPEX *n* pl. **-PICES** a soothsayer of ancient Rome

AUSPICE *n* pl. **-S** a favorable omen

AUSTERE *adj* **-TERER, -TEREST** grave in disposition or appearance

AUSTRAL *n* pl. **-ES** or **-S** a former monetary unit of Argentina

AUSUBO *n* pl. **-BOS** a tropical tree

AUTACOID *n* pl. **-S** a hormone

AUTARCH *n* pl. **-S** an absolute ruler

AUTARCHY *n* pl. **-CHIES** absolute rule

AUTARKY *n* pl. **-KIES** national economic self-sufficiency **AUTARKIC** *adj*

AUTECISM *n* pl. **-S** the development of the entire life cycle of a parasitic fungus on a single host

AUTEUR *n* pl. **-S** the creator of a film

AUTHOR *v* **-ED, -ING, -S** to write

AUTISM *n* pl. **-S** extreme withdrawal into fantasy

AUTIST *n* pl. **-S** an autistic

AUTISTIC *n* pl. **-S** one who is affected with autism

AUTO *v* **-ED, -ING, -S** to ride in an automobile

AUTOBAHN *n* pl. **-BAHNS** or **-BAHNEN** a German superhighway

AUTOBODY *n* pl. **-BODIES** the shell of a motor vehicle

AUTOBUS *n* pl. **-BUSES** or **-BUSSES** a bus

AUTOCADE *n* pl. **-S** a parade of automobiles

AUTOCOID *n* pl. **-S** autacoid

AUTOCRAT *n* pl. **-S** an absolute ruler

AUTODIAL *v* **-DIALED, -DIALING, -DIALS** or **-DIALLED, -DIALLING, -DIALS** to dial a telephone number automatically

AUTODYNE *n* pl. **-S** a type of electrical circuit

AUTOGAMY *n* pl. **-MIES** fertilization of a flower by its own pollen

AUTOGENY *n* pl. **-NIES** the production of living organisms from inanimate matter

AUTOGIRO *n* pl. **-ROS** a type of airplane

AUTOGYRO *n* pl. **-ROS** autogiro

AUTOHARP *n* pl. **-S** a type of zither

AUTOLOAD *adj* self-loading

AUTOLYSE *v* **-LYSED, -LYSING, -LYSES** to autolyze

AUTOLYZE *v* **-LYZED, -LYZING, -LYZES** to break down tissue by the action of self-contained enzymes

AUTOMAN *n* pl. **-MEN** an automobile maker

AUTOMAT *n* pl. **-S** a type of cafeteria

AUTOMATA *n/pl* robots

AUTOMATE *v* **-MATED, -MATING, -MATES** to convert to a system of automatic control

AUTOMEN *n* pl. of automan

AUTONOMY *n* pl. **-MIES** the state of being self-governing

AUTONYM *n* pl. **-S** a name by which a people refers to itself

AUTOPEN *n* pl. **-S** a device for imitating signatures

AUTOPSIC *adj* pertaining to an autopsy

AUTOPSY *v* **-SIED, -SYING, -SIES** to examine a dead body to determine the cause of death

AUTOSOME *n* pl. **-S** a type of chromosome

AUTOTOMY *n* pl. **-MIES** the shedding of a damaged body part

AUTOTYPE *n* pl. **-S** a type of photographic process

AUTOTYPY *n* pl. **-TYPIES** autotype

AUTUMN	*n* pl. **-S** a season of the year **AUTUMNAL** *adj*
AUTUNITE	*n* pl. **-S** a mineral
AUXESIS	*n* pl. **AUXESES** an increase in cell size without cell division
AUXETIC	*n* pl. **-S** a substance that promotes auxesis
AUXIN	*n* pl. **-S** a substance used to regulate plant growth **AUXINIC** *adj*
AVA	*adv* at all
AVADAVAT	*n* pl. **-S** a small songbird
AVAIL	*v* **-ED, -ING, -S** to be of use or advantage to
AVANT	*adj* culturally or stylistically new
AVARICE	*n* pl. **-S** greed
AVAST	*interj* — used as a command to stop
AVATAR	*n* pl. **-S** the incarnation of a Hindu deity
AVAUNT	*interj* — used as an order of dismissal
AVE	*n* pl. **-S** an expression of greeting or farewell
AVELLAN	*adj* having the four arms shaped like filberts — used of a heraldic cross
AVELLANE	*adj* avellan
AVENGE	*v* **AVENGED, AVENGING, AVENGES** to exact retribution for
AVENGER	*n* pl. **-S** one that avenges
AVENS	*n* pl. **-ES** a perennial herb
AVENTAIL	*n* pl. **-S** ventail
AVENUE	*n* pl. **-S** a wide street
AVER	*v* **AVERRED, AVERRING, AVERS** to declare positively
AVERAGE	*v* **-AGED, -AGING, -AGES** to calculate the arithmetic mean of
AVERMENT	*n* pl. **-S** the act of averring
AVERRED	past tense of aver
AVERRING	present participle of aver
AVERSE	*adj* opposed; reluctant **AVERSELY** *adv*
AVERSION	*n* pl. **-S** a feeling of repugnance
AVERSIVE	*n* pl. **-S** a punishment
AVERT	*v* **-ED, -ING, -S** to turn away
AVERTER	*n* pl. **-S** one that averts
AVGAS	*n* pl. **-GASES** or **-GASSES** gasoline for airplanes
AVIAN	*n* pl. **-S** a bird
AVIANIZE	*v* **-IZED, -IZING, -IZES** to make less severe by repeated culture in a chick embryo, as a virus
AVIARIST	*n* pl. **-S** the keeper of an aviary
AVIARY	*n* pl. **-ARIES** a large enclosure for live birds
AVIATE	*v* **-ATED, -ATING, -ATES** to fly an aircraft
AVIATION	*n* pl. **-S** the act of aviating **AVIATIC** *adj*
AVIATOR	*n* pl. **-S** one that aviates
AVIATRIX	*n* pl. **-TRICES** or **-TRIXES** a female aviator
AVICULAR	*adj* pertaining to birds
AVID	*adj* eager
AVIDIN	*n* pl. **-S** a protein found in egg white
AVIDITY	*n* pl. **-TIES** the state of being avid
AVIDLY	*adv* in an avid manner
AVIDNESS	*n* pl. **-ES** avidity
AVIFAUNA	*n* pl. **-NAS** or **-NAE** the bird life of a particular region
AVIGATOR	*n* pl. **-S** one that navigates aircraft
AVION	*n* pl. **-S** an airplane
AVIONICS	*n/pl* the science of electronics applied to aviation **AVIONIC** *adj*
AVISO	*n* pl. **-SOS** advice
AVO	*n* pl. **AVOS** a monetary unit of Macao
AVOCADO	*n* pl. **-DOS** or **-DOES** the edible fruit of a tropical tree
AVOCET	*n* pl. **-S** a shore bird
AVODIRE	*n* pl. **-S** an African tree
AVOID	*v* **-ED, -ING, -S** to keep away from
AVOIDER	*n* pl. **-S** one that avoids
AVOSET	*n* pl. **-S** avocet
AVOUCH	*v* **-ED, -ING, -ES** to affirm
AVOUCHER	*n* pl. **-S** one that avouches
AVOW	*v* **-ED, -ING, -S** to declare openly **AVOWABLE** *adj* **AVOWABLY, AVOWEDLY** *adv*
AVOWAL	*n* pl. **-S** an open declaration
AVOWER	*n* pl. **-S** one that avows
AVULSE	*v* **AVULSED, AVULSING, AVULSES** to tear off forcibly
AVULSION	*n* pl. **-S** the act of avulsing
AW	*interj* — used to express protest, disgust, or disbelief
AWA	*adv* away

AWAIT   v **-ED, -ING, -S** to wait for

AWAITER   n pl. **-S** one that awaits

AWAKE   v **AWAKED** or **AWOKE, AWOKEN, AWAKING, AWAKES** to wake up

AWAKEN   v **-ED, -ING, -S** to awake

AWAKENER   n pl. **-S** one that awakens

AWAKING   present participle of awake

AWARD   v **-ED, -ING, -S** to grant as due or merited

AWARDEE   n pl. **-S** one that is awarded something

AWARDER   n pl. **-S** one that awards

AWARE   adj having perception or knowledge

AWASH   adj covered with water

AWAY   adv from a certain place

AWAYNESS   n pl. **-ES** the state of being distant

AWE   v **AWED, AWING** or **AWEING, AWES** to inspire with awe (reverential fear)

AWEARY   adj weary

AWEATHER   adv toward the windward side of a vessel

AWED   past tense of awe

AWEE   adv awhile

AWEIGH   adj hanging just clear of the bottom — used of an anchor

AWELESS   adj lacking awe

AWESOME   adj inspiring awe

AWFUL   adj **-FULLER, -FULLEST** extremely bad or unpleasant **AWFULLY** adv

AWHILE   adv for a short time

AWHIRL   adj whirling

AWING   a present participle of awe

AWKWARD   adj **-WARDER, -WARDEST** lacking skill, dexterity, or grace

AWL   n pl. **-S** a pointed tool for making small holes

AWLESS   adj aweless

AWLWORT   n pl. **-S** an aquatic plant

AWMOUS   n pl. **AWMOUS** alms

AWN   n pl. **-S** a bristlelike appendage of certain grasses **AWNED, AWNLESS, AWNY** adj

AWNING   n pl. **-S** a rooflike canvas cover **AWNINGED** adj

AWOKE   a past tense of awake

AWOKEN   a past participle of awake

AWOL   n pl. **-S** one who is absent without leave

AWRY   adv with a turn or twist to one side

AX   v **-ED, -ING, -ES** to work on with an ax (a type of cutting tool)

AXAL   adj axial

AXE   v **AXED, AXING, AXES** to ax

AXEL   n pl. **-S** a jump in figure skating

AXEMAN   n pl. **-MEN** axman

AXENIC   adj free from germs

AXES   pl. of axis

AXIAL   adj pertaining to or forming an axis **AXIALLY** adv

AXIALITY   n pl. **-TIES** the state of being axial

AXIL   n pl. **-S** the angle between the upper side of a leaf and its supporting stem

AXILE   adj axial

AXILLA   n pl. **-LAE** or **-LAS** the armpit

AXILLAR   n pl. **-S** a feather on the undersurface of a bird's wing

AXILLARY   n pl. **-LARIES** an axillar

AXING   present participle of axe

AXIOLOGY   n pl. **-GIES** the study of values and value judgments

AXIOM   n pl. **-S** a self-evident truth

AXION   n pl. **-S** a hypothetical subatomic particle

AXIS   n pl. **AXES** a straight line about which a body rotates **AXISED** adj

AXIS   n pl. **AXISES** an Asian deer

AXITE   n pl. **-S** a fiber of an axon

AXLE   n pl. **-S** a shaft upon which a wheel revolves **AXLED** adj

AXLETREE   n pl. **-S** a type of axle

AXLIKE   adj resembling an ax

AXMAN   n pl. **-MEN** one who wields an ax

AXOLOTL   n pl. **-S** a salamander of Mexico and western United States

AXON   n pl. **-S** the central process of a neuron **AXONAL** adj

AXONE   n pl. **-S** axon

AXONEMAL   adj pertaining to an axoneme

AXONEME   n pl. **-S** a part of a cilium

AXONIC   adj pertaining to an axon

AXOPLASM   n pl. **-S** the protoplasm of an axon

AXSEED   n pl. **-S** a European herb

AY   *n* pl. **AYS** aye

AYAH   *n* pl. **-S** a native maid or nurse in India

AYAYA   *n* pl. **-S** a type of singing among the Inuit

AYE   *n* pl. **-S** an affirmative vote

AYIN   *n* pl. **-S** a Hebrew letter

AYURVEDA   *n* pl. **-S** a Hindu system of medicine

AZALEA   *n* pl. **-S** a flowering shrub

AZAN   *n* pl. **-S** a Muslim call to prayer

AZIDE   *n* pl. **-S** a type of chemical compound **AZIDO** *adj*

AZIMUTH   *n* pl. **-S** an angle of horizontal deviation

AZINE   *n* pl. **-S** a type of chemical compound

AZLON   *n* pl. **-S** a textile fiber

AZO   *adj* containing nitrogen

AZOIC   *adj* pertaining to geologic time before the appearance of life

AZOLE   *n* pl. **-S** a type of chemical compound

AZON   *n* pl. **-S** a radio-controlled aerial bomb

AZONAL   *adj* pertaining to a type of a soil group

AZONIC   *adj* not restricted to any particular zone

AZOTE   *n* pl. **-S** nitrogen **AZOTED** *adj*

AZOTEMIA   *n* pl. **-S** an excess of nitrogenous substances in the blood **AZOTEMIC** *adj*

AZOTH   *n* pl. **-S** mercury

AZOTIC   *adj* pertaining to azote

AZOTISE   *v* **-TISED, -TISING, -TISES** to azotize

AZOTIZE   *v* **-TIZED, -TIZING, -TIZES** to treat with nitrogen

AZOTURIA   *n* pl. **-S** an excess of nitrogenous substances in the urine

AZUKI   *n* pl. **-S** adzuki

AZULEJO   *n* pl. **-JOS** a type of ceramic tile

AZURE   *n* pl. **-S** a blue color

AZURITE   *n* pl. **-S** a mineral

AZYGOS   *n* pl. **-ES** an azygous anatomical part

AZYGOUS   *adj* not being one of a pair

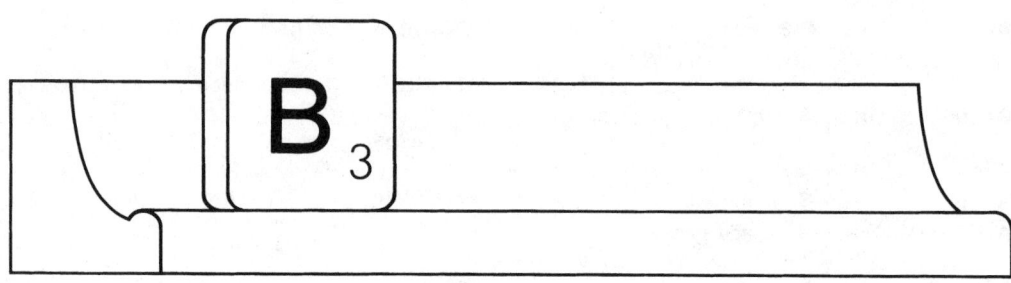

BA	*n* pl. **-S** the eternal soul, in Egyptian mythology
BAA	*v* **-ED, -ING, -S** to bleat
BAAL	*n* pl. **BAALS** or **BAALIM** a false god
BAALISM	*n* pl. **-S** the worship of a baal
BAAS	*n* pl. **-ES** master; boss
BAASKAAP	*n* pl. **-S** baaskap
BAASKAP	*n* pl. **-S** the policy of domination by white people in South Africa
BAASSKAP	*n* pl. **-S** baaskap
BABA	*n* pl. **-S** a rum cake
BABACU	*n* pl. **-S** babassu
BABASSU	*n* pl. **-S** a palm tree
BABBITRY	*n* pl. **-RIES** conventional middle-class attitudes and behavior stressing respectability and material success
BABBITT	*v* **-ED, -ING, -S** to line with babbitt (an alloy of tin, copper, and antimony)
BABBLE	*v* **-BLED, -BLING, -BLES** to talk idly or excessively
BABBLER	*n* pl. **-S** one that babbles
BABBLING	*n* pl. **-S** idle talk
BABE	*n* pl. **-S** a baby
BABEL	*n* pl. **-S** confusion
BABESIA	*n* pl. **-S** a parasitic protozoan
BABICHE	*n* pl. **-S** rawhide thongs
BABIED	past tense of baby
BABIER	comparative of baby
BABIES	present 3d person sing. of baby
BABIEST	superlative of baby
BABIRUSA	*n* pl. **-S** a wild pig
BABKA	*n* pl. **-S** a coffee cake
BABOO	*n* pl. **-BOOS** a Hindu gentleman
BABOOL	*n* pl. **-S** babul
BABOON	*n* pl. **-S** a large ape
BABOUCHE	*n* pl. **-S** a heelless slipper
BABU	*n* pl. **-S** baboo
BABUL	*n* pl. **-S** a North African tree
BABUSHKA	*n* pl. **-S** a woman's scarf
BABY	*adj* **BABIER, BABIEST** resembling a baby (an infant)
BABY	*v* **-BIED, -BYING, -BIES** to coddle
BABYDOLL	*n* pl. **-S** short, sheer pajamas for women
BABYHOOD	*n* pl. **-S** the state of being a baby
BABYISH	*adj* resembling a baby
BABYLIKE	*adj* resembling a baby
BABYSIT	*v* **-SAT, -SITTING, -SITS** to care for a child temporarily
BACALAO	*n* pl. **-LAOS** baccala
BACALHAU	*n* pl. **-S** baccala
BACCA	*n* pl. **-CAE** a berry
BACCALA	*n* pl. **-S** a codfish
BACCARA	*n* pl. **-S** baccarat
BACCARAT	*n* pl. **-S** a card game
BACCATE	*adj* pulpy like a berry
BACCATED	*adj* baccate
BACCHANT	*n* pl. **-S** or **-ES** a carouser
BACCHIC	*adj* riotous
BACCHIUS	*n* pl. **-CHII** a type of metrical foot
BACCY	*n* pl. **BACCIES** tobacco
BACH	*v* **-ED, -ING, -ES** to live as a bachelor
BACHELOR	*n* pl. **-S** an unmarried man
BACILLAR	*adj* rod-shaped
BACILLUS	*n* pl. **-LI** any of a class of rod-shaped bacteria
BACK	*v* **-ED, -ING, -S** to support
BACKACHE	*n* pl. **-S** a pain in the back

BACKBAR *n* pl. **-S** the space behind a bar with shelves for bottles

BACKBEAT *n* pl. **-S** a type of rhythm in music

BACKBEND *n* pl. **-S** an acrobatic feat

BACKBITE *v* **-BIT, -BITTEN, -BITING, -BITES** to slander

BACKBONE *n* pl. **-S** the spine

BACKCAST *n* pl. **-S** a backward movement in casting a fishing line

BACKCHAT *n* pl. **-S** repartee

BACKCOMB *v* **-ED, -ING, -S** to comb the hair from the ends to the scalp

BACKDATE *v* **-DATED, -DATING, -DATES** to predate

BACKDOOR *adj* secretive

BACKDOWN *n* pl. **-S** the act of backing down

BACKDROP *v* **-DROPPED** or **-DROPT, -DROPPING, -DROPS** to provide with a scenic background

BACKER *n* pl. **-S** a supporter

BACKFAT *n* pl. **-S** a layer of fat between the skin and muscle in animals

BACKFILL *v* **-ED, -ING, -S** to refill

BACKFIRE *v* **-FIRED, -FIRING, -FIRES** to produce undesirable effects

BACKFIT *v* **-FITTED, -FITTING, -FITS** to retrofit

BACKFLIP *v* **-FLIPPED, -FLIPPING, -FLIPS** to perform a backward somersault

BACKFLOW *n* pl. **-S** a flowing back toward a source

BACKHAND *v* **-ED, -ING, -S** to strike with the back of the hand

BACKHAUL *v* **-ED, -ING, -S** to return after delivering a load

BACKHOE *v* **-HOED, -HOEING, -HOES** to use a backhoe (a type of excavating machine)

BACKING *n* pl. **-S** support

BACKLAND *n* pl. **-S** a region remote from cities

BACKLASH *v* **-ED, -ING, -ES** to cause a reaction

BACKLESS *adj* having no back

BACKLIST *v* **-ED, -ING, -S** to include in a publisher's list of older book titles

BACKLIT *adj* illuminated from behind

BACKLOAD *v* **-ED, -ING, -S** to defer a financial obligation

BACKLOG *v* **-LOGGED, -LOGGING, -LOGS** to accumulate

BACKLOT *n* pl. **-S** an outdoor area in a movie studio

BACKMOST *adj* hindmost

BACKOUT *n* pl. **-S** a reversal of launching procedures

BACKPACK *v* **-ED, -ING, -S** to hike with a pack on one's back

BACKREST *n* pl. **-S** a back support

BACKROOM *n* pl. **-S** a place for meeting inconspicuously

BACKRUSH *n* pl. **-ES** the seaward return of water from a wave

BACKSAW *n* pl. **-S** a type of saw

BACKSEAT *n* pl. **-S** a rear seat

BACKSET *n* pl. **-S** a setback

BACKSIDE *n* pl. **-S** the hind part

BACKSLAP *v* **-SLAPPED, -SLAPPING, -SLAPS** to show much approval

BACKSLID past tense of backslide (to revert to sin)

BACKSPIN *n* pl. **-S** a backward rotation

BACKSTAB *v* **-STABBED, -STABBING, -STABS** to attack or betray behind one's back

BACKSTAY *n* pl. **-STAYS** a support for a mast

BACKSTOP *v* **-STOPPED, -STOPPING, -STOPS** to bolster

BACKTALK *n* pl. **-S** an impudent reply

BACKUP *n* pl. **-S** a substitute

BACKWARD *adv* toward the back

BACKWASH *v* **-ED, -ING, -ES** to spray water backward

BACKWIND *v* **-ED, -ING, -S** to deflect airflow into the back of a sail

BACKWOOD *adj* uncouth

BACKWRAP *n* pl. **-S** a wraparound garment that fastens in the back

BACKYARD *n* pl. **-S** an area at the rear of a house

BACLOFEN *n* pl. **-S** a muscle relaxant

BACON *n* pl. **-S** a side of a pig cured and smoked

BACTERIA *n* pl. **-S** a group of microscopic organisms

BACTERIN *n* pl. **-S** a vaccine prepared from dead bacteria

BACULINE *adj* pertaining to a rod

BACULUM *n* pl. **-LUMS** or **-LA** a bone in the penis of many mammals

BAD	*adj* **BADDER, BADDEST** very good
BAD	*adj* **WORSE, WORST** not good
BAD	*n* pl. **-S** something that is bad **BADDISH** *adj*
BADDIE	*n* pl. **-S** a bad person
BADDY	*n* pl. **-DIES** baddie
BADE	past tense of bid
BADGE	*v* **BADGED, BADGING, BADGES** to supply with an insignia
BADGER	*v* **-ED, -ING, -S** to harass
BADGERLY	*adj* bothersome
BADINAGE	*v* **-NAGED, -NAGING, -NAGES** to banter
BADLAND	*n* pl. **-S** a barren, hilly area
BADLY	*adv* in a bad manner
BADMAN	*n* pl. **-MEN** an outlaw
BADMOUTH	*v* **-ED, -ING, -S** to criticize
BADNESS	*n* pl. **-ES** the state of being bad
BAFF	*v* **-ED, -ING, -S** to strike under a golf ball
BAFFIES	pl. of baffy
BAFFLE	*v* **-FLED, -FLING, -FLES** to confuse
BAFFLER	*n* pl. **-S** one that baffles
BAFFY	*n* pl. **-FIES** a wooden golf club
BAG	*v* **BAGGED, BAGGING, BAGS** to put into a bag (a flexible container)
BAGASS	*n* pl. **-ES** bagasse
BAGASSE	*n* pl. **-S** crushed sugarcane
BAGEL	*n* pl. **-S** a ring-shaped roll
BAGFUL	*n* pl. **BAGFULS** or **BAGSFUL** as much as a bag can hold
BAGGAGE	*n* pl. **-S** luggage
BAGGED	past tense of bag
BAGGER	*n* pl. **-S** one that bags
BAGGIE	*n* pl. **-S** the stomach
BAGGING	*n* pl. **-S** material for making bags
BAGGY	*adj* **-GIER, -GIEST** loose-fitting **BAGGILY** *adv*
BAGHOUSE	*n* pl. **-S** a facility for removing particulates from exhaust gases
BAGLIKE	*adj* resembling a bag
BAGMAN	*n* pl. **-MEN** a traveling salesman
BAGNIO	*n* pl. **-NIOS** a brothel
BAGPIPE	*v* **-PIPED, -PIPING, -PIPES** to play a bagpipe (a wind instrument)
BAGPIPER	*n* pl. **-S** one that plays bagpipes
BAGSFUL	a pl. of bagful
BAGUET	*n* pl. **-S** baguette
BAGUETTE	*n* pl. **-S** a rectangular gem
BAGWIG	*n* pl. **-S** a type of wig
BAGWORM	*n* pl. **-S** the larva of certain moths
BAH	*interj* — used to express disgust
BAHADUR	*n* pl. **-S** a Hindu title of respect
BAHT	*n* pl. **-S** a monetary unit of Thailand
BAIDAR	*n* pl. **-S** bidarka
BAIDARKA	*n* pl. **-S** bidarka
BAIL	*v* **-ED, -ING, -S** to transfer property temporarily **BAILABLE** *adj*
BAILEE	*n* pl. **-S** a person to whom property is bailed
BAILER	*n* pl. **-S** bailor
BAILEY	*n* pl. **-LEYS** an outer castle wall
BAILIE	*n* pl. **-S** a Scottish magistrate
BAILIFF	*n* pl. **-S** a court officer
BAILMENT	*n* pl. **-S** the act of bailing
BAILOR	*n* pl. **-S** a person who bails property to another
BAILOUT	*n* pl. **-S** the act of parachuting from an aircraft
BAILSMAN	*n* pl. **-MEN** one who provides security for another
BAIRN	*n* pl. **-S** a child **BAIRNISH** *adj*
BAIRNLY	*adj* **-LIER, -LIEST** childish
BAIT	*v* **-ED, -ING, -S** to lure
BAITER	*n* pl. **-S** one that baits
BAITFISH	*n* pl. **-ES** a fish used as bait
BAITH	*adj* both
BAIZA	*n* pl. **-S** a monetary unit of Oman
BAIZE	*n* pl. **-S** a green, woolen fabric
BAKE	*v* **BAKED, BAKING, BAKES** to prepare food in an oven
BAKEMEAT	*n* pl. **-S** a pastry
BAKER	*n* pl. **-S** one that bakes
BAKERY	*n* pl. **-ERIES** a place where baked goods are sold
BAKESHOP	*n* pl. **-S** a bakery
BAKEWARE	*n* pl. **-S** dishes used for baking
BAKING	*n* pl. **-S** a quantity baked
BAKLAVA	*n* pl. **-S** a Turkish pastry
BAKLAWA	*n* pl. **-S** baklava
BAKSHISH	*v* **-ED, -ING, -ES** to give a tip
BAL	*n* pl. **-S** a balmoral

BALAFON _n_ pl. **-S** a musical instrument of Africa

BALANCE _v_ **-ANCED, -ANCING, -ANCES** to weigh

BALANCER _n_ pl. **-S** one that balances

BALAS _n_ pl. **-ES** a red variety of spinel

BALATA _n_ pl. **-S** a tropical tree

BALBOA _n_ pl. **-S** a monetary unit of Panama

BALCONY _n_ pl. **-NIES** an elevated platform

BALD _adj_ **BALDER, BALDEST** lacking hair

BALD _v_ **-ED, -ING, -S** to become bald

BALDHEAD _n_ pl. **-S** a bald person

BALDISH _adj_ somewhat bald

BALDLY _adv_ in a plain and blunt manner

BALDNESS _n_ pl. **-ES** the state of being bald

BALDPATE _n_ pl. **-S** a baldhead

BALDRIC _n_ pl. **-S** a shoulder belt

BALDRICK _n_ pl. **-S** baldric

BALDY _n_ pl. **BALDIES** a bald person

BALE _v_ **BALED, BALING, BALES** to form into tightly compressed bundles

BALEEN _n_ pl. **-S** whalebone

BALEFIRE _n_ pl. **-S** a bonfire

BALEFUL _adj_ menacing

BALER _n_ pl. **-S** one that bales

BALING _n_ pl. **-S** the forming of something into tight bundles

BALISAUR _n_ pl. **-S** a long-tailed badger

BALK _v_ **-ED, -ING, -S** to stop short and refuse to proceed

BALKER _n_ pl. **-S** one that balks

BALKLINE _n_ pl. **-S** the starting line in track events

BALKY _adj_ **BALKIER, BALKIEST** stubborn **BALKILY** _adv_

BALL _v_ **-ED, -ING, -S** to form into a ball (a spherical object)

BALLAD _n_ pl. **-S** a narrative poem or song **BALLADIC** _adj_

BALLADE _n_ pl. **-S** a type of poem

BALLADRY _n_ pl. **-RIES** ballad poetry

BALLAST _v_ **-ED, -ING, -S** to stabilize

BALLBOY _n_ pl. **-BOYS** a boy who retrieves balls during games

BALLCOCK _n_ pl. **-S** a type of valve

BALLER _n_ pl. **-S** one that balls

BALLET _n_ pl. **-S** a classical dance form **BALLETIC** _adj_

BALLGAME _n_ pl. **-S** a game played with a ball

BALLGIRL _n_ pl. **-S** a girl who retrieves balls during games

BALLHAWK _n_ pl. **-S** a very good defensive ballplayer

BALLIES pl. of bally

BALLISTA _n_ pl. **-TAE** or **-TAS** an ancient weapon

BALLON _n_ pl. **-S** lightness of movement

BALLONET _n_ pl. **-S** a small balloon

BALLONNE _n_ pl. **-S** a ballet jump

BALLOON _v_ **-ED, -ING, -S** to swell out

BALLOT _v_ **-ED, -ING, -S** to vote

BALLOTER _n_ pl. **-S** one that ballots

BALLPARK _n_ pl. **-S** a facility in which ballgames are played

BALLROOM _n_ pl. **-S** a large room for dancing

BALLS _v_ **-ED, -ING, -ES** to make a mistake in doing something

BALLUTE _n_ pl. **-S** a small inflatable parachute

BALLY _n_ pl. **-LIES** a noisy uproar

BALLYARD _n_ pl. **-S** a ballpark

BALLYHOO _v_ **-ED, -ING, -S** to promote by uproar

BALLYRAG _v_ **-RAGGED, -RAGGING, -RAGS** to bullyrag

BALM _n_ pl. **-S** a fragrant resin **BALMLIKE** _adj_

BALMORAL _n_ pl. **-S** a type of shoe

BALMY _adj_ **BALMIER, BALMIEST** mild **BALMILY** _adv_

BALNEAL _adj_ pertaining to baths

BALONEY _n_ pl. **-NEYS** bologna

BALSA _n_ pl. **-S** a tropical tree

BALSAM _v_ **-ED, -ING, -S** to anoint with balsam (an aromatic, resinous substance)

BALSAMIC _adj_ containing balsam

BALTI _n_ pl. **-S** a type of Pakistani cuisine

BALUSTER _n_ pl. **-S** a railing support

BAM _v_ **BAMMED, BAMMING, BAMS** to strike with a dull resounding noise

BAMBINO _n_ pl. **-NOS** or **-NI** a baby

BAMBOO _n_ pl. **-BOOS** a tropical grass

BAN _n_ pl. **BANI** a monetary unit of Romania

BAN	v **BANNED, BANNING, BANS** to prohibit
BANAL	adj ordinary **BANALLY** adv
BANALITY	n pl. **-TIES** something banal
BANALIZE	v **-IZED, -IZING, -IZES** to make banal
BANANA	n pl. **-S** an edible fruit
BANAUSIC	adj practical
BANC	n pl. **-S** a bench
BANCO	n pl. **-COS** a bet in certain gambling games
BAND	v **-ED, -ING, -S** to decorate with flexible strips of material
BANDA	n pl. **-S** a style of Mexican dance music
BANDAGE	v **-DAGED, -DAGING, -DAGES** to cover a wound with a strip of cloth
BANDAGER	n pl. **-S** one that bandages
BANDAID	adj providing superficial relief
BANDANA	n pl. **-S** bandanna
BANDANNA	n pl. **-S** a large, colored handkerchief
BANDBOX	n pl. **-ES** a lightweight box
BANDEAU	n pl. **-DEAUS** or **-DEAUX** a headband
BANDER	n pl. **-S** one that bands
BANDEROL	n pl. **-S** a streamer
BANDIED	past tense of bandy
BANDIES	present 3d person sing. of bandy
BANDING	n pl. **-S** the presence of stripes of contrasting colors
BANDIT	n pl. **-DITS** or **-DITTI** a robber
BANDITO	n pl. **-TOS** a bandit
BANDITRY	n pl. **-TRIES** robbery by bandits
BANDMATE	n pl. **-S** a fellow member of a band
BANDOG	n pl. **-S** a watchdog
BANDORA	n pl. **-S** bandore
BANDORE	n pl. **-S** an ancient lute
BANDPASS	n pl. **-ES** the range of frequencies transmitted through a filter
BANDSAW	n pl. **-S** a type of power saw
BANDSMAN	n pl. **-MEN** a member of a musical band
BANDURA	n pl. **-S** a Ukrainian stringed instrument
BANDY	v **-DIED, -DYING, -DIES** to throw to and fro
BANDY	adj **-DIER, -DIEST** curved apart at the knees
BANE	v **BANED, BANING, BANES** to kill with poison
BANEFUL	adj poisonous
BANG	v **-ED, -ING, -S** to hit sharply
BANGER	n pl. **-S** a sausage
BANGKOK	n pl. **-S** a straw hat
BANGLE	n pl. **-S** a bracelet
BANGTAIL	n pl. **-S** a racehorse
BANI	pl. of ban
BANIAN	n pl. **-S** a Hindu merchant
BANING	present participle of bane
BANISH	v **-ED, -ING, -ES** to expel
BANISHER	n pl. **-S** one that banishes
BANISTER	n pl. **-S** a handrail
BANJAX	v **-ED, -ING, -ES** to damage or ruin
BANJO	n pl. **-JOS** or **-JOES** a musical instrument
BANJOIST	n pl. **-S** one who plays the banjo
BANK	v **-ED, -ING, -S** to keep money in a bank (an institution dealing in money matters) **BANKABLE** adj
BANKBOOK	n pl. **-S** a depositor's book
BANKCARD	n pl. **-S** a credit card issued by a bank
BANKER	n pl. **-S** one who works in a bank **BANKERLY** adj
BANKING	n pl. **-S** the business of a bank
BANKIT	n pl. **-S** a raised sidewalk
BANKNOTE	n pl. **-S** a promissory note
BANKROLL	v **-ED, -ING, -S** to fund
BANKRUPT	v **-ED, -ING, -S** to impoverish
BANKSIA	n pl. **-S** an Australian plant
BANKSIDE	n pl. **-S** the slope of a river bank
BANNABLE	adj liable to be banned
BANNED	past tense of ban
BANNER	v **-ED, -ING, -S** to furnish with a flag
BANNERET	n pl. **-S** a small flag
BANNEROL	n pl. **-S** a banderol
BANNET	n pl. **-S** a bonnet
BANNING	present participle of ban
BANNOCK	n pl. **-S** a type of cake
BANNS	n/pl a marriage notice
BANQUET	v **-ED, -ING, -S** to feast
BANSHEE	n pl. **-S** a female spirit
BANSHIE	n pl. **-S** banshee

BANTAM	*n* pl. **-S** a small fowl
BANTENG	*n* pl. **-S** a wild ox
BANTER	*v* **-ED, -ING, -S** to exchange mildly teasing remarks
BANTERER	*n* pl. **-S** one that banters
BANTLING	*n* pl. **-S** a very young child
BANTY	*n* pl. **-TIES** a bantam
BANYAN	*n* pl. **-S** an East Indian tree
BANZAI	*n* pl. **-S** a Japanese battle cry
BAOBAB	*n* pl. **-S** a tropical tree
BAP	*n* pl. **-S** a small bun or roll
BAPTISE	*v* **-TISED, -TISING, -TISES** to baptize
BAPTISIA	*n* pl. **-S** a flowering plant
BAPTISM	*n* pl. **-S** a Christian ceremony
BAPTIST	*n* pl. **-S** one who baptizes
BAPTIZE	*v* **-TIZED, -TIZING, -TIZES** to administer baptism to
BAPTIZER	*n* pl. **-S** a baptist
BAR	*v* **BARRED, BARRING, BARS** to exclude
BARATHEA	*n* pl. **-S** a silk fabric
BARB	*v* **-ED, -ING, -S** to furnish with a barb (a sharp projection)
BARBAL	*adj* pertaining to the beard
BARBARIC	*adj* uncivilized
BARBASCO	*n* pl. **-COS** or **-COES** a tropical tree
BARBATE	*adj* bearded
BARBE	*n* pl. **-S** a medieval cloth headdress
BARBECUE	*v* **-CUED, -CUING, -CUES** to cook over live coals or an open fire
BARBEL	*n* pl. **-S** an organ of a fish
BARBELL	*n* pl. **-S** an exercise apparatus
BARBEQUE	*v* **-QUED, -QUING, -QUES** to barbecue
BARBER	*v* **-ED, -ING, -S** to cut hair
BARBERRY	*n* pl. **-RIES** a shrub
BARBET	*n* pl. **-S** a tropical bird
BARBETTE	*n* pl. **-S** a platform
BARBICAN	*n* pl. **-S** an outer fortification
BARBICEL	*n* pl. **-S** a part of a feather
BARBIE	*n* pl. **-S** a portable fireplace for cooking
BARBITAL	*n* pl. **-S** a sedative
BARBLESS	*adj* having no barbs
BARBOT	*n* pl. **-S** barbotte
BARBOTTE	*n* pl. **-S** a large catfish
BARBULE	*n* pl. **-S** a small barb
BARBUT	*n* pl. **-S** a type of helmet
BARBWIRE	*n* pl. **-S** barbed wire
BARCA	*n* pl. **-S** a double-ended boat
BARCHAN	*n* pl. **-S** a type of sand dune
BARD	*v* **-ED, -ING, -S** to armor a horse
BARDE	*v* **BARDED, BARDING, BARDES** to bard
BARDIC	*adj* poetic
BARE	*adj* **BARER, BAREST** naked
BARE	*v* **BARED, BARING, BARES** to expose
BAREBACK	*adv* without a saddle
BAREBOAT	*n* pl. **-S** a pleasure boat rented without personnel
BAREFIT	*adj* barefoot
BAREFOOT	*adj* being without shoes
BAREGE	*n* pl. **-S** a sheer fabric
BAREHAND	*v* **-ED, -ING, -S** to catch with a bare hand
BAREHEAD	*adv* without a hat
BARELY	*adv* scarcely
BARENESS	*n* pl. **-ES** the state of being bare
BARER	comparative of bare
BARESARK	*n* pl. **-S** an ancient warrior
BAREST	superlative of bare
BARF	*v* **-ED, -ING, -S** to vomit
BARFI	*n* pl. **-S** burfi
BARFLY	*n* pl. **-FLIES** a drinker who frequents bars
BARGAIN	*v* **-ED, -ING, -S** to discuss terms for selling or buying
BARGE	*v* **BARGED, BARGING, BARGES** to move by barge (a long, large boat)
BARGEE	*n* pl. **-S** a bargeman
BARGELLO	*n* pl. **-LOS** a needlepoint stitch that makes a zigzag pattern
BARGEMAN	*n* pl. **-MEN** the master or a crew member of a barge
BARGHEST	*n* pl. **-S** a goblin
BARGING	present participle of barge
BARGOON	*n* pl. **-S** a bargain
BARGUEST	*n* pl. **-S** barghest
BARHOP	*v* **-HOPPED, -HOPPING, -HOPS** to visit a number of bars during an evening

BARIC	*adj* pertaining to barium	**BAROQUE**	*n* pl. **-S** an ornate object
BARILLA	*n* pl. **-S** a chemical compound	**BAROSAUR**	*n* pl. **-S** a large dinosaur
BARING	present participle of bare	**BAROUCHE**	*n* pl. **-S** a type of carriage
BARISTA	*n* pl. **-S** one who makes and serves coffee to the public	**BARQUE**	*n* pl. **-S** a sailing vessel
		BARRABLE	*adj* capable of being barred
BARITE	*n* pl. **-S** a mineral	**BARRACK**	*v* **-ED, -ING, -S** to shout boisterously
BARITONE	*n* pl. **-S** a male singing voice		
BARIUM	*n* pl. **-S** a metallic element	**BARRAGE**	*v* **-RAGED, -RAGING, -RAGES** to subject to a massive attack
BARK	*v* **-ED, -ING, -S** to cry like a dog		
BARKEEP	*n* pl. **-S** a bartender	**BARRANCA**	*n* pl. **-S** a steep ravine
BARKER	*n* pl. **-S** one that barks	**BARRANCO**	*n* pl. **-COS** barranca
BARKLESS	*adj* having no bark; unable to bark	**BARRATER**	*n* pl. **-S** barrator
		BARRATOR	*n* pl. **-S** one who commits barratry
BARKY	*adj* **BARKIER, BARKIEST** covered with bark (tough outer covering of a root or stem)	**BARRATRY**	*n* pl. **-TRIES** fraud committed by a master or crew of a ship
BARLEDUC	*n* pl. **-S** a fruit jam	**BARRE**	*v* **BARRED, BARRING, BARRES** to play a type of guitar chord
BARLESS	*adj* having no restraints		
BARLEY	*n* pl. **-LEYS** a cereal grass	**BARRED**	past tense of bar
BARLOW	*n* pl. **-S** a jackknife	**BARREL**	*v* **-RELED, -RELING, -RELS** or **-RELLED, -RELLING, -RELS** to move fast
BARM	*n* pl. **-S** the foam on malt liquors		
BARMAID	*n* pl. **-S** a female bartender		
BARMAN	*n* pl. **-MEN** a male bartender	**BARREN**	*adj* **-RENER, -RENEST** unproductive **BARRENLY** *adv*
BARMIE	*adj* barmy		
BARMY	*adj* **BARMIER, BARMIEST** full of barm; frothy **BARMILY** *adv*	**BARREN**	*n* pl. **-S** a tract of barren land
		BARRET	*n* pl. **-S** a flat cap
BARN	*v* **-ED, -ING, -S** to store in a barn (a large storage building)	**BARRETOR**	*n* pl. **-S** barrator
		BARRETRY	*n* pl. **-TRIES** barratry
BARNACLE	*n* pl. **-S** a shellfish	**BARRETTE**	*n* pl. **-S** a hair clip
BARNEY	*n* pl. **-NEYS** a noisy argument	**BARRIER**	*n* pl. **-S** an obstacle
BARNLIKE	*adj* resembling a barn	**BARRING**	present participle of bar and barre
BARNWOOD	*n* pl. **-S** wide wood for building barns	**BARRIO**	*n* pl. **-RIOS** a district
		BARRIQUE	*n* pl. **-S** a wine barrel
BARNY	*adj* **BARNIER, BARNIEST** resembling a barn in size, shape, or smell	**BARROOM**	*n* pl. **-S** a room where liquor is sold
		BARROW	*n* pl. **-S** a type of cart
		BARRY	*adj* divided into horizontal bars
BARNYARD	*n* pl. **-S** a yard near a barn	**BARSTOOL**	*n* pl. **-S** a stool in a barroom
BAROGRAM	*n* pl. **-S** a barometric reading	**BARTEND**	*v* **-ED, -ING, -S** to tend a barroom
BARON	*n* pl. **-S** a lower member of nobility	**BARTER**	*v* **-ED, -ING, -S** to trade
BARONAGE	*n* pl. **-S** the rank of a baron	**BARTERER**	*n* pl. **-S** one that barters
BARONESS	*n* pl. **-ES** the wife of a baron	**BARTISAN**	*n* pl. **-S** bartizan
BARONET	*n* pl. **-S** the holder of a rank below that of a baron	**BARTIZAN**	*n* pl. **-S** a small turret
		BARWARE	*n* pl. **-S** barroom equipment
BARONG	*n* pl. **-S** a broad knife	**BARYE**	*n* pl. **-S** a unit of pressure
BARONIAL	*adj* pertaining to a baron	**BARYON**	*n* pl. **-S** a type of subatomic particle **BARYONIC** *adj*
BARONNE	*n* pl. **-S** a baroness		
BARONY	*n* pl. **-ONIES** the domain of a baron	**BARYTA**	*n* pl. **-S** a compound of barium **BARYTIC** *adj*

BARYTE *n* pl. **-S** barite

BARYTON *n* pl. **-S** a stringed instrument

BARYTONE *n* pl. **-S** baritone

BASAL *adj* pertaining to the foundation **BASALLY** *adv*

BASALT *n* pl. **-S** a volcanic rock **BASALTIC** *adj*

BASALTES *n* pl. **BASALTES** unglazed stoneware

BASCINET *n* pl. **-S** basinet

BASCULE *n* pl. **-S** a type of seesaw

BASE *adj* **BASER, BASEST** morally low

BASE *v* **BASED, BASING, BASES** to found

BASEBALL *n* pl. **-S** a type of ball

BASEBORN *adj* of low birth

BASED past tense of base

BASELESS *adj* having no foundation

BASELINE *n* pl. **-S** a line at either end of a court in certain sports

BASELOAD *n* pl. **-S** the permanent load on power supplies

BASELY *adv* in a base manner

BASEMAN *n* pl. **-MEN** a certain player in baseball

BASEMENT *n* pl. **-S** the part of a building below ground level

BASENESS *n* pl. **-ES** the state of being base

BASENJI *n* pl. **-S** a barkless dog

BASEPATH *n* pl. **-S** a base runner's path between bases

BASER comparative of base

BASES pl. of basis

BASEST superlative of base

BASH *v* **-ED, -ING, -ES** to smash

BASHAW *n* pl. **-S** a pasha

BASHER *n* pl. **-S** one that bashes

BASHFUL *adj* shy; timid

BASHING *n* pl. **-S** an act of beating

BASHLYK *n* pl. **-S** a cloth hood

BASIC *n* pl. **-S** a fundamental

BASICITY *n* pl. **-TIES** the state of being alkaline

BASIDIUM *n* pl. **-IA** a structure on a fungus **BASIDIAL** *adj*

BASIFIER *n* pl. **-S** one that basifies

BASIFY *v* **-FIED, -FYING, -FIES** to alkalize

BASIL *n* pl. **-S** an aromatic herb

BASILAR *adj* basal

BASILARY *adj* basilar

BASILECT *n* pl. **-S** the least prestigious language of an area

BASILIC *adj* pertaining to a basilica

BASILICA *n* pl. **-CAS** or **-CAE** an ancient Roman building

BASILISK *n* pl. **-S** a fabled serpent

BASIN *n* pl. **-S** a large bowl **BASINAL, BASINED** *adj*

BASINET *n* pl. **-S** a medieval helmet

BASINFUL *n* pl. **-S** as much as a basin can hold

BASING present participle of base

BASION *n* pl. **-S** a part of the skull

BASIS *n* pl. **BASES** the foundation of something

BASK *v* **-ED, -ING, -S** to lie in a pleasant warmth

BASKET *n* pl. **-S** a wooden container

BASKETRY *n* pl. **-RIES** basket weaving

BASMATI *n* pl. **-S** a long-grain rice

BASOPHIL *n* pl. **-S** a type of cell

BASQUE *n* pl. **-S** a bodice

BASS *n* pl. **-ES** an edible fish

BASS *adj* **BASSER, BASSEST** deep-sounding

BASSET *v* **-SETED, -SETING, -SETS** or **-SETTED, -SETTING, -SETS** to outcrop

BASSI a pl. of basso

BASSINET *n* pl. **-S** a basket used as a baby's crib

BASSIST *n* pl. **-S** a person who plays a double bass

BASSLY *adv* in a low-pitched manner

BASSNESS *n* pl. **-ES** lowness in pitch

BASSO *n* pl. **-SOS** or **-SI** a low-pitched singer

BASSOON *n* pl. **-S** a low-pitched instrument

BASSWOOD *n* pl. **-S** a linden tree

BASSY *adj* low in pitch

BAST *n* pl. **-S** a woody fiber

BASTARD *n* pl. **-S** an illegitimate child

BASTARDY *n* pl. **-TARDIES** the state of being a bastard

BASTE *v* **BASTED, BASTING, BASTES** to sew loosely together

BASTER *n* pl. **-S** one that bastes

BASTILE	*n* pl. **-S** bastille
BASTILLE	*n* pl. **-S** a prison
BASTING	*n* pl. **-S** the thread used by a baster
BASTION	*n* pl. **-S** a fortified place
BAT	*v* **BATTED, BATTING, BATS** to hit a baseball
BATARD	*n* pl. **-S** a birchbark canoe
BATATA	*n* pl. **-S** a sweet potato
BATBOY	*n* pl. **-BOYS** a boy who minds baseball equipment
BATCH	*v* **-ED, -ING, -ES** to bring together
BATCHER	*n* pl. **-S** one that batches
BATE	*v* **BATED, BATING, BATES** to reduce the force of
BATEAU	*n* pl. **-TEAUX** a flat-bottomed boat
BATFISH	*n* pl. **-ES** a batlike fish
BATFOWL	*v* **-ED, -ING, -S** to catch birds at night
BATGIRL	*n* pl. **-S** a girl who minds baseball equipment
BATH	*n* pl. **-S** a washing
BATHE	*v* **BATHED, BATHING, BATHES** to wash
BATHER	*n* pl. **-S** one that bathes
BATHETIC	*adj* trite
BATHING	*n* pl. **-S** the act of one that bathes
BATHLESS	*adj* not having had a bath
BATHMAT	*n* pl. **-S** a mat used in a bathroom
BATHOS	*n* pl. **-ES** triteness
BATHROBE	*n* pl. **-S** a housecoat
BATHROOM	*n* pl. **-S** a room in which to bathe
BATHTUB	*n* pl. **-S** a tub in which to bathe
BATHYAL	*adj* pertaining to deep water
BATIK	*v* **-ED, -ING, -S** to dye fabric by a particular process
BATING	present participle of bate
BATISTE	*n* pl. **-S** a sheer fabric
BATLIKE	*adj* resembling a bat (a flying mammal)
BATMAN	*n* pl. **-MEN** an orderly
BATON	*n* pl. **-S** a short rod
BATSMAN	*n* pl. **-MEN** one who bats
BATT	*n* pl. **-S** a sheet of cotton
BATTALIA	*n* pl. **-S** a military unit
BATTEAU	*n* pl. **-TEAUX** bateau
BATTED	past tense of bat

BATTEN	*v* **-ED, -ING, -S** to fasten with strips of wood
BATTENER	*n* pl. **-S** one that battens
BATTER	*v* **-ED, -ING, -S** to beat repeatedly
BATTERER	*n* pl. **-S** one that batters
BATTERIE	*n* pl. **-S** a ballet movement
BATTERY	*n* pl. **-TERIES** a device for generating an electric current
BATTIER	comparative of batty
BATTIEST	superlative of batty
BATTIK	*n* pl. **-S** a fabric dyed by batiking
BATTILY	*adv* in a batty manner
BATTING	*n* pl. **-S** a batt
BATTLE	*v* **-TLED, -TLING, -TLES** to fight
BATTLER	*n* pl. **-S** one that battles
BATTU	*adj* pertaining to a ballet movement
BATTUE	*n* pl. **-S** a type of hunt
BATTY	*adj* **-TIER, -TIEST** crazy
BATWING	*adj* shaped like a bat's wing
BAUBEE	*n* pl. **-S** bawbee
BAUBLE	*n* pl. **-S** a cheap trinket
BAUD	*n* pl. **-S** a unit of data transmission speed
BAUDEKIN	*n* pl. **-S** a brocaded fabric
BAUDRONS	*n* pl. **-ES** a cat
BAUHINIA	*n* pl. **-S** a small tropical tree
BAULK	*v* **-ED, -ING, -S** to balk
BAULKER	*n* pl. **-S** balker
BAULKY	*adj* **BAULKIER, BAULKIEST** balky
BAUSOND	*adj* having white marks
BAUXITE	*n* pl. **-S** an ore of aluminum **BAUXITIC** *adj*
BAWBEE	*n* pl. **-S** a Scottish coin
BAWCOCK	*n* pl. **-S** a fine fellow
BAWD	*n* pl. **-S** a madam
BAWDIER	comparative of bawdy
BAWDIES	pl. of bawdy
BAWDIEST	superlative of bawdy
BAWDILY	*adv* in a bawdy manner
BAWDRIC	*n* pl. **-S** baldric
BAWDRY	*n* pl. **-RIES** obscenity
BAWDY	*adj* **BAWDIER, BAWDIEST** obscene
BAWDY	*n* pl. **BAWDIES** obscene language
BAWK	*n* pl. **-S** an Atlantic seabird

BAWL	*v* **-ED, -ING, -S** to cry loudly
BAWLER	*n* pl. **-S** one that bawls
BAWN	*n* pl. **-S** a meadow for cows
BAWSUNT	*adj* bausond
BAWTIE	*n* pl. **-S** a dog
BAWTY	*n* pl. **-TIES** bawtie
BAY	*v* **-ED, -ING, -S** to howl
BAY	*adj* **BAYER, BAYEST** dark reddish-brown
BAYADEER	*n* pl. **-S** bayadere
BAYADERE	*n* pl. **-S** a dancing girl
BAYAMO	*n* pl. **-MOS** a strong wind
BAYARD	*n* pl. **-S** a horse
BAYBERRY	*n* pl. **-RIES** a berry tree
BAYFRONT	*n* pl. **-S** the shoreline of a bay (an inlet of the sea)
BAYMAN	*n* pl. **-MEN** a person who fishes on a bay
BAYNODDY	*n* pl. **-DIES** a bayman
BAYONET	*v* **-NETED, -NETING, -NETS** or **-NETTED, -NETTING, -NETS** to stab with a dagger-like weapon
BAYOU	*n* pl. **-S** a marshy body of water
BAYSIDE	*n* pl. **-S** the shore of a bay (an inlet of the sea)
BAYWOOD	*n* pl. **-S** a coarse mahogany
BAZAAR	*n* pl. **-S** a marketplace
BAZAR	*n* pl. **-S** bazaar
BAZOO	*n* pl. **-ZOOS** the mouth
BAZOOKA	*n* pl. **-S** a small rocket launcher
BAZZ	*v* **-ED, -ING, -ES** to throw (as a stone)
BDELLIUM	*n* pl. **-S** a gum resin
BE	*v* present sing. 1st person **AM**, 2d **ARE** or **ART**, 3d **IS**, past sing. 1st and 3d persons **WAS**, 2d **WERE** or **WAST** or **WERT**, past participle **BEEN**, present participle **BEING** to have actuality
BEACH	*v* **-ED, -ING, -ES** to drive ashore
BEACHBOY	*n* pl. **-BOYS** a male beach attendant
BEACHY	*adj* **BEACHIER, BEACHIEST** sandy or pebbly
BEACON	*v* **-ED, -ING, -S** to warn or guide
BEAD	*v* **-ED, -ING, -S** to adorn with beads (round pieces of glass)
BEADER	*n* pl. **-S** one that beads
BEADIER	comparative of beady
BEADIEST	superlative of beady
BEADILY	*adv* in a beady manner
BEADING	*n* pl. **-S** beaded material
BEADLE	*n* pl. **-S** a parish official
BEADLIKE	*adj* beady
BEADMAN	*n* pl. **-MEN** beadsman
BEADROLL	*n* pl. **-S** a list of names
BEADSMAN	*n* pl. **-MEN** one who prays for another
BEADWORK	*n* pl. **-S** beading
BEADY	*adj* **BEADIER, BEADIEST** resembling beads
BEAGLE	*v* **-GLED, -GLING, -GLES** to hunt with beagles (small hounds)
BEAGLER	*n* pl. **-S** one that hunts game with beagles
BEAGLING	*n* pl. **-S** the activity of hunting with beagles
BEAK	*n* pl. **-S** a bird's bill **BEAKED, BEAKLESS, BEAKLIKE** *adj*
BEAKER	*n* pl. **-S** a large cup
BEAKY	*adj* **BEAKIER, BEAKIEST** resembling a beak
BEAL	*n* pl. **-S** an infected sore (a painful place on the body)
BEALING	*n* pl. **-S** a beal
BEAM	*v* **-ED, -ING, -S** to emit in beams (rays of light)
BEAMIER	comparative of beamy
BEAMIEST	superlative of beamy
BEAMILY	*adv* in a beamy manner
BEAMISH	*adj* cheerful
BEAMLESS	*adj* having no beam
BEAMLIKE	*adj* resembling a beam
BEAMY	*adj* **BEAMIER, BEAMIEST** beaming
BEAN	*v* **-ED, -ING, -S** to hit on the head
BEANBAG	*n* pl. **-S** a small cloth bag
BEANBALL	*n* pl. **-S** a baseball thrown at the head
BEANERY	*n* pl. **-ERIES** a cheap restaurant
BEANIE	*n* pl. **-S** a small cap
BEANLIKE	*adj* resembling a bean
BEANO	*n* pl. **BEANOS** a form of bingo
BEANPOLE	*n* pl. **-S** a thin pole
BEAR	*v* **BORE, BORNE** or **BORN, BEARING, BEARS** to endure **BEARABLE** *adj* **BEARABLY** *adv*

BEARCAT	*n* pl. **-S** a small mammal
BEARD	*v* **-ED, -ING, -S** to oppose boldly
BEARER	*n* pl. **-S** one that bears
BEARHUG	*n* pl. **-S** a rough tight embrace
BEARING	*n* pl. **-S** demeanor
BEARISH	*adj* resembling a bear (a large mammal)
BEARLIKE	*adj* bearish
BEARPAW	*n* pl. **-S** the paw of a bear
BEARSKIN	*n* pl. **-S** the skin of a bear
BEARWOOD	*n* pl. **-S** a small tree of the buckthorn family
BEAST	*n* pl. **-S** an animal
BEASTIE	*n* pl. **-S** a tiny animal
BEASTLY	*adj* **-LIER, -LIEST** resembling a beast
BEAT	*v* **BEAT, BEATEN, BEATING, BEATS** to strike repeatedly **BEATABLE** *adj*
BEATBOX	*v* **-ED, -ING, -ES** to sing to the rhythm of rap music
BEATER	*n* pl. **-S** one that beats
BEATIFIC	*adj* blissful
BEATIFY	*v* **-FIED, -FYING, -FIES** to make happy
BEATING	*n* pl. **-S** a defeat
BEATLESS	*adj* having no rhythm
BEATNIK	*n* pl. **-S** a nonconformist
BEAU	*n* pl. **BEAUS** or **BEAUX** a boyfriend **BEAUISH** *adj*
BEAUCOUP	*n* pl. **-S** an abundance
BEAUT	*n* pl. **-S** something beautiful
BEAUT	*adj* **BEAUTER, BEAUTEST** beautiful
BEAUTIFY	*v* **-FIED, -FYING, -FIES** to make beautiful
BEAUTY	*n* pl. **-TIES** one that is lovely
BEAUX	a pl. of beau
BEAVER	*v* **-ED, -ING, -S** to work hard
BEBEERU	*n* pl. **-S** a tropical tree
BEBLOOD	*v* **-ED, -ING, -S** to cover with blood
BEBOP	*n* pl. **-S** a type of jazz
BEBOPPER	*n* pl. **-S** one that likes bebop
BECALM	*v* **-ED, -ING, -S** to make calm
BECAME	past tense of become
BECAP	*v* **-CAPPED, -CAPPING, -CAPS** to put a cap on

BECARPET	*v* **-ED, -ING, -S** to cover with a carpet
BECAUSE	*conj* for the reason that
BECHALK	*v* **-ED, -ING, -S** to cover with chalk
BECHAMEL	*n* pl. **-S** a white sauce
BECHANCE	*v* **-CHANCED, -CHANCING, -CHANCES** to befall
BECHARM	*v* **-ED, -ING, -S** to hold under a spell
BECK	*v* **-ED, -ING, -S** to beckon
BECKET	*n* pl. **-S** a securing rope
BECKON	*v* **-ED, -ING, -S** to signal by sign or gesture
BECKONER	*n* pl. **-S** one that beckons
BECLAMOR	*v* **-ED, -ING, -S** to clamor loudly
BECLASP	*v* **-ED, -ING, -S** to embrace
BECLOAK	*v* **-ED, -ING, -S** to place a cloak on
BECLOG	*v* **-CLOGGED, -CLOGGING, -CLOGS** to clog thoroughly
BECLOTHE	*v* **-CLOTHED, -CLOTHING, -CLOTHES** to clothe
BECLOUD	*v* **-ED, -ING, -S** to make cloudy
BECLOWN	*v* **-ED, -ING, -S** to cause to appear ridiculous
BECOME	*v* **-CAME, -COMING, -COMES** to come to be
BECOMING	*n* pl. **-S** a process of change
BECOWARD	*v* **-ED, -ING, -S** to accuse of cowardice
BECRAWL	*v* **-ED, -ING, -S** to crawl over
BECRIME	*v* **-CRIMED, -CRIMING, -CRIMES** to make guilty of a crime
BECROWD	*v* **-ED, -ING, -S** to crowd closely
BECRUST	*v* **-ED, -ING, -S** to cover with a crust
BECUDGEL	*v* **-GELLED, -GELLING, -GELS** or **-GELED, -GELING, -GELS** to cudgel thoroughly
BECURSE	*v* **-CURSED** or **-CURST, -CURSING, -CURSES** to curse severely
BED	*v* **BEDDED, BEDDING, BEDS** to provide with a bed (a piece of furniture used for sleeping)
BEDABBLE	*v* **-BLED, -BLING, -BLES** to soil
BEDAD	*interj* — used as a mild oath
BEDAMN	*v* **-ED, -ING, -S** to swear at
BEDARKEN	*v* **-ED, -ING, -S** to darken
BEDAUB	*v* **-ED, -ING, -S** to besmear

BEDAZZLE *v* **-ZLED, -ZLING, -ZLES** to confuse

BEDBOARD *n* pl. **-S** a board placed between a mattress and bedspring

BEDBUG *n* pl. **-S** a bloodsucking insect

BEDCHAIR *n* pl. **-S** a chair near a bed

BEDCOVER *n* pl. **-S** a cover for a bed

BEDDABLE *adj* suitable for taking to bed

BEDDED past tense of bed

BEDDER *n* pl. **-S** one that makes up beds

BEDDING *n* pl. **-S** material for making up a bed

BEDEAFEN *v* **-ED, -ING, -S** to deafen

BEDECK *v* **-ED, -ING, -S** to clothe with finery

BEDEL *n* pl. **-S** an English university officer

BEDELL *n* pl. **-S** bedel

BEDEMAN *n* pl. **-MEN** beadsman

BEDESMAN *n* pl. **-MEN** beadsman

BEDEVIL *v* **-ILED, -ILING, -ILS** or **-ILLED, -ILLING, -ILS** to harass

BEDEW *v* **-ED, -ING, -S** to wet with dew

BEDFAST *adj* confined to bed

BEDFRAME *n* pl. **-S** the frame of a bed

BEDGOWN *n* pl. **-S** a dressing gown

BEDHEAD *n* pl. **-S** an upright board at the head of a bed

BEDIAPER *v* **-ED, -ING, -S** to ornament with a kind of design

BEDIGHT *v* **-ED, -ING, -S** to bedeck

BEDIM *v* **-DIMMED, -DIMMING, -DIMS** to make dim

BEDIMPLE *v* **-PLED, -PLING, -PLES** to dimple

BEDIRTY *v* **-DIRTIED, -DIRTYING, -DIRTIES** to make dirty

BEDIZEN *v* **-ED, -ING, -S** to dress gaudily

BEDLAM *n* pl. **-S** confusion

BEDLAMER *n* pl. **-S** a young harp seal (an aquatic mammal)

BEDLAMP *n* pl. **-S** a lamp near a bed

BEDLESS *adj* having no bed

BEDLIKE *adj* resembling a bed

BEDLINER *n* pl. **-S** a protective covering for the bed of a truck

BEDMAKER *n* pl. **-S** one that makes beds

BEDMATE *n* pl. **-S** a bed companion

BEDOTTED *adj* covered with dots

BEDOUIN *n* pl. **-S** a nomadic Arab

BEDPAN *n* pl. **-S** a toilet pan

BEDPLATE *n* pl. **-S** a frame support

BEDPOST *n* pl. **-S** a post of a bed

BEDQUILT *n* pl. **-S** a quilt for a bed

BEDRAIL *n* pl. **-S** a board at bedside

BEDRAPE *v* **-DRAPED, -DRAPING, -DRAPES** to drape

BEDRENCH *v* **-ED, -ING, -ES** to drench thoroughly

BEDREST *n* pl. **-S** confinement to bed

BEDRID *adj* bedfast

BEDRIVEL *v* **-ELLED, -ELLING, -ELS** or **-ELED, -ELING, -ELS** to cover with saliva

BEDROCK *n* pl. **-S** the rock under soil

BEDROLL *n* pl. **-S** a portable roll of bedding

BEDROOM *n* pl. **-S** a room for sleeping

BEDRUG *v* **-DRUGGED, -DRUGGING, -DRUGS** to make sleepy

BEDSHEET *n* pl. **-S** a sheet for a bed

BEDSIDE *n* pl. **-S** the side of a bed

BEDSIT *n* pl. **-S** a one-room apartment

BEDSKIRT *n* pl. **-S** drapery attached to a bed frame

BEDSOCK *n* pl. **-S** a sock for wear in a bed

BEDSONIA *n* pl. **-S** a virus

BEDSORE *n* pl. **-S** a type of sore

BEDSTAND *n* pl. **-S** a table next to a bed

BEDSTEAD *n* pl. **-S** a support for a bed

BEDSTRAW *n* pl. **-S** a woody herb

BEDTICK *n* pl. **-S** the cloth case of a mattress

BEDTIME *n* pl. **-S** a time for going to bed

BEDU *n* pl. **BEDU** a bedouin

BEDUIN *n* pl. **-S** bedouin

BEDUMB *v* **-ED, -ING, -S** to render speechless

BEDUNCE *v* **-DUNCED, -DUNCING, -DUNCES** to make a dunce of

BEDWARD *adv* toward bed

BEDWARDS *adv* bedward

BEDWARF *v* **-ED, -ING, -S** to cause to appear small by comparison

BEE *n* pl. **-S** a winged insect

BEEBEE *n* pl. **-S** a pellet

BEEBREAD *n* pl. **-S** a pollen mixture

BEECH *n* pl. **-ES** a type of tree **BEECHEN** *adj*

BEECHNUT *n* pl. **-S** the nut of a beech

BEECHY *adj* **BEECHIER, BEECHIEST** abounding in beeches

BEEDI *n* pl. **-DIES** bidi

BEEF *n* pl. **BEEFS** or **BEEVES** a steer or cow fattened for food

BEEF *v* **-ED, -ING, -S** to add bulk to

BEEFALO *n* pl. **-LOS** or **-LOES** the offspring of an American buffalo and domestic cattle

BEEFCAKE *n* pl. **-S** pictures of male physiques

BEEFIER comparative of beefy

BEEFIEST superlative of beefy

BEEFILY *adv* in a beefy manner

BEEFLESS *adj* being without beef

BEEFWOOD *n* pl. **-S** a hardwood tree

BEEFY *adj* **BEEFIER, BEEFIEST** brawny

BEEHIVE *n* pl. **-S** a hive for bees

BEEHIVED *adj* having a hairdo shaped like a beehive

BEELIKE *adj* resembling a bee

BEELINE *v* **-LINED, -LINING, -LINES** to go in a straight direct course

BEEN past participle of be

BEEP *v* **-ED, -ING, -S** to honk a horn

BEEPER *n* pl. **-S** a signaling device

BEER *n* pl. **-S** an alcoholic beverage

BEERNUT *n* pl. **-S** a peanut with a sweet coating

BEERY *adj* **BEERIER, BEERIEST** affected by beer **BEERILY** *adv*

BEESWAX *v* **-ED, -ING, -ES** to polish furniture with a type of wax

BEESWING *n* pl. **-S** a crust that forms on wines

BEET *n* pl. **-S** a garden plant

BEETLE *v* **-TLED, -TLING, -TLES** to jut out

BEETLER *n* pl. **-S** one that operates a cloth-finishing machine

BEETROOT *n* pl. **-S** the root of the beet

BEEVES a pl. of beef

BEEYARD *n* pl. **-S** an apiary

BEEZER *n* pl. **-S** the nose

BEFALL *v* **-FELL, -FALLEN, -FALLING, -FALLS** to happen to

BEFINGER *v* **-ED, -ING, -S** to touch all over

BEFIT *v* **-FITTED, -FITTING, -FITS** to be suitable to

BEFLAG *v* **-FLAGGED, -FLAGGING, -FLAGS** to deck with flags

BEFLEA *v* **-ED, -ING, -S** to infest with fleas

BEFLECK *v* **-ED, -ING, -S** to fleck

BEFLOWER *v* **-ED, -ING, -S** to cover with flowers

BEFOG *v* **-FOGGED, -FOGGING, -FOGS** to envelop in fog

BEFOOL *v* **-ED, -ING, -S** to deceive

BEFORE *adv* previously

BEFOUL *v* **-ED, -ING, -S** to foul

BEFOULER *n* pl. **-S** one that befouls

BEFRET *v* **-FRETTED, -FRETTING, -FRETS** to gnaw

BEFRIEND *v* **-ED, -ING, -S** to act as a friend to

BEFRINGE *v* **-FRINGED, -FRINGING, -FRINGES** to border with a fringe

BEFUDDLE *v* **-DLED, -DLING, -DLES** to confuse

BEG *v* **BEGGED, BEGGING, BEGS** to plead

BEGAD *interj* — used as a mild oath

BEGALL *v* **-ED, -ING, -S** to make sore by rubbing

BEGAN past tense of begin

BEGAZE *v* **-GAZED, -GAZING, -GAZES** to gaze at

BEGEM *v* **-GEMMED, -GEMMING, -GEMS** to gem

BEGET *v* **-GOT** or **-GAT, -GOTTEN, -GETTING, -GETS** to cause to exist

BEGETTER *n* pl. **-S** one that begets

BEGGAR *v* **-ED, -ING, -S** to impoverish

BEGGARLY *adj* very poor

BEGGARY *n* pl. **-GARIES** extreme poverty

BEGGED past tense of beg

BEGGING present participle of beg

BEGIN *v* **-GAN, -GUN, -GINNING, -GINS** to start

BEGINNER *n* pl. **-S** one that begins

BEGIRD *v* **-GIRDED** or **-GIRT, -GIRDING, -GIRDS** to surround

BEGIRDLE *v* **-DLED, -DLING, -DLES** to surround

BEGLAD *v* **-GLADDED, -GLADDING, -GLADS** to gladden

BEGLAMOR *v* **-ED, -ING, -S** to dazzle with glamor

BEGLOOM *v* **-ED, -ING, -S** to make gloomy

BEGONE   *v* to go away — this is the only form in use

BEGONIA   *n* pl. **-S** a tropical herb

BEGORAH   *interj* begorra

BEGORRA   *interj* — used as a mild oath

BEGORRAH   *interj* begorra

BEGOT   a past tense of beget

BEGOTTEN   past participle of beget

BEGRIM   *v* **-GRIMMED, -GRIMMING, -GRIMS** to begrime

BEGRIME   *v* **-GRIMED, -GRIMING, -GRIMES** to dirty

BEGROAN   *v* **-ED, -ING, -S** to groan at

BEGRUDGE   *v* **-GRUDGED, -GRUDGING, -GRUDGES** to concede reluctantly

BEGUILE   *v* **-GUILED, -GUILING, -GUILES** to deceive

BEGUILER   *n* pl. **-S** one that beguiles

BEGUINE   *n* pl. **-S** a lively dance

BEGULF   *v* **-ED, -ING, -S** to engulf

BEGUM   *n* pl. **-S** a Muslim lady of high rank

BEGUN   past participle of begin

BEHALF   *n* pl. **-HALVES** interest, support, or benefit

BEHAVE   *v* **-HAVED, -HAVING, -HAVES** to act properly

BEHAVER   *n* pl. **-S** one that behaves

BEHAVIOR   *n* pl. **-S** demeanor

BEHEAD   *v* **-ED, -ING, -S** to cut off the head of

BEHEADAL   *n* pl. **-S** the act of beheading

BEHEADER   *n* pl. **-S** one that beheads

BEHELD   past tense of behold

BEHEMOTH   *n* pl. **-S** a large beast

BEHEST   *n* pl. **-S** a command

BEHIND   *n* pl. **-S** the buttocks

BEHOLD   *v* **-HELD, -HOLDING, -HOLDS** to view

BEHOLDEN   *adj* indebted

BEHOLDER   *n* pl. **-S** one that beholds

BEHOOF   *n* pl. **-HOOVES** use, advantage, or benefit

BEHOOVE   *v* **-HOOVED, -HOOVING, -HOOVES** to be proper for

BEHOVE   *v* **-HOVED, -HOVING, -HOVES** to behoove

BEHOWL   *v* **-ED, -ING, -S** to howl at

BEIGE   *n* pl. **-S** a tan color

BEIGE   *adj* **BEIGER, BEIGEST** of a tan color

BEIGNE   *n* pl. **-S** beignet

BEIGNET   *n* pl. **-S** a type of fritter or doughnut

BEIGY   *adj* of the color beige

BEING   *n* pl. **-S** something that exists

BEJABERS   *n* pl. **-SES** bejesus

BEJASUS   *n* pl. **-ES** bejesus

BEJEEZUS   *n* pl. **-ES** bejesus

BEJESUS   *n* pl. **-ES** an exclamation used as a mild oath

BEJEWEL   *v* **-ELED, -ELING, -ELS** or **-ELLED, -ELLING, -ELS** to adorn with jewels

BEJUMBLE   *v* **-BLED, -BLING, -BLES** to jumble

BEKISS   *v* **-ED, -ING, -ES** to cover with kisses

BEKNIGHT   *v* **-ED, -ING, -S** to raise to knighthood

BEKNOT   *v* **-KNOTTED, -KNOTTING, -KNOTS** to tie in knots

BEL   *n* pl. **-S** a unit of power

BELABOR   *v* **-ED, -ING, -S** to discuss for an absurd amount of time

BELABOUR   *v* **-ED, -ING, -S** to belabor

BELACED   *adj* adorned with lace

BELADY   *v* **-DIED, -DYING, -DIES** to apply the title of lady to

BELATED   *adj* late or too late

BELAUD   *v* **-ED, -ING, -S** to praise

BELAY   *v* **-ED, -ING, -S** to fasten a rope

BELAYER   *n* pl. **-S** one that belays

BELCH   *v* **-ED, -ING, -ES** to expel gas through the mouth

BELCHER   *n* pl. **-S** one that belches

BELDAM   *n* pl. **-S** an old woman

BELDAME   *n* pl. **-S** beldam

BELEAP   *v* **-LEAPED** or **-LEAPT, -LEAPING, -LEAPS** to leap upon

BELFRY   *n* pl. **-FRIES** a bell tower **BELFRIED** *adj*

BELGA   *n* pl. **-S** a former Belgian monetary unit

BELIE   *v* **-LIED, -LYING, -LIES** to misrepresent

BELIEF   *n* pl. **-S** acceptance of the truth or actuality of something

BELIER   *n* pl. **-S** one that belies

BELIEVE *v* **-LIEVED, -LIEVING, -LIEVES** to accept as true or real

BELIEVER *n* pl. **-S** one that believes

BELIKE *adv* perhaps

BELIQUOR *v* **-ED, -ING, -S** to soak with liquor

BELITTLE *v* **-TLED, -TLING, -TLES** to disparage

BELIVE *adv* in due time

BELL *v* **-ED, -ING, -S** to provide with a bell (a ringing device)

BELLBIRD *n* pl. **-S** a tropical bird

BELLBOY *n* pl. **-BOYS** a hotel's errand boy

BELLBUOY *n* pl. **-BUOYS** a buoy (a warning float) having a bell

BELLCAST *adj* designating a style of roof architecture

BELLE *n* pl. **-S** an attractive woman

BELLEEK *n* pl. **-S** a very thin translucent porcelain

BELLHOP *n* pl. **-S** a bellboy

BELLIED past tense of belly

BELLIES present 3d person sing. of belly

BELLING *n* pl. **-S** a mock serenade for newlyweds

BELLMAN *n* pl. **-MEN** a town crier

BELLOW *v* **-ED, -ING, -S** to shout in a deep voice

BELLOWER *n* pl. **-S** one that bellows

BELLPULL *n* pl. **-S** a cord pulled to ring a bell

BELLWORT *n* pl. **-S** a flowering plant

BELLY *v* **-LIED, -LYING, -LIES** to swell out

BELLYFUL *n* pl. **-S** an excessive amount

BELON *n* pl. **-S** a flat oyster

BELONG *v* **-ED, -ING, -S** to be a member of

BELOVED *n* pl. **-S** one who is loved

BELOW *n* pl. **-S** something that is beneath

BELT *v* **-ED, -ING, -S** to fasten with a belt (a strap or band worn around the waist)

BELTER *n* pl. **-S** one that belts

BELTING *n* pl. **-S** material for belts

BELTLESS *adj* having no belt

BELTLINE *n* pl. **-S** the waistline

BELTWAY *n* pl. **-WAYS** a highway around an urban area

BELUGA *n* pl. **-S** a white sturgeon

BELYING present participle of belie

BEMA *n* pl. **-MAS** or **-MATA** a platform in a synagogue

BEMADAM *v* **-ED, -ING, -S** to call by the title of madam

BEMADDEN *v* **-ED, -ING, -S** to madden

BEMEAN *v* **-ED, -ING, -S** to debase

BEMINGLE *v* **-GLED, -GLING, -GLES** to mix together

BEMIRE *v* **-MIRED, -MIRING, -MIRES** to soil with mud

BEMIST *v* **-ED, -ING, -S** to envelop in a mist

BEMIX *v* **-MIXED** or **-MIXT, -MIXING, -MIXES** to mix thoroughly

BEMOAN *v* **-ED, -ING, -S** to lament

BEMOCK *v* **-ED, -ING, -S** to mock

BEMUDDLE *v* **-DLED, -DLING, -DLES** to confuse completely

BEMURMUR *v* **-ED, -ING, -S** to murmur at

BEMUSE *v* **-MUSED, -MUSING, -MUSES** to confuse

BEMUZZLE *v* **-ZLED, -ZLING, -ZLES** to muzzle

BEN *n* pl. **-S** an inner room

BENAME *v* **-NAMED, -NEMPT** or **-NEMPTED, -NAMING, -NAMES** to name

BENCH *v* **-ED, -ING, -ES** to take a player out of a game (a team competition)

BENCHER *n* pl. **-S** a magistrate

BENCHTOP *adj* suitable for use on a workbench

BEND *v* **BENDED** or **BENT, BENDING, BENDS** to curve **BENDABLE** *adj*

BENDAY *v* **-ED, -ING, -S** to reproduce using a certain process

BENDEE *n* pl. **-S** bendy

BENDER *n* pl. **-S** one that bends

BENDWAYS *adv* bendwise

BENDWISE *adv* diagonally

BENDY *n* pl. **-DYS** okra

BENDY *adj* **BENDIER, BENDIEST** flexible

BENE *n* pl. **-S** benne

BENEATH *prep* under

BENEDICK *n* pl. **-S** benedict

BENEDICT *n* pl. **-S** a newly married man

BENEFIC *adj* kindly

BENEFICE *v* **-FICED, -FICING, -FICES** to endow with land

BENEFIT *v* **-FITED, -FITING, -FITS** or **-FITTED, -FITTING, -FITS** to be helpful or useful to

BENEMPT a past participle of bename

BENEMPTED a past participle of bename

BENIGN *adj* kind **BENIGNLY** *adv*

BENISON *n* pl. **-S** a blessing

BENJAMIN *n* pl. **-S** benzoin

BENNE *n* pl. **-S** the sesame plant

BENNET *n* pl. **-S** a perennial herb

BENNI *n* pl. **-S** benne

BENNY *n* pl. **-NIES** an amphetamine tablet

BENOMYL *n* pl. **-S** a chemical compound

BENT *n* pl. **-S** an inclination

BENTHAL *adj* benthic

BENTHIC *adj* pertaining to oceanic depths

BENTHON *n* pl. **-S** the organisms living in the benthos

BENTHOS *n* pl. **-ES** the bottom of the sea

BENTO *n* pl. **-TOS** obento

BENTWOOD *n* pl. **-S** wood bent for use in furniture

BENUMB *v* **-ED, -ING, -S** to make numb

BENZAL *adj* pertaining to a certain chemical group

BENZENE *n* pl. **-S** a volatile liquid

BENZIDIN *n* pl. **-S** a hydrocarbon

BENZIN *n* pl. **-S** benzine

BENZINE *n* pl. **-S** a volatile liquid

BENZOATE *n* pl. **-S** a chemical salt

BENZOIN *n* pl. **-S** a gum resin **BENZOIC** *adj*

BENZOL *n* pl. **-S** a benzene

BENZOLE *n* pl. **-S** benzol

BENZOYL *n* pl. **-S** a univalent chemical radical

BENZYL *n* pl. **-S** a univalent chemical radical **BENZYLIC** *adj*

BEPAINT *v* **-ED, -ING, -S** to tinge

BEPIMPLE *v* **-PLED, -PLING, -PLES** to cover with pimples

BEQUEATH *v* **-ED, -ING, -S** to grant by testament

BEQUEST *n* pl. **-S** a legacy

BERAKE *v* **-RAKED, -RAKING, -RAKES** to rake all over

BERASCAL *v* **-ED, -ING, -S** to accuse of being a rascal

BERATE *v* **-RATED, -RATING, -RATES** to scold severely

BERBER *n* pl. **-S** a type of carpet

BERBERIN *n* pl. **-S** a medicinal alkaloid

BERBERIS *n* pl. **-ES** a barberry

BERCEUSE *n* pl. **-S** a lullaby

BERDACHE *n* pl. **-S** a Native American male transvestite

BERDASH *n* pl. **-ES** berdache

BEREAVE *v* **-REAVED** or **-REFT, -REAVING, -REAVES** to deprive

BEREAVER *n* pl. **-S** one that bereaves

BERET *n* pl. **-S** a soft, flat cap

BERETTA *n* pl. **-S** biretta

BERG *n* pl. **-S** an iceberg

BERGAMOT *n* pl. **-S** a citrus tree

BERGENIA *n* pl. **-S** a flowering plant

BERGERE *n* pl. **-S** an upholstered armchair

BERHYME *v* **-RHYMED, -RHYMING, -RHYMES** to compose in rhyme

BERIBERI *n* pl. **-S** a thiamine deficiency disease

BERIMBAU *n* pl. **-S** a Brazilian musical instrument

BERIME *v* **-RIMED, -RIMING, -RIMES** to berhyme

BERINGED *adj* adorned with rings

BERK *n* pl. **-S** a foolish person

BERLIN *n* pl. **-S** a type of carriage

BERLINE *n* pl. **-S** a limousine

BERM *v* **-ED, -ING, -S** to provide with a berm (a ledge)

BERME *n* pl. **-S** berm

BERMUDAS *n/pl* knee-length walking shorts

BERNICLE *n* pl. **-S** a wild goose

BEROBED *adj* wearing a robe

BEROUGED *adj* obviously or thickly rouged

BERRETTA *n* pl. **-S** biretta

BERRY *v* **-RIED, -RYING, -RIES** to produce berries (fleshy fruits)

BERRYING *n* pl. **-S** the activity of gathering berries

BERSEEM *n* pl. **-S** a clover

BERSERK *n* pl. **-S** a fierce warrior

BERTH *v* **-ED, -ING, -S** to provide with a mooring

BERTHA *n* pl. **-S** a wide collar

BERTHING *n* pl. **-S** the action of mooring a ship

BERYL *n* pl. **-S** a green mineral **BERYLINE** *adj*

BES *n* pl. **BESES** beth

BESCORCH *v* **-ED, -ING, -ES** to scorch

BESCOUR *v* **-ED, -ING, -S** to scour thoroughly

BESCREEN *v* **-ED, -ING, -S** to screen

BESEECH *v* **-SEECHED** or **-SOUGHT, -SEECHING, -SEECHES** to implore

BESEEM *v* **-ED, -ING, -S** to be suitable

BESET *v* **-SET, -SETTING, -SETS** to assail

BESETTER *n* pl. **-S** one that besets

BESHADOW *v* **-ED, -ING, -S** to cast a shadow on

BESHAME *v* **-SHAMED, -SHAMING, -SHAMES** to put to shame

BESHIVER *v* **-ED, -ING, -S** to break into small pieces

BESHOUT *v* **-ED, -ING, -S** to shout at

BESHREW *v* **-ED, -ING, -S** to curse

BESHROUD *v* **-ED, -ING, -S** to cover

BESIDE *prep* next to

BESIDES *adv* in addition

BESIEGE *v* **-SIEGED, -SIEGING, -SIEGES** to surround

BESIEGER *n* pl. **-S** one that besieges

BESLAVED *adj* filled with slaves

BESLIME *v* **-SLIMED, -SLIMING, -SLIMES** to cover with slime

BESMEAR *v* **-ED, -ING, -S** to smear over

BESMILE *v* **-SMILED, -SMILING, -SMILES** to smile on

BESMIRCH *v* **-ED, -ING, -ES** to dirty

BESMOKE *v* **-SMOKED, -SMOKING, -SMOKES** to soil with smoke

BESMOOTH *v* **-ED, -ING, -S** to smooth

BESMUDGE *v* **-SMUDGED, -SMUDGING, -SMUDGES** to smudge

BESMUT *v* **-SMUTTED, -SMUTTING, -SMUTS** to blacken with smut

BESNOW *v* **-ED, -ING, -S** to cover with snow

BESOM *n* pl. **-S** a broom

BESOOTHE *v* **-SOOTHED, -SOOTHING, -SOOTHES** to soothe

BESOT *v* **-SOTTED, -SOTTING, -SOTS** to stupefy

BESOUGHT a past tense of beseech

BESPEAK *v* **-SPOKE** or **-SPAKE, -SPOKEN, -SPEAKING, -SPEAKS** to claim in advance

BESPOUSE *v* **-SPOUSED, -SPOUSING, -SPOUSES** to marry

BESPREAD *v* **-SPREAD, -SPREADING, -SPREADS** to spread over

BESPRENT *adj* sprinkled over

BEST *v* **-ED, -ING, -S** to outdo

BESTEAD *v* **-ED, -ING, -S** to help

BESTIAL *adj* pertaining to beasts

BESTIARY *n* pl. **-ARIES** a collection of animal fables

BESTIR *v* **-STIRRED, -STIRRING, -STIRS** to rouse

BESTOW *v* **-ED, -ING, -S** to present as a gift

BESTOWAL *n* pl. **-S** a gift

BESTOWER *n* pl. **-S** one that bestows

BESTREW *v* **-STREWED, -STREWN, -STREWING, -STREWS** to scatter

BESTRIDE *v* **-STRODE** or **-STRID, -STRIDDEN, -STRIDING, -STRIDES** to straddle

BESTROW *v* **-STROWED, -STROWN, -STROWING, -STROWS** to bestrew

BESTUD *v* **-STUDDED, -STUDDING, -STUDS** to dot

BESUITED *adj* wearing a suit

BESWARM *v* **-ED, -ING, -S** to swarm all over

BET *v* **BET** or **BETTED, BETTING, BETS** to wager

BETA *n* pl. **-S** a Greek letter

BETAINE *n* pl. **-S** an alkaloid

BETAKE *v* **-TOOK, -TAKEN, -TAKING, -TAKES** to cause to go

BETATRON *n* pl. **-S** an electron accelerator

BETATTER *v* **-ED, -ING, -S** to tatter

BETAXED *adj* burdened with taxes

BETEL *n* pl. **-S** a climbing plant

BETELNUT *n* pl. **-S** a seed chewed as a stimulant

BETH *n* pl. **-S** a Hebrew letter

BETHANK *v* **-ED, -ING, -S** to thank

BETHEL *n* pl. **-S** a holy place

BETHESDA *n* pl. **-S** a chapel

BETHINK *v* **-THOUGHT, -THINKING, -THINKS** to consider

BETHORN *v* **-ED, -ING, -S** to fill with thorns

BETHUMP	*v* **-ED, -ING, -S** to thump soundly
BETIDE	*v* **-TIDED, -TIDING, -TIDES** to befall
BETIME	*adv* betimes
BETIMES	*adv* soon
BETISE	*n* pl. **-S** stupidity
BETOKEN	*v* **-ED, -ING, -S** to indicate
BETON	*n* pl. **-S** a type of concrete
BETONY	*n* pl. **-NIES** a European herb
BETOOK	past tense of betake
BETRAY	*v* **-ED, -ING, -S** to aid an enemy of
BETRAYAL	*n* pl. **-S** the act of betraying
BETRAYER	*n* pl. **-S** one that betrays
BETROTH	*v* **-ED, -ING, -S** to engage to marry
BETTA	*n* pl. **-S** a freshwater fish
BETTED	a past tense of bet
BETTER	*v* **-ED, -ING, -S** to improve
BETTING	*n* pl. **-S** the act of gambling on the outcome of a race
BETTOR	*n* pl. **-S** one that bets
BETWEEN	*prep* in the space that separates
BETWIXT	*prep* between
BEUNCLED	*adj* having many uncles
BEVATRON	*n* pl. **-S** a proton accelerator
BEVEL	*v* **-ELED, -ELING, -ELS** or **-ELLED, -ELLING, -ELS** to cut at an angle
BEVELER	*n* pl. **-S** one that bevels
BEVELLER	*n* pl. **-S** beveler
BEVERAGE	*n* pl. **-S** a liquid for drinking
BEVIES	pl. of bevy
BEVOMIT	*v* **-ED, -ING, -S** to vomit all over
BEVOR	*n* pl. **-S** a piece of armor for the lower face
BEVVY	*n* pl. **BEVVIES** an alcoholic drink
BEVY	*n* pl. **BEVIES** a group
BEWAIL	*v* **-ED, -ING, -S** to lament
BEWAILER	*n* pl. **-S** one that bewails
BEWARE	*v* **-WARED, -WARING, -WARES** to be careful
BEWEARY	*v* **-WEARIED, -WEARYING, -WEARIES** to make weary
BEWEEP	*v* **-WEPT, -WEEPING, -WEEPS** to lament
BEWIG	*v* **-WIGGED, -WIGGING, -WIGS** to adorn with a wig
BEWILDER	*v* **-ED, -ING, -S** to confuse
BEWINGED	*adj* having wings
BEWITCH	*v* **-ED, -ING, -ES** to affect by witchcraft or magic
BEWORM	*v* **-ED, -ING, -S** to infest with worms
BEWORRY	*v* **-RIED, -RYING, -RIES** to worry
BEWRAP	*v* **-WRAPPED** or **-WRAPT, -WRAPPING, -WRAPS** to wrap completely
BEWRAY	*v* **-ED, -ING, -S** to divulge
BEWRAYER	*n* pl. **-S** one that bewrays
BEY	*n* pl. **BEYS** a Turkish ruler
BEYLIC	*n* pl. **-S** the domain of a bey
BEYLIK	*n* pl. **-S** beylic
BEYOND	*n* pl. **-S** something that lies farther ahead
BEZANT	*n* pl. **-S** a coin of ancient Rome
BEZAZZ	*n* pl. **-ES** pizazz
BEZEL	*n* pl. **-S** a slanted surface
BEZIL	*n* pl. **-S** bezel
BEZIQUE	*n* pl. **-S** a card game
BEZOAR	*n* pl. **-S** a gastric mass
BEZZANT	*n* pl. **-S** bezant
BHAJI	*n* pl. **-S** an Indian dish of fried vegetables
BHAKTA	*n* pl. **-S** one who practices bhakti
BHAKTI	*n* pl. **-S** a selfless devotion to a deity in Hinduism
BHANG	*n* pl. **-S** the hemp plant
BHANGRA	*n* pl. **-S** a form of popular Punjabi dance music
BHARAL	*n* pl. **-S** a goatlike Asian mammal
BHEESTIE	*n* pl. **-S** bheesty
BHEESTY	*n* pl. **-TIES** a water carrier
BHELPURI	*n* pl. **-S** a dish of rice, spices, and chutney
BHISTIE	*n* pl. **-S** bheesty
BHOOT	*n* pl. **-S** bhut
BHUT	*n* pl. **-S** a small whirlwind
BI	*n* pl. **-S** a bisexual
BIACETYL	*n* pl. **-S** a chemical flavor enhancer
BIALI	*n* pl. **-S** bialy
BIALY	*n* pl. **-ALYS** or **-ALIES** an onion roll
BIANNUAL	*adj* occurring twice a year
BIAS	*v* **-ASED, -ASING, -ASES** or **-ASSED, -ASSING, -ASSES** to prejudice **BIASEDLY** *adv*
BIASNESS	*n* pl. **-ES** the state of being slanted

BIATHLON   *n* pl. **-S** an athletic contest

BIAXAL   *adj* biaxial

BIAXIAL   *adj* having two axes

BIB   *v* **BIBBED, BIBBING, BIBS** to tipple

BIBASIC   *adj* dibasic

BIBB   *n* pl. **-S** a mast support

BIBBED   past tense of bib

BIBBER   *n* pl. **-S** a tippler

BIBBERY   *n* pl. **-BERIES** the act of tippling

BIBBING   *n* pl. **-S** the act of tippling

BIBCOCK   *n* pl. **-S** a type of faucet

BIBE   *n* pl. **-S** a creature whose crying is an omen of death

BIBELOT   *n* pl. **-S** a trinket

BIBLE   *n* pl. **-S** an authoritative publication **BIBLICAL** *adj*

BIBLESS   *adj* having no bib (a cloth covering)

BIBLIKE   *adj* resembling a bib

BIBLIST   *n* pl. **-S** one who takes the words of the Bible literally

BIBULOUS   *adj* given to drinking

BICARB   *n* pl. **-S** sodium bicarbonate

BICAUDAL   *adj* having two tails

BICE   *n* pl. **-S** a blue or green pigment

BICEP   *n* pl. **-S** biceps

BICEPS   *n* pl. **-ES** an arm muscle

BICHROME   *adj* two-colored

BICKER   *v* **-ED, -ING, -S** to argue

BICKERER   *n* pl. **-S** one that bickers

BICOLOR   *n* pl. **-S** something having two colors

BICOLOUR   *n* pl. **-S** bicolor

BICONVEX   *adj* convex on both sides

BICORN   *n* pl. **-S** bicorne

BICORNE   *n* pl. **-S** a type of hat

BICRON   *n* pl. **-S** one billionth of a meter

BICUSPID   *n* pl. **-S** a tooth

BICYCLE   *v* **-CLED, -CLING, -CLES** to ride a bicycle (a two-wheeled vehicle)

BICYCLER   *n* pl. **-S** one that bicycles

BICYCLIC   *adj* having two cycles

BID   *v* **BADE, BIDDEN, BIDDING, BIDS** to make a bid (an offer of a price)

BIDARKA   *n* pl. **-S** an Inuit canoe

BIDARKEE   *n* pl. **-S** bidarka

BIDDABLE   *adj* obedient **BIDDABLY** *adv*

BIDDEN   past participle of bid

BIDDER   *n* pl. **-S** one that bids

BIDDING   *n* pl. **-S** a command

BIDDY   *n* pl. **-DIES** a hen

BIDE   *v* **BIDED** or **BODE, BIDING, BIDES** to wait

BIDENTAL   *adj* having two teeth

BIDER   *n* pl. **-S** one that bides

BIDET   *n* pl. **-S** a low basin used for washing

BIDI   *n* pl. **-S** a cigarette of India

BIDING   present participle of bide

BIELD   *v* **-ED, -ING, -S** to shelter

BIENNALE   *n* pl. **-S** a biennial show

BIENNIAL   *n* pl. **-S** an event that occurs every two years

BIENNIUM   *n* pl. **-NIUMS** or **-NIA** a period of two years

BIER   *n* pl. **-S** a coffin stand

BIFACE   *n* pl. **-S** a stone tool having a cutting edge

BIFACIAL   *adj* having two faces

BIFF   *v* **-ED, -ING, -S** to hit

BIFFIN   *n* pl. **-S** a cooking apple

BIFFY   *n* pl. **-FIES** a toilet

BIFID   *adj* divided into two parts **BIFIDLY** *adv*

BIFIDITY   *n* pl. **-TIES** the state of being bifid

BIFIDUM   *n* pl. **-DA** a bacterium often added to yogurt

BIFILAR   *adj* having two threads

BIFLEX   *adj* bent in two places

BIFOCAL   *n* pl. **-S** a type of lens

BIFOLD   *n* pl. **-S** a two-piece door

BIFORATE   *adj* having two perforations

BIFORKED   *adj* divided into two branches

BIFORM   *adj* having two forms

BIFORMED   *adj* biform

BIG   *adj* **BIGGER, BIGGEST** of considerable size

BIG   *n* pl. **-S** one of great importance

BIGAMIES   pl. of bigamy

BIGAMIST   *n* pl. **-S** one who commits bigamy

BIGAMOUS   *adj* guilty of bigamy

BIGAMY   *n* pl. **-MIES** the crime of being married to two people at once

BIGARADE   *n* pl. **-S** a citrus tree

BIGAROON   *n* pl. **-S** a type of cherry

BIGEMINY   *n* pl. **-NIES** the state of having a double pulse

BIGEYE   *n* pl. **-S** a marine fish

BIGFOOT   *n* pl. **-FOOTS** or **-FEET** an influential person

BIGFOOT   *v* **-ED, -ING, -S** to apply one's influence as a bigfoot

BIGGER   comparative of big

BIGGEST   superlative of big

BIGGETY   *adj* biggity

BIGGIE   *n* pl. **-S** one that is big

BIGGIES   pl. of biggy

BIGGIN   *n* pl. **-S** a house

BIGGING   *n* pl. **-S** biggin

BIGGISH   *adj* somewhat big

BIGGITY   *adj* conceited

BIGGY   *n* pl. **-GIES** biggie

BIGHEAD   *n* pl. **-S** a disease of animals

BIGHORN   *n* pl. **-S** a wild sheep

BIGHT   *v* **-ED, -ING, -S** to fasten with a loop of rope

BIGLY   *adv* in a big manner

BIGMOUTH   *n* pl. **-S** a talkative person

BIGNESS   *n* pl. **-ES** the state of being big

BIGNONIA   *n* pl. **-S** a climbing plant

BIGOS   *n* pl. **-ES** a Polish stew

BIGOT   *n* pl. **-S** a prejudiced person

BIGOTED   *adj* intolerant

BIGOTRY   *n* pl. **-RIES** prejudice

BIGSTICK   *adj* threatening military force

BIGTIME   *adj* pertaining to the highest level

BIGUINE   *n* pl. **-S** beguine

BIGWIG   *n* pl. **-S** an important person

BIHOURLY   *adj* occurring every two hours

BIJOU   *n* pl. **-JOUS** or **-JOUX** a jewel

BIJUGATE   *adj* two-paired

BIJUGOUS   *adj* bijugate

BIJURAL   *adj* pertaining to a single jurisdiction with two legal systems

BIKE   *v* **BIKED, BIKING, BIKES** to bicycle

BIKER   *n* pl. **-S** one that bikes

BIKEWAY   *n* pl. **-WAYS** a route for bikes

BIKIE   *n* pl. **-S** biker

BIKING   present participle of bike

BIKINI   *n* pl. **-S** a type of two-piece bathing suit **BIKINIED** *adj*

BILABIAL   *n* pl. **-S** a sound articulated with both lips

BILANDER   *n* pl. **-S** a small ship

BILAYER   *n* pl. **-S** a film with two molecular layers

BILBERRY   *n* pl. **-RIES** an edible berry

BILBO   *n* pl. **-BOS** or **-BOES** a finely tempered sword

BILBOA   *n* pl. **-S** bilbo

BILBY   *n* pl. **-BIES** a small nocturnal mammal

BILE   *n* pl. **-S** a fluid secreted by the liver

BILEVEL   *n* pl. **-S** a house having two levels

BILGE   *v* **BILGED, BILGING, BILGES** to spring a leak

BILGY   *adj* **BILGIER, BILGIEST** smelling like seepage

BILIARY   *adj* pertaining to bile

BILINEAR   *adj* pertaining to two lines

BILIOUS   *adj* pertaining to bile

BILK   *v* **-ED, -ING, -S** to cheat

BILKER   *n* pl. **-S** one that bilks

BILL   *v* **-ED, -ING, -S** to present a statement of costs to **BILLABLE** *adj*

BILLBUG   *n* pl. **-S** a weevil

BILLER   *n* pl. **-S** one that bills

BILLET   *v* **-ED, -ING, -S** to lodge soldiers

BILLETEE   *n* pl. **-S** one that is billeted

BILLETER   *n* pl. **-S** one that billets

BILLFISH   *n* pl. **-ES** a fish with long, slender jaws

BILLFOLD   *n* pl. **-S** a wallet

BILLHEAD   *n* pl. **-S** a letterhead

BILLHOOK   *n* pl. **-S** a cutting tool

BILLIARD   *n* pl. **-S** a carom shot in billiards (a table game)

BILLIE   *n* pl. **-S** a comrade

BILLIES   pl. of billy

BILLING   *n* pl. **-S** the relative position in which a performer is listed

BILLION   *n* pl. **-S** a number

BILLON   *n* pl. **-S** an alloy of silver and copper

BILLOW   *v* **-ED, -ING, -S** to swell

BILLOWY _adj_ **-LOWIER, -LOWIEST** swelling; surging

BILLY _n_ pl. **-LIES** a short club

BILLYCAN _n_ pl. **-S** a pot for heating water

BILOBATE _adj_ having two lobes

BILOBED _adj_ bilobate

BILSTED _n_ pl. **-S** a hardwood tree

BILTONG _n_ pl. **-S** dried and cured meat

BIMA _n_ pl. **-S** bema

BIMAH _n_ pl. **-S** bema

BIMANOUS _adj_ two-handed

BIMANUAL _adj_ done with two hands

BIMBETTE _n_ pl. **-S** an attractive but empty-headed young woman

BIMBO _n_ pl. **-BOS** or **-BOES** a disreputable person

BIMENSAL _adj_ occurring every two months

BIMESTER _n_ pl. **-S** a two-month period

BIMETAL _n_ pl. **-S** something composed of two metals

BIMETHYL _n_ pl. **-S** ethane

BIMINI _n_ pl. **-S** a type of awning for a yacht

BIMODAL _adj_ having two statistical modes

BIMORPH _n_ pl. **-S** a device consisting of two crystals cemented together

BIN _v_ **BINNED, BINNING, BINS** to store in a large receptacle

BINAL _adj_ twofold

BINARISM _n_ pl. **-S** a mode of thought based on oppositions

BINARY _n_ pl. **-RIES** a combination of two things

BINATE _adj_ growing in pairs **BINATELY** _adv_

BINAURAL _adj_ hearing with both ears

BIND _v_ **BOUND, BINDING, BINDS** to tie or secure **BINDABLE** _adj_

BINDER _n_ pl. **-S** one that binds

BINDERY _n_ pl. **-ERIES** a place where books are bound

BINDI _n_ pl. **-S** a dot worn on the forehead by women in India

BINDING _n_ pl. **-S** the cover and fastenings of a book

BINDLE _n_ pl. **-S** a bundle

BINDWEED _n_ pl. **-S** a twining plant

BINE _n_ pl. **-S** a twining plant stem

BINER _n_ pl. **-S** a soldier armed with a carbine

BING _interj_ — used to indicate a sudden action

BINGE _v_ **BINGED, BINGEING** or **BINGING, BINGES** to indulge in something to excess

BINGEING _n_ pl. **-S** the act of indulging in something to excess

BINGER _n_ pl. **-S** one that binges

BINGING _n_ pl. **-S** bingeing

BINGO _n_ pl. **-GOS** or **-GOES** a game of chance

BINIT _n_ pl. **-S** a unit of computer information

BINMAN _n_ pl. **-MEN** a garbage collector

BINNACLE _n_ pl. **-S** a compass stand

BINNED past tense of bin

BINNING present participle of bin

BINOCLE _n_ pl. **-S** a binocular

BINOCS _n/pl_ binoculars

BINOMIAL _n_ pl. **-S** an algebraic expression

BINT _n_ pl. **-S** a woman

BIO _n_ pl. **BIOS** a biography

BIOASSAY _v_ **-ED, -ING, -S** to test a substance (as a drug) in order to determine its strength

BIOCHIP _n_ pl. **-S** a hypothetical computer component that uses proteins to store or process data

BIOCIDE _n_ pl. **-S** a substance destructive to living organisms **BIOCIDAL** _adj_

BIOCLEAN _adj_ free of harmful organisms

BIOCYCLE _n_ pl. **-S** a life-supporting region

BIOETHIC _adj_ pertaining to ethical questions arising from advances in biology

BIOFILM _n_ pl. **-S** a thin layer of microorganisms

BIOFUEL _n_ pl. **-S** fuel composed of biological raw materials

BIOG _n_ pl. **-S** a biography

BIOGAS _n_ pl. **-GASES** or **-GASSES** fuel gas produced by organic waste

BIOGEN _n_ pl. **-S** a hypothetical protein molecule

BIOGENIC _adj_ produced by living organisms

BIOGENY _n_ pl. **-NIES** the development of life from preexisting life

BIOHERM _n_ pl. **-S** a mass of marine fossils

BIOLOGIC   *n* pl. **-S** a drug obtained from an organic source

BIOLOGY   *n* pl. **-GIES** the science of life

BIOLYSIS   *n* pl. **-YSES** death **BIOLYTIC** *adj*

BIOMASS   *n* pl. **-ES** an amount of living matter

BIOME   *n* pl. **-S** an ecological community

BIOMETER   *n* pl. **-S** a device for measuring carbon dioxide given off by living matter

BIOMETRY   *n* pl. **-TRIES** the statistical study of biological data

BIOMORPH   *n* pl. **-S** an art form resembling a living organism in shape

BIONICS   *n/pl* a science joining biology and electronics **BIONIC** *adj*

BIONOMY   *n* pl. **-MIES** ecology **BIONOMIC** *adj*

BIONT   *n* pl. **-S** a living organism **BIONTIC** *adj*

BIOPIC   *n* pl. **-S** a biographical movie

BIOPLASM   *n* pl. **-S** living matter

BIOPSIC   *adj* pertaining to the examination of living tissue

BIOPSY   *v* **-SIED, -SYING, -SIES** to examine living tissue

BIOPTIC   *adj* biopsic

BIOSCOPE   *n* pl. **-S** an early movie projector

BIOSCOPY   *n* pl. **-PIES** a type of medical examination

BIOSOLID   *n* pl. **-S** solid organic matter obtained from treated sewage

BIOTA   *n* pl. **-S** flora and fauna

BIOTECH   *n* pl. **-S** applied biology

BIOTIC   *adj* pertaining to life

BIOTICAL   *adj* biotic

BIOTICS   *n/pl* a life science

BIOTIN   *n* pl. **-S** a B vitamin

BIOTITE   *n* pl. **-S** a form of mica **BIOTITIC** *adj*

BIOTOPE   *n* pl. **-S** a stable habitat

BIOTOXIN   *n* pl. **-S** poison made by a plant or animal

BIOTRON   *n* pl. **-S** a climate control chamber

BIOTYPE   *n* pl. **-S** a group of genetically similar organisms **BIOTYPIC** *adj*

BIOVULAR   *adj* derived from two ova

BIOWASTE   *n* pl. **-S** waste composed chiefly of organic matter

BIPACK   *n* pl. **-S** a pair of films

BIPAROUS   *adj* producing offspring in pairs

BIPARTED   *adj* having two parts

BIPARTY   *adj* of two parties

BIPED   *n* pl. **-S** a two-footed animal **BIPEDAL** *adj*

BIPHASIC   *adj* having two phases

BIPHENYL   *n* pl. **-S** a hydrocarbon

BIPLANE   *n* pl. **-S** a type of airplane

BIPOD   *n* pl. **-S** a two-legged support

BIPOLAR   *adj* having two poles

BIRACIAL   *adj* having members of two races

BIRADIAL   *adj* having dual symmetry

BIRAMOSE   *adj* biramous

BIRAMOUS   *adj* divided into two branches

BIRCH   *v* **-ED, -ING, -ES** to whip

BIRCHEN   *adj* made of birch wood

BIRD   *v* **-ED, -ING, -S** to hunt birds (winged, warm-blooded vertebrates)

BIRDBATH   *n* pl. **-S** a bath for birds

BIRDCAGE   *n* pl. **-S** a cage for birds

BIRDCALL   *n* pl. **-S** the call of a bird

BIRDDOG   *v* **-DOGGED, -DOGGING, -DOGS** to follow closely

BIRDER   *n* pl. **-S** a bird hunter

BIRDFARM   *n* pl. **-S** an aircraft carrier

BIRDFEED   *n* pl. **-S** birdseed

BIRDIE   *v* **BIRDIED, BIRDIEING, BIRDIES** to shoot in one stroke under par in golf

BIRDING   *n* pl. **-S** bird-watching

BIRDLIFE   *n* pl. **BIRDLIFE** avifauna

BIRDLIKE   *adj* resembling a bird

BIRDLIME   *v* **-LIMED, -LIMING, -LIMES** to trap small birds

BIRDMAN   *n* pl. **-MEN** one who keeps birds

BIRDSEED   *n* pl. **-S** a mixture of seeds used for feeding birds

BIRDSEYE   *n* pl. **-S** a flowering plant

BIRDSHOT   *n* pl. **-S** small shot for shooting birds

BIRDSONG   *n* pl. **-S** the song of a bird

BIREME   *n* pl. **-S** an ancient galley

BIRETTA   *n* pl. **-S** a cap worn by clergymen

BIRIANI   *n* pl. **-S** biryani

BIRK   *n* pl. **-S** a birch tree

BIRKIE   *n* pl. **-S** a lively person

BIRL   *v* **-ED, -ING, -S** to rotate a floating log

BIRLE   *v* **BIRLED, BIRLING, BIRLES** to carouse

BIRLER   *n* pl. **-S** one that birls

BIRLING   *n* pl. **-S** a lumberjack's game

BIRR   *n* pl. **BIRROTCH** a monetary unit of Ethiopia

BIRR   *v* **-ED, -ING, -S** to make a whirring noise

BIRRETTA   *n* pl. **-S** biretta

BIRSE   *n* pl. **-S** a bristle

BIRTH   *v* **-ED, -ING, -S** to originate

BIRTHDAY   *n* pl. **-DAYS** an anniversary of a birth

BIRTHING   *n* pl. **-S** the act of giving birth

BIRYANI   *n* pl. **-S** an Indian dish of meat, fish, or vegetables and rice

BIS   *adv* twice

BISCOTTO   *n* pl. **-COTTI** a crisp, anise-flavored cookie

BISCUIT   *n* pl. **-S** a small cake of shortened bread **BISCUITY** *adj*

BISE   *n* pl. **-S** a cold wind

BISECT   *v* **-ED, -ING, -S** to cut into two parts

BISECTOR   *n* pl. **-S** something that bisects

BISEXUAL   *n* pl. **-S** one who is attracted to both sexes

BISH   *n* pl. **-ES** a bishop

BISHOP   *v* **-ED, -ING, -S** to appoint as a bishop (the head of a diocese)

BISK   *n* pl. **-S** bisque

BISMARCK   *n* pl. **-S** a type of pastry

BISMUTH   *n* pl. **-S** a metallic element

BISNAGA   *n* pl. **-S** a type of cactus

BISON   *n* pl. **-S** an ox-like animal

BISQUE   *n* pl. **-S** a thick soup

BISTABLE   *n* pl. **-S** an electronic circuit that has two stable states

BISTATE   *adj* pertaining to two states

BISTER   *n* pl. **-S** a brown pigment **BISTERED** *adj*

BISTORT   *n* pl. **-S** a perennial herb with roots used as astringents

BISTOURY   *n* pl. **-RIES** a surgical knife

BISTRE   *n* pl. **-S** bister **BISTRED** *adj*

BISTRO   *n* pl. **-TROS** a small tavern **BISTROIC** *adj*

BIT   *v* **BITTED, BITTING, BITS** to restrain

BITABLE   *adj* capable of being bitten

BITCH   *v* **-ED, -ING, -ES** to complain

BITCHEN   *adj* excellent

BITCHERY   *n* pl. **-ERIES** bitchy behavior

BITCHY   *adj* **BITCHIER, BITCHIEST** malicious **BITCHILY** *adv*

BITE   *v* **BIT, BITTEN, BITING, BITES** to seize with the teeth **BITEABLE** *adj*

BITER   *n* pl. **-S** one that bites

BITEWING   *n* pl. **-S** a dental X-ray film

BITING   present participle of bite

BITINGLY   *adv* sarcastically

BITMAP   *n* pl. **-S** an array of binary data

BITSTOCK   *n* pl. **-S** a brace on a drill

BITSY   *adj* **-SIER, -SIEST** tiny

BITT   *v* **-ED, -ING, -S** to secure a cable around a post

BITTED   past tense of bit

BITTEN   a past participle of bite

BITTER   *adj* **-TERER, -TEREST** having a disagreeable taste **BITTERLY** *adv*

BITTER   *v* **-ED, -ING, -S** to make bitter

BITTERN   *n* pl. **-S** a wading bird

BITTIER   comparative of bitty

BITTIEST   superlative of bitty

BITTING   *n* pl. **-S** an indentation in a key

BITTOCK   *n* pl. **-S** a small amount

BITTY   *adj* **-TIER, -TIEST** tiny **BITTILY** *adv*

BITUMEN   *n* pl. **-S** an asphalt

BITWISE   *adj* denoting an operator in a computer program that deals with bits

BIUNIQUE   *adj* being a type of correspondence between two sets

BIVALENT   *n* pl. **-S** a pair of chromosomes

BIVALVE   *n* pl. **-S** a bivalved mollusk

BIVALVED   *adj* having a two-valved shell

BIVINYL   *n* pl. **-S** a flammable gas used in making synthetic rubber

BIVOUAC   *v* **-OUACKED, -OUACKING, -OUACKS** or **-OUACS** to make a camp

BIWEEKLY   *n* pl. **-LIES** a publication issued every two weeks

BIYEARLY   *adj* occurring every two years

BIZ   *n* pl. **BIZZES** business

BIZARRE *n pl.* **-S** a strangely striped flower

BIZARRO *n pl.* **-ROS** one that is strikingly unusual

BIZE *n pl.* **-S** bise

BIZNAGA *n pl.* **-S** bisnaga

BIZONE *n pl.* **-S** two combined zones **BIZONAL** *adj*

BLAB *v* **BLABBED, BLABBING, BLABS** to talk idly

BLABBER *v* **-ED, -ING, -S** to blab

BLABBY *adj* **-BIER, -BIEST** talkative

BLACK *adj* **BLACKER, BLACKEST** being of the darkest color

BLACK *v* **-ED, -ING, -S** to make black

BLACKBOY *n pl.* **-BOYS** an Australian plant

BLACKCAP *n pl.* **-S** a small European bird

BLACKEN *v* **-ED, -ING, -S** to make black

BLACKFIN *n pl.* **-S** a food fish

BLACKFLY *n pl.* **-FLIES** a biting fly

BLACKGUM *n pl.* **-S** a tupelo

BLACKING *n pl.* **-S** black shoe polish

BLACKISH *adj* somewhat black

BLACKLEG *n pl.* **-S** a cattle disease

BLACKLY *adv* in a black manner

BLACKOUT *n pl.* **-S** a power failure

BLACKTOP *v* **-TOPPED, -TOPPING, -TOPS** to pave with asphalt

BLADDER *n pl.* **-S** a saclike receptacle **BLADDERY** *adj*

BLADE *v* **BLADED, BLADING, BLADES** to skate on in-line skates

BLADER *n pl.* **-S** one that blades

BLADING *n pl.* **-S** the act of skating on in-line skates

BLAE *adj* bluish-black

BLAFF *n pl.* **-S** a West Indian stew

BLAG *v* **BLAGGED, BLAGGING, BLAGS** to rob with violence

BLAGGER *n pl.* **-S** one that blags

BLAGGING *n pl.* **-S** informal talk in public

BLAGUE *n pl.* **-S** pretentious nonsense

BLAH *n pl.* **-S** nonsense

BLAH *adj* **BLAHER, BLAHEST** dull, unexciting

BLAIN *n pl.* **-S** a blister

BLAM *v* **BLAMMED, BLAMMING, BLAMS** to make a loud sound like that of a gunshot

BLAMABLE *adj* being at fault **BLAMABLY** *adv*

BLAME *v* **BLAMED, BLAMING, BLAMES** to find fault with

BLAMEFUL *adj* blamable

BLAMER *n pl.* **-S** one that blames

BLAMING present participle of blame

BLANCH *v* **-ED, -ING, -ES** to whiten

BLANCHER *n pl.* **-S** a whitener

BLAND *adj* **BLANDER, BLANDEST** soothing **BLANDLY** *adv*

BLANDISH *v* **-ED, -ING, -ES** to coax by flattery

BLANK *adj* **BLANKER, BLANKEST** empty

BLANK *v* **-ED, -ING, -S** to delete

BLANKET *v* **-ED, -ING, -S** to cover uniformly

BLANKETY *n pl.* **-TIES** a euphemism for an unmentionable word

BLANKIE *n pl.* **-S** a child's blanket (a piece of fabric used as a cover)

BLANKLY *adv* in a blank manner

BLARE *v* **BLARED, BLARING, BLARES** to sound loudly

BLARNEY *v* **-NEYED, -NEYING, -NEYS** to beguile with flattery

BLASE *adj* indifferent

BLAST *v* **-ED, -ING, -S** to use an explosive

BLASTEMA *n pl.* **-MAS** or **-MATA** a region of embryonic cells

BLASTER *n pl.* **-S** one that blasts

BLASTIE *n pl.* **-S** a dwarf

BLASTIER comparative of blasty

BLASTIEST superlative of blasty

BLASTING *n pl.* **-S** the act of one that blasts

BLASTOFF *n pl.* **-S** the launching of a rocket

BLASTOMA *n pl.* **-MAS** or **-MATA** a type of tumor

BLASTULA *n pl.* **-LAS** or **-LAE** an early embryo

BLASTY *adj* **BLASTIER, BLASTIEST** gusty

BLAT *v* **BLATTED, BLATTING, BLATS** to bleat

BLATANCY *n pl.* **-CIES** something blatant

BLATANT *adj* obvious

BLATE *adj* timid

BLATHER *v* **-ED, -ING, -S** to talk foolishly

BLATTED past tense of blat

BLATTER *v* **-ED, -ING, -S** to chatter

BLATTING present participle of blat

BLAUBOK *n* pl. **-S** an extinct antelope

BLAW *v* **BLAWED, BLAWN, BLAWING, BLAWS** to blow

BLAZE *v* **BLAZED, BLAZING, BLAZES** to burn brightly

BLAZER *n* pl. **-S** a lightweight jacket **BLAZERED** *adj*

BLAZON *v* **-ED, -ING, -S** to proclaim

BLAZONER *n* pl. **-S** one that blazons

BLAZONRY *n* pl. **-RIES** a great display

BLEACH *v* **-ED, -ING, -ES** to whiten

BLEACHER *n* pl. **-S** one that bleaches

BLEAK *adj* **BLEAKER, BLEAKEST** dreary

BLEAK *n* pl. **-S** a freshwater fish

BLEAKISH *adj* somewhat bleak

BLEAKLY *adv* in a bleak manner

BLEAR *v* **-ED, -ING, -S** to dim

BLEARY *adj* **BLEARIER, BLEARIEST** dimmed **BLEARILY** *adv*

BLEAT *v* **-ED, -ING, -S** to utter the cry of a sheep

BLEATER *n* pl. **-S** one that bleats

BLEB *n* pl. **-S** a blister **BLEBBY** *adj*

BLEBBING *n* pl. **-S** the forming of a blister

BLECH *interj* — used to express disgust

BLEED *v* **BLED, BLEEDING, BLEEDS** to lose blood

BLEEDER *n* pl. **-S** one that bleeds

BLEEDING *n* pl. **-S** the act of losing blood

BLEEP *v* **-ED, -ING, -S** to blip

BLEEPER *n* pl. **-S** one that bleeps

BLELLUM *n* pl. **-S** a babbler

BLEMISH *v* **-ED, -ING, -ES** to mar

BLENCH *v* **-ED, -ING, -ES** to flinch

BLENCHER *n* pl. **-S** one that blenches

BLEND *v* **BLENDED** or **BLENT, BLENDING, BLENDS** to mix smoothly and inseparably together

BLENDE *n* pl. **-S** a shiny mineral

BLENDER *n* pl. **-S** one that blends

BLENDING *n* pl. **-S** the action of mixing together

BLENNY *n* pl. **-NIES** a marine fish

BLENT a past tense of blend

BLESBOK *n* pl. **-S** a large antelope

BLESBUCK *n* pl. **-S** blesbok

BLESS *v* **BLESSED** or **BLEST, BLESSING, BLESSES** to sanctify

BLESSED *adj* **-EDER, -EDEST** holy

BLESSER *n* pl. **-S** one that blesses

BLESSING *n* pl. **-S** a prayer

BLEST a past tense of bless

BLET *n* pl. **-S** a decay of fruit

BLETHER *v* **-ED, -ING, -S** to blather

BLEW past tense of blow

BLEWIT *n* pl. **-S** blewits

BLEWITS *n* pl. **-ES** a pale lilac mushroom

BLIGHT *v* **-ED, -ING, -S** to cause decay

BLIGHTER *n* pl. **-S** one that blights

BLIGHTY *n* pl. **BLIGHTIES** a wound causing one to be sent home to England

BLIMEY *interj* — used as an expression of surprise

BLIMP *n* pl. **-S** a nonrigid aircraft **BLIMPISH** *adj*

BLIMPERY *n* pl. **-ERIES** pompous behavior

BLIMY *interj* blimey

BLIN *n* pl. **BLINI** or **BLINIS** or **BLINY** a blintze

BLIND *adj* **BLINDER, BLINDEST** sightless

BLIND *v* **-ED, -ING, -S** to make sightless

BLINDAGE *n* pl. **-S** a protective screen

BLINDER *n* pl. **-S** an obstruction to sight

BLINDGUT *n* pl. **-S** a cecum

BLINDING *n* pl. **-S** the act of causing blindness

BLINDLY *adv* in a blind manner

BLING *v* **-ED, -ING, -S** to adopt a flamboyant appearance

BLINI a pl. of blin

BLINIS a pl. of blin

BLINK *v* **-ED, -ING, -S** to open and shut the eyes

BLINKARD *n* pl. **-S** one who habitually blinks

BLINKER *v* **-ED, -ING, -S** to put blinders on

BLINTZ *n* pl. **-ES** blintze

BLINTZE *n* pl. **-S** a thin pancake

BLINY a pl. of blin

BLIP *v* **BLIPPED, BLIPPING, BLIPS** to remove sound from a recording

BLISS *v* **-ED, -ING, -ES** to experience or produce ecstasy

BLISSFUL *adj* very happy

BLISTER   *v* **-ED, -ING, -S** to cause blisters (skin swellings)

BLISTERY   *adj* having blisters

BLITE   *n* pl. **-S** an annual herb

BLITHE   *adj* **BLITHER, BLITHEST** merry **BLITHELY** *adv*

BLITHER   *v* **-ED, -ING, -S** to blather

BLITZ   *v* **-ED, -ING, -ES** to subject to a sudden attack

BLITZER   *n* pl. **-S** one that blitzes

BLIZZARD   *n* pl. **-S** a heavy snowstorm

BLOAT   *v* **-ED, -ING, -S** to swell

BLOATER   *n* pl. **-S** a smoked herring

BLOATING   *n* pl. **-S** the state of being swollen

BLOB   *v* **BLOBBED, BLOBBING, BLOBS** to splotch

BLOBBY   *adj* **-BIER, -BIEST** splotchy

BLOC   *n* pl. **-S** a coalition

BLOCK   *v* **-ED, -ING, -S** to obstruct

BLOCKADE   *v* **-ADED, -ADING, -ADES** to block

BLOCKAGE   *n* pl. **-S** the act of blocking

BLOCKER   *n* pl. **-S** one that blocks

BLOCKING   *n* pl. **-S** the act of obstructing

BLOCKISH   *adj* blocky

BLOCKY   *adj* **BLOCKIER, BLOCKIEST** short and stout

BLOG   *v* **BLOGGED, BLOGGING, BLOGS** to record personal comments on a Web site

BLOGGER   *n* pl. **-S** one who blogs

BLOGGING   *n* pl. **-S** the act or practice of recording personal comments on a Web site

BLOKE   *n* pl. **-S** a fellow

BLOKEISH   *adj* resembling the typical behavior of a bloke

BLOKEY   *adj* **BLOKIER, BLOKIEST** blokeish

BLOND   *adj* **BLONDER, BLONDEST** light-colored

BLOND   *n* pl. **-S** a person with blond hair

BLONDE   *n* pl. **-S** blond

BLONDINE   *v* **-INED, -INING, -INES** to bleach hair blond

BLONDISH   *adj* somewhat blond

BLOOD   *v* **-ED, -ING, -S** to stain with blood (the fluid circulated by the heart)

BLOODFIN   *n* pl. **-S** a freshwater fish

BLOODIED   past tense of bloody

BLOODIER   comparative of bloody

BLOODIES   present 3d person sing. of bloody

BLOODIEST   superlative of bloody

BLOODILY   *adv* in a bloody manner

BLOODING   *n* pl. **-S** a fox hunting ceremony

BLOODRED   *adj* of the color of blood

BLOODY   *adj* **BLOODIER, BLOODIEST** stained with blood

BLOODY   *v* **BLOODIED, BLOODYING, BLOODIES** to make bloody

BLOOEY   *adj* being out of order

BLOOIE   *adj* blooey

BLOOM   *v* **-ED, -ING, -S** to bear flowers

BLOOMER   *n* pl. **-S** a blooming plant

BLOOMERY   *n* pl. **-ERIES** a furnace for smelting iron

BLOOMING   *n* pl. **-S** a process for smelting iron

BLOOMY   *adj* **BLOOMIER, BLOOMIEST** covered with flowers

BLOOP   *v* **-ED, -ING, -S** to hit a short fly ball

BLOOPER   *n* pl. **-S** a public blunder

BLOOPY   *adj* **BLOOPIER, BLOOPIEST** being a hit that is a short fly ball

BLOSSOM   *v* **-ED, -ING, -S** to bloom

BLOSSOMY   *adj* having blossoms

BLOT   *v* **BLOTTED, BLOTTING, BLOTS** to spot or stain

BLOTCH   *v* **-ED, -ING, -ES** to mark with large spots

BLOTCHY   *adj* **BLOTCHIER, BLOTCHIEST** blotched

BLOTLESS   *adj* spotless

BLOTTED   past tense of blot

BLOTTER   *n* pl. **-S** a piece of ink-absorbing paper

BLOTTIER   comparative of blotty

BLOTTIEST   superlative of blotty

BLOTTING   present participle of blot

BLOTTO   *adj* drunk

BLOTTY   *adj* **-TIER, -TIEST** spotty

BLOUSE   *v* **BLOUSED, BLOUSING, BLOUSES** to hang loosely

BLOUSON   *n* pl. **-S** a woman's garment

BLOUSY   *adj* **BLOUSIER, BLOUSIEST** blowsy **BLOUSILY** *adv*

BLOVIATE   *v* **-ATED, -ATING, -ATES** to speak pompously

BLOW	v **BLEW, BLOWED, BLOWING, BLOWS** to damn
BLOW	v **BLEW, BLOWN, BLOWING, BLOWS** to drive or impel by a current of air
BLOWBACK	n pl. **-S** an escape of gases
BLOWBALL	n pl. **-S** a fluffy seed ball
BLOWBY	n pl. **-BYS** leakage of exhaust fumes
BLOWDART	n pl. **-S** a dart shot from a blowpipe
BLOWDOWN	n pl. **-S** a tree blown down by the wind
BLOWER	n pl. **-S** one that blows
BLOWFISH	n pl. **-ES** a marine fish
BLOWFLY	n pl. **-FLIES** a type of fly
BLOWGUN	n pl. **-S** a tube through which darts may be blown
BLOWHARD	n pl. **-S** a braggart
BLOWHOLE	n pl. **-S** an air or gas vent
BLOWIER	comparative of blowy
BLOWIEST	superlative of blowy
BLOWLAMP	n pl. **-S** a blowtorch
BLOWN	past participle of blow
BLOWOFF	n pl. **-S** the expelling of gas
BLOWOUT	n pl. **-S** a sudden rupture
BLOWPIPE	n pl. **-S** a blowgun
BLOWSED	adj blowsy
BLOWSY	adj **-SIER, -SIEST** slovenly **BLOWSILY** adv
BLOWTUBE	n pl. **-S** a blowgun
BLOWUP	n pl. **-S** an explosion
BLOWY	adj **BLOWIER, BLOWIEST** windy
BLOWZED	adj blowzy
BLOWZY	adj **-ZIER, -ZIEST** blowsy **BLOWZILY** adv
BLUB	v **BLUBBED, BLUBBING, BLUBS** to blubber
BLUBBER	v **-ED, -ING, -S** to weep noisily
BLUBBERY	adj fat; swollen
BLUCHER	n pl. **-S** a half boot
BLUDGE	v **BLUDGED, BLUDGING, BLUDGES** to avoid work
BLUDGEON	v **-ED, -ING, -S** to hit with a club
BLUDGER	n pl. **-S** a loafer or shirker
BLUE	adj **BLUER, BLUEST** having the color of the clear sky
BLUE	v **BLUED, BLUEING** or **BLUING, BLUES** to make blue
BLUEBACK	n pl. **-S** a bird or fish having a bluish back
BLUEBALL	n pl. **-S** a medicinal herb
BLUEBEAT	n pl. **-S** ska
BLUEBELL	n pl. **-S** a flowering plant
BLUEBILL	n pl. **-S** the scaup duck
BLUEBIRD	n pl. **-S** a songbird
BLUEBOOK	n pl. **-S** an examination booklet
BLUECAP	n pl. **-S** a flowering plant
BLUECOAT	n pl. **-S** a police officer
BLUED	past tense of blue
BLUEFIN	n pl. **-S** a large tuna
BLUEFISH	n pl. **-ES** a marine fish
BLUEGILL	n pl. **-S** an edible sunfish
BLUEGUM	n pl. **-S** a timber tree
BLUEHEAD	n pl. **-S** a marine fish
BLUEING	n pl. **-S** bluing
BLUEISH	adj bluish
BLUEJACK	n pl. **-S** an oak tree
BLUEJAY	n pl. **-JAYS** a corvine bird
BLUELINE	n pl. **-S** a line that divides a hockey rink
BLUELY	adv in a blue manner
BLUENESS	n pl. **-ES** the state of being blue
BLUENOSE	n pl. **-S** a puritanical person
BLUER	comparative of blue
BLUESIER	comparative of bluesy
BLUESIEST	superlative of bluesy
BLUESMAN	n pl. **-MEN** one who plays the blues
BLUEST	superlative of blue
BLUESTEM	n pl. **-S** a prairie grass
BLUESY	adj **BLUESIER, BLUESIEST** resembling the blues (a musical form)
BLUET	n pl. **-S** a meadow flower
BLUETICK	n pl. **-S** a hunting dog
BLUEWEED	n pl. **-S** a bristly weed
BLUEWOOD	n pl. **-S** a shrub
BLUEY	n pl. **BLUEYS** a bag of clothing carried in travel
BLUFF	adj **BLUFFER, BLUFFEST** having a broad front **BLUFFLY** adv
BLUFF	v **-ED, -ING, -S** to mislead
BLUFFER	n pl. **-S** one that bluffs

BLUING	*n* pl. **-S** a fabric coloring
BLUISH	*adj* somewhat blue
BLUME	*v* **BLUMED, BLUMING, BLUMES** to blossom
BLUNDER	*v* **-ED, -ING, -S** to make a mistake
BLUNGE	*v* **BLUNGED, BLUNGING, BLUNGES** to mix clay with water
BLUNGER	*n* pl. **-S** one that blunges
BLUNT	*adj* **BLUNTER, BLUNTEST** not sharp or pointed **BLUNTLY** *adv*
BLUNT	*v* **-ED, -ING, -S** to make blunt
BLUR	*v* **BLURRED, BLURRING, BLURS** to make unclear
BLURB	*v* **-ED, -ING, -S** to praise in a publicity notice
BLURBIST	*n* pl. **-S** one that blurbs
BLURRY	*adj* **-RIER, -RIEST** unclear **BLURRILY** *adv*
BLURT	*v* **-ED, -ING, -S** to speak abruptly
BLURTER	*n* pl. **-S** one that blurts
BLUSH	*v* **-ED, -ING, -ES** to become red
BLUSHER	*n* pl. **-S** one that blushes
BLUSHFUL	*adj* of a red color
BLUSTER	*v* **-ED, -ING, -S** to blow violently
BLUSTERY	*adj* windy
BLYPE	*n* pl. **-S** a shred
BO	*n* pl. **BOS** a pal
BOA	*n* pl. **-S** a large snake
BOAR	*n* pl. **-S** a male pig
BOARD	*v* **-ED, -ING, -S** to take meals for a fixed price
BOARDER	*n* pl. **-S** one that boards
BOARDING	*n* pl. **-S** a surface of wooden boards
BOARDMAN	*n* pl. **-MEN** a board member
BOARFISH	*n* pl. **-ES** a marine fish
BOARISH	*adj* swinish; coarse
BOART	*n* pl. **-S** bort
BOAST	*v* **-ED, -ING, -S** to brag
BOASTER	*n* pl. **-S** one that boasts
BOASTFUL	*adj* given to boasting
BOAT	*v* **-ED, -ING, -S** to travel by boat (watercraft) **BOATABLE** *adj*
BOATBILL	*n* pl. **-S** a wading bird
BOATEL	*n* pl. **-S** a waterside hotel
BOATER	*n* pl. **-S** one that boats

BOATFUL	*n* pl. **-S** as much as a boat can hold
BOATHOOK	*n* pl. **-S** a pole with a metal hook for use aboard a boat
BOATING	*n* pl. **-S** the sport of traveling by boat
BOATLIFT	*v* **-ED, -ING, -S** to transport by boats
BOATLIKE	*adj* resembling a boat
BOATLOAD	*n* pl. **-S** the amount that a boat holds
BOATMAN	*n* pl. **-MEN** one who works on boats
BOATNECK	*n* pl. **-S** a wide neckline
BOATPORT	*n* pl. **-S** an enclosure for boats
BOATSMAN	*n* pl. **-MEN** boatman
BOATYARD	*n* pl. **-S** a marina
BOB	*v* **BOBBED, BOBBING, BOBS** to move up and down
BOBBER	*n* pl. **-S** one that bobs
BOBBERY	*n* pl. **-BERIES** a disturbance
BOBBIES	pl. of bobby
BOBBIN	*n* pl. **-S** a thread holder
BOBBINET	*n* pl. **-S** a machine-made net
BOBBING	present participle of bob
BOBBLE	*v* **-BLED, -BLING, -BLES** to fumble
BOBBLY	*adj* **-BLIER, -BLIEST** resembling a small ball of wool
BOBBY	*n* pl. **-BIES** a police officer
BOBBYSOX	*n/pl* girls' socks that reach above the ankle
BOBCAT	*n* pl. **-S** a lynx
BOBECHE	*n* pl. **-S** a glass collar on a candle holder
BOBO	*n* pl. **-BOS** a well-to-do person who holds bohemian values and leads a bourgeois life
BOBOLINK	*n* pl. **-S** a songbird
BOBSKATE	*n* pl. **-S** a child's skate having two parallel blades
BOBSLED	*v* **-SLEDDED, -SLEDDING, -SLEDS** to ride on a bobsled (a racing sled)
BOBSTAY	*n* pl. **-STAYS** a steadying rope
BOBTAIL	*v* **-ED, -ING, -S** to cut short
BOBWHITE	*n* pl. **-S** a game bird
BOCACCIO	*n* pl. **-CIOS** a rockfish
BOCCE	*n* pl. **-S** boccie

BOCCI	*n* pl. **-S** boccie	**BOGGIER**	comparative of boggy
BOCCIA	*n* pl. **-S** boccie	**BOGGIEST**	superlative of boggy
BOCCIE	*n* pl. **-S** an Italian bowling game	**BOGGING**	present participle of bog
BOCK	*n* pl. **-S** a dark beer	**BOGGISH**	*adj* boggy
BOD	*n* pl. **-S** a body	**BOGGLE**	*v* **-GLED, -GLING, -GLES** to hesitate
BODE	*v* **BODED, BODING, BODES** to be an omen of	**BOGGLER**	*n* pl. **-S** one that causes another to boggle
BODEGA	*n* pl. **-S** a grocery store	**BOGGY**	*adj* **-GIER, -GIEST** marshy
BODEMENT	*n* pl. **-S** an omen	**BOGHOLE**	*n* pl. **-S** a natural hole in the ground with a swampy bottom
BODHRAN	*n* pl. **-S** an Irish drum		
BODICE	*n* pl. **-S** a corset	**BOGIE**	*n* pl. **-S** bogy
BODIED	past tense of body	**BOGIES**	pl. of bogy
BODIES	present 3d person sing. of body	**BOGLAND**	*n* pl. **-S** an area of boggy land
BODILESS	*adj* lacking material form	**BOGLE**	*n* pl. **-S** a bogy
BODILY	*adj* of the body	**BOGUS**	*adj* not genuine; fake **BOGUSLY** *adv*
BODING	*n* pl. **-S** an omen		
BODINGLY	*adv* ominously	**BOGWOOD**	*n* pl. **-S** preserved tree wood
BODKIN	*n* pl. **-S** a sharp instrument	**BOGY**	*n* pl. **-GIES** a goblin
BODY	*v* **BODIED, BODYING, BODIES** to give form to	**BOGYISM**	*n* pl. **-S** behavior characteristic of a bogy
BODYMAN	*n* pl. **-MEN** one who repairs auto bodies	**BOGYMAN**	*n* pl. **-MEN** bogeyman
BODYSIDE	*n* pl. **-S** the side of the body of a vehicle	**BOHEA**	*n* pl. **-S** a black tea
		BOHEMIA	*n* pl. **-S** a community of bohemians
BODYSUIT	*n* pl. **-S** a one-piece garment for the torso	**BOHEMIAN**	*n* pl. **-S** an unconventional person
BODYSURF	*v* **-ED, -ING, -S** to ride a wave without a surfboard	**BOHO**	*n* pl. **-HOS** a bohemian
		BOHRIUM	*n* pl. **-S** a radioactive element
BODYWASH	*n* pl. **-ES** a liquid product for cleansing the body	**BOIL**	*v* **-ED, -ING, -S** to vaporize liquid **BOILABLE** *adj*
BODYWORK	*n* pl. **-S** a vehicle body	**BOILER**	*n* pl. **-S** a vessel for boiling
BOEHMITE	*n* pl. **-S** a mineral	**BOILOFF**	*n* pl. **-S** the vaporization of liquid
BOEUF	*n* pl. **-S** beef	**BOILOVER**	*n* pl. **-S** an overflowing while boiling
BOFF	*n* pl. **-S** a hearty laugh		
BOFFIN	*n* pl. **-S** a scientific expert **BOFFINY** *adj*	**BOING**	*v* **-ED, -ING, -S** to make the sound of reverberation or vibration
BOFFO	*n* pl. **-FOS** a boff	**BOISERIE**	*n* pl. **-S** wood paneling on a wall
BOFFOLA	*n* pl. **-S** a boff	**BOITE**	*n* pl. **-S** a nightclub
BOG	*v* **BOGGED, BOGGING, BOGS** to impede	**BOKKEN**	*n* pl. **-S** a wooden sword used for training
BOGAN	*n* pl. **-S** a backwater or tributary	**BOLA**	*n* pl. **-S** a throwing weapon
BOGART	*v* **-ED, -ING, -S** to use without sharing	**BOLAR**	*adj* pertaining to bole
		BOLAS	*n* pl. **-ES** bola
BOGBEAN	*n* pl. **-S** a marsh plant	**BOLD**	*adj* **BOLDER, BOLDEST** daring **BOLDLY** *adv*
BOGEY	*v* **-GEYED, -GEYING, -GEYS** to shoot in one stroke over par in golf	**BOLD**	*v* **-ED, -ING, -S** to boldface
BOGEYMAN	*n* pl. **-MEN** a terrifying creature	**BOLDFACE**	*v* **-FACED, -FACING, -FACES** to print in thick type
BOGGED	past tense of bog	**BOLDNESS**	*n* pl. **-ES** the quality of being bold

BOLE n pl. **-S** a fine clay

BOLERO n pl. **-ROS** a Spanish dance

BOLETE n pl. **-S** boletus

BOLETUS n pl. **-TUSES** or **-TI** a fungus

BOLIDE n pl. **-S** an exploding meteor

BOLIVAR n pl. **-S** or **-ES** a monetary unit of Venezuela

BOLIVIA n pl. **-S** a soft fabric

BOLL v **-ED, -ING, -S** to form pods

BOLLARD n pl. **-S** a thick post on a ship or wharf

BOLLIX v **-ED, -ING, -ES** to bungle

BOLLOX v **-ED, -ING, -ES** to bollix

BOLLWORM n pl. **-S** the larva of a certain moth

BOLO n pl. **-LOS** a machete

BOLOGNA n pl. **-S** a seasoned sausage

BOLONEY n pl. **-NEYS** bologna

BOLSHIE n pl. **-S** a Bolshevik

BOLSHY n pl. **-SHIES** bolshie

BOLSON n pl. **-S** a flat arid valley

BOLSTER v **-ED, -ING, -S** to support

BOLT v **-ED, -ING, -S** to sift

BOLTER n pl. **-S** a sifting machine

BOLTHEAD n pl. **-S** a matrass

BOLTHOLE n pl. **-S** a place or way of escape

BOLTLESS adj having no bolt (a type of metal fastener)

BOLTLIKE adj resembling a bolt

BOLTONIA n pl. **-S** a perennial herb

BOLTROPE n pl. **-S** a rope sewn to a sail

BOLUS n pl. **-ES** a large pill

BOMB v **-ED, -ING, -S** to attack with bombs (explosive projectiles) **BOMBABLE** adj

BOMBARD v **-ED, -ING, -S** to bomb

BOMBARDE n pl. **-S** a medieval shawm

BOMBAST n pl. **-S** pompous language

BOMBAX adj pertaining to a family of tropical trees

BOMBE n pl. **-S** a frozen dessert

BOMBER n pl. **-S** one that bombs

BOMBESIN n pl. **-S** a combination of amino acids

BOMBING n pl. **-S** an attack with bombs

BOMBLET n pl. **-S** a small bomb

BOMBLOAD n pl. **-S** the quantity of bombs being carried

BOMBORA n pl. **-S** a sea area over a ridge of rock

BOMBYCID n pl. **-S** a moth

BOMBYX n pl. **-ES** a silkworm

BONACI n pl. **-S** an edible fish

BONANZA n pl. **-S** a rich mine

BONBON n pl. **-S** a sugared candy

BONCE n pl. **-S** a person's head

BOND v **-ED, -ING, -S** to join together **BONDABLE** adj

BONDAGE n pl. **-S** slavery

BONDER n pl. **-S** one that bonds

BONDING n pl. **-S** the formation of a close personal relationship

BONDLESS adj having no bond

BONDMAID n pl. **-S** a female slave

BONDMAN n pl. **-MEN** a male slave

BONDSMAN n pl. **-MEN** bondman

BONDUC n pl. **-S** a prickly seed

BONE v **BONED, BONING, BONES** to debone

BONEBED n pl. **-S** an area containing dinosaur fossils

BONEFISH n pl. **-ES** a slender marine fish

BONEHEAD n pl. **-S** a stupid person

BONELESS adj having no bones (hard connective tissue)

BONEMEAL n pl. **-S** fertilizer or feed made from crushed bone

BONER n pl. **-S** a blunder

BONESET n pl. **-S** a perennial herb

BONEY adj **BONEYER, BONEYEST** bony

BONEYARD n pl. **-S** a junkyard

BONFIRE n pl. **-S** an open fire

BONG v **-ED, -ING, -S** to make a deep, ringing sound

BONGO n pl. **-GOS** or **-GOES** a small drum

BONGOIST n pl. **-S** a bongo player

BONHOMIE n pl. **-S** friendliness

BONIATO n pl. **-TOS** a sweet potato

BONIER comparative of bony

BONIEST superlative of bony

BONIFACE n pl. **-S** an innkeeper

BONINESS n pl. **-ES** the state of being bony

BONING present participle of bone

BONITA n pl. **-S** bonito

BONITO *n* pl. **-TOS** or **-TOES** a marine food fish

BONK *v* **-ED, -ING, -S** to hit on the head with a hollow blow

BONKERS *adj* crazy

BONNE *n* pl. **-S** a housemaid

BONNET *v* **-ED, -ING, -S** to provide with a bonnet (a type of hat)

BONNIE *adj* bonny

BONNOCK *n* pl. **-S** bannock

BONNY *adj* **-NIER, -NIEST** pretty **BONNILY** *adv*

BONNY *n* pl. **-NIES** a person that one loves

BONOBO *n* pl. **-BOS** an anthropoid ape

BONSAI *n* pl. **BONSAI** a potted shrub that has been dwarfed

BONSPELL *n* pl. **-S** bonspiel

BONSPIEL *n* pl. **-S** a curling match or tournament

BONTBOK *n* pl. **-S** bontebok

BONTEBOK *n* pl. **-S** an antelope

BONUS *n* pl. **-ES** an additional payment

BONUSING *n* pl. **-S** the act of subsidizing something

BONY *adj* **BONIER, BONIEST** full of bones

BONZE *n* pl. **-S** a Buddhist monk

BONZER *adj* very good

BOO *v* **-ED, -ING, -S** to cry "boo" to express disapproval or to startle

BOOB *v* **-ED, -ING, -S** to make a foolish mistake

BOOBIRD *n* pl. **-S** a fan who boos players of the home team

BOOBISH *adj* doltish

BOOBOO *n* pl. **-BOOS** a mistake

BOOBY *n* pl. **-BIES** a dolt

BOOCOO *n* pl. **-COOS** beaucoup

BOODLE *v* **-DLED, -DLING, -DLES** to take bribes

BOODLER *n* pl. **-S** one that boodles

BOOGALOO *v* **-ED, -ING, -S** to dance to rock music

BOOGER *n* pl. **-S** a bogeyman

BOOGEY *v* **-GEYED, -GEYING, -GEYS** to boogie

BOOGIE *v* **-GIED, -GIEING, -GIES** to dance to rock music

BOOGY *v* **-GIED, -GYING, -GIES** to boogie

BOOGYMAN *n* pl. **-MEN** bogeyman

BOOHOO *v* **-ED, -ING, -S** to weep noisily

BOOJUM *n* pl. **-S** a spiny desert tree

BOOK *v* **-ED, -ING, -S** to engage services **BOOKABLE** *adj*

BOOKBAG *n* pl. **-S** a bag for carrying books

BOOKCASE *n* pl. **-S** a case which holds books (literary volumes)

BOOKEND *v* **-ED, -ING, -S** to place something at either end of

BOOKER *n* pl. **-S** one that books

BOOKFUL *n* pl. **-S** as much as a book can hold

BOOKIE *n* pl. **-S** a bet taker

BOOKING *n* pl. **-S** an engagement

BOOKISH *adj* pertaining to books

BOOKLET *n* pl. **-S** a small book

BOOKLICE *n/pl* wingless insects that damage books

BOOKLORE *n* pl. **-S** book learning

BOOKMAN *n* pl. **-MEN** a scholar

BOOKMARK *v* **-ED, -ING, -S** to create a shortcut to a previously viewed website

BOOKOO *n* pl. **-KOOS** beaucoup

BOOKRACK *n* pl. **-S** a support for an open book

BOOKREST *n* pl. **-S** a bookrack

BOOKSHOP *n* pl. **-S** a store where books are sold

BOOKWORK *n* pl. **-S** the keeping of records of accounts

BOOKWORM *n* pl. **-S** an avid book reader

BOOM *v* **-ED, -ING, -S** to make a deep, resonant sound

BOOMBOX *n* pl. **-ES** a portable radio and tape or compact disc player

BOOMER *n* pl. **-S** one that booms

BOOMIER comparative of boomy

BOOMIEST superlative of boomy

BOOMKIN *n* pl. **-S** a bumkin

BOOMLET *n* pl. **-S** a small increase in prosperity

BOOMTOWN *n* pl. **-S** a prospering town

BOOMY *adj* **BOOMIER, BOOMIEST** prospering

BOON *n* pl. **-S** a timely benefit

BOONDOCK *adj* pertaining to a backwoods area

BOONIES *n/pl* a backwoods area

BOONLESS	*adj* having no boon
BOOR	*n* pl. **-S** a rude person
BOORISH	*adj* rude
BOOST	*v* **-ED, -ING, -S** to support
BOOSTER	*n* pl. **-S** one that boosts
BOOT	*v* **-ED, -ING, -S** to load a program into a computer **BOOTABLE** *adj*
BOOTEE	*n* pl. **-S** a baby's sock
BOOTERY	*n* pl. **-ERIES** a shoe store
BOOTH	*n* pl. **-S** a small enclosure
BOOTIE	*n* pl. **-S** bootee
BOOTIES	pl. of booty
BOOTJACK	*n* pl. **-S** a device for pulling off boots
BOOTLACE	*n* pl. **-S** a shoelace
BOOTLEG	*v* **-LEGGED, -LEGGING, -LEGS** to smuggle
BOOTLESS	*adj* useless
BOOTLICK	*v* **-ED, -ING, -S** to flatter servilely
BOOTY	*n* pl. **-TIES** a rich gain or prize
BOOZE	*v* **BOOZED, BOOZING, BOOZES** to drink liquor excessively
BOOZER	*n* pl. **-S** one that boozes
BOOZING	*n* pl. **-S** the act of drinking liquor excessively
BOOZY	*adj* **BOOZIER, BOOZIEST** drunken **BOOZILY** *adv*
BOP	*v* **BOPPED, BOPPING, BOPS** to hit or strike
BOPEEP	*n* pl. **-S** a game of peekaboo
BOPPER	*n* pl. **-S** a bebopper
BOPPISH	*adj* boppy
BOPPY	*adj* **-PIER, -PIEST** suggestive of bebop
BORA	*n* pl. **-S** a cold wind
BORACES	a pl. of borax
BORACIC	*adj* boric
BORACITE	*n* pl. **-S** a mineral
BORAGE	*n* pl. **-S** a medicinal herb
BORAL	*n* pl. **-S** a mixture of boron carbide and aluminum
BORANE	*n* pl. **-S** a chemical compound
BORATE	*v* **-RATED, -RATING, -RATES** to mix with borax or boric acid
BORAX	*n* pl. **-RAXES** or **-RACES** a white crystalline compound
BORAZON	*n* pl. **-S** a hard form of boron nitride

BORDEAUX	*n* pl. **BORDEAUX** a red or white wine
BORDEL	*n* pl. **-S** a brothel
BORDELLO	*n* pl. **-LOS** a brothel
BORDER	*v* **-ED, -ING, -S** to put a border (an edge) on
BORDERER	*n* pl. **-S** one that borders
BORDURE	*n* pl. **-S** a border around a shield
BORE	*v* **BORED, BORING, BORES** to pierce with a rotary tool
BOREAL	*adj* pertaining to the north
BOREAS	*n* pl. **-ES** the north wind
BORECOLE	*n* pl. **-S** kale
BORED	past tense of bore
BOREDOM	*n* pl. **-S** tedium
BOREEN	*n* pl. **-S** a lane in Ireland
BOREHOLE	*n* pl. **-S** a hole bored in the earth
BORER	*n* pl. **-S** one that bores
BORESOME	*adj* tedious
BORIC	*adj* pertaining to boron
BORIDE	*n* pl. **-S** a boron compound
BORING	*n* pl. **-S** an inner cavity
BORINGLY	*adv* tediously
BORK	*v* **-ED, -ING, -S** to attack a candidate in the media
BORKING	*n* pl. **-S** the act of attacking a candidate in the media
BORN	*adj* having particular qualities from birth
BORNE	a past participle of bear
BORNEOL	*n* pl. **-S** an alcohol
BORNITE	*n* pl. **-S** an ore of copper **BORNITIC** *adj*
BORON	*n* pl. **-S** a nonmetallic element **BORONIC** *adj*
BORONIA	*n* pl. **-S** an Australian shrub
BOROUGH	*n* pl. **-S** an incorporated town
BORRELIA	*n* pl. **-S** a coiled spirochete
BORROW	*v* **-ED, -ING, -S** to take on loan
BORROWER	*n* pl. **-S** one that borrows
BORSCH	*n* pl. **-ES** borscht
BORSCHT	*n* pl. **-S** a beet soup
BORSHT	*n* pl. **-S** borscht
BORSTAL	*n* pl. **-S** a reformatory
BORT	*n* pl. **-S** a low-quality diamond **BORTY** *adj*
BORTZ	*n* pl. **-ES** bort

BORZOI *n* pl. **-S** a Russian hound

BOSCAGE *n* pl. **-S** a thicket

BOSCHBOK *n* pl. **-S** bushbuck

BOSH *n* pl. **-ES** nonsense

BOSHBOK *n* pl. **-S** bushbuck

BOSHVARK *n* pl. **-S** a wild hog

BOSK *n* pl. **-S** a small wooded area

BOSKAGE *n* pl. **-S** boscage

BOSKER *adj* fine; very good

BOSKET *n* pl. **-S** a thicket

BOSKY *adj* **BOSKIER, BOSKIEST** wooded; bushy

BOSOM *v* **-ED, -ING, -S** to embrace

BOSOMY *adj* swelling outward

BOSON *n* pl. **-S** a subatomic particle **BOSONIC** *adj*

BOSQUE *n* pl. **-S** bosk

BOSQUET *n* pl. **-S** bosket

BOSS *v* **-ED, -ING, -ES** to supervise

BOSS *adj* **BOSSER, BOSSEST** first-rate, excellent

BOSSDOM *n* pl. **-S** the domain of a political boss

BOSSIES pl. of bossy

BOSSISM *n* pl. **-S** control by political bosses

BOSSY *adj* **BOSSIER, BOSSIEST** domineering **BOSSILY** *adv*

BOSSY *n* pl. **BOSSIES** a cow

BOSTON *n* pl. **-S** a card game

BOSUN *n* pl. **-S** a boatswain

BOT *n* pl. **-S** the larva of a botfly

BOTA *n* pl. **-S** a leather bottle

BOTANIC *adj* pertaining to botany

BOTANICA *n* pl. **-S** a shop that sells herbs and magic charms

BOTANIES pl. of botany

BOTANISE *v* **-NISED, -NISING, -NISES** to botanize

BOTANIST *n* pl. **-S** one skilled in botany

BOTANIZE *v* **-NIZED, -NIZING, -NIZES** to study plants

BOTANY *n* pl. **-NIES** the science of plants

BOTCH *v* **-ED, -ING, -ES** to bungle

BOTCHER *n* pl. **-S** one that botches

BOTCHERY *n* pl. **-ERIES** something botched

BOTCHY *adj* **BOTCHIER, BOTCHIEST** badly done **BOTCHILY** *adv*

BOTEL *n* pl. **-S** boatel

BOTFLY *n* pl. **-FLIES** a type of fly

BOTH *adj* being the two

BOTHER *v* **-ED, -ING, -S** to annoy

BOTHIE *n* pl. **-S** bothy

BOTHRIUM *n* pl. **-RIUMS** or **-RIA** a groove on a tapeworm

BOTHY *n* pl. **BOTHIES** a hut in Scotland

BOTONEE *adj* having arms ending in a trefoil — used of a heraldic cross

BOTONNEE *adj* botonee

BOTRYOID *adj* resembling a cluster of grapes

BOTRYOSE *adj* botryoid

BOTRYTIS *n* pl. **-TISES** a plant disease

BOTT *n* pl. **-S** bot

BOTTLE *v* **-TLED, -TLING, -TLES** to put into a bottle (a rigid container)

BOTTLER *n* pl. **-S** one that bottles

BOTTLING *n* pl. **-S** a bottled beverage

BOTTOM *v* **-ED, -ING, -S** to comprehend

BOTTOMER *n* pl. **-S** one that bottoms

BOTTOMRY *n* pl. **-RIES** a maritime contract

BOTULIN *n* pl. **-S** a nerve poison

BOTULISM *n* pl. **-S** botulin poisoning

BOUBOU *n* pl. **-S** a long flowing garment

BOUCHEE *n* pl. **-S** a small patty shell

BOUCLE *n* pl. **-S** a knitted fabric

BOUDIN *n* pl. **-S** a spicy Cajun sausage

BOUDOIR *n* pl. **-S** a woman's bedroom

BOUFFANT *n* pl. **-S** a woman's hairdo

BOUFFE *n* pl. **-S** a comic opera

BOUGH *n* pl. **-S** a tree branch **BOUGHED** *adj*

BOUGHPOT *n* pl. **-S** a large vase

BOUGHT past tense of buy

BOUGHTEN *adj* purchased

BOUGIE *n* pl. **-S** a wax candle

BOUILLON *n* pl. **-S** a clear broth

BOULDER *v* **-ED, -ING, -S** to climb up large rocks

BOULDERY *adj* characterized by large rocks

BOULE *n* pl. **-S** buhl

BOULLE *n* pl. **-S** buhl

BOULT *v* **-ED, -ING, -S** to bolt (sift)

BOUNCE *v* **BOUNCED, BOUNCING, BOUNCES** to spring back

BOUNCER	*n* pl. **-S** one that bounces
BOUNCY	*adj* **BOUNCIER, BOUNCIEST** tending to bounce **BOUNCILY** *adv*
BOUND	*v* **-ED, -ING, -S** to leap
BOUNDARY	*n* pl. **-ARIES** a dividing line
BOUNDEN	*adj* obliged
BOUNDER	*n* pl. **-S** one that bounds
BOUNTY	*n* pl. **-TIES** a reward **BOUNTIED** *adj*
BOUQUET	*n* pl. **-S** a bunch of flowers
BOURBON	*n* pl. **-S** a whiskey
BOURDON	*n* pl. **-S** a part of a bagpipe
BOURG	*n* pl. **-S** a medieval town
BOURGEON	*v* **-ED, -ING, -S** to burgeon
BOURN	*n* pl. **-S** a stream
BOURNE	*n* pl. **-S** bourn
BOURREE	*n* pl. **-S** an old French dance
BOURRIDE	*n* pl. **-S** a fish stew
BOURSE	*n* pl. **-S** a stock exchange
BOURTREE	*n* pl. **-S** a European tree
BOUSE	*v* **BOUSED, BOUSING, BOUSES** to haul by means of a tackle
BOUSOUKI	*n* pl. **-KIS** or **-KIA** bouzouki
BOUSY	*adj* boozy
BOUT	*n* pl. **-S** a contest
BOUTADE	*n* pl. **-S** a sudden outburst
BOUTIQUE	*n* pl. **-S** a small shop
BOUTON	*n* pl. **-S** an enlarged end of a nerve fiber
BOUVIER	*n* pl. **-S** a large dog
BOUZOUKI	*n* pl. **-KIS** or **-KIA** a stringed musical instrument
BOVID	*n* pl. **-S** a bovine
BOVINE	*n* pl. **-S** an ox-like animal
BOVINELY	*adv* stolidly
BOVINITY	*n* pl. **-TIES** the state of being a bovine
BOVVER	*n* pl. **-S** rowdy behavior
BOW	*v* **-ED, -ING, -S** to bend forward
BOWEL	*v* **-ELED, -ELING, -ELS** or **-ELLED, -ELLING, -ELS** to disbowel
BOWER	*v* **-ED, -ING, -S** to embower
BOWERY	*n* pl. **-ERIES** a colonial Dutch farm
BOWFIN	*n* pl. **-S** a freshwater fish
BOWFRONT	*adj* having a curved front
BOWHEAD	*n* pl. **-S** an arctic whale
BOWHUNT	*v* **-ED, -ING, -S** to hunt with a bow and arrow
BOWING	*n* pl. **-S** the technique of managing the bow of a stringed instrument
BOWINGLY	*adv* in a bowing manner
BOWKNOT	*n* pl. **-S** a type of knot
BOWL	*v* **-ED, -ING, -S** to play at bowling
BOWLDER	*n* pl. **-S** boulder
BOWLEG	*n* pl. **-S** an outwardly curved leg
BOWLER	*n* pl. **-S** one that bowls
BOWLESS	*adj* being without an archery bow
BOWLFUL	*n* pl. **-S** as much as a bowl can hold
BOWLIKE	*adj* curved
BOWLINE	*n* pl. **-S** a type of knot
BOWLING	*n* pl. **-S** a game in which balls are rolled at objects
BOWLLIKE	*adj* concave
BOWMAN	*n* pl. **-MEN** an archer
BOWPOT	*n* pl. **-S** boughpot
BOWSAW	*n* pl. **-S** a saw having a blade in a bow-shaped frame
BOWSE	*v* **BOWSED, BOWSING, BOWSES** to bouse
BOWSER	*n* pl. **-S** a truck having a tank for fuel or water
BOWSHOT	*n* pl. **-S** the distance an arrow is shot
BOWSMAN	*n* pl. **-MEN** a bowman
BOWSPRIT	*n* pl. **-S** a ship's spar
BOWWOOD	*n* pl. **-S** a deciduous tree
BOWWOW	*v* **-ED, -ING, -S** to bark like a dog
BOWYER	*n* pl. **-S** a maker of archery bows
BOX	*v* **-ED, -ING, -ES** to put in a box (a rectangular container)
BOXBALL	*n* pl. **-S** a form of handball
BOXBERRY	*n* pl. **-RIES** an evergreen plant
BOXBOARD	*n* pl. **-S** stiff paperboard
BOXCAR	*n* pl. **-S** a roofed freight car
BOXER	*n* pl. **-S** one that packs boxes
BOXFISH	*n* pl. **-ES** a marine fish
BOXFUL	*n* pl. **-S** as much as a box can hold
BOXHAUL	*v* **-ED, -ING, -S** to veer a ship around
BOXIER	comparative of boxy
BOXIEST	superlative of boxy
BOXINESS	*n* pl. **-ES** the state of being boxy

BOXING	*n* pl. **-S** a casing
BOXLA	*n* pl. **-S** a form of lacrosse played in an enclosed area
BOXLIKE	*adj* resembling a box
BOXTHORN	*n* pl. **-S** a thorny shrub
BOXWOOD	*n* pl. **-S** an evergreen shrub
BOXY	*adj* **BOXIER, BOXIEST** resembling a box **BOXILY** *adv*
BOY	*n* pl. **BOYS** a male child
BOYAR	*n* pl. **-S** a former Russian aristocrat
BOYARD	*n* pl. **-S** boyar
BOYARISM	*n* pl. **-S** the rule of boyars
BOYCHICK	*n* pl. **-S** boychik
BOYCHIK	*n* pl. **-S** a young man
BOYCOTT	*v* **-ED, -ING, -S** to refuse to buy
BOYHOOD	*n* pl. **-S** the state of being a boy
BOYISH	*adj* resembling a boy **BOYISHLY** *adv*
BOYLA	*n* pl. **-S** a witch doctor
BOYO	*n* pl. **BOYOS** a boy
BOZO	*n* pl. **-ZOS** a fellow
BRA	*n* pl. **-S** a brassiere
BRABBLE	*v* **-BLED, -BLING, -BLES** to quarrel noisily
BRABBLER	*n* pl. **-S** one that brabbles
BRACE	*v* **BRACED, BRACING, BRACES** to support
BRACELET	*n* pl. **-S** a wrist ornament
BRACER	*n* pl. **-S** one that braces
BRACERO	*n* pl. **-ROS** a Mexican laborer
BRACH	*n* pl. **-S** or **-ES** a hound bitch
BRACHET	*n* pl. **-S** a brach
BRACHIAL	*n* pl. **-S** a part of the arm
BRACHIUM	*n* pl. **-IA** the upper part of the arm
BRACING	*n* pl. **-S** a brace or reinforcement
BRACIOLA	*n* pl. **-S** a thin slice of meat
BRACIOLE	*n* pl. **-S** braciola
BRACKEN	*n* pl. **-S** a large fern
BRACKET	*v* **-ED, -ING, -S** to classify
BRACKISH	*adj* salty
BRACONID	*n* pl. **-S** any of a family of flies
BRACT	*n* pl. **-S** a leaflike plant part **BRACTEAL, BRACTED** *adj*
BRACTLET	*n* pl. **-S** a small bract
BRAD	*v* **BRADDED, BRADDING, BRADS** to fasten with thin nails
BRADAWL	*n* pl. **-S** a type of awl
BRADOON	*n* pl. **-S** bridoon
BRAE	*n* pl. **-S** a hillside
BRAG	*adj* **BRAGGER, BRAGGEST** first-rate
BRAG	*v* **BRAGGED, BRAGGING, BRAGS** to speak vainly of one's deeds
BRAGGART	*n* pl. **-S** one who brags
BRAGGER	*n* pl **-S** a braggart
BRAGGY	*adj* **-GIER, -GIEST** tending to brag
BRAHMA	*n* pl. **-S** a large domestic fowl
BRAHMAN	*n* pl. **-S** a member of the highest Hindu caste
BRAID	*v* **-ED, -ING, -S** to weave together
BRAIDER	*n* pl. **-S** one that braids
BRAIDING	*n* pl. **-S** something made of braided material
BRAIL	*v* **-ED, -ING, -S** to haul in a sail
BRAILLE	*v* **BRAILLED, BRAILLING, BRAILLES** to write in braille (raised writing for the blind)
BRAILLER	*n* pl. **-S** a machine for printing in braille
BRAIN	*v* **-ED, -ING, -S** to hit on the head
BRAINIAC	*n* pl. **-S** a very intelligent person
BRAINIER	comparative of brainy
BRAINIEST	superlative of brainy
BRAINILY	*adv* in a brainy manner
BRAINISH	*adj* impetuous
BRAINPAN	*n* pl. **-S** the skull
BRAINY	*adj* **BRAINIER, BRAINIEST** smart
BRAISE	*v* **BRAISED, BRAISING, BRAISES** to cook in fat
BRAIZE	*n* pl. **-S** a marine fish
BRAKE	*v* **BRAKED, BRAKING, BRAKES** to slow down or stop
BRAKEAGE	*n* pl. **-S** the act of braking
BRAKEMAN	*n* pl. **-MEN** a trainman
BRAKING	present participle of brake
BRAKY	*adj* **BRAKIER, BRAKIEST** abounding in shrubs or ferns
BRALESS	*adj* wearing no bra
BRAMBLE	*v* **-BLED, -BLING, -BLES** to gather berries
BRAMBLY	*adj* **-BLIER, -BLIEST** prickly

BRAN	*v* **BRANNED, BRANNING, BRANS** to soak in water mixed with bran (the outer coat of cereals)
BRANCH	*v* **-ED, -ING, -ES** to form branches (offshoots)
BRANCHIA	*n* pl. **-CHIAE** a respiratory organ of aquatic animals
BRANCHY	*adj* **BRANCHIER, BRANCHIEST** having many branches
BRAND	*v* **-ED, -ING, -S** to mark with a hot iron
BRANDADE	*n* pl. **-S** a dish of cod mixed with olive oil and milk
BRANDER	*n* pl. **-S** one that brands
BRANDING	*n* pl. **-S** the promoting of a product by associating it with a brand name
BRANDISH	*v* **-ED, -ING, -ES** to wave menacingly
BRANDY	*v* **-DIED, -DYING, -DIES** to mix with brandy (a liquor)
BRANK	*n* pl. **-S** a device used to restrain the tongue
BRANNED	past tense of bran
BRANNER	*n* pl. **-S** one that brans
BRANNING	present participle of bran
BRANNY	*adj* **-NIER, -NIEST** containing bran
BRANT	*n* pl. **-S** a wild goose
BRANTAIL	*n* pl. **-S** a singing bird
BRASH	*adj* **BRASHER, BRASHEST** rash; hasty **BRASHLY** *adv*
BRASH	*n* pl. **-ES** a mass of fragments
BRASHY	*adj* **BRASHIER, BRASHIEST** brash
BRASIER	*n* pl. **-S** brazier
BRASIL	*n* pl. **-S** brazil
BRASILIN	*n* pl. **-S** brazilin
BRASS	*v* **-ED, -ING, -ES** to coat with brass (an alloy of copper and zinc)
BRASSAGE	*n* pl. **-S** a fee for coining money
BRASSARD	*n* pl. **-S** an insignia
BRASSART	*n* pl. **-S** brassard
BRASSICA	*n* pl. **-S** a tall herb
BRASSIE	*n* pl. **-S** a golf club
BRASSISH	*adj* resembling brass
BRASSY	*adj* **BRASSIER, BRASSIEST** resembling brass **BRASSILY** *adv*
BRAT	*n* pl. **-S** a spoiled child **BRATTISH** *adj*
BRATTICE	*v* **-TICED, -TICING, -TICES** to partition
BRATTLE	*v* **-TLED, -TLING, -TLES** to clatter
BRATTY	*adj* **-TIER, -TIEST** resembling a brat
BRAUNITE	*n* pl. **-S** a mineral
BRAVA	*n* pl. **-S** a shout of approval
BRAVADO	*n* pl. **-DOS** or **-DOES** false bravery
BRAVE	*adj* **BRAVER, BRAVEST** showing courage **BRAVELY** *adv*
BRAVE	*v* **BRAVED, BRAVING, BRAVES** to face with courage
BRAVER	*n* pl. **-S** one that braves
BRAVERY	*n* pl. **-ERIES** courage
BRAVEST	superlative of brave
BRAVI	a pl. of bravo
BRAVING	present participle of brave
BRAVO	*n* pl. **-VOS** or **-VOES** or **-VI** a hired killer
BRAVO	*v* **-ED, -ING, -ES** to applaud by shouting "bravo"
BRAVURA	*n* pl. **-RAS** or **-RE** fine musical technique
BRAW	*adj* **BRAWER, BRAWEST** splendid
BRAWL	*v* **-ED, -ING, -S** to fight
BRAWLER	*n* pl. **-S** a fighter
BRAWLIE	*adv* splendidly
BRAWLY	*adj* **BRAWLIER, BRAWLIEST** inclined to brawl
BRAWN	*n* pl. **-S** muscular strength
BRAWNY	*adj* **BRAWNIER, BRAWNIEST** muscular **BRAWNILY** *adv*
BRAWS	*n/pl* fine clothes
BRAXY	*n* pl. **BRAXIES** a fever of sheep
BRAY	*v* **BRAYED, BRAYING, BRAYS** to utter a harsh cry
BRAYER	*n* pl. **-S** a roller used to spread ink
BRAZA	*n* pl. **-S** a Spanish unit of length
BRAZE	*v* **BRAZED, BRAZING, BRAZES** to solder together
BRAZEN	*v* **-ED, -ING, -S** to face boldly
BRAZENLY	*adv* boldly
BRAZER	*n* pl. **-S** one that brazes
BRAZIER	*n* pl. **-S** one who works in brass
BRAZIL	*n* pl. **-S** a dyewood
BRAZILIN	*n* pl. **-S** a chemical compound
BRAZING	present participle of braze

BREACH	v **-ED, -ING, -ES** to break through	**BREN**	n pl. **-S** a light machine gun
BREACHER	n pl. **-S** one that breaches	**BRENT**	n pl. **-S** brant
BREAD	v **-ED, -ING, -S** to cover with crumbs of bread (a baked foodstuff made from flour)	**BRESAOLA**	n pl. **-S** a dish of sliced dried beef
		BRETHREN	a pl. of brother
BREADBOX	n pl. **-ES** a container for bread	**BREVE**	n pl. **-S** a symbol used to indicate a short vowel
BREADNUT	n pl. **-S** a tropical fruit	**BREVET**	v **-VETED, -VETING, -VETS** or **-VETTED, -VETTING, -VETS** to confer an honorary rank upon
BREADTH	n pl. **-S** width		
BREADY	adj resembling or characteristic of bread		
		BREVETCY	n pl. **-CIES** an honorary rank
BREAK	v **BROKE, BROKEN, BREAKING, BREAKS** to reduce to fragments	**BREVIARY**	n pl. **-RIES** a prayer book
		BREVIER	n pl. **-S** a size of type
BREAKAGE	n pl. **-S** the act of breaking	**BREVITY**	n pl. **-TIES** shortness of duration
BREAKER	n pl. **-S** one that breaks	**BREW**	v **-ED, -ING, -S** to make beer or the like
BREAKING	n pl. **-S** the change of a pure vowel to a diphthong		
		BREWAGE	n pl. **-S** a brewed beverage
BREAKOUT	n pl. **-S** an escape	**BREWER**	n pl. **-S** one that brews
BREAKUP	n pl. **-S** the act of breaking up	**BREWERY**	n pl. **-ERIES** a place for brewing
BREAM	v **-ED, -ING, -S** to clean a ship's bottom	**BREWING**	n pl. **-S** a quantity brewed at one time
BREAST	v **-ED, -ING, -S** to confront boldly	**BREWIS**	n pl. **BREWISES** broth
BREATH	n pl. **-S** air inhaled and exhaled	**BREWPUB**	n pl. **-S** a restaurant that sells beverages brewed on the premises
BREATHE	v **BREATHED, BREATHING, BREATHES** to inhale and exhale air		
		BREWSKI	n pl. **-SKIES** or **-SKIS** a serving of beer
BREATHER	n pl. **-S** one that breathes		
BREATHY	adj **BREATHIER, BREATHIEST** marked by loud breathing	**BRIAR**	n pl. **-S** brier **BRIARY** adj
		BRIARD	n pl. **-S** a large dog
BRECCIA	n pl. **-S** a type of rock **BRECCIAL** adj	**BRIBE**	v **BRIBED, BRIBING, BRIBES** to practice bribery **BRIBABLE** adj
BRECHAM	n pl. **-S** a collar for a horse	**BRIBEE**	n pl. **-S** one that is bribed
BRECHAN	n pl. **-S** brecham	**BRIBER**	n pl. **-S** one that bribes
BRED	past tense of breed	**BRIBERY**	n pl. **-ERIES** an act of influencing corruptly
BREDE	n pl. **-S** a braid		
BREE	n pl. **-S** broth	**BRIBING**	present participle of bribe
BREECH	v **-ED, -ING, -ES** to clothe with breeches (trousers)	**BRICK**	v **-ED, -ING, -S** to build with bricks (blocks of clay)
BREED	v **BRED, BREEDING, BREEDS** to cause to give birth	**BRICKBAT**	n pl. **-S** a piece of brick
		BRICKLE	n pl. **-S** a brittle candy
BREEDER	n pl. **-S** one that breeds	**BRICKY**	adj **BRICKIER, BRICKIEST** made of bricks
BREEDING	n pl. **-S** upbringing		
BREEKS	n/pl breeches	**BRICOLE**	n pl. **-S** a cushion shot in billiards
BREEZE	v **BREEZED, BREEZING, BREEZES** to move swiftly	**BRIDAL**	n pl. **-S** a wedding
		BRIDALLY	adv in a manner befitting a bride
BREEZY	adj **BREEZIER, BREEZIEST** windy **BREEZILY** adv	**BRIDE**	n pl. **-S** a woman just married or about to be married
BREGMA	n pl. **-MATA** or **-MAS** a junction point of the skull **BREGMATE** adj	**BRIDGE**	v **BRIDGED, BRIDGING, BRIDGES** to connect
BREKKIE	n pl. **-S** breakfast	**BRIDGING**	n pl. **-S** a bracing

BRIDIE	*n* pl. **-S** a pastry filled with meat and onions
BRIDLE	*v* **-DLED, -DLING, -DLES** to control with a restraint
BRIDLER	*n* pl. **-S** one that bridles
BRIDOON	*n* pl. **-S** a device used to control a horse
BRIE	*n* pl. **-S** bree
BRIEF	*adj* **BRIEFER, BRIEFEST** short
BRIEF	*v* **-ED, -ING, -S** to summarize
BRIEFER	*n* pl. **-S** one that briefs
BRIEFING	*n* pl. **-S** a short lecture
BRIEFLY	*adv* in a brief manner
BRIER	*n* pl. **-S** a thorny shrub **BRIERY** *adj*
BRIG	*n* pl. **-S** a two-masted ship
BRIGADE	*v* **-GADED, -GADING, -GADES** to group together
BRIGAND	*n* pl. **-S** a bandit
BRIGHT	*adj* **BRIGHTER, BRIGHTEST** emitting much light **BRIGHTLY** *adv*
BRIGHT	*n* pl. **-S** a light-hued tobacco
BRIGHTEN	*v* **-ED, -ING, -S** to make bright
BRILL	*n* pl. **-S** an edible flatfish
BRIM	*v* **BRIMMED, BRIMMING, BRIMS** to fill to the top
BRIMFUL	*adj* ready to overflow
BRIMFULL	*adj* brimful
BRIMLESS	*adj* having no brim (an upper edge)
BRIMMED	past tense of brim
BRIMMER	*n* pl. **-S** a brimming cup or glass
BRIMMING	present participle of brim
BRIN	*n* pl. **-S** a rib of a fan
BRINDED	*adj* brindled
BRINDLE	*n* pl. **-S** a brindled color
BRINDLED	*adj* streaked
BRINE	*v* **BRINED, BRINING, BRINES** to treat with brine (salted water)
BRINER	*n* pl. **-S** one that brines
BRING	*v* **BROUGHT** or **BRUNG, BRINGING, BRINGS** to take with oneself to a place
BRINGER	*n* pl. **-S** one that brings
BRINIER	comparative of briny
BRINIES	pl. of briny
BRINIEST	superlative of briny
BRINING	present participle of brine

BRINISH	*adj* resembling brine
BRINK	*n* pl. **-S** an extreme edge
BRINY	*adj* **BRINIER, BRINIEST** salty
BRINY	*n* pl. **BRINIES** the sea
BRIO	*n* pl. **BRIOS** liveliness
BRIOCHE	*n* pl. **-S** a rich roll
BRIONY	*n* pl. **-NIES** bryony
BRIQUET	*v* **-QUETTED, -QUETTING, -QUETS** to mold into small bricks
BRIS	*n* pl. **-ES** a Jewish circumcision rite
BRISANCE	*n* pl. **-S** the shattering effect of an explosive **BRISANT** *adj*
BRISK	*adj* **BRISKER, BRISKEST** lively
BRISK	*v* **-ED, -ING, -S** to make brisk
BRISKET	*n* pl. **-S** the breast of an animal
BRISKLY	*adv* in a brisk manner
BRISLING	*n* pl. **-S** a small herring
BRISS	*n* pl. **-ES** bris
BRISTLE	*v* **-TLED, -TLING, -TLES** to rise stiffly
BRISTLY	*adj* **-TLIER, -TLIEST** stiffly erect
BRISTOL	*n* pl. **-S** a smooth cardboard
BRIT	*n* pl. **-S** a young herring
BRITCHES	*n/pl* breeches; trousers
BRITH	*n* pl. **-S** bris
BRITSKA	*n* pl. **-S** an open carriage
BRITT	*n* pl. **-S** brit
BRITTLE	*adj* **-TLER, -TLEST** likely to break
BRITTLE	*v* **-TLED, -TLING, -TLES** to become brittle
BRITTLY	*adv* in a brittle manner
BRITZKA	*n* pl. **-S** britska
BRITZSKA	*n* pl. **-S** britska
BRO	*n* pl. **BROS** a brother
BROACH	*v* **-ED, -ING, -ES** to pierce so as to withdraw a liquid
BROACHER	*n* pl. **-S** one that broaches
BROAD	*adj* **BROADER, BROADEST** wide
BROAD	*n* pl. **-S** an expansion of a river
BROADAX	*n* pl. **-ES** a broad-edged ax
BROADAXE	*n* pl. **-S** broadax
BROADEN	*v* **-ED, -ING, -S** to make broad
BROADISH	*adj* somewhat broad
BROADLY	*adv* in a broad manner
BROADWAY	*n* pl. **-WAYS** a large main road

BROAST   *v* **-ED, -ING, -S** to broil and roast food

BROCADE   *v* **-CADED, -CADING, -CADES** to weave with a raised design

BROCATEL   *n* pl. **-S** a heavy fabric

BROCCOLI   *n* pl. **-S** a vegetable related to the cabbage

BROCH   *n* pl. **-S** a prehistoric stone tower

BROCHE   *adj* brocaded

BROCHURE   *n* pl. **-S** a pamphlet

BROCK   *n* pl. **-S** a badger

BROCKAGE   *n* pl. **-S** an imperfectly minted coin

BROCKET   *n* pl. **-S** a small, red deer

BROCOLI   *n* pl. **-S** broccoli

BROGAN   *n* pl. **-S** a heavy shoe

BROGUE   *n* pl. **-S** an Irish accent

BROGUERY   *n* pl. **-ERIES** the use of an Irish accent

BROGUISH   *adj* resembling a brogue

BROIDER   *v* **-ED, -ING, -S** to adorn with needlework

BROIDERY   *n* pl. **-DERIES** the act of broidering

BROIL   *v* **-ED, -ING, -S** to cook by direct heat

BROILER   *n* pl. **-S** a device for broiling

BROKAGE   *n* pl. **-S** the business of a broker

BROKE   past tense of break

BROKEN   *adj* shattered **BROKENLY** *adv*

BROKER   *v* **-ED, -ING, -S** to act as a broker (an agent who buys and sells stocks)

BROKING   *n* pl. **-S** the business of a broker

BROLGA   *n* pl. **-S** a large Australian bird

BROLLY   *n* pl. **-LIES** an umbrella

BROMAL   *n* pl. **-S** a medicinal liquid

BROMANCE   *n* pl. **-S** a close nonsexual relationship between men

BROMATE   *v* **-MATED, -MATING, -MATES** to combine with bromine

BROME   *n* pl. **-S** a tall grass

BROMELIA   *n* pl. **-S** a tropical plant with stiff leaves

BROMELIN   *n* pl. **-S** an enzyme

BROMIC   *adj* containing bromine

BROMID   *n* pl. **-S** bromide

BROMIDE   *n* pl. **-S** a bromine compound

BROMIDIC   *adj* commonplace; trite

BROMIN   *n* pl. **-S** bromine

BROMINE   *n* pl. **-S** a volatile liquid element

BROMISM   *n* pl. **-S** a diseased condition of the skin

BROMIZE   *v* **-MIZED, -MIZING, -MIZES** to treat with bromine or a bromide

BROMO   *n* pl. **-MOS** a medicinal compound

BRONC   *n* pl. **-S** bronco

BRONCHI   pl. of bronchus

BRONCHIA   *n/pl* the main air passages of the lungs

BRONCHO   *n* pl. **-CHOS** bronco

BRONCHUS   *n* pl. **-CHI** a tracheal branch

BRONCO   *n* pl. **-COS** a wild horse

BRONZE   *v* **BRONZED, BRONZING, BRONZES** to make brown or tan

BRONZER   *n* pl. **-S** one that bronzes

BRONZING   *n* pl. **-S** a brownish coloring

BRONZY   *adj* **BRONZIER, BRONZIEST** of a brownish color

BROO   *n* pl. **BROOS** a bree

BROOCH   *n* pl. **-ES** a decorative pin

BROOD   *v* **-ED, -ING, -S** to ponder deeply

BROODER   *n* pl. **-S** one that broods

BROODY   *adj* **BROODIER, BROODIEST** tending to brood **BROODILY** *adv*

BROOK   *v* **-ED, -ING, -S** to tolerate

BROOKIE   *n* pl. **-S** a brook trout

BROOKITE   *n* pl. **-S** a mineral

BROOKLET   *n* pl. **-S** a small brook or creek

BROOM   *v* **-ED, -ING, -S** to sweep

BROOMY   *adj* **BROOMIER, BROOMIEST** abounding in broom (a type of shrub)

BROS   pl. of bro

BROSE   *n* pl. **-S** a porridge

BROSY   *adj* smeared with brose

BROTH   *n* pl. **-S** a thin clear soup

BROTHEL   *n* pl. **-S** a house of prostitution

BROTHER   *n* pl. **BROTHERS** or **BRETHREN** a male sibling

BROTHER   *v* **-ED, -ING, -S** to treat like a brother

BROTHY   *adj* resembling broth

BROUGHAM   *n* pl. **-S** a type of carriage

BROUGHT   past tense of bring

BROUHAHA   *n* pl. **-S** an uproar

BROW   *n* pl. **-S** the forehead **BROWED** *adj*

BROWBAND	*n* pl. **-S** a band designed to cross the forehead
BROWBEAT	*v* **-BEAT, -BEATEN, -BEATING, -BEATS** to intimidate
BROWBONE	*n* pl. **-S** the ridge of bone above the eye
BROWLESS	*adj* lacking eyebrows
BROWN	*adj* **BROWNER, BROWNEST** of a dark color
BROWN	*v* **-ED, -ING, -S** to make brown
BROWNER	*n* pl. **-S** a fawning person
BROWNIE	*n* pl. **-S** a small sprite
BROWNIER	comparative of browny
BROWNIEST	superlative of browny
BROWNING	*n* pl. **-S** brown flour used for coloring gravy
BROWNISH	*adj* somewhat brown
BROWNOUT	*n* pl. **-S** a power reduction
BROWNY	*adj* **BROWNIER, BROWNIEST** somewhat brown
BROWSE	*v* **BROWSED, BROWSING, BROWSES** to look at casually
BROWSER	*n* pl. **-S** one that browses
BRR	*interj* brrr
BRRR	*interj* — used to indicate that one feels cold
BRUCELLA	*n* pl. **-LAS** or **-LAE** any of a genus of harmful bacteria
BRUCIN	*n* pl. **-S** brucine
BRUCINE	*n* pl. **-S** a poisonous alkaloid
BRUCITE	*n* pl. **-S** a form of magnesium hydroxide
BRUGH	*n* pl. **-S** a borough
BRUIN	*n* pl. **-S** a bear
BRUISE	*v* **BRUISED, BRUISING, BRUISES** to injure without breaking the surface of the skin
BRUISER	*n* pl. **-S** a big, husky man
BRUISING	*n* pl. **-S** an injury that does not break the surface of the skin
BRUIT	*v* **-ED, -ING, -S** to spread news of
BRUITER	*n* pl. **-S** one that bruits
BRULOT	*n* pl. **-S** a biting fly
BRULYIE	*n* pl. **-S** a noisy quarrel
BRULZIE	*n* pl. **-S** brulyie
BRUMAL	*adj* wintry
BRUMBY	*n* pl. **-BIES** a wild horse
BRUME	*n* pl. **-S** fog **BRUMOUS** *adj*
BRUNCH	*v* **-ED, -ING, -ES** to eat a late morning meal
BRUNCHER	*n* pl. **-S** one that brunches
BRUNET	*n* pl. **-S** a dark-haired male
BRUNETTE	*n* pl. **-S** a dark-haired female
BRUNG	a past tense of bring
BRUNIZEM	*n* pl. **-S** a prairie soil
BRUNT	*n* pl. **-S** the main impact
BRUSH	*v* **-ED, -ING, -ES** to touch lightly
BRUSHER	*n* pl. **-S** one that brushes
BRUSHIER	comparative of brushy
BRUSHIEST	superlative of brushy
BRUSHOFF	*n* pl. **-S** an abrupt dismissal
BRUSHUP	*n* pl. **-S** a quick review
BRUSHY	*adj* **BRUSHIER, BRUSHIEST** shaggy; rough
BRUSK	*adj* **BRUSKER, BRUSKEST** brusque
BRUSQUE	*adj* **BRUSQUER, BRUSQUEST** abrupt in manner
BRUT	*n* pl. **-S** a very dry champagne
BRUTAL	*adj* cruel; savage **BRUTALLY** *adv*
BRUTE	*v* **BRUTED, BRUTING, BRUTES** to shape a diamond by rubbing it with another diamond
BRUTE	*adj* **BRUTER, BRUTEST** resembling an animal; cruel
BRUTELY	*adv* in a brutal manner
BRUTIFY	*v* **-FIED, -FYING, -FIES** to make brutal
BRUTISH	*adj* brutal
BRUTISM	*n* pl. **-S** the state of being brutal
BRUX	*v* **-ED, -ING, -ES** to grind the teeth
BRUXISM	*n* pl. **-S** a nervous grinding of the teeth
BRYOLOGY	*n* pl. **-GIES** the study of mosses
BRYONY	*n* pl. **-NIES** a climbing plant
BRYOZOAN	*n* pl. **-S** a type of small aquatic animal
BUB	*n* pl. **-S** young fellow
BUBAL	*n* pl. **-S** a large antelope
BUBALE	*n* pl. **-S** bubal
BUBALINE	*adj* pertaining to the bubal
BUBALIS	*n* pl. **-LISES** bubal
BUBBE	*n* pl. **-S** a Jewish grandmother
BUBBIE	*n* pl. **-S** bubbe

BUBBLE v **-BLED, -BLING, -BLES** to form bubbles (bodies of gas contained within a liquid)

BUBBLER n pl. **-S** a drinking fountain

BUBBLY adj **-BLIER, -BLIEST** full of bubbles

BUBBLY n pl. **-BLIES** champagne

BUBINGA n pl. **-S** an African tree

BUBKES n/pl the least amount

BUBO n pl. **-BOES** a swelling of a lymph gland **BUBOED** adj

BUBONIC adj pertaining to a bubo

BUBU n pl. **-S** boubou

BUCCAL adj pertaining to the cheek **BUCCALLY** adv

BUCK v **-ED, -ING, -S** to leap forward and upward suddenly

BUCKAROO n pl. **-ROOS** a cowboy

BUCKAYRO n pl. **-ROS** buckaroo

BUCKBEAN n pl. **-S** a marsh plant

BUCKEEN n pl. **-S** a poor man who acts as if wealthy

BUCKER n pl. **-S** a bucking horse

BUCKEROO n pl. **-ROOS** buckaroo

BUCKET v **-ED, -ING, -S** to hurry

BUCKEYE n pl. **-S** a nut-bearing tree

BUCKISH adj foppish

BUCKLE v **-LED, -LING, -LES** to bend under pressure

BUCKLER v **-ED, -ING, -S** to shield

BUCKO n pl. **BUCKOS** or **BUCKOES** a bully

BUCKRAM v **-ED, -ING, -S** to stiffen

BUCKSAW n pl. **-S** a wood-cutting saw

BUCKSHEE n pl. **-S** something extra obtained free

BUCKSHOT n pl. **-S** a large lead shot

BUCKSKIN n pl. **-S** the skin of a male deer

BUCKTAIL n pl. **-S** a fishing lure

BUCOLIC n pl. **-S** a pastoral poem

BUD v **BUDDED, BUDDING, BUDS** to put forth buds (undeveloped plant parts)

BUDDER n pl. **-S** one that buds

BUDDIED past tense of buddy

BUDDIES present 3d person sing. of buddy

BUDDING n pl. **-S** a type of asexual reproduction

BUDDLE n pl. **-S** an apparatus on which crushed ore is washed

BUDDLEIA n pl. **-S** a tropical shrub

BUDDY v **-DIED, -DYING, -DIES** to become close friends

BUDGE v **BUDGED, BUDGING, BUDGES** to move slightly

BUDGER n pl. **-S** one that budges

BUDGET v **-ED, -ING, -S** to estimate expenditures

BUDGETER n pl. **-S** one that budgets

BUDGIE n pl. **-S** a small parrot

BUDGING present participle of budge

BUDLESS adj being without buds

BUDLIKE adj resembling a bud

BUDWOOD n pl. **-S** a branch having buds that is used for grafting

BUDWORM n pl. **-S** a caterpillar that eats buds

BUFF adj **BUFFER, BUFFEST** having a muscular physique

BUFF v **-ED, -ING, -S** to polish **BUFFABLE** adj

BUFFALO n pl. **-LOS** or **-LOES** an ox-like animal

BUFFALO v **-ED, -ING, -ES** to intimidate

BUFFER v **-ED, -ING, -S** to cushion

BUFFET v **-ED, -ING, -S** to hit sharply

BUFFETER n pl. **-S** one that buffets

BUFFI a pl. of buffo

BUFFIER comparative of buffy

BUFFIEST superlative of buffy

BUFFO n pl. **-FOS** or **-FI** an operatic clown

BUFFOON n pl. **-S** a clown

BUFFY adj **BUFFIER, BUFFIEST** of a yellowish-brown color

BUG v **BUGGED, BUGGING, BUGS** to annoy

BUGABOO n pl. **-BOOS** a bugbear

BUGBANE n pl. **-S** a perennial herb

BUGBEAR n pl. **-S** an object or source of dread

BUGEYE n pl. **-S** a small boat

BUGGED past tense of bug

BUGGER v **-ED, -ING, -S** to damn

BUGGERY n pl. **-GERIES** sodomy

BUGGING present participle of bug

BUGGY adj **-GIER, -GIEST** infested with bugs

BUGGY	*n* pl. **-GIES** a light carriage
BUGHOUSE	*n* pl. **-S** an insane asylum
BUGLE	*v* **-GLED, -GLING, -GLES** to play a bugle (a brass wind instrument)
BUGLER	*n* pl. **-S** one that plays a bugle
BUGLOSS	*n* pl. **-ES** a coarse plant
BUGOUT	*n* pl. **-S** one that leaves hurriedly
BUGSEED	*n* pl. **-S** an annual herb
BUGSHA	*n* pl. **-S** buqsha
BUHL	*n* pl. **-S** a style of furniture decoration
BUHLWORK	*n* pl. **-S** buhl
BUHR	*n* pl. **-S** a heavy stone
BUILD	*v* **BUILT** or **BUILDED, BUILDING, BUILDS** to construct
BUILDER	*n* pl. **-S** one that builds
BUILDING	*n* pl. **-S** something that is built
BUILDUP	*n* pl. **-S** an accumulation
BUILT	a past tense of build
BUIRDLY	*adj* burly
BULB	*n* pl. **-S** an underground bud **BULBAR, BULBED** *adj*
BULBEL	*n* pl. **-S** bulbil
BULBIL	*n* pl. **-S** a small bulb
BULBLET	*n* pl. **-S** a small bulb
BULBOUS	*adj* bulb-shaped; bulging
BULBUL	*n* pl. **-S** a songbird
BULGAR	*n* pl. **-S** bulgur
BULGE	*v* **BULGED, BULGING, BULGES** to swell out
BULGER	*n* pl. **-S** a golf club
BULGHUR	*n* pl. **-S** bulgur
BULGUR	*n* pl. **-S** crushed wheat
BULGY	*adj* **BULGIER, BULGIEST** bulging
BULIMIA	*n* pl. **-S** insatiable appetite **BULIMIAC** *adj*
BULIMIC	*n* pl. **-S** one who is affected with bulimia
BULK	*v* **-ED, -ING, -S** to gather into a mass
BULKAGE	*n* pl. **-S** a peristaltic stimulant
BULKER	*n* pl. **-S** a ship that carries cargo in bulk (a mass)
BULKHEAD	*n* pl. **-S** a partition in a ship
BULKY	*adj* **BULKIER, BULKIEST** massive **BULKILY** *adv*
BULL	*v* **-ED, -ING, -S** to push ahead
BULLA	*n* pl. **-LAE** a large blister
BULLACE	*n* pl. **-S** a purple plum
BULLATE	*adj* blistered in appearance
BULLBAT	*n* pl. **-S** a nocturnal bird
BULLCOOK	*n* pl. **-S** a worker in a logging camp
BULLDOG	*v* **-DOGGED, -DOGGING, -DOGS** to throw a steer
BULLDOZE	*v* **-DOZED, -DOZING, -DOZES** to bully
BULLET	*v* **-ED, -ING, -S** to move swiftly
BULLETIN	*v* **-ED, -ING, -S** to issue a news item
BULLEY	*n* pl. **-LEYS** a two-masted fishing boat
BULLFROG	*n* pl. **-S** a large frog
BULLHEAD	*n* pl. **-S** a freshwater catfish
BULLHORN	*n* pl. **-S** an electric megaphone
BULLIED	past tense of bully
BULLIER	comparative of bully
BULLIES	present 3d person sing. of bully
BULLIEST	superlative of bully
BULLION	*n* pl. **-S** uncoined gold or silver
BULLISH	*adj* stubborn
BULLNECK	*n* pl. **-S** a thick neck
BULLNOSE	*n* pl. **-S** a disease of swine
BULLOCK	*n* pl. **-S** a castrated bull **BULLOCKY** *adj*
BULLOUS	*adj* resembling bullae
BULLPEN	*n* pl. **-S** an enclosure for bulls
BULLPOUT	*n* pl. **-S** a bullhead
BULLRING	*n* pl. **-S** a bullfight arena
BULLRUSH	*n* pl. **-ES** bulrush
BULLSEYE	*n* pl. **-S** the center of a target
BULLSHOT	*n* pl. **-S** a drink made of vodka and bouillon
BULLWEED	*n* pl. **-S** knapweed
BULLWHIP	*v* **-WHIPPED, -WHIPPING, -WHIPS** to strike with a long whip
BULLY	*adj* **-LIER, -LIEST** wonderful
BULLY	*v* **-LIED, -LYING, -LIES** to treat abusively
BULLYBOY	*n* pl. **-BOYS** a ruffian
BULLYRAG	*v* **-RAGGED, -RAGGING, -RAGS** to bully
BULRUSH	*n* pl. **-ES** a tall marsh plant
BULWARK	*v* **-ED, -ING, -S** to fortify with a defensive wall

BUM   *adj* **BUMMER, BUMMEST** of little value; worthless

BUM   *v* **BUMMED, BUMMING, BUMS** to live idly

BUMBAG   *n* pl. **-S** a pack that straps to the waist

BUMBLE   *v* **-BLED, -BLING, -BLES** to bungle

BUMBLER   *n* pl. **-S** one that bumbles

BUMBLING   *n* pl. **-S** an instance of clumsiness

BUMBOAT   *n* pl. **-S** a boat used to peddle wares to larger ships

BUMELIA   *n* pl. **-S** a thorny tree

BUMF   *n* pl. **-S** paperwork

BUMKIN   *n* pl. **-S** a ship's spar

BUMMALO   *n* pl. **-LOS** a small Asian fish

BUMMED   past tense of bum

BUMMER   *n* pl. **-S** one that bums

BUMMEST   superlative of bum

BUMMING   present participle of bum

BUMP   *v* **-ED, -ING, -S** to knock against

BUMPER   *v* **-ED, -ING, -S** to fill to the brim

BUMPH   *n* pl. **-S** bumf

BUMPKIN   *n* pl. **-S** an unsophisticated rustic

BUMPY   *adj* **BUMPIER, BUMPIEST** of uneven surface **BUMPILY** *adv*

BUN   *n* pl. **-S** a small bread roll

BUNA   *n* pl. **-S** a synthetic rubber

BUNCH   *v* **-ED, -ING, -ES** to group together

BUNCHER   *n* pl. **-S** one that gathers things together

BUNCHY   *adj* **BUNCHIER, BUNCHIEST** clustered **BUNCHILY** *adv*

BUNCO   *v* **-ED, -ING, -S** or **-ES** to swindle

BUNCOMBE   *n* pl. **-S** nonsense

BUND   *n* pl. **-S** a political association

BUNDIST   *n* pl. **-S** a member of a bund

BUNDLE   *v* **-DLED, -DLING, -DLES** to fasten a group of objects together

BUNDLER   *n* pl. **-S** one that bundles

BUNDLING   *n* pl. **-S** a former courtship custom

BUNDT   *n* pl. **-S** a type of cake pan

BUNFIGHT   *n* pl. **-S** a crowded boisterous party

BUNG   *v* **-ED, -ING, -S** to plug with a cork or stopper

BUNGALOW   *n* pl. **-S** a small cottage

BUNGEE   *n* pl. **-S** an elasticized cord

BUNGHOLE   *n* pl. **-S** a hole in a keg or barrel

BUNGLE   *v* **-GLED, -GLING, -GLES** to work, make, or do clumsily

BUNGLER   *n* pl. **-S** one that bungles

BUNGLING   *n* pl. **-S** something done clumsily

BUNHEAD   *n* pl. **-S** a female ballet dancer

BUNION   *n* pl. **-S** a painful swelling of the foot

BUNK   *v* **-ED, -ING, -S** to go to bed

BUNKER   *v* **-ED, -ING, -S** to store in a large bin

BUNKIE   *n* pl. **-S** a small separate building for guests

BUNKMATE   *n* pl. **-S** a person with whom sleeping quarters are shared

BUNKO   *v* **-ED, -ING, -S** to bunco

BUNKUM   *n* pl. **-S** nonsense

BUNN   *n* pl. **-S** bun

BUNNY   *n* pl. **-NIES** a rabbit

BUNRAKU   *n* pl. **-S** a Japanese puppet show

BUNT   *v* **-ED, -ING, -S** to butt

BUNTER   *n* pl. **-S** one that bunts

BUNTING   *n* pl. **-S** a fabric used for flags

BUNTLINE   *n* pl. **-S** a rope used to haul up a sail

BUNYA   *n* pl. **-S** an evergreen tree

BUNYIP   *n* pl. **-S** a fabulous monster of swamps

BUOY   *v* **-ED, -ING, -S** to mark with a buoy (a warning float)

BUOYAGE   *n* pl. **-S** a group of buoys

BUOYANCE   *n* pl. **-S** buoyancy

BUOYANCY   *n* pl. **-CIES** the tendency to float

BUOYANT   *adj* having buoyancy

BUPKES   *n/pl* bubkes

BUPKIS   *n/pl* bubkes

BUPKUS   *n/pl* bubkes

BUPPIE   *n* pl. **-S** a black professional person working in a city

BUPPY   *n* pl. **-PIES** buppie

BUQSHA   *n* pl. **-S** a monetary unit of Yemen

BUR   *v* **BURRED, BURRING, BURS** to burr

BURA   *n* pl. **-S** buran

BURAN   *n* pl. **-S** a violent windstorm

BURB   *n* pl. **-S** a suburb

BURBLE   *v* **-BLED, -BLING, -BLES** to speak quickly and excitedly

BURBLER	*n* pl. **-S** one that burbles
BURBLING	*n* pl. **-S** the breaking up of an airflow into turbulence
BURBLY	*adj* **-BLIER, -BLIEST** burbling
BURBOT	*n* pl. **-S** a freshwater fish
BURD	*n* pl. **-S** a maiden
BURDEN	*v* **-ED, -ING, -S** to load heavily
BURDENER	*n* pl. **-S** one that burdens
BURDIE	*n* pl. **-S** burd
BURDOCK	*n* pl. **-S** a coarse weed
BUREAU	*n* pl. **-REAUS** or **-REAUX** a chest of drawers
BURET	*n* pl. **-S** burette
BURETTE	*n* pl. **-S** a measuring tube
BURFI	*n* pl. **-S** a dessert made from milk solids and sugar
BURG	*n* pl. **-S** a city or town
BURGAGE	*n* pl. **-S** a feudal tenure
BURGEE	*n* pl. **-S** a small flag
BURGEON	*v* **-ED, -ING, -S** to develop rapidly
BURGER	*n* pl. **-S** a hamburger
BURGESS	*n* pl. **-ES** a citizen of an English borough
BURGH	*n* pl. **-S** a Scottish borough **BURGHAL** *adj*
BURGHER	*n* pl. **-S** a citizen of a borough
BURGLAR	*n* pl. **-S** one who commits burglary
BURGLARY	*n* pl. **-GLARIES** a felonious theft
BURGLE	*v* **-GLED, -GLING, -GLES** to commit burglary
BURGONET	*n* pl. **-S** an open helmet
BURGOO	*n* pl. **-GOOS** a thick oatmeal
BURGOUT	*n* pl. **-S** burgoo
BURGRAVE	*n* pl. **-S** a German nobleman
BURGUNDY	*n* pl. **-DIES** a red wine
BURIAL	*n* pl. **-S** the act of burying
BURIED	past tense of bury
BURIER	*n* pl. **-S** one that buries
BURIES	present 3d person sing. of bury
BURIN	*n* pl. **-S** an engraving tool
BURK	*n* pl. **-S** berk
BURKA	*n* pl. **-S** a long loose outer garment worn by some Muslim women
BURKE	*v* **BURKED, BURKING, BURKES** to murder by suffocation
BURKER	*n* pl. **-S** one that burkes
BURKHA	*n* pl. **-S** burka

BURKITE	*n* pl. **-S** a burker
BURL	*v* **-ED, -ING, -S** to finish cloth by removing lumps
BURLAP	*n* pl. **-S** a coarse fabric
BURLER	*n* pl. **-S** one that burls
BURLESK	*n* pl. **-S** a type of stage show
BURLEY	*n* pl. **-LEYS** a light tobacco
BURLY	*adj* **-LIER, -LIEST** heavy and muscular **BURLILY** *adv*
BURN	*v* **BURNED** or **BURNT, BURNING, BURNS** to destroy by fire
BURNABLE	*n* pl. **-S** something that can be burned
BURNER	*n* pl. **-S** one that burns
BURNET	*n* pl. **-S** a perennial herb
BURNIE	*n* pl. **-S** a brooklet
BURNING	*n* pl. **-S** the firing of ceramic materials
BURNISH	*v* **-ED, -ING, -ES** to polish
BURNOOSE	*n* pl. **-S** a hooded cloak
BURNOUS	*n* pl. **-ES** burnoose
BURNOUT	*n* pl. **-S** a destructive fire
BURNSIDE	*n* pl. **-S** a mustache and side whiskers on the cheeks
BURNT	a past tense of burn
BURP	*v* **-ED, -ING, -S** to belch
BURPEE	*n* pl. **-S** a physical exercise
BURQA	*n* pl. **-S** burka
BURR	*v* **-ED, -ING, -S** to remove a rough edge from
BURRED	past tense of bur
BURRER	*n* pl. **-S** one that burrs
BURRFISH	*n* pl. **-ES** a fish with erect spines
BURRIER	comparative of burry
BURRIEST	superlative of burry
BURRING	present participle of bur
BURRITO	*n* pl. **-TOS** a tortilla rolled around a filling
BURRO	*n* pl. **-ROS** a small donkey
BURROW	*v* **-ED, -ING, -S** to dig a hole or tunnel in the ground
BURROWER	*n* pl. **-S** one that burrows
BURRY	*adj* **-RIER, -RIEST** prickly
BURSA	*n* pl. **-SAS** or **-SAE** a bodily pouch **BURSAL** *adj*
BURSAR	*n* pl. **-S** a college treasurer
BURSARY	*n* pl. **-RIES** a college treasury

BURSATE	*adj* pertaining to a bursa
BURSE	*n* pl. **-S** a small bag or pouch
BURSEED	*n* pl. **-S** a coarse weed
BURSERA	*adj* designating a family of shrubs and trees
BURSITIS	*n* pl. **-TISES** inflammation of a bursa
BURST	*v* **BURSTED** or **BURST, BURSTING, BURSTS** to break open suddenly or violently
BURSTER	*n* pl. **-S** one that bursts
BURSTONE	*n* pl. **-S** a heavy stone
BURSTY	*adj* **BURSTIER, BURSTIEST** occurring in short sudden episodes or groups
BURTHEN	*v* **-ED, -ING, -S** to burden
BURTON	*n* pl. **-S** a hoisting tackle
BURWEED	*n* pl. **-S** a coarse weed
BURY	*v* **BURIED, BURYING, BURIES** to put in the ground and cover with earth
BUS	*v* **BUSED, BUSING, BUSES** or **BUSSED, BUSSING, BUSSES** to transport by bus (a large motor vehicle)
BUSBAR	*n* pl. **-S** a type of electrical conductor
BUSBOY	*n* pl. **-BOYS** a boy or man who is a server's assistant in a restaurant
BUSBY	*n* pl. **-BIES** a tall fur hat
BUSGIRL	*n* pl. **-S** a girl or woman who is a server's assistant in a restaurant
BUSH	*v* **-ED, -ING, -ES** to cover with bushes (shrubs)
BUSHBABY	*n* pl. **-BIES** a small tree-dwelling primate
BUSHBUCK	*n* pl. **-S** a small antelope
BUSHEL	*v* **-ELED, -ELING, -ELS** or **-ELLED, -ELLING, -ELS** to mend clothing
BUSHELER	*n* pl. **-S** one that bushels
BUSHER	*n* pl. **-S** a minor league baseball player
BUSHFIRE	*n* pl. **-S** a fire in a wooded area
BUSHGOAT	*n* pl. **-S** a bushbuck
BUSHIDO	*n* pl. **-DOS** the code of the samurai
BUSHIER	comparative of bushy
BUSHIES	pl. of bushy
BUSHIEST	superlative of bushy
BUSHILY	*adv* in a bushy manner

BUSHING	*n* pl. **-S** a lining for a hole
BUSHLAND	*n* pl. **-S** unsettled forest land
BUSHLESS	*adj* having no bushes
BUSHLIKE	*adj* resembling a bush
BUSHLOT	*n* pl. **-S** a woodlot
BUSHMAN	*n* pl. **-MEN** a woodsman
BUSHPIG	*n* pl. **-S** a wild African pig
BUSHTIT	*n* pl. **-S** a titmouse
BUSHVELD	*n* pl. **-S** a veld with shrubby vegetation
BUSHWA	*n* pl. **-S** nonsense
BUSHWAH	*n* pl. **-S** bushwa
BUSHY	*adj* **BUSHIER, BUSHIEST** covered with bushes
BUSHY	*n* pl. **BUSHIES** a person who lives in the bush (the wilderness)
BUSIED	past tense of busy
BUSIER	comparative of busy
BUSIES	present 3d person sing. of busy
BUSIEST	superlative of busy
BUSILY	*adv* in a busy manner
BUSINESS	*n* pl. **-ES** an occupation, profession, or trade
BUSING	*n* pl. **-S** the act of transporting by bus
BUSK	*v* **-ED, -ING, -S** to prepare
BUSKER	*n* pl. **-S** a roaming entertainer
BUSKIN	*n* pl. **-S** a high shoe **BUSKINED** *adj*
BUSKING	*n* pl. **-S** the act of performing as a busker
BUSLOAD	*n* pl. **-S** a load that fills a bus
BUSMAN	*n* pl. **-MEN** a bus operator
BUSS	*v* **-ED, -ING, -ES** to kiss
BUSSED	a past tense of bus
BUSSES	a present 3d person sing. of bus
BUSSING	*n* pl. **-S** busing
BUST	*v* **-ED, -ING, -S** to burst
BUSTARD	*n* pl. **-S** a game bird
BUSTEE	*n* pl. **-S** a slum in India
BUSTER	*n* pl. **-S** one that breaks up something
BUSTIC	*n* pl. **-S** a tropical tree
BUSTIER	*n* pl. **-S** a woman's undergarment
BUSTLE	*v* **-TLED, -TLING, -TLES** to move energetically
BUSTLER	*n* pl. **-S** one that bustles

BUSTLINE   *n* pl. **-S** the distance around the bust (the upper torso of a woman)

BUSTY   *adj* **BUSTIER, BUSTIEST** full-bosomed

BUSULFAN   *n* pl. **-S** a medicine

BUSY   *adj* **BUSIER, BUSIEST** occupied

BUSY   *v* **BUSIED, BUSYING, BUSIES** to make busy

BUSYBODY   *n* pl. **-BODIES** a nosy person

BUSYNESS   *n* pl. **-ES** the state of being busy

BUSYWORK   *n* pl. **-S** active but valueless work

BUT   *n* pl. **-S** a flatfish

BUTANE   *n* pl. **-S** a flammable gas

BUTANOL   *n* pl. **-S** a flammable alcohol

BUTANONE   *n* pl. **-S** a flammable ketone

BUTCH   *adj* **-ER, -EST** notably masculine in appearance or manner

BUTCHER   *v* **-ED, -ING, -S** to slaughter

BUTCHERY   *n* pl. **-ERIES** wanton or cruel killing

BUTE   *n* pl. **-S** a drug for treating arthritis

BUTENE   *n* pl. **-S** butylene

BUTEO   *n* pl. **-TEOS** a hawk

BUTLE   *v* **-LED, -LING, -LES** to buttle

BUTLER   *n* pl. **-S** a male servant

BUTLERY   *n* pl. **-LERIES** a storage room

BUTLES   present 3d person sing. of butle

BUTLING   present participle of butle

BUTOH   *n* pl. **-S** a style of modern Japanese dance

BUTT   *v* **-ED, -ING, -S** to hit with the head

BUTTALS   *n/pl* boundary lines

BUTTE   *n* pl. **-S** an isolated hill

BUTTER   *v* **-ED, -ING, -S** to spread with butter (a milk product)

BUTTERY   *adj* **-TERIER, -TERIEST** containing butter

BUTTERY   *n* pl. **-TERIES** a wine cellar

BUTTHEAD   *n* pl. **-S** a stupid person

BUTTIES   pl. of butty

BUTTLE   *v* **-TLED, -TLING, -TLES** to serve as a butler

BUTTOCK   *n* pl. **-S** either of the two rounded parts of the rump

BUTTON   *v* **-ED, -ING, -S** to fasten with a button (a small disk)

BUTTONER   *n* pl. **-S** one that buttons

BUTTONY   *adj* resembling a button

BUTTRESS   *v* **-ED, -ING, -ES** to prop up

BUTTY   *n* pl. **-TIES** a fellow workman

BUTUT   *n* pl. **-S** a monetary unit of Gambia

BUTYL   *n* pl. **-S** a hydrocarbon radical

BUTYLATE   *v* **-ATED, -ATING, -ATES** to add a butyl to

BUTYLENE   *n* pl. **-S** a gaseous hydrocarbon

BUTYRAL   *n* pl. **-S** a chemical compound

BUTYRATE   *n* pl. **-S** a chemical salt

BUTYRIC   *adj* derived from butter

BUTYRIN   *n* pl. **-S** a chemical compound

BUTYROUS   *adj* resembling butter

BUTYRYL   *n* pl. **-S** a radical of butyric acid

BUXOM   *adj* **-OMER, -OMEST** healthily plump **BUXOMLY** *adv*

BUY   *v* **BOUGHT, BUYING, BUYS** to purchase **BUYABLE** *adj*

BUYBACK   *n* pl. **-S** the repurchase by a corporation of its own stock

BUYER   *n* pl. **-S** one that buys

BUYOFF   *n* pl. **-S** a payment for a consideration

BUYOUT   *n* pl. **-S** the purchase of a business

BUZUKI   *n* pl. **-KIS** or **-KIA** bouzouki

BUZZ   *v* **-ED, -ING, -ES** to make a vibrating sound

BUZZARD   *n* pl. **-S** a large bird of prey

BUZZBAIT   *n* pl. **-S** a vibrating fishing lure

BUZZCUT   *n* pl. **-S** a very short haircut

BUZZER   *n* pl. **-S** a signaling device

BUZZIER   comparative of buzzy

BUZZIEST   superlative of buzzy

BUZZING   *n* pl. **-S** a vibrating sound

BUZZKILL   *n* pl. **-S** one that has a depressing or negative effect

BUZZWIG   *n* pl. **-S** a large, thick wig

BUZZWORD   *n* pl. **-S** a word used to impress someone

BUZZY   *adj* **BUZZIER, BUZZIEST** having a vibrating sound

BWANA   *n* pl. **-S** master; boss

BY   *n* pl. **BYS** a pass in certain card games

BYCATCH   *n* pl. **-ES** marine animals caught unintentionally

BYE   *n* pl. **-S** a side issue

BYELAW   *n* pl. **-S** bylaw

BYGONE   *n* pl. **-S** a past occurrence

BYLAW   *n* pl. **-S** a secondary law

BYLINE   *v* **-LINED, -LINING, -LINES** to write under a byline (a line giving the author's name)

BYLINER   *n* pl. **-S** one that writes under a byline

BYNAME   *n* pl. **-S** a secondary name

BYPASS   *v* **-ED, -ING, -ES** to avoid by going around

BYPAST   *adj* past; gone by

BYPATH   *n* pl. **-S** an indirect road

BYPLAY   *n* pl. **-PLAYS** secondary action

BYRE   *n* pl. **-S** a cowshed

BYRL   *v* **-ED, -ING, -S** to birle

BYRNIE   *n* pl. **-S** an armored shirt

BYROAD   *n* pl. **-S** a side road

BYSSUS   *n* pl. **BYSSUSES** or **BYSSI** a fine linen **BYSSAL** *adj*

BYSTREET   *n* pl. **-S** a side street

BYTALK   *n* pl. **-S** small talk

BYTE   *n* pl. **-S** a group of adjacent binary digits

BYWAY   *n* pl. **-WAYS** a side road

BYWORD   *n* pl. **-S** a well-known saying

BYWORK   *n* pl. **-S** work done during leisure time

BYZANT   *n* pl. **-S** bezant

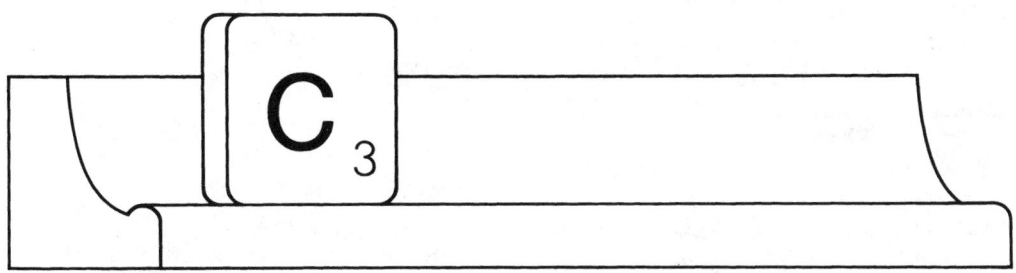

CAB	*v* **CABBED, CABBING, CABS** to take or drive a taxicab	**CABLET**	*n* pl. **-S** a small cable
CABAL	*v* **-BALLED, -BALLING, -BALS** to conspire	**CABLEWAY**	*n* pl. **-WAYS** a suspended cable
		CABLING	*n* pl. **-S** a cable or cables used for fastening something
CABALA	*n* pl. **-S** an occult or secret doctrine	**CABMAN**	*n* pl. **-MEN** a driver of a cab
CABALISM	*n* pl. **-S** adherence to a cabala	**CABOB**	*n* pl. **-S** kabob
CABALIST	*n* pl. **-S** one who practices cabalism	**CABOCHED**	*adj* full-faced — used of an animal's head in heraldry
CABALLED	past tense of cabal	**CABOCHON**	*n* pl. **-S** a precious stone
CABALLING	present participle of cabal	**CABOMBA**	*n* pl. **-S** an aquatic plant
CABANA	*n* pl. **-S** a small cabin	**CABOODLE**	*n* pl. **-S** a collection
CABARET	*n* pl. **-S** a music hall	**CABOOSE**	*n* pl. **-S** the last car of a freight train
CABBAGE	*v* **-BAGED, -BAGING, -BAGES** to steal	**CABOSHED**	*adj* caboched
CABBAGEY	*adj* resembling a cabbage (a leafy vegetable)	**CABOTAGE**	*n* pl. **-S** coastal trade
		CABOVER	*n* pl. **-S** a truck having the driver's compartment over the engine
CABBAGY	*adj* cabbagey		
CABBALA	*n* pl. **-S** cabala	**CABRESTA**	*n* pl. **-S** cabestro
CABBALAH	*n* pl. **-S** cabala	**CABRESTO**	*n* pl. **-TOS** cabestro
CABBED	past tense of cab	**CABRETTA**	*n* pl. **-S** a soft leather
CABBIE	*n* pl. **-S** cabby	**CABRILLA**	*n* pl. **-S** a sea bass
CABBING	present participle of cab	**CABRIOLE**	*n* pl. **-S** a curved furniture leg
CABBY	*n* pl. **-BIES** a driver of a cab	**CABSTAND**	*n* pl. **-S** a place where cabs await hire
CABER	*n* pl. **-S** a heavy pole thrown as a trial of strength	**CACA**	*n* pl. **-S** excrement
CABERNET	*n* pl. **-S** a dry red wine	**CACAO**	*n* pl. **-CAOS** a tropical tree
CABESTRO	*n* pl. **-TROS** a lasso	**CACHACA**	*n* pl. **-S** a Brazilian liquor
CABEZON	*n* pl. **-S** a large, edible fish	**CACHALOT**	*n* pl. **-S** a large whale
CABEZONE	*n* pl. **-S** cabezon	**CACHE**	*v* **CACHED, CACHING, CACHES** to store in a hiding place
CABILDO	*n* pl. **-DOS** a town council	**CACHEPOT**	*n* pl. **-S** an ornamental container for a flowerpot
CABIN	*v* **-ED, -ING, -S** to live in a cabin (a roughly built house)	**CACHET**	*v* **-ED, -ING, -S** to print a design on an envelope
CABINET	*n* pl. **-S** a piece of furniture with shelves and drawers	**CACHEXIA**	*n* pl. **-S** general ill health **CACHEXIC** *adj*
CABLE	*v* **-BLED, -BLING, -BLES** to fasten with a cable (a heavy rope)	**CACHEXY**	*n* pl. **-CHEXIES** cachexia
CABLER	*n* pl. **-S** one that supplies a cable	**CACHING**	present participle of cache

CACHOU *n* pl. **-S** catechu

CACHUCHA *n* pl. **-S** a Spanish dance

CACIQUE *n* pl. **-S** a tropical oriole

CACKLE *v* **-LED, -LING, -LES** to make the sound of a hen

CACKLER *n* pl. **-S** one that cackles

CACODYL *n* pl. **-S** a poisonous liquid

CACOMIXL *n* pl. **-S** a raccoon-like mammal

CACONYM *n* pl. **-S** an erroneous name

CACONYMY *n* pl. **-MIES** the state of having an erroneous name

CACTUS *n* pl. **-TUSES** or **-TI** a plant native to arid regions **CACTOID** *adj*

CAD *n* pl. **-S** an ungentlemanly man

CADASTER *n* pl. **-S** a public record of land ownership

CADASTRE *n* pl. **-S** cadaster

CADAVER *n* pl. **-S** a corpse

CADDICE *n* pl. **-S** caddis

CADDIE *v* **-DIED, -DYING, -DIES** to serve as a golfer's assistant

CADDIS *n* pl. **-DISES** a coarse woolen fabric **CADDISED** *adj*

CADDISH *adj* resembling a cad

CADDY *v* **-DIED, -DYING, -DIES** to caddie

CADE *n* pl. **-S** a European shrub

CADELLE *n* pl. **-S** a small, black beetle

CADENCE *v* **-DENCED, -DENCING, -DENCES** to make rhythmic

CADENCY *n* pl. **-CIES** a rhythm

CADENT *adj* having rhythm

CADENZA *n* pl. **-S** an elaborate musical passage

CADET *n* pl. **-S** a student at a military school

CADGE *v* **CADGED, CADGING, CADGES** to get by begging

CADGER *n* pl. **-S** one that cadges

CADGY *adj* cheerful

CADI *n* pl. **-S** a Muslim judge

CADMIUM *n* pl. **-S** a metallic element **CADMIC** *adj*

CADRE *n* pl. **-S** a nucleus of trained personnel

CADUCEUS *n* pl. **-CEI** a heraldic wand or staff **CADUCEAN** *adj*

CADUCITY *n* pl. **-TIES** senility

CADUCOUS *adj* transitory; perishable

CAECUM *n* pl. **-CA** cecum **CAECAL** *adj* **CAECALLY** *adv*

CAEOMA *n* pl. **-S** a spore-forming organ of a fungus

CAESAR *n* pl. **-S** an emperor

CAESIOUS *adj* bluish green

CAESIUM *n* pl. **-S** cesium

CAESTUS *n* pl. **-ES** cestus

CAESURA *n* pl. **-RAS** or **-RAE** a pause in a line of verse **CAESURAL, CAESURIC** *adj*

CAF *n* pl. **-S** a cafeteria or cafe

CAFARD *n* pl. **-S** a state of depression

CAFE *n* pl. **-S** a small restaurant

CAFF *n* pl. **-S** a caf

CAFFEIN *n* pl. **-S** caffeine

CAFFEINE *n* pl. **-S** a bitter alkaloid used as a stimulant

CAFTAN *n* pl. **-S** a full-length tunic **CAFTANED** *adj*

CAGE *v* **CAGED, CAGING, CAGES** to confine

CAGEFUL *n* pl. **-S** the number held in a cage (an enclosure)

CAGELIKE *adj* resembling a cage (an enclosure)

CAGELING *n* pl. **-S** a caged bird

CAGER *n* pl. **-S** a basketball player

CAGEY *adj* **CAGIER, CAGIEST** shrewd

CAGIER comparative of cagy

CAGIEST superlative of cagy

CAGILY *adv* in a cagey manner

CAGINESS *n* pl. **-ES** the quality of being cagey

CAGING present participle of cage

CAGOULE *n* pl. **-S** a hooded waterproof garment

CAGY *adj* **CAGIER, CAGIEST** cagey

CAHIER *n* pl. **-S** a notebook

CAHOOT *n* pl. **-S** partnership

CAHOUN *n* pl. **-S** cohune

CAHOW *n* pl. **-S** a sea bird

CAID *n* pl. **-S** a Muslim leader

CAIMAN *n* pl. **-S** a tropical reptile

CAIN *n* pl. **-S** kain

CAIQUE *n* pl. **-S** a long, narrow rowboat

CAIRD *n* pl. **-S** a gypsy

CAIRN   *n* pl. **-S** a mound of stones set up as a memorial **CAIRNED, CAIRNY** *adj*

CAISSON   *n* pl. **-S** a watertight chamber

CAITIFF   *n* pl. **-S** a despicable person

CAJAPUT   *n* pl. **-S** cajeput

CAJEPUT   *n* pl. **-S** an Australian tree

CAJOLE   *v* **-JOLED, -JOLING, -JOLES** to persuade by flattery

CAJOLER   *n* pl. **-S** one that cajoles

CAJOLERY   *n* pl. **-ERIES** persuasion by flattery

CAJON   *n* pl. **-ES** a steep-sided canyon

CAJUPUT   *n* pl. **-S** cajeput

CAKE   *v* **CAKED, CAKING, CAKES** to form into a hardened mass

CAKEBOX   *n* pl. **-ES** a container for a cake (a sweet baked food)

CAKEHOLE   *n* pl. **-S** a person's mouth

CAKEWALK   *v* **-ED, -ING, -S** to step stylishly

CAKEY   *adj* **CAKIER, CAKIEST** tending to form lumps

CAKINESS   *n* pl. **-ES** the state of being cakey

CAKY   *adj* **CAKIER, CAKIEST** cakey

CALABASH   *n* pl. **-ES** a gourd

CALABAZA   *n* pl. **-S** a large winter squash

CALADIUM   *n* pl. **-S** a tropical plant

CALAMAR   *n* pl. **-S** calamary

CALAMARI   *n* pl. **-S** squid used as food

CALAMARY   *n* pl. **-MARIES** a squid

CALAMATA   *n* pl. **-S** kalamata

CALAMI   pl. of calamus

CALAMINE   *v* **-MINED, -MINING, -MINES** to apply an ointment for skin ailments

CALAMINT   *n* pl. **-S** a perennial herb

CALAMITE   *n* pl. **-S** an extinct treelike plant

CALAMITY   *n* pl. **-TIES** a grievous misfortune

CALAMUS   *n* pl. **-MI** a marsh plant

CALANDO   *adj* gradually diminishing

CALASH   *n* pl. **-ES** a light carriage

CALATHEA   *n* pl. **-S** a plant with colorful leaves

CALATHOS   *n* pl. **-THI** a fruit basket

CALATHUS   *n* pl. **-THI** calathos

CALCANEA   *n/pl* calcanei

CALCANEI   *n/pl* bones of the heel

CALCAR   *n* pl. **-CARIA** an anatomical projection

CALCAR   *n* pl. **-S** a type of oven

CALCEATE   *adj* wearing shoes

CALCES   a pl. of calx

CALCIC   *adj* pertaining to lime or calcium

CALCIFIC   *adj* containing salts of calcium

CALCIFY   *v* **-FIED, -FYING, -FIES** to harden

CALCINE   *v* **-CINED, -CINING, -CINES** to reduce to a calx by heat

CALCITE   *n* pl. **-S** a mineral **CALCITIC** *adj*

CALCIUM   *n* pl. **-S** a metallic element

CALCRETE   *n* pl. **-S** a type of concrete made with calcium carbonate

CALCSPAR   *n* pl. **-S** a calcite

CALCTUFA   *n* pl. **-S** a mineral deposit

CALCTUFF   *n* pl. **-S** calctufa

CALCULUS   *n* pl. **-LUSES** or **-LI** a branch of mathematics

CALDARIA   *n/pl* rooms for taking hot baths

CALDERA   *n* pl. **-S** a large crater

CALDRON   *n* pl. **-S** a large kettle or boiler

CALECHE   *n* pl. **-S** calash

CALENDAL   *adj* pertaining to calends

CALENDAR   *v* **-ED, -ING, -S** to schedule

CALENDER   *v* **-ED, -ING, -S** to smooth by pressing between rollers

CALENDS   *n* pl. **CALENDS** the first day of the Roman month

CALESA   *n* pl. **-S** a calash

CALF   *n* pl. **CALVES** or **CALFS** a young cow or bull **CALFLIKE** *adj*

CALFHOOD   *n* pl. **-S** the state or time of being a calf

CALFSKIN   *n* pl. **-S** the skin of a calf

CALIBER   *n* pl. **-S** the diameter of a gun barrel

CALIBRE   *n* pl. **-S** caliber **CALIBRED** *adj*

CALICES   pl. of calix

CALICHE   *n* pl. **-S** a mineral deposit

CALICLE   *n* pl. **-S** a cup-shaped anatomical structure

CALICO   *n* pl. **-COS** or **-COES** a cotton fabric

CALIF   *n* pl. **-S** caliph

CALIFATE   *n* pl. **-S** the domain of a calif

CALIPASH   *n* pl. **-ES** an edible part of a turtle

CALIPEE   *n* pl. **-S** an edible part of a turtle

CALIPER   *v* **-ED, -ING, -S** to use a type of measuring device

CALIPH   *n* pl. **-S** a Muslim leader
CALIPHAL *adj*

CALISAYA   *n* pl. **-S** the medicinal bark of the cinchona

CALIX   *n* pl. **-LICES** or **-LIXES** a cup

CALK   *v* **-ED, -ING, -S** to caulk

CALKER   *n* pl. **-S** one that calks

CALKIN   *n* pl. **-S** a gripping projection on a horseshoe

CALKING   *n* pl. **-S** material used to calk

CALL   *v* **-ED, -ING, -S** to summon
CALLABLE *adj*

CALLA   *n* pl. **-S** a tropical plant

CALLALOO   *n* pl. **-LOOS** a crabmeat soup

CALLALOU   *n* pl. **-S** callaloo

CALLAN   *n* pl. **-S** callant

CALLANT   *n* pl. **-S** a lad

CALLBACK   *n* pl. **-S** a recall of a defective product

CALLBOY   *n* pl. **-BOYS** a bellboy

CALLEE   *n* pl. **-S** one that is called

CALLER   *n* pl. **-S** one that calls

CALLET   *n* pl. **-S** a prostitute

CALLING   *n* pl. **-S** a vocation or profession

CALLIOPE   *n* pl. **-S** a keyboard musical instrument

CALLIPEE   *n* pl. **-S** calipee

CALLIPER   *v* **-ED, -ING, -S** to caliper

CALLOSE   *n* pl. **-S** a part of a plant cell wall

CALLOUS   *v* **-ED, -ING, -ES** to make or become hard

CALLOUT   *n* pl. **-S** an inset in a printed article

CALLOW   *adj* **-LOWER, -LOWEST** immature
CALLOWLY *adv*

CALLUNA   *n* pl. **-S** an evergreen shrub

CALLUS   *v* **-ED, -ING, -ES** to form a hard growth

CALM   *adj* **CALMER, CALMEST** free from agitation **CALMLY** *adv*

CALM   *v* **-ED, -ING, -S** to make calm

CALMNESS   *n* pl. **-ES** the state of being calm

CALO   *n* pl. **-LOS** a Spanish argot used by Chicano youths

CALOMEL   *n* pl. **-S** a chemical compound used as a purgative

CALORIC   *n* pl. **-S** heat

CALORIE   *n* pl. **-S** a unit of heat

CALORIZE   *v* **-RIZED, -RIZING, -RIZES** to coat steel with aluminum

CALORY   *n* pl. **-RIES** calorie

CALOTTE   *n* pl. **-S** a skullcap

CALOTYPE   *n* pl. **-S** a kind of photograph

CALOYER   *n* pl. **-S** a monk of the Eastern Church

CALPAC   *n* pl. **-S** a sheepskin hat

CALPACK   *n* pl. **-S** calpac

CALPAIN   *n* pl. **-S** an enzyme for digesting proteins

CALQUE   *v* **CALQUED, CALQUING, CALQUES** to model a word's meaning upon that of an analogous word in another language

CALTHROP   *n* pl. **-S** caltrop

CALTRAP   *n* pl. **-S** caltrop

CALTROP   *n* pl. **-S** a spiny plant

CALUMET   *n* pl. **-S** a ceremonial pipe

CALUMNY   *v* **-NIED, -NYING, -NIES** to make a false and malicious accusation

CALUTRON   *n* pl. **-S** a device used for separating isotopes

CALVADOS   *n* pl. **-ES** a dry apple brandy

CALVARIA   *n* pl. **-S** the dome of the skull

CALVARY   *n* pl. **-RIES** a representation of the Crucifixion

CALVE   *v* **CALVED, CALVING, CALVES** to give birth to a calf

CALVES   a pl. of calf

CALX   *n* pl. **CALXES** or **CALCES** a mineral residue

CALYCATE   *adj* calycine

CALYCEAL   *adj* calycine

CALYCES   a pl. of calyx

CALYCINE   *adj* pertaining to a calyx

CALYCLE   *n* pl. **-S** an outer calyx

CALYCULI   *n/pl* small, cup-shaped structures

CALYPSO   *n* pl. **-SOS** or **-SOES** an improvised song

CALYPTER   *n* pl. **-S** calyptra

CALYPTRA   *n* pl. **-S** a hood-shaped organ of flowers

CALYX   *n* pl. **-LYXES** or **-LYCES** the outer protective covering of a flower

CALZONE   *n* pl. **-NES** or **-NI** a turnover with a savory filling

CAM   *n* pl. **-S** a rotating or sliding piece of machinery

CAMAIL *n* pl. **-S** a piece of armor for the neck **CAMAILED** *adj*

CAMAS *n* pl. **-ES** camass

CAMASS *n* pl. **-ES** a perennial herb

CAMBER *v* **-ED, -ING, -S** to arch slightly

CAMBIA a pl. of cambium

CAMBIAL *adj* pertaining to cambium

CAMBISM *n* pl. **-S** the theory and practice of exchange in commerce

CAMBIST *n* pl. **-S** a dealer in bills of exchange

CAMBIUM *n* pl. **-BIUMS** or **-BIA** a layer of plant tissue

CAMBOGIA *n* pl. **-S** a gum resin

CAMBOOSE *n* pl. **-S** a large cabin at a logging camp

CAMBRIC *n* pl. **-S** a fine linen

CAMCORD *v* **-ED, -ING, -S** to videotape with a portable camera

CAME *n* pl. **-S** a leaden window rod

CAMEL *n* pl. **-S** a large, humped mammal

CAMELEER *n* pl. **-S** a camel driver

CAMELIA *n* pl. **-S** camellia

CAMELID *n* pl. **-S** any of a family of 2-toed ruminant mammals

CAMELLIA *n* pl. **-S** a tropical shrub

CAMEO *v* **-ED, -ING, -S** to portray in sharp, delicate relief

CAMERA *n* pl. **-ERAS** or **-ERAE** a judge's chamber **CAMERAL** *adj*

CAMI *n* pl. **-S** a camisole

CAMION *n* pl. **-S** a military truck

CAMISA *n* pl. **-S** a shirt or chemise

CAMISADE *n* pl. **-S** camisado

CAMISADO *n* pl. **-DOS** or **-DOES** an attack made at night

CAMISE *n* pl. **-S** a loose shirt or gown

CAMISIA *n* pl. **-S** camise

CAMISOLE *n* pl. **-S** a brief negligee

CAMLET *n* pl. **-S** a durable fabric

CAMMIE *n* pl. **-S** camouflage

CAMO *n* pl. **CAMOS** a camouflage pattern

CAMOMILE *n* pl. **-S** a medicinal herb

CAMORRA *n* pl. **-S** an unscrupulous secret society

CAMP *v* **-ED, -ING, -S** to live in the open

CAMPAGNA *n* pl. **-PAGNE** a flat, open plain

CAMPAIGN *v* **-ED, -ING, -S** to conduct a series of operations to reach a specific goal

CAMPER *n* pl. **-S** one that camps

CAMPFIRE *n* pl. **-S** an outdoor fire

CAMPHENE *n* pl. **-S** camphine

CAMPHINE *n* pl. **-S** an explosive liquid

CAMPHIRE *n* pl. **-S** a flowering plant

CAMPHOL *n* pl. **-S** borneol

CAMPHOR *n* pl. **-S** a volatile compound

CAMPI pl. of campo

CAMPIER comparative of campy

CAMPIEST superlative of campy

CAMPILY *adv* in a campy manner

CAMPING *n* pl. **-S** the act of living outdoors

CAMPION *n* pl. **-S** an herb

CAMPO *n* pl. **-PI** an open space in a town

CAMPO *n* pl. **-POS** a level, grassy plain

CAMPONG *n* pl. **-S** kampong

CAMPOREE *n* pl. **-S** a gathering of Boy Scouts

CAMPOUT *n* pl. **-S** a camping out by a group

CAMPSITE *n* pl. **-S** an area suitable for camping

CAMPUS *v* **-ED, -ING, -ES** to restrict a student to the school grounds

CAMPY *adj* **CAMPIER, CAMPIEST** comically exaggerated

CAMSHAFT *n* pl. **-S** a shaft fitted with cams

CAMWOOD *n* pl. **-S** an African hardwood tree

CAN *v* **CANNED, CANNING, CANS** to put in a can (a cylindrical container)

CAN *v* present sing. 2d person **CAN** or **CANST,** past sing. 2d person **COULD** or **COULDEST** or **COULDST** — used as an auxiliary to express ability

CANAILLE *n* pl. **-S** the common people

CANAKIN *n* pl. **-S** cannikin

CANAL *v* **-NALLED, -NALLING, -NALS** or **-NALED, -NALING, -NALS** to dig an artificial waterway through

CANALISE *v* **-ISED, -ISING, -ISES** to canalize

CANALIZE *v* **-IZED, -IZING, -IZES** to canal

CANALLER *n* pl. **-S** a freight boat

CANALLING a present participle of canal

CANAPE *n* pl. **-S** a food served before a meal

CANARD *n* pl. **-S** a false story

CANARY n pl. **-NARIES** a songbird

CANASTA n pl. **-S** a card game

CANCAN n pl. **-S** a dance marked by high kicking

CANCEL v **-CELED, -CELING, -CELS** or **-CELLED, -CELLING, -CELS** to annul

CANCELER n pl. **-S** one that cancels

CANCER n pl. **-S** a malignant growth **CANCERED** adj

CANCHA n pl. **-S** a jai alai court

CANCROID n pl. **-S** a skin cancer

CANDELA n pl. **-S** a unit of light intensity

CANDENT adj glowing

CANDID adj **-DIDER, -DIDEST** frank and sincere

CANDID n pl. **-S** an unposed photograph

CANDIDA n pl. **-S** a parasitic fungus **CANDIDAL** adj

CANDIDLY adv in a candid manner

CANDIED past tense of candy

CANDIES present 3d person sing. of candy

CANDLE v **-DLED, -DLING, -DLES** to examine eggs in front of a light

CANDLER n pl. **-S** one that candles

CANDOR n pl. **-S** frankness; sincerity

CANDOUR n pl. **-S** candor

CANDY v **-DIED, -DYING, -DIES** to coat with sugar

CANDYMAN n pl. **-MEN** one who sells illegal drugs

CANE v **CANED, CANING, CANES** to weave or furnish with cane (hollow woody stems)

CANELLA n pl. **-S** a medicinal tree bark

CANEPHOR n pl. **-S** a Greek maiden bearing a basket on her head

CANER n pl. **-S** one that canes

CANEWARE n pl. **-S** a yellowish stoneware

CANFIELD n pl. **-S** a card game

CANFUL n pl. **CANFULS** or **CANSFUL** as much as a can holds

CANGUE n pl. **-S** an ancient Chinese punishing device

CANID n pl. **-S** any member of the dog family Canidae

CANIKIN n pl. **-S** cannikin

CANINE n pl. **-S** a dog

CANING n pl. **-S** punishment with a cane

CANINITY n pl. **-TIES** the state of being a canine

CANISTEL n pl. **-S** a tropical tree

CANISTER n pl. **-S** a small, metal box

CANITIES n pl. **CANITIES** the turning gray of the hair

CANKER v **-ED, -ING, -S** to affect with ulcerous sores

CANNA n pl. **-S** a tropical plant

CANNABIC adj pertaining to cannabis

CANNABIN n pl. **-S** a resin extracted from cannabis

CANNABIS n pl. **-BISES** hemp

CANNED past tense of can

CANNEL n pl. **-S** an oily, compact coal

CANNELON n pl. **-S** a stuffed roll

CANNER n pl. **-S** one that cans food

CANNERY n pl. **-NERIES** a place where food is canned

CANNIBAL n pl. **-S** one who eats his own kind

CANNIE adj **-NIER, -NIEST** canny

CANNIER comparative of canny

CANNIEST superlative of canny

CANNIKIN n pl. **-S** a small can or cup

CANNILY adv in a canny manner

CANNING n pl. **-S** the business of preserving food in airtight containers

CANNOLI n pl. **-S** a tube of pastry with a sweet filling

CANNON v **-ED, -ING, -S** to fire a cannon (a heavy firearm)

CANNONRY n pl. **-RIES** artillery

CANNOT the negative form of can

CANNULA n pl. **-LAS** or **-LAE** a tube inserted into a bodily cavity **CANNULAR** adj

CANNY adj **-NIER, -NIEST** prudent

CANOE v **-NOED, -NOEING, -NOES** to paddle a canoe (a light, slender boat)

CANOEING n pl. **-S** the action or sport of paddling a canoe

CANOEIST n pl. **-S** one who canoes

CANOEMAN n pl. **-MEN** a canoeist

CANOER n pl. **-S** one who canoes

CANOLA n pl. **-S** an oil from the seeds of a kind of herb

CANON n pl. **-S** a law decreed by a church council **CANONIC** adj

CANONESS *n pl.* **-ES** a woman who lives according to a canon

CANONISE *v* **-ISED, -ISING, -ISES** to canonize

CANONIST *n pl.* **-S** a specialist in canon law

CANONIZE *v* **-IZED, -IZING, -IZES** to declare to be a saint

CANONRY *n pl.* **-RIES** a clerical office

CANOODLE *v* **-DLED, -DLING, -DLES** to caress

CANOPIC *adj* pertaining to an Egyptian jar

CANOPY *v* **-PIED, -PYING, -PIES** to cover from above

CANOROUS *adj* melodic

CANSFUL a pl. of canful

CANSO *n pl.* **-SOS** a love song

CANST a present 2d person sing. of can

CANT *v* **-ED, -ING, -S** to tilt or slant

CANTAL *n pl.* **-S** a hard cheese of France

CANTALA *n pl.* **-S** a tropical plant

CANTATA *n pl.* **-S** a vocal composition

CANTDOG *n pl.* **-S** a device used to move logs

CANTEEN *n pl.* **-S** a small container for carrying water

CANTER *v* **-ED, -ING, -S** to ride a horse at a moderate pace

CANTHARI *n/pl* two-handled drinking cups

CANTHUS *n pl.* **-THI** a corner of the eye **CANTHAL, CANTHIC** *adj*

CANTIC *adj* slanted

CANTICLE *n pl.* **-S** a hymn

CANTINA *n pl.* **-S** a saloon

CANTLE *n pl.* **-S** the rear part of a saddle

CANTO *n pl.* **-TOS** a division of a long poem

CANTON *v* **-ED, -ING, -S** to divide into cantons (districts)

CANTONAL *adj* pertaining to a canton

CANTOR *n pl.* **-S** a religious singer

CANTORIS *adj* to be sung by the north side of the choir in a church

CANTRAIP *n pl.* **-S** cantrip

CANTRAP *n pl.* **-S** cantrip

CANTRIP *n pl.* **-S** a magic spell

CANTUS *n pl.* **CANTUS** a style of church music

CANTY *adj* cheerful

CANULA *n pl.* **-LAS** or **-LAE** cannula **CANULAR** *adj*

CANULATE *v* **-LATED, -LATING, -LATES** to insert a canula into

CANVAS *v* **-ED, -ING, -ES** to canvass

CANVASER *n pl.* **-S** one that canvases

CANVASS *v* **-ED, -ING, -ES** to examine thoroughly

CANYON *n pl.* **-S** a deep valley with steep sides

CANZONA *n pl.* **-S** canzone

CANZONE *n pl.* **-NES** or **-NI** a form of lyric poetry

CANZONET *n pl.* **-S** a short song

CAP *v* **CAPPED, CAPPING, CAPS** to provide with a cap (a type of head covering)

CAPABLE *adj* **-BLER, -BLEST** having ability **CAPABLY** *adv*

CAPACITY *n pl.* **-TIES** the ability to receive or contain

CAPE *v* **CAPED, CAPING, CAPES** to skin the head and neck of an animal

CAPEESH *interj* capisce

CAPELAN *n pl.* **-S** capelin

CAPELET *n pl.* **-S** a small cape

CAPELIN *n pl.* **-S** a small, edible fish

CAPER *v* **-ED, -ING, -S** to frolic

CAPERER *n pl.* **-S** one that capers

CAPESKIN *n pl.* **-S** a soft leather

CAPEWORK *n pl.* **-S** a bullfighting technique

CAPFUL *n pl.* **-S** as much as a cap can hold

CAPH *n pl.* **-S** kaph

CAPIAS *n pl.* **-ES** a judicial writ

CAPING present participle of cape

CAPISCE *interj* — used to ask if one understands

CAPITA pl. of caput

CAPITAL *n pl.* **-S** the upper part of a column

CAPITATE *n pl.* **-S** a bone of the wrist of primates

CAPITOL *n pl.* **-S** a building occupied by a state legislature

CAPITULA *n/pl* flower clusters

CAPIZ *n pl.* **-ES** a bivalve mollusk

CAPLESS *adj* being without a cap

CAPLET *n pl.* **-S** a coated tablet

CAPLIN *n pl.* **-S** capelin

CAPMAKER *n pl.* **-S** one that makes caps

CAPO _n_ pl. **-POS** a pitch-raising device for fretted instruments

CAPOEIRA _n_ pl. **-S** a Brazilian dance

CAPON _n_ pl. **-S** a gelded rooster

CAPONATA _n_ pl. **-S** a relish made with eggplant

CAPONIER _n_ pl. **-S** a type of defense

CAPONISE _v_ **-ISED, -ISING, -ISES** to caponize

CAPONIZE _v_ **-IZED, -IZING, -IZES** to geld a rooster

CAPORAL _n_ pl. **-S** a coarse tobacco

CAPOT _n_ pl. **-S** a capote

CAPOTE _n_ pl. **-S** a hooded cloak or overcoat

CAPOUCH _n_ pl. **-ES** capuche

CAPPED past tense of cap

CAPPER _n_ pl. **-S** a capmaker

CAPPING _n_ pl. **-S** a wax covering in a honeycomb

CAPRESE _n_ pl. **-S** a salad containing mozzarella, tomatoes, basil, and olive oil

CAPRI _n_ pl. **-S** a woman's tapered pants

CAPRIC _adj_ pertaining to a goat

CAPRICCI _n/pl_ caprices

CAPRICE _n_ pl. **-S** a whim

CAPRIFIG _n_ pl. **-S** a European tree

CAPRINE _adj_ capric

CAPRIOLE _v_ **-OLED, -OLING, -OLES** to leap

CAPRIS _n/pl_ pants for women

CAPROCK _n_ pl. **-S** an overlying rock layer

CAPSICIN _n_ pl. **-S** a liquid used as a flavoring

CAPSICUM _n_ pl. **-S** a tropical herb

CAPSID _n_ pl. **-S** the outer shell of a virus particle **CAPSIDAL** _adj_

CAPSIZE _v_ **-SIZED, -SIZING, -SIZES** to overturn

CAPSOMER _n_ pl. **-S** a protein forming the capsid

CAPSTAN _n_ pl. **-S** a machine used to hoist weights

CAPSTONE _n_ pl. **-S** the top stone of a structure

CAPSULAR _adj_ enclosed and compact

CAPSULE _v_ **-SULED, -SULING, -SULES** to condense into a brief form

CAPTAIN _v_ **-ED, -ING, -S** to lead or command

CAPTAN _n_ pl. **-S** a fungicide

CAPTION _v_ **-ED, -ING, -S** to provide with a title

CAPTIOUS _adj_ tending to find fault

CAPTIVE _n_ pl. **-S** a prisoner

CAPTOR _n_ pl. **-S** one who takes or holds a captive

CAPTURE _v_ **-TURED, -TURING, -TURES** to take by force or cunning

CAPTURER _n_ pl. **-S** one that captures

CAPUCHE _n_ pl. **-S** a hood or cowl **CAPUCHED** _adj_

CAPUCHIN _n_ pl. **-S** a long-tailed monkey

CAPUT _n_ pl. **CAPITA** a head or head-like part

CAPYBARA _n_ pl. **-S** a large rodent

CAR _n_ pl. **-S** an automobile

CARABAO _n_ pl. **-BAOS** a water buffalo

CARABID _n_ pl. **-S** a predatory beetle

CARABIN _n_ pl. **-S** carbine

CARABINE _n_ pl. **-S** carbine

CARACAL _n_ pl. **-S** an African lynx

CARACARA _n_ pl. **-S** a large hawk

CARACK _n_ pl. **-S** carrack

CARACOL _v_ **-COLLED, -COLLING, -COLS** to caracole

CARACOLE _v_ **-COLED, -COLING, -COLES** to perform a half turn on a horse

CARACUL _n_ pl. **-S** karakul

CARAFE _n_ pl. **-S** a glass bottle

CARAGANA _n_ pl. **-S** an Asian shrub

CARAGEEN _n_ pl. **-S** an edible seaweed

CARAMBA _interj_ — used to express surprise or dismay

CARAMEL _n_ pl. **-S** a chewy candy

CARANGID _n_ pl. **-S** a marine fish

CARAPACE _n_ pl. **-S** a hard, protective outer covering

CARAPAX _n_ pl. **-ES** carapace

CARASSOW _n_ pl. **-S** curassow

CARAT _n_ pl. **-S** a unit of weight for gems

CARATE _n_ pl. **-S** a tropical skin disease

CARAVAN _v_ **-VANED, -VANING, -VANS** or **-VANNED, -VANNING, -VANS** to travel in a group

CARAVEL _n_ pl. **-S** a small sailing ship

CARAWAY _n_ pl. **-WAYS** an herb used in cooking

CARB _n_ pl. **-S** a carburetor

CARBAMIC *adj* pertaining to a type of acid

CARBAMYL *n* pl. **-S** a chemical radical

CARBARN *n* pl. **-S** a garage for buses

CARBARYL *n* pl. **-S** an insecticide

CARBIDE *n* pl. **-S** a carbon compound

CARBINE *n* pl. **-S** a light rifle

CARBINOL *n* pl. **-S** an alcohol

CARBO *n* pl. **-BOS** a carbohydrate

CARBOLIC *n* pl. **-S** an acidic compound

CARBON *n* pl. **-S** a nonmetallic element **CARBONIC** *adj*

CARBONYL *n* pl. **-S** a chemical compound

CARBORA *n* pl. **-S** a wood-boring worm

CARBOXYL *n* pl. **-S** a univalent acid radical

CARBOY *n* pl. **-BOYS** a large bottle **CARBOYED** *adj*

CARBURET *v* **-RETED, -RETING, -RETS** or **-RETTED, -RETTING, -RETS** to combine chemically with carbon

CARCAJOU *n* pl. **-S** a carnivorous mammal

CARCANET *n* pl. **-S** a jeweled necklace

CARCASE *n* pl. **-S** carcass

CARCASS *n* pl. **-ES** the body of a dead animal

CARCEL *n* pl. **-S** a unit of illumination

CARCERAL *adj* pertaining to a prison

CARD *v* **-ED, -ING, -S** to provide with a card (a stiff piece of paper)

CARDAMOM *n* pl. **-S** a tropical herb

CARDAMON *n* pl. **-S** cardamom

CARDAMUM *n* pl. **-S** cardamom

CARDCASE *n* pl. **-S** a case for holding cards

CARDER *n* pl. **-S** one that does carding

CARDIA *n* pl. **-DIAS** or **-DIAE** an opening of the esophagus

CARDIAC *n* pl. **-S** a person with a heart disorder

CARDIGAN *n* pl. **-S** a type of sweater

CARDINAL *n* pl. **-S** a bright red bird

CARDING *n* pl. **-S** the process of combing and cleaning cotton fibers; cleaned and combed fibers

CARDIO *n* pl. **-DIOS** an exercise involving the heart and blood vessels

CARDIOID *n* pl. **-S** a heart-shaped curve

CARDITIS *n* pl. **-TISES** inflammation of the heart **CARDITIC** *adj*

CARDON *n* pl. **-S** cardoon

CARDOON *n* pl. **-S** a perennial plant

CARE *v* **CARED, CARING, CARES** to be concerned or interested

CAREEN *v* **-ED, -ING, -S** to lurch while moving

CAREENER *n* pl. **-S** one that careens

CAREER *v* **-ED, -ING, -S** to go at full speed

CAREERER *n* pl. **-S** one that careers

CAREFREE *adj* being without worry or anxiety

CAREFUL *adj* **-FULLER, -FULLEST** cautious

CARELESS *adj* inattentive; negligent

CARER *n* pl. **-S** one that cares

CARESS *v* **-ED, -ING, -ES** to touch lovingly

CARESSER *n* pl. **-S** one that caresses

CARET *n* pl. **-S** a proofreaders' symbol

CARETAKE *v* **-TOOK, -TAKEN, -TAKING, -TAKES** to take care of someone else's house or land

CAREWORN *adj* haggard

CAREX *n* pl. **CARICES** a marsh plant

CARFARE *n* pl. **-S** payment for a bus or car ride

CARFUL *n* pl. **-S** as much as a car can hold

CARGO *n* pl. **-GOS** or **-GOES** conveyed merchandise

CARHOP *v* **-HOPPED, -HOPPING, -HOPS** to serve customers at a drive-in restaurant

CARIBE *n* pl. **-S** the piranha

CARIBOO *n* pl. **-BOOS** a caribou

CARIBOU *n* pl. **-S** a large deer

CARICES pl. of carex

CARIES *n* pl. **CARIES** tooth decay **CARIED** *adj*

CARILLON *v* **-LONNED, -LONNING, -LONS** to play a set of bells

CARINA *n* pl. **-NAS** or **-NAE** a carinate anatomical part **CARINAL** *adj*

CARINATE *adj* shaped like the keel of a ship

CARING *n* pl. **-S** the work of looking after someone

CARINGLY *adv* in a caring manner

CARIOCA *n* pl. **-S** a South American dance

CARIOLE *n* pl. **-S** a small, open carriage

CARIOUS *adj* decayed

CARITAS *n* pl. **-ES** love for all people

CARJACK *v* **-ED, -ING, -S** to steal a vehicle from its driver by force

CARK	*v* **-ED, -ING, -S** to worry
CARL	*n* pl. **-S** a peasant
CARLE	*n* pl. **-S** carl
CARLESS	*adj* being without a car
CARLIN	*n* pl. **-S** an old woman
CARLINE	*n* pl. **-S** carling
CARLING	*n* pl. **-S** a beam supporting a ship's deck
CARLISH	*adj* resembling a carl
CARLOAD	*n* pl. **-S** as much as a car can hold
CARMAKER	*n* pl. **-S** an automobile manufacturer
CARMAN	*n* pl. **-MEN** a streetcar driver
CARMINE	*n* pl. **-S** a vivid red color
CARN	*n* pl. **-S** cairn
CARNAGE	*n* pl. **-S** great and bloody slaughter
CARNAL	*adj* pertaining to bodily appetites **CARNALLY** *adv*
CARNAUBA	*n* pl. **-S** a palm tree
CARNET	*n* pl. **-S** an official permit
CARNEY	*n* pl. **-NEYS** carny
CARNIE	*n* pl. **-S** carny
CARNIES	pl. of carny
CARNIFY	*v* **-FIED, -FYING, -FIES** to form into flesh
CARNIVAL	*n* pl. **-S** a traveling amusement show
CARNY	*n* pl. **-NIES** a carnival
CAROACH	*n* pl. **-ES** caroche
CAROB	*n* pl. **-S** an evergreen tree
CAROCH	*n* pl. **-ES** caroche
CAROCHE	*n* pl. **-S** a stately carriage
CAROL	*v* **-OLED, -OLING, -OLS** or **-OLLED, -OLLING, -OLS** to sing joyously
CAROLER	*n* pl. **-S** one that carols
CAROLI	a pl. of carolus
CAROLING	*n* pl. **-S** the act of singing joyously
CAROLLER	*n* pl. **-S** caroler
CAROLLING	a present participle of carol
CAROLUS	*n* pl. **-LUSES** or **-LI** an old English coin
CAROM	*v* **-ED, -ING, -S** to collide with and rebound
CAROTENE	*n* pl. **-S** a plant pigment
CAROTID	*n* pl. **-S** an artery in the neck
CAROTIN	*n* pl. **-S** carotene
CAROUSAL	*n* pl. **-S** a boisterous drinking party
CAROUSE	*v* **-ROUSED, -ROUSING, -ROUSES** to engage in a carousal
CAROUSEL	*n* pl. **-S** an amusement park ride
CAROUSER	*n* pl. **-S** one that carouses
CAROUSING	present participle of carouse
CARP	*v* **-ED, -ING, -S** to find fault unreasonably
CARPAL	*n* pl. **-S** carpale
CARPALE	*n* pl. **-LIA** a bone of the wrist
CARPEL	*n* pl. **-S** a simple pistil
CARPER	*n* pl. **-S** one that carps
CARPET	*v* **-ED, -ING, -S** to cover a floor with a heavy fabric
CARPI	pl. of carpus
CARPING	*n* pl. **-S** the act of one who carps
CARPOOL	*v* **-ED, -ING, -S** to take turns driving a group of commuters
CARPORT	*n* pl. **-S** a shelter for a car
CARPUS	*n* pl. **-PI** the wrist
CARR	*n* pl. **-S** a marsh
CARRACK	*n* pl. **-S** a type of merchant ship
CARREL	*n* pl. **-S** a desk in a library stack for solitary study
CARRELL	*n* pl. **-S** carrel
CARRIAGE	*n* pl. **-S** a wheeled, horse-drawn vehicle
CARRIED	past tense of carry
CARRIER	*n* pl. **-S** one that carries
CARRIES	present 3d person sing. of carry
CARRIOLE	*n* pl. **-S** cariole
CARRION	*n* pl. **-S** dead and putrefying flesh
CARRITCH	*n* pl. **-ES** a religious handbook
CARROCH	*n* pl. **-ES** caroche
CARROM	*v* **-ED, -ING, -S** to carom
CARROT	*n* pl. **-S** an edible orange root
CARROTIN	*n* pl. **-S** carotene
CARROTY	*adj* **-ROTIER, -ROTIEST** resembling a carrot in color
CARRY	*v* **-RIED, -RYING, -RIES** to convey from one place to another
CARRYALL	*n* pl. **-S** a light covered carriage
CARRYCOT	*n* pl. **-S** a portable baby's cot
CARRYON	*n* pl. **-S** a small piece of luggage
CARRYOUT	*n* pl. **-S** a take-out order of food
CARSE	*n* pl. **-S** low, fertile land along a river

CARSICK	adj nauseated from riding in a car
CARSPIEL	n pl. **-S** a curling match in which curlers compete for a car
CART	v **-ED, -ING, -S** to convey in a cart (a two-wheeled vehicle) **CARTABLE** adj
CARTAGE	n pl. **-S** the act of carting
CARTE	n pl. **-S** a menu
CARTEL	n pl. **-S** a business organization
CARTER	n pl. **-S** one that carts
CARTFUL	n pl. **-S** a cartload
CARTLOAD	n pl. **-S** as much as a cart can hold
CARTON	v **-ED, -ING, -S** to pack in a cardboard box
CARTOON	v **-ED, -ING, -S** to sketch a cartoon (a humorous representation) of
CARTOONY	adj resembling a cartoon
CARTOP	adj able to fit on top of a car
CARTOUCH	n pl. **-ES** a scroll-like tablet
CARUNCLE	n pl. **-S** a fleshy outgrowth
CARVE	v **CARVED, CARVING, CARVES** to form by cutting
CARVEL	n pl. **-S** caravel
CARVEN	adj carved
CARVER	n pl. **-S** one that carves
CARVERY	n pl. **-ERIES** a buffet restaurant serving roast beef
CARVING	n pl. **-S** a carved figure or design
CARWASH	n pl. **-ES** an establishment equipped to wash automobiles
CARYATIC	adj resembling a caryatid
CARYATID	n pl. **-S** or **-ES** a sculptured female figure used as a column
CARYOTIN	n pl. **-S** karyotin
CASA	n pl. **-S** a dwelling
CASABA	n pl. **-S** a variety of melon
CASAVA	n pl. **-S** cassava
CASBAH	n pl. **-S** the old section of a North African city
CASCABEL	n pl. **-S** the rear part of a cannon
CASCABLE	n pl. **-S** cascabel
CASCADE	v **-CADED, -CADING, -CADES** to fall like a waterfall
CASCARA	n pl. **-S** a medicinal tree bark
CASE	v **CASED, CASING, CASES** to put in a case (a container or receptacle)
CASEASE	n pl. **-S** an enzyme
CASEATE	v **-ATED, -ATING, -ATES** to become cheesy
CASEBOOK	n pl. **-S** a law textbook
CASED	past tense of case
CASEFY	v **-FIED, -FYING, -FIES** to caseate
CASEIN	n pl. **-S** a milk protein **CASEIC** adj
CASELAW	n pl. **-S** a law established by previous cases
CASELOAD	n pl. **-S** the number of cases being handled
CASEMATE	n pl. **-S** a bombproof shelter
CASEMENT	n pl. **-S** a type of window
CASEOSE	n pl. **-S** a proteose
CASEOUS	adj cheesy
CASERN	n pl. **-S** a barracks for soldiers
CASERNE	n pl. **-S** casern
CASETTE	n pl. **-S** cassette
CASEWORK	n pl. **-S** a form of social work
CASEWORM	n pl. **-S** an insect larva
CASH	v **-ED, -ING, -ES** to convert into cash (ready money) **CASHABLE** adj
CASHAW	n pl. **-S** cushaw
CASHBACK	n pl. **-S** an incentive of cash given back to a purchaser
CASHBOOK	n pl. **-S** a book of monetary records
CASHBOX	n pl. **-ES** a container for money
CASHEW	n pl. **-S** a nut-bearing tree
CASHIER	v **-ED, -ING, -S** to dismiss in disgrace
CASHLESS	adj having no cash
CASHMERE	n pl. **-S** a fine wool
CASHOO	n pl. **-SHOOS** catechu
CASIMERE	n pl. **-S** a woolen fabric
CASIMIRE	n pl. **-S** casimere
CASING	n pl. **-S** a protective outer covering
CASINO	n pl. **-NOS** or **-NI** a gambling room
CASITA	n pl. **-S** a small house
CASK	v **-ED, -ING, -S** to store in a cask (a strong barrel)
CASKET	v **-ED, -ING, -S** to place in a casket (a burial case)
CASKY	adj resembling a cask
CASQUE	n pl. **-S** a helmet **CASQUED** adj
CASSABA	n pl. **-S** casaba
CASSATA	n pl. **-S** an Italian ice cream

CASSAVA *n* pl. **-S** a tropical plant

CASSENA *n* pl. **-S** cassina

CASSENE *n* pl. **-S** cassina

CASSETTE *n* pl. **-S** a small case containing audiotape or videotape

CASSIA *n* pl. **-S** a variety of cinnamon

CASSINA *n* pl. **-S** an evergreen tree

CASSINE *n* pl. **-S** cassina

CASSINO *n* pl. **-NOS** a card game

CASSIOPE *n* pl. **-S** an evergreen shrub

CASSIS *n* pl. **-SISES** a European bush

CASSOCK *n* pl. **-S** a long garment worn by clergymen

CAST *v* **CAST, CASTING, CASTS** to throw with force **CASTABLE** *adj*

CASTANET *n* pl. **-S** a rhythm instrument

CASTAWAY *n* pl. **-AWAYS** an outcast

CASTE *n* pl. **-S** a system of distinct social classes

CASTEISM *n* pl. **-S** the use of a caste system

CASTER *n* pl. **-S** a small, swiveling wheel **CASTERED** *adj*

CASTING *n* pl. **-S** something made in a mold

CASTLE *v* **-TLED, -TLING, -TLES** to make a certain move in chess

CASTLING *n* pl. **-S** a certain move in chess

CASTOFF *n* pl. **-S** a discarded person or thing

CASTOR *n* pl. **-S** caster

CASTRATE *v* **-TRATED, -TRATING, -TRATES** to remove the testes of

CASTRATO *n* pl. **-TOS** or **-TI** a singer castrated in boyhood

CASUAL *n* pl. **-S** one who works occasionally

CASUALLY *adv* informally

CASUALTY *n* pl. **-TIES** a victim of war or disaster

CASUIST *n* pl. **-S** one who resolves ethical problems

CASUS *n* pl. **CASUS** a legal occurrence or event

CAT *v* **CATTED, CATTING, CATS** to hoist an anchor to the cathead

CATACOMB *n* pl. **-S** an underground cemetery

CATALASE *n* pl. **-S** an enzyme

CATALO *n* pl. **-LOS** or **-LOES** a hybrid between a buffalo and a cow

CATALOG *v* **-ED, -ING, -S** to classify information descriptively

CATALPA *n* pl. **-S** a tree

CATALYSE *v* **-LYSED, -LYSING, -LYSES** to catalyze

CATALYST *n* pl. **-S** a substance that accelerates a chemical reaction

CATALYZE *v* **-LYZED, -LYZING, -LYZES** to act as a catalyst

CATAMITE *n* pl. **-S** a boy used in sodomy

CATAPULT *v* **-ED, -ING, -S** to hurl through the air

CATARACT *n* pl. **-S** a tremendous waterfall

CATARRH *n* pl. **-S** inflammation of a mucous membrane

CATAWBA *n* pl. **-S** a variety of fox grape

CATBIRD *n* pl. **-S** a songbird

CATBOAT *n* pl. **-S** a small sailboat

CATBRIAR *n* pl. **-S** catbrier

CATBRIER *n* pl. **-S** a thorny vine

CATCALL *v* **-ED, -ING, -S** to deride by making shrill sounds

CATCH *v* **CAUGHT, CATCHING, CATCHES** to capture after pursuit

CATCHALL *n* pl. **-S** a container for odds and ends

CATCHER *n* pl. **-S** one that catches

CATCHFLY *n* pl. **-FLIES** an insect-catching plant

CATCHUP *n* pl. **-S** ketchup

CATCHY *adj* **CATCHIER, CATCHIEST** pleasing and easily remembered **CATCHILY** *adv*

CATCLAW *n* pl. **-S** a flowering shrub

CATE *n* pl. **-S** a choice food

CATECHIN *n* pl. **-S** a chemical used in dyeing

CATECHOL *n* pl. **-S** a chemical used in photography

CATECHU *n* pl. **-S** a resin used in tanning

CATEGORY *n* pl. **-RIES** a division in any system of classification

CATENA *n* pl. **-NAS** or **-NAE** a closely linked series

CATENARY *n* pl. **-NARIES** a mathematical curve

CATENATE *v* **-NATED, -NATING, -NATES** to link together

CATENOID *n* pl. **-S** a geometric surface

CATER *v* **-ED, -ING, -S** to provide food and service for

CATERAN	*n* pl. **-S** a brigand		**CATTIER**	comparative of catty
CATERER	*n* pl. **-S** one that caters		**CATTIEST**	superlative of catty
CATERESS	*n* pl. **-ES** a woman who caters		**CATTILY**	*adv* in a catty manner
CATERING	*n* pl. **-S** the work of a caterer		**CATTING**	present participle of cat
CATFACE	*n* pl. **-S** a deformity of fruit		**CATTISH**	*adj* catty
CATFALL	*n* pl. **-S** an anchor line		**CATTLE**	*n/pl* domesticated bovines
CATFIGHT	*n* pl. **-S** a fight between two women		**CATTLEYA**	*n* pl. **-S** a tropical orchid
CATFISH	*n* pl. **-ES** a scaleless, large-headed fish		**CATTY**	*adj* **-TIER, -TIEST** catlike; spiteful
CATGUT	*n* pl. **-S** a strong cord		**CATWALK**	*n* pl. **-S** a narrow walkway
CATHEAD	*n* pl. **-S** a beam projecting from a ship's bow		**CAUCUS**	*v* **-CUSED, -CUSING, -CUSES** or **-CUSSED, -CUSSING, -CUSSES** to hold a political meeting
CATHECT	*v* **-ED, -ING, -S** to invest with psychic energy		**CAUDAD**	*adv* toward the tail
CATHEDRA	*n* pl. **-DRAS** or **-DRAE** a bishop's throne		**CAUDAL**	*adj* taillike **CAUDALLY** *adv*
			CAUDATE	*n* pl. **-S** a basal ganglion of the brain
CATHETER	*n* pl. **-S** a medical instrument		**CAUDATED**	*adj* having a tail
CATHEXIS	*n* pl. **-THEXES** the concentration of psychic energy on a person or idea		**CAUDEX**	*n* pl. **-DEXES** or **-DICES** the woody base of some plants
			CAUDILLO	*n* pl. **-DILLOS** a military dictator
CATHODE	*n* pl. **-S** a negatively charged electrode **CATHODAL, CATHODIC** *adj*		**CAUDLE**	*n* pl. **-S** a warm beverage
			CAUGHT	past tense of catch
CATHOLIC	*n* pl **-S** a member of the universal Christian church		**CAUL**	*n* pl. **-S** a fetal membrane
			CAULD	*n* pl. **-S** cold
CATHOUSE	*n* pl. **-S** a brothel		**CAULDRON**	*n* pl. **-S** caldron
CATION	*n* pl. **-S** a positively charged ion **CATIONIC** *adj*		**CAULES**	pl. of caulis
			CAULICLE	*n* pl. **-S** a small stem
CATJANG	*n* pl. **-S** an African shrub		**CAULINE**	*adj* pertaining to a stem
CATKIN	*n* pl. **-S** a flower cluster		**CAULIS**	*n* pl. **-LES** a plant stem
CATLIKE	*adj* resembling a cat; stealthy; silent		**CAULK**	*v* **-ED, -ING, -S** to make the seams of a ship watertight
CATLIN	*n* pl. **-S** catling		**CAULKER**	*n* pl. **-S** one that caulks
CATLING	*n* pl. **-S** a surgical knife		**CAULKING**	*n* pl. **-S** the material used to caulk
CATMINT	*n* pl. **-S** catnip		**CAURI**	*n* pl. **-S** a former monetary unit of Guinea
CATNAP	*v* **-NAPPED, -NAPPING, -NAPS** to doze			
			CAUSABLE	*adj* capable of being caused
CATNAPER	*n* pl. **-S** one that steals cats		**CAUSAL**	*n* pl. **-S** a word expressing cause or reason
CATNIP	*n* pl. **-S** an aromatic herb			
CATSPAW	*n* pl. **-S** a light wind		**CAUSALLY**	*adv* by way of causing
CATSUIT	*n* pl. **-S** a close-fitting one-piece garment		**CAUSE**	*v* **CAUSED, CAUSING, CAUSES** to bring about
CATSUP	*n* pl. **-S** ketchup		**CAUSER**	*n* pl. **-S** one that causes
CATTAIL	*n* pl. **-S** a marsh plant		**CAUSERIE**	*n* pl. **-S** an informal conversation
CATTALO	*n* pl. **-LOS** or **-LOES** catalo		**CAUSEWAY**	*v* **-ED, -ING, -S** to build a causeway (a raised roadway) over
CATTED	past tense of cat			
CATTERY	*n* pl. **-TERIES** an establishment for breeding cats		**CAUSEY**	*n* pl. **-SEYS** a paved road
			CAUSING	present participle of cause
CATTIE	*n* pl. **-S** an Asian unit of weight		**CAUSTIC**	*n* pl. **-S** a corrosive substance

CAUTERY	*n* pl. **-TERIES** something used to destroy tissue
CAUTION	*v* **-ED, -ING, -S** to warn
CAUTIOUS	*adj* exercising prudence to avoid danger
CAVA	*n* pl. **-S** a sparkling Spanish wine
CAVALERO	*n* pl. **-ROS** a horseman
CAVALIER	*v* **-ED, -ING, -S** to behave haughtily
CAVALLA	*n* pl. **-S** a large food fish
CAVALLY	*n* pl. **-LIES** cavalla
CAVALRY	*n* pl. **-RIES** a mobile army unit
CAVATINA	*n* pl. **-NAS** or **-NE** a simple song
CAVE	*v* **CAVED, CAVING, CAVES** to hollow out
CAVEAT	*v* **-ED, -ING, -S** to enter a type of legal notice
CAVEATOR	*n* pl. **-S** one that files a caveat
CAVED	past tense of cave
CAVEFISH	*n* pl. **-ES** a sightless fish
CAVELIKE	*adj* resembling a cave (an underground chamber)
CAVEMAN	*n* pl. **-MEN** a cave dweller
CAVER	*n* pl. **-S** one that caves
CAVERN	*v* **-ED, -ING, -S** to hollow out
CAVETTO	*n* pl. **-TOS** or **-TI** a concave molding
CAVIAR	*n* pl. **-S** the roe of sturgeon
CAVIARE	*n* pl. **-S** caviar
CAVICORN	*adj* having hollow horns
CAVIE	*n* pl. **-S** a hencoop
CAVIES	pl. of cavy
CAVIL	*v* **-ILED, -ILING, -ILS** or **-ILLED, -ILLING, -ILS** to carp
CAVILER	*n* pl. **-S** one that cavils
CAVILLER	*n* pl. **-S** caviler
CAVILLING	a present participle of cavil
CAVING	*n* pl. **-S** the sport of exploring caves
CAVITARY	*adj* pertaining to the formation of cavities in tissue
CAVITATE	*v* **-TATED, -TATING, -TATES** to form cavities
CAVITY	*n* pl. **-TIES** an unfilled space within a mass **CAVITIED** *adj*
CAVORT	*v* **-ED, -ING, -S** to frolic
CAVORTER	*n* pl. **-S** one that cavorts
CAVY	*n* pl. **-VIES** a short-tailed rodent

CAW	*v* **-ED, -ING, -S** to utter the sound of a crow
CAY	*n* pl. **CAYS** a small low island
CAYENNE	*n* pl. **-S** a hot seasoning **CAYENNED** *adj*
CAYMAN	*n* pl. **-S** caiman
CAYUSE	*n* pl. **-S** an Indian pony
CAZH	*adj* casual
CAZIQUE	*n* pl. **-S** cacique
CEASE	*v* **CEASED, CEASING, CEASES** to stop
CEBID	*n* pl. **-S** ceboid
CEBOID	*n* pl. **-S** one of a family of monkeys
CECITY	*n* pl. **-TIES** blindness
CECROPIA	*n* pl. **-S** a large North American moth
CECUM	*n* pl. **CECA** a bodily cavity with one opening **CECAL** *adj* **CECALLY** *adv*
CEDAR	*n* pl. **-S** an evergreen tree **CEDARN, CEDARY** *adj*
CEDE	*v* **CEDED, CEDING, CEDES** to yield
CEDER	*n* pl. **-S** one that cedes
CEDI	*n* pl. **-S** a monetary unit of Ghana
CEDILLA	*n* pl. **-S** a pronunciation mark
CEDING	present participle of cede
CEDULA	*n* pl. **-S** a Philippine tax
CEE	*n* pl. **-S** the letter C
CEIBA	*n* pl. **-S** a tropical tree
CEIL	*v* **-ED, -ING, -S** to furnish with a ceiling
CEILER	*n* pl. **-S** one that ceils
CEILI	*n* pl. **-S** ceilidh
CEILIDH	*n* pl. **-S** an Irish or Scottish party
CEILING	*n* pl. **-S** the overhead lining of a room
CEINTURE	*n* pl. **-S** a belt for the waist
CEL	*n* pl. **-S** a sheet of celluloid used in animation
CELADON	*n* pl. **-S** a pale green color
CELEB	*n* pl. **-S** a celebrity; a famous person
CELERIAC	*n* pl. **-S** a variety of celery
CELERITY	*n* pl. **-TIES** swiftness
CELERY	*n* pl. **-ERIES** a plant with edible stalks
CELESTA	*n* pl. **-S** a keyboard instrument

CELESTE *n* pl. **-S** celesta

CELIAC *n* pl. **-S** one that has a chronic nutritional disturbance

CELIBACY *n* pl. **-CIES** abstention from sexual intercourse

CELIBATE *n* pl. **-S** one who lives a life of celibacy

CELL *v* **-ED, -ING, -S** to store in a honeycomb

CELLA *n* pl. **-LAE** the interior of an ancient temple

CELLAR *v* **-ED, -ING, -S** to store in an underground room

CELLARER *n* pl. **-S** the steward of a monastery

CELLARET *n* pl. **-S** a cabinet for wine bottles

CELLIST *n* pl. **-S** one who plays the cello

CELLMATE *n* pl. **-S** one of two or more prisoners sharing a cell

CELLO *n* pl. **-LOS** or **-LI** a stringed musical instrument

CELLULAR *n* pl. **-S** a cell phone

CELLULE *n* pl. **-S** a small cell

CELOM *n* pl. **-LOMS** or **-LOMATA** coelom

CELOSIA *n* pl. **-S** a flowering plant

CELT *n* pl. **-S** a primitive ax

CEMBALO *n* pl. **-LOS** or **-LI** a harpsichord

CEMENT *v* **-ED, -ING, -S** to bind firmly

CEMENTER *n* pl. **-S** one that cements

CEMENTUM *n* pl. **-TUMS** or **-TA** the hard tissue covering the roots of the teeth

CEMETERY *n* pl. **-TERIES** a burial ground

CENACLE *n* pl. **-S** a small dining room

CENOBITE *n* pl. **-S** a member of a religious order

CENOTAPH *n* pl. **-S** an empty tomb

CENOTE *n* pl. **-S** a sinkhole in limestone

CENSE *v* **CENSED, CENSING, CENSES** to perfume with incense

CENSER *n* pl. **-S** a vessel for burning incense

CENSOR *v* **-ED, -ING, -S** to delete an objectionable word or passage

CENSUAL *adj* pertaining to the act of censusing

CENSURE *v* **-SURED, -SURING, -SURES** to criticize severely

CENSURER *n* pl. **-S** one that censures

CENSUS *v* **-ED, -ING, -ES** to take an official count of

CENT *n* pl. **-S** the 100th part of a dollar

CENTAL *n* pl. **-S** a unit of weight

CENTARE *n* pl. **-S** a measure of land area

CENTAS *n* pl. **CENTAI** or **CENTU** a monetary unit of Lithuania

CENTAUR *n* pl. **-S** a mythological creature

CENTAURY *n* pl. **-RIES** a medicinal herb

CENTAVO *n* pl. **-VOS** a coin of various Spanish-American nations

CENTER *v* **-ED, -ING, -S** to place at the center (the midpoint)

CENTESIS *n* pl. **-TESES** a surgical puncture

CENTIARE *n* pl. **-S** centare

CENTILE *n* pl. **-S** a value of a statistical variable

CENTIME *n* pl. **-S** the 100th part of a franc

CENTIMO *n* pl. **-MOS** any of various small coins

CENTNER *n* pl. **-S** a unit of weight

CENTO *n* pl. **-TOS** or **-TONES** a literary work made up of parts from other works

CENTRA a pl. of centrum

CENTRAL *adj* **-TRALER, -TRALEST** situated at, in, or near the center

CENTRAL *n* pl. **-S** a telephone exchange

CENTRE *v* **-TRED, -TRING, -TRES** to center

CENTRIC *adj* situated at the center

CENTRING *n* pl. **-S** a temporary framework for an arch

CENTRISM *n* pl. **-S** a moderate political philosophy

CENTRIST *n* pl. **-S** an advocate of centrism

CENTROID *n* pl. **-S** the center of mass of an object

CENTRUM *n* pl. **-TRUMS** or **-TRA** the body of a vertebra

CENTU a pl. of centas

CENTUM *n* pl. **-S** one hundred

CENTUPLE *v* **-PLED, -PLING, -PLES** to increase a hundredfold

CENTURY *n* pl. **-RIES** a period of 100 years

CEORL *n* pl. **-S** a freeman of low birth **CEORLISH** *adj*

CEP *n* pl. **-S** cepe

CEPE *n* pl. **-S** a large mushroom

CEPHALAD *adv* toward the head

CEPHALIC *adj* pertaining to the head

CEPHALIN *n* pl. **-S** a bodily chemical

CEPHEID	*n* pl. **-S** a giant star
CERAMAL	*n* pl. **-S** a heat-resistant alloy
CERAMIC	*n* pl. **-S** an item made of baked clay
CERAMIDE	*n* pl. **-S** any of various lipids
CERAMIST	*n* pl. **-S** one who makes ceramics
CERASTES	*n* pl. **CERASTES** a venomous snake
CERATE	*n* pl. **-S** a medicated ointment
CERATED	*adj* covered with wax
CERATIN	*n* pl. **-S** keratin
CERATOID	*adj* hornlike
CERCARIA	*n* pl. **-IAS** or **-IAE** a parasitic worm
CERCIS	*n* pl. **-CISES** a shrub
CERCUS	*n* pl. **CERCI** a sensory appendage of an insect **CERCAL** *adj*
CERE	*v* **CERED, CERING, CERES** to wrap in a waxy cloth
CEREAL	*n* pl. **-S** a food made from grain
CEREBRAL	*n* pl. **-S** a kind of consonant
CEREBRUM	*n* pl. **-BRUMS** or **-BRA** a part of the brain **CEREBRIC** *adj*
CERED	past tense of cere
CEREMENT	*n* pl. **-S** a waxy cloth
CEREMONY	*n* pl. **-NIES** a formal observance
CERESIN	*n* pl. **-S** a hard whitish wax
CEREUS	*n* pl. **-ES** a tall cactus
CERIA	*n* pl. **-S** a chemical compound
CERIC	*adj* containing cerium
CERING	present participle of cere
CERIPH	*n* pl. **-S** serif
CERISE	*n* pl. **-S** a red color
CERITE	*n* pl. **-S** a mineral
CERIUM	*n* pl. **-S** a metallic element
CERMET	*n* pl. **-S** ceramal
CERNUOUS	*adj* drooping or nodding
CERO	*n* pl. **CEROS** a large food fish
CEROTIC	*adj* pertaining to beeswax
CEROTYPE	*n* pl. **-S** a process of engraving using wax
CEROUS	*adj* pertaining to cerium
CERT	*n* pl. **-S** an event considered certain to happen
CERTAIN	*adj* **-TAINER, -TAINEST** absolutely confident
CERTES	*adv* in truth
CERTIFY	*v* **-FIED, -FYING, -FIES** to confirm
CERULEAN	*n* pl. **-S** a blue color
CERUMEN	*n* pl. **-S** a waxy secretion of the ear
CERUSE	*n* pl. **-S** a lead compound
CERUSITE	*n* pl. **-S** a lead ore
CERVELAS	*n* pl. **-ES** cervelat
CERVELAT	*n* pl. **-S** a smoked sausage
CERVEZA	*n* pl. **-S** beer
CERVICAL	*adj* pertaining to the cervix
CERVID	*n* pl. **-S** a mammal of the deer family
CERVINE	*adj* pertaining to deer
CERVIX	*n* pl. **-VIXES** or **-VICES** the neck
CESAREAN	*n* pl. **-S** a method of child delivery
CESARIAN	*n* pl. **-S** cesarean
CESIUM	*n* pl. **-S** a metallic element
CESS	*v* **-ED, -ING, -ES** to tax or assess
CESSION	*n* pl. **-S** the act of ceding
CESSPIT	*n* pl. **-S** a cesspool
CESSPOOL	*n* pl. **-S** a covered well or pit for sewage
CESTA	*n* pl. **-S** a basket used in jai alai (a game played with a small hard ball)
CESTI	pl. of cestus
CESTODE	*n* pl. **-S** a tapeworm
CESTOID	*n* pl. **-S** cestode
CESTOS	*n* pl. **-TOI** cestus
CESTUS	*n* pl. **-ES** a hand covering for ancient Roman boxers
CESTUS	*n* pl. **-TI** a belt or girdle
CESURA	*n* pl. **-RAS** or **-RAE** caesura
CETACEAN	*n* pl. **-S** an aquatic mammal
CETANE	*n* pl. **-S** a diesel fuel
CETE	*n* pl. **-S** a group of badgers
CETOLOGY	*n* pl. **-GIES** the study of whales
CEVICHE	*n* pl. **-S** seviche
CHABLIS	*n* pl. **CHABLIS** a dry white wine
CHABOUK	*n* pl. **-S** a type of whip
CHABUK	*n* pl. **-S** chabouk
CHACHKA	*n* pl. **-S** chatchka
CHACMA	*n* pl. **-S** a large baboon
CHACONNE	*n* pl. **-S** an ancient dance
CHAD	*n* pl. **-S** a scrap of paper **CHADLESS** *adj*
CHADAR	*n* pl. **-DARS** or **-DRI** chador
CHADARIM	a pl. of cheder

CHADOR *n pl.* **-DORS** or **-DRI** a large shawl

CHAEBOL *n pl.* **-S** a group of businesses in Korea owned by one family

CHAETA *n pl.* **-TAE** a bristle or seta **CHAETAL** *adj*

CHAFE *v* **CHAFED, CHAFING, CHAFES** to warm by rubbing

CHAFER *n pl.* **-S** a large beetle

CHAFF *v* **-ED, -ING, -S** to poke fun at

CHAFFER *v* **-ED, -ING, -S** to bargain or haggle

CHAFFY *adj* **CHAFFIER, CHAFFIEST** worthless

CHAFING present participle of chafe

CHAGRIN *v* **-GRINED, -GRINING, -GRINS** or **-GRINNED, -GRINNING, -GRINS** to humiliate

CHAI *n pl.* **-S** spiced tea with honey and milk

CHAIN *v* **-ED, -ING, -S** to bind with a chain (a series of connected rings)

CHAINE *n pl.* **-S** a series of ballet turns

CHAINER *n pl.* **-S** a chainman

CHAINMAN *n pl.* **-MEN** a surveyor's assistant who uses a measuring chain

CHAINSAW *v* **-SAWED, -SAWING, -SAWS** to cut with a chain saw

CHAIR *v* **-ED, -ING, -S** to install in office

CHAIRMAN *n pl.* **-MEN** the presiding officer of a meeting

CHAIRMAN *v* **-MANED, -MANING, -MANS** or **-MANNED, -MANNING, -MANS** to act as chairman of

CHAISE *n pl.* **-S** a light carriage

CHAKRA *n pl.* **-S** a body center in yoga

CHALAH *n pl.* **-LAHS** or **-LOTH** or **-LOT** challah

CHALAZA *n pl.* **-ZAS** or **-ZAE** a band of tissue in an egg **CHALAZAL** *adj*

CHALAZIA *n/pl* tumors of the eyelid

CHALCID *n pl.* **-S** a tiny fly

CHALDRON *n pl.* **-S** a unit of dry measure

CHALEH *n pl.* **-S** challah

CHALET *n pl.* **-S** a Swiss cottage

CHALICE *n pl.* **-S** a drinking cup **CHALICED** *adj*

CHALK *v* **-ED, -ING, -S** to mark with chalk (a soft limestone)

CHALKY *adj* **CHALKIER, CHALKIEST** resembling chalk

CHALLA *n pl.* **-S** challah

CHALLAH *n pl.* **-LAHS** or **-LOTH** or **-LOT** a kind of bread

CHALLIE *n pl.* **-S** challis

CHALLIES pl. of chally

CHALLIS *n pl.* **-LISES** a light fabric

CHALLOT a pl. of challah

CHALLOTH a pl. of challah

CHALLY *n pl.* **-LIES** challis

CHALONE *n pl.* **-S** a hormone

CHALOT a pl. of chalah

CHALOTH a pl. of chalah

CHALUPA *n pl.* **-S** a fried corn tortilla spread with a savory mixture

CHALUTZ *n pl.* **-LUTZIM** halutz

CHAM *n pl.* **-S** a khan

CHAMADE *n pl.* **-S** a signal made with a drum

CHAMBER *v* **-ED, -ING, -S** to put in a chamber (a room)

CHAMBRAY *n pl.* **-BRAYS** a fine fabric

CHAMBRE *adj* brought (as wine) to room temperature

CHAMFER *v* **-ED, -ING, -S** to groove

CHAMFRON *n pl.* **-S** armor for a horse's head

CHAMISA *n pl.* **-S** a saltbush of the Southwest

CHAMISE *n pl.* **-S** chamiso

CHAMISO *n pl.* **-SOS** a flowering shrub

CHAMMY *v* **-MIED, -MYING, -MIES** to chamois

CHAMOIS *n pl.* **-OIX** a soft leather

CHAMOIS *v* **-ED, -ING, -ES** to prepare leather like chamois

CHAMP *v* **-ED, -ING, -S** to chew noisily

CHAMPAC *n pl.* **-S** champak

CHAMPACA *n pl.* **-S** champak

CHAMPAK *n pl.* **-S** an East Indian tree

CHAMPER *n pl.* **-S** one that champs

CHAMPION *v* **-ED, -ING, -S** to defend or support

CHAMPY *adj* broken up by the trampling of beasts

CHANA *n pl.* **-S** a snack of chick peas

CHANCE *v* **CHANCED, CHANCING, CHANCES** to risk

CHANCEL *n pl.* **-S** an area around a church altar

CHANCER *n pl.* **-S** an opportunist

CHANCERY *n* pl. **-CERIES** a court of public record

CHANCIER comparative of chancy

CHANCIEST superlative of chancy

CHANCILY *adv* in a chancy manner

CHANCING present participle of chance

CHANCRE *n* pl. **-S** a hard-based sore

CHANCY *adj* **CHANCIER, CHANCIEST** risky

CHANDLER *n* pl. **-S** a dealer in provisions

CHANFRON *n* pl. **-S** chamfron

CHANG *n* pl. **-S** a cattie

CHANGE *v* **CHANGED, CHANGING, CHANGES** to make different

CHANGER *n* pl. **-S** one that changes

CHANGEUP *n* pl. **-S** a slow pitch thrown like a fastball

CHANNEL *v* **-NELED, -NELING, -NELS** or **-NELLED, -NELLING, -NELS** to direct along some desired course

CHANOYU *n* pl. **-S** a Japanese tea ritual

CHANSON *n* pl. **-S** a song

CHANT *v* **-ED, -ING, -S** to sing

CHANTAGE *n* pl. **-S** blackmail

CHANTER *n* pl. **-S** one that chants

CHANTEY *n* pl. **-TEYS** a sailor's song

CHANTIES pl. of chanty

CHANTOR *n* pl. **-S** chanter

CHANTRY *n* pl. **-TRIES** an endowment given to a church

CHANTY *n* pl. **-TIES** chantey

CHAO *n* pl. **CHAO** a monetary unit of Vietnam

CHAOS *n* pl. **-ES** a state of total disorder; a confused mass **CHAOTIC** *adj*

CHAP *v* **CHAPPED** or **CHAPT, CHAPPING, CHAPS** to split, crack, or redden

CHAPATI *n* pl. **-S** an unleavened bread of India

CHAPATTI *n* pl. **-S** chapati

CHAPBOOK *n* pl. **-S** a small book of popular tales

CHAPE *n* pl. **-S** a part of a scabbard

CHAPEAU *n* pl. **-PEAUS** or **-PEAUX** a hat

CHAPEL *n* pl. **-S** a place of worship

CHAPERON *v* **-ED, -ING, -S** to accompany

CHAPITER *n* pl. **-S** the capital of a column

CHAPLAIN *n* pl. **-S** a clergyman for a chapel

CHAPLET *n* pl. **-S** a wreath for the head

CHAPMAN *n* pl. **-MEN** a peddler

CHAPPAL *n* pl. **-S** a sandal worn in India

CHAPPATI *n* pl. **-S** chapati

CHAPPED a past tense of chap

CHAPPIE *n* pl. **-S** a fellow

CHAPPING present participle of chap

CHAPT a past tense of chap

CHAPTER *v* **-ED, -ING, -S** to divide a book into chapters (main sections)

CHAQUETA *n* pl. **-S** a jacket worn by cowboys

CHAR *v* **CHARRED, CHARRING, CHARS** to burn slightly

CHARACID *n* pl. **-S** characin

CHARACIN *n* pl. **-S** a tropical fish

CHARADE *n* pl. **-S** a word represented by pantomime

CHARAS *n* pl. **-ES** hashish

CHARCOAL *v* **-ED, -ING, -S** to blacken with charcoal (a dark, porous carbon)

CHARD *n* pl. **-S** a variety of beet

CHARE *v* **CHARED, CHARING, CHARES** to do small jobs

CHARETTE *n* pl. **-S** a meeting for brainstorming

CHARGE *v* **CHARGED, CHARGING, CHARGES** to accuse formally

CHARGER *n* pl. **-S** one that charges

CHARGING *n* pl. **-S** an illegal play in hockey

CHARIER comparative of chary

CHARIEST superlative of chary

CHARILY *adv* in a chary manner

CHARING present participle of chare

CHARIOT *v* **-ED, -ING, -S** to ride in a chariot (a type of cart)

CHARISM *n* pl. **-S** charisma

CHARISMA *n* pl. **-MAS** or **-MATA** a special magnetic appeal

CHARITY *n* pl. **-TIES** something given to the needy

CHARK *v* **-ED, -ING, -S** to char

CHARKA *n* pl. **-S** charkha

CHARKHA *n* pl. **-S** a spinning wheel

CHARLADY *n* pl. **-DIES** a cleaning woman

CHARLEY *n* pl. **-LEYS** charlie

CHARLIE *n* pl. **-LIES** a fool

CHARLOCK *n* pl. **-S** a troublesome weed

CHARM v **-ED, -ING, -S** to attract irresistibly

CHARMER n pl. **-S** one that charms

CHARMING adj **-INGER, -INGEST** pleasing

CHARNEL n pl. **-S** a room where corpses are placed

CHARPAI n pl. **-S** charpoy

CHARPOY n pl. **-POYS** a bed used in India

CHARQUI n pl. **-S** a type of meat **CHARQUID** adj

CHARR n pl. **-S** a small-scaled trout

CHARRED past tense of char

CHARRIER comparative of charry

CHARRIEST superlative of charry

CHARRING present participle of char

CHARRO n pl. **-ROS** a cowboy

CHARRY adj **-RIER, -RIEST** resembling charcoal

CHART v **-ED, -ING, -S** to map out

CHARTER v **-ED, -ING, -S** to lease or hire

CHARTISM n pl. **-S** the use of financial charts to predict future trends

CHARTIST n pl. **-S** a stock market specialist

CHARY adj **CHARIER, CHARIEST** cautious

CHASE v **CHASED, CHASING, CHASES** to pursue

CHASER n pl. **-S** one that chases

CHASING n pl. **-S** a design engraved on metal

CHASM n pl. **-S** a deep cleft in the earth **CHASMAL, CHASMED, CHASMIC, CHASMY** adj

CHASSE v **CHASSED, CHASSEING, CHASSES** to perform a dance movement

CHASSEUR n pl. **-S** a cavalry soldier

CHASSIS n pl. **CHASSIS** the frame of a car

CHASTE adj **CHASTER, CHASTEST** morally pure **CHASTELY** adv

CHASTEN v **-ED, -ING, -S** to chastise

CHASTISE v **-TISED, -TISING, -TISES** to discipline by punishment

CHASTITY n pl. **-TIES** moral purity

CHASUBLE n pl. **-S** a sleeveless vestment

CHAT v **CHATTED, CHATTING, CHATS** to converse informally

CHATCHKA n pl. **-S** a knickknack

CHATCHKE n pl. **-S** chatchka

CHATEAU n pl. **-TEAUS** or **-TEAUX** a large country house

CHATLINE n pl. **-S** a telephone service that allows conversation among several callers

CHATROOM n pl. **-S** a real-time online discussion group

CHATTED past tense of chat

CHATTEL n pl. **-S** a slave

CHATTER v **-ED, -ING, -S** to talk rapidly and trivially **CHATTERY** adj

CHATTING present participle of chat

CHATTY adj **-TIER, -TIEST** talkative **CHATTILY** adv

CHAUFER n pl. **-S** chauffer

CHAUFFER n pl. **-S** a small furnace

CHAUNT v **-ED, -ING, -S** to chant

CHAUNTER n pl. **-S** one that chaunts

CHAUSSES n/pl medieval armor

CHAW v **-ED, -ING, -S** to chew

CHAWER n pl. **-S** one that chaws

CHAY n pl. **CHAYS** the root of an East Indian herb

CHAYOTE n pl. **-S** a tropical vine

CHAZAN n pl. **-ZANS** or **-ZANIM** a cantor

CHAZZAN n pl. **-ZANS** or **-ZANIM** chazan

CHAZZEN n pl. **-ZENS** or **-ZENIM** chazan

CHEAP adj **CHEAPER, CHEAPEST** inexpensive

CHEAP n pl. **-S** a market

CHEAPEN v **-ED, -ING, -S** to make cheap

CHEAPIE n pl. **-S** one that is cheap

CHEAPISH adj somewhat cheap

CHEAPLY adv in a cheap manner

CHEAPO n pl. **CHEAPOS** a cheapie

CHEAT v **-ED, -ING, -S** to defraud

CHEATER n pl. **-S** one that cheats

CHEBEC n pl. **-S** a small bird

CHECHAKO n pl. **-KOS** a newcomer

CHECK v **-ED, -ING, -S** to inspect

CHECKBOX n pl. **-ES** a small box on a computer screen to be clicked on to select a feature

CHECKER v **-ED, -ING, -S** to mark with squares

CHECKOFF n pl. **-S** a method of collecting union dues

CHECKOUT n pl. **-S** a test of a machine

CHECKROW v **-ED, -ING, -S** to plant in rows which divide the land into squares

CHECKSUM n pl. **-S** a sum derived from bits of computer data

CHECKUP n pl. **-S** an examination

CHEDDAR n pl. **-S** a type of cheese **CHEDDARY** adj

CHEDDITE n pl. **-S** chedite

CHEDER n pl. **CHEDERS** or **CHADARIM** or **CHEDARIM** heder

CHEDITE n pl. **-S** an explosive

CHEEK v **-ED, -ING, -S** to speak impudently to

CHEEKFUL n pl. **-S** the amount held in one's cheek

CHEEKY adj **CHEEKIER, CHEEKIEST** impudent **CHEEKILY** adv

CHEEP v **-ED, -ING, -S** to chirp

CHEEPER n pl. **-S** one that cheeps

CHEER v **-ED, -ING, -S** to applaud with shouts of approval

CHEERER n pl. **-S** one that cheers

CHEERFUL adj **-FULLER, -FULLEST** full of spirits

CHEERIER comparative of cheery

CHEERIEST superlative of cheery

CHEERILY adv in a cheery manner

CHEERIO n pl. **-IOS** a greeting

CHEERLED past tense of cheerlead

CHEERLY adv cheerily

CHEERO n pl. **CHEEROS** cheerio

CHEERY adj **CHEERIER, CHEERIEST** cheerful

CHEESE v **CHEESED, CHEESING, CHEESES** to stop

CHEESY adj **CHEESIER, CHEESIEST** resembling cheese (a food made from milk curds) **CHEESILY** adv

CHEETAH n pl. **-S** a swift-running wildcat

CHEF v **CHEFFED, CHEFFING, CHEFS** or **CHEFED, CHEFING, CHEFS** to work as a chef (a chief cook)

CHEFDOM n pl. **-S** the status of a chef

CHEGOE n pl. **-S** chigoe

CHELA n pl. **-LAE** a pincerlike claw

CHELA n pl. **-S** a pupil of a guru

CHELATE v **-LATED, -LATING, -LATES** to combine a metal ion with a compound

CHELATOR n pl. **-S** one that chelates

CHELIPED n pl. **-S** a claw-bearing leg

CHELOID n pl. **-S** keloid

CHEM n pl. **-S** a chemistry class or course

CHEMIC n pl. **-S** a chemist

CHEMICAL n pl. **-S** a substance obtained by a process of chemistry

CHEMISE n pl. **-S** a loose dress

CHEMISM n pl. **-S** chemical attraction

CHEMIST n pl. **-S** one versed in chemistry

CHEMO n pl. **-S** treatment (as of disease) with chemical agents

CHEMURGY n pl. **-GIES** a branch of applied chemistry

CHENILLE n pl. **-S** a soft fabric

CHENOPOD n pl. **-S** a flowering plant

CHEQUE n pl. **-S** a written order directing a bank to pay money

CHEQUER v **-ED, -ING, -S** to checker

CHERISH v **-ED, -ING, -ES** to hold dear

CHEROOT n pl. **-S** a square-cut cigar

CHERRY n pl. **-RIES** a fruit

CHERRY adj **-RIER, -RIEST** of a light red color

CHERT n pl. **-S** a compact rock

CHERTY adj **CHERTIER, CHERTIEST** resembling chert

CHERUB n pl. **-UBS** or **-UBIM** or **-UBIMS** an angel **CHERUBIC** adj

CHERVIL n pl. **-S** an aromatic herb

CHESHIRE n pl. **-S** a hard English cheese

CHESS n pl. **-ES** a weed

CHESSMAN n pl. **-MEN** one of the pieces used in chess (a board game for two players)

CHEST n pl. **-S** a part of the body **CHESTED** adj

CHESTFUL n pl. **-S** as much as a chest or box can hold

CHESTNUT n pl. **-S** an edible nut

CHESTY adj **CHESTIER, CHESTIEST** proud **CHESTILY** adv

CHETAH n pl. **-S** cheetah

CHETH n pl. **-S** heth

CHETRUM n pl. **-S** a monetary unit of Bhutan

CHEVALET n pl. **-S** a part of a stringed instrument

CHEVERON n pl. **-S** chevron

CHEVET	*n* pl. **-S** the apsidal end of a church
CHEVIED	past tense of chevy
CHEVIES	present 3d person sing. of chevy
CHEVIOT	*n* pl. **-S** a coarse fabric
CHEVRE	*n* pl. **-S** a cheese made from goat's milk
CHEVRET	*n* pl. **-S** chevre
CHEVRON	*n* pl. **-S** a V-shaped pattern
CHEVY	*v* **CHEVIED, CHEVYING, CHEVIES** to chase about
CHEW	*v* **-ED, -ING, -S** to crush or grind with the teeth **CHEWABLE** *adj*
CHEWER	*n* pl. **-S** one that chews
CHEWINK	*n* pl. **-S** a common finch
CHEWY	*adj* **CHEWIER, CHEWIEST** not easily chewed
CHEZ	*prep* at the home of
CHI	*n* pl. **-S** a Greek letter
CHIA	*n* pl. **-S** a Mexican herb
CHIANTI	*n* pl. **-S** a dry red wine
CHIAO	*n* pl. **CHIAO** a monetary unit of China
CHIASM	*n* pl. **-S** chiasma
CHIASMA	*n* pl. **-MAS** or **-MATA** an anatomical junction **CHIASMAL, CHIASMIC** *adj*
CHIASMUS	*n* pl. **-MI** a reversal of word order between parallel phrases **CHIASTIC** *adj*
CHIAUS	*n* pl. **-ES** a Turkish messenger
CHIBOUK	*n* pl. **-S** a Turkish tobacco pipe
CHIC	*adj* **CHICER, CHICEST** smartly stylish
CHIC	*n* pl. **-S** elegance of dress or manner
CHICA	*n* pl. **-S** a girl or young woman
CHICANE	*v* **-CANED, -CANING, -CANES** to trick by a clever ruse
CHICANER	*n* pl. **-S** one that chicanes
CHICANO	*n* pl. **-NOS** an American of Mexican descent
CHICCORY	*n* pl. **-RIES** chicory
CHICHI	*adj* **CHICHIER, CHICHIEST** showily stylish
CHICHI	*n* pl. **-S** elaborate ornamentation
CHICK	*n* pl. **-S** a young bird
CHICKEE	*n* pl. **-S** a stilt house of the Seminole Indians
CHICKEN	*v* **-ED, -ING, -S** to lose one's nerve
CHICKORY	*n* pl. **-RIES** chicory
CHICKPEA	*n* pl. **-S** an Asian herb
CHICLE	*n* pl. **-S** a tree gum
CHICLY	*adv* in an elegant manner
CHICNESS	*n* pl. **-ES** elegance
CHICO	*n* pl. **-COS** a prickly shrub
CHICORY	*n* pl. **-RIES** a perennial herb
CHICOT	*n* pl. **-S** a dead tree
CHIDE	*v* **CHIDED** or **CHID, CHIDDEN, CHIDING, CHIDES** to scold
CHIDER	*n* pl. **-S** one that chides
CHIEF	*adj* **CHIEFER, CHIEFEST** highest in authority
CHIEF	*n* pl. **-S** the person highest in authority
CHIEFDOM	*n* pl. **-S** the domain of a chief
CHIEFLY	*adv* above all
CHIEL	*n* pl. **-S** chield
CHIELD	*n* pl. **-S** a young man
CHIFFON	*n* pl. **-S** a sheer fabric
CHIGETAI	*n* pl. **-S** a wild ass
CHIGGER	*n* pl. **-S** a parasitic mite
CHIGNON	*n* pl. **-S** a woman's hairdo
CHIGOE	*n* pl. **-S** a tropical flea
CHILD	*n* pl. **CHILDREN** a young person
CHILDBED	*n* pl. **-S** the state of a woman giving birth
CHILDE	*n* pl. **-S** a youth of noble birth
CHILDING	*adj* pregnant
CHILDISH	*adj* resembling a child
CHILDLY	*adj* **-LIER, -LIEST** resembling a child
CHILDREN	pl. of child
CHILE	*n* pl. **-S** chili
CHILI	*n* pl. **-S** or **-ES** a hot pepper
CHILIAD	*n* pl. **-S** a group of one thousand
CHILIASM	*n* pl. **-S** a religious doctrine
CHILIAST	*n* pl. **-S** a supporter of chiliasm
CHILIDOG	*n* pl. **-S** a hot dog topped with chili
CHILL	*adj* **CHILLER, CHILLEST** cool
CHILL	*v* **-ED, -ING, -S** to make cold
CHILLAX	*v* **-ED, -ING, -ES** to calm down
CHILLER	*n* pl. **-S** one that chills
CHILLI	*n* pl. **-ES** or **-S** chili
CHILLUM	*n* pl. **-S** a part of a water pipe

CHILLY *adj* **CHILLIER, CHILLIEST** cool **CHILLILY** *adv*

CHILOPOD *n* pl. **-S** a multi-legged insect

CHIMAERA *n* pl. **-S** a marine fish

CHIMAR *n* pl. **-S** chimere

CHIMB *n* pl. **-S** the rim of a cask

CHIMBLEY *n* pl. **-BLEYS** chimley

CHIMBLY *n* pl. **-BLIES** chimley

CHIME *v* **CHIMED, CHIMING, CHIMES** to ring harmoniously

CHIMENEA *n* pl. **-S** an outdoor fireplace shaped like a lightbulb

CHIMER *n* pl. **-S** one that chimes

CHIMERA *n* pl. **-S** an imaginary monster

CHIMERE *n* pl. **-S** a bishop's robe

CHIMERIC *adj* imaginary; unreal

CHIMINEA *n* pl. **-S** chimenea

CHIMING present participle of chime

CHIMLA *n* pl. **-S** chimley

CHIMLEY *n* pl. **-LEYS** a chimney

CHIMNEY *n* pl. **-NEYS** a flue

CHIMP *n* pl. **-S** a chimpanzee

CHIN *v* **CHINNED, CHINNING, CHINS** to hold with the chin (the lower part of the face)

CHINA *n* pl. **-S** fine porcelain ware

CHINBONE *n* pl. **-S** the lower jaw

CHINCH *v* **-ED, -ING, -ES** to chinse

CHINCHY *adj* **CHINCHIER, CHINCHIEST** stingy

CHINE *v* **CHINED, CHINING, CHINES** to cut through the backbone of

CHING *n* pl. **-S** a high-pitched ringing sound

CHINK *v* **-ED, -ING, -S** to fill cracks or fissures in

CHINKY *adj* **CHINKIER, CHINKIEST** full of cracks

CHINLESS *adj* lacking a chin

CHINNED past tense of chin

CHINNING present participle of chin

CHINO *n* pl. **-NOS** a strong fabric

CHINOIS *n* pl. **-NOISES** a cone-shaped sieve

CHINONE *n* pl. **-S** quinone

CHINOOK *n* pl. **-S** a warm wind

CHINSE *v* **CHINSED, CHINSING, CHINSES** to fill the seams in a boat or cabin

CHINTS *n* pl. **-ES** chintz

CHINTZ *n* pl. **-ES** a cotton fabric

CHINTZY *adj* **CHINTZIER, CHINTZIEST** gaudy; cheap

CHINWAG *v* **-WAGGED, -WAGGING, -WAGS** to gossip

CHIP *v* **CHIPPED, CHIPPING, CHIPS** to break a small piece from

CHIPMUCK *n* pl. **-S** a chipmunk

CHIPMUNK *n* pl. **-S** a small rodent

CHIPOTLE *n* pl. **-S** a smoked and dried jalapeno pepper

CHIPPED past tense of chip

CHIPPER *v* **-ED, -ING, -S** to chirp

CHIPPIE *n* pl. **-S** chippy

CHIPPING present participle of chip

CHIPPY *adj* **-PIER, -PIEST** belligerent

CHIPPY *n* pl. **-PIES** a prostitute

CHIPSET *n* pl. **-S** a set of integrated circuits

CHIRAL *adj* pertaining to an asymmetrical molecule

CHIRK *adj* **CHIRKER, CHIRKEST** cheerful

CHIRK *v* **-ED, -ING, -S** to make a shrill noise

CHIRM *v* **-ED, -ING, -S** to chirp

CHIRO *n* pl. **-ROS** a marine fish

CHIRP *v* **-ED, -ING, -S** to utter a short, shrill sound

CHIRPER *n* pl. **-S** one that chirps

CHIRPY *adj* **CHIRPIER, CHIRPIEST** cheerful **CHIRPILY** *adv*

CHIRR *v* **-ED, -ING, -S** to make a harsh, vibrant sound

CHIRRE *v* **CHIRRED, CHIRRING, CHIRRES** to chirr

CHIRREN *n/pl* children

CHIRRUP *v* **-ED, -ING, -S** to chirp repeatedly **CHIRRUPY** *adj*

CHIRU *n* pl. **-S** a Tibetan antelope

CHISEL *v* **-ELED, -ELING, -ELS** or **-ELLED, -ELLING, -ELS** to use a chisel (a cutting tool)

CHISELER *n* pl. **-S** one that chisels

CHIT *n* pl. **-S** a short letter

CHITAL *n* pl. **-S** an Asian deer

CHITCHAT *v* **-CHATTED, -CHATTING, -CHATS** to indulge in small talk

CHITIN	*n* pl. **-S** the main component of insect shells
CHITLIN	*n* pl. **-S** chitling
CHITLING	*n* pl. **-S** a part of the small intestine of swine
CHITON	*n* pl. **-S** a tunic worn in ancient Greece
CHITOSAN	*n* pl. **-S** a compound derived from chitin
CHITTER	*v* **-ED, -ING, -S** to twitter
CHITTY	*n* pl. **-TIES** a chit
CHIVALRY	*n* pl. **-RIES** knightly behavior and skill
CHIVAREE	*v* **-REED, -REEING, -REES** to perform a mock serenade
CHIVARI	*v* **-RIED, -RIING, -RIES** to chivaree
CHIVE	*n* pl. **-S** an herb used as a seasoning
CHIVVY	*v* **-VIED, -VYING, -VIES** to chevy
CHIVY	*v* **CHIVIED, CHIVYING, CHIVIES** to chevy
CHLAMYS	*n* pl. **-MYSES** or **-MYDES** a garment worn in ancient Greece
CHLOASMA	*n* pl. **-MAS** or **-MATA** a skin discoloration
CHLORAL	*n* pl. **-S** a chemical compound
CHLORATE	*n* pl. **-S** a chemical salt
CHLORDAN	*n* pl. **-S** a toxic compound of chlorine
CHLORIC	*adj* pertaining to chlorine
CHLORID	*n* pl. **-S** chloride
CHLORIDE	*n* pl. **-S** a chlorine compound
CHLORIN	*n* pl. **-S** chlorine
CHLORINE	*n* pl. **-S** a gaseous element
CHLORITE	*n* pl. **-S** a mineral group
CHLOROUS	*adj* pertaining to chlorine
CHOANA	*n* pl. **-NAE** a funnel-shaped opening
CHOC	*n* pl. **-S** a chocolate
CHOCK	*v* **-ED, -ING, -S** to secure with a wedge of wood or metal
CHOCKFUL	*adj* full to the limit
CHOICE	*adj* **CHOICER, CHOICEST** of fine quality **CHOICELY** *adv*
CHOICE	*n* pl. **-S** one that is chosen
CHOIL	*n* pl. **-S** the end of a knife blade nearer the handle
CHOIR	*v* **-ED, -ING, -S** to sing in unison
CHOIRBOY	*n* pl. **-BOYS** a boy who sings in a choir (a body of church singers)
CHOKE	*v* **CHOKED, CHOKING, CHOKES** to impede the breathing of
CHOKER	*n* pl. **-S** one that chokes
CHOKEY	*adj* **CHOKIER, CHOKIEST** choky
CHOKEY	*n* pl. **CHOKEYS** choky
CHOKY	*adj* **CHOKIER, CHOKIEST** tending to cause choking
CHOKY	*n* pl. **CHOKIES** a prison
CHOLATE	*n* pl. **-S** a chemical salt
CHOLENT	*n* pl. **-S** a traditional Jewish stew
CHOLER	*n* pl. **-S** anger
CHOLERA	*n* pl. **-S** an acute disease
CHOLERIC	*adj* bad-tempered
CHOLI	*n* pl. **-S** a bodice worn by some Hindu women
CHOLIAMB	*n* pl. **-S** a type of poetic meter
CHOLINE	*n* pl. **-S** a B vitamin
CHOLLA	*n* pl. **-S** a treelike cactus
CHOMP	*v* **-ED, -ING, -S** to champ
CHOMPER	*n* pl. **-S** one that chomps
CHON	*n* pl. **CHON** a monetary unit of North and South Korea
CHOOK	*n* pl. **-S** a chicken
CHOOSE	*v* **CHOSE, CHOSEN, CHOOSING, CHOOSES** to take by preference
CHOOSER	*n* pl. **-S** one that chooses
CHOOSEY	*adj* **CHOOSIER, CHOOSIEST** choosy
CHOOSY	*adj* **CHOOSIER, CHOOSIEST** hard to please **CHOOSILY** *adv*
CHOP	*v* **CHOPPED, CHOPPING, CHOPS** to sever with a sharp tool
CHOPIN	*n* pl. **-S** chopine
CHOPINE	*n* pl. **-S** a type of shoe
CHOPPED	past tense of chop
CHOPPER	*v* **-ED, -ING, -S** to travel by helicopter
CHOPPING	present participle of chop
CHOPPY	*adj* **CHOPPIER, CHOPPIEST** full of short, rough waves **CHOPPILY** *adv*
CHORAGUS	*n* pl. **-GUSES** or **-GI** the leader of a chorus or choir **CHORAGIC** *adj*
CHORAL	*n* pl. **-S** chorale
CHORALE	*n* pl. **-S** a hymn that is sung in unison
CHORALLY	*adv* harmoniously

CHORD *v* **-ED, -ING, -S** to play a chord (a combination of three or more musical tones)

CHORDAL *adj* pertaining to a chord

CHORDATE *n* pl. **-S** any of a large phylum of animals

CHORDING *n* pl. **-S** the act of playing a chord

CHORE *v* **CHORED, CHORING, CHORES** to do small jobs

CHOREA *n* pl. **-S** a nervous disorder **CHOREAL, CHOREIC** *adj*

CHOREBOY *n* pl. **-BOYS** a boy employed to do odd jobs

CHOREGUS *n* pl. **-GUSES** or **-GI** choragus

CHOREMAN *n* pl. **-MEN** a menial worker

CHOREOID *adj* resembling chorea

CHORIAL *adj* pertaining to the chorion

CHORIAMB *n* pl. **-S** a type of metrical foot

CHORIC *adj* pertaining to a chorus

CHORINE *n* pl. **-S** a chorus girl

CHORING present participle of chore

CHORIOID *n* pl. **-S** choroid

CHORION *n* pl. **-S** an embryonic membrane

CHORIZO *n* pl. **-ZOS** a highly seasoned sausage

CHOROID *n* pl. **-S** a membrane of the eye

CHORTEN *n* pl. **-S** a Tibetan shrine

CHORTLE *v* **-TLED, -TLING, -TLES** to chuckle with glee

CHORTLER *n* pl. **-S** one that chortles

CHORUS *v* **-RUSED, -RUSING, -RUSES** or **-RUSSED, -RUSSING, -RUSSES** to sing in unison

CHOSE *n* pl. **-S** an item of personal property

CHOSEN past participle of choose

CHOTT *n* pl. **-S** a saline lake

CHOUGH *n* pl. **-S** a crow-like bird

CHOUSE *v* **CHOUSED, CHOUSING, CHOUSES** to swindle

CHOUSER *n* pl. **-S** one that chouses

CHOUSH *n* pl. **-ES** chiaus

CHOW *v* **-ED, -ING, -S** to eat

CHOWCHOW *n* pl. **-S** a relish of mixed pickles in mustard

CHOWDER *v* **-ED, -ING, -S** to make a thick soup of

CHOWSE *v* **CHOWSED, CHOWSING, CHOWSES** to chouse

CHOWTIME *n* pl. **-S** mealtime

CHRESARD *n* pl. **-S** the available water of the soil

CHRISM *n* pl. **-S** a consecrated oil **CHRISMAL** *adj*

CHRISMON *n* pl. **-MONS** or **-MA** a Christian monogram

CHRISOM *n* pl. **-S** chrism

CHRISTEN *v* **-ED, -ING, -S** to baptize

CHRISTIE *n* pl. **-S** christy

CHRISTY *n* pl. **-TIES** a skiing turn

CHROMA *n* pl. **-S** the purity of a color

CHROMATE *n* pl. **-S** a chemical salt

CHROME *v* **CHROMED, CHROMING, CHROMES** to plate with chromium

CHROMIC *adj* pertaining to chromium

CHROMIDE *n* pl. **-S** a tropical fish

CHROMING *n* pl. **-S** a chromium ore

CHROMITE *n* pl. **-S** a chromium ore

CHROMIUM *n* pl. **-S** a metallic element

CHROMIZE *v* **-MIZED, -MIZING, -MIZES** to chrome

CHROMO *n* pl. **-MOS** a type of color picture

CHROMOLY *n* pl. **-LIES** a steel alloy made of chromium and molybdenum

CHROMOUS *adj* pertaining to chromium

CHROMY *adj* **CHROMIER, CHROMIEST** decorated with chrome

CHROMYL *n* pl. **-S** a bivalent radical

CHRONAXY *n* pl. **-AXIES** the time required to excite a nerve cell electrically

CHRONIC *n* pl. **-S** one that suffers from a long-lasting disease

CHRONON *n* pl. **-S** a hypothetical unit of time

CHTHONIC *adj* pertaining to the gods of the underworld

CHUB *n* pl. **-S** a freshwater fish

CHUBASCO *n* pl. **-COS** a violent thunderstorm

CHUBBY *adj* **-BIER, -BIEST** plump **CHUBBILY** *adv*

CHUCK *v* **-ED, -ING, -S** to throw

CHUCKER *n* pl. **-S** one that chucks

CHUCKIES pl. of chucky

CHUCKLE *v* **-LED, -LING, -LES** to laugh quietly

CHUCKLER *n* pl. **-S** one that chuckles

CHUCKY *n* pl. **CHUCKIES** a little chick

CHUDDAH *n* pl. **-S** chuddar

CHUDDAR *n* pl. **-S** a large, square shawl

CHUDDER *n* pl. **-S** chuddar

CHUFA *n* pl. **-S** a European sedge

CHUFF *adj* **CHUFFER, CHUFFEST** gruff

CHUFF *v* **-ED, -ING, -S** to chug

CHUFFY *adj* **-FIER, -FIEST** plump

CHUG *v* **CHUGGED, CHUGGING, CHUGS** to move with a dull explosive sound

CHUGALUG *v* **-LUGGED, -LUGGING, -LUGS** to drink without pause

CHUGGER *n* pl. **-S** one that chugs

CHUKAR *n* pl. **-S** a game bird

CHUKKA *n* pl. **-S** a type of boot

CHUKKAR *n* pl. **-S** a chukker

CHUKKER *n* pl. **-S** a period of play in polo

CHUM *v* **CHUMMED, CHUMMING, CHUMS** to be close friends with someone

CHUMMY *adj* **-MIER, -MIEST** friendly **CHUMMILY** *adv*

CHUMP *v* **-ED, -ING, -S** to munch

CHUMSHIP *n* pl. **-S** friendship

CHUNDER *v* **-ED, -ING, -S** to vomit

CHUNK *v* **-ED, -ING, -S** to make a dull explosive sound

CHUNKY *adj* **CHUNKIER, CHUNKIEST** stocky **CHUNKILY** *adv*

CHUNNEL *n* pl. **-S** a tunnel under the English Channel

CHUNTER *v* **-ED, -ING, -S** to mutter

CHUPPA *n* pl. **CHUPPAS** or **CHUPPOT** chuppah

CHUPPAH *n* pl. **CHUPPAHS** or **CHUPPOT** a canopy used at a Jewish wedding

CHURCH *v* **-ED, -ING, -ES** to bring to church (a building for Christian worship)

CHURCHLY *adj* **-LIER, -LIEST** pertaining to a church

CHURCHY *adj* **CHURCHIER, CHURCHIEST** churchly

CHURINGA *n* pl. **-S** a sacred object of Australian Aboriginals

CHURL *n* pl. **-S** a rude person **CHURLISH** *adj*

CHURN *v* **-ED, -ING, -S** to stir briskly in order to make butter

CHURNER *n* pl. **-S** one that churns

CHURNING *n* pl. **-S** the butter churned at one time

CHURR *v* **-ED, -ING, -S** to make a vibrant sound

CHURRO *n* pl. **-ROS** a Spanish and Mexican pastry

CHUSE *v* **CHUSED, CHUSING, CHUSES** to choose

CHUTE *v* **CHUTED, CHUTING, CHUTES** to convey by chute (a vertical passage)

CHUTIST *n* pl. **-S** a parachutist

CHUTNEE *n* pl. **-S** chutney

CHUTNEY *n* pl. **-NEYS** a sweet and sour sauce

CHUTZPA *n* pl. **-S** chutzpah

CHUTZPAH *n* pl. **-S** supreme self-confidence

CHYLE *n* pl. **-S** a digestive fluid **CHYLOUS** *adj*

CHYME *n* pl. **-S** semi-digested food

CHYMIC *n* pl. **-S** chemic

CHYMIST *n* pl. **-S** chemist

CHYMOSIN *n* pl. **-S** rennin

CHYMOUS *adj* pertaining to chyme

CHYTRID *n* pl. **-S** an aquatic or soil fungus

CIABATTA *n* pl. **-S** a type of Italian bread

CIAO *interj* — used as an expression of greeting and farewell

CIBOL *n* pl. **-S** a variety of onion

CIBORIUM *n* pl. **-RIA** a vessel for holding holy bread

CIBOULE *n* pl. **-S** cibol

CICADA *n* pl. **-DAS** or **-DAE** a winged insect

CICALA *n* pl. **-LAS** or **-LE** cicada

CICATRIX *n* pl. **-TRIXES** or **-TRICES** scar tissue

CICELY *n* pl. **-LIES** a fragrant herb

CICERO *n* pl. **-ROS** a unit of measure in printing

CICERONE *n* pl. **-NES** or **-NI** a tour guide

CICHLID *n* pl. **-LIDS** or **-LIDAE** a tropical fish

CICISBEO *n* pl. **-BEOS** or **-BEI** a lover of a married woman

CICOREE *n* pl. **-S** a perennial herb

CIDER *n* pl. **-S** the juice pressed from apples

CIG *n* pl. **-S** a cigarette

CIGAR *n* pl. **-S** a roll of tobacco leaf for smoking

CIGARET *n* pl. **-S** a cigarette

CIGGIE *n* pl. **-S** a cigarette

CIGGY *n* pl. **CIGGIES** ciggie

CILANTRO *n* pl. **-TROS** an herb used in cooking

CILIA pl. of cilium

CILIARY *adj* pertaining to cilia

CILIATE *n* pl. **-S** one of a class of ciliated protozoans

CILIATED *adj* having cilia

CILICE *n* pl. **-S** a coarse cloth

CILIUM *n* pl. **CILIA** a short, hairlike projection

CIMBALOM *n* pl. **-S** a Hungarian dulcimer

CIMEX *n* pl. **-MICES** a bedbug

CINCH *v* **-ED, -ING, -ES** to girth

CINCHONA *n* pl. **-S** a Peruvian tree

CINCTURE *v* **-TURED, -TURING, -TURES** to gird or encircle

CINDER *v* **-ED, -ING, -S** to reduce to cinders (ashes)

CINDERY *adj* containing cinders

CINE *n* pl. **-S** a motion picture

CINEAST *n* pl. **-S** a devotee of motion pictures

CINEASTE *n* pl. **-S** cineast

CINEMA *n* pl. **-S** a motion-picture theater

CINEOL *n* pl. **-S** a liquid used as an antiseptic

CINEOLE *n* pl. **-S** cineol

CINERARY *adj* used for cremated ashes

CINERIN *n* pl. **-S** a compound used in insecticides

CINGULUM *n* pl. **-LA** an anatomical band or girdle **CINGULAR** *adj*

CINNABAR *n* pl. **-S** the principal ore of mercury

CINNAMON *n* pl. **-S** a spice obtained from tree bark **CINNAMIC** *adj*

CINNAMYL *n* pl. **-S** a chemical used to make soap

CINQ *n* pl. **-S** cinque

CINQUAIN *n* pl. **-S** a stanza of five lines

CINQUE *n* pl. **-S** the number five

CION *n* pl. **-S** a cutting from a plant or tree

CIOPPINO *n* pl. **-NOS** a spicy fish stew

CIPAILLE *n* pl. **-S** a pie with layers of meat and pastry

CIPHER *v* **-ED, -ING, -S** to solve problems in arithmetic

CIPHERER *n* pl. **-S** one that ciphers

CIPHONY *n* pl. **-NIES** the electronic scrambling of voice transmissions

CIPOLIN *n* pl. **-S** a type of marble

CIRCA *prep* about; around

CIRCLE *v* **-CLED, -CLING, -CLES** to move or revolve around

CIRCLER *n* pl. **-S** one that circles

CIRCLET *n* pl. **-S** a small ring or ring-shaped object

CIRCS *n/pl* circumstances

CIRCUIT *v* **-ED, -ING, -S** to move around

CIRCUITY *n* pl. **-ITIES** lack of straightforwardness

CIRCULAR *n* pl. **-S** a leaflet intended for wide distribution

CIRCUS *n* pl. **-ES** a public entertainment **CIRCUSY** *adj*

CIRE *n* pl. **-S** a highly glazed finish for fabrics

CIRQUE *n* pl. **-S** a deep, steep-walled basin on a mountain

CIRRATE *adj* having cirri

CIRRI pl. of cirrus

CIRRIPED *n* pl. **-S** any of an order of crustaceans

CIRROSE *adj* cirrous

CIRROUS *adj* having cirri

CIRRUS *n* pl. **-RI** a tendril or similar part

CIRSOID *adj* varicose

CIS *adj* having certain atoms on the same side of the molecule

CISCO *n* pl. **-COS** or **-COES** a freshwater fish

CISLUNAR *adj* situated between the earth and the moon

CISSOID *n* pl. **-S** a type of geometric curve

CISSY *n* pl. **-SIES** sissy

CIST *n* pl. **-S** a prehistoric stone coffin **CISTED** *adj*

CISTERN *n* pl. **-S** a water tank

CISTERNA *n* pl. **-NAE** a fluid-containing sac

CISTRON *n* pl. **-S** a segment of DNA

CISTUS *n* pl. **-ES** a flowering shrub

CITABLE *adj* citeable

CITADEL	*n* pl. **-S** a fortress or stronghold
CITATION	*n* pl. **-S** the act of citing **CITATORY** *adj*
CITATOR	*n* pl. **-S** one that cites
CITE	*v* **CITED, CITING, CITES** to quote as an authority or example
CITEABLE	*adj* suitable for citation
CITER	*n* pl. **-S** one that cites
CITHARA	*n* pl. **-S** an ancient stringed instrument
CITHER	*n* pl. **-S** cittern
CITHERN	*n* pl. **-S** cittern
CITHREN	*n* pl. **-S** cittern
CITIED	*adj* having cities
CITIES	pl. of city
CITIFY	*v* **-FIED, -FYING, -FIES** to urbanize
CITING	present participle of cite
CITIZEN	*n* pl. **-S** a resident of a city or town
CITOLA	*n* pl. **-S** a cittern
CITOLE	*n* pl. **-S** citola
CITRAL	*n* pl. **-S** a lemon flavoring
CITRATE	*n* pl. **-S** a salt of citric acid **CITRATED** *adj*
CITREOUS	*adj* having a lemonlike color
CITRIC	*adj* derived from citrus fruits
CITRIN	*n* pl. **-S** a citric vitamin
CITRINE	*n* pl. **-S** a variety of quartz
CITRININ	*n* pl. **-S** an antibiotic
CITRON	*n* pl. **-S** a lemonlike fruit
CITROUS	*adj* pertaining to a citrus tree
CITRUS	*n* pl. **-ES** any of a genus of tropical, fruit-bearing trees **CITRUSY** *adj*
CITTERN	*n* pl. **-S** a pear-shaped guitar
CITY	*n* pl. **CITIES** a large town
CITYFIED	*adj* having the customs and manners of city people
CITYWARD	*adv* toward the city
CITYWIDE	*adj* including all parts of a city
CIVET	*n* pl. **-S** a catlike mammal
CIVIC	*adj* pertaining to a city
CIVICISM	*n* pl. **-S** a system of government based upon individual rights
CIVICS	*n/pl* the science of civic affairs
CIVIE	*n* pl. **-S** civvy
CIVIL	*adj* pertaining to citizens
CIVILIAN	*n* pl. **-S** a nonmilitary person

CIVILISE	*v* **-LISED, -LISING, -LISES** to civilize
CIVILITY	*n* pl. **-TIES** courtesy; politeness
CIVILIZE	*v* **-LIZED, -LIZING, -LIZES** to bring out of savagery
CIVILLY	*adv* politely
CIVISM	*n* pl. **-S** good citizenship
CIVVY	*n* pl. **-VIES** a civilian
CLABBER	*v* **-ED, -ING, -S** to curdle
CLACH	*n* pl. **-S** clachan
CLACHAN	*n* pl. **-S** a hamlet
CLACK	*v* **-ED, -ING, -S** to make an abrupt, dry sound
CLACKER	*n* pl. **-S** one that clacks
CLAD	*v* **CLADDED, CLADDING, CLADS** to coat one metal over another
CLADDAGH	*n* pl. **-S** a ring designed with two hands clasping
CLADDING	*n* pl. **-S** something that overlays
CLADE	*n* pl. **-S** a group of biological taxa
CLADISM	*n* pl. **-S** the method of a cladist
CLADIST	*n* pl. **-S** a taxonomist who uses clades in classifying life-forms
CLADODE	*n* pl. **-S** a leaflike part of a stem
CLAFOUTI	*n* pl. **-S** a dessert consisting of a layer of fruit topped with batter and baked
CLAG	*v* **CLAGGED, CLAGGING, CLAGS** to clog
CLAIM	*v* **-ED, -ING, -S** to demand as one's due
CLAIMANT	*n* pl. **-S** one that asserts a right or title
CLAIMER	*n* pl. **-S** one that claims
CLAM	*v* **CLAMMED, CLAMMING, CLAMS** to dig for clams (bivalve mollusks)
CLAMANT	*adj* noisy
CLAMBAKE	*n* pl. **-S** a beach picnic
CLAMBER	*v* **-ED, -ING, -S** to climb awkwardly
CLAMLIKE	*adj* resembling a clam
CLAMMED	past tense of clam
CLAMMER	*n* pl. **-S** one that clams
CLAMMING	present participle of clam
CLAMMY	*adj* **-MIER, -MIEST** cold and damp **CLAMMILY** *adv*
CLAMOR	*v* **-ED, -ING, -S** to make loud outcries
CLAMORER	*n* pl. **-S** one that clamors

CLAMOUR v **-ED, -ING, -S** to clamor

CLAMP v **-ED, -ING, -S** to fasten with a clamp (a securing device)

CLAMPER n pl. **-S** a device worn on shoes to prevent slipping on ice

CLAMWORM n pl. **-S** a marine worm

CLAN n pl. **-S** a united group of families

CLANG v **-ED, -ING, -S** to ring loudly

CLANGER n pl. **-S** a blunder

CLANGOR v **-ED, -ING, -S** to clang repeatedly

CLANGOUR v **-ED, -ING, -S** to clangor

CLANK v **-ED, -ING, -S** to make a sharp, metallic sound

CLANKY adj **CLANKIER, CLANKIEST** making a sharp, metallic sound

CLANNISH adj characteristic of a clan

CLANSMAN n pl. **-MEN** a member of a clan

CLAP v **CLAPPED** or **CLAPT, CLAPPING, CLAPS** to strike one palm against the other

CLAPPER n pl. **-S** one that claps

CLAPTRAP n pl. **-S** pretentious language

CLAQUE n pl. **-S** a group of hired applauders

CLAQUER n pl. **-S** claqueur

CLAQUEUR n pl. **-S** a member of a claque

CLARENCE n pl. **-S** a closed carriage

CLARET n pl. **-S** a dry red wine

CLARIES pl. of clary

CLARIFY v **-FIED, -FYING, -FIES** to make clear

CLARINET n pl. **-S** a woodwind instrument

CLARION v **-ED, -ING, -S** to proclaim by blowing a medieval trumpet

CLARITY n pl. **-TIES** the state of being clear

CLARKIA n pl. **-S** an annual herb

CLARO n pl. **-ROS** or **-ROES** a mild cigar

CLARY n pl. **CLARIES** an aromatic herb

CLASH v **-ED, -ING, -ES** to conflict or disagree

CLASHER n pl. **-S** one that clashes

CLASP v **CLASPED** or **CLASPT, CLASPING, CLASPS** to embrace tightly

CLASPER n pl. **-S** one that clasps

CLASS v **-ED, -ING, -ES** to classify

CLASSER n pl. **-S** one that classes

CLASSES pl. of classis

CLASSIC n pl. **-S** a work of enduring excellence

CLASSICO adj made from grapes grown in a certain part of Italy

CLASSIER comparative of classy

CLASSIEST superlative of classy

CLASSIFY v **-FIED, -FYING, -FIES** to arrange according to characteristics

CLASSILY adv in a classy manner

CLASSIS n pl. **CLASSES** a governing body in certain churches

CLASSISM n pl. **-S** discrimination based on social class

CLASSIST n pl. **-S** an advocate of classism

CLASSON n pl. **-S** a subatomic particle

CLASSY adj **CLASSIER, CLASSIEST** stylish; elegant

CLAST n pl. **-S** a fragment of rock

CLASTIC n pl. **-S** a rock made up of other rocks

CLATTER v **-ED, -ING, -S** to move with a rattling noise

CLATTERY adj having a rattling noise

CLAUCHT a past tense of cleek

CLAUGHT v **-ED, -ING, -S** to clutch

CLAUSE n pl. **-S** a distinct part of a composition **CLAUSAL** adj

CLAUSTRA n/pl basal ganglia in the brain

CLAVATE adj shaped like a club

CLAVE n pl. **-S** one of a pair of percussion sticks

CLAVER v **-ED, -ING, -S** to gossip

CLAVI pl. of clavus

CLAVICLE n pl. **-S** a bone of the shoulder

CLAVIER n pl. **-S** a keyboard instrument

CLAVUS n pl. **-VI** a horny thickening of the skin

CLAW v **-ED, -ING, -S** to scratch with claws (sharp, curved toenails)

CLAWBACK n pl. **-S** money taken back by taxation

CLAWER n pl. **-S** one that claws

CLAWLESS adj having no claws

CLAWLIKE adj resembling a claw

CLAXON n pl. **-S** klaxon

CLAY v **-ED, -ING, -S** to treat with clay (a fine-grained, earthy material)

CLAYBANK n pl. **-S** a yellow-brown color

CLAYEY *adj* **CLAYIER, CLAYIEST** resembling clay

CLAYISH *adj* resembling or containing clay

CLAYLIKE *adj* resembling clay

CLAYMORE *n* pl. **-S** a type of sword

CLAYPAN *n* pl. **-S** a shallow natural depression

CLAYWARE *n* pl. **-S** pottery

CLEAN *adj* **CLEANER, CLEANEST** free from dirt or stain **CLEANISH** *adj*

CLEAN *v* **-ED, -ING, -S** to rid of dirt or stain

CLEANER *n* pl. **-S** one that cleans

CLEANING *n* pl. **-S** the act of ridding of dirt or stain

CLEANLY *adj* **-LIER, -LIEST** habitually clean

CLEANOUT *n* pl. **-S** the act of cleaning something out

CLEANSE *v* **CLEANSED, CLEANSING, CLEANSES** to clean

CLEANSER *n* pl. **-S** one that cleanses

CLEANUP *n* pl. **-S** an act of cleaning

CLEAR *adj* **CLEARER, CLEAREST** clean and pure

CLEAR *v* **-ED, -ING, -S** to remove obstructions

CLEARCUT *v* **-CUT, -CUTTING, -CUTS** to cut a forest completely

CLEARER *n* pl. **-S** one that clears

CLEARING *n* pl. **-S** an open space

CLEARLY *adv* in a clear manner

CLEAROUT *n* pl. **-S** the action of removing unwanted material from a place

CLEARWAY *n* pl. **-WAYS** a road on which stopping is not permitted

CLEAT *v* **-ED, -ING, -S** to strengthen with a strip of wood or iron

CLEAVAGE *n* pl. **-S** the act of cleaving

CLEAVE *v* **CLEAVED** or **CLEFT** or **CLOVE** or **CLAVE, CLOVEN, CLEAVING, CLEAVES** to split or divide

CLEAVER *n* pl. **-S** a heavy knife

CLEEK *v* **CLAUCHT** or **CLEEKED, CLEEKING, CLEEKS** to clutch

CLEF *n* pl. **-S** a musical symbol

CLEFT *v* **-ED, -ING, -S** to insert a scion into the stock of a plant

CLEG *n* pl. **-S** a horsefly

CLEIDOIC *adj* enclosed in a shell

CLEMATIS *n* pl. **-TISES** a flowering vine

CLEMENCY *n* pl. **-CIES** mercy

CLEMENT *adj* merciful

CLENCH *v* **-ED, -ING, -ES** to grasp firmly

CLENCHER *n* pl. **-S** one that clenches

CLEOME *n* pl. **-S** a tropical plant

CLEPE *v* **CLEPED** or **CLEPT, CLEPING, CLEPES** to call by name

CLERGY *n* pl. **-GIES** the body of persons ordained for religious service

CLERIC *n* pl. **-S** a member of the clergy

CLERICAL *n* pl. **-S** a cleric

CLERID *n* pl. **-S** a predatory beetle

CLERIHEW *n* pl. **-S** a humorous poem

CLERISY *n* pl. **-SIES** the well-educated class

CLERK *v* **-ED, -ING, -S** to serve as a clerk (an office worker)

CLERKDOM *n* pl. **-S** the status or function of a clerk

CLERKISH *adj* resembling or suitable to a clerk

CLERKLY *adj* **-LIER, -LIEST** pertaining to a clerk

CLEVEITE *n* pl. **-S** a radioactive mineral

CLEVER *adj* **-ERER, -EREST** mentally keen **CLEVERLY** *adv*

CLEVIS *n* pl. **-ISES** a metal fastening device

CLEW *v* **-ED, -ING, -S** to roll into a ball

CLICHE *n* pl. **-S** a trite expression **CLICHED** *adj*

CLICK *v* **-ED, -ING, -S** to make a short, sharp sound

CLICKER *n* pl. **-S** one that clicks

CLIENT *n* pl. **-S** a customer **CLIENTAL** *adj*

CLIFF *n* pl. **-S** a high, steep face of rock

CLIFFTOP *n* pl. **-S** the top of a cliff

CLIFFY *adj* **CLIFFIER, CLIFFIEST** abounding in cliffs

CLIFT *n* pl. **-S** cliff

CLIMATE *n* pl. **-S** the weather conditions characteristic of an area **CLIMATAL, CLIMATIC** *adj*

CLIMAX *v* **-ED, -ING, -ES** to reach a high or dramatic point

CLIMB *v* **CLIMBED** or **CLOMB, CLIMBING, CLIMBS** to ascend

CLIMBER *n* pl. **-S** one that climbs

CLIMBING n pl. **-S** the sport or activity of ascending mountains

CLIME n pl. **-S** climate

CLINAL adj pertaining to a cline

CLINALLY adv in a clinal manner

CLINCH v **-ED, -ING, -ES** to settle a matter decisively

CLINCHER n pl. **-S** a decisive fact or remark

CLINE n pl. **-S** a series of changes within a species

CLING v **-ED, -ING, -S** to make a high-pitched ringing sound

CLING v **CLUNG, CLINGING, CLINGS** to adhere closely

CLINGER n pl. **-S** one that clings

CLINGY adj **CLINGIER, CLINGIEST** adhesive

CLINIC n pl. **-S** a medical facility **CLINICAL** adj

CLINK v **-ED, -ING, -S** to make a soft, sharp, ringing sound

CLINKER v **-ED, -ING, -S** to form fused residue in burning

CLIP v **CLIPPED** or **CLIPT, CLIPPING, CLIPS** to trim by cutting

CLIPPER n pl. **-S** one that clips

CLIPPING n pl. **-S** something that is clipped out or off

CLIPT a past participle of clip

CLIQUE v **CLIQUED, CLIQUING, CLIQUES** to form a clique (an exclusive group of persons)

CLIQUEY adj **CLIQUIER, CLIQUIEST** inclined to form cliques

CLIQUISH adj cliquey

CLIQUY adj **CLIQUIER, CLIQUIEST** cliquey

CLITELLA n/pl regions in the body walls of certain annelids

CLITIC n pl. **-S** a word pronounced as part of a neighboring word

CLITORIS n pl. **-RISES** or **-RIDES** a sex organ **CLITORAL, CLITORIC** adj

CLITTER v **-ED, -ING, -S** to make a thin rattling sound

CLIVERS n pl. **CLIVERS** an annual herb

CLIVIA n pl. **-S** a flowering plant

CLOACA n pl. **-ACAS** or **-ACAE** a sewer **CLOACAL** adj

CLOAK v **-ED, -ING, -S** to conceal

CLOBBER v **-ED, -ING, -S** to trounce

CLOCHARD n pl. **-S** a vagrant

CLOCHE n pl. **-S** a bell-shaped hat

CLOCK v **-ED, -ING, -S** to time with a stopwatch

CLOCKER n pl. **-S** one that clocks

CLOD n pl. **-S** a dolt **CLODDISH** adj

CLODDY adj **-DIER, -DIEST** lumpy

CLODPATE n pl. **-S** a stupid person

CLODPOLE n pl. **-S** clodpate

CLODPOLL n pl. **-S** clodpate

CLOG v **CLOGGED, CLOGGING, CLOGS** to block up or obstruct

CLOGGER n pl. **-S** one that clogs

CLOGGING n pl. **-S** the act of dancing while wearing shoes with thick wooden soles

CLOGGY adj **-GIER, -GIEST** clogging or able to clog **CLOGGILY** adv

CLOISTER v **-ED, -ING, -S** to seclude

CLOMB a past tense of climb

CLOMP v **-ED, -ING, -S** to walk heavily and clumsily

CLON n pl. **-S** a group of asexually derived organisms **CLONAL** adj **CLONALLY** adv

CLONE v **CLONED, CLONING, CLONES** to reproduce by asexual means

CLONER n pl. **-S** one that clones

CLONIC adj pertaining to clonus

CLONING n pl. **-S** a technique for reproducing by asexual means

CLONISM n pl. **-S** the condition of having clonus

CLONK v **-ED, -ING, -S** to make a dull thumping sound

CLONKY adj **CLONKIER, CLONKIEST** making a dull thumping sound

CLONUS n pl. **-ES** a form of muscular spasm

CLOOT n pl. **-S** a cloven hoof

CLOP v **CLOPPED, CLOPPING, CLOPS** to make the sound of a hoof striking pavement

CLOQUE n pl. **-S** a fabric with an embossed design

CLOSE adj **CLOSER, CLOSEST** near **CLOSELY** adv

CLOSE v **CLOSED, CLOSING, CLOSES** to block against entry or passage **CLOSABLE** adj

CLOSEOUT n pl. **-S** a clearance sale

CLOSER	*n* pl. **-S** one that closes	**CLUB**	*v* **CLUBBED, CLUBBING, CLUBS** to form a club (an organized group of persons)
CLOSEST	superlative of close		
CLOSET	*v* **-ED, -ING, -S** to enclose in a private room	**CLUBABLE**	*adj* sociable
CLOSEUP	*n* pl. **-S** a photograph taken at close range	**CLUBBER**	*n* pl. **-S** a member of a club
		CLUBBING	*n* pl. **-S** the practice of frequenting nightclubs
CLOSING	*n* pl. **-S** a concluding part	**CLUBBISH**	*adj* clubby
CLOSURE	*v* **-SURED, -SURING, -SURES** to cloture	**CLUBBY**	*adj* **-BIER, -BIEST** characteristic of a club
CLOT	*v* **CLOTTED, CLOTTING, CLOTS** to form into a clot (a thick mass)	**CLUBFACE**	*n* pl. **-S** the striking surface of a clubhead
CLOTBUR	*n* pl. **-S** a type of plant with prickly seeds	**CLUBFOOT**	*n* pl. **-FEET** a deformed foot
		CLUBHAND	*n* pl. **-S** a deformed hand
CLOTH	*n* pl. **-S** fabric	**CLUBHAUL**	*v* **-ED, -ING, -S** to put a vessel about
CLOTHE	*v* **CLOTHED** or **CLAD, CLOTHING, CLOTHES** to provide with clothing	**CLUBHEAD**	*n* pl. **-S** the part of a golf club that strikes the ball
CLOTHIER	*n* pl. **-S** one who makes or sells clothing	**CLUBLAND**	*n* pl. **-S** an area having many nightclubs
CLOTHING	*n* pl. **-S** wearing apparel	**CLUBMAN**	*n* pl. **-MEN** a male member of a club
CLOTTED	past tense of clot	**CLUBMATE**	*n* pl. **-S** a fellow member of a club
CLOTTING	present participle of clot	**CLUBMOSS**	*n* pl. **-ES** a green plant resembling a large moss
CLOTTY	*adj* tending to clot		
CLOTURE	*v* **-TURED, -TURING, -TURES** to end a debate by calling for a vote	**CLUBROOM**	*n* pl. **-S** a room for a club's meetings
CLOUD	*v* **-ED, -ING, -S** to cover with clouds (masses of visible vapor)	**CLUBROOT**	*n* pl. **-S** a plant disease
		CLUCK	*v* **-ED, -ING, -S** to make the sound of a hen
CLOUDLET	*n* pl. **-S** a small cloud		
CLOUDY	*adj* **CLOUDIER, CLOUDIEST** overcast with clouds **CLOUDILY** *adv*	**CLUCKER**	*n* pl. **-S** a chicken
		CLUE	*v* **CLUED, CLUEING** or **CLUING, CLUES** to give guiding information
CLOUGH	*n* pl. **-S** a ravine	**CLUELESS**	*adj* hopelessly confused or ignorant
CLOUR	*v* **-ED, -ING, -S** to knock or bump		
CLOUT	*v* **-ED, -ING, -S** to hit with the hand	**CLUMBER**	*n* pl. **-S** a stocky spaniel
CLOUTER	*n* pl. **-S** one that clouts	**CLUMP**	*v* **-ED, -ING, -S** to form into a thick mass
CLOVE	*n* pl. **-S** a spice	**CLUMPER**	*n* pl. **-S** a large floating chunk of ice
CLOVEN	a past participle of cleave	**CLUMPET**	*n* pl. **-S** a clumper
CLOVER	*n* pl. **-S** a plant **CLOVERED, CLOVERY** *adj*	**CLUMPISH**	*adj* resembling a clump (a thick mass)
CLOWDER	*n* pl. **-S** a group of cats	**CLUMPY**	*adj* **CLUMPIER, CLUMPIEST** lumpy
CLOWN	*v* **-ED, -ING, -S** to act like a clown (a humorous performer)	**CLUMSY**	*adj* **-SIER, -SIEST** awkward **CLUMSILY** *adv*
CLOWNERY	*n* pl. **-ERIES** clownish behavior		
CLOWNISH	*adj* resembling or befitting a clown	**CLUNG**	past tense of cling
CLOY	*v* **-ED, -ING, -S** to gratify beyond desire	**CLUNK**	*v* **-ED, -ING, -S** to thump
		CLUNKER	*n* pl. **-S** a jalopy
CLOZE	*n* pl. **-S** a test of reading comprehension	**CLUNKY**	*adj* **CLUNKIER, CLUNKIEST** clumsy in style

CLUPEID *n* pl. **-S** a fish of the herring family

CLUPEOID *n* pl. **-S** a clupeid

CLUSTER *v* **-ED, -ING, -S** to form into a cluster (a group of similar objects)

CLUSTERY *adj* pertaining to a cluster

CLUTCH *v* **-ED, -ING, -ES** to grasp and hold tightly

CLUTCHY *adj* tending to clutch

CLUTTER *v* **-ED, -ING, -S** to pile in a disorderly state

CLUTTERY *adj* characterized by disorder

CLYPEUS *n* pl. **CLYPEI** a shield-like structure **CLYPEAL, CLYPEATE** *adj*

CLYSTER *n* pl. **-S** an enema

CNIDA *n* pl. **-DAE** a stinging organ in a jellyfish

COACH *v* **-ED, -ING, -ES** to tutor or train

COACHER *n* pl. **-S** one that coaches

COACHING *n* pl. **-S** the work of one that coaches

COACHMAN *n* pl. **-MEN** one who drives a coach or carriage

COACT *v* **-ED, -ING, -S** to act together

COACTION *n* pl. **-S** joint action

COACTIVE *adj* mutually active

COACTOR *n* pl. **-S** a fellow actor in a production

COADMIRE *v* **-MIRED, -MIRING, -MIRES** to admire together

COADMIT *v* **-MITTED, -MITTING, -MITS** to admit several things equally

COADY *n* pl. **-DIES** a sauce made from molasses

COAEVAL *n* pl. **-S** coeval

COAGENCY *n* pl. **-CIES** a joint agency

COAGENT *n* pl. **-S** a person, force, or other agent working together with another

COAGULUM *n* pl. **-LUMS** or **-LA** a clot

COAL *v* **-ED, -ING, -S** to supply with coal (a carbon fuel)

COALA *n* pl. **-S** koala

COALBIN *n* pl. **-S** a bin for storing coal

COALBOX *n* pl. **-ES** a box for storing coal

COALER *n* pl. **-S** one that supplies coal

COALESCE *v* **-ALESCED, -ALESCING, -ALESCES** to blend

COALFACE *n* pl. **-S** the place where coal is cut out of the rock

COALFISH *n* pl. **-ES** a blackish fish

COALHOLE *n* pl. **-S** a compartment for storing coal

COALIER comparative of coaly

COALIEST superlative of coaly

COALIFY *v* **-FIED, -FYING, -FIES** to convert into coal

COALLESS *adj* lacking coal

COALPIT *n* pl. **-S** a pit from which coal is obtained

COALSACK *n* pl. **-S** a dark region of the Milky Way

COALSHED *n* pl. **-S** a shed for storing coal

COALY *adj* **COALIER, COALIEST** containing coal

COALYARD *n* pl. **-S** a yard for storing coal

COAMING *n* pl. **-S** a raised border

COANCHOR *v* **-ED, -ING, -S** to present televised news reports jointly

COANNEX *v* **-ED, -ING, -ES** to annex jointly

COAPPEAR *v* **-ED, -ING, -S** to appear together or at the same time

COAPT *v* **-ED, -ING, -S** to fit together and make fast

COARSE *adj* **COARSER, COARSEST** rough **COARSELY** *adv* **COARSISH** *adj*

COARSEN *v* **-ED, -ING, -S** to make coarse

COASSIST *v* **-ED, -ING, -S** to assist jointly

COASSUME *v* **-SUMED, -SUMING, -SUMES** to assume together

COAST *v* **-ED, -ING, -S** to slide down a hill

COASTAL *adj* pertaining to or located near a seashore

COASTER *n* pl. **-S** a sled

COASTING *n* pl. **-S** coastal trade

COAT *v* **-ED, -ING, -S** to cover with a coat (an outer garment)

COATEE *n* pl. **-S** a small coat

COATER *n* pl. **-S** one that coats

COATI *n* pl. **-S** a tropical mammal

COATING *n* pl. **-S** a covering layer

COATLESS *adj* lacking a coat

COATRACK *n* pl. **-S** a rack or stand for coats

COATROOM *n* pl. **-S** a room for storing coats

COATTAIL *n* pl. **-S** the back lower portion of a coat

COATTEND *v* **-ED, -ING, -S** to attend together

COATTEST *v* **-ED, -ING, -S** to attest jointly

COAUTHOR	v -**ED, -ING, -S** to write together
COAX	v -**ED, -ING, -ES** to cajole
COAXAL	adj coaxial
COAXER	n pl. -**S** one that coaxes
COAXIAL	adj having a common axis
COAXING	n pl. -**S** an act of cajoling
COB	n pl. -**S** a corncob
COBALT	n pl. -**S** a metallic element **COBALTIC** adj
COBB	n pl. -**S** a seagull
COBBER	n pl. -**S** a comrade
COBBIER	comparative of cobby
COBBIEST	superlative of cobby
COBBLE	v -**BLED, -BLING, -BLES** to mend
COBBLER	n pl. -**S** a mender of shoes
COBBY	adj -**BIER, -BIEST** stocky
COBIA	n pl. -**S** a large game fish
COBLE	n pl. -**S** a small fishing boat
COBNUT	n pl. -**S** an edible nut
COBRA	n pl. -**S** a venomous snake
COBWEB	v -**WEBBED, -WEBBING, -WEBS** to cover with cobwebs (spider webs)
COBWEBBY	adj -**BIER, -BIEST** covered with cobwebs
COCA	n pl. -**S** a South American shrub
COCAIN	n pl. -**S** cocaine
COCAINE	n pl. -**S** a narcotic alkaloid
COCCAL	adj pertaining to a coccus
COCCI	pl. of coccus
COCCIC	adj coccal
COCCID	n pl. -**S** an insect
COCCIDIA	n/pl parasitic protozoans
COCCOID	n pl. -**S** a spherical cell or body
COCCUS	n pl. **COCCI** a spherical bacterium **COCCOUS** adj
COCCYX	n pl. -**CYXES** or -**CYGES** a bone of the spine
COCHAIR	v -**ED, -ING, -S** to serve jointly as chairman of
COCHIN	n pl. -**S** a large domestic chicken
COCHLEA	n pl. -**CHLEAS** or -**CHLEAE** a part of the ear **COCHLEAR** adj
COCINERA	n pl. -**S** a cook
COCK	v -**ED, -ING, -S** to tilt to one side
COCKADE	n pl. -**S** an ornament worn on a hat **COCKADED** adj
COCKAPOO	n pl. -**POOS** a hybrid between a cocker spaniel and a poodle
COCKATOO	n pl. -**TOOS** a parrot
COCKBILL	v -**ED, -ING, -S** to raise the yardarm on a ship
COCKBOAT	n pl. -**S** a small boat
COCKCROW	n pl. -**S** daybreak
COCKER	v -**ED, -ING, -S** to pamper
COCKEREL	n pl. -**S** a young rooster
COCKEYE	n pl. -**S** a squinting eye **COCKEYED** adj
COCKIER	comparative of cocky
COCKIES	pl. of cocky
COCKIEST	superlative of cocky
COCKILY	adv in a cocky manner
COCKISH	adj cocky
COCKLE	v -**LED, -LING, -LES** to wrinkle or pucker
COCKLIKE	adj resembling a rooster
COCKLOFT	n pl. -**S** a small attic
COCKNEY	n pl. -**NEYS** a resident of the East End of London
COCKPIT	n pl. -**S** a pilot's compartment in certain airplanes
COCKSHUT	n pl. -**S** the close of day
COCKSHY	n pl. -**SHIES** a target in a throwing contest
COCKSPUR	n pl. -**S** a thorny plant
COCKSURE	adj certain
COCKTAIL	v -**ED, -ING, -S** to drink alcoholic beverages
COCKUP	n pl. -**S** a turned-up part of something
COCKY	adj **COCKIER, COCKIEST** arrogantly self-confident
COCKY	n pl. **COCKIES** a cockatoo
COCO	n pl. -**COS** a tall palm tree
COCOA	n pl. -**S** chocolate
COCOANUT	n pl. -**S** coconut
COCOBOLA	n pl. -**S** cocobolo
COCOBOLO	n pl. -**LOS** a tropical tree
COCOMAT	n pl. -**S** a matting made from coir
COCONUT	n pl. -**S** the fruit of the coco
COCOON	v -**ED, -ING, -S** to wrap or envelop tightly
COCOONER	n pl. -**S** one who retreats to the private world of the family
COCOPLUM	n pl. -**S** an evergreen shrub

COCOTTE *n* pl. **-S** a prostitute

COCOYAM *n* pl. **-S** a tropical plant having edible rootstocks

COCREATE *v* **-ATED, -ATING, -ATES** to create together

COD *v* **CODDED, CODDING, CODS** to fool

CODA *n* pl. **-S** a passage at the end of a musical composition

CODABLE *adj* capable of being coded

CODDER *n* pl. **-S** a cod fisherman

CODDING present participle of cod

CODDLE *v* **-DLED, -DLING, -DLES** to pamper

CODDLER *n* pl. **-S** one that coddles

CODE *v* **CODED, CODING, CODES** to convert into symbols

CODEBOOK *n* pl. **-S** a book listing words and their coded equivalents

CODEBTOR *n* pl. **-S** one that shares a debt

CODEC *n* pl. **-S** an integrated circuit

CODED past tense of code

CODEIA *n* pl. **-S** codeine

CODEIN *n* pl. **-S** codeine

CODEINA *n* pl. **-S** codeine

CODEINE *n* pl. **-S** a narcotic alkaloid

CODELESS *adj* being without a set of laws

CODEN *n* pl. **-S** a coding classification

CODER *n* pl. **-S** one that codes

CODERIVE *v* **-RIVED, -RIVING, -RIVES** to derive jointly

CODESIGN *v* **-ED, -ING, -S** to design jointly

CODEX *n* pl. **-DICES** or **-DEXES** an ancient manuscript

CODFISH *n* pl. **-ES** a marine food fish

CODGER *n* pl. **-S** an old man

CODICES pl. of codex

CODICIL *n* pl. **-S** a supplement to a will

CODIFIER *n* pl. **-S** one that codifies

CODIFY *v* **-FIED, -FYING, -FIES** to arrange or systematize

CODING *n* pl. **-S** the process of converting into symbols

CODIRECT *v* **-ED, -ING, -S** to direct jointly

CODLIN *n* pl. **-S** codling

CODLING *n* pl. **-S** an unripe apple

CODOMAIN *n* pl. **-S** a mathematical set

CODON *n* pl. **-S** a triplet of nucleotides (basic components of DNA)

CODPIECE *n* pl. **-S** a cover for the crotch in men's breeches

CODRIVE *v* **-DROVE, -DRIVEN, -DRIVING, -DRIVES** to work as a codriver

CODRIVER *n* pl. **-S** one who takes turns driving a vehicle

COED *n* pl. **-S** a female student

COEDIT *v* **-ED, -ING, -S** to edit with another person

COEDITOR *n* pl. **-S** one that coedits

COEFFECT *n* pl. **-S** an accompanying effect

COELIAC *n* pl. **-S** celiac

COELOM *n* pl. **-LOMS** or **-LOMATA** a body cavity in some animals **COELOMIC** *adj*

COELOME *n* pl. **-S** coelom

COEMBODY *v* **-BODIED, -BODYING, -BODIES** to embody jointly

COEMPLOY *v* **-ED, -ING, -S** to employ together

COEMPT *v* **-ED, -ING, -S** to buy up the entire supply of a product

COENACT *v* **-ED, -ING, -S** to enact jointly or at the same time

COENAMOR *v* **-ED, -ING, -S** to inflame with mutual love

COENDURE *v* **-DURED, -DURING, -DURES** to endure together

COENURE *n* pl. **-S** coenurus

COENURUS *n* pl. **-RI** a tapeworm larva

COENZYME *n* pl. **-S** a substance necessary for the functioning of certain enzymes

COEQUAL *n* pl. **-S** one who is equal with another

COEQUATE *v* **-QUATED, -QUATING, -QUATES** to equate with something else

COERCE *v* **-ERCED, -ERCING, -ERCES** to compel by force or threat

COERCER *n* pl. **-S** one that coerces

COERCION *n* pl. **-S** the act of coercing

COERCIVE *adj* serving to coerce

COERECT *v* **-ED, -ING, -S** to erect together

COESITE *n* pl. **-S** a type of silica

COEVAL *n* pl. **-S** one of the same era or period as another

COEVALLY *adv* contemporarily

COEVOLVE *v* **-VOLVED, -VOLVING, -VOLVES** to evolve together

COEXERT *v* **-ED, -ING, -S** to exert jointly

COEXIST	v **-ED, -ING, -S** to exist together
COEXTEND	v **-ED, -ING, -S** to extend through the same space or time as another
COFACTOR	n pl. **-S** a coenzyme
COFF	v **COFT, COFFING, COFFS** to buy
COFFEE	n pl. **-S** an aromatic, mildly stimulating beverage
COFFER	v **-ED, -ING, -S** to put in a strongbox
COFFIN	v **-ED, -ING, -S** to put in a coffin (a burial case)
COFFING	present participle of coff
COFFLE	v **-FLED, -FLING, -FLES** to chain slaves together
COFFRET	n pl. **-S** a small strongbox
COFOUND	v **-ED, -ING, -S** to found jointly
COFT	past tense of coff
COG	v **COGGED, COGGING, COGS** to cheat at dice
COGENCY	n pl. **-CIES** the state of being cogent
COGENT	adj convincing **COGENTLY** adv
COGITATE	v **-TATED, -TATING, -TATES** to ponder
COGITO	n pl. **-TOS** a philosophical principle
COGNAC	n pl. **-S** a brandy
COGNATE	n pl. **-S** one that is related to another
COGNISE	v **-NISED, -NISING, -NISES** to cognize
COGNIZE	v **-NIZED, -NIZING, -NIZES** to become aware of in one's mind
COGNIZER	n pl. **-S** one that cognizes
COGNOMEN	n pl. **-MENS** or **-MINA** a family name
COGNOVIT	n pl. **-S** a written admission of liability
COGON	n pl. **-S** a tall tropical grass
COGWAY	n pl. **-WAYS** a railway operating on steep slopes
COGWHEEL	n pl. **-S** a toothed wheel
COHABIT	v **-ED, -ING, -S** to live together as man and wife while unmarried
COHEAD	v **-ED, -ING, -S** to head jointly
COHEIR	n pl. **-S** a joint heir
COHERE	v **-HERED, -HERING, -HERES** to stick together
COHERENT	adj sticking together

COHERER	n pl. **-S** a device used to detect radio waves
COHESION	n pl. **-S** the act or state of cohering **COHESIVE** adj
COHO	n pl. **-HOS** a small salmon
COHOBATE	v **-BATED, -BATING, -BATES** to distill again
COHOE	n pl. **-S** coho
COHOG	n pl. **-S** a quahog
COHOLDER	n pl. **-S** an athlete who holds a record with another
COHORT	n pl. **-S** a companion or associate
COHOSH	n pl. **-ES** a medicinal plant
COHOST	v **-ED, -ING, -S** to host jointly
COHUNE	n pl. **-S** a palm tree
COIF	v **-ED, -ING, -S** to style the hair
COIFFE	v **COIFFED, COIFFING, COIFFES** to coif
COIFFEUR	n pl. **-S** a male hairdresser
COIFFURE	v **-FURED, -FURING, -FURES** to coif
COIGN	v **-ED, -ING, -S** to quoin
COIGNE	v **COIGNED, COIGNING, COIGNES** to quoin
COIL	v **-ED, -ING, -S** to wind in even rings
COILER	n pl. **-S** one that coils
COIN	v **-ED, -ING, -S** to make coins (metal currency) **COINABLE** adj
COINAGE	n pl. **-S** the act of making coins
COINCIDE	v **-CIDED, -CIDING, -CIDES** to be in the same place
COINER	n pl. **-S** one that coins
COINFECT	v **-ED, -ING, -S** to infect with two organisms
COINFER	v **-FERRED, -FERRING, -FERS** to infer jointly
COINHERE	v **-HERED, -HERING, -HERES** to inhere jointly
COINMATE	n pl. **-S** a fellow inmate
COINSURE	v **-SURED, -SURING, -SURES** to insure with another
COINTER	v **-TERRED, -TERRING, -TERS** to bury together
COINVENT	v **-ED, -ING, -S** to invent together
COIR	n pl. **-S** a fiber obtained from coconut husks
COISTREL	n pl. **-S** a knave
COISTRIL	n pl. **-S** coistrel

COITION   *n* pl. **-S** coitus

COITUS   *n* pl. **-ES** sexual intercourse **COITAL** *adj* **COITALLY** *adv*

COJOIN   *v* **-ED, -ING, -S** to join together

COKE   *v* **COKED, COKING, COKES** to change into a carbon fuel

COKEHEAD   *n* pl. **-S** a cocaine addict

COKELIKE   *adj* resembling coke (a carbon fuel)

COKING   *n* pl. **-S** the process of converting coal into coke (a carbon fuel)

COKY   *adj* cokelike

COL   *n* pl. **-S** a depression between two mountains

COLA   *n* pl. **-S** a carbonated beverage

COLANDER   *n* pl. **-S** a kitchen utensil for draining off liquids

COLBY   *n* pl. **-BYS** a mild cheese

COLD   *adj* **COLDER, COLDEST** having little or no warmth

COLD   *n* pl. **-S** the relative lack of heat; a chill

COLDCOCK   *v* **-ED, -ING, -S** to knock unconscious

COLDISH   *adj* somewhat cold

COLDLY   *adv* in a cold manner

COLDNESS   *n* pl. **-ES** the state of being cold

COLE   *n* pl. **-S** a plant of the cabbage family

COLEAD   *v* **-LED, -LEADING, -LEADS** to lead jointly

COLEADER   *n* pl. **-S** one that coleads

COLESEED   *n* pl. **-S** colza

COLESLAW   *n* pl. **-S** a salad made of shredded raw cabbage

COLESSEE   *n* pl. **-S** a joint lessee

COLESSOR   *n* pl. **-S** a joint lessor

COLEUS   *n* pl. **-ES** a tropical plant

COLEWORT   *n* pl. **-S** cole

COLIC   *n* pl. **-S** acute abdominal pain

COLICIN   *n* pl. **-S** an antibacterial substance

COLICINE   *n* pl. **-S** colicin

COLICKY   *adj* pertaining to or associated with colic

COLIES   pl. of coly

COLIFORM   *n* pl. **-S** a bacillus of the colon

COLIN   *n* pl. **-S** the bobwhite

COLINEAR   *adj* lying in the same straight line

COLISEUM   *n* pl. **-S** a large structure for public entertainment

COLISTIN   *n* pl. **-S** an antibiotic

COLITIS   *n* pl. **-TISES** inflammation of the colon **COLITIC** *adj*

COLLAGE   *v* **-LAGED, -LAGING, -LAGES** to arrange materials in a collage (a kind of artistic composition)

COLLAGEN   *n* pl. **-S** a protein

COLLAPSE   *v* **-LAPSED, -LAPSING, -LAPSES** to crumble suddenly

COLLAR   *v* **-ED, -ING, -S** to provide with a collar (something worn around the neck)

COLLARD   *n* pl. **-S** a variety of kale

COLLARET   *n* pl. **-S** a small collar

COLLATE   *v* **-LATED, -LATING, -LATES** to compare critically

COLLATOR   *n* pl. **-S** one that collates

COLLECT   *v* **-ED, -ING, -S** to bring together in a group

COLLEEN   *n* pl. **-S** an Irish girl

COLLEGE   *n* pl. **-S** a school of higher learning

COLLEGER   *n* pl. **-S** a student supported by funds from his college

COLLEGIA   *n/pl* soviet executive councils

COLLET   *v* **-ED, -ING, -S** to set a gem in a rim or ring

COLLIDE   *v* **-LIDED, -LIDING, -LIDES** to come together with violent impact

COLLIDER   *n* pl. **-S** a type of particle accelerator

COLLIE   *n* pl. **-S** a large dog

COLLIED   past tense of colly

COLLIER   *n* pl. **-S** a coal miner

COLLIERY   *n* pl. **-LIERIES** a coal mine

COLLIES   present 3d person sing. of colly

COLLINS   *n* pl. **-ES** an alcoholic beverage

COLLOGUE   *v* **-LOGUED, -LOGUING, -LOGUES** to conspire

COLLOID   *n* pl. **-S** a type of chemical suspension

COLLOP   *n* pl. **-S** a small portion of meat

COLLOQUY   *n* pl. **-QUIES** a conversation

COLLUDE   *v* **-LUDED, -LUDING, -LUDES** to conspire

COLLUDER   *n* pl. **-S** one that colludes

COLLUVIA   *n/pl* rock debris

COLLY   *v* **-LIED, -LYING, -LIES** to blacken with coal dust

COLLYRIA *n/pl* medicinal lotions

COLOBOMA *n* pl. **-MATA** or **-MAS** a lesion of the eye

COLOBUS *n* pl. **-BUSES** or **-BI** a large African monkey

COLOCATE *v* **-CATED, -CATING, -CATES** to place two or more housing units in close proximity

COLOG *n* pl. **-S** the logarithm of the reciprocal of a number

COLOGNE *n* pl. **-S** a scented liquid **COLOGNED** *adj*

COLON *n* pl. **-ES** a monetary unit of Costa Rica

COLON *n* pl. **-S** a section of the large intestine

COLONE *n* pl. **-S** colon

COLONEL *n* pl. **-S** a military officer

COLONI pl. of colonus

COLONIAL *n* pl. **-S** a citizen of a colony

COLONIC *n* pl. **-S** irrigation of the colon

COLONIES pl. of colony

COLONISE *v* **-NISED, -NISING, -NISES** to colonize

COLONIST *n* pl. **-S** one who settles a colony

COLONIZE *v* **-NIZED, -NIZING, -NIZES** to establish a colony

COLONUS *n* pl. **-NI** a freeborn serf

COLONY *n* pl. **-NIES** a group of emigrants living in a new land

COLOPHON *n* pl. **-S** an inscription placed at the end of a book

COLOR *v* **-ED, -ING, -S** to give color (a visual attribute of objects) to

COLORADO *adj* of medium strength and color — used of cigars

COLORANT *n* pl. **-S** a pigment or dye

COLORED *adj* having color

COLORER *n* pl. **-S** one that colors

COLORFUL *adj* full of color

COLORING *n* pl. **-S** appearance in regard to color

COLORISE *v* **-ISED, -ISING, -ISES** to colorize

COLORISM *n* pl. **-S** coloring

COLORIST *n* pl. **-S** a person skilled in the use of color

COLORIZE *v* **-IZED, -IZING, -IZES** to give color to a black-and-white film

COLORMAN *n* pl. **-MEN** a sportscaster who provides commentary during a game

COLORWAY *n* pl. **-WAYS** an arrangement of colors

COLOSSAL *adj* gigantic

COLOSSUS *n* pl. **-LOSSUSES** or **-LOSSI** a gigantic statue

COLOTOMY *n* pl. **-MIES** a surgical incision of the colon

COLOUR *v* **-ED, -ING, -S** to color

COLOURER *n* pl. **-S** colorer

COLPITIS *n* pl. **-TISES** a vaginal inflammation

COLT *n* pl. **-S** a young male horse **COLTISH** *adj*

COLTAN *n* pl. **-S** a black ore containing columbite and tantalite

COLTER *n* pl. **-S** a blade on a plow

COLTHOOD *n* pl. **-S** the state or time of being a colt

COLUBRID *n* pl. **-S** any of a large family of snakes

COLUGO *n* pl. **-GOS** a small mammal

COLUMBIC *adj* pertaining to niobium

COLUMEL *n* pl. **-S** a small column-like anatomical part

COLUMN *n* pl. **-S** a vertical cylindrical support **COLUMNAL, COLUMNAR, COLUMNED** *adj*

COLUMNEA *n* pl. **-S** a bushy tropical plant

COLURE *n* pl. **-S** an astronomical circle

COLY *n* pl. **COLIES** an African bird

COLZA *n* pl. **-S** a plant of the cabbage family

COMA *n* pl. **-MAE** a tuft of silky hairs

COMA *n* pl. **-S** a condition of prolonged unconsciousness

COMAKE *v* **-MADE, -MAKING, -MAKES** to serve as comaker for another's loan

COMAKER *n* pl. **-S** one who assumes financial responsibility for another's default

COMAL *adj* comose

COMANAGE *v* **-AGED, -AGING, -AGES** to manage jointly

COMATE *n* pl. **-S** a companion

COMATIC *adj* having blurred vision as a result of coma

COMATIK *n* pl. **-S** komatik

COMATOSE *adj* affected with coma

COMATULA *n* pl. **-LAE** a marine animal

COMB *v* **-ED, -ING, -S** to arrange or clean with a comb (a toothed instrument)

COMBAT *v* **-BATED, -BATING, -BATS** or **-BATTED, -BATTING, -BATS** to fight against

COMBATER *n* pl. **-S** one that combats

COMBE *n* pl. **-S** a narrow valley

COMBER *n* pl. **-S** one that combs

COMBI *n* pl. **-S** a machine having a combined function

COMBINE *v* **-BINED, -BINING, -BINES** to blend

COMBINED *n* pl. **-S** a skiing competition combining two events

COMBINER *n* pl. **-S** one that combines

COMBINGS *n/pl* hair removed by a comb

COMBINING present participle of combine

COMBLIKE *adj* resembling a comb

COMBO *n* pl. **-BOS** a small jazz band

COMBOVER *n* pl. **-S** hair that is combed over a bald spot

COMBUST *v* **-ED, -ING, -S** to burn

COME *v* **CAME, COMING, COMES** or **COMETH** to move toward something or someone

COMEBACK *n* pl. **-S** a return to former prosperity

COMEDIAN *n* pl. **-S** a humorous entertainer

COMEDIC *adj* pertaining to comedy

COMEDIES pl. of comedy

COMEDIST *n* pl. **-S** a writer of comedies

COMEDO *n* pl. **-DOS** or **-DONES** a skin blemish

COMEDOWN *n* pl. **-S** a drop in status

COMEDY *n* pl. **-DIES** a humorous play, movie, or other work

COMELY *adj* **-LIER, -LIEST** pleasing to look at **COMELILY** *adv*

COMEMBER *n* pl. **-S** one that shares membership

COMER *n* pl. **-S** one showing great promise

COMET *n* pl. **-S** a celestial body **COMETARY** *adj*

COMETH a present 3d person sing. of come

COMETHER *n* pl. **-S** an affair or matter

COMETIC *adj* pertaining to a comet

COMFIER comparative of comfy

COMFIEST superlative of comfy

COMFIT *n* pl. **-S** a candy

COMFORT *v* **-ED, -ING, -S** to soothe in time of grief

COMFREY *n* pl. **-FREYS** a coarse herb

COMFY *adj* **-FIER, -FIEST** comfortable **COMFILY** *adv*

COMIC *n* pl. **-S** a comedian

COMICAL *adj* funny

COMING *n* pl. **-S** arrival

COMINGLE *v* **-GLED, -GLING, -GLES** to blend thoroughly

COMITIA *n* pl. **COMITIA** a public assembly in ancient Rome **COMITIAL** *adj*

COMITY *n* pl. **-TIES** civility

COMIX *n/pl* comic books or strips

COMM *n* pl. **-S** communication

COMMA *n* pl. **-MAS** or **-MATA** a fragment of a few words or feet in ancient prosody

COMMAND *v* **-ED, -ING, -S** to direct with authority

COMMANDO *n* pl. **-DOS** or **-DOES** a military unit

COMMATA a pl. of comma

COMMENCE *v* **-MENCED, -MENCING, -MENCES** to begin

COMMEND *v* **-ED, -ING, -S** to praise

COMMENT *v* **-ED, -ING, -S** to remark

COMMERCE *v* **-MERCED, -MERCING, -MERCES** to commune

COMMIE *n* pl. **-S** a Communist

COMMIES pl. of commy

COMMIS *n* pl. **COMMIS** a junior chef

COMMISH *n* pl. **-ES** a commissioner

COMMIT *v* **-MITTED, -MITTING, -MITS** to do, perform, or perpetrate

COMMIX *v* **-MIXED** or **-MIXT, -MIXING, -MIXES** to mix together

COMMO *n* pl. **-MOS** communication

COMMODE *n* pl. **-S** a cabinet

COMMON *adj* **-MONER, -MONEST** ordinary

COMMON *n* pl. **-S** a tract of publicly used land

COMMONER *n* pl. **-S** one of the common people

COMMONLY *adv* in a common manner

COMMOVE *v* **-MOVED, -MOVING, -MOVES** to move violently

COMMUNAL *adj* belonging to a community; public

COMMUNE *v* **-MUNED, -MUNING, -MUNES** to converse intimately

COMMUNER *n* pl. **-S** one that communes

COMMUTE *v* **-MUTED, -MUTING, -MUTES** to exchange

COMMUTER *n* pl. **-S** one that commutes

COMMY *n* pl. **-MIES** commie

COMORBID *adj* existing simultaneously with another medical condition

COMOSE *adj* bearing a tuft of silky hairs

COMOUS *adj* comose

COMP *v* **-ED, -ING, -S** to play a jazz accompaniment

COMPACT *adj* **-PACTER, -PACTEST** closely and firmly united

COMPACT *v* **-ED, -ING, -S** to pack closely together

COMPADRE *n* pl. **-S** a close friend

COMPANY *v* **-NIED, -NYING, -NIES** to associate with

COMPARE *v* **-PARED, -PARING, -PARES** to represent as similar

COMPARER *n* pl. **-S** one that compares

COMPART *v* **-ED, -ING, -S** to divide into parts

COMPAS *n* a popular music of Haiti

COMPASS *v* **-ED, -ING, -ES** to go around

COMPEER *v* **-ED, -ING, -S** to equal or match

COMPEL *v* **-PELLED, -PELLING, -PELS** to urge forcefully

COMPEND *n* pl. **-S** a brief summary

COMPERE *v* **-PERED, -PERING, -PERES** to act as master of ceremonies

COMPETE *v* **-PETED, -PETING, -PETES** to vie

COMPILE *v* **-PILED, -PILING, -PILES** to collect into a volume

COMPILER *n* pl. **-S** one that compiles

COMPING *n* pl. **-S** the playing of a jazz accompaniment

COMPLAIN *v* **-ED, -ING, -S** to express discontent

COMPLEAT *v* **-ED, -ING, -S** to complete

COMPLECT *v* **-ED, -ING, -S** to weave together

COMPLETE *adj* **-PLETER, -PLETEST** having all necessary parts

COMPLETE *v* **-PLETED, -PLETING, -PLETES** to bring to an end

COMPLEX *adj* **-PLEXER, -PLEXEST** complicated

COMPLEX *v* **-ED, -ING, -ES** to make complex

COMPLICE *n* pl. **-S** an associate

COMPLIED past tense of comply

COMPLIER *n* pl. **-S** one that complies

COMPLIES present 3d person sing. of comply

COMPLIN *n* pl. **-S** compline

COMPLINE *n* pl. **-S** the last liturgical prayer of the day

COMPLOT *v* **-PLOTTED, -PLOTTING, -PLOTS** to conspire

COMPLY *v* **-PLIED, -PLYING, -PLIES** to obey

COMPO *n* pl. **-POS** a mixed substance

COMPONE *adj* compony

COMPONY *adj* composed of squares of alternating colors

COMPORT *v* **-ED, -ING, -S** to conduct oneself in a certain way

COMPOSE *v* **-POSED, -POSING, -POSES** to form the substance of

COMPOSER *n* pl. **-S** one that writes music

COMPOST *v* **-ED, -ING, -S** to fertilize

COMPOTE *n* pl. **-S** fruit stewed in syrup

COMPOUND *v* **-ED, -ING, -S** to add to

COMPRESS *v* **-ED, -ING, -ES** to compact

COMPRISE *v* **-PRISED, -PRISING, -PRISES** to include or contain

COMPRIZE *v* **-PRIZED, -PRIZING, -PRIZES** to comprise

COMPT *v* **-ED, -ING, -S** to count

COMPUTE *v* **-PUTED, -PUTING, -PUTES** to calculate

COMPUTER *n* pl. **-S** a machine that computes automatically

COMRADE *n* pl. **-S** a close friend

COMTE *n* pl. **-S** a French nobleman

CON *v* **CONNED, CONNING, CONS** to study carefully

CONATION *n* pl. **-S** the inclination to act purposefully **CONATIVE** *adj*

CONATUS *n* pl. **CONATUS** an effort

CONCAVE *v* **-CAVED, -CAVING, -CAVES** to make concave (curving inward)

CONCEAL *v* **-ED, -ING, -S** to keep from sight or discovery

CONCEDE *v* **-CEDED, -CEDING, -CEDES** to acknowledge as true

CONCEDER *n* pl. **-S** one that concedes

CONCEIT *v* **-ED, -ING, -S** to imagine

CONCEIVE   v **-CEIVED, -CEIVING, -CEIVES** to understand

CONCENT   n pl. **-S** harmony

CONCEPT   n pl. **-S** a general idea

CONCEPTI   n/pl fertilized eggs

CONCERN   v **-ED, -ING, -S** to be of interest to

CONCERT   v **-ED, -ING, -S** to plan

CONCERTO   n pl. **-TOS** or **-TI** a musical composition

CONCH   n pl. **-S** or **-ES** a marine mollusk

CONCHA   n pl. **-S** an ornamental disk

CONCHA   n pl. **-CHAE** an anatomical shell-like structure **CONCHAL** adj

CONCHIE   n pl. **-S** conchy

CONCHO   n pl. **-CHOS** concha (ornamental disk)

CONCHOID   n pl. **-S** a type of geometric curve

CONCHY   n pl. **-CHIES** a conscientious objector

CONCISE   adj **-CISER, -CISEST** succinct

CONCLAVE   n pl. **-S** a secret meeting

CONCLUDE   v **-CLUDED, -CLUDING, -CLUDES** to finish

CONCOCT   v **-ED, -ING, -S** to prepare by combining ingredients

CONCORD   n pl. **-S** a state of agreement

CONCOURS   n pl. **CONCOURS** a public competition

CONCRETE   v **-CRETED, -CRETING, -CRETES** to solidify

CONCUR   v **-CURRED, -CURRING, -CURS** to agree

CONCUSS   v **-ED, -ING, -ES** to injure the brain by a violent blow

CONDEMN   v **-ED, -ING, -S** to criticize severely

CONDENSE   v **-DENSED, -DENSING, -DENSES** to compress

CONDIGN   adj deserved; appropriate

CONDO   n pl. **-DOS** or **-DOES** an individually owned unit in a multiunit structure

CONDOLE   v **-DOLED, -DOLING, -DOLES** to mourn

CONDOLER   n pl. **-S** one that condoles

CONDOM   n pl. **-S** a prophylactic

CONDONE   v **-DONED, -DONING, -DONES** to forgive or overlook

CONDONER   n pl. **-S** one that condones

CONDOR   n pl. **-S** or **-ES** a coin of Chile

CONDUCE   v **-DUCED, -DUCING, -DUCES** to contribute to a result

CONDUCER   n pl. **-S** one that conduces

CONDUCT   v **-ED, -ING, -S** to lead or guide

CONDUIT   n pl. **-S** a channel or pipe for conveying fluids

CONDYLE   n pl. **-S** a protuberance on a bone **CONDYLAR** adj

CONE   v **CONED, CONING, CONES** to shape like a cone (a geometric solid)

CONELRAD   n pl. **-S** a system of defense in the event of air attack

CONENOSE   n pl. **-S** a bloodsucking insect

CONEPATE   n pl. **-S** a skunk

CONEPATL   n pl. **-S** conepate

CONEY   n pl. **-NEYS** cony

CONFAB   v **-FABBED, -FABBING, -FABS** to chat

CONFECT   v **-ED, -ING, -S** to prepare from various ingredients

CONFER   v **-FERRED, -FERRING, -FERS** to bestow

CONFEREE   n pl. **-S** one upon whom something is conferred

CONFERVA   n pl. **-VAS** or **-VAE** a freshwater alga

CONFESS   v **-ED, -ING, -ES** to acknowledge or disclose

CONFETTO   n pl. **-TI** a bonbon

CONFIDE   v **-FIDED, -FIDING, -FIDES** to reveal in trust or confidence

CONFIDER   n pl. **-S** one that confides

CONFINE   v **-FINED, -FINING, -FINES** to shut within an enclosure

CONFINER   n pl. **-S** one that confines

CONFIRM   v **-ED, -ING, -S** to assure the validity of

CONFIT   n pl. **-S** meat cooked and preserved in its own fat

CONFLATE   v **-FLATED, -FLATING, -FLATES** to blend

CONFLICT   v **-ED, -ING, -S** to come into opposition

CONFLUX   n pl. **-ES** a flowing together of streams

CONFOCAL   adj having the same focus or foci

CONFORM   v **-ED, -ING, -S** to become the same or similar

CONFOUND   v **-ED, -ING, -S** to confuse

CONFRERE   n pl. **-S** a colleague

CONFRONT *v* **-ED, -ING, -S** to face defiantly

CONFUSE *v* **-FUSED, -FUSING, -FUSES** to mix up mentally

CONFUTE *v* **-FUTED, -FUTING, -FUTES** to disprove

CONFUTER *n* pl. **-S** one that confutes

CONGA *v* **-ED, -ING, -S** to perform a conga (Latin-American dance)

CONGE *n* pl. **-S** permission to depart

CONGEAL *v* **-ED, -ING, -S** to change from a fluid to a solid

CONGEE *v* **-GEED, -GEEING, -GEES** to bow politely

CONGENER *n* pl. **-S** one of the same kind or class

CONGER *n* pl. **-S** a marine eel

CONGEST *v* **-ED, -ING, -S** to fill to excess

CONGIUS *n* pl. **-GII** an ancient unit of measure

CONGLOBE *v* **-GLOBED, -GLOBING, -GLOBES** to become a globule

CONGO *n* pl. **-GOES** an eellike amphibian

CONGO *n* pl. **-GOS** congou

CONGOU *n* pl. **-S** a Chinese tea

CONGRATS *n/pl* congratulations

CONGRESS *v* **-ED, -ING, -ES** to assemble together

CONI pl. of conus

CONIC *n* pl. **-S** a geometric curve

CONICAL *adj* shaped like a cone

CONICITY *n* pl. **-TIES** the state of being conical

CONIDIUM *n* pl. **-NIDIA** a fungus spore **CONIDIAL, CONIDIAN** *adj*

CONIES pl. of cony

CONIFER *n* pl. **-S** an evergreen tree

CONIINE *n* pl. **-S** a poisonous alkaloid

CONIN *n* pl. **-S** coniine

CONINE *n* pl. **-S** coniine

CONING present participle of cone

CONIOSIS *n* pl. **-OSES** an infection caused by the inhalation of dust

CONIUM *n* pl. **-S** a poisonous herb

CONJOIN *v* **-ED, -ING, -S** to join together **CONJOINT** *adj*

CONJUGAL *adj* pertaining to marriage

CONJUNCT *n* pl. **-S** one that is joined with another

CONJUNTO *n* pl. **-TOS** a style of dance music along the Mexican border

CONJURE *v* **-JURED, -JURING, -JURES** to summon a spirit

CONJURER *n* pl. **-S** a sorcerer

CONJUROR *n* pl. **-S** conjurer

CONK *v* **-ED, -ING, -S** to hit on the head

CONKER *n* pl. **-S** a chestnut used in a British game

CONKY *adj* full of a tree fungus

CONN *v* **-ED, -ING, -S** to direct the steering of a ship

CONNATE *adj* innate

CONNECT *v* **-ED, -ING, -S** to join together

CONNED past tense of con

CONNER *n* pl. **-S** one that cons

CONNING present participle of con

CONNIVE *v* **-NIVED, -NIVING, -NIVES** to feign ignorance of wrongdoing

CONNIVER *n* pl. **-S** one that connives

CONNOR *n* pl. **-S** a saltwater fish

CONNOTE *v* **-NOTED, -NOTING, -NOTES** to imply another meaning besides the literal one

CONODONT *n* pl. **-S** a fossil

CONOID *n* pl. **-S** a geometric solid **CONOIDAL** *adj*

CONQUER *v* **-ED, -ING, -S** to overcome by force

CONQUEST *n* pl. **-S** the act of conquering

CONQUIAN *n* pl. **-S** a card game

CONSENT *v* **-ED, -ING, -S** to permit or approve

CONSERVE *v* **-SERVED, -SERVING, -SERVES** to protect from loss or depletion

CONSIDER *v* **-ED, -ING, -S** to think about

CONSIGN *v* **-ED, -ING, -S** to give over to another's care

CONSIST *v* **-ED, -ING, -S** to be made up or composed

CONSOL *n* pl. **-S** a government bond

CONSOLE *v* **-SOLED, -SOLING, -SOLES** to comfort

CONSOLER *n* pl. **-S** one that consoles

CONSOMME *n* pl. **-S** a clear soup

CONSORT *v* **-ED, -ING, -S** to keep company

CONSPIRE *v* **-SPIRED, -SPIRING, -SPIRES** to plan secretly with another

CONSTANT *n* pl. **-S** something that does not vary

CONSTRUE *v* **-STRUED, -STRUING, -STRUES** to interpret

CONSUL *n* pl. **-S** an official serving abroad **CONSULAR** *adj*

CONSULT *v* **-ED, -ING, -S** to ask an opinion of

CONSUME *v* **-SUMED, -SUMING, -SUMES** to use up

CONSUMER *n* pl. **-S** one that consumes

CONTACT *v* **-ED, -ING, -S** to communicate with

CONTAGIA *n/pl* causative agents of infectious diseases

CONTAIN *v* **-ED, -ING, -S** to hold within

CONTANGO *n* pl. **-GOS** postponement of the transfer of stock

CONTE *n* pl. **-S** a short story

CONTEMN *v* **-ED, -ING, -S** to scorn

CONTEMPO *adj* contemporary

CONTEMPT *n* pl. **-S** the feeling of one who views something as mean, vile, or worthless

CONTEND *v* **-ED, -ING, -S** to vie

CONTENT *v* **-ED, -ING, -S** to satisfy

CONTESSA *n* pl. **-S** an Italian countess

CONTEST *v* **-ED, -ING, -S** to compete for

CONTEXT *n* pl. **-S** the part of a discourse in which a particular word or phrase appears

CONTINUA *n/pl* mathematical sets

CONTINUE *v* **-UED, -UING, -UES** to go on with

CONTINUO *n* pl. **-UOS** a type of instrumental part

CONTO *n* pl. **-TOS** a Portuguese money of account

CONTORT *v* **-ED, -ING, -S** to twist out of shape

CONTOUR *v* **-ED, -ING, -S** to make the outline of

CONTRA *n* pl. **-S** a Nicaraguan revolutionary

CONTRACT *v* **-ED, -ING, -S** to decrease in size or volume

CONTRAIL *n* pl. **-S** a visible trail of water vapor from an aircraft

CONTRARY *n* pl. **-TRARIES** an opposite

CONTRAST *v* **-ED, -ING, -S** to place in opposition to set off differences

CONTRITE *adj* deeply sorry for one's sins

CONTRIVE *v* **-TRIVED, -TRIVING, -TRIVES** to devise

CONTROL *v* **-TROLLED, -TROLLING, -TROLS** to exercise authority over

CONTUSE *v* **-TUSED, -TUSING, -TUSES** to bruise

CONURE *n* pl. **-S** a tropical American parakeet

CONUS *n* pl. **CONI** an anatomical part in mammals

CONVECT *v* **-ED, -ING, -S** to transfer heat by a process of circulation

CONVENE *v* **-VENED, -VENING, -VENES** to assemble

CONVENER *n* pl. **-S** one that convenes

CONVENOR *n* pl. **-S** convener

CONVENT *v* **-ED, -ING, -S** to convene

CONVERGE *v* **-VERGED, -VERGING, -VERGES** to come together

CONVERSE *v* **-VERSED, -VERSING, -VERSES** to speak together

CONVERSO *n* pl. **-SOS** a Jew who converted to Christianity

CONVERT *v* **-ED, -ING, -S** to change into another form

CONVEX *n* pl. **-ES** a surface or body that is convex (curving outward)

CONVEXLY *adv* in a convex manner

CONVEY *v* **-ED, -ING, -S** to transport

CONVEYER *n* pl. **-S** one that conveys

CONVEYOR *n* pl. **-S** conveyer

CONVICT *v* **-ED, -ING, -S** to prove guilty

CONVINCE *v* **-VINCED, -VINCING, -VINCES** to cause to believe something

CONVOKE *v* **-VOKED, -VOKING, -VOKES** to cause to assemble

CONVOKER *n* pl. **-S** one that convokes

CONVOLVE *v* **-VOLVED, -VOLVING, -VOLVES** to roll together

CONVOY *v* **-ED, -ING, -S** to escort

CONVULSE *v* **-VULSED, -VULSING, -VULSES** to shake violently

CONY *n* pl. **CONIES** a rabbit

COO *v* **-ED, -ING, -S** to make the sound of a dove

COOCH *n* pl. **-ES** a sinuous dance

COOCOO *adj* crazy

COOEE *v* **COOEED, COOEEING, COOEES** to cry out shrilly

COOER *n* pl. **-S** one that coos

COOEY	*v* **-EYED, -EYING, -EYS** to cooee
COOF	*n* pl. **-S** a dolt
COOING	present participle of coo
COOINGLY	*adv* in the manner of cooing doves; affectionately
COOK	*v* **-ED, -ING, -S** to prepare food by heating **COOKABLE** *adj*
COOKBOOK	*n* pl. **-S** a book of recipes
COOKER	*n* pl. **-S** one that cooks
COOKERY	*n* pl. **-ERIES** the art of cooking
COOKEY	*n* pl. **-EYS** cookie
COOKIE	*n* pl. **-S** a small, flat cake
COOKING	*n* pl. **-S** the act of one that cooks
COOKLESS	*adj* having no person that cooks
COOKOFF	*n* pl. **-S** a cooking contest
COOKOUT	*n* pl. **-S** a meal eaten and prepared outdoors
COOKSHOP	*n* pl. **-S** a shop that sells cooked food
COOKTOP	*n* pl. **-S** a counter-top cooking apparatus
COOKWARE	*n* pl. **-S** utensils used in cooking
COOKY	*n* pl. **COOKIES** cookie
COOL	*adj* **COOLER, COOLEST** moderately cold
COOL	*v* **-ED, -ING, -S** to make less warm
COOLABAH	*n* pl. **-S** an Australian gum tree
COOLANT	*n* pl. **-S** a fluid used to cool engines
COOLDOWN	*n* pl. **-S** a gradual return of physiological functions to normal levels after strenuous exercise
COOLER	*n* pl. **-S** something that cools
COOLIBAH	*n* pl. **-S** coolabah
COOLIE	*n* pl. **-S** a laborer in or from the Far East
COOLIES	pl. of cooly
COOLISH	*adj* somewhat cool
COOLLY	*adv* in a cool manner
COOLNESS	*n* pl. **-ES** the state of being cool
COOLTH	*n* pl. **-S** coolness
COOLY	*n* pl. **COOLIES** coolie
COOMB	*n* pl. **-S** combe
COOMBE	*n* pl. **-S** combe
COON	*n* pl. **-S** a raccoon
COONCAN	*n* pl. **-S** conquian
COONSKIN	*n* pl. **-S** the pelt of a raccoon
COONTIE	*n* pl. **-S** a tropical plant
COOP	*v* **-ED, -ING, -S** to confine
COOPER	*v* **-ED, -ING, -S** to make or mend barrels
COOPERY	*n* pl. **-ERIES** the trade of coopering
COOPT	*v* **-ED, -ING, -S** to elect or appoint
COOPTION	*n* pl. **-S** the act of coopting
COOT	*n* pl. **-S** an aquatic bird
COOTER	*n* pl. **-S** a turtle
COOTIE	*n* pl. **-S** a body louse
COP	*v* **COPPED, COPPING, COPS** to steal
COPAIBA	*n* pl. **-S** a resin
COPAL	*n* pl. **-S** a resin
COPALM	*n* pl. **-S** a hardwood tree
COPARENT	*v* **-ED, -ING, -S** to share in the custody of one's child
COPASTOR	*n* pl. **-S** one that shares the duties of a pastor
COPATRON	*n* pl. **-S** a fellow patron
COPAY	*n* pl. **-PAYS** a fee required by a health insurer to be paid by the patient
COPE	*v* **COPED, COPING, COPES** to contend or strive
COPECK	*n* pl. **-S** kopeck
COPEMATE	*n* pl. **-S** an antagonist
COPEN	*n* pl. **-S** a blue color
COPEPOD	*n* pl. **-S** a minute crustacean
COPER	*n* pl. **-S** a horse dealer
COPIABLE	*adj* capable of being copied
COPIED	past tense of copy
COPIER	*n* pl. **-S** one that copies
COPIES	present 3d person sing. of copy
COPIHUE	*n* pl. **-S** a climbing vine
COPILOT	*v* **-ED, -ING, -S** to act as an assistant pilot
COPING	*n* pl. **-S** the top part of a wall
COPIOUS	*adj* abundant
COPLANAR	*adj* lying in the same plane
COPLOT	*v* **-PLOTTED, -PLOTTING, -PLOTS** to plot together
COPOUT	*n* pl. **-S** a backing out of a responsibility
COPPED	past tense of cop
COPPER	*v* **-ED, -ING, -S** to cover with copper (a metallic element)

COPPERAH *n pl.* **-S** copra

COPPERAS *n pl.* **-ES** a compound used in making inks

COPPERY *adj* resembling copper

COPPICE *v* **-PICED, -PICING, -PICES** to cause to grow in the form of a coppice (a thicket)

COPPING present participle of cop

COPPRA *n pl.* **-S** copra

COPRA *n pl.* **-S** dried coconut meat

COPRAH *n pl.* **-S** copra

COPREMIA *n pl.* **-S** a form of blood poisoning **COPREMIC** *adj*

COPRINCE *n pl.* **-S** one of two princes ruling jointly

COPSE *n pl.* **-S** a coppice **COPSY** *adj*

COPTER *n pl.* **-S** a helicopter

COPULA *n pl.* **-LAS** or **-LAE** something that links **COPULAR** *adj*

COPULATE *v* **-LATED, -LATING, -LATES** to engage in coitus

COPURIFY *v* **-FIED, -FYING, -FIES** to become purified with another substance

COPY *v* **COPIED, COPYING, COPIES** to imitate **COPYABLE** *adj*

COPYBOOK *n pl.* **-S** a book used in teaching penmanship

COPYBOY *n pl.* **-BOYS** a boy who runs errands in a newspaper office

COPYCAT *v* **-CATTED, -CATTING, -CATS** to imitate

COPYDESK *n pl.* **-S** an editor's desk in a newspaper office

COPYEDIT *v* **-ED, -ING, -S** to prepare copy for the printer

COPYGIRL *n pl.* **-S** a girl who runs errands in a newspaper office

COPYHOLD *n pl.* **-S** a type of ownership of land

COPYIST *n pl.* **-S** an imitator

COPYLEFT *n pl.* **-S** a license that allows free use of copyrighted software

COPYREAD *v* **-READ, -READING, -READS** to copyedit

COQUET *v* **-QUETTED, -QUETTING, -QUETS** to flirt

COQUETRY *n pl.* **-TRIES** flirtatious behavior

COQUETTE *v* **-QUETTED, -QUETTING, -QUETTES** to coquet

COQUI *n pl.* **-S** a small arboreal frog

COQUILLE *n pl.* **-S** a cooking utensil

COQUINA *n pl.* **-S** a small marine clam

COQUITO *n pl.* **-TOS** a palm tree

COR *n pl.* **-S** an ancient unit of measure

CORACLE *n pl.* **-S** a small boat

CORACOID *n pl.* **-S** a bone of the shoulder girdle

CORAL *n pl.* **-S** a mass of marine animal skeletons

CORANTO *n pl.* **-TOS** or **-TOES** courante

CORBAN *n pl.* **-S** an offering to God

CORBEIL *n pl.* **-S** a sculptured fruit basket

CORBEL *v* **-BELED, -BELING, -BELS** or **-BELLED, -BELLING, -BELS** to provide a wall with a bracket

CORBIE *n pl.* **-S** a raven or crow

CORBINA *n pl.* **-S** a food and game fish

CORBY *n pl.* **CORBIES** corbie

CORD *v* **-ED, -ING, -S** to fasten with a cord (a thin rope)

CORDAGE *n pl.* **-S** the amount of wood in an area

CORDATE *adj* heart-shaped

CORDELLE *v* **-DELLED, -DELLING, -DELLES** to tow a boat with a cordelle (a towrope)

CORDER *n pl.* **-S** one that cords

CORDIAL *n pl.* **-S** a liqueur

CORDING *n pl.* **-S** the ribbed surface of cloth

CORDITE *n pl.* **-S** an explosive powder

CORDLESS *n pl.* **-ES** an electrical device with its own power supply

CORDLIKE *adj* resembling a cord

CORDOBA *n pl.* **-S** a monetary unit of Nicaragua

CORDON *v* **-ED, -ING, -S** to form a barrier around

CORDOVAN *n pl.* **-S** a fine leather

CORDUROY *v* **-ED, -ING, -S** to build a type of road

CORDWAIN *n pl.* **-S** cordovan

CORDWOOD *n pl.* **-S** wood used for fuel

CORE *v* **CORED, CORING, CORES** to remove the core (the central part) of

COREDEEM *v* **-ED, -ING, -S** to redeem jointly

COREIGN *n pl.* **-S** a joint reign

CORELATE *v* **-LATED, -LATING, -LATES** to place into mutual or reciprocal relation

CORELESS *adj* having no core

CORELLA *n* pl. **-S** a small cockatoo

COREMIUM *n* pl. **-MIA** an organ of certain fungi

CORER *n* pl. **-S** a utensil for coring apples

CORF *n* pl. **CORVES** a wagon used in a mine

CORGI *n* pl. **-S** a short-legged dog

CORING present participle of core

CORIUM *n* pl. **-RIA** a skin layer

CORK *v* **-ED, -ING, -S** to stop up

CORKAGE *n* pl. **-S** a charge for wine in a restaurant

CORKER *n* pl. **-S** one that corks

CORKIER comparative of corky

CORKIEST superlative of corky

CORKLIKE *adj* resembling cork (a porous tree bark)

CORKWOOD *n* pl. **-S** a small tree

CORKY *adj* **CORKIER, CORKIEST** corklike

CORM *n* pl. **-S** a stem of certain plants **CORMLIKE, CORMOID, CORMOUS** *adj*

CORMEL *n* pl. **-S** a small corm

CORMLET *n* pl. **-S** a small corm

CORN *v* **-ED, -ING, -S** to preserve with salt

CORNBALL *n* pl. **-S** a hick

CORNCAKE *n* pl. **-S** a cake made of cornmeal

CORNCOB *n* pl. **-S** the woody core of an ear of corn

CORNCRIB *n* pl. **-S** a building in which corn is stored

CORNEA *n* pl. **-S** a part of the eye **CORNEAL** *adj*

CORNEL *n* pl. **-S** a hardwood tree or shrub

CORNEOUS *adj* of a hornlike texture

CORNER *v* **-ED, -ING, -S** to gain control of

CORNET *n* pl. **-S** a trumpetlike instrument

CORNETCY *n* **-CIES** a rank in the British cavalry

CORNETT *n* pl. **-S** cornetto

CORNETTO *n* pl. **-TOS** or **-TI** a musical wind instrument

CORNFED *adj* fed on corn

CORNHUSK *n* pl. **-S** the husk covering an ear of corn

CORNICE *v* **-NICED, -NICING, -NICES** to decorate with a molding

CORNICHE *n* pl. **-S** a road built along a cliff

CORNICLE *n* pl. **-S** a part of an aphid

CORNIER comparative of corny

CORNIEST superlative of corny

CORNIFY *v* **-FIED, -FYING, -FIES** to form keratin

CORNILY *adv* in a corny manner

CORNMEAL *n* pl. **-S** meal made from corn

CORNPONE *n* pl. **-S** a bread made with cornmeal

CORNROW *v* **-ED, -ING, -S** to braid hair tightly in rows close to the scalp

CORNSILK *n* pl. **-S** a silky thread on an ear of corn

CORNU *n* pl. **-NUA** a hornlike bone formation **CORNUAL** *adj*

CORNUS *n* pl. **-ES** a cornel

CORNUTE *adj* horn-shaped

CORNUTED *adj* cornute

CORNUTO *n* pl. **-TOS** the husband of an unfaithful wife

CORNY *adj* **CORNIER, CORNIEST** trite

CORODY *n* pl. **-DIES** an allowance of food or clothes

COROLLA *n* pl. **-S** a protective covering of a flower

CORONA *n* pl. **-NAS** or **-NAE** a luminous circle around a celestial body

CORONACH *n* pl. **-S** a dirge

CORONAL *n* pl. **-S** a wreath worn on the head

CORONARY *n* pl. **-NARIES** an artery supplying blood to the heart

CORONATE *v* **-NATED, -NATING, -NATES** to crown

CORONEL *n* pl. **-S** coronal

CORONER *n* pl. **-S** an officer who investigates questionable deaths

CORONET *n* pl. **-S** a small crown

CORONOID *adj* crown-shaped

COROTATE *v* **-TATED, -TATING, -TATES** to rotate together

COROZO *n* pl. **-ZOS** a tropical palm tree

CORPORA a pl. of corpus

CORPORAL *n* pl. **-S** a military rank

CORPS *n* pl. **CORPS** a military unit

CORPSE *n* pl. **-S** a dead body

CORPSMAN *n* pl. **-MEN** an enlisted man trained in first aid

CORPUS *n* pl. **-PORA** or **-PUSES** a human or animal body

CORRADE *v* **-RADED, -RADING, -RADES** to erode

CORRAL *v* **-RALLED, -RALLING, -RALS** to place livestock in a corral (an enclosure)

CORRECT *adj* **-RECTER, -RECTEST** free from error

CORRECT *v* **-ED, -ING, -S** to make free from error

CORRETTO *n* pl. **-TOS** espresso mixed with brandy or liqueur

CORRIDA *n* pl. **-S** a bullfight

CORRIDOR *n* pl. **-S** a narrow hallway

CORRIE *n* pl. **-S** a cirque

CORRIVAL *n* pl. **-S** a rival or opponent

CORRODE *v* **-RODED, -RODING, -RODES** to eat away gradually

CORRODY *n* pl. **-DIES** corody

CORRUPT *adj* **-RUPTER, -RUPTEST** dishonest and venal

CORRUPT *v* **-ED, -ING, -S** to subvert the honesty or integrity of

CORSAC *n* pl. **-S** an Asian fox

CORSAGE *n* pl. **-S** a small bouquet of flowers

CORSAIR *n* pl. **-S** a pirate

CORSE *n* pl. **-S** a corpse

CORSELET *n* pl. **-S** a piece of body armor

CORSET *v* **-ED, -ING, -S** to fit with a corset (a supporting undergarment)

CORSETRY *n* pl. **-RIES** the work of making corsets

CORSLET *n* pl. **-S** corselet

CORTEGE *n* pl. **-S** a retinue

CORTEX *n* pl. **-TEXES** or **-TICES** the outer layer of an organ **CORTICAL** *adj*

CORTIN *n* pl. **-S** a hormone

CORTINA *n* pl. **-S** a membrane on some mushrooms

CORTISOL *n* pl. **-S** a hormone

CORULER *n* pl. **-S** one that rules jointly

CORUNDUM *n* pl. **-S** a hard mineral

CORVEE *n* pl. **-S** an obligation to perform feudal service

CORVES pl. of corf

CORVET *n* pl. **-S** corvette

CORVETTE *n* pl. **-S** a small, swift warship

CORVID *n* pl. **-S** any of a family of passerine birds

CORVINA *n* pl. **-S** corbina

CORVINE *adj* pertaining or belonging to the crow family of birds

CORY *n* pl. **CORY** a former monetary unit of Guinea

CORYBANT *n* pl. **-BANTS** or **-BANTES** a reveler

CORYMB *n* pl. **-S** a flower cluster **CORYMBED** *adj*

CORYPHEE *n* pl. **-S** a ballet dancer

CORYZA *n* pl. **-S** a head cold **CORYZAL** *adj*

COS *n* pl. **-ES** a variety of lettuce

COSCRIPT *v* **-ED, -ING, -S** to collaborate in preparing a script for

COSEC *n* pl. **-S** cosecant

COSECANT *n* pl. **-S** a trigonometric function of an angle

COSET *n* pl. **-S** a mathematical subset

COSEY *n* pl. **-SEYS** a covering for a teapot

COSH *v* **-ED, -ING, -ES** to bludgeon

COSHER *v* **-ED, -ING, -S** to coddle

COSIE *n* pl. **-S** cosey

COSIED past tense of cosy

COSIER comparative of cosy

COSIES present 3d person sing. of cosy

COSIEST superlative of cosy

COSIGN *v* **-ED, -ING, -S** to sign jointly

COSIGNER *n* pl. **-S** one that cosigns

COSILY *adv* in a cosy manner

COSINE *n* pl. **-S** a trigonometric function of an angle

COSINESS *n* pl. **-ES** coziness

COSMETIC *n* pl. **-S** a beauty preparation

COSMIC *adj* pertaining to the cosmos

COSMICAL *adj* cosmic

COSMID *n* pl. **-S** a hybrid vector used in cloning

COSMISM *n* pl. **-S** a philosophical theory

COSMIST *n* pl. **-S** a supporter of cosmism

COSMOS *n* pl. **-ES** the universe regarded as an orderly system

COSS *n* pl. **COSS** kos

COSSACK *n* pl. **-S** a Russian cavalryman

COSSET *v* **-ED, -ING, -S** to fondle

COST	v **COST** or **COSTED, COSTING, COSTS** to estimate a price for production of	**COTTAGE**	v **-TAGED, -TAGING, -TAGES** to vacation at a small house
COSTA	n pl. **-TAE** a rib **COSTAL** adj **COSTALLY** adv	**COTTAGER**	n pl. **-S** one that lives in a small house
COSTAR	v **-STARRED, -STARRING, -STARS** to star with another actor	**COTTAGEY**	adj resembling a small house
COSTARD	n pl. **-S** a large cooking apple	**COTTAR**	n pl. **-S** a tenant farmer
COSTATE	adj having a rib or ribs	**COTTER**	n pl. **-S** a pin or wedge used for fastening parts together **COTTERED** adj
COSTER	n pl. **-S** a hawker of fruit or vegetables	**COTTIER**	n pl. **-S** cottar
COSTING	n pl. **-S** an estimation of the price of the production of something	**COTTON**	v **-ED, -ING, -S** to take a liking
COSTIVE	adj constipated	**COTTONY**	adj resembling cotton (a soft, fibrous material)
COSTLESS	adj free of charge	**COTURNIX**	n pl. **-ES** a small quail
COSTLY	adj **-LIER, -LIEST** expensive	**COTYLOID**	adj cup-shaped
COSTMARY	n pl. **-MARIES** an herb used in salads	**COTYPE**	n pl. **-S** a taxonomic type
COSTREL	n pl. **-S** a flask	**COUCH**	v **-ED, -ING, -ES** to put into words
COSTUME	v **-TUMED, -TUMING, -TUMES** to supply with a costume (a style of dress)	**COUCHANT**	adj lying down
		COUCHER	n pl. **-S** one that couches
COSTUMER	n pl. **-S** one that costumes	**COUCHING**	n pl. **-S** a form of embroidery
COSTUMEY	adj of or pertaining to a costume	**COUDE**	n pl. **-S** a type of telescope
COSY	adj **COSIER, COSIEST** cozy	**COUGAR**	n pl. **-S** a mountain lion
COSY	v **COSIED, COSYING, COSIES** to cozy	**COUGH**	v **-ED, -ING, -S** to expel air from the lungs noisily
COT	n pl. **-S** a light, narrow bed	**COUGHER**	n pl. **-S** one that coughs
COTAN	n pl. **-S** a trigonometric function of an angle	**COULD**	past tense of can
		COULDEST	a past 2d person sing. of can
COTE	v **COTED, COTING, COTES** to pass by	**COULDST**	a past 2d person sing. of can
		COULEE	n pl. **-S** a small ravine
COTEAU	n pl. **-TEAUX** the higher ground of a region	**COULIS**	n pl. **COULIS** a thick sauce of pureed vegetable or fruit
COTENANT	n pl. **-S** one who is a tenant with another in the same place	**COULISSE**	n pl. **-S** a side scene of a theatre stage
COTERIE	n pl. **-S** a clique	**COULOIR**	n pl. **-S** a deep gorge or gully
COTHURN	n pl. **-S** a buskin worn by ancient Roman actors	**COULOMB**	n pl. **-S** an electrical measure
		COULTER	n pl. **-S** colter
COTHURNI	n/pl cothurns	**COUMARIN**	n pl. **-S** a chemical compound **COUMARIC** adj
COTIDAL	adj indicating coincidence of the tides	**COUMAROU**	n pl. **-S** the seed of a tropical tree
COTILLON	n pl. **-S** a ballroom dance	**COUNCIL**	n pl. **-S** a group of persons appointed for a certain function
COTING	present participle of cote	**COUNSEL**	v **-SELED, -SELING, -SELS** or **-SELLED, -SELLING, -SELS** to advise
COTINGA	n pl. **-S** a tropical bird		
COTININE	n pl. **-S** an alkaloid produced by nicotine in the body	**COUNT**	v **-ED, -ING, -S** to list or mention the units of one by one to ascertain the total
COTQUEAN	n pl. **-S** a vulgar woman	**COUNTER**	v **-ED, -ING, -S** to oppose
COTTA	n pl. **-TAS** or **-TAE** a short surplice	**COUNTESS**	n pl. **-ES** a noblewoman

COUNTIAN *n* pl. **-S** a resident of a county

COUNTRY *n* pl. **-TRIES** the territory of a nation

COUNTY *n* pl. **-TIES** an administrative division of a state

COUP *v* **-ED, -ING, -S** to overturn

COUPE *n* pl. **-S** an automobile with two doors

COUPLE *v* **-PLED, -PLING, -PLES** to unite in pairs

COUPLER *n* pl. **-S** one that couples

COUPLET *n* pl. **-S** a pair of successive lines of verse

COUPLING *n* pl. **-S** a joining device

COUPON *n* pl. **-S** a certificate entitling the holder to certain benefits

COURAGE *n* pl. **-S** the quality that enables one to face danger fearlessly; spirit

COURANT *n* pl. **-S** courante

COURANTE *n* pl. **-S** an old, lively dance

COURANTO *n* pl. **-TOS** or **-TOES** courante

COURIER *v* **-ED, -ING, -S** to send or transport by a messenger

COURLAN *n* pl. **-S** a wading bird

COURSE *v* **COURSED, COURSING, COURSES** to cause hounds to chase game

COURSER *n* pl. **-S** one that courses

COURSING *n* pl. **-S** the pursuit of game by hounds

COURT *v* **-ED, -ING, -S** to woo

COURTER *n* pl. **-S** one that courts

COURTESY *v* **-SIED, -SYING, -SIES** to curtsy

COURTIER *n* pl. **-S** one who attends a royal court

COURTLY *adj* **-LIER, -LIEST** stately

COUSCOUS *n* pl. **-ES** a North African cereal

COUSIN *n* pl. **-S** a child of one's aunt or uncle **COUSINLY** *adj*

COUSINRY *n* pl. **-RIES** cousins collectively

COUTEAU *n* pl. **-TEAUX** a knife

COUTER *n* pl. **-S** a piece of armor for the elbow

COUTH *adj* **COUTHER, COUTHEST** sophisticated

COUTH *n* pl. **-S** refinement

COUTHIE *adj* **COUTHIER, COUTHIEST** friendly

COUTURE *n* pl. **-S** the business of dressmaking

COUVADE *n* pl. **-S** a primitive birth ritual

COVALENT *adj* sharing electron pairs

COVARY *v* **-VARIED, -VARYING, -VARIES** to exhibit variation of two or more variables

COVE *v* **COVED, COVING, COVES** to curve over or inward

COVEN *n* pl. **-S** a group of witches

COVENANT *v* **-ED, -ING, -S** to enter into a binding agreement

COVER *v* **-ED, -ING, -S** to place something over or upon

COVERAGE *n* pl. **-S** the extent to which something is covered

COVERALL *n* pl. **-S** a one-piece work garment

COVERER *n* pl. **-S** one that covers

COVERING *n* pl. **-S** something that covers

COVERLET *n* pl. **-S** a bed covering

COVERLID *n* pl. **-S** a coverlet

COVERT *n* pl. **-S** a hiding place

COVERTLY *adv* secretly

COVERUP *n* pl. **-S** something used to conceal improper activity

COVET *v* **-ED, -ING, -S** to desire greatly

COVETER *n* pl. **-S** one that covets

COVETOUS *adj* excessively desirous

COVEY *n* pl. **-EYS** a flock of birds

COVIN *n* pl. **-S** a conspiracy to defraud

COVINE *n* pl. **-S** covin

COVING *n* pl. **-S** a concave molding

COW *v* **-ED, -ING, -S** to intimidate

COWAGE *n* pl. **-S** a tropical vine

COWARD *n* pl. **-S** one who lacks courage

COWARDLY *adj* lacking courage

COWBANE *n* pl. **-S** a poisonous plant

COWBELL *n* pl. **-S** a bell around a cow's neck

COWBERRY *n* pl. **-RIES** a pasture shrub

COWBIND *n* pl. **-S** a species of bryony

COWBIRD *n* pl. **-S** a blackbird

COWBOY *v* **-BOYED, -BOYING, -BOYS** to tend cattle or horses

COWEDLY *adv* in a cowed manner

COWER *v* **-ED, -ING, -S** to cringe

COWFISH *n* pl. **-ES** an aquatic mammal

COWFLAP *n* pl. **-S** cowflop

COWFLOP *n* pl. **-S** a cowpat

COWGIRL *n* pl. **-S** a female ranch worker

COWHAGE   *n* pl. **-S** cowage

COWHAND   *n* pl. **-S** a ranch worker

COWHERB   *n* pl. **-S** an annual herb

COWHERD   *n* pl. **-S** one who tends cattle

COWHIDE   *v* **-HIDED, -HIDING, -HIDES** to flog with a leather whip

COWIER   comparative of cowy

COWIEST   superlative of cowy

COWINNER   *n* pl. **-S** one of two or more winners

COWL   *v* **-ED, -ING, -S** to cover with a hood

COWLICK   *n* pl. **-S** a lock of unruly hair

COWLIKE   *adj* resembling a cow

COWLING   *n* pl. **-S** a covering for an aircraft engine

COWMAN   *n* pl. **-MEN** one who owns cattle

COWORKER   *n* pl. **-S** a fellow worker

COWPAT   *n* pl. **-S** a dropping of cow dung

COWPEA   *n* pl. **-S** a black-eyed pea

COWPIE   *n* pl. **-S** a cowpat

COWPLOP   *n* pl. **-S** a cowpat

COWPOKE   *n* pl. **-S** a cowhand

COWPOX   *n* pl. **-ES** a cattle disease

COWPUNK   *n* pl. **-S** music combining country and western styles with punk rock

COWRIE   *n* pl. **-S** cowry

COWRITE   *v* **-WROTE, -WRITTEN, -WRITING, -WRITES** to collaborate in writing

COWRITER   *n* pl. **-S** one that cowrites

COWRY   *n* pl. **-RIES** a glossy seashell

COWSHED   *n* pl. **-S** a shelter for cows

COWSKIN   *n* pl. **-S** the hide of a cow

COWSLIP   *n* pl. **-S** a flowering plant

COWTOWN   *n* pl. **-S** a town or city in a cattle-raising area

COWY   *adj* **COWIER, COWIEST** suggestive of a cow

COX   *v* **-ED, -ING, -ES** to coxswain

COXA   *n* pl. **COXAE** the hip or hip joint **COXAL** *adj*

COXALGIA   *n* pl. **-S** pain in the hip **COXALGIC** *adj*

COXALGY   *n* pl. **-GIES** coxalgia

COXCOMB   *n* pl. **-S** a conceited dandy

COXITIS   *n* pl. **COXITIDES** inflammation of the hip joint

COXLESS   *adj* having no coxswain (the director of the crew of a racing rowboat)

COXSWAIN   *v* **-ED, -ING, -S** to direct (a crew) as coxswain

COY   *adj* **COYER, COYEST** shy

COY   *v* **-ED, -ING, -S** to caress

COYAU   *n* pl. **-S** a steep roof design

COYDOG   *n* pl. **-S** a hybrid between a coyote and a wild dog

COYISH   *adj* somewhat coy

COYLY   *adv* in a coy manner

COYNESS   *n* pl. **-ES** the state of being coy

COYOTE   *n* pl. **-S** a small wolf

COYPOU   *n* pl. **-S** a coypu

COYPU   *n* pl. **-S** an aquatic rodent

COZ   *n* pl. **COZES** or **COZZES** a cousin

COZEN   *v* **-ED, -ING, -S** to deceive

COZENAGE   *n* pl. **-S** the practice of cozening

COZENER   *n* pl. **-S** one that cozens

COZEY   *n* pl. **-ZEYS** a cover for a teapot

COZIE   *n* pl. **-S** a cozey

COZIED   past tense of cozy

COZIER   comparative of cozy

COZIES   present 3d person sing. of cozy

COZINESS   *n* pl. **-ES** the state of being cozy

COZY   *adj* **COZIER, COZIEST** snug and comfortable **COZILY** *adv*

COZY   *v* **COZIED, COZYING, COZIES** to attempt to get on friendly terms

COZZES   a pl. of coz

CRAAL   *v* **-ED, -ING, -S** to kraal

CRAB   *v* **CRABBED, CRABBING, CRABS** to complain

CRABBER   *n* pl. **-S** one that crabs

CRABBY   *adj* **-BIER, -BIEST** grumpy **CRABBILY** *adv*

CRABLIKE   *adj* resembling a crab

CRABMEAT   *n* pl. **-S** the edible part of a crab

CRABWISE   *adv* sideways

CRACK   *v* **-ED, -ING, -S** to break without dividing into parts

CRACKER   *n* pl. **-S** a thin, crisp biscuit

CRACKIE   *n* pl. **-S** a small dog of mixed breed

CRACKING   *n* pl. **-S** a chemical process

CRACKLE   *v* **-LED, -LING, -LES** to make a succession of snapping sounds

CRACKLY *adj* **-LIER, -LIEST** brittle

CRACKNEL *n* pl. **-S** a hard, crisp biscuit

CRACKPOT *n* pl. **-S** an eccentric person

CRACKUP *n* pl. **-S** a collision

CRACKY *adj* **CRACKIER, CRACKIEST** having cracks

CRADLE *v* **-DLED, -DLING, -DLES** to nurture during infancy

CRADLER *n* pl. **-S** one that cradles

CRADLING *n* pl. **-S** a framework in a ceiling

CRAFT *v* **-ED, -ING, -S** to make by hand

CRAFTER *n* pl. **-S** one that crafts

CRAFTY *adj* **CRAFTIER, CRAFTIEST** skillful in deceiving **CRAFTILY** *adv*

CRAG *n* pl. **-S** a large jagged rock **CRAGGED** *adj*

CRAGGY *adj* **-GIER, -GIEST** full of crags **CRAGGILY** *adv*

CRAGSMAN *n* pl. **-MEN** one who climbs crags

CRAKE *n* pl. **-S** a small, harsh-voiced bird

CRAM *v* **CRAMMED, CRAMMING, CRAMS** to fill or pack tightly

CRAMBE *n* pl. **-S** an annual herb

CRAMBO *n* pl. **-BOS** or **-BOES** a word game

CRAMMER *n* pl. **-S** one that crams

CRAMMING *n* pl. **-S** the fraudulent adding to the charges of a phone bill

CRAMOISY *n* pl. **-SIES** crimson cloth

CRAMP *v* **-ED, -ING, -S** to restrain or confine

CRAMPIT *n* pl. **-S** a piece of equipment used in curling

CRAMPON *n* pl. **-S** a device for raising heavy objects

CRAMPOON *n* pl. **-S** crampon

CRAMPY *adj* **CRAMPIER, CRAMPIEST** affected with a cramp

CRANCH *v* **-ED, -ING, -ES** to craunch

CRANE *v* **CRANED, CRANING, CRANES** to stretch out one's neck

CRANIA a pl. of cranium

CRANIAL *adj* pertaining to the skull

CRANIATE *n* pl. **-S** one that has a skull

CRANING present participle of crane

CRANIUM *n* pl. **-NIUMS** or **-NIA** the skull

CRANK *adj* **CRANKER, CRANKEST** lively

CRANK *v* **-ED, -ING, -S** to start manually

CRANKIER comparative of cranky

CRANKIEST superlative of cranky

CRANKILY *adv* in a cranky manner

CRANKISH *adj* eccentric

CRANKLE *v* **-KLED, -KLING, -KLES** to crinkle

CRANKLY *adv* in a crank manner

CRANKOUS *adj* cranky

CRANKPIN *n* pl. **-S** the handle of a crank

CRANKY *adj* **CRANKIER, CRANKIEST** grumpy

CRANNIES pl. of cranny

CRANNOG *n* pl. **-S** an artificial island

CRANNOGE *n* pl. **-S** crannog

CRANNY *n* pl. **-NIES** a crevice **CRANNIED** *adj*

CRAP *v* **CRAPPED, CRAPPING, CRAPS** to throw a 2, 3, or 12 in a dice game

CRAPE *v* **CRAPED, CRAPING, CRAPES** to crepe

CRAPOLA *n* pl. **-S** nonsense, drivel

CRAPPIE *n* pl. **-S** an edible fish

CRAPPY *adj* **-PIER, -PIEST** markedly inferior in quality

CRASH *v* **-ED, -ING, -ES** to collide noisily

CRASHER *n* pl. **-S** one that crashes

CRASIS *n* pl. **CRASES** a vowel contraction

CRASS *adj* **CRASSER, CRASSEST** grossly vulgar or stupid **CRASSLY** *adv*

CRATCH *n* pl. **-ES** a manger

CRATE *v* **CRATED, CRATING, CRATES** to put in a packing box

CRATEFUL *n* pl. **-S** as much as a crate can hold

CRATER *v* **-ED, -ING, -S** to form cavities in a surface

CRATON *n* pl. **-S** a part of the earth's crust **CRATONIC** *adj*

CRAUNCH *v* **-ED, -ING, -ES** to crunch

CRAVAT *n* pl. **-S** a necktie

CRAVE *v* **CRAVED, CRAVING, CRAVES** to desire greatly

CRAVEN *v* **-ED, -ING, -S** to make cowardly

CRAVENLY *adv* in a cowardly manner

CRAVER *n* pl. **-S** one that craves

CRAVING *n* pl. **-S** a great desire

CRAW *n* pl. **-S** the stomach of an animal

CRAWDAD *n* pl. **-S** a crayfish

CRAWFISH v -ED, -ING, -ES to back out or retreat

CRAWL v -ED, -ING, -S to move with the body on or near the ground

CRAWLER n pl. -S one that crawls

CRAWLWAY n pl. -WAYS a small, low tunnel

CRAWLY adj CRAWLIER, CRAWLIEST creepy

CRAYFISH n pl. -ES a crustacean

CRAYON v -ED, -ING, -S to use a drawing implement

CRAYONER n pl. -S one that crayons

CRAZE v CRAZED, CRAZING, CRAZES to make insane

CRAZING n pl. -S a fine surface crack on pottery

CRAZY adj -ZIER, -ZIEST insane CRAZILY adv

CRAZY n pl. -ZIES a crazy person

CREAK v -ED, -ING, -S to squeak

CREAKY adj CREAKIER, CREAKIEST creaking CREAKILY adv

CREAM v -ED, -ING, -S to form cream (a part of milk)

CREAMER n pl. -S a cream pitcher

CREAMERY n pl. -ERIES a dairy

CREAMY adj CREAMIER, CREAMIEST rich in cream CREAMILY adv

CREASE v CREASED, CREASING, CREASES to make a fold or wrinkle in

CREASER n pl. -S one that creases

CREASY adj CREASIER, CREASIEST having folds or wrinkles

CREATE v -ATED, -ATING, -ATES to cause to exist

CREATIN n pl. -S creatine

CREATINE n pl. -S a chemical compound

CREATION n pl. -S something created

CREATIVE n pl. -S one who has the ability to create

CREATOR n pl. -S one that creates

CREATURE n pl. -S a living being

CRECHE n pl. -S a day nursery

CRED n pl. -S credibility

CREDAL adj pertaining to a creed

CREDENCE n pl. -S belief

CREDENDA n/pl articles of faith

CREDENT adj believing

CREDENZA n pl. -S a piece of furniture

CREDIBLE adj believable CREDIBLY adv

CREDIT v -ED, -ING, -S to accept as true

CREDITOR n pl. -S one to whom money is owed

CREDO n pl. -DOS a creed

CREED n pl. -S a statement of belief CREEDAL adj

CREEK n pl. -S a watercourse smaller than a river

CREEL v -ED, -ING, -S to put fish in a creel (a fish basket)

CREEP v CREPT or CREEPED, CREEPING, CREEPS to crawl

CREEPAGE n pl. -S gradual movement

CREEPER n pl. -S one that creeps

CREEPIE n pl. -S a low stool

CREEPING present participle of creep

CREEPY adj CREEPIER, CREEPIEST repugnant CREEPILY adv

CREESE n pl. -S kris

CREESH v -ED, -ING, -ES to grease

CREMAINS n/pl the ashes of a cremated body

CREMATE v -MATED, -MATING, -MATES to reduce to ashes by burning

CREMATOR n pl. -S one that cremates

CREME n pl. -S cream

CREMINI n pl. -S a brown mushroom

CRENATE adj having an edge with rounded projections

CRENATED adj crenate

CRENEL v -ELED, -ELING, -ELS or -ELLED, -ELLING, -ELS to provide with crenelles

CRENELLE n pl. -S a rounded projection

CRENSHAW n pl. -S a variety of honeydew melon

CREODONT n pl. -S an extinct carnivore

CREOLE n pl. -S a type of mixed language

CREOLISE v -ISED, -ISING, -ISES to creolize

CREOLIZE v -IZED, -IZING, -IZES to cause a language to become a creole

CREOSOL n pl. -S a chemical compound

CREOSOTE v -SOTED, -SOTING, -SOTES to treat with a wood preservative

CREPE v CREPED, CREPING, CREPES to frizz the hair

CREPERIE   *n* pl. **-S** a restaurant that serves crepes (thin pancakes)

CREPEY   *adj* **CREPIER, CREPIEST** crinkly

CREPITUS   *n* pl. **CREPITUS** a grating sound made in breathing

CREPON   *n* pl. **-S** a crinkled fabric

CREPT   past tense of creep

CREPY   *adj* **CREPIER, CREPIEST** crepey

CRESCENT   *n* pl. **-S** the figure of the moon in its first or last quarter

CRESCIVE   *adj* increasing

CRESOL   *n* pl. **-S** a chemical disinfectant

CRESS   *n* pl. **-ES** a plant used in salads **CRESSY** *adj*

CRESSET   *n* pl. **-S** a metal cup for burning oil

CREST   *v* **-ED, -ING, -S** to reach a crest (a peak)

CRESTAL   *adj* pertaining to a crest

CRESTING   *n* pl. **-S** a decorative coping

CRESYL   *n* pl. **-S** tolyl

CRESYLIC   *adj* pertaining to cresol

CRETIC   *n* pl. **-S** a type of metrical foot

CRETIN   *n* pl. **-S** an idiot

CRETONNE   *n* pl. **-S** a heavy fabric

CRETONS   *n/pl* a spread of shredded pork and onions

CREVALLE   *n* pl. **-S** a food and game fish

CREVASSE   *v* **-VASSED, -VASSING, -VASSES** to fissure

CREVICE   *n* pl. **-S** a cleft **CREVICED** *adj*

CREW   *v* **-ED, -ING, -S** to serve aboard a ship

CREWCUT   *n* pl. **-S** a short haircut

CREWEL   *n* pl. **-S** a woolen yarn

CREWLESS   *adj* being without any crewmen

CREWMAN   *n* pl. **-MEN** one who serves on a ship

CREWMATE   *n* pl. **-S** a fellow crewman

CREWNECK   *n* pl. **-S** a sweater with a collarless neckline

CRIB   *v* **CRIBBED, CRIBBING, CRIBS** to confine closely

CRIBBAGE   *n* pl. **-S** a card game

CRIBBER   *n* pl. **-S** one that cribs

CRIBBING   *n* pl. **-S** a supporting framework

CRIBBLED   *adj* covered with dots

CRIBROUS   *adj* pierced with small holes

CRIBWORK   *n* pl. **-S** a framework of logs

CRICETID   *n* pl. **-S** a small rodent

CRICK   *v* **-ED, -ING, -S** to cause a spasm of the neck

CRICKET   *v* **-ED, -ING, -S** to play cricket (a ball game)

CRICKEY   *interj* — used as a mild oath

CRICOID   *n* pl. **-S** a cartilage of the larynx

CRIED   past tense of cry

CRIER   *n* pl. **-S** one that cries

CRIES   present 3d person sing. of cry

CRIKEY   *interj* — used as a mild oath

CRIME   *n* pl. **-S** a violation of the law

CRIMINAL   *n* pl. **-S** one who has committed a crime

CRIMINE   *interj* — used to express surprise or anger

CRIMINI   *n* pl. **-S** cremini

CRIMINY   *interj* crimine

CRIMMER   *n* pl. **-S** krimmer

CRIMP   *v* **-ED, -ING, -S** to pleat

CRIMPER   *n* pl. **-S** one that crimps

CRIMPLE   *v* **-PLED, -PLING, -PLES** to wrinkle

CRIMPY   *adj* **CRIMPIER, CRIMPIEST** wavy

CRIMSON   *v* **-ED, -ING, -S** to make crimson (a red color)

CRINGE   *v* **CRINGED, CRINGING, CRINGES** to shrink in fear

CRINGER   *n* pl. **-S** one that cringes

CRINGLE   *n* pl. **-S** a small loop of rope

CRINITE   *n* pl. **-S** a fossil crinoid

CRINKLE   *v* **-KLED, -KLING, -KLES** to wrinkle

CRINKLY   *adj* **-KLIER, -KLIEST** crinkled

CRINOID   *n* pl. **-S** a marine animal

CRINUM   *n* pl. **-S** a tropical herb

CRIOLLO   *n* pl. **-LOS** a person of Spanish ancestry

CRIPE   *interj* — used as a mild oath

CRIPES   *interj* — used as a mild oath

CRIPPLE   *v* **-PLED, -PLING, -PLES** to disable or impair

CRIPPLER   *n* pl. **-S** one that cripples

CRIS   *n* pl. **-ES** kris

CRISIS   *n* pl. **CRISES** a crucial turning point **CRISIC** *adj*

CRISP   *adj* **CRISPER, CRISPEST** brittle

CRISP   *v* **-ED, -ING, -S** to make crisp

CRISPATE	*adj* curled
CRISPEN	*v* **-ED, -ING, -S** to make crisp
CRISPER	*n* pl. **-S** one that crisps
CRISPLY	*adv* in a crisp manner
CRISPY	*adj* **CRISPIER, CRISPIEST** crisp **CRISPILY** *adv*
CRISSUM	*n* pl. **CRISSA** a region of feathers on a bird **CRISSAL** *adj*
CRISTA	*n* pl. **-TAE** a part of a cell
CRISTATE	*adj* having a projection on the head
CRIT	*n* pl. **-S** criticism
CRITERIA	*n/pl* standards of judgment
CRITIC	*n* pl. **-S** one who judges the merits of something **CRITICAL** *adj*
CRITIQUE	*v* **-TIQUED, -TIQUING, -TIQUES** to judge as a critic
CRITTER	*n* pl. **-S** a creature
CRITTUR	*n* pl. **-S** critter
CROAK	*v* **-ED, -ING, -S** to utter a low, hoarse sound
CROAKER	*n* pl. **-S** one that croaks
CROAKY	*adj* **CROAKIER, CROAKIEST** low and hoarse **CROAKILY** *adv*
CROC	*n* pl. **-S** a crocodile
CROCEIN	*n* pl. **-S** a red dye
CROCEINE	*n* pl. **-S** crocein
CROCHET	*v* **-ED, -ING, -S** to do a type of needlework
CROCI	a pl. of crocus
CROCINE	*adj* pertaining to the crocus
CROCK	*v* **-ED, -ING, -S** to soil
CROCKERY	*n* pl. **-ERIES** pottery
CROCKET	*n* pl. **-S** an architectural ornament
CROCKPOT	*n* pl. **-S** an electric cooking pot
CROCOITE	*n* pl. **-S** a mineral
CROCUS	*n* pl. **-CUSES** or **-CI** a flowering plant
CROFT	*v* **-ED, -ING, -S** to farm on a small tenant farm
CROFTER	*n* pl. **-S** a tenant farmer
CROJIK	*n* pl. **-S** a triangular sail
CROMLECH	*n* pl. **-S** a dolmen
CRONE	*n* pl. **-S** a withered old woman **CRONISH** *adj*
CRONY	*n* pl. **CRONIES** a close friend
CRONYISM	*n* pl. **-S** a kind of political favoritism
CROOK	*adj* **CROOKER, CROOKEST** sick

CROOK	*v* **-ED, -ING, -S** to bend
CROOKED	*adj* **-EDER, -EDEST** dishonest
CROOKERY	*n* pl. **-ERIES** crooked activity
CROON	*v* **-ED, -ING, -S** to sing softly
CROONER	*n* pl. **-S** one that croons
CROONY	*adj* **-NIER, -NIEST** having or being a soft singing style
CROP	*v* **CROPPED, CROPPING, CROPS** to cut off short
CROPLAND	*n* pl. **-S** farmland
CROPLESS	*adj* being without crops (agricultural produce)
CROPPER	*n* pl. **-S** one that crops
CROPPIE	*n* pl. **-S** crappie
CROPPING	present participle of crop
CROQUET	*v* **-ED, -ING, -S** to drive a ball away in a certain game
CROQUIS	*n* pl. **CROQUIS** a sketch
CRORE	*n* pl. **-S** a monetary unit of India
CROSIER	*n* pl. **-S** a bishop's staff
CROSS	*adj* **CROSSER, CROSSEST** ill-tempered
CROSS	*v* **-ED, -ING, -ES** to intersect
CROSSARM	*n* pl. **-S** a horizontal bar
CROSSBAR	*v* **-BARRED, -BARRING, -BARS** to fasten with crossarms
CROSSBOW	*n* pl. **-S** a kind of weapon
CROSSCUT	*v* **-CUT, -CUTTING, -CUTS** to cut across
CROSSE	*n* pl. **-S** a lacrosse stick
CROSSER	*n* pl. **-S** one that crosses
CROSSING	*n* pl. **-S** an intersection
CROSSLET	*n* pl. **-S** a heraldic symbol
CROSSLY	*adv* in a cross manner
CROSSPLY	*adj* having layers of fabric with cords lying crosswise in a tire
CROSSTIE	*n* pl. **-S** a transverse beam
CROSSWAY	*n* pl. **-WAYS** a road that crosses another road
CROSTATA	*n* pl. **-S** a type of fruit tart
CROSTINO	*n* pl. **-NI** a small piece of toast topped with a spread
CROTALE	*n* pl. **-S** a small cymbal
CROTCH	*n* pl. **-ES** an angle formed by two diverging parts **CROTCHED** *adj*
CROTCHET	*n* pl. **-S** a small hook
CROTON	*n* pl. **-S** a tropical plant
CROUCH	*v* **-ED, -ING, -ES** to stoop

CROUP *n* pl. **-S** a disease of the throat

CROUPE *n* pl. **-S** the rump of certain animals

CROUPIER *n* pl. **-S** an attendant in a casino

CROUPOUS *adj* pertaining to croup

CROUPY *adj* **CROUPIER, CROUPIEST** affected with croup **CROUPILY** *adv*

CROUSE *adj* lively **CROUSELY** *adv*

CROUTE *n* pl. **-S** a pastry case

CROUTON *n* pl. **-S** a small cube of toasted bread

CROW *v* **-ED, -ING, -S** to boast

CROWBAIT *n* pl. **-S** an old horse

CROWBAR *v* **-BARRED, -BARRING, -BARS** to use a steel bar as a lever

CROWD *v* **-ED, -ING, -S** to press into an insufficient space

CROWDER *n* pl. **-S** one that crowds

CROWDIE *n* pl. **-S** crowdy

CROWDY *n* pl. **-DIES** porridge

CROWER *n* pl. **-S** one that crows

CROWFOOT *n* pl. **-FOOTS** or **-FEET** a flowering plant

CROWN *v* **-ED, -ING, -S** to supply with a crown (a royal headpiece)

CROWNER *n* pl. **-S** a coroner

CROWNET *n* pl. **-S** a coronet

CROWSTEP *n* pl. **-S** a step on top of a wall

CROZE *n* pl. **-S** a tool used in barrel-making

CROZER *n* pl. **-S** a croze

CROZIER *n* pl. **-S** crosier

CRU *n* pl. **-S** a grade or class of wine

CRUCES a pl. of crux

CRUCIAL *adj* of supreme importance

CRUCIAN *n* pl. **-S** a European fish

CRUCIATE *adj* cross-shaped

CRUCIBLE *n* pl. **-S** a heat-resistant vessel

CRUCIFER *n* pl. **-S** one who carries a cross

CRUCIFIX *n* pl. **-ES** a cross bearing an image of Christ

CRUCIFY *v* **-FIED, -FYING, -FIES** to put to death on a cross

CRUCK *n* pl. **-S** a curved roof timber

CRUD *v* **CRUDDED, CRUDDING, CRUDS** to curd

CRUDDY *adj* **-DIER, -DIEST** filthy; contemptible

CRUDE *adj* **CRUDER, CRUDEST** unrefined **CRUDELY** *adv*

CRUDE *n* pl. **-S** unrefined petroleum

CRUDITES *n/pl* pieces of raw vegetables served with a dip

CRUDITY *n* pl. **-TIES** the state of being crude

CRUDO *n* pl. **CRUDOS** sliced, uncooked seafood often served with a sauce

CRUEL *adj* **CRUELER, CRUELEST** or **CRUELLER, CRUELLEST** indifferent to the pain of others **CRUELLY** *adv*

CRUELTY *n* pl. **-TIES** a cruel act

CRUET *n* pl. **-S** a glass bottle

CRUFT *n* pl. **-S** technical material that is redundant, old, or inferior

CRUISE *v* **CRUISED, CRUISING, CRUISES** to sail about touching at several ports

CRUISER *n* pl. **-S** a boat that cruises

CRUISEY *adj* **CRUISIER, CRUISIEST** cruisy

CRUISING *n* pl. **-S** the act of driving around in search of fun

CRUISY *adj* **CRUISIER, CRUISIEST** frequented by homosexuals seeking partners

CRULLER *n* pl. **-S** a small sweet cake

CRUMB *v* **-ED, -ING, -S** to break into crumbs (small pieces)

CRUMBER *n* pl. **-S** one that crumbs

CRUMBIER comparative of crumby

CRUMBIEST superlative of crumby

CRUMBLE *v* **-BLED, -BLING, -BLES** to break into small pieces

CRUMBLY *adj* **-BLIER, -BLIEST** easily crumbled

CRUMBUM *n* pl. **-S** a despicable person

CRUMBY *adj* **CRUMBIER, CRUMBIEST** full of crumbs

CRUMHORN *n* pl. **-S** a double-reed woodwind instrument

CRUMMIE *n* pl. **-S** a cow with crooked horns

CRUMMY *adj* **-MIER, -MIEST** of little or no value **CRUMMILY** *adv*

CRUMP *v* **-ED, -ING, -S** to crunch

CRUMPET *n* pl. **-S** a small cake cooked on a griddle

CRUMPLE *v* **-PLED, -PLING, -PLES** to wrinkle

CRUMPLY *adj* **-PLIER, -PLIEST** easily wrinkled

CRUNCH   *v* **-ED, -ING, -ES** to chew with a crackling sound

CRUNCHER   *n* pl. **-S** one that crunches

CRUNCHY   *adj* **CRUNCHIER, CRUNCHIEST** crisp

CRUNCHY   *n* pl. **CRUNCHIES** something that makes a crackling sound when eaten

CRUNK   *n* pl. **-S** a type of rap music

CRUNODE   *n* pl. **-S** a point at which a curve crosses itself **CRUNODAL** *adj*

CRUOR   *n* pl. **-S** clotted blood

CRUPPER   *n* pl. **-S** the rump of a horse

CRURAL   *adj* pertaining to the thigh or leg

CRUS   *n* pl. **CRURA** a part of the leg

CRUSADE   *v* **-SADED, -SADING, -SADES** to engage in a holy war

CRUSADER   *n* pl. **-S** one that crusades

CRUSADO   *n* pl. **-DOS** or **-DOES** an old Portuguese coin

CRUSE   *n* pl. **-S** a small bottle

CRUSET   *n* pl. **-S** a melting pot

CRUSH   *v* **-ED, -ING, -ES** to press or squeeze out of shape

CRUSHER   *n* pl. **-S** one that crushes

CRUSILY   *adj* covered with crosslets

CRUST   *v* **-ED, -ING, -S** to form a crust (a hardened outer surface)

CRUSTAL   *adj* pertaining to the earth's crust

CRUSTOSE   *adj* forming a thin, brittle crust

CRUSTY   *adj* **CRUSTIER, CRUSTIEST** surly **CRUSTILY** *adv*

CRUTCH   *v* **-ED, -ING, -ES** to prop up or support

CRUX   *n* pl. **CRUXES** or **CRUCES** a basic or decisive point

CRUZADO   *n* pl. **-DOS** or **-DOES** crusado

CRUZEIRO   *n* pl. **-ROS** a former monetary unit of Brazil

CRWTH   *n* pl. **-S** an ancient stringed musical instrument

CRY   *v* **CRIED, CRYING, CRIES** to weep **CRYINGLY** *adv*

CRYBABY   *n* pl. **-BIES** a person who cries easily

CRYER   *n* pl. **-S** crier

CRYOBANK   *n* pl. **-S** a place for storing human tissue at very low temperatures

CRYOGEN   *n* pl. **-S** a substance for producing low temperatures

CRYOGENY   *n* pl. **-NIES** a branch of physics

CRYOLITE   *n* pl. **-S** a mineral

CRYONICS   *n/pl* the practice of freezing dead bodies for future revival **CRYONIC** *adj*

CRYOSTAT   *n* pl. **-S** a refrigerating device

CRYOTRON   *n* pl. **-S** an electronic device

CRYPT   *n* pl. **-S** a burial vault **CRYPTAL** *adj*

CRYPTIC   *adj* mysterious

CRYPTO   *n* pl. **-TOS** one who belongs secretly to a group

CRYSTAL   *n* pl. **-S** a transparent mineral

CSARDAS   *n* pl. **-ES** czardas

CTENIDIA   *n/pl* comblike anatomical structures

CTENOID   *adj* comblike

CUATRO   *n* pl. **-ROS** a small guitar of Latin America

CUB   *v* **CUBBED, CUBBING, CUBS** to give birth to the young of certain animals

CUBAGE   *n* pl. **-S** cubature

CUBATURE   *n* pl. **-S** cubical content

CUBBISH   *adj* resembling a cub

CUBBY   *n* pl. **-BIES** a small, enclosed space

CUBE   *v* **CUBED, CUBING, CUBES** to form into a cube (a regular solid)

CUBEB   *n* pl. **-S** a woody vine

CUBER   *n* pl. **-S** one that cubes

CUBIC   *n* pl. **-S** a mathematical equation or expression

CUBICAL   *adj* shaped like a cube

CUBICITY   *n* pl. **-TIES** the state of being cubical

CUBICLE   *n* pl. **-S** a small chamber

CUBICLY   *adv* in the form of a cube

CUBICULA   *n/pl* burial chambers

CUBIFORM   *adj* shaped like a cube

CUBING   present participle of cube

CUBISM   *n* pl. **-S** a style of art **CUBISTIC** *adj*

CUBIST   *n* pl. **-S** an adherent of cubism

CUBIT   *n* pl. **-S** an ancient measure of length **CUBITAL** *adj*

CUBITUS   *n* pl. **-TI** the forearm

CUBOID   *n* pl. **-S** a bone of the foot **CUBOIDAL** *adj*

CUCKOLD   *v* **-ED, -ING, -S** to make a cuckold (a cornuto) of

CUCKOO   *v* **-ED, -ING, -S** to repeat monotonously

CUCUMBER   *n* pl. **-S** a garden vegetable

CUCURBIT   *n* pl. **-S** a gourd

CUD   *n* pl. **-S** a portion of food to be chewed again

CUDBEAR   *n* pl. **-S** a red dye

CUDDIE   *n* pl. **-S** cuddy

CUDDIES   pl. of cuddy

CUDDLE   *v* **-DLED, -DLING, -DLES** to hug tenderly

CUDDLER   *n* pl. **-S** one that cuddles

CUDDLY   *adj* **-DLIER, -DLIEST** fit for cuddling

CUDDY   *n* pl. **-DIES** a donkey

CUDGEL   *v* **-ELED, -ELING, -ELS** or **-ELLED, -ELLING, -ELS** to beat with a heavy club

CUDGELER   *n* pl. **-S** one that cudgels

CUDWEED   *n* pl. **-S** a perennial herb

CUE   *v* **CUED, CUING** or **CUEING, CUES** to give a signal to an actor

CUEIST   *n* pl. **-S** one that uses a cue (a straight tapering rod) in billiards

CUESTA   *n* pl. **-S** a type of land elevation

CUFF   *v* **-ED, -ING, -S** to furnish with a cuff (a part of a sleeve)

CUFFABLE   *adj* intended to be folded down to the ankle — used of a sock

CUFFLESS   *adj* having no cuff

CUFFLINK   *n* pl. **-S** a fastening for a shirt cuff

CUIF   *n* pl. **-S** coof

CUING   a present participle of cue

CUIRASS   *v* **-ED, -ING, -ES** to cover with a type of armor

CUISH   *n* pl. **-ES** cuisse

CUISINE   *n* pl. **-S** a style of cooking

CUISSE   *n* pl. **-S** a piece of armor for the thigh

CUITTLE   *v* **-TLED, -TLING, -TLES** to coax

CUKE   *n* pl. **-S** a cucumber

CULCH   *n* pl. **-ES** an oyster bed

CULET   *n* pl. **-S** a piece of armor for the lower back

CULEX   *n* pl. **CULEXES** or **CULICES** a mosquito

CULICID   *n* pl. **-S** a culicine

CULICINE   *n* pl. **-S** a mosquito

CULINARY   *adj* pertaining to cookery

CULL   *v* **-ED, -ING, -S** to select from others

CULLAY   *n* pl. **-LAYS** quillai

CULLER   *n* pl. **-S** one that culls

CULLET   *n* pl. **-S** broken glass gathered for remelting

CULLIED   past tense of cully

CULLION   *n* pl. **-S** a vile fellow

CULLIS   *n* pl. **-LISES** a gutter in a roof

CULLY   *v* **-LIED, -LYING, -LIES** to trick

CULM   *v* **-ED, -ING, -S** to form a hollow stem

CULMEN   *n* pl. **-MINA** the upper ridge of a bird's beak

CULOTTE   *n* pl. **-S** a divided skirt

CULPA   *n* pl. **-PAE** negligence for which one is liable

CULPABLE   *adj* deserving blame or censure **CULPABLY** *adv*

CULPRIT   *n* pl. **-S** one that is guilty

CULT   *n* pl. **-S** a group of zealous devotees

CULTCH   *n* pl. **-ES** culch

CULTI   a pl. of cultus

CULTIC   *adj* pertaining to a cult

CULTIGEN   *n* pl. **-S** a cultivar

CULTISH   *adj* pertaining to a cult

CULTISM   *n* pl. **-S** devotion to a cult

CULTIST   *n* pl. **-S** a member of a cult

CULTIVAR   *n* pl. **-S** a variety of plant originating under cultivation

CULTLIKE   *adj* resembling a cult

CULTRATE   *adj* sharp-edged and pointed

CULTURAL   *adj* produced by breeding

CULTURE   *v* **-TURED, -TURING, -TURES** to make fit for raising crops

CULTUS   *n* pl. **-TUSES** or **-TI** a cult

CULVER   *n* pl. **-S** a pigeon

CULVERIN   *n* pl. **-S** a medieval musket

CULVERT   *v* **-ED, -ING, -S** to channel a stream through a conduit

CUM   *prep* together with

CUMARIN   *n* pl. **-S** coumarin

CUMBER   *v* **-ED, -ING, -S** to hinder

CUMBERER   *n* pl. **-S** one that cumbers

CUMBIA   *n* pl. **-S** a Latin-American dance

CUMBROUS   *adj* unwieldy

CUMIN *n* pl. **-S** a plant used in cooking

CUMMER *n* pl. **-S** a godmother

CUMMIN *n* pl. **-S** cumin

CUMQUAT *n* pl. **-S** kumquat

CUMSHAW *n* pl. **-S** a gift

CUMULATE *v* **-LATED, -LATING, -LATES** to heap

CUMULUS *n* pl. **-LI** a type of cloud **CUMULOUS** *adj*

CUNDUM *n* pl. **-S** condom

CUNEAL *adj* cuneate

CUNEATE *adj* wedge-shaped; triangular

CUNEATED *adj* cuneate

CUNEATIC *adj* cuneate

CUNIFORM *n* pl. **-S** wedge-shaped writing characters

CUNIT *n* pl. **-S** 100 cubic feet (2.83 cubic meters) of wood

CUNNER *n* pl. **-S** a marine fish

CUNNING *adj* **-NINGER, -NINGEST** crafty

CUNNING *n* pl. **-S** skill in deception

CUP *v* **CUPPED, CUPPING, CUPS** to place in a cup (a small, open container)

CUPBOARD *n* pl. **-S** a cabinet

CUPCAKE *n* pl. **-S** a small cake

CUPEL *v* **-PELED, -PELING, -PELS** or **-PELLED, -PELLING, -PELS** to refine gold or silver in a cuplike vessel

CUPELER *n* pl. **-S** cupeller

CUPELLER *n* pl. **-S** one that cupels

CUPFUL *n* pl. **CUPFULS** or **CUPSFUL** as much as a cup can hold

CUPID *n* pl. **-S** a naked, winged representation of the Roman god of love

CUPIDITY *n* pl. **-TIES** greed; lust

CUPLIKE *adj* resembling a cup

CUPOLA *v* **-ED, -ING, -S** to shape like a dome

CUPPA *n* pl. **-S** a cup of tea

CUPPED past tense of cup

CUPPER *n* pl. **-S** one that performs cupping

CUPPING *n* pl. **-S** an archaic medical process

CUPPY *adj* **-PIER, -PIEST** cuplike

CUPREOUS *adj* containing copper

CUPRIC *adj* containing copper

CUPRITE *n* pl. **-S** an ore of copper

CUPROUS *adj* containing copper

CUPRUM *n* pl. **-S** copper

CUPSFUL a pl. of cupful

CUPULA *n* pl. **-LAE** cupule

CUPULAR *adj* cupulate

CUPULATE *adj* cup-shaped

CUPULE *n* pl. **-S** a cup-shaped anatomical structure

CUR *n* pl. **-S** a mongrel dog

CURABLE *adj* capable of being cured **CURABLY** *adv*

CURACAO *n* pl. **-S** a type of liqueur

CURACOA *n* pl. **-S** curacao

CURACY *n* pl. **-CIES** the office of a curate

CURAGH *n* pl. **-S** currach

CURARA *n* pl. **-S** curare

CURARE *n* pl. **-S** an arrow poison

CURARI *n* pl. **-S** curare

CURARINE *n* pl. **-S** a poisonous alkaloid

CURARIZE *v* **-RIZED, -RIZING, -RIZES** to poison with curare

CURASSOW *n* pl. **-S** a turkey-like bird

CURATE *v* **-RATED, -RATING, -RATES** to act as curator of

CURATION *n* pl. **-S** the work of a curator

CURATIVE *n* pl. **-S** something that cures

CURATOR *n* pl. **-S** a museum manager

CURB *v* **-ED, -ING, -S** to restrain **CURBABLE** *adj*

CURBER *n* pl. **-S** one that curbs

CURBING *n* pl. **-S** a concrete border along a street

CURBSIDE *n* pl. **-S** the side of a pavement bordered by a curbing

CURCH *n* pl. **-ES** a kerchief

CURCULIO *n* pl. **-LIOS** a weevil

CURCUMA *n* pl. **-S** a tropical plant

CURCUMIN *n* pl. **-S** the coloring ingredient of the spice turmeric

CURD *v* **-ED, -ING, -S** to curdle

CURDLE *v* **-DLED, -DLING, -DLES** to congeal

CURDLER *n* pl. **-S** one that curdles

CURDY *adj* **CURDIER, CURDIEST** curdled

CURE *v* **CURED, CURING, CURES** to restore to health

CURELESS	*adj* not curable	**CURSE**	*v* **CURSED** or **CURST, CURSING, CURSES** to wish evil upon
CURER	*n* pl. **-S** one that cures	**CURSED**	*adj* **CURSEDER, CURSEDEST** wicked **CURSEDLY** *adv*
CURET	*n* pl. **-S** a surgical instrument		
CURETTE	*v* **-RETTED, -RETTING, -RETTES** to treat with a curet	**CURSER**	*n* pl. **-S** one that curses
		CURSILLO	*n* pl. **-LOS** a type of spiritual retreat (seclusion with a group)
CURF	*n* pl. **-S** an incision made by a cutting tool		
		CURSING	present participle of curse
CURFEW	*n* pl. **-S** a regulation concerning the hours which one may keep	**CURSIVE**	*n* pl. **-S** a style of print
		CURSOR	*n* pl. **-S** a light indicator on a computer display
CURIA	*n* pl. **-RIAE** a court of justice **CURIAL** *adj*		
		CURSORY	*adj* hasty and superficial
CURIE	*n* pl. **-S** a unit of radioactivity	**CURST**	a past tense of curse
CURING	present participle of cure	**CURT**	*adj* **CURTER, CURTEST** abrupt
CURIO	*n* pl. **-RIOS** an unusual art object	**CURTAIL**	*v* **-ED, -ING, -S** to cut short
CURIOSA	*n/pl* pornographic books	**CURTAIN**	*v* **-ED, -ING, -S** to provide with a hanging piece of fabric
CURIOUS	*adj* **-OUSER, -OUSEST** eager for information		
		CURTAL	*n* pl. **-S** an animal with a clipped tail
CURITE	*n* pl. **-S** a radioactive mineral		
CURIUM	*n* pl. **-S** a radioactive element	**CURTALAX**	*n* pl. **-ES** a cutlass
CURL	*v* **-ED, -ING, -S** to form into ringlets	**CURTANA**	*n* pl. **-S** a type of English sword
CURLER	*n* pl. **-S** one that curls	**CURTATE**	*adj* shortened
CURLEW	*n* pl. **-S** a shore bird	**CURTESY**	*n* pl. **-SIES** a type of legal tenure
CURLICUE	*v* **-CUED, -CUING, -CUES** to decorate with curlicues (fancy spiral figures)	**CURTLY**	*adv* in a curt manner
		CURTNESS	*n* pl. **-ES** the quality of being curt
CURLING	*n* pl. **-S** a game played on ice	**CURTSEY**	*v* **-ED, -ING, -S** to curtsy
CURLY	*adj* **CURLIER, CURLIEST** tending to curl **CURLILY** *adv*	**CURTSY**	*v* **-SIED, -SYING, -SIES** to bow politely
CURLYCUE	*n* pl. **-S** curlicue	**CURULE**	*adj* of the highest rank
CURN	*n* pl. **-S** grain	**CURVE**	*v* **CURVED, CURVING, CURVES** to deviate from straightness **CURVEDLY** *adv*
CURR	*v* **-ED, -ING, -S** to purr		
CURRACH	*n* pl. **-S** a coracle		
CURRAGH	*n* pl. **-S** currach	**CURVET**	*v* **-VETED, -VETING, -VETS** or **-VETTED, -VETTING, -VETS** to prance
CURRAN	*n* pl. **-S** curn		
CURRANT	*n* pl. **-S** an edible berry	**CURVEY**	*adj* **CURVIER, CURVIEST** curvy
CURRENCY	*n* pl. **-CIES** money	**CURVING**	present participle of curve
CURRENT	*n* pl. **-S** a continuous flow	**CURVY**	*adj* **CURVIER, CURVIEST** curved
CURRICLE	*n* pl. **-S** a light carriage	**CUSCUS**	*n* pl. **-ES** an arboreal mammal
CURRIE	*v* **-RIED, -RYING, -RIES** to prepare food a certain way	**CUSEC**	*n* pl. **-S** a volumetric unit of flow of liquids
CURRIED	past tense of curry	**CUSHAT**	*n* pl. **-S** a pigeon
CURRIER	*n* pl. **-S** one that curries leather	**CUSHAW**	*n* pl. **-S** a variety of squash
CURRIERY	*n* pl. **-ERIES** the shop of a currier	**CUSHIER**	comparative of cushy
CURRISH	*adj* resembling a cur	**CUSHIEST**	superlative of cushy
CURRY	*v* **-RIED, -RYING, -RIES** to prepare leather for use or sale	**CUSHILY**	*adv* in a cushy manner
		CUSHION	*v* **-ED, -ING, -S** to pad with soft material
CURRYING	present participle of currie		

CUSHIONY	*adj* soft
CUSHY	*adj* **CUSHIER, CUSHIEST** easy
CUSK	*n* pl. **-S** a marine food fish
CUSP	*n* pl. **-S** a pointed end **CUSPAL, CUSPATE, CUSPATED, CUSPED** *adj*
CUSPID	*n* pl. **-S** a pointed tooth
CUSPIDAL	*adj* having a cusp
CUSPIDOR	*n* pl. **-S** a spittoon
CUSPIS	*n* pl. **-PIDES** a cusp
CUSS	*v* **-ED, -ING, -ES** to curse
CUSSEDLY	*adv* in a cranky manner
CUSSER	*n* pl. **-S** one that cusses
CUSSO	*n* pl. **-SOS** an Ethiopian tree
CUSSWORD	*n* pl. **-S** a profane or obscene word
CUSTARD	*n* pl. **-S** a thick, soft dessert **CUSTARDY** *adj*
CUSTODES	pl. of custos
CUSTODY	*n* pl. **-DIES** guardianship
CUSTOM	*n* pl. **-S** a habitual practice
CUSTOMER	*n* pl. **-S** one who buys something
CUSTOS	*n* pl. **-TODES** a guardian or keeper
CUSTUMAL	*n* pl. **-S** a written record of laws and customs
CUT	*v* **CUT, CUTTING, CUTS** to divide into parts with a sharp-edged instrument
CUTAWAY	*n* pl. **-AWAYS** a type of coat
CUTBACK	*n* pl. **-S** a reduction
CUTBANK	*n* pl. **-S** a steep stream bank
CUTBLOCK	*n* pl. **-S** a limited area authorized for logging
CUTCH	*n* pl. **-ES** catechu
CUTCHERY	*n* pl. **-CHERIES** a judicial office in India
CUTDOWN	*n* pl. **-S** a reduction
CUTE	*adj* **CUTER, CUTEST** pleasingly attractive **CUTELY** *adv*
CUTENESS	*n* pl. **-ES** the quality of being cute
CUTES	a pl. of cutis
CUTESIE	*adj* **-SIER, -SIEST** cutesy
CUTEST	superlative of cute
CUTESY	*adj* **-SIER, -SIEST** self-consciously cute
CUTEY	*n* pl. **-TEYS** cutie
CUTGRASS	*n* pl. **-ES** a swamp grass
CUTICLE	*n* pl. **-S** the epidermis
CUTICULA	*n* pl. **-LAE** the outer hard covering of an insect
CUTIE	*n* pl. **-S** a cute person
CUTIN	*n* pl. **-S** a waxy substance found on plants
CUTINISE	*v* **-ISED, -ISING, -ISES** to cutinize
CUTINIZE	*v* **-IZED, -IZING, -IZES** to become coated with cutin
CUTIS	*n* pl. **-TISES** or **-TES** the corium
CUTLAS	*n* pl. **-ES** cutlass
CUTLASS	*n* pl. **-ES** a short sword
CUTLER	*n* pl. **-S** one who sells and repairs cutting tools
CUTLERY	*n* pl. **-LERIES** the occupation of a cutler
CUTLET	*n* pl. **-S** a slice of meat
CUTLETTE	*n* pl. **-S** a breaded patty of chopped meat
CUTLINE	*n* pl. **-S** a caption
CUTOFF	*n* pl. **-S** the point at which something terminates
CUTOUT	*n* pl. **-S** something cut out
CUTOVER	*n* pl. **-S** land cleared of trees
CUTPURSE	*n* pl. **-S** a pickpocket
CUTSCENE	*n* pl. **-S** a type of scene in computer games
CUTTABLE	*adj* capable of being cut
CUTTAGE	*n* pl. **-S** a means of plant propagation
CUTTER	*n* pl. **-S** one that cuts
CUTTIES	pl. of cutty
CUTTING	*n* pl. **-S** a section cut from a plant
CUTTLE	*v* **-TLED, -TLING, -TLES** to fold cloth in a particular fashion
CUTTY	*n* pl. **-TIES** a thickset girl
CUTUP	*n* pl. **-S** a mischievous person
CUTWATER	*n* pl. **-S** the front part of a ship's prow
CUTWORK	*n* pl. **-S** a type of embroidery
CUTWORM	*n* pl. **-S** a caterpillar
CUVEE	*n* pl. **-S** wine blended in casks
CUVETTE	*n* pl. **-S** a small tube or vessel
CUZ	*n* pl. **CUZZES** or **CUZES** a cousin
CWM	*n* pl. **-S** a cirque
CYAN	*n* pl. **-S** a blue color
CYANAMID	*n* pl. **-S** a chemical compound
CYANATE	*n* pl. **-S** a chemical salt
CYANIC	*adj* blue or bluish

CYANID   *n* pl. **-S** a compound of cyanogen

CYANIDE   *v* **-NIDED, -NIDING, -NIDES** to treat an ore with cyanid

CYANIN   *n* pl. **-S** cyanine

CYANINE   *n* pl. **-S** a blue dye

CYANITE   *n* pl. **-S** a mineral **CYANITIC** *adj*

CYANO   *adj* pertaining to cyanogen

CYANOGEN   *n* pl. **-S** a reactive compound of carbon and nitrogen

CYANOSIS   *n* pl. **-NOSES** bluish discoloration of the skin **CYANOSED, CYANOTIC** *adj*

CYATHIUM   *n* pl. **-ATHIA** the flower head of certain plants

CYBER   *adj* pertaining to computers

CYBERSEX   *n* pl. **-ES** an online sex-oriented conversation

CYBERWAR   *n* pl. **-S** a conflict in which enemies try to gain access to each other's computer systems

CYBORG   *n* pl. **-S** a human linked to a mechanical device for life support

CYCAD   *n* pl. **-S** a tropical plant

CYCAS   *n* pl. **-ES** a tropical plant

CYCASIN   *n* pl. **-S** a sugar derivative

CYCLAMEN   *n* pl. **-S** a flowering plant

CYCLASE   *n* pl. **-S** an enzyme

CYCLE   *v* **-CLED, -CLING, -CLES** to ride a bicycle

CYCLECAR   *n* pl. **-S** a type of motor vehicle

CYCLER   *n* pl. **-S** a cyclist

CYCLERY   *n* pl. **-RIES** a bicycle shop

CYCLEWAY   *n* pl. **-WAYS** a bikeway

CYCLIC   *adj* moving in complete circles **CYCLICLY** *adv*

CYCLICAL   *n* pl. **-S** a stock whose earnings fluctuate widely with variations in the economy

CYCLIN   *n* pl. **-S** any of a group of proteins that control the cell cycle

CYCLING   *n* pl. **-S** the act of riding a bicycle

CYCLIST   *n* pl. **-S** one who rides a bicycle

CYCLITOL   *n* pl. **-S** a chemical compound

CYCLIZE   *v* **-CLIZED, -CLIZING, -CLIZES** to form one or more rings in a chemical compound

CYCLO   *n* pl. **-CLOS** a three-wheeled motor vehicle

CYCLOID   *n* pl. **-S** a geometric curve

CYCLONE   *n* pl. **-S** a rotating system of winds **CYCLONAL, CYCLONIC** *adj*

CYCLOPS   *n* pl. **CYCLOPS** a minute one-eyed crustacean

CYCLOSIS   *n* pl. **-CLOSES** the circulation of protoplasm within a cell

CYDER   *n* pl. **-S** cider

CYESIS   *n* pl. **CYESES** pregnancy

CYGNET   *n* pl. **-S** a young swan

CYLINDER   *v* **-ED, -ING, -S** to furnish with a cylinder (a chamber in an engine)

CYLIX   *n* pl. **CYLICES** kylix

CYMA   *n* pl. **-MAS** or **-MAE** a curved molding

CYMAR   *n* pl. **-S** simar

CYMATIUM   *n* pl. **-TIA** a cyma

CYMBAL   *n* pl. **-S** a percussion instrument

CYMBALER   *n* pl. **-S** one that plays the cymbals

CYMBALOM   *n* pl. **-S** cimbalom

CYMBIDIA   *n/pl* tropical orchids

CYMBLING   *n* pl. **-S** cymling

CYME   *n* pl. **-S** a flower cluster

CYMENE   *n* pl. **-S** a hydrocarbon

CYMLIN   *n* pl. **-S** cymling

CYMLING   *n* pl. **-S** a variety of squash

CYMOGENE   *n* pl. **-S** a volatile compound

CYMOID   *adj* resembling a cyma

CYMOL   *n* pl. **-S** cymene

CYMOSE   *adj* resembling a cyme **CYMOSELY** *adv*

CYMOUS   *adj* cymose

CYNIC   *n* pl. **-S** a cynical person

CYNICAL   *adj* distrusting the motives of others

CYNICISM   *n* pl. **-S** cynical quality

CYNODONT   *n* pl. **-S** a type of fossil reptile

CYNOSURE   *n* pl. **-S** a center of attraction

CYPHER   *v* **-ED, -ING, -S** to cipher

CYPRES   *n* pl. **-ES** a legal doctrine

CYPRESS   *n* pl. **-ES** a thin fabric

CYPRIAN   *n* pl. **-S** a prostitute

CYPRINID   *n* pl. **-S** a small freshwater fish

CYPRUS   *n* pl. **-ES** cypress

CYPSELA   *n* pl. **-LAE** an achene in certain plants

CYST   *n* pl. **-S** a sac

CYSTEIN   *n* pl. **-S** cysteine

CYSTEINE   *n* pl. **-S** an amino acid

CYSTIC   *adj* pertaining to a cyst

CYSTINE   *n* pl. **-S** an amino acid

CYSTITIS   *n* pl. **-TITIDES** inflammation of the urinary bladder

CYSTOID   *n* pl. **-S** a cyst-like structure

CYTASTER   *n* pl. **-S** a structure formed in a cell during mitosis

CYTIDINE   *n* pl. **-S** a compound containing cytosine

CYTOGENY   *n* pl. **-NIES** the formation of cells

CYTOKINE   *n* pl. **-S** a kind of substance secreted by cells of the immune system

CYTOLOGY   *n* pl. **-GIES** a study of cells

CYTON   *n* pl. **-S** the body of a nerve cell

CYTOSINE   *n* pl. **-S** a component of DNA and RNA

CYTOSOL   *n* pl. **-S** the fluid portion of cell material

CZAR   *n* pl. **-S** an emperor or king

CZARDAS   *n* pl. **-ES** a Hungarian dance

CZARDOM   *n* pl. **-S** the domain of a czar

CZAREVNA   *n* pl. **-S** the daughter of a czar

CZARINA   *n* pl. **-S** the wife of a czar

CZARISM   *n* pl. **-S** autocratic government

CZARIST   *n* pl. **-S** a supporter of czarism

CZARITZA   *n* pl. **-S** a czarina

DA	*n* pl. **-S** dad
DAB	*v* **DABBED, DABBING, DABS** to touch lightly
DABBER	*n* pl. **-S** one that dabs
DABBLE	*v* **-BLED, -BLING, -BLES** to involve oneself in a superficial interest
DABBLER	*n* pl. **-S** one that dabbles
DABBLING	*n* pl. **-S** a superficial interest
DABCHICK	*n* pl. **-S** a small grebe
DABSTER	*n* pl. **-S** a dabbler
DACE	*n* pl. **-S** a freshwater fish
DACHA	*n* pl. **-S** a Russian cottage
DACITE	*n* pl. **-S** a light gray rock
DACKER	*v* **-ED, -ING, -S** to waver
DACOIT	*n* pl. **-S** a bandit in India
DACOITY	*n* pl. **-COITIES** robbery by dacoits
DACTYL	*n* pl. **-S** a type of metrical foot
DACTYLIC	*n* pl. **-S** a verse consisting of dactyls
DACTYLUS	*n* pl. **-LI** a leg joint of certain insects
DAD	*n* pl. **-S** father
DADA	*n* pl. **-S** an artistic and literary movement
DADAISM	*n* pl. **-S** the dada movement
DADAIST	*n* pl. **-S** a follower of dadaism
DADDLE	*v* **-DLED, -DLING, -DLES** to diddle
DADDY	*n* pl. **-DIES** father
DADGUM	*adj* — used as an intensive
DADO	*v* **-ED, -ING, -S** or **-ES** to set into a groove
DAEDAL	*adj* skillful
DAEMON	*n* pl. **-S** demon **DAEMONIC** *adj*
DAEMON	*n* pl. **-S** or **-ES** daimon
DAFF	*v* **-ED, -ING, -S** to thrust aside
DAFFODIL	*n* pl. **-S** a flowering plant
DAFFY	*adj* **-FIER, -FIEST** silly **DAFFILY** *adv*
DAFT	*adj* **DAFTER, DAFTEST** insane **DAFTLY** *adv*
DAFTNESS	*n* pl. **-ES** the quality of being daft
DAG	*n* pl. **-S** a hanging end or shred
DAGGA	*n* pl. **-S** marijuana
DAGGER	*v* **-ED, -ING, -S** to stab with a small knife
DAGGLE	*v* **-GLED, -GLING, -GLES** to drag in mud
DAGLOCK	*n* pl. **-S** a dirty or tangled lock of wool
DAGOBA	*n* pl. **-S** a Buddhist shrine
DAGWOOD	*n* pl. **-S** a large sandwich
DAH	*n* pl. **-S** a dash in Morse code
DAHABEAH	*n* pl. **-S** a large passenger boat
DAHABIAH	*n* pl. **-S** dahabeah
DAHABIEH	*n* pl. **-S** dahabeah
DAHABIYA	*n* pl. **-S** dahabeah
DAHL	*n* pl. **-S** dal
DAHLIA	*n* pl. **-S** a flowering plant
DAHOON	*n* pl. **-S** an evergreen tree
DAIDZEIN	*n* pl. **-S** a chemical found chiefly in soybeans
DAIKER	*v* **-ED, -ING, -S** to dacker
DAIKON	*n* pl. **-S** a Japanese radish
DAILY	*n* pl. **-LIES** a newspaper published every weekday
DAIMEN	*adj* occasional
DAIMIO	*n* pl. **-MIOS** a former Japanese nobleman
DAIMON	*n* pl. **-S** or **-ES** an attendant spirit **DAIMONIC** *adj*
DAIMYO	*n* pl. **-MYOS** daimio
DAINTY	*adj* **-TIER, -TIEST** delicately pretty **DAINTILY** *adv*
DAINTY	*n* pl. **-TIES** something delicious

DAIQUIRI	*n* pl. **-S** a cocktail
DAIRY	*n* pl. **DAIRIES** an establishment dealing in milk products
DAIRYING	*n* pl. **-S** the business of a dairy
DAIRYMAN	*n* pl. **-MEN** a man who works in or owns a dairy
DAIS	*n* pl. **-ISES** a raised platform
DAISHIKI	*n* pl. **-S** dashiki
DAISY	*n* pl. **-SIES** a flowering plant **DAISIED** *adj*
DAK	*n* pl. **-S** transportation by relays of men and horses
DAKERHEN	*n* pl. **-S** a European bird
DAKOIT	*n* pl. **-S** dacoit
DAKOITY	*n* pl. **-TIES** dacoity
DAL	*n* pl. **-S** a dish of lentils and spices in India
DALAPON	*n* pl. **-S** an herbicide used on unwanted grasses
DALASI	*n* pl. **-S** a unit of Gambian currency
DALE	*n* pl. **-S** a valley
DALEDH	*n* pl. **-S** daleth
DALESMAN	*n* pl. **-MEN** one living in a dale
DALETH	*n* pl. **-S** a Hebrew letter
DALLES	*n/pl* rapids
DALLIER	*n* pl. **-S** one that dallies
DALLY	*v* **-LIED, -LYING, -LIES** to waste time
DALMATIC	*n* pl. **-S** a wide-sleeved vestment
DALTON	*n* pl. **-S** a unit of atomic mass
DALTONIC	*adj* pertaining to a form of color blindness
DAM	*v* **DAMMED, DAMMING, DAMS** to build a barrier to obstruct the flow of water
DAMAGE	*v* **-AGED, -AGING, -AGES** to injure
DAMAGER	*n* pl. **-S** one that damages
DAMAN	*n* pl. **-S** a small mammal
DAMAR	*n* pl. **-S** dammar
DAMASK	*v* **-ED, -ING, -S** to weave with elaborate design
DAME	*n* pl. **-S** a matron
DAMEWORT	*n* pl. **-S** a flowering plant
DAMFOOL	*n* pl. **-S** a stupid or foolish person
DAMIANA	*n* pl. **-S** a tropical American shrub
DAMMAR	*n* pl. **-S** a hard resin
DAMMED	past tense of dam
DAMMER	*n* pl. **-S** dammar

DAMMING	present participle of dam
DAMMIT	*interj* — used to express anger
DAMN	*v* **-ED, -ING, -S** to curse
DAMNABLE	*adj* detestable **DAMNABLY** *adv*
DAMNDEST	*n* pl. **-S** utmost
DAMNED	*adj* **DAMNEDER, DAMNEDEST** or **DAMNDEST** damnable
DAMNER	*n* pl. **-S** one that damns
DAMNEST	*n* pl. **-S** damndest
DAMNIFY	*v* **-FIED, -FYING, -FIES** to cause loss or damage to
DAMOSEL	*n* pl. **-S** damsel
DAMOZEL	*n* pl. **-S** damsel
DAMP	*adj* **DAMPER, DAMPEST** moist
DAMP	*v* **-ED, -ING, -S** to lessen in intensity
DAMPEN	*v* **-ED, -ING, -S** to moisten
DAMPENER	*n* pl. **-S** one that dampens
DAMPER	*n* pl. **-S** one that damps
DAMPING	*n* pl. **-S** the ability of a device to prevent instability
DAMPISH	*adj* somewhat damp
DAMPLY	*adv* in a damp manner
DAMPNESS	*n* pl. **-ES** the state of being damp
DAMSEL	*n* pl. **-S** a maiden
DAMSON	*n* pl. **-S** a small purple plum
DAN	*n* pl. **-S** a level of skill in martial arts
DANAZOL	*n* pl. **-S** a synthetic androgen
DANCE	*v* **DANCED, DANCING, DANCES** to move rhythmically to music
DANCER	*n* pl. **-S** one that dances
DANCEY	*adj* **DANCIER, DANCIEST** suitable for dancing
DANDER	*v* **-ED, -ING, -S** to stroll
DANDIER	comparative of dandy
DANDIES	pl. of dandy
DANDIEST	superlative of dandy
DANDIFY	*v* **-FIED, -FYING, -FIES** to cause to resemble a dandy
DANDILY	*adv* in a dandy manner
DANDLE	*v* **-DLED, -DLING, -DLES** to fondle
DANDLER	*n* pl. **-S** one that dandles
DANDRIFF	*n* pl. **-S** dandruff
DANDRUFF	*n* pl. **-S** a scurf that forms on the scalp
DANDY	*adj* **-DIER, -DIEST** fine

DANDY *n pl.* **-DIES** a man who is overly concerned about his appearance

DANDYISH *adj* suggestive of a dandy

DANDYISM *n pl.* **-S** the style or conduct of a dandy

DANEGELD *n pl.* **-S** an annual tax in medieval England

DANEGELT *n pl.* **-S** danegeld

DANEWEED *n pl.* **-S** a danewort

DANEWORT *n pl.* **-S** a flowering plant

DANG *v* **-ED, -ING, -S** to damn

DANGER *v* **-ED, -ING, -S** to endanger

DANGLE *v* **-GLED, -GLING, -GLES** to hang loosely

DANGLER *n pl.* **-S** one that dangles

DANGLY *adj* **-GLIER, -GLIEST** dangling

DANIO *n pl.* **-NIOS** an aquarium fish

DANISH *n pl.* **-ES** a pastry of raised dough

DANK *adj* **DANKER, DANKEST** unpleasantly damp **DANKLY** *adv*

DANKNESS *n pl.* **-ES** the state of being dank

DANSAK *n pl.* **-S** dhansak

DANSEUR *n pl.* **-S** a male ballet dancer

DANSEUSE *n pl.* **-S** a female ballet dancer

DAP *v* **DAPPED, DAPPING, DAPS** to dip lightly or quickly into water

DAPHNE *n pl.* **-S** a flowering shrub

DAPHNIA *n pl.* **-S** a minute crustacean

DAPPER *adj* **-PERER, -PEREST** looking neat and trim **DAPPERLY** *adv*

DAPPING present participle of dap

DAPPLE *v* **-PLED, -PLING, -PLES** to mark with spots

DAPSONE *n pl.* **-S** a medicinal substance

DARB *n pl.* **-S** something considered extraordinary

DARBAR *n pl.* **-S** durbar

DARBIES *n/pl* handcuffs

DARE *v* **DARED** or **DURST, DARING, DARES** to have the necessary courage

DAREFUL *adj* brave

DARER *n pl.* **-S** one that dares

DARESAY *v* to venture to say — DARESAY is the only form of this verb; it is not conjugated

DARIC *n pl.* **-S** an ancient Persian coin

DARING *n pl.* **-S** bravery

DARINGLY *adv* in a brave manner

DARIOLE *n pl.* **-S** a type of pastry filled with cream, custard, or jelly

DARK *adj* **DARKER, DARKEST** having little or no light

DARK *v* **-ED, -ING, -S** to darken

DARKEN *v* **-ED, -ING, -S** to make dark

DARKENER *n pl.* **-S** one that darkens

DARKISH *adj* somewhat dark

DARKLE *v* **-KLED, -KLING, -KLES** to become dark

DARKLING *n pl.* **-S** the dark

DARKLY *adv* **-LIER, -LIEST** in a dark manner

DARKNESS *n pl.* **-ES** the state of being dark

DARKROOM *n pl.* **-S** a room in which film is processed

DARKSOME *adj* dark

DARLING *n pl.* **-S** a much-loved person

DARN *v* **-ED, -ING, -S** to mend with interlacing stitches

DARNDEST *n pl.* **-S** damndest

DARNED *adj* **DARNEDER, DARNEDEST** or **DARNDEST** damned

DARNEL *n pl.* **-S** an annual grass

DARNER *n pl.* **-S** one that darns

DARNEST *n pl.* **-S** damndest

DARNING *n pl.* **-S** things to be darned

DARSHAN *n pl.* **-S** a Hindu blessing

DART *v* **-ED, -ING, -S** to move suddenly or swiftly

DARTER *n pl.* **-S** one that darts

DARTLE *v* **-TLED, -TLING, -TLES** to dart repeatedly

DASH *v* **-ED, -ING, -ES** to strike violently

DASHEEN *n pl.* **-S** a tropical plant

DASHER *n pl.* **-S** one that dashes

DASHI *n pl.* **-S** a fish broth

DASHIER comparative of dashy

DASHIEST superlative of dashy

DASHIKI *n pl.* **-S** an African tunic

DASHPOT *n pl.* **-S** a shock absorber

DASHY *adj* **DASHIER, DASHIEST** stylish

DASSIE *n pl.* **-S** a hyrax

DASTARD *n pl.* **-S** a base coward

DASYURE *n pl.* **-S** a flesh-eating mammal

DATA *a pl.* of datum

DATABANK *n* pl. **-S** a database

DATABASE *v* **-BASED, -BASING, -BASES** to put data into a database (a collection of data in a computer)

DATABLE *adj* capable of being dated

DATARY *n* pl. **-RIES** a cardinal in the Roman Catholic Church

DATCHA *n* pl. **-S** dacha

DATE *v* **DATED, DATING, DATES** to determine or record the date of **DATEABLE** *adj*

DATEBOOK *n* pl. **-S** a notebook for listing appointments

DATEDLY *adv* in an old-fashioned manner

DATELESS *adj* having no date

DATELINE *v* **-LINED, -LINING, -LINES** to provide a news story with its date and place of origin

DATER *n* pl. **-S** one that dates

DATING *n* pl. **-S** the act of one that dates

DATIVE *n* pl. **-S** a grammatical case **DATIVAL** *adj* **DATIVELY** *adv*

DATO *n* pl. **-TOS** datto

DATTO *n* pl. **-TOS** a Philippine tribal chief

DATUM *n* pl. **-TUMS** or **-TA** something used as a basis for calculating

DATURA *n* pl. **-S** a flowering plant **DATURIC** *adj*

DAUB *v* **-ED, -ING, -S** to smear

DAUBE *n* pl. **-S** a braised meat stew

DAUBER *n* pl. **-S** one that daubs

DAUBERY *n* pl. **-ERIES** a bad or inexpert painting

DAUBRY *n* pl. **-RIES** daubery

DAUBY *adj* **DAUBIER, DAUBIEST** smeary

DAUGHTER *n* pl. **-S** a female child

DAUNDER *v* **-ED, -ING, -S** to dander

DAUNT *v* **-ED, -ING, -S** to intimidate

DAUNTER *n* pl. **-S** one that daunts

DAUPHIN *n* pl. **-S** the eldest son of a French king

DAUPHINE *n* pl. **-S** the wife of a dauphin

DAUT *v* **-ED, -ING, -S** to fondle

DAUTIE *n* pl. **-S** a small pet

DAVEN *v* **-ED, -ING, -S** to utter Jewish prayers

DAVIT *n* pl. **-S** a hoisting device on a ship

DAVY *n* pl. **-VIES** a safety lamp

DAW *v* **DAWED, DAWEN, DAWING, DAWS** to dawn

DAWDLE *v* **-DLED, -DLING, -DLES** to waste time

DAWDLER *n* pl. **-S** one that dawdles

DAWK *n* pl. **-S** dak

DAWN *v* **-ED, -ING, -S** to begin to grow light in the morning

DAWNING *n* pl. **-S** daybreak

DAWNLIKE *adj* suggestive of daybreak

DAWT *v* **-ED, -ING, -S** to daut

DAWTIE *n* pl. **-S** dautie

DAY *n* pl. **DAYS** the time between sunrise and sunset

DAYBED *n* pl. **-S** a couch that can be converted into a bed

DAYBOOK *n* pl. **-S** a diary

DAYBREAK *n* pl. **-S** the first appearance of light in the morning

DAYCARE *n* pl. **-S** care for children and disabled adults during the day

DAYDREAM *v* **-DREAMED** or **-DREAMT, -DREAMING, -DREAMS** to fantasize

DAYFLY *n* pl. **-FLIES** a mayfly

DAYGLOW *n* pl. **-S** airglow seen during the day

DAYLIGHT *v* **-LIGHTED** or **-LIT, -LIGHTING, -LIGHTS** to illuminate with the light of day

DAYLILY *n* pl. **-LILIES** a flowering plant

DAYLONG *adj* lasting all day

DAYMARE *n* pl. **-S** a nightmarish fantasy experienced while awake

DAYPACK *n* pl. **-S** a bag carrying things that is strapped on one's back

DAYROOM *n* pl. **-S** a room for reading and recreation

DAYSAIL *v* **-ED, -ING, -S** to sail a yacht for a day

DAYSIDE *n* pl. **-S** the sun side of a planet or the moon

DAYSMAN *n* pl. **-MEN** an arbiter

DAYSTAR *n* pl. **-S** a planet visible in the east just before sunrise

DAYTIME *n* pl. **-S** day

DAYWEAR *n* pl. **DAYWEAR** clothing suitable for informal occasions

DAYWORK *n* pl. **-S** work done on a daily basis

DAZE *v* **DAZED, DAZING, DAZES** to stun **DAZEDLY** *adv*

DAZZLE v **-ZLED, -ZLING, -ZLES** to blind by bright light

DAZZLER n pl. **-S** one that dazzles

DE prep of; from — used in names

DEACON v **-ED, -ING, -S** to read a hymn aloud

DEACONRY n pl. **-RIES** a clerical office

DEAD adj **DEADER, DEADEST** deprived of life

DEAD n pl. **-S** the period of greatest intensity

DEADBEAT n pl. **-S** a loafer

DEADBOLT n pl. **-S** a lock for a door

DEADEN v **-ED, -ING, -S** to diminish the sensitivity or vigor of

DEADENER n pl. **-S** one that deadens

DEADEYE n pl. **-S** an expert marksman

DEADFALL n pl. **-S** a type of animal trap

DEADHEAD v **-ED, -ING, -S** to travel without freight

DEADLIER comparative of deadly

DEADLIEST superlative of deadly

DEADLIFT v **-ED, -ING, -S** to execute a type of lift in weight lifting

DEADLINE v **-LINED, -LINING, -LINES** to set a time limit on something

DEADLOCK v **-ED, -ING, -S** to come to a standstill

DEADLY adj **-LIER, -LIEST** fatal

DEADMAN n pl. **-MEN** an anchor for securing a rope in mountain climbing

DEADNESS n pl. **-ES** the state of being dead

DEADPAN v **-PANNED, -PANNING, -PANS** to act without emotion

DEADWOOD n pl. **-S** a reinforcement in a ship's keel

DEAERATE v **-ATED, -ATING, -ATES** to remove air or gas from

DEAF adj **DEAFER, DEAFEST** lacking the sense of hearing

DEAFEN v **-ED, -ING, -S** to make deaf

DEAFISH adj somewhat deaf

DEAFLY adv in a deaf manner

DEAFNESS n pl. **-ES** the state of being deaf

DEAIR v **-ED, -ING, -S** to remove air from

DEAL v **DEALT, DEALING, DEALS** to trade or do business

DEALATE n pl. **-S** an insect divested of its wings **DEALATED** adj

DEALER n pl. **-S** one that deals

DEALFISH n pl. **-ES** a marine fish

DEALIGN v **-ED, -ING, -S** to withdraw allegiance to a political party

DEALING n pl. **-S** a business transaction

DEALT past tense of deal

DEAN v **-ED, -ING, -S** to serve as dean (the head of a faculty)

DEANERY n pl. **-ERIES** the office of a dean

DEANSHIP n pl. **-S** deanery

DEAR adj **DEARER, DEAREST** greatly loved

DEAR n pl. **-S** a loved one

DEAREST n pl. **-S** a much-loved person

DEARIE n pl. **-S** deary

DEARIES pl. of deary

DEARLY adv in a dear manner

DEARNESS n pl. **-ES** the state of being dear

DEARTH n pl. **-S** scarcity

DEARY n pl. **DEARIES** darling

DEASH v **-ED, -ING, -ES** to remove ash from

DEASIL adv clockwise

DEATH n pl. **-S** the end of life

DEATHBED n pl. **-S** the bed on which a person dies

DEATHCUP n pl. **-S** a poisonous mushroom

DEATHFUL adj fatal

DEATHLY adj **-LIER, -LIEST** resembling or suggestive of death

DEATHY adj deathly

DEAVE v **DEAVED, DEAVING, DEAVES** to deafen

DEB n pl. **-S** a debutante

DEBACLE n pl. **-S** a sudden collapse

DEBAG v **-BAGGED, -BAGGING, -BAGS** to remove the pants from someone

DEBAR v **-BARRED, -BARRING, -BARS** to exclude

DEBARK v **-ED, -ING, -S** to unload from a ship

DEBARKER n pl. **-S** one that removes bark (the outer covering of woody plants)

DEBASE v **-BASED, -BASING, -BASES** to lower in character, quality, or value

DEBASER n pl. **-S** one that debases

DEBATE v **-BATED, -BATING, -BATES** to argue about

DEBATER *n* pl. **-S** one that debates

DEBAUCH *v* **-ED, -ING, -ES** to corrupt

DEBEAK *v* **-ED, -ING, -S** to remove the tip of the upper beak of

DEBEARD *v* **-ED, -ING, -S** to remove filaments from a mussel

DEBILITY *n* pl. **-TIES** weakness

DEBIT *v* **-ED, -ING, -S** to charge with a debt

DEBONAIR *adj* suave

DEBONE *v* **-BONED, -BONING, -BONES** to remove the bones from

DEBONER *n* pl. **-S** a bone remover

DEBOUCH *v* **-ED, -ING, -ES** to march into the open

DEBOUCHE *n* pl. **-S** an opening for the passage of troops

DEBRIDE *v* **-BRIDED, -BRIDING, -BRIDES** to remove dead tissue surgically

DEBRIEF *v* **-ED, -ING, -S** to question after a mission

DEBRIS *n* pl. **DEBRIS** fragments or scattered remains

DEBRUISE *v* **-BRUISED, -BRUISING, -BRUISES** to cross a coat of arms

DEBT *n* pl. **-S** something that is owed **DEBTLESS** *adj*

DEBTOR *n* pl. **-S** one who owes something to another

DEBUG *v* **-BUGGED, -BUGGING, -BUGS** to remove bugs from

DEBUGGER *n* pl. **-S** one that debugs

DEBUNK *v* **-ED, -ING, -S** to expose the sham or falseness of

DEBUNKER *n* pl. **-S** one that debunks

DEBUR *v* **-BURRED, -BURRING, -BURS** deburr

DEBURR *v* **-BURRED, -BURRING, -BURRS** to remove rough edges from

DEBUT *v* **-ED, -ING, -S** to make one's first public appearance

DEBUTANT *n* pl. **-S** one who is debuting

DEBYE *n* pl. **-S** a unit of measure for electric dipole moments

DECADE *n* pl. **-S** a period of ten years **DECADAL** *adj*

DECADENT *n* pl. **-S** one in a state of mental or moral decay

DECAF *n* pl. **-S** decaffeinated coffee

DECAGON *n* pl. **-S** a ten-sided polygon

DECAGRAM *n* pl. **-S** dekagram

DECAL *n* pl. **-S** a picture or design made to be transferred from specially prepared paper

DECALOG *n* pl. **-S** the Ten Commandments

DECAMP *v* **-ED, -ING, -S** to depart from a camping ground

DECAN *n* pl. **-S** one of three equal 10-degree divisions of a sign of the zodiac

DECANAL *adj* pertaining to a dean

DECANE *n* pl. **-S** a hydrocarbon

DECANI *adj* to be sung by the right side of the choir

DECANT *v* **-ED, -ING, -S** to pour from one container into another

DECANTER *n* pl. **-S** a decorative bottle

DECAPOD *n* pl. **-S** a ten-legged crustacean

DECARE *n* pl. **-S** dekare

DECAY *v* **-ED, -ING, -S** to decompose

DECAYER *n* pl. **-S** one that decays

DECEASE *v* **-CEASED, -CEASING, -CEASES** to die

DECEASED *n* pl. **-S** a deceased person

DECEDENT *n* pl. **-S** a deceased person

DECEIT *n* pl. **-S** the act of deceiving

DECEIVE *v* **-CEIVED, -CEIVING, -CEIVES** to mislead by falsehood

DECEIVER *n* pl. **-S** one that deceives

DECEMVIR *n* pl. **-VIRS** or **-VIRI** one of a body of ten Roman magistrates

DECENARY *n* pl. **-RIES** a tithing

DECENCY *n* pl. **-CIES** the state of being decent

DECENNIA *n/pl* decades

DECENT *adj* **-CENTER, -CENTEST** conforming to recognized standards of propriety **DECENTLY** *adv*

DECENTER *v* **-ED, -ING, -S** to put out of center

DECENTRE *v* **-TRED, -TRING, -TRES** to decenter

DECERN *v* **-ED, -ING, -S** to decree by judicial sentence

DECIARE *n* pl. **-S** a metric unit of area

DECIBEL *n* pl. **-S** a unit of sound intensity

DECIDE *v* **-CIDED, -CIDING, -CIDES** to make a choice or judgment

DECIDER *n* pl. **-S** one that decides

DECIDUA   *n* pl. **-UAS** or **-UAE** a mucous membrane of the uterus **DECIDUAL** *adj*

DECIGRAM   *n* pl. **-S** one tenth of a gram

DECILE   *n* pl. **-S** a statistical interval

DECIMAL   *n* pl. **-S** a fraction whose denominator is some power of ten

DECIMATE   *v* **-MATED, -MATING, -MATES** to destroy a large part of

DECIPHER   *v* **-ED, -ING, -S** to decode

DECISION   *v* **-ED, -ING, -S** to win a victory over a boxing opponent on points

DECISIVE   *adj* conclusive

DECK   *v* **-ED, -ING, -S** to adorn

DECKEL   *n* pl. **-S** deckle

DECKER   *n* pl. **-S** something having a specified number of levels, floors, or layers

DECKHAND   *n* pl. **-S** a seaman who performs manual duties

DECKING   *n* pl. **-S** material for a ship's deck (the platform serving as a floor)

DECKLE   *n* pl. **-S** a frame used in making paper by hand

DECKLESS   *adj* lacking a deck

DECLAIM   *v* **-ED, -ING, -S** to speak formally

DECLARE   *v* **-CLARED, -CLARING, -CLARES** to make known clearly

DECLARER   *n* pl. **-S** one that declares

DECLASS   *v* **-ED, -ING, -ES** to lower in status

DECLASSE   *adj* lowered in status

DECLAW   *v* **-CLAWED, -CLAWING, -CLAWS** to surgically remove the claws of

DECLINE   *v* **-CLINED, -CLINING, -CLINES** to refuse

DECLINER   *n* pl. **-S** one that declines

DECLUTCH   *v* **-ED, -ING, -ES** to disengage the clutch (a coupling mechanism) of a motor vehicle

DECO   *n* pl. **DECOS** a decorative style

DECOCT   *v* **-ED, -ING, -S** to extract the flavor of by boiling

DECODE   *v* **-CODED, -CODING, -CODES** to convert a coded message into plain language

DECODER   *n* pl. **-S** one that decodes

DECOLOR   *v* **-ED, -ING, -S** to deprive of color

DECOLOUR   *v* **-ED, -ING, -S** to decolor

DECOR   *n* pl. **-S** style or mode of decoration

DECORATE   *v* **-RATED, -RATING, -RATES** to adorn

DECOROUS   *adj* proper

DECORUM   *n* pl. **-S** conformity to social conventions

DECOUPLE   *v* **-PLED, -PLING, -PLES** to disconnect

DECOY   *v* **-ED, -ING, -S** to lure into a trap

DECOYER   *n* pl. **-S** one that decoys

DECREASE   *v* **-CREASED, -CREASING, -CREASES** to diminish

DECREE   *v* **-CREED, -CREEING, -CREES** to order or establish by law or edict

DECREER   *n* pl. **-S** one that decrees

DECREPIT   *adj* worn out by long use

DECRETAL   *n* pl. **-S** a papal edict

DECRIAL   *n* pl. **-S** the act of decrying

DECRIED   past tense of decry

DECRIER   *n* pl. **-S** one that decries

DECROWN   *v* **-ED, -ING, -S** to deprive of a crown; depose

DECRY   *v* **-CRIED, -CRYING, -CRIES** to denounce

DECRYPT   *v* **-ED, -ING, -S** to decode

DECUMAN   *adj* extremely large

DECUPLE   *v* **-PLED, -PLING, -PLES** to increase tenfold

DECURIES   pl. of decury

DECURION   *n* pl. **-S** a commander of a decury

DECURVE   *v* **-CURVED, -CURVING, -CURVES** to curve downward

DECURY   *n* pl. **-RIES** a group of ten soldiers in ancient Rome

DEDAL   *adj* daedal

DEDANS   *n* pl. **DEDANS** a gallery for tennis spectators

DEDENDUM   *n* pl. **-DUMS** or **-DA** the root of a gear tooth

DEDICATE   *v* **-CATED, -CATING, -CATES** to set apart for some special use

DEDUCE   *v* **-DUCED, -DUCING, -DUCES** to infer

DEDUCT   *v* **-ED, -ING, -S** to subtract

DEE   *n* pl. **-S** the letter D

DEED   *v* **-ED, -ING, -S** to transfer by deed (a legal document)

DEEDLESS   *adj* being without deeds

DEEDY   *adj* **DEEDIER, DEEDIEST** industrious

DEEJAY	v **-JAYED, -JAYING, -JAYS** to work as a disc jockey
DEEM	v **-ED, -ING, -S** to hold as an opinion
DEEMSTER	n pl. **-S** a judicial officer of the Isle of Man
DEEP	adj **DEEPER, DEEPEST** extending far down from a surface
DEEP	n pl. **-S** a place or thing of great depth
DEEPEN	v **-ED, -ING, -S** to make deep
DEEPENER	n pl. **-S** one that deepens
DEEPLY	adv at or to a great depth
DEEPNESS	n pl. **-ES** the quality of being deep
DEER	n pl. **-S** a ruminant mammal **DEERLIKE** adj
DEERFLY	n pl. **-FLIES** a bloodsucking fly
DEERSKIN	n pl. **-S** the skin of a deer
DEERWEED	n pl. **-S** a bushlike herb
DEERYARD	n pl. **-S** an area where deer herd in winter
DEET	n pl. **-S** an insect repellent
DEEWAN	n pl. **-S** dewan
DEF	adj **DEFFER, DEFFEST** excellent
DEFACE	v **-FACED, -FACING, -FACES** to mar the appearance of
DEFACER	n pl. **-S** one that defaces
DEFAME	v **-FAMED, -FAMING, -FAMES** to attack the good name of
DEFAMER	n pl. **-S** one that defames
DEFANG	v **-ED, -ING, -S** to make harmless
DEFAT	v **-FATTED, -FATTING, -FATS** to remove fat from
DEFAULT	v **-ED, -ING, -S** to fail to do something required
DEFEAT	v **-ED, -ING, -S** to win victory over
DEFEATER	n pl. **-S** one that defeats
DEFECATE	v **-CATED, -CATING, -CATES** to discharge feces
DEFECT	v **-ED, -ING, -S** to desert an allegiance
DEFECTOR	n pl. **-S** one that defects
DEFENCE	v **-FENCED, -FENCING, -FENCES** to defense
DEFEND	v **-ED, -ING, -S** to protect
DEFENDER	n pl. **-S** one that defends
DEFENSE	v **-FENSED, -FENSING, -FENSES** to guard against a specific attack
DEFER	v **-FERRED, -FERRING, -FERS** to postpone
DEFERENT	n pl. **-S** an imaginary circle around the earth
DEFERRAL	n pl. **-S** the act of deferring
DEFERRER	n pl. **-S** one that defers
DEFERRING	present participle of defer
DEFFER	comparative of def
DEFFEST	superlative of def
DEFI	n pl. **-S** a challenge
DEFIANCE	n pl. **-S** bold opposition
DEFIANT	adj showing defiance
DEFICIT	n pl. **-S** a shortage
DEFIED	past tense of defy
DEFIER	n pl. **-S** one that defies
DEFIES	present 3d person sing. of defy
DEFILADE	v **-LADED, -LADING, -LADES** to shield from enemy fire
DEFILE	v **-FILED, -FILING, -FILES** to make dirty
DEFILER	n pl. **-S** one that defiles
DEFINE	v **-FINED, -FINING, -FINES** to state the meaning of
DEFINER	n pl. **-S** one that defines
DEFINITE	n pl. **-S** something that is known for certain
DEFLATE	v **-FLATED, -FLATING, -FLATES** to release the air or gas from
DEFLATER	n pl. **-S** one that deflates
DEFLATOR	n pl. **-S** one that deflates
DEFLEA	v **-ED, -ING, -S** to rid of fleas
DEFLECT	v **-ED, -ING, -S** to turn aside
DEFLEXED	adj bent downward
DEFLOWER	v **-ED, -ING, -S** to deprive of flowers
DEFOAM	v **-ED, -ING, -S** to remove foam from
DEFOAMER	n pl. **-S** one that defoams
DEFOCUS	v **-CUSED, -CUSING, -CUSES** or **-CUSSED, -CUSSING, -CUSSES** to cause to go out of focus
DEFOG	v **-FOGGED, -FOGGING, -FOGS** to remove fog from
DEFOGGER	n pl. **-S** one that defogs
DEFORCE	v **-FORCED, -FORCING, -FORCES** to withhold by force
DEFORCER	n pl. **-S** one that deforces
DEFOREST	v **-ED, -ING, -S** to clear of forests

DEFORM v **-ED, -ING, -S** to spoil the form of

DEFORMER n pl. **-S** one that deforms

DEFRAG v **-FRAGGED, -FRAGGING, -FRAGS** to eliminate fragmentation in a computer file

DEFRAUD v **-ED, -ING, -S** to swindle

DEFRAY v **-ED, -ING, -S** to pay

DEFRAYAL n pl. **-S** the act of defraying

DEFRAYER n pl. **-S** one that defrays

DEFRIEND v **-ED, -ING, -S** to remove (a person's name) from a list of friends

DEFROCK v **-ED, -ING, -S** to unfrock

DEFROST v **-ED, -ING, -S** to remove frost from

DEFT adj **DEFTER, DEFTEST** skillful **DEFTLY** adv

DEFTNESS n pl. **-ES** the quality of being deft

DEFUEL v **-ELED, -ELING, -ELS** or **-ELLED, -ELLING, -ELS** to remove fuel from

DEFUNCT adj deceased

DEFUND v **-ED, -ING, -S** to withdraw funding from

DEFUSE v **-FUSED, -FUSING, -FUSES** to remove the fuse from

DEFUSER n pl. **-S** one that defuses

DEFUZE v **-FUZED, -FUZING, -FUZES** to defuse

DEFY v **-FIED, -FYING, -FIES** to resist openly and boldly

DEGAGE adj free and relaxed in manner

DEGAME n pl. **-S** a tropical tree

DEGAMI n pl. **-S** degame

DEGAS v **-GASSED, -GASSING, -GASES** or **-GASSES** to remove gas from

DEGASSER n pl. **-S** one that degasses

DEGAUSS v **-ED, -ING, -ES** to demagnetize

DEGENDER v **-ED, -ING, -S** to remove references to a person's gender

DEGERM v **-ED, -ING, -S** to remove germs from

DEGLAZE v **-GLAZED, -GLAZING, -GLAZES** to remove the glaze from

DEGRADE v **-GRADED, -GRADING, -GRADES** to debase

DEGRADER n pl. **-S** one that degrades

DEGREASE v **-GREASED, -GREASING, -GREASES** to remove the grease from

DEGREE n pl. **-S** one of a series of stages **DEGREED** adj

DEGUM v **-GUMMED, -GUMMING, -GUMS** to free from gum

DEGUST v **-ED, -ING, -S** to taste with pleasure

DEHAIR v **-ED, -ING, -S** to remove the hair from

DEHISCE v **-HISCED, -HISCING, -HISCES** to split open

DEHORN v **-ED, -ING, -S** to deprive of horns

DEHORNER n pl. **-S** one that dehorns

DEHORS prep other than

DEHORT v **-ED, -ING, -S** to try to dissuade

DEICE v **-ICED, -ICING, -ICES** to free from ice

DEICER n pl. **-S** one that deices

DEICIDE n pl. **-S** the killing of a god **DEICIDAL** adj

DEICTIC n pl. **-S** a word or phrase that specifies identity or location

DEIFIC adj godlike

DEIFICAL adj deific

DEIFIED past tense of deify

DEIFIER n pl. **-S** one that deifies

DEIFORM adj having the form of a god

DEIFY v **-FIED, -FYING, -FIES** to make a god of

DEIGN v **-ED, -ING, -S** to lower oneself to do something

DEIL n pl. **-S** the devil

DEIONISE v **-ISED, -ISING, -ISES** to deionize

DEIONISER n pl. **-S** deionizer

DEIONIZE v **-IZED, -IZING, -IZES** to remove ions from

DEIONIZER n pl. **-S** one that deionizes

DEISM n pl. **-S** a religious philosophy

DEIST n pl. **-S** an adherent of deism **DEISTIC** adj

DEITY n pl. **-TIES** a god or goddess

DEIXIS n pl. **DEIXISES** the specifying function of some words

DEJECT v **-ED, -ING, -S** to depress

DEJECTA n/pl excrements

DEJEUNER n pl. **-S** a late breakfast

DEKAGRAM n pl. **-S** a measure equal to ten grams

DEKARE n pl. **-S** a measure equal to ten ares

DEKE	*v* **DEKED, DEKING** or **DEKEING, DEKES** to fake an opponent out of position
DEKKO	*n* pl. **-KOS** a look
DEL	*n* pl. **-S** an operator in differential calculus
DELAINE	*n* pl. **-S** a wool fabric
DELATE	*v* **-LATED, -LATING, -LATES** to accuse
DELATION	*n* pl. **-S** the act of delating
DELATOR	*n* pl. **-S** one that delates
DELAY	*v* **-ED, -ING, -S** to put off to a later time
DELAYER	*n* pl. **-S** one that delays
DELE	*v* **DELED, DELEING, DELES** to delete
DELEAD	*v* **-ED, -ING, -S** to remove lead from
DELEAVE	*v* **-LEAVED, -LEAVING, -LEAVES** to separate the copies of
DELEGACY	*n* pl. **-CIES** the act of delegating
DELEGATE	*v* **-GATED, -GATING, -GATES** to appoint as one's representative
DELETE	*v* **-LETED, -LETING, -LETES** to remove written or printed matter
DELETION	*n* pl. **-S** the act of deleting
DELF	*n* pl. **-S** delft
DELFT	*n* pl. **-S** an earthenware
DELI	*n* pl. **DELIS** a delicatessen
DELICACY	*n* pl. **-CIES** a choice food
DELICATE	*n* pl. **-S** a delicacy
DELICT	*n* pl. **-S** an offense against civil law
DELIGHT	*v* **-ED, -ING, -S** to give great pleasure to
DELIME	*v* **-LIMED, -LIMING, -LIMES** to free from lime
DELIMIT	*v* **-ED, -ING, -S** to mark the boundaries of
DELINK	*v* **-ED, -ING, -S** to break a connection between
DELIRIUM	*n* pl. **-IUMS** or **-IA** wild frenzy
DELISH	*adj* delicious
DELIST	*v* **-ED, -ING, -S** to remove from a list
DELIVER	*v* **-ED, -ING, -S** to take to the intended recipient
DELIVERY	*n* pl. **-ERIES** the act of delivering
DELL	*n* pl. **-S** a small, wooded valley
DELLY	*n* pl. **DELLIES** deli
DELOUSE	*v* **-LOUSED, -LOUSING, -LOUSES** to remove lice from
DELOUSER	*n* pl. **-S** one that gets rid of lice
DELPHIC	*adj* ambiguous
DELT	*n* pl. **-S** a deltoid
DELTA	*n* pl. **-S** an alluvial deposit at the mouth of a river **DELTAIC, DELTIC** *adj*
DELTOID	*n* pl. **-S** a shoulder muscle
DELUDE	*v* **-LUDED, -LUDING, -LUDES** to mislead the mind or judgment of
DELUDER	*n* pl. **-S** one that deludes
DELUGE	*v* **-UGED, -UGING, -UGES** to flood
DELUSION	*n* pl. **-S** the act of deluding
DELUSIVE	*adj* tending to delude
DELUSORY	*adj* delusive
DELUSTER	*v* **-ED, -ING, -S** to lessen the sheen of
DELUXE	*adj* of special elegance or luxury
DELVE	*v* **DELVED, DELVING, DELVES** to search in depth
DELVER	*n* pl. **-S** one that delves
DEMAGOG	*v* **-ED, -ING, -S** to behave like a demagog (a leader who appeals to emotions and prejudices)
DEMAGOGY	*n* pl. **-GOGIES** the rule of a demagog
DEMAND	*v* **-ED, -ING, -S** to ask for with authority
DEMANDER	*n* pl. **-S** one that demands
DEMARCHE	*n* pl. **-S** a procedure
DEMARK	*v* **-ED, -ING, -S** to delimit
DEMAST	*v* **-ED, -ING, -S** to strip masts from
DEME	*n* pl. **-S** a Greek district
DEMEAN	*v* **-ED, -ING, -S** to conduct oneself in a particular manner
DEMEANOR	*n* pl. **-S** the manner in which one conducts oneself
DEMENT	*v* **-ED, -ING, -S** to make insane
DEMENTI	*n* pl. **-S** an official denial of a published statement
DEMENTIA	*n* pl. **-S** mental illness
DEMERARA	*n* pl. **-S** a coarse light-brown sugar
DEMERGE	*v* **-MERGED, -MERGING, -MERGES** to remove a division from a corporation
DEMERGER	*v* **-ED, -ING, -S** to demerge
DEMERIT	*v* **-ED, -ING, -S** to lower in rank or status

DEMERSAL	*adj* found at the bottom of the sea
DEMESNE	*n* pl. **-S** the legal possession of land as one's own
DEMETON	*n* pl. **-S** an insecticide
DEMIC	*adj* pertaining to a deme
DEMIES	pl. of demy
DEMIGOD	*n* pl. **-S** a lesser god
DEMIJOHN	*n* pl. **-S** a narrow-necked jug
DEMILUNE	*n* pl. **-S** a half-moon
DEMINER	*n* pl. **-S** one that removes mines (explosive devices)
DEMINING	*n* pl. **-S** the removal of mines
DEMIREP	*n* pl. **-S** a prostitute
DEMISE	*v* **-MISED, -MISING, -MISES** to bequeath
DEMIST	*v* **-ED, -ING, -S** to defog
DEMISTER	*n* pl. **-S** one that defogs
DEMIT	*v* **-MITTED, -MITTING, -MITS** to resign
DEMIURGE	*n* pl. **-S** a magistrate of ancient Greece
DEMIVOLT	*n* pl. **-S** a half turn made by a horse
DEMO	*v* **-ED, -ING, -S** to demonstrate
DEMOB	*v* **-MOBBED, -MOBBING, -MOBS** to discharge from military service
DEMOCRAT	*n* pl. **-S** one who believes in political and social equality
DEMODE	*adj* demoded
DEMODED	*adj* out-of-date
DEMOI	*n* pl. of demos
DEMOLISH	*v* **-ED, -ING, -ES** to destroy
DEMON	*n* pl. **-S** an evil spirit
DEMONESS	*n* pl. **-ES** a female demon
DEMONIAC	*n* pl. **-S** one regarded as possessed by a demon
DEMONIAN	*adj* demonic
DEMONIC	*adj* characteristic of a demon
DEMONISE	*v* **-ISED, -ISING, -ISES** to demonize
DEMONISM	*n* pl. **-S** belief in demons
DEMONIST	*n* pl. **-S** one who believes in demons
DEMONIZE	*v* **-IZED, -IZING, -IZES** to make a demon of
DEMOS	*n* pl. **-MOI** the people of an ancient Greek state
DEMOTE	*v* **-MOTED, -MOTING, -MOTES** to lower in rank or grade
DEMOTIC	*adj* pertaining to a simplified form of ancient Egyptian writing
DEMOTICS	*n/pl* the study of people in society
DEMOTION	*n* pl. **-S** the act of demoting
DEMOTIST	*n* pl. **-S** a student of demotic writings
DEMOUNT	*v* **-ED, -ING, -S** to remove from a mounting
DEMPSTER	*n* pl. **-S** a deemster
DEMUR	*v* **-MURRED, -MURRING, -MURS** to object
DEMURE	*adj* **-MURER, -MUREST** shy and modest **DEMURELY** *adv*
DEMURRAL	*n* pl. **-S** the act of demurring
DEMURRER	*n* pl. **-S** one that demurs
DEMURRING	present participle of demur
DEMY	*n* pl. **-MIES** a size of paper
DEN	*v* **DENNED, DENNING, DENS** to live in a lair
DENAR	*n* pl. **-NARS** or **-NARI** a monetary unit of Macedonia
DENARIUS	*n* pl. **DENARII** a coin of ancient Rome
DENARY	*adj* containing ten
DENATURE	*v* **-TURED, -TURING, -TURES** to deprive of natural qualities
DENAZIFY	*v* **-FIED, -FYING, -FIES** to rid of Nazism
DENDRITE	*n* pl. **-S** a branched part of a nerve cell
DENDROID	*n* pl. **-S** a fossil marine invertebrate
DENDRON	*n* pl. **-S** a dendrite
DENE	*n* pl. **-S** a valley
DENGUE	*n* pl. **-S** a tropical disease
DENI	*n* pl. **DENI** a monetary unit of Macedonia
DENIABLE	*adj* capable of being denied **DENIABLY** *adv*
DENIAL	*n* pl. **-S** the act of denying
DENIED	past tense of deny
DENIER	*n* pl. **-S** one that denies
DENIES	present 3d person sing. of deny
DENIM	*n* pl. **-S** a durable fabric **DENIMED** *adj*
DENIZEN	*v* **-ED, -ING, -S** to make a citizen of
DENNED	past tense of den
DENNING	present participle of den
DENOTE	*v* **-NOTED, -NOTING, -NOTES** to indicate **DENOTIVE** *adj*

DENOUNCE *v* **-NOUNCED, -NOUNCING, -NOUNCES** to condemn openly

DENSE *adj* **DENSER, DENSEST** compact **DENSELY** *adv*

DENSIFY *v* **-FIED, -FYING, -FIES** to make denser

DENSITY *n* pl. **-TIES** the state of being dense

DENT *v* **-ED, -ING, -S** to make a depression in

DENTAL *n* pl. **-S** a dentally produced sound

DENTALIA *n/pl* mollusks with long, tapering shells

DENTALLY *adv* with the tip of the tongue against the upper front teeth

DENTARY *n* pl. **-RIES** the lower jaw in mammals

DENTATE *adj* having teeth

DENTATED *adj* dentate

DENTELLE *n* pl. **-S** a lacy style of book-cover decoration

DENTICLE *n* pl. **-S** a small tooth

DENTIL *n* pl. **-S** a small rectangular block **DENTILED** *adj*

DENTIN *n* pl. **-S** the hard substance forming the body of a tooth **DENTINAL** *adj*

DENTINE *n* pl. **-S** dentin

DENTIST *n* pl. **-S** one who treats the teeth

DENTOID *adj* resembling a tooth

DENTURE *n* pl. **-S** a set of teeth **DENTURAL** *adj*

DENUDATE *v* **-DATED, -DATING, -DATES** to denude

DENUDE *v* **-NUDED, -NUDING, -NUDES** to strip of all covering

DENUDER *n* pl. **-S** one that denudes

DENY *v* **-NIED, -NYING, -NIES** to declare to be untrue

DEODAND *n* pl. **-S** property forfeited to the crown under a former English law

DEODAR *n* pl. **-S** an East Indian cedar

DEODARA *n* pl. **-S** deodar

DEONTIC *adj* pertaining to moral obligation

DEORBIT *v* **-ED, -ING, -S** to come out of an orbit

DEOXY *adj* having less oxygen than the compound from which it is derived

DEP *n* pl. **-S** a convenience store

DEPAINT *v* **-ED, -ING, -S** to depict

DEPART *v* **-ED, -ING, -S** to go away

DEPARTED *n* pl. **-S** one that has died

DEPARTEE *n* pl. **-S** one that departs

DEPEND *v* **-ED, -ING, -S** to rely

DEPEOPLE *v* **-PLED, -PLING, -PLES** to reduce the population of

DEPERM *v* **-ED, -ING, -S** to demagnetize

DEPICT *v* **-ED, -ING, -S** to portray

DEPICTER *n* pl. **-S** one that depicts

DEPICTOR *n* pl. **-S** depicter

DEPILATE *v* **-LATED, -LATING, -LATES** to remove hair from

DEPLANE *v* **-PLANED, -PLANING, -PLANES** to get off an airplane

DEPLETE *v* **-PLETED, -PLETING, -PLETES** to lessen or exhaust the supply of

DEPLETER *n* pl. **-S** one that depletes

DEPLORE *v* **-PLORED, -PLORING, -PLORES** to regret strongly

DEPLORER *n* pl. **-S** one that deplores

DEPLOY *v* **-ED, -ING, -S** to position troops for battle

DEPLOYER *n* pl. **-S** one that deploys

DEPLUME *v* **-PLUMED, -PLUMING, -PLUMES** to deprive of feathers

DEPOLISH *v* **-ED, -ING, -ES** to remove the gloss or polish of

DEPONE *v* **-PONED, -PONING, -PONES** to testify under oath

DEPONENT *n* pl. **-S** one that depones

DEPORT *v* **-ED, -ING, -S** to expel from a country

DEPORTEE *n* pl. **-S** one who is deported

DEPORTER *n* pl. **-S** one that deports

DEPOSAL *n* pl. **-S** the act of deposing

DEPOSE *v* **-POSED, -POSING, -POSES** to remove from office

DEPOSER *n* pl. **-S** one that deposes

DEPOSIT *v* **-ED, -ING, -S** to place

DEPOT *n* pl. **-S** a railroad or bus station

DEPRAVE *v* **-PRAVED, -PRAVING, -PRAVES** to corrupt in morals

DEPRAVER *n* pl. **-S** one that depraves

DEPRENYL *n* pl. **-S** a drug for treating Parkinson's disease

DEPRESS *v* **-ED, -ING, -ES** to make sad

DEPRIVAL *n* pl. **-S** the act of depriving

DEPRIVE *v* **-PRIVED, -PRIVING, -PRIVES** to take something away from

DEPRIVER   *n* pl. **-S** one that deprives

DEPSIDE   *n* pl. **-S** an aromatic compound

DEPTH   *n* pl. **-S** deepness

DEPURATE   *v* **-RATED, -RATING, -RATES** to free from impurities

DEPUTE   *v* **-PUTED, -PUTING, -PUTES** to delegate

DEPUTISE   *v* **-TISED, -TISING, -TISES** to deputize

DEPUTIZE   *v* **-TIZED, -TIZING, -TIZES** to appoint as a deputy

DEPUTY   *n* pl. **-TIES** one appointed to act for another

DERACINE   *n* pl. **-S** a displaced person

DERAIGN   *v* **-ED, -ING, -S** to dispute a claim

DERAIL   *v* **-ED, -ING, -S** to run off the rails of a track

DERANGE   *v* **-RANGED, -RANGING, -RANGES** to disorder

DERANGER   *n* pl. **-S** one that deranges

DERAT   *v* **-RATTED, -RATTING, -RATS** to rid of rats

DERATE   *v* **-RATED, -RATING, -RATES** to lower the rated capability of

DERATION   *v* **-ED, -ING, -S** to free (as food) from rationing

DERAY   *n* pl. **-RAYS** disorderly revelry

DERBY   *n* pl. **-BIES** a type of hat

DERE   *adj* dire

DERECHO   *n* pl. **-CHOS** a line of intense widespread windstorms

DERELICT   *n* pl. **-S** something abandoned

DERIDE   *v* **-RIDED, -RIDING, -RIDES** to ridicule

DERIDER   *n* pl. **-S** one that derides

DERINGER   *n* pl. **-S** a short-barreled pistol

DERISION   *n* pl. **-S** the act of deriding

DERISIVE   *adj* expressing derision

DERISORY   *adj* derisive

DERIVATE   *n* pl. **-S** something derived

DERIVE   *v* **-RIVED, -RIVING, -RIVES** to obtain or receive from a source

DERIVER   *n* pl. **-S** one that derives

DERM   *n* pl. **-S** derma

DERMA   *n* pl. **-S** a layer of the skin **DERMAL** *adj*

DERMIS   *n* pl. **-MISES** derma **DERMIC** *adj*

DERMOID   *n* pl. **-S** a cystic tumor

DERNIER   *adj* last

DEROGATE   *v* **-GATED, -GATING, -GATES** to detract

DERRICK   *n* pl. **-S** a hoisting apparatus

DERRIERE   *n* pl. **-S** the buttocks

DERRIS   *n* pl. **-RISES** a climbing plant

DERRY   *n* pl. **-RIES** a meaningless word used in the chorus of old songs

DERVISH   *n* pl. **-ES** a member of a Muslim religious order

DESALT   *v* **-ED, -ING, -S** to remove the salt from

DESALTER   *n* pl. **-S** one that desalts

DESAND   *v* **-ED, -ING, -S** to remove sand from

DESCALE   *v* **-SCALED, -SCALING, -SCALES** to remove the scales from

DESCANT   *v* **-ED, -ING, -S** to sing a counterpoint to a melody

DESCEND   *v* **-ED, -ING, -S** to come or go down

DESCENT   *n* pl. **-S** the act of descending

DESCRIBE   *v* **-SCRIBED, -SCRIBING, -SCRIBES** to give a verbal account of

DESCRIER   *n* pl. **-S** one that descries

DESCRY   *v* **-SCRIED, -SCRYING, -SCRIES** to discern

DESEED   *v* **-ED, -ING, -S** to remove the seeds from

DESEEDER   *n* pl. **-S** one that deseeds

DESELECT   *v* **-ED, -ING, -S** to dismiss from a training program

DESERT   *v* **-ED, -ING, -S** to abandon

DESERTER   *n* pl. **-S** one that deserts

DESERTIC   *adj* arid and barren

DESERVE   *v* **-SERVED, -SERVING, -SERVES** to be entitled to or worthy of

DESERVER   *n* pl. **-S** one that deserves

DESEX   *v* **-ED, -ING, -ES** to castrate or spay

DESHI   *n* pl. **-S** desi

DESI   *n* pl. **-S** a person of Indian, Pakistani, or Bangladeshi birth who lives abroad

DESIGN   *v* **-ED, -ING, -S** to conceive and plan out

DESIGNEE   *n* pl. **-S** one who is designated

DESIGNER   *n* pl. **-S** one that designs

DESILVER   *v* **-ED, -ING, -S** to remove the silver from

DESINENT	*adj* terminating
DESIRE	*v* **-SIRED, -SIRING, -SIRES** to wish for
DESIRER	*n* pl. **-S** one that desires
DESIROUS	*adj* desiring
DESIST	*v* **-ED, -ING, -S** to cease doing something
DESK	*n* pl. **-S** a writing table
DESKILL	*v* **-ED, -ING, -S** to reduce the level of skill required
DESKMAN	*n* pl. **-MEN** one who works at a desk
DESKTOP	*n* pl. **-S** the top of a desk
DESMAN	*n* pl. **-S** an aquatic mammal
DESMID	*n* pl. **-S** a freshwater alga
DESMOID	*n* pl. **-S** a very hard tumor
DESOLATE	*v* **-LATED, -LATING, -LATES** to lay waste
DESORB	*v* **-ED, -ING, -S** to remove by the reverse of absorption
DESORBER	*n* pl. **-S** one that desorbs
DESOXY	*adj* deoxy
DESPAIR	*v* **-ED, -ING, -S** to lose all hope
DESPATCH	*v* **-ED, -ING, -ES** to dispatch
DESPISAL	*n* pl. **-S** intense dislike
DESPISE	*v* **-SPISED, -SPISING, -SPISES** to loathe
DESPISER	*n* pl. **-S** one that despises
DESPITE	*v* **-SPITED, -SPITING, -SPITES** to treat with contempt
DESPOIL	*v* **-ED, -ING, -S** to plunder
DESPOND	*v* **-ED, -ING, -S** to lose spirit or hope
DESPOT	*n* pl. **-S** a tyrant **DESPOTIC** *adj*
DESSERT	*n* pl. **-S** something served as the last course of a meal
DESTAIN	*v* **-ED, -ING, -S** to remove stain from
DESTINE	*v* **-TINED, -TINING, -TINES** to determine beforehand
DESTINY	*n* pl. **-NIES** the fate or fortune to which one is destined
DESTREAM	*v* **-ED, -ING, -S** to reverse the categorizing of students
DESTRESS	*v* **-ED, -ING, -ES** to remove stress from
DESTRIER	*n* pl. **-S** a warhorse
DESTROY	*v* **-ED, -ING, -S** to damage beyond repair or renewal
DESTRUCT	*v* **-ED, -ING, -S** to destroy
DESUGAR	*v* **-ED, -ING, -S** to remove sugar from
DESULFUR	*v* **-ED, -ING, -S** to free from sulfur
DETACH	*v* **-ED, -ING, -ES** to unfasten and separate
DETACHER	*n* pl. **-S** one that detaches
DETAIL	*v* **-ED, -ING, -S** to report with complete particulars
DETAILER	*n* pl. **-S** one that details
DETAIN	*v* **-ED, -ING, -S** to hold in custody
DETAINEE	*n* pl. **-S** one who is detained
DETAINER	*n* pl. **-S** the unlawful withholding of another's property
DETANGLE	*v* **-GLED, -GLING, -GLES** to remove knots from
DETANGLER	*n* pl, **-S** one that detangles
DETASSEL	*v* **-SELED, -SELING, -SELS** or **-SELLED, -SELLING, -SELS** to remove tassels from
DETECT	*v* **-ED, -ING, -S** to discover or perceive
DETECTER	*n* pl. **-S** detector
DETECTOR	*n* pl. **-S** one that detects
DETENT	*n* pl. **-S** a locking or unlocking mechanism
DETENTE	*n* pl. **-S** an easing of international tension
DETER	*v* **-TERRED, -TERRING, -TERS** to stop from proceeding
DETERGE	*v* **-TERGED, -TERGING, -TERGES** to cleanse
DETERGER	*n* pl. **-S** one that deterges
DETERRER	*n* pl. **-S** one that deters
DETERRING	present participle of deter
DETEST	*v* **-ED, -ING, -S** to dislike intensely
DETESTER	*n* pl. **-S** one that detests
DETHATCH	*v* **-ED, -ING, -ES** to remove thatch from
DETHRONE	*v* **-THRONED, -THRONING, -THRONES** to remove from a throne
DETICK	*v* **-ED, -ING, -S** to remove ticks from
DETICKER	*n* pl. **-S** one that deticks
DETINUE	*n* pl. **-S** an action to recover property wrongfully detained
DETONATE	*v* **-NATED, -NATING, -NATES** to cause to explode

DETOUR v **-ED, -ING, -S** to take an indirect route

DETOX v **-ED, -ING, -ES** to detoxify

DETOXIFY v **-FIED, -FYING, -FIES** to remove a toxin from

DETRACT v **-ED, -ING, -S** to take away

DETRAIN v **-ED, -ING, -S** to get off a railroad train

DETRITUS n pl. **DETRITUS** particles of rock **DETRITAL** adj

DETRUDE v **-TRUDED, -TRUDING, -TRUDES** to thrust out

DETUNE v **-TUNED, -TUNING, -TUNES** to adjust (an instrument) so that it is no longer in tune

DEUCE v **DEUCED, DEUCING, DEUCES** to bring a tennis score to a tie

DEUCEDLY adv extremely

DEUTERIC adj pertaining to heavy hydrogen

DEUTERON n pl. **-S** an atomic particle

DEUTZIA n pl. **-S** an ornamental shrub

DEV n pl. **-S** deva

DEVA n pl. **-S** a Hindu god

DEVALUE v **-UED, -UING, -UES** to lessen the worth of

DEVEIN v **-ED, -ING, -S** to remove the dorsal vein from

DEVEL v **-ED, -ING, -S** to strike forcibly

DEVELOP v **-ED, -ING, -S** to bring to a more advanced or effective state

DEVELOPE v **-OPED, -OPING, -OPES** to develop

DEVERBAL n pl. **-S** a word derived from a verb

DEVEST v **-ED, -ING, -S** to divest

DEVI n pl. **-S** a Hindu goddess

DEVIANCE n pl. **-S** the behavior of a deviant

DEVIANCY n pl. **-CIES** deviance

DEVIANT n pl. **-S** one that deviates from a norm

DEVIATE v **-ATED, -ATING, -ATES** to turn aside from a course or norm

DEVIATOR n pl. **-S** one that deviates

DEVICE n pl. **-S** something devised or constructed for a specific purpose

DEVIL v **-ILED, -ILING, -ILS** or **-ILLED, -ILLING, -ILS** to prepare food with pungent seasoning

DEVILISH adj fiendish

DEVILKIN n pl. **-S** a small demon

DEVILRY n pl. **-RIES** deviltry

DEVILTRY n pl. **-TRIES** mischief

DEVIOUS adj indirect

DEVISAL n pl. **-S** the act of devising

DEVISE v **-VISED, -VISING, -VISES** to form in the mind

DEVISEE n pl. **-S** one to whom a will is made

DEVISER n pl. **-S** one that devises

DEVISOR n pl. **-S** one who makes a will

DEVOICE v **-VOICED, -VOICING, -VOICES** to unvoice

DEVOID adj completely lacking

DEVOIR n pl. **-S** an act of civility or respect

DEVOLVE v **-VOLVED, -VOLVING, -VOLVES** to transfer from one person to another

DEVON n pl. **-S** one of a breed of small, hardy cattle

DEVOTE v **-VOTED, -VOTING, -VOTES** to give oneself wholly to

DEVOTEE n pl. **-S** an ardent follower or supporter

DEVOTION n pl. **-S** the act of devoting

DEVOUR v **-ED, -ING, -S** to eat up voraciously

DEVOURER n pl. **-S** one that devours

DEVOUT adj **-VOUTER, -VOUTEST** pious **DEVOUTLY** adv

DEW v **-ED, -ING, -S** to wet with dew (condensed moisture)

DEWAN n pl. **-S** an official in India

DEWAR n pl. **-S** a double-walled flask

DEWATER v **-ED, -ING, -S** to remove water from

DEWAX v **-ED, -ING, -ES** to remove wax from

DEWBERRY n pl. **-RIES** an edible berry

DEWCLAW n pl. **-S** a vestigial toe

DEWDROP n pl. **-S** a drop of dew

DEWFALL n pl. **-S** the formation of dew

DEWIER comparative of dewy

DEWIEST superlative of dewy

DEWILY adv in a dewy manner

DEWINESS n pl. **-ES** the state of being dewy

DEWLAP n pl. **-S** a fold of loose skin under the neck

DEWLESS adj having no dew

DEWOOL v **-ED, -ING, -S** to remove the wool from

DEWORM v **-ED, -ING, -S** to rid of worms

DEWORMER *n* pl. **-S** one that deworms

DEWY *adj* **DEWIER, DEWIEST** moist with dew

DEX *n* pl. **-ES** a sulfate used as a central nervous system stimulant

DEXIE *n* pl. **-S** a tablet of dex

DEXIES pl. of dexy

DEXTER *n* pl. **-S** an animal of a breed of Irish cattle

DEXTRAL *n* pl. **-S** a right-handed person

DEXTRAN *n* pl. **-S** a substance used as a blood plasma substitute

DEXTRIN *n* pl. **-S** a substance used as an adhesive

DEXTRINE *n* pl. **-S** dextrin

DEXTRO *adj* turning to the right

DEXTROSE *n* pl. **-S** a form of glucose

DEXTROUS *adj* adroit

DEXY *n* pl. **DEXIES** dexie

DEY *n* pl. **DEYS** a former North African ruler

DEZINC *v* **-ZINCKED, -ZINCKING, -ZINCS** or **-ZINCED, -ZINCING, -ZINCS** to remove zinc from

DHAK *n* pl. **-S** an Asian tree

DHAL *n* pl. **-S** dal

DHANSAK *n* pl. **-S** a casserole of meats and vegetables

DHARMA *n* pl. **-S** conformity to Hindu law **DHARMIC** *adj*

DHARNA *n* pl. **-S** a form of protest in India

DHIKR *n* pl. **-S** a Sufi religious ceremony

DHOBI *n* pl. **-S** a person who does laundry in India

DHOLAK *n* pl. **-S** a two-headed drum

DHOLE *n* pl. **-S** a wild dog of India

DHOOLY *n* pl. **-LIES** doolee

DHOORA *n* pl. **-S** durra

DHOOTI *n* pl. **-S** dhoti

DHOOTIE *n* pl. **-S** dhoti

DHOTI *n* pl. **-S** a loincloth worn by Hindu men

DHOURRA *n* pl. **-S** durra

DHOW *n* pl. **-S** an Arabian sailing vessel

DHURNA *n* pl. **-S** dharna

DHURRA *n* pl. **-S** durra

DHURRIE *n* pl. **-S** a cotton rug made in India

DHUTI *n* pl. **-S** dhoti

DHYANA *n* pl. **-S** profound meditation in Hinduism

DIABASE *n* pl. **-S** an igneous rock **DIABASIC** *adj*

DIABETES *n* pl. **DIABETES** a metabolic disorder

DIABETIC *n* pl. **-S** one who has diabetes

DIABLERY *n* pl. **-RIES** sorcery

DIABOLIC *adj* devilish

DIABOLO *n* pl. **-LOS** a game requiring manual dexterity

DIACETYL *n* pl. **-S** biacetyl

DIACID *n* pl. **-S** a type of acid **DIACIDIC** *adj*

DIACONAL *adj* pertaining to a deacon

DIADEM *v* **-ED, -ING, -S** to adorn with a crown

DIAGNOSE *v* **-NOSED, -NOSING, -NOSES** to recognize a disease by its signs and symptoms

DIAGONAL *n* pl. **-S** an oblique line

DIAGRAM *v* **-GRAMED, -GRAMING, -GRAMS** or **-GRAMMED, -GRAMMING, -GRAMS** to illustrate by a diagram (a graphic design)

DIAGRAPH *n* pl. **-S** a drawing device

DIAL *v* **DIALED, DIALING, DIALS** or **DIALLED, DIALLING, DIALS** to manipulate a calibrated disk

DIALECT *n* pl. **-S** a regional variety of a language

DIALER *n* pl. **-S** one that dials

DIALING *n* pl. **-S** the measurement of time by sundials

DIALIST *n* pl. **-S** a dialer

DIALLAGE *n* pl. **-S** a mineral

DIALLED a past tense of dial

DIALLEL *adj* pertaining to a genetic crossing

DIALLER *n* pl. **-S** dialer

DIALLING *n* pl. **-S** dialing

DIALLIST *n* pl. **-S** dialist

DIALOG *v* **-ED, -ING, -S** to dialogue

DIALOGER *n* pl. **-S** one that dialogs

DIALOGIC *adj* conversational

DIALOGUE *v* **-LOGUED, -LOGUING, -LOGUES** to carry on a conversation

DIALYSE *v* **-LYSED, -LYSING, -LYSES** to dialyze

DIALYSER *n pl.* **-S** dialyzer

DIALYSIS *n pl.* **-YSES** the separation of substances in a solution by diffusion through a membrane

DIALYTIC *adj* pertaining to dialysis

DIALYZE *v* **-LYZED, -LYZING, -LYZES** to subject to dialysis

DIALYZER *n pl.* **-S** an apparatus used for dialysis

DIAMANTE *n pl.* **-S** a sparkling decoration

DIAMETER *n pl.* **-S** a straight line passing through the center of a circle and ending at the periphery

DIAMIDE *n pl.* **-S** a chemical compound

DIAMIN *n pl.* **-S** diamine

DIAMINE *n pl.* **-S** a chemical compound

DIAMOND *v* **-ED, -ING, -S** to adorn with diamonds (precious gems)

DIANTHUS *n pl.* **-ES** an ornamental herb

DIAPASON *n pl.* **-S** a burst of harmonious sound

DIAPAUSE *v* **-PAUSED, -PAUSING, -PAUSES** to undergo dormancy

DIAPER *v* **-ED, -ING, -S** to put a diaper (a baby's breechcloth) on

DIAPHONE *n pl.* **-S** a low-pitched foghorn

DIAPHONY *n pl.* **-NIES** organum

DIAPIR *n pl.* **-S** a bend in a layer of rock **DIAPIRIC** *adj*

DIAPSID *n pl.* **-S** a reptile with two pairs of temporal openings in the skull

DIARCHY *n pl.* **-CHIES** a government with two rulers **DIARCHIC** *adj* **DIARCHAL** *adj*

DIARIES pl. of diary

DIARIST *n pl.* **-S** one who keeps a diary

DIARRHEA *n pl.* **-S** an intestinal disorder

DIARY *n pl.* **-RIES** a personal journal

DIASPORA *n pl.* **-S** migration

DIASPORE *n pl.* **-S** a mineral

DIASTASE *n pl.* **-S** an enzyme

DIASTEM *n pl.* **-S** an interruption in the deposition of sediment

DIASTEMA *n pl.* **-MAS** or **-MATA** a space between teeth

DIASTER *n pl.* **-S** a stage in mitosis **DIASTRAL** *adj*

DIASTOLE *n pl.* **-S** the normal rhythmical dilation of the heart

DIATOM *n pl.* **-S** any of a class of algae

DIATOMIC *adj* composed of two atoms

DIATONIC *adj* pertaining to a type of musical scale

DIATREME *n pl.* **-S** a volcanic vent produced by gaseous explosions

DIATRIBE *n pl.* **-S** a bitter and abusive criticism

DIATRON *n pl.* **-S** a circuitry design that uses diodes

DIAZEPAM *n pl.* **-S** a tranquilizer

DIAZIN *n pl.* **-S** diazine

DIAZINE *n pl.* **-S** a chemical compound

DIAZINON *n pl.* **-S** an insecticide

DIAZO *n pl.* **-AZOS** a type of coloring or copying process

DIAZOLE *n pl.* **-S** a chemical compound

DIB *v* **DIBBED, DIBBING, DIBS** to fish by letting the bait bob lightly on the water

DIBASIC *adj* having two replaceable hydrogen atoms

DIBBER *n pl.* **-S** a planting implement

DIBBLE *v* **-BLED, -BLING, -BLES** to dib

DIBBLER *n pl.* **-S** one that dibbles

DIBBUK *n pl.* **-BUKS** or **-BUKIM** dybbuk

DICAMBA *n pl.* **-S** an herbicide

DICAST *n pl.* **-S** a judge of ancient Athens **DICASTIC** *adj*

DICE *v* **DICED, DICING, DICES** to cut into small cubes

DICENTRA *n pl.* **-S** a perennial herb

DICER *n pl.* **-S** a device that dices food

DICEY *adj* **DICIER, DICIEST** dangerous

DICHASIA *n/pl* flower clusters

DICHOTIC *adj* affecting the two ears differently

DICHROIC *adj* having two colors

DICIER comparative of dicey

DICIEST superlative of dicey

DICING present participle of dice

DICK *n pl.* **-S** a detective

DICKENS *n pl.* **-ES** devil

DICKER *v* **-ED, -ING, -S** to bargain

DICKERER *n pl.* **-S** one who dickers

DICKEY *n pl.* **-EYS** a blouse front

DICKIE *n pl.* **-S** dickey

DICKY *adj* **DICKIER, DICKIEST** poor in condition

DICKY   *n* pl. **DICKIES** dickey

DICLINY   *n* pl. **-NIES** the state of having stamens and pistils in separate flowers

DICOT   *n* pl. **-S** a plant with two seed leaves

DICOTYL   *n* pl. **-S** dicot

DICROTAL   *adj* dicrotic

DICROTIC   *adj* having a double pulse beat

DICTA   a pl. of dictum

DICTATE   *v* **-TATED, -TATING, -TATES** to read aloud for recording

DICTATOR   *n* pl. **-S** one that dictates

DICTION   *n* pl. **-S** choice and use of words in speech or writing

DICTUM   *n* pl. **-TUMS** or **-TA** an authoritative statement

DICTY   *adj* **-TIER, -TIEST** snobbish

DICYCLIC   *adj* having two maxima of population each year

DICYCLY   *n* pl. **-CLIES** the state of being dicyclic

DID   a past tense of do

DIDACT   *n* pl. **-S** a didactic person

DIDACTIC   *adj* instructive

DIDACTYL   *adj* having two digits at the end of each limb

DIDAPPER   *n* pl. **-S** a dabchick

DIDDLE   *v* **-DLED, -DLING, -DLES** to swindle

DIDDLER   *n* pl. **-S** one that diddles

DIDDLEY   *n* pl. **-DLEYS** diddly

DIDDLY   *n* pl. **-DLIES** the least amount

DIDDUMS   *interj* — used to express sympathy to a child

DIDIE   *n* pl. **-S** didy

DIDIES   pl. of didy

DIDO   *n* pl. **-DOS** or **-DOES** a mischievous act

DIDST   a past tense of do

DIDY   *n* pl. **-DIES** a diaper

DIDYMIUM   *n* pl. **-S** a mixture of rare-earth elements

DIDYMOUS   *adj* occurring in pairs

DIDYNAMY   *n* pl. **-MIES** the state of having four stamens in pairs of unequal length

DIE   *v* **DIED, DIEING, DIES** to cut with a die (a device for shaping material)

DIE   *v* **DIED, DYING, DIES** to cease living

DIEBACK   *n* pl. **-S** a gradual dying of plant shoots

DIECIOUS   *adj* dioicous

DIED   past tense of die

DIEHARD   *n* pl. **-S** a stubborn person

DIEL   *adj* involving a full day

DIELDRIN   *n* pl. **-S** an insecticide

DIEMAKER   *n* pl. **-S** one that makes dies

DIENE   *n* pl. **-S** a chemical compound

DIEOFF   *n* pl. **-S** a sudden decline in a population

DIERESIS   *n* pl. **DIERESES** the separation of two vowels into two syllables **DIERETIC** *adj*

DIESEL   *v* **-ED, -ING, -S** to continue running after the ignition is turned off

DIESIS   *n* pl. **DIESES** a reference mark in printing

DIESTER   *n* pl. **-S** a type of chemical compound

DIESTOCK   *n* pl. **-S** a frame for holding dies

DIESTRUM   *n* pl. **-S** diestrus

DIESTRUS   *n* pl. **-ES** a period of sexual inactivity

DIET   *v* **-ED, -ING, -S** to regulate one's daily sustenance

DIETARY   *n* pl. **-ETARIES** a system of dieting

DIETER   *n* pl. **-S** one that diets

DIETETIC   *adj* pertaining to diet

DIETHER   *n* pl. **-S** a chemical compound

DIF   *n* pl. **-S** diff

DIFF   *n* pl. **-S** a difference

DIFFER   *v* **-ED, -ING, -S** to be unlike

DIFFRACT   *v* **-ED, -ING, -S** to separate into parts

DIFFUSE   *v* **-FUSED, -FUSING, -FUSES** to spread widely or thinly

DIFFUSER   *n* pl. **-S** one that diffuses

DIFFUSOR   *n* pl. **-S** diffuser

DIG   *v* **DUG** or **DIGGED, DIGGING, DIGS** to break up, turn over, or remove earth

DIGAMIES   pl. of digamy

DIGAMIST   *n* pl. **-S** one who practices digamy

DIGAMMA   *n* pl. **-S** a Greek letter

DIGAMY   *n* pl. **-MIES** a second legal marriage **DIGAMOUS** *adj*

DIGERATI *n/pl* persons skilled in the use of computers

DIGEST *v* **-ED, -ING, -S** to render food usable for the body

DIGESTER *n* pl. **-S** an apparatus in which substances are softened or decomposed

DIGESTIF *n* pl. **-S** an alcoholic drink taken after a meal

DIGESTOR *n* pl. **-S** digester

DIGGED a past tense of dig

DIGGER *n* pl. **-S** one that digs

DIGGING present participle of dig

DIGGINGS *n/pl* an excavation site

DIGHT *v* **-ED, -ING, -S** to adorn

DIGICAM *n* pl. **-S** a digital camera

DIGIT *n* pl. **-S** a finger or toe

DIGITAL *n* pl. **-S** a piano key

DIGITATE *adj* having digits

DIGITISE *v* **-TISED, -TISING, -TISES** to digitize

DIGITIZE *v* **-TIZED, -TIZING, -TIZES** to put data into digital notation

DIGLOT *n* pl. **-S** a bilingual book or edition

DIGNIFY *v* **-FIED, -FYING, -FIES** to add dignity to

DIGNITY *n* pl. **-TIES** stateliness and nobility of manner

DIGOXIN *n* pl. **-S** a drug to improve heart function

DIGRAPH *n* pl. **-S** a pair of letters representing a single speech sound

DIGRESS *v* **-ED, -ING, -ES** to stray from the main topic

DIHEDRAL *n* pl. **-S** a dihedron

DIHEDRON *n* pl. **-S** a figure formed by two intersecting planes

DIHYBRID *n* pl. **-S** an offspring of parents differing in two pairs of genes

DIHYDRIC *adj* containing two hydroxyl radicals

DIKDIK *n* pl. **-S** a small antelope

DIKE *v* **DIKED, DIKING, DIKES** to furnish with an embankment

DIKER *n* pl. **-S** one that dikes

DIKTAT *n* pl. **-S** a harsh settlement imposed on a defeated nation

DILATANT *n* pl. **-S** a dilator

DILATATE *adj* dilated

DILATE *v* **-LATED, -LATING, -LATES** to make wider or larger

DILATER *n* pl. **-S** dilator

DILATION *n* pl. **-S** the act of dilating

DILATIVE *adj* tending to dilate

DILATOR *n* pl. **-S** one that dilates

DILATORY *adj* tending to delay

DILDO *n* pl. **-DOS** an object used as a penis substitute

DILDOE *n* pl. **-S** dildo

DILEMMA *n* pl. **-S** a perplexing situation **DILEMMIC** *adj*

DILIGENT *adj* persevering

DILL *n* pl. **-S** an annual herb

DILLED *adj* flavored with dill

DILLWEED *n* pl. **-S** the leaves of the dill plant

DILLY *n* pl. **DILLIES** something remarkable

DILUENT *n* pl. **-S** a diluting substance

DILUTE *v* **-LUTED, -LUTING, -LUTES** to thin or reduce the concentration of

DILUTER *n* pl. **-S** one that dilutes

DILUTION *n* pl. **-S** the act of diluting

DILUTIVE *adj* tending to dilute

DILUTOR *n* pl. **-S** diluter

DILUVIA a pl. of diluvium

DILUVIAL *adj* pertaining to a flood

DILUVIAN *adj* diluvial

DILUVION *n* pl. **-S** diluvium

DILUVIUM *n* pl. **-VIUMS** or **-VIA** coarse rock material deposited by glaciers

DIM *adj* **DIMMER, DIMMEST** obscure **DIMMISH** *adj*

DIM *v* **DIMMED, DIMMING, DIMS** to make dim

DIME *n* pl. **-S** a coin of the United States

DIMER *n* pl. **-S** a molecule composed of two identical molecules

DIMERIC *adj* dimerous

DIMERISM *n* pl. **-S** the state of being dimerous

DIMERIZE *v* **-IZED, -IZING, -IZES** to form a dimer

DIMEROUS *adj* composed of two parts

DIMETER *n* pl. **-S** a verse of two metrical feet

DIMETHYL *n* pl. **-S** ethane

DIMETRIC *adj* pertaining to a type of crystal system

DIMINISH *v* **-ED, -ING, -ES** to lessen

DIMITY	*n* pl. **-TIES** a cotton fabric	**DINGY**	*n* pl. **-GIES** dinghy
DIMLY	*adv* in a dim manner	**DINING**	*n* pl. **-S** the activity of eating dinner
DIMMABLE	*adj* capable of being dimmed	**DINITRO**	*adj* containing two nitro groups
DIMMED	past tense of dim	**DINK**	*v* **-ED, -ING, -S** to adorn
DIMMER	*n* pl. **-S** a device for varying the intensity of illumination	**DINKEY**	*n* pl. **-KEYS** a small locomotive
		DINKIER	comparative of dinky
DIMMEST	superlative of dim	**DINKIES**	pl. of dinky
DIMMING	present participle of dim	**DINKIEST**	superlative of dinky
DIMMISH	*adj* somewhat dim	**DINKLY**	*adv* neatly
DIMNESS	*n* pl. **-ES** the state of being dim	**DINKUM**	*n* pl. **-S** the truth
DIMORPH	*n* pl. **-S** either of two distinct forms	**DINKY**	*adj* **-KIER, -KIEST** small
DIMOUT	*n* pl. **-S** a condition of partial darkness	**DINKY**	*n* pl. **-KIES** dinkey
		DINNED	past tense of din
DIMPLE	*v* **-PLED, -PLING, -PLES** to mark with indentations	**DINNER**	*n* pl. **-S** the main meal of the day
		DINNING	present participle of din
DIMPLY	*adj* **-PLIER, -PLIEST** dimpled	**DINO**	*n* pl. **-NOS** a dinosaur
DIMWIT	*n* pl. **-S** a dunce	**DINOSAUR**	*n* pl. **-S** one of a group of extinct reptiles
DIN	*v* **DINNED, DINNING, DINS** to make a loud noise	**DINT**	*v* **-ED, -ING, -S** to dent
DINAR	*n* pl. **-S** an ancient gold coin of Muslim areas	**DIOBOL**	*n* pl. **-S** a coin of ancient Greece
		DIOBOLON	*n* pl. **-S** diobol
DINDLE	*v* **-DLED, -DLING, -DLES** to tingle	**DIOCESAN**	*n* pl. **-S** a bishop
DINE	*v* **DINED, DINING, DINES** to eat dinner	**DIOCESE**	*n* pl. **-S** an ecclesiastical district
		DIODE	*n* pl. **-S** a type of electron tube
DINER	*n* pl. **-S** one that dines	**DIOECISM**	*n* pl. **-S** the state of being dioicous
DINERIC	*adj* pertaining to the interface between two immiscible liquids	**DIOECY**	*n* pl. **DIOECIES** dioecism
DINERO	*n* pl. **-ROS** a former silver coin of Peru	**DIOICOUS**	*adj* unisexual
		DIOL	*n* pl. **-S** a chemical compound
DINETTE	*n* pl. **-S** a small dining room	**DIOLEFIN**	*n* pl. **-S** a hydrocarbon
DING	*v* **-ED, -ING, -S** to ring	**DIOPSIDE**	*n* pl. **-S** a mineral
DINGBAT	*n* pl. **-S** a typographical ornament	**DIOPTASE**	*n* pl. **-S** a mineral
DINGDONG	*v* **-ED, -ING, -S** to make a ringing sound	**DIOPTER**	*n* pl. **-S** a measure of refractive power **DIOPTRAL** *adj*
DINGE	*n* pl. **-S** the condition of being dingy	**DIOPTRE**	*n* pl. **-S** diopter
		DIOPTRIC	*adj* aiding the vision by refraction
DINGER	*n* pl. **-S** a home run	**DIORAMA**	*n* pl. **-S** a three-dimensional exhibit **DIORAMIC** *adj*
DINGEY	*n* pl. **-GEYS** dinghy		
DINGHY	*n* pl. **-GHIES** a small boat	**DIORITE**	*n* pl. **-S** an igneous rock **DIORITIC** *adj*
DINGIER	comparative of dingy		
DINGIES	pl. of dingy	**DIOXAN**	*n* pl. **-S** dioxane
DINGIEST	superlative of dingy	**DIOXANE**	*n* pl. **-S** a flammable liquid
DINGILY	*adv* in a dingy manner	**DIOXID**	*n* pl. **-S** dioxide
DINGLE	*n* pl. **-S** a dell	**DIOXIDE**	*n* pl. **-S** a type of oxide
DINGO	*n* pl. **-GOES** or **-GOS** a wild dog of Australia	**DIOXIN**	*n* pl. **-S** a toxic solid hydrocarbon
DINGUS	*n* pl. **-ES** a doodad	**DIP**	*v* **DIPPED** or **DIPT, DIPPING, DIPS** to immerse briefly
DINGY	*adj* **-GIER, -GIEST** grimy		

DIPHASE   *adj* having two phases

DIPHASIC   *adj* diphase

DIPHENYL   *n* pl. **-S** biphenyl

DIPLEGIA   *n* pl. **-S** paralysis of the same part on both sides of the body **DIPLEGIC** *adj*

DIPLEX   *adj* pertaining to the simultaneous transmission or reception of two radio signals

DIPLEXER   *n* pl. **-S** a coupling device

DIPLOE   *n* pl. **-S** a bony tissue of the cranium **DIPLOIC** *adj*

DIPLOID   *n* pl. **-S** a cell having the basic chromosome number doubled

DIPLOIDY   *n* pl. **-DIES** the condition of being a diploid

DIPLOMA   *n* pl. **-MAS** or **-MATA** a certificate of an academic degree

DIPLOMA   *v* **-ED, -ING, -S** to furnish with a diploma

DIPLOMAT   *n* pl. **-S** a governmental official

DIPLONT   *n* pl. **-S** an organism having a particular chromosomal structure

DIPLOPIA   *n* pl. **-S** double vision **DIPLOPIC** *adj*

DIPLOPOD   *n* pl. **-S** a multi-legged insect

DIPLOSIS   *n* pl. **-LOSES** a method of chromosome formation

DIPNET   *v* **-NETTED, -NETTING, -NETS** to scoop fish with a type of net

DIPNOAN   *n* pl. **-S** a lungfish

DIPODY   *n* pl. **-DIES** a dimeter **DIPODIC** *adj*

DIPOLE   *n* pl. **-S** a pair of equal and opposite electric charges **DIPOLAR** *adj*

DIPPABLE   *adj* capable of being dipped

DIPPED   a past tense of dip

DIPPER   *n* pl. **-S** one that dips

DIPPING   present participle of dip

DIPPY   *adj* **-PIER, -PIEST** foolish

DIPROTIC   *adj* having two hydrogen ions to donate to bases

DIPSAS   *n* pl. **DIPSADES** a fabled serpent

DIPSO   *n* pl. **-SOS** a person who craves alcoholic liquors

DIPSTICK   *n* pl. **-S** a measuring rod

DIPT   a past tense of dip

DIPTERA   pl. of dipteron

DIPTERAL   *adj* having two rows or columns

DIPTERAN   *n* pl. **-S** a two-winged fly

DIPTERON   *n* pl. **-TERA** dipteran

DIPTYCA   *n* pl. **-S** diptych

DIPTYCH   *n* pl. **-S** an ancient writing tablet

DIQUAT   *n* pl. **-S** an herbicide

DIRAM   *n* pl. **-S** a monetary unit of Tajikistan

DIRDUM   *n* pl. **-S** blame

DIRE   *adj* **DIRER, DIREST** disastrous

DIRECT   *adj* **-RECTER, -RECTEST** straightforward **DIRECTLY** *adv*

DIRECT   *v* **-ED, -ING, -S** to control or conduct the affairs of

DIRECTOR   *n* pl. **-S** one that directs

DIREFUL   *adj* dreadful

DIRELY   *adv* in a dire manner

DIRENESS   *n* pl. **-ES** the state of being dire

DIRER   comparative of dire

DIREST   superlative of dire

DIRGE   *n* pl. **-S** a funeral song **DIRGEFUL** *adj*

DIRHAM   *n* pl. **-S** a monetary unit of Morocco

DIRIMENT   *adj* nullifying

DIRK   *v* **-ED, -ING, -S** to stab with a small knife

DIRL   *v* **-ED, -ING, -S** to tremble

DIRNDL   *n* pl. **-S** a woman's dress

DIRT   *n* pl. **-S** earth or soil

DIRTBAG   *n* pl. **-S** a dirty or contemptible person

DIRTBALL   *n* pl. **-S** a dirty or contemptible person

DIRTY   *adj* **DIRTIER, DIRTIEST** unclean **DIRTILY** *adv*

DIRTY   *v* **DIRTIED, DIRTYING, DIRTIES** to make dirty

DIS   *v* **DISSED, DISSING, DISSES** to insult or criticize

DISABLE   *v* **-ABLED, -ABLING, -ABLES** to render incapable or unable

DISABLER   *n* pl. **-S** one that disables

DISABUSE   *v* **-ABUSED, -ABUSING, -ABUSES** to free from false or mistaken ideas

DISAGREE   *v* **-AGREED, -AGREEING, -AGREES** to differ in opinion

DISALLOW   *v* **-ED, -ING, -S** to refuse to allow

DISANNUL   *v* **-NULLED, -NULLING, -NULS** to annul

DISARM v -**ED, -ING, -S** to deprive of weapons

DISARMER n pl. -**S** one that disarms

DISARRAY v -**ED, -ING, -S** to disorder

DISASTER n pl. -**S** a calamity

DISAVOW v -**ED, -ING, -S** to disclaim responsibility for

DISBAND v -**ED, -ING, -S** to break up

DISBAR v -**BARRED, -BARRING, -BARS** to expel from the legal profession

DISBOSOM v -**ED, -ING, -S** to confess

DISBOUND adj not having a binding

DISBOWEL v -**ELED, -ELING, -ELS** or -**ELLED, -ELLING, -ELS** to remove the intestines of

DISBUD v -**BUDDED, -BUDDING, -BUDS** to remove buds from

DISBURSE v -**BURSED, -BURSING, -BURSES** to pay out

DISC v -**ED, -ING, -S** to disk

DISCANT v -**ED, -ING, -S** to descant

DISCARD v -**ED, -ING, -S** to throw away

DISCASE v -**CASED, -CASING, -CASES** to remove the case of

DISCEPT v -**ED, -ING, -S** to debate

DISCERN v -**ED, -ING, -S** to perceive

DISCI a pl. of discus

DISCIPLE v -**PLED, -PLING, -PLES** to cause to become a follower

DISCLAIM v -**ED, -ING, -S** to renounce any claim to or connection with

DISCLESS adj diskless

DISCLIKE adj disklike

DISCLOSE v -**CLOSED, -CLOSING, -CLOSES** to reveal

DISCO v -**ED, -ING, -S** or -**ES** to dance at a discotheque

DISCOID n pl. -**S** a disk

DISCOLOR v -**ED, -ING, -S** to alter the color of

DISCORD v -**ED, -ING, -S** to disagree

DISCOUNT v -**ED, -ING, -S** to reduce the price of

DISCOVER v -**ED, -ING, -S** to gain sight or knowledge of

DISCREET adj -**CREETER, -CREETEST** tactful

DISCRETE adj separate

DISCROWN v -**ED, -ING, -S** to deprive of a crown

DISCUS n pl. -**CUSES** or -**CI** a disk hurled in athletic competition

DISCUSS v -**ED, -ING, -ES** to talk over or write about

DISDAIN v -**ED, -ING, -S** to scorn

DISEASE v -**EASED, -EASING, -EASES** to make unhealthy

DISENDOW v -**ED, -ING, -S** to deprive of endowment

DISEUR n pl. -**S** a skilled reciter

DISEUSE n pl. -**S** a female entertainer

DISFAVOR v -**ED, -ING, -S** to regard with disapproval

DISFROCK v -**ED, -ING, -S** to unfrock

DISGORGE v -**GORGED, -GORGING, -GORGES** to vomit

DISGRACE v -**GRACED, -GRACING, -GRACES** to bring shame or discredit upon

DISGUISE v -**GUISED, -GUISING, -GUISES** to alter the appearance of

DISGUST v -**ED, -ING, -S** to cause nausea or loathing in

DISH v -**ED, -ING, -ES** to put into a dish (a concave vessel)

DISHELM v -**ED, -ING, -S** to deprive of a helmet

DISHERIT v -**ED, -ING, -S** to deprive of an inheritance

DISHEVEL v -**ELED, -ELING, -ELS** or -**ELLED, -ELLING, -ELS** to make messy

DISHFUL n pl. -**S** as much as a dish can hold

DISHIER comparative of dishy

DISHIEST superlative of dishy

DISHLIKE adj resembling a dish

DISHONOR v -**ED, -ING, -S** to deprive of honor

DISHPAN n pl. -**S** a pan for washing dishes

DISHRAG n pl. -**S** a cloth for washing dishes

DISHWARE n pl. -**S** tableware used in serving food

DISHY adj **DISHIER, DISHIEST** attractive

DISINTER v -**TERRED, -TERRING, -TERS** to exhume

DISJECT v -**ED, -ING, -S** to disperse

DISJOIN v -**ED, -ING, -S** to separate

DISJOINT v -**ED, -ING, -S** to put out of order

DISJUNCT n pl. -**S** an alternative in a logical disjunction

DISK	*v* **-ED, -ING, -S** to break up land with a type of farm implement
DISKER	*n* pl. **-S** one that disks
DISKETTE	*n* pl. **-S** a floppy disk for a computer
DISKLESS	*adj* having no disk (a round, flat storage device for a computer)
DISKLIKE	*adj* resembling a disk (a flat, circular plate)
DISLIKE	*v* **-LIKED, -LIKING, -LIKES** to regard with aversion
DISLIKER	*n* pl. **-S** one that dislikes
DISLIMN	*v* **-ED, -ING, -S** to make dim
DISLODGE	*v* **-LODGED, -LODGING, -LODGES** to remove from a firm position
DISLOYAL	*adj* not loyal
DISMAL	*adj* **-MALER, -MALEST** cheerless and depressing **DISMALLY** *adv*
DISMAL	*n* pl. **-S** a track of swampy land
DISMAST	*v* **-ED, -ING, -S** to remove the mast of
DISMAY	*v* **-ED, -ING, -S** to deprive of courage or resolution
DISME	*n* pl. **-S** a former coin of the United States
DISMISS	*v* **-ED, -ING, -ES** to permit or cause to leave
DISMOUNT	*v* **-ED, -ING, -S** to get down from an elevated position
DISOBEY	*v* **-ED, -ING, -S** to fail to obey
DISOMIC	*adj* having a number of chromosomes duplicated
DISOMY	*n* pl. **-MIES** the condition of being disomic
DISORDER	*v* **-ED, -ING, -S** to put out of order
DISOWN	*v* **-ED, -ING, -S** to deny the ownership of
DISOWNER	*n* pl. **-S** one that disowns
DISPART	*v* **-ED, -ING, -S** to separate
DISPATCH	*v* **-ED, -ING, -ES** to send off with speed
DISPEL	*v* **-PELLED, -PELLING, -PELS** to drive off in various directions
DISPEND	*v* **-ED, -ING, -S** to squander
DISPENSE	*v* **-PENSED, -PENSING, -PENSES** to distribute
DISPERSE	*v* **-PERSED, -PERSING, -PERSES** to scatter
DISPIRIT	*v* **-ED, -ING, -S** to lower in spirit

DISPLACE	*v* **-PLACED, -PLACING, -PLACES** to remove from the usual or proper place
DISPLANT	*v* **-ED, -ING, -S** to dislodge
DISPLAY	*v* **-ED, -ING, -S** to make evident or obvious
DISPLODE	*v* **-PLODED, -PLODING, -PLODES** to explode
DISPLUME	*v* **-PLUMED, -PLUMING, -PLUMES** to deplume
DISPORT	*v* **-ED, -ING, -S** to amuse oneself
DISPOSAL	*n* pl. **-S** the act of disposing
DISPOSE	*v* **-POSED, -POSING, -POSES** to put in place
DISPOSER	*n* pl. **-S** one that disposes
DISPREAD	*v* **-SPREAD, -SPREADING, -SPREADS** to spread out
DISPRIZE	*v* **-PRIZED, -PRIZING, -PRIZES** to disdain
DISPROOF	*n* pl. **-S** the act of disproving
DISPROVE	*v* **-PROVED, -PROVEN, -PROVING, -PROVES** to refute
DISPUTE	*v* **-PUTED, -PUTING, -PUTES** to argue about
DISPUTER	*n* pl. **-S** one that disputes
DISQUIET	*v* **-ED, -ING, -S** to deprive of quiet, rest, or peace
DISRATE	*v* **-RATED, -RATING, -RATES** to lower in rating or rank
DISROBE	*v* **-ROBED, -ROBING, -ROBES** to undress
DISROBER	*n* pl. **-S** one that disrobes
DISROOT	*v* **-ED, -ING, -S** to uproot
DISRUPT	*v* **-ED, -ING, -S** to throw into confusion
DISS	*v* **-ED, -ING, -ES** to dis
DISSAVE	*v* **-SAVED, -SAVING, -SAVES** to use savings for current expenses
DISSAVER	*n* pl. **-S** one that dissaves
DISSEAT	*v* **-ED, -ING, -S** to unseat
DISSECT	*v* **-ED, -ING, -S** to cut apart for scientific examination
DISSED	past tense of dis
DISSEISE	*v* **-SEISED, -SEISING, -SEISES** to deprive
DISSEIZE	*v* **-SEIZED, -SEIZING, -SEIZES** to disseise
DISSENT	*v* **-ED, -ING, -S** to disagree
DISSERT	*v* **-ED, -ING, -S** to discuss in a learned or formal manner

DISSERVE	*v* **-SERVED, -SERVING, -SERVES** to treat badly
DISSES	present 3d person sing. of dis
DISSEVER	*v* **-ED, -ING, -S** to sever
DISSING	present participle of dis
DISSOLVE	*v* **-SOLVED, -SOLVING, -SOLVES** to make into a solution
DISSUADE	*v* **-SUADED, -SUADING, -SUADES** to persuade not to do something
DISTAFF	*n* pl. **-TAFFS** or **-TAVES** a type of staff
DISTAIN	*v* **-ED, -ING, -S** to stain
DISTAL	*adj* located far from the point of origin **DISTALLY** *adv*
DISTANCE	*v* **-TANCED, -TANCING, -TANCES** to leave behind
DISTANT	*adj* far off or apart
DISTASTE	*v* **-TASTED, -TASTING, -TASTES** to dislike
DISTAVES	a pl. of distaff
DISTEND	*v* **-ED, -ING, -S** to swell
DISTENT	*adj* distended
DISTICH	*n* pl. **-S** a couplet
DISTIL	*v* **-TILLED, -TILLING, -TILS** to distill
DISTILL	*v* **-ED, -ING, -S** to extract by vaporization and condensation
DISTINCT	*adj* **-TINCTER, -TINCTEST** clearly different
DISTOME	*n* pl. **-S** a parasitic flatworm
DISTORT	*v* **-ED, -ING, -S** to put out of shape
DISTRACT	*v* **-ED, -ING, -S** to divert the attention of
DISTRAIN	*v* **-ED, -ING, -S** to seize and hold property as security
DISTRAIT	*adj* absentminded
DISTRESS	*v* **-ED, -ING, -ES** to cause anxiety or suffering to
DISTRICT	*v* **-ED, -ING, -S** to divide into localities
DISTRUST	*v* **-ED, -ING, -S** to have no trust in
DISTURB	*v* **-ED, -ING, -S** to interrupt the quiet, rest, or peace of
DISULFID	*n* pl. **-S** a chemical compound
DISUNION	*n* pl. **-S** the state of being disunited
DISUNITE	*v* **-UNITED, -UNITING, -UNITES** to separate
DISUNITY	*n* pl. **-TIES** lack of unity
DISUSE	*v* **-USED, -USING, -USES** to stop using
DISVALUE	*v* **-UED, -UING, -UES** to treat as of little value
DISYOKE	*v* **-YOKED, -YOKING, -YOKES** to free from a yoke
DIT	*n* pl. **-S** a dot in Morse code
DITA	*n* pl. **-S** a Philippine tree
DITCH	*v* **-ED, -ING, -ES** to dig a long, narrow excavation in the ground
DITCHER	*n* pl. **-S** one that ditches
DITE	*n* pl. **-S** a small amount
DITHEISM	*n* pl. **-S** belief in two coequal gods
DITHEIST	*n* pl. **-S** an adherent of ditheism
DITHER	*v* **-ED, -ING, -S** to act nervously or indecisively
DITHERER	*n* pl. **-S** one that dithers
DITHERY	*adj* nervously excited
DITHIOL	*adj* containing two chemical groups both of which include sulfur and hydrogen
DITSY	*adj* **-SIER, -SIEST** silly, eccentric
DITTANY	*n* pl. **-NIES** a perennial herb
DITTO	*v* **-ED, -ING, -S** to repeat
DITTY	*n* pl. **-TIES** a short, simple song
DITZ	*n* pl. **-ES** a ditsy person
DITZY	*adj* **-ZIER, -ZIEST** ditsy
DIURESIS	*n* pl. **DIURESES** excessive discharge of urine
DIURETIC	*n* pl. **-S** a drug which increases urinary discharge
DIURNAL	*n* pl. **-S** a diary
DIURON	*n* pl. **-S** an herbicide
DIVA	*n* pl. **-S** a distinguished female operatic singer
DIVAGATE	*v* **-GATED, -GATING, -GATES** to wander
DIVALENT	*adj* having a valence of two
DIVAN	*n* pl. **-S** a sofa or couch
DIVE	*v* **DIVED** or **DOVE, DIVING, DIVES** to plunge headfirst into water
DIVEBOMB	*v* **-ED, -ING, -S** to drop bombs on a target from a diving airplane
DIVER	*n* pl. **-S** one that dives
DIVERGE	*v* **-VERGED, -VERGING, -VERGES** to move in different directions from a common point
DIVERSE	*adj* different
DIVERT	*v* **-ED, -ING, -S** to turn aside
DIVERTER	*n* pl. **-S** one that diverts

DIVEST *v* **-ED, -ING, -S** to strip or deprive of anything

DIVIDE *v* **-VIDED, -VIDING, -VIDES** to separate into parts, areas, or groups

DIVIDEND *n* pl. **-S** a quantity to be divided

DIVIDER *n* pl. **-S** one that divides

DIVIDING present participle of divide

DIVIDUAL *adj* capable of being divided

DIVINE *adj* **-VINER, -VINEST** pertaining to or characteristic of a god **DIVINELY** *adv*

DIVINE *v* **-VINED, -VINING, -VINES** to foretell by occult means

DIVINER *n* pl. **-S** one that divines

DIVING *n* pl. **-S** the act or sport of plunging headfirst into water

DIVINING present participle of divine

DIVINISE *v* **-NISED, -NISING, -NISES** to divinize

DIVINITY *n* pl. **-TIES** the state of being divine

DIVINIZE *v* **-NIZED, -NIZING, -NIZES** to make divine

DIVISION *n* pl. **-S** the act of dividing

DIVISIVE *adj* causing disunity or dissension

DIVISOR *n* pl. **-S** a number by which a dividend is divided

DIVORCE *v* **-VORCED, -VORCING, -VORCES** to terminate the marriage contract between

DIVORCEE *n* pl. **-S** a divorced woman

DIVORCER *n* pl. **-S** one that divorces

DIVOT *n* pl. **-S** a piece of turf

DIVULGE *v* **-VULGED, -VULGING, -VULGES** to reveal

DIVULGER *n* pl. **-S** one that divulges

DIVULSE *v* **-VULSED, -VULSING, -VULSES** to tear away

DIVVY *v* **-VIED, -VYING, -VIES** to divide

DIWAN *n* pl. **-S** dewan

DIXIT *n* pl. **-S** a statement

DIZEN *v* **-ED, -ING, -S** to dress in fine clothes

DIZYGOUS *adj* developed from two fertilized ova

DIZZY *adj* **-ZIER, -ZIEST** having a sensation of whirling **DIZZILY** *adv*

DIZZY *v* **-ZIED, -ZYING, -ZIES** to make dizzy

DJEBEL *n* pl. **-S** jebel

DJELLABA *n* pl. **-S** a long hooded garment

DJEMBE *n* pl. **-S** a type of African hand drum

DJIBBA *n* pl. **-S** jibba

DJIBBAH *n* pl. **-S** jibba

DJIN *n* pl. **-S** jinni

DJINN *n* pl. **-S** jinni

DJINNI *n* pl. **DJINN** jinni

DJINNY *n* pl. **DJINN** jinni

DO *n* pl. **DOS** the first tone of the diatonic musical scale

DO *v* **DID** or **DIDST, DONE, DOING,** present sing. 2d person **DO** or **DOEST** or **DOST,** 3d person **DOES** or **DOETH** or **DOTH** to begin and carry through to completion

DOABLE *adj* able to be done

DOAT *v* **-ED, -ING, -S** to dote

DOBBER *n* pl. **-S** a float for a fishing line

DOBBIN *n* pl. **-S** a farm horse

DOBBY *n* pl. **-BIES** a fool

DOBE *n* pl. **-S** adobe

DOBIE *n* pl. **-S** adobe

DOBIES pl. of doby

DOBLA *n* pl. **-S** a former gold coin of Spain

DOBLON *n* pl. **-S** or **-ES** a former gold coin of Spain and Spanish America

DOBRA *n* pl. **-S** a former gold coin of Portugal

DOBSON *n* pl. **-S** an aquatic insect larva

DOBY *n* pl. **-BIES** dobie

DOC *n* pl. **-S** doctor

DOCENT *n* pl. **-S** a college or university lecturer

DOCETIC *adj* pertaining to a religious doctrine

DOCILE *adj* easily trained **DOCILELY** *adv*

DOCILITY *n* pl. **-TIES** the quality of being docile

DOCK *v* **-ED, -ING, -S** to bring into a dock (a wharf)

DOCKAGE *n* pl. **-S** a charge for the use of a dock

DOCKER *n* pl. **-S** a dock worker

DOCKET *v* **-ED, -ING, -S** to supply with an identifying statement

DOCKHAND *n* pl. **-S** a docker

DOCKLAND	*n* pl. **-S** the part of a port occupied by docks
DOCKSIDE	*n* pl. **-S** the area adjacent to a dock
DOCKYARD	*n* pl. **-S** a shipyard
DOCTOR	*v* **-ED, -ING, -S** to treat medically **DOCTORLY** *adj*
DOCTORAL	*adj* pertaining to a doctor
DOCTRINE	*n* pl. **-S** a belief or set of beliefs taught or advocated
DOCUMENT	*v* **-ED, -ING, -S** to support by conclusive information or evidence
DOCUSOAP	*n* pl. **-S** a television series about the activities of real people
DODDER	*v* **-ED, -ING, -S** to totter
DODDERER	*n* pl. **-S** one that dodders
DODDERY	*adj* feeble
DODDLE	*n* pl. **-S** an easy task
DODGE	*v* **DODGED, DODGING, DODGES** to evade
DODGEM	*n* pl. **-S** an amusement park ride
DODGER	*n* pl. **-S** one that dodges
DODGERY	*n* pl. **-ERIES** evasion
DODGING	present participle of dodge
DODGY	*adj* **DODGIER, DODGIEST** evasive
DODO	*n* pl. **-DOS** or **-DOES** an extinct flightless bird
DODOISM	*n* pl. **-S** a stupid remark
DOE	*n* pl. **-S** a female deer
DOER	*n* pl. **-S** one that does something
DOES	a present 3d person sing. of do
DOESKIN	*n* pl. **-S** the skin of a doe
DOEST	a present 2d person sing. of do
DOETH	a present 3d person sing. of do
DOFF	*v* **-ED, -ING, -S** to take off
DOFFER	*n* pl. **-S** one that doffs
DOG	*v* **DOGGED, DOGGING, DOGS** to follow after like a dog (a domesticated, carnivorous mammal)
DOGBANE	*n* pl. **-S** a perennial herb
DOGBERRY	*n* pl. **-RIES** a wild berry
DOGCART	*n* pl. **-S** a one-horse carriage
DOGDOM	*n* pl. **-S** the world of dogs
DOGE	*n* pl. **-S** the chief magistrate in the former republics of Venice and Genoa
DOGEAR	*v* **-ED, -ING, -S** to turn down a corner of a page
DOGEDOM	*n* pl. **-S** the domain of a doge
DOGESHIP	*n* pl. **-S** the office of a doge
DOGEY	*n* pl. **-GEYS** dogie
DOGFACE	*n* pl. **-S** a soldier in the U.S. Army
DOGFIGHT	*v* **-FOUGHT, -FIGHTING, -FIGHTS** to engage in an aerial battle
DOGFISH	*n* pl. **-ES** a small shark
DOGGED	past tense of dog
DOGGEDLY	*adv* stubbornly
DOGGER	*n* pl. **-S** a fishing vessel
DOGGEREL	*n* pl. **-S** trivial, awkwardly written verse
DOGGERY	*n* pl. **-GERIES** surly behavior
DOGGIE	*n* pl. **-S** doggy
DOGGIER	comparative of doggy
DOGGIES	pl. of doggy
DOGGIEST	superlative of doggy
DOGGING	present participle of dog
DOGGISH	*adj* doglike
DOGGO	*adv* in hiding
DOGGONE	*adj* **-GONER, -GONEST** damned
DOGGONE	*v* **-GONED, -GONING, -GONES** to damn
DOGGONED	*adj* **-GONEDER, -GONEDEST** damned
DOGGREL	*n* pl. **-S** doggerel
DOGGY	*adj* **-GIER, -GIEST** resembling or suggestive of a dog
DOGGY	*n* pl. **-GIES** a small dog
DOGHOUSE	*n* pl. **-S** a shelter for a dog
DOGIE	*n* pl. **-S** a stray calf
DOGIES	pl. of dogy
DOGLEG	*v* **-LEGGED, -LEGGING, -LEGS** to move along a bent course
DOGLIKE	*adj* resembling a dog
DOGMA	*n* pl. **-MAS** or **-MATA** a principle or belief put forth as authoritative **DOGMATIC** *adj*
DOGNAP	*v* **-NAPED, -NAPING, -NAPS** or **-NAPPED, -NAPPING, -NAPS** to steal a dog
DOGNAPER	*n* pl. **-S** one that dognaps
DOGSBODY	*n* pl. **-BODIES** a menial worker
DOGSKIN	*n* pl. **-S** leather made from the skin of a dog

DOGSLED *v* -**SLEDDED**, -**SLEDDING**, -**SLEDS** to move on a sled drawn by dogs

DOGSTAIL *n* pl. -**S** a grass with spiky flower heads

DOGTAIL *n* pl. -**S** a type of grass

DOGTOOTH *n* pl. -**TEETH** a cuspid

DOGTROT *v* -**TROTTED**, -**TROTTING**, -**TROTS** to move at a steady trot

DOGVANE *n* pl. -**S** a small vane

DOGWATCH *n* pl. -**ES** a short period of watch duty on a ship

DOGWOOD *n* pl. -**S** a tree

DOGY *n* pl. -**GIES** dogie

DOH *n* pl. -**S** the first tone of the diatonic scale

DOILED *adj* dazed

DOILY *n* pl. -**LIES** a small napkin

DOING *n* pl. -**S** an action

DOIT *n* pl. -**S** a former Dutch coin

DOITED *adj* old and feeble

DOJO *n* pl. -**JOS** a school that teaches judo or karate

DOL *n* pl. -**S** a unit of pain intensity

DOLCE *n* pl. -**CI** a soft-toned organ stop

DOLCETTO *n* pl. -**TOS** a red wine of Italy

DOLDRUMS *n/pl* a slump or slack period

DOLE *v* **DOLED**, **DOLING**, **DOLES** to distribute in small portions

DOLEFUL *adj* -**FULLER**, -**FULLEST** mournful

DOLERITE *n* pl. -**S** a variety of basalt

DOLESOME *adj* doleful

DOLING present participle of dole

DOLL *v* -**ED**, -**ING**, -**S** to dress stylishly

DOLLAR *n* pl. -**S** a monetary unit of the United States

DOLLIED past tense of dolly

DOLLIES present 3d person sing. of dolly

DOLLISH *adj* pretty

DOLLOP *v* -**ED**, -**ING**, -**S** to dispense in small amounts

DOLLY *v* -**LIED**, -**LYING**, -**LIES** to move on a wheeled platform

DOLMA *n* pl. -**MAS** or -**MADES** a stuffed grape leaf

DOLMAN *n* pl. -**S** a Turkish robe

DOLMEN *n* pl. -**S** a prehistoric monument **DOLMENIC** *adj*

DOLOMITE *n* pl. -**S** a mineral

DOLOR *n* pl. -**S** grief

DOLOROSO *adj* having a mournful musical quality

DOLOROUS *adj* mournful

DOLOUR *n* pl. -**S** dolor

DOLPHIN *n* pl. -**S** a marine mammal

DOLT *n* pl. -**S** a stupid person **DOLTISH** *adj*

DOM *n* pl. -**S** a title given to certain monks

DOMAIN *n* pl. -**S** an area of control

DOMAINE *n* pl. -**S** a vineyard in Burgundy

DOMAL *adj* domical

DOME *v* **DOMED**, **DOMING**, **DOMES** to cover with a dome (a rounded roof)

DOMELIKE *adj* resembling a dome

DOMESDAY *n* pl. -**DAYS** doomsday

DOMESTIC *n* pl. -**S** a household servant

DOMIC *adj* domical

DOMICAL *adj* shaped like a dome

DOMICIL *v* -**ED**, -**ING**, -**S** to domicile

DOMICILE *v* -**CILED**, -**CILING**, -**CILES** to establish in a residence

DOMINANT *n* pl. -**S** a controlling genetic character

DOMINATE *v* -**NATED**, -**NATING**, -**NATES** to control

DOMINE *n* pl. -**S** master

DOMINEER *v* -**ED**, -**ING**, -**S** to tyrannize

DOMING present participle of dome

DOMINICK *n* pl. -**S** one of an American breed of chickens

DOMINIE *n* pl. -**S** a clergyman

DOMINION *n* pl. -**S** supreme authority

DOMINIUM *n* pl. -**S** the right of ownership and control of property

DOMINO *n* pl. -**NOS** or -**NOES** a small mask

DON *v* **DONNED**, **DONNING**, **DONS** to put on

DONA *n* pl. -**S** a Spanish lady

DONAIR *n* pl. -**S** sliced lamb rolled in pita bread

DONATE *v* -**NATED**, -**NATING**, -**NATES** to contribute

DONATION *n* pl. -**S** something donated

DONATIVE *n* pl. -**S** a donation

DONATOR *n* pl. -**S** a donor

DONE	past participle of do
DONEE	*n* pl. **-S** a recipient of a gift
DONEGAL	*n* pl. **-S** a type of tweed
DONENESS	*n* pl. **-ES** the state of being cooked enough
DONG	*v* **-ED, -ING, -S** to make a deep sound like that of a large bell
DONGA	*n* pl. **-S** a gully in a veldt
DONGLE	*n* pl. **-S** a device for a computer
DONGOLA	*n* pl. **-S** a type of leather
DONJON	*n* pl. **-S** the main tower of a castle
DONKEY	*n* pl. **-KEYS** the domestic ass
DONNA	*n* pl. **DONNAS** or **DONNE** an Italian lady
DONNED	past tense of don
DONNEE	*n* pl. **-S** the set of assumptions upon which a story proceeds
DONNERD	*adj* donnered
DONNERED	*adj* dazed
DONNERT	*adj* donnered
DONNIKER	*n* pl. **-S** a bathroom or privy
DONNING	present participle of don
DONNISH	*adj* scholarly
DONOR	*n* pl. **-S** one that donates
DONSHIP	*n* pl. **-S** the position of a don (a senior member of a British university)
DONSIE	*adj* unlucky
DONSY	*adj* donsie
DONUT	*n* pl. **-S** doughnut
DONZEL	*n* pl. **-S** a young squire
DOOB	*n* pl. **-S** a doobie
DOOBIE	*n* pl. **-S** a marijuana cigarette
DOODAD	*n* pl. **-S** an article whose name is unknown or forgotten
DOODAH	*n* pl. **-S** a small useful device
DOODLE	*v* **-DLED, -DLING, -DLES** to draw or scribble aimlessly
DOODLER	*n* pl. **-S** one that doodles
DOODOO	*n* pl. **-DOOS** feces
DOODY	*n* pl. **-DIES** feces
DOOFUS	*n* pl. **-ES** a stupid or foolish person
DOOLEE	*n* pl. **-S** a stretcher for the sick or wounded
DOOLIE	*n* pl. **-S** doolee
DOOLY	*n* pl. **-LIES** doolee

DOOM	*v* **-ED, -ING, -S** to destine to an unhappy fate
DOOMFUL	*adj* ominous
DOOMSDAY	*n* pl. **-DAYS** judgment day
DOOMSTER	*n* pl. **-S** a judge
DOOMY	*adj* **DOOMIER, DOOMIEST** doomful **DOOMILY** *adv*
DOOR	*n* pl. **-S** a movable barrier at an entranceway **DOORED** *adj*
DOORBELL	*n* pl. **-S** a bell at a door
DOORCASE	*n* pl. **-S** the frame for a door
DOORJAMB	*n* pl. **-S** a vertical piece at the side of a doorway
DOORKNOB	*n* pl. **-S** a handle for opening a door
DOORLESS	*adj* having no door
DOORMAN	*n* pl. **-MEN** the door attendant of a building
DOORMAT	*n* pl. **-S** a mat placed in front of a door
DOORNAIL	*n* pl. **-S** a large-headed nail
DOORPOST	*n* pl. **-S** a doorjamb
DOORSILL	*n* pl. **-S** the sill of a door
DOORSTEP	*n* pl. **-S** a step leading to a door
DOORSTOP	*n* pl. **-S** an object used for holding a door open
DOORWAY	*n* pl. **-WAYS** the entranceway to a room or building
DOORYARD	*n* pl. **-S** a yard in front of a house
DOOWOP	*n* pl. **-S** a singing style
DOOZER	*n* pl. **-S** doozy
DOOZIE	*n* pl. **-S** doozy
DOOZY	*n* pl. **-ZIES** an extraordinary one of its kind
DOPA	*n* pl. **-S** a drug to treat Parkinson's disease
DOPAMINE	*n* pl. **-S** a form of dopa used to stimulate the heart
DOPANT	*n* pl. **-S** an impurity added to a pure substance
DOPE	*v* **DOPED, DOPING, DOPES** to give a narcotic to
DOPE	*adj* **DOPER, DOPEST** excellent, outstanding
DOPER	*n* pl. **-S** one that dopes
DOPESTER	*n* pl. **-S** one who predicts the outcomes of contests
DOPEY	*adj* **DOPIER, DOPIEST** lethargic; stupid **DOPILY** *adv*
DOPIER	comparative of dopy

DOPIEST	superlative of dopy	**DOSA**	*n* pl. **DOSAS** or **DOSAI** a pancake made from rice flour
DOPINESS	*n* pl. **-ES** the state of being dopey	**DOSAGE**	*n* pl. **-S** the amount of medicine to be given
DOPING	*n* pl. **-S** the use of drugs by athletes	**DOSE**	*v* **DOSED, DOSING, DOSES** to give a specified quantity of medicine to
DOPY	*adj* **DOPIER, DOPIEST** dopey		
DOR	*n* pl. **-S** a black European beetle	**DOSER**	*n* pl. **-S** one that doses
DORADO	*n* pl. **-DOS** a marine fish	**DOSH**	*n* money
DORBUG	*n* pl. **-S** a dor	**DOSHA**	*n* pl. **-S** each of three energies believed to circulate in the body
DORE	*n* pl. **-S** a large freshwater fish		
DORHAWK	*n* pl. **-S** a nocturnal bird	**DOSS**	*v* **-ED, -ING, -ES** to sleep in any convenient place
DORIES	pl. of dory		
DORK	*n* pl. **-S** a stupid or foolish person	**DOSSAL**	*n* pl. **-S** an ornamental cloth hung behind an altar
DORKY	*adj* **DORKIER, DORKIEST** stupid, foolish	**DOSSEL**	*n* pl. **-S** dossal
DORM	*n* pl. **-S** a dormitory	**DOSSER**	*n* pl. **-S** a basket carried on the back
DORMANCY	*n* pl. **-CIES** the state of being dormant	**DOSSERET**	*n* pl. **-S** a block resting on the capital of a column
DORMANT	*adj* lying asleep	**DOSSIER**	*n* pl. **-S** a file of papers on a single subject
DORMER	*n* pl. **-S** a type of window **DORMERED** *adj*		
DORMICE	pl. of dormouse	**DOSSIL**	*n* pl. **-S** a cloth roll for wiping ink
DORMIE	*adj* being ahead by as many holes in golf as remain to be played	**DOST**	a present 2d person sing. of do
		DOT	*v* **DOTTED, DOTTING, DOTS** to cover with dots (tiny round marks)
DORMIENT	*adj* dormant		
DORMIN	*n* pl. **-S** a plant hormone	**DOTAGE**	*n* pl. **-S** a state of senility
DORMOUSE	*n* pl. **-MICE** a small rodent	**DOTAL**	*adj* pertaining to a dowry
DORMY	*adj* dormie	**DOTARD**	*n* pl. **-S** a senile person **DOTARDLY** *adj*
DORNECK	*n* pl. **-S** dornick		
DORNICK	*n* pl. **-S** a heavy linen fabric	**DOTATION**	*n* pl. **-S** an endowment
DORNOCK	*n* pl. **-S** dornick	**DOTE**	*v* **DOTED, DOTING, DOTES** to show excessive affection
DORP	*n* pl. **-S** a village		
DORPER	*n* pl. **-S** one of a breed of mutton-producing sheep	**DOTER**	*n* pl. **-S** one that dotes
		DOTH	a present 3d person sing. of do
DORR	*n* pl. **-S** dor	**DOTIER**	comparative of doty
DORSA	pl. of dorsum	**DOTIEST**	superlative of doty
DORSAD	*adv* dorsally	**DOTING**	present participle of dote
DORSAL	*n* pl. **-S** a dorsally located anatomical part	**DOTINGLY**	*adv* in an excessively affectionate manner
DORSALLY	*adv* toward the back		
DORSEL	*n* pl. **-S** a dossal	**DOTTED**	past tense of dot
DORSER	*n* pl. **-S** dosser	**DOTTEL**	*n* pl. **-S** dottle
DORSUM	*n* pl. **-SA** the back	**DOTTER**	*n* pl. **-S** one that dots
DORTY	*adj* sullen	**DOTTEREL**	*n* pl. **-S** a shorebird
DORY	*n* pl. **-RIES** a flat-bottomed boat	**DOTTIER**	comparative of dotty
DORYMAN	*n* pl. **-MEN** one that fishes from a dory	**DOTTIEST**	superlative of dotty
		DOTTILY	*adv* in a dotty manner
		DOTTING	present participle of dot

DOTTLE	*n* pl. **-S** a mass of half-burnt pipe tobacco
DOTTREL	*n* pl. **-S** dotterel
DOTTY	*adj* **-TIER, -TIEST** crazy
DOTY	*adj* **DOTIER, DOTIEST** stained by decay
DOUBLE	*v* **-BLED, -BLING, -BLES** to make twice as great
DOUBLER	*n* pl. **-S** one that doubles
DOUBLET	*n* pl. **-S** a close-fitting jacket
DOUBLING	present participle of double
DOUBLOON	*n* pl. **-S** a former Spanish gold coin
DOUBLURE	*n* pl. **-S** the lining of a book cover
DOUBLY	*adv* to twice the degree
DOUBT	*v* **-ED, -ING, -S** to be uncertain about
DOUBTER	*n* pl. **-S** one that doubts
DOUBTFUL	*adj* uncertain
DOUCE	*adj* **DOUCER, DOUCEST** sober, sedate **DOUCELY** *adv*
DOUCEUR	*n* pl. **-S** a gratuity
DOUCHE	*v* **DOUCHED, DOUCHING, DOUCHES** to cleanse with a jet of water
DOUCHING	*n* pl. **-S** a cleansing with a jet of water
DOUGH	*n* pl. **-S** a flour mixture
DOUGHBOY	*n* pl. **-BOYS** an infantryman
DOUGHIER	comparative of doughy
DOUGHIEST	superlative of doughy
DOUGHNUT	*n* pl. **-S** a ring-shaped cake
DOUGHT	a past tense of dow
DOUGHTY	*adj* **-TIER, -TIEST** courageous
DOUGHY	*adj* **DOUGHIER, DOUGHIEST** resembling dough
DOULA	*n* pl. **-S** a woman who assists another woman during childbirth
DOUM	*n* pl. **-S** an African palm tree
DOUMA	*n* pl. **-S** duma
DOUPIONI	*n* pl. **-S** a silk yarn
DOUR	*adj* **DOURER, DOUREST** sullen
DOURA	*n* pl. **-S** durra
DOURAH	*n* pl. **-S** durra
DOURINE	*n* pl. **-S** a disease of horses
DOURLY	*adv* in a dour manner
DOURNESS	*n* pl. **-ES** the state of being dour
DOUSE	*v* **DOUSED, DOUSING, DOUSES** to plunge into water

DOUSER	*n* pl. **-S** one that douses
DOUT	*v* **-ED, -ING, -S** to extinguish (as a fire)
DOUX	*adj* very sweet — used of champagne
DOUZEPER	*n* pl. **-S** one of twelve legendary knights
DOVE	*n* pl. **-S** a bird of the pigeon family
DOVECOT	*n* pl. **-S** dovecote
DOVECOTE	*n* pl. **-S** a roost for domesticated pigeons
DOVEKEY	*n* pl. **-KEYS** dovekie
DOVEKIE	*n* pl. **-S** a seabird
DOVELIKE	*adj* resembling or suggestive of a dove
DOVEN	*v* **-ED, -ING, -S** to daven
DOVETAIL	*v* **-ED, -ING, -S** to fit together closely
DOVISH	*adj* not warlike
DOW	*v* **DOWED** or **DOUGHT, DOWING, DOWS** to prosper
DOWABLE	*adj* entitled to an endowment
DOWAGER	*n* pl. **-S** a dignified elderly woman
DOWDY	*adj* **DOWDIER, DOWDIEST** lacking in stylishness or neatness **DOWDILY** *adv* **DOWDYISH** *adj*
DOWDY	*n* pl. **DOWDIES** a dowdy woman
DOWEL	*v* **-ELED, -ELING, -ELS** or **-ELLED, -ELLING, -ELS** to fasten with wooden pins
DOWELING	*n* pl. **-S** a cylindrical rod
DOWER	*v* **-ED, -ING, -S** to provide with a dowry
DOWERY	*n* pl. **-ERIES** dowry
DOWIE	*adj* dreary
DOWN	*v* **-ED, -ING, -S** to cause to fall
DOWNBEAT	*n* pl. **-S** the first beat of a musical measure
DOWNBOW	*n* pl. **-S** a type of stroke in playing a bowed instrument
DOWNCAST	*n* pl. **-S** an overthrow or ruin
DOWNCOME	*n* pl. **-S** downfall
DOWNER	*n* pl. **-S** a depressant drug
DOWNFALL	*n* pl. **-S** a sudden fall
DOWNHAUL	*n* pl. **-S** a rope for hauling down sails
DOWNHILL	*n* pl. **-S** a downward slope
DOWNHOLE	*adj* used down or in an oil well
DOWNIER	comparative of downy

DOWNIEST superlative of downy

DOWNILY *adv* in a downy manner

DOWNLAND *n* pl. **-S** a rolling treeless upland

DOWNLESS *adj* having no down (soft furry feathers)

DOWNLIKE *adj* resembling down

DOWNLINK *v* **-ED, -ING, -S** to transmit data from a satellite to earth

DOWNLOAD *v* **-ED, -ING, -S** to transfer data from a large computer to a smaller one

DOWNPIPE *n* pl. **-S** a pipe for draining water from a roof

DOWNPLAY *v* **-ED, -ING, -S** to de-emphasize

DOWNPOUR *n* pl. **-S** a heavy rain

DOWNRATE *v* **-RATED, -RATING, -RATES** to make lower in value

DOWNSIDE *n* pl. **-S** a negative aspect

DOWNSIZE *v* **-SIZED, -SIZING, -SIZES** to produce in a smaller size

DOWNSPIN *n* pl. **-S** a spinning motion

DOWNTICK *n* pl. **-S** a stock market transaction

DOWNTIME *n* pl. **-S** the time when a machine or factory is inactive

DOWNTOWN *n* pl. **-S** the business district of a city

DOWNTROD *adj* oppressed

DOWNTURN *n* pl. **-S** a downward turn

DOWNWARD *adv* from a higher to a lower place

DOWNWARP *n* pl. **-S** a broad surface depression

DOWNWASH *n* pl. **-ES** a downward deflection of air

DOWNWIND *adv* in the direction that the wind blows

DOWNY *adj* **DOWNIER, DOWNIEST** soft

DOWNZONE *v* **-ZONED, -ZONING, -ZONES** to reduce or limit the number of buildings permitted

DOWRY *n* pl. **-RIES** the money or property a wife brings to her husband at marriage

DOWSABEL *n* pl. **-S** a sweetheart

DOWSE *v* **DOWSED, DOWSING, DOWSES** to search for underground water with a divining rod

DOWSER *n* pl. **-S** one that dowses

DOWSING *n* pl. **-S** a technique for searching for underground water

DOXIE *n* pl. **-S** doxy

DOXOLOGY *n* pl. **-GIES** a hymn or verse of praise to God

DOXY *n* pl. **DOXIES** a doctrine

DOYEN *n* pl. **-S** the senior member of a group

DOYENNE *n* pl. **-S** a female doyen

DOYLEY *n* pl. **-LEYS** doily

DOYLY *n* pl. **-LIES** doily

DOZE *v* **DOZED, DOZING, DOZES** to sleep lightly

DOZEN *v* **-ED, -ING, -S** to stun

DOZENTH *n* pl. **-S** twelfth

DOZER *n* pl. **-S** one that dozes

DOZIER comparative of dozy

DOZIEST superlative of dozy

DOZILY *adv* in a dozy manner

DOZINESS *n* pl. **-ES** the state of being dozy

DOZING present participle of doze

DOZY *adj* **DOZIER, DOZIEST** drowsy

DRAB *adj* **DRABBER, DRABBEST** cheerless

DRAB *v* **DRABBED, DRABBING, DRABS** to consort with prostitutes

DRABBET *n* pl. **-S** a coarse linen fabric

DRABBLE *v* **-BLED, -BLING, -BLES** to draggle

DRABLY *adv* in a drab manner

DRABNESS *n* pl. **-ES** the quality of being drab

DRACAENA *n* pl. **-S** a tropical plant

DRACENA *n* pl. **-S** dracaena

DRACHM *n* pl. **-S** a unit of weight

DRACHMA *n* pl. **-MAS, -MAE** or **-MAI** a former monetary unit of Greece

DRACONIC *adj* pertaining to a dragon

DRAFF *n* pl. **-S** the damp remains of malt after brewing

DRAFFISH *adj* draffy

DRAFFY *adj* **DRAFFIER, DRAFFIEST** worthless

DRAFT *v* **-ED, -ING, -S** to conscript for military service

DRAFTEE *n* pl. **-S** one that is drafted

DRAFTER *n* pl. **-S** one that drafts

DRAFTING *n* pl. **-S** mechanical drawing

DRAFTY *adj* **DRAFTIER, DRAFTIEST** having or exposed to currents of air **DRAFTILY** *adv*

DRAG *v* **DRAGGED, DRAGGING, DRAGS** to pull along the ground

DRAGEE *n* pl. **-S** a sugarcoated candy

DRAGGER *n* pl. **-S** one that drags

DRAGGIER comparative of draggy

DRAGGIEST superlative of draggy

DRAGGING present participle of drag

DRAGGLE *v* **-GLED, -GLING, -GLES** to make wet and dirty

DRAGGY *adj* **-GIER, -GIEST** sluggish

DRAGLINE *n* pl. **-S** a line used for dragging

DRAGNET *n* pl. **-S** a net for trawling

DRAGOMAN *n* pl. **-MANS** or **-MEN** an interpreter in Near Eastern countries

DRAGON *n* pl. **-S** a mythical monster resembling a serpent

DRAGONET *n* pl. **-S** a marine fish

DRAGOON *v* **-ED, -ING, -S** to harass by the use of troops

DRAGROPE *n* pl. **-S** a rope used for dragging

DRAGSTER *n* pl. **-S** a vehicle used in drag racing

DRAIL *n* pl. **-S** a heavy fishhook

DRAIN *v* **-ED, -ING, -S** to draw off a liquid

DRAINAGE *n* pl. **-S** the act of draining

DRAINER *n* pl. **-S** one that drains

DRAKE *n* pl. **-S** a male duck

DRAM *v* **DRAMMED, DRAMMING, DRAMS** to tipple

DRAMA *n* pl. **-S** a composition written for theatrical performance

DRAMADY *n* pl. **-DIES** dramedy

DRAMATIC *adj* pertaining to drama

DRAMEDY *n* pl. **-DIES** a sitcom having dramatic scenes

DRAMMED past tense of dram

DRAMMING present participle of dram

DRAMMOCK *n* pl. **-S** raw oatmeal mixed with cold water

DRAMSHOP *n* pl. **-S** a barroom

DRANK past tense of drink

DRAPE *v* **DRAPED, DRAPING, DRAPES** to arrange in graceful folds **DRAPABLE** *adj*

DRAPER *n* pl. **-S** a dealer in cloth

DRAPERY *n* pl. **-ERIES** cloth arranged in graceful folds

DRAPEY *adj* characterized by graceful folds

DRAPING present participle of drape

DRASTIC *adj* extremely severe

DRAT *v* **DRATTED, DRATTING, DRATS** to damn

DRAUGHT *v* **-ED, -ING, -S** to draft

DRAUGHTY *adj* **DRAUGHTIER, DRAUGHTIEST** drafty

DRAVE a past tense of drive

DRAW *v* **DREW, DRAWN, DRAWING, DRAWS** to move by pulling **DRAWABLE** *adj*

DRAWBACK *n* pl. **-S** a hindrance

DRAWBAR *n* pl. **-S** a railroad coupler

DRAWBORE *n* pl. **-S** a hole for joining a mortise and tenon

DRAWCORD *n* pl. **-S** a cord for drawing a garment tight

DRAWDOWN *n* pl. **-S** a lowering of a water level

DRAWEE *n* pl. **-S** the person on whom a bill of exchange is drawn

DRAWER *n* pl. **-S** one that draws

DRAWING *n* pl. **-S** a portrayal in lines of a form or figure

DRAWL *v* **-ED, -ING, -S** to speak slowly with vowels greatly prolonged

DRAWLER *n* pl. **-S** one that drawls

DRAWLY *adj* **DRAWLIER, DRAWLIEST** marked by drawling

DRAWN past participle of draw

DRAWTUBE *n* pl. **-S** a tube that slides within another tube

DRAY *v* **-ED, -ING, -S** to transport by dray (a low, strong cart)

DRAYAGE *n* pl. **-S** transportation by dray

DRAYMAN *n* pl. **-MEN** one who drives a dray

DREAD *v* **-ED, -ING, -S** to fear greatly

DREAD *adj* **DREADER, DREADEST** frightening

DREADFUL *n* pl. **-S** a publication containing sensational material

DREAM *v* **DREAMED** or **DREAMT, DREAMING, DREAMS** to have a dream (a series of images occurring during sleep)

DREAMER *n* pl. **-S** one that dreams

DREAMFUL *adj* dreamy

DREAMY *adj* **DREAMIER, DREAMIEST** full of dreams **DREAMILY** *adv*

DREAR *n* pl. **-S** the state of being dreary

DREAR *adj* **DREARER, DREAREST** dreary

DREARY *adj* **DREARIER, DREARIEST** dismal **DREARILY** *adv*

DREARY *n* pl. **DREARIES** a dismal person

DRECK *n* pl. **-S** rubbish **DRECKISH** *adj*

DRECKY *adj* **DRECKIER, DRECKIEST** trashy

DREDGE *v* **DREDGED, DREDGING, DREDGES** to clear with a dredge (a machine for scooping mud)

DREDGER *n* pl. **-S** one that dredges

DREDGING *n* pl. **-S** matter that is dredged up

DREE *v* **DREED, DREEING, DREES** to suffer

DREG *n* pl. **-S** the sediment of liquors **DREGGISH** *adj*

DREGGY *adj* **-GIER, -GIEST** full of dregs

DREICH *adj* dreary

DREIDEL *n* pl. **-S** a spinning toy

DREIDL *n* pl. **-S** dreidel

DREIGH *adj* dreich

DREK *n* pl. **-S** dreck

DREKKY *adj* **DREKKIER, DREKKIEST** drecky

DRENCH *v* **-ED, -ING, -ES** to wet thoroughly

DRENCHER *n* pl. **-S** one that drenches

DRESS *v* **DRESSED** or **DREST, DRESSING, DRESSES** to put clothes on

DRESSAGE *n* pl. **-S** the training of a horse in obedience and deportment

DRESSER *n* pl. **-S** one that dresses

DRESSING *n* pl. **-S** material applied to cover a wound

DRESSY *adj* **DRESSIER, DRESSIEST** stylish **DRESSILY** *adv*

DREST a past tense of dress

DREW past tense of draw

DRIB *v* **DRIBBED, DRIBBING, DRIBS** to drip

DRIBBLE *v* **-BLED, -BLING, -BLES** to drivel

DRIBBLER *n* pl. **-S** one that dribbles

DRIBBLET *n* pl. **-S** driblet

DRIBBLING present participle of dribble

DRIBBLY *adj* tending to dribble

DRIBLET *n* pl. **-S** a small drop of liquid

DRIED past tense of dry

DRIEGH *adj* dreary

DRIER *n* pl. **-S** one that dries

DRIES present 3d person sing. of dry

DRIEST a superlative of dry

DRIFT *v* **-ED, -ING, -S** to move along in a current

DRIFTAGE *n* pl. **-S** the act of drifting

DRIFTER *n* pl. **-S** one that drifts

DRIFTNET *n* pl. **-S** a large fishnet arranged to drift with the tide or current

DRIFTPIN *n* pl. **-S** a metal rod for securing timbers

DRIFTY *adj* **DRIFTIER, DRIFTIEST** full of drifts (masses of wind-driven snow)

DRILL *v* **-ED, -ING, -S** to bore a hole in

DRILLER *n* pl. **-S** one that drills

DRILLING *n* pl. **-S** a heavy twilled cotton fabric

DRILY *adv* dryly

DRINK *v* **DRANK, DRUNK, DRINKING, DRINKS** to swallow liquid

DRINKER *n* pl. **-S** one that drinks

DRINKING *n* pl. **-S** a habit of drinking alcoholic beverages

DRIP *v* **DRIPPED** or **DRIPT, DRIPPING, DRIPS** to fall in drops

DRIPLESS *adj* designed not to drip

DRIPPER *n* pl. **-S** something from which a liquid drips

DRIPPING *n* pl. **-S** juice drawn from meat during cooking

DRIPPY *adj* **-PIER, -PIEST** very wet **DRIPPILY** *adv*

DRIPT a past tense of drip

DRIVE *v* **DROVE** or **DRAVE, DRIVEN, DRIVING, DRIVES** to urge or propel forward **DRIVABLE** *adj*

DRIVEL *v* **-ELED, -ELING, -ELS** or **-ELLED, -ELLING, -ELS** to let saliva flow from the mouth

DRIVELER *n* pl. **-S** one that drivels

DRIVER *n* pl. **-S** one that drives

DRIVEWAY *n* pl. **-WAYS** a private road providing access to a building

DRIVING *n* pl. **-S** management of a motor vehicle

DRIZZLE *v* **-ZLED, -ZLING, -ZLES** to rain lightly

DRIZZLY *adj* **-ZLIER, -ZLIEST** characterized by light rain

DROGUE *n* pl. **-S** a sea anchor

DROID	*n* pl. **-S** an android
DROIT	*n* pl. **-S** a legal right
DROKE	*n* pl. **-S** a grove of trees
DROLL	*adj* **DROLLER, DROLLEST** comical
DROLL	*v* **-ED, -ING, -S** to jest
DROLLERY	*n* pl. **-ERIES** something droll
DROLLY	*adv* in a droll manner
DROMON	*n* pl. **-S** dromond
DROMOND	*n* pl. **-S** a large fast-sailing medieval galley
DRONE	*v* **DRONED, DRONING, DRONES** to make a continuous low sound
DRONER	*n* pl. **-S** one that drones
DRONGO	*n* pl. **-GOS** or **-GOES** a tropical bird
DRONISH	*adj* habitually lazy
DROOL	*v* **-ED, -ING, -S** to drivel
DROOLY	*adj* **DROOLIER, DROOLIEST** drooling
DROOP	*v* **-ED, -ING, -S** to hang downward
DROOPY	*adj* **DROOPIER, DROOPIEST** drooping **DROOPILY** *adv*
DROP	*v* **DROPPED** or **DROPT, DROPPING, DROPS** to fall in drops (globules)
DROPHEAD	*n* pl. **-S** a convertible car
DROPKICK	*n* pl. **-S** a type of kick in football
DROPLET	*n* pl. **-S** a tiny drop
DROPOUT	*n* pl. **-S** one who quits school prematurely
DROPPED	a past tense of drop
DROPPER	*n* pl. **-S** a tube for dispensing liquid in drops
DROPPING	*n* pl. **-S** something that has been dropped
DROPSEED	*n* pl. **-S** a type of grass
DROPSHOT	*n* pl. **-S** a type of shot in tennis
DROPSY	*n* pl. **-SIES** an excessive accumulation of serous fluid **DROPSIED** *adj*
DROPT	a past tense of drop
DROPTOP	*n* pl. **-S** a convertible automobile
DROPWORT	*n* pl. **-S** a perennial herb
DROSERA	*n* pl. **-S** a sundew
DROSHKY	*n* pl. **-KIES** an open carriage
DROSKY	*n* pl. **-KIES** droshky
DROSS	*n* pl. **-ES** waste matter
DROSSY	*adj* **DROSSIER, DROSSIEST** worthless
DROUGHT	*n* pl. **-S** a dry period
DROUGHTY	*adj* **DROUGHTIER, DROUGHTIEST** dry
DROUK	*v* **-ED, -ING, -S** to drench
DROUTH	*n* pl. **-S** drought
DROUTHY	*adj* **DROUTHIER, DROUTHIEST** droughty
DROVE	*v* **DROVED, DROVING, DROVES** to drive cattle or sheep
DROVER	*n* pl. **-S** a driver of cattle or sheep
DROVING	*n* pl. **-S** the work of a drover
DROWN	*v* **-ED, -ING, -S** to suffocate in water
DROWND	*v* **-ED, -ING, -S** to drown
DROWNER	*n* pl. **-S** one that drowns
DROWSE	*v* **DROWSED, DROWSING, DROWSES** to doze
DROWSY	*adj* **DROWSIER, DROWSIEST** sleepy **DROWSILY** *adv*
DRUB	*v* **DRUBBED, DRUBBING, DRUBS** to beat severely
DRUBBER	*n* pl. **-S** one that drubs
DRUBBING	*n* pl. **-S** a severe beating
DRUDGE	*v* **DRUDGED, DRUDGING, DRUDGES** to do hard, menial, or tedious work
DRUDGER	*n* pl. **-S** one that drudges
DRUDGERY	*n* pl. **-ERIES** hard, menial, or tedious work
DRUG	*v* **DRUGGED, DRUGGING, DRUGS** to affect with a drug (a medicinal substance)
DRUGGET	*n* pl. **-S** a coarse woolen fabric
DRUGGIE	*n* pl. **-S** a drug addict
DRUGGIST	*n* pl. **-S** a pharmacist
DRUGGY	*adj* **-GIER, -GIEST** affected by drugs
DRUGLESS	*adj* being without drugs
DRUID	*n* pl. **-S** one of an ancient Celtic order of priests **DRUIDIC** *adj*
DRUIDESS	*n* pl. **-ES** a female druid
DRUIDISM	*n* pl. **-S** the religious system of the druids
DRUM	*v* **DRUMMED, DRUMMING, DRUMS** to beat a drum (a percussion instrument)
DRUMBEAT	*n* pl. **-S** the sound of a drum

DRUMBLE *v* **-BLED, -BLING, -BLES** to move slowly

DRUMFIRE *n* pl. **-S** heavy, continuous gunfire

DRUMFISH *n* pl. **-ES** a fish that makes a drumming sound

DRUMHEAD *n* pl. **-S** the material stretched over the end of a drum

DRUMLIKE *adj* resembling the head of a drum

DRUMLIN *n* pl. **-S** a long hill of glacial drift

DRUMLY *adj* **-LIER, -LIEST** dark and gloomy

DRUMMED past tense of drum

DRUMMER *n* pl. **-S** one that drums

DRUMMING *n* pl. **-S** the act of beating a drum

DRUMROLL *n* pl. **-S** a roll played on a drum

DRUNK *adj* **DRUNKER, DRUNKEST** intoxicated

DRUNK *n* pl. **-S** a drunken person

DRUNKARD *n* pl. **-S** one who is habitually drunk

DRUNKEN *adj* drunk

DRUNKISH *adj* somewhat drunk

DRUPE *n* pl. **-S** a fleshy fruit

DRUPEL *n* pl. **-S** drupelet

DRUPELET *n* pl. **-S** a small drupe

DRUSE *n* pl. **-S** a crust of small crystals lining a rock cavity

DRUTHER *n* pl. **-S** one's preference

DRY *adj* **DRIER, DRIEST** or **DRYER, DRYEST** having no moisture

DRY *n* pl. **DRYS** a prohibitionist

DRY *v* **DRIED, DRYING, DRIES** to make dry **DRYABLE** *adj*

DRYAD *n* pl. **-S** or **-ES** a nymph of the woods **DRYADIC** *adj*

DRYAS *n* pl. **DRYAS** a flowering alpine plant

DRYER *n* pl. **-S** drier

DRYISH *adj* somewhat dry

DRYLAND *n* pl. **-S** an arid region

DRYLOT *n* pl. **-S** an enclosure for livestock

DRYLY *adv* in a dry manner

DRYNESS *n* pl. **-ES** the state of being dry

DRYPOINT *n* pl. **-S** a method of engraving

DRYSTONE *adj* constructed of stone without mortar

DRYSUIT *n* pl. **-S** a waterproof rubber suit worn by divers

DRYWALL *v* **-ED, -ING, -S** to cover a wall with plasterboard

DRYWELL *n* pl. **-S** a hole for receiving drainage from a roof

DUAD *n* pl. **-S** a pair

DUAL *n* pl. **-S** a linguistic form

DUALISE *v* **-ISED, -ISING, -ISES** to dualize

DUALISM *n* pl. **-S** a philosophical theory

DUALIST *n* pl. **-S** an adherent of dualism

DUALITY *n* pl. **-TIES** the state of being twofold

DUALIZE *v* **-IZED, -IZING, -IZES** to make twofold

DUALLIE *n* pl. **-S** dually

DUALLY *n* pl. **-LIES** a pickup truck with double rear wheels

DUATHLON *n* pl. **-S** a long-distance race involving running and bicycling

DUB *v* **DUBBED, DUBBING, DUBS** to confer knighthood on

DUBBER *n* pl. **-S** one that dubs

DUBBIN *v* **-ED, -ING, -S** to apply dubbing to leather

DUBBING *n* pl. **-S** material for softening and waterproofing leather

DUBIETY *n* pl. **-ETIES** the state of being dubious

DUBIOUS *adj* doubtful

DUBNIUM *n* pl. **-S** a radioactive element

DUBONNET *n* pl. **-S** a red color

DUBSTEP *n* pl. **-S** a type of electronic dance music

DUCAL *adj* pertaining to a duke (a high-ranking nobleman) **DUCALLY** *adv*

DUCAT *n* pl. **-S** any of several gold coins formerly used in Europe

DUCE *n* pl. **DUCES** or **DUCI** a leader

DUCHESS *n* pl. **-ES** the wife or widow of a duke

DUCHY *n* pl. **DUCHIES** the domain of a duke

DUCI a pl. of duce

DUCK *v* **-ED, -ING, -S** to lower quickly

DUCKBILL *n* pl. **-S** a platypus

DUCKER *n* pl. **-S** one that ducks

DUCKIE *adj* ducky

DUCKIER comparative of ducky

DUCKIES pl. of ducky

DUCKIEST superlative of ducky

DUCKISH	*n* pl. **-ES** dusk
DUCKLING	*n* pl. **-S** a young duck
DUCKPIN	*n* pl. **-S** a type of bowling pin
DUCKTAIL	*n* pl. **-S** a style of haircut
DUCKWALK	*v* **-ED, -ING, -S** to walk in a squatting position
DUCKWEED	*n* pl. **-S** an aquatic plant
DUCKY	*adj* **DUCKIER, DUCKIEST** excellent
DUCKY	*n* pl. **DUCKIES** a darling
DUCT	*v* **-ED, -ING, -S** to convey through a duct (a tubular passage)
DUCTAL	*adj* made up of ducts
DUCTILE	*adj* easily molded or shaped
DUCTING	*n* pl. **-S** a system of ducts
DUCTLESS	*adj* being without a duct
DUCTULE	*n* pl. **-S** a small duct
DUCTWORK	*n* pl. **-S** a system of ducts
DUD	*n* pl. **-S** a bomb that fails to explode
DUDDIE	*adj* ragged
DUDDY	*adj* duddie
DUDE	*v* **DUDED, DUDING, DUDES** to dress up in flashy clothes
DUDEEN	*n* pl. **-S** a short tobacco pipe
DUDENESS	*n* pl. **-ES** the state of being a dude (a dandy)
DUDETTE	*n* pl. **-S** a dudish female
DUDGEON	*n* pl. **-S** a feeling of resentment
DUDING	present participle of dude
DUDISH	*adj* resembling a dude (a dandy)
DUDISHLY	*adv* in the manner of a dude
DUE	*n* pl. **-S** something that is owed
DUECENTO	*n* pl. **-TOS** the thirteenth century
DUEL	*v* **DUELED, DUELING, DUELS** or **DUELLED, DUELLING, DUELS** to fight formally
DUELER	*n* pl. **-S** one that duels
DUELING	*n* pl. **-S** a contest between two persons with deadly weapons
DUELIST	*n* pl. **-S** a dueler
DUELLER	*n* pl. **-S** dueler
DUELLI	a pl. of duello
DUELLING	*n* pl. **-S** dueling
DUELLIST	*n* pl. **-S** duelist
DUELLO	*n* pl. **-LOS** or **-LI** the art of dueling; a duel

DUENDE	*n* pl. **-S** charisma
DUENESS	*n* pl. **-ES** the state of being owed
DUENNA	*n* pl. **-S** a governess
DUET	*v* **DUETED, DUETING, DUETS** or **DUETTED, DUETTING, DUETS** to perform a duet (a musical composition for two)
DUETTIST	*n* pl. **-S** a participant in a duet
DUFF	*v* **-ED, -ING, -S** to mishit a ball in golf
DUFF	*adj* **DUFFER, DUFFEST** worthless, useless
DUFFEL	*n* pl. **-S** a coarse woolen fabric
DUFFER	*n* pl. **-S** a clumsy person
DUFFLE	*n* pl. **-S** duffel
DUFUS	*n* pl. **-ES** doofus
DUG	*n* pl. **-S** the teat or udder of a female mammal
DUGONG	*n* pl. **-S** an aquatic mammal
DUGOUT	*n* pl. **-S** a canoe made by hollowing out a log
DUH	*interj* — used to indicate that something just stated is too obvious
DUI	a pl. of duo
DUIKER	*n* pl. **-S** a small antelope
DUIT	*n* pl. **-S** doit
DUKE	*v* **DUKED, DUKING, DUKES** to fight
DUKEDOM	*n* pl. **-S** a duchy
DULCE	*n* pl. **-S** a sweet food or drink
DULCET	*n* pl. **-S** a soft-toned organ stop
DULCETLY	*adv* melodiously
DULCIAN	*n* pl. **-S** an early type of bassoon
DULCIANA	*n* pl. **-S** a soft-toned organ stop
DULCIFY	*v* **-FIED, -FYING, -FIES** to sweeten
DULCIMER	*n* pl. **-S** a stringed instrument
DULCINEA	*n* pl. **-S** a sweetheart
DULIA	*n* pl. **-S** veneration of saints
DULL	*adj* **DULLER, DULLEST** mentally slow
DULL	*v* **-ED, -ING, -S** to make less sharp
DULLARD	*n* pl. **-S** a dolt
DULLISH	*adj* somewhat dull
DULLNESS	*n* pl. **-ES** the state of being dull
DULLY	*adv* in a dull manner
DULNESS	*n* pl. **-ES** dullness
DULSE	*n* pl. **-S** an edible seaweed

DULY   *adv* rightfully

DUM   *adj* cooked with steam

DUMA   *n* pl. **-S** a Russian council

DUMB   *adj* **DUMBER, DUMBEST** incapable of speech

DUMB   *v* **-ED, -ING, -S** to make silent

DUMBBELL   *n* pl. **-S** a weight lifted for muscular exercise

DUMBCANE   *n* pl. **-S** a tropical plant

DUMBHEAD   *n* pl. **-S** a stupid person

DUMBLY   *adv* in a dumb manner

DUMBNESS   *n* pl. **-ES** the state of being dumb

DUMBO   *n* pl. **-BOS** a stupid person

DUMBSHOW   *n* pl. **-S** a presentation in which communication is solely by signs and gestures

DUMBSIZE   *v* **-SIZED, -SIZING, -SIZES** to reduce the workforce so low that work cannot be done effectively

DUMDUM   *n* pl. **-S** a type of bullet

DUMFOUND   *v* **-ED, -ING, -S** to astonish

DUMKA   *n* pl. **-KAS** or **-KY** a Slavic folk ballad

DUMMKOPF   *n* pl. **-S** a dolt

DUMMY   *v* **-MIED, -MYING, -MIES** to make a representation of

DUMP   *v* **-ED, -ING, -S** to let fall heavily

DUMPCART   *n* pl. **-S** a type of cart

DUMPER   *n* pl. **-S** one that dumps

DUMPIER   comparative of dumpy

DUMPIEST   superlative of dumpy

DUMPILY   *adv* in a dumpy manner

DUMPING   *n* pl. **-S** the selling of large quantities of goods at below the market price

DUMPISH   *adj* sad

DUMPLING   *n* pl. **-S** a ball of dough cooked with stew or soup

DUMPSITE   *n* pl. **-S** a place for dumping rubbish

DUMPY   *adj* **DUMPIER, DUMPIEST** short and thick

DUN   *adj* **DUNNER, DUNNEST** of a dull brown color

DUN   *v* **DUNNED, DUNNING, DUNS** to make demands upon for payment of a debt

DUNAM   *n* pl. **-S** a unit of land measure in Israel

DUNCE   *n* pl. **-S** a stupid person **DUNCICAL, DUNCISH** *adj*

DUNCH   *n* pl. **-ES** a push

DUNE   *n* pl. **-S** a hill of sand **DUNELIKE** *adj*

DUNELAND   *n* pl. **-S** an area having many dunes

DUNG   *v* **-ED, -ING, -S** to fertilize with manure

DUNGAREE   *n* pl. **-S** a coarse cotton fabric

DUNGEON   *v* **-ED, -ING, -S** to confine in a dungeon (an underground prison)

DUNGHEAP   *n* pl. **-S** a dunghill

DUNGHILL   *n* pl. **-S** a heap of manure

DUNGY   *adj* **DUNGIER, DUNGIEST** filthy

DUNITE   *n* pl. **-S** an igneous rock **DUNITIC** *adj*

DUNK   *v* **-ED, -ING, -S** to dip into liquid

DUNKER   *n* pl. **-S** one that dunks

DUNKING   *n* pl. **-S** the act of dipping something into liquid

DUNLIN   *n* pl. **-S** a wading bird

DUNNAGE   *n* pl. **-S** packing material used to protect cargo

DUNNED   past tense of dun

DUNNER   comparative of dun

DUNNESS   *n* pl. **-ES** the state of being dun

DUNNEST   superlative of dun

DUNNING   present participle of dun

DUNNITE   *n* pl. **-S** an explosive

DUNT   *v* **-ED, -ING, -S** to strike with a heavy blow

DUO   *n* pl. **DUOS** or **DUI** an instrumental duet

DUODENUM   *n* pl. **-DENUMS** or **-DENA** the first portion of the small intestine **DUODENAL** *adj*

DUOLOG   *n* pl. **-S** duologue

DUOLOGUE   *n* pl. **-S** a conversation between two persons

DUOMO   *n* pl. **-MOS** or **-MI** a cathedral

DUOPOLY   *n* pl. **-LIES** the market condition existing when there are two sellers only

DUOPSONY   *n* pl. **-NIES** the market condition existing when there are two buyers only

DUOTONE   *n* pl. **-S** an illustration in two tones

DUP   *v* **DUPPED, DUPPING, DUPS** to open

DUPATTA	*n* pl. **-S** a scarf or headdress worn by some Muslim women
DUPE	*v* **DUPED, DUPING, DUPES** to deceive **DUPABLE** *adj*
DUPER	*n* pl. **-S** one that dupes
DUPERY	*n* pl. **-ERIES** the act of duping
DUPING	*n* pl. **-S** the act of duplicating something
DUPION	*n* pl. **-S** a type of silk fabric
DUPLE	*adj* having two parts or elements
DUPLET	*n* pl. **-S** a set of two of one kind
DUPLEX	*v* **-ED, -ING, -ES** to make duple
DUPLEXER	*n* pl. **-S** an electronic switching device
DUPPED	past tense of dup
DUPPING	present participle of dup
DURA	*n* pl. **-S** durra
DURABLE	*adj* able to withstand wear or decay **DURABLY** *adv*
DURABLES	*n/pl* durable goods
DURAL	*adj* of the dura mater (a brain membrane)
DURAMEN	*n* pl. **-S** the central wood of a tree
DURANCE	*n* pl. **-S** restraint by or as if by physical force
DURATION	*n* pl. **-S** continuance in time
DURATIVE	*n* pl. **-S** a type of verb
DURBAR	*n* pl. **-S** the court of a native ruler in India
DURE	*v* **DURED, DURING, DURES** to endure
DURESS	*n* pl. **-ES** compulsion by threat
DURIAN	*n* pl. **-S** an East Indian tree
DURION	*n* pl. **-S** durian
DURMAST	*n* pl. **-S** a European oak
DURN	*v* **-ED, -ING, -S** to damn
DURNED	*adj* **DURNEDER, DURNEDEST** or **DURNDEST** damned
DURO	*n* pl. **-ROS** a Spanish silver dollar
DUROC	*n* pl. **-S** a large red hog
DURR	*n* pl. **-S** durra
DURRA	*n* pl. **-S** a cereal grain
DURRIE	*n* pl. **-S** dhurrie
DURST	a past tense of dare
DURUM	*n* pl. **-S** a kind of wheat
DUSK	*v* **-ED, -ING, -S** to become dark
DUSKISH	*adj* dusky

DUSKY	*adj* **DUSKIER, DUSKIEST** somewhat dark **DUSKILY** *adv*
DUST	*v* **-ED, -ING, -S** to make free of dust (minute particles of matter)
DUSTBALL	*n* pl. **-S** a ball of dust
DUSTBIN	*n* pl. **-S** a trash can
DUSTCART	*n* pl. **-S** a garbage truck
DUSTER	*n* pl. **-S** one that dusts
DUSTHEAP	*n* pl. **-S** a pile of trash
DUSTIER	comparative of dusty
DUSTIEST	superlative of dusty
DUSTILY	*adv* in a dusty manner
DUSTING	*n* pl. **-S** a light sprinkling
DUSTLESS	*adj* being without dust
DUSTLIKE	*adj* resembling dust
DUSTMAN	*n* pl. **-MEN** a trashman
DUSTOFF	*n* pl. **-S** a military helicopter for evacuating the wounded
DUSTPAN	*n* pl. **-S** a pan for holding swept dust
DUSTRAG	*n* pl. **-S** a rag used for dusting
DUSTUP	*n* pl. **-S** an argument
DUSTY	*adj* **DUSTIER, DUSTIEST** full of dust
DUTCH	*adv* with each person paying for himself
DUTCHMAN	*n* pl. **-MEN** something used to hide structural defects
DUTEOUS	*adj* dutiful
DUTIABLE	*adj* subject to import tax
DUTIFUL	*adj* obedient
DUTY	*n* pl. **-TIES** a moral or legal obligation
DUUMVIR	*n* pl. **-VIRS** or **-VIRI** a magistrate of ancient Rome
DUVET	*n* pl. **-S** a down-filled bed covering
DUVETINE	*n* pl. **-S** duvetyn
DUVETYN	*n* pl. **-S** a soft fabric
DUVETYNE	*n* pl. **-S** duvetyn
DUXELLES	*n* pl. **DUXELLES** a garnish or sauce with minced mushrooms
DUYKER	*n* pl. **-S** duiker
DWALE	*n* **-S** a poisonous plant with purple flowers
DWARF	*adj* **DWARFER, DWARFEST** extremely small
DWARF	*n* pl. **DWARFS** or **DWARVES** an extremely small person

DWARF   *v* **-ED, -ING, -S** to cause to appear small

DWARFISH   *adj* resembling a dwarf

DWARFISM   *n* pl. **-S** a condition of stunted growth

DWARVES   a pl. of dwarf

DWEEB   *n* pl. **-S** an unattractive or inept person **DWEEBISH** *adj*

DWEEBY   *adj* **DWEEBIER, DWEEBIEST** socially inept

DWELL   *v* **DWELT** or **DWELLED, DWELLING, DWELLS** to reside

DWELLER   *n* pl. **-S** one that dwells

DWELLING   *n* pl. **-S** a place of residence

DWINDLE   *v* **-DLED, -DLING, -DLES** to decrease steadily

DWINE   *v* **DWINED, DWINING, DWINES** to pine or waste away

DYABLE   *adj* dyeable

DYAD   *n* pl. **-S** a pair of units

DYADIC   *n* pl. **-S** a sum of mathematical dyads

DYARCHY   *n* pl. **-CHIES** diarchy **DYARCHAL, DYARCHIC** *adj*

DYBBUK   *n* pl. **-BUKS** or **-BUKIM** a wandering soul in Jewish folklore

DYE   *v* **DYED, DYEING, DYES** to treat with a dye (a coloring matter)

DYEABLE   *adj* capable of being dyed

DYEING   *n* pl. **-S** something colored with a dye

DYER   *n* pl. **-S** one that dyes

DYESTUFF   *n* pl. **-S** a dye

DYEWEED   *n* pl. **-S** a shrub that yields a yellow dye

DYEWOOD   *n* pl. **-S** a wood from which a dye is extracted

DYING   *n* pl. **-S** a passing out of existence

DYKE   *v* **DYKED, DYKING, DYKES** to dike

DYNAMIC   *n* pl. **-S** a physical force

DYNAMISM   *n* pl. **-S** a theory that explains the universe in terms of force or energy

DYNAMIST   *n* pl. **-S** an adherent of dynamism

DYNAMITE   *v* **-MITED, -MITING, -MITES** to blow up with a powerful explosive

DYNAMO   *n* pl. **-MOS** a generator

DYNAST   *n* pl. **-S** a ruler

DYNASTY   *n* pl. **-TIES** a succession of rulers from the same line of descent **DYNASTIC** *adj*

DYNATRON   *n* pl. **-S** a type of electron tube

DYNE   *n* pl. **-S** a unit of force

DYNEIN   *n* pl. **-S** an enzyme involved in cell movement

DYNEL   *n* pl. **-S** a synthetic fiber

DYNODE   *n* pl. **-S** a type of electrode

DYSGENIC   *adj* causing the deterioration of hereditary qualities

DYSLALIA   *n* pl. **-S** the inability to articulate speech

DYSLEXIA   *n* pl. **-S** impairment of the ability to read

DYSLEXIC   *n* pl. **-S** one who is affected with dyslexia

DYSPEPSY   *n* pl. **-SIES** indigestion

DYSPNEA   *n* pl. **-S** labored breathing **DYSPNEAL, DYSPNEIC** *adj*

DYSPNOEA   *n* pl. **-S** dyspnea **DYSPNOIC** *adj*

DYSTAXIA   *n* pl. **-S** a form of muscular tremor

DYSTOCIA   *n* pl. **-S** difficult labor and delivery in childbirth

DYSTONIA   *n* pl. **-S** a condition of disordered tonicity of muscle tissue **DYSTONIC** *adj*

DYSTOPIA   *n* pl. **-S** a wretched place

DYSURIA   *n* pl. **-S** painful urination **DYSURIC** *adj*

DYVOUR   *n* pl. **-S** one who is bankrupt

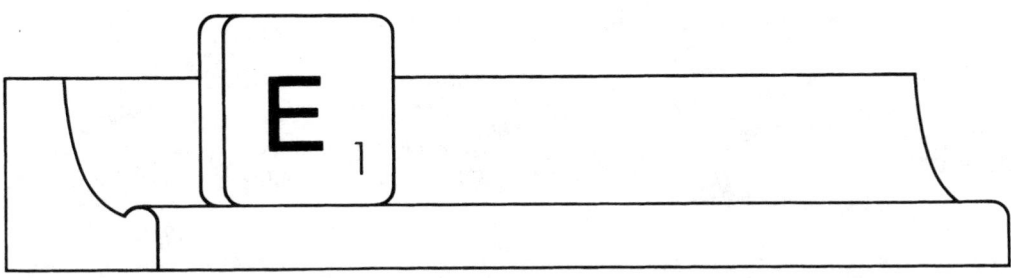

EACH	*adj* being one of two or more distinct individuals
EAGER	*adj* **-GERER, -GEREST** impatiently longing **EAGERLY** *adv*
EAGER	*n* pl. **-S** eagre
EAGLE	*v* **EAGLED, EAGLING, EAGLES** to score an eagle (two strokes under par) on a hole in golf
EAGLET	*n* pl. **-S** a young eagle
EAGRE	*n* pl. **-S** a tidal flood
EANLING	*n* pl. **-S** yeanling
EAR	*v* **-ED, -ING, -S** to form the fruiting head of a cereal
EARACHE	*n* pl. **-S** a pain in the ear (an organ of hearing)
EARBUD	*n* pl. **-S** a small earphone
EARDROP	*n* pl. **-S** an earring
EARDRUM	*n* pl. **-S** the tympanic membrane
EARED	*adj* having ears
EARFLAP	*n* pl. **-S** a part of a cap designed to cover the ears
EARFUL	*n* pl. **-S** a flow of information
EARHOLE	*n* pl. **-S** the external opening of the ear
EARING	*n* pl. **-S** a line on a ship
EARL	*n* pl. **-S** a British nobleman
EARLAP	*n* pl. **-S** an earflap
EARLDOM	*n* pl. **-S** the rank of an earl
EARLESS	*adj* lacking ears
EARLIER	comparative of early
EARLIEST	superlative of early
EARLOBE	*n* pl. **-S** a part of the ear
EARLOCK	*n* pl. **-S** a curl of hair by the ear
EARLSHIP	*n* pl. **-S** earldom
EARLY	*adv* **-LIER, -LIEST** near the beginning of a period of time or a series of events
EARMARK	*v* **-ED, -ING, -S** to designate for a specific use
EARMUFF	*n* pl. **-S** one of a pair of ear coverings
EARN	*v* **-ED, -ING, -S** to gain or deserve for one's labor or service
EARNER	*n* pl. **-S** one that earns
EARNEST	*n* pl. **-S** a down payment
EARNINGS	*n/pl* something earned
EARPHONE	*n* pl. **-S** a listening device worn over the ear
EARPIECE	*n* pl. **-S** an earphone
EARPLUG	*n* pl. **-S** a plug for the ear
EARRING	*n* pl. **-S** an ornament for the earlobe
EARSHOT	*n* pl. **-S** the range within which sound can be heard
EARSTONE	*n* pl. **-S** an otolith
EARTH	*v* **-ED, -ING, -S** to cover with earth (soil)
EARTHEN	*adj* made of earth
EARTHIER	comparative of earthy
EARTHIEST	superlative of earthy
EARTHILY	*adv* in an earthy manner
EARTHLY	*adj* **-LIER, -LIEST** worldly
EARTHMAN	*n* pl. **-MEN** a person from the planet earth
EARTHNUT	*n* pl. **-S** a European herb
EARTHPEA	*n* pl. **-S** a twining plant
EARTHSET	*n* pl. **-S** the setting of the earth as seen from the moon
EARTHY	*adj* **EARTHIER, EARTHIEST** composed of, resembling, or suggestive of earth
EARWAX	*n* pl. **-ES** cerumen
EARWIG	*v* **-WIGGED, -WIGGING, -WIGS** to insinuate against in secret
EARWORM	*n* pl. **-S** a bollworm

EASE	v **EASED, EASING, EASES** to give rest or relief to
EASEFUL	adj restful
EASEL	n pl. **-S** a three-legged frame **EASELED** adj
EASEMENT	n pl. **-S** relief
EASER	v pl. **-S** one that eases
EASIER	comparative of easy
EASIES	pl. of easy
EASIEST	superlative of easy
EASILY	adv without difficulty
EASINESS	n pl. **-ES** the state of being easy
EASING	present participle of ease
EAST	n pl. **-S** a cardinal point of the compass
EASTER	n pl. **-S** a wind or storm from the east
EASTERLY	n pl. **-LIES** a wind from the east
EASTERN	adj being to, toward, or in the east
EASTING	n pl. **-S** a movement toward the east
EASTWARD	n pl. **-S** a direction toward the east
EASY	adj **EASIER, EASIEST** not difficult
EASY	n pl. **EASIES** a communications code word for the letter E
EAT	v **ATE** or **ET, EATEN, EATING, EATS** to consume food
EATABLE	n pl. **-S** an edible
EATER	n pl. **-S** one that eats
EATERY	n pl. **-ERIES** a lunchroom
EATH	adj easy
EATING	n pl. **-S** the act of consuming food
EAU	n pl. **EAUX** water (a transparent, tasteless, odorless liquid)
EAVE	n pl. **-S** the lower projecting edge of a roof **EAVED** adj
EBB	v **-ED, -ING, -S** to recede
EBBET	n pl. **-S** a common green newt
EBON	n pl. **-S** ebony
EBONICS	n/pl a dialect of English spoken by some African-Americans
EBONIES	pl. of ebony
EBONISE	v **-ISED, -ISING, -ISES** to ebonize
EBONITE	n pl. **-S** a hard rubber
EBONIZE	v **-IZED, -IZING, -IZES** to stain black in imitation of ebony
EBONY	n pl. **-NIES** a hard, heavy wood

EBOOK	n pl. **-S** a device for reading books in electronic format
ECARTE	n pl. **-S** a card game
ECAUDATE	adj having no tail
ECBOLIC	n pl. **-S** a type of drug
ECCLESIA	n pl. **-SIAE** an assembly in ancient Greece
ECCRINE	adj producing secretions externally
ECDYSIS	n pl. **-DYSES** the shedding of an outer layer of skin **ECDYSIAL** adj
ECDYSON	n pl. **-S** ecdysone
ECDYSONE	n pl. **-S** an insect hormone
ECESIS	n pl. **-SISES** the establishment of a plant or animal in a new environment **ECESIC** adj
ECHAPPE	adj moving from a closed to an open position of the feet in ballet
ECHARD	n pl. **-S** the water in the soil not available to plants
ECHE	v **ECHED, ECHING, ECHES** to increase
ECHELLE	n pl. **-S** a device for spreading light into its component colors
ECHELON	v **-ED, -ING, -S** to group in a particular formation
ECHIDNA	n pl. **-NAS** or **-NAE** a spiny anteater
ECHINATE	adj spiny
ECHING	present participle of eche
ECHINOID	n pl. **-S** a spiny marine animal
ECHINUS	n pl. **-NI** an echinoid
ECHO	n pl. **ECHOS** or **ECHOES** a repetition of sound by reflection of sound waves
ECHO	v **-ED, -ING, -ES** to produce an echo
ECHOER	n pl. **-S** one that echoes
ECHOEY	adj full of echoes
ECHOGRAM	n pl. **-S** a record produced by a device that uses ultrasonic waves
ECHOIC	adj resembling an echo
ECHOISM	n pl. **-S** the formation of words in imitation of sounds
ECHOLESS	adj producing no echo
ECHT	adj genuine
ECLAIR	n pl. **-S** a type of pastry
ECLAT	n pl. **-S** brilliance
ECLECTIC	n pl. **-S** one who draws his beliefs from various sources

ECLIPSE   *v* **ECLIPSED, ECLIPSING, ECLIPSES** to obscure

ECLIPSER   *n* pl. **-S** one that eclipses

ECLIPSIS   *n* pl. **ECLIPSISES** or **ECLIPSES** an ellipsis

ECLIPTIC   *n* pl. **-S** an astronomical plane

ECLOGITE   *n* pl. **-S** a type of rock

ECLOGUE   *n* pl. **-S** a pastoral poem

ECLOSE   *v* **ECLOSED, ECLOSING, ECLOSES** to emerge as a larva from an egg

ECLOSION   *n* pl. **-S** the emergence of an insect larva from an egg

ECO   *n* pl. **-S** ecology

ECOCIDE   *n* pl. **-S** the destruction of the natural environment **ECOCIDAL** *adj*

ECOFREAK   *n* pl. **-S** a zealous environmentalist

ECOGIFT   *n* pl. **-S** a donation of land to a government for ecological purposes

ECOLOGY   *n* pl. **-GIES** an environmental science **ECOLOGIC** *adj*

ECONOBOX   *n* pl. **-ES** a small economical car

ECONOMIC   *adj* pertaining to financial matters

ECONOMY   *n* pl. **-MIES** thrift

ECORCHE   *n* pl. **-S** an anatomical figure with the skin removed to show the musculature

ECOTAGE   *n* pl. **-S** obstructive action in defense of the natural environment

ECOTONE   *n* pl. **-S** a type of ecological zone **ECOTONAL** *adj*

ECOTOPIA   *n* pl. **-S** an ecologically ideal region or form of society

ECOTOUR   *n* pl. **-S** a tour of a natural habitat

ECOTYPE   *n* pl. **-S** a subspecies adapted to specific environmental conditions **ECOTYPIC** *adj*

ECOZONE   *n* pl. **-S** a regional ecosystem

ECRASEUR   *n* pl. **-S** a surgical instrument

ECRU   *n* pl. **-S** a yellowish brown color

ECSTASY   *n* pl. **-SIES** a state of exaltation

ECSTATIC   *n* pl. **-S** one that is subject to ecstasies

ECTASIS   *n* pl. **-TASES** the lengthening of a usually short syllable **ECTATIC** *adj*

ECTHYMA   *n* pl. **-MATA** a virus disease

ECTODERM   *n* pl. **-S** the outermost germ layer of an embryo

ECTOGENE   *n* pl. **-S** a gene involved in the development of an embryo in artificial conditions

ECTOMERE   *n* pl. **-S** a cell that develops into ectoderm

ECTOPIA   *n* pl. **-S** congenital displacement of parts or organs **ECTOPIC** *adj*

ECTOSARC   *n* pl. **-S** the outermost layer of protoplasm of certain protozoans

ECTOZOAN   *n* pl. **-S** ectozoon

ECTOZOON   *n* pl. **-ZOA** a parasite on the body of an animal

ECTYPE   *n* pl. **-S** a copy **ECTYPAL** *adj*

ECU   *n* pl. **-S** an old French coin

ECUMENE   *n* pl. **-S** an inhabited area

ECUMENIC   *adj* universal

ECZEMA   *n* pl. **-S** a skin disease

ED   *n* pl. **-S** education

EDACIOUS   *adj* voracious

EDACITY   *n* pl. **-TIES** gluttony

EDAMAME   *n* pl. **-S** green soybeans in a pod

EDAPHIC   *adj* pertaining to the soil

EDDO   *n* pl. **-DOES** a tropical plant

EDDY   *v* **-DIED, -DYING, -DIES** to move against the main current

EDEMA   *n* pl. **-MAS** or **-MATA** an excessive accumulation of serous fluid

EDENIC   *adj* pertaining to a paradise

EDENTATE   *n* pl. **-S** a toothless mammal

EDGE   *v* **EDGED, EDGING, EDGES** to provide with an edge (a bounding or dividing line)

EDGELESS   *adj* lacking an edge

EDGER   *n* pl. **-S** a tool used to trim a lawn's edge

EDGEWAYS   *adv* edgewise

EDGEWISE   *adv* sideways

EDGIER   comparative of edgy

EDGIEST   superlative of edgy

EDGILY   *adv* in an edgy manner

EDGINESS   *n* pl. **-ES** the state of being edgy

EDGING   *n* pl. **-S** something that forms or serves as an edge

EDGY   *adj* **EDGIER, EDGIEST** tense, nervous, or irritable

EDH   *n* pl. **-S** an Old English letter

EDIBLE   *n* pl. **-S** something fit to be eaten

EDICT *n* pl. **-S** an authoritative order having the force of law **EDICTAL** *adj*

EDIFICE *n* pl. **-S** a building

EDIFIER *n* pl. **-S** one that edifies

EDIFY *v* **-FIED, -FYING, -FIES** to enlighten

EDILE *n* pl. **-S** aedile

EDIT *v* **-ED, -ING, -S** to correct and prepare for publication **EDITABLE** *adj*

EDITION *n* pl. **-S** a particular series of printed material

EDITOR *n* pl. **-S** one that edits

EDITRESS *n* pl. **-ES** a female editor

EDITRIX *n* pl. **-TRIXES** or **-TRICES** a female editor

EDUCABLE *n* pl. **-S** a mildly retarded person

EDUCATE *v* **-CATED, -CATING, -CATES** to teach

EDUCATOR *n* pl. **-S** one that educates

EDUCE *v* **EDUCED, EDUCING, EDUCES** to draw forth or bring out **EDUCIBLE** *adj*

EDUCT *n* pl. **-S** something educed

EDUCTION *n* pl. **-S** the act of educing **EDUCTIVE** *adj*

EDUCTOR *n* pl. **-S** one that educes

EEEW *interj* — used to express disgust

EEJIT *n* pl. **-S** an idiot

EEK *interj* — used to express sudden fright

EEL *n* pl. **-S** a snakelike fish

EELGRASS *n* pl. **-ES** an aquatic plant

EELIER comparative of eely

EELIEST superlative of eely

EELLIKE *adj* resembling an eel

EELPOUT *n* pl. **-S** a marine fish

EELWORM *n* pl. **-S** a small roundworm

EELY *adj* **EELIER, EELIEST** resembling an eel

EENSY *adj* **-SIER, -SIEST** tiny

EERIE *adj* **-RIER, -RIEST** weird **EERILY** *adv*

EERINESS *n* pl. **-ES** the state of being eerie

EERY *adj* **-RIER, -RIEST** eerie

EEW *interj* eeew

EF *n* pl. **-S** the letter F

EFF *n* pl. **-S** ef

EFFABLE *adj* capable of being uttered or expressed

EFFACE *v* **-FACED, -FACING, -FACES** to rub or wipe out

EFFACER *n* pl. **-S** one that effaces

EFFECT *v* **-ED, -ING, -S** to bring about

EFFECTER *n* pl. **-S** effector

EFFECTOR *n* pl. **-S** a bodily organ that responds to a nerve impulse

EFFENDI *n* pl. **-S** a Turkish title of respect

EFFERENT *n* pl. **-S** an organ or part conveying nervous impulses to an effector

EFFETE *adj* exhausted of vigor or energy **EFFETELY** *adv*

EFFICACY *n* pl. **-CIES** effectiveness

EFFIGIAL *adj* resembling an effigy

EFFIGY *n* pl. **-GIES** a likeness or representation

EFFLUENT *n* pl. **-S** an outflow

EFFLUVIA *n/pl* byproducts in the form of waste

EFFLUX *n* pl. **-ES** an outflow

EFFORT *n* pl. **-S** a deliberate exertion

EFFULGE *v* **-FULGED, -FULGING, -FULGES** to shine forth

EFFUSE *v* **-FUSED, -FUSING, -FUSES** to pour forth

EFFUSION *n* pl. **-S** an outpouring of emotion

EFFUSIVE *adj* pouring forth

EFT *n* pl. **-S** a newt

EFTSOON *adv* soon afterward

EFTSOONS *adv* eftsoon

EGAD *interj* — used as a mild oath

EGADS *interj* egad

EGAL *adj* equal

EGALITE *n* pl. **-S** equality

EGER *n* pl. **-S** eagre

EGEST *v* **-ED, -ING, -S** to discharge from the body

EGESTA *n/pl* egested matter

EGESTION *n* pl. **-S** the act of egesting **EGESTIVE** *adj*

EGG *v* **-ED, -ING, -S** to incite or urge

EGGAR *n* pl. **-S** egger

EGGCUP *n* pl. **-S** a cup from which an egg is eaten

EGGER *n* pl. **-S** a kind of moth

EGGFRUIT *n* pl. **-S** a tropical tree

EGGHEAD	*n* pl. **-S** an intellectual
EGGIER	comparative of eggy
EGGIEST	superlative of eggy
EGGLESS	*adj* lacking eggs
EGGNOG	*n* pl. **-S** a beverage
EGGPLANT	*n* pl. **-S** a perennial herb yielding edible fruit
EGGSHELL	*n* pl. **-S** the hard exterior of a bird's egg
EGGY	*adj* **EGGIER, EGGIEST** tasting or smelling of egg
EGIS	*n* pl. **EGISES** aegis
EGLATERE	*n* pl. **-S** a wild rose
EGLOMISE	*adj* made of glass with a painted picture on the back
EGO	*n* pl. **EGOS** the conscious self
EGOISM	*n* pl. **-S** extreme devotion to self-interest
EGOIST	*n* pl. **-S** one who practices egoism **EGOISTIC** *adj*
EGOLESS	*adj* not characterized by egoism
EGOMANIA	*n* pl. **-S** extreme egotism
EGOTISM	*n* pl. **-S** self-conceit
EGOTIST	*n* pl. **-S** a conceited person
EGOTIZE	*v* **-TIZED, -TIZING, -TIZES** to talk and think about oneself excessively
EGRESS	*v* **-ED, -ING, -ES** to go out
EGRET	*n* pl. **-S** a wading bird
EGYPTIAN	*n* pl. **-S** a typeface with squared serifs
EH	*interj* — used to express doubt or surprise
EIDE	pl. of eidos
EIDER	*n* pl. **-S** a large sea duck
EIDETIC	*n* pl. **-S** a person able to recall vivid images
EIDOLIC	*adj* pertaining to an eidolon
EIDOLON	*n* pl. **-LONS** or **-LA** a phantom
EIDOS	*n* pl. **EIDE** an essence
EIGHT	*n* pl. **-S** a number
EIGHTEEN	*n* pl. **-S** a number
EIGHTH	*n* pl. **-S** one of eight equal parts
EIGHTHLY	*adv* in the eighth place
EIGHTVO	*n* pl. **-VOS** octavo
EIGHTY	*n* pl. **EIGHTIES** a number
EIKON	*n* pl. **-S** or **-ES** icon
EINKORN	*n* pl. **-S** a variety of wheat
EINSTEIN	*n* pl. **-S** a very intelligent person
EIRENIC	*adj* irenic
EIRENICS	*n/pl* irenics
EISWEIN	*n* pl. **-S** a sweet German wine
EITHER	*adj* being one or the other
EJECT	*v* **-ED, -ING, -S** to throw out forcibly
EJECTA	*n/pl* ejected material
EJECTION	*n* pl. **-S** the act of ejecting
EJECTIVE	*n* pl. **-S** a sound produced with air compressed above the closed glottis
EJECTOR	*n* pl. **-S** one that ejects
EJIDO	*n* pl. **-DOS** a piece of land farmed communally in Mexico
EKE	*v* **EKED, EKING, EKES** to supplement with great effort
EKISTICS	*n/pl* a science dealing with human habitats **EKISTIC** *adj*
EKKA	*n* pl. **-S** a one-horse vehicle of India
EKPWELE	*n* pl. **-S** a former monetary unit of Equatorial Guinea
EKTEXINE	*n* pl. **-S** an outer layer of the exine
EKUELE	*n* pl. **EKUELE** ekpwele
EL	*n* pl. **-S** an elevated railroad or train
ELAIN	*n* pl. **-S** olein
ELAN	*n* pl. **-S** enthusiasm
ELAND	*n* pl. **-S** a large antelope
ELAPHINE	*adj* pertaining to a genus of deer
ELAPID	*n* pl. **-S** a venomous snake
ELAPINE	*adj* pertaining to a family of snakes
ELAPSE	*v* **ELAPSED, ELAPSING, ELAPSES** to pass away
ELASTANE	*n* pl. **-S** spandex
ELASTASE	*n* pl. **-S** an enzyme
ELASTIC	*n* pl. **-S** a stretchable material
ELASTIN	*n* pl. **-S** a bodily protein
ELATE	*v* **ELATED, ELATING, ELATES** to raise the spirits of **ELATEDLY** *adv*
ELATER	*n* pl. **-S** a click beetle
ELATERID	*n* pl. **-S** an elater
ELATERIN	*n* pl. **-S** a chemical compound
ELATING	present participle of elate
ELATION	*n* pl. **-S** a feeling of great joy
ELATIVE	*n* pl. **-S** an adjectival form in some languages
ELBOW	*v* **-ED, -ING, -S** to jostle

ELBOWING *n* pl. **-S** the act of fouling an opponent with an elbow (a joint of the arm)

ELD *n* pl. **-S** old age

ELDER *n* pl. **-S** an older person

ELDERLY *n* pl. **-LIES** a rather old person

ELDEST *n* pl. **-S** the oldest one of three or more

ELDORADO *n* pl. **-DOS** a place of great abundance

ELDRESS *n* pl. **-ES** a female elder (a church officer)

ELDRICH *adj* eldritch

ELDRITCH *adj* weird

ELECT *v* **-ED, -ING, -S** to select by vote for an office

ELECTEE *n* pl. **-S** a person who has been elected

ELECTION *n* pl. **-S** the act of electing

ELECTIVE *n* pl. **-S** an optional course of study

ELECTOR *n* pl. **-S** one that elects

ELECTRET *n* pl. **-S** a type of nonconductor

ELECTRIC *n* pl. **-S** something run by electricity

ELECTRO *v* **-ED, -ING, -S** to make a metallic copy of a page of type for printing

ELECTRON *n* pl. **-S** an elementary particle

ELECTRUM *n* pl. **-S** an alloy of gold and silver

ELEGANCE *n* pl. **-S** tasteful opulence

ELEGANCY *n* pl. **-CIES** elegance

ELEGANT *adj* tastefully opulent

ELEGIAC *n* pl. **-S** a type of verse

ELEGIES pl. of elegy

ELEGISE *v* **-GISED, -GISING, -GISES** to elegize

ELEGIST *n* pl. **-S** one that writes elegies

ELEGIT *n* pl. **-S** a type of judicial writ

ELEGIZE *v* **-GIZED, -GIZING, -GIZES** to write an elegy

ELEGY *n* pl. **-GIES** a mournful poem for one who is dead

ELEMENT *n* pl. **-S** a substance that cannot be separated into simpler substances by chemical means

ELEMI *n* pl. **-S** a fragrant resin

ELENCHUS *n* pl. **-CHI** a logical refutation **ELENCHIC, ELENCTIC** *adj*

ELEPHANT *n* pl. **-S** a large mammal

ELEVATE *v* **-VATED, -VATING, -VATES** to raise

ELEVATED *n* pl. **-S** a railway that operates on a raised structure

ELEVATOR *n* pl. **-S** one that elevates

ELEVEN *n* pl. **-S** a number

ELEVENTH *n* pl. **-S** one of eleven equal parts

ELEVON *n* pl. **-S** a type of airplane control surface

ELF *n* pl. **ELVES** a small, often mischievous fairy **ELFLIKE** *adj*

ELFIN *n* pl. **-S** an elf

ELFISH *adj* resembling an elf **ELFISHLY** *adv*

ELFLOCK *n* pl. **-S** a lock of tangled hair

ELHI *adj* pertaining to school grades 1 through 12

ELICIT *v* **-ED, -ING, -S** to educe

ELICITOR *n* pl. **-S** one that elicits

ELIDE *v* **ELIDED, ELIDING, ELIDES** to omit **ELIDIBLE** *adj*

ELIGIBLE *n* pl. **-S** one that is qualified to be chosen

ELIGIBLY *adv* in a qualified manner

ELINT *n* pl. **-S** the gathering of intelligence by electronic devices

ELISION *n* pl. **-S** the act of eliding

ELITE *n* pl. **-S** a socially superior group

ELITISM *n* pl. **-S** belief in rule by an elite

ELITIST *n* pl. **-S** an adherent of elitism

ELIXIR *n* pl. **-S** a medicinal beverage

ELK *n* pl. **-S** a large deer

ELKHOUND *n* pl. **-S** a hunting dog

ELL *n* pl. **-S** the letter L

ELLIPSE *n* pl. **-S** a type of plane curve

ELLIPSIS *n* pl. **-LIPSES** an omission of a word or words in a sentence

ELLIPTIC *adj* having the shape of an ellipse

ELM *n* pl. **-S** a deciduous tree

ELMWOOD *n* pl. **-S** the wood of an elm

ELMY *adj* **-MIER, -MIEST** abounding in elms

ELODEA *n* pl. **-S** an aquatic herb

ELOIGN *v* **-ED, -ING, -S** to remove to a distant place

ELOIGNER *n* pl. **-S** one that eloigns

ELOIN *v* **-ED, -ING, -S** to eloign

ELOINER *n* pl. **-S** one that eloins

ELONGATE   v **-GATED, -GATING, -GATES** to lengthen

ELOPE   v **ELOPED, ELOPING, ELOPES** to run off secretly to be married

ELOPER   n pl. **-S** one that elopes

ELOQUENT   adj fluent and convincing in speech

ELSE   adv in a different place, time, or way

ELUANT   n pl. **-S** a solvent

ELUATE   n pl. **-S** the material obtained by eluting

ELUDE   v **ELUDED, ELUDING, ELUDES** to evade

ELUDER   n pl. **-S** one that eludes

ELUENT   n pl. **-S** eluant

ELUSION   n pl. **-S** the act of eluding

ELUSIVE   adj tending to elude

ELUSORY   adj elusive

ELUTE   v **ELUTED, ELUTING, ELUTES** to remove by means of a solvent

ELUTION   n pl. **-S** the act of eluting

ELUVIA   a pl. of eluvium

ELUVIAL   adj pertaining to an eluvium

ELUVIATE   v **-ATED, -ATING, -ATES** to undergo a transfer of materials in the soil

ELUVIUM   n pl. **-VIUMS** or **-VIA** a soil deposit

ELVEN   adj resembling an elf

ELVER   n pl. **-S** a young eel

ELVES   pl. of elf

ELVISH   adj elfish **ELVISHLY** adv

ELYSIAN   adj delightful

ELYTRON   n pl. **-TRA** a hardened forewing of certain insects **ELYTROID, ELYTROUS** adj

ELYTRUM   n pl. **-TRA** elytron

EM   n pl. **-S** the letter M

EMACIATE   v **-ATED, -ATING, -ATES** to make thin

EMAIL   v **-ED, -ING, -S** to send a message to by computer

EMANANT   adj issuing from a source

EMANATE   v **-NATED, -NATING, -NATES** to send forth

EMANATOR   n pl. **-S** one that emanates

EMBALM   v **-ED, -ING, -S** to treat so as to protect from decay

EMBALMER   n pl. **-S** one that embalms

EMBANK   v **-ED, -ING, -S** to confine or protect with a raised structure

EMBAR   v **-BARRED, -BARRING, -BARS** to imprison

EMBARGO   v **-ED, -ING, -ES** to restrain trade by a governmental order

EMBARK   v **-ED, -ING, -S** to make a start

EMBASSY   n pl. **-SIES** the headquarters of an ambassador

EMBATTLE   v **-TLED, -TLING, -TLES** to prepare for battle

EMBAY   v **-ED, -ING, -S** to enclose in a bay

EMBED   v **-BEDDED, -BEDDING, -BEDS** to fix firmly into a surrounding mass

EMBER   n pl. **-S** a glowing fragment from a fire

EMBEZZLE   v **-ZLED, -ZLING, -ZLES** to appropriate fraudulently to one's own use

EMBITTER   v **-ED, -ING, -S** to make bitter

EMBLAZE   v **-BLAZED, -BLAZING, -BLAZES** to set on fire

EMBLAZER   n pl. **-S** one that emblazes

EMBLAZON   v **-ED, -ING, -S** to decorate with brilliant colors

EMBLEM   v **-ED, -ING, -S** to represent with an emblem (a graphical symbol)

EMBODIER   n pl. **-S** one that embodies

EMBODY   v **-BODIED, -BODYING, -BODIES** to provide with a body

EMBOLDEN   v **-ED, -ING, -S** to instill with courage

EMBOLI   pl. of embolus

EMBOLIES   pl. of emboly

EMBOLISM   n pl. **-S** the obstruction of a blood vessel by an embolus **EMBOLIC** adj

EMBOLUS   n pl. **-LI** an abnormal particle circulating in the blood

EMBOLY   n pl. **-LIES** a phase of embryonic growth

EMBORDER   v **-ED, -ING, -S** to provide with a border

EMBOSK   v **-ED, -ING, -S** to conceal with foliage

EMBOSOM   v **-ED, -ING, -S** to embrace

EMBOSS   v **-ED, -ING, -ES** to decorate with raised designs

EMBOSSER   n pl. **-S** one that embosses

EMBOW   v **-ED, -ING, -S** to arch

EMBOWEL	*v* **-ELED, -ELING, -ELS** or **-ELLED, -ELLING, -ELS** to disbowel
EMBOWER	*v* **-ED, -ING, -S** to surround with foliage
EMBRACE	*v* **-BRACED, -BRACING, -BRACES** to hug
EMBRACER	*n* pl. **-S** one that embraces
EMBROIL	*v* **-ED, -ING, -S** to involve in conflict
EMBROWN	*v* **-ED, -ING, -S** to make brown
EMBRUE	*v* **-BRUED, -BRUING, -BRUES** to imbrue
EMBRUTE	*v* **-BRUTED, -BRUTING, -BRUTES** to imbrute
EMBRYO	*n* pl. **-BRYOS** an organism in its early stages of development
EMBRYOID	*n* pl. **-S** a mass of tissue that resembles an embryo
EMBRYON	*n* pl. **-S** an embryo
EMCEE	*v* **-CEED, -CEEING, -CEES** to serve as master of ceremonies
EMDASH	*n* pl. **-ES** a mark in writing that indicates a break in thought or structure
EME	*n* pl. **-S** an uncle
EMEER	*n* pl. **-S** emir
EMEERATE	*n* pl. **-S** emirate
EMEND	*v* **-ED, -ING, -S** to correct
EMENDATE	*v* **-DATED, -DATING, -DATES** to emend
EMENDER	*n* pl. **-S** one that emends
EMERALD	*n* pl. **-S** a green gem
EMERG	*n* pl. **-S** the section of a hospital that deals with emergencies
EMERGE	*v* **EMERGED, EMERGING, EMERGES** to come out into view
EMERGENT	*n* pl. **-S** a type of aquatic plant
EMERIES	pl. of emery
EMERITA	*n* pl. **-TAS** or **-TAE** a retired woman who retains an honorary title
EMERITUS	*n* pl. **-TI** a retired person who retains an honorary title
EMEROD	*n* pl. **-S** a tumor
EMEROID	*n* pl. **-S** emerod
EMERSED	*adj* standing out of water
EMERSION	*n* pl. **-S** the act of emerging
EMERY	*n* pl. **-ERIES** a granular corundum
EMESIS	*n* pl. **EMESES** the act of vomiting
EMETIC	*n* pl. **-S** a substance which induces vomiting
EMETIN	*n* pl. **-S** emetine
EMETINE	*n* pl. **-S** an alkaloid
EMEU	*n* pl. **-S** emu
EMEUTE	*n* pl. **-S** a riot
EMICS	*n/pl* a type of linguistic analysis **EMIC** *adj*
EMIGRANT	*n* pl. **-S** one that emigrates
EMIGRATE	*v* **-GRATED, -GRATING, -GRATES** to leave one country or region to settle in another
EMIGRE	*n* pl. **-S** an emigrant
EMINENCE	*n* pl. **-S** high station or rank
EMINENCY	*n* pl. **-CIES** eminence
EMINENT	*adj* of high station or rank
EMIR	*n* pl. **-S** an Arab chieftain or prince
EMIRATE	*n* pl. **-S** the rank of an emir
EMISSARY	*n* pl. **-SARIES** a person sent on a mission
EMISSION	*n* pl. **-S** the act of emitting **EMISSIVE** *adj*
EMIT	*v* **EMITTED, EMITTING, EMITS** to send forth
EMITTER	*n* pl. **-S** one that emits
EMMER	*n* pl. **-S** a type of wheat
EMMET	*n* pl. **-S** an ant
EMO	*n* pl. **EMOS** a style of rock music with emotional lyrics
EMOCORE	*n* pl. **-S** emo
EMODIN	*n* pl. **-S** a chemical compound
EMOTE	*v* **EMOTED, EMOTING, EMOTES** to express emotion in an exaggerated manner
EMOTER	*n* pl. **-S** one that emotes
EMOTICON	*n* pl. **-S** a group of keyboard characters used to suggest a facial expression or an emotion
EMOTION	*n* pl. **-S** an affective state of consciousness
EMOTIVE	*adj* pertaining to emotion
EMPALE	*v* **-PALED, -PALING, -PALES** to impale
EMPALER	*n* pl. **-S** one that empales
EMPANADA	*n* pl. **-S** a pastry turnover
EMPANEL	*v* **-ELED, -ELING, -ELS** or **-ELLED, -ELLING, -ELS** to impanel
EMPATHY	*n* pl. **-THIES** imaginative identification with another's thoughts and feelings **EMPATHIC** *adj*

EMPEROR   *n* pl. **-S** the ruler of an empire

EMPERY   *n* pl. **-PERIES** absolute dominion

EMPHASIS   *n* pl. **-PHASES** special significance imparted to something

EMPHATIC   *adj* strongly expressive

EMPIRE   *n* pl. **-S** a major political unit

EMPIRIC   *n* pl. **-S** one who relies on practical experience

EMPLACE   *v* **-PLACED, -PLACING, -PLACES** to position

EMPLANE   *v* **-PLANED, -PLANING, -PLANES** to enplane

EMPLOY   *v* **-ED, -ING, -S** to hire

EMPLOYE   *n* pl. **-S** employee

EMPLOYEE   *n* pl. **-S** a person who is employed

EMPLOYER   *n* pl. **-S** one that employs

EMPOISON   *v* **-ED, -ING, -S** to embitter

EMPORIUM   *n* pl. **-RIUMS** or **-RIA** a trading or market center

EMPOWER   *v* **-ED, -ING, -S** to give legal power to

EMPRESS   *n* pl. **-ES** a female ruler of an empire

EMPRISE   *n* pl. **-S** an adventurous undertaking

EMPRIZE   *n* pl. **-S** emprise

EMPTIED   past tense of empty

EMPTIER   *n* pl. **-S** one that empties

EMPTIES   present 3d person sing. of empty

EMPTIEST   superlative of empty

EMPTILY   *adv* in an empty manner

EMPTINGS   *n/pl* emptins

EMPTINS   *n/pl* a liquid leavening

EMPTY   *adj* **-TIER, -TIEST** containing nothing

EMPTY   *v* **-TIED, -TYING, -TIES** to remove the contents of

EMPURPLE   *v* **-PLED, -PLING, -PLES** to tinge with purple

EMPYEMA   *n* pl. **-EMAS** or **-EMATA** a collection of pus in a body cavity **EMPYEMIC** *adj*

EMPYREAL   *adj* pertaining to the sky

EMPYREAN   *n* pl. **-S** the highest heaven

EMU   *n* pl. **-S** a large, flightless bird

EMULATE   *v* **-LATED, -LATING, -LATES** to try to equal or surpass

EMULATOR   *n* pl. **-S** one that emulates

EMULOUS   *adj* eager to equal or surpass another

EMULSIFY   *v* **-FIED, -FYING, -FIES** to make into an emulsion

EMULSION   *n* pl. **-S** a type of liquid mixture **EMULSIVE** *adj*

EMULSOID   *n* pl. **-S** a liquid dispersed in another liquid

EMYD   *n* pl. **-S** a freshwater tortoise

EMYDE   *n* pl. **-S** emyd

EN   *n* pl. **-S** the letter N

ENABLE   *v* **-BLED, -BLING, -BLES** to make possible

ENABLER   *n* pl. **-S** one that enables

ENACT   *v* **-ED, -ING, -S** to make into a law

ENACTION   *n* pl. **-S** the action of enacting

ENACTIVE   *adj* having the power to enact

ENACTOR   *n* pl. **-S** one that enacts

ENACTORY   *adj* pertaining to the enactment of law

ENAMEL   *v* **-ELED, -ELING, -ELS** or **-ELLED, -ELLING, -ELS** to cover with a hard, glossy surface

ENAMELER   *n* pl. **-S** one that enamels

ENAMINE   *n* pl. **-S** a type of amine

ENAMOR   *v* **-ED, -ING, -S** to inspire with love

ENAMOUR   *v* **-ED, -ING, -S** to enamor

ENATE   *n* pl. **-S** a relative on the mother's side **ENATIC** *adj*

ENATION   *n* pl. **-S** an outgrowth from the surface of an organ

ENCAENIA   *n/pl* annual university ceremonies

ENCAGE   *v* **-CAGED, -CAGING, -CAGES** to confine in a cage

ENCAMP   *v* **-ED, -ING, -S** to set up a camp

ENCASE   *v* **-CASED, -CASING, -CASES** to enclose in a case

ENCASH   *v* **-ED, -ING, -ES** to cash

ENCEINTE   *n* pl. **-S** an encircling fortification

ENCHAIN   *v* **-ED, -ING, -S** to bind with chains

ENCHANT   *v* **-ED, -ING, -S** to delight

ENCHASE   *v* **-CHASED, -CHASING, -CHASES** to place in an ornamental setting

ENCHASER   *n* pl. **-S** one that enchases

ENCHORIC   *adj* belonging to a particular country

ENCINA   *n* pl. **-S** an evergreen oak **ENCINAL** *adj*

ENCIPHER *v* **-ED, -ING, -S** to write in characters of hidden meaning

ENCIRCLE *v* **-CLED, -CLING, -CLES** to form a circle around

ENCLASP *v* **-ED, -ING, -S** to embrace

ENCLAVE *v* **-CLAVED, -CLAVING, -CLAVES** to enclose within a foreign territory

ENCLITIC *n* pl. **-S** a word pronounced as part of the preceding word

ENCLOSE *v* **-CLOSED, -CLOSING, -CLOSES** to close in on all sides

ENCLOSER *n* pl. **-S** one that encloses

ENCODE *v* **-CODED, -CODING, -CODES** to put into code

ENCODER *n* pl. **-S** one that encodes

ENCOMIUM *n* pl. **-MIUMS** or **-MIA** a eulogy

ENCORE *v* **-CORED, -CORING, -CORES** to call for the reappearance of a performer

ENCROACH *v* **-ED, -ING, -ES** to advance beyond the proper limits

ENCRUST *v* **-ED, -ING, -S** to cover with a crust

ENCRYPT *v* **-ED, -ING, -S** to encipher

ENCUMBER *v* **-ED, -ING, -S** to hinder in action or movement

ENCYCLIC *n* pl. **-S** a letter addressed by the pope to the bishops of the world

ENCYST *v* **-ED, -ING, -S** to enclose in a cyst

END *v* **-ED, -ING, -S** to terminate

ENDAMAGE *v* **-AGED, -AGING, -AGES** to damage

ENDAMEBA *n* pl. **-BAS** or **-BAE** a parasitic ameba

ENDANGER *v* **-ED, -ING, -S** to imperil

ENDARCH *adj* formed from the center outward

ENDARCHY *n* pl. **-CHIES** the condition of being endarch

ENDASH *n* pl. **-ES** a mark in writing used to connect elements of a compound

ENDBRAIN *n* pl. **-S** a part of the brain

ENDCAP *n* pl. **-S** a display of products at the end of an aisle in a store

ENDEAR *v* **-ED, -ING, -S** to make dear or beloved

ENDEAVOR *v* **-ED, -ING, -S** to make an effort

ENDEMIAL *adj* peculiar to a country or people

ENDEMIC *n* pl. **-S** an endemial disease

ENDEMISM *n* pl. **-S** the state of being endemial

ENDER *n* pl. **-S** one that ends something

ENDERMIC *adj* acting by absorption through the skin

ENDEXINE *n* pl. **-S** an inner layer of the exine

ENDGAME *n* pl. **-S** the last stage of a chess game

ENDING *n* pl. **-S** a termination

ENDITE *v* **-DITED, -DITING, -DITES** to indite

ENDIVE *n* pl. **-S** an herb cultivated as a salad plant

ENDLEAF *n* pl. **-LEAVES** or **-LEAFS** an endpaper

ENDLESS *adj* enduring forever

ENDLONG *adv* lengthwise

ENDMOST *adj* farthest

ENDNOTE *n* pl. **-S** a note placed at the end of the text

ENDOCARP *n* pl. **-S** the inner layer of a pericarp

ENDOCAST *n* pl. **-S** a cast of the cranial cavity

ENDODERM *n* pl. **-S** the innermost germ layer of an embryo

ENDOGAMY *n* pl. **-MIES** marriage within a particular group

ENDOGEN *n* pl. **-S** a type of plant

ENDOGENY *n* pl. **-NIES** growth from within

ENDOPOD *n* pl. **-S** a branch of a crustacean limb

ENDORSE *v* **-DORSED, -DORSING, -DORSES** to sign the back of a negotiable document

ENDORSEE *n* pl. **-S** one to whom a document is transferred by endorsement

ENDORSER *n* pl. **-S** one that endorses

ENDORSOR *n* pl. **-S** endorser

ENDOSARC *n* pl. **-S** a portion of a cell

ENDOSMOS *n* pl. **-ES** a form of osmosis

ENDOSOME *n* pl. **-S** a cellular particle

ENDOSTEA *n/pl* bone membranes

ENDOW *v* **-ED, -ING, -S** to provide with something

ENDOWER *n* pl. **-S** one that endows

ENDOZOIC *adj* involving passage through an animal

ENDPAPER *n* pl. **-S** a sheet of paper used in bookbinding

ENDPLATE *n* pl. **-S** a type of nerve terminal

ENDPLAY *v* **-ED, -ING, -S** to force (an opponent in bridge) to lead

ENDPOINT *n* pl. **-S** either of two points that mark the end of a line segment

ENDRIN *n* pl. **-S** an insecticide

ENDUE *v* **-DUED, -DUING, -DUES** to provide with some quality or gift

ENDURE *v* **-DURED, -DURING, -DURES** to last

ENDURER *n* pl. **-S** one that endures

ENDURO *n* pl. **-DUROS** a long race

ENDWAYS *adv* endwise

ENDWISE *adv* lengthwise

ENEMA *n* pl. **-MAS** or **-MATA** a liquid injected into the rectum

ENEMY *n* pl. **-MIES** one that is antagonistic toward another

ENERGID *n* pl. **-S** a nucleus and the body of cytoplasm with which it interacts

ENERGIES pl. of energy

ENERGISE *v* **-GISED, -GISING, -GISES** to energize

ENERGIZE *v* **-GIZED, -GIZING, -GIZES** to give energy to

ENERGY *n* **-GIES** the capacity for vigorous activity

ENERVATE *v* **-VATED, -VATING, -VATES** to deprive of strength or vitality

ENFACE *v* **-FACED, -FACING, -FACES** to write on the front of

ENFEEBLE *v* **-BLED, -BLING, -BLES** to make feeble

ENFEOFF *v* **-ED, -ING, -S** to invest with a feudal estate

ENFETTER *v* **-ED, -ING, -S** to enchain

ENFEVER *v* **-ED, -ING, -S** to fever

ENFILADE *v* **-LADED, -LADING, -LADES** to direct heavy gunfire along the length of

ENFLAME *v* **-FLAMED, -FLAMING, -FLAMES** to inflame

ENFOLD *v* **-ED, -ING, -S** to envelop

ENFOLDER *n* pl. **-S** one that enfolds

ENFORCE *v* **-FORCED, -FORCING, -FORCES** to compel obedience to

ENFORCER *n* pl. **-S** one that enforces

ENFRAME *v* **-FRAMED, -FRAMING, -FRAMES** to frame

ENG *n* pl. **-S** a phonetic symbol

ENGAGE *v* **-GAGED, -GAGING, -GAGES** to employ

ENGAGER *n* pl. **-S** one that engages

ENGENDER *v* **-ED, -ING, -S** to bring into existence

ENGILD *v* **-ED, -ING, -S** to brighten

ENGINE *v* **-GINED, -GINING, -GINES** to equip with machinery

ENGINEER *v* **-ED, -ING, -S** to carry through or manage by contrivance

ENGINERY *n* pl. **-RIES** machinery

ENGINING present participle of engine

ENGINOUS *adj* ingenious

ENGIRD *v* **-GIRT** or **-GIRDED, -GIRDING, -GIRDS** to gird

ENGIRDLE *v* **-DLED, -DLING, -DLES** to engird

ENGLISH *v* **-ED, -ING, -ES** to cause a billiard ball to spin around its vertical axis

ENGLUT *v* **-GLUTTED, -GLUTTING, -GLUTS** to gulp down

ENGORGE *v* **-GORGED, -GORGING, -GORGES** to fill with blood

ENGRAFT *v* **-ED, -ING, -S** to graft for propagation

ENGRAIL *v* **-ED, -ING, -S** to ornament the edge of with curved indentations

ENGRAIN *v* **-ED, -ING, -S** to ingrain

ENGRAM *n* pl. **-S** the durable mark caused by a stimulus upon protoplasm

ENGRAMME *n* pl. **-S** engram

ENGRAVE *v* **-GRAVED, -GRAVING, -GRAVES** to form by incision

ENGRAVER *n* pl. **-S** one that engraves

ENGROSS *v* **-ED, -ING, -ES** to occupy completely

ENGULF *v* **-ED, -ING, -S** to surround completely

ENHALO *v* **-ED, -ING, -S** or **-ES** to surround with a halo

ENHANCE *v* **-HANCED, -HANCING, -HANCES** to raise to a higher degree

ENHANCER *n* pl. **-S** one that enhances

ENIGMA *n* pl. **-MAS** or **-MATA** something that is hard to understand or explain

ENISLE *v* **-ISLED, -ISLING, -ISLES** to isolate

ENJAMB *v* **-ED, -ING, -S** to continue a sentence from one line of a poem to the next

ENJOIN *v* **-ED, -ING, -S** to command

ENJOINER *n* pl. **-S** one that enjoins

ENJOY *v* **-ED, -ING, -S** to receive pleasure from

ENJOYER *n* pl. **-S** one that enjoys

ENKINDLE *v* **-DLED, -DLING, -DLES** to set on fire

ENLACE *v* **-LACED, -LACING, -LACES** to bind with laces

ENLARGE *v* **-LARGED, -LARGING, -LARGES** to make or become larger

ENLARGER *n* pl. **-S** a device used to enlarge photographs

ENLIST *v* **-ED, -ING, -S** to engage for military service

ENLISTEE *n* pl. **-S** one that is enlisted

ENLISTER *n* pl. **-S** one that enlists

ENLIVEN *v* **-ED, -ING, -S** to make lively

ENMESH *v* **-ED, -ING, -ES** to ensnare or entangle in a net

ENMITY *n* pl. **-TIES** hostility

ENNEAD *n* pl. **-S** a group of nine **ENNEADIC** *adj*

ENNEAGON *n* pl. **-S** a nonagon

ENNOBLE *v* **-BLED, -BLING, -BLES** to make noble

ENNOBLER *n* pl. **-S** one that ennobles

ENNUI *n* pl. **-S** a feeling of weariness and discontent

ENNUYE *adj* oppressed with ennui

ENNUYEE *adj* ennuye

ENOKI *n* pl. **-S** a small mushroom

ENOL *n* pl. **-S** a chemical compound **ENOLIC** *adj*

ENOLASE *n* pl. **-S** an enzyme

ENOLOGY *n* pl. **-GIES** oenology

ENOPHILE *n* pl. **-S** oenophile

ENORM *adj* enormous

ENORMITY *n* pl. **-TIES** great wickedness

ENORMOUS *adj* huge

ENOSIS *n* pl. **-SISES** union

ENOUGH *n* pl. **-S** a sufficient supply

ENOUNCE *v* **ENOUNCED, ENOUNCING, ENOUNCES** to announce

ENOW *n* pl. **-S** enough

ENPLANE *v* **-PLANED, -PLANING, -PLANES** to board an airplane

ENQUIRE *v* **-QUIRED, -QUIRING, -QUIRES** to inquire

ENQUIRER *n* pl. **-S** one that inquires

ENQUIRY *n* pl. **-RIES** inquiry

ENRAGE *v* **-RAGED, -RAGING, -RAGES** to make very angry

ENRAPT *adj* rapt

ENRAVISH *v* **-ED, -ING, -ES** to delight greatly

ENRICH *v* **-ED, -ING, -ES** to add desirable elements to

ENRICHER *n* pl. **-S** one that enriches

ENROBE *v* **-ROBED, -ROBING, -ROBES** to dress

ENROBER *n* pl. **-S** one that enrobes

ENROL *v* **-ROLLED, -ROLLING, -ROLS** to enroll

ENROLL *v* **-ED, -ING, -S** to enter the name of in a register, record, or roll

ENROLLEE *n* pl. **-S** one that is enrolled

ENROLLER *n* pl. **-S** one that enrolls

ENROLLING present participle of enrol

ENROOT *v* **-ED, -ING, -S** to implant

ENS *n* pl. **ENTIA** an entity

ENSAMPLE *n* pl. **-S** an example

ENSCONCE *v* **-SCONCED, -SCONCING, -SCONCES** to settle securely or comfortably

ENSCROLL *v* **-ED, -ING, -S** to write on a scroll

ENSEMBLE *n* pl. **-S** a group of complementary parts

ENSERF *v* **-ED, -ING, -S** to make a serf of

ENSHEATH *v* **-ED, -ING, -S** to enclose in a sheath

ENSHRINE *v* **-SHRINED, -SHRINING, -SHRINES** to place in a shrine

ENSHROUD *v* **-ED, -ING, -S** to conceal

ENSIFORM *adj* sword-shaped

ENSIGN *n* pl. **-S** a navy officer

ENSIGNCY *n* pl. **-CIES** the rank of an ensign

ENSILAGE *v* **-LAGED, -LAGING, -LAGES** to ensile

ENSILE *v* **-SILED, -SILING, -SILES** to store in a silo

ENSKY *v* **-SKIED** or **-SKYED, -SKYING, -SKIES** to raise to the skies

ENSLAVE *v* **-SLAVED, -SLAVING, -SLAVES** to make a slave of

ENSLAVER *n* pl. **-S** one that enslaves

ENSNARE *v* **-SNARED, -SNARING, -SNARES** to trap

ENSNARER *n* pl. **-S** one that ensnares

ENSNARL *v* **-ED, -ING, -S** to tangle

ENSORCEL _v_ **-ED, -ING, -S** to bewitch

ENSOUL _v_ **-ED, -ING, -S** to endow with a soul

ENSPHERE _v_ **-SPHERED, -SPHERING, -SPHERES** to enclose in a sphere

ENSUE _v_ **-SUED, -SUING, -SUES** to occur afterward or as a result

ENSUITE _n_ pl. **-S** a room (as a bathroom) adjoining another room

ENSURE _v_ **-SURED, -SURING, -SURES** to make certain

ENSURER _n_ pl. **-S** one that ensures

ENSWATHE _v_ **-SWATHED, -SWATHING, -SWATHES** to swathe

ENTAIL _v_ **-ED, -ING, -S** to restrict the inheritance of to a specified line of heirs

ENTAILER _n_ pl. **-S** one that entails

ENTAMEBA _n_ pl. **-BAS** or **-BAE** endameba

ENTANGLE _v_ **-TANGLED, -TANGLING, -TANGLES** to tangle

ENTASIA _n_ pl. **-S** spasmodic contraction of a muscle

ENTASIS _n_ pl. **-TASES** a slight convexity in a column **ENTASTIC** _adj_

ENTELLUS _n_ pl. **-ES** a hanuman

ENTENTE _n_ pl. **-S** an agreement between nations

ENTER _v_ **-ED, -ING, -S** to come or go into

ENTERA a pl. of enteron

ENTERAL _adj_ enteric

ENTERER _n_ pl. **-S** one that enters

ENTERIC _adj_ pertaining to the enteron

ENTERICS _n/pl_ a family of bacteria

ENTERON _n_ pl. **-TERONS** or **-TERA** the alimentary canal

ENTHALPY _n_ pl. **-PIES** a thermodynamic measure of heat

ENTHETIC _adj_ introduced from outside

ENTHRAL _v_ **-THRALLED, -THRALLING, -THRALS** to enthrall

ENTHRALL _v_ **-ED, -ING, -S** to charm

ENTHRONE _v_ **-THRONED, -THRONING, -THRONES** to place on a throne

ENTHUSE _v_ **-THUSED, -THUSING, -THUSES** to show enthusiasm

ENTIA pl. of ens

ENTICE _v_ **-TICED, -TICING, -TICES** to allure

ENTICER _n_ pl. **-S** one that entices

ENTIRE _n_ pl. **-S** the whole of something

ENTIRELY _adv_ completely

ENTIRETY _n_ pl. **-TIES** completeness

ENTITLE _v_ **-TLED, -TLING, -TLES** to give a title to

ENTITY _n_ pl. **-TIES** something that has a real existence

ENTODERM _n_ pl. **-S** endoderm

ENTOIL _v_ **-ED, -ING, -S** to entrap

ENTOMB _v_ **-ED, -ING, -S** to place in a tomb

ENTOPIC _adj_ situated in the normal place

ENTOZOA pl. of entozoon

ENTOZOAL _adj_ entozoic

ENTOZOAN _n_ pl. **-S** an entozoic parasite

ENTOZOIC _adj_ living within an animal

ENTOZOON _n_ pl. **-ZOA** entozoan

ENTRAILS _n/pl_ the internal organs

ENTRAIN _v_ **-ED, -ING, -S** to board a train

ENTRANCE _v_ **-TRANCED, -TRANCING, -TRANCES** to fill with delight or wonder

ENTRANT _n_ pl. **-S** one that enters

ENTRAP _v_ **-TRAPPED, -TRAPPING, -TRAPS** to trap

ENTREAT _v_ **-ED, -ING, -S** to ask for earnestly

ENTREATY _n_ pl. **-TREATIES** an earnest request

ENTREE _n_ pl. **-S** the principal dish of a meal

ENTRENCH _v_ **-ED, -ING, -ES** to establish firmly

ENTREPOT _n_ pl. **-S** a warehouse

ENTRESOL _n_ pl. **-S** a mezzanine

ENTRIES pl. of entry

ENTROPY _n_ pl. **-PIES** a thermodynamic measure of disorder **ENTROPIC** _adj_

ENTRUST _v_ **-ED, -ING, -S** to give over for safekeeping

ENTRY _n_ pl. **-TRIES** a place of entrance

ENTRYWAY _n_ pl. **-WAYS** a passage serving as an entrance

ENTWINE _v_ **-TWINED, -TWINING, -TWINES** to twine around

ENTWIST _v_ **-ED, -ING, -S** to twist together

ENURE _v_ **-URED, -URING, -URES** to inure

ENURESIS _n_ pl. **-RESES** involuntary urination

ENURETIC _n_ pl. **-S** one who is affected with enuresis

ENVELOP _v_ **-ED, -ING, -S** to cover completely

ENVELOPE	*n* pl. **-S** a paper container
ENVENOM	*v* **-ED, -ING, -S** to put venom into
ENVIABLE	*adj* desirable **ENVIABLY** *adv*
ENVIED	past tense of envy
ENVIER	*n* pl. **-S** one that envies
ENVIES	present 3d person sing. of envy
ENVIOUS	*adj* resentful and desirous of another's possessions or qualities
ENVIRO	*n* pl. **-ROS** an advocate for the preservation of the natural environment
ENVIRON	*v* **-ED, -ING, -S** to encircle
ENVISAGE	*v* **-AGED, -AGING, -AGES** to form a mental image of
ENVISION	*v* **-ED, -ING, -S** to envisage
ENVOI	*n* pl. **-S** the closing of a poem or prose work
ENVOY	*n* pl. **-VOYS** a representative
ENVY	*v* **-VIED, -VYING, -VIES** to be envious of
ENWHEEL	*v* **-ED, -ING, -S** to encircle
ENWIND	*v* **-WOUND, -WINDING, -WINDS** to wind around
ENWOMB	*v* **-ED, -ING, -S** to enclose as if in a womb
ENWRAP	*v* **-WRAPPED, -WRAPPING, -WRAPS** to envelop
ENZOOTIC	*n* pl. **-S** a type of animal disease
ENZYM	*n* pl. **-S** enzyme
ENZYME	*n* pl. **-S** a complex protein **ENZYMIC** *adj*
EOBIONT	*n* pl. **-S** a type of basic organism
EOHIPPUS	*n* pl. **-ES** an extinct horse
EOLIAN	*adj* pertaining to the wind
EOLIPILE	*n* pl. **-S** a type of engine
EOLITH	*n* pl. **-S** a prehistoric stone tool **EOLITHIC** *adj*
EOLOPILE	*n* pl. **-S** eolipile
EON	*n* pl. **-S** an indefinitely long period of time
EONIAN	*adj* everlasting
EONISM	*n* pl. **-S** adoption of the dress and mannerisms of the opposite sex
EOSIN	*n* pl. **-S** a red dye **EOSINIC** *adj*
EOSINE	*n* pl. **-S** eosin
EPACT	*n* pl. **-S** the difference between the lengths of the solar and lunar years
EPARCH	*n* pl. **-S** the head of an eparchy

EPARCHY	*n* pl. **-CHIES** a district of modern Greece
EPATER	*v* **-ED, -ING, -S** to shock complacent people
EPAULET	*n* pl. **-S** a shoulder ornament
EPAZOTE	*n* pl. **-S** an herb of the goosefoot family
EPEE	*n* pl. **-S** a type of sword
EPEEIST	*n* pl. **-S** one who fences with an epee
EPEIRIC	*adj* pertaining to vertical movement of the earth's crust
EPENDYMA	*n* pl. **-S** a membrane lining certain body cavities
EPERGNE	*n* pl. **-S** an ornamental dish
EPHA	*n* pl. **-S** ephah
EPHAH	*n* pl. **-S** a Hebrew unit of dry measure
EPHEBE	*n* pl. **-S** ephebus **EPHEBIC** *adj*
EPHEBOS	*n* pl. **-BOI** ephebus
EPHEBUS	*n* pl. **-BI** a young man of ancient Greece
EPHEDRA	*n* pl. **-S** a desert shrub
EPHEDRIN	*n* pl. **-S** an alkaloid used to treat allergies
EPHEMERA	*n* pl. **-ERAS** or **-ERAE** something of very short life or duration
EPHOD	*n* pl. **-S** an ancient Hebrew vestment
EPHOR	*n* pl. **-ORS** or **-ORI** a magistrate of ancient Greece **EPHORAL** *adj*
EPHORATE	*n* pl. **-S** the office of ephor
EPIBLAST	*n* pl. **-S** the ectoderm
EPIBOLY	*n* pl. **-LIES** the growth of one part around another **EPIBOLIC** *adj*
EPIC	*n* pl. **-S** a long narrative poem **EPICAL** *adj* **EPICALLY** *adv*
EPICALYX	*n* pl. **-LYXES** or **-LYCES** a set of bracts close to and resembling a calyx
EPICARP	*n* pl. **-S** the outer layer of a pericarp
EPICEDIA	*n/pl* funeral songs
EPICENE	*n* pl. **-S** one having both male and female characteristics
EPICLIKE	*adj* resembling an epic
EPICOTYL	*n* pl. **-S** a part of a plant embryo
EPICURE	*n* pl. **-S** a gourmet
EPICYCLE	*n* pl. **-S** a circle that rolls on the circumference of another circle

EPIDEMIC *n* pl. **-S** a rapid spread of a disease

EPIDERM *n* pl. **-S** the outer layer of skin

EPIDOTE *n* pl. **-S** a mineral **EPIDOTIC** *adj*

EPIDURAL *n* pl. **-S** an injection to produce loss of sensation

EPIFAUNA *n* pl. **-FAUNAS** or **-FAUNAE** fauna living on a hard sea floor

EPIFOCAL *adj* pertaining to the point of origin of an earthquake

EPIGEAL *adj* epigeous

EPIGEAN *adj* epigeous

EPIGEIC *adj* epigeous

EPIGENE *adj* occurring near the surface of the earth

EPIGENIC *adj* pertaining to change in the mineral character of a rock

EPIGEOUS *adj* growing on or close to the ground

EPIGON *n* pl. **-S** epigone

EPIGONE *n* pl. **-S** an inferior imitator **EPIGONIC** *adj*

EPIGONUS *n* pl. **-NI** epigone

EPIGRAM *n* pl. **-S** a brief, witty remark

EPIGRAPH *n* pl. **-S** an engraved inscription

EPIGYNY *n* pl. **-NIES** the state of having floral organs near the top of the ovary

EPILATE *v* **-LATED, -LATING, -LATES** to remove hair from

EPILATOR *n* pl. **-S** an agent for removing hair

EPILEPSY *n* pl. **-SIES** a disorder of the nervous system

EPILOG *n* pl. **-S** a concluding section

EPILOGUE *v* **-LOGUED, -LOGUING, -LOGUES** to provide with a concluding section

EPIMER *n* pl. **-S** a type of sugar compound **EPIMERIC** *adj*

EPIMERE *n* pl. **-S** a part of an embryo

EPIMYSIA *n/pl* muscle sheaths

EPINAOS *n* pl. **-NAOI** a rear vestibule

EPINASTY *n* pl. **-TIES** a downward bending of plant parts

EPIPHANY *n* pl. **-NIES** an appearance of a deity

EPIPHYTE *n* pl. **-S** a plant growing upon another plant

EPISCIA *n* pl. **-S** a tropical herb

EPISCOPE *n* pl. **-S** a type of projector

EPISODE *n* pl. **-S** an incident in the course of a continuous experience **EPISODIC** *adj*

EPISOME *n* pl. **-S** a genetic determinant **EPISOMAL** *adj*

EPISTASY *n* pl. **-SIES** a suppression of genetic effect

EPISTLE *n* pl. **-S** a long or formal letter

EPISTLER *n* pl. **-S** one that writes epistles

EPISTOME *n* pl. **-S** a structure covering the mouth of various invertebrates

EPISTYLE *n* pl. **-S** a part of a classical building

EPITAPH *n* pl. **-S** an inscription on a tomb

EPITASIS *n* pl. **-ASES** the main part of a classical drama

EPITAXY *n* pl. **-TAXIES** a type of crystalline growth **EPITAXIC** *adj*

EPITHET *n* pl. **-S** a term used to characterize a person or thing

EPITOME *n* pl. **-S** a typical or ideal example **EPITOMIC** *adj*

EPITOPE *n* pl. **-S** a region on the surface of an antigen

EPIZOA pl. of epizoon

EPIZOIC *adj* living on the body of an animal

EPIZOISM *n* pl. **-S** the state of being epizoic

EPIZOITE *n* pl. **-S** an epizoic organism

EPIZOON *n* pl. **-ZOA** an epizoic parasite

EPIZOOTY *n* pl. **-TIES** a type of animal disease

EPOCH *n* pl. **-S** a particular period of time **EPOCHAL** *adj*

EPODE *n* pl. **-S** a type of poem

EPONYM *n* pl. **-S** the person for whom something is named **EPONYMIC** *adj*

EPONYMY *n* pl. **-MIES** the derivation of an eponymic name

EPOPEE *n* pl. **-S** an epic poem

EPOPOEIA *n* pl. **-S** epopee

EPOS *n* pl. **-ES** an epic poem

EPOXIDE *n* pl. **-S** an epoxy compound

EPOXY *v* **EPOXIED** or **EPOXYED, EPOXYING, EPOXIES** to glue with epoxy (a type of resin)

EPSILON *n* pl. **-S** a Greek letter

EQUABLE *adj* not changing or varying greatly **EQUABLY** *adv*

EQUAL *adj* having the same capability, quantity, or effect as another

EQUAL	*v* **EQUALED, EQUALING, EQUALS** or **EQUALLED, EQUALLING, EQUALS** to be equal to
EQUALISE	*v* **-ISED, -ISING, -ISES** to equalize
EQUALITY	*n* pl. **-TIES** the state of being equal
EQUALIZE	*v* **-IZED, -IZING, -IZES** to make equal
EQUALLED	a past tense of equal
EQUALLING	a past participle of equal
EQUALLY	*adv* in an equal manner
EQUATE	*v* **EQUATED, EQUATING, EQUATES** to make equal
EQUATION	*n* pl. **-S** the act of equating
EQUATIVE	*adj* denoting a sentence in which one term is identified with another
EQUATOR	*n* pl. **-S** a great circle of spherical celestial bodies
EQUERRY	*n* pl. **-RIES** an officer in charge of the care of horses
EQUES	*n* pl. **EQUITES** a member of a privileged military class of ancient Rome
EQUID	*n* pl. **-S** an animal of the horse family
EQUINE	*n* pl. **-S** a horse
EQUINELY	*adv* in a horselike manner
EQUINITY	*n* pl. **-TIES** the state of being like a horse
EQUINOX	*n* pl. **-ES** a point on the celestial sphere
EQUIP	*v* **EQUIPPED, EQUIPPING, EQUIPS** to provide with whatever is needed
EQUIPAGE	*n* pl. **-S** a carriage
EQUIPPER	*n* pl. **-S** one that equips
EQUISETA	*n/pl* rushlike plants
EQUITANT	*adj* overlapping
EQUITES	pl. of eques
EQUITY	*n* pl. **-TIES** fairness or impartiality
EQUIVOKE	*n* pl. **-S** a play on words
ER	*interj* — used to express hesitation
ERA	*n* pl. **-S** an epoch
ERADIATE	*v* **-ATED, -ATING, -ATES** to radiate
ERASE	*v* **ERASED, ERASING, ERASES** to rub or scrape out **ERASABLE** *adj*
ERASER	*n* pl. **-S** one that erases
ERASION	*n* pl. **-S** an erasure
ERASURE	*n* pl. **-S** the act of erasing
ERBIUM	*n* pl. **-S** a metallic element
ERE	*prep* previous to; before
ERECT	*v* **-ED, -ING, -S** to build
ERECTER	*n* pl. **-S** erector
ERECTILE	*adj* capable of being raised upright
ERECTION	*n* pl. **-S** the act of erecting
ERECTIVE	*adj* tending to erect
ERECTLY	*adv* in an upright manner
ERECTOR	*n* pl. **-S** one that erects
ERELONG	*adv* soon
EREMITE	*n* pl. **-S** a hermit **EREMITIC** *adj*
EREMURUS	*n* pl. **-URUSES** or **-URI** a perennial herb
ERENOW	*adv* before this time
EREPSIN	*n* pl. **-S** a mixture of enzymes in the small intestine
ERETHISM	*n* pl. **-S** abnormal irritability **ERETHIC** *adj*
EREWHILE	*adv* some time ago
ERG	*n* pl. **-S** a unit of work or energy
ERGASTIC	*adj* constituting the nonliving by-products of protoplasmic activity
ERGATE	*n* pl. **-S** a worker ant
ERGATIVE	*n* pl. **-S** a type of verb
ERGO	*conj* therefore
ERGODIC	*adj* pertaining to the probability that any state will recur
ERGOT	*n* pl. **-S** a fungus **ERGOTIC** *adj*
ERGOTISM	*n* pl. **-S** poisoning produced by eating ergot-infected grain
ERICA	*n* pl. **-S** a shrub of the heath family
ERICOID	*adj* resembling heath
ERIGERON	*n* pl. **-S** an herb
ERINGO	*n* pl. **-GOS** or **-GOES** eryngo
ERISTIC	*n* pl. **-S** an expert in debate
ERLKING	*n* pl. **-S** an evil spirit of Germanic folklore
ERMINE	*n* pl. **-S** the fur of certain weasels **ERMINED** *adj*
ERN	*n* pl. **-S** erne
ERNE	*n* pl. **-S** a sea eagle
ERODABLE	*adj* erosible
ERODE	*v* **ERODED, ERODING, ERODES** to wear away by constant friction
ERODENT	*adj* erosive
ERODIBLE	*adj* erosible

EROGENIC *adj* arousing sexual desire

EROS *n* pl. **-ES** sexual desire

EROSE *adj* uneven **EROSELY** *adv*

EROSIBLE *adj* capable of being eroded

EROSION *n* pl. **-S** the act of eroding

EROSIVE *adj* causing erosion

EROTIC *n* pl. **-S** an amatory poem **EROTICAL** *adj*

EROTICA *n/pl* literature or art dealing with sexual love

EROTISM *n* pl. **-S** sexual excitement

EROTIZE *v* **-TIZED, -TIZING, -TIZES** to give a sexual meaning to

ERR *v* **-ED, -ING, -S** to make a mistake **ERRABLE** *adj*

ERRANCY *n* pl. **-CIES** an instance of erring

ERRAND *n* pl. **-S** a short trip made for a particular purpose

ERRANT *n* pl. **-S** a wanderer

ERRANTLY *adv* in a wandering manner

ERRANTRY *n* pl. **-RIES** the state of wandering

ERRATA *n* pl. **-S** a list of printing errors

ERRATIC *n* pl. **-S** an eccentric person

ERRATUM *n* pl. **-TA** a printing error

ERRHINE *n* pl. **-S** a substance that promotes nasal discharge

ERRINGLY *adv* in a mistaken manner

ERROR *n* pl. **-S** a mistake

ERS *n* pl. **-ES** ervil

ERSATZ *n* pl. **-ES** a substitute

ERST *adv* formerly

ERUCT *v* **-ED, -ING, -S** to belch

ERUCTATE *v* **-TATED, -TATING, -TATES** to eruct

ERUDITE *adj* scholarly

ERUGO *n* pl. **-GOS** aerugo

ERUMPENT *adj* bursting forth

ERUPT *v* **-ED, -ING, -S** to burst forth

ERUPTION *n* pl. **-S** the act of erupting

ERUPTIVE *n* pl. **-S** a type of rock

ERUV *n* pl. **ERUVIM** or **ERUVS** an enclosed area in which Jews are permitted to carry on activities normally forbidden on the Sabbath

ERVIL *n* pl. **-S** a European vetch

ERYNGIUM *n* pl. **-S** a plant of the parsley family

ERYNGO *n* pl. **-GOS** or **-GOES** a medicinal herb

ERYTHEMA *n* pl. **-S** a redness of the skin

ERYTHRON *n* pl. **-S** a bodily organ consisting of the red blood cells

ES *n* pl. **ESES** ess

ESCALADE *v* **-LADED, -LADING, -LADES** to enter by means of ladders

ESCALATE *v* **-LATED, -LATING, -LATES** to increase

ESCALLOP *v* **-ED, -ING, -S** to scallop

ESCALOP *v* **-ED, -ING, -S** to escallop

ESCALOPE *n* pl. **-S** a thin slice of meat or fish

ESCAPADE *n* pl. **-S** a reckless adventure

ESCAPE *v* **-CAPED, -CAPING, -CAPES** to get away

ESCAPEE *n* pl. **-S** one that has escaped

ESCAPER *n* pl. **-S** one that escapes

ESCAPISM *n* pl. **-S** the avoidance of reality by diversion of the mind

ESCAPIST *n* pl. **-S** one given to escapism

ESCAR *n* pl. **-S** esker

ESCARGOT *n* pl. **-S** an edible snail

ESCAROLE *n* pl. **-S** a variety of endive

ESCARP *v* **-ED, -ING, -S** to cause to slope steeply

ESCHALOT *n* pl. **-S** a shallot

ESCHAR *n* pl. **-S** a hard, dry scab

ESCHEAT *v* **-ED, -ING, -S** to confiscate

ESCHEW *v* **-ED, -ING, -S** to avoid

ESCHEWAL *n* pl. **-S** the act of eschewing

ESCHEWER *n* pl. **-S** one that avoids something

ESCOLAR *n* pl. **-S** a food fish

ESCORT *v* **-ED, -ING, -S** to accompany

ESCOT *v* **-ED, -ING, -S** to provide support for

ESCROW *v* **-ED, -ING, -S** to place in the custody of a third party

ESCUAGE *n* pl. **-S** scutage

ESCUDO *n* pl. **-DOS** a former monetary unit of Portugal

ESCULENT *n* pl. **-S** something that is edible

ESERINE *n* pl. **-S** a toxic alkaloid

ESKAR *n* pl. **-S** esker

ESKER *n* pl. **-S** a narrow ridge of gravel and sand

ESNE *n* pl. **-S** a laborer in Anglo-Saxon England

ESOPHAGI *n/pl* tubes connecting the mouth to the stomach

ESOTERIC *adj* designed for a select few

ESPALIER *v* **-ED, -ING, -S** to furnish with a trellis

ESPANOL *n* pl. **-ES** a native of Spain

ESPARTO *n* pl. **-TOS** a perennial grass

ESPECIAL *adj* special

ESPIAL *n* pl. **-S** the act of espying

ESPIED past tense of espy

ESPIEGLE *adj* playful

ESPIES present 3d person sing. of espy

ESPOIR *n* pl. **-S** a category of wrestlers

ESPOUSAL *n* pl. **-S** a marriage ceremony

ESPOUSE *v* **-POUSED, -POUSING, -POUSES** to marry

ESPOUSER *n* pl. **-S** one that espouses

ESPRESSO *n* pl. **-SOS** a strong coffee

ESPRIT *n* pl. **-S** spirit

ESPY *v* **-PIED, -PYING, -PIES** to catch sight of

ESQUIRE *v* **-QUIRED, -QUIRING, -QUIRES** to escort

ESS *n* pl. **-ES** the letter S

ESSAY *v* **-ED, -ING, -S** to try

ESSAYER *n* pl. **-S** one that essays

ESSAYIST *n* pl. **-S** a writer of essays (prose compositions)

ESSE *n* pl. **-S** essential nature

ESSENCE *n* pl. **-S** a fundamental nature or quality

ESSOIN *n* pl. **-S** an excuse

ESSONITE *n* pl. **-S** a variety of garnet

EST *n* pl. **-S** a group technique for raising self-awareness

ESTANCIA *n* pl. **-S** a cattle ranch

ESTATE *v* **-TATED, -TATING, -TATES** to provide with landed property

ESTEEM *v* **-ED, -ING, -S** to have a high opinion of

ESTER *n* pl. **-S** a type of chemical compound

ESTERASE *n* pl. **-S** a type of enzyme

ESTERIFY *v* **-FIED, -FYING, -FIES** to convert into an ester

ESTHESIA *n* pl. **-S** the ability to receive sensation

ESTHESIS *n* pl. **-THESISES** or **-THESES** esthesia

ESTHETE *n* pl. **-S** an esthetic person

ESTHETIC *n* pl. **-S** a conception of beauty

ESTIMATE *v* **-MATED, -MATING, -MATES** to make an approximate judgment of

ESTIVAL *adj* pertaining to summer

ESTIVATE *v* **-VATED, -VATING, -VATES** to spend the summer

ESTOP *v* **-TOPPED, -TOPPING, -TOPS** to impede by estoppel

ESTOPPEL *n* pl. **-S** a legal restraint preventing a person from contradicting his own previous statement

ESTOVERS *n/pl* necessities allowed by law

ESTRAGON *n* pl. **-S** tarragon

ESTRAL *adj* estrous

ESTRANGE *v* **-TRANGED, -TRANGING, -TRANGES** to alienate

ESTRAY *v* **-ED, -ING, -S** to stray

ESTREAT *v* **-ED, -ING, -S** to copy from court records for use in prosecution

ESTRIN *n* pl. **-S** estrone

ESTRIOL *n* pl. **-S** an estrogen

ESTROGEN *n* pl. **-S** a female sex hormone promoting or producing estrus

ESTRONE *n* pl. **-S** an estrogen

ESTROUS *adj* pertaining to estrus

ESTRUAL *adj* estrous

ESTRUM *n* pl. **-S** estrus

ESTRUS *n* pl. **-ES** the period of heat in female mammals

ESTUARY *n* pl. **-ARIES** an inlet of the sea at a river's lower end

ESURIENT *adj* greedy

ET a past tense of eat

ETA *n* pl. **-S** a Greek letter

ETAGERE *n* pl. **-S** an ornamental stand

ETALON *n* pl. **-S** an optical instrument

ETAMIN *n* pl. **-S** etamine

ETAMINE *n* pl. **-S** a loosely woven fabric

ETAPE *n* pl. **-S** a warehouse

ETATISM *n* pl. **-S** state socialism **ETATIST** *adj*

ETCETERA *n* pl. **-S** a number of additional items

ETCH *v* **-ED, -ING, -ES** to engrave with acid

ETCHANT *n* pl. **-S** a substance used in etching

ETCHER *n* pl. **-S** one that etches

ETCHING *n* pl. **-S** an etched design

ETERNAL *n* pl. **-S** something lasting forever

ETERNE *adj* everlasting

ETERNISE *v* **-NISED, -NISING, -NISES** to eternize

ETERNITY *n* pl. **-TIES** infinite time

ETERNIZE *v* **-NIZED, -NIZING, -NIZES** to make everlasting

ETESIAN *n* pl. **-S** an annually recurring wind

ETH *n* pl. **-S** edh

ETHANAL *n* pl. **-S** a volatile liquid compound

ETHANE *n* pl. **-S** a gaseous hydrocarbon

ETHANOL *n* pl. **-S** an alcohol

ETHENE *n* pl. **-S** ethylene

ETHEPHON *n* pl. **-S** a synthetic plant growth regulator

ETHER *n* pl. **-S** a volatile liquid used as an anesthetic **ETHERIC** *adj*

ETHEREAL *adj* airy

ETHERIFY *v* **-FIED, -FYING, -FIES** to convert into ether

ETHERISE *v* **-ISED, -ISING, -ISES** to etherize

ETHERISH *adj* resembling ether

ETHERIZE *v* **-IZED, -IZING, -IZES** to treat with ether

ETHIC *n* pl. **-S** a body of moral principles

ETHICAL *n* pl. **-S** a drug sold by prescription only

ETHICIAN *n* pl. **-S** an ethicist

ETHICIST *n* pl. **-S** a specialist in ethics

ETHICIZE *v* **-CIZED, -CIZING, -CIZES** to make ethical

ETHINYL *n* pl. **-S** ethynyl

ETHION *n* pl. **-S** a pesticide

ETHMOID *n* pl. **-S** a bone of the nasal cavity

ETHNARCH *n* pl. **-S** the ruler of a people or province

ETHNIC *n* pl. **-S** a member of a particular ethnos **ETHNICAL** *adj*

ETHNONYM *n* pl. **-S** the name of an ethnic group

ETHNOS *n* pl. **-ES** a group of people who share a common and distinctive culture

ETHOGRAM *n* pl. **-S** a list of the behavior patterns of a species

ETHOLOGY *n* pl. **-GIES** the study of animal behavior

ETHOS *n* pl. **-ES** the fundamental character of a culture

ETHOXY *n* pl. **-OXIES** ethoxyl

ETHOXYL *n* pl. **-S** a univalent chemical radical

ETHYL *n* pl. **-S** a univalent chemical radical

ETHYLATE *v* **-ATED, -ATING, -ATES** to introduce the ethyl group into

ETHYLENE *n* pl. **-S** a flammable gas

ETHYLIC *adj* pertaining to ethyl

ETHYNE *n* pl. **-S** a flammable gas

ETHYNYL *n* pl. **-S** a univalent chemical radical

ETICS *n/pl* a type of linguistic analysis **ETIC** *adj*

ETIOLATE *v* **-LATED, -LATING, -LATES** to whiten

ETIOLOGY *n* pl. **-GIES** the study of the causes of diseases

ETNA *n* pl. **-S** a container for heating liquids

ETOILE *n* pl. **-S** a star

ETOUFFEE *n* pl. **-S** a Cajun stew

ETRIER *n* pl. **-S** a short rope ladder

ETUDE *n* pl. **-S** a piece of music for the practice of a point of technique

ETUI *n* pl. **-S** a case for holding small articles

ETWEE *n* pl. **-S** etui

ETYMON *n* pl. **-MONS** or **-MA** the earliest known form of a word

EUCAINE *n* pl. **-S** an anesthetic

EUCALYPT *n* pl. **-S** an evergreen tree

EUCHARIS *n* pl. **-RISES** a flowering plant

EUCHRE *v* **-CHRED, -CHRING, -CHRES** to prevent from winning three tricks in euchre (a card game)

EUCLASE *n* pl. **-S** a mineral

EUCRITE *n* pl. **-S** a type of meteorite **EUCRITIC** *adj*

EUDAEMON *n* pl. **-S** eudemon

EUDAIMON *n* pl. **-S** eudemon

EUDEMON *n* pl. **-S** a good spirit

EUGENIA *n* pl. **-S** a tropical evergreen tree

EUGENICS *n/pl* the science of hereditary improvement **EUGENIC** *adj*

EUGENIST *n* pl. **-S** a student of eugenics

EUGENOL *n* pl. **-S** an aromatic liquid

EUGLENA	*n* pl. **-S** a freshwater protozoan
EUGLENID	*n* pl. **-S** a euglena
EULACHAN	*n* pl. **-S** eulachon
EULACHON	*n* pl. **-S** a marine food fish
EULOGIA	*n* pl. **-GIAE** holy bread
EULOGIA	*n* pl. **-S** a blessing
EULOGIES	pl. of eulogy
EULOGISE	*v* **-GISED, -GISING, -GISES** to eulogize
EULOGIST	*n* pl. **-S** one that eulogizes
EULOGIUM	*n* pl. **-GIUMS** or **-GIA** a eulogy
EULOGIZE	*v* **-GIZED, -GIZING, -GIZES** to praise highly
EULOGY	*n* pl. **-GIES** a formal expression of high praise
EUNUCH	*n* pl. **-S** a castrated man
EUONYMUS	*n* pl. **-ES** any of a genus of shrubs or small trees
EUPATRID	*n* pl. **-RIDS** or **-RIDAE** an aristocrat of ancient Athens
EUPEPSIA	*n* pl. **-S** good digestion **EUPEPTIC** *adj*
EUPEPSY	*n* pl. **-SIES** eupepsia
EUPHENIC	*adj* dealing with biological improvement
EUPHONY	*n* pl. **-NIES** pleasant sound **EUPHONIC** *adj*
EUPHORIA	*n* pl. **-S** a feeling of well-being **EUPHORIC** *adj*
EUPHOTIC	*adj* pertaining to the upper layer of a body of water
EUPHRASY	*n* pl. **-SIES** an annual herb
EUPHROE	*n* pl. **-S** a device used to adjust a shipboard awning
EUPHUISM	*n* pl. **-S** an artificially elegant style of speech or writing
EUPHUIST	*n* pl. **-S** one given to euphuism
EUPLOID	*n* pl. **-S** a cell having three or more identical genomes
EUPLOIDY	*n* pl. **-DIES** the state of being a euploid
EUPNEA	*n* pl. **-S** normal breathing **EUPNEIC** *adj*
EUPNOEA	*n* pl. **-S** eupnea **EUPNOEIC** *adj*
EUREKA	*n* pl. **-S** a fortunate discovery
EURIPUS	*n* pl. **-PI** a swift sea channel
EURO	*n* pl. **EUROS** the unit of currency used by most European countries
EUROKY	*n* pl. **-KIES** the ability of an organism to live under variable conditions **EUROKOUS** *adj*
EUROLAND	*n* pl. **-S** the eurozone
EUROPIUM	*n* pl. **-S** a metallic element
EUROZONE	*n* pl. **-S** the area formed by the countries using the euro
EURYBATH	*n* pl. **-S** an organism that can live in a wide range of water depths
EURYOKY	*n* pl. **-KIES** euroky
EURYTHMY	*n* pl. **-MIES** harmony of movement or structure
EUSOCIAL	*adj* pertaining to an animal society marked by specialization of tasks
EUSTACY	*n* pl. **-CIES** a worldwide change in sea level **EUSTATIC** *adj*
EUSTASY	*n* pl. **-SIES** eustacy
EUSTELE	*n* pl. **-S** a plant part
EUTAXY	*n* pl. **-TAXIES** good order
EUTECTIC	*n* pl. **-S** an alloy that has the lowest possible melting point
EUTROPHY	*n* pl. **-PHIES** healthful nutrition
EUXENITE	*n* pl. **-S** a mineral
EVACUANT	*n* pl. **-S** a cathartic medicine
EVACUATE	*v* **-ATED, -ATING, -ATES** to remove from a dangerous area
EVACUEE	*n* pl. **-S** one that is evacuated
EVADE	*v* **EVADED, EVADING, EVADES** to escape or avoid by cleverness or deceit **EVADABLE, EVADIBLE** *adj*
EVADER	*n* pl. **-S** one that evades
EVALUATE	*v* **-ATED, -ATING, -ATES** to determine the value of
EVANESCE	*v* **-NESCED, -NESCING, -NESCES** to fade away
EVANGEL	*n* pl. **-S** a preacher of the gospel
EVANISH	*v* **-ED, -ING, -ES** to vanish
EVASION	*n* pl. **-S** the act of evading
EVASIVE	*adj* tending to evade
EVE	*n* pl. **-S** evening
EVECTION	*n* pl. **-S** irregularity in the moon's motion
EVEN	*adj* **EVENER, EVENEST** flat and smooth
EVEN	*v* **-ED, -ING, -S** to make even
EVENER	*n* pl. **-S** one that evens
EVENFALL	*n* pl. **-S** twilight
EVENING	*n* pl. **-S** the latter part of the day and early part of the night

EVENLY	*adv* in an even manner
EVENNESS	*n* pl. **-ES** the state of being even
EVENSONG	*n* pl. **-S** an evening prayer service
EVENT	*n* pl. **-S** something that occurs
EVENTER	*n* pl. **-S** a horse or rider competing in eventing
EVENTFUL	*adj* momentous
EVENTIDE	*n* pl. **-S** evening
EVENTING	*n* pl. **-S** an equestrian competition
EVENTIVE	*adj* denoting an event
EVENTUAL	*adj* occurring at a later time
EVER	*adv* at all times
EVERMORE	*adv* forever
EVERSION	*n* pl. **-S** the act of everting
EVERT	*v* **-ED, -ING, -S** to turn outward or inside out
EVERTOR	*n* pl. **-S** a muscle that turns a part outward
EVERY	*adj* each without exception
EVERYDAY	*n* pl. **-S** the routine day
EVERYMAN	*n* pl. **-MEN** the typical or ordinary man
EVERYONE	*pron* every person
EVERYWAY	*adv* in every way
EVICT	*v* **-ED, -ING, -S** to expel by legal process
EVICTEE	*n* pl. **-S** one that is evicted
EVICTION	*n* pl. **-S** the act of evicting
EVICTOR	*n* pl. **-S** one that evicts
EVIDENCE	*v* **-DENCED, -DENCING, -DENCES** to indicate clearly
EVIDENT	*adj* clear to the vision or understanding
EVIL	*adj* **EVILER, EVILEST** or **EVILLER, EVILLEST** morally bad
EVIL	*n* pl. **-S** something that is evil
EVILDOER	*n* pl. **-S** one that does evil
EVILLY	*adv* in an evil manner
EVILNESS	*n* pl. **-ES** the quality of being evil
EVINCE	*v* **EVINCED, EVINCING, EVINCES** to show clearly **EVINCIVE** *adj*
EVITE	*v* **EVITED, EVITING, EVITES** to avoid **EVITABLE** *adj*
EVOCABLE	*adj* capable of being evoked
EVOCATOR	*n* pl. **-S** one that evokes
EVOKE	*v* **EVOKED, EVOKING, EVOKES** to call forth
EVOKER	*n* pl. **-S** an evocator

EVOLUTE	*n* pl. **-S** a type of geometric curve
EVOLVE	*v* **EVOLVED, EVOLVING, EVOLVES** to develop
EVOLVER	*n* pl. **-S** one that evolves
EVONYMUS	*n* pl. **-ES** euonymus
EVULSE	*v* **EVULSED, EVULSING, EVULSES** to extract forcibly
EVULSION	*n* pl. **-S** the act of pulling out
EVZONE	*n* pl. **-S** a Greek soldier
EWE	*n* pl. **-S** a female sheep
EWER	*n* pl. **-S** a large pitcher
EX	*v* **-ED, -ING, -ES** to cross out
EXABYTE	*n* pl. **-S** one quintillion bytes
EXACT	*adj* **-ACTER, -ACTEST** precise
EXACT	*v* **-ED, -ING, -S** to force the payment or yielding of
EXACTA	*n* pl. **-S** a type of horse racing bet
EXACTER	*n* pl. **-S** one that exacts
EXACTION	*n* pl. **-S** the act of exacting
EXACTLY	*adv* in an exact manner
EXACTOR	*n* pl. **-S** exacter
EXAHERTZ	*n* pl. **EXAHERTZ** one quintillion hertz
EXALT	*v* **-ED, -ING, -S** to raise
EXALTER	*n* pl. **-S** one that exalts
EXAM	*n* pl. **-S** an examination
EXAMEN	*n* pl. **-S** a critical study
EXAMINE	*v* **-INED, -INING, -INES** to inspect
EXAMINEE	*n* pl. **-S** one that is taking an examination
EXAMINER	*n* pl. **-S** one that examines
EXAMPLE	*v* **-PLED, -PLING, -PLES** to show by representation
EXANTHEM	*n* pl. **-S** a skin eruption
EXAPTED	*adj* utilized for a function other than the one developed through natural selection
EXAPTIVE	*adj* pertaining to an exapted function
EXARCH	*n* pl. **-S** the ruler of a province in the Byzantine Empire **EXARCHAL** *adj*
EXARCHY	*n* pl. **-CHIES** the domain of an exarch
EXCAVATE	*v* **-VATED, -VATING, -VATES** to dig out
EXCEED	*v* **-ED, -ING, -S** to go beyond
EXCEEDER	*n* pl. **-S** one that exceeds

EXCEL v -CELLED, -CELLING, -CELS to surpass others

EXCEPT v -ED, -ING, -S to leave out

EXCERPT v -ED, -ING, -S to pick out a passage from for quoting

EXCESS v -ED, -ING, -ES to eliminate the position of

EXCHANGE v -CHANGED, -CHANGING, -CHANGES to give and receive reciprocally

EXCIDE v -CIDED, -CIDING, -CIDES to excise

EXCIMER n pl. -S a dimer that exists in an excited state

EXCIPLE n pl. -S a rim around the hymenium of various lichens

EXCISE v -CISED, -CISING, -CISES to remove by cutting out

EXCISION n pl. -S the act of excising

EXCITANT n pl. -S a stimulant

EXCITE v -CITED, -CITING, -CITES to arouse the emotions of

EXCITER n pl. -S one that excites

EXCITON n pl. -S a phenomenon occurring in an excited crystal

EXCITOR n pl. -S exciter

EXCLAIM v -ED, -ING, -S to cry out suddenly

EXCLAVE n pl. -S a portion of a country which is isolated in foreign territory

EXCLUDE v -CLUDED, -CLUDING, -CLUDES to shut out

EXCLUDER n pl. -S one that excludes

EXCRETA n/pl excreted matter **EXCRETAL** adj

EXCRETE v -CRETED, -CRETING, -CRETES to separate and eliminate from an organic body

EXCRETER n pl. -S one that excretes

EXCURSUS n pl. -ES a long appended exposition of a topic

EXCUSE v -CUSED, -CUSING, -CUSES to apologize for

EXCUSER n pl. -S one that excuses

EXEC n pl. -S an executive officer

EXECRATE v -CRATED, -CRATING, -CRATES to curse

EXECUTE v -CUTED, -CUTING, -CUTES to carry out

EXECUTER n pl. -S executor

EXECUTOR n pl. -S one that executes

EXEDRA n pl. -DRAS or -DRAE a curved outdoor bench

EXEGESIS n pl. -GESES critical explanation or analysis **EXEGETIC** adj

EXEGETE n pl. -S one skilled in exegesis

EXEMPLAR n pl. -S one that is worthy of being copied

EXEMPLUM n pl. -PLA an example

EXEMPT v -ED, -ING, -S to free from an obligation required of others

EXEQUY n pl. -QUIES a funeral procession **EXEQUIAL** adj

EXERCISE v -CISED, -CISING, -CISES to make use of

EXERGUE n pl. -S a space on a coin **EXERGUAL** adj

EXERT v -ED, -ING, -S to put into action

EXERTION n pl. -S the act of exerting

EXERTIVE adj tending to exert

EXEUNT v they leave the stage — used as a stage direction

EXHALANT n pl. -S something that exhales

EXHALE v -HALED, -HALING, -HALES to expel air or vapor

EXHALENT n pl. -S exhalant

EXHAUST v -ED, -ING, -S to use up

EXHEDRA n pl. -DRAE exedra

EXHIBIT v -ED, -ING, -S to present for public viewing

EXHORT v -ED, -ING, -S to advise urgently

EXHORTER n pl. -S one that exhorts

EXHUME v -HUMED, -HUMING, -HUMES to dig out of the earth

EXHUMER n pl. -S one that exhumes

EXIGENCE n pl. -S exigency

EXIGENCY n pl. -CIES urgency

EXIGENT adj urgent

EXIGIBLE adj liable to be demanded

EXIGUITY n pl. -ITIES the state of being exiguous

EXIGUOUS adj meager

EXILE v -ILED, -ILING, -ILES to banish from one's own country **EXILABLE** adj

EXILER n pl. -S one that exiles

EXILIAN adj exilic

EXILIC adj pertaining to exile (banishment from one's own country)

EXILING present participle of exile

EXIMIOUS   *adj* excellent

EXINE   *n* pl. **-S** the outer layer of certain spores

EXIST   *v* **-ED, -ING, -S** to be

EXISTENT   *n* pl. **-S** something that exists

EXIT   *v* **-ED, -ING, -S** to go out

EXITLESS   *adj* lacking a way out

EXOCARP   *n* pl. **-S** the epicarp

EXOCRINE   *n* pl. **-S** an external secretion

EXOCYTIC   *adj* pertaining to cellular excretion

EXODERM   *n* pl. **-S** the ectoderm

EXODOS   *n* pl. **-DOI** a concluding dramatic scene

EXODUS   *n* pl. **-ES** a movement away

EXOERGIC   *adj* releasing energy

EXOGAMY   *n* pl. **-MIES** marriage outside of a particular group **EXOGAMIC** *adj*

EXOGEN   *n* pl. **-S** a type of plant

EXOGENIC   *adj* formed or occurring on the surface of the earth

EXON   *n* pl. **-S** a sequence in the genetic code **EXONIC** *adj*

EXONUMIA   *n/pl* collectible items other than coins or paper money

EXONYM   *n* pl. **-S** a name for a people used by outsiders and not by the people themselves

EXORABLE   *adj* persuadable

EXORCISE   *v* **-CISED, -CISING, -CISES** to free of an evil spirit

EXORCISM   *n* pl. **-S** the act of exorcising

EXORCIST   *n* pl. **-S** one who practices exorcism

EXORCIZE   *v* **-CIZED, -CIZING, -CIZES** to exorcise

EXORDIUM   *n* pl. **-DIUMS** or **-DIA** a beginning **EXORDIAL** *adj*

EXOSMOSE   *n* pl. **-S** a form of osmosis **EXOSMIC** *adj*

EXOSPORE   *n* pl. **-S** the outer coat of a spore

EXOTERIC   *adj* suitable for the public

EXOTIC   *n* pl. **-S** something from another part of the world

EXOTICA   *n/pl* things excitingly different or unusual

EXOTISM   *n* pl. **-S** an exotic

EXOTOXIN   *n* pl. **-S** an excreted toxin **EXOTOXIC** *adj*

EXPAND   *v* **-ED, -ING, -S** to increase in size or volume

EXPANDER   *n* pl. **-S** one that expands

EXPANDOR   *n* pl. **-S** a type of transducer

EXPANSE   *n* pl. **-S** a wide, continuous area

EXPAT   *n* pl. **-S** an expatriate person

EXPECT   *v* **-ED, -ING, -S** to anticipate

EXPECTER   *n* pl. **-S** one that expects

EXPEDITE   *v* **-DITED, -DITING, -DITES** to speed up the progress of

EXPEL   *v* **-PELLED, -PELLING, -PELS** to force out

EXPELLEE   *n* pl. **-S** a deportee

EXPELLER   *n* pl. **-S** one that expels

EXPEND   *v* **-ED, -ING, -S** to use up

EXPENDER   *n* pl. **-S** one that expends

EXPENSE   *v* **-PENSED, -PENSING, -PENSES** to charge with costs

EXPERT   *v* **-ED, -ING, -S** to serve as an authority

EXPERTLY   *adv* skillfully

EXPIABLE   *adj* capable of being expiated

EXPIATE   *v* **-ATED, -ATING, -ATES** to atone for

EXPIATOR   *n* pl. **-S** one that expiates

EXPIRE   *v* **-PIRED, -PIRING, -PIRES** to come to an end

EXPIRER   *n* pl. **-S** one that expires

EXPIRY   *n* pl. **-RIES** a termination

EXPLAIN   *v* **-ED, -ING, -S** to make plain or understandable

EXPLANT   *v* **-ED, -ING, -S** to remove from the natural site of growth and place in a medium

EXPLICIT   *n* pl. **-S** a statement formerly used at the close of a book

EXPLODE   *v* **-PLODED, -PLODING, -PLODES** to blow up

EXPLODER   *n* pl. **-S** one that explodes

EXPLOIT   *v* **-ED, -ING, -S** to take advantage of

EXPLORE   *v* **-PLORED, -PLORING, -PLORES** to travel through for the purpose of discovery

EXPLORER   *n* pl. **-S** one that explores

EXPO   *n* pl. **-POS** a public exhibition

EXPONENT   *n* pl. **-S** one who expounds

EXPORT   *v* **-ED, -ING, -S** to send to other countries for commercial purposes

EXPORTER   *n* pl. **-S** one that exports

EXPOSAL   *n* pl. **-S** an exposure

EXPOSE   *v* **-POSED, -POSING, -POSES** to lay open to view

EXPOSER   *n* pl. **-S** one that exposes

EXPOSIT   *v* **-ED, -ING, -S** to expound

EXPOSURE   *n* pl. **-S** the act of exposing

EXPOUND   *v* **-ED, -ING, -S** to explain in detail

EXPRESS   *v* **-ED, -ING, -ES** to set forth in words

EXPRESSO   *n* pl. **-SOS** espresso

EXPULSE   *v* **-PULSED, -PULSING, -PULSES** to expel

EXPUNGE   *v* **-PUNGED, -PUNGING, -PUNGES** to delete

EXPUNGER   *n* pl. **-S** one that expunges

EXSCIND   *v* **-ED, -ING, -S** to cut out

EXSECANT   *n* pl. **-S** a trigonometric function of an angle

EXSECT   *v* **-ED, -ING, -S** to cut out

EXSERT   *v* **-ED, -ING, -S** to thrust out

EXTANT   *adj* still in existence

EXTEND   *v* **-ED, -ING, -S** to stretch out to full length

EXTENDER   *n* pl. **-S** a substance added to another substance

EXTENSOR   *n* pl. **-S** a muscle that extends a limb

EXTENT   *n* pl. **-S** the range over which something extends

EXTERIOR   *n* pl. **-S** a part or surface that is outside

EXTERN   *n* pl. **-S** a nonresident of an institution

EXTERNAL   *n* pl. **-S** an exterior

EXTERNE   *n* pl. **-S** extern

EXTINCT   *v* **-ED, -ING, -S** to extinguish

EXTOL   *v* **-TOLLED, -TOLLING, -TOLS** to praise highly

EXTOLL   *v* **-ED, -ING, -S** to extol

EXTOLLER   *n* pl. **-S** one that extols

EXTORT   *v* **-ED, -ING, -S** to obtain from a person by violence or intimidation

EXTORTER   *n* pl. **-S** one that extorts

EXTRA   *n* pl. **-S** something additional

EXTRACT   *v* **-ED, -ING, -S** to pull or draw out

EXTRADOS   *n* pl. **-ES** the outer curve of an arch

EXTRANET   *n* pl. **-S** an intranet that permits limited access by outsiders

EXTREMA   pl. of extremum

EXTREME   *adj* **-TREMER, -TREMEST** existing in a very high degree

EXTREME   *n* pl. **-S** the highest degree

EXTREMUM   *n* pl. **-MA** a maximum or a minimum of a mathematical function

EXTROPY   *n* pl. **-PIES** the prediction that human intelligence will enable life to expand throughout the universe

EXTRORSE   *adj* facing outward

EXTRUDE   *v* **-TRUDED, -TRUDING, -TRUDES** to force, thrust, or push out

EXTRUDER   *n* pl. **-S** one that extrudes

EXTUBATE   *v* **-BATED, -BATING, -BATES** to remove a tube from

EXUDATE   *n* pl. **-S** an exuded substance

EXUDE   *v* **-UDED, -UDING, -UDES** to ooze forth

EXULT   *v* **-ED, -ING, -S** to rejoice greatly

EXULTANT   *adj* exulting

EXURB   *n* pl. **-S** a residential area lying beyond the suburbs of a city **EXURBAN** *adj*

EXURBIA   *n* pl. **-S** an exurb

EXUVIATE   *v* **-ATED, -ATING, -ATES** to molt

EXUVIUM   *n* pl. **-VIAE** or **-VIA** the molted covering of an animal **EXUVIAL** *adj*

EYAS   *n* pl. **-ES** a young hawk

EYASS   *n* pl. **-ES** eyas

EYE   *n* pl. **EYES** or **EYEN** or **EYNE** the organ of sight

EYE   *v* **EYED, EYING** or **EYEING, EYES** to watch closely **EYEABLE** *adj*

EYEBALL   *v* **-ED, -ING, -S** to eye

EYEBAR   *n* pl. **-S** a metal bar with a loop at one or both ends

EYEBEAM   *n* pl. **-S** a glance

EYEBLACK   *n* pl. **-S** a dark pigment applied under the eyes

EYEBLINK   *n* pl. **-S** an instant

EYEBOLT   *n* pl. **-S** a type of bolt or screw

EYEBROW   *n* pl. **-S** the ridge over the eye

EYECUP   *n* pl. **-S** a cup used for applying lotions to the eyes

EYED   past tense of eye

EYEDNESS   *n* pl. **-ES** preference for the use of one eye over the other

EYEDROPS   *n/pl* a medicated solution for the eyes applied in drops

EYEFOLD	*n* pl. **-S** a fold of skin of the upper eyelid	**EYESHINE**	*n* pl. **-S** a reflection from the eyes of some animals
EYEFUL	*n* pl. **-S** a complete view	**EYESHOT**	*n* pl. **-S** the range of vision
EYEGLASS	*n* pl. **-ES** a lens used to aid vision	**EYESIGHT**	*n* pl. **-S** the ability to see
EYEHOLE	*n* pl. **-S** a small opening	**EYESOME**	*adj* pleasant to look at
EYEHOOK	*n* pl. **-S** a type of hook	**EYESORE**	*n* pl. **-S** something offensive to the sight
EYELASH	*n* pl. **-ES** a hair growing on the edge of an eyelid	**EYESPOT**	*n* pl. **-S** a simple visual organ of lower animals
EYELESS	*adj* lacking eyes	**EYESTALK**	*n* pl. **-S** a stalklike structure with an eye at its tip
EYELET	*v* **-LETTED, -LETTING, -LETS** or **-LETED, -LETING, -LETS** to make a small hole in	**EYESTONE**	*n* pl. **-S** a disk used to remove foreign matter from the eye
EYELID	*n* pl. **-S** the lid of skin that can be closed over an eyeball	**EYETOOTH**	*n* pl. **-TEETH** a cuspid
		EYEWASH	*n* pl. **-ES** an eye lotion
EYELIFT	*n* pl. **-S** plastic surgery of the eyelid	**EYEWATER**	*n* pl. **-S** an eyewash
EYELIKE	*adj* resembling an eye	**EYEWEAR**	*n* pl. **EYEWEAR** a device worn on or over the eyes
EYELINER	*n* pl. **-S** makeup for the eyes		
EYEN	a pl. of eye	**EYEWINK**	*n* pl. **-S** a wink of the eye
EYEPATCH	*n* pl. **-ES** a patch worn to protect an injured eye	**EYING**	a present participle of eye
EYEPIECE	*n* pl. **-S** the lens or lens group nearest the eye in an optical instrument	**EYNE**	a pl. of eye
		EYRA	*n* pl. **-S** a wild cat of tropical America
EYEPOINT	*n* pl. **-S** the point at which an eye is placed in using an optical instrument	**EYRE**	*n* pl. **-S** a journey
		EYRIE	*n* pl. **-S** aerie
EYER	*n* pl. **-S** one that eyes	**EYRIR**	*n* pl. **AURAR** a monetary unit of Iceland
EYESHADE	*n* pl. **-S** a visor for shading the eyes	**EYRY**	*n* pl. **-RIES** aerie

FA   *n* pl. **-S** the fourth tone of the diatonic musical scale

FAB   *n* pl. **-S** something created or constructed

FAB   *adj* **FABBER, FABBEST** fabulous

FABLE   *v* **-BLED, -BLING, -BLES** to compose or tell fictitious tales

FABLER   *n* pl. **-S** one that fables

FABLIAU   *n* pl. **-AUX** a short metrical tale popular in medieval France

FABLING   present participle of fable

FABRIC   *n* pl. **-S** a woven, felted, or knitted material

FABRIQUE   *n* pl. **-S** a parish group that deals with church property

FABULAR   *adj* legendary

FABULATE   *v* **-LATED, -LATING, -LATES** to compose fables

FABULISM   *n* pl. **-S** the placing of fantastical elements into everyday settings

FABULIST   *n* pl. **-S** a liar

FABULOUS   *adj* almost unbelievable

FACADE   *n* pl. **-S** the front of a building

FACE   *v* **FACED, FACING, FACES** to oppose or meet defiantly **FACEABLE** *adj*

FACEDOWN   *n* pl. **-S** a confrontation between opponents

FACELESS   *adj* lacking personal distinction or identity

FACELIFT   *v* **-ED, -ING, -S** to perform plastic surgery on the face

FACEMASK   *n* pl. **-S** a device to shield the face

FACEOFF   *n* pl. **-S** the action that starts a hockey game

FACER   *n* pl. **-S** one that faces

FACET   *v* **-ETED, -ETING, -ETS** or **-ETTED, -ETTING, -ETS** to cut small plane surfaces on

FACETE   *adj* witty **FACETELY** *adv*

FACETIAE   *n/pl* witty sayings or writings

FACETING   *n* pl. **-S** a surface of a cut gemstone

FACEUP   *adv* with the front part up

FACIA   *n* pl. **-CIAE** or **-CIAS** fascia

FACIAL   *n* pl. **-S** a treatment for the face

FACIALLY   *adv* with respect to the face

FACIEND   *n* pl. **-S** a number to be multiplied by another

FACIES   *n* pl. **FACIES** general appearance

FACILE   *adj* easily achieved or performed **FACILELY** *adv*

FACILITY   *n* pl. **-TIES** the quality of being facile

FACING   *n* pl. **-S** a lining at the edge of a garment

FACT   *n* pl. **-S** something known with certainty **FACTFUL** *adj*

FACTICE   *n* pl. **-S** a rubber-like material

FACTION   *n* pl. **-S** a clique within a larger group

FACTIOUS   *adj* promoting dissension

FACTOID   *n* pl. **-S** a brief news item

FACTOR   *v* **-ED, -ING, -S** to express as a product of two or more quantities

FACTORY   *n* pl. **-RIES** a building or group of buildings in which goods are manufactured

FACTOTUM   *n* pl. **-S** a person employed to do many kinds of work

FACTUAL   *adj* pertaining to facts

FACTUM   *n* pl. **-TUMS** or **-TA** a statement of the facts of a case being appealed

FACTURE   *n* pl. **-S** the act of making something

FACULA   *n* pl. **-LAE** an unusually bright spot on the sun's surface **FACULAR** *adj*

FACULTY   *n* pl. **-TIES** an inherent power or ability

FAD   *n* pl. **-S** a practice or interest that enjoys brief popularity

FADABLE   *adj* capable of fading

FADDIER   comparative of faddy

FADDIEST   superlative of faddy

FADDISH   *adj* inclined to take up fads

FADDISM   *n* pl. **-S** inclination to take up fads

FADDIST   *n* pl. **-S** a faddish person

FADDY   *adj* **-DIER, -DIEST** faddish

FADE   *v* **FADED, FADING, FADES** to lose color or brightness **FADEDLY** *adv*

FADEAWAY   *n* pl. **-AWAYS** a type of pitch in baseball

FADEIN   *n* pl. **-S** a gradual increase in the brightness of an image

FADELESS   *adj* not fading

FADEOUT   *n* pl. **-S** a gradual disappearance of an image

FADER   *n* pl. **-S** one that fades

FADGE   *v* **FADGED, FADGING, FADGES** to succeed

FADING   *n* pl. **-S** an Irish dance

FADLIKE   *adj* resembling a fad

FADO   *n* pl. **-DOS** a Portuguese folk song

FAECES   *n/pl* feces **FAECAL** *adj*

FAENA   *n* pl. **-S** a series of passes made by a matador in a bullfight

FAERIE   *n* pl. **-S** a fairy

FAERY   *n* pl. **-ERIES** faerie

FAFF   *v* **-ED, -ING, -S** to make a fuss

FAG   *v* **FAGGED, FAGGING, FAGS** to make weary by hard work

FAGGOT   *v* **-ED, -ING, -S** to fagot

FAGIN   *n* pl. **-S** a person who instructs others in crime

FAGOT   *v* **-ED, -ING, -S** to bind together into a bundle

FAGOTER   *n* pl. **-S** one that fagots

FAGOTING   *n* pl. **-S** a type of embroidery

FAH   *n* pl. **-S** fa

FAHLBAND   *n* pl. **-S** a band or stratum of rock impregnated with metallic sulfides

FAIENCE   *n* pl. **-S** a variety of glazed pottery

FAIL   *v* **-ED, -ING, -S** to be unsuccessful in an attempt

FAILING   *n* pl. **-S** a minor fault or weakness

FAILLE   *n* pl. **-S** a woven fabric

FAILURE   *n* pl. **-S** the act of failing

FAIN   *adj* **FAINER, FAINEST** glad

FAINEANT   *n* pl. **-S** a lazy person

FAINT   *adj* **FAINTER, FAINTEST** lacking strength or vigor

FAINT   *v* **-ED, -ING, -S** to lose consciousness

FAINTER   *n* pl. **-S** one that faints

FAINTISH   *adj* somewhat faint

FAINTLY   *adv* in a faint manner

FAIR   *adj* **FAIRER, FAIREST** free from bias, dishonesty, or injustice

FAIR   *v* **-ED, -ING, -S** to make smooth

FAIRGOER   *n* pl. **-S** one who attends a fair

FAIRIES   pl. of fairy

FAIRING   *n* pl. **-S** a structure on an aircraft serving to reduce drag

FAIRISH   *adj* moderately good

FAIRLEAD   *n* pl. **-S** a device used to hold a ship's rigging in place

FAIRLY   *adv* in a fair manner

FAIRNESS   *n* pl. **-ES** the quality of being fair

FAIRWAY   *n* pl. **-WAYS** the mowed part of a golf course between tee and green

FAIRY   *n* pl. **FAIRIES** an imaginary supernatural being

FAIRY   *adj* **FAIRIER, FAIRIEST** pertaining to or resembling a fairy

FAIRYISM   *n* pl. **-S** the quality of being like a fairy

FAITH   *v* **-ED, -ING, -S** to believe or trust

FAITHFUL   *n* pl. **-S** a loyal follower or member

FAITOUR   *n* pl. **-S** an impostor

FAJITA   *n* pl. **-S** marinated and grilled beef, chicken, or shrimp served with a flour tortilla

FAKE   *v* **FAKED, FAKING, FAKES** to contrive and present as genuine

FAKEER   *n* pl. **-S** fakir

FAKER   *n* pl. **-S** one that fakes

FAKERY   *n* pl. **-ERIES** the practice of faking

FAKEY   *adj* not genuine; phony

FAKIE   *n* pl. **-S** a movement in skateboarding and snowboarding

FAKING   present participle of fake

FAKIR   *n* pl. **-S** a Hindu ascetic

FALAFEL   *n* pl. **-S** ground spiced vegetables formed into patties

FALBALA   *n* pl. **-S** a trimming for a woman's garment

FALCATE	*adj* curved and tapering to a point
FALCATED	*adj* falcate
FALCES	pl. of falx
FALCHION	*n* pl. **-S** a broad-bladed sword
FALCON	*n* pl. **-S** a bird of prey
FALCONER	*n* pl. **-S** one that hunts with hawks
FALCONET	*n* pl. **-S** a small falcon
FALCONRY	*n* pl. **-RIES** the sport of hunting with falcons
FALDERAL	*n* pl. **-S** nonsense
FALDEROL	*n* pl. **-S** falderal
FALL	*v* **FELL, FALLEN, FALLING, FALLS** to descend under the force of gravity
FALLACY	*n* pl. **-CIES** a false idea
FALLAL	*n* pl. **-S** a showy article of dress
FALLAWAY	*n* pl. **-AWAYS** a shot in basketball
FALLBACK	*n* pl. **-S** an act of retreating
FALLEN	past participle of fall
FALLER	*n* pl. **-S** one that falls
FALLFISH	*n* pl. **-ES** a freshwater fish
FALLIBLE	*adj* capable of erring **FALLIBLY** *adv*
FALLING	*n* pl. **-S** the felling of trees for timber
FALLOFF	*n* pl. **-S** a decline in quantity or quality
FALLOUT	*n* pl. **-S** radioactive debris resulting from a nuclear explosion
FALLOW	*v* **-ED, -ING, -S** to plow and leave unseeded
FALSE	*adj* **FALSER, FALSEST** contrary to truth or fact **FALSELY** *adv*
FALSETTO	*n* pl. **-TOS** an artificially high voice
FALSIE	*n* pl. **-S** a pad worn within a brassiere
FALSIFY	*v* **-FIED, -FYING, -FIES** to represent falsely
FALSITY	*n* pl. **-TIES** something false
FALTBOAT	*n* pl. **-S** a collapsible boat resembling a kayak
FALTER	*v* **-ED, -ING, -S** to hesitate
FALTERER	*n* pl. **-S** one that falters
FALX	*n* pl. **FALCES** a sickle-shaped structure
FAME	*v* **FAMED, FAMING, FAMES** to make famous
FAMELESS	*adj* not famous
FAMILIAL	*adj* pertaining to a family

FAMILIAR	*n* pl. **-S** a close friend or associate
FAMILISM	*n* pl. **-S** a social structure in which the family takes precedence over the individual **FAMILIST** *adj*
FAMILY	*n* pl. **-LIES** a group of persons related by blood or marriage
FAMINE	*n* pl. **-S** a widespread scarcity of food
FAMING	present participle of fame
FAMISH	*v* **-ED, -ING, -ES** to suffer extreme hunger
FAMOUS	*adj* well-known **FAMOUSLY** *adv*
FAMULUS	*n* pl. **-LI** a servant or attendant
FAN	*v* **FANNED, FANNING, FANS** to cool or refresh with a fan (a device for putting air into motion)
FANATIC	*n* pl. **-S** a zealot
FANBOY	*n* pl. **-BOYS** a male who is an enthusiastic devotee of something
FANCIED	past tense of fancy
FANCIER	*n* pl. **-S** one that has a special liking for something
FANCIES	present 3d person sing. of fancy
FANCIFUL	*adj* unrealistic
FANCIFY	*v* **-FIED, -FYING, -FIES** to make fancy
FANCY	*adj* **-CIER, -CIEST** ornamental **FANCILY** *adv*
FANCY	*v* **-CIED, -CYING, -CIES** to take a liking to
FANDANGO	*n* pl. **-GOS** or **-GOES** a lively Spanish dance
FANDOM	*n* pl. **-S** an aggregate of enthusiastic devotees
FANE	*n* pl. **-S** a temple
FANEGA	*n* pl. **-S** a Spanish unit of dry measure
FANEGADA	*n* pl. **-S** a Spanish unit of area
FANFARE	*n* pl. **-S** a short, lively musical flourish
FANFARON	*n* pl. **-S** a braggart
FANFIC	*n* pl. **-S** fiction written by fans of an admired work
FANFOLD	*v* **-ED, -ING, -S** to fold paper like a fan
FANG	*n* pl. **-S** a long, pointed tooth **FANGED, FANGLESS, FANGLIKE** *adj*
FANGA	*n* pl. **-S** fanega
FANGIRL	*n* pl. **-S** a female who is an enthusiastic devotee of something

FANION *n* pl. **-S** a small flag

FANJET *n* pl. **-S** a type of jet engine

FANLIGHT *n* pl. **-S** a type of window

FANLIKE *adj* resembling a fan

FANNED past tense of fan

FANNER *n* pl. **-S** one that fans

FANNING present participle of fan

FANNY *n* pl. **-NIES** the buttocks

FANO *n* pl. **FANOS** a fanon

FANON *n* pl. **-S** a cape worn by the pope

FANTAIL *n* pl. **-S** a fan-shaped tail or end

FANTASIA *n* pl. **-S** a free-form musical composition

FANTASIE *n* pl. **-S** a fantasia

FANTASIED past tense of fantasy

FANTASM *n* pl. **-S** phantasm

FANTAST *n* pl. **-S** an impractical person

FANTASY *v* **-SIED, -SYING, -SIES** to imagine

FANTOD *n* pl. **-S** an emotional outburst

FANTOM *n* pl. **-S** phantom

FANUM *n* pl. **-S** fanon

FANWISE *adj* spread out like an open fan

FANWORT *n* pl. **-S** an aquatic plant

FANZINE *n* pl. **-S** a magazine written by and for enthusiastic devotees

FAQIR *n* pl. **-S** fakir

FAQUIR *n* pl. **-S** fakir

FAR *adv* **FARTHER, FARTHEST** or **FURTHER, FURTHEST** at or to a great distance

FARAD *n* pl. **-S** a unit of electrical capacitance

FARADAIC *adj* faradic

FARADAY *n* pl. **-DAYS** a unit of electricity

FARADIC *adj* pertaining to a type of electric current

FARADISE *v* **-DISED, -DISING, -DISES** to faradize

FARADISM *n* pl. **-S** the use of faradic current for therapeutic purposes

FARADIZE *v* **-DIZED, -DIZING, -DIZES** to treat by faradism

FARAWAY *adj* distant

FARCE *v* **FARCED, FARCING, FARCES** to fill out with witty material

FARCER *n* pl. **-S** farceur

FARCEUR *n* pl. **-S** a joker

FARCI *adj* stuffed with finely chopped meat

FARCICAL *adj* absurd

FARCIE *adj* farci

FARCING present participle of farce

FARCY *n* pl. **-CIES** a disease of horses

FARD *v* **-ED, -ING, -S** to apply cosmetics to

FARDEL *n* pl. **-S** a bundle

FARE *v* **FARED, FARING, FARES** to get along

FAREBOX *n* pl. **-ES** a receptacle for fares on a bus

FARER *n* pl. **-S** a traveler

FAREWELL *v* **-ED, -ING, -S** to say goodby

FARFAL *n* pl. **-S** farfel

FARFALLE *n* pl. **-S** pasta in the shape of bow ties

FARFEL *n* pl. **-S** noodles in the form of small pellets or granules

FARINA *n* pl. **-S** a fine meal made from cereal grain

FARING present participle of fare

FARINHA *n* pl. **-S** a meal made from the root of the cassava

FARINOSE *adj* resembling farina

FARL *n* pl. **-S** a thin oatmeal cake

FARLE *n* pl. **-S** farl

FARM *v* **-ED, -ING, -S** to manage and cultivate as a farm (a tract of land devoted to agriculture) **FARMABLE** *adj*

FARMER *n* pl. **-S** one that farms

FARMHAND *n* pl. **-S** a farm laborer

FARMING *n* pl. **-S** the business of operating a farm

FARMLAND *n* pl. **-S** cultivated land

FARMWIFE *n* pl. **-WIVES** a farmer's wife

FARMWORK *n* pl. **-S** labor done on a farm

FARMYARD *n* pl. **-S** an area surrounded by farm buildings

FARNESOL *n* pl. **-S** an alcohol used in perfumes

FARNESS *n* pl. **-ES** the state of being far off or apart

FARO *n* pl. **FAROS** a card game

FAROLITO *n* pl. **-TOS** a candle in a paper bag weighted with sand

FAROUCHE *adj* sullenly shy

FARRAGO *n* pl. **-GOES** or **-GOS** a confused mixture

FARRIER *n* pl. **-S** one that shoes horses

FARRIERY *n* pl. **-ERIES** the trade of a farrier

FARROW *v* **-ED, -ING, -S** to give birth to a litter of pigs

FARSIDE *n* pl. **-S** the farther side

FARTHER a comparative of far

FARTHEST a superlative of far

FARTHING *n* pl. **-S** a former British coin

FARTLEK *n* pl. **-S** an athletic training technique

FASCES *n* pl. **FASCES** an ancient Roman symbol of power

FASCIA *n* pl. **-CIAS** or **-CIAE** a broad and distinct band of color **FASCIAL, FASCIATE** *adj*

FASCICLE *n* pl. **-S** a small bundle

FASCINE *n* pl. **-S** a bundle of sticks used in building fortifications

FASCISM *n* pl. **-S** an oppressive political system

FASCIST *n* pl. **-S** an advocate of fascism

FASCITIS *n* pl. **-TISES** inflammation of a connective tissue

FASH *v* **-ED, -ING, -ES** to annoy

FASHION *v* **-ED, -ING, -S** to give a particular shape or form to

FASHIONY *adj* fashionable, trendy

FASHIOUS *adj* annoying

FAST *adj* **FASTER, FASTEST** moving or able to move quickly

FAST *v* **-ED, -ING, -S** to abstain from eating

FASTBACK *n* pl. **-S** a type of automobile roof

FASTBALL *n* pl. **-S** a type of pitch in baseball

FASTEN *v* **-ED, -ING, -S** to secure

FASTENER *n* pl. **-S** one that fastens

FASTING *n* pl. **-S** abstention from eating

FASTNESS *n* pl. **-ES** the quality of being fast

FASTUOUS *adj* arrogant

FAT *adj* **FATTER, FATTEST** having an abundance of flesh

FAT *v* **FATTED, FATTING, FATS** to make fat

FATAL *adj* causing or capable of causing death

FATALISM *n* pl. **-S** the doctrine that all events are predetermined

FATALIST *n* pl. **-S** a believer in fatalism

FATALITY *n* pl. **-TIES** a death resulting from an unexpected occurrence

FATALLY *adv* in a fatal manner

FATBACK *n* pl. **-S** a marine fish

FATBIRD *n* pl. **-S** a wading bird

FATE *v* **FATED, FATING, FATES** to destine

FATEFUL *adj* decisively important

FATHEAD *n* pl. **-S** a dolt

FATHER *v* **-ED, -ING, -S** to cause to exist

FATHERLY *adj* paternal

FATHOM *v* **-ED, -ING, -S** to understand

FATHOMER *n* pl. **-S** one that fathoms

FATIDIC *adj* pertaining to prophecy

FATIGUE *v* **-TIGUED, -TIGUING, -TIGUES** to weary

FATING present participle of fate

FATLESS *adj* having no fat

FATLIKE *adj* resembling fat

FATLING *n* pl. **-S** a young animal fattened for slaughter

FATLY *adv* in the manner of one that is fat

FATNESS *n* pl. **-ES** the state of being fat

FATSTOCK *n* pl. **-S** livestock that is fat and ready for market

FATTED past tense of fat

FATTEN *v* **-ED, -ING, -S** to make fat

FATTENER *n* pl. **-S** one that fattens

FATTER comparative of fat

FATTEST superlative of fat

FATTIER comparative of fatty

FATTIES pl. of fatty

FATTIEST superlative of fatty

FATTILY *adv* in a fatty manner

FATTING present participle of fat

FATTISH *adj* somewhat fat

FATTY *adj* **-TIER, -TIEST** greasy; oily

FATTY *n* pl. **-TIES** one that is fat

FATUITY *n* pl. **-ITIES** something foolish or stupid

FATUOUS *adj* smugly stupid

FATWA *n* pl. **-S** an Islamic legal decree

FATWOOD *n* pl. **-S** wood used for kindling

FAUBOURG *n* pl. **-S** a suburb

FAUCAL   *n* pl. **-S** a sound produced in the fauces

FAUCES   *n/pl* the passage from the mouth to the pharynx

FAUCET   *n* pl. **-S** a device for controlling the flow of liquid from a pipe

FAUCETRY   *n* pl. **-TRIES** an array of faucets

FAUCIAL   *adj* pertaining to the fauces

FAUGH   *interj* — used to express disgust

FAULD   *n* pl. **-S** a piece of armor below the breastplate

FAULT   *v* **-ED, -ING, -S** to criticize

FAULTY   *adj* **FAULTIER, FAULTIEST** imperfect **FAULTILY** *adv*

FAUN   *n* pl. **-S** a woodland deity of Roman mythology **FAUNLIKE** *adj*

FAUNA   *n* pl. **-NAS** or **-NAE** the animal life of a particular region **FAUNAL** *adj* **FAUNALLY** *adv*

FAUNIST   *n* pl. **-S** a specialist on faunas

FAUTEUIL   *n* pl. **-S** an armchair

FAUVE   *n* pl. **-S** a fauvist

FAUVISM   *n* pl. **-S** a movement in painting

FAUVIST   *n* pl. **-S** an advocate of fauvism

FAUX   *adj* not genuine; fake

FAVA   *n* pl. **-S** the edible seed of a climbing vine

FAVE   *n* pl. **-S** a favorite

FAVELA   *n* pl. **-S** a slum area

FAVELLA   *n* pl. **-S** favela

FAVISM   *n* pl. **-S** an acute anemia

FAVONIAN   *adj* pertaining to the west wind

FAVOR   *v* **-ED, -ING, -S** to regard with approval

FAVORER   *n* pl. **-S** one that favors

FAVORITE   *n* pl. **-S** a person or thing preferred above all others

FAVOUR   *v* **-ED, -ING, -S** to favor

FAVOURER   *n* pl. **-S** favorer

FAVUS   *n* pl. **-ES** a skin disease

FAWN   *v* **-ED, -ING, -S** to seek notice or favor by servile demeanor

FAWNER   *n* pl. **-S** one that fawns

FAWNLIKE   *adj* resembling a young deer

FAWNY   *adj* **FAWNIER, FAWNIEST** of a yellowish-brown color

FAX   *v* **-ED, -ING, -ES** to transmit and reproduce by electronic means **FAXABLE** *adj*

FAY   *v* **-ED, -ING, -S** to join closely

FAYALITE   *n* pl. **-S** a mineral

FAZE   *v* **FAZED, FAZING, FAZES** to disturb the composure of

FAZENDA   *n* pl. **-S** a Brazilian plantation

FE   *n* pl. **-S** a Hebrew letter

FEAL   *adj* loyal

FEALTY   *n* pl. **-TIES** loyalty

FEAR   *v* **-ED, -ING, -S** to be afraid of

FEARER   *n* pl. **-S** one that fears

FEARFUL   *adj* **-FULLER, -FULLEST** afraid

FEARLESS   *adj* unafraid

FEARSOME   *adj* frightening

FEASANCE   *n* pl. **-S** the performance of a condition, obligation, or duty

FEASE   *v* **FEASED, FEASING, FEASES** to faze

FEASIBLE   *adj* capable of being done **FEASIBLY** *adv*

FEAST   *v* **-ED, -ING, -S** to eat sumptuously

FEASTER   *n* pl. **-S** one that feasts

FEASTFUL   *adj* festive

FEAT   *adj* **FEATER, FEATEST** skillful

FEAT   *n* pl. **-S** a notable act or achievement

FEATHER   *v* **-ED, -ING, -S** to cover with feathers (horny structures that form the principal covering of birds)

FEATHERY   *adj* **-ERIER, -ERIEST** resembling feathers

FEATLY   *adj* **-LIER, -LIEST** graceful

FEATURE   *v* **-TURED, -TURING, -TURES** to give special prominence to

FEAZE   *v* **FEAZED, FEAZING, FEAZES** to faze

FEBRIFIC   *adj* feverish

FEBRILE   *adj* feverish

FECAL   *adj* pertaining to feces

FECES   *n/pl* bodily waste discharged through the anus

FECIAL   *n* pl. **-S** fetial

FECK   *n* pl. **-S** value

FECKLESS   *adj* worthless

FECKLY   *adv* almost

FECULA   *n* pl. **-LAE** fecal matter

FECULENT   *adj* foul with impurities

FECUND   *adj* fruitful

FED   *n* pl. **-S** a federal agent

FEDAYEE *n pl.* **-YEEN** an Arab commando

FEDERACY *n pl.* **-CIES** an alliance

FEDERAL *n pl.* **-S** a supporter of a type of central government

FEDERATE *v* **-ATED, -ATING, -ATES** to unite in an alliance

FEDEX *v* **-ED, -ING, -ES** to send by Federal Express

FEDORA *n pl.* **-S** a type of hat

FEE *v* **FEED, FEEING, FEES** to pay a fee (a fixed charge) to

FEEB *n pl.* **-S** a wimp (a weak or ineffective person)

FEEBLE *adj* **-BLER, -BLEST** weak **FEEBLY** *adv*

FEEBLISH *adj* somewhat feeble

FEED *v* **FED, FEEDING, FEEDS** to give food to **FEEDABLE** *adj*

FEEDBACK *n pl.* **-S** the return of a portion of the output to the input

FEEDBAG *n pl.* **-S** a bag for feeding horses

FEEDBOX *n pl.* **-ES** a box for animal feed

FEEDER *n pl.* **-S** one that feeds

FEEDHOLE *n pl.* **-S** one of a series of holes in paper tape

FEEDING *n pl.* **-S** the act of giving food to a person or animal

FEEDLOT *n pl.* **-S** a plot of land on which livestock is fattened

FEEDYARD *n pl.* **-S** a feedlot

FEEL *v* **FELT, FEELING, FEELS** to perceive through the sense of touch

FEELER *n pl.* **-S** a tactile organ

FEELESS *adj* requiring no fee

FEELING *n pl.* **-S** the function or power of perceiving by touch

FEET pl. of foot

FEETLESS *adj* having no feet

FEEZE *v* **FEEZED, FEEZING, FEEZES** to faze

FEH *n pl.* **-S** peh

FEIGN *v* **-ED, -ING, -S** to pretend

FEIGNER *n pl.* **-S** one that feigns

FEIJOA *n pl.* **-S** a green edible fruit

FEINT *v* **-ED, -ING, -S** to make a deceptive movement

FEIRIE *adj* nimble

FEIST *n pl.* **-S** a small dog of mixed breed

FEISTY *adj* **FEISTIER, FEISTIEST** full of nervous energy **FEISTILY** *adv*

FELAFEL *n pl.* **-S** falafel

FELDSHER *n pl.* **-S** a medical worker in Russia

FELDSPAR *n pl.* **-S** a mineral

FELICITY *n pl.* **-TIES** happiness

FELID *n pl.* **-S** a feline

FELINE *n pl.* **-S** an animal of the cat family

FELINELY *adv* in a catlike manner

FELINITY *n pl.* **-TIES** the quality of being catlike

FELL *adj* **FELLER, FELLEST** cruel

FELL *v* **-ED, -ING, -S** to cause to fall

FELLA *n pl.* **-S** a man or boy

FELLABLE *adj* capable of being felled

FELLAH *n pl.* **-LAHS, -LAHIN** or **-LAHEEN** a peasant or laborer in Arab countries

FELLATE *v* **-LATED, -LATING, -LATES** to perform fellatio

FELLATIO *n pl.* **-TIOS** oral stimulation of the penis

FELLATOR *n pl.* **-S** one that fellates

FELLER *n pl.* **-S** one that fells

FELLIES pl. of felly

FELLNESS *n pl.* **-ES** extreme cruelty

FELLOE *n pl.* **-S** the rim of a wheel

FELLOW *v* **-ED, -ING, -S** to produce an equal to

FELLOWLY *adj* friendly

FELLY *n pl.* **-LIES** a felloe

FELON *n pl.* **-S** a person who has committed a felony

FELONRY *n pl.* **-RIES** the whole class of felons

FELONY *n pl.* **-NIES** a grave crime

FELSIC *adj* consisting of feldspar and silicates

FELSITE *n pl.* **-S** an igneous rock **FELSITIC** *adj*

FELSPAR *n pl.* **-S** feldspar

FELSTONE *n pl.* **-S** felsite

FELT *v* **-ED, -ING, -S** to mat together

FELTING *n pl.* **-S** felted material

FELTLIKE *adj* like a cloth made from wool

FELTY *adj* **FELTIER, FELTIEST** resembling a cloth made from wool

FELUCCA *n pl.* **-S** a swift sailing vessel

FELWORT *n* pl. **-S** a flowering plant

FEM *n* pl. **-S** a passive homosexual

FEMALE *n* pl. **-S** an individual that bears young or produces ova

FEME *n* pl. **-S** a wife

FEMINACY *n* pl. **-CIES** the state of being a female

FEMINIE *n/pl* women collectively

FEMININE *n* pl. **-S** a word or form having feminine gender

FEMINISE *v* **-NISED, -NISING, -NISES** to feminize

FEMINISM *n* pl. **-S** a doctrine advocating rights for women equal to those of men

FEMINIST *n* pl. **-S** a supporter of feminism

FEMINITY *n* pl. **-TIES** the quality of being womanly

FEMINIZE *v* **-NIZED, -NIZING, -NIZES** to make womanly

FEMME *n* pl. **-S** a woman

FEMORAL *adj* pertaining to the femur

FEMUR *n* pl. **-MURS** or **-MORA** a bone of the leg

FEN *n* pl. **-S** a marsh

FENAGLE *v* **-GLED, -GLING, -GLES** to finagle

FENCE *v* **FENCED, FENCING, FENCES** to practice the art of fencing

FENCER *n* pl. **-S** one that fences

FENCEROW *n* pl. **-S** the land occupied by a fence

FENCIBLE *n* pl. **-S** a soldier enlisted for home service only

FENCING *n* pl. **-S** the art of using a sword in attack and defense

FEND *v* **-ED, -ING, -S** to ward off

FENDER *n* pl. **-S** a metal guard over the wheel of a motor vehicle **FENDERED** *adj*

FENESTRA *n* pl. **-TRAE** a small anatomical opening

FENING *n* pl. **-S** a monetary unit of Bosnia and Herzegovina

FENLAND *n* pl. **-S** marshy ground

FENNEC *n* pl. **-S** an African fox

FENNEL *n* pl. **-S** a perennial herb

FENNY *adj* **-NIER, -NIEST** marshy

FENTANYL *n* pl. **-S** a narcotic opioid

FENTHION *n* pl. **-S** an insecticide

FENURON *n* pl. **-S** an herbicide

FEOD *n* pl. **-S** a fief

FEODARY *n* pl. **-RIES** a vassal

FEOFF *v* **-ED, -ING, -S** to grant a fief to

FEOFFEE *n* pl. **-S** one to whom a fief is granted

FEOFFER *n* pl. **-S** one that grants a fief to another

FEOFFOR *n* pl. **-S** feoffer

FER *prep* for

FERACITY *n* pl. **-TIES** the state of being fruitful

FERAL *n* pl. **-S** a wild beast

FERBAM *n* pl. **-S** a fungicide

FERE *n* pl. **-S** a companion

FERETORY *n* pl. **-RIES** a receptacle in which sacred relics are kept

FERIA *n* pl. **-RIAS** or **-RIAE** a weekday of a church calendar on which no feast is celebrated **FERIAL** *adj*

FERINE *adj* feral

FERITY *n* pl. **-TIES** wildness

FERLIE *n* pl. **-S** a strange sight

FERLY *n* pl. **-LIES** ferlie

FERMATA *n* pl. **-TAS** or **-TE** the sustaining of a musical note, chord, or rest beyond its written time value

FERMENT *v* **-ED, -ING, -S** to undergo a type of chemical reaction

FERMI *n* pl. **-S** a unit of length

FERMION *n* pl. **-S** a type of atomic particle

FERMIUM *n* pl. **-S** a radioactive element

FERN *n* pl. **-S** a flowerless vascular plant **FERNLESS, FERNLIKE** *adj*

FERNERY *n* pl. **-ERIES** a place in which ferns are grown

FERNINST *prep* near to

FERNY *adj* **FERNIER, FERNIEST** abounding in ferns

FEROCITY *n* pl. **-TIES** fierceness

FERRATE *n* pl. **-S** a chemical salt

FERREL *v* **-RELED, -RELING, -RELS** or **-RELLED, -RELLING, -RELS** to ferrule

FERREOUS *adj* containing iron

FERRET *v* **-ED, -ING, -S** to search out by careful investigation

FERRETER *n* pl. **-S** one that ferrets

FERRETY *adj* suggestive of a ferret (a polecat)

FERRIAGE *n* pl. **-S** transportation by ferry

FERRIC *adj* pertaining to iron

FERRIED past tense of ferry

FERRIES present 3d person sing. of ferry

FERRITE *n* pl. **-S** a magnetic substance **FERRITIC** *adj*

FERRITIN *n* pl. **-S** a protein that contains iron

FERROUS *adj* pertaining to iron

FERRULE *v* **-RULED, -RULING, -RULES** to furnish with a metal ring or cap to prevent splitting

FERRUM *n* pl. **-S** iron

FERRY *v* **-RIED, -RYING, -RIES** to transport by ferry (a type of boat)

FERRYMAN *n* pl. **-MEN** one who operates a ferry

FERTILE *adj* capable of reproducing

FERULA *n* pl. **-LAS** or **-LAE** a flat piece of wood

FERULE *v* **-ULED, -ULING, -ULES** to ferrule

FERVENCY *n* pl. **-CIES** fervor

FERVENT *adj* marked by fervor

FERVID *adj* fervent **FERVIDLY** *adv*

FERVOR *n* pl. **-S** great warmth or intensity

FERVOUR *n* pl. **-S** fervor

FESCUE *n* pl. **-S** a perennial grass

FESS *v* **-ED, -ING, -ES** to confess

FESSE *n* pl. **-S** a horizontal band across the middle of a heraldic shield

FESSWISE *adv* horizontally

FEST *n* pl. **-S** a gathering for an activity

FESTA *n* pl. **-S** a religious festival

FESTAL *adj* festive **FESTALLY** *adv*

FESTER *v* **-ED, -ING, -S** to generate pus

FESTIVAL *n* pl. **-S** a day or time of celebration

FESTIVE *adj* of or befitting a festival

FESTOON *v* **-ED, -ING, -S** to hang decorative chains or strips on

FET *v* **FETTED, FETTING, FETS** to fetch

FETA *n* pl. **-S** a Greek cheese

FETAL *adj* pertaining to a fetus

FETATION *n* pl. **-S** the development of a fetus

FETCH *v* **-ED, -ING, -ES** to go after and bring back

FETCHER *n* pl. **-S** one that fetches

FETE *v* **FETED, FETING, FETES** to honor with a celebration

FETERITA *n* pl. **-S** a cereal grass

FETIAL *n* pl. **-S** a priest of ancient Rome

FETIALIS *n* pl. **-LES** fetial

FETICH *n* pl. **-ES** fetish

FETICIDE *n* pl. **-S** the killing of a fetus

FETID *adj* having an offensive odor **FETIDLY** *adv*

FETIDITY *n* pl. **-TIES** the state of being fetid

FETING present participle of fete

FETISH *n* pl. **-ES** an object believed to have magical power

FETLOCK *n* pl. **-S** a joint of a horse's leg

FETOLOGY *n* pl. **-GIES** the branch of medicine dealing with the fetus

FETOR *n* pl. **-S** an offensive odor

FETTED past tense of fet

FETTER *v* **-ED, -ING, -S** to shackle

FETTERER *n* pl. **-S** one that fetters

FETTING present participle of fet

FETTLE *v* **-TLED, -TLING, -TLES** to cover the hearth of with fettling

FETTLER *n* pl. **-S** one who fettles

FETTLING *n* pl. **-S** loose material thrown on the hearth of a furnace to protect it

FETUS *n* pl. **-ES** the unborn organism carried within the womb in the later stages of its development

FEU *v* **-ED, -ING, -S** to grant land to under Scottish feudal law

FEUAR *n* pl. **-S** one granted land under Scottish feudal law

FEUD *v* **-ED, -ING, -S** to engage in a feud (a bitter, continuous hostility)

FEUDAL *adj* pertaining to a political and economic system of medieval Europe **FEUDALLY** *adv*

FEUDARY *n* pl. **-RIES** a vassal

FEUDIST *n* pl. **-S** one that feuds

FEVER *v* **-ED, -ING, -S** to affect with fever (abnormal elevation of the body temperature)

FEVERFEW *n* pl. **-S** a perennial herb

FEVERISH *adj* having a fever

FEVEROUS *adj* feverish

FEW *adj* **FEWER, FEWEST** amounting to or consisting of a small number

FEWNESS *n* pl. **-ES** the state of being few

FEWTRILS *n/pl* things of little value

FEY *adj* **FEYER, FEYEST** crazy **FEYLY** *adv*

FEYNESS *n* pl. **-ES** the state of being fey

FEZ *n* pl. **FEZES** or **FEZZES** a brimless cap worn by men in the Near East **FEZZED, FEZZY** *adj*

FIACRE *n* pl. **-S** a small carriage

FIANCE *n* pl. **-S** a man engaged to be married

FIANCEE *n* pl. **-S** a woman engaged to be married

FIAR *n* pl. **-S** the holder of a type of absolute ownership of land under Scottish law

FIASCO *n* pl. **-COES** or **-CHI** a wine bottle

FIASCO *n* pl. **-COS** or **-COES** a complete failure

FIAT *n* pl. **-S** an authoritative order

FIB *v* **FIBBED, FIBBING, FIBS** to tell a trivial lie

FIBBER *n* pl. **-S** one that fibs

FIBER *n* pl. **-S** a thread or threadlike object or structure **FIBERED** *adj*

FIBERIZE *v* **-IZED, -IZING, -IZES** to break into fibers

FIBRANNE *n* pl. **-S** a fabric made of spun-rayon yarn

FIBRE *n* pl. **-S** fiber **FIBRED** *adj*

FIBRIL *n* pl. **-S** a small fiber

FIBRILLA *n* pl. **-LAE** a fibril

FIBRIN *n* pl. **-S** an insoluble protein

FIBROID *n* pl. **-S** a fibroma

FIBROIN *n* pl. **-S** an insoluble protein

FIBROMA *n* pl. **-MAS** or **-MATA** a benign tumor composed of fibrous tissue

FIBROSIS *n* pl. **-BROSES** the development of excess fibrous tissue in a bodily organ **FIBROTIC** *adj*

FIBROUS *adj* containing, consisting of, or resembling fibers

FIBSTER *n* pl. **-S** one that fibs

FIBULA *n* pl. **-LAS** or **-LAE** a bone of the leg **FIBULAR** *adj*

FICE *n* pl. **-S** a feist

FICHE *n* pl. **-S** a sheet of microfilm

FICHU *n* pl. **-S** a woman's scarf

FICIN *n* pl. **-S** an enzyme

FICKLE *adj* **-LER, -LEST** not constant or loyal **FICKLY** *adv*

FICO *n* pl. **-COES** something of little worth

FICTILE *adj* moldable

FICTION *n* pl. **-S** a literary work whose content is produced by the imagination

FICTIVE *adj* imaginary

FICUS *n* pl. **-ES** a tropical tree

FID *n* pl. **-S** a square bar used as a support for a topmast

FIDDLE *v* **-DLED, -DLING, -DLES** to play a violin

FIDDLER *n* pl. **-S** one that fiddles

FIDDLING *n* pl. **-S** the action of playing a violin

FIDDLY *adj* **FIDDLIER, FIDDLIEST** intricately difficult to handle

FIDEISM *n* pl. **-S** reliance on faith rather than reason

FIDEIST *n* pl. **-S** a believer in fideism

FIDELITY *n* pl. **-TIES** loyalty

FIDGE *v* **FIDGED, FIDGING, FIDGES** to fidget

FIDGET *v* **-ED, -ING, -S** to move nervously or restlessly

FIDGETER *n* pl. **-S** one that fidgets

FIDGETY *adj* nervously restless

FIDGING present participle of fidge

FIDO *n* pl. **-DOS** a defective coin

FIDUCIAL *adj* based on faith or trust

FIE *interj* — used to express disapproval

FIEF *n* pl. **-S** a feudal estate

FIEFDOM *n* pl. **-S** a fief

FIELD *v* **-ED, -ING, -S** to play as a fielder

FIELDER *n* pl. **-S** one that catches or picks up a ball in play

FIEND *n* pl. **-S** a demon

FIENDISH *adj* extremely wicked or cruel

FIERCE *adj* **FIERCER, FIERCEST** violently hostile or aggressive **FIERCELY** *adv*

FIERY *adj* **-ERIER, -ERIEST** intensely hot **FIERILY** *adv*

FIESTA *n* pl. **-S** a festival

FIFE *v* **FIFED, FIFING, FIFES** to play a fife (a high-pitched flute)

FIFER *n* pl. **-S** one that plays a fife

FIFTEEN *n* pl. **-S** a number

FIFTH   *n* pl. **-S** one of five equal parts

FIFTHLY   *adv* in the fifth place

FIFTIETH   *n* pl. **-S** one of fifty equal parts

FIFTY   *n* pl. **-TIES** a number

FIFTYISH   *adj* being about fifty years old

FIG   *v* **FIGGED, FIGGING, FIGS** to adorn

FIGEATER   *n* pl. **-S** a large beetle

FIGHT   *v* **FOUGHT, FIGHTING, FIGHTS** to attempt to defeat an adversary

FIGHTER   *n* pl. **-S** one that fights

FIGHTING   *n* pl. **-S** the act of one that fights

FIGMENT   *n* pl. **-S** a product of mental invention

FIGTREE   *n* pl. **-S** a tree that bears figs (soft, sweet dark fruits)

FIGULINE   *n* pl. **-S** a piece of pottery

FIGURAL   *adj* consisting of human or animal form

FIGURANT   *n* pl. **-S** a ballet dancer who dances only in groups

FIGURATE   *adj* having a definite shape

FIGURE   *v* **-URED, -URING, -URES** to compute

FIGURER   *n* pl. **-S** one that figures

FIGURINE   *n* pl. **-S** a small statue

FIGWORT   *n* pl. **-S** a flowering plant

FIL   *n* pl. **-S** a coin of Iraq and Jordan

FILA   pl. of filum

FILAGREE   *v* **-GREED, -GREEING, -GREES** to filigree

FILAMENT   *n* pl. **-S** a very thin thread or threadlike structure

FILAR   *adj* pertaining to a thread

FILAREE   *n* pl. **-S** a European weed

FILARIA   *n* pl. **-IAE** a parasitic worm **FILARIAL, FILARIAN** *adj*

FILARIID   *n* pl. **-S** filaria

FILATURE   *n* pl. **-S** the reeling of silk from cocoons

FILBERT   *n* pl. **-S** the edible nut of a European shrub

FILCH   *v* **-ED, -ING, -ES** to steal

FILCHER   *n* pl. **-S** one that filches

FILE   *v* **FILED, FILING, FILES** to arrange in order for future reference **FILEABLE** *adj*

FILEFISH   *n* pl. **-ES** a marine fish

FILEMOT   *adj* of a brownish yellow color

FILENAME   *n* pl. **-S** the name of a computer file

FILER   *n* pl. **-S** one that files

FILET   *v* **-ED, -ING, -S** to fillet

FILIAL   *adj* pertaining to a son or daughter **FILIALLY** *adv*

FILIATE   *v* **-ATED, -ATING, -ATES** to bring into close association

FILIBEG   *n* pl. **-S** a pleated skirt worn by Scottish Highlanders

FILICIDE   *n* pl. **-S** the killing of one's child

FILIFORM   *adj* shaped like a filament

FILIGREE   *v* **-GREED, -GREEING, -GREES** to adorn with intricate ornamental work

FILING   *n* pl. **-S** a particle removed by a file

FILISTER   *n* pl. **-S** a groove on a window frame

FILK   *n* pl. **-S** a type of popular music that parodies folk songs

FILL   *v* **-ED, -ING, -S** to put as much as can be held into **FILLABLE** *adj*

FILLE   *n* pl. **-S** a girl

FILLER   *n* pl. **-S** one that fills

FILLET   *v* **-ED, -ING, -S** to cut boneless slices from

FILLETER   *n* pl. **-S** one who fillets

FILLIES   pl. of filly

FILLING   *n* pl. **-S** that which is used to fill something

FILLIP   *v* **-ED, -ING, -S** to strike sharply

FILLO   *n* pl. **-LOS** phyllo

FILLY   *n* pl. **-LIES** a young female horse

FILM   *v* **-ED, -ING, -S** to make a motion picture **FILMABLE** *adj*

FILMCARD   *n* pl. **-S** a fiche

FILMDOM   *n* pl. **-S** the motion-picture industry

FILMER   *n* pl. **-S** one that films

FILMFEST   *n* pl. **-S** a festival at which many films are shown

FILMGOER   *n* pl. **-S** one that goes to see motion pictures

FILMI   *n* pl. **-S** music composed for Indian films

FILMIC   *adj* pertaining to motion pictures

FILMIER   comparative of filmy

FILMIEST   superlative of filmy

FILMILY   *adv* in a filmy manner

FILMLAND   *n* pl. **-S** filmdom

FILMLESS   *adj* having no film

FILMLIKE *adj* resembling film

FILMSET *v* -**SET, -SETTING, -SETS** to photoset

FILMY *adj* **FILMIER, FILMIEST** resembling or covered with film; hazy

FILO *n* pl. -**LOS** phyllo

FILOSE *adj* resembling a thread

FILTER *v* -**ED, -ING, -S** to pass through a filter (a device for removing suspended matter)

FILTERER *n* pl. -**S** one that filters

FILTH *n* pl. -**S** foul or dirty matter

FILTHY *adj* **FILTHIER, FILTHIEST** offensively dirty **FILTHILY** *adv*

FILTRATE *v* -**TRATED, -TRATING, -TRATES** to filter

FILUM *n* pl. -**LA** a threadlike anatomical structure

FIMBLE *n* pl. -**S** the male hemp plant

FIMBRIA *n* pl. -**BRIAE** a fringe or fringe-like structure **FIMBRIAL** *adj*

FIN *v* **FINNED, FINNING, FINS** to equip with fins (external paddle-like structures)

FINABLE *adj* subject to the payment of a fine

FINAGLE *v* -**GLED, -GLING, -GLES** to obtain by trickery

FINAGLER *n* pl. -**S** one that finagles

FINAL *n* pl. -**S** the last examination of an academic course

FINALE *n* pl. -**S** a close or termination of something

FINALIS *n* pl. -**LES** a type of tone in medieval music

FINALISE *v* -**ISED, -ISING, -ISES** finalize

FINALISM *n* pl. -**S** the doctrine that all events are determined by ultimate purposes

FINALIST *n* pl. -**S** a contestant who reaches the last part of a competition

FINALITY *n* pl. -**TIES** the state of being conclusive

FINALIZE *v* -**IZED, -IZING, -IZES** to put into finished form

FINALLY *adv* at the end

FINANCE *v* -**NANCED, -NANCING, -NANCES** to supply the money for

FINBACK *n* pl. -**S** the rorqual

FINCA *n* pl. -**S** an estate in Spanish America

FINCH *n* pl. -**ES** a small bird

FIND *v* **FOUND, FINDING, FINDS** to come upon after a search **FINDABLE** *adj*

FINDER *n* pl. -**S** one that finds

FINDING *n* pl. -**S** something that is found

FINE *adj* **FINER, FINEST** excellent

FINE *v* **FINED, FINING, FINES** to subject to a fine (a monetary penalty)

FINEABLE *adj* finable

FINELY *adv* in a fine manner

FINENESS *n* pl. -**ES** the quality of being fine

FINER comparative of fine

FINERY *n* pl. -**ERIES** elaborate adornment

FINESPUN *adj* developed with extreme care

FINESSE *v* -**NESSED, -NESSING, -NESSES** to bring about by adroit maneuvering

FINEST *n* pl. -**S** the police of a specified city

FINFISH *n* pl. -**ES** a true fish

FINFOOT *n* pl. -**S** an aquatic bird

FINGER *v* -**ED, -ING, -S** to touch with the fingers (the terminating members of the hand)

FINGERER *n* pl. -**S** one that fingers

FINIAL *n* pl. -**S** a crowning ornament **FINIALED** *adj*

FINICAL *adj* finicky

FINICKIN *adj* finicky

FINICKY *adj* -**ICKIER, -ICKIEST** difficult to please

FINIKIN *adj* finicky

FINIKING *adj* finicky

FINING *n* pl. -**S** the clarifying of wines

FINIS *n* pl. -**NISES** the end

FINISH *v* -**ED, -ING, -ES** to bring to an end

FINISHER *n* pl. -**S** one that finishes

FINITE *n* pl. -**S** something that is finite (having definite limits)

FINITELY *adv* to a finite extent

FINITISM *n* pl. -**S** the belief that a particular entity is finite

FINITIST *n* pl. -**S** an advocate of finitism

FINITO *adj* finished

FINITUDE *n* pl. -**S** the state of being finite

FINK *v* -**ED, -ING, -S** to inform to the police

FINLESS	*adj* having no fins
FINLIKE	*adj* resembling a fin
FINMARK	*n* pl. **-S** a former monetary unit of Finland
FINNAN	*n* pl. **-S** smoked haddock
FINNED	past tense of fin
FINNICKY	*adj* **-NICKIER, -NICKIEST** finicky
FINNIER	comparative of finny
FINNIEST	superlative of finny
FINNING	present participle of fin
FINNMARK	*n* pl. **-S** finmark
FINNY	*adj* **-NIER, -NIEST** having or characterized by fins
FINO	*n* pl. **-NOS** a very dry sherry
FINOCHIO	*n* pl. **-CHIOS** a perennial herb
FIORD	*n* pl. **-S** fjord
FIPPLE	*n* pl. **-S** a plug of wood at the mouth of certain wind instruments
FIQUE	*n* pl. **-S** a tropical plant
FIR	*n* pl. **-S** an evergreen tree
FIRE	*v* **FIRED, FIRING, FIRES** to project by discharging from a gun **FIREABLE** *adj*
FIREARM	*n* pl. **-S** a weapon from which a shot is discharged by gunpowder
FIREBACK	*n* pl. **-S** a cast-iron plate along the back of a fireplace
FIREBALL	*n* pl. **-S** a luminous meteor
FIREBASE	*n* pl. **-S** a military base from which fire is directed against the enemy
FIREBIRD	*n* pl. **-S** a brightly colored bird
FIREBOAT	*n* pl. **-S** a boat equipped with fire-fighting apparatus
FIREBOMB	*v* **-ED, -ING, -S** to attack with incendiary bombs
FIREBOX	*n* pl. **-ES** a chamber in which fuel is burned
FIREBRAT	*n* pl. **-S** a small, wingless insect
FIREBUG	*n* pl. **-S** an arsonist
FIRECLAY	*n* pl. **-CLAYS** a heat-resistant clay
FIRED	past tense of fire
FIREDAMP	*n* pl. **-S** a combustible gas
FIREDOG	*n* pl. **-S** an andiron
FIREFANG	*v* **-ED, -ING, -S** to decompose by oxidation
FIREFLY	*n* pl. **-FLIES** a luminous insect
FIREHALL	*n* pl. **-S** a fire station
FIREHOSE	*n* pl. **-S** a hose used by firefighters
FIRELESS	*adj* having no fire
FIRELIT	*adj* lighted by firelight
FIRELOCK	*n* pl. **-S** a type of gun
FIREMAN	*n* pl. **-MEN** a man employed to extinguish fires
FIREPAN	*n* pl. **-S** an open pan for holding live coals
FIREPINK	*n* pl. **-S** a flowering plant
FIREPIT	*n* pl. **-S** a depression dug in the ground in which a fire is made
FIREPLUG	*n* pl. **-S** a hydrant
FIREPOT	*n* pl. **-S** a clay pot filled with burning items
FIRER	*n* pl. **-S** one that fires
FIREREEL	*n* pl. **-S** a fire engine
FIREROOM	*n* pl. **-S** a room containing a ship's boilers
FIRESHIP	*n* pl. **-S** a burning ship sent among the enemy's ships
FIRESIDE	*n* pl. **-S** the area immediately surrounding a fireplace
FIRETRAP	*n* pl. **-S** a building that is likely to catch on fire
FIREWALL	*n* pl. **-S** a computer component that prevents unauthorized access to data
FIREWEED	*n* pl. **-S** a perennial herb
FIREWOOD	*n* pl. **-S** wood used as fuel
FIREWORK	*n* pl. **-S** a device for producing a striking display of light or a loud noise
FIREWORM	*n* pl. **-S** a glowworm
FIRING	*n* pl. **-S** the process of maturing ceramic products by heat
FIRKIN	*n* pl. **-S** a British unit of capacity
FIRM	*adj* **FIRMER, FIRMEST** unyielding to pressure
FIRM	*v* **-ED, -ING, -S** to make firm
FIRMAN	*n* pl. **-S** an edict issued by a Middle Eastern sovereign
FIRMER	*n* pl. **-S** a woodworking tool
FIRMLY	*adv* in a firm manner
FIRMNESS	*n* pl. **-ES** the state of being firm
FIRMWARE	*n* pl. **-S** computer programs permanently stored on a microchip
FIRN	*n* pl. **-S** neve
FIRRY	*adj* **-RIER, -RIEST** abounding in firs
FIRST	*n* pl. **-S** something that precedes all others

FIRSTLY	*adv* before all others	**FISSILE**	*adj* capable of being split
FIRTH	*n* pl. **-S** an inlet of the sea	**FISSION**	*v* **-ED, -ING, -S** to split into parts
FISC	*n* pl. **-S** a state or royal treasury	**FISSIPED**	*n* pl. **-S** a mammal that has separated toes
FISCAL	*n* pl. **-S** a public prosecutor	**FISSURAL**	*adj* pertaining to a long narrow opening
FISCALLY	*adv* with regard to financial matters	**FISSURE**	*v* **-SURED, -SURING, -SURES** to split
FISH	*v* **-ED, -ING, -ES** to catch or try to catch fish (cold-blooded aquatic vertebrates)	**FIST**	*v* **-ED, -ING, -S** to strike with the fist (the hand closed tightly)
FISHABLE	*adj* suitable for fishing	**FISTFUL**	*n* pl. **-S** a handful
FISHBOAT	*n* pl. **-S** a watercraft used for fishing	**FISTIC**	*adj* pertaining to pugilism
FISHBOLT	*n* pl. **-S** a type of bolt	**FISTNOTE**	*n* pl. **-S** a part of a text to which attention is drawn by an index mark
FISHBONE	*n* pl. **-S** a bone of a fish	**FISTULA**	*n* pl. **-LAS** or **-LAE** a duct formed by the imperfect closing of a wound **FISTULAR** *adj*
FISHBOWL	*n* pl. **-S** a bowl in which live fish are kept		
FISHER	*n* pl. **-S** one that fishes	**FIT**	*adj* **FITTER, FITTEST** healthy
FISHERY	*n* pl. **-ERIES** a place for catching fish	**FIT**	*v* **FITTED, FITTING, FITS** to bring to a required form and size
FISHEYE	*n* pl. **-S** a suspicious stare	**FITCH**	*n* pl. **-ES** a polecat
FISHGIG	*n* pl. **-S** a pronged implement for spearing fish	**FITCHEE**	*adj* fitchy
FISHHOOK	*n* pl. **-S** a barbed hook for catching fish	**FITCHET**	*n* pl. **-S** a fitch
		FITCHEW	*n* pl. **-S** a fitch
FISHIER	comparative of fishy	**FITCHY**	*adj* having the arms ending in a point — used of a heraldic cross
FISHIEST	superlative of fishy		
FISHILY	*adv* in a fishy manner	**FITFUL**	*adj* recurring irregularly **FITFULLY** *adv*
FISHING	*n* pl. **-S** the occupation or pastime of catching fish		
FISHKILL	*n* pl. **-S** the sudden destruction of large numbers of fish	**FITLY**	*adv* in a fit manner
		FITMENT	*n* pl. **-S** equipment
FISHLESS	*adj* having no fish	**FITNESS**	*n* pl. **-ES** the state of being fit
FISHLIKE	*adj* resembling a fish	**FITTABLE**	*adj* capable of being fitted
FISHLINE	*n* pl. **-S** a line used in fishing	**FITTED**	past tense of fit
FISHMEAL	*n* pl. **-S** ground dried fish	**FITTER**	*n* pl. **-S** one that fits
FISHNET	*n* pl. **-S** a net for catching fish	**FITTEST**	superlative of fit
FISHPOLE	*n* pl. **-S** a fishing rod	**FITTING**	*n* pl. **-S** a small often standardized accessory part
FISHPOND	*n* pl. **-S** a pond abounding in edible fish		
FISHTAIL	*v* **-ED, -ING, -S** to have the rear end of a moving vehicle slide from side to side	**FIVE**	*n* pl. **-S** a number
		FIVEFOLD	*adj* five times as great
		FIVEPINS	*n/pl* a bowling game
FISHWAY	*n* pl. **-WAYS** a device for enabling fish to pass around a dam	**FIVER**	*n* pl. **-S** a five-dollar bill
FISHWIFE	*n* pl. **-WIVES** a woman who sells fish	**FIX**	*v* **FIXED** or **FIXT, FIXING, FIXES** to repair **FIXABLE** *adj*
FISHWORM	*n* pl. **-S** a worm used as bait	**FIXATE**	*v* **-ATED, -ATING, -ATES** to make stable or stationary
FISHY	*adj* **FISHIER, FISHIEST** of or resembling fish		
		FIXATIF	*n* pl. **-S** fixative
FISSATE	*adj* deeply split	**FIXATION**	*n* pl. **-S** the act of fixating

FIXATIVE   *n* pl. **-S** a substance for preserving paintings or drawings

FIXEDLY   *adv* firmly

FIXER   *n* pl. **-S** one that fixes

FIXINGS   *n/pl* accompaniments to the main dish of a meal

FIXIT   *n* pl. **-S** a person known for fixing things

FIXITY   *n* pl. **-TIES** stability

FIXT   a past tense of fix

FIXTURE   *n* pl. **-S** a permanent part or appendage of a house

FIXURE   *n* pl. **-S** firmness

FIZ   *n* pl. **FIZZES** a hissing or sputtering sound

FIZGIG   *n* pl. **-S** fishgig

FIZZ   *v* **-ED, -ING, -ES** to make a hissing or sputtering sound

FIZZER   *n* pl. **-S** one that fizzes

FIZZES   pl. of fiz

FIZZLE   *v* **-ZLED, -ZLING, -ZLES** to fizz

FIZZY   *adj* **FIZZIER, FIZZIEST** fizzing **FIZZILY** *adv*

FJELD   *n* pl. **-S** a high, barren plateau

FJORD   *n* pl. **-S** a narrow inlet of the sea between steep cliffs **FJORDIC** *adj*

FLAB   *n* pl. **-S** flabby body tissue

FLABBY   *adj* **-BIER, -BIEST** flaccid **FLABBILY** *adv*

FLABELLA   *n/pl* fan-shaped anatomical structures

FLACCID   *adj* lacking firmness

FLACK   *v* **-ED, -ING, -S** to work as a press agent

FLACKERY   *n* pl. **-ERIES** publicity

FLACON   *n* pl. **-S** a small stoppered bottle

FLAG   *v* **FLAGGED, FLAGGING, FLAGS** to mark with a flag (a piece of cloth used as a symbol)

FLAGELLA   *n/pl* long, slender plant shoots

FLAGGER   *n* pl. **-S** one that flags

FLAGGING   *n* pl. **-S** a type of pavement

FLAGGY   *adj* **-GIER, -GIEST** drooping

FLAGLESS   *adj* having no flag

FLAGMAN   *n* pl. **-MEN** one who carries a flag

FLAGON   *n* pl. **-S** a large bulging bottle

FLAGPOLE   *n* pl. **-S** a pole on which a flag is displayed

FLAGRANT   *adj* extremely conspicuous

FLAGSHIP   *n* pl. **-S** a ship bearing the flag of a fleet

FLAIL   *v* **-ED, -ING, -S** to swing freely

FLAIR   *n* pl. **-S** a natural aptitude

FLAK   *n* pl. **FLAK** antiaircraft fire

FLAKE   *v* **FLAKED, FLAKING, FLAKES** to peel off in flakes (flat, thin pieces)

FLAKER   *n* pl. **-S** one that flakes

FLAKEY   *adj* **FLAKIER, FLAKIEST** flaky

FLAKY   *adj* **FLAKIER, FLAKIEST** resembling flakes **FLAKILY** *adv*

FLAM   *v* **FLAMMED, FLAMMING, FLAMS** to deceive

FLAMBE   *v* **-BEED, -BEING, -BES** to douse with a liqueur and ignite

FLAMBEAU   *n* pl. **-BEAUS** or **-BEAUX** a flaming torch

FLAMBEE   *adj* flaming

FLAME   *v* **FLAMED, FLAMING, FLAMES** to burn brightly

FLAMEN   *n* pl. **-MENS** or **-MINES** a priest of ancient Rome

FLAMENCO   *n* pl. **-COS** a strongly rhythmic style of dancing

FLAMEOUT   *n* pl. **-S** a failure of a jet engine in flight

FLAMER   *n* pl. **-S** one that flames

FLAMIER   comparative of flamy

FLAMIEST   superlative of flamy

FLAMINES   a pl. of flamen

FLAMING   present participle of flame

FLAMINGO   *n* pl. **-GOS** or **-GOES** a wading bird

FLAMMED   past tense of flam

FLAMMING   present participle of flam

FLAMY   *adj* **FLAMIER, FLAMIEST** flaming

FLAN   *n* pl. **-S** or **-ES** a type of custard

FLANCARD   *n* pl. **-S** a piece of armor for the side of a horse

FLANERIE   *n* pl. **-S** idleness

FLANEUR   *n* pl. **-S** an idler

FLANGE   *v* **FLANGED, FLANGING, FLANGES** to provide with a protecting rim

FLANGER   *n* pl. **-S** one that flanges

FLANGING   *n* pl. **-S** the providing of a protecting rim on an object

FLANK   *v* **-ED, -ING, -S** to be located at the side of

FLANKEN *n/pl* beef cut from the sides that is boiled with vegetables

FLANKER *n* pl. **-S** one that flanks

FLANNEL *v* **-NELED, -NELING, -NELS** or **-NELLED, -NELLING, -NELS** to cover with flannel (a soft fabric)

FLAP *v* **FLAPPED, FLAPPING, FLAPS** to wave up and down

FLAPERON *n* pl. **-S** an airfoil that functions as a flap and an aileron

FLAPJACK *n* pl. **-S** a pancake

FLAPLESS *adj* having no flap (a flat appendage)

FLAPPED past tense of flap

FLAPPER *n* pl. **-S** one that flaps

FLAPPING present participle of flap

FLAPPY *adj* **-PIER, -PIEST** flapping

FLARE *v* **FLARED, FLARING, FLARES** to burn with a bright, wavering light

FLAREUP *n* pl. **-S** a sudden outbreak

FLASH *v* **-ED, -ING, -ES** to send forth a sudden burst of light

FLASHER *n* pl. **-S** one that flashes

FLASHGUN *n* pl. **-S** a photographic apparatus

FLASHING *n* pl. **-S** sheet metal used in waterproofing a roof

FLASHY *adj* **FLASHIER, FLASHIEST** gaudy **FLASHILY** *adv*

FLASK *n* pl. **-S** a narrow-necked container

FLASKET *n* pl. **-S** a small flask

FLAT *adj* **FLATTER, FLATTEST** having a smooth or even surface

FLAT *v* **FLATTED, FLATTING, FLATS** to flatten

FLATBED *n* pl. **-S** a type of truck or trailer

FLATBOAT *n* pl. **-S** a flat-bottomed boat

FLATCAP *n* pl. **-S** a type of hat

FLATCAR *n* pl. **-S** a railroad car without sides or roof

FLATFISH *n* pl. **-ES** any of an order of marine fishes

FLATFOOT *n* pl. **-FEET** a foot condition

FLATFOOT *v* **-ED, -ING, -S** to walk with a dragging gait

FLATHEAD *n* pl. **-S** a marine food fish

FLATIRON *n* pl. **-S** a device for pressing clothes

FLATLAND *n* pl. **-S** land lacking significant variation in elevation

FLATLET *n* pl. **-S** a type of apartment

FLATLINE *v* **-LINED, -LINING, -LINES** to register as having no brain waves or heartbeat

FLATLING *adv* with a flat side or edge

FLATLONG *adv* flatling

FLATLY *adv* in a flat manner

FLATMATE *n* pl. **-S** one with whom an apartment is shared

FLATNESS *n* pl. **-ES** the state of being flat

FLATPACK *n* pl. **-S** a package for an integrated circuit

FLATTED past tense of flat

FLATTEN *v* **-ED, -ING, -S** to make or become flat

FLATTER *v* **-ED, -ING, -S** to praise excessively

FLATTERY *n* pl. **-TERIES** the act of flattering

FLATTEST superlative of flat

FLATTIE *n* pl. **-S** a flat-heeled shoe

FLATTING present participle of flat

FLATTISH *adj* somewhat flat

FLATTOP *n* pl. **-S** an aircraft carrier

FLATUS *n* pl. **-ES** intestinal gas

FLATWARE *n* pl. **-S** tableware that is fairly flat

FLATWASH *n* pl. **-ES** flatwork

FLATWAYS *adv* flatwise

FLATWISE *adv* with the flat side in a particular position

FLATWORK *n* pl. **-S** laundry that can be ironed mechanically

FLATWORM *n* pl. **-S** a flat-bodied worm

FLAUNT *v* **-ED, -ING, -S** to exhibit in a gaudy manner

FLAUNTER *n* pl. **-S** one that flaunts

FLAUNTY *adj* **FLAUNTIER, FLAUNTIEST** gaudy

FLAUTA *n* pl. **-S** a tortilla rolled around a filling and fried

FLAUTIST *n* pl. **-S** flutist

FLAVA *n* pl. **-S** a style of hip-hop music

FLAVANOL *n* pl. **-S** flavonol

FLAVIN *n* pl. **-S** a yellow pigment

FLAVINE *n* pl. **-S** flavin

FLAVONE *n* pl. **-S** a chemical compound

FLAVONOL *n* pl. **-S** a derivative of flavone

FLAVOR *v* **-ED, -ING, -S** to give flavor (distinctive taste) to

FLAVORER *n* pl. **-S** one that flavors

FLAVORY *adj* full of flavor

FLAVOUR *v* **-ED, -ING, -S** to flavor

FLAVOURY *adj* flavory

FLAW *v* **-ED, -ING, -S** to produce a flaw (an imperfection) in

FLAWLESS *adj* having no flaw

FLAWY *adj* **FLAWIER, FLAWIEST** full of flaws

FLAX *n* pl. **-ES** an annual herb

FLAXEN *adj* of a pale yellow color

FLAXSEED *n* pl. **-S** the seed of flax

FLAXY *adj* **FLAXIER, FLAXIEST** flaxen

FLAY *v* **-ED, -ING, -S** to strip off the skin of

FLAYER *n* pl. **-S** one that flays

FLEA *n* pl. **-S** a parasitic insect

FLEABAG *n* pl. **-S** an inferior hotel

FLEABANE *n* pl. **-S** a flowering plant

FLEABITE *n* pl. **-S** the bite of a flea

FLEAM *n* pl. **-S** a surgical instrument

FLEAPIT *n* pl. **-S** a run-down movie theater

FLEAWORT *n* pl. **-S** a European herb

FLECHE *n* pl. **-S** a steeple

FLECK *v* **-ED, -ING, -S** to mark with flecks (tiny streaks or spots)

FLECKY *adj* flecked

FLECTION *n* pl. **-S** the act of bending

FLED past tense of flee

FLEDGE *v* **FLEDGED, FLEDGING, FLEDGES** to furnish with feathers

FLEDGY *adj* **FLEDGIER, FLEDGIEST** covered with feathers

FLEE *v* **FLED, FLEEING, FLEES** to run away

FLEECE *v* **FLEECED, FLEECING, FLEECES** to remove the coat of wool from

FLEECER *n* pl. **-S** one that fleeces

FLEECH *v* **-ED, -ING, -ES** to coax

FLEECY *adj* **FLEECIER, FLEECIEST** woolly **FLEECILY** *adv*

FLEER *v* **-ED, -ING, -S** to deride

FLEET *adj* **FLEETER, FLEETEST** swift **FLEETLY** *adv*

FLEET *v* **-ED, -ING, -S** to move swiftly

FLEHMEN *v* **-ED, -ING, -S** to inhale with the mouth open and upper lip curled

FLEISHIG *adj* made of meat or meat products

FLEMISH *v* **-ED, -ING, -ES** to coil rope in a certain manner

FLENCH *v* **-ED, -ING, -ES** to flense

FLENSE *v* **FLENSED, FLENSING, FLENSES** to strip the blubber or skin from

FLENSER *n* pl. **-S** one that flenses

FLESH *v* **-ED, -ING, -ES** to plunge into the flesh (soft body tissue)

FLESHER *n* pl. **-S** one that removes flesh from animal hides

FLESHIER comparative of fleshy

FLESHIEST superlative of fleshy

FLESHING *n* pl. **-S** the distribution of the lean and fat on an animal

FLESHLY *adj* **-LIER, -LIEST** pertaining to the body

FLESHPOT *n* pl. **-S** a pot for cooking meat

FLESHY *adj* **FLESHIER, FLESHIEST** having much flesh **FLESHILY** *adv*

FLETCH *v* **-ED, -ING, -ES** to fledge

FLETCHER *n* pl. **-S** one that makes arrows

FLEURON *n* pl. **-S** a floral ornament

FLEURY *adj* having the arms terminating in three leaves — used of a heraldic cross

FLEW *n* pl. **-S** a fishing net

FLEX *v* **-ED, -ING, -ES** to bend

FLEXAGON *n* pl. **-S** a folded paper construction

FLEXIBLE *adj* capable of being bent **FLEXIBLY** *adv*

FLEXILE *adj* flexible

FLEXION *n* pl. **-S** flection

FLEXOR *n* pl. **-S** a muscle that serves to bend a bodily part

FLEXTIME *n* pl. **-S** a system that allows flexible working hours

FLEXUOSE *adj* flexuous

FLEXUOUS *adj* winding

FLEXURE *n* pl. **-S** the act of bending **FLEXURAL** *adj*

FLEXWING *n* pl. **-S** a collapsible fabric wing used in hang gliders

FLEY *v* **-ED, -ING, -S** to frighten

FLIC *n* pl. **-S** a Parisian policeman

FLICHTER *v* **-ED, -ING, -S** to flicker

FLICK *v* **-ED, -ING, -S** to strike with a quick, light blow

FLICKER *v* **-ED, -ING, -S** to move waveringly

FLICKERY *adj* flickering

FLIED a past tense of fly

FLIER *n* pl. **-S** one that flies

FLIES present 3d person sing. of fly

FLIEST superlative of fly

FLIGHT *v* **-ED, -ING, -S** to fly in a flock

FLIGHTY *adj* **FLIGHTIER, FLIGHTIEST** fickle

FLIMFLAM *v* **-FLAMMED, -FLAMMING, -FLAMS** to swindle

FLIMSY *adj* **-SIER, -SIEST** lacking solidity or strength **FLIMSILY** *adv*

FLIMSY *n* pl. **-SIES** a thin paper

FLINCH *v* **-ED, -ING, -ES** to shrink back involuntarily

FLINCHER *n* pl. **-S** one that flinches

FLINDER *n* pl. **-S** a small fragment

FLING *v* **FLUNG, FLINGING, FLINGS** to throw with force

FLINGER *n* pl. **-S** one that flings

FLINKITE *n* pl. **-S** a mineral

FLINT *v* **-ED, -ING, -S** to provide with flint (a spark-producing rock)

FLINTY *adj* **FLINTIER, FLINTIEST** resembling flint **FLINTILY** *adv*

FLIP *adj* **FLIPPER, FLIPPEST** flippant

FLIP *v* **FLIPPED, FLIPPING, FLIPS** to throw with a brisk motion

FLIPBOOK *n* pl. **-S** a book of a series of images that when flipped give the illusion of movement

FLIPFLOP *v* **-FLOPPED, -FLOPPING, -FLOPS** to perform a backward somersault

FLIPPANT *adj* impudent

FLIPPED past tense of flip

FLIPPER *n* pl. **-S** a broad, flat limb adapted for swimming

FLIPPEST superlative of flip

FLIPPING present participle of flip

FLIPPY *adj* **FLIPPIER, FLIPPIEST** flaring at the bottom

FLIR *n* pl. **-S** an electronic heat sensor

FLIRT *v* **-ED, -ING, -S** to behave amorously without serious intent

FLIRTER *n* pl. **-S** one that flirts

FLIRTY *adj* **FLIRTIER, FLIRTIEST** given to flirting

FLIT *v* **FLITTED, FLITTING, FLITS** to move lightly and swiftly

FLITCH *v* **-ED, -ING, -ES** to cut into strips

FLITE *v* **FLITED, FLITING, FLITES** to quarrel

FLITTED past tense of flit

FLITTER *v* **-ED, -ING, -S** to flutter

FLITTING present participle of flit

FLIVVER *n* pl. **-S** an old, battered car

FLIXWEED *n* pl. **-S** a plant of the mustard family

FLOAT *v* **-ED, -ING, -S** to rest or remain on the surface of a liquid

FLOATAGE *n* pl. **-S** flotage

FLOATEL *n* pl. **-S** a houseboat used as a hotel

FLOATER *n* pl. **-S** one that floats

FLOATY *adj* **FLOATIER, FLOATIEST** tending to float

FLOC *v* **FLOCCED, FLOCCING, FLOCS** to aggregate into floccules

FLOCCI pl. of floccus

FLOCCOSE *adj* having woolly tufts

FLOCCULE *n* pl. **-S** a tuft-like mass

FLOCCULI *n/pl* small, loosely aggregated masses

FLOCCUS *n* pl. **FLOCCI** a floccule

FLOCK *v* **-ED, -ING, -S** to gather or move in a crowd

FLOCKING *n* pl. **-S** a velvety design in short fibers on cloth or paper

FLOCKY *adj* **FLOCKIER, FLOCKIEST** woolly

FLOE *n* pl. **-S** a large mass of floating ice

FLOG *v* **FLOGGED, FLOGGING, FLOGS** to beat with a whip or rod

FLOGGER *n* pl. **-S** one that flogs

FLOGGING *n* pl. **-S** a whipping

FLOKATI *n* pl. **-S** a Greek handwoven rug

FLONG *n* pl. **-S** a sheet of a certain type of paper

FLOOD *v* **-ED, -ING, -S** to inundate

FLOODER *n* pl. **-S** one that floods

FLOODING *n* pl. **-S** a filling with fluid to excess

FLOODLIT *adj* illuminated by floodlights

FLOODWAY *n* pl. **-WAYS** an overflow channel

FLOOEY *adj* awry

FLOOIE	*adj* flooey
FLOOR	*v* **-ED, -ING, -S** to provide with a floor (the level base of a room)
FLOORAGE	*n* pl. **-S** floor space
FLOORER	*n* pl. **-S** one that floors
FLOORING	*n* pl. **-S** a floor
FLOORPAN	*n* pl. **-S** the bottom part of the interior of a motor vehicle
FLOOSIE	*n* pl. **-S** floozy
FLOOSY	*n* pl. **-SIES** floozy
FLOOZIE	*n* pl. **-S** floozy
FLOOZY	*n* pl. **-ZIES** a prostitute
FLOP	*v* **FLOPPED, FLOPPING, FLOPS** to fall heavily and noisily
FLOPOVER	*n* pl. **-S** a defect in television reception
FLOPPER	*n* pl. **-S** one that flops
FLOPPING	present participle of flop
FLOPPY	*adj* **-PIER, -PIEST** soft and flexible **FLOPPILY** *adv*
FLOPPY	*n* pl. **-PIES** a type of computer disk
FLOPS	*n* pl. **FLOPS** a measure of computer speed
FLORA	*n* pl. **-RAS** or **-RAE** the plant life of a particular region
FLORAL	*n* pl. **-S** a design having flowers
FLORALLY	*adv* in a manner like that of a flower
FLOREAT	*v* may he/she/it flourish
FLORENCE	*n* pl. **-S** florin
FLORET	*n* pl. **-S** a small flower
FLORID	*adj* ruddy **FLORIDLY** *adv*
FLORIGEN	*n* pl. **-S** a plant hormone
FLORIN	*n* pl. **-S** a former gold coin of Europe
FLORIST	*n* pl. **-S** a grower or seller of flowers
FLORUIT	*n* pl. **-S** a period of flourishing
FLOSS	*v* **-ED, -ING, -ES** to clean between the teeth with a thread
FLOSSER	*n* pl. **-S** one that flosses
FLOSSIE	*n* pl. **-S** a floozy
FLOSSING	*n* pl. **-S** the act of one that flosses
FLOSSY	*adj* **FLOSSIER, FLOSSIEST** resembling floss (a soft, light fiber) **FLOSSILY** *adv*
FLOTA	*n* pl. **-S** a fleet of Spanish ships
FLOTAGE	*n* pl. **-S** the act of floating
FLOTEL	*n* pl. **-S** floatel
FLOTILLA	*n* pl. **-S** a fleet of ships
FLOTSAM	*n* pl. **-S** floating wreckage of a ship or its cargo
FLOUNCE	*v* **FLOUNCED, FLOUNCING, FLOUNCES** to move with exaggerated motions
FLOUNCY	*adj* **FLOUNCIER, FLOUNCIEST** flouncing
FLOUNDER	*v* **-ED, -ING, -S** to struggle clumsily
FLOUR	*v* **-ED, -ING, -S** to cover with flour (a finely ground meal of grain)
FLOURISH	*v* **-ED, -ING, -ES** to thrive
FLOURY	*adj* **FLOURIER, FLOURIEST** resembling flour
FLOUT	*v* **-ED, -ING, -S** to treat with contempt
FLOUTER	*n* pl. **-S** one that flouts
FLOW	*v* **-ED, -ING, -S** to move steadily and smoothly along **FLOWABLE** *adj*
FLOWAGE	*n* pl. **-S** the act of flowing
FLOWER	*v* **-ED, -ING, -S** to put forth flowers (reproductive structures of seed-bearing plants)
FLOWERER	*n* pl. **-S** a plant that flowers at a certain time
FLOWERET	*n* pl. **-S** a floret
FLOWERY	*adj* **-ERIER, -ERIEST** abounding in flowers
FLOWN	a past participle of fly
FLU	*n* pl. **-S** a virus disease
FLUB	*v* **FLUBBED, FLUBBING, FLUBS** to bungle
FLUBBER	*n* pl. **-S** one that flubs
FLUBDUB	*n* pl. **-S** pretentious nonsense
FLUE	*n* pl. **-S** an enclosed passageway for directing a current **FLUED** *adj*
FLUENCY	*n* pl. **-CIES** the quality of being fluent
FLUENT	*adj* spoken or written with effortless ease **FLUENTLY** *adv*
FLUERICS	*n/pl* fluidics **FLUERIC** *adj*
FLUFF	*v* **-ED, -ING, -S** to make fluffy
FLUFFER	*n* pl. **-S** one that fluffs
FLUFFY	*adj* **FLUFFIER, FLUFFIEST** light and soft **FLUFFILY** *adv*
FLUID	*n* pl. **-S** a substance that tends to flow **FLUIDAL** *adj*
FLUIDICS	*n/pl* a branch of mechanical engineering **FLUIDIC** *adj*

FLUIDISE *v* **-ISED, -ISING, -ISES** to fluidize

FLUIDITY *n* pl. **-TIES** the quality of being able to flow

FLUIDIZE *v* **-IZED, -IZING, -IZES** to cause to flow like a fluid

FLUIDLY *adv* with fluidity

FLUIDRAM *n* pl. **-S** a unit of liquid capacity

FLUISH *adj* having symptoms like those of the flu

FLUKE *v* **FLUKED, FLUKING, FLUKES** to obtain by chance

FLUKEY *adj* **FLUKIER, FLUKIEST** fluky

FLUKY *adj* **FLUKIER, FLUKIEST** happening by or depending on chance **FLUKILY** *adv*

FLUME *v* **FLUMED, FLUMING, FLUMES** to convey by means of an artificial water channel

FLUMMERY *n* pl. **-MERIES** a sweet dessert

FLUMMOX *v* **-ED, -ING, -ES** to confuse

FLUMP *v* **-ED, -ING, -S** to fall heavily

FLUNG past tense of fling

FLUNK *v* **-ED, -ING, -S** to fail an examination or course

FLUNKER *n* pl. **-S** one that flunks

FLUNKEY *n* pl. **-KEYS** flunky

FLUNKIE *n* pl. **-S** flunky

FLUNKY *n* pl. **-KIES** a servile follower

FLUOR *n* pl. **-S** fluorite **FLUORIC** *adj*

FLUORENE *n* pl. **-S** a chemical compound

FLUORID *n* pl. **-S** fluoride

FLUORIDE *n* pl. **-S** a compound of fluorine

FLUORIN *n* pl. **-S** fluorine

FLUORINE *n* pl. **-S** a gaseous element

FLUORITE *n* pl. **-S** a mineral

FLURRY *v* **-RIED, -RYING, -RIES** to confuse

FLUSH *adj* **FLUSHER, FLUSHEST** ruddy

FLUSH *v* **-ED, -ING, -ES** to blush

FLUSHER *n* pl. **-S** one that flushes

FLUSHING *n* pl. **-S** the act of blushing

FLUSTER *v* **-ED, -ING, -S** to put into a state of nervous confusion

FLUTE *v* **FLUTED, FLUTING, FLUTES** to play on a flute (a woodwind instrument)

FLUTER *n* pl. **-S** a flutist

FLUTEY *adj* **FLUTEYER, FLUTEYEST** or **FLUTIER, FLUTIEST** fluty

FLUTING *n* pl. **-S** a series of parallel grooves

FLUTIST *n* pl. **-S** one who plays the flute

FLUTTER *v* **-ED, -ING, -S** to wave rapidly and irregularly

FLUTTERY *adj* marked by fluttering

FLUTY *adj* **FLUTIER, FLUTIEST** resembling a flute in sound

FLUVIAL *adj* pertaining to a river

FLUX *v* **-ED, -ING, -ES** to melt

FLUXGATE *n* pl. **-S** a device to measure a magnetic field

FLUXION *n* pl. **-S** the act of flowing

FLUYT *n* pl. **-S** a type of ship

FLY *adj* **FLIER, FLIEST** clever

FLY *v* **FLEW, FLOWN, FLYING, FLIES** to move through the air

FLY *v* **FLIED, FLYING, FLIES** to hit a ball high into the air in baseball

FLYABLE *adj* suitable for flying

FLYAWAY *n* pl. **-AWAYS** one that is elusive

FLYBELT *n* pl. **-S** an area infested with tsetse flies

FLYBLOW *v* **-BLEW, -BLOWN, -BLOWING, -BLOWS** to taint

FLYBOAT *n* pl. **-S** a small, fast boat

FLYBOY *n* pl. **-BOYS** a pilot in an air force

FLYBY *n* pl. **-BYS** a flight of aircraft close to a specified place

FLYER *n* pl. **-S** flier

FLYING *n* pl. **-S** the operation of an aircraft

FLYLEAF *n* pl. **-LEAVES** a blank leaf at the beginning or end of a book

FLYLESS *adj* free of flies (winged insects)

FLYLINE *n* pl. **-S** a type of line used in fly fishing

FLYMAN *n* pl. **-MEN** a stage worker in a theater

FLYOFF *n* pl. **-S** a competitive testing of model aircraft

FLYOVER *n* pl. **-S** a flight of aircraft over a specific location

FLYPAPER *n* pl. **-S** paper designed to catch or kill flies

FLYPAST *n* pl. **-S** a flyby

FLYSCH *n* pl. **-ES** a sandstone deposit

FLYSHEET *n* pl. **-S** a circular

FLYSPECK *v* **-ED, -ING, -S** to mark with minute spots

FLYTE	*v* **FLYTED, FLYTING, FLYTES** to flite
FLYTIER	*n* pl. **-S** a maker of fishing flies
FLYTING	*n* pl. **-S** a dispute in verse form
FLYTRAP	*n* pl. **-S** a trap for catching flies
FLYWAY	*n* pl. **-WAYS** an established air route of migratory birds
FLYWHEEL	*n* pl. **-S** a heavy disk used in machinery
FOAL	*v* **-ED, -ING, -S** to give birth to a horse
FOALING	*n* pl. **-S** the act of giving birth to a horse
FOAM	*v* **-ED, -ING, -S** to form foam (a light, bubbly, gas and liquid mass) **FOAMABLE** *adj*
FOAMER	*n* pl. **-S** one that foams
FOAMIER	comparative of foamy
FOAMIEST	superlative of foamy
FOAMILY	*adv* in a foamy manner
FOAMLESS	*adj* being without foam
FOAMLIKE	*adj* resembling foam
FOAMY	*adj* **FOAMIER, FOAMIEST** covered with foam
FOB	*v* **FOBBED, FOBBING, FOBS** to deceive
FOCACCIA	*n* pl. **-S** a flat Italian bread
FOCAL	*adj* pertaining to a focus
FOCALISE	*v* **-ISED, -ISING, -ISES** to focalize
FOCALIZE	*v* **-IZED, -IZING, -IZES** to focus
FOCALLY	*adv* with regard to focus
FOCUS	*n* pl. **-CUSES** or **-CI** a point at which rays converge or from which they diverge
FOCUS	*v* **-CUSED, -CUSING, -CUSES** or **-CUSSED, -CUSSING, -CUSSES** to bring to a focus
FOCUSER	*n* pl. **-S** one that focuses
FODDER	*v* **-ED, -ING, -S** to feed with coarse food
FODGEL	*adj* plump
FOE	*n* pl. **-S** an enemy
FOEHN	*n* pl. **-S** a warm, dry wind
FOEMAN	*n* pl. **-MEN** an enemy in war
FOETAL	*adj* fetal
FOETID	*adj* fetid **FOETIDLY** *adv*
FOETOR	*n* pl. **-S** fetor
FOETUS	*n* pl. **-ES** fetus
FOG	*v* **FOGGED, FOGGING, FOGS** to cover with fog (condensed water vapor near the earth's surface)
FOGBOUND	*adj* surrounded by fog
FOGBOW	*n* pl. **-S** a nebulous arc of light sometimes seen in a fog
FOGDOG	*n* pl. **-S** a fogbow
FOGEY	*n* pl. **-GEYS** fogy **FOGEYISH** *adj*
FOGEYDOM	*n* pl. **-S** fogydom
FOGEYISM	*n* pl. **-S** fogyism
FOGFRUIT	*n* pl. **-S** a flowering plant
FOGGAGE	*n* pl. **-S** a second growth of grass
FOGGED	past tense of fog
FOGGER	*n* pl. **-S** one that fogs
FOGGING	*n* pl. **-S** the covering with fog
FOGGY	*adj* **-GIER, -GIEST** filled with fog **FOGGILY** *adv*
FOGHORN	*n* pl. **-S** a horn sounded in a fog
FOGIE	*n* pl. **-S** fogy
FOGLESS	*adj* having no fog
FOGLIGHT	*n* pl. **-S** a motor-vehicle light used in foggy conditions
FOGY	*n* pl. **-GIES** an old-fashioned person **FOGYISH** *adj*
FOGYDOM	*n* pl. **-S** all the fogies
FOGYISM	*n* pl. **-S** old-fashioned behavior
FOH	*interj* faugh
FOHN	*n* pl. **-S** foehn
FOIBLE	*n* pl. **-S** a minor weakness
FOIL	*v* **-ED, -ING, -S** to prevent the success of **FOILABLE** *adj*
FOILIST	*n* pl. **-S** one who fences with a foil (a sword without cutting edges)
FOILSMAN	*n* pl. **-MEN** a fencer
FOIN	*v* **-ED, -ING, -S** to thrust with a pointed weapon
FOISON	*n* pl. **-S** strength
FOIST	*v* **-ED, -ING, -S** to force upon slyly
FOLACIN	*n* pl. **-S** a B vitamin
FOLATE	*n* pl. **-S** folacin
FOLD	*v* **-ED, -ING, -S** to lay one part over another part of **FOLDABLE** *adj*
FOLDAWAY	*n* pl. **-S** an object designed to be folded out of the way
FOLDAWAY	*adj* designed to fold out of the way
FOLDBOAT	*n* pl. **-S** a faltboat
FOLDER	*n* pl. **-S** one that folds
FOLDEROL	*n* pl. **-S** falderal

FOLDOUT *n* pl. **-S** a gatefold

FOLDUP *n* pl. **-S** an object that folds up

FOLEY *n* pl. **-LEYS** a process for creating sounds for films

FOLIA a pl. of folium

FOLIAGE *n* pl. **-S** the growth of leaves of a plant **FOLIAGED** *adj*

FOLIAR *adj* pertaining to a leaf

FOLIATE *v* **-ATED, -ATING, -ATES** to hammer into thin plates

FOLIC *adj* derived from folic acid

FOLIO *v* **-ED, -ING, -S** to number the pages of

FOLIOSE *adj* having leaves

FOLIOUS *adj* foliose

FOLIUM *n* pl. **-LIUMS** or **-LIA** a thin layer

FOLK *n* pl. **-S** a people or tribe

FOLKIE *adj* **FOLKIER, FOLKIEST** being in the style of folk music

FOLKIE *n* pl. **-S** a performer of folk music

FOLKISH *adj* characteristic of the common people

FOLKLIFE *n* pl. **-LIVES** the traditions, skills, and products of a people

FOLKLIKE *adj* folkish

FOLKLORE *n* pl. **-S** the lore of a people

FOLKMOOT *n* pl. **-S** a general assembly of the people in early England

FOLKMOT *n* pl. **-S** folkmoot

FOLKMOTE *n* pl. **-S** folkmoot

FOLKSONG *n* pl. **-S** a song of the folk music of an area

FOLKSY *adj* **FOLKSIER, FOLKSIEST** friendly **FOLKSILY** *adv*

FOLKTALE *n* pl. **-S** a tale forming part of the oral tradition of a people

FOLKWAY *n* pl. **-WAYS** a traditional custom of a people

FOLKY *adj* **FOLKIER, FOLKIEST** folkie

FOLKY *n* pl. **FOLKIES** folkie

FOLLES pl. of follis

FOLLICLE *n* pl. **-S** a small bodily cavity

FOLLIES pl. of folly

FOLLIS *n* pl. **-LES** a coin of ancient Rome

FOLLOW *v* **-ED, -ING, -S** to come or go after

FOLLOWER *n* pl. **-S** one that follows

FOLLOWUP *n* pl. **-S** a news article that adds information to a previous article

FOLLY *n* pl. **-LIES** a foolish idea or action

FOMENT *v* **-ED, -ING, -S** to promote the development of

FOMENTER *n* pl. **-S** one that foments

FOMITE *n* pl. **-S** an inanimate object that serves to transmit infectious organisms

FON *n* pl. **-S** foehn

FOND *adj* **FONDER, FONDEST** having an affection

FOND *v* **-ED, -ING, -S** to display affection

FONDANT *n* pl. **-S** a soft, creamy candy

FONDLE *v* **-DLED, -DLING, -DLES** to caress

FONDLER *n* pl. **-S** one that fondles

FONDLING *n* pl. **-S** one that is fondled

FONDLY *adv* in a fond manner

FONDNESS *n* pl. **-ES** affection

FONDU *n* pl. **-S** a dish of melted cheese

FONDUE *v* **-DUED, -DUING** or **-DUEING, -DUES** to cook in a pot of melted cheese

FONT *n* pl. **-S** a receptacle for the water used in baptism **FONTAL** *adj*

FONTANEL *n* pl. **-S** a space in the fetal and infantile skull

FONTINA *n* pl. **-S** an Italian cheese

FOO *n* pl. **FOOS** a name for temporary computer variables or files

FOOD *n* pl. **-S** a substance taken into the body to maintain life and growth **FOODLESS** *adj*

FOODERY *n* pl. **-ERIES** a restaurant

FOODIE *n* pl. **-S** an enthusiast of foods and their preparation

FOODLAND *n* pl. **-S** land for the production of food

FOODWAYS *n/pl* the eating habits of a people

FOOFARAW *n* pl. **-S** excessive ornamentation

FOOL *v* **-ED, -ING, -S** to deceive

FOOLERY *n* pl. **-ERIES** foolish behavior or speech

FOOLFISH *n* pl. **-ES** a marine fish

FOOLISH *adj* **-ISHER, -ISHEST** lacking good sense or judgment

FOOLSCAP *n* pl. **-S** a paper size

FOOSBALL *n* pl. **-S** a table game resembling soccer

FOOT *n* pl. **FEET** the terminal part of the leg on which the body stands and moves

FOOT	*v* **-ED, -ING, -S** to walk	**FOOTWAY**	*n* pl. **-WAYS** a footpath
FOOTAGE	*n* pl. **-S** a length or quantity expressed in feet	**FOOTWEAR**	*n* pl. **FOOTWEAR** wearing apparel for the feet
FOOTBAG	*n* pl. **-S** a small bag filled with pellets that is kept aloft with the feet	**FOOTWELL**	*n* pl. **-S** a space for the feet in a motor vehicle
FOOTBALL	*n* pl. **-S** a type of ball	**FOOTWORK**	*n* pl. **-S** the use of the feet
FOOTBATH	*n* pl. **-S** a bath for the feet	**FOOTWORN**	*adj* footsore
FOOTBED	*n* pl. **-S** an insole in a boot or shoe	**FOOTY**	*adj* **-TIER, -TIEST** paltry
FOOTBOY	*n* pl. **-BOYS** a serving boy	**FOOZLE**	*v* **-ZLED, -ZLING, -ZLES** to bungle
FOOTER	*n* pl. **-S** one that walks	**FOOZLER**	*n* pl. **-S** one that foozles
FOOTFALL	*n* pl. **-S** the sound of a footstep	**FOP**	*v* **FOPPED, FOPPING, FOPS** to deceive
FOOTGEAR	*n* pl. **FOOTGEAR** footwear	**FOPPERY**	*n* pl. **-PERIES** foppish behavior
FOOTHILL	*n* pl. **-S** a low hill at the foot of higher hills	**FOPPISH**	*adj* characteristic of a dandy
FOOTHOLD	*n* pl. **-S** a secure support for the feet	**FOR**	*prep* directed or sent to
FOOTIE	*n* pl. **-S** footsie	**FORA**	a pl. of forum
FOOTIER	comparative of footy	**FORAGE**	*v* **-AGED, -AGING, -AGES** to search about
FOOTIEST	superlative of footy	**FORAGER**	*n* pl. **-S** one that forages
FOOTING	*n* pl. **-S** a foothold	**FORAM**	*n* pl. **-S** a marine rhizopod
FOOTLE	*v* **-TLED, -TLING, -TLES** to waste time	**FORAMEN**	*n* pl. **-MENS** or **-MINA** a small anatomical opening
FOOTLER	*n* pl. **-S** one that footles	**FORAY**	*v* **-ED, -ING, -S** to raid
FOOTLESS	*adj* having no feet	**FORAYER**	*n* pl. **-S** one that forays
FOOTLIKE	*adj* resembling a foot	**FORB**	*n* pl. **-S** an herb other than grass
FOOTLING	present participle of footle	**FORBEAR**	*v* **-BORE** or **-BARE, -BORNE, -BEARING, -BEARS** to refrain from
FOOTLONG	*n* pl. **-S** a hot dog one foot long		
FOOTMAN	*n* pl. **-MEN** a male servant	**FORBID**	*v* **-BADE** or **-BAD, -BIDDEN, -BIDDING, -BIDS** to command not to do something
FOOTMARK	*n* pl. **-S** a mark left by the foot on a surface		
FOOTNOTE	*v* **-NOTED, -NOTING, -NOTES** to furnish with explanatory notes	**FORBIDAL**	*n* pl. **-S** the act of forbidding
		FORBODE	*v* **-BODED, -BODING, -BODES** to forebode
FOOTPACE	*n* pl. **-S** a walking pace		
FOOTPAD	*n* pl. **-S** one who robs a pedestrian	**FORBORE**	past tense of forbear
FOOTPATH	*n* pl. **-S** a path for pedestrians	**FORBORNE**	past participle of forbear
FOOTRACE	*n* pl. **-S** a race run on foot	**FORBY**	*prep* close by
FOOTREST	*n* pl. **-S** a support for the feet	**FORBYE**	*prep* forby
FOOTROPE	*n* pl. **-S** a rope used in sailing	**FORCE**	*v* **FORCED, FORCING, FORCES** to overcome resistance by the exertion of strength **FORCEDLY** *adv*
FOOTSIE	*n* pl. **-S** a flirting game played with the feet		
FOOTSLOG	*v* **-SLOGGED, -SLOGGING, -SLOGS** to march through mud	**FORCEFUL**	*adj* strong
		FORCEOUT	*n* pl. **-S** a play by which a runner in baseball is put out
FOOTSORE	*adj* having sore or tired feet		
FOOTSTEP	*n* pl. **-S** a step with the foot	**FORCEPS**	*n* pl. **-CIPES** an instrument for seizing and holding objects
FOOTSY	*n* pl. **-SIES** footsie		
FOOTWALL	*n* pl. **-S** the layer of rock beneath a vein of ore	**FORCER**	*n* pl. **-S** one that forces

FORCIBLE *adj* effected by force **FORCIBLY** *adv*

FORCING present participle of force

FORCIPES pl. of forceps

FORD *v* **-ED, -ING, -S** to cross by wading **FORDABLE** *adj*

FORDLESS *adj* unable to be forded

FORDO *v* **-DID, -DONE, -DOING, -DOES** to destroy

FORE *n* pl. **-S** the front part of something

FOREARM *v* **-ED, -ING, -S** to arm in advance

FOREBAY *n* pl. **-BAYS** a reservoir from which water is taken to run equipment

FOREBEAR *n* pl. **-S** an ancestor

FOREBODE *v* **-BODED, -BODING, -BODES** to indicate in advance

FOREBODY *n* pl. **-BODIES** the forward part of a ship

FOREBOOM *n* pl. **-S** the boom of a ship's foremast

FOREBY *prep* forby

FOREBYE *prep* forby

FORECAST *v* **-ED, -ING, -S** to estimate or calculate in advance

FOREDATE *v* **-DATED, -DATING, -DATES** to antedate

FOREDECK *n* pl. **-S** the forward part of a ship's deck

FOREDO *v* **-DID, -DONE, -DOING, -DOES** to fordo

FOREDOOM *v* **-ED, -ING, -S** to doom in advance

FOREFACE *n* pl. **-S** the front part of the head of a quadruped

FOREFEEL *v* **-FELT, -FEELING, -FEELS** to have a premonition of

FOREFEND *v* **-ED, -ING, -S** to forfend

FOREFOOT *n* pl. **-FEET** one of the front feet of an animal

FOREGO *v* **-WENT, -GONE, -GOING, -GOES** to go before

FOREGOER *n* pl. **-S** one that foregoes

FOREGUT *n* pl. **-S** the front part of the embryonic alimentary canal

FOREHAND *n* pl. **-S** a type of tennis stroke

FOREHEAD *n* pl. **-S** the part of the face above the eyes

FOREHOOF *n* pl. **-HOOFS** or **-HOOVES** the hoof of a forefoot

FOREIGN *adj* situated outside a place or country

FOREKNOW *v* **-KNEW, -KNOWN, -KNOWING, -KNOWS** to know in advance

FORELADY *n* pl. **-DIES** a woman who supervises workers

FORELAND *n* pl. **-S** a projecting mass of land

FORELEG *n* pl. **-S** one of the front legs of an animal

FORELIMB *n* pl. **-S** a foreleg

FORELOCK *v* **-ED, -ING, -S** to fasten with a linchpin

FOREMAN *n* pl. **-MEN** a man who supervises workers

FOREMAST *n* pl. **-S** the forward mast of a ship

FOREMILK *n* pl. **-S** the milk secreted immediately after childbirth

FOREMOST *adj* first in position

FORENAME *n* pl. **-S** a first name

FORENOON *n* pl. **-S** the period of daylight before noon

FORENSIC *n* pl. **-S** an argumentative exercise

FOREPART *n* pl. **-S** the front part

FOREPAST *adj* already in the past

FOREPAW *n* pl. **-S** the paw of a foreleg

FOREPEAK *n* pl. **-S** the forward part of a ship's hold

FOREPLAY *n* pl. **-PLAYS** erotic stimulation preceding sexual intercourse

FORERANK *n* pl. **-S** the first rank

FORERUN *v* **-RAN, -RUNNING, -RUNS** to run in advance of

FORESAID *adj* previously said

FORESAIL *n* pl. **-S** the lowest sail on a foremast

FORESEE *v* **-SAW, -SEEN, -SEEING, -SEES** to see in advance

FORESEER *n* pl. **-S** one that foresees

FORESHOW *v* **-SHOWED, -SHOWN, -SHOWING, -SHOWS** to show in advance

FORESIDE *n* pl. **-S** the front side

FORESKIN *n* pl. **-S** the prepuce

FOREST *v* **-ED, -ING, -S** to convert into a forest (a densely wooded area)

FORESTAL *adj* of or pertaining to a forest

FORESTAY *n* pl. **-STAYS** a wire or rope used to support a foremast

FORESTER *n* pl. **-S** one skilled in forestry

FORESTRY *n* pl. **-RIES** the science of planting and managing forests

FORETELL   *v* **-TOLD, -TELLING, -TELLS** to tell of or about in advance

FORETIME   *n* pl. **-S** the past

FORETOP   *n* pl. **-S** a platform at the head of a ship's foremast

FOREVER   *n* pl. **-S** an indefinite length of time

FOREWARN   *v* **-ED, -ING, -S** to warn in advance

FOREWENT   past tense of forego

FOREWING   *n* pl. **-S** an anterior wing of an insect

FOREWORD   *n* pl. **-S** an introductory statement

FOREWORN   *adj* forworn

FOREX   *n* pl. **-ES** a foreign exchange

FOREYARD   *n* pl. **-S** the lowest yard on a foremast

FORFEIT   *v* **-ED, -ING, -S** to lose as a penalty

FORFEND   *v* **-ED, -ING, -S** to protect

FORGAT   a past tense of forget

FORGAVE   past tense of forgive

FORGE   *v* **FORGED, FORGING, FORGES** to fashion or reproduce for fraudulent purposes

FORGER   *n* pl. **-S** one that forges

FORGERY   *n* pl. **-ERIES** the act of forging

FORGET   *v* **-GOT** or **-GAT, -GOTTEN, -GETTING, -GETS** to fail to remember

FORGING   *n* pl. **-S** a forgery

FORGIVE   *v* **-GAVE, -GIVEN, -GIVING, -GIVES** to pardon

FORGIVER   *n* pl. **-S** one that forgives

FORGO   *v* **-WENT, -GONE, -GOING, -GOES** to refrain from

FORGOER   *n* pl. **-S** one that forgoes

FORGOT   a past tense of forget

FORGOTTEN   past participle of forget

FORINT   *n* pl. **-S** a monetary unit of Hungary

FORJUDGE   *v* **-JUDGED, -JUDGING, -JUDGES** to deprive by judgment of a court

FORK   *v* **-ED, -ING, -S** to work with a fork (a pronged implement) **FORKEDLY** *adv*

FORKBALL   *n* pl. **-S** a breaking pitch in baseball

FORKER   *n* pl. **-S** one that forks

FORKFUL   *n* pl. **FORKFULS** or **FORKSFUL** as much as a fork will hold

FORKIER   comparative of forky

FORKIEST   superlative of forky

FORKLESS   *adj* having no fork

FORKLIFT   *v* **-ED, -ING, -S** to raise or transport by means of a forklift (a machine with projecting prongs)

FORKLIKE   *adj* resembling a fork

FORKSFUL   a pl. of forkful

FORKY   *adj* **FORKIER, FORKIEST** resembling a fork

FORLORN   *adj* **-LORNER, -LORNEST** dreary

FORM   *v* **-ED, -ING, -S** to produce **FORMABLE** *adj* **FORMABLY** *adv*

FORMAL   *n* pl. **-S** a social event that requires evening dress

FORMALIN   *n* pl. **-S** an aqueous solution of formaldehyde

FORMALLY   *adv* in a prescribed or customary manner

FORMANT   *n* pl. **-S** a characteristic component of the quality of a speech sound

FORMAT   *v* **-MATTED, -MATTING, -MATS** to produce in a specified style

FORMATE   *n* pl. **-S** a chemical salt

FORME   *n* pl. **-S** an assemblage of printing type secured in a metal frame

FORMEE   *adj* having the arms narrow at the center and expanding toward the ends — used of a heraldic cross

FORMER   *n* pl. **-S** one that forms

FORMERLY   *adv* previously

FORMFUL   *adj* exhibiting good form

FORMIC   *adj* pertaining to ants

FORMLESS   *adj* lacking structure

FORMOL   *n* pl. **-S** formalin

FORMULA   *n* pl. **-LAS** or **-LAE** an exact method for doing something

FORMWORK   *n* pl. **-S** a set of forms to hold concrete until it sets

FORMYL   *n* pl. **-S** a univalent chemical radical

FORNENT   *prep* near to

FORNIX   *n* pl. **-NICES** an arched anatomical structure **FORNICAL** *adj*

FORRADER   *adv* further ahead

FORRIT   *adv* toward the front

FORSAKE   *v* **-SOOK, -SAKEN, -SAKING, -SAKES** to quit or leave entirely

FORSAKER   *n* pl. **-S** one that forsakes

FORSOOTH   *adv* in truth

FORSPENT   *adj* worn out

FORSWEAR *v* **-SWORE, -SWORN, -SWEARING, -SWEARS** to deny under oath

FORT *n* pl. **-S** a fortified enclosure or structure

FORTE *n* pl. **-S** a strong point

FORTES pl. of fortis

FORTH *adv* onward in time, place, or order

FORTIES pl. of forty

FORTIETH *n* pl. **-S** one of forty equal parts

FORTIFY *v* **-FIED, -FYING, -FIES** to strengthen against attack

FORTIS *n* pl. **-TES** a consonant pronounced with relatively strong release of breath

FORTRESS *v* **-ED, -ING, -ES** to fortify

FORTUITY *n* pl. **-ITIES** an accidental occurrence

FORTUNE *v* **-TUNED, -TUNING, -TUNES** to endow with wealth

FORTY *n* pl. **-TIES** a number

FORTYISH *adj* being about forty years old

FORUM *n* pl. **-RUMS** or **-RA** a public meeting place

FORWARD *adj* **-WARDER, -WARDEST** being at a point in advance

FORWARD *v* **-ED, -ING, -S** to help onward

FORWENT past tense of forgo

FORWHY *adv* for what reason

FORWORN *adj* worn out

FORZANDO *n* pl. **-DOS** or **-DI** sforzato

FOSS *n* pl. **-ES** fosse

FOSSA *n* pl. **-S** a catlike mammal

FOSSA *n* pl. **-SAE** an anatomical depression **FOSSATE** *adj*

FOSSE *n* pl. **-S** a ditch

FOSSETTE *n* pl. **-S** a small fossa

FOSSICK *v* **-ED, -ING, -S** to search for gold

FOSSIL *n* pl. **-S** the remains of an animal or plant preserved in the earth's crust

FOSTER *v* **-ED, -ING, -S** to promote the growth of

FOSTERER *n* pl. **-S** one that fosters

FOU *adj* drunk

FOUETTE *n* pl. **-S** a movement in ballet

FOUGHT past tense of fight

FOUGHTEN *adj* exhausted especially from fighting

FOUL *adj* **FOULER, FOULEST** offensive to the senses

FOUL *v* **-ED, -ING, -S** to make foul

FOULARD *n* pl. **-S** a soft fabric

FOULING *n* pl. **-S** a deposit or crust

FOULLY *adv* in a foul manner

FOULNESS *n* pl. **-ES** the state of being foul

FOUND *v* **-ED, -ING, -S** to establish

FOUNDER *v* **-ED, -ING, -S** to become disabled

FOUNDRY *n* pl. **-RIES** an establishment in which metal is cast

FOUNT *n* pl. **-S** a fountain

FOUNTAIN *v* **-ED, -ING, -S** to flow like a fountain (a spring of water)

FOUR *n* pl. **-S** a number

FOURCHEE *adj* having the end of each arm forked — used of a heraldic cross

FOUREYED *adj* wearing eyeglasses

FOURFOLD *adj* four times as great

FOURGON *n* pl. **-S** a wagon for carrying baggage

FOURPLEX *n* pl. **-ES** quadplex

FOURSOME *n* pl. **-S** a group of four

FOURTEEN *n* pl. **-S** a number

FOURTH *n* pl. **-S** one of four equal parts

FOURTHLY *adv* in the fourth place

FOUSTY *adj* **FOUSTIER, FOUSTIEST** moldy

FOVEA *n* pl. **-VEAS** or **-VEAE** a shallow anatomical depression **FOVEAL, FOVEATE, FOVEATED** *adj*

FOVEOLA *n* pl. **-LAS** or **-LAE** a small fovea **FOVEOLAR** *adj*

FOVEOLE *n* pl. **-S** a foveola

FOVEOLET *n* pl. **-S** a foveola

FOWL *v* **-ED, -ING, -S** to hunt birds

FOWLER *n* pl. **-S** one that fowls

FOWLING *n* pl. **-S** the hunting of birds

FOWLPOX *n* pl. **-ES** a virus disease of poultry

FOX *v* **-ED, -ING, -ES** to outwit

FOXBERRY *n* pl. **-RIES** a cowberry

FOXFIRE *n* pl. **-S** a glow produced by certain fungi on decaying wood

FOXFISH *n* pl. **-ES** a large shark

FOXGLOVE *n* pl. **-S** a flowering plant

FOXHOLE *n* pl. **-S** a small pit used for cover in a battle area

FOXHOUND   *n* pl. **-S** a hunting dog

FOXHUNT   *v* **-ED, -ING, -S** to hunt with hounds for a fox

FOXIER   comparative of foxy

FOXIEST   superlative of foxy

FOXILY   *adv* in a foxy manner

FOXINESS   *n* pl. **-ES** the state of being foxy

FOXING   *n* pl. **-S** a piece of material used to cover the upper portion of a shoe

FOXLIKE   *adj* resembling a fox (a carnivorous mammal)

FOXSKIN   *n* pl. **-S** the skin of a fox

FOXTAIL   *n* pl. **-S** the tail of a fox

FOXTROT   *v* **-TROTTED, -TROTTING, -TROTS** to dance the fox trot (a dance for couples)

FOXY   *adj* **FOXIER, FOXIEST** crafty

FOY   *n* pl. **FOYS** a farewell feast or gift

FOYER   *n* pl. **-S** an entrance room or hall

FOZINESS   *n* pl. **-ES** the state of being fozy

FOZY   *adj* **-ZIER, -ZIEST** too ripe

FRABJOUS   *adj* splendid

FRACAS   *n* pl. **-ES** a brawl

FRACK   *v* **-ED, -ING, -S** to engage in fracking

FRACKING   *n* pl. **-S** the injection of fluid into shale beds in order to free up petroleum reserves

FRACTAL   *n* pl. **-S** a complex geometric curve

FRACTED   *adj* broken

FRACTI   pl. of fractus

FRACTION   *v* **-ED, -ING, -S** to divide into portions

FRACTUR   *n* pl. **-S** fraktur

FRACTURE   *v* **-TURED, -TURING, -TURES** to break

FRACTUS   *n* pl. **-TI** a ragged cloud

FRAE   *prep* from

FRAENUM   *n* pl. **-NUMS** or **-NA** frenum

FRAG   *v* **FRAGGED, FRAGGING, FRAGS** to injure with a type of grenade

FRAGGING   *n* pl. **-S** the act of one that frags

FRAGILE   *adj* easily broken or damaged

FRAGMENT   *v* **-ED, -ING, -S** to break into pieces

FRAGRANT   *adj* having a pleasant odor

FRAIL   *adj* **FRAILER, FRAILEST** fragile **FRAILLY** *adv*

FRAIL   *n* pl. **-S** a basket for holding dried fruits

FRAILTY   *n* pl. **-TIES** a weakness of character

FRAISE   *n* pl. **-S** a barrier of pointed stakes

FRAKTUR   *n* pl. **-S** a style of type

FRAME   *v* **FRAMED, FRAMING, FRAMES** to construct by putting together the various parts **FRAMABLE** *adj*

FRAMER   *n* pl. **-S** one that frames

FRAMING   *n* pl. **-S** framework

FRANC   *n* pl. **-S** a former monetary unit of France

FRANCISE   *v* **-CISED, -CISING, -CISES** to francize

FRANCIUM   *n* pl. **-S** a radioactive element

FRANCIZE   *v* **-CIZED, -CIZING, -CIZES** to force to adopt French customs and language

FRANK   *adj* **FRANKER, FRANKEST** honest and unreserved in speech

FRANK   *v* **-ED, -ING, -S** to mark (a piece of mail) for free delivery

FRANKER   *n* pl. **-S** one that franks

FRANKLIN   *n* pl. **-S** a medieval English landowner

FRANKLY   *adv* in a frank manner

FRANKUM   *n* pl. **-S** the hardened resin of a spruce tree

FRANTIC   *adj* wildly excited

FRAP   *v* **FRAPPED, FRAPPING, FRAPS** to bind firmly

FRAPPE   *n* pl. **-S** a partly frozen drink

FRASCATI   *n* pl. **-S** an Italian white wine

FRASS   *n* pl. **-ES** debris made by insects

FRAT   *n* pl. **-S** a college fraternity

FRATER   *n* pl. **-S** a comrade

FRAUD   *n* pl. **-S** trickery

FRAUGHT   *v* **-ED, -ING, -S** to load down

FRAULEIN   *n* pl. **-S** a German governess

FRAY   *v* **-ED, -ING, -S** to wear off by rubbing

FRAYING   *n* pl. **-S** something worn off by rubbing

FRAZIL   *n* pl. **-S** tiny ice crystals formed in supercooled waters

FRAZZLE   *v* **-ZLED, -ZLING, -ZLES** to fray

FREAK   *v* **-ED, -ING, -S** to streak with color

FREAKIER   comparative of freaky

FREAKIEST superlative of freaky

FREAKILY *adv* in a freaky manner

FREAKISH *adj* unusual

FREAKOUT *n* pl. **-S** an event marked by wild excitement

FREAKY *adj* **FREAKIER, FREAKIEST** freakish

FRECKLE *v* **-LED, -LING, -LES** to mark with freckles (small, brownish spots)

FRECKLY *adj* **-LIER, -LIEST** marked with freckles

FREE *adj* **FREER, FREEST** not subject to restriction or control

FREE *v* **FREED, FREEING, FREES** to make free

FREEBASE *v* **-BASED, -BASING, -BASES** to use a form of cocaine that is inhaled

FREEBEE *n* pl. **-S** freebie

FREEBIE *n* pl. **-S** something given or received without charge

FREEBOOT *v* **-ED, -ING, -S** to plunder

FREEBORN *adj* born free

FREED past tense of free

FREEDMAN *n* pl. **-MEN** a man who has been freed from slavery

FREEDOM *n* pl. **-S** the state of being free

FREEFORM *adj* having a free-flowing design or shape

FREEGAN *n* pl. **-S** an activist who scavenges for free food to reduce consumption of resources

FREEHAND *adj* drawn by hand without mechanical aids

FREEHOLD *n* pl. **-S** a form of tenure of real property

FREELOAD *v* **-ED, -ING, -S** to live at the expense of others

FREELY *adv* in a free manner

FREEMAN *n* pl. **-MEN** one who is free

FREENESS *n* pl. **-ES** freedom

FREER *n* pl. **-S** one that frees

FREERIDE *n* pl. **-S** a type of snowboard

FREESIA *n* pl. **-S** an African herb

FREEST superlative of free

FREEWARE *n* pl. **-S** software distributed without charge

FREEWAY *n* pl. **-WAYS** an express highway

FREEWILL *adj* voluntary

FREEZE *v* **FROZE, FROZEN, FREEZING, FREEZES** to become hardened into a solid body by loss of heat

FREEZER *n* pl. **-S** an apparatus for freezing food

FREEZING *n* pl. **-S** the method by which foods are frozen to preserve them

FREIGHT *v* **-ED, -ING, -S** to load with goods for transportation

FREMD *adj* strange

FREMITUS *n* pl. **-ES** a palpable vibration

FRENA a pl. of frenum

FRENCH *v* **-ED, -ING, -ES** to cut into thin strips before cooking

FRENEMY *n* pl. **-MIES** one who pretends to be a friend but is actually an enemy

FRENETIC *n* pl. **-S** a frantic person

FRENULUM *n* pl. **-LUMS** or **-LA** a frenum **FRENULAR** *adj*

FRENUM *n* pl. **-NUMS** or **-NA** a connecting fold of membrane

FRENZILY *adv* in a frantic manner

FRENZY *v* **-ZIED, -ZYING, -ZIES** to make frantic

FREQUENT *adj* **-QUENTER, -QUENTEST** occurring again and again

FREQUENT *v* **-ED, -ING, -S** to be in or at often

FRERE *n* pl. **-S** brother

FRESCO *v* **-ED, -ING, -S** or **-ES** to paint on a surface of plaster

FRESCOER *n* pl. **-S** one that frescoes

FRESH *adj* **FRESHER, FRESHEST** new

FRESH *v* **-ED, -ING, -ES** to freshen

FRESHEN *v* **-ED, -ING, -S** to make or become fresh

FRESHER *n* pl. **-S** a freshman

FRESHET *n* pl. **-S** a sudden overflow of a stream

FRESHLY *adv* in a fresh manner

FRESHMAN *n* pl. **-MEN** a first-year student at a high school, university, or college

FRESNEL *n* pl. **-S** a type of lens used in lights

FRET *v* **FRETTED, FRETTING, FRETS** to worry

FRETFUL *adj* inclined to fret

FRETLESS *adj* having no fretwork

FRETSAW *n* pl. **-S** a narrow-bladed saw

FRETSOME *adj* fretful

FRETTED past tense of fret

FRETTER	*n* pl. **-S** one that frets
FRETTING	present participle of fret
FRETTY	*adj* **-TIER, -TIEST** fretful
FRETWORK	*n* pl. **-S** ornamental work consisting of interlacing parts
FRIABLE	*adj* easily crumbled
FRIAR	*n* pl. **-S** a member of a religious order **FRIARLY** *adj*
FRIARY	*n* pl. **-ARIES** a monastery of friars
FRIBBLE	*v* **-BLED, -BLING, -BLES** to act foolishly
FRIBBLER	*n* pl. **-S** one that fribbles
FRICANDO	*n* pl. **-DOES** a roasted loin of veal
FRICOT	*n* pl. **-S** a stew with potatoes and meat or fish
FRICTION	*n* pl. **-S** the rubbing of one body against another
FRIDGE	*n* pl. **-S** a refrigerator
FRIED	past tense of fry
FRIEND	*v* **-ED, -ING, -S** to enter into a warm association with
FRIENDLY	*adj* **-LIER, -LIEST** inclined to approve, help, or support
FRIENDLY	*n* pl. **-LIES** one who is friendly
FRIER	*n* pl. **-S** fryer
FRIES	present 3d person sing. of fry
FRIEZE	*n* pl. **-S** a coarse woolen fabric
FRIG	*n* pl. **-ES** a refrigerator
FRIG	*v* **FRIGGED, FRIGGING, FRIGS** to cheat or trick
FRIGATE	*n* pl. **-S** a sailing vessel
FRIGHT	*v* **-ED, -ING, -S** to frighten
FRIGHTEN	*v* **-ED, -ING, -S** to make afraid
FRIGID	*adj* very cold **FRIGIDLY** *adv*
FRIJOL	*n* pl. **-ES** a bean used as food
FRIJOLE	*n* pl. **-S** frijol
FRILL	*v* **-ED, -ING, -S** to provide with a frill (an ornamental ruffled edge)
FRILLER	*n* pl. **-S** one that frills
FRILLERY	*n* pl. **-ERIES** an arrangement of frills
FRILLIES	*n/pl* an item of women's underwear
FRILLING	*n* pl. **-S** an arrangement of frills
FRILLY	*adj* **FRILLIER, FRILLIEST** having frills
FRINGE	*v* **FRINGED, FRINGING, FRINGES** to provide with a fringe (an ornamental border)
FRINGING	*n* pl. **-S** an ornamental border of loose short strips
FRINGY	*adj* **FRINGIER, FRINGIEST** resembling a fringe
FRIPPERY	*n* pl. **-PERIES** excessive ornamentation
FRISE	*n* pl. **-S** frieze
FRISEE	*n* pl. **-S** curly leaves of endive
FRISETTE	*n* pl. **-S** frizette
FRISEUR	*n* pl. **-S** a hairdresser
FRISK	*v* **-ED, -ING, -S** to move or leap about playfully
FRISKER	*n* pl. **-S** one that frisks
FRISKET	*n* pl. **-S** a frame used to protect paper in a printing press
FRISKY	*adj* **FRISKIER, FRISKIEST** lively and playful **FRISKILY** *adv*
FRISSON	*n* pl. **-S** a shudder
FRIT	*v* **FRITTED, FRITTING, FRITS** to fuse into a vitreous substance
FRITES	*n/pl* french fries
FRITH	*n* pl. **-S** firth
FRITT	*v* **-ED, -ING, -S** to frit
FRITTATA	*n* pl. **-S** an unfolded omelet with chopped vegetables or meat
FRITTED	past tense of frit
FRITTER	*v* **-ED, -ING, -S** to squander little by little
FRITTING	present participle of frit
FRITZ	*n* pl. **-ES** a nonfunctioning state
FRIULANO	*n* pl. **-NOS** a mild Italian cheese
FRIVOL	*v* **-OLED, -OLING, -OLS** or **-OLLED, -OLLING, -OLS** to behave playfully
FRIVOLER	*n* pl. **-S** one that frivols
FRIZ	*v* **-ED, -ING, -ES** to frizz
FRIZER	*n* pl. **-S** frizzer
FRIZETTE	*n* pl. **-S** a frizzed fringe of hair
FRIZZ	*v* **-ED, -ING, -ES** to form into small, tight curls
FRIZZER	*n* pl. **-S** one that frizzes
FRIZZIER	comparative of frizzy
FRIZZIES	*n/pl* frizzy hair
FRIZZIEST	superlative of frizzy
FRIZZILY	*adv* in a frizzy manner
FRIZZLE	*v* **-ZLED, -ZLING, -ZLES** to frizz
FRIZZLER	*n* pl. **-S** one that frizzles
FRIZZLY	*adj* **-ZLIER, -ZLIEST** frizzy

FRIZZY	*adj* **FRIZZIER, FRIZZIEST** tightly curled
FRO	*adv* away
FROCK	*v* **-ED, -ING, -S** to clothe in a long, loose outer garment
FROE	*n* pl. **-S** a cleaving tool
FROG	*v* **FROGGED, FROGGING, FROGS** to hunt frogs (web-footed, tailless amphibians)
FROGEYE	*n* pl. **-S** a plant disease **FROGEYED** *adj*
FROGFISH	*n* pl. **-ES** a marine fish
FROGGED	past tense of frog
FROGGING	*n* pl. **-S** a type of ornamental coat fastener
FROGGY	*adj* **-GIER, -GIEST** abounding in frogs
FROGLET	*n* pl. **-S** a young frog
FROGLIKE	*adj* resembling a frog
FROGMAN	*n* pl. **-MEN** a person equipped for extended periods of underwater swimming
FROLIC	*v* **-ICKED, -ICKING, -ICS** to play and run about merrily **FROLICKY** *adj*
FROM	*prep* starting at
FROMAGE	*n* pl. **-S** cheese
FROMENTY	*n* pl. **-TIES** frumenty
FROND	*n* pl. **-S** a type of leaf **FRONDED, FRONDOSE** *adj*
FRONDEUR	*n* pl. **-S** a rebel
FRONS	*n* pl. **FRONTES** the upper anterior portion of an insect's head
FRONT	*adj* **FRONTER, FRONTEST** pertaining to or situated at the forward part of a surface
FRONT	*v* **-ED, -ING, -S** to provide with a front (a forward part)
FRONTAGE	*n* pl. **-S** the front of a building or lot
FRONTAL	*n* pl. **-S** a bone of the skull
FRONTES	pl. of frons
FRONTIER	*n* pl. **-S** a border between two countries
FRONTLET	*n* pl. **-S** a decorative band worn across the forehead
FRONTMAN	*n* pl. **-MEN** the most prominent member of a group of musicians
FRONTON	*n* pl. **-S** a jai alai arena
FRORE	*adj* frozen
FROSH	*n* pl. **-ES** a freshman
FROST	*v* **-ED, -ING, -S** to cover with frost (a deposit of minute ice crystals)
FROSTBIT	*adj* injured by extreme cold
FROSTED	*n* pl. **-S** a type of milk shake
FROSTING	*n* pl. **-S** icing
FROSTNIP	*n* pl. **-S** the freezing of outer skin layers
FROSTY	*adj* **FROSTIER, FROSTIEST** covered with frost **FROSTILY** *adv*
FROTH	*v* **-ED, -ING, -S** to foam
FROTHER	*n* pl. **-S** one that froths
FROTHING	*n* pl. **-S** a layer of foam in a liquid or solid
FROTHY	*adj* **FROTHIER, FROTHIEST** foamy **FROTHILY** *adv*
FROTTAGE	*n* pl. **-S** masturbation by rubbing against another person
FROTTEUR	*n* pl. **-S** one who practices frottage
FROUFROU	*n* pl. **-S** a rustling sound
FROUNCE	*v* **FROUNCED, FROUNCING, FROUNCES** to pleat
FROUZY	*adj* **-ZIER, -ZIEST** frowzy
FROW	*n* pl. **-S** froe
FROWARD	*adj* disobedient
FROWN	*v* **-ED, -ING, -S** to contract the brow in displeasure
FROWNER	*n* pl. **-S** one that frowns
FROWST	*v* **-ED, -ING, -S** to lounge in a stuffy room
FROWSTY	*adj* **-TIER, -TIEST** musty
FROWSY	*adj* **-SIER, -SIEST** frowzy
FROWZY	*adj* **-ZIER, -ZIEST** unkempt **FROWZILY** *adv*
FROZE	past tense of freeze
FROZEN	*adj* very cold **FROZENLY** *adv*
FRUCTIFY	*v* **-FIED, -FYING, -FIES** to bear fruit
FRUCTOSE	*n* pl. **-S** a sugar found in various fruits
FRUG	*v* **FRUGGED, FRUGGING, FRUGS** to perform a type of vigorous dance
FRUGAL	*adj* thrifty **FRUGALLY** *adv*
FRUIT	*v* **-ED, -ING, -S** to bear fruit (usually edible reproductive bodies of a seed plant)
FRUITAGE	*n* pl. **-S** the process of bearing fruit
FRUITER	*n* pl. **-S** one that grows or sells fruit
FRUITFUL	*adj* **-FULLER, -FULLEST** producing abundantly

FRUITIER comparative of fruity

FRUITIEST superlative of fruity

FRUITING *n* pl. **-S** the production of fruit on a tree

FRUITION *n* pl. **-S** the accomplishment of something desired

FRUITLET *n* pl. **-S** a small fruit

FRUITY *adj* **FRUITIER, FRUITIEST** suggestive of fruit **FRUITILY** *adv*

FRUMENTY *n* pl. **-TIES** a dish of wheat boiled in milk and sweetened with sugar

FRUMP *n* pl. **-S** a dowdy woman **FRUMPISH** *adj*

FRUMPY *adj* **FRUMPIER, FRUMPIEST** dowdy **FRUMPILY** *adv*

FRUSTULE *n* pl. **-S** the shell of a diatom

FRUSTUM *n* pl. **-TUMS** or **-TA** a part of a conical solid

FRY *v* **FRIED, FRYING, FRIES** to cook over direct heat in hot fat or oil **FRYABLE** *adj*

FRYBREAD *n* pl. **-S** a fried bread

FRYER *n* pl. **-S** one that fries

FRYPAN *n* pl. **-S** a pan for frying food

FUB *v* **FUBBED, FUBBING, FUBS** to fob

FUBSY *adj* **FUBSIER, FUBSIEST** chubby and somewhat squat

FUCHSIA *n* pl. **-S** a flowering shrub

FUCHSIN *n* pl. **-S** a red dye

FUCHSINE *n* pl. **-S** fuchsin

FUCI a pl. of fucus

FUCOID *n* pl. **-S** a brown seaweed **FUCOIDAL** *adj*

FUCOSE *n* pl. **-S** a type of sugar

FUCOUS *adj* of or pertaining to fucoids

FUCUS *n* pl. **-CUSES** or **-CI** any of a genus of brown algae

FUD *n* pl. **-S** an old-fashioned person

FUDDLE *v* **-DLED, -DLING, -DLES** to confuse

FUDDY *n* pl. **-DIES** a fussy person

FUDGE *v* **FUDGED, FUDGING, FUDGES** to falsify

FUDGY *adj* **-GIER, -GIEST** resembling fudge (a soft, sweet candy)

FUEHRER *n* pl. **-S** fuhrer

FUEL *v* **-ELED, -ELING, -ELS** or **-ELLED, -ELLING, -ELS** to provide with fuel (material used to produce energy)

FUELER *n* pl. **-S** one that fuels

FUELLER *n* pl. **-S** fueler

FUELWOOD *n* pl. **-S** firewood

FUG *v* **FUGGED, FUGGING, FUGS** to make stuffy and odorous

FUGACITY *n* pl. **-TIES** lack of enduring qualities

FUGAL *adj* being in the style of a fugue **FUGALLY** *adv*

FUGATO *n* pl. **-TOS** a fugal composition

FUGGED past tense of fug

FUGGING present participle of fug

FUGGY *adj* **-GIER, -GIEST** stuffy and odorous **FUGGILY** *adv*

FUGIO *n* pl. **-GIOS** a former coin of the United States

FUGITIVE *n* pl. **-S** one who flees

FUGLE *v* **-GLED, -GLING, -GLES** to lead by setting an example

FUGLEMAN *n* pl. **-MEN** a leader

FUGU *n* pl. **-S** a toxin-containing fish

FUGUE *v* **FUGUED, FUGUING, FUGUES** to compose a fugue (a type of musical composition)

FUGUIST *n* pl. **-S** one who composes fugues

FUHRER *n* pl. **-S** a leader

FUJI *n* pl. **-S** a silk fabric

FULCRUM *n* pl. **-CRUMS** or **-CRA** a support for a lever

FULFIL *v* **-FILLED, -FILLING, -FILS** to fulfill

FULFILL *v* **-ED, -ING, -S** to bring about the accomplishment of

FULGENT *adj* shining brightly

FULGID *adj* fulgent

FULHAM *n* pl. **-S** a loaded die

FULL *adj* **FULLER, FULLEST** filled completely

FULL *v* **-ED, -ING, -S** to shrink and thicken, as cloth

FULLAM *n* pl. **-S** fulham

FULLBACK *n* pl. **-S** an offensive back in football

FULLER *v* **-ED, -ING, -S** to groove with a type of hammer

FULLERY   *n* pl. **-ERIES** a place for fulling cloth

FULLFACE   *n* pl. **-S** a heavy-faced type

FULLNESS   *n* pl. **-ES** the state of being full

FULLY   *adv* in a full manner

FULMAR   *n* pl. **-S** an arctic seabird

FULMINE   *v* **-MINED, -MINING, -MINES** to explode loudly

FULMINIC   *adj* highly explosive

FULNESS   *n* pl. **-ES** fullness

FULSOME   *adj* repulsive

FULVOUS   *adj* of a brownish yellow color

FUMARASE   *n* pl. **-S** an enzyme

FUMARATE   *n* pl. **-S** a chemical salt

FUMARIC   *adj* pertaining to a certain acid

FUMAROLE   *n* pl. **-S** a hole from which volcanic vapors issue

FUMATORY   *n* pl. **-RIES** a fumigation chamber

FUMBLE   *v* **-BLED, -BLING, -BLES** to handle clumsily

FUMBLER   *n* pl. **-S** one that fumbles

FUME   *v* **FUMED, FUMING, FUMES** to give off fumes (gaseous exhalations)

FUMELESS   *adj* having no fumes

FUMELIKE   *adj* resembling fumes

FUMER   *n* pl. **-S** one that fumes

FUMET   *n* pl. **-S** the odor of meat while cooking

FUMETTE   *n* pl. **-S** fumet

FUMIER   comparative of fumy

FUMIEST   superlative of fumy

FUMIGANT   *n* pl. **-S** a substance used in fumigating

FUMIGATE   *v* **-GATED, -GATING, -GATES** to subject to fumes in order to destroy pests

FUMING   present participle of fume

FUMINGLY   *adv* angrily

FUMITORY   *n* pl. **-RIES** a climbing plant

FUMULUS   *n* pl. **-LI** a thin cloud

FUMY   *adj* **FUMIER, FUMIEST** producing or full of fumes

FUN   *adj* **FUNNER, FUNNEST** providing enjoyment

FUN   *v* **FUNNED, FUNNING, FUNS** to act playfully

FUNCTION   *v* **-ED, -ING, -S** to be in action

FUNCTOR   *n* pl. **-S** one that functions

FUND   *v* **-ED, -ING, -S** to provide money for **FUNDABLE** *adj*

FUNDER   *n* pl. **-S** a provider of money

FUNDING   *n* pl. **-S** money provided for a particular purpose

FUNDUS   *n* pl. **-DI** the inner basal surface of a bodily organ **FUNDIC** *adj*

FUNERAL   *n* pl. **-S** a ceremony held for a dead person

FUNERARY   *adj* pertaining to a funeral

FUNEREAL   *adj* funerary

FUNEST   *adj* portending death or evil

FUNFAIR   *n* pl. **-S** an amusement park

FUNFEST   *n* pl. **-S** a party for fun

FUNGAL   *n* pl. **-S** a fungus

FUNGI   a pl. of fungus

FUNGIBLE   *n* pl. **-S** something that may be exchanged for an equivalent unit of the same class

FUNGIC   *adj* fungous

FUNGO   *n* pl. **-GOES** or **-GOS** a fly ball hit to a fielder for practice in baseball

FUNGOID   *n* pl. **-S** a growth resembling a fungus

FUNGOUS   *adj* pertaining to a fungus

FUNGUS   *n* pl. **-GUSES** or **-GI** any of a major group of lower plants

FUNHOUSE   *n* pl. **-S** an amusement park attraction

FUNICLE   *n* pl. **-S** a cordlike anatomical structure

FUNICULI   *n/pl* funicles

FUNK   *v* **-ED, -ING, -S** to shrink back in fear

FUNKER   *n* pl. **-S** one that funks

FUNKIA   *n* pl. **-S** a flowering plant

FUNKSTER   *n* pl. **-S** a fan or performer of earthy, bluesy music

FUNKY   *adj* **FUNKIER, FUNKIEST** having an offensive odor **FUNKILY** *adv*

FUNNED   past tense of fun

FUNNEL   *v* **-NELED, -NELING, -NELS** or **-NELLED, -NELLING, -NELS** to pass through a funnel (a cone-shaped utensil)

FUNNER   comparative of fun

FUNNEST   superlative of fun

FUNNING   present participle of fun

FUNNY *adj* **-NIER, -NIEST** causing laughter or amusement **FUNNILY** *adv*

FUNNY *n* pl. **-NIES** a comic strip

FUNNYMAN *n* pl. **-MEN** a comedian

FUNPLEX *n* pl. **-ES** a building with facilities for sports and games

FUNSTER *n* pl. **-S** one that makes fun; a comedian

FUR *v* **FURRED, FURRING, FURS** to cover with fur (a dressed animal pelt)

FURAN *n* pl. **-S** a flammable liquid

FURANE *n* pl. **-S** furan

FURANOSE *n* pl. **-S** a type of sugar

FURBALL *n* pl. **-S** a ball of fur regurgitated by a cat

FURBELOW *v* **-ED, -ING, -S** to decorate with ruffles

FURBISH *v* **-ED, -ING, -ES** to polish

FURCATE *v* **-CATED, -CATING, -CATES** to divide into branches

FURCRAEA *n* pl. **-S** a tropical plant

FURCULA *n* pl. **-LAE** a forked bone **FURCULAR** *adj*

FURCULUM *n* pl. **-LA** a furcula

FURFUR *n* pl. **-ES** dandruff

FURFURAL *n* pl. **-S** a chemical compound

FURFURAN *n* pl. **-S** furan

FURIBUND *adj* furious

FURIES pl. of fury

FURIOSO *adv* with great force — used as a musical direction

FURIOUS *adj* extremely angry

FURL *v* **-ED, -ING, -S** to roll up **FURLABLE** *adj*

FURLER *n* pl. **-S** one that furls

FURLESS *adj* having no fur

FURLONG *n* pl. **-S** a unit of distance

FURLOUGH *v* **-ED, -ING, -S** to grant a leave of absence to

FURMENTY *n* pl. **-TIES** frumenty

FURMETY *n* pl. **-TIES** frumenty

FURMITY *n* pl. **-TIES** frumenty

FURNACE *v* **-NACED, -NACING, -NACES** to subject to heat

FURNISH *v* **-ED, -ING, -ES** to equip

FUROR *n* pl. **-S** an uproar

FURORE *n* pl. **-S** furor

FURPIECE *n* pl. **-S** an item of clothing made out of fur

FURRED past tense of fur

FURRIER *n* pl. **-S** one that deals in furs

FURRIERY *n* pl. **-ERIES** the business of a furrier

FURRIEST superlative of furry

FURRILY *adv* in a furry manner

FURRINER *n* pl. **-S** a foreigner

FURRING *n* pl. **-S** a trimming or lining of fur

FURROW *v* **-ED, -ING, -S** to make furrows (narrow depressions) in

FURROWER *n* pl. **-S** one that furrows

FURROWY *adj* marked by furrows

FURRY *adj* **-RIER, -RIEST** covered with fur

FURTHER *v* **-ED, -ING, -S** to help forward

FURTHEST a superlative of far

FURTIVE *adj* stealthy

FURUNCLE *n* pl. **-S** a painful swelling of the skin

FURY *n* pl. **-RIES** violent anger

FURZE *n* pl. **-S** a spiny shrub

FURZY *adj* **FURZIER, FURZIEST** abounding in furze

FUSAIN *n* pl. **-S** a fine charcoal used in drawing

FUSARIUM *n* pl. **-SARIUMS** or **-SARIA** a disease-causing fungus

FUSCOUS *adj* of a dusky color

FUSE *v* **FUSED, FUSING, FUSES** to equip with a fuse (a detonating device)

FUSEE *n* pl. **-S** a large-headed friction match

FUSEL *n* pl. **-S** an oily liquid

FUSELAGE *n* pl. **-S** the body of an airplane

FUSELESS *adj* lacking a fuse

FUSELIKE *adj* resembling a fuse

FUSIBLE *adj* capable of being melted **FUSIBLY** *adv*

FUSIFORM *adj* tapering toward each end

FUSIL *n* pl. **-S** a type of musket

FUSILE *adj* formed by melting

FUSILEER *n* pl. **-S** fusilier

FUSILIER *n* pl. **-S** a soldier armed with a fusil

FUSILLI *n* pl. **-S** spiral-shaped pasta

FUSING present participle of fuse

FUSION — *n* pl. **-S** the act of melting together **FUSIONAL** *adj*

FUSS — *v* **-ED, -ING, -ES** to be overly concerned with small details

FUSSER — *n* pl. **-S** one that fusses

FUSSPOT — *n* pl. **-S** a fusser

FUSSY — *adj* **FUSSIER, FUSSIEST** overly concerned with small details **FUSSILY** *adv*

FUSTIAN — *n* pl. **-S** a cotton fabric

FUSTIC — *n* pl. **-S** a tropical tree

FUSTY — *adj* **-TIER, -TIEST** musty **FUSTILY** *adv*

FUSUMA — *n* pl. **FUSUMA** a sliding partition in a Japanese house

FUTHARC — *n* pl. **-S** futhark

FUTHARK — *n* pl. **-S** an ancient alphabet

FUTHORC — *n* pl. **-S** futhark

FUTHORK — *n* pl. **-S** futhark

FUTILE — *adj* having no useful result **FUTILELY** *adv*

FUTILITY — *n* pl. **-TIES** the quality of being futile

FUTON — *n* pl. **-S** a cotton-filled mattress for use as a bed

FUTTOCK — *n* pl. **-S** a curved timber in the frame of a wooden ship

FUTURE — *n* pl. **-S** the time yet to come **FUTURAL** *adj*

FUTURISM — *n* pl. **-S** an artistic and literary movement

FUTURIST — *n* pl. **-S** an advocate of futurism

FUTURITY — *n* pl. **-TIES** the future

FUTZ — *v* **-ED, -ING, -ES** to spend time aimlessly

FUZE — *v* **FUZED, FUZING, FUZES** to fuse

FUZEE — *n* pl. **-S** fusee

FUZELESS — *adj* fuseless

FUZIL — *n* pl. **-S** fusil

FUZING — present participle of fuze

FUZZ — *v* **-ED, -ING, -ES** to become fuzzy

FUZZBALL — *n* pl. **-S** a ball of fuzz (a fluffy mass of hair or fiber)

FUZZTONE — *n* pl. **-S** a blurred audio effect

FUZZY — *adj* **FUZZIER, FUZZIEST** blurry **FUZZILY** *adv*

FYCE — *n* pl. **-S** feist

FYKE — *n* pl. **-S** a bag-shaped fishnet

FYLFOT — *n* pl. **-S** a swastika

FYNBOS — *n* pl. **FYNBOS** a type of biome in South Africa

FYTTE — *n* pl. **-S** a division of a poem or song

GAB	v **GABBED, GABBING, GABS** to chatter	**GADGET**	n pl. **-S** a mechanical device **GADGETY** adj
GABBA	n pl. **-S** aggressive sounding music with a very fast beat	**GADGETRY**	n pl. **-RIES** the devising or constructing of gadgets
GABBARD	n pl. **-S** a barge	**GADI**	n pl. **-S** gaddi
GABBART	n pl. **-S** gabbard	**GADID**	n pl. **-S** gadoid
GABBED	past tense of gab	**GADOID**	n pl. **-S** a type of fish
GABBER	n pl. **-S** one that gabs	**GADROON**	v **-ED, -ING, -S** to decorate with bands of fluted or reeded molding
GABBIER	comparative of gabby		
GABBIEST	superlative of gabby	**GADWALL**	n pl. **-S** a wild duck
GABBING	present participle of gab	**GADZOOKS**	interj — used as a mild oath
GABBLE	v **-BLED, -BLING, -BLES** to jabber	**GAE**	v **GAED, GANE** or **GAEN, GAEING** or **GAUN, GAES** to go
GABBLER	n pl. **-S** one that gabbles	**GAFF**	v **-ED, -ING, -S** to catch a fish with a sharp hook
GABBRO	n pl. **-BROS** a type of rock **GABBROIC, GABBROID** adj		
GABBY	adj **-BIER, -BIEST** talkative	**GAFFE**	n pl. **-S** a social blunder
GABELLE	n pl. **-S** a tax on salt **GABELLED** adj	**GAFFER**	n pl. **-S** an old man
		GAG	v **GAGGED, GAGGING, GAGS** to stop up the mouth
GABFEST	n pl. **-S** an informal gathering for general talk	**GAGA**	adj crazy
GABIES	pl. of gaby	**GAGAKU**	n pl. **-S** ancient court music of Japan
GABION	n pl. **-S** a type of basket		
GABLE	v **-BLED, -BLING, -BLES** to form a triangular section of a wall	**GAGE**	v **GAGED, GAGING, GAGES** to pledge as security
GABOON	n pl. **-S** a spittoon	**GAGER**	n pl. **-S** gauger
GABY	n pl. **-BIES** a dolt	**GAGGED**	past tense of gag
GACH	v **-ED, -ING, -ES** to gatch	**GAGGER**	n pl. **-S** one that gags
GACHER	n pl. **-S** gatcher	**GAGGING**	present participle of gag
GAD	v **GADDED, GADDING, GADS** to roam about restlessly	**GAGGLE**	v **-GLED, -GLING, -GLES** to cackle
GADABOUT	n pl. **-S** one that gads about	**GAGING**	present participle of gage
GADARENE	adj headlong	**GAGMAN**	n pl. **-MEN** one who writes jokes
GADDED	past tense of gad	**GAGSTER**	n pl. **-S** a gagman
GADDER	n pl. **-S** one that gads about	**GAHNITE**	n pl. **-S** a mineral
GADDI	n pl. **-S** a hassock	**GAIETY**	n pl. **-ETIES** festive activity
GADDING	present participle of gad	**GAIJIN**	n pl. **GAIJIN** a foreigner in Japan
GADFLY	n pl. **-FLIES** a biting fly	**GAILY**	adv in a gay manner

GAIN   *v* **-ED, -ING, -S** to acquire **GAINABLE** *adj*

GAINER   *n* pl. **-S** one that gains

GAINFUL   *adj* profitable

GAINLESS   *adj* profitless

GAINLY   *adj* **-LIER, -LIEST** graceful

GAINSAY   *v* **-SAID, -SAYING, -SAYS** to deny

GAINST   *prep* against

GAIT   *v* **-ED, -ING, -S** to train a horse to move in a particular way

GAITER   *n* pl. **-S** a covering for the lower leg **GAITERED** *adj*

GAL   *n* pl. **-S** a girl

GALA   *n* pl. **-S** a celebration

GALABIA   *n* pl. **-S** djellaba

GALABIEH   *n* pl. **-S** djellaba

GALABIYA   *n* pl. **-S** djellaba

GALACTIC   *adj* pertaining to a galaxy

GALAGO   *n* pl. **-GOS** a small primate

GALAH   *n* pl. **-S** a cockatoo

GALANGA   *n* pl. **-S** galangal

GALANGAL   *n* pl. **-S** a medicinal plant

GALATEA   *n* pl. **-S** a strong cotton fabric

GALAVANT   *v* **-ED, -ING, -S** to gad about

GALAX   *n* pl. **-ES** an evergreen herb

GALAXY   *n* pl. **-AXIES** a large system of celestial bodies

GALBANUM   *n* pl. **-S** a gum resin

GALE   *v* **GALED, GALING, GALES** to frolic playfully

GALEA   *n* pl. **-LEAS** or **-LEAE** a helmet-shaped anatomical part **GALEATE, GALEATED** *adj*

GALENA   *n* pl. **-S** the principal ore of lead **GALENIC** *adj*

GALENITE   *n* pl. **-S** galena

GALERE   *n* pl. **-S** a group of people having a common quality

GALETTE   *n* pl. **-S** a flat round cake

GALILEE   *n* pl. **-S** a type of porch

GALING   present participle of gale

GALIOT   *n* pl. **-S** galliot

GALIPOT   *n* pl. **-S** a type of turpentine

GALIVANT   *v* **-ED, -ING, -S** to gad about

GALL   *v* **-ED, -ING, -S** to vex or irritate

GALLANT   *v* **-ED, -ING, -S** to court a woman

GALLATE   *n* pl. **-S** a chemical salt

GALLEASS   *n* pl. **-ES** a large war galley

GALLEIN   *n* pl. **-S** a green dye

GALLEON   *n* pl. **-S** a large sailing vessel

GALLERIA   *n* pl. **-S** a roofed promenade or court

GALLERY   *v* **-LERIED, -LERYING, -LERIES** to provide with a long covered area

GALLET   *v* **-ED, -ING, -S** to fill in mortar joints with stone chips

GALLETA   *n* pl. **-S** a perennial grass

GALLEY   *n* pl. **-LEYS** a long, low medieval ship

GALLFLY   *n* pl. **-FLIES** a small insect

GALLIARD   *n* pl. **-S** a lively dance

GALLIASS   *n* pl. **-ES** galleass

GALLIC   *adj* containing gallium

GALLICA   *n* pl. **-S** a European rose

GALLICAN   *adj* pertaining to a French religious movement

GALLIED   past tense of gally

GALLIES   present 3d person sing. of gally

GALLIOT   *n* pl. **-S** a small galley

GALLIPOT   *n* pl. **-S** a small earthen jar

GALLIUM   *n* pl. **-S** a metallic element

GALLNUT   *n* pl. **-S** an abnormal swelling of plant tissue

GALLON   *n* pl. **-S** a unit of liquid measure

GALLOON   *n* pl. **-S** an ornamental braid

GALLOOT   *n* pl. **-S** galoot

GALLOP   *v* **-ED, -ING, -S** to ride a horse at full speed

GALLOPER   *n* pl. **-S** one that gallops

GALLOUS   *adj* containing gallium

GALLOWAY   *n* pl. **-WAYS** a breed of hornless cattle

GALLOWS   *n* pl. **-ES** a structure used for hanging a condemned person

GALLUS   *n* pl. **-ES** a suspender for trousers **GALLUSED** *adj*

GALLY   *v* **-LIED, -LYING, -LIES** to frighten

GALOOT   *n* pl. **-S** an awkward or uncouth person

GALOP   *v* **-ED, -ING, -S** to dance a galop (a lively round dance)

GALOPADE   *n* pl. **-S** a lively round dance

GALORE   *n* pl. **-S** abundance

GALOSH   *n* pl. **-ES** an overshoe **GALOSHED** *adj*

GALOSHE	*n* pl. **-S** galosh
GALUMPH	*v* **-ED, -ING, -S** to move clumsily
GALVANIC	*adj* pertaining to a direct electric current
GALYAC	*n* pl. **-S** galyak
GALYAK	*n* pl. **-S** a fur made from lambskin
GAM	*v* **GAMMED, GAMMING, GAMS** to visit socially
GAMA	*n* pl. **-S** a pasture grass
GAMASHES	*n/pl* boots worn by horseback riders
GAMAY	*n* pl. **-MAYS** a red grape
GAMB	*n* pl. **-S** a leg
GAMBA	*n* pl. **-S** a bass viol
GAMBADE	*n* pl. **-S** a gambado
GAMBADO	*n* pl. **-DOS** or **-DOES** a leap made by a horse
GAMBE	*n* pl. **-S** gamb
GAMBESON	*n* pl. **-S** a medieval coat
GAMBIA	*n* pl. **-S** gambier
GAMBIER	*n* pl. **-S** an extract obtained from an Asian vine
GAMBIR	*n* pl. **-S** gambier
GAMBIT	*n* pl. **-S** a type of chess opening
GAMBLE	*v* **-BLED, -BLING, -BLES** to play a game of chance for money or valuables
GAMBLER	*n* pl. **-S** one that gambles
GAMBOGE	*n* pl. **-S** a gum resin
GAMBOL	*v* **-BOLED, -BOLING, -BOLS** or **-BOLLED, -BOLLING, -BOLS** to leap about playfully
GAMBREL	*n* pl. **-S** a part of a horse's leg
GAMBUSIA	*n* pl. **-S** a small fish
GAME	*adj* **GAMER, GAMEST** plucky
GAME	*v* **GAMED, GAMING, GAMES** to gamble
GAMEBOOK	*n* pl. **-S** a book of strategies used by a sports team
GAMECOCK	*n* pl. **-S** a rooster trained for fighting
GAMEFISH	*n* pl. **-ES** a fish caught for sport
GAMEFOWL	*n* pl. **-S** a gamecock
GAMELAN	*n* pl. **-S** a type of orchestra
GAMELIKE	*adj* similar to a game (a contest governed by a set of rules)
GAMELY	*adv* in a game manner
GAMENESS	*n* pl. **-ES** the quality of being game
GAMEPLAY	*n* pl. **-S** the way a computer or video game is played
GAMER	*n* pl. **-S** an avid game player
GAMESMAN	*n* pl. **-MEN** one who plays games
GAMESOME	*adj* playful
GAMEST	superlative of game
GAMESTER	*n* pl. **-S** a gambler
GAMETE	*n* pl. **-S** a mature reproductive cell **GAMETAL, GAMETIC** *adj*
GAMEY	*adj* **GAMIER, GAMIEST** gamy
GAMIC	*adj* requiring fertilization
GAMIER	comparative of gamy
GAMIEST	superlative of gamy
GAMILY	*adv* in a game manner
GAMIN	*n* pl. **-S** an urchin
GAMINE	*n* pl. **-S** a tomboy
GAMINESS	*n* pl. **-ES** the quality of being gamy
GAMING	*n* pl. **-S** the practice of gambling
GAMMA	*n* pl. **-S** a Greek letter
GAMMADIA	*n/pl* Greek ornamental designs
GAMMED	past tense of gam
GAMMER	*n* pl. **-S** an old woman
GAMMIER	comparative of gammy
GAMMIEST	superlative of gammy
GAMMING	present participle of gam
GAMMON	*v* **-ED, -ING, -S** to mislead by deceptive talk
GAMMONER	*n* pl. **-S** one that gammons
GAMMY	*adj* **-MIER, -MIEST** lame
GAMODEME	*n* pl. **-S** a somewhat isolated breeding community of organisms
GAMP	*n* pl. **-S** a large umbrella
GAMUT	*n* pl. **-S** an entire range
GAMY	*adj* **GAMIER, GAMIEST** plucky
GAN	past tense of gin
GANACHE	*n* pl. **-S** creamy chocolate mixture
GANDER	*v* **-ED, -ING, -S** to wander
GANE	a past participle of gae
GANEF	*n* pl. **-S** a thief
GANEV	*n* pl. **-S** ganef
GANG	*v* **-ED, -ING, -S** to form into a gang (a group)
GANGBANG	*v* **-ED, -ING, -S** to participate in gang-related activities
GANGER	*n* pl. **-S** a foreman of a gang of laborers

GANGLAND *n* pl. **-S** the criminal underworld

GANGLE *v* **-GLED, -GLING, -GLES** to move awkwardly

GANGLIA a pl. of ganglion

GANGLIAL *adj* gangliar

GANGLIAR *adj* pertaining to a ganglion

GANGLIER comparative of gangly

GANGLIEST superlative of gangly

GANGLING *adj* awkwardly tall and lanky

GANGLION *n* pl. **-GLIONS** or **-GLIA** a group of nerve cells

GANGLY *adj* **-GLIER, -GLIEST** gangling

GANGPLOW *n* pl. **-S** an agricultural implement

GANGREL *n* pl. **-S** a vagabond

GANGRENE *v* **-GRENED, -GRENING, -GRENES** to suffer the loss of tissue in part of the body

GANGSTA *n* pl. **-S** a member of a street gang

GANGSTER *n* pl. **-S** a member of a criminal gang

GANGUE *n* pl. **-S** the worthless rock in which valuable minerals are found

GANGWAY *n* pl. **-WAYS** a passageway

GANISTER *n* pl. **-S** a type of rock

GANJA *n* pl. **-S** cannabis used for smoking

GANJAH *n* pl. **-S** ganja

GANNET *n* pl. **-S** a large seabird

GANNETRY *n* pl. **-RIES** a place where gannets breed

GANOF *n* pl. **-S** ganef

GANOID *n* pl. **-S** a type of fish

GANTLET *v* **-ED, -ING, -S** to overlap railroad tracks

GANTLINE *n* pl. **-S** a rope on a ship

GANTLOPE *n* pl. **-S** a former military punishment

GANTRY *n* pl. **-TRIES** a structure for supporting railroad signals

GANYMEDE *n* pl. **-S** a youth who serves liquors

GANZFELD *n* pl. **-S** a technique of controlled sensory input used in parapsychology

GAOL *v* **-ED, -ING, -S** to jail

GAOLBIRD *n* pl. **-S** jailbird

GAOLER *n* pl. **-S** jailer

GAP *v* **GAPPED, GAPPING, GAPS** to make an opening in

GAPE *v* **GAPED, GAPING, GAPES** to stare with open mouth

GAPER *n* pl. **-S** one that gapes

GAPESEED *n* pl. **-S** something that causes wonder

GAPEWORM *n* pl. **-S** a worm that causes a disease of young birds

GAPING present participle of gape

GAPINGLY *adv* in a gaping manner

GAPLESS *adj* having no gap

GAPOSIS *n* pl. **-SISES** a gap in a row of buttons or snaps

GAPPED past tense of gap

GAPPING present participle of gap

GAPPY *adj* **-PIER, -PIEST** having openings

GAPY *adj* infested with gapeworms

GAR *v* **GARRED, GARRING, GARS** to cause or compel

GARAGE *v* **-RAGED, -RAGING, -RAGES** to put in a garage (a car shelter)

GARB *v* **-ED, -ING, -S** to clothe

GARBAGE *n* pl. **-S** food waste **GARBAGEY, GARBAGY** *adj*

GARBANZO *n* pl. **-ZOS** a chickpea

GARBLE *v* **-BLED, -BLING, -BLES** to distort the meaning of

GARBLER *n* pl. **-S** one that garbles

GARBLESS *adj* being without clothing

GARBOARD *n* pl. **-S** a plank on a ship's bottom

GARBOIL *n* pl. **-S** turmoil

GARCON *n* pl. **-S** a waiter

GARDA *n* pl. **-DAI** a police officer in Ireland

GARDANT *adj* turned directly toward the observer — used of a heraldic animal

GARDEN *v* **-ED, -ING, -S** to cultivate a plot of ground

GARDENER *n* pl. **-S** one that gardens

GARDENIA *n* pl. **-S** a tropical shrub or tree

GARDYLOO *interj* — used as a warning cry

GARFISH *n* pl. **-ES** a freshwater fish

GARGANEY *n* pl. **-NEYS** a small duck

GARGET *n* pl. **-S** mastitis of domestic animals **GARGETY** *adj*

GARGLE *v* **-GLED, -GLING, -GLES** to rinse the mouth or throat

GARGLER *n* pl. **-S** one that gargles

GARGOYLE *n* pl. **-S** an ornamental figure

GARIGUE *n* pl. **-S** a low scrubland

GARISH	*adj* gaudy **GARISHLY** *adv*
GARLAND	*v* **-ED, -ING, -S** to deck with wreaths of flowers
GARLIC	*v* **-LICKED, -LICKING, -LICS** to season with garlic (an herb used in cooking)
GARLICKY	*adj* **-LICKIER, -LICKIEST** smelling or tasting of garlic
GARMENT	*v* **-ED, -ING, -S** to clothe
GARNER	*v* **-ED, -ING, -S** to gather and store
GARNET	*n* pl. **-S** a mineral
GARNI	*adj* garnished
GARNISH	*v* **-ED, -ING, -ES** to decorate
GAROTE	*v* **-ROTED, -ROTING, -ROTES** to garrote
GAROTTE	*v* **-ROTTED, -ROTTING, -ROTTES** to garrote
GAROTTER	*n* pl. **-S** one that garottes
GARPIKE	*n* pl. **-S** a garfish
GARRED	past tense of gar
GARRET	*n* pl. **-S** an attic **GARRETED** *adj*
GARRING	present participle of gar
GARRISON	*v* **-ED, -ING, -S** to assign to a military post
GARRON	*n* pl. **-S** a small, sturdy horse
GARROTE	*v* **-ROTED, -ROTING, -ROTES** to execute by strangling
GARROTER	*n* pl. **-S** one that garrotes
GARROTTE	*v* **-ROTTED, -ROTTING, -ROTTES** to garrote
GARTER	*v* **-ED, -ING, -S** to fasten with an elastic band
GARTH	*n* pl. **-S** a yard or garden
GARVEY	*n* pl. **-VEYS** a small scow
GAS	*v* **GASSED, GASSING, GASES** or **GASSES** to supply with gas (a substance capable of indefinite expansion)
GASALIER	*n* pl. **-S** gaselier
GASBAG	*n* pl. **-S** a bag for holding gas
GASCON	*n* pl. **-S** a boaster
GASEITY	*n* pl. **-TIES** the state of being a gas
GASELIER	*n* pl. **-S** a gaslight chandelier
GASEOUS	*adj* pertaining to gas
GASH	*adj* **GASHER, GASHEST** knowing
GASH	*v* **-ED, -ING, -ES** to make a long deep cut in
GASHOUSE	*n* pl. **-S** a gasworks
GASIFIED	past tense of gasify
GASIFIER	*n* pl. **-S** one that gasifies
GASIFORM	*adj* having the form of gas
GASIFY	*v* **-IFIED, -IFYING, -IFIES** to convert into gas
GASKET	*n* pl. **-S** packing for making something fluid-tight **GASKETED** *adj*
GASKIN	*n* pl. **-S** a part of a horse's leg
GASKING	*n* pl. **-S** a gasket
GASLESS	*adj* having no gas
GASLIGHT	*n* pl. **-S** light made by burning gas
GASLIT	*adj* illuminated by gaslight
GASMAN	*n* pl. **-MEN** an employee of a gas company
GASOGENE	*n* pl. **-S** gazogene
GASOHOL	*n* pl. **-S** a fuel mixture of gasoline and ethyl alcohol
GASOLENE	*n* pl. **-S** gasoline
GASOLIER	*n* pl. **-S** gaselier
GASOLINE	*n* pl. **-S** a liquid fuel
GASP	*v* **-ED, -ING, -S** to breathe convulsively
GASPER	*n* pl. **-S** a cigarette
GASSED	past tense of gas
GASSER	*n* pl. **-S** one that gasses
GASSES	a present 3d person sing. of gas
GASSING	*n* pl. **-S** a poisoning by noxious gas
GASSY	*adj* **-SIER, -SIEST** containing gas **GASSILY** *adv*
GAST	*v* **-ED, -ING, -S** to scare
GASTER	*n* pl. **-S** the enlarged part of the abdomen in some insects
GASTHAUS	*n* pl. **-ES** or **-ER** a small hotel in Germany
GASTIGHT	*adj* not allowing gas to escape or enter
GASTNESS	*n* pl. **-ES** fright
GASTRAEA	*n* pl. **-S** a type of metazoan
GASTRAL	*adj* pertaining to the stomach
GASTREA	*n* pl. **-S** gastraea
GASTRIC	*adj* pertaining to the stomach
GASTRIN	*n* pl. **-S** a hormone
GASTRULA	*n* pl. **-LAS** or **-LAE** a metazoan embryo
GASWORKS	*n* pl. **GASWORKS** a factory where gas is produced
GAT	*n* pl. **-S** a pistol

GATCH	v **-ED, -ING, -ES** to behave boastfully
GATCHER	n pl. **-S** one that gatches
GATE	v **GATED, GATING, GATES** to supply with a gate (a movable barrier)
GATEAU	n pl. **-TEAUS** or **-TEAUX** a fancy cake
GATEFOLD	n pl. **-S** a folded insert in a book or magazine
GATELEG	n pl. **-S** a table with extensions supported by movable legs
GATELESS	adj lacking a gate
GATELIKE	adj resembling a gate
GATEMAN	n pl. **-MEN** a person in charge of a gate
GATEPOST	n pl. **-S** a post from which a gate is hung
GATER	n pl. **-S** gator
GATEWAY	n pl. **-WAYS** a passage that may be closed by a gate
GATHER	v **-ED, -ING, -S** to bring together into one place or group
GATHERER	n pl. **-S** one that gathers
GATING	n pl. **-S** the process of opening and closing a channel
GATOR	n pl. **-S** an alligator
GAUCH	v **-ED, -ING, -ES** to gatch
GAUCHE	adj **GAUCHER, GAUCHEST** lacking social grace **GAUCHELY** adv
GAUCHER	n pl. **-S** gatcher
GAUCHO	n pl. **-CHOS** a cowboy of the South American pampas
GAUD	n pl. **-S** a showy ornament
GAUDERY	n pl. **-ERIES** finery
GAUDY	adj **GAUDIER, GAUDIEST** tastelessly showy **GAUDILY** adv
GAUDY	n pl. **-DIES** a festival
GAUFFER	v **-ED, -ING, -S** to goffer
GAUGE	v **GAUGED, GAUGING, GAUGES** to measure precisely
GAUGER	n pl. **-S** one that gauges
GAULT	n pl. **-S** a heavy, thick clay soil
GAUM	v **-ED, -ING, -S** to smear
GAUN	present participle of gae
GAUNCH	n pl. **-ES** underpants
GAUNT	adj **GAUNTER, GAUNTEST** emaciated **GAUNTLY** adv
GAUNTLET	v **-ED, -ING, -S** to gantlet

GAUNTRY	n pl. **-TRIES** gantry
GAUR	n pl. **-S** a wild ox
GAUSS	n pl. **-ES** a unit of magnetic induction
GAUZE	n pl. **-S** a transparent fabric
GAUZY	adj **GAUZIER, GAUZIEST** resembling gauze **GAUZILY** adv
GAVAGE	n pl. **-S** introduction of material into the stomach by a tube
GAVE	past tense of give
GAVEL	v **-ELED, -ELING, -ELS** or **-ELLED, -ELLING, -ELS** to signal for attention or order by use of a gavel (a small mallet)
GAVELOCK	n pl. **-S** a crowbar
GAVIAL	n pl. **-S** a large reptile
GAVOT	n pl. **-S** a French dance
GAVOTTE	v **-VOTTED, -VOTTING, -VOTTES** to dance a gavot
GAWK	v **-ED, -ING, -S** to stare stupidly
GAWKER	n pl. **-S** one that gawks
GAWKIER	comparative of gawky
GAWKIES	pl. of gawky
GAWKISH	adj gawky
GAWKY	adj **GAWKIER, GAWKIEST** awkward **GAWKILY** adv
GAWKY	n pl. **GAWKIES** an awkward person
GAWMOGE	n pl. **-S** a clownish person
GAWP	v **-ED, -ING, -S** to stare stupidly
GAWPER	n pl. **-S** one that gawps
GAWSIE	adj well-fed and healthy looking
GAWSY	adj gawsie
GAY	adj **GAYER, GAYEST** 1. merry 2. homosexual
GAY	n pl. **GAYS** a homosexual
GAYAL	n pl. **-S** a domesticated ox
GAYDAR	n pl. **-S** the ability to recognize that a person is homosexual
GAYETY	n pl. **-ETIES** gaiety
GAYLY	adv in a gay manner
GAYNESS	n pl. **-ES** the state of being gay
GAYWINGS	n pl. **GAYWINGS** a perennial herb
GAZABO	n pl. **-BOS** or **-BOES** a fellow
GAZANIA	n pl. **-S** a South African herb
GAZAR	n pl. **-S** silky sheer fabric
GAZE	v **GAZED, GAZING, GAZES** to look intently

GAZEBO   *n* pl. **-BOS** or **-BOES** a roofed structure open on the sides

GAZELLE   *n* pl. **-S** a small antelope

GAZER   *n* pl. **-S** one that gazes

GAZETTE   *v* **-ZETTED, -ZETTING, -ZETTES** to announce in an official journal

GAZING   present participle of gaze

GAZOGENE   *n* pl. **-S** an apparatus for carbonating liquids

GAZPACHO   *n* pl. **-CHOS** a cold, spicy soup

GAZUMP   *v* **-ED, -ING, -S** to cheat by raising the price originally agreed upon

GAZUMPER   *n* pl. **-S** one that gazumps

GAZUNDER   *v* **-ED, -ING, -S** to lower the buyer's offer to a seller of a property

GEAN   *n* pl **-S** a wild sweet cherry

GEAR   *v* **-ED, -ING, -S** to provide with gears (toothed machine parts)

GEARBOX   *n* pl. **-ES** an automotive transmission

GEARCASE   *n* pl. **-S** a casing for gears

GEARHEAD   *n* pl. **-S** a mechanically inclined person

GEARING   *n* pl. **-S** a system of gears

GEARLESS   *adj* being without gears

GECK   *v* **-ED, -ING, -S** to mock

GECKO   *n* pl. **GECKOS** or **GECKOES** a small lizard

GED   *n* pl. **-S** a food fish

GEE   *v* **GEED, GEEING, GEES** to turn to the right

GEEGAW   *n* pl. **-S** gewgaw

GEEK   *n* pl. **-S** a single-minded enthusiast or expert

GEEKDOM   *n* pl. **-S** the world of geeks

GEEKED   *adj* filled with enthusiasm

GEEKISH   *adj* geeky

GEEKY   *adj* **GEEKIER, GEEKIEST** socially awkward or unappealing

GEEPOUND   *n* pl. **-S** a unit of mass

GEESE   pl. of goose

GEEST   *n* pl. **-S** old alluvial matter

GEEZ   *interj* jeez

GEEZER   *n* pl. **-S** an eccentric man

GEISHA   *n* pl. **-S** a Japanese girl trained to entertain

GEL   *v* **GELLED, GELLING, GELS** to become like jelly **GELABLE** *adj*

GELADA   *n* pl. **-S** a baboon

GELANT   *n* pl. **-S** gellant

GELATE   *v* **-ATED, -ATING, -ATES** to gel

GELATI   *n* pl. **-S** gelato

GELATIN   *n* pl. **-S** a glutinous substance

GELATINE   *n* pl. **-S** gelatin

GELATING   present participle of gelate

GELATION   *n* pl. **-S** the process of gelling

GELATO   *n* pl. **-TOS** or **-TI** Italian ice cream

GELCAP   *n* pl. **-S** a tablet coated with gelatin

GELCOAT   *n* pl. **-S** a surface layer of polyester resin

GELD   *v* **-ED, -ING, -S** to castrate

GELDER   *n* pl. **-S** one that gelds

GELDING   *n* pl. **-S** a castrated animal

GELEE   *n* pl. **-S** a cosmetic gel

GELID   *adj* icy **GELIDLY** *adv*

GELIDITY   *n* pl. **-TIES** iciness

GELLANT   *n* pl. **-S** a substance used to produce gelling

GELLED   past tense of gel

GELLING   present participle of gel

GELLY   *n* pl. **GELLIES** gelignite (a high explosive)

GELSEMIA   *n/pl* medicinal plant roots

GELT   *n* pl. **-S** money

GEM   *v* **GEMMED, GEMMING, GEMS** to adorn with gems (precious stones)

GEMATRIA   *n* pl. **-S** a cabalistic method of interpreting the Scriptures

GEMINAL   *adj* of or pertaining to two substituents on the same atom

GEMINATE   *v* **-NATED, -NATING, -NATES** to arrange in pairs

GEMLIKE   *adj* resembling a gem

GEMMA   *n* pl. **-MAE** an asexual reproductive structure

GEMMATE   *v* **-MATED, -MATING, -MATES** to produce gemmae

GEMMED   past tense of gem

GEMMIER   comparative of gemmy

GEMMIEST   superlative of gemmy

GEMMILY   *adv* in a manner suggesting a gem

GEMMING   present participle of gem

GEMMULE   *n* pl. **-S** a small gemma

GEMMY   *adj* **-MIER, -MIEST** resembling a gem

GEMOLOGY   *n* pl. **-GIES** the science of gems

GEMOT   *n* pl. **-S** a public meeting in Anglo-Saxon England

GEMOTE	*n* pl. **-S** gemot
GEMSBOK	*n* pl. **-S** a large antelope
GEMSBUCK	*n* pl. **-S** gemsbok
GEMSTONE	*n* pl. **-S** a precious stone
GEN	*v* **GENNED, GENNING, GENS** to provide or obtain information
GENDARME	*n* pl. **-S** a policeman
GENDER	*v* **-ED, -ING, -S** to engender
GENE	*n* pl. **-S** a hereditary unit
GENERA	a pl. of genus
GENERAL	*n* pl. **-S** a military officer
GENERATE	*v* **-ATED, -ATING, -ATES** to bring into existence
GENERIC	*n* pl. **-S** a type of drug
GENEROUS	*adj* willing to give
GENESIS	*n* pl. **GENESES** an origin
GENET	*n* pl. **-S** a carnivorous mammal
GENETIC	*adj* pertaining to genetics
GENETICS	*n/pl* the science of heredity
GENETTE	*n* pl. **-S** genet
GENEVA	*n* pl. **-S** a liquor
GENIAL	*adj* having a pleasant or friendly manner **GENIALLY** *adv*
GENIC	*adj* pertaining to genes
GENIE	*n* pl. **-S** jinni
GENII	a pl. of genius
GENIP	*n* pl. **-S** a tropical tree
GENIPAP	*n* pl. **-S** a tropical tree
GENIPAPO	*n* pl. **-POS** genipap
GENISTA	*n* pl. **-S** a shrub with yellow flowers
GENITAL	*adj* pertaining to reproduction
GENITALS	*n/pl* the sexual organs
GENITIVE	*n* pl. **-S** a grammatical case
GENITOR	*n* pl. **-S** a male parent
GENITURE	*n* pl. **-S** birth
GENIUS	*n* pl. **GENIUSES** or **GENII** an exceptional natural aptitude
GENLOCK	*n* pl. **-S** a device for synchronizing different video signals
GENNAKER	*n* pl. **-S** a spinnaker sail
GENNED	past tense of gen
GENNING	present participle of gen
GENOA	*n* pl. **-S** a triangular sail
GENOCIDE	*n* pl. **-S** the deliberate extermination of a national or racial group
GENOGRAM	*n* pl. **-S** a diagram of the history of behavior patterns of a family
GENOISE	*n* pl. **-S** a rich sponge cake
GENOM	*n* pl. **-S** genome
GENOME	*n* pl. **-S** a haploid set of chromosomes **GENOMIC** *adj*
GENOMICS	*n/pl* the study of genomes
GENOTYPE	*n* pl. **-S** the genetic constitution of an organism
GENRE	*n* pl. **-S** a type or kind
GENRO	*n* pl. **-ROS** a group of elder statesmen in Japan
GENS	*n* pl. **GENTES** a type of clan
GENSENG	*n* pl. **-S** ginseng
GENT	*n* pl. **-S** a gentleman
GENTEEL	*adj* **-TEELER, -TEELEST** well-bred or refined
GENTES	pl. of gens
GENTIAN	*n* pl. **-S** a flowering plant
GENTIL	*adj* kind
GENTILE	*n* pl. **-S** a non-Jewish person
GENTLE	*adj* **-TLER, -TLEST** mild **GENTLY** *adv*
GENTLE	*v* **-TLED, -TLING, -TLES** to tame
GENTOO	*n* pl. **-TOOS** a gray-backed penguin
GENTRICE	*n* pl. **-S** good breeding
GENTRIFY	*v* **-FIED, -FYING, -FIES** to renew a decayed urban area so as to attract middle-class residents
GENTRY	*n* pl. **-TRIES** people of high social class
GENTS	*n/pl* a public men's room
GENU	*n* pl. **GENUA** the knee
GENUINE	*adj* authentic
GENUS	*n* pl. **GENUSES** or **GENERA** a kind, sort, or class
GEOCACHE	*v* **-CACHED, -CACHING, -CACHES** to search for hidden items by using a Global Positioning System device as part of a game
GEODE	*n* pl. **-S** a type of rock
GEODESIC	*n* pl. **-S** a geometric line
GEODESY	*n* pl. **-SIES** geographical surveying
GEODETIC	*adj* pertaining to geodesy
GEODIC	*adj* of or pertaining to a geode
GEODUCK	*n* pl. **-S** a large, edible clam
GEOGNOSY	*n* pl. **-SIES** a branch of geology
GEOID	*n* pl. **-S** a hypothetical surface of the earth **GEOIDAL** *adj*

GEOLOGER	*n* pl. **-S** a specialist in geology	**GERONTIC**	*adj* pertaining to old age
GEOLOGY	*n* pl. **-GIES** the science that deals with the origin and structure of the earth **GEOLOGIC** *adj*	**GERUND**	*n* pl. **-S** a verbal noun
		GESNERIA	*adj* designating a type of flowering plant
GEOMANCY	*n* pl. **-CIES** a method of foretelling the future by geographical features	**GESSO**	*n* pl. **-SOES** a plaster mixture
GEOMETER	*n* pl. **-S** a specialist in geometry	**GESSOED**	*adj* having gesso as a coating
GEOMETRY	*n* pl. **-TRIES** a branch of mathematics	**GEST**	*n* pl. **-S** a feat
		GESTALT	*n* pl. **-STALTS** or **-STALTEN** a unified whole
GEOPHAGY	*n* pl. **-GIES** the practice of eating earthy substances	**GESTAPO**	*n* pl. **-POS** a secret-police organization
GEOPHONE	*n* pl. **-S** a device that detects vibrations in the earth	**GESTATE**	*v* **-TATED, -TATING, -TATES** to carry in the uterus during pregnancy
GEOPHYTE	*n* pl. **-S** a plant having underground buds		
GEOPONIC	*adj* pertaining to farming	**GESTE**	*n* pl. **-S** gest
GEOPROBE	*n* pl. **-S** a spacecraft for exploring space near the earth	**GESTIC**	*adj* pertaining to bodily motion
		GESTICAL	*adj* gestic
GEORGIC	*n* pl. **-S** a poem about farming	**GESTURAL**	*adj* pertaining to or consisting of gestures (expressive bodily motions)
GEOTAXIS	*n* pl. **-TAXES** the movement of an organism in response to gravity		
GERAH	*n* pl. **-S** a Hebrew unit of weight	**GESTURE**	*v* **-TURED, -TURING, -TURES** to express by bodily motion
GERANIAL	*n* pl. **-S** citral		
GERANIOL	*n* pl. **-S** an alcohol used in perfumes	**GESTURER**	*n* pl. **-S** one that gestures
		GET	*n* pl. **GITTIN** a divorce by Jewish law
GERANIUM	*n* pl. **-S** a flowering plant		
GERARDIA	*n* pl. **-S** an herb	**GET**	*v* **GOT, GOTTEN, GETTING, GETS** to obtain or acquire **GETABLE, GETTABLE** *adj*
GERBERA	*n* pl. **-S** an herb		
GERBIL	*n* pl. **-S** a burrowing rodent	**GETA**	*n* pl. **-S** a Japanese wooden clog
GERBILLE	*n* pl. **-S** gerbil	**GETAWAY**	*n* pl. **-AWAYS** an escape
GERENT	*n* pl. **-S** a ruler or manager	**GETOUT**	*n* pl. **-S** an excuse to avoid doing something
GERENUK	*n* pl. **-S** a long-necked antelope		
GERM	*n* pl. **-S** a microorganism that causes disease	**GETTER**	*v* **-ED, -ING, -S** to purify with a chemically active substance
GERMAN	*n* pl. **-S** an elaborate dance	**GETTING**	present participle of get
GERMANE	*adj* relevant	**GETUP**	*n* pl. **-S** a costume
GERMANIC	*adj* containing germanium (a metallic element)	**GEUM**	*n* pl. **-S** a perennial herb
		GEWGAW	*n* pl. **-S** a showy trinket **GEWGAWED** *adj*
GERMEN	*n* pl. **-MENS** or **-MINA** something that serves as an origin		
		GEY	*adv* very
GERMFREE	*adj* free from germs	**GEYSER**	*v* **-ED, -ING, -S** to eject jets of hot water and steam
GERMIER	comparative of germy		
GERMIEST	superlative of germy	**GHARIAL**	*n* pl. **-S** a large reptile
GERMINA	a pl. of germen	**GHARRI**	*n* pl. **-S** gharry
GERMINAL	*adj* being in the earliest stage of development	**GHARRY**	*n* pl. **-RIES** a carriage used in India
		GHAST	*adj* ghastly
GERMLIKE	*adj* resembling a germ	**GHASTFUL**	*adj* frightful
GERMY	*adj* **GERMIER, GERMIEST** full of germs	**GHASTLY**	*adj* **-LIER, -LIEST** terrifying
		GHAT	*n* pl. **-S** a passage to a river

GHAUT	*n* pl. **-S** ghat
GHAZAL	*n* pl. **-S** an amatory lyric poem
GHAZI	*n* pl. **-S** or **-ES** a Muslim war hero
GHEE	*n* pl. **-S** a kind of liquid butter
GHERAO	*v* **-ED, -ING, -ES** to coerce by physical means
GHERKIN	*n* pl. **-S** a small cucumber
GHETTO	*v* **-ED, -ING, -S** or **-ES** to isolate in a slum
GHI	*n* pl. **-S** ghee
GHIBLI	*n* pl. **-S** a hot desert wind
GHILLIE	*n* pl. **-S** a type of shoe
GHOST	*v* **-ED, -ING, -S** to haunt
GHOSTING	*n* pl. **-S** a false image on a television screen
GHOSTLY	*adj* **-LIER, -LIEST** spectral
GHOSTY	*adj* **GHOSTIER, GHOSTIEST** ghostly
GHOUL	*n* pl. **-S** a demon **GHOULISH** *adj*
GHOULIE	*n* pl. **-S** a ghoul
GHYLL	*n* pl. **-S** a ravine
GI	*n* pl. **-S** a white garment worn in martial arts
GIANT	*n* pl. **-S** a person or thing of great size
GIANTESS	*n* pl. **-ES** a female giant
GIANTISM	*n* pl. **-S** the condition of being a giant
GIAOUR	*n* pl. **-S** a non-Muslim
GIARDIA	*n* pl. **-S** a protozoan inhabiting the intestines
GIB	*v* **GIBBED, GIBBING, GIBS** to fasten with a wedge of wood or metal
GIBBER	*v* **-ED, -ING, -S** to jabber
GIBBET	*v* **-BETED, -BETING, -BETS** or **-BETTED, -BETTING, -BETS** to execute by hanging
GIBBON	*n* pl. **-S** an arboreal ape
GIBBOSE	*adj* gibbous
GIBBOUS	*adj* irregularly rounded
GIBBSITE	*n* pl. **-S** a mineral
GIBE	*v* **GIBED, GIBING, GIBES** to jeer **GIBINGLY** *adv*
GIBER	*n* pl. **-S** one that gibes
GIBLET	*n* pl. **-S** an edible part of a fowl
GIBSON	*n* pl. **-S** a martini served with a tiny onion
GID	*n* pl. **-S** a disease of sheep
GIDDAP	*interj* — used as a command to a horse to go faster
GIDDY	*adj* **-DIER, -DIEST** dizzy **GIDDILY** *adv*
GIDDY	*v* **-DIED, -DYING, -DIES** to make giddy
GIDDYAP	*interj* giddap
GIDDYUP	*interj* giddap
GIE	*v* **GIED, GIEN, GIEING, GIES** to give
GIF	*n* pl. **-S** a computer file in a format for images
GIFT	*v* **-ED, -ING, -S** to present with a gift (something given without charge)
GIFTABLE	*n* pl. **-S** something appropriate for a gift
GIFTEDLY	*adv* in a talented manner
GIFTEE	*n* pl. **-S** one that receives a gift
GIFTING	*n* pl. **-S** the act of presenting with a gift
GIFTLESS	*adj* being without a gift
GIFTWARE	*n* pl. **-S** wares suitable for gifts
GIFTWRAP	*v* **-WRAPPED, -WRAPPING, -WRAPS** to wrap with decorative paper
GIG	*v* **GIGGED, GIGGING, GIGS** to catch fish with a pronged spear
GIGA	*n* pl. **GIGHE** a gigue
GIGABIT	*n* pl. **-S** a unit of information
GIGABYTE	*n* pl. **-S** 1,073,741,824 bytes
GIGAFLOP	*n* pl. **-S** a measure of computing speed
GIGANTIC	*adj* huge
GIGAS	*adj* pertaining to variations in plant development
GIGATON	*n* pl. **-S** a unit of weight
GIGAWATT	*n* pl. **-S** a unit of power
GIGGED	past tense of gig
GIGGING	present participle of gig
GIGGLE	*v* **-GLED, -GLING, -GLES** to laugh in a silly manner
GIGGLER	*n* pl. **-S** one that giggles
GIGGLY	*adj* **-GLIER, -GLIEST** tending to giggle
GIGHE	pl. of giga
GIGLET	*n* pl. **-S** a playful girl
GIGLOT	*n* pl. **-S** giglet
GIGOLO	*n* pl. **-LOS** a man supported financially by a woman

GIGOT	*n* pl. **-S** a leg of lamb
GIGUE	*n* pl. **-S** a lively dance
GILBERT	*n* pl. **-S** a unit of magnetomotive force
GILD	*v* **GILDED** or **GILT, GILDING, GILDS** to cover with a thin layer of gold
GILDER	*n* pl. **-S** one that gilds
GILDHALL	*n* pl. **-S** a town hall
GILDING	*n* pl. **-S** the application of gilt
GILL	*v* **-ED, -ING, -S** to catch fish with a type of net
GILLER	*n* pl. **-S** one that gills
GILLIE	*n* pl. **-S** ghillie
GILLNET	*v* **-NETTED, -NETTING, -NETS** to gill
GILLY	*v* **-LIED, -LYING, -LIES** to transport on a type of wagon
GILT	*n* pl. **-S** the gold with which something is gilded
GILTHEAD	*n* pl. **-S** a marine fish
GIMBAL	*v* **-BALED, -BALING, -BALS** or **-BALLED, -BALLING, -BALS** to support on a set of rings
GIMCRACK	*n* pl. **-S** a gewgaw
GIMEL	*n* pl. **-S** a Hebrew letter
GIMLET	*v* **-ED, -ING, -S** to pierce with a boring tool
GIMMAL	*n* pl. **-S** a pair of interlocked rings
GIMME	*n* pl. **-S** something easily won
GIMMICK	*v* **-ED, -ING, -S** to provide with a gimmick (a novel or tricky feature)
GIMMICKY	*adj* having or being like a gimmick
GIMMIE	*n* pl. **-MIES** an easy golf putt conceded to an opponent
GIMP	*v* **-ED, -ING, -S** to limp
GIMPIER	comparative of gimpy
GIMPIEST	superlative of gimpy
GIMPY	*adj* **GIMPIER, GIMPIEST** limping
GIN	*v* **GAN, GUNNEN, GINNING, GINS** to begin
GIN	*v* **GINNED, GINNING, GINS** to remove seeds from cotton
GINCH	*n* pl. **-ES** gotch
GINGAL	*n* pl. **-S** jingal
GINGALL	*n* pl. **-S** jingal
GINGELEY	*n* pl. **-LEYS** gingelly
GINGELI	*n* pl. **-S** gingelly
GINGELIES	pl. of gingely
GINGELLI	*n* pl. **-S** gingelly
GINGELLY	*n* pl. **-LIES** the sesame seed or its oil
GINGELY	*n* pl. **-LIES** gingelly
GINGER	*v* **-ED, -ING, -S** to flavor with ginger (a pungent spice)
GINGERLY	*adv* in a careful manner
GINGERY	*adj* having the characteristics of ginger
GINGHAM	*n* pl. **-S** a cotton fabric
GINGILI	*n* pl. **-LIS** gingelly
GINGILLI	*n* pl. **-S** gingelly
GINGIVA	*n* pl. **-VAE** the fleshy tissue that surrounds the teeth **GINGIVAL** *adj*
GINGKO	*n* pl. **-KOS** or **-KOES** ginkgo
GINK	*n* pl. **-S** a fellow
GINKGO	*n* pl. **-GOS** or **-GOES** an ornamental tree
GINNED	past tense of gin
GINNER	*n* pl. **-S** one that gins cotton
GINNING	*n* pl. **-S** cotton as it comes from a gin
GINNY	*adj* **GINNIER, GINNIEST** affected with gin (a strong liquor)
GINSENG	*n* pl. **-S** a perennial herb
GIP	*v* **GIPPED, GIPPING, GIPS** to gyp
GIPON	*n* pl. **-S** jupon
GIPPER	*n* pl. **-S** one that gips
GIPSY	*v* **-SIED, -SYING, -SIES** to gypsy
GIPSYDOM	*n* pl. **-S** gypsydom
GIRAFFE	*n* pl. **-S** a long-necked mammal
GIRASOL	*n* pl. **-S** a variety of opal
GIRASOLE	*n* pl. **-S** girasol
GIRD	*v* **GIRDED** or **GIRT, GIRDING, GIRDS** to surround
GIRDER	*n* pl. **-S** a horizontal support
GIRDLE	*v* **-DLED, -DLING, -DLES** to encircle with a belt
GIRDLER	*n* pl. **-S** one that girdles
GIRL	*n* pl. **-S** a female child
GIRLHOOD	*n* pl. **-S** the state of being a girl
GIRLIE	*adj* **GIRLIER, GIRLIEST** girlish
GIRLISH	*adj* of, pertaining to, or having the characteristics of a girl
GIRLY	*adj* **GIRLIER, GIRLIEST** girlie
GIRN	*v* **-ED, -ING, -S** to snarl
GIRO	*n* pl. **-ROS** an autogiro

GIROLLE	*n* pl. **-S** an edible mushroom
GIRON	*n* pl. **-S** gyron
GIROSOL	*n* pl. **-S** girasol
GIRSH	*n* pl. **-ES** qursh
GIRT	*v* **-ED, -ING, -S** to gird
GIRTH	*v* **-ED, -ING, -S** to encircle
GISARME	*n* pl. **-S** a medieval weapon
GISMO	*n* pl. **-MOS** a gadget
GIST	*n* pl. **-S** the main point
GIT	*v* **GITTED, GITTING, GITS** to get
GITANO	*n* pl. **-NOS** a Spanish gypsy
GITCH	*n* pl. **-ES** gotch
GITE	*n* pl. **-S** a vacation retreat in France
GITTED	past tense of git
GITTERN	*n* pl. **-S** a medieval guitar
GITTIN	pl. of get
GITTING	present participle of git
GIVE	*v* **GAVE, GIVEN, GIVING, GIVES** to transfer freely to another's possession **GIVEABLE** *adj*
GIVEAWAY	*n* pl. **-AWAYS** something given away free of charge
GIVEBACK	*n* pl. **-S** a worker's benefit given back to management
GIVEN	*n* pl. **-S** something assigned as a basis for a calculation
GIVER	*n* pl. **-S** one that gives
GIVING	present participle of give
GIZMO	*n* pl. **-MOS** gismo
GIZZARD	*n* pl. **-S** a digestive organ
GJETOST	*n* pl. **-S** a hard brown cheese
GLABELLA	*n* pl. **-BELLAE** the smooth area between the eyebrows
GLABRATE	*adj* glabrous
GLABROUS	*adj* smooth
GLACE	*v* **-CEED** or **-CED, -CEING, -CES** to cover with icing
GLACIAL	*adj* of or pertaining to glaciers
GLACIATE	*v* **-ATED, -ATING, -ATES** to cover with glaciers
GLACIER	*n* pl. **-S** a huge mass of ice
GLACIS	*n* pl. **-CISES** a slope
GLAD	*adj* **GLADDER, GLADDEST** feeling pleasure
GLAD	*v* **GLADDED, GLADDING, GLADS** to gladden
GLADDEN	*v* **-ED, -ING, -S** to make glad
GLADDER	comparative of glad
GLADDEST	superlative of glad
GLADDING	present participle of glad
GLADE	*n* pl. **-S** an open space in a forest
GLADIATE	*adj* shaped like a sword
GLADIER	comparative of glady
GLADIEST	superlative of glady
GLADIOLA	*n* pl. **-S** a flowering plant
GLADIOLI	*n/pl* segments of the sternum
GLADLY	*adv* **-LIER, -LIEST** in a glad manner
GLADNESS	*n* pl. **-ES** the state of being glad
GLADSOME	*adj* **-SOMER, -SOMEST** glad
GLADY	*adj* **GLADIER, GLADIEST** having glades
GLAIKET	*adj* glaikit
GLAIKIT	*adj* foolish
GLAIR	*v* **-ED, -ING, -S** to coat with egg white
GLAIRE	*v* **GLAIRED, GLAIRING, GLAIRES** to glair
GLAIRY	*adj* **GLAIRIER, GLAIRIEST** resembling egg white
GLAIVE	*n* pl. **-S** a sword **GLAIVED** *adj*
GLAM	*v* **GLAMMED, GLAMMING, GLAMS** to make oneself look alluringly attractive
GLAM	*adj* **GLAMMER, GLAMMEST** characterized by extravagant glamor
GLAMMY	*adj* **GLAMMIER, GLAMMIEST** alluringly attractive
GLAMOR	*n* pl. **-S** alluring attractiveness
GLAMOUR	*v* **-ED, -ING, -S** to bewitch
GLANCE	*v* **GLANCED, GLANCING, GLANCES** to look quickly
GLANCER	*n* pl. **-S** one that glances
GLAND	*n* pl. **-S** a secreting organ
GLANDERS	*n/pl* a disease of horses
GLANDULE	*n* pl. **-S** a small gland
GLANS	*n* pl. **GLANDES** the tip of the penis or clitoris
GLARE	*v* **GLARED, GLARING, GLARES** to shine with a harshly brilliant light
GLARY	*adj* **GLARIER, GLARIEST** glaring
GLASNOST	*n* pl. **-S** a Soviet policy of open political discussion
GLASS	*v* **-ED, -ING, -ES** to encase in glass (a transparent substance)

GLASSFUL *n pl.* **-FULS** as much as a drinking glass will hold

GLASSIE *n pl.* **-S** a type of playing marble

GLASSIER comparative of glassy

GLASSIEST superlative of glassy

GLASSILY *adv* in a glassy manner

GLASSINE *n pl.* **-S** a type of paper

GLASSMAN *n pl.* **-MEN** a glazier

GLASSY *adj* **GLASSIER, GLASSIEST** resembling glass

GLAUCOMA *n pl.* **-S** a disease of the eye

GLAUCOUS *adj* bluish green

GLAZE *v* **GLAZED, GLAZING, GLAZES** to fit windows with glass panes

GLAZER *n pl.* **-S** a glazier

GLAZIER *n pl.* **-S** one that glazes

GLAZIERY *n pl.* **-ZIERIES** the work of a glazier

GLAZING *n pl.* **-S** glaziery

GLAZY *adj* **GLAZIER, GLAZIEST** covered with a smooth, glossy coating **GLAZILY** *adv*

GLEAM *v* **-ED, -ING, -S** to shine with a soft radiance

GLEAMER *n pl.* **-S** one that gleams

GLEAMY *adj* **GLEAMIER, GLEAMIEST** gleaming

GLEAN *v* **-ED, -ING, -S** to gather little by little

GLEANER *n pl.* **-S** one that gleans

GLEANING *n pl.* **-S** something that is gleaned

GLEBA *n pl.* **-BAE** a spore-bearing mass of some fungi

GLEBE *n pl.* **-S** the soil or earth

GLED *n pl.* **-S** glede

GLEDE *n pl.* **-S** a bird of prey

GLEE *n pl.* **-S** an unaccompanied song

GLEED *n pl.* **-S** a glowing coal

GLEEFUL *adj* merry

GLEEK *v* **-ED, -ING, -S** to gibe

GLEEMAN *n pl.* **-MEN** a minstrel

GLEESOME *adj* gleeful

GLEET *v* **-ED, -ING, -S** to discharge mucus from the urethra

GLEETY *adj* **GLEETIER, GLEETIEST** resembling mucus

GLEG *adj* alert **GLEGLY** *adv*

GLEGNESS *n pl.* **-ES** alertness

GLEN *n pl.* **-S** a small valley **GLENLIKE** *adj*

GLENOID *adj* having the shallow or slightly cupped form of a bone socket

GLEY *n pl.* **GLEYS** a clay soil layer **GLEYED** *adj*

GLEYING *n pl.* **-S** development of gley

GLIA *n pl.* **-S** supporting tissue that binds nerve tissue

GLIADIN *n pl.* **-S** a simple protein

GLIADINE *n pl.* **-S** gliadin

GLIAL *adj* pertaining to the supporting tissue of the central nervous system

GLIB *adj* **GLIBBER, GLIBBEST** fluent **GLIBLY** *adv*

GLIBNESS *n pl.* **-ES** the quality of being glib

GLIDE *v* **GLIDED, GLIDING, GLIDES** to move effortlessly

GLIDER *n pl.* **-S** a type of aircraft

GLIFF *n pl.* **-S** a brief moment

GLIM *n pl.* **-S** a light or lamp

GLIME *v* **GLIMED, GLIMING, GLIMES** to glance slyly

GLIMMER *v* **-ED, -ING, -S** to shine faintly or unsteadily

GLIMPSE *v* **GLIMPSED, GLIMPSING, GLIMPSES** to see for an instant

GLIMPSER *n pl.* **-S** one that glimpses

GLINT *v* **-ED, -ING, -S** to glitter

GLINTY *adj* **GLINTIER, GLINTIEST** glittering

GLIOMA *n pl.* **-MAS** or **-MATA** a type of tumor

GLIOSIS *n pl.* **-OSES** pathological proliferation of glial cells

GLISSADE *v* **-SADED, -SADING, -SADES** to perform a gliding dance step

GLISSE *n pl.* **-S** a dance step

GLISTEN *v* **-ED, -ING, -S** to shine by reflection

GLISTER *v* **-ED, -ING, -S** to glisten

GLITCH *n pl.* **-ES** a malfunction

GLITCHY *adj* **GLITCHIER, GLITCHIEST** characterized by glitches

GLITTER *v* **-ED, -ING, -S** to sparkle

GLITTERY *adj* glittering

GLITZ *v* **-ED, -ING, -ES** to make flashy in appearance

GLITZY *adj* **GLITZIER, GLITZIEST** showy **GLITZILY** *adv*

GLOAM *n* pl. **-S** twilight

GLOAMING *n* pl. **-S** twilight

GLOAT *v* **-ED, -ING, -S** to regard with great or excessive satisfaction

GLOATER *n* pl. **-S** one that gloats

GLOB *n* pl. **-S** a rounded mass

GLOBAL *adj* spherical **GLOBALLY** *adv*

GLOBATE *adj* spherical

GLOBATED *adj* spherical

GLOBBY *adj* **-BIER, -BIEST** full of globs

GLOBE *v* **GLOBED, GLOBING, GLOBES** to form into a perfectly round body

GLOBIN *n* pl. **-S** a simple protein

GLOBOID *n* pl. **-S** a spheroid

GLOBOSE *adj* spherical

GLOBOUS *adj* spherical

GLOBULAR *n* pl. **-S** a spherical cluster of stars

GLOBULE *n* pl. **-S** a small spherical mass

GLOBULIN *n* pl. **-S** a simple protein

GLOCHID *n* pl. **-S** a barbed hair on some plants

GLOGG *n* pl. **-S** an alcoholic beverage

GLOM *v* **GLOMMED, GLOMMING, GLOMS** to steal

GLOMUS *n* pl. **-MERA** a type of vascular tuft

GLONOIN *n* pl. **-S** nitroglycerin

GLOOM *v* **-ED, -ING, -S** to become dark

GLOOMFUL *adj* gloomy

GLOOMING *n* pl. **-S** gloaming

GLOOMY *adj* **GLOOMIER, GLOOMIEST** dismally dark **GLOOMILY** *adv*

GLOOP *n* pl. **-S** sticky material

GLOOPY *adj* **GLOOPIER, GLOOPIEST** resembling gloop

GLOP *v* **GLOPPED, GLOPPING, GLOPS** to cover with glop (a messy mass or mixture)

GLOPPY *adj* **-PIER, -PIEST** resembling glop

GLORIA *n* pl. **-S** a halo

GLORIED past tense of glory

GLORIES present 3d person sing. of glory

GLORIFY *v* **-FIED, -FYING, -FIES** to bestow honor or praise on

GLORIOLE *n* pl. **-S** a halo

GLORIOUS *adj* magnificent

GLORY *v* **-RIED, -RYING, -RIES** to rejoice proudly

GLOSS *v* **-ED, -ING, -ES** to make lustrous

GLOSSA *n* pl. **-SAS** or **-SAE** the tongue **GLOSSAL** *adj*

GLOSSARY *n* pl. **-RIES** a list of terms and their definitions

GLOSSEME *n* pl. **-S** the smallest linguistic unit that signals a meaning

GLOSSER *n* pl. **-S** one that glosses

GLOSSIES pl. of glossy

GLOSSINA *n* pl. **-S** a tsetse fly

GLOSSY *adj* **GLOSSIER, GLOSSIEST** lustrous **GLOSSILY** *adv*

GLOSSY *n* pl. **GLOSSIES** a type of photograph

GLOST *n* pl. **-S** pottery that has been coated with a glassy surface

GLOTTIS *n* pl. **-TISES** or **-TIDES** the opening between the vocal cords **GLOTTAL, GLOTTIC** *adj*

GLOUT *v* **-ED, -ING, -S** to scowl

GLOVE *v* **GLOVED, GLOVING, GLOVES** to furnish with gloves (hand coverings)

GLOVEBOX *n* pl. **-ES** a small compartment in the dashboard of a vehicle

GLOVER *n* pl. **-S** a maker or seller of gloves

GLOW *v* **-ED, -ING, -S** to emit light and heat

GLOWER *v* **-ED, -ING, -S** to scowl

GLOWFLY *n* pl. **-FLIES** a firefly

GLOWWORM *n* pl. **-S** a luminous insect

GLOXINIA *n* pl. **-S** a tropical plant

GLOZE *v* **GLOZED, GLOZING, GLOZES** to explain away

GLUCAGON *n* pl. **-S** a hormone

GLUCAN *n* pl. **-S** a polymer of glucose

GLUCINUM *n* pl. **-S** a metallic element **GLUCINIC** *adj*

GLUCOSE *n* pl. **-S** a sugar **GLUCOSIC** *adj*

GLUE *v* **GLUED, GLUING** or **GLUEING, GLUES** to fasten with glue (an adhesive substance)

GLUELIKE *adj* resembling glue

GLUEPOT *n* pl. **-S** a pot for melting glue

GLUER *n* pl. **-S** one that glues

GLUEY *adj* **GLUIER, GLUIEST** resembling glue **GLUILY** *adv*

GLUG	*v* **GLUGGED, GLUGGING, GLUGS** to make a gurgling sound
GLUHWEIN	*n* pl. **-S** wine flavored with spices
GLUINESS	*n* pl. **-ES** the state of being gluey
GLUING	present participle of glue
GLUM	*n* pl. **-S** glumness
GLUM	*adj* **GLUMMER, GLUMMEST** being in low spirits **GLUMLY** *adv*
GLUME	*n* pl. **-S** a bract on grassy plants
GLUMNESS	*n* pl. **-ES** the state of being glum
GLUMPY	*adj* **GLUMPIER, GLUMPIEST** glum **GLUMPILY** *adv*
GLUNCH	*v* **-ED, -ING, -ES** to frown
GLUON	*n* pl. **-S** a hypothetical massless particle binding quarks together
GLUT	*v* **GLUTTED, GLUTTING, GLUTS** to feed or fill to excess
GLUTCH	*v* **-ED, -ING, -ES** to gulp or swallow
GLUTE	*n* pl. **-S** a gluteus
GLUTEAL	*adj* of or pertaining to the buttock muscles
GLUTEI	pl. of gluteus
GLUTELIN	*n* pl. **-S** any of a group of proteins occurring in cereal grains
GLUTEN	*n* pl. **-S** a sticky component of grain flours that contains glutenin
GLUTENIN	*n* pl. **-S** a protein of cereal grains that gives adhesiveness to bread dough
GLUTEUS	*n* pl. **-TEI** a buttock muscle
GLUTTED	past tense of glut
GLUTTING	present participle of glut
GLUTTON	*n* pl. **-S** a person who eats to excess
GLUTTONY	*n* pl. **-TONIES** excessive eating
GLYCAN	*n* pl. **-S** a carbohydrate
GLYCEMIA	*n* pl. **-S** the presence of glucose in the blood **GLYCEMIC** *adj*
GLYCERIN	*n* pl. **-S** a glycerol **GLYCERIC** *adj*
GLYCEROL	*n* pl. **-S** a syrupy alcohol
GLYCERYL	*n* pl. **-S** a radical derived from glycerol
GLYCIN	*n* pl. **-S** a compound used in photography
GLYCINE	*n* pl. **-S** an amino acid
GLYCOGEN	*n* pl. **-S** a carbohydrate
GLYCOL	*n* pl. **-S** an alcohol **GLYCOLIC** *adj*
GLYCONIC	*n* pl. **-S** a type of verse line
GLYCOSYL	*n* pl. **-S** a radical derived from glucose
GLYCYL	*n* pl. **-S** a radical derived from glycine
GLYPH	*n* pl. **-S** an ornamental groove **GLYPHIC** *adj*
GLYPTIC	*n* pl. **-S** the art or process of engraving on gems
GNAR	*v* **GNARRED, GNARRING, GNARS** to snarl
GNARL	*v* **-ED, -ING, -S** to twist into a state of deformity
GNARLY	*adj* **GNARLIER, GNARLIEST** gnarled
GNARR	*v* **-ED, -ING, -S** to gnar
GNARRED	past tense of gnar
GNARRING	present participle of gnar
GNASH	*v* **-ED, -ING, -ES** to grind the teeth together
GNAT	*n* pl. **-S** a small winged insect
GNATHAL	*adj* gnathic
GNATHIC	*adj* of or pertaining to the jaw
GNATHION	*n* pl. **-S** the tip of the chin
GNATHITE	*n* pl. **-S** a jawlike appendage of an insect
GNATLIKE	*adj* resembling a gnat
GNATTY	*adj* **-TIER, -TIEST** infested with gnats
GNAW	*v* **GNAWED, GNAWN, GNAWING, GNAWS** to wear away by persistent biting **GNAWABLE** *adj*
GNAWER	*n* pl. **-S** one that gnaws
GNAWING	*n* pl. **-S** a persistent dull pain
GNEISS	*n* pl. **-ES** a type of rock **GNEISSIC** *adj*
GNOCCHI	*n/pl* dumplings made of pasta
GNOME	*n* pl. **-S** a dwarf
GNOMIC	*adj* resembling or containing aphorisms
GNOMICAL	*adj* gnomic
GNOMISH	*adj* resembling a gnome
GNOMIST	*n* pl. **-S** a writer of aphorisms
GNOMON	*n* pl. **-S** a part of a sundial **GNOMONIC** *adj*
GNOSIS	*n* pl. **GNOSES** mystical knowledge
GNOSTIC	*n* pl. **-S** an adherent of gnosticism
GNU	*n* pl. **-S** a large antelope
GO	*v* **WENT, GONE, GOING** or **GWINE, GOES** to move along

GO	*n* pl. **GOS** a Japanese board game	**GOBONEE**	*adj* gobony
GOA	*n* pl. **-S** an Asian gazelle	**GOBONY**	*adj* compony
GOAD	*v* **-ED, -ING, -S** to drive animals with a goad (a pointed stick)	**GOBY**	*n* pl. **GOBIES** a small fish
GOADLIKE	*adj* resembling a goad	**GOD**	*v* **GODDED, GODDING, GODS** to treat as a god (a supernatural being)
GOAL	*v* **-ED, -ING, -S** to score a goal (a point-scoring play in some games)	**GODAWFUL**	*adj* extremely unpleasant
GOALBALL	*n* pl. **-S** a ball thrown at a goal to score	**GODCHILD**	*n* pl. **-CHILDREN** one whom a person sponsors at baptism
GOALIE	*n* pl. **-S** a player who defends against goals	**GODDED**	past tense of god
GOALLESS	*adj* having no goal	**GODDESS**	*n* pl. **-ES** a female god
GOALPOST	*n* pl. **-S** a post that marks a boundary of the scoring area in some games	**GODDING**	present participle of god
		GODET	*n* pl. **-S** insert of cloth in a seam
		GODETIA	*n* pl. **-S** a showy annual herb
GOALWARD	*adv* toward a goal (a point-scoring area)	**GODHEAD**	*n* pl. **-S** godhood
GOANNA	*n* pl. **-S** a large monitor lizard	**GODHOOD**	*n* pl. **-S** the state of being a god
GOAT	*n* pl. **-S** a horned mammal	**GODLESS**	*adj* worshiping no god
GOATEE	*n* pl. **-S** a small pointed beard **GOATEED** *adj*	**GODLIKE**	*adj* divine
		GODLING	*n* pl. **-S** a lesser god
GOATFISH	*n* pl. **-ES** a tropical fish	**GODLY**	*adj* **-LIER, -LIEST** pious **GODLILY** *adv*
GOATHERD	*n* pl. **-S** one who tends goats		
GOATIER	comparative of goaty	**GODOWN**	*n* pl. **-S** an Asian warehouse
GOATIEST	superlative of goaty	**GODROON**	*n* pl. **-S** gadroon
GOATISH	*adj* resembling a goat	**GODSEND**	*n* pl. **-S** an unexpected boon
GOATLIKE	*adj* goatish	**GODSHIP**	*n* pl. **-S** the rank of a god
GOATSKIN	*n* pl. **-S** the hide of a goat	**GODSON**	*n* pl. **-S** a male godchild
GOATY	*adj* **GOATIER, GOATIEST** suggestive of a goat	**GODWARD**	*adv* toward God
		GODWARDS	*adv* Godward
GOB	*v* **GOBBED, GOBBING, GOBS** to fill a mine pit with waste material	**GODWIT**	*n* pl. **-S** a wading bird
		GOER	*n* pl. **-S** one that goes
GOBAN	*n* pl. **-S** gobang	**GOEST**	*v* a 2d person sing. of go
GOBANG	*n* pl. **-S** a Japanese game	**GOETH**	*v* a 3d person sing. of go
GOBBED	past tense of gob	**GOETHITE**	*n* pl. **-S** an ore of iron
GOBBET	*n* pl. **-S** a piece of raw meat	**GOFER**	*n* pl. **-S** an employee who runs errands
GOBBING	present participle of gob		
GOBBLE	*v* **-BLED, -BLING, -BLES** to eat hastily	**GOFFER**	*v* **-ED, -ING, -S** to press ridges or pleats into
GOBBLER	*n* pl. **-S** a male turkey	**GOGGLE**	*v* **-GLED, -GLING, -GLES** to stare with wide eyes
GOBIES	pl. of goby		
GOBIOID	*n* pl. **-S** a fish of the goby family	**GOGGLER**	*n* pl. **-S** one that goggles
GOBLET	*n* pl. **-S** a drinking vessel	**GOGGLY**	*adj* **-GLIER, -GLIEST** wide-eyed
GOBLIN	*n* pl. **-S** an evil or mischievous creature	**GOGLET**	*n* pl. **-S** a long-necked jar
		GOGO	*n* pl. **-GOS** a discotheque
GOBO	*n* pl. **-BOS** or **-BOES** a device used to shield a microphone from extraneous sounds	**GOING**	*n* pl. **-S** an advance toward an objective

GOITER	*n* pl. **-S** an enlargement of the thyroid gland **GOITERED** *adj* **GOITROUS** *adj*
GOITRE	*n* pl. **-S** goiter **GOITRED** *adj*
GOJI	*n* pl. **-S** the red berry of an Asian shrub
GOLCONDA	*n* pl. **-S** a source of great wealth
GOLD	*adj* **GOLDER, GOLDEST** golden
GOLD	*n* pl. **-S** a gold medal
GOLDARN	*n* pl. **-S** an expression of anger
GOLDBUG	*n* pl. **-S** a gold beetle
GOLDEN	*adj* **-ENER, -ENEST** of the color of gold **GOLDENLY** *adv*
GOLDEYE	*n* pl. **-S** a freshwater fish
GOLDFISH	*n* pl. **-ES** a freshwater fish
GOLDTONE	*adj* made to resemble gold
GOLDURN	*n* pl. **-S** goldarn
GOLEM	*n* pl. **-S** a legendary creature
GOLF	*v* **-ED, -ING, -S** to play golf (a type of ball game)
GOLFER	*n* pl. **-S** one that golfs
GOLFING	*n* pl. **-S** the game of golf
GOLGOTHA	*n* pl. **-S** a place of burial
GOLIARD	*n* pl. **-S** a wandering student
GOLIATH	*n* pl. **-S** a person considered to be a giant
GOLLIWOG	*n* pl. **-S** a grotesque doll
GOLLY	*interj* — used as a mild oath
GOLLYWOG	*n* pl. **-S** golliwog
GOLOSH	*n* pl. **-ES** galosh
GOLOSHE	*n* pl. **-S** galosh
GOMBEEN	*n* pl. **-S** usury
GOMBO	*n* pl. **-BOS** gumbo
GOMBROON	*n* pl. **-S** a kind of Persian pottery
GOMER	*n* pl. **-S** an undesirable hospital patient
GOMERAL	*n* pl. **-S** a fool
GOMEREL	*n* pl. **-S** gomeral
GOMERIL	*n* pl. **-S** gomeral
GOMUTI	*n* pl. **-S** a palm tree
GONAD	*n* pl. **-S** a sex gland **GONADAL, GONADIAL, GONADIC** *adj*
GONCH	*n* pl. **-ES** gaunch
GONDOLA	*n* pl. **-S** a long, narrow boat
GONE	*adj* departed
GONEF	*n* pl. **-S** ganef
GONENESS	*n* pl. **-ES** a state of exhaustion
GONER	*n* pl. **-S** one who is in a hopeless situation
GONFALON	*n* pl. **-S** a banner
GONFANON	*n* pl. **-S** gonfalon
GONG	*v* **-ED, -ING, -S** to make the sound of a gong (a disk-shaped percussion instrument)
GONGLIKE	*adj* resembling a gong
GONIA	pl. of gonion and of gonium
GONIDIUM	*n* pl. **-IA** an asexual reproductive cell **GONIDIAL, GONIDIC** *adj*
GONIF	*n* pl. **-S** ganef
GONIFF	*n* pl. **-S** ganef
GONION	*n* pl. **-NIA** a part of the lower jaw
GONIUM	*n* pl. **-NIA** an immature reproductive cell
GONOCYTE	*n* pl. **-S** a cell that produces gametes
GONOF	*n* pl. **-S** ganef
GONOPH	*n* pl. **-S** ganef
GONOPORE	*n* pl. **-S** a genital pore
GONZO	*adj* bizarre
GOO	*n* pl. **GOOS** a sticky or viscid substance
GOOBER	*n* pl. **-S** a peanut
GOOD	*adj* **BETTER, BEST** having positive or desirable qualities
GOOD	*n* pl. **-S** something that is good
GOODBY	*n* pl. **-BYS** goodbye
GOODBYE	*n* pl. **-S** a concluding remark or gesture at parting
GOODIE	*n* pl. **-S** goody
GOODIES	pl. of goody
GOODISH	*adj* somewhat good
GOODLY	*adj* **-LIER, -LIEST** of pleasing appearance
GOODMAN	*n* pl. **-MEN** the master of a household
GOODNESS	*n* pl. **-ES** the state of being good
GOODWIFE	*n* pl. **-WIVES** the mistress of a household
GOODWILL	*n* pl. **-S** an attitude of friendliness
GOODY	*n* pl. **GOODIES** a desirable food
GOOEY	*adj* **GOOIER, GOOIEST** sticky or viscid
GOOF	*v* **-ED, -ING, -S** to blunder
GOOFBALL	*n* pl. **-S** a sleeping pill
GOOFUS	*n* pl. **-ES** a foolish or stupid person

GOOFY	*adj* **GOOFIER, GOOFIEST** silly **GOOFILY** *adv*
GOOGLE	*v* **-GLED, -GLING, -GLES** to use an Internet search engine
GOOGLY	*n* pl. **-GLIES** a type of bowled ball in cricket
GOOGOL	*n* pl. **-S** an enormous number
GOOIER	comparative of gooey
GOOIEST	superlative of gooey
GOOK	*n* pl. **-S** goo **GOOKY** *adj*
GOOMBAH	*n* pl. **-S** an older man who is a friend
GOOMBAY	*n* pl. **-BAYS** calypso music of the Bahamas
GOON	*n* pl. **-S** a hired thug
GOONDA	*n* pl. **-S** a hired thug
GOONERY	*n* pl. **-ERIES** thuggish behavior
GOONEY	*n* pl. **-NEYS** an albatross
GOONIE	*n* pl. **-S** gooney
GOONY	*n* pl. **-NIES** gooney
GOONY	*adj* **GOONIER, GOONIEST** stupid
GOOP	*n* pl. **-S** goo, gunk
GOOPY	*adj* **GOOPIER, GOOPIEST** sticky, gooey
GOORAL	*n* pl. **-S** goral
GOOSE	*n* pl. **GEESE** a swimming bird
GOOSE	*v* **GOOSED, GOOSING, GOOSES** to poke between the buttocks
GOOSEY	*adj* **GOOSIER, GOOSIEST** goosy
GOOSY	*adj* **GOOSIER, GOOSIEST** resembling a goose
GOPHER	*n* pl. **-S** a burrowing rodent
GOPIK	*n* pl. **-S** a monetary unit of Azerbaijan
GOR	*interj* — used as a mild oath
GORAL	*n* pl. **-S** a goat antelope
GORBELLY	*n* pl. **-LIES** a potbelly
GORBLIMY	*interj* blimey
GORCOCK	*n* pl. **-S** the male red grouse
GORDITA	*n* pl. **-S** a stuffed and fried pocket of cornmeal dough
GORE	*v* **GORED, GORING, GORES** to pierce with a horn or tusk
GOREFEST	*n* pl. **-S** a movie featuring much bloodshed
GORGE	*v* **GORGED, GORGING, GORGES** to stuff with food **GORGEDLY** *adv*
GORGEOUS	*adj* beautiful
GORGER	*n* pl. **-S** one that gorges
GORGERIN	*n* pl. **-S** a part of a column
GORGET	*n* pl. **-S** a piece of armor for the throat **GORGETED** *adj*
GORGING	present participle of gorge
GORGON	*n* pl. **-S** an ugly woman
GORHEN	*n* pl. **-S** the female red grouse
GORIER	comparative of gory
GORIEST	superlative of gory
GORILLA	*n* pl. **-S** a large ape
GORILY	*adv* in a gory manner
GORINESS	*n* pl. **-ES** the state of being gory
GORING	present participle of gore
GORM	*v* **-ED, -ING, -S** to gaum
GORMAND	*n* pl. **-S** gourmand
GORMLESS	*adj* stupid
GORP	*n* pl. **-S** a snack for quick energy
GORSE	*n* pl. **-S** furze
GORSY	*adj* **GORSIER, GORSIEST** abounding in gorse
GORY	*adj* **GORIER, GORIEST** bloody
GOSH	*interj* — used as an exclamation of surprise
GOSHAWK	*n* pl. **-S** a large hawk
GOSLING	*n* pl. **-S** a young goose
GOSPEL	*n* pl. **-S** the message concerning Christ, the kingdom of God, and salvation
GOSPELER	*n* pl. **-S** one that teaches the gospel
GOSPELLY	*adj* having characteristics of gospel music
GOSPORT	*n* pl. **-S** a communication device in an airplane
GOSSAMER	*n* pl. **-S** a fine film of cobwebs
GOSSAN	*n* pl. **-S** a type of decomposed rock
GOSSIP	*v* **-SIPED, -SIPING, -SIPS** or **-SIPPED, -SIPPING, -SIPS** to talk idly about the affairs of others
GOSSIPER	*n* pl. **-S** one that gossips
GOSSIPRY	*n* pl. **-RIES** the practice of gossiping
GOSSIPY	*adj* inclined to gossip
GOSSOON	*n* pl. **-S** a boy
GOSSYPOL	*n* pl. **-S** a toxic pigment
GOT	past tense of get
GOTCH	*n* pl. **-ES** underpants

GOTCHA	*n* pl. **-S** an instance of catching a person out in a deceit or wrongdoing
GOTCHIES	*n/pl* underpants
GOTH	*n* pl. **-S** a morbid style of rock music
GOTHIC	*n* pl. **-S** a style of printing
GOTHITE	*n* pl. **-S** goethite
GOTTEN	past participle of get
GOUACHE	*n* pl. **-S** a method of painting
GOUGE	*v* **GOUGED, GOUGING, GOUGES** to cut or scoop out
GOUGER	*n* pl. **-S** one that gouges
GOULASH	*n* pl. **-ES** a beef stew
GOURAMI	*n* pl. **-S** or **-ES** a food fish
GOURD	*n* pl. **-S** a hard-shelled fruit
GOURDE	*n* pl. **-S** a monetary unit of Haiti
GOURDFUL	*n* pl. **-S** as much as a hollowed gourd can hold
GOURMAND	*n* pl. **-S** one who loves to eat
GOURMET	*n* pl. **-S** a connoisseur of fine food and drink
GOUT	*n* pl. **-S** a metabolic disease
GOUTWEED	*n* pl. **-S** a plant with white flowers
GOUTY	*adj* **GOUTIER, GOUTIEST** affected with gout **GOUTILY** *adv*
GOVERN	*v* **-ED, -ING, -S** to rule or direct
GOVERNOR	*n* pl. **-S** one that governs
GOWAN	*n* pl. **-S** a daisy **GOWANED, GOWANY** *adj*
GOWD	*n* pl. **-S** gold
GOWK	*n* pl. **-S** a fool
GOWN	*v* **-ED, -ING, -S** to dress in a gown (a long, loose outer garment)
GOWNSMAN	*n* pl. **-MEN** a professional or academic person
GOX	*n* pl. **-ES** gaseous oxygen
GRAAL	*n* pl. **-S** grail
GRAB	*v* **GRABBED, GRABBING, GRABS** to grasp suddenly
GRABBER	*n* pl. **-S** one that grabs
GRABBIER	comparative of grabby
GRABBIEST	superlative of grabby
GRABBING	present participle of grab
GRABBLE	*v* **-BLED, -BLING, -BLES** to grope
GRABBLER	*n* pl. **-S** one that grabbles
GRABBY	*adj* **-BIER, -BIEST** tending to grab

GRABEN	*n* pl. **-S** a depression of the earth's crust
GRACE	*v* **GRACED, GRACING, GRACES** to give beauty to
GRACEFUL	*adj* **-FULLER, -FULLEST** having beauty of form or movement
GRACILE	*adj* gracefully slender
GRACILIS	*n* pl. **-LES** a thigh muscle
GRACING	present participle of grace
GRACIOSO	*n* pl. **-SOS** a clown in Spanish comedy
GRACIOUS	*adj* marked by kindness and courtesy
GRACKLE	*n* pl. **-S** a blackbird
GRAD	*n* pl. **-S** a graduate
GRADATE	*v* **-DATED, -DATING, -DATES** to change by degrees
GRADE	*v* **GRADED, GRADING, GRADES** to arrange in steps or degrees **GRADABLE** *adj*
GRADER	*n* pl. **-S** one that grades
GRADIENT	*n* pl. **-S** a rate of inclination
GRADIN	*n* pl. **-S** gradine
GRADINE	*n* pl. **-S** one of a series of steps
GRADING	present participle of grade
GRADUAL	*n* pl. **-S** a hymn sung in alternate parts
GRADUAND	*n* pl. **-S** one who is about to graduate
GRADUATE	*v* **-ATED, -ATING, -ATES** to receive an academic degree or diploma
GRADUS	*n* pl. **-ES** a dictionary of prosody
GRAECIZE	*v* **-CIZED, -CIZING, -CIZES** to grecize
GRAFFITI	*v* **-TIED, -TIING** or **-TING, -TIS** to draw graffiti on
GRAFFITO	*n* pl. **-TI** an inscription or drawing made on a rock or wall
GRAFT	*v* **-ED, -ING, -S** to unite with a growing plant by insertion
GRAFTAGE	*n* pl. **-S** the process of grafting
GRAFTER	*n* pl. **-S** one that grafts
GRAHAM	*n* pl. **-S** whole-wheat flour
GRAIL	*n* pl. **-S** the object of a long quest
GRAIN	*v* **-ED, -ING, -S** to form into small particles
GRAINER	*n* pl. **-S** one that grains
GRAINY	*adj* **GRAINIER, GRAINIEST** granular
GRAM	*n* pl. **-S** a unit of mass and weight

GRAMA *n* pl. **-S** a pasture grass

GRAMARY *n* pl. **-RIES** gramarye

GRAMARYE *n* pl. **-S** occult learning; magic

GRAMERCY *n* pl. **-CIES** an expression of gratitude

GRAMMA *n* pl. **-S** grama

GRAMMAR *n* pl. **-S** the study of the formal features of a language

GRAMME *n* pl. **-S** gram

GRAMP *n* pl. **-S** grandfather

GRAMPA *n* pl. **-S** a grandfather

GRAMPUS *n* pl. **-ES** a marine mammal

GRAMPY *n* pl. **-PIES** grampa

GRAN *n* pl. **-S** a grandmother

GRANA pl. of granum

GRANARY *n* pl. **-RIES** a storehouse for grain

GRAND *adj* **GRANDER, GRANDEST** large and impressive

GRAND *n* pl. **-S** a type of piano

GRANDAD *n* pl. **-S** granddad

GRANDAM *n* pl. **-S** a grandmother

GRANDAME *n* pl. **-S** grandam

GRANDDAD *n* pl. **-S** a grandfather

GRANDDAM *n* pl. **-S** the female parent of an animal with offspring

GRANDEE *n* pl. **-S** man of high social position

GRANDEUR *n* pl. **-S** the state of being grand

GRANDKID *n* pl. **-S** the child of one's son or daughter

GRANDLY *adv* in a grand manner

GRANDMA *n* pl. **-S** a grandmother

GRANDPA *n* pl. **-S** a grandfather

GRANDSIR *n* pl. **-S** a grandfather

GRANDSON *n* pl. **-S** a son of one's son or daughter

GRANGE *n* pl. **-S** a farm

GRANGER *n* pl. **-S** a farmer

GRANITA *n* pl. **-S** an iced dessert

GRANITE *n* pl. **-S** a type of rock **GRANITIC** *adj*

GRANNIE *n* pl. **-S** granny

GRANNY *n* pl. **-NIES** a grandmother

GRANOLA *n* pl. **-S** a breakfast cereal

GRANT *v* **-ED, -ING, -S** to bestow upon

GRANTEE *n* pl. **-S** one to whom something is granted

GRANTER *n* pl. **-S** one that grants

GRANTOR *n* pl. **-S** granter

GRANULAR *adj* composed of granules

GRANULE *n* pl. **-S** a small particle

GRANUM *n* pl. **GRANA** a part of a plant chloroplast

GRAPE *n* pl. **-S** an edible berry

GRAPERY *n* pl. **-ERIES** a vinery

GRAPEY *adj* **GRAPIER, GRAPIEST** grapy

GRAPH *v* **-ED, -ING, -S** to represent by means of a diagram

GRAPHEME *n* pl. **-S** a unit of a writing system

GRAPHIC *n* pl. **-S** a product of the art of representation

GRAPHITE *n* pl. **-S** a variety of carbon

GRAPIER comparative of grapy

GRAPIEST superlative of grapy

GRAPLIN *n* pl. **-S** a grapnel

GRAPLINE *n* pl. **-S** graplin

GRAPNEL *n* pl. **-S** a type of anchor

GRAPPA *n* pl. **-S** an Italian brandy

GRAPPLE *v* **-PLED, -PLING, -PLES** to struggle or contend

GRAPPLER *n* pl. **-S** one that grapples

GRAPY *adj* **GRAPIER, GRAPIEST** resembling grapes

GRASP *v* **-ED, -ING, -S** to seize firmly with the hand

GRASPER *n* pl. **-S** one that grasps

GRASS *v* **-ED, -ING, -ES** to cover with grass (herbaceous plants)

GRASSY *adj* **GRASSIER, GRASSIEST** of, resembling, or pertaining to grass **GRASSILY** *adv*

GRAT past tense of greet (to weep)

GRATE *v* **GRATED, GRATING, GRATES** to reduce to shreds by rubbing

GRATEFUL *adj* **-FULLER, -FULLEST** deeply thankful

GRATER *n* pl. **-S** one that grates

GRATIFY *v* **-FIED, -FYING, -FIES** to satisfy

GRATIN *n* pl. **-S** a type of food crust

GRATINE *adj* covered with a crust

GRATINEE *v* **-NEED, -NEEING, -NEES** to cook food that is covered with a crust

GRATING *n* pl. **-S** a network of bars covering an opening

GRATIS *adj* free of charge

GRATUITY *n* pl. **-ITIES** a gift of money

GRAUPEL *n* pl. **-S** granular snow pellets

GRAVAMEN *n* pl. **-MENS** or **-MINA** the most serious part of an accusation

GRAVE *adj* **GRAVER, GRAVEST** extremely serious

GRAVE *v* **GRAVED, GRAVEN, GRAVING, GRAVES** to engrave

GRAVEL *v* **-ELED, -ELING, -ELS** or **-ELLED, -ELLING, -ELS** to pave with gravel (a mixture of rock fragments)

GRAVELLY *adj* containing gravel

GRAVELY *adv* in a grave manner

GRAVEN past participle of grave

GRAVER *n* pl. **-S** an engraver

GRAVEST superlative of grave

GRAVID *adj* pregnant **GRAVIDLY** *adv*

GRAVIDA *n* pl. **-DAS** or **-DAE** a pregnant woman

GRAVIES pl. of gravy

GRAVING present participle of grave

GRAVITAS *n* pl. **-ES** reserved, dignified behavior

GRAVITON *n* pl. **-S** a hypothetical particle

GRAVITY *n* pl. **-TIES** the force of attraction toward the earth's center

GRAVLAKS *n* pl. **GRAVLAKS** gravlax

GRAVLAX *n* pl. **GRAVLAX** cured salmon

GRAVURE *n* pl. **-S** a printing process

GRAVY *n* pl. **-VIES** a sauce of the fat and juices from cooked meat

GRAY *adj* **GRAYER, GRAYEST** of a color between white and black

GRAY *v* **-ED, -ING, -S** to make gray

GRAYBACK *n* pl. **-S** a gray bird

GRAYFISH *n* pl. **-ES** a dogfish

GRAYISH *adj* somewhat gray

GRAYLAG *n* pl. **-S** a wild goose

GRAYLING *n* pl. **-S** a food fish

GRAYLY *adv* in a gray manner

GRAYMAIL *n* pl. **-S** pressure on an official to reveal sensitive information

GRAYNESS *n* pl. **-ES** the state of being gray

GRAYOUT *n* pl. **-S** a temporary blurring of vision

GRAZE *v* **GRAZED, GRAZING, GRAZES** to feed on growing grass **GRAZABLE** *adj*

GRAZER *n* pl. **-S** one that grazes

GRAZIER *n* pl. **-S** one that grazes cattle

GRAZING *n* pl. **-S** land used for the feeding of animals

GRAZIOSO *adj* graceful in style

GREASE *v* **GREASED, GREASING, GREASES** to smear with grease (a lubricating substance)

GREASER *n* pl. **-S** one that greases

GREASY *adj* **GREASIER, GREASIEST** containing or resembling grease **GREASILY** *adv*

GREAT *adj* **GREATER, GREATEST** large

GREAT *n* pl. **-S** a distinguished or outstanding person

GREATEN *v* **-ED, -ING, -S** to make greater

GREATLY *adv* in a great manner

GREAVE *n* pl. **-S** a piece of armor for the leg **GREAVED** *adj*

GREBE *n* pl. **-S** a diving bird

GRECIZE *v* **-CIZED, -CIZING, -CIZES** to provide with a Greek style

GREE *v* **GREED, GREEING, GREES** to agree

GREED *n* pl. **-S** excessive desire for gain or wealth

GREEDY *adj* **GREEDIER, GREEDIEST** marked by greed **GREEDILY** *adv*

GREEGREE *n* pl. **-S** grigri

GREEK *n* pl. **GREEK** something unintelligible

GREEN *adj* **GREENER, GREENEST** of the color of growing foliage

GREEN *v* **-ED, -ING, -S** to become green

GREENBUG *n* pl. **-S** a green aphid

GREENERY *n* pl. **-ERIES** green vegetation

GREENFLY *n* pl. **-FLIES** a green aphid

GREENIE *n* pl. **-S** an amphetamine pill

GREENIER comparative of greeny

GREENIEST superlative of greeny

GREENING *n* pl. **-S** a variety of apple

GREENISH *adj* somewhat green

GREENLET *n* pl. **-S** a vireo

GREENLIT a past tense of greenlight (to give approval for)

GREENLY *adv* in a green manner

GREENTH *n* pl. **-S** verdure

GREENWAY *n* pl. **-WAYS** piece of undeveloped land in a city

GREENY *adj* **GREENIER, GREENIEST** somewhat green

GREET *v* **-ED, -ING, -S** to address in a friendly and courteous way

GREET *v* **GRAT, GRUTTEN, GREETING, GREETS** to weep

GREETER *n* pl. **-S** one that greets

GREETING *n* pl. **-S** a salutation

GREGO *n* pl. **-GOS** a hooded coat

GREIGE *n* pl. **-S** fabric in a gray state

GREISEN *n* pl. **-S** a type of rock

GREMIAL *n* pl. **-S** a lap cloth used by a bishop during a service

GREMLIN *n* pl. **-S** a mischievous creature

GREMMIE *n* pl. **-S** an inexperienced surfer

GREMMY *n* pl. **-MIES** gremmie

GRENADE *n* pl. **-S** an explosive device

GREW past tense of grow

GREWSOME *adj* **-SOMER, -SOMEST** gruesome

GREY *adj* **GREYER, GREYEST** gray

GREY *v* **-ED, -ING, -S** to gray

GREYHEN *n* pl. **-S** the female black grouse

GREYISH *adj* grayish

GREYLAG *n* pl. **-S** graylag

GREYLY *adv* grayly

GREYNESS *n* pl. **-ES** grayness

GRIBBLE *n* pl. **-S** a marine isopod

GRID *v* **GRIDDED, GRIDDING, GRIDS** to put into or set out as a framework of bars or lines

GRIDDER *n* pl. **-S** a football player

GRIDDLE *v* **-DLED, -DLING, -DLES** to cook on a flat pan

GRIDE *v* **GRIDED, GRIDING, GRIDES** to scrape harshly

GRIDIRON *v* **-ED, -ING, -S** to mark off into squares

GRIDLOCK *v* **-ED, -ING, -S** to bring to a standstill

GRIEF *n* pl. **-S** intense mental distress

GRIEVANT *n* pl. **-S** one that submits a complaint for arbitration

GRIEVE *v* **GRIEVED, GRIEVING, GRIEVES** to feel grief

GRIEVER *n* pl. **-S** one that grieves

GRIEVOUS *adj* causing grief

GRIFF *n* pl. **-S** griffe

GRIFFE *n* pl. **-S** the offspring of a black person and a mulatto

GRIFFIN *n* pl. **-S** a mythological creature

GRIFFON *n* pl. **-S** griffin

GRIFT *v* **-ED, -ING, -S** to swindle

GRIFTER *n* pl. **-S** a swindler

GRIG *n* pl. **-S** a lively person

GRIGRI *n* pl. **-S** a fetish or amulet

GRILL *v* **-ED, -ING, -S** to broil on a gridiron

GRILLADE *n* pl. **-S** a dish of grilled meat

GRILLAGE *n* pl. **-S** a framework of timber

GRILLE *n* pl. **-S** a grating

GRILLER *n* pl. **-S** one that grills

GRILLERY *n* pl. **-ERIES** a place where grilled foods are served

GRILSE *n* pl. **-S** a young salmon

GRIM *adj* **GRIMMER, GRIMMEST** stern and unrelenting

GRIMACE *v* **-MACED, -MACING, -MACES** to contort the facial features

GRIMACER *n* pl. **-S** one that grimaces

GRIME *v* **GRIMED, GRIMING, GRIMES** to make dirty

GRIMIER comparative of grimy

GRIMIEST superlative of grimy

GRIMILY *adv* in a grimy manner

GRIMING present participle of grime

GRIMLY *adv* in a grim manner

GRIMMER comparative of grim

GRIMMEST superlative of grim

GRIMNESS *n* pl. **-ES** the quality of being grim

GRIMOIRE *n* pl. **-S** a book of magic spells

GRIMY *adj* **GRIMIER, GRIMIEST** dirty

GRIN *v* **GRINNED, GRINNING, GRINS** to smile broadly

GRINCH *n* pl. **-ES** one who spoils the fun of others

GRIND *v* **GROUND** or **GRINDED, GRINDING, GRINDS** to wear, smooth, or sharpen by friction

GRINDER *n* pl. **-S** one that grinds

GRINDERY *n* pl. **-ERIES** a place where tools are ground

GRINNED past tense of grin

GRINNER *n* pl. **-S** one that grins

GRINNING present participle of grin

GRIOT   *n* pl. **-S** a tribal entertainer in West Africa

GRIP   *v* **GRIPPED** or **GRIPT, GRIPPING, GRIPS** to grasp

GRIPE   *v* **GRIPED, GRIPING, GRIPES** to complain peevishly

GRIPER   *n* pl. **-S** one that gripes

GRIPEY   *adj* **GRIPIER, GRIPIEST** gripy

GRIPIER   comparative of gripy

GRIPIEST   superlative of gripy

GRIPING   present participle of gripe

GRIPINGLY   *adv* in a complaining manner

GRIPMAN   *n* pl. **-MEN** a cable car operator

GRIPPE   *n* pl. **-S** a virus disease

GRIPPED   a past tense of grip

GRIPPER   *n* pl. **-S** one that grips

GRIPPING   present participle of grip

GRIPPLE   *adj* greedy

GRIPPY   *adj* **GRIPPIER, GRIPPIEST** affected with the grippe

GRIPSACK   *n* pl. **-S** a valise

GRIPT   a past tense of grip

GRIPY   *adj* **GRIPIER, GRIPIEST** causing sharp pains in the bowels

GRISEOUS   *adj* grayish

GRISETTE   *n* pl. **-S** a young French working-class girl

GRISKIN   *n* pl. **-S** the lean part of a loin of pork

GRISLY   *adj* **-LIER, -LIEST** horrifying

GRISON   *n* pl. **-S** a carnivorous mammal

GRIST   *n* pl. **-S** grain for grinding

GRISTER   *n* pl. **-S** one that grinds grain

GRISTLE   *n* pl. **-S** the tough part of meat

GRISTLY   *adj* **-TLIER, -TLIEST** containing gristle

GRIT   *v* **GRITTED, GRITTING, GRITS** to press the teeth together

GRITH   *n* pl. **-S** sanctuary for a limited period of time

GRITTER   *n* pl. **-S** one that grits

GRITTY   *adj* **-TIER, -TIEST** plucky **GRITTILY** *adv*

GRIVET   *n* pl. **-S** a small monkey

GRIZ   *n* pl. **GRIZ** a grizzly

GRIZZLE   *v* **-ZLED, -ZLING, -ZLES** to complain

GRIZZLER   *n* pl. **-S** one that grizzles

GRIZZLY   *adj* **-ZLIER, -ZLIEST** grayish

GRIZZLY   *n* pl. **-ZLIES** a large bear

GROAN   *v* **-ED, -ING, -S** to utter a low, mournful sound

GROANER   *n* pl. **-S** one that groans

GROAT   *n* pl. **-S** an old English coin

GROCER   *n* pl. **-S** a dealer in foodstuffs and household supplies

GROCERY   *n* pl. **-CERIES** a grocer's store

GRODY   *adj* **GRODIER, GRODIEST** sleazy

GROG   *n* pl. **-S** a mixture of liquor and water

GROGGERY   *n* pl. **-GERIES** a barroom

GROGGY   *adj* **-GIER, -GIEST** dazed **GROGGILY** *adv*

GROGRAM   *n* pl. **-S** a coarse silk fabric

GROGSHOP   *n* pl. **-S** a groggery

GROIN   *v* **-ED, -ING, -S** to build with intersecting arches

GROK   *v* **GROKKED, GROKKING, GROKS** to understand intuitively

GROMMET   *v* **-ED, -ING, -S** to fasten with a reinforcing ring of metal

GROMWELL   *n* pl. **-S** an herb

GROOM   *v* **-ED, -ING, -S** to clean and care for

GROOMER   *n* pl. **-S** one that grooms

GROOVE   *v* **GROOVED, GROOVING, GROOVES** to form a groove (a long, narrow depression)

GROOVER   *n* pl. **-S** one that grooves

GROOVY   *adj* **GROOVIER, GROOVIEST** marvelous **GROOVILY** *adv*

GROPE   *v* **GROPED, GROPING, GROPES** to feel about with the hands

GROPER   *n* pl. **-S** one that gropes

GROSBEAK   *n* pl. **-S** a finch

GROSCHEN   *n* pl. **GROSCHEN** a formerly used Austrian coin

GROSS   *adj* **GROSSER, GROSSEST** flagrant

GROSS   *v* **-ED, -ING, -ES** to earn exclusive of deductions

GROSSER   *n* pl. **-S** a product yielding a large volume of business

GROSSLY   *adv* in a gross manner

GROSZ   *n* pl. **GROSZY** a Polish coin

GROSZE   *n* pl. **GROSZY** grosz

GROT   *n* pl. **-S** a grotto

GROTTO *n* pl. **-TOS** or **-TOES** a cave **GROTTOED** *adj*

GROTTY *adj* **-TIER, -TIEST** wretched

GROUCH *v* **-ED, -ING, -ES** to complain

GROUCHY *adj* **GROUCHIER, GROUCHIEST** ill-tempered

GROUND *v* **-ED, -ING, -S** to place on a foundation

GROUNDER *n* pl. **-S** a type of batted baseball

GROUP *v* **-ED, -ING, -S** to arrange in a group (an assemblage of persons or things)

GROUPAGE *n* pl. **-S** the arranging of persons or things into groups

GROUPER *n* pl. **-S** a food fish

GROUPIE *n* pl. **-S** a follower of rock groups

GROUPING *n* pl. **-S** a set of objects

GROUPOID *n* pl. **-S** a type of mathematical set

GROUSE *v* **GROUSED, GROUSING, GROUSES** to complain

GROUSER *n* pl. **-S** one that grouses

GROUT *v* **-ED, -ING, -S** to fill with a thin mortar

GROUTER *n* pl. **-S** one that grouts

GROUTY *adj* **GROUTIER, GROUTIEST** surly

GROVE *n* pl. **-S** a small forested area **GROVED** *adj*

GROVEL *v* **-ELED, -ELING, -ELS** or **-ELLED, -ELLING, -ELS** to crawl in an abject manner

GROVELER *n* pl. **-S** one that grovels

GROVY *adj* **GROVIER, GROVIEST** resembling or suggestive of a grove

GROW *v* **GREW, GROWN, GROWING, GROWS** to cultivate **GROWABLE** *adj*

GROWER *n* pl. **-S** one that grows

GROWL *v* **-ED, -ING, -S** to utter a deep, harsh sound

GROWLER *n* pl. **-S** one that growls

GROWLY *adj* **GROWLIER, GROWLIEST** deep and harsh in speech

GROWN *adj* mature

GROWNUP *n* pl. **-S** a mature person

GROWTH *n* pl. **-S** development

GROWTHY *adj* **GROWTHIER, GROWTHIEST** fast-growing

GROYNE *n* pl. **-S** a structure built to protect a shore from erosion

GRR *interj* — used to express anger or annoyance

GRRRL *n* pl. **-S** a young woman who resists the exploitation of women

GRUB *v* **GRUBBED, GRUBBING, GRUBS** to dig

GRUBBER *n* pl. **-S** one that grubs

GRUBBY *adj* **-BIER, -BIEST** dirty **GRUBBILY** *adv*

GRUBWORM *n* pl. **-S** the larva of some insects

GRUDGE *v* **GRUDGED, GRUDGING, GRUDGES** to be unwilling to give or admit

GRUDGER *n* pl. **-S** one that grudges

GRUE *n* pl. **-S** a shudder of fear

GRUEL *v* **-ELED, -ELING, -ELS** or **-ELLED, -ELLING, -ELS** to disable by hard work

GRUELER *n* pl. **-S** one that gruels

GRUELING *n* pl. **-S** an exhausting experience

GRUELLED a past tense of gruel

GRUELLER *n* pl. **-S** grueler

GRUELLING present participle of gruel

GRUESOME *adj* **-SOMER, -SOMEST** repugnant

GRUFF *adj* **GRUFFER, GRUFFEST** low and harsh in speech

GRUFF *v* **-ED, -ING, -S** to utter in a gruff voice

GRUFFIER comparative of gruffy

GRUFFIEST superlative of gruffy

GRUFFILY *adv* in a gruffy manner

GRUFFISH *adj* somewhat gruff

GRUFFLY *adv* in a gruff manner

GRUFFY *adj* **GRUFFIER, GRUFFIEST** gruff

GRUGRU *n* pl. **-S** a palm tree

GRUIFORM *adj* designating an order of birds

GRUM *adj* **GRUMMER, GRUMMEST** morose

GRUMBLE *v* **-BLED, -BLING, -BLES** to mutter in discontent

GRUMBLER *n* pl. **-S** one that grumbles

GRUMBLY *adj* **-BLIER, -BLIEST** given to grumbling

GRUME *n* pl. **-S** a thick, viscid substance

GRUMMER comparative of grum

GRUMMEST superlative of grum

GRUMMET *v* **-ED, -ING, -S** to grommet

GRUMOSE *adj* grumous

GRUMOUS	*adj* consisting of clustered grains
GRUMP	*v* **-ED, -ING, -S** to complain
GRUMPHIE	*n* pl. **-S** a pig
GRUMPHY	*n* pl. **GRUMPHIES** grumphie
GRUMPISH	*adj* grumpy
GRUMPY	*adj* **GRUMPIER, GRUMPIEST** ill-tempered **GRUMPILY** *adv*
GRUNGE	*n* pl. **-S** dirt
GRUNGER	*n* pl. **-S** a fan of a style of rock music and associated fashions
GRUNGY	*adj* **-GIER, -GIEST** dirty
GRUNION	*n* pl. **-S** a small food fish
GRUNT	*v* **-ED, -ING, -S** to utter a deep, guttural sound
GRUNTER	*n* pl. **-S** one that grunts
GRUNTLE	*v* **-TLED, -TLING, -TLES** to put in a good humor
GRUSHIE	*adj* thriving
GRUTCH	*v* **-ED, -ING, -ES** to grudge
GRUTTEN	past participle of greet (to weep)
GRUYERE	*n* pl. **-S** a Swiss cheese
GRYPHON	*n* pl. **-S** griffin
GUACHARO	*n* pl. **-ROS** or **-ROES** a tropical bird
GUACO	*n* pl. **-COS** a tropical plant
GUAIAC	*n* pl. **-S** guaiacum
GUAIACOL	*n* pl. **-S** a chemical compound
GUAIACUM	*n* pl. **-S** a medicinal resin
GUAIOCUM	*n* pl. **-S** guaiacum
GUAN	*n* pl. **-S** a large bird
GUANACO	*n* pl. **-COS** a South American mammal
GUANASE	*n* pl. **-S** an enzyme
GUANAY	*n* pl. **-NAYS** a Peruvian cormorant
GUANIDIN	*n* pl. **-S** a chemical compound
GUANIN	*n* pl. **-S** guanine
GUANINE	*n* pl. **-S** a chemical compound
GUANO	*n* pl. **-NOS** the accumulated excrement of seabirds
GUAR	*n* pl. **-S** a drought-tolerant legume
GUARACHE	*n* pl. **-S** huarache
GUARANA	*n* pl. **-S** a South American shrub
GUARANI	*n* pl. **-NIS** or **-NIES** a monetary unit of Paraguay
GUARANTY	*v* **-TIED, -TYING, -TIES** to assume responsibility for the quality of
GUARD	*v* **-ED, -ING, -S** to protect

GUARDANT	*n* pl. **-S** a guardian
GUARDDOG	*n* pl. **-S** a dog trained to guard persons or property
GUARDER	*n* pl. **-S** one that guards
GUARDIAN	*n* pl. **-S** one that guards
GUAVA	*n* pl. **-S** a tropical shrub
GUAYULE	*n* pl. **-S** a shrub that is a source of rubber
GUBBINS	*n* pl. **GUBBINSES** a trivial object
GUCK	*n* pl. **-S** a messy substance
GUDE	*n* pl. **-S** good
GUDGEON	*v* **-ED, -ING, -S** to dupe
GUENON	*n* pl. **-S** a long-tailed monkey
GUERDON	*v* **-ED, -ING, -S** to reward
GUERIDON	*n* pl. **-S** a small stand or table
GUERILLA	*n* pl. **-S** a member of a small independent band of soldiers
GUERNSEY	*n* pl. **-SEYS** a woolen shirt
GUESS	*v* **-ED, -ING, -ES** to form an opinion from little or no evidence
GUESSER	*n* pl. **-S** one that guesses
GUEST	*v* **-ED, -ING, -S** to appear as a visitor
GUFF	*n* pl. **-S** foolish talk
GUFFAW	*v* **-ED, -ING, -S** to laugh loudly
GUGGLE	*v* **-GLED, -GLING, -GLES** to gurgle
GUGLET	*n* pl. **-S** goglet
GUID	*n* pl. **-S** good
GUIDANCE	*n* pl. **-S** advice
GUIDE	*v* **GUIDED, GUIDING, GUIDES** to show the way to **GUIDABLE** *adj*
GUIDER	*n* pl. **-S** one that guides
GUIDEWAY	*n* pl. **-WAYS** a track for controlling the line of motion of something
GUIDON	*n* pl. **-S** a small flag
GUILD	*n* pl. **-S** an association of people of the same trade
GUILDER	*n* pl. **-S** a former monetary unit of the Netherlands
GUILE	*v* **GUILED, GUILING, GUILES** to beguile
GUILEFUL	*adj* cunning
GUILT	*v* **-ED, -ING, -S** to cause (someone) to feel guilty
GUILTY	*adj* **GUILTIER, GUILTIEST** worthy of blame for an offense **GUILTILY** *adv*
GUIMPE	*n* pl. **-S** a short blouse

GUINEA   *n* pl. **-S** a formerly used British coin

GUINEP   *n* pl. **-S** genip

GUIPURE   *n* pl. **-S** a type of lace

GUIRO   *n* pl. **-ROS** a percussion instrument

GUISARD   *n* pl. **-S** a masker

GUISE   *v* **GUISED, GUISING, GUISES** to disguise

GUITAR   *n* pl. **-S** a stringed musical instrument

GUITGUIT   *n* pl. **-S** a tropical American bird

GUL   *n* pl. **-S** a design in oriental carpets

GULAG   *n* pl. **-S** a forced-labor camp

GULAR   *n* pl. **-S** a scale on the throat of a reptile or fish

GULCH   *n* pl. **-ES** a deep, narrow ravine

GULDEN   *n* pl. **-S** a guilder

GULES   *n* pl. **GULES** the color red

GULF   *v* **-ED, -ING, -S** to swallow up

GULFIER   comparative of gulfy

GULFIEST   superlative of gulfy

GULFLIKE   *adj* resembling a deep chasm

GULFWEED   *n* pl. **-S** a brownish seaweed

GULFY   *adj* **GULFIER, GULFIEST** full of whirlpools

GULL   *v* **-ED, -ING, -S** to deceive

GULLABLE   *adj* gullible **GULLABLY** *adv*

GULLERY   *n* pl. **-ERIES** a place where gulls (web-footed seabirds) breed

GULLET   *n* pl. **-S** the throat

GULLEY   *n* pl. **-LEYS** a ravine

GULLIBLE   *adj* easily deceived **GULLIBLY** *adv*

GULLWING   *adj* hinged at the top to swing upward

GULLY   *v* **-LIED, -LYING, -LIES** to form ravines by the action of water

GULOSITY   *n* pl. **-TIES** gluttony

GULP   *v* **-ED, -ING, -S** to swallow rapidly

GULPER   *n* pl. **-S** one that gulps

GULPY   *adj* **GULPIER, GULPIEST** marked by gulping

GUM   *v* **GUMMED, GUMMING, GUMS** to smear, seal, or clog with gum (a sticky, viscid substance)

GUMBALL   *n* pl. **-S** a small ball of chewing gum

GUMBO   *n* pl. **-BOS** the okra plant

GUMBOIL   *n* pl. **-S** an abscess in the gum

GUMBOOT   *n* pl. **-S** a rubber boot

GUMBOTIL   *n* pl. **-S** a sticky clay

GUMDROP   *n* pl. **-S** a chewy candy

GUMLESS   *adj* having no gum

GUMLIKE   *adj* resembling gum

GUMLINE   *n* pl. **-S** the edge of the gums meeting the teeth

GUMMA   *n* pl. **-MAS** or **-MATA** a soft tumor

GUMMED   past tense of gum

GUMMER   *n* pl. **-S** one that gums

GUMMI   *n* pl. **-S** a rubbery, flavored candy

GUMMIER   comparative of gummy

GUMMIEST   superlative of gummy

GUMMILY   *adv* in a toothless manner

GUMMING   present participle of gum

GUMMITE   *n* pl. **-S** a mixture of various minerals

GUMMOSE   *adj* gummy

GUMMOSIS   *n* pl. **-MOSES** a disease of plants

GUMMOUS   *adj* gummy

GUMMY   *adj* **-MIER, -MIEST** resembling gum

GUMPTION   *n* pl. **-S** shrewdness

GUMSHOE   *v* **-SHOED, -SHOEING, -SHOES** to investigate stealthily

GUMTREE   *n* pl. **-S** a tree that yields gum

GUMWEED   *n* pl. **-S** a plant covered with a gummy substance

GUMWOOD   *n* pl. **-S** the wood of a gumtree

GUN   *v* **GUNNED, GUNNING, GUNS** to shoot with a gun (a portable firearm)

GUNBOAT   *n* pl. **-S** an armed vessel

GUNDOG   *n* pl. **-S** a hunting dog

GUNFIGHT   *v* **-FOUGHT, -FIGHTING, -FIGHTS** to fight with guns

GUNFIRE   *n* pl. **-S** the firing of guns

GUNFLINT   *n* pl. **-S** the flint in a flintlock

GUNGE   *v* **GUNGED, GUNGING, GUNGES** to obstruct with gunky material

GUNGY   *adj* **GUNGIER, GUNGIEST** gunky

GUNITE   *n* pl. **-S** a mixture of cement, sand, and water

GUNK   *v* **-ED, -ING, -S** to cause something to be gunky

GUNKHOLE   *v* **-HOLED, -HOLING, -HOLES** to make a series of short boat trips

GUNKY	*adj* **GUNKIER, GUNKIEST** filthy, sticky, or greasy
GUNLESS	*adj* having no gun
GUNLOCK	*n* pl. **-S** the mechanism which ignites the charge of a gun
GUNMAN	*n* pl. **-MEN** one who is armed with a gun
GUNMETAL	*n* pl. **-S** a dark gray color
GUNNED	past tense of gun
GUNNEL	*n* pl. **-S** a marine fish
GUNNEN	past participle of gin
GUNNER	*n* pl. **-S** one that operates a gun
GUNNERA	*n* pl. **-S** a plant with large leaves
GUNNERY	*n* pl. **-NERIES** the use of guns
GUNNING	*n* pl. **-S** the sport of hunting with a gun
GUNNY	*n* pl. **-NIES** a coarse fabric
GUNNYBAG	*n* pl. **-S** a bag made of gunny
GUNPAPER	*n* pl. **-S** a type of explosive paper
GUNPLAY	*n* pl. **-PLAYS** the shooting of guns
GUNPOINT	*n* pl. **-S** the point or aim of a gun
GUNPORT	*n* pl. **-S** an opening in a ship or airplane for a gun
GUNROOM	*n* pl. **-S** a room on a British warship
GUNSEL	*n* pl. **-S** a gunman
GUNSHIP	*n* pl. **-S** an armed helicopter
GUNSHOT	*n* pl. **-S** a projectile fired from a gun
GUNSIGHT	*n* pl. **-S** a device on a gun for aiming
GUNSMITH	*n* pl. **-S** one who makes or repairs firearms
GUNSTOCK	*n* pl. **-S** the rear wooden part of a rifle
GUNTER	*n* pl. **-S** a type of sail
GUNWALE	*n* pl. **-S** the upper edge of a ship's side
GUPPY	*n* pl. **-PIES** a small, tropical fish
GURDWARA	*n* pl. **-S** a Sikh temple
GURDY	*n* pl. **-DIES** a winch on a fishing boat
GURGE	*v* **GURGED, GURGING, GURGES** to swirl
GURGLE	*v* **-GLED, -GLING, -GLES** to flow with bubbling sounds
GURGLET	*n* pl. **-S** goglet
GURGLY	*adj* **-GLIER, -GLIEST** making bubbling sounds
GURNARD	*n* pl. **-S** a marine fish
GURNET	*n* pl. **-S** a gurnard
GURNEY	*n* pl. **-NEYS** a wheeled cot
GURRY	*n* pl. **-RIES** fish offal
GURSH	*n* pl. **-ES** qursh
GURU	*n* pl. **-S** a Hindu spiritual teacher
GURUSHIP	*n* pl. **-S** the office of a guru
GUSH	*v* **-ED, -ING, -ES** to flow forth forcefully
GUSHER	*n* pl. **-S** a gushing oil well
GUSHY	*adj* **GUSHIER, GUSHIEST** overly sentimental **GUSHILY** *adv*
GUSSET	*v* **-ED, -ING, -S** to furnish with a reinforcing piece of material
GUSSIE	*v* **-SIED, -SYING, -SIES** to gussy
GUSSY	*v* **-SIED, -SYING, -SIES** to dress up in fine or showy clothes
GUST	*v* **-ED, -ING, -S** to blow in gusts (sudden blasts of wind)
GUSTABLE	*n* pl. **-S** a savory food
GUSTIER	comparative of gusty
GUSTIEST	superlative of gusty
GUSTILY	*adv* in a gusty manner
GUSTLESS	*adj* having no gusts
GUSTO	*n* pl. **-TOES** or **-TOS** vigorous enjoyment
GUSTY	*adj* **GUSTIER, GUSTIEST** blowing in gusts
GUT	*v* **GUTTED, GUTTING, GUTS** to remove the guts (intestines) of
GUTFUL	*n* pl. **-S** an excessive amount
GUTLESS	*adj* lacking courage
GUTLIKE	*adj* resembling guts
GUTSILY	*adv* in a gutsy manner
GUTSY	*adj* **GUTSIER, GUTSIEST** brave
GUTTA	*n* pl. **-TAE** a drop of liquid
GUTTATE	*adj* resembling a drop
GUTTATED	*adj* guttate
GUTTED	past tense of gut
GUTTER	*v* **-ED, -ING, -S** to form channels for draining off water
GUTTERY	*adj* marked by extreme vulgarity or indecency
GUTTIER	comparative of gutty
GUTTIEST	superlative of gutty
GUTTING	present participle of gut
GUTTLE	*v* **-TLED, -TLING, -TLES** to eat rapidly
GUTTLER	*n* pl. **-S** one that guttles

GUTTURAL   *n* pl. **-S** a throaty sound

GUTTY   *adj* **-TIER, -TIEST** marked by courage

GUV   *n* pl. **-S** a governor

GUY   *v* **-ED, -ING, -S** to ridicule

GUYLINE   *n* pl. **-S** a rope, chain, or wire used as a brace

GUYOT   *n* pl. **-S** a flat-topped seamount

GUZZLE   *v* **-ZLED, -ZLING, -ZLES** to drink rapidly

GUZZLER   *n* pl. **-S** one that guzzles

GWEDUC   *n* pl. **-S** geoduck

GWEDUCK   *n* pl. **-S** geoduck

GWINE   a present participle of go

GYBE   *v* **GYBED, GYBING, GYBES** to shift from side to side while sailing

GYM   *n* pl. **-S** a room for athletic activities

GYMKHANA   *n* pl. **-S** an athletic meet

GYMNASIA   *n/pl* gyms

GYMNAST   *n* pl. **-S** one who is skilled in physical exercises

GYMSLIP   *n* pl. **-S** a sleeveless tunic often worn by schoolgirls

GYNAECEA   *n/pl* gynecia

GYNAECIA   *n/pl* gynecia

GYNANDRY   *n* pl. **-DRIES** the condition of having both male and female sexual organs

GYNARCHY   *n* pl. **-CHIES** government by women

GYNECIC   *adj* pertaining to women

GYNECIUM   *n* pl. **-CIA** the pistil of a flower

GYNECOID   *adj* resembling a woman

GYNIATRY   *n* pl. **-TRIES** the treatment of women's diseases

GYNIE   *n* pl. **-S** a gynecologist

GYNO   *n* pl. **GYNOS** a gynecologist

GYNOECIA   *n/pl* gynecia

GYOZA   *n* pl. **-S** a stuffed and fried pocket of dough

GYP   *v* **GYPPED, GYPPING, GYPS** to swindle

GYPLURE   *n* pl. **-S** a synthetic attractant to trap gypsy moths

GYPO   *n* pl. **GYPOS** a small-time logging operator

GYPPER   *n* pl. **-S** one that gyps

GYPPO   *n* pl. **GYPPOS** gypo

GYPSEIAN   *adj* of or pertaining to gypsies

GYPSEOUS   *adj* containing gypsum

GYPSTER   *n* pl. **-S** one that gyps

GYPSUM   *n* pl. **-S** a mineral

GYPSY   *v* **-SIED, -SYING, -SIES** to live like a gypsy (a wanderer)

GYPSYDOM   *n* pl. **-S** the realm of gypsies

GYPSYISH   *adj* resembling a gypsy

GYPSYISM   *n* pl. **-S** the mode of life of gypsies

GYRAL   *adj* gyratory **GYRALLY** *adv*

GYRASE   *n* pl. **-S** an enzyme

GYRATE   *v* **-RATED, -RATING, -RATES** to revolve or rotate

GYRATION   *n* pl. **-S** the act of gyrating

GYRATOR   *n* pl. **-S** one that gyrates

GYRATORY   *adj* moving in a circle or spiral

GYRE   *v* **GYRED, GYRING, GYRES** to move in a circle or spiral

GYRENE   *n* pl. **-S** a marine

GYRI   pl. of gyrus

GYRO   *n* pl. **-ROS** a gyroscope

GYROIDAL   *adj* spiral in arrangement

GYRON   *n* pl. **-S** a heraldic design

GYROSE   *adj* marked with wavy lines

GYROSTAT   *n* pl. **-S** a type of stabilizing device

GYRUS   *n* pl. **-RI** a ridge in the brain

GYTTJA   *n* pl. **-S** an organically rich mud

GYVE   *v* **GYVED, GYVING, GYVES** to shackle

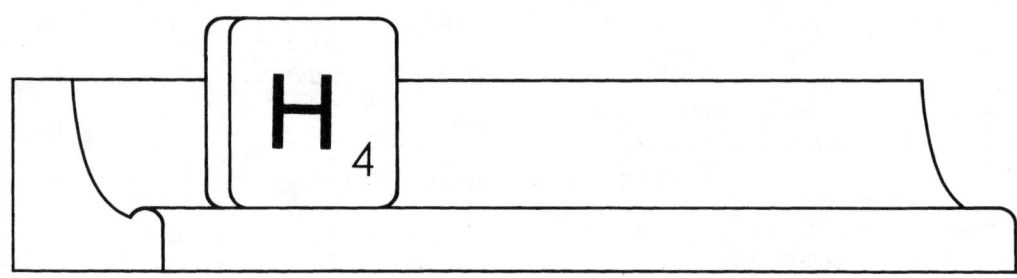

HA	*n* pl. **-S** a sound of surprise	**HACKLE**	*v* **-LED, -LING, -LES** to hack
HAAF	*n* pl. **-S** a deep-sea fishing ground	**HACKLER**	*n* pl. **-S** one that hackles
HAAR	*n* pl. **-S** a fog	**HACKLY**	*adj* **-LIER, -LIEST** jagged
HABANERA	*n* pl. **-S** a Cuban dance	**HACKMAN**	*n* pl. **-MEN** a hackie
HABANERO	*n* pl. **-ROS** a hot chili pepper	**HACKNEY**	*v* **-NEYED, -NEYING, -NEYS** to make common
HABDALAH	*n* pl. **-S** a Jewish ceremony	**HACKSAW**	*v* **-SAWED, -SAWN, -SAWING, -SAWS** to use a saw having a fine-toothed blade
HABENDUM	*n* pl. **-S** the part of a deed that limits the extent of ownership		
HABILE	*adj* skillful	**HACKWORK**	*n* pl. **-S** artistic work done according to formula
HABIT	*v* **-ED, -ING, -S** to clothe or dress	**HAD**	a past tense of have
HABITAN	*n* pl. **-S** a French settler	**HADAL**	*adj* pertaining to deep parts of the ocean
HABITANT	*n* pl. **-S** an inhabitant		
HABITAT	*n* pl. **-S** the natural environment of an organism	**HADARIM**	a pl. of heder
HABITUAL	*adj* occurring frequently or constantly	**HADDEST**	a past 2d person sing. of have
		HADDOCK	*n* pl. **-S** a food fish
HABITUDE	*n* pl. **-S** a usual course of action	**HADE**	*v* **HADED, HADING, HADES** to incline
HABITUE	*n* pl. **-S** a frequent customer		
HABITUS	*n* pl. **HABITUS** bodily build and constitution	**HADITH**	*n* pl. **HADITH** or **HADITHS** a record of the sayings of Muhammed
HABOOB	*n* pl. **-S** a violent sandstorm	**HADJ**	*n* pl. **-ES** a pilgrimage to Mecca
HABU	*n* pl. **-S** a poisonous snake	**HADJEE**	*n* pl. **-S** hadji
HACEK	*n* pl. **-S** a mark placed over a letter to modify it	**HADJI**	*n* pl. **-S** one who has made a hadj
HACHURE	*v* **-CHURED, -CHURING, -CHURES** to make a hatching on a map	**HADRON**	*n* pl. **-S** an elementary particle **HADRONIC** *adj*
		HADST	a past 2d person sing. of have
HACIENDA	*n* pl. **-S** an estate	**HAE**	*v* **HAED, HAEN, HAEING, HAES** to have
HACK	*v* **-ED, -ING, -S** to cut or chop roughly **HACKABLE** *adj*	**HAEM**	*n* pl. **-S** heme
HACKBUT	*n* pl. **-S** a type of gun	**HAEMAL**	*adj* hemal
HACKEE	*n* pl. **-S** a chipmunk	**HAEMATAL**	*adj* hemal
HACKER	*n* pl. **-S** one that hacks	**HAEMATIC**	*n* pl. **-S** hematic
HACKERY	*n* pl. **-ERIES** dull, unoriginal writing	**HAEMATIN**	*n* pl. **-S** hematin
HACKIE	*n* pl. **-S** a taxicab driver	**HAEMIC**	*adj* hemic
HACKING	*n* pl. **-S** the activity of riding a horse for pleasure	**HAEMIN**	*n* pl. **-S** hemin
		HAEMOID	*adj* hemoid

HAEN	past participle of hae
HAERES	*n* pl. **-REDES** heres
HAET	*n* pl. **-S** a small amount
HAFFET	*n* pl. **-S** the cheekbone and temple
HAFFIT	*n* pl. **-S** haffet
HAFIZ	*n* pl. **-ES** a Muslim who knows the Koran by heart
HAFNIUM	*n* pl. **-S** a metallic element
HAFT	*v* **-ED, -ING, -S** to supply with a handle
HAFTARA	*n* pl. **-RAS** or **-ROT** or **-ROTH** haphtara
HAFTARAH	*n* pl. **-RAHS** or **-ROS** or **-ROT** or **-ROTH** haphtara
HAFTER	*n* pl. **-S** one that hafts
HAFTORAH	*n* pl. **-RAHS** or **-ROT** or **-ROTH** haphtara
HAG	*v* **HAGGED, HAGGING, HAGS** to hack
HAGADIC	*adj* haggadic
HAGADIST	*n* pl. **-S** a haggadic scholar
HAGBERRY	*n* pl. **-RIES** a small cherry
HAGBORN	*adj* born of a witch
HAGBUSH	*n* pl. **-ES** a large tree
HAGBUT	*n* pl. **-S** hackbut
HAGDON	*n* pl. **-S** a seabird
HAGFISH	*n* pl. **-ES** an eellike fish
HAGGADA	*n* pl. **-DAS, -DOT** or **-DOTH** haggadah
HAGGADAH	*n* pl. **-DAHS** or **-DOT** or **-DOTH** a biblical narrative **HAGGADIC** *adj*
HAGGARD	*n* pl. **-S** an adult hawk
HAGGED	past tense of hag
HAGGING	present participle of hag
HAGGIS	*n* pl. **-GISES** a Scottish dish made of a sheep's inner organs, which are cut up, spiced, and cooked in a bag
HAGGISH	*adj* resembling a hag
HAGGLE	*v* **-GLED, -GLING, -GLES** to bargain
HAGGLER	*n* pl. **-S** one that haggles
HAGGLING	*n* pl. **-S** a bargaining about a price
HAGRIDE	*v* **-RODE, -RIDDEN, -RIDING, -RIDES** to harass
HAGRIDER	*n* pl. **-S** one that hagrides
HAH	*n* pl. **-S** ha
HAHA	*n* pl. **-S** a fence set in a ditch
HAHNIUM	*n* pl. **-S** a radioactive element
HAICK	*n* pl. **-S** haik
HAIK	*n* pl. **HAIKS** or **HAIKA** an outer garment worn by Arabs
HAIKU	*n* pl. **-S** a Japanese poem
HAIL	*v* **-ED, -ING, -S** to welcome
HAILER	*n* pl. **-S** one that hails
HAIMISH	*adj* homey, unpretentious
HAINT	*n* pl. **-S** a ghost
HAIR	*n* pl. **-S** a threadlike growth
HAIRBALL	*n* pl. **-S** a ball of hair
HAIRBAND	*n* pl. **-S** a headband
HAIRCAP	*n* pl. **-S** a hat
HAIRCUT	*n* pl. **-S** a cutting of the hair
HAIRDO	*n* pl. **-DOS** a style of wearing the hair
HAIRED	*adj* having hair
HAIRGRIP	*n* pl. **-S** a bobby pin
HAIRIER	comparative of hairy
HAIRIEST	superlative of hairy
HAIRILY	*adv* in a hairy manner
HAIRLESS	*adj* having no hair
HAIRLIKE	*adj* resembling a hair
HAIRLINE	*n* pl. **-S** a very thin line
HAIRLOCK	*n* pl. **-S** a lock of hair
HAIRNET	*n* pl. **-S** a net worn to keep the hair in place
HAIRPIN	*n* pl. **-S** a hair fastener
HAIRWING	*n* pl. **-S** a fishing lure tied with hair
HAIRWORK	*n* pl. **-S** the making of articles from hair
HAIRWORM	*n* pl. **-S** a parasitic worm
HAIRY	*adj* **HAIRIER, HAIRIEST** covered with hair
HAJ	*n* pl. **-ES** hadj
HAJI	*n* pl. **-S** hadji
HAJJ	*n* pl. **-ES** hadj
HAJJI	*n* pl. **-S** hadji
HAKE	*n* pl. **-S** a marine fish
HAKEEM	*n* pl. **-S** hakim
HAKIM	*n* pl. **-S** a Muslim physician
HAKU	*n* pl. **-S** a crown of flowers
HALACHA	*n* pl. **-CHAS** or **-CHOT** or **-CHOTH** the legal part of the Talmud **HALACHIC** *adj*
HALAKAH	*n* pl. **-KAHS** or **-KOTH** halacha **HALAKIC** *adj*

HALAKHA *n* pl. **-KHAS** or **-KHOT** halacha **HALAKHIC** *adj*

HALAKHAH *n* pl. **-KHAHS** or **-KHOTH** or **-KHOT** halacha **HALAKHIC** *adj*

HALAKIST *n* pl. **-S** a halakic writer

HALAKOTH a pl. of halakah

HALAL *n* pl. **-S** meat prepared in accordance with Islamic law

HALALA *n* pl. **-S** a Saudi Arabian coin

HALALAH *n* pl. **-S** halala

HALATION *n* pl. **-S** a blurring of light in photographs

HALAVAH *n* pl. **-S** halvah

HALAZONE *n* pl. **-S** a disinfectant for drinking water

HALBERD *n* pl. **-S** an axlike weapon of the 15th and 16th centuries

HALBERT *n* pl. **-S** halberd

HALCYON *n* pl. **-S** a mythical bird

HALE *adj* **HALER, HALEST** healthy

HALE *v* **HALED, HALING, HALES** to compel to go

HALENESS *n* pl. **-ES** the state of being hale

HALER *n* pl. **-LERS** or **-LERU** a coin of the Czech Republic

HALEST superlative of hale

HALF *n* pl. **HALVES** one of two equal parts

HALFBACK *n* pl. **-S** a football player

HALFBEAK *n* pl. **-S** a marine fish

HALFLIFE *n* pl. **-LIVES** a measure of radioactive decay

HALFNESS *n* pl. **-ES** the state of being half

HALFPIPE *n* pl. **-S** a U-shaped course used for skateboarding

HALFTIME *n* pl. **-S** an intermission in a football game

HALFTONE *n* pl. **-S** a shade between light and dark

HALFWAY *adj* being in the middle

HALFWIT *n* pl. **-S** a foolish or stupid person

HALIBUT *n* pl. **-S** a flatfish

HALID *n* pl. **-S** halide

HALIDE *n* pl. **-S** a chemical compound

HALIDOM *n* pl. **-S** something holy

HALIDOME *n* pl. **-S** halidom

HALIER *n* pl. **HALIERS** or **HALIEROV** a former monetary unit of Slovakia

HALING present participle of hale

HALIOTIS *n* pl. **HALIOTIS** a mollusk with an ear-shaped shell

HALITE *n* pl. **-S** a mineral

HALITUS *n* pl. **-ES** an exhalation

HALL *n* pl. **-S** a large room for assembly

HALLAH *n* pl. **-LAHS** or **-LOTH** or **-LOT** challah

HALLAL *adj* prepared according to Islamic law

HALLEL *n* pl. **-S** a chant of praise

HALLIARD *n* pl. **-S** halyard

HALLMARK *v* **-ED, -ING, -S** to mark with an official stamp

HALLO *v* **-ED, -ING, -S** or **-ES** to shout

HALLOA *v* **-ED, -ING, -S** to hallo

HALLOO *v* **-ED, -ING, -S** to hallo

HALLOT a pl. of hallah

HALLOTH a pl. of hallah

HALLOW *v* **-ED, -ING, -S** to make holy

HALLOWER *n* pl. **-S** one that hallows

HALLUX *n* pl. **-LUCES** the big toe **HALLUCAL** *adj*

HALLWAY *n* pl. **-WAYS** a hall

HALM *n* pl. **-S** haulm

HALMA *n* pl. **-S** a board game

HALO *v* **-ED, -ING, -S** or **-ES** to form a halo (a ring of light)

HALOGEN *n* pl. **-S** a nonmetallic element

HALOID *n* pl. **-S** a chemical salt

HALOLIKE *adj* resembling a halo

HALON *n* pl. **-S** a compound of carbon and bromine

HALT *v* **-ED, -ING, -S** to stop

HALTER *v* **-ED, -ING, -S** to put restraint upon

HALTERE *n* pl. **-S** a pair of wings of an insect

HALTLESS *adj* not hesitant

HALUTZ *n* pl. **-LUTZIM** an Israeli farmer

HALVA *n* pl. **-S** halvah

HALVAH *n* pl. **-S** a Turkish confection

HALVE *v* **HALVED, HALVING, HALVES** to divide into two equal parts

HALVERS *n* pl. **HALVERS** half shares

HALVES pl. of half

HALVING *n* pl. **-S** the act of fitting timbers together by cutting out half the thickness of each

HALWA *n* pl. **-S** a sweet Indian dish

HALYARD	*n* pl. **-S** a line used to hoist a sail		**HANDBILL**	*n* pl. **-S** a circular
HAM	*v* **HAMMED, HAMMING, HAMS** to overact		**HANDBOOK**	*n* pl. **-S** a manual
HAMADA	*n* pl. **-S** hammada		**HANDCAR**	*n* pl. **-S** a hand-operated railroad car
HAMAL	*n* pl. **-S** a porter in eastern countries		**HANDCART**	*n* pl. **-S** a cart pushed by hand
HAMARTIA	*n* pl. **-S** a defect of character		**HANDCLAP**	*n* pl. **-S** a striking together of the palms of the hands
HAMATE	*n* pl. **-S** a wrist bone		**HANDCUFF**	*v* **-ED, -ING, -S** to fetter with restraining cuffs
HAMATSA	*n* pl. **-S** a dance inspired by the spirit of a man-eating monster		**HANDER**	*n* pl. **-S** one that hands
HAMAUL	*n* pl. **-S** hamal		**HANDFAST**	*v* **-ED, -ING, -S** to grip securely
HAMBONE	*v* **-BONED, -BONING, -BONES** to overact		**HANDFUL**	*n* pl. **HANDFULS** or **HANDSFUL** as much as the hand can hold
HAMBURG	*n* pl. **-S** a patty of ground beef		**HANDGRIP**	*n* pl. **-S** a grip by the hand or hands
HAME	*n* pl. **-S** a part of a horse collar		**HANDGUN**	*n* pl. **-S** a small firearm
HAMFAT	*n* pl. **-S** an amateurish performer		**HANDHELD**	*n* pl. **-S** something held in the hand
HAMLET	*n* pl. **-S** a small town		**HANDHOLD**	*n* pl. **-S** a handgrip
HAMMADA	*n* pl. **-S** a desert plateau of bedrock		**HANDICAP**	*v* **-CAPPED, -CAPPING, -CAPS** to hinder
HAMMAL	*n* pl. **-S** hamal		**HANDIER**	comparative of handy
HAMMAM	*n* pl. **-S** a Turkish bath		**HANDIEST**	superlative of handy
HAMMED	past tense of ham		**HANDILY**	*adv* in a handy manner
HAMMER	*v* **-ED, -ING, -S** to strike repeatedly		**HANDLE**	*v* **-DLED, -DLING, -DLES** to touch with the hands
HAMMERER	*n* pl. **-S** one that hammers		**HANDLER**	*n* pl. **-S** one that handles
HAMMIER	comparative of hammy		**HANDLESS**	*adj* having no hands
HAMMIEST	superlative of hammy		**HANDLIKE**	*adj* resembling a hand
HAMMILY	*adv* in a hammy manner		**HANDLINE**	*n* pl. **-S** a fishing line worked by hand
HAMMING	present participle of ham			
HAMMOCK	*n* pl. **-S** a hanging cot		**HANDLING**	*n* pl. **-S** the manner in which something is handled
HAMMY	*adj* **-MIER, -MIEST** overly theatrical		**HANDLIST**	*n* pl. **-S** a reference list
HAMPER	*v* **-ED, -ING, -S** to hinder		**HANDLOOM**	*n* pl. **-S** a manually operated loom
HAMPERER	*n* pl. **-S** one that hampers		**HANDMADE**	*adj* made by hand
HAMSTER	*n* pl. **-S** a burrowing rodent		**HANDMAID**	*n* pl. **-S** a female servant
HAMULUS	*n* pl. **-LI** a small hook **HAMULAR, HAMULATE, HAMULOSE, HAMULOUS** *adj*		**HANDOFF**	*n* pl. **-S** a play in football
			HANDOUT	*n* pl. **-S** something given out free
HAMZA	*n* pl. **-S** an Arabic diacritical mark		**HANDOVER**	*n* pl. **-S** an instance of giving up control
HAMZAH	*n* pl. **-S** hamza			
HANAPER	*n* pl. **-S** a wicker receptacle		**HANDPICK**	*v* **-ED, -ING, -S** to choose carefully
HANCE	*n* pl. **-S** a side of an arch		**HANDRAIL**	*n* pl. **-S** a railing used for support
HAND	*v* **-ED, -ING, -S** to present with the hand (the end of the forearm)		**HANDSAW**	*n* pl. **-S** a saw used manually
HANDAX	*n* pl. **-ES** a short-handled ax		**HANDSEL**	*v* **-SELED, -SELING, -SELS** or **-SELLED, -SELLING, -SELS** to give a gift to
HANDBAG	*n* pl. **-S** a small carrying bag			
HANDBALL	*n* pl. **-S** a small rubber ball		**HANDSET**	*n* pl. **-S** a type of telephone
HANDBELL	*n* pl. **-S** a small bell with a handle		**HANDSEWN**	*adj* sewn by hand

HANDSFUL a pl. of handful

HANDSOME *adj* **-SOMER, -SOMEST** attractive

HANDWORK *n* pl. **-S** manual labor

HANDWRIT *adj* written by hand

HANDY *adj* **HANDIER, HANDIEST** convenient for handling

HANDYMAN *n* pl. **-MEN** a man who does odd jobs

HANG *v* **HUNG** or **HANGED, HANGING, HANGS** to attach from above only **HANGABLE** *adj*

HANGAR *v* **-ED, -ING, -S** to place in an aircraft shelter

HANGBIRD *n* pl. **-S** a type of bird

HANGDOG *n* pl. **-S** a sneaky person

HANGER *n* pl. **-S** one that hangs

HANGFIRE *n* pl. **-S** a delay in detonation

HANGING *n* pl. **-S** an execution by strangling with a suspended noose

HANGMAN *n* pl. **-MEN** an executioner

HANGNAIL *n* pl. **-S** an agnail

HANGNEST *n* pl. **-S** a hangbird

HANGOUT *n* pl. **-S** a place often visited

HANGOVER *n* pl. **-S** the physical effects following a drinking binge

HANGTAG *n* pl. **-S** a type of tag used commercially

HANGUL *n* the Korean alphabetic script

HANGUP *n* pl. **-S** an inhibition or obsession

HANIWA *n/pl* Japanese clay sculptures

HANK *v* **-ED, -ING, -S** to fasten a sail

HANKER *v* **-ED, -ING, -S** to long for

HANKERER *n* pl. **-S** one that hankers

HANKIE *n* pl. **-S** hanky

HANKY *n* pl. **-KIES** a handkerchief

HANSA *n* pl. **-S** hanse

HANSE *n* pl. **-S** a guild of merchants

HANSEL *v* **-SELED, -SELING, -SELS** or **-SELLED, -SELLING, -SELS** to handsel

HANSOM *n* pl. **-S** a light carriage

HANT *v* **-ED, -ING, -S** to haunt

HANTLE *n* pl. **-S** a large amount

HANUMAN *n* pl. **-S** an East Indian monkey

HAO *n* pl. **HAO** a monetary unit of Vietnam

HAP *v* **HAPPED, HAPPING, HAPS** to happen

HAPAX *n* pl. **-ES** a word that occurs only once

HAPHTARA *n* pl. **-RAS** or **-ROT** or **-ROTH** a biblical selection

HAPKIDO *n* pl. **-DOS** a Korean martial art

HAPLESS *adj* luckless

HAPLITE *n* pl. **-S** aplite

HAPLOID *n* pl. **-S** a cell having only one set of chromosomes

HAPLOIDY *n* pl. **-DIES** the state of being a haploid

HAPLONT *n* pl. **-S** an organism having a particular chromosomal structure

HAPLOPIA *n* pl. **-S** normal vision

HAPLOSIS *n* pl. **-LOSES** the halving of the chromosome number

HAPLY *adv* by chance

HAPPED past tense of hap

HAPPEN *v* **-ED, -ING, -S** to occur

HAPPI *n* pl. **-S** a loose Japanese coat

HAPPING present participle of hap

HAPPY *adj* **-PIER, -PIEST** marked by joy **HAPPILY** *adv*

HAPTEN *n* pl. **-S** a substance similar to an antigen **HAPTENIC** *adj*

HAPTENE *n* pl. **-S** hapten

HAPTIC *adj* pertaining to the sense of touch

HAPTICAL *adj* haptic

HARAM *adj* forbidden by Islamic law

HARANGUE *v* **-RANGUED, -RANGUING, -RANGUES** to deliver a tirade to

HARASS *v* **-ED, -ING, -ES** to bother persistently

HARASSER *n* pl. **-S** one that harasses

HARBOR *v* **-ED, -ING, -S** to shelter

HARBORER *n* pl. **-S** one that harbors

HARBOUR *v* **-ED, -ING, -S** to harbor

HARD *adj* **HARDER, HARDEST** firm and unyielding

HARDBACK *n* pl. **-S** a hardcover book

HARDBALL *n* pl. **-S** baseball

HARDBODY *n* pl. **-DIES** an attractive person with a muscular body

HARDBOOT *n* pl. **-S** a horseman

HARDCASE *n* pl. **-S** a tough or obstinate person

HARDCORE *n* pl. **-S** hard material used in foundations

HARDEDGE *n* pl. **-S** a geometric painting

HARDEN *v* **-ED, -ING, -S** to make hard

HARDENER *n* pl. **-S** one that hardens

HARDHACK *n* pl. **-S** a woody plant

HARDHAT *n* pl. **-S** a conservative

HARDHEAD *n* pl. **-S** a practical person

HARDIER comparative of hardy

HARDIES pl. of hardy

HARDIEST superlative of hardy

HARDILY *adv* in a hardy manner

HARDISH *adj* somewhat hard

HARDLINE *adj* unyielding

HARDLY *adv* scarcely

HARDNESS *n* pl. **-ES** the state of being hard

HARDNOSE *n* pl. **-S** a stubborn person

HARDPACK *n* pl. **-S** compacted snow

HARDPAN *n* pl. **-S** a layer of hard subsoil

HARDS *n/pl* the coarse refuse of flax

HARDSET *adj* rigid

HARDSHIP *n* pl. **-S** a difficult, painful condition

HARDTACK *n* pl. **-S** a hard biscuit

HARDTOP *n* pl. **-S** a type of car

HARDWARE *n* pl. **-S** metal goods

HARDWIRE *v* **-WIRED, -WIRING, -WIRES** to permanently connect electronic components

HARDWOOD *n* pl. **-S** the hard, compact wood of various trees

HARDY *adj* **-DIER, -DIEST** very sturdy

HARDY *n* pl. **-DIES** a blacksmith's chisel

HARE *v* **HARED, HARING, HARES** to run

HAREBELL *n* pl. **-S** a perennial herb

HAREEM *n* pl. **-S** harem

HARELIKE *adj* resembling a hare (a long-eared mammal)

HARELIP *n* pl. **-S** a deformity of the upper lip

HAREM *n* pl. **-S** the section of a Muslim household reserved for women

HAREWOOD *n* pl. **-S** sycamore wood used for furniture

HARIANA *n* pl. **-S** a breed of cattle

HARICOT *n* pl. **-S** the seed of various string beans

HARIJAN *n* pl. **-S** an outcaste in India

HARING present participle of hare

HARISSA *n* pl. **-S** a spicy North African sauce

HARK *v* **-ED, -ING, -S** to listen to

HARKEN *v* **-ED, -ING, -S** to hearken

HARKENER *n* pl. **-S** one that harkens

HARL *n* pl. **-S** a herl

HARLOT *n* pl. **-S** a prostitute

HARLOTRY *n* pl. **-RIES** prostitution

HARM *v* **-ED, -ING, -S** to injure

HARMER *n* pl. **-S** one that harms

HARMFUL *adj* capable of harming

HARMIN *n* pl. **-S** harmine

HARMINE *n* pl. **-S** an alkaloid used as a stimulant

HARMLESS *adj* not harmful

HARMONIC *n* pl. **-S** an overtone

HARMONY *n* pl. **-NIES** agreement

HARNESS *v* **-ED, -ING, -ES** to put tackle on a draft animal

HARP *v* **-ED, -ING, -S** to play on a harp (a type of stringed musical instrument)

HARPER *n* pl. **-S** a harpist

HARPIES pl. of harpy

HARPIN *n* pl. **-S** harping

HARPING *n* pl. **-S** a wooden plank used in shipbuilding

HARPIST *n* pl. **-S** one that plays the harp

HARPOON *v* **-ED, -ING, -S** to strike with a barbed spear

HARPY *n* pl. **-PIES** a shrewish person

HARRIDAN *n* pl. **-S** a haggard woman

HARRIED past tense of harry

HARRIER *n* pl. **-S** a hunting dog

HARRIES present 3d person sing. of harry

HARROW *v* **-ED, -ING, -S** to break up and level soil

HARROWER *n* pl. **-S** one that harrows

HARRUMPH *v* **-ED, -ING, -S** to make a guttural sound

HARRY *v* **-RIED, -RYING, -RIES** to pillage

HARSH *adj* **HARSHER, HARSHEST** severe **HARSHLY** *adv*

HARSHEN *v* **-ED, -ING, -S** to make harsh

HARSLET *n* pl. **-S** haslet

HART *n* pl. **-S** a male deer

HARTAL *n* pl. **-S** a stoppage of work

HARUMPH *v* **-ED, -ING, -S** to harrumph

HARUSPEX *n pl.* **-PICES** a soothsayer of ancient Rome

HARVEST *v* **-ED, -ING, -S** to gather a crop

HAS a present 3d person sing. of have

HASH *v* **-ED, -ING, -ES** to mince

HASHEESH *n pl.* **-ES** hashish

HASHHEAD *n pl.* **-S** a hashish addict

HASHISH *n pl.* **-ES** a mild narcotic

HASHTAG *n pl.* **-S** a word or phrase preceded by the symbol # that categorizes the accompanying text

HASLET *n pl.* **-S** the edible viscera of an animal

HASP *v* **-ED, -ING, -S** to fasten with a clasp

HASSEL *n pl.* **-S** an argument

HASSIUM *n pl.* **-S** a radioactive element

HASSLE *v* **-SLED, -SLING, -SLES** to argue

HASSOCK *n pl.* **-S** a footstool

HAST a present 2d person sing. of have

HASTATE *adj* triangular

HASTE *v* **HASTED, HASTING, HASTES** to hasten

HASTEFUL *adj* hasty

HASTEN *v* **-ED, -ING, -S** to hurry

HASTENER *n pl.* **-S** one that hastens

HASTING present participle of haste

HASTY *adj* **HASTIER, HASTIEST** speedy **HASTILY** *adv*

HAT *v* **HATTED, HATTING, HATS** to provide with a hat (a covering for the head)

HATABLE *adj* hateable

HATBAND *n pl.* **-S** a band worn on a hat

HATBOX *n pl.* **-ES** a box for a hat

HATCH *v* **-ED, -ING, -ES** to bring forth young from an egg

HATCHECK *n pl.* **-S** a room for the temporary keeping of hats

HATCHEL *v* **-ELED, -ELING, -ELS** or **-ELLED, -ELLING, -ELS** to separate flax fibers with a comb

HATCHER *n pl.* **-S** one that hatches

HATCHERY *n pl.* **-ERIES** a place for hatching eggs

HATCHET *n pl.* **-S** a small ax

HATCHING *n pl.* **-S** a series of lines used to show shading

HATCHWAY *n pl.* **-WAYS** an opening in the deck of a ship

HATE *v* **HATED, HATING, HATES** to despise

HATEABLE *adj* meriting hatred

HATEFUL *adj* detestable

HATER *n pl.* **-S** one that hates

HATFUL *n pl.* **HATFULS** or **HATSFUL** as much as a hat can hold

HATH a present 3d person sing. of have

HATING present participle of hate

HATLESS *adj* lacking a hat

HATLIKE *adj* resembling a hat

HATMAKER *n pl.* **-S** one that makes hats

HATPIN *n pl.* **-S** a pin for securing a hat

HATRACK *n pl.* **-S** a rack for hats

HATRED *n pl.* **-S** intense dislike or aversion

HATSFUL a pl. of hatful

HATTED past tense of hat

HATTER *n pl.* **-S** a hatmaker

HATTERIA *n pl.* **-S** a reptile

HATTING present participle of hat

HAUBERK *n pl.* **-S** a coat of armor

HAUGH *n pl.* **-S** a low-lying meadow

HAUGHTY *adj* **-TIER, -TIEST** arrogant

HAUL *v* **-ED, -ING, -S** to pull with force

HAULAGE *n pl.* **-S** the act of hauling

HAULBACK *n pl.* **-S** a line for drawing a cable back

HAULER *n pl.* **-S** one that hauls

HAULIER *n pl.* **-S** hauler

HAULING *n pl.* **-S** the action of transporting logs

HAULM *n pl.* **-S** a plant stem

HAULMY *adj* **HAULMIER, HAULMIEST** having haulms

HAULOUT *n pl.* **-S** the action of hauling a boat out of water

HAULYARD *n pl.* **-S** halyard

HAUNCH *n pl.* **-ES** the hindquarter **HAUNCHED** *adj*

HAUNT *v* **-ED, -ING, -S** to visit frequently

HAUNTER *n pl.* **-S** one that haunts

HAUNTING *n pl.* **-S** a visitation by a ghost

HAUSEN *n pl.* **-S** a Russian sturgeon

HAUSFRAU *n pl.* **-FRAUS** or **-FRAUEN** a housewife

HAUT	*adj* haute
HAUTBOIS	*n* pl. **HAUTBOIS** hautboy
HAUTBOY	*n* pl. **-BOYS** an oboe
HAUTE	*adj* **HAUTER, HAUTEST** high-class
HAUTEUR	*n* pl. **-S** haughty manner or spirit
HAVARTI	*n* pl. **-S** a Danish cheese
HAVDALAH	*n* pl. **-S** habdalah
HAVE	*v* **HAD, HAVING, HAS** to hold as a possession, privilege, or entitlement
HAVE	*n* pl. **-S** a wealthy person
HAVELOCK	*n* pl. **-S** a covering for a cap
HAVEN	*v* **-ED, -ING, -S** to shelter
HAVER	*v* **-ED, -ING, -S** to hem and haw
HAVEREL	*n* pl. **-S** a fool
HAVING	present participle of have
HAVIOR	*n* pl. **-S** behavior
HAVIOUR	*n* pl. **-S** havior
HAVOC	*v* **-OCKED, -OCKING, -OCS** to destroy
HAVOCKER	*n* pl. **-S** one that havocs
HAW	*v* **-ED, -ING, -S** to turn left
HAWALA	*n* pl. **-S** a type of financial arrangement in Islamic societies
HAWEATER	*n* pl. **-S** a resident of Manitoulin Island, Ontario
HAWFINCH	*n* pl. **-ES** a Eurasian finch
HAWK	*v* **-ED, -ING, -S** to peddle
HAWKBILL	*n* pl. **-S** a sea turtle
HAWKER	*n* pl. **-S** one that hawks
HAWKEY	*n* pl. **-EYS** a hawkie
HAWKEYED	*adj* having keen sight
HAWKIE	*n* pl. **-S** a white-faced cow
HAWKING	*n* pl. **-S** falconry
HAWKISH	*adj* warlike
HAWKLIKE	*adj* resembling a hawk (a bird of prey)
HAWKMOTH	*n* pl. **-S** a large moth
HAWKNOSE	*n* pl. **-S** a large, curved nose
HAWKSHAW	*n* pl. **-S** a detective
HAWKWEED	*n* pl. **-S** a weedlike herb
HAWSE	*n* pl. **-S** a part of a ship's bow
HAWSER	*n* pl. **-S** a mooring rope
HAWTHORN	*n* pl. **-S** a thorny shrub
HAY	*v* **-ED, -ING, -S** to convert into hay (grass, cut and dried for fodder)
HAYCOCK	*n* pl. **-S** a pile of hay
HAYER	*n* pl. **-S** one that hays
HAYEY	*adj* resembling hay
HAYFIELD	*n* pl. **-S** a field where grasses for hay are grown
HAYFORK	*n* pl. **-S** a tool for pitching hay
HAYING	*n* pl. **-S** the season for harvesting hay
HAYLAGE	*n* pl. **-S** a type of hay
HAYLOFT	*n* pl. **-S** a loft for hay storage
HAYMAKER	*n* pl. **-S** one that makes hay
HAYMOW	*n* pl. **-S** a hayloft
HAYRACK	*n* pl. **-S** a frame used in hauling hay
HAYRICK	*n* pl. **-S** a haystack
HAYRIDE	*n* pl. **-S** a wagon ride
HAYSEED	*n* pl. **-S** a bumpkin
HAYSTACK	*n* pl. **-S** a pile of hay
HAYWARD	*n* pl. **-S** an officer who tends cattle
HAYWIRE	*n* pl. **-S** wire used in baling hay
HAZAN	*n* pl. **-ZANS** or **-ZANIM** a cantor
HAZARD	*v* **-ED, -ING, -S** to venture
HAZARDER	*n* pl. **-S** one that hazards
HAZE	*v* **HAZED, HAZING, HAZES** to subject to a humiliating initiation
HAZEL	*n* pl. **-S** a shrub
HAZELHEN	*n* pl. **-S** a European grouse
HAZELLY	*adj* yellowish brown
HAZELNUT	*n* pl. **-S** an edible nut
HAZER	*n* pl. **-S** one that hazes
HAZIER	comparative of hazy
HAZIEST	superlative of hazy
HAZILY	*adv* in a hazy manner
HAZINESS	*n* pl. **-ES** the state of being hazy
HAZING	*n* pl. **-S** an attempt to embarrass or ridicule
HAZMAT	*n* pl. **-S** hazardous material
HAZY	*adj* **HAZIER, HAZIEST** unclear
HAZZAN	*n* pl. **HAZZANS** or **HAZZANIM** hazan
HE	*n* pl. **-S** a male person
HEAD	*v* **-ED, -ING, -S** to be chief of
HEADACHE	*n* pl. **-S** a pain inside the head
HEADACHY	*adj* **-ACHIER, -ACHIEST** having a headache
HEADBAND	*n* pl. **-S** a band worn on the head

HEADEND *n* pl. **-S** a facility that receives and distributes communications signals

HEADER *n* pl. **-S** a grain harvester

HEADFISH *n* pl. **-ES** a marine fish

HEADFUL *n* pl. **-S** a great amount of knowledge

HEADGATE *n* pl. **-S** a gate to control the flow of water

HEADGEAR *n* pl. **HEADGEAR** a covering for the head

HEADHUNT *v* **-ED, -ING, -S** to seek out, decapitate, and preserve the heads of enemies

HEADIER comparative of heady

HEADIEST superlative of heady

HEADILY *adv* in a heady manner

HEADING *n* pl. **-S** a title

HEADLAMP *n* pl. **-S** a light on the front of a car

HEADLAND *n* pl. **-S** a cliff

HEADLESS *adj* lacking a head

HEADLINE *v* **-LINED, -LINING, -LINES** to provide with a title

HEADLOCK *n* pl. **-S** a wrestling hold

HEADLONG *adj* rash; impetuous

HEADMAN *n* pl. **-MEN** a foreman

HEADMOST *adj* foremost

HEADNOTE *n* pl. **-S** a prefixed note

HEADPIN *n* pl. **-S** a bowling pin

HEADPOND *n* pl. **-S** a pond created behind a dam

HEADRACE *n* pl. **-S** a water channel

HEADRAIL *n* pl. **-S** a horizontal rail at the top of something

HEADREST *n* pl. **-S** a support for the head

HEADROOM *n* pl. **-S** clear vertical space

HEADSAIL *n* pl. **-S** a type of sail

HEADSET *n* pl. **-S** a pair of earphones

HEADSHIP *n* pl. **-S** the position of a leader

HEADSHOT *n* pl. **-S** a photograph of a person from the neck up

HEADSMAN *n* pl. **-MEN** an executioner

HEADSTAY *n* pl. **-STAYS** a support for a ship's foremast

HEADWARD *adv* toward the head

HEADWAY *n* pl. **-WAYS** forward movement

HEADWIND *n* pl. **-S** an oncoming wind

HEADWORD *n* pl. **-S** a word put at the beginning

HEADWORK *n* pl. **-S** mental work

HEADY *adj* **HEADIER, HEADIEST** intoxicating

HEAL *v* **-ED, -ING, -S** to make sound or whole **HEALABLE** *adj*

HEALER *n* pl. **-S** one that heals

HEALING *n* pl. **-S** the process of becoming healthy again

HEALTH *n* pl. **-S** the physical condition of an organism

HEALTHY *adj* **HEALTHIER, HEALTHIEST** having good health

HEAP *v* **-ED, -ING, -S** to pile up

HEAPER *n* pl. **-S** one that heaps

HEAPY *adj* resembling a heap (a group of things piled one on another)

HEAR *v* **HEARD, HEARING, HEARS** to perceive by the ear **HEARABLE** *adj*

HEARER *n* pl. **-S** one that hears

HEARING *n* pl. **-S** a preliminary examination

HEARKEN *v* **-ED, -ING, -S** to listen to

HEARSAY *n* pl. **-SAYS** secondhand information

HEARSE *v* **HEARSED, HEARSING, HEARSES** to transport in a hearse (a vehicle for conveying corpses)

HEART *v* **-ED, -ING, -S** to hearten

HEARTEN *v* **-ED, -ING, -S** to give courage to

HEARTH *n* pl. **-S** the floor of a fireplace

HEARTY *adj* **HEARTIER, HEARTIEST** very friendly **HEARTILY** *adv*

HEARTY *n* pl. **HEARTIES** a comrade

HEAT *v* **HEATED** or **HET, HEATING, HEATS** to make hot **HEATABLE** *adj*

HEATEDLY *adv* in an inflamed or excited manner

HEATER *n* pl. **-S** an apparatus for heating

HEATH *n* pl. **-S** an evergreen shrub

HEATHEN *n* pl. **-S** an uncivilized person

HEATHER *n* pl. **-S** an evergreen shrub **HEATHERY** *adj*

HEATHY *adj* **HEATHIER, HEATHIEST** abounding in heath

HEATING *n* pl. **-S** the act of making something hot

HEATLESS *adj* having no warmth

HEAUME *n* pl. **-S** a medieval helmet

HEAVE   *v* **HEAVED** or **HOVE, HEAVING, HEAVES** to lift forcefully

HEAVEN   *n* pl. **-S** the sky

HEAVENLY   *adj* **-LIER, -LIEST** full of beauty and peace

HEAVER   *n* pl. **-S** one that heaves

HEAVIER   comparative of heavy

HEAVIES   pl. of heavy

HEAVING   present participle of heave

HEAVY   *adj* **HEAVIER, HEAVIEST** having much weight **HEAVILY** *adv*

HEAVY   *n* pl. **HEAVIES** a villain

HEAVYISH   *adj* somewhat heavy

HEAVYSET   *adj* solidly built; stocky

HEBDOMAD   *n* pl. **-S** the number seven

HEBETATE   *v* **-TATED, -TATING, -TATES** to make dull

HEBETIC   *adj* pertaining to puberty

HEBETUDE   *n* pl. **-S** mental dullness

HEBRAIZE   *v* **-IZED, -IZING, -IZES** to make Hebrew

HECATOMB   *n* pl. **-S** a great sacrifice or slaughter

HECK   *n* pl. **-S** hell (a place or state of misery)

HECKLE   *v* **-LED, -LING, -LES** to harass a speaker

HECKLER   *n* pl. **-S** one that heckles

HECTARE   *n* pl. **-S** a unit of area

HECTIC   *adj* filled with turmoil **HECTICLY** *adv*

HECTIC   *n* pl. **-S** a fever accompanied by flushed cheeks

HECTICAL   *adj* hectic

HECTOR   *v* **-ED, -ING, -S** to bully

HEDDLE   *n* pl. **-S** a part of a loom

HEDER   *n* pl. **HEDERS** or **HADARIM** or **HEDARIM** a Jewish school

HEDGE   *v* **HEDGED, HEDGING, HEDGES** to surround with a hedge (a dense row of shrubs)

HEDGEHOG   *n* pl. **-S** a small mammal

HEDGEHOP   *v* **-HOPPED, -HOPPING, -HOPS** to fly near the ground

HEDGEPIG   *n* pl. **-S** a hedgehog

HEDGER   *n* pl. **-S** one that hedges

HEDGEROW   *n* pl. **-S** a row of bushes

HEDGING   present participle of hedge

HEDGY   *adj* **HEDGIER, HEDGIEST** abounding in hedges

HEDONIC   *adj* pertaining to pleasure

HEDONICS   *n/pl* a branch of psychology

HEDONISM   *n* pl. **-S** the pursuit of pleasure

HEDONIST   *n* pl. **-S** a follower of hedonism

HEED   *v* **-ED, -ING, -S** to pay attention to

HEEDER   *n* pl. **-S** one that heeds

HEEDFUL   *adj* paying close attention

HEEDLESS   *adj* paying little or no attention

HEEHAW   *v* **-ED, -ING, -S** to guffaw

HEEL   *v* **-ED, -ING, -S** to supply with a heel (the raised part of a shoe)

HEELBALL   *n* pl. **-S** a composition used for polishing

HEELER   *n* pl. **-S** one that puts heels on shoes

HEELING   *n* pl. **-S** the act of inclining laterally

HEELLESS   *adj* lacking heels

HEELPOST   *n* pl. **-S** a post fitted to the end of something

HEELTAP   *n* pl. **-S** material put on the heel of a shoe

HEEZE   *v* **HEEZED, HEEZING, HEEZES** to hoist

HEFT   *v* **-ED, -ING, -S** to lift up

HEFTER   *n* pl. **-S** one that hefts

HEFTY   *adj* **HEFTIER, HEFTIEST** heavy **HEFTILY** *adv*

HEGARI   *n* pl. **-S** a grain

HEGEMON   *n* pl. **-S** a political state having hegemony

HEGEMONY   *n* pl. **-NIES** great authority

HEGIRA   *n* pl. **-S** an exodus

HEGUMEN   *n* pl. **-S** the head of a monastery

HEGUMENE   *n* pl. **-S** the head of a nunnery

HEGUMENY   *n* pl. **-NIES** the office of a hegumen

HEH   *n* pl. **-S** a Hebrew letter

HEIFER   *n* pl. **-S** a young cow

HEIGH   *interj* — used to attract attention

HEIGHT   *n* pl. **-S** the highest point

HEIGHTEN   *v* **-ED, -ING, -S** to raise

HEIGHTH   *n* pl. **-S** height

HEIL   *v* **-ED, -ING, -S** to salute

HEIMISH   *adj* haimish

HEINIE   *n* pl. **-S** the buttocks

HEINOUS   *adj* very wicked

HEIR *v* **-ED, -ING, -S** to inherit

HEIRDOM *n* pl. **-S** heirship

HEIRESS *n* pl. **-ES** a female inheritor

HEIRLESS *adj* having no inheritors

HEIRLOOM *n* pl. **-S** an inherited possession

HEIRSHIP *n* pl. **-S** the right to inheritance

HEISHI *n/pl* tiny beads made from shells

HEIST *v* **-ED, -ING, -S** to steal

HEISTER *n* pl. **-S** one that heists

HEJIRA *n* pl. **-S** hegira

HEKTARE *n* pl. **-S** hectare

HELD past tense of hold

HELENIUM *n* pl. **-S** a plant with daisy-like flowers

HELIAC *adj* heliacal

HELIACAL *adj* pertaining to the sun

HELIAST *n* pl. **-S** an Athenian judge

HELICAL *adj* shaped like a helix

HELICES a pl. of helix

HELICITY *n* pl. **-TIES** a component of a particle's spin

HELICOID *n* pl. **-S** a type of geometrical surface

HELICON *n* pl. **-S** a large bass tuba

HELICOPT *v* **-ED, -ING, -S** to travel by helicopter

HELILIFT *v* **-ED, -ING, -S** to transport by helicopter

HELIO *n* pl. **-LIOS** a signaling mirror

HELIPAD *n* pl. **-S** a heliport

HELIPORT *n* pl. **-S** an airport for helicopters

HELISKI *v* **-ED, -ING, -S** to ski downhill on mountains reached by helicopter

HELISTOP *n* pl. **-S** a heliport

HELITACK *n* pl. **-S** the use of helicopters to fight forest fires

HELIUM *n* pl. **-S** a gaseous element

HELIX *n* pl. **-LIXES** or **-LICES** something spiral in form

HELL *v* **-ED, -ING, -S** to behave raucously

HELLBENT *adj* stubbornly determined

HELLBOX *n* pl. **-ES** a printer's receptacle

HELLCAT *n* pl. **-S** a shrewish person

HELLER *n* pl. **-S** a hellion

HELLERI *n* pl. **-S** or **-ES** a tropical fish

HELLERY *n* pl. **-LERIES** rough play

HELLFIRE *n* pl. **-S** the torment of hell (a place of great suffering)

HELLHOLE *n* pl. **-S** a horrible place

HELLION *n* pl. **-S** a troublesome person

HELLISH *adj* horrible

HELLKITE *n* pl. **-S** a cruel person

HELLO *v* **-ED, -ING, -S** or **-ES** to greet

HELLUVA *adj* disagreeable

HELLWARD *adv* toward hell (a place of great suffering))

HELM *v* **-ED, -ING, -S** to steer a ship

HELMET *v* **-ED, -ING, -S** to supply with a helmet (a protective covering for the head)

HELMINTH *n* pl. **-S** a worm

HELMLESS *adj* lacking a helm (a steering system)

HELMSMAN *n* pl. **-MEN** one that steers a ship

HELO *n* pl. **HELOS** a helicopter

HELOT *n* pl. **-S** a slave or serf

HELOTAGE *n* pl. **-S** helotism

HELOTISM *n* pl. **-S** slavery or serfdom

HELOTRY *n* pl. **-RIES** helotism

HELP *v* **HELPED** or **HOLP, HELPED** or **HOLPEN, HELPING, HELPS** to give assistance to **HELPABLE** *adj*

HELPDESK *n* pl. **-S** a service that helps customers with problems

HELPER *n* pl. **-S** one that helps

HELPFUL *adj* being of service or assistance

HELPING *n* pl. **-S** a portion of food

HELPLESS *adj* defenseless

HELPLINE *n* pl. **-S** a telephone service that provides advice

HELPMATE *n* pl. **-S** a helpful companion

HELPMEET *n* pl. **-S** a helpmate

HELVE *v* **HELVED, HELVING, HELVES** to provide with a handle

HEM *v* **HEMMED, HEMMING, HEMS** to provide with an edge

HEMAGOG *n* pl. **-S** an agent that promotes blood flow

HEMAL *adj* pertaining to the blood

HEMATAL *adj* hemal

HEMATEIN *n* pl. **-S** a chemical compound

HEMATIC *n* pl. **-S** a medicine for a blood disease

HEMATIN *n* pl. **-S** heme

HEMATINE *n* pl. **-S** hematin

HEMATITE *n* pl. **-S** an ore of iron

HEMATOID *adj* resembling blood

HEMATOMA *n* pl. **-MAS** or **-MATA** a swelling filled with blood

HEME *n* pl. **-S** a component of hemoglobin

HEMIC *adj* hemal

HEMIN *n* pl. **-S** a chloride of heme

HEMIOLA *n* pl. **-S** a rhythmic alteration in music

HEMIOLIA *n* pl. **-S** hemiola

HEMIPTER *n* pl. **-S** an insect

HEMLINE *n* pl. **-S** the bottom edge of a garment

HEMLOCK *n* pl. **-S** a poisonous herb

HEMMED past tense of hem

HEMMER *n* pl. **-S** one that hems

HEMMING present participle of hem

HEMOCOEL *n* pl. **-S** a body cavity

HEMOCYTE *n* pl. **-S** a blood cell

HEMOID *adj* hemal

HEMOLYZE *v* **-LYZED, -LYZING, -LYZES** to break down red blood cells

HEMOSTAT *n* pl. **-S** an instrument for reducing bleeding

HEMP *n* pl. **-S** a tall herb

HEMPEN *adj* made of hemp

HEMPIE *adj* **HEMPIER, HEMPIEST** hempy

HEMPIER comparative of hempy

HEMPIEST superlative of hempy

HEMPLIKE *adj* resembling hemp

HEMPSEED *n* pl. **-S** the seed of hemp

HEMPWEED *n* pl. **-S** a climbing plant

HEMPY *adj* **HEMPIER, HEMPIEST** mischievous

HEN *n* pl. **-S** a female chicken

HENBANE *n* pl. **-S** a poisonous herb

HENBIT *n* pl. **-S** a perennial herb

HENCE *adv* consequently

HENCHMAN *n* pl. **-MEN** an unscrupulous supporter

HENCOOP *n* pl. **-S** a cage for hens

HENEQUEN *n* pl. **-S** a fiber used to make ropes

HENEQUIN *n* pl. **-S** henequen

HENGE *n* pl. **-S** a circular Bronze Age structure in England

HENHOUSE *n* pl. **-S** a shelter for poultry

HENIQUEN *n* pl. **-S** henequen

HENLEY *n* pl. **-LEYS** a type of knit shirt

HENLIKE *adj* resembling a hen

HENNA *v* **-ED, -ING, -S** to dye with a reddish coloring

HENNERY *n* pl. **-NERIES** a poultry farm

HENNISH *adj* resembling a hen

HENPECK *v* **-ED, -ING, -S** to dominate by nagging

HENRY *n* pl. **-RYS** or **-RIES** a unit of inductance

HENT *v* **-ED, -ING, -S** to grasp

HEP *adj* **HEPPER, HEPPEST** hip

HEP *n* pl. **-S** hepatitis (inflammation of the liver)

HEPARIN *n* pl. **-S** a biochemical

HEPATIC *n* pl. **-S** a drug acting on the liver

HEPATICA *n* pl. **-CAS** or **-CAE** a perennial herb

HEPATIZE *v* **-TIZED, -TIZING, -TIZES** to convert tissue into a firm mass

HEPATOMA *n* pl. **-MAS** or **-MATA** a tumor of the liver

HEPCAT *n* pl. **-S** a jazz enthusiast

HEPTAD *n* pl. **-S** a group of seven

HEPTAGON *n* pl. **-S** a seven-sided polygon

HEPTANE *n* pl. **-S** a hydrocarbon used as a solvent

HEPTARCH *n* pl. **-S** one of a group of seven rulers

HEPTOSE *n* pl. **-S** a chemical compound

HER *pron* the objective or possessive case of the pronoun she

HERALD *v* **-ED, -ING, -S** to proclaim

HERALDIC *adj* pertaining to heraldry

HERALDRY *n* pl. **-RIES** the art or science of armorial bearings

HERB *n* pl. **-S** a flowering plant with a nonwoody stem

HERBAGE *n* pl. **-S** nonwoody plant life **HERBAGED** *adj*

HERBAL *n* pl. **-S** a book about herbs and plants

HERBARIA *n/pl* collections of dried plants

HERBED *adj* flavored with herbs

HERBLESS *adj* lacking herbs

HERBLIKE *adj* resembling an herb

HERBY *adj* **HERBIER, HERBIEST** abounding in herbs

HERCULES *n* pl. **-LESES** any man of great size and strength

HERD *v* **-ED, -ING, -S** to bring together in a herd (a group of animals)

HERDER *n* pl. **-S** one who tends a herd

HERDIC *n* pl. **-S** a type of carriage

HERDING *n* pl. **-S** the work of tending or moving livestock

HERDLIKE *adj* resembling a herd

HERDMAN *n* pl. **-MEN** herdsman

HERDSMAN *n* pl. **-MEN** a herder

HERE *n* pl. **-S** this place

HEREAT *adv* at this time

HEREAWAY *adv* in this vicinity

HEREBY *adv* by this means

HEREDES pl. of heres

HEREDITY *n* pl. **-TIES** the genetic transmission of characteristics

HEREIN *adv* in this

HEREINTO *adv* into this place

HEREOF *adv* of this

HEREON *adv* on this

HERES *n* pl. **HEREDES** an heir

HERESY *n* pl. **-SIES** a belief contrary to a church doctrine

HERETIC *n* pl. **-S** one that upholds heresy

HERETO *adv* to this matter

HERETRIX *n* pl. **-TRIXES** or **-TRICES** heritrix

HEREUNTO *adv* hereto

HEREUPON *adv* immediately following this

HEREWITH *adv* along with this

HERIOT *n* pl. **-S** a feudal tribute or payment

HERITAGE *n* pl. **-S** something that is inherited

HERITOR *n* pl. **-S** one that inherits

HERITRIX *n* pl. **-TRIXES** or **-TRICES** a female heritor

HERL *n* pl. **-S** a feathered fishing lure

HERM *n* pl. **-S** a type of statue

HERMA *n* pl. **-MAE** or **-MAI** a herm **HERMAEAN** *adj*

HERMETIC *adj* airtight

HERMIT *n* pl. **-S** a recluse **HERMITIC** *adj*

HERMITRY *n* pl. **-RIES** the state of being a hermit

HERN *n* pl. **-S** a heron

HERNIA *n* pl. **-NIAS** or **-NIAE** the protrusion of an organ through its surrounding wall **HERNIAL** *adj*

HERNIATE *v* **-ATED, -ATING, -ATES** to protrude through an abnormal bodily opening

HERO *n* pl. **-ROS** or **-ROES** a hoagie

HEROIC *n* pl. **-S** an epic verse

HEROICAL *adj* courageous; noble

HEROIN *n* pl. **-S** an addictive narcotic

HEROINE *n* pl. **-S** a brave woman

HEROISM *n* pl. **-S** heroic behavior

HEROIZE *v* **-IZED, -IZING, -IZES** to make heroic

HERON *n* pl. **-S** a wading bird

HERONRY *n* pl. **-RIES** a place where herons breed

HERPES *n* pl. **HERPES** a skin infection **HERPETIC** *adj*

HERRING *n* pl. **-S** a food fish

HERRY *v* **-RIED, -RYING, -RIES** to harry

HERS *pron* the possessive case of the pronoun she

HERSELF *pron* a form of the 3d person sing. feminine pronoun

HERSTORY *n* pl. **-RIES** history with a feminist viewpoint

HERTZ *n* pl. **HERTZ** a unit of frequency

HESITANT *adj* tending to hesitate

HESITATE *v* **-TATED, -TATING, -TATES** to hold back in uncertainty

HESSIAN *n* pl. **-S** a coarse cloth

HESSITE *n* pl. **-S** a mineral

HEST *n* pl. **-S** a command

HET *n* pl. **-S** heth

HETAERA *n* pl. **-RAS** or **-RAE** a concubine **HETAERIC** *adj*

HETAIRA *n* pl. **-RAS** or **-RAI** hetaera

HETERO *n* pl. **-EROS** a heterosexual

HETH *n* pl. **-S** a Hebrew letter

HETMAN *n* pl. **-MANS** a cossack leader

HEUCH *n* pl. **-S** heugh

HEUCHERA *n* pl. **-S** a North American plant

HEUGH *n* pl. **-S** a steep cliff

HEVEA *n* pl. **-S** a tree yielding sap used for rubber

HEW *v* **HEWED, HEWN, HEWING, HEWS** to cut with an ax **HEWABLE** *adj*

HEWER   *n* pl. **-S** one that hews

HEX   *v* **-ED, -ING, -ES** to cast an evil spell upon

HEXAD   *n* pl. **-S** a group of six **HEXADIC** *adj*

HEXADE   *n* pl. **-S** hexad

HEXAGON   *n* pl. **-S** a polygon having six sides

HEXAGRAM   *n* pl. **-S** a six-pointed star

HEXAMINE   *n* pl. **-S** a chemical compound

HEXANE   *n* pl. **-S** a volatile liquid

HEXAPLA   *n* pl. **-S** an edition in which six texts are set in parallel columns **HEXAPLAR** *adj*

HEXAPOD   *n* pl. **-S** a six-legged insect

HEXAPODY   *n* pl. **-DIES** a line of verse with six feet

HEXARCHY   *n* pl. **-CHIES** a group of six separate states

HEXER   *n* pl. **-S** one that hexes

HEXEREI   *n* pl. **-S** witchcraft

HEXONE   *n* pl. **-S** a hydrocarbon solvent

HEXOSAN   *n* pl. **-S** a carbohydrate

HEXOSE   *n* pl. **-S** a simple sugar

HEXYL   *n* pl. **-S** a hydrocarbon radical **HEXYLIC** *adj*

HEY   *interj* — used to attract attention

HEYDAY   *n* pl. **-DAYS** the period of one's greatest success

HEYDEY   *n* pl. **-DEYS** heyday

HI   *interj* — used as a greeting

HIATUS   *n* pl. **-ES** a gap or missing section **HIATAL** *adj*

HIBACHI   *n* pl. **-S** a cooking device

HIBERNAL   *adj* pertaining to winter

HIBISCUS   *n* pl. **-ES** a tropical plant

HIC   *interj* — used to represent a hiccup

HICCOUGH   *v* **-ED, -ING, -S** to hiccup

HICCUP   *v* **-CUPED, -CUPING, -CUPS** or **-CUPPED, -CUPPING, -CUPS** to make a peculiar-sounding, spasmodic inhalation

HICCUPY   *adj* having hiccups (spasmodic inhalations)

HICK   *n* pl. **-S** a rural person **HICKISH** *adj*

HICK   *adj* **HICKER, HICKEST** characteristic of rural people

HICKEY   *n* pl. **HICKEYS** or **HICKIES** a gadget

HICKIE   *n* pl. **-S** hickey

HICKORY   *n* pl. **-RIES** a hardwood tree

HID   a past tense of hide

HIDABLE   *adj* able to be hidden

HIDALGO   *n* pl. **-GOS** a minor Spanish nobleman

HIDDEN   *adj* concealed; obscure **HIDDENLY** *adv*

HIDE   *v* **HID, HIDDEN, HIDING, HIDES** to conceal

HIDE   *v* **HIDED, HIDING, HIDES** to flog

HIDEAWAY   *n* pl. **-AWAYS** a hideout

HIDELESS   *adj* lacking a skin

HIDEOUS   *adj* very ugly

HIDEOUT   *n* pl. **-S** a place of refuge

HIDER   *n* pl. **-S** one that hides

HIDING   *n* pl. **-S** a beating

HIDROSIS   *n* pl. **-DROSES** abnormal perspiration

HIDROTIC   *n* pl. **-S** a drug that induces perspiration

HIE   *v* **HIED, HIEING** or **HYING, HIES** to hurry

HIEMAL   *adj* pertaining to winter

HIERARCH   *n* pl. **-S** a religious leader

HIERATIC   *adj* pertaining to priests

HIERURGY   *n* pl. **-GIES** a rite of worship

HIGGLE   *v* **-GLED, -GLING, -GLES** to haggle

HIGGLER   *n* pl. **-S** one that higgles

HIGH   *adj* **HIGHER, HIGHEST** reaching far upward

HIGH   *n* pl. **-S** a high level

HIGHBALL   *v* **-ED, -ING, -S** to go at full speed

HIGHBORN   *adj* of noble birth

HIGHBOY   *n* pl. **-BOYS** a tall chest of drawers

HIGHBRED   *adj* highborn

HIGHBROW   *n* pl. **-S** a person who has superior tastes

HIGHBUSH   *adj* forming a tall bush

HIGHJACK   *v* **-ED, -ING, -S** to hijack

HIGHLAND   *n* pl. **-S** an elevated region

HIGHLIFE   *n* pl. **-S** the lifestyle of fashionable society

HIGHLY   *adv* to a high degree

HIGHNESS   *n* pl. **-ES** the state of being high

HIGHRISE   *n* pl. **-S** a building with many stories (horizontal divisions)

HIGHROAD n pl. **-S** a highway

HIGHSPOT n pl. **-S** an event of major importance

HIGHT v **-ED, -ING, -S** to command

HIGHTAIL v **-ED, -ING, -S** to retreat rapidly

HIGHTH n pl. **-S** height

HIGHTOP n pl. **-S** a sports shoe extending over the ankle

HIGHWAY n pl. **-WAYS** a main road

HIJAB n pl. **-S** a head covering worn by Muslim women

HIJACK v **-ED, -ING, -S** to seize a vehicle while in transit

HIJACKER n pl. **-S** one that hijacks

HIJINKS n/pl mischievous fun

HIJRA n pl. **-S** hegira

HIJRAH n pl. **-S** hegira

HIKE v **HIKED, HIKING, HIKES** to walk a long distance

HIKER n pl. **-S** one that hikes

HILA pl. of hilum

HILAR adj pertaining to a hilum

HILARITY n pl. **-TIES** noisy merriment

HILDING n pl. **-S** a vile person

HILI pl. of hilus

HILL v **-ED, -ING, -S** to form into a hill (a rounded elevation)

HILLER n pl. **-S** one that hills

HILLIER comparative of hilly

HILLIEST superlative of hilly

HILLO v **-ED, -ING, -S** or **-ES** to hallo

HILLOA v **-ED, -ING, -S** to hallo

HILLOCK n pl. **-S** a small hill **HILLOCKY** adj

HILLSIDE n pl. **-S** the side of a hill

HILLTOP n pl. **-S** the top of a hill

HILLY adj **HILLIER, HILLIEST** abounding in hills

HILT v **-ED, -ING, -S** to provide with a hilt (a handle for a weapon)

HILTLESS adj having no hilt

HILUM n pl. **HILA** a small opening in a bodily organ

HILUS n pl. **HILI** hilum

HIM n pl. **-S** a male

HIMATION n pl. **-MATIONS** or **-MATIA** a loose outer garment

HIMBO n pl. **-BOS** an attractive but unintelligent man

HIMSELF pron a form of the 3d person sing. masculine pronoun

HIN n pl. **-S** a Hebrew unit of liquid measure

HIND n pl. **-S** a female red deer

HINDER v **-ED, -ING, -S** to impede

HINDERER n pl. **-S** one that hinders

HINDGUT n pl. **-S** the rear part of the alimentary canal

HINDMILK n pl. **-S** breast milk exuded after the first part of a feeding

HINDMOST adj farthest to the rear

HINDWING n pl. **-S** a posterior wing of an insect

HINGE v **HINGED, HINGING, HINGES** to attach a jointed device

HINGER n pl. **-S** one that hinges

HINKY adj **HINKIER, HINKIEST** suspicious

HINNIE n pl **-S** darling, sweetheart

HINNY v **-NIED, -NYING, -NIES** to whinny

HINT v **-ED, -ING, -S** to suggest indirectly

HINTER n pl. **-S** one that hints

HIP adj **HIPPER, HIPPEST** aware of the most current styles and trends

HIP v **HIPPED, HIPPING, HIPS** to build a type of roof

HIPBONE n pl. **-S** a pelvic bone

HIPLESS adj lacking a hip (the pelvic joint)

HIPLIKE adj suggestive of a hip

HIPLINE n pl. **-S** the distance around the hips

HIPLY adv in a hip manner

HIPNESS n pl. **-ES** the state of being hip

HIPPARCH n pl. **-S** a cavalry commander in ancient Greece

HIPPED past tense of hip

HIPPER comparative of hip

HIPPEST superlative of hip

HIPPIE n pl. **-S** a nonconformist

HIPPIER comparative of hippy

HIPPIEST superlative of hippy

HIPPING present participle of hip

HIPPISH adj depressed; sad

HIPPO n pl. **-POS** a hippopotamus

HIPPY adj **-PIER, -PIEST** having big hips

HIPPYISH *adj* relating to or resembling a hippie

HIPSHOT *adj* lame; awkward

HIPSTER *n* pl. **-S** one that is hip

HIRABLE *adj* available for hire

HIRAGANA *n* pl. **-S** a Japanese cursive script

HIRCINE *adj* pertaining to a goat

HIRE *v* **HIRED, HIRING, HIRES** to engage the services of for payment **HIREABLE** *adj*

HIREE *n* pl. **-S** one that is hired

HIRELING *n* pl. **-S** one that works for money only

HIRER *n* pl. **-S** one that hires

HIRPLE *v* **-PLED, -PLING, -PLES** to limp

HIRSEL *v* **-SELED, -SELING, -SELS** or **-SELLED, -SELLING, -SELS** to herd sheep

HIRSLE *v* **-SLED, -SLING, -SLES** to slide along

HIRSUTE *adj* hairy

HIRUDIN *n* pl. **-S** an anticoagulant

HIS *pron* the possessive form of the pronoun he

HISN *pron* his

HISPID *adj* covered with stiff hairs

HISS *v* **-ED, -ING, -ES** to make a sibilant sound

HISSELF *pron* himself

HISSER *n* pl. **-S** one that hisses

HISSING *n* pl. **-S** an object of scorn

HISSY *adj* **HISSIER, HISSIEST** characterized by a hissing sound

HISSY *n* pl. **HISSIES** a tantrum

HIST *v* **-ED, -ING, -S** to hoist

HISTAMIN *n* pl. **-S** an amine released in allergic reactions

HISTIDIN *n* pl. **-S** an amino acid

HISTOGEN *n* pl. **-S** interior plant tissue

HISTOID *adj* pertaining to connective tissue

HISTONE *n* pl. **-S** a simple protein

HISTORIC *adj* important in history

HISTORY *n* pl. **-RIES** a chronological record of past events

HIT *v* **HIT, HITTING, HITS** to strike forcibly

HITCH *v* **-ED, -ING, -ES** to fasten with a knot or hook

HITCHER *n* pl. **-S** one that hitches

HITHER *adv* toward this place

HITHERTO *adv* up to now

HITLESS *adj* being without a hit

HITMAKER *n* pl. **-S** a musician who produces best-selling records

HITMAN *n* pl. **-MEN** a professional killer

HITTABLE *adj* capable of being hit

HITTER *n* pl. **-S** one that hits

HITTING present participle of hit

HIVE *v* **HIVED, HIVING, HIVES** to cause to enter a hive (a bee's nest)

HIVELESS *adj* lacking a hive

HIYA *interj* — used as an informal greeting

HIZZONER *n* pl. **-S** — used as a title for a mayor

HM *interj* hmm

HMM *interj* — used to express thoughtful consideration

HMMM *interj* hmm

HO *interj* — used to express surprise

HOACTZIN *n* pl. **-S** or **-ES** hoatzin

HOAGIE *n* pl. **-S** a long sandwich

HOAGY *n* pl. **-GIES** hoagie

HOAR *n* pl. **-S** a white coating

HOARD *v* **-ED, -ING, -S** to gather and store away

HOARDER *n* pl. **-S** one that hoards

HOARDING *n* pl. **-S** something hoarded

HOARIER comparative of hoary

HOARIEST superlative of hoary

HOARILY *adv* in a hoary manner

HOARSE *adj* **HOARSER, HOARSEST** low and rough in sound **HOARSELY** *adv*

HOARSEN *v* **-ED, -ING, -S** to make hoarse

HOARY *adj* **HOARIER, HOARIEST** white with age

HOATZIN *n* pl. **-S** or **-ES** a tropical bird

HOAX *v* **-ED, -ING, -ES** to deceive

HOAXER *n* pl. **-S** one that hoaxes

HOB *v* **HOBBED, HOBBING, HOBS** to furnish with hobnails

HOBBER *n* pl. **-S** one that hobs

HOBBIES pl. of hobby

HOBBIT *n* pl. **-S** a fictitious creature that lives underground

HOBBLE *v* **-BLED, -BLING, -BLES** to limp

HOBBLER *n* pl. **-S** one that hobbles

HOBBY   *n* pl. **-BIES** a recreational pastime

HOBBYIST   *n* pl. **-S** one that pursues a hobby

HOBLIKE   *adj* suggestive of an elf

HOBNAIL   *v* **-ED, -ING, -S** to put hobnails (short nails with a broad head) on a shoe sole

HOBNOB   *v* **-NOBBED, -NOBBING, -NOBS** to associate in a friendly way

HOBO   *v* **-ED, -ING, -S** or **-ES** to live like a hobo (a vagrant or tramp)

HOBOISM   *n* pl. **-S** the state of being a hobo

HOCK   *v* **-ED, -ING, -S** to pawn

HOCKER   *n* pl. **-S** one that hocks

HOCKEY   *n* pl. **-EYS** a game played on ice

HOCKSHOP   *n* pl. **-S** a pawnshop

HOCUS   *v* **-CUSED, -CUSING, -CUSES** or **-CUSSED, -CUSSING, -CUSSES** to deceive or cheat

HOD   *n* pl. **-S** a portable trough

HODAD   *n* pl. **-S** one who is not a surfer

HODADDY   *n* pl. **-DIES** hodad

HODDEN   *n* pl. **-S** a coarse cloth

HODDIN   *n* pl. **-S** hodden

HOE   *v* **HOED, HOEING, HOES** to use a hoe (a gardening tool)

HOECAKE   *n* pl. **-S** a cornmeal cake

HOEDOWN   *n* pl. **-S** a square dance

HOELIKE   *adj* resembling a hoe

HOER   *n* pl. **-S** one that hoes

HOG   *v* **HOGGED, HOGGING, HOGS** to take more than one's share

HOGAN   *n* pl. **-S** a Navaho Indian dwelling

HOGBACK   *n* pl. **-S** a sharp ridge

HOGFISH   *n* pl. **-ES** a tropical fish

HOGG   *n* pl. **-S** a young sheep

HOGGED   past tense of hog

HOGGER   *n* pl. **-S** one that hogs

HOGGERY   *n* pl. **-GERIES** a pigpen

HOGGET   *n* pl. **-S** a young unshorn sheep

HOGGING   present participle of hog

HOGGISH   *adj* coarsely selfish

HOGLIKE   *adj* hoggish

HOGMANAY   *n* pl. **-NAYS** a Scottish celebration

HOGMANE   *n* pl. **-S** hogmanay

HOGMENAY   *n* pl. **-NAYS** hogmanay

HOGNOSE   *n* pl. **-S** a nonvenomous snake

HOGNUT   *n* pl. **-S** a hickory nut

HOGSHEAD   *n* pl. **-S** a large cask

HOGTIE   *v* **-TIED, -TIEING** or **-TYING, -TIES** to tie together the legs of

HOGWASH   *n* pl. **-ES** meaningless talk

HOGWEED   *n* pl. **-S** a coarse plant

HOICK   *v* **-ED, -ING, -S** to change directions abruptly

HOIDEN   *v* **-ED, -ING, -S** to hoyden

HOISE   *v* **HOISED, HOISING, HOISES** to hoist

HOISIN   *n* pl. **-S** a spicy brown sauce

HOIST   *v* **-ED, -ING, -S** to haul up by some mechanical means

HOISTER   *n* pl. **-S** one that hoists

HOKE   *v* **HOKED, HOKING, HOKES** to give false value to

HOKEY   *adj* **HOKIER, HOKIEST** false; contrived **HOKILY** *adv*

HOKINESS   *n* pl. **-ES** the state of being hokey

HOKKU   *n* pl. **HOKKU** haiku

HOKUM   *n* pl. **-S** nonsense

HOKYPOKY   *n* pl. **-KIES** trickery

HOLARD   *n* pl. **-S** the total quantity of water in the soil

HOLD   *v* **HELD, HOLDEN, HOLDING, HOLDS** to maintain possession of **HOLDABLE** *adj*

HOLDALL   *n* pl. **-S** a carrying case

HOLDBACK   *n* pl. **-S** a restraining device

HOLDDOWN   *n* pl. **-S** a clamp for holding an object in place

HOLDEN   a past participle of hold

HOLDER   *n* pl. **-S** one that holds

HOLDFAST   *n* pl. **-S** a fastening device

HOLDING   *n* pl. **-S** something held

HOLDOUT   *n* pl. **-S** one who delays signing a contract

HOLDOVER   *n* pl. **-S** something left over

HOLDUP   *n* pl. **-S** a delay

HOLE   *v* **HOLED, HOLING, HOLES** to make a hole (a cavity in a solid)

HOLELESS   *adj* lacking a hole

HOLEY   *adj* full of holes

HOLIBUT   *n* pl. **-S** halibut

HOLIDAY   *v* **-ED, -ING, -S** to take a vacation

HOLIER   comparative of holy

HOLIES   pl. of holy

HOLIEST   superlative of holy

HOLILY	*adv* in a holy manner
HOLINESS	*n* pl. **-ES** the state of being holy
HOLING	present participle of hole
HOLISM	*n* pl. **-S** a philosophical theory
HOLIST	*n* pl. **-S** one who adheres to the theory of holism **HOLISTIC** *adj*
HOLK	*v* **-ED, -ING, -S** to howk
HOLLA	*v* **-ED, -ING, -S** to hallo
HOLLAND	*n* pl. **-S** a cotton fabric
HOLLER	*v* **-ED, -ING, -S** to yell
HOLLIES	pl. of holly
HOLLO	*v* **-ED, -ING, -S** or **-ES** to hallo
HOLLOA	*v* **-ED, -ING, -S** to hallo
HOLLOO	*v* **-ED, -ING, -S** to hallo
HOLLOW	*adj* **-LOWER, -LOWEST** not solid **HOLLOWLY** *adv*
HOLLOW	*v* **-ED, -ING, -S** to make hollow
HOLLY	*n* pl. **-LIES** a tree
HOLM	*n* pl. **-S** an island in a river
HOLME	*n* pl. **-S** holm
HOLMIUM	*n* pl. **-S** a metallic element **HOLMIC** *adj*
HOLO	*n* pl. **-S** a hologram
HOLOGAMY	*n* pl. **-MIES** the state of having gametes of the same size and form as other cells
HOLOGRAM	*n* pl. **-S** a three-dimensional photograph
HOLOGYNY	*n* pl. **-NIES** a trait transmitted solely in the female line
HOLOTYPE	*n* pl. **-S** an animal or plant specimen
HOLOZOIC	*adj* eating solid foods
HOLP	a past tense of help
HOLPEN	a past participle of help
HOLS	*n/pl* a vacation
HOLSTEIN	*n* pl. **-S** a breed of cattle
HOLSTER	*v* **-ED, -ING, -S** to put in a holster (a case for a pistol)
HOLT	*n* pl. **-S** a grove
HOLUBTSI	*n/pl* cabbage rolls
HOLY	*adj* **-LIER, -LIEST** having a divine nature or origin
HOLY	*n* pl. **-LIES** a holy place
HOLYDAY	*n* pl. **-DAYS** a religious holiday
HOLYTIDE	*n* pl. **-S** a time of religious observance

HOM	*n* pl. **-S** a sacred plant of the ancient Persians
HOMA	*n* pl. **-S** a hom
HOMAGE	*v* **-AGED, -AGING, -AGES** to pay tribute to
HOMAGER	*n* pl. **-S** a feudal vassal
HOMBRE	*n* pl. **-S** a fellow
HOMBURG	*n* pl. **-S** a felt hat
HOME	*v* **HOMED, HOMING, HOMES** to return to one's home (place of residence)
HOMEBODY	*n* pl. **-BODIES** one who likes to stay at home
HOMEBOY	*n* pl. **-BOYS** a boy or man from one's neighborhood
HOMEBRED	*n* pl. **-S** a native athlete
HOMEBREW	*n* pl. **-S** an alcoholic beverage made at home
HOMED	past tense of home
HOMEGIRL	*n* pl. **-S** a girl or woman from one's neighborhood
HOMELAND	*n* pl. **-S** one's native land
HOMELESS	*adj* lacking a home
HOMELIKE	*adj* suggestive of a home
HOMELY	*adj* **-LIER, -LIEST** unattractive
HOMEMADE	*adj* made at home
HOMEOBOX	*n* pl. **-ES** a short DNA sequence
HOMEOTIC	*adj* being a gene producing a shift in development
HOMEPAGE	*n* pl. **-S** the main page of a website
HOMEPORT	*v* **-ED, -ING, -S** to assign a ship to a port
HOMER	*v* **-ED, -ING, -S** to hit a home run
HOMERIC	*adj* having a large or grand quality
HOMEROOM	*n* pl. **-S** the classroom where pupils report before classes begin
HOMESICK	*adj* longing for home
HOMESITE	*n* pl. **-S** a location for a house
HOMESPUN	*n* pl. **-S** a loosely woven fabric
HOMESTAY	*n* pl. **-STAYS** a period during which a visitor in a foreign country lives with a local family
HOMETOWN	*n* pl. **-S** the town of one's birth or residence
HOMEWARD	*adv* toward home
HOMEWORK	*n* pl. **-S** work done at home
HOMEY	*adj* **HOMIER, HOMIEST** homelike
HOMEY	*n* pl. **HOMEYS** a person from one's neighborhood

HOMICIDE *n* pl. **-S** the killing of one person by another

HOMIE *n* pl. **-S** homey

HOMIER comparative of homy

HOMIEST superlative of homy

HOMILIST *n* pl. **-S** one that delivers a homily

HOMILY *n* pl. **-LIES** a sermon

HOMINES a pl. of homo

HOMINESS *n* pl. **-ES** the quality of being homey

HOMING present participle of home

HOMINIAN *n* pl. **-S** a hominid

HOMINID *n* pl. **-S** a manlike creature

HOMINIES pl. of hominy

HOMININ *n* pl. **-S** a hominid of a tribe that includes recent humans and extinct related forms

HOMININE *adj* characteristic of man

HOMINIZE *v* **-NIZED, -NIZING, -NIZES** to alter the environment to conform with evolving man

HOMINOID *n* pl. **-S** a manlike animal

HOMINY *n* pl. **-NIES** hulled, dried corn

HOMMOCK *n* pl. **-S** a ridge in an ice field

HOMMOS *n* pl. **-ES** hummus

HOMO *n* pl. **HOMOS** or **HOMINES** a member of the genus that includes modern man

HOMOGAMY *n* pl. **-MIES** the bearing of sexually similar flowers

HOMOGENY *n* pl. **-NIES** correspondence in form or structure

HOMOGONY *n* pl. **-NIES** the condition of having flowers with uniform stamens and pistils

HOMOLOG *n* pl. **-S** something that exhibits homology

HOMOLOGY *n* pl. **-GIES** similarity in structure

HOMONYM *n* pl. **-S** a namesake

HOMONYMY *n* pl. **-MIES** the condition of having the same name

HOMOSEX *n* pl. **-ES** homosexuality

HOMY *adj* **HOMIER, HOMIEST** homey

HON *n* pl. **-S** a honeybun

HONAN *n* pl. **-S** a fine silk

HONCHO *v* **-ED, -ING, -S** or **-ES** to take charge of

HONDA *n* pl. **-S** a part of a lariat

HONDLE *v* **-DLED, -DLING, -DLES** to haggle

HONE *v* **HONED, HONING, HONES** to sharpen

HONER *n* pl. **-S** one that hones

HONEST *adj* **-ESTER, -ESTEST** truthful **HONESTLY** *adv*

HONESTY *n* pl. **-TIES** truthfulness

HONEWORT *n* pl. **-S** a perennial herb

HONEY *v* **HONEYED** or **HONIED, HONEYING, HONEYS** to sweeten with honey (a sweet, viscid fluid)

HONEYBEE *n* pl. **-S** a type of bee

HONEYBUN *n* pl. **-S** a sweetheart

HONEYDEW *n* pl. **-S** a sweet fluid

HONEYFUL *adj* containing much honey

HONEYPOT *n* pl. **-S** one that is attractive or desirable

HONG *n* pl. **-S** a Chinese factory

HONGI *v* **-GIED, -GIING, -GIES** to greet another by pressing noses together

HONIED a past tense of honey

HONING present participle of hone

HONK *v* **-ED, -ING, -S** to emit a cry like that of a goose

HONKER *n* pl. **-S** one that honks

HONOR *v* **-ED, -ING, -S** to respect

HONORAND *n* pl. **-S** an honoree

HONORARY *n* pl. **-ARIES** an honor society

HONOREE *n* pl. **-S** one that receives an honor

HONORER *n* pl. **-S** one that honors

HONOUR *v* **-ED, -ING, -S** to honor

HONOUREE *n* pl. **-S** honoree

HONOURER *n* pl. **-S** honorer

HOO *interj* — used to express surprise or apprehension

HOOCH *n* pl. **-ES** cheap whiskey

HOOCHIE *n* pl. **-S** a promiscuous young woman

HOOD *v* **-ED, -ING, -S** to furnish with a hood (a covering for the head)

HOODIE *n* pl. **-S** a gray crow of Europe

HOODIER comparative of hoody

HOODIEST superlative of hoody

HOODLESS *adj* lacking a hood

HOODLIKE *adj* resembling a hood

HOODLUM *n* pl. **-S** a thug

HOODMOLD *n* pl. **-S** a protective projection on a cornice

HOODOO *v* **-ED, -ING, -S** to jinx

HOODWINK *v* **-ED, -ING, -S** to trick

HOODY *adj* **HOODIER, HOODIEST** resembling a hoodlum

HOOEY *n* pl. **-EYS** nonsense

HOOF *n* pl. **HOOVES** or **HOOFS** the hard covering on the feet of certain animals

HOOF *v* **-ED, -ING, -S** to dance

HOOFBEAT *n* pl. **-S** the sound of hooves striking the ground

HOOFER *n* pl. **-S** a professional dancer

HOOFLESS *adj* lacking hooves

HOOFLIKE *adj* resembling a hoof

HOOK *v* **-ED, -ING, -S** to catch with a hook (a bent piece of metal)

HOOKA *n* pl. **-S** hookah

HOOKAH *n* pl. **-S** a water pipe

HOOKER *n* pl. **-S** a prostitute

HOOKEY *n* pl. **-EYS** hooky

HOOKIER comparative of hooky

HOOKIES pl. of hooky

HOOKIEST superlative of hooky

HOOKING *n* pl. **-S** an illegal move in hockey involving the blade of the stick

HOOKLESS *adj* lacking a hook

HOOKLET *n* pl. **-S** a small hook

HOOKLIKE *adj* resembling a hook

HOOKNOSE *n* pl. **-S** an aquiline nose

HOOKUP *n* pl. **-S** an electrical assemblage

HOOKWORM *n* pl. **-S** a parasitic worm

HOOKY *adj* **HOOKIER, HOOKIEST** full of hooks

HOOKY *n* pl. **HOOKIES** truancy

HOOLIE *adj* easy; slow

HOOLIGAN *n* pl. **-S** a hoodlum

HOOLY *adj* hoolie

HOOP *v* **-ED, -ING, -S** to fasten with a hoop (a circular band of metal)

HOOPER *n* pl. **-S** one that hoops

HOOPLA *n* pl. **-S** commotion

HOOPLESS *adj* lacking a hoop

HOOPLIKE *adj* suggestive of a hoop

HOOPOE *n* pl. **-S** a European bird

HOOPOO *n* pl. **-POOS** hoopoe

HOOPSTER *n* pl. **-S** a basketball player

HOORAH *v* **-ED, -ING, -S** to hurrah

HOORAY *v* **-ED, -ING, -S** to hurrah

HOOSEGOW *n* pl. **-S** a jail

HOOSGOW *n* pl. **-S** hoosegow

HOOT *v* **-ED, -ING, -S** to cry like an owl

HOOTCH *n* pl. **-ES** hooch

HOOTER *n* pl. **-S** one that hoots

HOOTY *adj* **HOOTIER, HOOTIEST** sounding like the cry of an owl

HOOVED *adj* having hooves

HOOVER *v* **-ED, -ING, -S** to clean with a vacuum cleaner

HOOVES a pl. of hoof

HOP *v* **HOPPED, HOPPING, HOPS** to move by jumping on one foot

HOPAK *n* pl. **-S** a Ukrainian dance

HOPE *v* **HOPED, HOPING, HOPES** to have a desire or expectation

HOPEFUL *n* pl. **-S** one that aspires

HOPELESS *adj* despairing

HOPER *n* pl. **-S** one that hopes

HOPHEAD *n* pl. **-S** a drug addict

HOPING present participle of hope

HOPINGLY *adv* in a hopeful manner

HOPLITE *n* pl. **-S** a foot soldier of ancient Greece **HOPLITIC** *adj*

HOPPED past tense of hop

HOPPER *n* pl. **-S** one that hops

HOPPING *n* pl. **-S** a going from one place to another of the same kind

HOPPLE *v* **-PLED, -PLING, -PLES** to hobble

HOPPY *adj* **-PIER, -PIEST** having the taste of hops (catkins of a particular vine)

HOPSACK *n* pl. **-S** a coarse fabric

HOPTOAD *n* pl. **-S** a toad

HORA *n* pl. **-S** an Israeli dance

HORAH *n* pl. **-S** hora

HORAL *adj* hourly

HORARY *adj* hourly

HORDE *v* **HORDED, HORDING, HORDES** to gather in a large group

HORDEIN *n* pl. **-S** a simple protein

HORDEOLA *n/pl* swellings of the eyelid

HORIZON *n* pl. **-S** the line where the sky seems to meet the earth

HORK v **-ED, -ING, -S** to spit

HORMONE n pl. **-S** a secretion of the endocrine organs **HORMONAL, HORMONIC** adj

HORN v **-ED, -ING, -S** to form a horn (a hard projection of the head)

HORNBEAM n pl. **-S** a small tree

HORNBILL n pl. **-S** a large-billed bird

HORNBOOK n pl. **-S** a primer

HORNDOG n pl. **-S** a sexually aggressive man

HORNET n pl. **-S** a stinging insect

HORNFELS n pl. **HORNFELS** a silicate rock

HORNIER comparative of horny

HORNIEST superlative of horny

HORNILY adv in a horny manner

HORNING n pl. **-S** a mock serenade for newlyweds

HORNIST n pl. **-S** a French horn player

HORNITO n pl. **-TOS** a mound of volcanic matter

HORNLESS adj lacking a horn

HORNLIKE adj resembling a horn

HORNPIPE n pl. **-S** a musical instrument

HORNPOUT n pl. **-S** a catfish

HORNTAIL n pl. **-S** a wasplike insect

HORNWORM n pl. **-S** the larva of a hawkmoth

HORNWORT n pl. **-S** an aquatic herb

HORNY adj **HORNIER, HORNIEST** hornlike in hardness

HOROLOGE n pl. **-S** a timepiece

HOROLOGY n pl. **-GIES** the science of measuring time

HORRENT adj bristling; standing erect

HORRIBLE n pl. **-S** something that causes horror

HORRIBLY adv dreadfully

HORRID adj **-RIDER, -RIDEST** repulsive **HORRIDLY** adv

HORRIFIC adj causing horror

HORRIFY v **-FIED, -FYING, -FIES** to cause to feel horror

HORROR n pl. **-S** a feeling of intense fear or repugnance

HORSE v **HORSED, HORSING, HORSES** to provide with a horse (a large, hoofed mammal)

HORSEBOX n pl. **-ES** a closed vehicle for transporting horses

HORSECAR n pl. **-S** a streetcar drawn by a horse

HORSEFLY n pl. **-FLIES** a large fly

HORSEMAN n pl. **-MEN** one who rides a horse

HORSEPOX n pl. **-ES** a skin disease of horses

HORSEY adj **HORSIER, HORSIEST** horsy

HORSIE n pl. **-S** a child's name for a horse

HORSIER comparative of horsy

HORSIEST superlative of horsy

HORSILY adv in a horsy manner

HORSING present participle of horse

HORST n pl. **-S** a portion of the earth's crust

HORSTE n pl. **-S** horst

HORSY adj **HORSIER, HORSIEST** resembling a horse

HOSANNA v **-ED, -ING, -S** to praise

HOSANNAH n pl. **-S** a shout of fervent praise

HOSE n pl. **HOSEN** stockings or socks

HOSE v **HOSED, HOSING, HOSES** to spray with water

HOSEL n pl. **-S** a part of a golf club

HOSELIKE adj resembling a hose

HOSEPIPE n pl. **-S** a flexible tube for conveying fluids

HOSER n pl. **-S** an uncouth man

HOSEY v **-SEYED, -SEYING, -SEYS** to choose sides for a children's game

HOSIER n pl. **-S** one that makes hose

HOSIERY n pl. **-SIERIES** hose

HOSING present participle of hose

HOSPICE n pl. **-S** a shelter

HOSPITAL n pl. **-S** a medical institution

HOSPITIA n/pl places of shelter

HOSPODAR n pl. **-S** a governor of a region under Turkish rule

HOST v **-ED, -ING, -S** to entertain socially

HOSTA n pl. **-S** a plantain lily

HOSTAGE n pl. **-S** a person held as security

HOSTEL v **-TELED, -TELING, -TELS** or **-TELLED, -TELLING, -TELS** to stay at inns overnight while traveling

HOSTELER n pl. **-S** an innkeeper

HOSTELRY n pl. **-RIES** an inn

HOSTESS v **-ED, -ING, -ES** to act as a hostess (a woman who entertains socially)

HOSTILE   *n* pl. **-S** an unfriendly person

HOSTLER   *n* pl. **-S** a person who tends horses or mules

HOSTLY   *adj* pertaining to one who hosts

HOT   *adj* **HOTTER, HOTTEST** having a high temperature

HOT   *v* **HOTTED, HOTTING, HOTS** to heat

HOTBED   *n* pl. **-S** a bed of rich soil

HOTBLOOD   *n* pl. **-S** a thoroughbred horse

HOTBOX   *n* pl. **-ES** an overheated bearing of a railroad car

HOTCAKE   *n* pl. **-S** a pancake

HOTCH   *v* **-ED, -ING, -ES** to wiggle

HOTCHPOT   *n* pl. **-S** the combining of properties in order to divide them equally among heirs

HOTDOG   *v* **-DOGGED, -DOGGING, -DOGS** to perform showily

HOTEL   *n* pl. **-S** a public lodging

HOTELDOM   *n* pl. **-S** hotels and hotel workers

HOTELIER   *n* pl. **-S** a hotel manager

HOTELMAN   *n* pl. **-MEN** a hotelier

HOTFOOT   *v* **-FOOTED, -FOOTING, -FOOTS** to hurry

HOTHEAD   *n* pl. **-S** a quick-tempered person

HOTHOUSE   *v* **-HOUSED, -HOUSING, -HOUSES** to grow in a hothouse (a heated greenhouse)

HOTLINE   *n* pl. **-S** a direct communications system for immediate contact

HOTLINER   *n* pl. **-S** a person who runs a radio phone-in show

HOTLINK   *n* pl. **-S** a connection between two computer files

HOTLY   *adv* in a hot manner

HOTNESS   *n* pl. **-ES** the state of being hot

HOTPOT   *n* pl. **-S** a casserole of meat and vegetables

HOTPRESS   *v* **-ED, -ING, -ES** to subject to heat and pressure

HOTROD   *n* pl. **-S** a car modified for high speeds

HOTSHOT   *n* pl. **-S** a showily skillful person

HOTSPOT   *n* pl. **-S** an area known for violence or unrest

HOTSPUR   *n* pl. **-S** a hothead

HOTTED   past tense of hot

HOTTER   comparative of hot

HOTTEST   superlative of hot

HOTTIE   *n* pl. **-S** an attractive person

HOTTING   present participle of hot

HOTTISH   *adj* somewhat hot

HOTTY   *n* pl. **-TIES** a hottie

HOUDAH   *n* pl. **-S** howdah

HOUMMOS   *n* pl. **-ES** hummus

HOUND   *v* **-ED, -ING, -S** to pursue relentlessly

HOUNDER   *n* pl. **-S** one that hounds

HOUNGAN   *n* pl. **-S** a voodoo priest

HOUR   *n* pl. **-S** a period of sixty minutes

HOURI   *n* pl. **-S** a beautiful maiden in Muslim belief

HOURLONG   *adj* lasting an hour

HOURLY   *n* pl. **-LIES** a worker paid by the hour

HOUSE   *v* **HOUSED, HOUSING, HOUSES** to lodge in a house (a building in which people live)

HOUSEBOY   *n* pl. **-BOYS** a male servant

HOUSEFLY   *n* pl. **-FLIES** a common fly

HOUSEFUL   *n* pl. **-S** as much as a house will hold

HOUSEL   *v* **-SELED, -SELING, -SELS** or **-SELLED, -SELLING, -SELS** to administer the Eucharist to

HOUSEMAN   *n* pl. **-MEN** a male servant

HOUSER   *n* pl. **-S** one who organizes housing projects

HOUSESIT   *v* **-SAT, -SITTING, -SITS** to occupy a dwelling while the tenants are away

HOUSETOP   *n* pl. **-S** the roof of a house

HOUSEY   *adj* **HOUSIER, HOUSIEST** being in the style of house music

HOUSING   *n* pl. **-S** any dwelling place

HOVE   a past tense of heave

HOVEL   *v* **-ELED, -ELING, -ELS** or **-ELLED, -ELLING, -ELS** to live in a small, miserable dwelling

HOVER   *v* **-ED, -ING, -S** to hang suspended in the air

HOVERER   *n* pl. **-S** something that hovers

HOVERFLY   *n* pl. **-FLIES** a fly noted for hovering

HOW   *n* pl. **-S** a method of doing something

HOWBEIT   *adv* nevertheless

HOWDAH   *n* pl. **-S** a seat on an elephant or camel for riders

HOWDIE   *n* pl. **-S** a midwife

HOWDY   *v* **-DIED, -DYING, -DIES** to greet with the words ``how do you do''

HOWE   *n* pl. **-S** a valley

HOWEVER   *adv* nevertheless

HOWF   *n* pl. **-S** a place frequently visited

HOWFF   *n* pl. **-S** howf

HOWITZER   *n* pl. **-S** a short cannon

HOWK   *v* **-ED, -ING, -S** to dig

HOWL   *v* **-ED, -ING, -S** to cry like a dog

HOWLER   *n* pl. **-S** one that howls

HOWLET   *n* pl. **-S** an owl

HOY   *n* pl. **HOYS** a heavy barge or scow

HOYA   *n* pl. **-S** a flowering plant

HOYDEN   *v* **-ED, -ING, -S** to act like a tomboy

HOYLE   *n* pl. **-S** a rule book

HRYVNA   *n* pl. **-S** hryvnia

HRYVNIA   *n* pl. **-S** a monetary unit of Ukraine

HRYVNYA   *n* pl. **-S** hryvnia

HUARACHE   *n* pl. **-S** a flat-heeled sandal

HUARACHO   *n* pl. **-CHOS** huarache

HUB   *n* pl. **-S** the center of a wheel

HUBBLY   *adj* having an uneven surface

HUBBUB   *n* pl. **-S** an uproar

HUBBY   *n* pl. **-BIES** a husband

HUBCAP   *n* pl. **-S** a covering for the hub of a wheel

HUBLESS   *adj* lacking a hub

HUBRIS   *n* pl. **-BRISES** arrogance

HUCK   *n* pl. **-S** a durable fabric

HUCKLE   *n* pl. **-S** the hip

HUCKSTER   *v* **-ED, -ING, -S** to peddle

HUDDLE   *v* **-DLED, -DLING, -DLES** to crowd together

HUDDLER   *n* pl. **-S** one that huddles

HUE   *n* pl. **-S** color **HUED, HUELESS** *adj*

HUFF   *v* **-ED, -ING, -S** to breathe heavily

HUFFISH   *adj* sulky

HUFFY   *adj* **HUFFIER, HUFFIEST** easily offended **HUFFILY** *adv*

HUG   *v* **HUGGED, HUGGING, HUGS** to clasp tightly in the arms

HUGE   *adj* **HUGER, HUGEST** very large **HUGELY** *adv*

HUGENESS   *n* pl. **-ES** the quality of being huge

HUGEOUS   *adj* huge

HUGGABLE   *adj* cuddlesome

HUGGED   past tense of hug

HUGGER   *n* pl. **-S** one that hugs

HUGGING   present participle of hug

HUGGY   *adj* **HUGGIER, HUGGIEST** involving or given to hugging

HUH   *interj* — used to express surprise

HUIC   *interj* — used to encourage hunting hounds

HUIPIL   *n* pl. **-S** or **-ES** an embroidered blouse or dress of Mexico

HUISACHE   *n* pl. **-S** a flowering plant

HULA   *n* pl. **-S** a Hawaiian dance

HULK   *v* **-ED, -ING, -S** to appear impressively large

HULKY   *adj* **HULKIER, HULKIEST** massive

HULL   *v* **-ED, -ING, -S** to remove the shell from a seed

HULLER   *n* pl. **-S** one that hulls

HULLO   *v* **-ED, -ING, -S** or **-ES** to hallo

HULLOA   *v* **-ED, -ING, -S** to hallo

HULLOO   *v* **-ED, -ING, -S** to hallo

HUM   *v* **HUMMED, HUMMING, HUMS** to sing without opening the lips or saying words

HUMAN   *n* pl. **-S** a person

HUMANE   *adj* **-MANER, -MANEST** compassionate **HUMANELY** *adv*

HUMANISE   *v* **-ISED, -ISING, -ISES** to humanize

HUMANISM   *n* pl. **-S** the quality of being human

HUMANIST   *n* pl. **-S** one who studies human nature

HUMANITY   *n* pl. **-TIES** the human race

HUMANIZE   *v* **-IZED, -IZING, -IZES** to make human

HUMANLY   *adv* in a human manner

HUMANOID   *n* pl. **-S** something having human form

HUMATE   *n* pl. **-S** a chemical salt

HUMBLE   *adj* **-BLER, -BLEST** modest

HUMBLE   *v* **-BLED, -BLING, -BLES** to reduce the pride of

HUMBLER   *n* pl. **-S** one that humbles

HUMBLEST   superlative of humble

HUMBLING   present participle of humble

HUMBLY   *adv* in a humble manner

HUMBUG   *v* **-BUGGED, -BUGGING, -BUGS** to deceive

HUMDRUM *n* pl. **-S** a dull, boring person

HUMERAL *n* pl. **-S** a bone of the shoulder

HUMERUS *n* pl. **-MERI** the large bone of the upper arm

HUMIC *adj* derived from humus

HUMID *adj* having much humidity

HUMIDEX *n* pl. **-ES** an index of discomfort

HUMIDIFY *v* **-FIED, -FYING, -FIES** to make humid

HUMIDITY *n* pl. **-TIES** moisture of the air

HUMIDLY *adv* in a humid manner

HUMIDOR *n* pl. **-S** a cigar case

HUMIFIED *adj* converted into humus

HUMILITY *n* pl. **-TIES** the quality of being humble

HUMINT *n* pl. **-S** secret intelligence-gathering by agents

HUMITURE *n* pl. **-S** a combined measurement of temperature and humidity

HUMMABLE *adj* capable of being hummed

HUMMED past tense of hum

HUMMER *n* pl. **-S** one that hums

HUMMING present participle of hum

HUMMOCK *v* **-ED, -ING, -S** to form into hummocks (small rounded hills)

HUMMOCKY *adj* abounding in hummocks

HUMMUS *n* pl. **-ES** a paste of pureed chickpeas and tahini

HUMOR *v* **-ED, -ING, -S** to indulge

HUMORAL *adj* pertaining to bodily fluids

HUMORFUL *adj* humorous

HUMORIST *n* pl. **-S** a humorous writer or entertainer

HUMOROUS *adj* funny; witty

HUMOUR *v* **-ED, -ING, -S** to humor

HUMOUS *n* pl. **-ES** hummus

HUMP *v* **-ED, -ING, -S** to arch into a hump (a rounded protuberance)

HUMPBACK *n* pl. **-S** a humped back

HUMPER *n* pl. **-S** one that humps

HUMPH *v* **-ED, -ING, -S** to utter a grunt

HUMPLESS *adj* lacking a hump

HUMPY *adj* **HUMPIER, HUMPIEST** full of humps

HUMPY *n* pl. **HUMPIES** a primitive hut in Australia

HUMUS *n* pl. **-ES** decomposed organic matter

HUMUSY *adj* resembling humus

HUMVEE *n* pl. **-S** a type of motor vehicle

HUN *n* pl. **-S** a barbarous, destructive person

HUNCH *v* **-ED, -ING, -ES** to arch forward

HUNDRED *n* pl. **-S** a number

HUNG a past tense of hang

HUNGER *v* **-ED, -ING, -S** to crave

HUNGOVER *adj* suffering from a hangover

HUNGRY *adj* **-GRIER, -GRIEST** wanting food **HUNGRILY** *adv*

HUNH *interj* — used to ask for a repetition of an utterance

HUNK *n* pl. **-S** a large piece

HUNKER *v* **-ED, -ING, -S** to squat

HUNKY *adj* **HUNKIER, HUNKIEST** muscular and attractive

HUNNISH *adj* resembling a hun

HUNT *v* **-ED, -ING, -S** to pursue for food or sport **HUNTABLE** *adj* **HUNTEDLY** *adv*

HUNTER *n* pl. **-S** one that hunts

HUNTING *n* pl. **-S** an instance of searching

HUNTRESS *n* pl. **-ES** a female hunter

HUNTSMAN *n* pl. **-MEN** a hunter

HUP *interj* — used to mark a marching cadence

HUPPAH *n* pl. **HUPPAHS** or **CHUPPOT** chuppah

HURDIES *n/pl* the buttocks

HURDLE *v* **-DLED, -DLING, -DLES** to jump over

HURDLER *n* pl. **-S** one that hurdles

HURDS *n/pl* hards

HURL *v* **-ED, -ING, -S** to throw with great force

HURLER *n* pl. **-S** one that hurls

HURLEY *n* pl. **-LEYS** hurling

HURLING *n* pl. **-S** an Irish game

HURLY *n* pl. **-LIES** commotion

HURRAH *v* **-ED, -ING, -S** to cheer

HURRAY *v* **-ED, -ING, -S** to hurrah

HURRIER *n* pl. **-S** one that hurries

HURRY *v* **-RIED, -RYING, -RIES** to move swiftly

HURST *n* pl. **-S** a small hill

HURT *v* **HURT, HURTING, HURTS** to injure

HURTER	*n* pl. **-S** one that hurts
HURTFUL	*adj* causing injury
HURTLE	*v* **-TLED, -TLING, -TLES** to rush violently
HURTLESS	*adj* harmless
HUSBAND	*v* **-ED, -ING, -S** to spend wisely
HUSH	*v* **-ED, -ING, -ES** to quiet **HUSHEDLY** *adv*
HUSHABY	*v* go to sleep — used imperatively to soothe a child
HUSHABYE	*v* hushaby
HUSHFUL	*adj* quiet
HUSK	*v* **-ED, -ING, -S** to remove the husk (the outer covering) from
HUSKER	*n* pl. **-S** one that husks
HUSKIER	comparative of husky
HUSKIES	pl. of husky
HUSKIEST	superlative of husky
HUSKILY	*adv* in a husky manner
HUSKING	*n* pl. **-S** a gathering of families to husk corn
HUSKLIKE	*adj* resembling a husk
HUSKY	*adj* **-KIER, -KIEST** hoarse
HUSKY	*n* pl. **-KIES** a dog of the arctic region
HUSSAR	*n* pl. **-S** a cavalry soldier
HUSSY	*n* pl. **-SIES** a lewd woman
HUSTINGS	*n* pl. **HUSTINGS** a British court
HUSTLE	*v* **-TLED, -TLING, -TLES** to hurry
HUSTLER	*n* pl. **-S** one that hustles
HUSWIFE	*n* pl. **-WIVES** or **-WIFES** a sewing kit
HUT	*v* **HUTTED, HUTTING, HUTS** to live in a hut (a simple shelter)
HUTCH	*v* **-ED, -ING, -ES** to store away
HUTLIKE	*adj* resembling a hut
HUTMENT	*n* pl. **-S** a group of huts
HUTTED	past tense of hut
HUTTING	present participle of hut
HUTZPA	*n* pl. **-S** chutzpah
HUTZPAH	*n* pl. **-S** chutzpah
HUZZA	*v* **-ED, -ING, -S** to cheer
HUZZAH	*v* **-ED, -ING, -S** to huzza
HWAN	*n* pl. **HWAN** a monetary unit of South Korea
HWYL	*n* pl. **-S** an emotion that inspires impassioned eloquence

HYACINTH	*n* pl. **-S** a flowering plant
HYAENA	*n* pl. **-S** hyena **HYAENIC** *adj*
HYALIN	*n* pl. **-S** hyaline
HYALINE	*n* pl. **-S** a transparent substance
HYALITE	*n* pl. **-S** a colorless opal
HYALOGEN	*n* pl. **-S** a substance found in animal cells
HYALOID	*n* pl. **-S** a membrane of the eye
HYBRID	*n* pl. **-S** the offspring of genetically dissimilar parents
HYBRIS	*n* pl. **-BRISES** hubris
HYDATID	*n* pl. **-S** a cyst caused by a tapeworm
HYDRA	*n* pl. **-DRAS** or **-DRAE** a freshwater polyp
HYDRACID	*n* pl. **-S** an acid
HYDRAGOG	*n* pl. **-S** a purgative causing watery discharges
HYDRANT	*n* pl. **-S** an outlet from a water main
HYDRANTH	*n* pl. **-S** the oral opening of a hydra
HYDRASE	*n* pl. **-S** an enzyme
HYDRATE	*v* **-DRATED, -DRATING, -DRATES** to combine with water
HYDRATOR	*n* pl. **-S** one that hydrates
HYDRIA	*n* pl. **-DRIAE** a water jar
HYDRIC	*adj* pertaining to moisture
HYDRID	*n* pl. **-S** hydride
HYDRIDE	*n* pl. **-S** a chemical compound
HYDRILLA	*n* pl. **-S** an aquatic Asian plant
HYDRO	*n* pl. **-DROS** electricity produced by waterpower
HYDROGEL	*n* pl. **-S** a colloid
HYDROGEN	*n* pl. **-S** a gaseous element
HYDROID	*n* pl. **-S** a polyp
HYDROMEL	*n* pl. **-S** a mixture of honey and water
HYDRONIC	*adj* pertaining to heating and cooling by water
HYDROPIC	*adj* affected with hydropsy
HYDROPS	*n* pl. **-ES** hydropsy
HYDROPSY	*n* pl. **-SIES** dropsy
HYDROSKI	*n* pl. **-S** a plate attached to a seaplane to facilitate takeoffs and landings
HYDROSOL	*n* pl. **-S** an aqueous solution of a colloid
HYDROUS	*adj* containing water
HYDROXY	*adj* containing hydroxyl
HYDROXYL	*n* pl. **-S** the radical or group containing oxygen and hydrogen

HYENA   *n* pl. **-S** a wolflike mammal
HYENIC, HYENINE, HYENOID *adj*

HYETAL   *adj* pertaining to rain

HYGEIST   *n* pl. **-S** an expert in hygiene

HYGIEIST   *n* pl. **-S** hygeist

HYGIENE   *n* pl. **-S** the science of health
HYGIENIC *adj*

HYING   present participle of hie

HYLA   *n* pl. **-S** a tree frog

HYLOZOIC   *adj* pertaining to the doctrine that
life and matter are inseparable

HYMEN   *n* pl. **-S** a vaginal membrane
HYMENAL *adj*

HYMENEAL   *n* pl. **-S** a wedding song or poem

HYMENIUM   *n* pl. **-NIUMS** or **-NIA** a layer in
certain fungi **HYMENIAL** *adj*

HYMN   *v* **-ED, -ING, -S** to sing a hymn (a
song of praise to God)

HYMNAL   *n* pl. **-S** a book of hymns

HYMNARY   *n* pl. **-RIES** a hymnal

HYMNBOOK   *n* pl. **-S** a hymnal

HYMNIC   *adj* pertaining to a hymn

HYMNIST   *n* pl. **-S** one who composes hymns

HYMNLESS   *adj* lacking a hymn

HYMNLIKE   *adj* resembling a hymn

HYMNODY   *n* pl. **-DIES** the singing of hymns

HYOID   *n* pl. **-S** a bone of the tongue
HYOIDAL, HYOIDEAN *adj*

HYOSCINE   *n* pl. **-S** a sedative

HYP   *n* pl. **-S** hypochondria

HYPE   *v* **HYPED, HYPING, HYPES** to
promote extravagantly

HYPER   *n* pl. **-S** one that hypes

HYPERGOL   *n* pl. **-S** a rocket fuel

HYPERNYM   *n* pl. **-S** a word that denotes a
broad category that includes more
specific words

HYPERON   *n* pl. **-S** an atomic particle

HYPEROPE   *n* pl. **-S** a farsighted person

HYPHA   *n* pl. **-PHAE** a threadlike element
of a fungus **HYPHAL** *adj*

HYPHEMIA   *n* pl. **-S** deficiency of blood

HYPHEN   *v* **-ED, -ING, -S** to connect words
or syllables with a hyphen (a mark
of punctuation) **HYPHENIC** *adj*

HYPING   present participle of hype

HYPNIC   *adj* pertaining to sleep

HYPNOID   *adj* pertaining to hypnosis or
sleep

HYPNOSIS   *n* pl. **-NOSES** an artificially
induced state resembling sleep

HYPNOTIC   *n* pl. **-S** a sleep-inducing drug

HYPO   *v* **-ED, -ING, -S** to inject with a
hypodermic needle

HYPOACID   *adj* having a lower than normal
degree of acidity

HYPODERM   *n* pl. **-S** a skin layer

HYPOGEA   pl. of hypogeum

HYPOGEAL   *adj* underground

HYPOGEAN   *adj* hypogeal

HYPOGENE   *adj* formed underground

HYPOGEUM   *n* pl. **-GEA** an underground
chamber

HYPOGYNY   *n* pl. **-NIES** the condition of having
flowers with organs situated below
the ovary

HYPOID   *n* pl. **-S** a type of toothed
wheel

HYPONEA   *n* pl. **-S** hyponoia

HYPONOIA   *n* pl. **-S** dulled mental activity

HYPONYM   *n* pl. **-S** a word that denotes a
subcategory

HYPONYMY   *n* pl. **-MIES** the state of being a
hyponym

HYPOPNEA   *n* pl. **-S** abnormally shallow
breathing

HYPOPYON   *n* pl. **-S** an accumulation of pus in
the eye

HYPOTHEC   *n* pl. **-S** a type of mortgage

HYPOXIA   *n* pl. **-S** a deficiency of oxygen in
body tissue **HYPOXIC** *adj*

HYRACOID   *n* pl. **-S** a hyrax

HYRAX   *n* pl. **-RAXES** or **-RACES** a small,
harelike mammal

HYSON   *n* pl. **-S** a Chinese tea

HYSSOP   *n* pl. **-S** a medicinal herb

HYSTERIA   *n* pl. **-S** uncontrollable excitement
or fear

HYSTERIC   *n* pl. **-S** one who is subject to fits of
hysteria

HYTE   *adj* insane

IAMB   *n* pl. **-S** a type of metrical foot

IAMBIC   *n* pl. **-S** an iamb

IAMBUS   *n* pl. **-BUSES** or **-BI** an iamb

IATRIC   *adj* pertaining to medicine

IATRICAL   *adj* iatric

IBEX   *n* pl. **IBEXES** or **IBICES** a wild goat

IBIDEM   *adv* in the same place

IBIS   *n* pl. **IBISES** a wading bird

IBOGAINE   *n* pl. **-S** an alkaloid used as an antidepressant

ICE   *v* **ICED, ICING, ICES** to cover with ice (frozen water)

ICEBERG   *n* pl. **-S** a large floating body of ice

ICEBLINK   *n* pl. **-S** a glare over an icefield

ICEBOAT   *v* **-ED, -ING, -S** to travel in a vehicle that sails on ice

ICEBOUND   *adj* surrounded by ice

ICEBOX   *n* pl. **-ES** a cabinet for cooling food

ICECAP   *n* pl. **-S** a covering of ice and snow

ICED   past tense of ice

ICEFALL   *n* pl. **-S** a kind of frozen waterfall

ICEFIELD   *n* pl. **-S** a large area of ice

ICEFISH   *v* **-ED, -ING, -ES** to fish through holes in the ice on a lake or river

ICEHOUSE   *n* pl. **-S** a building for storing ice

ICEKHANA   *n* pl. **-S** an automotive event held on a frozen lake

ICELESS   *adj* having no ice

ICELIKE   *adj* resembling ice

ICEMAKER   *n* pl. **-S** an appliance that makes ice

ICEMAN   *n* pl. **-MEN** a man who supplies ice

ICESCAPE   *n* pl. **-S** landscape covered with ice

ICEWINE   *n* pl. **-S** sweet wine made from grapes frozen on the vine

ICEWORM   *n* pl. **-S** a small worm found in glaciers

ICH   *n* pl. **ICHS** a disease of certain fishes

ICHNITE   *n* pl. **-S** a fossil footprint

ICHOR   *n* pl. **-S** a watery discharge from a wound **ICHOROUS** *adj*

ICHTHYIC   *adj* pertaining to fishes

ICICLE   *n* pl. **-S** a hanging spike of ice **ICICLED** *adj*

ICIER   comparative of icy

ICIEST   superlative of icy

ICILY   *adv* in an icy manner

ICINESS   *n* pl. **-ES** the state of being icy

ICING   *n* pl. **-S** a sweet mixture for covering cakes

ICK   *n* pl. **-S** something sticky or disgusting

ICKER   *n* pl. **-S** a head of grain

ICKINESS   *n* pl. **-ES** the state of being icky

ICKY   *adj* **ICKIER, ICKIEST** repulsive **ICKILY** *adv*

ICON   *n* pl. **-S** or **-ES** a representation **ICONIC, ICONICAL** *adj*

ICTERIC   *n* pl. **-S** a remedy for icterus

ICTERUS   *n* pl. **-ES** a diseased condition of the liver

ICTUS   *n* pl. **-ES** a recurring stress or beat in a poetical form **ICTIC** *adj*

ICY   *adj* **ICIER, ICIEST** covered with ice

ID   *n* pl. **-S** a part of the psyche

IDEA   *n* pl. **-S** a conception existing in the mind **IDEALESS** *adj*

IDEAL   *n* pl. **-S** a standard of perfection

IDEALISE   *v* **-ISED, -ISING, -ISES** to idealize

IDEALISM   *n* pl. **-S** the pursuit of noble goals

IDEALIST   *n* pl. **-S** an adherent of idealism

IDEALITY *n* pl. **-TIES** the state of being perfect; something idealized

IDEALIZE *v* **-IZED, -IZING, -IZES** to regard as perfect

IDEALLY *adv* perfectly

IDEALOGY *n* pl. **-GIES** ideology

IDEATE *v* **-ATED, -ATING, -ATES** to form an idea

IDEATION *n* pl. **-S** the act of ideating

IDEATIVE *adj* pertaining to ideation

IDEM *adj* the same

IDENT *n* pl. **-S** identification

IDENTIC *adj* identical

IDENTIFY *v* **-FIED, -FYING, -FIES** to establish the identity of

IDENTITY *n* pl. **-TIES** the essential character of a person or thing

IDEOGRAM *n* pl. **-S** a type of written symbol

IDEOLOGY *n* pl. **-GIES** a systematic body of ideas

IDES *n* pl. **IDES** a certain day in the ancient Roman calendar

IDIOCY *n* pl. **-CIES** the condition of being an idiot

IDIOLECT *n* pl. **-S** one's speech pattern

IDIOM *n* pl. **-S** an expression peculiar to a language

IDIOT *n* pl. **-S** a mentally deficient person **IDIOTIC** *adj*

IDIOTISM *n* pl. **-S** idiocy

IDIOTYPE *n* pl. **-S** a structure of an antibody

IDLE *adj* **IDLER, IDLEST** inactive

IDLE *v* **IDLED, IDLING, IDLES** to pass time idly

IDLENESS *n* pl. **-ES** the state of being idle

IDLER *n* pl. **-S** one that idles

IDLESSE *n* pl. **-S** idleness

IDLEST superlative of idle

IDLING present participle of idle

IDLY *adv* in an idle manner

IDOCRASE *n* pl. **-S** a mineral

IDOL *n* pl. **-S** an object of worship

IDOLATER *n* pl. **-S** one that worships idols

IDOLATOR *n* pl. **-S** idolater

IDOLATRY *n* pl. **-TRIES** the worship of idols

IDOLISE *v* **-ISED, -ISING, -ISES** to idolize

IDOLISER *n* pl. **-S** one that idolises

IDOLISM *n* pl. **-S** idolatry

IDOLIZE *v* **-IZED, -IZING, -IZES** to worship

IDOLIZER *n* pl. **-S** one that idolizes

IDONEITY *n* pl. **-TIES** the state of being idoneous

IDONEOUS *adj* suitable

IDYL *n* pl. **-S** a poem or prose work depicting scenes of rural simplicity

IDYLIST *n* pl. **-S** a writer of idyls

IDYLL *n* pl. **-S** idyl **IDYLLIC** *adj*

IDYLLIST *n* pl. **-S** idylist

IF *n* pl. **-S** a possibility

IFF *conj* if and only if

IFFINESS *n* pl. **-ES** the state of being iffy

IFFY *adj* **IFFIER, IFFIEST** full of uncertainty **IFFILY** *adv*

IGG *v* **-ED, -ING, -S** to ignore

IGLOO *n* pl. **-LOOS** an Inuit dwelling

IGLU *n* pl. **-S** igloo

IGNATIA *n* pl. **-S** a medicinal seed

IGNEOUS *adj* pertaining to fire

IGNIFY *v* **-FIED, -FYING, -FIES** to burn

IGNITE *v* **-NITED, -NITING, -NITES** to set on fire

IGNITER *n* pl. **-S** one that ignites

IGNITION *n* pl. **-S** the act of igniting

IGNITOR *n* pl. **-S** igniter

IGNITRON *n* pl. **-S** a type of rectifier tube

IGNOBLE *adj* **-NOBLER, -NOBLEST** of low character **IGNOBLY** *adv*

IGNOMINY *n* pl. **-NIES** disgrace or dishonor

IGNORAMI *n/pl* utterly ignorant persons

IGNORANT *adj* having no knowledge

IGNORE *v* **-NORED, -NORING, -NORES** to refuse to notice

IGNORER *n* pl. **-S** one that ignores

IGUANA *n* pl. **-S** a tropical lizard

IGUANIAN *n* pl. **-S** a lizard related to the iguana

IGUANID *n* pl. **-S** a long-tailed lizard

IHRAM *n* pl. **-S** the garb worn by Muslim pilgrims

IKAT *n* pl. **-S** a fabric of tie-dyed yarns

IKEBANA *n* pl. **-S** the Japanese art of flower arranging

IKON *n* pl. **-S** icon

ILEA pl. of ileum

ILEAC *adj* pertaining to the ileum

ILEAL	*adj* ileac	**IMAGINE**	*v* **-INED, -INING, -INES** to form a mental picture of
ILEITIS	*n* pl. **ILEITIDES** or **ILEITISES** inflammation of the ileum	**IMAGINER**	*n* pl. **-S** one that imagines
ILEUM	*n* pl. **ILEA** a part of the small intestine	**IMAGING**	*n* pl. **-S** the action of producing a visible representation
ILEUS	*n* pl. **-ES** intestinal obstruction	**IMAGINING**	present participle of imagine
ILEX	*n* pl. **-ES** a holly	**IMAGISM**	*n* pl. **-S** a movement in poetry
ILIA	pl. of ilium	**IMAGIST**	*n* pl. **-S** an adherent of imagism
ILIAC	*adj* pertaining to the ilium	**IMAGO**	*n* pl. **-GOS** or **-GOES** an adult insect
ILIAD	*n* pl. **-S** a long poem		
ILIAL	*adj* iliac	**IMAM**	*n* pl. **-S** a Muslim priest
ILIUM	*n* pl. **ILIA** a bone of the pelvis	**IMAMATE**	*n* pl. **-S** the office of an imam
ILK	*n* pl. **-S** a class or kind	**IMARET**	*n* pl. **-S** a Turkish inn
ILKA	*adj* each	**IMAUM**	*n* pl. **-S** imam
ILL	*adj* **ILLER, ILLEST** not well	**IMBALM**	*v* **-ED, -ING, -S** to embalm
ILL	*n* pl. **-S** an evil	**IMBALMER**	*n* pl. **-S** embalmer
ILLATION	*n* pl. **-S** the act of inferring	**IMBARK**	*v* **-ED, -ING, -S** to embark
ILLATIVE	*n* pl. **-S** a word or phrase introducing an inference	**IMBECILE**	*n* pl. **-S** a mentally deficient person
ILLEGAL	*n* pl. **-S** a person who enters a country without authorization	**IMBED**	*v* **-BEDDED, -BEDDING, -BEDS** to embed
ILLICIT	*adj* not permitted	**IMBIBE**	*v* **-BIBED, -BIBING, -BIBES** to drink
ILLINIUM	*n* pl. **-S** a radioactive element	**IMBIBER**	*n* pl. **-S** one that imbibes
ILLIQUID	*adj* not being cash	**IMBITTER**	*v* **-ED, -ING, -S** to embitter
ILLITE	*n* pl. **-S** a group of minerals **ILLITIC** *adj*	**IMBLAZE**	*v* **-BLAZED, -BLAZING, -BLAZES** to emblaze
ILLNESS	*n* pl. **-ES** sickness	**IMBODY**	*v* **-BODIED, -BODYING, -BODIES** to embody
ILLOGIC	*n* pl. **-S** absence of logic		
ILLUDE	*v* **-LUDED, -LUDING, -LUDES** to deceive	**IMBOLDEN**	*v* **-ED, -ING, -S** to embolden
		IMBOSOM	*v* **-ED, -ING, -S** to embosom
ILLUME	*v* **-LUMED, -LUMING, -LUMES** to illuminate	**IMBOWER**	*v* **-ED, -ING, -S** to embower
		IMBROWN	*v* **-ED, -ING, -S** to embrown
ILLUMINE	*v* **-MINED, -MINING, -MINES** to illuminate	**IMBRUE**	*v* **-BRUED, -BRUING, -BRUES** to stain
ILLUSION	*n* pl. **-S** a false perception	**IMBRUTE**	*v* **-BRUTED, -BRUTING, -BRUTES** to make brutal
ILLUSIVE	*adj* illusory		
ILLUSORY	*adj* based on illusion	**IMBUE**	*v* **-BUED, -BUING, -BUES** to make thoroughly wet
ILLUVIUM	*n* pl. **-VIUMS** or **-VIA** a type of material accumulated in soil **ILLUVIAL** *adj*	**IMID**	*n* pl. **-S** imide
		IMIDE	*n* pl. **-S** a chemical compound **IMIDIC** *adj*
ILLY	*adv* badly	**IMIDO**	*adj* containing an imide
ILMENITE	*n* pl. **-S** a mineral	**IMINE**	*n* pl. **-S** a chemical compound
IMAGE	*v* **-AGED, -AGING, -AGES** to imagine	**IMINO**	*adj* containing an imine
		IMITABLE	*adj* capable of being imitated
IMAGER	*n* pl. **-S** one that images	**IMITATE**	*v* **-TATED, -TATING, -TATES** to behave in the same way as
IMAGERY	*n* pl. **-ERIES** mental pictures		
IMAGINAL	*adj* pertaining to an imago	**IMITATOR**	*n* pl. **-S** one that imitates

IMMANE   *adj* great in size

IMMANENT   *adj* existing within

IMMATURE   *n* pl. **-S** an individual that is not fully grown or developed

IMMENSE   *adj* **-MENSER, -MENSEST** great in size

IMMERGE   *v* **-MERGED, -MERGING, -MERGES** to immerse

IMMERSE   *v* **-MERSED, -MERSING, -MERSES** to plunge into a liquid

IMMESH   *v* **-ED, -ING, -ES** to enmesh

IMMIES   pl. of immy

IMMINENT   *adj* ready to take place

IMMINGLE   *v* **-GLED, -GLING, -GLES** to blend

IMMIX   *v* **-ED, -ING, -ES** to mix in

IMMOBILE   *adj* incapable of being moved

IMMODEST   *adj* not modest

IMMOLATE   *v* **-LATED, -LATING, -LATES** to kill as a sacrifice

IMMORAL   *adj* contrary to established morality

IMMORTAL   *n* pl. **-S** one who is not subject to death

IMMOTILE   *adj* lacking mobility

IMMUNE   *n* pl. **-S** one who is protected from a disease

IMMUNISE   *v* **-NISED, -NISING, -NISES** to immunize

IMMUNITY   *n* pl. **-TIES** the state of being protected from a disease

IMMUNIZE   *v* **-NIZED, -NIZING, -NIZES** to protect from a disease

IMMURE   *v* **-MURED, -MURING, -MURES** to imprison

IMMY   *n* pl. **-MIES** a type of playing marble

IMP   *v* **-ED, -ING, -S** to graft feathers onto a bird's wing

IMPACT   *v* **-ED, -ING, -S** to pack firmly together

IMPACTER   *n* pl. **-S** one that impacts

IMPACTOR   *n* pl. **-S** impacter

IMPAINT   *v* **-ED, -ING, -S** to paint or depict

IMPAIR   *v* **-ED, -ING, -S** to make worse

IMPAIRER   *n* pl. **-S** one that impairs

IMPALA   *n* pl. **-S** an African antelope

IMPALE   *v* **-PALED, -PALING, -PALES** to pierce with a pointed object

IMPALER   *n* pl. **-S** one that impales

IMPANEL   *v* **-ELED, -ELING, -ELS** or **-ELLED, -ELLING, -ELS** to enter on a list for jury duty

IMPARITY   *n* pl. **-TIES** lack of equality

IMPARK   *v* **-ED, -ING, -S** to confine in a park

IMPART   *v* **-ED, -ING, -S** to make known

IMPARTER   *n* pl. **-S** one that imparts

IMPASSE   *n* pl. **-S** a road or passage having no exit

IMPASTE   *v* **-PASTED, -PASTING, -PASTES** to make into a paste

IMPASTO   *n* pl. **-TOS** a painting technique

IMPAVID   *adj* brave

IMPAWN   *v* **-ED, -ING, -S** to pawn

IMPEACH   *v* **-ED, -ING, -ES** to charge with misconduct in office

IMPEARL   *v* **-ED, -ING, -S** to make pearly

IMPEDE   *v* **-PEDED, -PEDING, -PEDES** to obstruct the progress of

IMPEDER   *n* pl. **-S** one that impedes

IMPEL   *v* **-PELLED, -PELLING, -PELS** to force into action

IMPELLER   *n* pl. **-S** one that impels

IMPELLOR   *n* pl. **-S** impeller

IMPEND   *v* **-ED, -ING, -S** to be imminent

IMPERIA   a pl. of imperium

IMPERIAL   *n* pl. **-S** an emperor or empress

IMPERIL   *v* **-ILED, -ILING, -ILS** or **-ILLED, -ILLING, -ILS** to place in jeopardy

IMPERIUM   *n* pl. **-RIUMS** or **-RIA** absolute power

IMPETIGO   *n* pl. **-GOS** a skin disease

IMPETUS   *n* pl. **-ES** an impelling force

IMPHEE   *n* pl. **-S** an African grass

IMPI   *n* pl. **-S** a body of warriors

IMPIETY   *n* pl. **-TIES** lack of piety

IMPING   *n* pl. **-S** the process of grafting

IMPINGE   *v* **-PINGED, -PINGING, -PINGES** to collide

IMPINGER   *n* pl. **-S** one that impinges

IMPIOUS   *adj* not pious

IMPISH   *adj* mischievous **IMPISHLY** *adv*

IMPLANT   *v* **-ED, -ING, -S** to set securely

IMPLEAD   *v* **-PLEADED** or **-PLED, -PLEADING, -PLEADS** to sue in a court of law

IMPLEDGE   *v* **-PLEDGED, -PLEDGING, -PLEDGES** to pawn

IMPLICIT	*adj* implied	**IMPUGN**	*v* **-ED, -ING, -S** to make insinuations against
IMPLIED	past tense of imply	**IMPUGNER**	*n* pl. **-S** one that impugns
IMPLIES	present 3d person sing. of imply	**IMPULSE**	*v* **-PULSED, -PULSING, -PULSES** to give impetus to
IMPLODE	*v* **-PLODED, -PLODING, -PLODES** to collapse inward	**IMPUNITY**	*n* pl. **-TIES** exemption from penalty
IMPLORE	*v* **-PLORED, -PLORING, -PLORES** to beg for urgently	**IMPURE**	*adj* **-PURER, -PUREST** not pure
IMPLORER	*n* pl. **-S** one that implores	**IMPURE**	*adj* not pure **IMPURELY** *adv*
IMPLY	*v* **-PLIED, -PLYING, -PLIES** to indicate or suggest indirectly	**IMPURITY**	*n* pl. **-TIES** something that is impure
IMPOLICY	*n* pl. **-CIES** an unwise course of action	**IMPUTE**	*v* **-PUTED, -PUTING, -PUTES** to credit to a person or a cause
IMPOLITE	*adj* not polite	**IMPUTER**	*n* pl. **-S** one that imputes
IMPONE	*v* **-PONED, -PONING, -PONES** to wager	**IN**	*v* **INNED, INNING, INS** to harvest
IMPOROUS	*adj* extremely dense	**INACTION**	*n* pl. **-S** lack of action
IMPORT	*v* **-ED, -ING, -S** to bring into a country from abroad	**INACTIVE**	*adj* not active
IMPORTER	*n* pl. **-S** one that imports	**INANE**	*adj* **INANER, INANEST** nonsensical **INANELY** *adv*
IMPOSE	*v* **-POSED, -POSING, -POSES** to establish as compulsory	**INANE**	*n* pl. **-S** empty space
IMPOSER	*n* pl. **-S** one that imposes	**INANITY**	*n* pl. **-TIES** something that is inane
IMPOST	*v* **-ED, -ING, -S** to determine customs duties	**INAPT**	*adj* not apt **INAPTLY** *adv*
IMPOSTER	*n* pl. **-S** impostor	**INARABLE**	*adj* not arable
IMPOSTOR	*n* pl. **-S** one that poses as another for deceptive purposes	**INARCH**	*v* **-ED, -ING, -ES** to graft with in a certain way
IMPOTENT	*n* pl. **-S** one that is powerless	**INARM**	*v* **-ED, -ING, -S** to encircle with the arms
IMPOUND	*v* **-ED, -ING, -S** to seize and retain in legal custody	**INASMUCH**	*adv* to the extent that
IMPOWER	*v* **-ED, -ING, -S** to empower	**INBEING**	*n* pl. **-S** the state of being inherent
IMPREGN	*v* **-ED, -ING, -S** to make pregnant	**INBOARD**	*n* pl. **-S** a type of boat motor
IMPRESA	*n* pl. **-S** a type of emblem	**INBORN**	*adj* existing in one from birth
IMPRESE	*n* pl. **-S** impresa	**INBOUND**	*v* **-ED, -ING, -S** to put a basketball in play from out of bounds
IMPRESS	*v* **-ED, -ING, -ES** to affect strongly	**INBOUNDS**	*adj* being within certain boundaries
IMPREST	*n* pl. **-S** a loan or advance of money	**INBOX**	*n* pl. **-ES** a window in which electronic mail is displayed
IMPRIMIS	*adv* in the first place	**INBRED**	*n* pl. **-S** a product of inbreeding
IMPRINT	*v* **-ED, -ING, -S** to produce a mark by pressure	**INBREED**	*v* **-BRED, -BREEDING, -BREEDS** to breed closely related stock
IMPRISON	*v* **-ED, -ING, -S** to confine	**INBUILT**	*adj* forming an integral part of a structure
IMPRO	*n* pl. **IMPROS** improv	**INBURST**	*n* pl. **-S** the act of bursting inward
IMPROPER	*adj* not proper	**INBY**	*adv* inward
IMPROV	*n* pl. **-S** improvisation	**INBYE**	*adv* inby
IMPROVE	*v* **-PROVED, -PROVING, -PROVES** to make better	**INCAGE**	*v* **-CAGED, -CAGING, -CAGES** to encage
IMPROVER	*n* pl. **-S** one that improves	**INCANT**	*v* **-ED, -ING, -S** to utter ritually
IMPUDENT	*adj* offensively bold or disrespectful	**INCASE**	*v* **-CASED, -CASING, -CASES** to encase

INCENSE   v **-CENSED, -CENSING, -CENSES** to make angry

INCENT   v **-ED, -ING, -S** to provide with an incentive

INCENTER   n pl. **-S** the point where the three lines bisecting the angles of a triangle meet

INCEPT   v **-ED, -ING, -S** to take in

INCEPTOR   n pl. **-S** one that incepts

INCEST   n pl. **-S** sexual intercourse between closely related persons

INCH   v **-ED, -ING, -ES** to move very slowly

INCHER   n pl. **-S** something having a specified number of inches

INCHMEAL   adv little by little

INCHOATE   adj being in an early stage

INCHWORM   n pl. **-S** a type of worm

INCIDENT   n pl. **-S** an event

INCIPIT   n pl. **-S** the opening words of a text

INCISAL   adj being the cutting edge of a tooth

INCISE   v **-CISED, -CISING, -CISES** to cut into

INCISION   n pl. **-S** the act of incising

INCISIVE   adj penetrating

INCISOR   n pl. **-S** a cutting tooth

INCISORY   adj adapted for cutting

INCISURE   n pl. **-S** a notch or cleft of a body part

INCITANT   n pl. **-S** something that incites

INCITE   v **-CITED, -CITING, -CITES** to arouse to action

INCITER   n pl. **-S** one that incites

INCIVIL   adj discourteous

INCLASP   v **-ED, -ING, -S** to enclasp

INCLINE   v **-CLINED, -CLINING, -CLINES** to slant

INCLINER   n pl. **-S** one that inclines

INCLIP   v **-CLIPPED, -CLIPPING, -CLIPS** to clasp

INCLOSE   v **-CLOSED, -CLOSING, -CLOSES** to enclose

INCLOSER   n pl. **-S** one that incloses

INCLUDE   v **-CLUDED, -CLUDING, -CLUDES** to have as a part

INCOG   n pl. **-S** a disguised person

INCOME   n pl. **-S** a sum of money earned regularly

INCOMER   n pl. **-S** one that comes in

INCOMING   n pl. **-S** an arrival

INCONNU   n pl. **-S** a large food fish

INCONY   adj pretty

INCORPSE   v **-CORPSED, -CORPSING, -CORPSES** to become combined with

INCREASE   v **-CREASED, -CREASING, -CREASES** to make or become greater

INCREATE   adj not created

INCROSS   v **-ED, -ING, -ES** to inbreed

INCRUST   v **-ED, -ING, -S** to encrust

INCUBATE   v **-BATED, -BATING, -BATES** to warm eggs for hatching

INCUBUS   n pl. **-BUSES** or **-BI** a demon

INCUDAL   adj pertaining to the incus

INCUDATE   adj incudal

INCUDES   pl. of incus

INCULT   adj uncultivated

INCUMBER   v **-ED, -ING, -S** to encumber

INCUR   v **-CURRED, -CURRING, -CURS** to bring upon oneself

INCURVE   v **-CURVED, -CURVING, -CURVES** to curve inward

INCUS   n pl. **INCUDES** a bone in the middle ear

INCUSE   v **-CUSED, -CUSING, -CUSES** to mark by stamping

INDABA   n pl. **-S** a meeting of South African tribes

INDAGATE   v **-GATED, -GATING, -GATES** to investigate

INDAMIN   n pl. **-S** indamine

INDAMINE   n pl. **-S** a chemical compound

INDEBTED   adj owing something to another

INDECENT   adj **-CENTER, -CENTEST** not decent

INDEED   adv in truth

INDEEDY   interj — used to emphasize an affirmative

INDENE   n pl. **-S** a hydrocarbon

INDENT   v **-ED, -ING, -S** to cut or tear irregularly

INDENTER   n pl. **-S** one that indents

INDENTOR   n pl. **-S** indenter

INDEVOUT   adj not devout

INDEX   *n* pl. **INDEXES** or **INDICES** a type of reference guide at the end of a book

INDEX   *v* **-ED, -ING, -ES** to provide with an index

INDEXER   *n* pl. **-S** one that indexes

INDEXING   *n* pl. **-S** the linking of wages and prices to cost-of-living levels

INDICAN   *n* pl. **-S** a chemical compound

INDICANT   *n* pl. **-S** something that indicates

INDICATE   *v* **-CATED, -CATING, -CATES** to point out

INDICES   a pl. of index

INDICIA   *n* pl. **-S** a distinctive mark

INDICIUM   *n* pl. **-S** an indicia

INDICT   *v* **-ED, -ING, -S** to charge with a crime

INDICTEE   *n* pl. **-S** one that is indicted

INDICTER   *n* pl. **-S** one that indicts

INDICTOR   *n* pl. **-S** indicter

INDIE   *n* pl. **-S** a person who is independent

INDIGEN   *n* pl. **-S** indigene

INDIGENE   *n* pl. **-S** a native

INDIGENT   *n* pl. **-S** a needy person

INDIGN   *adj* disgraceful **INDIGNLY** *adv*

INDIGO   *n* pl. **-GOS** or **-GOES** a blue dye

INDIGOID   *n* pl. **-S** a blue dye

INDIRECT   *adj* not direct

INDITE   *v* **-DITED, -DITING, -DITES** to write or compose

INDITER   *n* pl. **-S** one that indites

INDIUM   *n* pl. **-S** a metallic element

INDOCILE   *adj* not docile

INDOL   *n* pl. **-S** indole

INDOLE   *n* pl. **-S** a chemical compound

INDOLENT   *adj* lazy

INDOOR   *adj* pertaining to the interior of a building

INDOORS   *adv* in or into a house

INDORSE   *v* **-DORSED, -DORSING, -DORSES** to endorse

INDORSEE   *n* pl. **-S** endorsee

INDORSER   *n* pl. **-S** endorser

INDORSING   present participle of indorse

INDORSOR   *n* pl. **-S** endorsor

INDOW   *v* **-ED, -ING, -S** to endow

INDOXYL   *n* pl. **-S** a chemical compound

INDRAFT   *n* pl. **-S** an inward flow or current

INDRAWN   *adj* drawn in

INDRI   *n* pl. **-S** a short-tailed lemur

INDUCE   *v* **-DUCED, -DUCING, -DUCES** to influence into doing something

INDUCER   *n* pl. **-S** one that induces

INDUCT   *v* **-ED, -ING, -S** to bring into military service

INDUCTEE   *n* pl. **-S** one that is inducted

INDUCTOR   *n* pl. **-S** one that inducts

INDUE   *v* **-DUED, -DUING, -DUES** to endue

INDULGE   *v* **-DULGED, -DULGING, -DULGES** to yield to the desire of

INDULGER   *n* pl. **-S** one that indulges

INDULIN   *n* pl. **-S** induline

INDULINE   *n* pl. **-S** a blue dye

INDULT   *n* pl. **-S** a privilege granted by the pope

INDUNA   *n* pl. **-S** a tribal overseer in Africa

INDURATE   *v* **-RATED, -RATING, -RATES** to make hard

INDUSIUM   *n* pl. **-SIA** an enclosing membrane **INDUSIAL** *adj*

INDUSTRY   *n* pl. **-TRIES** a group of productive enterprises

INDWELL   *v* **-DWELT, -DWELLING, -DWELLS** to live within

INEARTH   *v* **-ED, -ING, -S** to bury

INEDIBLE   *adj* not fit to be eaten **INEDIBLY** *adv*

INEDITA   *n/pl* unpublished literary works

INEDITED   *adj* not published

INEPT   *adj* not suitable **INEPTLY** *adv*

INEQUITY   *n* pl. **-TIES** unfairness

INERRANT   *adj* free from error

INERT   *n* pl. **-S** something that lacks active properties

INERTIA   *n* pl. **-TIAS** or **-TIAE** the tendency of a body to resist acceleration **INERTIAL** *adj*

INERTLY   *adv* inactively

INEXACT   *adj* not exact

INEXPERT   *n* pl. **-S** a novice

INFALL   *n* pl. **-S** movement under the influence of gravity toward a celestial object

INFAMOUS   *adj* having a vile reputation

INFAMY   *n* pl. **-MIES** the state of being infamous

INFANCY   *n* pl. **-CIES** the state of being an infant

INFANT   *n* pl. **-S** a child in the earliest stages of life

INFANTA   *n* pl. **-S** a daughter of a Spanish or Portuguese monarch

INFANTE   *n* pl. **-S** a younger son of a Spanish or Portuguese monarch

INFANTRY   *n* pl. **-TRIES** a branch of the army composed of foot soldiers

INFARCT   *n* pl. **-S** an area of dead or dying tissue

INFARE   *n* pl. **-S** a reception for newlyweds

INFAUNA   *n* pl. **-NAS** or **-NAE** fauna living on a soft sea floor **INFAUNAL** *adj*

INFECT   *v* **-ED, -ING, -S** to contaminate with disease-producing germs

INFECTER   *n* pl. **-S** one that infects

INFECTOR   *n* pl. **-S** infecter

INFECUND   *adj* barren

INFEED   *n* pl. **-S** the action of supplying material to a machine

INFEOFF   *v* **-ED, -ING, -S** to enfeoff

INFER   *v* **-FERRED, -FERRING, -FERS** to reach or derive by reasoning

INFERIOR   *n* pl. **-S** one of lesser rank

INFERNAL   *adj* pertaining to hell

INFERNO   *n* pl. **-NOS** a place that resembles or suggests hell

INFERRED   past tense of infer

INFERRER   *n* pl. **-S** one that infers

INFERRING   present participle of infer

INFEST   *v* **-ED, -ING, -S** to overrun in large numbers

INFESTER   *n* pl. **-S** one that infests

INFIDEL   *n* pl. **-S** one who has no religious faith

INFIELD   *n* pl. **-S** a part of a baseball field

INFIGHT   *v* **-FOUGHT, -FIGHTING, -FIGHTS** to contend with others within the same group

INFILL   *v* **-ED, -ING, -S** to fill in (a hole)

INFINITE   *n* pl. **-S** something that has no limits

INFINITY   *n* pl. **-TIES** the state of having no limits

INFIRM   *v* **-ED, -ING, -S** to weaken or destroy the validity of

INFIRMLY   *adv* in a feeble manner

INFIX   *v* **-ED, -ING, -ES** to implant

INFIXION   *n* pl. **-S** the act of infixing

INFLAME   *v* **-FLAMED, -FLAMING, -FLAMES** to set on fire

INFLAMER   *n* pl. **-S** one that inflames

INFLATE   *v* **-FLATED, -FLATING, -FLATES** to cause to expand by filling with gas or air

INFLATER   *n* pl. **-S** one that inflates

INFLATOR   *n* pl. **-S** inflater

INFLECT   *v* **-ED, -ING, -S** to bend

INFLEXED   *adj* bent inward

INFLICT   *v* **-ED, -ING, -S** to cause to be endured; impose

INFLIGHT   *adj* done during an air voyage

INFLOW   *n* pl. **-S** the act of flowing in

INFLUENT   *n* pl. **-S** a tributary

INFLUX   *n* pl. **-ES** a flowing in

INFO   *n* pl. **-FOS** information

INFOBAHN   *n* pl. **-S** an electronic communications network

INFOLD   *v* **-ED, -ING, -S** to fold inward

INFOLDER   *n* pl. **-S** one that infolds

INFORM   *v* **-ED, -ING, -S** to supply with information

INFORMAL   *adj* marked by the absence of formality or ceremony

INFORMER   *n* pl. **-S** one that informs

INFOTECH   *n* pl. **-S** computer technology for distributing data

INFOUGHT   past tense of infight

INFRA   *adv* below

INFRACT   *v* **-ED, -ING, -S** to break a legal rule

INFRARED   *n* pl. **-S** a part of the invisible spectrum

INFRINGE   *v* **-FRINGED, -FRINGING, -FRINGES** to violate an oath or a law

INFRUGAL   *adj* not frugal

INFULA   *n* pl. **INFULAE** either of the two ribbons on a bishop's miter

INFUSE   *v* **-FUSED, -FUSING, -FUSES** to permeate with something

INFUSER   *n* pl. **-S** one that infuses

INFUSION   *n* pl. **-S** the act of infusing

INFUSIVE   *adj* capable of infusing

INGATE   *n* pl. **-S** a channel by which molten metal enters a mold

INGATHER   *v* **-ED, -ING, -S** to gather in

INGENUE   *n* pl. **-S** a naive young woman

INGEST   *v* **-ED, -ING, -S** to take into the body

INGESTA   *n/pl* ingested material

INGLE   *n* pl. **-S** a fire

INGOING   *adj* entering

INGOT   *v* **-ED, -ING, -S** to shape into a convenient form for storage

INGRAFT   *v* **-ED, -ING, -S** to engraft

INGRAIN   *v* **-ED, -ING, -S** to impress firmly on the mind

INGRATE   *n* pl. **-S** an ungrateful person

INGRESS   *n* pl. **-ES** the act of entering

INGROUND   *adj* built into the ground

INGROUP   *n* pl. **-S** a group with which one feels a sense of solidarity

INGROWN   *adj* grown into the flesh

INGROWTH   *n* pl. **-S** growth inward

INGUINAL   *adj* pertaining to the groin

INGULF   *v* **-ED, -ING, -S** to engulf

INHABIT   *v* **-ED, -ING, -S** to live in

INHALANT   *n* pl. **-S** something that is inhaled

INHALE   *v* **-HALED, -HALING, -HALES** to take into the lungs

INHALER   *n* pl. **-S** one that inhales

INHAUL   *n* pl. **-S** a line for bringing in a sail

INHAULER   *n* pl. **-S** an inhaul

INHERE   *v* **-HERED, -HERING, -HERES** to be inherent

INHERENT   *adj* existing in something as an essential characteristic

INHERIT   *v* **-ED, -ING, -S** to receive by legal succession

INHESION   *n* pl. **-S** the state of inhering

INHIBIN   *n* pl. **-S** a human hormone

INHIBIT   *v* **-ED, -ING, -S** to restrain or hold back

INHOLDER   *n* pl. **-S** one that owns a tract of land within a national park

INHUMAN   *adj* lacking desirable human qualities

INHUMANE   *adj* not humane

INHUME   *v* **-HUMED, -HUMING, -HUMES** to bury

INHUMER   *n* pl. **-S** one that inhumes

INIMICAL   *adj* unfriendly

INION   *n* pl. **INIA** a part of the skull

INIQUITY   *n* pl. **-TIES** a gross injustice

INITIAL   *v* **-TIALED, -TIALING, -TIALS** or **-TIALLED, -TIALLING, -TIALS** to mark with the first letters of one's name

INITIATE   *v* **-ATED, -ATING, -ATES** to originate

INJECT   *v* **-ED, -ING, -S** to force a fluid into

INJECTOR   *n* pl. **-S** one that injects

INJERA   *n* pl. **-S** a type of Ethiopian bread

INJURE   *v* **-JURED, -JURING, -JURES** to do or cause injury to

INJURER   *n* pl. **-S** one that injures

INJURY   *n* pl. **-RIES** harm inflicted or suffered

INK   *v* **-ED, -ING, -S** to mark with ink (a colored fluid used for writing)

INKBERRY   *n* pl. **-RIES** a small shrub

INKBLOT   *n* pl. **-S** a blotted pattern of spilled ink

INKER   *n* pl. **-S** one that inks

INKHORN   *n* pl. **-S** a small container for ink

INKIER   comparative of inky

INKIEST   superlative of inky

INKINESS   *n* pl. **-ES** the state of being inky

INKJET   *n* pl. **-S** a printer that spurts ink to form letters

INKLE   *n* pl. **-S** a tape used for trimming

INKLESS   *adj* being without ink

INKLIKE   *adj* resembling ink

INKLING   *n* pl. **-S** a slight suggestion

INKPOT   *n* pl. **-S** an inkwell

INKSTAND   *n* pl. **-S** an inkwell

INKSTONE   *n* pl. **-S** a stone on which dry ink and water are mixed

INKWELL   *n* pl. **-S** a small container for ink

INKWOOD   *n* pl. **-S** an evergreen tree

INKY   *adj* **INKIER, INKIEST** resembling ink

INLACE   *v* **-LACED, -LACING, -LACES** to enlace

INLAID   past tense of inlay

INLAND   *n* pl. **-S** the interior of a region

INLANDER   *n* pl. **-S** one living in the interior of a region

INLAY   *v* **-LAID, -LAYING, -LAYS** to set into a surface

INLAYER   *n* pl. **-S** one that inlays

INLET   *v* **-LET, -LETTING, -LETS** to insert

INLIER   *n* pl. **-S** a type of rock formation

INLY   *adv* inwardly

INLYING   *adj* located farther in

INMATE   *n* pl. **-S** one who is confined to an institution

INMESH   *v* **-ED, -ING, -ES** to enmesh

INMOST   *adj* farthest within

INN   *v* **-ED, -ING, -S** to put up at an inn (a public lodging house)

INNAGE   *n* pl. **-S** the quantity of goods remaining in a container after shipment

INNARDS   *n/pl* the internal organs

INNATE   *adj* inborn **INNATELY** *adv*

INNED   past tense of in

INNER   *n* pl. **-S** something that is within

INNERLY   *adv* inwardly

INNERVE   *v* **-NERVED, -NERVING, -NERVES** to stimulate

INNING   *n* pl. **-S** a division of a baseball game

INNINGS   *n* pl. **-ES** a part of the game of cricket

INNLESS   *adj* having no inns

INNOCENT   *adj* **-CENTER, -CENTEST** free from guilt or sin

INNOCENT   *n* pl. **-S** an innocent person

INNOVATE   *v* **-VATED, -VATING, -VATES** to introduce something new

INNUENDO   *v* **-ED, -ING, -S** or **-ES** to make a derogatory implication

INOCULUM   *n* pl. **-LUMS** or **-LA** the material used in an inoculation

INOSINE   *n* pl. **-S** a compound of hypoxanthine and ribose

INOSITE   *n* pl. **-S** inositol

INOSITOL   *n* pl. **-S** an alcohol found in plant and animal tissue

INOTROPE   *n* pl. **-S** a drug for controlling the force of muscular contractions

INPHASE   *adj* having matching electrical phases

INPOUR   *v* **-ED, -ING, -S** to pour in

INPUT   *v* **-PUTTED, -PUTTING, -PUTS** to enter data into a computer

INPUTTER   *n* pl. **-S** one that inputs

INQUEST   *n* pl. **-S** a legal inquiry

INQUIET   *v* **-ED, -ING, -S** to disturb

INQUIRE   *v* **-QUIRED, -QUIRING, -QUIRES** to ask about

INQUIRER   *n* pl. **-S** one that inquires

INQUIRY   *n* pl. **-RIES** a question

INRO   *n* pl. **INRO** a Japanese ornamental container

INROAD   *n* pl. **-S** a hostile invasion

INRUN   *n* pl. **-S** the approach ramp of a ski jump

INRUSH   *n* pl. **-ES** a rushing in

INSANE   *adj* **-SANER, -SANEST** mentally unsound **INSANELY** *adv*

INSANITY   *n* pl. **-TIES** the state of being insane; something utterly foolish

INSCAPE   *n* pl. **-S** the inner essential quality of something

INSCRIBE   *v* **-SCRIBED, -SCRIBING, -SCRIBES** to write or engrave as a lasting record

INSCROLL   *v* **-ED, -ING, -S** to enscroll

INSCULP   *v* **-ED, -ING, -S** to engrave

INSEAM   *n* pl. **-S** an inner seam

INSECT   *n* pl. **-S** any of a class of small invertebrate animals

INSECTAN   *adj* pertaining to insects

INSECURE   *adj* unsafe

INSERT   *v* **-ED, -ING, -S** to put in

INSERTER   *n* pl. **-S** one that inserts

INSET   *v* **-SETTED, -SETTING, -SETS** to insert

INSETTER   *n* pl. **-S** one that inserts

INSHEATH   *v* **-ED, -ING, -S** to ensheath

INSHORE   *adj* near the shore

INSHRINE   *v* **-SHRINED, -SHRINING, -SHRINES** to enshrine

INSIDE   *n* pl. **-S** something that lies within

INSIDER   *n* pl. **-S** an accepted member of a clique

INSIGHT   *n* pl. **-S** a perception of the inner nature of things

INSIGNE   *n* pl. **INSIGNIA** an insignia

INSIGNIA   *n* pl. **-S** an emblem of authority or honor

INSIPID   *adj* dull and uninteresting

INSIST   *v* **-ED, -ING, -S** to be resolute on some matter

INSISTER   *n* pl. **-S** one that insists

INSNARE v -**SNARED, -SNARING, -SNARES** to ensnare

INSNARER n pl. **-S** ensnarer

INSOFAR adv to such an extent

INSOLATE v -**LATED, -LATING, -LATES** to expose to sunlight

INSOLE n pl. **-S** the inner sole of a boot or shoe

INSOLENT n pl. **-S** an extremely rude person

INSOMNIA n pl. **-S** chronic inability to sleep

INSOMUCH adv to such a degree

INSOUL v -**ED, -ING, -S** to ensoul

INSOURCE v -**SOURCED, -SOURCING, -SOURCES** to procure goods and services from within one's own country

INSPAN v -**SPANNED, -SPANNING, -SPANS** to harness or yoke to a vehicle

INSPECT v -**ED, -ING, -S** to look carefully at or over

INSPHERE v -**SPHERED, -SPHERING, -SPHERES** to ensphere

INSPIRE v -**SPIRED, -SPIRING, -SPIRES** to animate the mind or emotions of

INSPIRER n pl. **-S** one that inspires

INSPIRIT v -**ED, -ING, -S** to fill with spirit or life

INSTABLE adj unstable

INSTAL v -**STALLED, -STALLING, -STALS** to install

INSTALL v -**ED, -ING, -S** to place in position for use

INSTANCE v -**STANCED, -STANCING, -STANCES** to cite as an example

INSTANCY n pl. **-CIES** urgency

INSTANT n pl. **-S** a very short time

INSTAR v -**STARRED, -STARRING, -STARS** to adorn with stars

INSTATE v -**STATED, -STATING, -STATES** to place in office

INSTEAD adv as a substitute or equivalent

INSTEP n pl. **-S** a part of the foot

INSTIL v -**STILLED, -STILLING, -STILS** to instill

INSTILL v -**ED, -ING, -S** to infuse slowly

INSTINCT n pl. **-S** an inborn behavioral pattern

INSTROKE n pl. **-S** an inward stroke

INSTRUCT v -**ED, -ING, -S** to supply with knowledge

INSULA n pl. **-LAE** a region of the brain

INSULANT n pl. **-S** an insulating material

INSULAR n pl. **-S** an islander

INSULATE v -**LATED, -LATING, -LATES** to separate with nonconducting material

INSULIN n pl. **-S** a hormone

INSULT v -**ED, -ING, -S** to treat offensively

INSULTER n pl. **-S** one that insults

INSURANT n pl. **-S** one who is insured

INSURE v -**SURED, -SURING, -SURES** to guarantee against loss

INSURED n pl. **-S** one who is insured

INSURER n pl. **-S** one that insures

INSURING present participle of insure

INSWATHE v -**SWATHED, -SWATHING, -SWATHES** to enswathe

INSWEPT adj narrowed in front

INTACT adj not damaged in any way **INTACTLY** adv

INTAGLIO n pl. **-GLIOS** or **-GLI** an incised or sunken design

INTAGLIO v -**ED, -ING, -S** or **-ES** to engrave in intaglio

INTAKE n pl. **-S** the act of taking in

INTARSIA n pl. **-S** a decorative technique

INTEGER n pl. **-S** a whole number

INTEGRAL n pl. **-S** a total unit

INTEGRIN n pl. **-S** a class of animal proteins

INTEND v -**ED, -ING, -S** to have as a specific aim or purpose

INTENDED n pl. **-S** one's spouse to-be

INTENDER n pl. **-S** one that intends

INTENSE adj -**TENSER, -TENSEST** existing in an extreme degree

INTENT n pl. **-S** a purpose

INTENTLY adv in an unwavering manner

INTER v -**TERRED, -TERRING, -TERS** to bury

INTERACT v -**ED, -ING, -S** to act on each other

INTERAGE adj including persons of various ages

INTERBED v -**BEDDED, -BEDDING, -BEDS** to insert between other layers

INTERCOM n pl. **-S** a type of communication system

INTERCUT v -**CUT, -CUTTING, -CUTS** to alternate camera shots

INTEREST	*v* -**ED**, -**ING**, -**S** to engage the attention of
INTERIM	*n* pl. -**S** an interval
INTERIOR	*n* pl. -**S** the inside
INTERLAP	*v* -**LAPPED**, -**LAPPING**, -**LAPS** to lap one over another
INTERLAY	*v* -**LAID**, -**LAYING**, -**LAYS** to place between
INTERMAT	*v* -**MATTED**, -**MATTING**, -**MATS** to mat fibers together
INTERMIT	*v* -**MITTED**, -**MITTING**, -**MITS** to stop temporarily
INTERMIX	*v* -**ED**, -**ING**, -**ES** to mix together
INTERN	*v* -**ED**, -**ING**, -**S** to confine during a war
INTERNAL	*n* pl. -**S** an inner attribute
INTERNE	*n* pl. -**S** a recent medical school graduate on a hospital staff
INTERNEE	*n* pl. -**S** one who has been interned
INTERRED	past tense of inter
INTERREX	*n* pl. -**REGES** a type of sovereign
INTERRING	present participle of inter
INTERROW	*adj* existing between rows
INTERSEX	*n* pl. -**ES** a person having characteristics of both sexes
INTERTIE	*n* pl. -**S** a type of electrical connection
INTERVAL	*n* pl. -**S** a space of time between periods or events
INTERWAR	*adj* happening between wars
INTHRAL	*v* -**THRALLED**, -**THRALLING**, -**THRALS** to enthrall
INTHRALL	*v* -**ED**, -**ING**, -**S** to enthrall
INTHRONE	*v* -**THRONED**, -**THRONING**, -**THRONES** to enthrone
INTI	*n* pl. -**S** a former monetary unit of Peru
INTIFADA	*n* pl. -**S** an uprising of Palestinians against Israelis
INTIMA	*n* pl. -**MAS** or -**MAE** the innermost layer of an organ **INTIMAL** *adj*
INTIMACY	*n* pl. -**CIES** the state of being closely associated
INTIMATE	*v* -**MATED**, -**MATING**, -**MATES** to make known indirectly
INTIME	*adj* cozy
INTIMIST	*n* pl. -**S** a writer or artist who deals with deep personal experiences
INTINE	*n* pl. -**S** the inner wall of a spore
INTITLE	*v* -**TLED**, -**TLING**, -**TLES** to entitle

INTITULE	*v* -**ULED**, -**ULING**, -**ULES** to entitle
INTO	*prep* to the inside of
INTOMB	*v* -**ED**, -**ING**, -**S** to entomb
INTONATE	*v* -**NATED**, -**NATING**, -**NATES** to intone
INTONE	*v* -**TONED**, -**TONING**, -**TONES** to speak in a singing voice
INTONER	*n* pl. -**S** one that intones
INTORT	*v* -**ED**, -**ING**, -**S** to twist inward
INTOWN	*adj* located in the center of a city
INTRADAY	*adj* occurring within a single day
INTRADOS	*n* pl. -**ES** the inner curve of an arch
INTRANET	*n* pl. -**S** a computer network with restricted access
INTRANT	*n* pl. -**S** an entrant
INTREAT	*v* -**ED**, -**ING**, -**S** to entreat
INTRENCH	*v* -**ED**, -**ING**, -**ES** to entrench
INTREPID	*adj* fearless
INTRIGUE	*v* -**TRIGUED**, -**TRIGUING**, -**TRIGUES** to arouse the curiosity of
INTRO	*n* pl. -**TROS** an introduction
INTROFY	*v* -**FIED**, -**FYING**, -**FIES** to increase the wetting properties of
INTROIT	*n* pl. -**S** music sung at the beginning of a worship service
INTROMIT	*v* -**MITTED**, -**MITTING**, -**MITS** to put in
INTRON	*n* pl. -**S** an intervening sequence in the genetic code **INTRONIC** *adj*
INTRORSE	*adj* facing inward
INTRUDE	*v* -**TRUDED**, -**TRUDING**, -**TRUDES** to thrust or force oneself in
INTRUDER	*n* pl. -**S** one that intrudes
INTRUST	*v* -**ED**, -**ING**, -**S** to entrust
INTUBATE	*v* -**BATED**, -**BATING**, -**BATES** to insert a tube into
INTUIT	*v* -**ED**, -**ING**, -**S** to know without conscious reasoning
INTURN	*n* pl. -**S** a turning inward **INTURNED** *adj*
INTWINE	*v* -**TWINED**, -**TWINING**, -**TWINES** to entwine
INTWIST	*v* -**ED**, -**ING**, -**S** to entwist
INUKSHUK	*n* pl. -**S** a figure of a human made of stones
INUKSUK	*n* pl. **INUKSUKS** or **INUKSUIT** an inukshuk
INULASE	*n* pl. -**S** an enzyme
INULIN	*n* pl. -**S** a chemical compound

INUNDANT   *adj* inundating

INUNDATE   *v* **-DATED, -DATING, -DATES** to overwhelm with water

INURBANE   *adj* not urbane

INURE   *v* **-URED, -URING, -URES** to accustom to accept something undesirable

INURN   *v* **-ED, -ING, -S** to put in an urn

INUTILE   *adj* useless

INVADE   *v* **-VADED, -VADING, -VADES** to enter for conquest or plunder

INVADER   *n* pl. **-S** one that invades

INVALID   *v* **-ED, -ING, -S** to disable physically

INVAR   *n* pl. **-S** an iron-nickel alloy

INVASION   *n* pl. **-S** the act of invading **INVASIVE** *adj*

INVECTED   *adj* edged by convex curves

INVEIGH   *v* **-ED, -ING, -S** to protest angrily

INVEIGLE   *v* **-GLED, -GLING, -GLES** to induce by guile or flattery

INVENT   *v* **-ED, -ING, -S** to devise originally

INVENTER   *n* pl. **-S** inventor

INVENTOR   *n* pl. **-S** one that invents

INVERITY   *n* pl. **-TIES** lack of truth

INVERSE   *v* **-VERSED, -VERSING, -VERSES** to reverse

INVERT   *v* **-ED, -ING, -S** to turn upside down

INVERTER   *n* pl. **-S** one that inverts

INVERTIN   *n* pl. **-S** an enzyme

INVERTOR   *n* pl. **-S** a type of electrical device

INVEST   *v* **-ED, -ING, -S** to commit something of value for future profit

INVESTOR   *n* pl. **-S** one that invests

INVIABLE   *adj* not viable **INVIABLY** *adv*

INVIRILE   *adj* not virile

INVISCID   *adj* not viscid

INVITAL   *adj* not vital

INVITE   *v* **-VITED, -VITING, -VITES** to request the presence of

INVITEE   *n* pl. **-S** one that is invited

INVITER   *n* pl. **-S** one that invites

INVITING   present participle of invite

INVOCATE   *v* **-CATED, -CATING, -CATES** to invoke

INVOICE   *v* **-VOICED, -VOICING, -VOICES** to bill

INVOKE   *v* **-VOKED, -VOKING, -VOKES** to appeal to for aid

INVOKER   *n* pl. **-S** one that invokes

INVOLUTE   *v* **-LUTED, -LUTING, -LUTES** to roll or curl up

INVOLVE   *v* **-VOLVED, -VOLVING, -VOLVES** to contain or include as a part

INVOLVER   *n* pl. **-S** one that involves

INWALL   *v* **-ED, -ING, -S** to surround with a wall

INWARD   *adv* toward the inside

INWARDLY   *adv* on the inside

INWARDS   *adv* inward

INWEAVE   *v* **-WOVE** or **-WEAVED, -WOVEN, -WEAVING, -WEAVES** to weave together

INWIND   *v* **-WOUND, -WINDING, -WINDS** to enwind

INWRAP   *v* **-WRAPPED, -WRAPPING, -WRAPS** to enwrap

IODATE   *v* **-DATED, -DATING, -DATES** to iodize

IODATION   *n* pl. **-S** the act of iodating

IODIC   *adj* pertaining to iodine

IODID   *n* pl. **-S** iodide

IODIDE   *n* pl. **-S** a compound of iodine

IODIN   *n* pl. **-S** iodine

IODINATE   *v* **-ATED, -ATING, -ATES** to iodize

IODINE   *n* pl. **-S** a nonmetallic element

IODISE   *v* **-DISED, -DISING, -DISES** to iodize

IODISM   *n* pl. **-S** iodine poisoning

IODIZE   *v* **-DIZED, -DIZING, -DIZES** to treat with iodine

IODIZER   *n* pl. **-S** one that iodizes

IODOFORM   *n* pl. **-S** an iodine compound

IODOPHOR   *n* pl. **-S** an iodine compound

IODOPSIN   *n* pl. **-S** a pigment in the retina

IODOUS   *adj* pertaining to iodine

IOLITE   *n* pl. **-S** a mineral

ION   *n* pl. **-S** an electrically charged atom

IONIC   *n* pl. **-S** a style of type

IONIC   *adj* pertaining to or using ions

IONICITY   *n* pl. **-TIES** the state of existing as or like an ion

IONISE   *v* **-ISED, -ISING, -ISES** to ionize

IONISER   *n* pl. **-S** ionizer

IONIUM   *n* pl. **-S** an isotope of thorium

IONIZE   *v* **-IZED, -IZING, -IZES** to convert into ions

IONIZER   *n* pl. **-S** one that ionizes

IONOGEN   *n* pl. **-S** a compound capable of forming ions

IONOMER   *n* pl. **-S** a type of plastic

IONONE   *n* pl. **-S** a chemical compound

IOTA   *n* pl. **-S** a Greek letter

IOTACISM   *n* pl. **-S** excessive use of the letter iota

IPECAC   *n* pl. **-S** a medicinal plant

IPOMOEA   *n* pl. **-S** a flowering plant

IRACUND   *adj* easily angered

IRADE   *n* pl. **-S** a decree of a Muslim ruler

IRATE   *adj* **IRATER, IRATEST** angry **IRATELY** *adv*

IRE   *v* **IRED, IRING, IRES** to anger

IREFUL   *adj* angry **IREFULLY** *adv*

IRELESS   *adj* not angry

IRENIC   *adj* peaceful in purpose

IRENICAL   *adj* irenic

IRENICS   *n/pl* a branch of theology

IRID   *n* pl. **-S** a plant of the iris family

IRIDES   a pl. of iris

IRIDIC   *adj* pertaining to iridium

IRIDIUM   *n* pl. **-S** a metallic element

IRING   present participle of ire

IRIS   *n* pl. **IRISES** or **IRIDES** a part of the eye

IRIS   *v* **-ED, -ING, -ES** to give the form of a rainbow to

IRITIS   *n* pl. **-TISES** inflammation of the iris **IRITIC** *adj*

IRK   *v* **-ED, -ING, -S** to annoy or weary

IRKSOME   *adj* tending to irk

IROKO   *n* pl. **-KOS** a large African tree

IRON   *v* **-ED, -ING, -S** to furnish with iron (a metallic element)

IRONBARK   *n* pl. **-S** a timber tree

IRONCLAD   *n* pl. **-S** an armored warship

IRONE   *n* pl. **-S** an aromatic oil

IRONER   *n* pl. **-S** a machine for pressing clothes

IRONIC   *adj* pertaining to irony

IRONICAL   *adj* ironic

IRONIES   pl. of irony

IRONING   *n* pl. **-S** clothes pressed or to be pressed

IRONISE   *v* **-NISED, -NISING, -NISES** to ironize

IRONIST   *n* pl. **-S** one who uses irony

IRONIZE   *v* **-NIZED, -NIZING, -NIZES** to mix with nutritional iron

IRONLESS   *adj* having no iron

IRONLIKE   *adj* resembling iron

IRONMAN   *n* pl. **-MEN** a man of great strength and stamina

IRONNESS   *n* pl. **-ES** the state of being iron

IRONSIDE   *n* pl. **-S** a man of great strength

IRONWARE   *n* pl. **-S** articles made of iron

IRONWEED   *n* pl. **-S** a shrub

IRONWOOD   *n* pl. **-S** a hardwood tree

IRONWORK   *n* pl. **-S** objects made of iron

IRONY   *n* pl. **-NIES** the use of words to express the opposite of what is literally said

IRREAL   *adj* not real

IRRIGATE   *v* **-GATED, -GATING, -GATES** to supply with water by artificial means

IRRITANT   *n* pl. **-S** something that irritates

IRRITATE   *v* **-TATED, -TATING, -TATES** to excite to impatience or anger

IRRUPT   *v* **-ED, -ING, -S** to rush in forcibly

IS   present 3d person sing. of be

ISAGOGE   *n* pl. **-S** a type of introduction to a branch of study

ISAGOGIC   *n* pl. **-S** a branch of theology

ISARITHM   *n* pl. **-S** an isopleth

ISATIN   *n* pl. **-S** a chemical compound **ISATINIC** *adj*

ISATINE   *n* pl. **-S** isatin

ISBA   *n* pl. **-S** a Russian log hut

ISCHEMIA   *n* pl. **-S** a type of anemia **ISCHEMIC** *adj*

ISCHIUM   *n* pl. **-CHIA** a pelvic bone **ISCHIAL** *adj*

ISLAND   *v* **-ED, -ING, -S** to make into an island (a land area entirely surrounded by water)

ISLANDER   *n* pl. **-S** one that lives on an island

ISLE   *v* **ISLED, ISLING, ISLES** to place on an isle (a small island)

ISLELESS   *adj* lacking an isle

ISLET   *n* pl. **-S** a small island **ISLETED** *adj*

ISM   *n* pl. **-S** a distinctive theory or doctrine

ISOBAR   *n* pl. **-S** a type of atom **ISOBARIC** *adj*

ISOBARE   *n* pl. **-S** isobar

ISOBATH   *n* pl. **-S** a line on a map connecting points of equal water depth

ISOBUTYL   *n* pl. **-S** a hydrocarbon radical

ISOCHEIM   *n* pl. **-S** a type of isotherm

ISOCHIME   *n* pl. **-S** isocheim

ISOCHOR   *n* pl. **-S** isochore

ISOCHORE   *n* pl. **-S** a curve used to show a relationship between pressure and temperature

ISOCHRON   *n* pl. **-S** a line on a chart connecting points representing the same time

ISOCLINE   *n* pl. **-S** a type of rock formation

ISOCRACY   *n* pl. **-CIES** a form of government

ISODOSE   *adj* pertaining to zones that receive equal doses of radiation

ISOFORM   *n* pl. **-S** one of two or more proteins having a similar form

ISOGAMY   *n* pl. **-MIES** the fusion of two similar gametes

ISOGENIC   *adj* genetically similar

ISOGENY   *n* pl. **-NIES** the state of being of similar origin

ISOGLOSS   *n* pl. **-ES** a line on a map between linguistically varied areas

ISOGON   *n* pl. **-S** a polygon having equal angles

ISOGONAL   *n* pl. **-S** isogone

ISOGONE   *n* pl. **-S** a line on a map used to show characteristics of the earth's magnetic field

ISOGONIC   *n* pl. **-S** isogone

ISOGONY   *n* pl. **-NIES** an equivalent relative growth of parts

ISOGRAFT   *v* **-ED, -ING, -S** to transplant from one individual to another of the same species

ISOGRAM   *n* pl. **-S** a line on a map connecting points of equal value

ISOGRAPH   *n* pl. **-S** a line on a map indicating areas that are linguistically similar

ISOGRIV   *n* pl. **-S** a line drawn on a map such that all points have equal grid variation

ISOHEL   *n* pl. **-S** a line on a map connecting points receiving equal sunshine

ISOHYET   *n* pl. **-S** a line on a map connecting points having equal rainfall

ISOLABLE   *adj* capable of being isolated

ISOLATE   *v* **-LATED, -LATING, -LATES** to set apart from others

ISOLATOR   *n* pl. **-S** one that isolates

ISOLEAD   *n* pl. **-S** a line on a ballistic graph

ISOLINE   *n* pl. **-S** an isogram

ISOLOG   *n* pl. **-S** isologue

ISOLOGUE   *n* pl. **-S** a type of chemical compound

ISOMER   *n* pl. **-S** a type of chemical compound **ISOMERIC** *adj*

ISOMETRY   *n* pl. **-TRIES** equality of measure

ISOMORPH   *n* pl. **-S** something similar to something else in form

ISONOMY   *n* pl. **-MIES** equality of civil rights **ISONOMIC** *adj*

ISOPACH   *n* pl. **-S** an isogram connecting points of equal thickness

ISOPHOTE   *n* pl. **-S** a curve on a chart joining points of equal light intensity

ISOPLETH   *n* pl. **-S** a type of isogram

ISOPOD   *n* pl. **-S** a kind of crustacean

ISOPODAN   *n* pl. **-S** an isopod

ISOPRENE   *n* pl. **-S** a volatile liquid

ISOSPIN   *n* pl. **-S** a type of quantum number

ISOSPORY   *n* pl. **-RIES** the condition of producing sexual or asexual spores of but one kind

ISOSTACY   *n* pl. **-CIES** isostasy

ISOSTASY   *n* pl. **-SIES** the state of balance in the earth's crust

ISOTACH   *n* pl. **-S** a line on a map connecting points of equal wind velocity

ISOTHERE   *n* pl. **-S** a type of isotherm

ISOTHERM   *n* pl. **-S** a line on a map connecting points of equal mean temperature

ISOTONE   *n* pl. **-S** a type of atom

ISOTONIC   *adj* of equal tension

ISOTOPE   *n* pl. **-S** a form of an element **ISOTOPIC** *adj*

ISOTOPY   *n* pl. **-PIES** the state of being an isotope

ISOTROPY   *n* pl. **-PIES** the state of being identical in all directions

ISOTYPE   *n* pl. **-S** a type of diagram **ISOTYPIC** *adj*

ISOZYME   *n* pl. **-S** a type of enzyme **ISOZYMIC** *adj*

ISSEI	*n* pl. **-S** a Japanese immigrant to the United States	**ITEMIZE**	*v* **-IZED, -IZING, -IZES** to set down the particulars of
ISSUABLE	*adj* authorized for issuing **ISSUABLY** *adv*	**ITEMIZER**	*n* pl. **-S** one that itemizes
ISSUANCE	*n* pl. **-S** the act of issuing	**ITERANCE**	*n* pl. **-S** repetition
ISSUANT	*adj* coming forth	**ITERANT**	*adj* repeating
ISSUE	*v* **-SUED, -SUING, -SUES** to come forth	**ITERATE**	*v* **-ATED, -ATING, -ATES** to repeat
ISSUER	*n* pl. **-S** one that issues	**ITERUM**	*adv* again; once more
ISTHMI	a pl. of isthmus	**ITHER**	*adj* other
ISTHMIAN	*n* pl. **-S** a native of an isthmus	**ITS**	*pron* the possessive form of the pronoun it
ISTHMIC	*adj* pertaining to an isthmus	**ITSELF**	*pron* a reflexive form of the pronoun it
ISTHMOID	*adj* isthmic	**IVORY**	*n* pl. **-RIES** a hard white substance found in elephant tusks **IVORIED** *adj*
ISTHMUS	*n* pl. **-MUSES** or **-MI** a strip of land connecting two larger land masses	**IVY**	*n* pl. **IVIES** a climbing vine **IVYLIKE** *adj* **IVIED** *adj*
ISTLE	*n* pl. **-S** a strong fiber	**IWIS**	*adv* certainly
IT	*pron* the 3d person sing. neuter pronoun	**IXIA**	*n* pl. **-S** a flowering plant
		IXNAY	*interj* no
ITALIC	*n* pl. **-S** a style of print	**IXODID**	*n* pl. **-S** a bloodsucking insect
ITCH	*v* **-ED, -ING, -ES** to have an uneasy or tingling skin sensation		
ITCHING	*n* pl. **-S** an uneasy or tingling skin sensation	**IXORA**	*n* pl. **-S** a flowering plant
		IXTLE	*n* pl. **-S** istle
ITCHY	*adj* **ITCHIER, ITCHIEST** causing an itching sensation **ITCHILY** *adv*	**IZAR**	*n* pl. **-S** an outer garment worn by Muslim women
ITEM	*v* **-ED, -ING, -S** to itemize	**IZARD**	*n* pl. **-S** a goatlike antelope
ITEMISE	*v* **-ISED, -ISING, -ISES** to itemize	**IZZARD**	*n* pl. **-S** the letter Z

JAB	*v* **JABBED, JABBING, JABS** to poke sharply
JABBER	*v* **-ED, -ING, -S** to talk rapidly
JABBERER	*n* pl. **-S** one that jabbers
JABIRU	*n* pl. **-S** a wading bird
JABOT	*n* pl. **-S** a decoration on a shirt
JACAL	*n* pl. **-S** or **-ES** a hut
JACAMAR	*n* pl. **-S** a tropical bird
JACANA	*n* pl. **-S** a wading bird
JACINTH	*n* pl. **-S** a variety of zircon
JACINTHE	*n* pl. **-S** an orange color
JACK	*v* **-ED, -ING, -S** to raise with a type of lever
JACKAL	*n* pl. **-S** a doglike mammal
JACKAROO	*n* pl. **-ROOS** jackeroo
JACKASS	*n* pl. **-ES** a male donkey
JACKBOOT	*n* pl. **-S** a heavy boot
JACKDAW	*n* pl. **-S** a bird resembling a crow
JACKER	*n* pl. **-S** one that jacks
JACKEROO	*n* pl. **-ROOS** an inexperienced ranch hand
JACKET	*v* **-ED, -ING, -S** to provide with a jacket (a short coat)
JACKFISH	*n* pl. **-ES** a food fish
JACKIES	pl. of jacky
JACKLEG	*n* pl. **-S** an unskilled worker
JACKPOT	*n* pl. **-S** a top prize or reward
JACKROLL	*v* **-ED, -ING, -S** to rob a drunken or sleeping person
JACKSTAY	*n* pl. **-STAYS** a rope on a ship
JACKY	*n* pl. **JACKIES** a sailor
JACOBIN	*n* pl. **-S** a pigeon
JACOBUS	*n* pl. **-ES** an old English coin
JACONET	*n* pl. **-S** a cotton cloth
JACQUARD	*n* pl. **-S** a fabric of intricate weave
JACULATE	*v* **-LATED, -LATING, -LATES** to throw
JADE	*v* **JADED, JADING, JADES** to weary **JADEDLY** *adv*
JADEITE	*n* pl. **-S** a mineral **JADITIC** *adj*
JADELIKE	*adj* resembling jade (a green gemstone)
JADISH	*adj* worn-out **JADISHLY** *adv*
JAEGER	*n* pl. **-S** a hunter
JAG	*v* **JAGGED, JAGGING, JAGS** to cut unevenly
JAGER	*n* pl. **-S** jaeger
JAGG	*v* **-ED, -ING, -S** to jag
JAGGARY	*n* pl. **-RIES** jaggery
JAGGED	*adj* **-GEDER, -GEDEST** having a sharply uneven edge or surface **JAGGEDLY** *adv*
JAGGER	*n* pl. **-S** one that jags
JAGGERY	*n* pl. **-GERIES** a coarse, dark sugar
JAGGHERY	*n* pl. **-GHERIES** jaggery
JAGGIES	*n/pl* a jagged effect on a curved line
JAGGING	present participle of jag
JAGGY	*adj* **-GIER, -GIEST** jagged
JAGLESS	*adj* smooth and even
JAGRA	*n* pl. **-S** jaggery
JAGUAR	*n* pl. **-S** a large feline animal
JAIL	*v* **-ED, -ING, -S** to put in jail (a place of confinement) **JAILABLE** *adj*
JAILBIRD	*n* pl. **-S** a prisoner
JAILER	*n* pl. **-S** a keeper of a jail
JAILOR	*n* pl. **-S** jailer
JAKE	*adj* all right; fine

JAKES *n/pl* an outhouse

JALAP *n* pl. **-S** a Mexican plant **JALAPIC** *adj*

JALAPENO *n* pl. **-NOS** a hot pepper

JALAPIN *n* pl. **-S** a medicinal substance contained in jalap

JALOP *n* pl. **-S** jalap

JALOPPY *n* pl. **-PIES** jalopy

JALOPY *n* pl. **-LOPIES** a decrepit car

JALOUSIE *n* pl. **-S** a type of window

JAM *v* **JAMMED, JAMMING, JAMS** to force together tightly **JAMMABLE** *adj*

JAMB *v* **-ED, -ING, -S** to jam

JAMBE *n* pl. **-S** a jambeau

JAMBEAU *n* pl. **-BEAUX** or **-BEAUS** a piece of armor for the leg

JAMBOREE *n* pl. **-S** a noisy celebration

JAMLIKE *adj* resembling jam

JAMMED past tense of jam

JAMMER *n* pl. **-S** one that jams

JAMMIES *n/pl* pajamas

JAMMING present participle of jam

JAMMY *adj* **-MIER, -MIEST** sticky with jam (boiled fruit and sugar)

JANE *n* pl. **-S** a girl or woman

JANGLE *v* **-GLED, -GLING, -GLES** to make a harsh, metallic sound

JANGLER *n* pl. **-S** one that jangles

JANGLY *adj* **-GLIER, -GLIEST** jangling

JANIFORM *adj* hypocritical

JANISARY *n* pl. **-SARIES** janizary

JANITOR *n* pl. **-S** a maintenance man

JANIZARY *n* pl. **-ZARIES** a Turkish soldier

JANNEY *v* **-ED, -ING, -S** to janny

JANNY *v* **-NIED, -NYING, -NIES** to act as a disguised merrymaker at Christmas

JANNYING *n* pl. **-S** the action of one that jannies

JANTY *adj* jaunty

JAPAN *v* **-PANNED, -PANNING, -PANS** to coat with a glossy, black lacquer

JAPANIZE *v* **-NIZED, -NIZING, -NIZES** to make Japanese

JAPANNER *n* pl. **-S** one that japans

JAPE *v* **JAPED, JAPING, JAPES** to mock

JAPER *n* pl. **-S** one that japes

JAPERY *n* pl. **-ERIES** mockery

JAPING present participle of jape

JAPINGLY *adv* in a japing manner

JAPONICA *n* pl. **-S** an Asian shrub

JAR *v* **JARRED, JARRING, JARS** to cause to shake

JARFUL *n* pl. **JARFULS** or **JARSFUL** the quantity held by a jar (a cylindrical container)

JARGON *v* **-ED, -ING, -S** to speak or write an obscure and often pretentious kind of language

JARGONEL *n* pl. **-S** a variety of pear

JARGONY *adj* characterized by the use of obscure language

JARGOON *n* pl. **-S** a variety of zircon

JARHEAD *n* pl. **-S** a marine soldier

JARINA *n* pl. **-S** the hard seed of a palm tree

JARL *n* pl. **-S** a Scandinavian nobleman

JARLDOM *n* pl. **-S** the domain of a jarl

JAROSITE *n* pl. **-S** a mineral

JAROVIZE *v* **-VIZED, -VIZING, -VIZES** to hasten the flowering of a plant

JARRAH *n* pl. **-S** an evergreen tree

JARRED past tense of jar

JARRING present participle of jar

JARSFUL a pl. of jarful

JARVEY *n* pl. **-VEYS** the driver of a carriage for hire

JASMIN *n* pl. **-S** jasmine

JASMINE *n* pl. **-S** a climbing shrub

JASPER *n* pl. **-S** a variety of quartz **JASPERY** *adj*

JASSID *n* pl. **-S** any of a family of plant pests

JATO *n* pl. **-TOS** a takeoff aided by jet propulsion

JAUK *v* **-ED, -ING, -S** to dawdle

JAUNCE *v* **JAUNCED, JAUNCING, JAUNCES** to prance

JAUNDICE *v* **-DICED, -DICING, -DICES** to prejudice unfavorably

JAUNT *v* **-ED, -ING, -S** to make a pleasure trip

JAUNTY *adj* **-TIER, -TIEST** having a lively and self-confident manner **JAUNTILY** *adv*

JAUP *v* **-ED, -ING, -S** to splash

JAVA	*n* pl. **-S** coffee
JAVELIN	*v* **-ED, -ING, -S** to pierce with a javelin (a light spear)
JAVELINA	*n* pl. **-S** a peccary
JAW	*v* **-ED, -ING, -S** to jabber
JAWAN	*n* pl. **-S** a soldier of India
JAWBONE	*v* **-BONED, -BONING, -BONES** to attempt to convince
JAWBONER	*n* pl. **-S** one that jawbones
JAWLESS	*adj* having no jaw (a bony structure bordering the mouth)
JAWLIKE	*adj* resembling the jaw (the framework of the mouth)
JAWLINE	*n* pl. **-S** the outline of the lower jaw
JAY	*n* pl. **JAYS** a corvine bird
JAYBIRD	*n* pl. **-S** a jay
JAYGEE	*n* pl. **-S** a military officer
JAYVEE	*n* pl. **-S** a junior varsity player
JAYWALK	*v* **-ED, -ING, -S** to cross a street recklessly
JAZZ	*v* **-ED, -ING, -ES** to enliven
JAZZBO	*n* pl. **-BOS** a devotee of jazz (a style of lively syncopated music)
JAZZER	*n* pl. **-S** one that jazzes
JAZZLIKE	*adj* resembling a type of music
JAZZMAN	*n* pl. **-MEN** a type of musician
JAZZY	*adj* **JAZZIER, JAZZIEST** lively **JAZZILY** *adv*
JEALOUS	*adj* resentful of another's advantages
JEALOUSY	*n* pl. **-SIES** a jealous feeling
JEAN	*n* pl. **-S** a durable cotton fabric **JEANED** *adj*
JEBEL	*n* pl. **-S** a mountain
JEE	*v* **JEED, JEEING, JEES** to gee
JEEP	*v* **-ED, -ING, -S** to travel by a small type of motor vehicle
JEEPERS	*interj* — used as a mild oath
JEEPNEY	*n* pl. **-NEYS** a Philippine jitney
JEER	*v* **-ED, -ING, -S** to mock
JEERER	*n* pl. **-S** one that jeers
JEESLY	*adj* jeezly
JEEZ	*interj* — used as a mild oath
JEEZE	*interj* jeez
JEEZELY	*adj* jeezly
JEEZLY	*adj* used as an intensifier
JEFE	*n* pl. **-S** a chief
JEHAD	*n* pl. **-S** jihad
JEHADI	*n* pl. **-S** jihadi
JEHADIST	*n* pl. **-S** jihadist
JEHU	*n* pl. **-S** a fast driver
JEJUNA	pl. of jejunum
JEJUNAL	*adj* pertaining to the jejunum
JEJUNE	*adj* uninteresting; childish **JEJUNELY** *adv*
JEJUNITY	*n* pl. **-TIES** something that is jejune
JEJUNUM	*n* pl. **-NA** or **-NUMS** a part of the small intestine
JELL	*v* **-ED, -ING, -S** to congeal
JELLABA	*n* pl. **-S** djellaba
JELLIFY	*v* **-FIED, -FYING, -FIES** to jelly
JELLY	*v* **-LIED, -LYING, -LIES** to make into a jelly (a soft, semisolid substance)
JELUTONG	*n* pl. **-S** a tropical tree
JEMADAR	*n* pl. **-S** an officer in the army of India
JEMIDAR	*n* pl. **-S** jemadar
JEMMY	*v* **-MIED, -MYING, -MIES** to jimmy
JENNET	*n* pl. **-S** a small horse
JENNY	*n* pl. **-NIES** a female donkey
JEON	*n* pl. **JEON** a monetary unit of South Korea
JEOPARD	*v* **-ED, -ING, -S** to imperil
JEOPARDY	*n* pl. **-DIES** risk of loss or injury
JERBOA	*n* pl. **-S** a small rodent
JEREED	*n* pl. **-S** a wooden javelin
JEREMIAD	*n* pl. **-S** a tale of woe
JERID	*n* pl. **-S** jereed
JERK	*v* **-ED, -ING, -S** to move with a sharp, sudden motion
JERKER	*n* pl. **-S** one that jerks
JERKIN	*n* pl. **-S** a sleeveless jacket
JERKY	*adj* **JERKIER, JERKIEST** characterized by jerking movements **JERKILY** *adv*
JERKY	*n* pl. **-KIES** dried meat
JEROBOAM	*n* pl. **-S** a wine bottle
JERREED	*n* pl. **-S** jereed
JERRICAN	*n* pl. **-S** jerrycan
JERRID	*n* pl. **-S** jereed
JERRY	*n* pl. **-RIES** a German soldier
JERRYCAN	*n* pl. **-S** a fuel container
JERSEY	*n* pl. **-SEYS** a close-fitting knitted shirt **JERSEYED** *adj*

JESS	*v* **-ED, -ING, -ES** to fasten straps around the legs of a hawk	**JEZAIL**	*n* pl. **-S** a type of firearm
JESSANT	*adj* shooting forth	**JEZEBEL**	*n* pl. **-S** a scheming, wicked woman
JESSE	*v* **JESSED, JESSING, JESSES** to jess	**JIAO**	*n* pl. **JIAO** chiao
JEST	*v* **-ED, -ING, -S** to joke	**JIB**	*v* **JIBBED, JIBBING, JIBS** to refuse to proceed further
JESTER	*n* pl. **-S** one that jests	**JIBB**	*v* **-ED, -ING, -S** to shift from side to side while sailing
JESTFUL	*adj* tending to jest		
JESTING	*n* pl. **-S** the act of one who jests	**JIBBA**	*n* pl. **-S** a long coat worn by Muslim men
JET	*v* **JETTED, JETTING, JETS** to spurt forth in a stream	**JIBBAH**	*n* pl. **-S** jibba
JETBEAD	*n* pl. **-S** an ornamental shrub	**JIBBER**	*n* pl. **-S** a horse that jibs
JETE	*n* pl. **-S** a ballet leap	**JIBBOOM**	*n* pl. **-S** a ship's spar
JETFOIL	*n* pl. **-S** a jet-powered hydrofoil (a boat with winglike structures for lifting the hull above the water)	**JIBE**	*v* **JIBED, JIBING, JIBES** to gibe **JIBINGLY** *adv*
		JIBER	*n* pl. **-S** one that jibes
JETLAG	*n* pl. **-S** the disruption of body rhythms after a flight through several time zones	**JICAMA**	*n* pl. **-S** a tropical plant with edible roots
		JIFF	*n* pl. **-S** jiffy
JETLIKE	*adj* resembling a jet airplane	**JIFFY**	*n* pl. **-FIES** a short time
JETLINER	*n* pl. **-S** a type of aircraft	**JIG**	*v* **JIGGED, JIGGING, JIGS** to bob
JETON	*n* pl. **-S** jetton	**JIGGER**	*v* **-ED, -ING, -S** to jerk up and down
JETPACK	*n* pl. **-S** a backpack with jets to transport the wearer		
		JIGGERED	*adj* damned
JETPORT	*n* pl. **-S** a type of airport	**JIGGIER**	comparative of jiggy
JETSAM	*n* pl. **-S** goods cast overboard	**JIGGIEST**	superlative of jiggy
JETSOM	*n* pl. **-S** jetsam	**JIGGISH**	*adj* suitable for a jig (a lively dance)
JETTED	past tense of jet		
JETTIED	past tense of jetty	**JIGGLE**	*v* **-GLED, -GLING, -GLES** to shake lightly
JETTIER	comparative of jetty		
JETTIES	present 3d person sing. of jetty	**JIGGLY**	*adj* **-GLIER, -GLIEST** unsteady
JETTIEST	superlative of jetty	**JIGGY**	*adj* **-GIER, -GIEST** pleasurably excited
JETTING	present participle of jet		
JETTISON	*v* **-ED, -ING, -S** to cast overboard	**JIGLIKE**	*adj* resembling a jig
JETTON	*n* pl. **-S** a piece used in counting	**JIGSAW**	*v* **-SAWED, -SAWN, -SAWING, -SAWS** to cut with a type of saw
JETTY	*adj* **-TIER, -TIEST** having the color jet black		
		JIHAD	*n* pl. **-S** a Muslim holy war
JETTY	*v* **-TIED, -TYING, -TIES** to jut	**JIHADI**	*n* pl. **-S** a Muslim who participates in a jihad
JEU	*n* pl. **JEUX** a game		
JEWEL	*v* **-ELED, -ELING, -ELS** or **-ELLED, -ELLING, -ELS** to adorn or equip with jewels (precious stones)	**JIHADIST**	*n* pl. **-S** a jihadi
		JILL	*n* pl. **-S** a unit of liquid measure
		JILLION	*n* pl. **-S** a very large number
		JILT	*v* **-ED, -ING, -S** to reject a lover
JEWELER	*n* pl. **-S** a dealer or maker of jewelry	**JILTER**	*n* pl. **-S** one that jilts
		JIMINY	*interj* — used to express surprise
JEWELLER	*n* pl. **-S** jeweler	**JIMJAMS**	*n/pl* violent delirium
JEWELRY	*n* pl. **-RIES** an article or articles for personal adornment	**JIMMIE**	*n* pl. **-S** a tiny bit of candy for decorating ice cream
JEWFISH	*n* pl. **-ES** a large marine fish		

JIMMINY   *interj* jiminy

JIMMY   *v* **-MIED, -MYING, -MIES** to pry open with a crowbar

JIMP   *adj* **JIMPER, JIMPEST** natty **JIMPLY** *adv*

JIMPY   *adj* jimp

JIMSON   *n* pl. **-S** a tall poisonous weed

JIN   *n* pl. **-S** jinn

JINGAL   *n* pl. **-S** a heavy musket

JINGALL   *n* pl. **-S** jingal

JINGKO   *n* pl. **-KOES** ginkgo

JINGLE   *v* **-GLED, -GLING, -GLES** to make a tinkling sound

JINGLER   *n* pl. **-S** one that jingles

JINGLY   *adj* **-GLIER, -GLIEST** jingling

JINGO   *n* pl. **-GOES** a zealous patriot **JINGOISH** *adj*

JINGOISM   *n* pl. **-S** the spirit or policy of jingoes

JINGOIST   *n* pl. **-S** a jingo

JINK   *v* **-ED, -ING, -S** to move quickly out of the way

JINKER   *n* pl. **-S** one that jinks

JINN   *n* pl. **-S** a supernatural being in Muslim mythology

JINNEE   *n* pl. **JINN** jinn

JINNI   *n* pl. **-S** jinn

JINX   *v* **-ED, -ING, -ES** to bring bad luck to

JIPIJAPA   *n* pl. **-S** a tropical plant

JIRD   *n* pl. **-S** a long-tailed rodent

JITNEY   *n* pl. **-NEYS** a small bus

JITTER   *v* **-ED, -ING, -S** to fidget

JITTERY   *adj* **-TERIER, -TERIEST** extremely nervous

JIUJITSU   *n* pl. **-S** jujitsu

JIUJUTSU   *n* pl. **-S** jujitsu

JIVE   *v* **JIVED, JIVING, JIVES** to play jazz or swing music

JIVE   *adj* **JIVER, JIVEST** deceitful

JIVER   *n* pl. **-S** one that jives

JIVEY   *adj* **JIVIER, JIVIEST** jazzy, lively

JIVING   present participle of jive

JIVY   *adj* jivey

JNANA   *n* pl. **-S** knowledge acquired through meditation

JO   *n* pl. **JOES** a sweetheart

JOANNES   *n* pl. **JOANNES** johannes

JOB   *v* **JOBBED, JOBBING, JOBS** to work by the piece

JOBBER   *n* pl. **-S** a pieceworker

JOBBERY   *n* pl. **-BERIES** corruption in public office

JOBBIE   *n* pl. **-S** an example of its type

JOBLESS   *adj* having no job

JOBNAME   *n* pl. **-S** a computer code for a job instruction

JOCK   *n* pl. **-S** an athletic supporter

JOCKDOM   *n* pl. **-S** the world of athletes

JOCKETTE   *n* pl. **-S** a woman who rides horses in races

JOCKEY   *v* **-EYED, -EYING, -EYS** to maneuver for an advantage

JOCKISH   *adj* characteristic of an athlete

JOCKO   *n* pl. **JOCKOS** a monkey

JOCKY   *adj* **JOCKIER, JOCKIEST** resembling an athlete

JOCOSE   *adj* humorous **JOCOSELY** *adv*

JOCOSITY   *n* pl. **-TIES** the state of being jocose

JOCULAR   *adj* given to joking

JOCUND   *adj* cheerful **JOCUNDLY** *adv*

JODHPUR   *n* pl. **-S** a type of boot

JOE   *n* pl. **-S** a fellow

JOEY   *n* pl. **-EYS** a young kangaroo

JOG   *v* **JOGGED, JOGGING, JOGS** to run at a slow, steady pace

JOGGER   *n* pl. **-S** one that jogs

JOGGING   *n* pl. **-S** the practice of running at a slow, steady pace

JOGGLE   *v* **-GLED, -GLING, -GLES** to shake slightly

JOGGLER   *n* pl. **-S** one that joggles

JOGTROT   *n* pl. **-S** a slow regular way of walking or running

JOHANNES   *n* pl. **JOHANNES** a Portuguese coin

JOHN   *n* pl. **-S** a toilet

JOHNBOAT   *n* pl. **-S** a narrow square-ended boat

JOHNNIE   *n* pl. **-S** johnny

JOHNNY   *n* pl. **-NIES** a sleeveless hospital gown

JOIN   *v* **-ED, -ING, -S** to unite **JOINABLE** *adj*

JOINDER   *n* pl. **-S** a joining of parties in a lawsuit

JOINER	*n* pl. **-S** a carpenter
JOINERY	*n* pl. **-ERIES** the trade of a joiner
JOINING	*n* pl. **-S** a juncture
JOINT	*v* **-ED, -ING, -S** to fit together by means of a junction
JOINTER	*n* pl. **-S** one that joints
JOINTLY	*adv* together
JOINTURE	*v* **-TURED, -TURING, -TURES** to set aside property as an inheritance
JOIST	*v* **-ED, -ING, -S** to support with horizontal beams
JOJOBA	*n* pl. **-S** a small tree
JOKE	*v* **JOKED, JOKING, JOKES** to say something amusing
JOKER	*n* pl. **-S** one that jokes
JOKESTER	*n* pl. **-S** a practical joker
JOKEY	*adj* **JOKIER, JOKIEST** amusing **JOKILY** *adv*
JOKIER	comparative of joky
JOKIEST	superlative of joky
JOKINESS	*n* pl. **-ES** the state of being jokey
JOKING	present participle of joke
JOKINGLY	*adv* in a joking manner
JOKY	*adj* **JOKIER, JOKIEST** jokey
JOLE	*n* pl. **-S** jowl
JOLLIED	past tense of jolly
JOLLIER	*n* pl. **-S** one who puts others in good humor
JOLLIES	present 3d person sing. of jolly
JOLLIEST	superlative of jolly
JOLLIFY	*v* **-FIED, -FYING, -FIES** to make jolly
JOLLITY	*n* pl. **-TIES** mirth
JOLLY	*adj* **-LIER, -LIEST** cheerful **JOLLILY** *adv*
JOLLY	*v* **-LIED, -LYING, -LIES** to put in a good humor for one's own purposes
JOLT	*v* **-ED, -ING, -S** to jar or shake roughly
JOLTER	*n* pl. **-S** one that jolts
JOLTY	*adj* **JOLTIER, JOLTIEST** marked by a jolting motion **JOLTILY** *adv*
JOMON	*adj* pertaining to a Japanese cultural period
JONES	*v* **-ED, -ING, -ES** to have a strong craving for something
JONGLEUR	*n* pl. **-S** a minstrel
JONQUIL	*n* pl. **-S** a perennial herb
JOOK	*n* pl. **-S** a tavern that has a jukebox
JORAM	*n* pl. **-S** jorum
JORDAN	*n* pl. **-S** a type of container
JORUM	*n* pl. **-S** a large drinking bowl
JOSEPH	*n* pl. **-S** a woman's long cloak
JOSH	*v* **-ED, -ING, -ES** to tease
JOSHER	*n* pl. **-S** one that joshes
JOSHING	*n* pl. **-S** the act of teasing
JOSS	*n* pl. **-ES** a Chinese idol
JOSTLE	*v* **-TLED, -TLING, -TLES** to bump or push roughly
JOSTLER	*n* pl. **-S** one that jostles
JOT	*v* **JOTTED, JOTTING, JOTS** to write down quickly
JOTA	*n* pl. **-S** a Spanish dance
JOTTER	*n* pl. **-S** one that jots
JOTTING	*n* pl. **-S** a brief note
JOTTY	*adj* written down quickly
JOUAL	*n* pl. **-S** a dialect of Canadian French
JOUK	*v* **-ED, -ING, -S** to dodge
JOULE	*n* pl. **-S** a unit of energy
JOUNCE	*v* **JOUNCED, JOUNCING, JOUNCES** to move roughly up and down
JOUNCY	*adj* **JOUNCIER, JOUNCIEST** marked by a jouncing motion
JOURNAL	*v* **-ED, -ING, -S** to enter in a daily record
JOURNEY	*v* **-ED, -ING, -S** to travel
JOURNO	*n* pl. **-NOS** a writer for a news medium
JOUST	*v* **-ED, -ING, -S** to engage in personal combat
JOUSTER	*n* pl. **-S** one that jousts
JOVIAL	*adj* good-humored **JOVIALLY** *adv*
JOVIALTY	*n* pl. **-TIES** the quality or state of being jovial
JOW	*v* **-ED, -ING, -S** to toll
JOWAR	*n* pl. **-S** a durra grown in India
JOWL	*n* pl. **-S** the fleshy part under the lower jaw **JOWLED** *adj*
JOWLY	*adj* **JOWLIER, JOWLIEST** having prominent jowls
JOY	*v* **-ED, -ING, -S** to rejoice
JOYANCE	*n* pl. **-S** gladness

JOYFUL	*adj* **-FULLER, -FULLEST** happy **JOYFULLY** *adv*
JOYLESS	*adj* being without gladness
JOYOUS	*adj* joyful **JOYOUSLY** *adv*
JOYPAD	*n* pl. **-S** a device with buttons to control computer images
JOYPOP	*v* **-POPPED, -POPPING, -POPS** to use habit-forming drugs occasionally
JOYRIDE	*v* **-RODE, -RIDDEN, -RIDING, -RIDES** to take an automobile ride for pleasure
JOYRIDER	*n* pl. **-S** one that joyrides
JOYSTICK	*n* pl. **-S** the control stick in an airplane
JUBA	*n* pl. **-S** a lively dance
JUBBAH	*n* pl. **-S** a loose outer garment
JUBE	*n* pl. **-S** a platform in a church
JUBHAH	*n* pl. **-S** jubbah
JUBILANT	*adj* exultant
JUBILATE	*v* **-LATED, -LATING, -LATES** to exult
JUBILE	*n* pl. **-S** jubilee
JUBILEE	*n* pl. **-S** a celebration
JUCO	*n* pl. **-COS** a junior college
JUDAS	*n* pl. **-ES** a peephole
JUDDER	*v* **-ED, -ING, -S** to vibrate
JUDDERY	*adj* vibrating
JUDGE	*v* **JUDGED, JUDGING, JUDGES** to decide on critically
JUDGER	*n* pl. **-S** one that judges
JUDGMENT	*n* pl. **-S** an authoritative opinion
JUDICARE	*n* pl. **-S** legal aid whereby lawyers are paid by the government for services to poor clients
JUDICIAL	*adj* pertaining to courts of law
JUDIES	pl. of judy
JUDO	*n* pl. **-DOS** a form of jujitsu
JUDOIST	*n* pl. **-S** one skilled in judo
JUDOKA	*n* pl. **-S** a judoist
JUDY	*n* pl. **JUDIES** a woman
JUG	*v* **JUGGED, JUGGING, JUGS** to put into a jug (a large, deep container with a narrow mouth and a handle)
JUGA	a pl. of jugum
JUGAL	*adj* pertaining to the cheek or cheekbone
JUGATE	*adj* occurring in pairs
JUGFUL	*n* pl. **JUGFULS** or **JUGSFUL** as much as a jug will hold
JUGGED	past tense of jug
JUGGING	present participle of jug
JUGGLE	*v* **-GLED, -GLING, -GLES** to perform feats of manual dexterity
JUGGLER	*n* pl. **-S** one that juggles
JUGGLERY	*n* pl. **-GLERIES** the art of a juggler
JUGGLING	*n* pl. **-S** jugglery
JUGHEAD	*n* pl. **-S** a dolt
JUGSFUL	a pl. of jugful
JUGULA	pl. of jugulum
JUGULAR	*n* pl. **-S** a vein of the neck
JUGULATE	*v* **-LATED, -LATING, -LATES** to suppress a disease by extreme measures
JUGULUM	*n* pl. **-LA** a part of a bird's neck
JUGUM	*n* pl. **-GUMS** or **-GA** a pair of the opposite leaflets of a pinnate leaf
JUICE	*v* **JUICED, JUICING, JUICES** to extract the juice (the liquid part of a fruit or vegetable) from
JUICER	*n* pl. **-S** a juice extractor
JUICY	*adj* **JUICIER, JUICIEST** full of juice **JUICILY** *adv*
JUJITSU	*n* pl. **-S** a Japanese art of self-defense
JUJU	*n* pl. **-S** an object regarded as having magical power
JUJUBE	*n* pl. **-S** a fruit-flavored candy
JUJUISM	*n* pl. **-S** the system of beliefs connected with jujus
JUJUIST	*n* pl. **-S** a follower of jujuism
JUJUTSU	*n* pl. **-S** jujitsu
JUKE	*v* **JUKED, JUKING, JUKES** to fake out of position
JUKEBOX	*n* pl. **-ES** a coin-operated phonograph
JUKU	*n* pl. **-S** an additional school in Japan for preparing students for college
JULEP	*n* pl. **-S** a sweet drink
JULIENNE	*v* **-ENNED, -ENNING, -ENNES** to cut food into long thin strips
JUMAR	*v* **-MARED, -MARING, -MARS** or **-MARRED, -MARRING, -MARS** to climb with ropes using a type of clamp
JUMBAL	*n* pl. **-S** a ring-shaped cookie
JUMBIE	*n* pl. **-S** a spirit of a dead person

JUMBLE   v **-BLED, -BLING, -BLES** to mix in a disordered manner

JUMBLER   n pl. **-S** one that jumbles

JUMBO   n pl. **-BOS** a very large specimen of its kind

JUMBUCK   n pl. **-S** a sheep

JUMP   v **-ED, -ING, -S** to spring off the ground **JUMPABLE** adj

JUMPER   n pl. **-S** one that jumps

JUMPING   n pl. **-S** the act of one that jumps

JUMPOFF   n pl. **-S** a starting point

JUMPROPE   n pl. **-S** a rope used in children's games for jumping

JUMPSHOT   n pl. **-S** a type of shot in basketball

JUMPSIES   n/pl a game involving jumping over a taut rope

JUMPSUIT   n pl. **-S** a one-piece garment

JUMPY   adj **JUMPIER, JUMPIEST** nervous **JUMPILY** adv

JUN   n pl. **JUN** a coin of North Korea

JUNCO   n pl. **-COS** or **-COES** a small finch

JUNCTION   n pl. **-S** a place where things join

JUNCTURE   n pl. **-S** the act of joining

JUNGLE   n pl. **-S** land covered with dense tropical vegetation **JUNGLED** adj

JUNGLIST   n pl. **-S** a performer of a style of fast dance music

JUNGLY   adj **-GLIER, -GLIEST** resembling a jungle

JUNIOR   n pl. **-S** a person who is younger than another

JUNIPER   n pl. **-S** an evergreen tree

JUNK   v **-ED, -ING, -S** to discard as trash

JUNKER   n pl. **-S** something ready for junking

JUNKET   v **-ED, -ING, -S** to banquet

JUNKETER   n pl. **-S** one that junkets

JUNKIE   n pl. **-S** a drug addict

JUNKMAN   n pl. **-MEN** one who buys and sells junk

JUNKY   adj **JUNKIER, JUNKIEST** worthless

JUNKYARD   n pl. **-S** a place where junk is stored

JUNTA   n pl. **-S** a political or governmental council

JUNTO   n pl. **-TOS** a political faction

JUPE   n pl. **-S** a woman's jacket

JUPON   n pl. **-S** a tunic

JURA   pl. of jus

JURAL   adj pertaining to law **JURALLY** adv

JURANT   n pl. **-S** one that takes an oath

JURAT   n pl. **-S** a statement on an affidavit

JURATORY   adj pertaining to an oath

JUREL   n pl. **-S** a food fish

JURIDIC   adj pertaining to the law

JURIST   n pl. **-S** one versed in the law **JURISTIC** adj

JUROR   n pl. **-S** a member of a jury (a committee for selecting material for exhibition)

JURY   v **-RIED, -RYING, -RIES** to select material for exhibition

JURYLESS   adj being without a jury

JURYMAN   n pl. **-MEN** a juror

JUS   n pl. **JURA** a legal right

JUSSIVE   n pl. **-S** a word used to express command

JUST   adj **JUSTER, JUSTEST** acting in conformity with what is morally good

JUST   v **-ED, -ING, -S** to joust

JUSTER   n pl. **-S** jouster

JUSTICE   n pl. **-S** a judge

JUSTIFY   v **-FIED, -FYING, -FIES** to show to be just, right, or valid

JUSTLE   v **-TLED, -TLING, -TLES** to jostle

JUSTLY   adv in a just manner

JUSTNESS   n pl. **-ES** the quality of being just

JUT   v **JUTTED, JUTTING, JUTS** to protrude

JUTE   n pl. **-S** a strong, coarse fiber

JUTELIKE   adj resembling jute

JUTTY   v **-TIED, -TYING, -TIES** to jut

JUVENAL   n pl. **-S** a young bird's plumage

JUVENILE   n pl. **-S** a young person

JUVIE   n pl. **-S** a juvenile delinquent

KA — *n* pl. **-S** the spiritual self of a human being in Egyptian religion

KAAS — *n* pl. **KAAS** kas

KAB — *n* pl. **-S** an ancient Hebrew unit of measure

KABAB — *n* pl. **-S** kabob

KABADDI — *n* pl. **-S** a tackling sport of South Asia played by two teams

KABAKA — *n* pl. **-S** a Ugandan emperor

KABALA — *n* pl. **-S** cabala

KABALISM — *n* pl. **-S** cabalism

KABALIST — *n* pl. **-S** cabalist

KABAR — *n* pl. **-S** caber

KABAYA — *n* pl. **-S** a cotton jacket

KABBALA — *n* pl. **-S** cabala

KABBALAH — *n* pl. **-S** cabala

KABELJOU — *n* pl. **-S** a large food fish

KABIKI — *n* pl. **-S** a tropical tree

KABLOOEY — *interj* — used to indicate an abrupt happening

KABLOOIE — *interj* kablooey

KABLOONA — *n* pl. **KABLOONAS** or **KABLOONAT** a person who is not an Inuit

KABOB — *n* pl. **-S** cubes of meat cooked on a skewer

KABOCHA — *n* pl. **-S** a type of Japanese pumpkin or squash

KABOODLE — *n* pl. **-S** caboodle

KABOOM — *n* pl. **-S** the sound of a loud explosion

KABUKI — *n* pl. **-S** a form of Japanese theater

KACHINA — *n* pl. **-S** an ancestral spirit

KADDISH — *n* pl. **-DISHES** or **-DISHIM** a Jewish prayer

KADI — *n* pl. **-S** cadi

KAE — *n* pl. **-S** a bird resembling a crow

KAF — *n* pl. **-S** kaph

KAFFIR — *n* pl. **-S** kafir

KAFFIYAH — *n* pl. **-S** kaffiyeh

KAFFIYEH — *n* pl. **-S** a large, square kerchief

KAFIR — *n* pl. **-S** a cereal grass

KAFTAN — *n* pl. **-S** caftan

KAFUFFLE — *n* pl. **-S** a disturbance or commotion

KAGU — *n* pl. **-S** a flightless bird

KAHUNA — *n* pl. **-S** a medicine man

KAIAK — *n* pl. **-S** kayak

KAIF — *n* pl. **-S** kef

KAIL — *n* pl. **-S** kale

KAILYARD — *n* pl. **-S** kaleyard

KAIN — *n* pl. **-S** a tax paid in produce or livestock

KAINIT — *n* pl. **-S** kainite

KAINITE — *n* pl. **-S** a mineral salt

KAISER — *n* pl. **-S** an emperor

KAISERIN — *n* pl. **-S** a kaiser's wife

KAIZEN — *n* pl. **-S** a Japanese business practice of continuous improvement

KAJEPUT — *n* pl. **-S** cajuput

KAKA — *n* pl. **-S** a parrot

KAKAPO — *n* pl. **-POS** a flightless parrot

KAKEMONO — *n* pl. **-NOS** a Japanese scroll

KAKI — *n* pl. **-S** a Japanese tree

KAKIEMON — *n* pl. **-S** a Japanese porcelain

KAKIVAK — *n* pl. **-S** a fish spear used by the Inuits

KALAM — *n* pl. **-S** a type of Muslim theology

KALAMATA — *n* pl. **-S** a black olive grown in Greece

KALE — *n* pl. **-S** a variety of cabbage

KALENDS — *n* pl. **KALENDS** calends

KALEWIFE — *n* pl. **-WIVES** a female vegetable vendor

KALEYARD *n* pl. **-S** a kitchen garden

KALIAN *n* pl. **-S** a hookah

KALIF *n* pl. **-S** caliph

KALIFATE *n* pl. **-S** califate

KALIMBA *n* pl. **-S** an African musical instrument

KALIPH *n* pl. **-S** caliph

KALIUM *n* pl. **-S** potassium

KALLIDIN *n* pl. **-S** a hormone

KALMIA *n* pl. **-S** an evergreen shrub

KALONG *n* pl. **-S** a fruit-eating bat

KALPA *n* pl. **-S** a period of time in Hindu religion

KALPAC *n* pl. **-S** calpac

KALPAK *n* pl. **-S** calpac

KALYPTRA *n* pl. **-S** a thin veil

KAMAAINA *n* pl. **-S** a longtime resident of Hawaii

KAMACITE *n* pl. **-S** an alloy of nickel and iron

KAMALA *n* pl. **-S** an Asian tree

KAME *n* pl. **-S** a mound of detrital material

KAMEEZ *n* pl. **-ES** a long tunic worn by some people of India

KAMI *n* pl. **KAMI** a sacred power or force

KAMIK *n* pl. **-S** a type of boot

KAMIKAZE *n* pl. **-S** a plane to be flown in a suicide crash on a target

KAMOTIK *n* pl. **-S** komatik

KAMOTIQ *n* pl. **-S** komatik

KAMPONG *n* pl. **-S** a small village

KAMSEEN *n* pl. **-S** khamsin

KAMSIN *n* pl. **-S** khamsin

KANA *n* pl. **-S** the Japanese syllabic script

KANBAN *n* pl. **-S** a manufacturing strategy wherein parts are delivered only as needed

KANE *n* pl. **-S** kain

KANGAROO *n* pl. **-ROOS** an Australian mammal

KANJI *n* pl. **-S** a system of Japanese writing

KANTAR *n* pl. **-S** a unit of weight

KANTELE *n* pl. **-S** a type of harp

KANZU *n* pl. **-S** a long white garment worn in Africa

KAOLIANG *n* pl. **-S** an Asian sorghum

KAOLIN *n* pl. **-S** a fine white clay **KAOLINIC** *adj*

KAOLINE *n* pl. **-S** kaolin

KAON *n* pl. **-S** a type of meson **KAONIC** *adj*

KAPA *n* pl. **-S** a coarse cloth

KAPEYKA *n* pl. **KAPEEK** a monetary unit of Belarus

KAPH *n* pl. **-S** a Hebrew letter

KAPOK *n* pl. **-S** a mass of silky fibers

KAPOW *n* pl. **-S** a sudden sharp sound

KAPPA *n* pl. **-S** a Greek letter

KAPU *n* pl. **-S** a Hawaiian set of rules for daily life

KAPUT *adj* ruined

KAPUTT *adj* kaput

KARAHI *n* pl. **-S** a small frying pan used in India

KARAKUL *n* pl. **-S** an Asian sheep

KARAOKE *n* pl. **-S** a musical device to which a user sings along

KARAT *n* pl. **-S** a unit of quality for gold

KARATE *n* pl. **-S** a Japanese art of self-defense

KARMA *n* pl. **-S** the force generated by a person's actions **KARMIC** *adj*

KARN *n* pl. **-S** cairn

KAROO *n* pl. **-ROOS** karroo

KAROSS *n* pl. **-ES** an African garment

KARRI *n* pl. **-S** an Australian eucalyptus

KARROO *n* pl. **-ROOS** a dry plateau

KARST *n* pl. **-S** a limestone region **KARSTIC** *adj*

KART *n* pl. **-S** a small motor vehicle

KARTING *n* pl. **-S** the sport of racing karts

KARYOTIN *n* pl. **-S** the nuclear material of a cell

KAS *n* pl. **KAS** a large cupboard

KASBAH *n* pl. **-S** casbah

KASHA *n* pl. **-S** a cooked cereal

KASHER *v* **-ED, -ING, -S** to kosher

KASHMIR *n* pl. **-S** cashmere

KASHRUT *n* pl. **-S** kashruth

KASHRUTH *n* pl. **-S** the Jewish dietary laws

KAT *n* pl. **-S** an evergreen shrub

KATA *n* pl. **-S** an exercise of set movements

KATAKANA *n* pl. **-S** a Japanese syllabic symbol

KATANA *n* pl. **-S** a Japanese single-edged sword

KATCHINA *n* pl. **-S** kachina

KATCINA *n* pl. **-S** kachina

KATHODE *n* pl. **-S** cathode **KATHODAL, KATHODIC** *adj*

KATHUMP *n* pl. **-S** a loud thudding sound

KATION *n* pl. **-S** cation

KATSINA *n* pl. **-NAM** or **-NAS** kachina

KATSURA *n* pl. **-S** a deciduous tree of Japan and China

KATYDID *n* pl. **-S** a grasshopper

KAURI *n* pl. **-S** a timber tree

KAURY *n* pl. **-RIES** kauri

KAVA *n* pl. **-S** a tropical shrub

KAVAKAVA *n* pl. **-S** kava

KAVASS *n* pl. **-ES** a Turkish policeman

KAY *n* pl. **KAYS** the letter K

KAYAK *v* **-ED, -ING, -S** to travel in a kayak (an Inuit canoe)

KAYAKER *n* pl. **-S** one that rides in a kayak

KAYAKING *n* pl. **-S** the act or skill of managing a kayak

KAYLES *n/pl* a British game

KAYO *v* **-ED, -ING, -S** or **-ES** to knock out

KAZACHOC *n* pl. **-S** kazachok

KAZACHOK *n* pl. **-ZACHKI** a Russian folk dance

KAZATSKI *n* pl. **-ES** kazachok

KAZATSKY *n* pl. **-SKIES** kazachok

KAZOO *n* pl. **-ZOOS** a toy musical instrument

KBAR *n* pl. **-S** a kilobar

KEA *n* pl. **-S** a parrot

KEBAB *n* pl. **-S** kabob

KEBAR *n* pl. **-S** caber

KEBBIE *n* pl. **-S** a rough walking stick

KEBBOCK *n* pl. **-S** kebbuck

KEBBUCK *n* pl. **-S** a whole cheese

KEBLAH *n* pl. **-S** kiblah

KEBOB *n* pl. **-S** kabob

KECK *v* **-ED, -ING, -S** to retch

KECKLE *v* **-LED, -LING, -LES** to wind with rope to prevent chafing

KEDDAH *n* pl. **-S** an enclosure for elephants

KEDGE *v* **KEDGED, KEDGING, KEDGES** to move a vessel with the use of an anchor

KEDGEREE *n* pl. **-S** a food in India

KEEF *n* pl. **-S** kef

KEEK *v* **-ED, -ING, -S** to peep

KEEL *v* **-ED, -ING, -S** to capsize

KEELAGE *n* pl. **-S** the amount paid to keep a boat in a harbor

KEELBOAT *n* pl. **-S** a freight boat

KEELHALE *v* **-HALED, -HALING, -HALES** to keelhaul

KEELHAUL *v* **-ED, -ING, -S** to rebuke severely

KEELLESS *adj* having no keel (the main structural part of a ship)

KEELSON *n* pl. **-S** a beam in a ship

KEEN *adj* **KEENER, KEENEST** enthusiastic

KEEN *v* **-ED, -ING, -S** to wail loudly over the dead

KEENER *n* pl. **-S** one that keens

KEENING *n* pl. **-S** the act of wailing loudly over the dead

KEENLY *adv* in a keen manner

KEENNESS *n* pl. **-ES** sharpness

KEEP *v* **KEPT, KEEPING, KEEPS** to continue to possess **KEEPABLE** *adj*

KEEPER *n* pl. **-S** one that keeps

KEEPING *n* pl. **-S** custody

KEEPSAKE *n* pl. **-S** a memento

KEESHOND *n* pl. **-HONDS** or **-HONDEN** a small, heavy-coated dog

KEESTER *n* pl. **-S** keister

KEET *n* pl. **-S** a young guinea fowl

KEEVE *n* pl. **-S** a tub or vat

KEF *n* pl. **-S** hemp smoked to produce euphoria

KEFFIYAH *n* pl. **-S** kaffiyeh

KEFFIYEH *n* pl. **-S** kaffiyeh

KEFIR *n* pl. **-S** a fermented beverage made from cow's milk

KEG *v* **KEGGED, KEGGING, KEGS** to store in a keg (a small barrel)

KEGELER *n* pl. **-S** kegler

KEGGER *n* pl. **-S** a party having one or more kegs of beer

KEGLER *n* pl. **-S** a bowler

KEGLING *n* pl. **-S** bowling

KEIR   *n* pl. **-S** kier

KEIRETSU   *n* pl. **-S** a coalition of business groups in Japan

KEISTER   *n* pl. **-S** the buttocks

KEITLOA   *n* pl. **-S** a rhinoceros

KELEP   *n* pl. **-S** a stinging ant

KELIM   *n* pl. **-S** kilim

KELLY   *n* pl. **-LIES** a bright green color

KELOID   *n* pl. **-S** a scar caused by excessive growth of fibrous tissue **KELOIDAL** *adj*

KELP   *v* **-ED, -ING, -S** to burn a type of seaweed

KELPFISH   *n* pl. **-ES** a fish that lives among seaweed

KELPIE   *n* pl. **-S** a water sprite

KELPY   *n* pl. **-PIES** kelpie

KELSON   *n* pl. **-S** keelson

KELT   *n* pl. **-S** a salmon that has spawned

KELTER   *n* pl. **-S** kilter

KELVIN   *n* pl. **-S** a unit of temperature

KEMP   *n* pl. **-S** a champion

KEMPT   *adj* neatly kept

KEMPY   *adj* **KEMPIER, KEMPIEST** having coarse hair or fibers

KEN   *v* **KENNED** or **KENT, KENNING, KENS** to know

KENAF   *n* pl. **-S** an East Indian plant

KENCH   *n* pl. **-ES** a bin for salting fish

KENDO   *n* pl. **-DOS** a Japanese sport

KENDOIST   *n* pl. **-S** one skilled in kendo

KENNED   a past tense of ken

KENNEL   *v* **-NELED, -NELING, -NELS** or **-NELLED, -NELLING, -NELS** to keep in a shelter for dogs

KENNING   *n* pl. **-S** a metaphorical compound word or phrase

KENO   *n* pl. **-NOS** a game of chance

KENOSIS   *n* pl. **-SISES** the incarnation of Christ **KENOTIC** *adj*

KENOTRON   *n* pl. **-S** a type of diode

KENT   a past tense of ken

KENTE   *n* pl. **-S** a colorful fabric made in Ghana

KEP   *v* **KEPPED, KEPPEN** or **KIPPEN, KEPPING, KEPS** to catch

KEPHALIN   *n* pl. **-S** cephalin

KEPI   *n* pl. **-S** a type of cap

KEPT   past tense of keep

KERAMIC   *n* pl. **-S** ceramic

KERATIN   *n* pl. **-S** a fibrous protein

KERATOID   *adj* horny

KERATOMA   *n* pl. **-MAS** or **-MATA** a skin disease

KERATOSE   *adj* of or resembling horny tissue

KERB   *v* **-ED, -ING, -S** to provide with curbing

KERBSIDE   *n* pl. **-S** curbside

KERCHIEF   *n* pl. **-CHIEFS** or **-CHIEVES** a cloth worn as a head covering

KERCHOO   *interj* ahchoo

KERF   *v* **-ED, -ING, -S** to make an incision with a cutting tool

KERMES   *n* pl. **KERMESES** a red dye

KERMESS   *n* pl. **-ES** kermis

KERMESSE   *n* pl. **-S** kermis

KERMIS   *n* pl. **-MISES** a festival

KERMODE   *n* pl. **-S** a type of black bear

KERN   *v* **-ED, -ING, -S** to be formed with a projecting typeface

KERNE   *n* pl. **-S** a medieval foot soldier

KERNEL   *v* **-NELED, -NELING, -NELS** or **-NELLED, -NELLING, -NELS** to envelop as a kernel (the inner part of a nut)

KERNELLY   *adj* resembling kernels

KERNING   *n* pl. **-S** the act of forming a projecting part of a typeface

KERNITE   *n* pl. **-S** a mineral

KEROGEN   *n* pl. **-S** a substance found in shale

KEROSENE   *n* pl. **-S** a fuel oil

KEROSINE   *n* pl. **-S** kerosene

KERPLUNK   *v* **-ED, -ING, -S** to fall or drop with a heavy sound

KERRIA   *n* pl. **-S** a Chinese shrub

KERRY   *n* pl. **-RIES** one of an Irish breed of cattle

KERSEY   *n* pl. **-SEYS** a woolen cloth

KERYGMA   *n* pl. **-MAS** or **-MATA** the preaching of the gospel

KESTREL   *n* pl. **-S** a small falcon

KETA   *n* pl. **-S** a type of salmon

KETAINE   *adj* being in poor taste

KETAMINE   *n* pl. **-S** a general anesthetic

KETCH   *n* pl. **-ES** a sailing vessel

KETCHUP	*n* pl. **-S** a spicy tomato sauce **KETCHUPY** *adj*
KETENE	*n* pl. **-S** a toxic gas
KETO	*adj* of or pertaining to ketone
KETOL	*n* pl. **-S** a chemical compound
KETONE	*n* pl. **-S** a type of chemical compound **KETONIC** *adj*
KETOSE	*n* pl. **-S** a simple sugar
KETOSIS	*n* pl. **-TOSES** a buildup of ketones in the body **KETOTIC** *adj*
KETTLE	*n* pl. **-S** a vessel for boiling liquids
KEVEL	*n* pl. **-S** a belaying cleat or peg
KEVIL	*n* pl. **-S** kevel
KEX	*n* pl. **-ES** a dry, hollow stalk
KEY	*v* **-ED, -ING, -S** to provide with a key (a device used to turn the bolt in a lock)
KEYBOARD	*v* **-ED, -ING, -S** to operate a machine by means of a keyset
KEYCARD	*n* pl. **-S** a coded card for operating a device
KEYER	*n* pl. **-S** a device that turns an electronic circuit on or off
KEYFRAME	*n* pl. **-S** the frozen image in a sequence of animation
KEYHOLE	*n* pl. **-S** a hole for a key
KEYLESS	*adj* being without a key
KEYNOTE	*v* **-NOTED, -NOTING, -NOTES** to deliver the main speech at a function
KEYNOTER	*n* pl. **-S** one that keynotes
KEYPAD	*n* pl. **-S** a small keyboard
KEYPAL	*n* pl. **-S** a person with whom one corresponds by email
KEYPRESS	*n* pl. **-ES** a single depression of a key on a keyset
KEYPUNCH	*v* **-ED, -ING, -ES** to perforate with a machine
KEYSET	*n* pl. **-S** a system of finger levers
KEYSTER	*n* pl. **-S** keister
KEYSTONE	*n* pl. **-S** the central stone of an arch
KEYWAY	*n* pl. **-WAYS** a slot for a key
KEYWORD	*n* pl. **-S** a significant word
KHADDAR	*n* pl. **-S** a cotton cloth
KHADI	*n* pl. **-S** khaddar
KHAF	*n* pl. **-S** kaph
KHAKI	*n* pl. **-S** a durable cloth
KHALIF	*n* pl. **-S** caliph
KHALIFA	*n* pl. **-S** caliph
KHAMSEEN	*n* pl. **-S** khamsin
KHAMSIN	*n* pl. **-S** a hot, dry wind
KHAN	*n* pl. **-S** an Asian ruler
KHANATE	*n* pl. **-S** the domain of a khan
KHAPH	*n* pl. **-S** kaph
KHAT	*n* pl. **-S** kat
KHAZEN	*n* pl. **-ZENS** or **-ZENIM** hazzan
KHEDA	*n* pl. **-S** keddah
KHEDAH	*n* pl. **-S** keddah
KHEDIVE	*n* pl. **-S** a Turkish viceroy **KHEDIVAL** *adj*
KHET	*n* pl. **-S** heth
KHETH	*n* pl. **-S** heth
KHI	*n* pl. **-S** chi
KHIRKAH	*n* pl. **-S** a patchwork garment
KHOUM	*n* pl. **-S** a monetary unit of Mauritania
KI	*n* pl. **KIS** qi
KIACK	*n* pl. **-S** a fish of the herring family
KIANG	*n* pl. **-S** a wild ass
KIAUGH	*n* pl. **-S** trouble; worry
KIBBE	*n* pl. **-S** a Near Eastern dish of ground lamb and bulgur
KIBBEH	*n* pl. **-S** kibbe
KIBBI	*n* pl. **-S** kibbe
KIBBITZ	*v* **-ED, -ING, -ES** to kibitz
KIBBLE	*v* **-BLED, -BLING, -BLES** to grind coarsely
KIBBUTZ	*n* pl. **-BUTZIM** a collective farm in Israel
KIBE	*n* pl. **-S** a sore caused by exposure to cold
KIBEI	*n* pl. **-S** one born in America of immigrant Japanese parents and educated in Japan
KIBITKA	*n* pl. **-S** a type of Russian sled or wagon
KIBITZ	*v* **-ED, -ING, -ES** to meddle
KIBITZER	*n* pl. **-S** one that kibitzes
KIBLA	*n* pl. **-S** kiblah
KIBLAH	*n* pl. **-S** the direction toward which Muslims face while praying
KIBOSH	*v* **-ED, -ING, -ES** to stop
KICK	*v* **-ED, -ING, -S** to strike out with the foot or feet **KICKABLE** *adj*
KICKBACK	*n* pl. **-S** a strong reaction
KICKBALL	*n* pl. **-S** baseball using an inflated ball that is kicked

KICKBOX v **-ED, -ING, -ES** to box in a style that allows kicking

KICKER n pl. **-S** one that kicks

KICKIER comparative of kicky

KICKIEST superlative of kicky

KICKING n pl. **-S** the act of striking with the foot

KICKOFF n pl. **-S** the kick that begins play in football

KICKSHAW n pl. **-S** a trifle or trinket

KICKUP n pl. **-S** a noisy argument

KICKY adj **KICKIER, KICKIEST** exciting

KID v **KIDDED, KIDDING, KIDS** to tease

KIDDER n pl. **-S** one that kids

KIDDIE n pl. **-S** a small child

KIDDIES pl. of kiddy

KIDDING present participle of kid

KIDDISH adj childish

KIDDO n pl. **-DOS** or **-DOES** — used as a form of familiar address

KIDDUSH n pl. **-ES** a Jewish prayer

KIDDY n pl. **-DIES** kiddie

KIDLIKE adj resembling a child

KIDLIT n pl. **-S** literature for children

KIDNAP v **-NAPED, -NAPING, -NAPS** or **-NAPPED, -NAPPING, -NAPS** to take a person by force and often for ransom

KIDNAPEE n pl. **-S** one that is kidnaped

KIDNAPER n pl. **-S** one that kidnaps

KIDNAPPER n pl. **-S** kidnaper

KIDNAPPING present participle of kidnap

KIDNEY n pl. **-NEYS** a bodily organ

KIDSKIN n pl. **-S** a type of leather

KIDVID n pl. **-S** television programs for children

KIEF n pl. **-S** kef

KIELBASA n pl. **-BASAS, -BASI** or **-BASY** a smoked sausage

KIER n pl. **-S** a vat for boiling and dyeing fabrics

KIESTER n pl. **-S** keister

KIF n pl. **-S** kef

KIKUYU n pl. **-S** a type of grass

KILIM n pl. **-S** an oriental tapestry

KILL v **-ED, -ING, -S** to cause to die
KILLABLE adj

KILLDEE n pl. **-S** killdeer

KILLDEER n pl. **-S** a wading bird

KILLER n pl. **-S** one that kills

KILLICK n pl. **-S** a small anchor

KILLIE n pl. **-S** a freshwater fish

KILLING n pl. **-S** a sudden notable success

KILLJOY n pl. **-JOYS** one who spoils the fun of others

KILLOCK n pl. **-S** killick

KILN v **-ED, -ING, -S** to bake in a type of oven

KILO n pl. **KILOS** a kilogram or kilometer

KILOBAR n pl. **-S** a unit of atmospheric pressure

KILOBASE n pl. **-S** unit of measure of a nucleic-acid chain

KILOBAUD n pl. **-S** a unit of data transmission speed

KILOBIT n pl. **-S** a unit of computer information

KILOBYTE n pl. **-S** 1,024 bytes

KILOGRAM n pl. **-S** a unit of mass and weight

KILOMOLE n pl. **-S** one thousand moles

KILORAD n pl. **-S** a unit of nuclear radiation

KILOTON n pl. **-S** a unit of weight

KILOVOLT n pl. **-S** a unit of electromotive force

KILOWATT n pl. **-S** a unit of power

KILT v **-ED, -ING, -S** to make creases or pleats in

KILTER n pl. **-S** good condition

KILTIE n pl. **-S** one who wears a kilt (a type of skirt)

KILTING n pl. **-S** an arrangement of kilt pleats

KILTLIKE adj resembling a kilt

KILTY n pl. **KILTIES** kiltie

KIMCHEE n pl. **-S** kimchi

KIMCHI n pl. **-S** a spicy Korean dish of pickled cabbage

KIMONO n pl. **-NOS** a loose robe
KIMONOED adj

KIN n pl. **-S** a group of persons of common ancestry

KINA n pl. **-S** a monetary unit of Papua New Guinea

KINARA n pl. **-S** a candelabra with seven candlesticks

KINASE n pl. **-S** an enzyme

KIND   adj **KINDER, KINDEST** having a gentle, giving nature

KIND   n pl. **-S** a class of similar or related objects or individuals

KINDLE   v **-DLED, -DLING, -DLES** to cause to burn

KINDLER   n pl. **-S** one that kindles

KINDLESS   adj lacking kindness

KINDLING   n pl. **-S** material that is easily ignited

KINDLY   adj **-LIER, -LIEST** kind

KINDNESS   n pl. **-ES** the quality of being kind

KINDRED   n pl. **-S** a natural grouping

KINE   n pl. **-S** a type of television tube

KINEMA   n pl. **-S** cinema

KINESIC   adj pertaining to kinesics

KINESICS   n/pl the study of body motion in relation to communication

KINESIS   n pl. **-NESES** a type of movement

KINETIC   adj pertaining to motion

KINETICS   n/pl a branch of science dealing with motion

KINETIN   n pl. **-S** a substance that increases plant growth

KINFOLK   n/pl relatives

KINFOLKS   n/pl kinfolk

KING   v **-ED, -ING, -S** to reign as king (a male monarch)

KINGBIRD   n pl. **-S** an American bird

KINGBOLT   n pl. **-S** a kingpin

KINGCUP   n pl. **-S** a marsh plant

KINGDOM   n pl. **-S** the area ruled by a king

KINGFISH   n pl. **-ES** a marine food fish

KINGHOOD   n pl. **-S** the office of a king

KINGLESS   adj having no king

KINGLET   n pl. **-S** a king who rules over a small area

KINGLIKE   adj resembling a king

KINGLY   adj **-LIER, -LIEST** of or befitting a king

KINGPIN   n pl. **-S** a central bolt connecting an axle to a vehicle

KINGPOST   n pl. **-S** a supporting structure of a roof

KINGSHIP   n pl. **-S** the power or position of a king

KINGSIDE   n pl. **-S** a part of a chessboard

KINGWOOD   n pl. **-S** a hardwood tree

KININ   n pl. **-S** a hormone

KINK   v **-ED, -ING, -S** to form a tight curl or bend in

KINKAJOU   n pl. **-S** an arboreal mammal

KINKY   adj **KINKIER, KINKIEST** tightly curled **KINKILY** adv

KINLESS   adj having no kin

KINO   n pl. **-NOS** a gum resin

KINSFOLK   n/pl kinfolk

KINSHIP   n pl. **-S** relationship

KINSMAN   n pl. **-MEN** a male relative

KIOSK   n pl. **-S** an open booth

KIP   v **KIPPED, KIPPING, KIPS** to sleep

KIPPA   n pl. **-S** a yarmulke

KIPPAH   n pl. **-S** kippa

KIPPEN   a past participle of kep

KIPPER   v **-ED, -ING, -S** to cure fish by salting and smoking

KIPPERER   n pl. **-S** one that kippers

KIPPING   present participle of kip

KIPSKIN   n pl. **-S** an animal hide that has not been tanned

KIR   n pl. **-S** an alcoholic beverage

KIRIGAMI   n pl. **-S** the Japanese art of folding paper

KIRK   n pl. **-S** a church

KIRKMAN   n pl. **-MEN** a member of a church

KIRMESS   n pl. **-ES** kermis

KIRN   v **-ED, -ING, -S** to churn

KIRPAN   n pl. **-S** a dagger carried by Sikhs

KIRSCH   n pl. **-ES** a kind of brandy

KIRTLE   n pl. **-S** a man's tunic or coat **KIRTLED** adj

KISHKA   n pl. **-S** kishke

KISHKE   n pl. **-S** a sausage

KISKADEE   n pl. **-S** a large flycatcher

KISMAT   n pl. **-S** kismet

KISMET   n pl. **-S** destiny **KISMETIC** adj

KISS   v **-ED, -ING, -ES** to touch with the lips as a sign of affection **KISSABLE** adj **KISSABLY** adv

KISSER   n pl. **-S** one that kisses

KISSY   adj **KISSIER, KISSIEST** inclined to kiss

KIST   n pl. **-S** a chest, box, or coffin

KISTFUL   n pl. **-S** as much as a kist can hold

KIT	v **KITTED, KITTING, KITS** to equip
KITBAG	n pl. **-S** a knapsack
KITCHEN	n pl. **-S** a room where food is cooked
KITE	v **KITED, KITING, KITES** to obtain money or credit fraudulently
KITELIKE	adj resembling a kite (a light, covered frame flown in the wind)
KITER	n pl. **-S** one that kites
KITH	n pl. **-S** one's friends and neighbors
KITHARA	n pl. **-S** cithara
KITHE	v **KITHED, KITHING, KITHES** to make known
KITING	n pl. **-S** the act of flying a kite
KITLING	n pl. **-S** a young animal
KITSCH	n pl. **-ES** garish art or literature
KITSCHY	adj **KITSCHIER, KITSCHIEST** garish; gaudy
KITTED	past tense of kit
KITTEL	n pl. **KITTEL** a Jewish ceremonial robe
KITTEN	v **-ED, -ING, -S** to bear kittens (young cats)
KITTIES	pl. of kitty
KITTING	present participle of kit
KITTLE	adj **-TLER, -TLEST** ticklish
KITTLE	v **-TLED, -TLING, -TLES** to tickle
KITTY	n pl. **-TIES** a kitten or cat
KIVA	n pl. **-S** an underground ceremonial chamber
KIWI	n pl. **-S** a flightless bird
KLATCH	n pl. **-ES** a social gathering
KLATSCH	n pl. **-ES** klatch
KLAVERN	n pl. **-S** a local branch of the Ku Klux Klan
KLAXON	n pl. **-S** a low-pitched horn
KLEAGLE	n pl. **-S** an official in the Ku Klux Klan
KLEPHT	n pl. **-S** a Greek guerrilla **KLEPHTIC** adj
KLEPTO	n pl. **-TOS** one that steals impulsively
KLEZMER	n pl. **-MERS** or **-MORIM** a Jewish folk musician
KLICK	n pl. **-S** a kilometer
KLIEG	n pl. **-S** an electric lamp used in filming
KLIK	n pl. **-S** klick
KLISTER	n pl. **-S** a wax for skis
KLONDIKE	n pl. **-S** a card game
KLONG	n pl. **-S** a canal
KLOOF	n pl. **-S** a ravine
KLUDGE	v **KLUDGED, KLUDGING, KLUDGES** to put together from ill-fitting components
KLUDGEY	adj **KLUDGIER, KLUDGIEST** kludgy
KLUDGY	adj **KLUDGIER, KLUDGIEST** involving or put together with ill-fitting components
KLUGE	v **KLUGED, KLUGING, KLUGES** to kludge
KLUTZ	n pl. **-ES** a clumsy person
KLUTZY	adj **KLUTZIER, KLUTZIEST** clumsy
KLYSTRON	n pl. **-S** a type of electron tube
KNACK	v **-ED, -ING, -S** to strike sharply
KNACKER	n pl. **-S** one that buys old livestock
KNACKERY	n pl. **-ERIES** the place of business of a knacker
KNAIDEL	n pl. **KNAIDLACH** or **KNAIDELS** a type of dumpling
KNAP	v **KNAPPED, KNAPPING, KNAPS** to strike sharply
KNAPPER	n pl. **-S** one that knaps
KNAPSACK	n pl. **-S** a bag carried on the back
KNAPWEED	n pl. **-S** a meadow plant
KNAR	n pl. **-S** a bump on a tree **KNARRED, KNARRY** adj
KNAUR	n pl. **-S** knar
KNAVE	n pl. **-S** a dishonest person **KNAVISH** adj
KNAVERY	n pl. **-ERIES** trickery
KNAWE	n pl. **-S** knawel
KNAWEL	n pl. **-S** a Eurasian plant
KNEAD	v **-ED, -ING, -S** to work into a uniform mixture with the hands
KNEADER	n pl. **-S** one that kneads
KNEE	v **KNEED, KNEEING, KNEES** to strike with the knee (a joint of the leg)
KNEECAP	v **-CAPPED, -CAPPING, -CAPS** to maim by shooting in the kneecap (a bone at the front of the knee)

KNEEHOLE	*n* pl. **-S** a space for the knees
KNEEL	*v* **KNELT** or **KNEELED, KNEELING, KNEELS** to rest on the knees
KNEELER	*n* pl. **-S** one that kneels
KNEEPAD	*n* pl. **-S** a covering for a knee
KNEEPAN	*n* pl. **-S** the kneecap
KNEESIES	*n/pl* the pressing of one's knees against another person's knees
KNEESOCK	*n* pl. **-S** a sock reaching up to the knee
KNEIDEL	*n* pl. **KNEIDLACH** or **KNEIDELS** knaidel
KNELL	*v* **-ED, -ING, -S** to sound a bell
KNELT	a past tense of kneel
KNESSET	*n* pl. **-S** the Israeli parliament
KNEW	past tense of know
KNICKERS	*n/pl* loose-fitting pants gathered at the knee
KNIFE	*n* pl. **KNIVES** a sharp-edged instrument used for cutting
KNIFE	*v* **KNIFED, KNIFING, KNIFES** to cut with a knife
KNIFER	*n* pl. **-S** one that knifes
KNIFING	*n* pl. **-S** the act of stabbing with a knife
KNIGHT	*v* **-ED, -ING, -S** to make a knight (a medieval gentleman-soldier) of
KNIGHTLY	*adj* of or befitting a knight
KNISH	*n* pl. **-ES** dough stuffed with filling and fried
KNIT	*v* **KNITTED, KNITTING, KNITS** to make a fabric or garment by joining loops of yarn
KNITBONE	*n* pl. **-S** a comfrey
KNITTER	*n* pl. **-S** one that knits
KNITTING	*n* pl. **-S** work done by a knitter
KNITWEAR	*n* pl. **KNITWEAR** knitted clothing
KNIVES	pl. of knife
KNOB	*v* **KNOBBED, KNOBBING, KNOBS** to provide with a knob (a rounded protuberance)
KNOBBLY	*adj* **-BLIER, -BLIEST** having very small knobs
KNOBBY	*adj* **-BIER, -BIEST** full of knobs
KNOBLIKE	*adj* resembling a knob
KNOCK	*v* **-ED, -ING, -S** to strike sharply
KNOCKER	*n* pl. **-S** one that knocks
KNOCKOFF	*n* pl. **-S** a copy that sells for less than the original
KNOCKOUT	*n* pl. **-S** a blow that induces unconsciousness
KNOLL	*v* **-ED, -ING, -S** to knell
KNOLLER	*n* pl. **-S** one that knolls
KNOLLY	*adj* hilly
KNOP	*n* pl. **-S** a knob **KNOPPED** *adj*
KNOSP	*n* pl. **-S** a knob
KNOT	*v* **KNOTTED, KNOTTING, KNOTS** to tie in a knot (a closed loop)
KNOTHEAD	*n* pl. **-S** a stupid person
KNOTHOLE	*n* pl. **-S** a hole in a plank
KNOTLESS	*adj* having no knots
KNOTLIKE	*adj* resembling a knot
KNOTTED	past tense of knot
KNOTTER	*n* pl. **-S** one that knots
KNOTTING	*n* pl. **-S** a fringe made of knotted threads
KNOTTY	*adj* **-TIER, -TIEST** full of knots **KNOTTILY** *adv*
KNOTWEED	*n* pl. **-S** a common weed
KNOUT	*v* **-ED, -ING, -S** to flog with a leather whip
KNOW	*v* **KNEW, KNOWN, KNOWING, KNOWS** to have a true understanding of **KNOWABLE** *adj*
KNOWER	*n* pl. **-S** one that knows
KNOWING	*adj* **-INGER, -INGEST** astute
KNOWING	*n* pl. **-S** knowledge
KNOWN	*n* pl. **-S** a mathematical quantity whose value is given
KNUBBY	*adj* **-BIER, -BIEST** nubby
KNUCKLE	*v* **-LED, -LING, -LES** to hit with the knuckles (the joints of the fingers)
KNUCKLER	*n* pl. **-S** a type of baseball pitch
KNUCKLY	*adj* **-LIER, -LIEST** having prominent knuckles
KNUR	*n* pl. **-S** a bump on a tree
KNURL	*v* **-ED, -ING, -S** to make grooves or ridges in
KNURLY	*adj* **KNURLIER, KNURLIEST** gnarly
KNURR	*n* pl. **-S** knur
KOA	*n* pl. **-S** a timber tree
KOALA	*n* pl. **-S** an Australian mammal

KOAN *n* pl. **-S** a paradox meditated on by Buddhist monks

KOB *n* pl. **-S** a reddish brown antelope

KOBO *n* pl. **-BOS** a monetary unit of Nigeria

KOBOLD *n* pl. **-S** an elf

KOCHIA *n* pl. **-S** a Eurasian plant

KOEL *n* pl. **-S** an Australian bird

KOFTA *n* pl. **-S** a spiced ball of meat or fish in Indian cooking

KOHL *n* pl. **-S** a type of eye makeup

KOHLRABI *n* pl. **-ES** a variety of cabbage

KOI *n* pl. **-S** a large and colorful fish

KOINE *n* pl. **-S** a type of dialect

KOJI *n* pl. **-S** a fungus used to start fermentation

KOKAM *n* pl. **-S** kokum

KOKANEE *n* pl. **-S** a food fish

KOKUM *n* pl. **-S** an East Indian tree

KOLA *n* pl. **-S** cola

KOLACKY *n* pl. **KOLACKY** a kind of pastry

KOLBASI *n* pl. **-S** kielbasa

KOLBASSA *n* pl. **-S** kielbasa

KOLBASSI *n* pl. **-S** kielbasa

KOLHOZ *n* pl. **-HOZES** or **-HOZY** kolkhoz

KOLINSKI *n* pl. **-ES** kolinsky

KOLINSKY *n* pl. **-SKIES** an Asian mink

KOLKHOS *n* pl. **-KHOSES** or **-KHOSY** kolkhoz

KOLKHOZ *n* pl. **-KHOZES** or **-KHOZY** a collective farm in Russia

KOLKOZ *n* pl. **-KOZES** or **-KOZY** kolkhoz

KOLO *n* pl. **-LOS** a European folk dance

KOMATIK *n* pl. **-S** an Inuit sledge

KOMBU *n* pl. **-S** kelp used in Japanese cooking

KOMONDOR *n* pl. **-DORS** or **-DOROK** or **-DOROCK** a large, shaggy-coated dog

KONGONI *n* pl. **KONGONI** an African antelope

KONK *v* **-ED, -ING, -S** to conk

KOODOO *n* pl. **-DOOS** kudu

KOOK *n* pl. **-S** an eccentric person

KOOKIE *adj* **KOOKIER, KOOKIEST** kooky

KOOKUM *n* pl. **-S** kokum

KOOKY *adj* **KOOKIER, KOOKIEST** eccentric **KOOKILY** *adv*

KOP *n* pl. **-S** a hill

KOPECK *n* pl. **-S** a Russian coin

KOPEK *n* pl. **-S** kopeck

KOPH *n* pl. **-S** a Hebrew letter

KOPIYKA *n* pl. **-S** a monetary unit of Ukraine

KOPJE *n* pl. **-S** a small hill

KOPPA *n* pl. **-S** a Greek letter

KOPPIE *n* pl. **-S** kopje

KOR *n* pl. **-S** a Hebrew unit of measure

KORA *n* pl. **-S** a stringed African musical instrument

KORAT *n* pl. **-S** a cat having a silver-blue coat

KORE *n* pl. **-RAI** an ancient Greek statue of a young woman

KORMA *n* pl. **-S** an Indian dish of meat or vegetables with spices

KORUNA *n* pl. **KORUNAS** or **KORUNY** or **KORUN** a monetary unit of the Czech Republic

KOS *n* pl. **KOS** a land measure in India

KOSHER *v* **-ED, -ING, -S** to make fit to be eaten according to Jewish dietary laws

KOSS *n* pl. **KOSS** kos

KOTO *n* pl. **-TOS** a musical instrument

KOTOW *v* **-ED, -ING, -S** to kowtow

KOTOWER *n* pl. **-S** one that kotows

KOUMIS *n* pl. **-MISES** koumiss

KOUMISS *n* pl. **-ES** a beverage made from camel's milk

KOUMYS *n* pl. **-ES** koumiss

KOUMYSS *n* pl. **-ES** koumiss

KOUPREY *n* pl. **-PREYS** a short-haired ox

KOUROS *n* pl. **-ROI** an ancient Greek statue of a young man

KOUSSO *n* pl. **-SOS** cusso

KOWTOW *v* **-ED, -ING, -S** to behave in a servile manner

KOWTOWER *n* pl. **-S** one that kowtows

KRAAL *v* **-ED, -ING, -S** to pen in a type of enclosure

KRAFT *n* pl. **-S** a strong paper

KRAI *n* pl. **-S** an administrative territory of Russia

KRAIT *n* pl. **-S** a venomous snake

KRAKEN *n* pl. **-S** a legendary sea monster

KRATER *n* pl. **-S** a type of vase

KRAUT *n* pl. **-S** sauerkraut

KRAY *n* pl. **KRAYS** krai

KREEP *n* pl. **-S** a basaltic lunar rock

KREMLIN *n* pl. **-S** a Russian citadel

KREPLACH *n* pl. **KREPLACH** dumplings filled with ground meat or cheese

KREPLECH *n* pl. **KREPLECH** kreplach

KREUTZER *n* pl. **-S** a former monetary unit of Austria

KREUZER *n* pl. **-S** kreutzer

KREWE *n* pl. **-S** a private group participating in the New Orleans Mardi Gras

KRILL *n* pl. **-S** an aggregate of small marine crustaceans

KRIMMER *n* pl. **-S** a kind of fur

KRIS *n* pl. **-ES** a short sword

KRONA *n* pl. **KRONOR** a monetary unit of Sweden

KRONA *n* pl. **KRONUR** a monetary unit of Iceland

KRONE *n* pl. **KRONEN** a former monetary unit of Austria

KRONE *n* pl. **KRONER** a monetary unit of Denmark

KRONOR pl. of krona

KRONUR pl. of krona

KROON *n* pl. **KROONS** or **KROONI** a former monetary unit of Estonia

KRUBI *n* pl. **-S** a tropical plant

KRUBUT *n* pl. **-S** krubi

KRULLER *n* pl. **-S** cruller

KRUMHORN *n* pl. **-S** crumhorn

KRUMKAKE *n* pl. **-S** a large thin cookie

KRYOLITE *n* pl. **-S** cryolite

KRYOLITH *n* pl. **-S** cryolite

KRYPTON *n* pl. **-S** a gaseous element

KUBASA *n* pl. **-S** a Ukrainian sausage

KUBIE *n* pl. **-S** a kubasa on a bun

KUCHEN *n* pl. **-S** a coffee cake

KUDLIK *n* pl. **-S** an Inuit oil lamp

KUDO *n* pl. **-DOS** award; honor

KUDU *n* pl. **-S** a large antelope

KUDZU *n* pl. **-S** an Asian vine

KUE *n* pl. **-S** the letter Q

KUFI *n* pl. **-S** a brimless hat

KUGEL *n* pl. **-S** a baked pudding of potatoes or noodles

KUKRI *n* pl. **-S** a long, curved knife of Nepal

KULAK *n* pl. **-LAKS** or **-LAKI** a rich Russian peasant

KULFI *n* pl. **-S** an Indian dessert resembling ice cream

KULTUR *n* pl. **-S** culture; civilization

KUMIS *n* pl. **-ES** koumiss

KUMISS *n* pl. **-ES** koumiss

KUMKUM *n* pl. **-S** a red powder used by Hindu women

KUMMEL *n* pl. **-S** a type of liqueur

KUMQUAT *n* pl. **-S** a citrus fruit

KUMYS *n* pl. **-ES** koumiss

KUNA *n* pl. **KUNE** a monetary unit of Croatia

KUNZITE *n* pl. **-S** a mineral

KURBASH *v* **-ED, -ING, -ES** to flog with a leather whip

KURGAN *n* pl. **-S** a mound of earth over a grave

KURTA *n* pl. **-S** a shirt worn in India

KURTOSIS *n* pl. **-TOSES** the relative degree of curvature in a statistical curve

KURU *n* pl. **-S** a disease of the nervous system

KURUSH *n* pl. **-ES** a monetary unit of Turkey

KUSSO *n* pl. **-SOS** cusso

KUVASZ *n* pl. **-VASZOK** a large dog having a white coat

KVAS *n* pl. **-ES** kvass

KVASS *n* pl. **-ES** a Russian beer

KVELL *v* **-ED, -ING, -S** to exclaim joyfully

KVETCH *v* **-ED, -ING, -ES** to complain

KVETCHER *n* pl. **-S** one that kvetches

KVETCHY *adj* **KVETCHIER, KVETCHIEST** habitually complaining

KWACHA *n* pl. **-S** a monetary unit of Malawi and Zambia

KWANZA *n* pl. **-S** a monetary unit of Angola

KYACK *n* pl. **-S** a packsack

KYAK *n* pl. **-S** a kayak (an Inuit canoe)

KYANISE *v* **-ISED, -ISING, -ISES** to kyanize

KYANITE *n* pl. **-S** cyanite **KYANITIC** *adj*

KYANIZE *v* **-IZED, -IZING, -IZES** to treat wood with a type of preservative

KYAR *n* pl. **-S** coir

KYAT *n* pl. **-S** a monetary unit of Myanmar (Burma)

KYBOSH   *v* **-ED, -ING, -ES** to kibosh

KYE   *n* pl. **-S** a private Korean-American banking club

KYLIN   *n* pl. **-S** a composite mythical animal

KYLIX   *n* pl. **-LIKES** or **-LIXES** a drinking vessel

KYMOGRAM   *n* pl. **-S** a record of fluid pressure

KYPHOSIS   *n* pl. **-PHOSES** abnormal curvature of the spine **KYPHOTIC** *adj*

KYRIE   *n* pl. **-S** a religious petition for mercy

KYTE   *n* pl. **-S** the stomach

KYTHE   *v* **KYTHED, KYTHING, KYTHES** to kithe

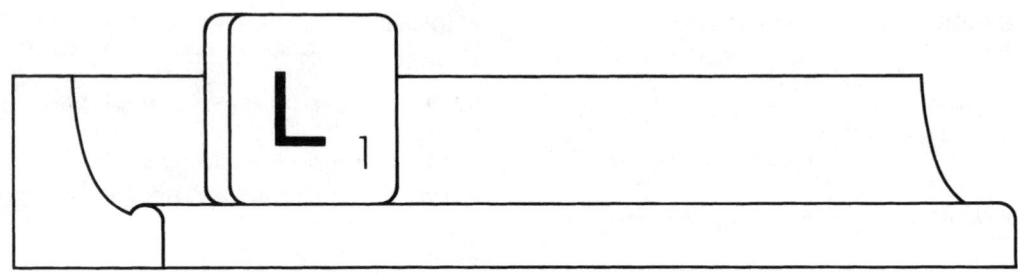

LA   *n* pl. **-S** the sixth tone of the diatonic musical scale

LAAGER   *v* **-ED, -ING, -S** to form a defensive encampment

LAARI   *n* pl. **-S** a monetary unit of the Maldives

LAB   *n* pl. **-S** a laboratory

LABARUM   *n* pl. **-RUMS** or **-RA** an ecclesiastical banner

LABDANUM   *n* pl. **-S** a fragrant resin

LABEL   *v* **-BELED, -BELING, -BELS** or **-BELLED, -BELLING, -BELS** to describe or designate

LABELER   *n* pl. **-S** one that labels

LABELLA   pl. of labellum

LABELLER   *n* pl. **-S** labeler

LABELLING   a present participle of label

LABELLUM   *n* pl. **-LA** the lower petal of an orchid

LABIA   pl. of labium

LABIAL   *n* pl. **-S** a labially produced sound

LABIALLY   *adv* by means of the lips

LABIATE   *n* pl. **-S** a labiated plant

LABIATED   *adj* having corollas that are divided into two liplike parts

LABILE   *adj* likely to change

LABILITY   *n* pl. **-TIES** the state of being labile

LABIUM   *n* pl. **-BIA** a fold of the vulva

LABOR   *v* **-ED, -ING, -S** to work

LABORER   *n* pl. **-S** one that labors

LABORITE   *n* pl. **-S** a supporter of labor interests

LABOUR   *v* **-ED, -ING, -S** to labor

LABOURER   *n* pl. **-S** laborer

LABRA   a pl. of labrum

LABRADOR   *n* pl. **-S** a hunting dog

LABRET   *n* pl. **-S** an ornament worn in a perforation of the lip

LABROID   *n* pl. **-S** a marine fish

LABRUM   *n* pl. **-BRUMS** or **-BRA** a lip or liplike structure **LABRAL** *adj*

LABRUSCA   *n* pl. **-S** a fox grape

LABURNUM   *n* pl. **-S** an ornamental tree

LAC   *n* pl. **-S** a resinous substance secreted by certain insects

LACE   *v* **LACED, LACING, LACES** to fasten by means of a lace (a cord for drawing together two edges)

LACELESS   *adj* lacking lace

LACELIKE   *adj* resembling lace

LACER   *n* pl. **-S** one that laces

LACERATE   *v* **-ATED, -ATING, -ATES** to tear roughly

LACERTID   *n* pl. **-S** a type of lizard

LACEWING   *n* pl. **-S** a winged insect

LACEWOOD   *n* pl. **-S** an Australian tree

LACEWORK   *n* pl. **-S** a delicate openwork fabric

LACEY   *adj* **LACIER, LACIEST** lacy

LACHES   *n* pl. **LACHES** undue delay in asserting a legal right

LACIER   comparative of lacy

LACIEST   superlative of lacy

LACILY   *adv* in a lacy manner

LACINESS   *n* pl. **-ES** the quality of being lacy

LACING   *n* pl. **-S** a contrasting marginal band of color

LACK   *v* **-ED, -ING, -S** to be without

LACKADAY   *interj* — used to express regret

LACKER   *v* **-ED, -ING, -S** to lacquer

LACKEY   *v* **-ED, -ING, -S** to act in a servile manner

LACONIC   *adj* using a minimum of words

LACONISM   *n* pl. **-S** brevity of expression

LACQUER   *v* **-ED, -ING, -S** to coat with a glossy substance

LACQUEY	*v* **-ED, -ING, -S** to lackey
LACRIMAL	*n* pl. **-S** a small bone of the eye socket
LACROSSE	*n* pl. **-S** a type of ball game
LACRYMAL	*n* pl. **-S** lacrimal
LACTAM	*n* pl. **-S** a chemical compound
LACTARY	*adj* pertaining to milk
LACTASE	*n* pl. **-S** an enzyme
LACTATE	*v* **-TATED, -TATING, -TATES** to secrete milk
LACTEAL	*n* pl. **-S** a lymphatic vessel
LACTEAN	*adj* lacteous
LACTEOUS	*adj* resembling milk
LACTIC	*adj* derived from milk
LACTITOL	*n* pl. **-S** an artificial sweetener
LACTONE	*n* pl. **-S** any of a group of esters **LACTONIC** *adj*
LACTOSE	*n* pl. **-S** a lactic sugar
LACUNA	*n* pl. **-NAS** or **-NAE** an empty space or missing part **LACUNAL, LACUNARY, LACUNATE** *adj*
LACUNAR	*n* pl. **-NARS** or **-NARIA** a ceiling with recessed panels
LACUNE	*n* pl. **-S** lacuna
LACUNOSE	*adj* marked by shallow depressions
LACY	*adj* **LACIER, LACIEST** resembling lacework
LAD	*n* pl. **-S** a boy or youth **LADDISH** *adj*
LADANUM	*n* pl. **-S** labdanum
LADDER	*v* **-ED, -ING, -S** to cause a run in a stocking
LADDIE	*n* pl. **-S** a lad
LADDISH	*adj* characteristic of boisterous lads
LADDISM	*n* pl. **-S** boisterous macho behavior by lads
LADDY	*adj* **LADDIER, LADDIEST** laddish in behavior
LADE	*v* **LADED, LADEN, LADING, LADES** to load with a cargo
LADEN	*v* **-ED, -ING, -S** to lade
LADER	*n* pl. **-S** one that lades
LADHOOD	*n* pl. **-S** the state of being a lad
LADIES	pl. of lady
LADING	*n* pl. **-S** cargo; freight
LADINO	*n* pl. **-NOS** a fast-growing clover
LADLE	*v* **-DLED, -DLING, -DLES** to lift out with a ladle (a type of spoon)
LADLEFUL	*n* pl. **-S** as much as a ladle will hold
LADLER	*n* pl. **-S** one that ladles
LADLING	present participle of ladle
LADRON	*n* pl. **-S** ladrone
LADRONE	*n* pl. **-S** a thief
LADY	*n* pl. **-DIES** a woman of refinement and gentle manners
LADYBIRD	*n* pl. **-S** a ladybug
LADYBUG	*n* pl. **-S** a small beetle
LADYFISH	*n* pl. **-ES** a bonefish
LADYHOOD	*n* pl. **-S** the state of being a lady
LADYISH	*adj* somewhat ladylike
LADYKIN	*n* pl. **-S** a small lady
LADYLIKE	*adj* resembling or suitable to a lady
LADYLOVE	*n* pl. **-S** a sweetheart
LADYNESS	*n* pl. **-ES** the quality or state of being a lady
LADYPALM	*n* pl. **-S** a palm tree
LADYSHIP	*n* pl. **-S** the condition of being a lady
LAETRILE	*n* pl. **-S** a drug derived from apricot pits
LAEVO	*adj* levo
LAG	*v* **LAGGED, LAGGING, LAGS** to stay or fall behind
LAGAN	*n* pl. **-S** goods thrown into the sea with a buoy attached to enable recovery
LAGEND	*n* pl. **-S** lagan
LAGER	*v* **-ED, -ING, -S** to laager
LAGGARD	*n* pl. **-S** one that lags
LAGGED	past tense of lag
LAGGER	*n* pl. **-S** a laggard
LAGGING	*n* pl. **-S** an insulating material
LAGNAPPE	*n* pl. **-S** a small gift given to a customer with his purchase
LAGOON	*n* pl. **-S** a shallow body of water **LAGOONAL** *adj*
LAGUNA	*n* pl. **-S** lagoon
LAGUNE	*n* pl. **-S** lagoon
LAH	*n* pl. **-S** la
LAHAL	*n* pl. **-S** a team game played by indigenous peoples of the Pacific Northwest
LAHAR	*n* pl. **-S** a flowing mass of volcanic debris

LAIC *n* pl. **-S** a layman **LAICAL** *adj* **LAICALLY** *adv*

LAICH *n* pl. **-S** laigh

LAICISE *v* **-ICISED, -ICISING, -ICISES** to laicize

LAICISM *n* pl. **-S** a political system free from clerical control

LAICIZE *v* **-ICIZED, -ICIZING, -ICIZES** to free from clerical control

LAID a past tense of lay

LAIGH *n* pl. **-S** a lowland

LAIN past participle of lie

LAIR *v* **-ED, -ING, -S** to live in a lair (a wild animal's resting or dwelling place)

LAIRAGE *n* pl. **-S** a place where cattle are housed at markets

LAIRD *n* pl. **-S** the owner of a landed estate **LAIRDLY** *adj*

LAIRY *adj* **-RIER, -RIEST** unpleasantly loud

LAITANCE *n* pl. **-S** a milky deposit on the surface of fresh concrete

LAITH *adj* loath **LAITHLY** *adv*

LAITY *n* pl. **-ITIES** the nonclerical membership of a religious faith

LAKE *n* pl. **-S** a sizable inland body of water **LAKELIKE** *adj*

LAKEBED *n* pl. **-S** the floor of a lake

LAKED *adj* subjected to the process of laking

LAKEFILL *n* pl. **-S** an area of land built by filling a lake

LAKEHEAD *n* pl. **-S** the shore of a lake farthest from the outlet

LAKELAND *n* pl. **-S** an area with many lakes

LAKEPORT *n* pl. **-S** a city located on the shore of a lake

LAKER *n* pl. **-S** a lake fish

LAKESIDE *n* pl. **-S** the land along the edge of a lake

LAKEVIEW *adj* overlooking a lake

LAKEWARD *adj* facing a lake

LAKH *n* pl. **-S** the sum of one hundred thousand

LAKING *n* pl. **-S** the reddening of blood plasma by the release of hemoglobin from the red corpuscles

LAKY *adj* **LAKIER, LAKIEST** of the color of blood

LALIQUE *n* pl. **-S** a style of cut glass or crystal

LALL *v* **-ED, -ING, -S** to articulate the letter *r* as *l*

LALLAN *n* pl. **-S** a lowland

LALLAND *n* pl. **-S** a lowland

LALLYGAG *v* **-GAGGED, -GAGGING, -GAGS** to dawdle

LAM *v* **LAMMED, LAMMING, LAMS** to flee hastily

LAMA *n* pl. **-S** a Buddhist monk

LAMASERY *n* pl. **-SERIES** a monastery of lamas

LAMB *v* **-ED, -ING, -S** to give birth to a lamb (a young sheep)

LAMBADA *n* pl. **-S** a Brazilian dance

LAMBAST *v* **-ED, -ING, -S** to lambaste

LAMBASTE *v* **-BASTED, -BASTING, -BASTES** to beat severely

LAMBDA *n* pl. **-S** a Greek letter **LAMBDOID** *adj*

LAMBENCY *n* pl. **-CIES** the quality or an instance of being lambent

LAMBENT *adj* flickering lightly and gently over a surface

LAMBER *n* pl. **-S** a ewe that is lambing

LAMBERT *n* pl. **-S** a unit of brightness

LAMBIE *n* pl. **-S** a lambkin

LAMBIER comparative of lamby

LAMBIEST superlative of lamby

LAMBING *n* pl. **-S** the birth of lambs on a farm

LAMBKILL *n* pl. **-S** an evergreen shrub

LAMBKIN *n* pl. **-S** a small lamb

LAMBLIKE *adj* resembling a lamb

LAMBSKIN *n* pl. **-S** the skin of a lamb

LAMBY *adj* **LAMBIER, LAMBIEST** resembling a lamb

LAME *adj* **LAMER, LAMEST** physically disabled

LAME *v* **LAMED, LAMING, LAMES** to make lame

LAMED *n* pl. **-S** a Hebrew letter

LAMEDH *n* pl. **-S** lamed

LAMELLA *n* pl. **-LAS** or **-LAE** a thin plate, scale, or membrane **LAMELLAR** *adj*

LAMELY *adv* in a lame manner

LAMENESS *n* pl. **-ES** the state of being lame

LAMENT *v* **-ED, -ING, -S** to express sorrow or regret for

LAMENTER *n* pl. **-S** one that laments

LAMER comparative of lame

LAMEST superlative of lame

LAMIA *n* pl. **-MIAS** or **-MIAE** a female demon

LAMINA *n* pl. **-NAS** or **-NAE** a thin plate, scale, or layer **LAMINAR, LAMINARY** *adj*

LAMINAL *n* pl. **-S** a speech sound articulated with the blade of the tongue

LAMINATE *v* **-NATED, -NATING, -NATES** to compress into a thin plate

LAMING present participle of lame

LAMININ *n* pl. **-S** a glycoprotein

LAMINOSE *adj* composed of laminae

LAMINOUS *adj* laminose

LAMISTER *n* pl. **-S** lamster

LAMMED past tense of lam

LAMMING present participle of lam

LAMP *v* **-ED, -ING, -S** to look at

LAMPAD *n* pl. **-S** a candlestick

LAMPAS *n* pl. **-ES** inflammation of the roof of a horse's mouth

LAMPERS *n* pl. **-ES** lampas

LAMPION *n* pl. **-S** a type of light-generating device

LAMPLESS *adj* lacking a lamp (a device for giving light)

LAMPLIT *adj* lighted by a lamp

LAMPOON *v* **-ED, -ING, -S** to ridicule in a satirical composition

LAMPPOST *n* pl. **-S** a post supporting a streetlight

LAMPREY *n* pl. **-PREYS** an eellike fish

LAMPYRID *n* pl. **-S** any of a family of beetles

LAMSTER *n* pl. **-S** a fugitive

LANAI *n* pl. **-S** a veranda

LANATE *adj* covered with wool

LANATED *adj* lanate

LANCE *v* **LANCED, LANCING, LANCES** to pierce with a lance (a spearlike weapon)

LANCELET *n* pl. **-S** a small marine organism

LANCER *n* pl. **-S** a cavalryman armed with a lance

LANCET *n* pl. **-S** a narrow, pointed arch **LANCETED** *adj*

LANCH *v* **-ED, -ING, -ES** to haul a boat over ice

LANCIERS *n* pl. **LANCIERS** a French dance

LANCING present participle of lance

LAND *v* **-ED, -ING, -S** to set down upon land (solid ground)

LANDAU *n* pl. **-S** a type of carriage

LANDER *n* pl. **-S** one that lands

LANDFALL *n* pl. **-S** a sighting or approach to land

LANDFAST *adj* attached to the shore — used of ice

LANDFILL *v* **-ED, -ING, -S** to build up an area by burying refuse

LANDFORM *n* pl. **-S** a natural feature of the earth's surface

LANDGRAB *n* pl. **-S** a swift and often fraudulent seizure of land

LANDING *n* pl. **-S** a place for discharging or taking on passengers or cargo

LANDLADY *n* pl. **-DIES** a female landlord

LANDLER *n* pl. **-S** a slow Austrian dance

LANDLESS *adj* owning no land

LANDLINE *n* pl. **-S** a line of communication on land

LANDLORD *n* pl. **-S** one who owns and rents out real estate

LANDMAN *n* pl. **-MEN** one who lives and works on land

LANDMARK *v* **-ED, -ING, -S** to designate a building or site as a place of historical or aesthetic importance

LANDMASS *n* pl. **-ES** a large area of land

LANDMEN pl. of landman

LANDSIDE *n* pl. **-S** a part of a plow

LANDSKIP *n* pl. **-S** landscape

LANDSLID past tense of landslide (to win an election by an overwhelming majority)

LANDSLIP *n* pl. **-S** the fall of a mass of earth

LANDSMAN *n* pl. **-MEN** landman

LANDSMAN *n* pl. **LANDSLEIT** a fellow Jew coming from one's own section of Eastern Europe

LANDWARD *adv* toward the land

LANDWASH *n* pl. **-ES** the shore area between the high-water mark and the sea

LANE *n* pl. **-S** a narrow passageway

LANELY *adj* lonely

LANEWAY *n* pl. **-WAYS** a lane

LANG *adj* long

LANGLAUF *n* pl. **-S** a cross-country ski run

LANGLEY *n* pl. **-LEYS** a unit of illumination

LANGRAGE *n* pl. **-S** a shot formerly used in naval warfare

LANGREL *n* pl. **-S** langrage

LANGSHAN *n* pl. **-S** any of a breed of large domestic fowl

LANGSYNE *n* pl. **-S** time long past

LANGUAGE *n* pl. **-S** a body of words and systems serving as a means of communication

LANGUE *n* pl. **-S** a type of language

LANGUED *adj* having the tongue of a specified color

LANGUET *n* pl. **-S** a tonguelike part

LANGUID *adj* lacking in vigor or vitality

LANGUISH *v* **-ED, -ING, -ES** to lose vigor or vitality

LANGUOR *n* pl. **-S** the state of being languid

LANGUR *n* pl. **-S** an Asian monkey

LANIARD *n* pl. **-S** lanyard

LANIARY *n* pl. **-ARIES** a cuspid

LANITAL *n* pl. **-S** a woollike fiber

LANK *adj* **LANKER, LANKEST** long and slender **LANKLY** *adv*

LANKNESS *n* pl. **-ES** the state of being lank

LANKY *adj* **LANKIER, LANKIEST** ungracefully tall and thin **LANKILY** *adv*

LANNER *n* pl. **-S** a falcon of Europe and Asia

LANNERET *n* pl. **-S** a male lanner

LANOLIN *n* pl. **-S** a fatty substance obtained from wool

LANOLINE *n* pl. **-S** lanolin

LANOSE *adj* lanate

LANOSITY *n* pl. **-TIES** the state of being lanose

LANTANA *n* pl. **-S** a tropical shrub

LANTERN *n* pl. **-S** a protective case for a light

LANTHORN *n* pl. **-S** a lantern

LANUGO *n* pl. **-GOS** fine, soft hair

LANYARD *n* pl. **-S** a fastening rope on a ship

LAOGAI *n* pl. **-S** the system of forced-labor camps in China

LAP *v* **LAPPED, LAPPING, LAPS** to fold over or around something

LAPBOARD *n* pl. **-S** a flat board used as a table or desk

LAPDOG *n* pl. **-S** a small dog

LAPEL *n* pl. **-S** an extension of the collar of a garment **LAPELED, LAPELLED** *adj*

LAPFUL *n* pl. **-S** as much as the lap can hold

LAPIDARY *n* pl. **-DARIES** one who works with precious stones

LAPIDATE *v* **-DATED, -DATING, -DATES** to hurl stones at

LAPIDIFY *v* **-FIED, -FYING, -FIES** to turn to stone

LAPIDIST *n* pl. **-S** a lapidary

LAPILLUS *n* pl. **-LI** a small fragment of lava

LAPIN *n* pl. **-S** a rabbit

LAPIS *n* pl. **-PISES, -PIDES** a semiprecious stone

LAPPED past tense of lap

LAPPER *v* **-ED, -ING, -S** to lopper

LAPPET *n* pl. **-S** a decorative flap on a garment **LAPPETED** *adj*

LAPPING present participle of lap

LAPSE *v* **LAPSED, LAPSING, LAPSES** to fall from a previous standard **LAPSABLE, LAPSIBLE** *adj*

LAPSER *n* pl. **-S** one that lapses

LAPSUS *n* pl. **LAPSUS** a mistake

LAPTOP *n* pl. **-S** a small computer for use on one's lap

LAPWING *n* pl. **-S** a shore bird

LAR *n* pl. **-S** or **-ES** a tutelary god or spirit of an ancient Roman household

LARBOARD *n* pl. **-S** the left-hand side of a ship

LARCENER *n* pl. **-S** one that commits larceny

LARCENY *n* pl. **-NIES** the felonious taking and removal of another's personal goods

LARCH *n* pl. **-ES** a coniferous tree **LARCHEN** *adj*

LARD *v* **-ED, -ING, -S** to coat with lard (the melted fat of hogs)

LARDER *n* pl. **-S** a place where food is stored

LARDIER comparative of lardy

LARDIEST superlative of lardy

LARDLIKE *adj* resembling lard

LARDON *n* pl. **-S** a thin slice of bacon or pork

LARDOON n pl. **-S** lardon

LARDY adj **LARDIER, LARDIEST** resembling lard

LAREE n pl. **-S** lari

LARES a pl. of lar

LARGANDO adj becoming gradually slower — used as a musical direction

LARGE adj **LARGER, LARGEST** of considerable size or quantity **LARGELY** adv

LARGE n pl. **-S** generosity

LARGESS n pl. **-ES** generosity

LARGESSE n pl. **-S** largess

LARGEST superlative of large

LARGISH adj somewhat large

LARGO n pl. **-GOS** a slow musical movement

LARI n pl. **-S** a monetary unit of the Republic of Georgia

LARIAT v **-ED, -ING, -S** to lasso

LARIGAN n pl. **-S** a leather boot

LARINE adj resembling a gull

LARK v **-ED, -ING, -S** to behave playfully

LARKER n pl. **-S** one that larks

LARKIER comparative of larky

LARKIEST superlative of larky

LARKISH adj playful

LARKSOME adj playful

LARKSPUR n pl. **-S** a flowering plant

LARKY adj **LARKIER, LARKIEST** playful

LARN v **LARNED** or **LARNT, LARNING, LARNS** to learn

LARRIGAN n pl. **-S** larigan

LARRIKIN n pl. **-S** a rowdy

LARRUP v **-ED, -ING, -S** to beat or thrash

LARRUPER n pl. **-S** one that larrups

LARUM n pl. **-S** an alarm

LARVA n pl. **-VAS** or **-VAE** the immature form of various insects and animals when newly hatched **LARVAL** adj

LARYNGAL n pl. **-S** a speech sound articulated in the larynx

LARYNX n pl. **LARYNXES** or **LARYNGES** an organ of the respiratory tract

LASAGNA n pl. **-S** an Italian baked dish

LASAGNE n pl. **-S** lasagna

LASCAR n pl. **-S** an East Indian sailor

LASE v **LASED, LASING, LASES** to function as a laser

LASER v **-ED, -ING, -S** to treat with a laser (a device that amplifies light waves)

LASH v **-ED, -ING, -ES** to strike with a whip

LASHER n pl. **-S** one that lashes

LASHING n pl. **-S** a flogging

LASHINS n/pl an abundance

LASHKAR n pl. **-S** lascar

LASHLESS adj lacking a lash (a whip)

LASING present participle of lase

LASS n pl. **-ES** a young woman

LASSI n pl. **-S** a beverage of yogurt, water, and flavorings

LASSIE n pl. **-S** a lass

LASSO v **-ED, -ING, -S** or **-ES** to catch with a lasso (a long rope with a running noose)

LASSOER n pl. **-S** one that lassos

LASSY n pl. **LASSIES** molasses

LAST v **-ED, -ING, -S** to continue in existence

LASTBORN n pl. **-S** a child born last in a family

LASTER n pl. **-S** one that lasts

LASTING n pl. **-S** a durable fabric

LASTLY adv in conclusion

LAT n pl. **-S** a muscle of the back

LATAKIA n pl. **-S** a variety of Turkish tobacco

LATCH v **-ED, -ING, -ES** to close with a type of fastening device

LATCHET n pl. **-S** a thong used to fasten a shoe

LATCHKEY n pl. **-KEYS** a key for opening a latched door

LATE adj **LATER, LATEST** coming or occurring after the expected time

LATED adj belated

LATEEN n pl. **-S** a sailing vessel

LATEENER n pl. **-S** a lateen

LATELY adv not long ago

LATEN v **-ED, -ING, -S** to become late

LATENCY n pl. **-CIES** the state of being present but not manifest

LATENESS n pl. **-ES** the state of being late

LATENT n pl. **-S** a barely visible fingerprint that can be developed for study

LATENTLY adv in a dormant manner

LATER comparative of late

LATERAD *adv* toward the side

LATERAL *v* **-ALED, -ALING, -ALS** or **-ALLED, -ALLING, -ALS** to execute a type of pass in football

LATERITE *n* pl. **-S** a type of soil

LATERIZE *v* **-IZED, -IZING, -IZES** to convert to laterite

LATEST *n* pl. **-S** the most recent development

LATEWOOD *n* pl. **-S** a part of an annual ring of wood

LATEX *n* pl. **LATEXES** or **LATICES** a milky liquid of certain plants

LATH *v* **-ED, -ING, -S** to cover with laths (thin strips of wood)

LATHE *v* **LATHED, LATHING, LATHES** to cut or shape on a type of machine

LATHER *v* **-ED, -ING, -S** to cover with lather (a light foam)

LATHERER *n* pl. **-S** one that lathers

LATHERY *adj* covered with lather

LATHI *n* pl. **-S** a heavy stick of bamboo and iron in India

LATHING *n* pl. **-S** work made of or using laths

LATHWORK *n* pl. **-S** lathing

LATHY *adj* **LATHIER, LATHIEST** long and slender

LATI a pl. of lats

LATICES a pl. of latex

LATIGO *n* pl. **-GOS** or **-GOES** a strap used to fasten a saddle

LATILLA *n* pl. **-S** a peeled limb used in ceilings

LATINA *n* pl **-S** a Latin-American woman or girl

LATINITY *n* pl. **-TIES** a manner of writing or speaking Latin

LATINIZE *v* **-IZED, -IZING, -IZES** to translate into Latin

LATINO *n* pl. **-NOS** a Latin American

LATISH *adj* somewhat late

LATITUDE *n* pl. **-S** freedom from narrow restrictions

LATKE *n* pl. **-S** a potato pancake

LATOSOL *n* pl. **-S** a tropical soil

LATRIA *n* pl. **-S** the supreme worship given to God only, in Roman Catholicism

LATRINE *n* pl. **-S** a type of toilet

LATS *n* pl. **LATI** or **LATU** a monetary unit of Latvia

LATTE *n* pl. **-S** espresso coffee with milk

LATTEN *n* pl. **-S** a brass-like alloy

LATTER *n* pl. **-S** the second mentioned person or thing of two

LATTERLY *adv* lately

LATTICE *v* **-TICED, -TICING, -TICES** to form a structure consisting of interlaced strips of material

LATTIN *n* pl. **-S** latten

LATU a pl. of lats

LAUAN *n* pl. **-S** a Philippine timber

LAUD *v* **-ED, -ING, -S** to praise

LAUDABLE *adj* worthy of praise **LAUDABLY** *adv*

LAUDANUM *n* pl. **-S** a type of opium preparation

LAUDATOR *n* pl. **-S** a lauder

LAUDER *n* pl. **-S** one that lauds

LAUGH *v* **-ED, -ING, -S** to express emotion, typically mirth, by a series of inarticulate sounds

LAUGHER *n* pl. **-S** one that laughs

LAUGHING *n* pl. **-S** laughter

LAUGHTER *n* pl. **-S** the act or sound of one that laughs

LAUNCE *n* pl. **-S** a marine fish

LAUNCH *v* **-ED, -ING, -ES** to set in motion

LAUNCHER *n* pl. **-S** a launching device

LAUNDER *v* **-ED, -ING, -S** to wash clothes

LAUNDRY *n* pl. **-DRIES** a collection of clothes to be washed

LAURA *n* pl. **-RAS** or **-RAE** a type of monastery

LAUREATE *v* **-ATED, -ATING, -ATES** to laurel

LAUREL *v* **-RELED, -RELING, -RELS** or **-RELLED, -RELLING, -RELS** to crown with a wreath of evergreen leaves

LAUWINE *n* pl. **-S** an avalanche

LAV *n* pl. **-S** a lavatory

LAVA *n* pl. **-S** molten rock that issues from a volcano

LAVABO *n* pl. **-BOS** or **-BOES** a ceremonial washing in certain Christian churches

LAVAGE *n* pl. **-S** a washing

LAVALAVA *n* pl. **-S** a Polynesian garment

LAVALIER *n* pl. **-S** a pendant worn on a chain around the neck

LAVALIKE *adj* resembling lava

LAVASH *n* pl. **-ES** a thin flat bread of Armenian origin

LAVATERA *n* pl. **-S** a plant of the mallow family

LAVATION *n* pl. **-S** the acting of washing

LAVATORY *n* pl. **-RIES** a room equipped with washing and toilet facilities

LAVE *v* **LAVED, LAVING, LAVES** to wash

LAVEER *v* **-ED, -ING, -S** to sail against the wind

LAVENDER *v* **-ED, -ING, -S** to sprinkle with a type of perfume

LAVER *n* pl. **-S** a vessel used for ancient Hebrew ceremonial washings

LAVEROCK *n* pl. **-S** a songbird

LAVING present participle of lave

LAVISH *adj* **-ISHER, -ISHEST** expending or giving in great amounts **LAVISHLY** *adv*

LAVISH *v* **-ED, -ING, -ES** to expend or give in great amounts

LAVISHER *n* pl. **-S** one that lavishes

LAVROCK *n* pl. **-S** laverock

LAW *v* **-ED, -ING, -S** to take a complaint to court for settlement

LAWBOOK *n* pl. **-S** a book containing or dealing with laws

LAWFUL *adj* allowed by law (the body of rules governing the affairs of a community) **LAWFULLY** *adv*

LAWGIVER *n* pl. **-S** one who institutes a legal system

LAWINE *n* pl. **-S** lauwine

LAWING *n* pl. **-S** a bill for food or drink in a tavern

LAWLESS *adj* having no system of laws

LAWLIKE *adj* being like the law

LAWMAKER *n* pl. **-S** a legislator

LAWMAN *n* pl. **-MEN** a law-enforcement officer

LAWN *n* pl. **-S** an area of grass-covered land **LAWNY** *adj*

LAWNED *adj* having a lawn

LAWSUIT *n* pl. **-S** a legal action

LAWYER *v* **-ED, -ING, -S** to work as a member of the legal profession

LAWYERLY *adj* befitting a member of the legal profession

LAX *adj* **LAXER, LAXEST** not strict or stringent

LAX *n* pl. **-ES** a vowel articulated with relatively relaxed muscles

LAXATION *n* pl. **-S** the act of relaxing

LAXATIVE *n* pl. **-S** a drug that stimulates evacuation of the bowels

LAXITY *n* pl. **-ITIES** the state of being lax

LAXLY *adv* in a lax manner

LAXNESS *n* pl. **-ES** laxity

LAY *v* **LAID** or **LAYED, LAYING, LAYS** to deposit as a wager

LAYABOUT *n* pl. **-S** a lazy person

LAYAWAY *n* pl. **-AWAYS** an item that has been reserved with a down payment

LAYER *v* **-ED, -ING, -S** to form a layer (a single thickness, coating, or covering)

LAYERAGE *n* pl. **-S** a method of plant propagation

LAYERING *n* pl. **-S** layerage

LAYETTE *n* pl. **-S** an outfit of clothing and equipment for a newborn child

LAYIN *n* pl. **-S** a type of shot in basketball

LAYMAN *n* pl. **-MEN** a member of the laity

LAYOFF *n* pl. **-S** the suspension or dismissal of employees

LAYOUT *n* pl. **-S** an arrangement or plan

LAYOVER *n* pl. **-S** a stopover

LAYUP *n* pl. **-S** a shot in basketball

LAYWOMAN *n* pl. **-WOMEN** a female member of the laity

LAZAR *n* pl. **-S** a beggar afflicted with a loathsome disease

LAZARET *n* pl. **-S** a hospital treating contagious diseases

LAZE *v* **LAZED, LAZING, LAZES** to pass time lazily

LAZIED past tense of lazy

LAZIER comparative of lazy

LAZIES present 3d person sing. of lazy

LAZIEST superlative of lazy

LAZILY *adv* in a lazy manner

LAZINESS *n* pl. **-ES** the state of being lazy

LAZING present participle of laze

LAZULI *n* pl. **-S** a mineral

LAZULITE *n* pl. **-S** a mineral

LAZURITE *n* pl. **-S** a mineral

LAZY   *adj* **LAZIER, LAZIEST** disinclined toward work or exertion

LAZY   *v* **LAZIED, LAZYING, LAZIES** to move or lie lazily

LAZYISH   *adj* somewhat lazy

LEA   *n* pl. **-S** a meadow

LEACH   *v* **-ED, -ING, -ES** to subject to the filtering action of a liquid

LEACHATE   *n* pl. **-S** a solution obtained by leaching

LEACHER   *n* pl. **-S** one that leaches

LEACHY   *adj* **LEACHIER, LEACHIEST** porous

LEAD   *v* **-ED, -ING, -S** to cover with lead (a heavy metallic element)

LEAD   *v* **LED, LEADING, LEADS** to show the way to by going in advance **LEADABLE** *adj*

LEADEN   *v* **-ED, -ING, -S** to make dull or sluggish **LEADENLY** *adv*

LEADER   *n* pl. **-S** one that leads or guides

LEADIER   comparative of leady

LEADIEST   superlative of leady

LEADING   *n* pl. **-S** a covering or border of lead

LEADLESS   *adj* having no lead

LEADMAN   *n* pl. **-MEN** a worker in charge of other workers

LEADOFF   *n* pl. **-S** an opening play or move

LEADSMAN   *n* pl. **-MEN** a seaman who measures the depth of water

LEADWORK   *n* pl. **-S** something made of lead

LEADWORT   *n* pl. **-S** a tropical plant

LEADY   *adj* **LEADIER, LEADIEST** resembling lead

LEAF   *n* pl. **LEAVES** a usually green, flattened organ of vascular plants

LEAF   *v* **-ED, -ING, -S** to turn pages rapidly

LEAFAGE   *n* pl. **-S** foliage

LEAFIER   comparative of leafy

LEAFIEST   superlative of leafy

LEAFLESS   *adj* having no leaves

LEAFLET   *v* **-LETED, -LETING, -LETS** or **-LETTED, -LETTING, -LETS** to distribute printed sheets of paper

LEAFLIKE   *adj* resembling a leaf

LEAFMOLD   *n* pl. **-S** soil composed mostly of decayed leaves

LEAFROLL   *n* pl. **-S** a virus disease of potatoes

LEAFWORM   *n* pl. **-S** a moth larva that feeds on leaves

LEAFY   *adj* **LEAFIER, LEAFIEST** covered with leaves

LEAGUE   *v* **LEAGUED, LEAGUING, LEAGUES** to come together for a common purpose

LEAGUER   *v* **-ED, -ING, -S** to besiege

LEAK   *v* **-ED, -ING, -S** to permit the escape of something through a breach or flaw

LEAKAGE   *n* pl. **-S** the act or an instance of leaking

LEAKER   *n* pl. **-S** one that leaks

LEAKLESS   *adj* designed not to leak

LEAKY   *adj* **LEAKIER, LEAKIEST** tending to leak **LEAKILY** *adv*

LEAL   *adj* loyal **LEALLY** *adv*

LEALTY   *n* pl. **-TIES** loyalty

LEAN   *adj* **LEANER, LEANEST** having little fat **LEANLY** *adv*

LEAN   *v* **LEANED** or **LEANT, LEANING, LEANS** to deviate from a vertical position

LEANER   *n* pl. **-S** one that leans

LEANING   *n* pl. **-S** a tendency

LEANNESS   *n* pl. **-ES** the state of being lean

LEANT   a past tense of lean

LEAP   *v* **LEAPED** or **LEAPT** or **LEPT, LEAPING, LEAPS** to spring off the ground

LEAPER   *n* pl. **-S** one that leaps

LEAPFROG   *v* **-FROGGED, -FROGGING, -FROGS** to jump over with the legs wide apart

LEAR   *n* pl. **-S** learning

LEARIER   comparative of leary

LEARIEST   superlative of leary

LEARN   *v* **LEARNED** or **LEARNT, LEARNING, LEARNS** to gain knowledge by experience, instruction, or study

LEARNER   *n* pl. **-S** one that learns

LEARNING   *n* pl. **-S** acquired knowledge

LEARY   *adj* **LEARIER, LEARIEST** leery

LEASE   *v* **LEASED, LEASING, LEASES** to grant temporary use of in exchange for rent **LEASABLE** *adj*

LEASER   *n* pl. **-S** one that leases

LEASH   *v* **-ED, -ING, -ES** to restrain an animal with a line or thong

LEASING *n* pl. **-S** a falsehood

LEAST *n* pl. **-S** something that is smallest in size or degree

LEATHER *v* **-ED, -ING, -S** to cover with leather (the dressed or tanned hide of an animal)

LEATHERN *adj* made of leather

LEATHERY *adj* resembling leather

LEAVE *v* **LEFT, LEAVING, LEAVES** to go away from

LEAVED *adj* having a leaf or leaves

LEAVEN *v* **-ED, -ING, -S** to produce fermentation in

LEAVENER *n* pl. **-S** one that has a tempering influence

LEAVER *n* pl. **-S** one that leaves

LEAVES pl. of leaf

LEAVING *n* pl. **-S** a leftover

LEAVY *adj* **LEAVIER, LEAVIEST** leafy

LEBEN *n* pl. **-S** a type of liquid food

LECH *v* **-ED, -ING, -ES** to engage in lechery

LECHAYIM *n* pl. **-S** lehayim

LECHER *v* **-ED, -ING, -S** to engage in lechery

LECHERY *n* pl. **-ERIES** excessive sexual indulgence

LECHWE *n* pl. **-S** an African antelope

LECITHIN *n* pl. **-S** any of a group of fatty substances found in plant and animal tissues

LECTERN *n* pl. **-S** a reading desk

LECTIN *n* pl. **-S** a protein that binds to a sugar molecule

LECTION *n* pl. **-S** a portion of sacred writing read in a church service

LECTOR *n* pl. **-S** a reader of the lessons in a church service

LECTURE *v* **-TURED, -TURING, -TURES** to expound on a specific subject

LECTURER *n* pl. **-S** one that lectures

LECYTHIS *adj* designating a family of tropical shrubs

LECYTHUS *n* pl. **-THI** lekythos

LED past tense of lead

LEDE *n* pl. **-S** the introductory section of a news story

LEDGE *n* pl. **-S** a narrow, shelflike projection

LEDGER *n* pl. **-S** an account book of final entry

LEDGY *adj* **LEDGIER, LEDGIEST** abounding in ledges

LEE *n* pl. **-S** shelter from the wind

LEEBOARD *n* pl. **-S** a board attached to a sailing vessel to prevent leeway

LEECH *v* **-ED, -ING, -ES** to cling to and feed upon or drain

LEEK *n* pl. **-S** an herb used in cookery

LEER *v* **-ED, -ING, -S** to look with a sideways glance

LEERY *adj* **LEERIER, LEERIEST** suspicious **LEERILY** *adv*

LEET *n* pl. **-S** a former English court for petty offenses

LEEWARD *n* pl. **-S** the direction toward which the wind is blowing

LEEWAY *n* pl. **-WAYS** the lateral drift of a ship

LEFT *adj* **LEFTER, LEFTEST** pertaining to the side of the body to the north when one faces east

LEFT *n* pl. **-S** the left side or hand

LEFTIE *n* pl. **-S** lefty

LEFTISH *adj* inclined to be a leftist

LEFTISM *n* pl. **-S** a liberal political philosophy

LEFTIST *n* pl. **-S** an advocate of leftism

LEFTMOST *adj* farthest on the left

LEFTOVER *n* pl. **-S** an unused or unconsumed portion

LEFTWARD *adv* toward the left

LEFTWING *adj* favoring leftism

LEFTY *n* pl. **LEFTIES** a left-handed person

LEG *v* **LEGGED, LEGGING, LEGS** to move with the legs (appendages that serve as a means of support and locomotion)

LEGACY *n* pl. **-CIES** something bequeathed

LEGAL *n* pl. **-S** an authorized investment that may be made by investors such as savings banks

LEGALESE *n* pl. **-S** the specialized language of lawyers

LEGALISE *v* **-ISED, -ISING, -ISES** to legalize

LEGALISM *n* pl. **-S** strict conformity to the law

LEGALIST *n* pl. **-S** an adherent of legalism

LEGALITY *n* pl. **-TIES** the condition of being lawful

LEGALIZE *v* **-IZED, -IZING, -IZES** to make lawful

LEGALLY *adv* in a lawful manner

LEGATE *v* **-GATED, -GATING, -GATES** to bequeath

LEGATEE *n* pl. **-S** the inheritor of a legacy

LEGATINE *adj* pertaining to an official envoy

LEGATING present participle of legate

LEGATION *n* pl. **-S** the sending of an official envoy

LEGATO *n* pl. **-TOS** a smooth and flowing musical style

LEGATOR *n* pl. **-S** one that legates

LEGEND *n* pl. **-S** an unverified story from earlier times

LEGENDRY *n* pl. **-RIES** a collection of legends

LEGER *n* pl. **-S** fishing bait made to lie on the bottom

LEGERITY *n* pl. **-TIES** quickness of the mind or body

LEGES pl. of lex

LEGGED past tense of leg

LEGGIER comparative of leggy

LEGGIERO *adv* in a light or graceful manner — used as a musical direction

LEGGIEST superlative of leggy

LEGGIN *n* pl. **-S** legging

LEGGING *n* pl. **-S** a covering for the leg

LEGGY *adj* **-GIER, -GIEST** having long legs

LEGHOLD *n* pl. **-S** a trap that catches an animal by its leg

LEGHORN *n* pl. **-S** a smooth, plaited straw

LEGIBLE *adj* capable of being read **LEGIBLY** *adv*

LEGION *n* pl. **-S** a large military force

LEGIST *n* pl. **-S** one learned or skilled in the law

LEGIT *n* pl. **-S** legitimate drama

LEGLESS *adj* having no legs

LEGLIKE *adj* resembling a leg

LEGMAN *n* pl. **-MEN** a newspaperman assigned to gather information

LEGONG *n* pl. **-S** a Balinese dance

LEGROOM *n* pl. **-S** space in which to extend the legs

LEGUME *n* pl. **-S** a type of plant

LEGUMIN *n* pl. **-S** a plant protein

LEGWORK *n* pl. **-S** work that involves extensive walking

LEHAYIM *n* pl. **-S** a traditional Jewish toast

LEHR *n* pl. **-S** a type of oven

LEHUA *n* pl. **-S** a tropical tree

LEI *n* pl. **-S** a wreath of flowers

LEISTER *v* **-ED, -ING, -S** to spear with a three-pronged fishing implement

LEISURE *n* pl. **-S** freedom from the demands of work or duty **LEISURED** *adj*

LEK *n* pl. **LEKS** or **LEKE** or **LEKU** a monetary unit of Albania

LEK *v* **LEKKED, LEKKING, LEKS** to assemble for competitive displays during the mating season

LEKVAR *n* pl. **-S** a prune butter

LEKYTHOS *n* pl. **-THOI** an oil jar used in ancient Greece

LEKYTHUS *n* pl. **-THI** lekythos

LEMAN *n* pl. **-S** a lover

LEMMA *n* pl. **-MAS** or **-MATA** a type of proposition in logic

LEMMING *n* pl. **-S** a mouselike rodent

LEMNISCI *n/pl* bands of nerve fibers

LEMON *n* pl. **-S** a citrus fruit **LEMONISH, LEMONY** *adj*

LEMONADE *n* pl. **-S** a beverage

LEMPIRA *n* pl. **-S** a monetary unit of Honduras

LEMUR *n* pl. **-S** an arboreal mammal related to the monkeys

LEMURES *n/pl* the ghosts of the dead in ancient Roman religion

LEMURINE *adj* pertaining to a lemur

LEMUROID *n* pl. **-S** a lemur

LEND *v* **LENT, LENDING, LENDS** to give the temporary use of **LENDABLE** *adj*

LENDER *n* pl. **-S** one that lends

LENDING *n* pl. **-S** the act of giving something temporarily

LENES pl. of lenis

LENGTH *n* pl. **-S** the longer or longest dimension of an object

LENGTHEN *v* **-ED, -ING, -S** to make or become longer

LENGTHY *adj* **LENGTHIER, LENGTHIEST** very long

LENIENCE *n* pl. **-S** leniency

LENIENCY *n* pl. **-CIES** the quality of being lenient

LENIENT *adj* gently tolerant

LENIS *n* pl. **LENES** a speech sound pronounced with little or no aspiration

LENITE *v* **-NITED, -NITING, -NITES** to articulate a lenis

LENITION *n* pl. **-S** a change in articulation

LENITIVE *n* pl. **-S** a soothing medicine

LENITY *n* pl. **-TIES** leniency

LENO *n* pl. **-NOS** a style of weaving

LENS *n* pl. **-ES** a piece of transparent material used in changing the convergence of light rays **LENSLESS** *adj*

LENS *v* **-ED, -ING, -ES** to make a film of

LENSE *n* pl. **-S** lens

LENSING *n* pl. **-S** the act or an instance of filming a motion picture

LENSMAN *n* pl. **-MEN** a photographer

LENT past tense of lend

LENTANDO *adv* becoming slower — used as a musical direction

LENTEN *adj* meager

LENTIC *adj* pertaining to still water

LENTICEL *n* pl. **-S** a mass of cells on a plant stem

LENTIGO *n* pl. **-TIGINES** a freckle

LENTIL *n* pl. **-S** a Eurasian annual plant

LENTISK *n* pl. **-S** an evergreen tree

LENTO *n* pl. **-TOS** a slow musical movement

LENTOID *n* pl. **-S** an object shaped like a lens

LEONE *n* pl. **-S** a monetary unit of Sierra Leone

LEONINE *adj* pertaining to a lion

LEOPARD *n* pl. **-S** a large, carnivorous feline mammal

LEOTARD *n* pl. **-S** a close-fitting garment

LEPER *n* pl. **-S** one affected with leprosy

LEPIDOTE *n* pl. **-S** a flowering shrub

LEPORID *n* pl. **-RIDS** or **-RIDAE** a gnawing mammal

LEPORINE *adj* resembling a rabbit or hare

LEPROSE *adj* leprous

LEPROSY *n* pl. **-SIES** a chronic disease characterized by skin lesions and deformities

LEPROTIC *adj* leprous

LEPROUS *adj* affected with leprosy

LEPT a past tense of leap

LEPTIN *n* pl. **-S** a hormone released by fat cells

LEPTON *n* pl. **-S** a subatomic particle **LEPTONIC** *adj*

LEPTON *n* pl. **-TA** a former monetary unit of Greece

LESBIAN *n* pl. **-S** a female homosexual

LESBIGAY *n* pl. **-GAYS** a lesbian, bisexual, or male homosexual

LESION *v* **-ED, -ING, -S** to cause an abnormal change in the structure of an organ

LESS *adj* **LESSER, LEAST** not as great in quantity or degree

LESSEE *n* pl. **-S** one to whom a lease is granted

LESSEN *v* **-ED, -ING, -S** to make or become less

LESSER *adj* not as large or important

LESSON *v* **-ED, -ING, -S** to instruct

LESSOR *n* pl. **-S** one that grants a lease

LEST *conj* for fear that

LET *v* **LETTED, LETTING, LETS** to hinder

LETCH *v* **-ED, -ING, -ES** to lech

LETDOWN *n* pl. **-S** a decrease

LETHAL *n* pl. **-S** a death-causing genetic defect

LETHALLY *adv* in a deadly manner

LETHARGY *n* pl. **-GIES** drowsiness; sluggishness

LETHE *n* pl. **-S** forgetfulness **LETHEAN** *adj*

LETOUT *n* pl. **-S** something that makes it possible to avoid doing something

LETTED past tense of let

LETTER *v* **-ED, -ING, -S** to mark with letters (written symbols representing speech sounds)

LETTERER *n* pl. **-S** one that letters

LETTING present participle of let

LETTUCE *n* pl. **-S** an herb cultivated as a salad plant

LETUP *n* pl. **-S** a lessening or relaxation

LEU *n* pl. **LEI** a monetary unit of Romania

LEUCEMIA *n* pl. **-S** leukemia **LEUCEMIC** *adj*

LEUCIN *n* pl. **-S** leucine

LEUCINE *n* pl. **-S** an amino acid

LEUCITE *n* pl. **-S** a mineral **LEUCITIC** *adj*

LEUCOMA *n* pl. **-S** leukoma

LEUCON *n* pl. **-S** a sponge of complex structure

LEUCOSIS *n* pl. **-COSES** leukosis **LEUCOTIC** *adj*

LEUD *n* pl. **-S** or **-ES** a feudal vassal

LEUKEMIA *n* pl. **-S** a disease of the blood-forming organs

LEUKEMIC *n* pl. **-S** one affected with leukemia

LEUKOMA *n* pl. **-S** an opacity of the cornea

LEUKON *n* pl. **-S** a bodily organ consisting of the white blood cells

LEUKOSIS *n* pl. **-KOSES** leukemia **LEUKOTIC** *adj*

LEV *n* pl. **LEVA** or **LEVAS** or **LEVS** a monetary unit of Bulgaria

LEVANT *v* **-ED, -ING, -S** to avoid a debt

LEVANTER *n* pl. **-S** an easterly Mediterranean wind

LEVATOR *n* pl. **-S** or **-ES** a muscle that raises an organ or part

LEVEE *v* **LEVEED, LEVEEING, LEVEES** to provide with an embankment

LEVEL *v* **-ELED, -ELING, -ELS** or **-ELLED, -ELLING, -ELS** to make even

LEVELER *n* pl. **-S** one that levels

LEVELLER *n* pl. **-S** leveler

LEVELLING a present participle of level

LEVELLY *adv* in an even manner

LEVER *v* **-ED, -ING, -S** to move with a lever (a rigid body used to lift weight)

LEVERAGE *v* **-AGED, -AGING, -AGES** to provide with a type of economic advantage

LEVERET *n* pl. **-S** a young hare

LEVIABLE *adj* liable to be levied

LEVIED past tense of levy

LEVIER *n* pl. **-S** one that levies

LEVIES present 3d person sing. of levy

LEVIGATE *v* **-GATED, -GATING, -GATES** to reduce to a fine powder

LEVIN *n* pl. **-S** lightning

LEVIRATE *n* pl. **-S** the custom of marrying the widow of one's brother

LEVITATE *v* **-TATED, -TATING, -TATES** to rise and float in the air

LEVITY *n* pl. **-TIES** conduct characterized by a lack of seriousness

LEVO *adj* turning toward the left

LEVODOPA *n* pl. **-S** a form of dopa

LEVOGYRE *adj* turning toward the left

LEVULIN *n* pl. **-S** a chemical compound

LEVULOSE *n* pl. **-S** a very sweet sugar

LEVY *v* **LEVIED, LEVYING, LEVIES** to impose or collect by legal authority

LEWD *adj* **LEWDER, LEWDEST** obscene **LEWDLY** *adv*

LEWDNESS *n* pl. **-ES** the state of being lewd

LEWIS *n* pl. **-ISES** a hoisting device

LEWISITE *n* pl. **-S** a vesicant liquid

LEWISSON *n* pl. **-S** lewis

LEX *n* pl. **LEGES** law

LEXEME *n* pl. **-S** a linguistic unit **LEXEMIC** *adj*

LEXICAL *adj* pertaining to the words of a language

LEXICON *n* pl. **-CONS** or **-CA** a dictionary

LEXIGRAM *n* pl. **-S** a symbol representing a word

LEXIS *n* pl. **LEXES** the vocabulary of a language, a group, or a subject field

LEY *n* pl. **LEYS** lea

LI *n* pl. **-S** a Chinese unit of distance

LIABLE *adj* subject or susceptible to something possible or likely

LIAISE *v* **LIAISED, LIAISING, LIAISES** to establish liaison

LIAISON *n* pl. **-S** a means for maintaining communication

LIANA *n* pl. **-S** a tropical vine

LIANE *n* pl. **-S** liana

LIANG *n* pl. **-S** a Chinese unit of weight

LIANOID *adj* pertaining to a liana

LIAR *n* pl. **-S** one that speaks falsely

LIARD *n* pl. **-S** a former silver coin of France

LIAS *n* pl. **LIASES** a blue limestone rock **LIASSIC** *adj*

LIATRIS *n* pl. **-ATRISES** an herb with tubular flowers

LIB *n* pl. **-S** liberation

LIBATION *n* pl. **-S** a ceremonial pouring of a liquid

LIBECCIO	*n* pl. **-CIOS** a southwest wind
LIBEL	*v* **-BELED, -BELING, -BELS** or **-BELLED, -BELLING, -BELS** to make or publish a defamatory statement about
LIBELANT	*n* pl. **-S** a plaintiff in a type of lawsuit
LIBELEE	*n* pl. **-S** a defendant in a type of lawsuit
LIBELER	*n* pl. **-S** one that libels
LIBELIST	*n* pl. **-S** a libeler
LIBELLED	a past tense of libel
LIBELLEE	*n* pl. **-S** libelee
LIBELLER	*n* pl. **-S** libeler
LIBELLING	a present participle of libel
LIBELOUS	*adj* defamatory
LIBER	*n* pl. **LIBERS** or **LIBRI** a book of public records
LIBERAL	*n* pl. **-S** a person favorable to progress or reform
LIBERATE	*v* **-ATED, -ATING, -ATES** to set free
LIBERTY	*n* pl. **-TIES** the state of being free
LIBIDO	*n* pl. **-DOS** the energy derived from instinctual biological drives
LIBLAB	*n* pl. **-S** a person supporting a coalition of liberal and labor groups
LIBRA	*n* pl. **-BRAE** an ancient Roman unit of weight
LIBRA	*n* pl. **-S** a former gold coin of Peru
LIBRARY	*n* pl. **-BRARIES** a place where literary materials are kept for reading and reference
LIBRATE	*v* **-BRATED, -BRATING, -BRATES** to move from side to side
LIBRETTO	*n* pl. **-TOS** or **-TI** the text of an opera
LIBRI	a pl. of liber
LICE	pl. of louse
LICENCE	*v* **-CENCED, -CENCING, -CENCES** to license
LICENCEE	*n* pl. **-S** licensee
LICENCER	*n* pl. **-S** licenser
LICENSE	*v* **-CENSED, -CENSING, -CENSES** to issue or grant authoritative permission to
LICENSEE	*n* pl. **-S** one that is licensed
LICENSER	*n* pl. **-S** one that licenses
LICENSOR	*n* pl. **-S** licenser

LICENTE	a pl. of sente
LICH	*n* pl. **-ES** a corpse
LICHEE	*n* pl. **-S** litchi
LICHEN	*v* **-ED, -ING, -S** to cover with lichens (flowerless plants)
LICHENIN	*n* pl. **-S** a chemical compound
LICHGATE	*n* pl. **-S** lychgate
LICHI	*n* pl. **-S** litchi
LICHT	*v* **-ED, -ING, -S** to light
LICHTLY	*adv* lightly
LICIT	*adj* lawful **LICITLY** *adv*
LICK	*v* **-ED, -ING, -S** to pass the tongue over the surface of
LICKER	*n* pl. **-S** one that licks
LICKING	*n* pl. **-S** a thrashing or beating
LICKSPIT	*n* pl. **-S** a fawning person
LICORICE	*n* pl. **-S** a perennial herb
LICTOR	*n* pl. **-S** a magistrate's attendant in ancient Rome
LID	*v* **LIDDED, LIDDING, LIDS** to provide with a lid (a movable cover)
LIDAR	*n* pl. **-S** an electronic locating device
LIDLESS	*adj* having no lid
LIDO	*n* pl. **-DOS** a fashionable beach resort
LIE	*v* **LAY, LAIN, LYING, LIES** to be in or get into a horizontal position
LIE	*v* **LIED, LYING, LIES** to speak falsely
LIED	*n* pl. **LIEDER** a German song
LIEF	*adj* **LIEFER, LIEFEST** willing **LIEFLY** *adv*
LIEGE	*n* pl. **-S** a feudal lord
LIEGEMAN	*n* pl. **-MEN** a feudal vassal
LIEN	*n* pl. **-S** a legal right to hold or sell a debtor's property
LIENABLE	*adj* capable of being subjected to a lien
LIENAL	*adj* pertaining to the spleen
LIENTERY	*n* pl. **-TERIES** a form of diarrhea
LIER	*n* pl. **-S** one that lies or reclines
LIERNE	*n* pl. **-S** a connecting part in Gothic vaulting
LIEU	*n* pl. **-S** place; stead
LIEVE	*adv* **LIEVER, LIEVEST** gladly

LIFE	*n pl.* **LIVES** the quality that distinguishes animals and plants from inanimate matter
LIFEBELT	*n pl.* **-S** a life preserver shaped like a belt
LIFEBOAT	*n pl.* **-S** a small rescue boat
LIFEBUOY	*n pl.* **-S** a life preserver shaped like a ring
LIFECARE	*n pl.* **-S** housing and health services for the elderly
LIFEFUL	*adj* full of life
LIFELESS	*adj* having no life
LIFELIKE	*adj* resembling a living thing
LIFELINE	*n pl.* **-S** a rope used to aid a person in distress
LIFELONG	*adj* lasting for a lifetime
LIFER	*n pl.* **-S** a prisoner serving a life sentence
LIFESPAN	*n pl.* **-S** a lifetime
LIFETIME	*n pl.* **-S** the period of living existence
LIFEWAY	*n pl.* **-WAYS** a way of living
LIFEWORK	*n pl.* **-S** the major work of one's lifetime
LIFT	*v* **-ED, -ING, -S** to move to a higher position **LIFTABLE** *adj*
LIFTER	*n pl.* **-S** one that lifts
LIFTGATE	*n pl.* **-S** a rear panel on a station wagon that opens upward
LIFTMAN	*n pl.* **-MEN** an elevator operator
LIFTOFF	*n pl.* **-S** the vertical takeoff of a rocket
LIGAMENT	*n pl.* **-S** a band of firm, fibrous tissue
LIGAN	*n pl.* **-S** lagan
LIGAND	*n pl.* **-S** a type of ion or molecule
LIGASE	*n pl.* **-S** an enzyme
LIGATE	*v* **-GATED, -GATING, -GATES** to bind
LIGATION	*n pl.* **-S** the act of ligating **LIGATIVE** *adj*
LIGATURE	*v* **-TURED, -TURING, -TURES** to ligate
LIGER	*n pl.* **-S** the offspring of a male lion and a female tiger
LIGHT	*adj* **LIGHTER, LIGHTEST** having little weight
LIGHT	*v* **LIGHTED** or **LIT, LIGHTING, LIGHTS** to illuminate
LIGHTEN	*v* **-ED, -ING, -S** to reduce the weight of
LIGHTER	*v* **-ED, -ING, -S** to convey in a type of barge
LIGHTFUL	*adj* brightly illuminated
LIGHTING	*n pl.* **-S** illumination
LIGHTISH	*adj* somewhat light
LIGHTLY	*adv* to a moderate degree
LIGNAN	*n pl.* **-S** a type of polymer
LIGNEOUS	*adj* of or resembling wood
LIGNIFY	*v* **-FIED, -FYING, -FIES** to convert into wood
LIGNIN	*n pl.* **-S** an essential part of woody tissue
LIGNITE	*n pl.* **-S** a type of coal **LIGNITIC** *adj*
LIGROIN	*n pl.* **-S** a flammable liquid
LIGROINE	*n pl.* **-S** ligroin
LIGULA	*n pl.* **-LAS** or **-LAE** a strap-shaped organ or part **LIGULAR, LIGULATE, LIGULOID** *adj*
LIGULE	*n pl.* **-S** a strap-shaped plant part
LIGURE	*n pl.* **-S** a precious stone
LIKABLE	*adj* pleasant **LIKABLY** *adv*
LIKE	*adj* **LIKER, LIKEST** possessing the same or almost the same characteristics
LIKE	*v* **LIKED, LIKING, LIKES** to find pleasant
LIKEABLE	*adj* likable **LIKEABLY** *adv*
LIKED	past tense of like
LIKELY	*adj* **-LIER, -LIEST** probable
LIKEN	*v* **-ED, -ING, -S** to represent as similar
LIKENESS	*n pl.* **-ES** a pictorial representation
LIKER	*n pl.* **-S** one that likes
LIKEST	superlative of like
LIKEWISE	*adv* in a similar manner
LIKING	*n pl.* **-S** a feeling of attraction or affection
LIKUTA	*n pl.* **MAKUTA** a former monetary unit of Zaire
LILAC	*n pl.* **-S** a flowering shrub
LILIED	*adj* covered with lilies
LILIES	pl. of lily
LILLIPUT	*n pl.* **-S** a very small person
LILT	*v* **-ED, -ING, -S** to sing or speak rhythmically
LILY	*n pl.* **LILIES** a flowering plant **LILYLIKE** *adj*

LIMA   *n* pl. **-S** the edible seed of a tropical American plant

LIMACINE   *adj* resembling a type of mollusk

LIMACON   *n* pl. **-S** a type of geometric curve

LIMAN   *n* pl. **-S** a lagoon

LIMB   *v* **-ED, -ING, -S** to cut off the arms or legs of

LIMBA   *n* pl. **-S** an African tree

LIMBATE   *adj* having an edge of a different color

LIMBECK   *n* pl. **-S** alembic

LIMBER   *adj* **-BERER, -BEREST** flexible **LIMBERLY** *adv*

LIMBER   *v* **-ED, -ING, -S** to make flexible

LIMBI   a pl. of limbus

LIMBIC   *adj* pertaining to a system of the brain

LIMBIER   comparative of limby

LIMBIEST   superlative of limby

LIMBLESS   *adj* having no arms or legs

LIMBO   *v* **-BOED, -BOING, -BOS** to perform a West Indian dance

LIMBUS   *n* pl. **-BUSES** or **-BI** a distinctive border

LIMBY   *adj* **LIMBIER, LIMBIEST** having many large branches

LIME   *v* **LIMED, LIMING, LIMES** to treat with lime (a calcium compound)

LIMEADE   *n* pl. **-S** a beverage

LIMEKILN   *n* pl. **-S** a furnace in which shells are burned to produce lime

LIMELESS   *adj* having no lime

LIMEN   *n* pl. **-MENS** or **-MINA** a sensory threshold

LIMERICK   *n* pl. **-S** a humorous verse

LIMES   *n* pl. **LIMITES** a fortified boundary

LIMEWASH   *n* pl. **-ES** a mixture of lime and water for coating walls

LIMEY   *n* pl. **-EYS** a British sailor

LIMIER   comparative of limy

LIMIEST   superlative of limy

LIMINA   a pl. of limen

LIMINAL   *adj* pertaining to the limen

LIMINESS   *n* pl. **-ES** the state of being limy

LIMING   present participle of lime

LIMIT   *v* **-ED, -ING, -S** to restrict

LIMITARY   *adj* limiting

LIMITED   *n* pl. **-S** a train or bus making few stops

LIMITER   *n* pl. **-S** one that limits

LIMITES   pl. of limes

LIMMER   *n* pl. **-S** a scoundrel

LIMN   *v* **-ED, -ING, -S** to depict by painting or drawing

LIMNER   *n* pl. **-S** one that limns

LIMNETIC   *adj* pertaining to the open water of a lake or pond

LIMNIC   *adj* limnetic

LIMO   *n* pl. **LIMOS** a limousine

LIMONENE   *n* pl. **-S** a chemical compound

LIMONITE   *n* pl. **-S** a major ore of iron

LIMONIUM   *n* pl. **-S** a sea plant of brightly colored funnel-like flowers

LIMP   *adj* **LIMPER, LIMPEST** lacking rigidity

LIMP   *v* **-ED, -ING, -S** to walk lamely

LIMPA   *n* pl. **-S** rye bread made with molasses

LIMPER   *n* pl. **-S** one that limps

LIMPET   *n* pl. **-S** a type of mollusk

LIMPID   *adj* transparent **LIMPIDLY** *adv*

LIMPKIN   *n* pl. **-S** a wading bird

LIMPLY   *adv* in a limp manner

LIMPNESS   *n* pl. **-ES** the state of being limp

LIMPSEY   *adj* **-SIER, -SIEST** limpsy

LIMPSY   *adj* **-SIER, -SIEST** lacking strength or vigor

LIMULOID   *n* pl. **-S** a horseshoe crab

LIMULUS   *n* pl. **-LI** a horseshoe crab

LIMY   *adj* **LIMIER, LIMIEST** resembling or containing lime

LIN   *n* pl. **-S** linn

LINABLE   *adj* lineable

LINAC   *n* pl. **-S** a device for imparting high velocities to charged particles

LINAGE   *n* pl. **-S** the number of lines of printed material

LINALOL   *n* pl. **-S** linalool

LINALOOL   *n* pl. **-S** a fragrant alcohol

LINCHPIN   *n* pl. **-S** a locking pin inserted in the end of a shaft

LINCTUS   *n* pl. **-TUSES** a syrupy medicine

LINDANE   *n* pl. **-S** an insecticide

LINDEN   *n* pl. **-S** a tall forest tree

LINDY — *v* **-DIED, -DYING, -DIES** to perform a fast, lively dance

LINE — *v* **LINED, LINING, LINES** to mark with lines (slender, continuous marks)

LINEABLE — *adj* lying in a straight line

LINEAGE — *n* pl. **-S** direct descent from an ancestor

LINEAL — *adj* being directly descended from an ancestor **LINEALLY** *adv*

LINEAR — *adj* of or resembling a straight line **LINEARLY** *adv*

LINEATE — *adj* marked with lines

LINEATED — *adj* lineate

LINEBRED — *adj* produced by interbreeding within a particular line of descent

LINECUT — *n* pl. **-S** a type of printing plate

LINED — past tense of line

LINELESS — *adj* having no lines

LINELIKE — *adj* resembling a line

LINEMAN — *n* pl. **-MEN** one who installs or repairs telephone wires

LINEMATE — *n* pl. **-S** a hockey player on the same line as another

LINEN — *n* pl. **-S** a fabric woven from the fibers of flax **LINENY** *adj*

LINER — *n* pl. **-S** a commercial ship or airplane

LINESMAN — *n* pl. **-MEN** a football official

LINEUP — *n* pl. **-S** a row of persons

LINEY — *adj* **LINIER, LINIEST** liny

LING — *n* pl. **-S** a heath plant

LINGA — *n* pl. **-S** lingam

LINGAM — *n* pl. **-S** a Hindu phallic symbol

LINGCOD — *n* pl. **-S** a marine food fish

LINGER — *v* **-ED, -ING, -S** to delay leaving

LINGERER — *n* pl. **-S** one that lingers

LINGERIE — *n* pl. **-S** women's underwear

LINGIER — comparative of lingy

LINGIEST — superlative of lingy

LINGO — *n* pl. **-GOES** or **-GOS** strange or incomprehensible language

LINGUA — *n* pl. **-GUAE** the tongue or a tonguelike part

LINGUAL — *n* pl. **-S** a sound articulated with the tongue

LINGUICA — *n* pl. **-S** a spicy Portuguese sausage

LINGUINE — *n* pl. **-S** linguini

LINGUINI — *n* pl. **-S** a type of pasta

LINGUISA — *n* pl. **-S** linguica

LINGUIST — *n* pl. **-S** a person skilled in several languages

LINGULA — *n* pl. **-LAE** an organ or process shaped like a tongue **LINGULAR** *adj*

LINGY — *adj* **LINGIER, LINGIEST** covered with heaths

LINHAY — *n* pl. **-HAYS** linny

LINIER — comparative of liney and liny

LINIEST — superlative of liney and liny

LINIMENT — *n* pl. **-S** a medicinal liquid

LININ — *n* pl. **-S** a substance in the nucleus of a cell

LINING — *n* pl. **-S** an inner layer

LINK — *v* **-ED, -ING, -S** to connect **LINKABLE** *adj*

LINKAGE — *n* pl. **-S** the act of linking

LINKBOY — *n* pl. **-BOYS** a man or boy hired to carry a torch to light the way along dark streets

LINKER — *n* pl. **-S** one that links

LINKMAN — *n* pl. **-MEN** a linkboy

LINKSMAN — *n* pl. **-MEN** a golfer

LINKUP — *n* pl. **-S** something that serves as a linking device

LINKWORK — *n* pl. **-S** something composed of interlocking rings

LINKY — *adj* full of interlocking rings

LINN — *n* pl. **-S** a waterfall

LINNET — *n* pl. **-S** a European songbird

LINNEY — *n* pl. **-NEYS** linny

LINNY — *n* pl. **-NIES** a row of rooms across the back of a house

LINO — *n* pl. **-NOS** linoleum

LINOCUT — *n* pl. **-S** a print made from a design cut into linoleum

LINOLEUM — *n* pl. **-S** a durable material used as a floor covering

LINOTYPE — *v* **-TYPED, -TYPING, -TYPES** to set type with a machine

LINSANG — *n* pl. **-S** a carnivorous mammal

LINSEED — *n* pl. **-S** flaxseed

LINSEY — *n* pl. **-SEYS** a coarse fabric

LINSTOCK — *n* pl. **-S** a stick having one end divided to hold a match

LINT — *v* **-ED, -ING, -S** to give off lint (bits of fiber or fluff)

LINTEL — *n* pl. **-S** a horizontal supporting beam **LINTELED** *adj*

LINTER — *n pl.* **-S** a machine for removing fibers from cotton seeds

LINTIER — comparative of linty

LINTIEST — superlative of linty

LINTLESS — *adj* free from lint

LINTOL — *n pl.* **-S** lintel

LINTY — *adj* **LINTIER, LINTIEST** covered with lint

LINUM — *n pl.* **-S** a plant of the flax family

LINURON — *n pl.* **-S** an herbicide

LINY — *adj* **LINIER, LINIEST** resembling a line

LION — *n pl.* **-S** a large, carnivorous feline mammal

LIONESS — *n pl.* **-ES** a female lion

LIONFISH — *n pl.* **-ES** a tropical fish

LIONISE — *v* **-ISED, -ISING, -ISES** to lionize

LIONISER — *n pl.* **-S** one that lionises

LIONIZE — *v* **-IZED, -IZING, -IZES** to treat or regard as a celebrity

LIONIZER — *n pl.* **-S** one that lionizes

LIONLIKE — *adj* resembling a lion

LIP — *v* **LIPPED, LIPPING, LIPS** to touch with the lips (the folds of flesh around the mouth)

LIPA — *n pl.* **LIPE** or **LIPAS** a monetary unit of Croatia

LIPASE — *n pl.* **-S** an enzyme

LIPGLOSS — *n pl.* **-ES** a cosmetic for making lips glossy

LIPID — *n pl.* **-S** any of a class of fatty substances **LIPIDIC** *adj*

LIPIDE — *n pl.* **-S** lipid

LIPIN — *n pl.* **-S** a lipid

LIPLESS — *adj* having no lips

LIPLIKE — *adj* resembling a lip

LIPLINER — *n pl.* **-S** a cosmetic applied to outline the lips

LIPO — *n pl.* **-POS** liposuction

LIPOCYTE — *n pl.* **-S** a fat-producing cell

LIPOGRAM — *n pl.* **-S** a writing in which a certain letter of the alphabet is omitted

LIPOID — *n pl.* **-S** a lipid **LIPOIDAL** *adj*

LIPOMA — *n pl.* **-MAS** or **-MATA** a tumor of fatty tissue

LIPOSOME — *n pl.* **-S** a microscopic globule composed of lipids

LIPPED — past tense of lip

LIPPEN — *v* **-ED, -ING, -S** to trust

LIPPER — *v* **-ED, -ING, -S** to ripple

LIPPING — *n pl.* **-S** a liplike outgrowth of bone

LIPPY — *adj* **-PIER, -PIEST** impudent

LIPREAD — *n pl.* **-READ, -READING, -READS** to understand spoken words by interpreting the lip movements of a speaker

LIPSTICK — *n pl.* **-S** a cosmetic used to color the lips

LIQUATE — *v* **-QUATED, -QUATING, -QUATES** to purify metal by heating

LIQUEFY — *v* **-FIED, -FYING, -FIES** to make or become liquid

LIQUEUR — *n pl.* **-S** a sweetened alcoholic beverage

LIQUID — *n pl.* **-S** a substance that flows freely **LIQUIDY** *adj*

LIQUIDLY — *adv* in a free-flowing manner

LIQUIFY — *v* **-FIED, -FYING, -FIES** to liquefy

LIQUOR — *v* **-ED, -ING, -S** to intoxicate with liquor (an alcoholic beverage)

LIRA — *n pl.* **LIRAS** or **LIRE** a former monetary unit of Italy

LIRA — *n pl.* **LIRI** a former monetary unit of Malta

LIRA — *n pl.* **LIROTH** or **LIROT** a former monetary unit of Israel

LIRIOPE — *n pl.* **-S** a stemless Asian herb

LIRIPIPE — *n pl.* **-S** a long scarf

LISENTE — a pl. of sente

LISLE — *n pl.* **-S** a fine, tightly twisted cotton thread

LISP — *v* **-ED, -ING, -S** to pronounce the letters s and z imperfectly

LISPER — *n pl.* **-S** one that lisps

LISPING — *n pl.* **-S** the act or an instance of pronouncing the letters s or z imperfectly

LISSOM — *adj* lissome **LISSOMLY** *adv*

LISSOME — *adj* lithe

LIST — *v* **-ED, -ING, -S** to write down in a particular order **LISTABLE** *adj*

LISTBOX — *n pl.* **-ES** a box on a computer screen that contains a list of options

LISTEE — *n pl.* **-S** one that is on a list

LISTEL — *n pl.* **-S** a narrow molding

LISTEN — *v* **-ED, -ING, -S** to make conscious use of the sense of hearing

LISTENER — *n pl.* **-S** one that listens

LISTER — *n pl.* **-S** a type of plow

LISTERIA *n* pl. **-S** a rod-shaped bacterium

LISTING *n* pl. **-S** something that is listed

LISTLESS *adj* languid

LISTSERV *n* pl. **-S** an email system that automatically sends messages to all subscribers

LIT *n* pl. **-S** the litas

LITANY *n* pl. **-NIES** a ceremonial form of prayer

LITAS *n* pl. **LITAI** or **LITU** a monetary unit of Lithuania

LITCHI *n* pl. **-S** the edible fruit of a Chinese tree

LITE *n* pl. **-S** a beer having relatively few calories

LITENESS *n* pl. **-ES** the state of being lite

LITER *n* pl. **-S** a unit of capacity

LITERACY *n* pl. **-CIES** the ability to read and write

LITERAL *n* pl. **-S** a small error in printing or writing

LITERARY *adj* of, pertaining to, or having the characteristics of books and writings

LITERATE *n* pl. **-S** one who can read and write

LITERATI *n/pl* scholars collectively

LITHARGE *n* pl. **-S** a monoxide of lead

LITHE *adj* **LITHER, LITHEST** bending easily **LITHELY** *adv*

LITHEMIA *n* pl. **-S** an excess of uric acid in the blood **LITHEMIC** *adj*

LITHIA *n* pl. **-S** an oxide of lithium

LITHIC *adj* pertaining to lithium

LITHIFY *v* **-FIED, -FYING, -FIES** to petrify

LITHIUM *n* pl. **-S** a metallic element

LITHO *v* **-ED, -ING, -S** or **-ES** to make prints by lithography

LITHOID *adj* resembling stone

LITHOPS *n* pl. **LITHOPS** a succulent African plant

LITHOSOL *n* pl. **-S** a type of soil

LITIGANT *n* pl. **-S** one who is engaged in a lawsuit

LITIGATE *v* **-GATED, -GATING, -GATES** to subject to legal proceedings

LITMUS *n* pl. **-ES** a blue coloring matter

LITORAL *adj* pertaining to a coastal region

LITOTES *n* pl. **LITOTES** a figure of speech in which an assertion is made by the negation of its opposite **LITOTIC** *adj*

LITRE *n* pl. **-S** liter

LITTEN *adj* lighted

LITTER *v* **-ED, -ING, -S** to scatter rubbish about

LITTERER *n* pl. **-S** one that litters

LITTERY *adj* covered with rubbish

LITTLE *adj* **-TLER, -TLEST** small

LITTLE *n* pl. **-S** a small amount

LITTLISH *adj* somewhat little

LITTORAL *n* pl. **-S** a coastal region

LITU a pl. of litas

LITURGY *n* pl. **-GIES** a prescribed system of public worship **LITURGIC** *adj*

LIVABLE *adj* suitable for living in

LIVE *adj* **LIVER, LIVEST** having life

LIVE *v* **LIVED, LIVING, LIVES** to function as an animal or plant

LIVEABLE *adj* livable

LIVELONG *adj* long in passing

LIVELY *adj* **-LIER, -LIEST** full of energy **LIVELILY** *adv*

LIVEN *v* **-ED, -ING, -S** to make lively

LIVENER *n* pl. **-S** one that livens

LIVENESS *n* pl. **-ES** the state of being live

LIVER *v* **-ED, -ING, -S** to thicken or gel

LIVERIED *adj* wearing a livery

LIVERISH *adj* having a disorder of the liver (a bodily organ)

LIVERY *n* pl. **-ERIES** a uniform worn by servants

LIVES pl. of life

LIVEST superlative of live

LIVETRAP *v* **-TRAPPED, -TRAPPING, -TRAPS** to capture in a type of animal trap

LIVEWARE *n* pl. **-S** working personnel

LIVEWELL *n* pl. **-S** a container of water in a boat for keeping fish alive

LIVEYER *n* pl. **-S** livyer

LIVID *adj* having the skin abnormally discolored **LIVIDLY** *adv*

LIVIDITY *n* pl. **-TIES** the state of being livid

LIVIER *n* pl. **-S** livyer

LIVING *n* pl. **-S** a means of subsistence

LIVINGLY *adv* realistically

LIVRE *n* pl. **-S** a former monetary unit of France

LIVYER *n* pl. **-S** a permanent resident of Newfoundland

LIXIVIUM *n* pl. **-IUMS** or **-IA** a solution obtained by leaching **LIXIVIAL** *adj*

LIZARD *n* pl. **-S** any of a suborder of reptiles

LLAMA *n* pl. **-S** a ruminant mammal

LLANO *n* pl. **-NOS** an open, grassy plain

LO *interj* — used to attract attention or to express surprise

LOACH *n* pl. **-ES** a freshwater fish

LOAD *v* **-ED, -ING, -S** to place in or on a means of conveyance **LOADABLE** *adj*

LOADER *n* pl. **-S** one that loads

LOADING *n* pl. **-S** a burden

LOADSTAR *n* pl. **-S** lodestar

LOAF *n* pl. **LOAVES** a shaped mass of bread

LOAF *v* **-ED, -ING, -S** to pass time idly

LOAFER *n* pl. **-S** one that loafs

LOAFING *n* pl. **-S** a place where cattle are allowed to roam freely

LOAM *v* **-ED, -ING, -S** to cover with loam (a type of soil)

LOAMLESS *adj* having no loam

LOAMY *adj* **LOAMIER, LOAMIEST** resembling loam

LOAN *v* **-ED, -ING, -S** to lend **LOANABLE** *adj*

LOANEE *n* pl. **-S** one that receives a loan

LOANER *n* pl. **-S** one that loans

LOANING *n* pl. **-S** a lane

LOANWORD *n* pl. **-S** a word taken from another language

LOATH *adj* unwilling

LOATHE *v* **LOATHED, LOATHING, LOATHES** to detest greatly

LOATHER *n* pl. **-S** one that loathes

LOATHFUL *adj* repulsive

LOATHING *n* pl. **-S** extreme dislike

LOATHLY *adj* repulsive

LOAVES pl. of loaf

LOB *v* **LOBBED, LOBBING, LOBS** to throw or hit in a high arc

LOBAR *adj* pertaining to a lobe

LOBATE *adj* having lobes **LOBATELY** *adv*

LOBATED *adj* lobate

LOBATION *n* pl. **-S** the formation of lobes

LOBBED past tense of lob

LOBBER *n* pl. **-S** one that lobs

LOBBING present participle of lob

LOBBY *v* **-BIED, -BYING, -BIES** to attempt to influence legislators

LOBBYER *n* pl. **-S** a lobbyist

LOBBYGOW *n* pl. **-S** an errand boy

LOBBYING *n* pl. **-S** the soliciting of support of an influential person

LOBBYISM *n* pl. **-S** the practice of lobbying

LOBBYIST *n* pl. **-S** one who lobbies

LOBE *n* pl. **-S** a rounded, projecting anatomical part **LOBED** *adj*

LOBEFIN *n* pl. **-S** a bony fish

LOBELESS *adj* lacking a lobe

LOBELIA *n* pl. **-S** a flowering plant

LOBELINE *n* pl. **-S** a poisonous alkaloid

LOBLOLLY *n* pl. **-LIES** a pine tree

LOBO *n* pl. **-BOS** the timber wolf

LOBOTOMY *n* pl. **-MIES** a type of surgical operation

LOBSTER *v* **-ED, -ING, -S** to fish for lobsters (marine crustaceans)

LOBSTICK *n* pl. **-S** a tree with its lower branches trimmed

LOBTAIL *v* **-ED, -ING, -S** (of a whale) to slap its tail against the surface of the water

LOBULE *n* pl. **-S** a small lobe **LOBULAR, LOBULATE, LOBULOSE** *adj*

LOBWORM *n* pl. **-S** a lugworm

LOCA a pl. of locus

LOCAL *n* pl. **-S** a train or bus making all stops

LOCALE *n* pl. **-S** a locality

LOCALISE *v* **-ISED, -ISING, -ISES** to localize

LOCALISM *n* pl. **-S** a custom or mannerism peculiar to a locality

LOCALIST *n* pl. **-S** one who is strongly concerned with the matters of a locality

LOCALITE *n* pl. **-S** a resident of a locality

LOCALITY *n* pl. **-TIES** an area or neighborhood

LOCALIZE *v* **-IZED, -IZING, -IZES** to confine to a particular area

LOCALLY	*adv* in a particular area
LOCATE	*v* **-CATED, -CATING, -CATES** to determine the position of
LOCATER	*n* pl. **-S** one that locates
LOCATION	*n* pl. **-S** the place where something is at a given moment
LOCATIVE	*n* pl. **-S** a type of grammatical case
LOCATOR	*n* pl. **-S** locater
LOCAVORE	*n* pl. **-S** one who eats foods grown locally when possible
LOCH	*n* pl. **-S** a lake
LOCHAN	*n* pl. **-S** a small lake
LOCHE	*n* pl. **-S** a fish of the cod family
LOCHIA	*n* pl. **-S** a vaginal discharge following childbirth **LOCHIAL** *adj*
LOCI	*n* pl. **-S** an engine used in logging
LOCIE	*n* pl. **-S** loci
LOCK	*v* **-ED, -ING, -S** to secure by means of a mechanical fastening device **LOCKABLE** *adj*
LOCKAGE	*n* pl. **-S** a toll on a ship passing through a canal
LOCKBOX	*n* pl. **-ES** a box that locks
LOCKDOWN	*n* pl. **-S** the confinement of prisoners to their cells
LOCKER	*n* pl. **-S** an enclosure that may be locked
LOCKET	*n* pl. **-S** a small ornamental case
LOCKJAW	*n* pl. **-S** a form of tetanus
LOCKLESS	*adj* lacking a lock (a mechanical fastening device)
LOCKNUT	*n* pl. **-S** a nut which keeps another from loosening
LOCKOUT	*n* pl. **-S** a closing of a business to coerce employees to agree to terms
LOCKRAM	*n* pl. **-S** a coarse, linen fabric
LOCKSET	*n* pl. **-S** a set of hardware for locking a door
LOCKSTEP	*n* pl. **-S** a mode of marching in close file
LOCKUP	*n* pl. **-S** a jail
LOCO	*n* pl. **-COS** or **-COES** locoweed
LOCO	*v* **-ED, -ING, -S** to poison with locoweed
LOCOFOCO	*n* pl. **-COS** a type of friction match
LOCOISM	*n* pl. **-S** a disease of livestock
LOCOMOTE	*v* **-MOTED, -MOTING, -MOTES** to move about
LOCOWEED	*n* pl. **-S** a plant that causes poisoning when eaten by livestock
LOCULAR	*adj* having or divided into loculi
LOCULATE	*adj* locular
LOCULE	*n* pl. **-S** loculus **LOCULED** *adj*
LOCULUS	*n* pl. **-LI** a small, cell-like chamber
LOCUM	*n* pl. **-S** a temporary substitute
LOCUS	*n* pl. **LOCI** or **LOCA** a place
LOCUST	*n* pl. **-S** a migratory grasshopper
LOCUSTA	*n* pl. **-TAE** a spikelet **LOCUSTAL** *adj*
LOCUTION	*n* pl. **-S** a particular form of expression
LOCUTORY	*n* pl. **-RIES** a room in a monastery
LODE	*n* pl. **-S** a deposit of ore
LODEN	*n* pl. **-S** a thick, woolen fabric
LODESTAR	*n* pl. **-S** a star used as a point of reference
LODGE	*v* **LODGED, LODGING, LODGES** to furnish with temporary quarters
LODGER	*n* pl. **-S** one that resides in rented quarters
LODGING	*n* pl. **-S** a temporary place to live
LODGMENT	*n* pl. **-S** a lodging
LODICULE	*n* pl. **-S** a scale at the base of the ovary of a grass
LOESS	*n* pl. **-ES** a soil deposit **LOESSAL, LOESSIAL, LOESSIC** *adj*
LOFT	*v* **-ED, -ING, -S** to store in a loft (an upper room)
LOFTER	*n* pl. **-S** a type of golf club
LOFTIER	comparative of lofty
LOFTIEST	superlative of lofty
LOFTILY	*adv* in a lofty manner
LOFTLESS	*adj* having no loft
LOFTLIKE	*adj* resembling a loft
LOFTY	*adj* **LOFTIER, LOFTIEST** extending high in the air
LOG	*v* **LOGGED, LOGGING, LOGS** to cut down trees for timber
LOGAN	*n* pl. **-S** a stone balanced to permit easy movement
LOGANIA	*adj* designating a family of flowering plants
LOGBOOK	*n* pl. **-S** a record book of a ship or aircraft
LOGE	*n* pl. **-S** a small compartment
LOGGATS	*n/pl* loggets
LOGGED	past tense of log

LOGGER *n* pl. **-S** one that logs

LOGGETS *n/pl* an old English throwing game

LOGGIA *n* pl. **-GIAS** or **-GIE** an open gallery

LOGGING *n* pl. **-S** the business of cutting down trees for timber

LOGGISH *adj* resembling a log

LOGGY *adj* **-GIER, -GIEST** logy

LOGIA a pl. of logion

LOGIC *n* pl. **-S** the science of reasoning

LOGICAL *adj* pertaining to logic

LOGICIAN *n* pl. **-S** one who is skilled in logic

LOGICISE *v* **-CISED, -CISING, -CISES** to logicize

LOGICIZE *v* **-CIZED, -CIZING, -CIZES** to reason

LOGIER comparative of logy

LOGIEST superlative of logy

LOGILY *adv* in a logy manner

LOGIN *n* pl. **-S** the process of identifying oneself to a computer

LOGINESS *n* pl. **-ES** the state of being logy

LOGION *n* pl. **-GIONS** or **-GIA** a saying attributed to Jesus

LOGISTIC *n* pl. **-S** symbolic logic

LOGJAM *v* **-JAMMED, -JAMMING, -JAMS** to cause to become tangled in a mass

LOGO *n* pl. **LOGOS** an identifying symbol **LOGOED** *adj*

LOGOFF *n* pl. **-S** a logout

LOGOGRAM *n* pl. **-S** a symbol used to represent an entire word

LOGOMACH *n* pl. **-S** one given to arguing about words

LOGON *n* pl. **-S** login

LOGOS *n* pl. **-GOI** the rational principle that governs the universe in ancient Greek philosophy

LOGOTYPE *n* pl. **-S** a piece of type bearing a syllable, word, or words

LOGOTYPY *n* pl. **-TYPIES** the use of logotypes

LOGOUT *n* pl. **-S** the act of ending a connection with a computer system

LOGROLL *v* **-ED, -ING, -S** to obtain passage of by exchanging political favors

LOGWAY *n* pl. **-WAYS** a ramp used in logging

LOGWOOD *n* pl. **-S** a tropical tree

LOGY *adj* **-GIER, -GIEST** sluggish

LOIASIS *n* pl. **-ASES** a tropical African disease

LOID *v* **-ED, -ING, -S** to open a spring lock by using a piece of celluloid

LOIN *n* pl. **-S** a part of the side and back between the ribs and the hipbone

LOITER *v* **-ED, -ING, -S** to stand idly about

LOITERER *n* pl. **-S** one that loiters

LOLL *v* **-ED, -ING, -S** to lounge

LOLLER *n* pl. **-S** one that lolls

LOLLIES pl. of lolly

LOLLIPOP *n* pl. **-S** a piece of candy on the end of a stick

LOLLOP *v* **-ED, -ING, -S** to loll

LOLLOPY *adj* characterized by a bobbing motion

LOLLY *n* pl. **-LIES** a lollipop

LOLLYGAG *v* **-GAGGED, -GAGGING, -GAGS** to lallygag

LOLLYPOP *n* pl. **-S** lollipop

LOMEIN *n* pl. **-S** a Chinese dish of noodles, meat, and vegetables

LOMENT *n* pl. **-S** a type of plant pod

LOMENTUM *n* pl. **-TUMS** or **-TA** loment

LONE *adj* having no companions

LONELY *adj* **-LIER, -LIEST** sad from lack of companionship **LONELILY** *adv*

LONENESS *n* pl. **-ES** the state of being lone

LONER *n* pl. **-S** one that avoids others

LONESOME *n* pl. **-S** self

LONG *adj* **LONGER, LONGEST** extending for a considerable distance

LONG *v* **-ED, -ING, -S** to desire strongly

LONGAN *n* pl. **-S** the edible fruit of a Chinese tree

LONGBOAT *n* pl. **-S** the largest boat carried by a sailing vessel

LONGBOW *n* pl. **-S** a type of archery bow

LONGE *v* **LONGED, LONGEING, LONGES** to guide a horse by means of a long rope

LONGER *n* pl. **-S** one that longs

LONGERON *n* pl. **-S** a longitudinal support of an airplane

LONGHAIR *n* pl. **-S** an intellectual

LONGHAND *n* pl. **-S** ordinary handwriting

LONGHEAD *n* pl. **-S** a person having a long skull

LONGHORN *n* pl. **-S** one of a breed of long-horned cattle

LONGIES *n/pl* long underwear

LONGING *n* pl. **-S** a strong desire

LONGISH *adj* somewhat long

LONGJUMP *v* **-ED, -ING, -S** to jump for distance from a running start

LONGLEAF *n* pl. **-LEAVES** an evergreen tree

LONGLINE *n* pl. **-S** a type of fishing line

LONGLY *adv* for a considerable distance

LONGNECK *n* pl. **-S** a beer bottle with a long neck

LONGNESS *n* pl. **-ES** the state of being long

LONGSHIP *n* pl. **-S** a medieval ship

LONGSOME *adj* tediously long

LONGSPUR *n* pl. **-S** a long-clawed finch

LONGTIME *adj* of long duration

LONGUEUR *n* pl. **-S** a dull and tedious section

LONGWAYS *adv* longwise

LONGWISE *adv* lengthwise

LONICERA *n* pl. **-S** a shrub with fragrant flowers

LOO *v* **-ED, -ING, -S** to subject to a forfeit at loo (a card game)

LOOBY *n* pl. **-BIES** a large, awkward person

LOOEY *n* pl. **-EYS** looie

LOOF *n* pl. **-S** the palm of the hand

LOOFA *n* pl. **-S** loofah

LOOFAH *n* pl. **-S** a tropical vine

LOOIE *n* pl. **-S** a lieutenant of the armed forces

LOOK *v* **-ED, -ING, -S** to use one's eyes in seeing

LOOKDOWN *n* pl. **-S** a marine fish

LOOKER *n* pl. **-S** one that looks

LOOKIE *interj* looky

LOOKISM *n* pl. **-S** discrimination based on physical appearance

LOOKIST *n* pl. **-S** one that practices lookism

LOOKIT *interj* — used to draw attention to something

LOOKOUT *n* pl. **-S** one engaged in keeping watch

LOOKSISM *n* pl. **-S** lookism

LOOKUP *n* pl. **-S** the process of looking something up

LOOKY *interj* — used to draw attention to something

LOOM *v* **-ED, -ING, -S** to appear in an enlarged and indistinct form

LOON *n* pl. **-S** a diving waterfowl

LOONEY *adj* **-NIER, -NIEST** loony

LOONEY *n* pl. **-EYS** loony

LOONIE *n* pl. **-S** a coin worth one Canadian dollar

LOONY *adj* **-NIER, -NIEST** crazy **LOONILY** *adv*

LOONY *n* pl. **-NIES** a loony person

LOOP *v* **-ED, -ING, -S** to form loops (circular or oval openings)

LOOPER *n* pl. **-S** one that loops

LOOPHOLE *v* **-HOLED, -HOLING, -HOLES** to make small openings in

LOOPY *adj* **LOOPIER, LOOPIEST** full of loops **LOOPILY** *adv*

LOOSE *adj* **LOOSER, LOOSEST** not firm, taut, or rigid **LOOSELY** *adv*

LOOSE *v* **LOOSED, LOOSING, LOOSES** to set free

LOOSEN *v* **-ED, -ING, -S** to make looser

LOOSENER *n* pl. **-S** one that loosens

LOOSER comparative of loose

LOOSEST superlative of loose

LOOSING present participle of loose

LOOT *v* **-ED, -ING, -S** to plunder

LOOTER *n* pl. **-S** one that loots

LOOTING *n* pl. **-S** the act of stealing goods left unprotected

LOP *v* **LOPPED, LOPPING, LOPS** to cut off branches or twigs from

LOPE *v* **LOPED, LOPING, LOPES** to run with a steady, easy gait

LOPER *n* pl. **-S** one that lopes

LOPINGLY *adv* in the manner of one that lopes

LOPPED past tense of lop

LOPPER *v* **-ED, -ING, -S** to curdle

LOPPET *n* pl. **-S** a long-distance cross-country ski race

LOPPING present participle of lop

LOPPY *adj* **-PIER, -PIEST** hanging limply

LOPSIDED *adj* leaning to one side

LOPSTICK *n* pl. **-S** lobstick

LOQUAT *n* pl. **-S** a small yellow fruit

LOQUITUR *v* he or she speaks

LOR *interj* — used to express surprise or dismay

LORAL *adj* pertaining to the space between the eye and bill of a bird

LORAN *n* pl. **-S** a type of navigational system

LORD *v* **-ED, -ING, -S** to invest with the power of a lord (a person having dominion over others)

LORDING *n* pl. **-S** a lordling

LORDLESS *adj* having no lord

LORDLIER comparative of lordly

LORDLIEST superlative of lordly

LORDLIKE *adj* lordly

LORDLING *n* pl. **-S** a young or unimportant lord

LORDLY *adj* **-LIER, -LIEST** of or befitting a lord

LORDOMA *n* pl. **-S** lordosis

LORDOSIS *n* pl. **-DOSES** a curvature of the spinal column **LORDOTIC** *adj*

LORDSHIP *n* pl. **-S** the power of a lord

LORE *n* pl. **-S** traditional knowledge or belief

LOREAL *adj* loral

LORGNON *n* pl. **-S** a pair of eyeglasses with a handle

LORICA *n* pl. **-CAE** or **-CAS** a protective covering or shell

LORICATE *n* pl. **-S** an animal having a lorica

LORIES pl. of lory

LORIKEET *n* pl. **-S** a small parrot

LORIMER *n* pl. **-S** a maker of implements for harnesses and saddles

LORINER *n* pl. **-S** lorimer

LORIS *n* pl. **-RISES** an Asian lemur

LORN *adj* abandoned

LORNNESS *n* pl. **-ES** the state of being lorn

LORRY *n* pl. **-RIES** a type of wagon or truck

LORY *n* pl. **-RIES** a small parrot

LOSE *v* **LOST, LOSING, LOSES** to come to be without and be unable to find **LOSABLE** *adj*

LOSEL *n* pl. **-S** a worthless person

LOSER *n* pl. **-S** one that loses

LOSING *n* pl. **-S** a loss

LOSINGLY *adv* in a manner characterized by defeat

LOSS *n* pl. **-ES** the act of one that loses

LOSSLESS *adj* done or being without loss

LOSSY *adj* causing dissipation of electrical energy

LOST *adj* not to be found or recovered

LOSTNESS *n* pl. **-ES** the state of being lost

LOT *v* **LOTTED, LOTTING, LOTS** to distribute proportionately

LOTA *n* pl. **-S** lotah

LOTAH *n* pl. **-S** a small water vessel used in India

LOTH *adj* loath

LOTHARIO *n* pl. **-IOS** a seducer of women

LOTHSOME *adj* repulsive

LOTI *n* pl. **MALOTI** a monetary unit of Lesotho

LOTIC *adj* pertaining to moving water

LOTION *n* pl. **-S** a liquid preparation for external application

LOTO *n* pl. **-S** lotto

LOTOS *n* pl. **-ES** lotus

LOTTE *n* pl. **-S** a monkfish

LOTTED past tense of lot

LOTTER *n* pl. **-S** one who assembles merchandise into salable lots

LOTTERY *n* pl. **-TERIES** a type of gambling game

LOTTING present participle of lot

LOTTO *n* pl. **-TOS** a game of chance

LOTUS *n* pl. **-ES** an aquatic plant

LOUCHE *adj* not reputable

LOUD *adj* **LOUDER, LOUDEST** strongly audible

LOUDEN *v* **-ED, -ING, -S** to make or become louder

LOUDISH *adj* somewhat loud

LOUDLY *adv* **-LIER, -LIEST** in a loud manner

LOUDNESS *n* pl. **-ES** the quality of being loud

LOUGH *n* pl. **-S** a lake

LOUIE *n* pl. **-S** looie

LOUIS *n* pl. **LOUIS** a former gold coin of France

LOUMA *n* pl. **-S** luma

LOUNGE *v* **LOUNGED, LOUNGING, LOUNGES** to recline or lean in a relaxed, lazy manner

LOUNGER *n* pl. **-S** one that lounges

LOUNGEY *adj* loungy

LOUNGY *adj* **LOUNGIER, LOUNGIEST** suitable for lounging

LOUP   v **LOUPED, LOUPEN, LOUPING, LOUPS** to leap

LOUPE   n pl. **-S** a small magnifying glass

LOUR   v **-ED, -ING, -S** to lower

LOURY   adj lowery

LOUSE   n pl. **LICE** a parasitic insect

LOUSE   v **LOUSED, LOUSING, LOUSES** to spoil or bungle

LOUSY   adj **LOUSIER, LOUSIEST** mean or contemptible **LOUSILY** adv

LOUT   v **-ED, -ING, -S** to bow in respect

LOUTISH   adj clumsy

LOUVER   n pl. **-S** a type of window **LOUVERED** adj

LOUVRE   n pl. **-S** louver **LOUVRED** adj

LOVABLE   adj having qualities that attract love **LOVABLY** adv

LOVAGE   n pl. **-S** a perennial herb

LOVAT   n pl. **-S** a chiefly green color mixture in fabrics

LOVE   v **LOVED, LOVING, LOVES** to feel great affection for

LOVEABLE   adj lovable **LOVEABLY** adv

LOVEBIRD   n pl. **-S** a small parrot

LOVEBUG   n pl. **-S** a small black fly that swarms along highways

LOVED   past tense of love

LOVEFEST   n pl. **-S** a gathering to promote good feeling

LOVELESS   adj feeling no love

LOVELIER   comparative of lovely

LOVELIES   pl. of lovely

LOVELIEST   superlative of lovely

LOVELILY   adv in a lovely manner

LOVELOCK   n pl. **-S** a lock of hair hanging separately

LOVELORN   adj not loved

LOVELY   adj **-LIER, -LIEST** beautiful

LOVELY   n pl. **-LIES** a beautiful woman

LOVER   n pl. **-S** one that loves another **LOVERLY** adj

LOVESEAT   n pl. **-S** a small sofa for two persons

LOVESICK   adj languishing with love

LOVESOME   adj lovely

LOVEVINE   n pl. **-S** a twining herb

LOVEY   n pl. **LOVEYS** a sweetheart

LOVEY   adj **LOVIER, LOVIEST** fondly affectionate

LOVING   n pl. **-S** the act of expressing love

LOVINGLY   adv in a loving manner

LOW   adj **LOWER, LOWEST** having relatively little upward extension

LOW   v **-ED, -ING, -S** to utter the sound characteristic of cattle

LOWBALL   v **-ED, -ING, -S** to give a customer a deceptively low price

LOWBORN   adj of humble birth

LOWBOY   n pl. **-BOYS** a low chest of drawers

LOWBRED   adj lowborn

LOWBROW   n pl. **-S** an uncultivated person

LOWBUSH   n pl **-ES** a bush with sweet blueberries

LOWDOWN   n pl. **-S** the whole truth

LOWE   v **LOWED, LOWING, LOWES** to blaze

LOWER   v **-ED, -ING, -S** to appear dark and threatening

LOWERY   adj dark and threatening

LOWING   n pl. **-S** the sound characteristic of cattle

LOWISH   adj somewhat low

LOWLAND   n pl. **-S** an area of land lying lower than the adjacent country

LOWLIFE   n pl. **-LIFES** or **-LIVES** a despicable person

LOWLIFER   n pl. **-S** a lowlife

LOWLIGHT   n pl. **-S** an unpleasant event, detail, or part

LOWLY   adj **-LIER, -LIEST** low in position or rank **LOWLILY** adv

LOWN   adj peaceful

LOWNESS   n pl. **-ES** the state of being low

LOWPASS   adj being a type of filter

LOWRIDER   n pl. **-S** a car having a lowered suspension

LOWSE   adj loose

LOX   v **-ED, -ING, -ES** to supply with lox (liquid oxygen)

LOYAL   adj **-ALER, -ALEST** faithful to one's allegiance

LOYALISM   n pl. **-S** loyalty

LOYALIST   n pl. **-S** one who is loyal

LOYALLY   adv in a loyal manner

LOYALTY   n pl. **-TIES** the state of being loyal

LOZENGE   *n* pl. **-S** a small, often medicated candy

LUAU   *n* pl. **-S** a Hawaiian feast

LUBBER   *n* pl. **-S** a clumsy person **LUBBERLY** *adj*

LUBE   *v* **LUBED, LUBING, LUBES** to lubricate

LUBRIC   *adj* slippery

LUBRICAL   *adj* lubric

LUCARNE   *n* pl. **-S** a type of window

LUCE   *n* pl. **-S** a freshwater fish

LUCENCE   *n* pl. **-S** lucency

LUCENCY   *n* pl. **-CIES** the quality of being lucent

LUCENT   *adj* giving off light **LUCENTLY** *adv*

LUCERN   *n* pl. **-S** lucerne

LUCERNE   *n* pl. **-S** alfalfa

LUCES   a pl. of lux

LUCID   *adj* easily understood **LUCIDLY** *adv*

LUCIDITY   *n* pl. **-TIES** the quality of being lucid

LUCIFER   *n* pl. **-S** a friction match

LUCK   *v* **-ED, -ING, -S** to succeed by chance or good fortune

LUCKIE   *n* pl. **-S** an old woman

LUCKLESS   *adj* unlucky

LUCKY   *adj* **LUCKIER, LUCKIEST** having good fortune **LUCKILY** *adv*

LUCRE   *n* pl. **-S** monetary gain

LUCULENT   *adj* lucid

LUD   *n* pl. **-S** a form of address to a judge in a court

LUDE   *n* pl. **-S** a methaqualone pill

LUDIC   *adj* aimlessly playful

LUDO   *n* pl. **-DOS** a simple board game

LUES   *n* pl. **LUES** syphilis

LUETIC   *n* pl. **-S** one infected with syphilis

LUFF   *v* **-ED, -ING, -S** to steer a sailing vessel nearer into the wind

LUFFA   *n* pl. **-S** loofah

LUG   *v* **LUGGED, LUGGING, LUGS** to carry or pull with effort

LUGE   *v* **LUGED, LUGEING** or **LUGING, LUGES** to race on a luge (a small sled)

LUGER   *n* pl. **-S** one that luges

LUGGAGE   *n* pl. **-S** articles containing a traveler's belongings

LUGGED   past tense of lug

LUGGER   *n* pl. **-S** a small sailing vessel

LUGGIE   *n* pl. **-S** a small wooden dish or pail

LUGGING   present participle of lug

LUGSAIL   *n* pl. **-S** a type of sail

LUGWORM   *n* pl. **-S** a burrowing marine worm

LUKEWARM   *adj* moderately warm

LULL   *v* **-ED, -ING, -S** to cause to sleep or rest

LULLABY   *v* **-BIED, -BYING, -BIES** to lull with a soothing song

LULLER   *n* pl. **-S** one that lulls

LULU   *n* pl. **-S** something remarkable

LUM   *n* pl. **-S** a chimney

LUMA   *n* pl. **-S** a monetary unit of Armenia

LUMBAGO   *n* pl. **-GOS** pain in the lower back

LUMBAR   *n* pl. **-S** an anatomical part situated near the loins

LUMBER   *v* **-ED, -ING, -S** to cut down and prepare timber for market

LUMBERER   *n* pl. **-S** one that lumbers

LUMBERLY   *adj* moving slowly with a heavy gait

LUMEN   *n* pl. **-MENS** or **-MINA** the inner passage of a tubular organ **LUMENAL, LUMINAL** *adj*

LUMINARY   *n* pl. **-NARIES** a body that gives light

LUMINISM   *n* pl. **-S** a style of painting

LUMINIST   *n* pl. **-S** a painter who uses the effects of light

LUMINOUS   *adj* giving off light

LUMMOX   *n* pl. **-ES** a clumsy person

LUMP   *v* **-ED, -ING, -S** to make into lumps (shapeless masses)

LUMPEN   *n* pl. **-S** an uprooted individual

LUMPER   *n* pl. **-S** a laborer employed to load and unload ships

LUMPFISH   *n* pl. **-ES** a marine fish

LUMPIA   *n* pl. **-S** an Indonesian spring roll

LUMPISH   *adj* stupid

LUMPY   *adj* **LUMPIER, LUMPIEST** full of lumps **LUMPILY** *adv*

LUN   *n* pl. **-S** a lee

LUNA   *n* pl. **-S** an alchemical designation for silver

LUNACY   *n* pl. **-CIES** insanity

LUNAR   *n* pl. **-S** an observation of the moon taken for navigational purposes

LUNARIAN *n* pl. **-S** a supposed inhabitant of the moon

LUNATE *adj* crescent-shaped **LUNATELY** *adv*

LUNATED *adj* lunate

LUNATIC *n* pl. **-S** an insane person

LUNATION *n* pl. **-S** the interval between two successive new moons

LUNCH *v* **-ED, -ING, -ES** to eat a noonday meal

LUNCHBOX *n* pl. **-ES** a container for carrying meals to school or work

LUNCHEON *n* pl. **-S** a noonday meal

LUNCHER *n* pl. **-S** one that lunches

LUNE *n* pl. **-S** a crescent-shaped figure

LUNET *n* pl. **-S** lunette

LUNETTE *n* pl. **-S** a crescent-shaped object

LUNG *n* pl. **-S** a respiratory organ

LUNGAN *n* pl. **-S** longan

LUNGE *v* **LUNGED, LUNGING** or **LUNGEING, LUNGES** to make a forceful forward movement

LUNGEE *n* pl. **-S** lungi

LUNGER *n* pl. **-S** one that lunges

LUNGFISH *n* pl. **-ES** a type of fish

LUNGFUL *n* pl. **-S** as much as the lungs can hold

LUNGI *n* pl. **-S** a loincloth worn by men in India

LUNGING a present participle of lunge

LUNGLESS *adj* having no lung

LUNGWORM *n* pl. **-S** a parasitic worm

LUNGWORT *n* pl. **-S** a European herb

LUNGYI *n* pl. **-S** lungi

LUNIER comparative of luny

LUNIES pl. of luny

LUNIEST superlative of luny

LUNK *n* pl. **-S** a lunkhead

LUNKER *n* pl. **-S** a large game fish

LUNKHEAD *n* pl. **-S** a stupid person

LUNT *v* **-ED, -ING, -S** to emit smoke

LUNULA *n* pl. **-LAE** a small crescent-shaped structure **LUNULAR, LUNULATE** *adj*

LUNULE *n* pl. **-S** lunula

LUNY *adj* **-NIER, -NIEST** loony

LUNY *n* pl. **-NIES** a loony

LUPANAR *n* pl. **-S** a brothel

LUPIN *n* pl. **-S** lupine

LUPINE *n* pl. **-S** a flowering plant

LUPULIN *n* pl. **-S** a medicinal powder obtained from the hop plant

LUPUS *n* pl. **-ES** a skin disease **LUPOID, LUPOUS** *adj*

LURCH *v* **-ED, -ING, -ES** to sway abruptly

LURCHER *n* pl. **-S** one that lurks or prowls

LURDAN *n* pl. **-S** a lazy or stupid person

LURDANE *n* pl. **-S** lurdan

LURE *v* **LURED, LURING, LURES** to attract with something desirable

LURER *n* pl. **-S** one that lures

LURID *adj* causing shock or horror **LURIDLY** *adv*

LURINGLY *adv* in an enticing manner

LURK *v* **-ED, -ING, -S** to wait in concealment

LURKER *n* pl. **-S** one that lurks

LUSCIOUS *adj* having a very pleasing taste or smell

LUSH *adj* **LUSHER, LUSHEST** abounding in vegetation **LUSHLY** *adv*

LUSH *v* **-ED, -ING, -ES** to drink to excess

LUSHNESS *n* pl. **-ES** the state of being lush

LUST *v* **-ED, -ING, -S** to have an intense desire

LUSTER *v* **-ED, -ING, -S** to make or become lustrous

LUSTFUL *adj* marked by excessive sexual desire

LUSTIER comparative of lusty

LUSTIEST superlative of lusty

LUSTILY *adv* in a lusty manner

LUSTRA a pl. of lustrum

LUSTRAL *adj* pertaining to a lustrum

LUSTRATE *v* **-TRATED, -TRATING, -TRATES** to purify ceremonially

LUSTRE *v* **-TRED, -TRING, -TRES** to luster

LUSTRINE *n* pl. **-S** lustring

LUSTRING *n* pl. **-S** a glossy silk fabric

LUSTROUS *adj* reflecting light evenly and efficiently

LUSTRUM *n* pl. **-TRUMS** or **-TRA** a ceremonial purification of the population in ancient Rome

LUSTY *adj* **LUSTIER, LUSTIEST** full of vigor

LUSUS   *n* pl. **-ES** an abnormality

LUTANIST   *n* pl. **-S** one who plays the lute

LUTE   *v* **LUTED, LUTING, LUTES** to play a lute (a stringed musical instrument)

LUTEA   pl. of luteum

LUTEAL   *adj* pertaining to the luteum

LUTECIUM   *n* pl. **-S** lutetium

LUTED   past tense of lute

LUTEFISK   *n* pl. **-S** dried codfish

LUTEIN   *n* pl. **-S** a yellow pigment

LUTENIST   *n* pl. **-S** lutanist

LUTEOLIN   *n* pl. **-S** a yellow pigment

LUTEOUS   *adj* light to moderate greenish yellow in color

LUTETIUM   *n* pl. **-S** a metallic element

LUTEUM   *n* pl. **-TEA** a hormone-secreting body

LUTFISK   *n* pl. **-S** lutefisk

LUTHERN   *n* pl. **-S** a type of window

LUTHIER   *n* pl. **-S** one who makes stringed instruments

LUTING   *n* pl. **-S** a substance used as a sealant

LUTIST   *n* pl. **-S** a lutanist

LUTZ   *n* pl. **-ES** a jump in figure skating

LUV   *v* **LUVVED, LUVVING, LUVS** to love

LUVVIE   *n* pl. **-S** lovey

LUVVY   *n* pl. **LUVVIES** lovey

LUX   *n* pl. **LUXES** or **LUCES** a unit of illumination

LUXATE   *v* **-ATED, -ATING, -ATES** to put out of joint

LUXATION   *n* pl. **-S** the act of luxating

LUXE   *n* pl. **-S** luxury

LUXE   *adj* **LUXER, LUXEST** deluxe

LUXURY   *n* pl. **-RIES** free indulgence in that which affords pleasure or comfort

LWEI   *n* pl. **-S** a monetary unit of Angola

LYARD   *adj* streaked with gray

LYART   *adj* lyard

LYASE   *n* pl. **-S** an enzyme

LYCEE   *n* pl. **-S** a French secondary school

LYCEUM   *n* pl. **-CEUMS** or **-CEA** a hall for public lectures or discussions

LYCH   *n* pl. **-ES** lich

LYCHEE   *n* pl. **-S** litchi

LYCHGATE   *n* pl. **-S** a roofed gateway to a churchyard

LYCHNIS   *n* pl. **-NISES** a flowering plant

LYCOPENE   *n* pl. **-S** a red pigment

LYCOPOD   *n* pl. **-S** an evergreen plant

LYCOPSID   *n* pl. **-S** a type of club moss

LYDDITE   *n* pl. **-S** an explosive

LYE   *n* pl. **-S** a solution used in making soap

LYING   *n* pl. **-S** the act of telling lies

LYINGLY   *adv* falsely

LYMPH   *n* pl. **-S** a body fluid containing white blood cells **LYMPHOID, LYMPHOUS** *adj*

LYMPHOMA   *n* pl. **-MAS** or **-MATA** a type of tumor

LYNCEAN   *adj* of or resembling a lynx

LYNCH   *v* **-ED, -ING, -ES** to put to death without legal sanction

LYNCHER   *n* pl. **-S** one that lynches

LYNCHING   *n* pl. **-S** the act of one who lynches

LYNCHPIN   *n* pl. **-S** linchpin

LYNX   *n* pl. **-ES** a short-tailed wildcat

LYOPHILE   *adj* pertaining to a type of colloid

LYRATE   *adj* having the shape of a lyre **LYRATELY** *adv*

LYRATED   *adj* lyrate

LYRE   *n* pl. **-S** an ancient harp-like instrument

LYREBIRD   *n* pl. **-S** an Australian bird

LYRIC   *n* pl. **-S** a lyrical poem

LYRICAL   *adj* having the form of a song

LYRICISE   *v* **-CISED, -CISING, -CISES** to lyricize

LYRICISM   *n* pl. **-S** the quality of being lyrics

LYRICIST   *n* pl. **-S** one who writes the words for songs

LYRICIZE   *v* **-CIZED, -CIZING, -CIZES** to write lyrics

LYRICON   *n* pl. **-S** an electronic wind instrument

LYRIFORM   *adj* lyrate

LYRISM   *n* pl. **-S** lyricism

LYRIST   *n* pl. **-S** one who plays the lyre

LYSATE   *n* pl. **-S** a product of lysis

LYSE *v* **LYSED, LYSING, LYSES** to cause to undergo lysis

LYSIN *n* pl. **-S** a substance capable of disintegrating blood cells or bacteria

LYSINE *n* pl. **-S** an amino acid

LYSING present participle of lyse

LYSIS *n* pl. **LYSES** the disintegration of cells by lysins

LYSOGEN *n* pl. **-S** a type of antigen

LYSOGENY *n* pl. **-NIES** the state of being like a lysogen

LYSOSOME *n* pl. **-S** a saclike part of a cell

LYSOZYME *n* pl. **-S** an enzyme

LYSSA *n* pl. **-S** rabies

LYTIC *adj* pertaining to lysis

LYTTA *n* pl. **-TAS** or **-TAE** a fibrous band in the tongue of certain carnivorous mammals

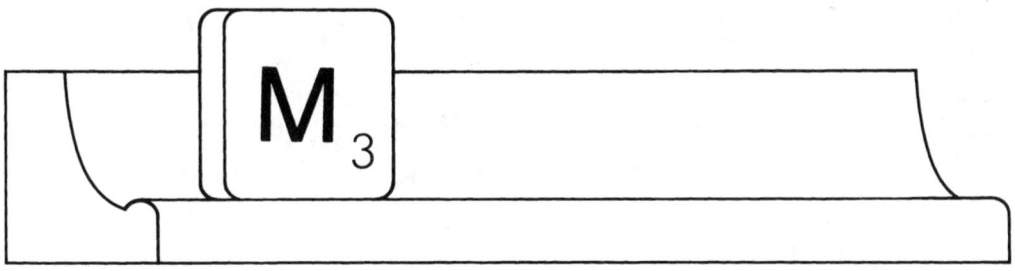

MA	*n* pl. **-S** mother
MAAR	*n* pl. **-S** a volcanic crater
MABE	*n* pl. **-S** a cultured pearl
MAC	*n* pl. **-S** a raincoat
MACABER	*adj* macabre
MACABRE	*adj* gruesome
MACACO	*n* pl. **-COS** a lemur
MACADAM	*n* pl. **-S** a type of pavement
MACAQUE	*n* pl. **-S** a short-tailed monkey
MACARONI	*n* pl. **-NIS** or **-NIES** a tubular pasta
MACAROON	*n* pl. **-S** a type of cookie
MACAW	*n* pl. **-S** a large parrot
MACCABAW	*n* pl. **-S** maccaboy
MACCABOY	*n* pl. **-BOYS** a type of snuff
MACCHIA	*n* pl. **-CHIE** a dense growth of small trees and shrubs
MACCOBOY	*n* pl. **-BOYS** maccaboy
MACE	*v* **MACED, MACING, MACES** to attack with a weapon resembling a club (a heavy piece of wood)
MACER	*n* pl. **-S** an official who carries a ceremonial staff
MACERATE	*v* **-ATED, -ATING, -ATES** to soften by soaking in liquid
MACH	*n* pl. **-S** a number indicating the ratio of the speed of a body to the speed of sound
MACHACA	*n* pl. **-S** a Mexican dish featuring shredded meat fried with vegetables
MACHE	*n* pl. **-S** a European herb
MACHER	*n* pl. **-S** a person known for getting things done
MACHETE	*n* pl. **-S** a large, heavy knife
MACHINE	*v* **-CHINED, -CHINING, -CHINES** to process by machine (a mechanical device)
MACHISMO	*n* pl. **-MOS** strong masculinity
MACHO	*n* pl. **-CHOS** a person who exhibits machismo
MACHOISM	*n* pl. **-S** machismo
MACHREE	*n* pl. **-S** dear
MACHZOR	*n* pl. **-ZORS** or **-ZORIM** mahzor
MACING	present participle of mace
MACK	*n* pl. **-S** mac
MACKEREL	*n* pl. **-S** a marine food fish
MACKINAW	*n* pl. **-S** a woolen fabric
MACKLE	*v* **-LED, -LING, -LES** to blur in printing
MACLE	*n* pl. **-S** a spot or discoloration in a mineral **MACLED** *adj*
MACON	*n* pl. **-S** a red or white French wine
MACRAME	*n* pl. **-S** a trimming of knotted thread or cord
MACRO	*n* pl. **-ROS** a type of computer instruction
MACRON	*n* pl. **-S** a symbol placed over a vowel to show that it has a long sound
MACROPOD	*n* pl. **-S** a plant-eating marsupial mammal
MACRURAL	*adj* pertaining to macruran
MACRURAN	*n* pl. **-S** any of a suborder of crustaceans
MACULA	*n* pl. **-LAS** or **-LAE** a spot **MACULAR** *adj*
MACULATE	*v* **-LATED, -LATING, -LATES** to mark with spots
MACULE	*v* **-ULED, -ULING, -ULES** to mackle
MACUMBA	*n* pl. **-S** a religion practiced in Brazil
MAD	*adj* **MADDER, MADDEST** insane
MAD	*v* **MADDED, MADDING, MADS** to madden
MADAM	*n* pl. **-S** a woman who manages a brothel

MADAME   *n* pl. **-S** madam

MADAME   *n* pl. **MESDAMES** the French title of respect for a married woman

MADCAP   *n* pl. **-S** an impulsive person

MADDED   past tense of mad

MADDEN   *v* **-ED, -ING, -S** to make or become mad

MADDER   *n* pl. **-S** a perennial herb

MADDEST   superlative of mad

MADDING   present participle of mad

MADDISH   *adj* somewhat mad

MADE   past tense of make

MADEIRA   *n* pl. **-S** a white wine

MADERIZE   *v* **-IZED, -IZING, -IZES** to turn brown — used of white wine

MADHOUSE   *n* pl. **-S** an insane asylum

MADLY   *adv* in a mad manner

MADMAN   *n* pl. **-MEN** a man who is insane

MADNESS   *n* pl. **-ES** the state of being mad

MADONNA   *n* pl. **-S** a former Italian title of respect for a woman

MADRAS   *n* pl. **-ES** a cotton fabric

MADRASA   *n* pl. **-S** madrassa

MADRASAH   *n* pl. **-S** madrassa

MADRASSA   *n* pl. **-S** a Muslim school

MADRE   *n* pl. **-S** mother

MADRIGAL   *n* pl. **-S** a short lyric poem

MADRONA   *n* pl. **-S** an evergreen tree

MADRONE   *n* pl. **-S** madrona

MADRONO   *n* pl. **-NOS** madrona

MADTOM   *n* pl. **-S** a North American catfish

MADURO   *n* pl. **-ROS** a dark-colored, relatively strong cigar

MADWOMAN   *n* pl. **-WOMEN** a woman who is insane

MADWORT   *n* pl. **-S** a flowering plant

MADZOON   *n* pl. **-S** matzoon

MAE   *n* pl. **-S** more

MAENAD   *n* pl. **-S** or **-ES** a female participant in ancient Greek orgies **MAENADIC** *adj*

MAESTOSO   *n* pl. **-SOS** a stately musical passage

MAESTRO   *n* pl. **-STROS** or **-STRI** a master of an art

MAFFIA   *n* pl. **-S** mafia

MAFFICK   *v* **-ED, -ING, -S** to celebrate boisterously

MAFIA   *n* pl. **-S** a secret criminal organization

MAFIC   *adj* pertaining to minerals rich in magnesium and iron

MAFIOSO   *n* pl. **-SOS** or **-SI** a member of the mafia

MAFTIR   *n* pl. **-S** the concluding section of a parashah

MAG   *n* pl. **-S** a magazine

MAGALOG   *n* pl. **-S** a sales catalog resembling a magazine

MAGAZINE   *n* pl. **-S** a type of periodical publication

MAGDALEN   *n* pl. **-S** a reformed prostitute

MAGE   *n* pl. **-S** a magician

MAGENTA   *n* pl. **-S** a purplish red dye

MAGGOT   *n* pl. **-S** the legless larva of certain insects **MAGGOTY** *adj*

MAGI   pl. of magus

MAGIAN   *n* pl. **-S** a magus

MAGIC   *v* **-ICKED, -ICKING, -ICS** to affect by magic (sorcery)

MAGICAL   *adj* resembling magic

MAGICIAN   *n* pl. **-S** one skilled in magic

MAGICKED   past tense of magic

MAGICKING   present participle of magic

MAGILP   *n* pl. **-S** megilp

MAGISTER   *n* pl. **-S** a master or teacher

MAGLEV   *n* pl. **-S** a train using magnets to move above the tracks

MAGMA   *n* pl. **-MAS** or **-MATA** the molten matter from which igneous rock is formed **MAGMATIC** *adj*

MAGNATE   *n* pl. **-S** a powerful or influential person

MAGNESIA   *n* pl. **-S** a medicinal compound **MAGNESIC** *adj*

MAGNET   *n* pl. **-S** a body that possesses the property of attracting iron

MAGNETIC   *n* pl. **-S** a magnet

MAGNETO   *n* pl. **-TOS** a type of electric generator

MAGNETON   *n* pl. **-S** a unit of magnetic moment

MAGNIFIC   *adj* magnificent

MAGNIFY   *v* **-FIED, -FYING, -FIES** to increase the perceived size of

MAGNOLIA   *n* pl. **-S** a flowering shrub or tree

MAGNOX   *n* pl. **-ES** a magnesium-based alloy

MAGNUM   *n* pl. **-S** a large wine bottle

MAGOT	n pl. **-S** a tailless ape	**MAILROOM**	n pl. **-S** a room for processing mail
MAGPIE	n pl. **-S** a corvine bird	**MAILSHOT**	n pl. **-S** something mailed to many people at one time
MAGUEY	n pl. **-GUEYS** a tropical plant	**MAIM**	v **-ED, -ING, -S** to injure so as to cause lasting damage
MAGUS	n pl. **-GI** a magician		
MAHANT	n pl. **-S** a chief Hindu priest	**MAIMER**	n pl. **-S** one that maims
MAHARAJA	n pl. **-S** a king or prince in India	**MAIN**	n pl. **-S** the principal part
MAHARANI	n pl. **-S** the wife of a maharaja	**MAINLAND**	n pl. **-S** a principal land mass
MAHATMA	n pl. **-S** a Hindu sage	**MAINLINE**	v **-LINED, -LINING, -LINES** to inject a narcotic into a major vein
MAHIMAHI	n pl. **-S** a food fish in Hawaii		
MAHJONG	n pl. **-S** a game of Chinese origin	**MAINLY**	adv for the most part
MAHJONGG	n pl. **-S** mahjong	**MAINMAST**	n pl. **-S** the principal mast of a vessel
MAHOE	n pl. **-S** a tropical tree	**MAINSAIL**	n pl. **-S** the principal sail of a vessel
MAHOGANY	n pl. **-NIES** a tropical tree		
MAHONIA	n pl. **-S** a flowering shrub	**MAINSTAY**	n pl. **-STAYS** a principal support
MAHOUT	n pl. **-S** the keeper and driver of an elephant	**MAINTAIN**	v **-ED, -ING, -S** to keep in proper condition
MAHUA	n pl. **-S** an Indian tree	**MAINTOP**	n pl. **-S** a platform at the head of a mainmast
MAHUANG	n pl. **-S** an Asian plant		
MAHWA	n pl. **-S** mahua	**MAIOLICA**	n pl. **-S** majolica
MAHZOR	n pl. **-ZORS** or **-ZORIM** a Jewish prayer book	**MAIR**	n pl. **-S** more
		MAIST	n pl. **-S** most
MAIASAUR	n pl. **-S** an herbivorous dinosaur	**MAIZE**	n pl. **-S** an American cereal grass
MAID	n pl. **-S** a maiden **MAIDISH** adj	**MAJAGUA**	n pl. **-S** a tropical tree
MAIDAN	n pl. **-S** an open space in or near a town	**MAJESTIC**	adj having majesty
		MAJESTY	n pl. **-TIES** regal dignity
MAIDEN	n pl. **-S** a young unmarried woman **MAIDENLY** adj	**MAJLIS**	n pl. **-ES** the parliament in various North African and Middle Eastern countries
MAIDHOOD	n pl. **-S** the state of being a maiden		
MAIEUTIC	adj pertaining to a method of eliciting knowledge	**MAJOLICA**	n pl. **-S** a type of pottery
		MAJOR	v **-ED, -ING, -S** to pursue a specific principal course of study
MAIGRE	adj containing neither flesh nor its juices		
		MAJORITY	n pl. **-TIES** the greater number or part
MAIHEM	n pl. **-S** mayhem		
MAIL	v **-ED, -ING, -S** to send by a governmental postal system **MAILABLE** adj	**MAJORLY**	adv mainly
		MAKAR	n pl. **-S** a poet
		MAKE	v **MADE, MAKING, MAKES** to cause to exist **MAKABLE, MAKEABLE** adj
MAILBAG	n pl. **-S** a bag for carrying mail (postal material)		
MAILBOX	n pl. **-ES** a box for depositing mail	**MAKEBATE**	n pl. **-S** one that encourages quarrels
MAILE	n pl. **-S** a Pacific island vine	**MAKEFAST**	n pl. **-S** an object to which a boat is tied
MAILER	n pl. **-S** one that mails		
MAILING	n pl. **-S** a rented farm	**MAKEOVER**	n pl. **-S** a changing of appearance
MAILL	n pl. **-S** a payment	**MAKER**	n pl. **-S** one that makes
MAILLESS	adj having no armor	**MAKEUP**	n pl. **-S** the way in which the parts or ingredients of something are put together
MAILLOT	n pl. **-S** a woman's one-piece bathing suit		
MAILMAN	n pl. **-MEN** a man who carries and delivers mail		

MAKI *n* pl. **-S** a dish of sushi and raw vegetables wrapped in seaweed

MAKIMONO *n* pl. **-NOS** a Japanese ornamental scroll

MAKING *n* pl. **-S** material from which something can be developed

MAKO *n* pl. **-KOS** a large shark

MAKUTA pl. of likuta

MALACCA *n* pl. **-S** the cane of an Asian rattan palm

MALADY *n* pl. **-DIES** an illness

MALAISE *n* pl. **-S** a feeling of vague discomfort

MALAMUTE *n* pl. **-S** an Alaskan sled dog

MALANGA *n* pl. **-S** a yautia

MALAPERT *n* pl. **-S** an impudent person

MALAPROP *n* pl. **-S** a humorous misuse of a word

MALAR *n* pl. **-S** the cheekbone

MALARIA *n* pl. **-S** an infectious disease **MALARIAL, MALARIAN** *adj*

MALARKEY *n* pl. **-KEYS** nonsense

MALARKY *n* pl. **-KIES** malarkey

MALAROMA *n* pl. **-S** a malodor

MALATE *n* pl. **-S** a chemical salt

MALE *n* pl. **-S** an individual that begets young by fertilizing the female

MALEATE *n* pl. **-S** a chemical salt

MALEDICT *v* **-ED, -ING, -S** to curse

MALEFIC *adj* producing or causing evil

MALEMIUT *n* pl. **-S** malamute

MALEMUTE *n* pl. **-S** malamute

MALENESS *n* pl. **-ES** the quality of being a male

MALFED *adj* badly fed

MALGRE *prep* in spite of

MALIC *adj* pertaining to apples

MALICE *n* pl. **-S** a desire to injure another

MALIGN *v* **-ED, -ING, -S** to speak evil of

MALIGNER *n* pl. **-S** one that maligns

MALIGNLY *adv* in an evil manner

MALIHINI *n* pl. **-S** a newcomer to Hawaii

MALINE *n* pl. **-S** a delicate net used for veils

MALINGER *v* **-ED, -ING, -S** to feign illness in order to avoid duty or work

MALISON *n* pl. **-S** a curse

MALKIN *n* pl. **-S** an untidy woman

MALL *v* **-ED, -ING, -S** to maul

MALLARD *n* pl. **-S** a wild duck

MALLEE *n* pl. **-S** an evergreen tree

MALLEI pl. of malleus

MALLEOLI *n/pl* bony protuberances of the ankle

MALLET *n* pl. **-S** a type of hammer

MALLEUS *n* pl. **-LEI** a bone of the middle ear

MALLING *n* pl. **-S** the practice of shopping at malls (large buildings with many shops)

MALLOW *n* pl. **-S** a flowering plant

MALM *n* pl. **-S** a soft, friable limestone

MALMSEY *n* pl. **-SEYS** a white wine

MALMY *adj* **MALMIER, MALMIEST** resembling malm

MALODOR *n* pl. **-S** an offensive odor

MALONATE *n* pl. **-S** a salt or ester of malonic acid

MALOTI pl. of loti

MALPOSED *adj* being in the wrong position

MALT *v* **-ED, -ING, -S** to treat or combine with malt (germinated grain)

MALTASE *n* pl. **-S** an enzyme

MALTED *n* pl. **-S** a sweet beverage

MALTHA *n* pl. **-S** a natural tar

MALTIER comparative of malty

MALTIEST superlative of malty

MALTING *n* pl. **-S** the process of preparing grain for brewing

MALTOL *n* pl. **-S** a chemical compound

MALTOSE *n* pl. **-S** a type of sugar

MALTREAT *v* **-ED, -ING, -S** to treat badly

MALTSTER *n* pl. **-S** one that makes malt

MALTY *adj* **MALTIER, MALTIEST** resembling malt

MALVASIA *n* pl. **-S** malmsey

MALWARE *n* pl. **-S** software designed to disable computers

MAM *n* pl. **-S** mother

MAMA *n* pl. **-S** mother

MAMALIGA *n* pl. **-S** a cornmeal porridge

MAMASAN *n* pl. **-S** a Japanese woman in a position of authority

MAMATEEK *n* pl. **-S** a type of wigwam

MAMBA *n* pl. **-S** a venomous snake

MAMBO *v* **-ED, -ING, -ES** or **-S** to perform a ballroom dance

MAMEE _n_ pl. **-S** mamey

MAMELUKE _n_ pl. **-S** a slave in Muslim countries

MAMEY _n_ pl. **-MEYS** or **-MEYES** a tropical tree

MAMIE _n_ pl. **-S** mamey

MAMILLA _n_ pl. **-LAE** mammilla

MAMLUK _n_ pl. **-S** mameluke

MAMMA _n_ pl. **-MAE** a milk-secreting organ

MAMMA _n_ pl. **-S** mama

MAMMAL _n_ pl. **-S** any of a class of warm-blooded vertebrates

MAMMARY _adj_ pertaining to the mammae

MAMMATE _adj_ having mammae

MAMMATUS _n_ pl. **-TI** a type of cloud

MAMMEE _n_ pl. **-S** mamey

MAMMER _v_ **-ED, -ING, -S** to hesitate

MAMMET _n_ pl. **-S** maumet

MAMMEY _n_ pl. **-MEYS** mamey

MAMMIE _n_ pl. **-S** mammy

MAMMIES pl. of mammy

MAMMILLA _n_ pl. **-LAE** a nipple

MAMMITIS _n_ pl. **-MITIDES** mastitis

MAMMOCK _v_ **-ED, -ING, -S** to shred

MAMMON _n_ pl. **-S** material wealth

MAMMOTH _n_ pl. **-S** an extinct elephant

MAMMY _n_ pl. **-MIES** mother

MAMZER _n_ pl. **-S** a bastard

MAN _n_ pl. **MEN** an adult human male

MAN _v_ **MANNED, MANNING, MANS** to supply with men

MANA _n_ pl. **-S** a supernatural force in certain Pacific island religions

MANACLE _v_ **-CLED, -CLING, -CLES** to handcuff

MANAGE _v_ **-AGED, -AGING, -AGES** to control or direct

MANAGER _n_ pl. **-S** one that manages

MANAKIN _n_ pl. **-S** a tropical bird

MANANA _n_ pl. **-S** tomorrow

MANAT _n_ pl. **-S** a monetary unit of Azerbaijan

MANATEE _n_ pl. **-S** an aquatic mammal **MANATOID** _adj_

MANCHE _n_ pl. **-S** a heraldic design

MANCHET _n_ pl. **-S** a small loaf of fine white bread

MANCIPLE _n_ pl. **-S** an officer authorized to purchase provisions

MANDALA _n_ pl. **-S** a Hindu or Buddhist graphic symbol of the universe **MANDALIC** _adj_

MANDAMUS _v_ **-ED, -ING, -ES** to command by means of writ issued by a superior court

MANDARIN _n_ pl. **-S** a citrus fruit

MANDATE _v_ **-DATED, -DATING, -DATES** to authorize or decree

MANDATOR _n_ pl. **-S** one that mandates

MANDIBLE _n_ pl. **-S** the bone of the lower jaw

MANDIOCA _n_ pl. **-S** manioc

MANDOLA _n_ pl. **-S** an ancient lute

MANDOLIN _n_ pl. **-S** a stringed musical instrument

MANDORA _n_ pl. **-S** a stringed musical instrument

MANDORLA _n_ pl. **-S** a pointed oval figure

MANDRAKE _n_ pl. **-S** a European herb

MANDREL _n_ pl. **-S** a shaft on which a tool is mounted

MANDRIL _n_ pl. **-S** mandrel

MANDRILL _n_ pl. **-S** a large baboon

MANE _n_ pl. **-S** the long hair growing on and about the neck of some animals **MANED, MANELESS** _adj_

MANEB _n_ pl. **-S** a powder for killing fungi

MANEGE _n_ pl. **-S** the art of training and riding horses

MANEUVER _v_ **-ED, -ING, -S** to change the position of for a specific purpose

MANFUL _adj_ courageous **MANFULLY** _adv_

MANGA _n_ pl. **-S** a Japanese graphic novel

MANGABEY _n_ pl. **-BEYS** a long-tailed monkey

MANGABY _n_ pl. **-BIES** mangabey

MANGANIC _adj_ containing manganese (a metallic element)

MANGANIN _n_ pl. **-S** an alloy of copper, manganese, and nickel

MANGE _n_ pl. **-S** a skin disease of domestic animals

MANGEL _n_ pl. **-S** a variety of beet

MANGER _n_ pl. **-S** a trough or box from which horses or cattle eat

MANGEY _adj_ **MANGIER, MANGIEST** mangy

MANGIER comparative of mangy

MANGIEST superlative of mangy

MANGILY _adv_ in a mangy manner

MANGLE	*v* **-GLED, -GLING, -GLES** to cut, slash, or crush so as to disfigure
MANGLER	*n* pl. **-S** one that mangles
MANGO	*n* pl. **-GOS** or **-GOES** an edible tropical fruit
MANGOLD	*n* pl. **-S** mangel
MANGONEL	*n* pl. **-S** a medieval military device for hurling stones
MANGROVE	*n* pl. **-S** a tropical tree or shrub
MANGY	*adj* **MANGIER, MANGIEST** affected with mange
MANHOLE	*n* pl. **-S** a hole providing entrance to an underground or enclosed structure
MANHOOD	*n* pl. **-S** the state of being a man
MANHUNT	*n* pl. **-S** an intensive search for a person
MANIA	*n* pl. **-S** an excessive interest or enthusiasm
MANIAC	*n* pl. **-S** an insane person **MANIACAL** *adj*
MANIC	*n* pl. **-S** one that is affected with mania
MANICURE	*v* **-CURED, -CURING, -CURES** to trim and polish the fingernails of
MANIFEST	*v* **-ED, -ING, -S** to show clearly
MANIFOLD	*v* **-ED, -ING, -S** to make several copies of
MANIHOT	*n* pl. **-S** a tropical plant
MANIKIN	*n* pl. **-S** an anatomical model of the human body
MANILA	*n* pl. **-S** a strong paper
MANILLA	*n* pl. **-S** manila
MANILLE	*n* pl. **-S** the second highest trump in certain card games
MANIOC	*n* pl. **-S** a tropical plant
MANIOCA	*n* pl. **-S** manioc
MANIPLE	*n* pl. **-S** a silk band worn on the left arm as a vestment
MANITO	*n* pl. **-TOS** manitou
MANITOU	*n* pl. **-S** an Algonquian Indian deity
MANITU	*n* pl. **-S** manitou
MANKIND	*n* pl. **MANKIND** the human race
MANKY	*adj* **MANKIER, MANKIEST** inferior, defective
MANLESS	*adj* having no men
MANLIKE	*adj* resembling a man
MANLY	*adj* **-LIER, -LIEST** having the qualities of a man **MANLILY** *adv*
MANMADE	*adj* made by man
MANNA	*n* pl. **-S** divinely supplied food
MANNAN	*n* pl. **-S** a type of sugar
MANNED	past tense of man
MANNER	*n* pl. **-S** a way of acting **MANNERED** *adj*
MANNERLY	*adj* polite
MANNIKIN	*n* pl. **-S** manikin
MANNING	present participle of man
MANNISH	*adj* resembling or characteristic of a man
MANNITE	*n* pl. **-S** mannitol **MANNITIC** *adj*
MANNITOL	*n* pl. **-S** an alcohol
MANNOSE	*n* pl. **-S** a type of sugar
MANO	*n* pl. **-NOS** a stone used for grinding foods
MANOR	*n* pl. **-S** a landed estate or territorial unit **MANORIAL** *adj*
MANPACK	*adj* designed to be carried by one person
MANPOWER	*n* pl. **-S** the number of men available for service
MANQUE	*adj* frustrated in the fulfillment of one's aspirations
MANROPE	*n* pl. **-S** a rope used as a handrail
MANSARD	*n* pl. **-S** a type of roof
MANSCAPE	*v* **-SCAPED, -SCAPING, -SCAPES** to trim or shave a man's body hair to enhance appearance
MANSE	*n* pl. **-S** a clergyman's house
MANSION	*n* pl. **-S** a large, impressive house
MANTA	*n* pl. **-S** a cotton fabric
MANTEAU	*n* pl. **-TEAUS** or **-TEAUX** a loose cloak
MANTEL	*n* pl. **-S** a shelf above a fireplace
MANTELET	*n* pl. **-S** a mobile screen used to protect soldiers
MANTES	a pl. of mantis
MANTIC	*adj* having powers of prophecy
MANTID	*n* pl. **-S** mantis
MANTILLA	*n* pl. **-S** a woman's scarf
MANTIS	*n* pl. **-TISES** or **-TES** a predatory insect
MANTISSA	*n* pl. **-S** the decimal part of a logarithm
MANTLE	*v* **-TLED, -TLING, -TLES** to cloak
MANTLET	*n* pl. **-S** mantelet
MANTLING	*n* pl. **-S** an ornamental cloth

MANTRA   *n* pl. **-S** a mystical formula of prayer or incantation in Hinduism **MANTRIC** *adj*

MANTRAM   *n* pl. **-S** mantra

MANTRAP   *n* pl. **-S** a trap for catching men

MANTUA   *n* pl. **-S** a woman's gown

MANUAL   *n* pl. **-S** a small reference book

MANUALLY   *adv* by means of the hands

MANUARY   *adj* involving the hands

MANUBRIA   *n/pl* handle-shaped anatomical parts

MANUCODE   *n* pl. **-S** a bird of paradise

MANUKA   *n* pl. **-S** a small tree of New Zealand

MANUMIT   *v* **-MITTED, -MITTING, -MITS** to free from slavery

MANURE   *v* **-NURED, -NURING, -NURES** to fertilize with manure (animal excrement)

MANURER   *n* pl. **-S** one that manures

MANURIAL   *adj* of or pertaining to manure

MANURING   present participle of manure

MANUS   *n* pl. **MANUS** the end of the forelimb in vertebrates

MANWARD   *adv* toward man

MANWARDS   *adv* manward

MANWISE   *adv* in a manner characteristic of man

MANY   *adj* **MORE, MOST** consisting of or amounting to a large number

MANYFOLD   *adv* by many times

MAP   *v* **MAPPED, MAPPING, MAPS** to delineate on a map (a representation of a region)

MAPLE   *n* pl. **-S** a hardwood tree

MAPLESS   *adj* lacking a map

MAPLIKE   *adj* resembling a map

MAPMAKER   *n* pl. **-S** one that makes maps

MAPPABLE   *adj* capable of being mapped

MAPPED   past tense of map

MAPPER   *n* pl. **-S** one that maps

MAPPING   *n* pl. **-S** a mathematical correspondence

MAQUETTE   *n* pl. **-S** a small preliminary model

MAQUI   *n* pl. **-S** maquis

MAQUILA   *n* pl. **-S** a foreign-owned assembly factory in Mexico

MAQUIS   *n* pl. **MAQUIS** a thick underbrush

MAR   *v* **MARRED, MARRING, MARS** to detract from the perfection or wholeness of

MARA   *n* pl. **-S** a cavy of Argentina

MARABOU   *n* pl. **-S** an African stork

MARABOUT   *n* pl. **-S** a marabou

MARACA   *n* pl. **-S** a percussion instrument

MARANTA   *n* pl. **-S** a tropical plant

MARASCA   *n* pl. **-S** a wild cherry

MARASMUS   *n* pl. **-ES** a wasting away of the body **MARASMIC** *adj*

MARATHON   *n* pl. **-S** a long-distance race

MARAUD   *v* **-ED, -ING, -S** to rove in search of booty

MARAUDER   *n* pl. **-S** one that marauds

MARAVEDI   *n* pl. **-S** a former coin of Spain

MARBLE   *v* **-BLED, -BLING, -BLES** to give a mottled appearance to

MARBLER   *n* pl. **-S** one that marbles

MARBLING   *n* pl. **-S** an intermixture of fat and lean in meat

MARBLY   *adj* **-BLIER, -BLIEST** mottled

MARC   *n* pl. **-S** the residue remaining after a fruit has been pressed

MARCATO   *n* pl. **-TOS** a musical passage played with strong accentuation

MARCEL   *v* **-CELLED, -CELLING, -CELS** to make a deep, soft wave in the hair

MARCH   *v* **-ED, -ING, -ES** to walk in a formal military manner

MARCHEN   *n* pl. **MARCHEN** a folktale

MARCHER   *n* pl. **-S** one that marches

MARCHESA   *n* pl. **-CHESE** the wife or widow of a marchese

MARCHESE   *n* pl. **-CHESI** an Italian nobleman

MARCONI   *n* pl. **-S** a two-way radio

MARE   *n* pl. **-RIA** a dark area on the surface of the moon or Mars

MARE   *n* pl. **-S** a mature female horse

MAREMMA   *n* pl. **-REMME** a marshy coastal region

MARENGO   *adj* served with a sauce of mushrooms, tomatoes, oil, and wine

MARGARIC   *adj* pearly

MARGARIN   *n* pl. **-S** a butter substitute

MARGATE   *n* pl. **-S** a tropical fish

MARGAY   *n* pl. **-GAYS** a small American wildcat

MARGE	*n* pl. **-S** a margin
MARGENT	*v* **-ED, -ING, -S** to margin
MARGIN	*v* **-ED, -ING, -S** to provide with a margin (a border)
MARGINAL	*n* pl. **-S** one considered to be at a lower or outer limit
MARGRAVE	*n* pl. **-S** the military governor of a medieval German border province
MARIA	pl. of mare
MARIACHI	*n* pl. **-S** a Mexican musical band
MARIGOLD	*n* pl. **-S** a flowering plant
MARIMBA	*n* pl. **-S** a percussion instrument
MARINA	*n* pl. **-S** a docking area for small boats
MARINADE	*v* **-NADED, -NADING, -NADES** to marinate
MARINARA	*n* pl. **-S** a seasoned tomato sauce
MARINATE	*v* **-NATED, -NATING, -NATES** to soak in a seasoned liquid before cooking
MARINE	*n* pl. **-S** a soldier trained for service at sea and on land
MARINER	*n* pl. **-S** a sailor
MARIPOSA	*n* pl. **-S** a flowering plant
MARISH	*n* pl. **-ES** a marsh
MARITAL	*adj* pertaining to marriage
MARITIME	*adj* pertaining to navigation or commerce on the sea
MARJORAM	*n* pl. **-S** a fragrant herb
MARK	*v* **-ED, -ING, -S** to make a visible impression on
MARKA	*n* pl. **-S** a monetary unit of Bosnia and Herzegovina
MARKDOWN	*n* pl. **-S** a reduction in price
MARKEDLY	*adv* in an evident manner
MARKER	*n* pl. **-S** one that marks
MARKET	*v* **-ED, -ING, -S** to offer for sale
MARKETER	*n* pl. **-S** one that markets
MARKHOOR	*n* pl. **-S** markhor
MARKHOR	*n* pl. **-S** a wild goat
MARKING	*n* pl. **-S** a pattern of marks
MARKKA	*n* pl. **-KAS** or **-KAA** a former monetary unit of Finland
MARKSMAN	*n* pl. **-MEN** a person skillful at hitting a target
MARKUP	*n* pl. **-S** an increase in price
MARL	*v* **-ED, -ING, -S** to fertilize with marl (an earthy deposit containing lime, clay, and sand)

MARLIER	comparative of marly
MARLIEST	superlative of marly
MARLIN	*n* pl. **-S** a marine game fish
MARLINE	*n* pl. **-S** a rope used on a ship
MARLING	*n* pl. **-S** marline
MARLITE	*n* pl. **-S** a type of marl **MARLITIC** *adj*
MARLY	*adj* **MARLIER, MARLIEST** abounding with marl
MARMITE	*n* pl. **-S** a large soup kettle
MARMOSET	*n* pl. **-S** a small monkey
MARMOT	*n* pl. **-S** a burrowing rodent
MAROCAIN	*n* pl. **-S** a light crinkled fabric
MAROON	*v* **-ED, -ING, -S** to abandon in an isolated place
MARPLOT	*n* pl. **-S** one that ruins a plan by meddling
MARQUE	*n* pl. **-S** reprisal
MARQUEE	*n* pl. **-S** a rooflike structure projecting over an entrance
MARQUESS	*n* pl. **-ES** marquis
MARQUIS	*n* pl. **-ES** a European nobleman
MARQUISE	*n* pl. **-S** the wife or widow of a marquis
MARRAM	*n* pl. **-S** a beach grass
MARRANO	*n* pl. **-NOS** a Jew in Spain who professed Christianity to avoid persecution
MARRED	past tense of mar
MARRER	*n* pl. **-S** one that mars
MARRIAGE	*n* pl. **-S** the legal union of two persons of the opposiite or same sex
MARRIED	*n* pl. **-S** one who has entered into marriage
MARRIER	*n* pl. **-S** one that marries
MARRIES	present 3d person sing. of marry
MARRING	present participle of mar
MARRON	*n* pl. **-S** a variety of chestnut
MARROW	*v* **-ED, -ING, -S** to marry
MARROWY	*adj* pithy
MARRY	*v* **-RIED, -RYING, -RIES** to enter into marriage
MARSALA	*n* pl. **-S** a Sicilian wine
MARSE	*n* pl. **-S** master
MARSH	*n* pl. **-ES** a tract of low, wet land **MARSHED** *adj*
MARSHAL	*v* **-ED, -ING, -S** to put in proper order

MARSHALL	*v* **-ED, -ING, -S** to marshal
MARSHY	*adj* **MARSHIER, MARSHIEST** resembling a marsh
MARSUPIA	*n/pl* abdominal pouches of certain mammals
MART	*v* **-ED, -ING, -S** to market
MARTAGON	*n* pl. **-S** a flowering plant
MARTELLO	*n* pl. **-LOS** a circular fort
MARTEN	*n* pl. **-S** a carnivorous mammal
MARTIAL	*adj* pertaining to war
MARTIAN	*n* pl. **-S** a supposed inhabitant of the planet Mars
MARTIN	*n* pl. **-S** a small bird
MARTINET	*n* pl. **-S** one who demands rigid adherence to rules
MARTINI	*n* pl. **-S** an alcoholic beverage
MARTLET	*n* pl. **-S** a martin
MARTYR	*v* **-ED, -ING, -S** to put to death for adhering to a belief
MARTYRLY	*adj* resembling a martyr
MARTYRY	*n* pl. **-TYRIES** a shrine erected in honor of a martyred person
MARVEL	*v* **-VELED, -VELING, -VELS** or **-VELLED, -VELLING, -VELS** to be filled with wonder or astonishment
MARVELER	*n* pl. **-S** one who marvels
MARVY	*adj* marvelous
MARYJANE	*n* pl. **-S** marijuana
MARZIPAN	*n* pl. **-S** an almond candy
MASA	*n* pl. **-S** dough made of dried corn
MASALA	*n* pl. **-S** a blend of spices used in Indian cooking
MASCARA	*v* **-ED, -ING, -S** to color the eyelashes or eyebrows with a cosmetic
MASCON	*n* pl. **-S** a concentration of dense mass beneath the moon's surface
MASCOT	*n* pl. **-S** a person, animal, or object believed to bring good luck
MASER	*n* pl. **-S** a device for amplifying electrical impulses
MASH	*v* **-ED, -ING, -ES** to reduce to a pulpy mass
MASHER	*n* pl. **-S** one that mashes
MASHGIAH	*n* pl. **-GIHIM** an inspector of kosher establishments
MASHIE	*n* pl. **-S** a golf club
MASHY	*n* pl. **MASHIES** mashie
MASJID	*n* pl. **-S** a mosque

MASK	*v* **-ED, -ING, -S** to cover with a mask (a covering used to disguise the face) **MASKABLE** *adj*
MASKEG	*n* pl. **-S** muskeg
MASKER	*n* pl. **-S** one that wears a mask
MASKING	*n* pl. **-S** a piece of scenery used to conceal parts of a stage from the audience
MASKLIKE	*adj* suggestive of a mask
MASON	*v* **-ED, -ING, -S** to build with stone or brick
MASONIC	*adj* pertaining to masonry
MASONRY	*n* pl. **-RIES** a structure built of stone or brick
MASQUE	*n* pl. **-S** a dramatic entertainment formerly popular in England
MASQUER	*n* pl. **-S** masker
MASS	*v* **-ED, -ING, -ES** to assemble in a mass (a body of coherent matter)
MASSA	*n* pl. **-S** master
MASSACRE	*v* **-CRED, -CRING, -CRES** to kill indiscriminately
MASSAGE	*v* **-SAGED, -SAGING, -SAGES** to manipulate parts of the body for remedial or hygienic purposes
MASSAGER	*n* pl. **-S** one that massages
MASSCULT	*n* pl. **-S** culture as popularized by the mass media
MASSE	*n* pl. **-S** a type of shot in billiards
MASSEDLY	*adv* in a massed manner
MASSETER	*n* pl. **-S** a muscle that raises the lower jaw
MASSEUR	*n* pl. **-S** a man who massages
MASSEUSE	*n* pl. **-S** a woman who massages
MASSICOT	*n* pl. **-S** a yellow pigment
MASSIER	comparative of massy
MASSIEST	superlative of massy
MASSIF	*n* pl. **-S** a principal mountain mass
MASSIVE	*adj* of considerable size
MASSLESS	*adj* having no mass
MASSY	*adj* **MASSIER, MASSIEST** massive
MAST	*v* **-ED, -ING, -S** to provide with a mast (a long pole on a ship that supports the sails and rigging)
MASTABA	*n* pl. **-S** an ancient Egyptian tomb
MASTABAH	*n* pl. **-S** mastaba
MASTER	*v* **-ED, -ING, -S** to become skilled in
MASTERLY	*adj* very skillful

MASTERY   n pl. **-TERIES** superior knowledge or skill

MASTHEAD   v **-ED, -ING, -S** to raise to the top of a mast

MASTIC   n pl. **-S** an aromatic resin

MASTICHE   n pl. **-S** mastic

MASTIFF   n pl. **-S** a large, short-haired dog

MASTITIS   n pl. **-TITIDES** inflammation of the breast **MASTITIC** adj

MASTIX   n pl. **-ES** mastic

MASTLESS   adj having no mast

MASTLIKE   adj resembling a mast

MASTODON   n pl. **-S** an extinct elephant-like mammal

MASTOID   n pl. **-S** the rear portion of the temporal bone

MASURIUM   n pl. **-S** a metallic element

MAT   v **MATTED, MATTING, MATS** to pack down into a dense mass

MATADOR   n pl. **-S** the bullfighter who kills the bull in a bullfight

MATAMBALA   a pl. of tambala

MATCH   v **-ED, -ING, -ES** to set in competition or opposition

MATCHBOX   n pl. **-ES** a small box

MATCHER   n pl. **-S** one that matches

MATCHUP   n pl. **-S** a setting of two players against each other

MATE   v **MATED, MATING, MATES** to join as mates (partners in a union)

MATELESS   adj having no mate

MATELOT   n pl. **-S** a sailor

MATELOTE   n pl. **-S** a fish stew

MATER   n pl. **-TERS** or **-TRES** mother

MATERIAL   n pl. **-S** the substance of which anything is or may be composed

MATERIEL   n pl. **-S** the aggregate of equipment and supplies used by an organization

MATERNAL   adj pertaining to or characteristic of a mother

MATESHIP   n pl. **-S** the state of being a mate

MATEY   n pl. **-EYS** a friend

MATEY   adj **MATIER, MATIEST** companionable

MATH   n pl. **-S** mathematics

MATILDA   n pl. **-S** a hobo's bundle

MATIN   n pl. **-S** a morning song, as of birds

MATINAL   adj pertaining to the morning

MATINEE   n pl. **-S** a daytime performance

MATINESS   n pl. **-ES** friendliness

MATING   n pl. **-S** the period during which a seasonal-breeding animal can mate

MATLESS   adj having no mats (small floor coverings)

MATRASS   n pl. **-ES** a long-necked glass vessel

MATRES   a pl. of mater

MATRIC   n pl. **-S** matriculation (admission into a university)

MATRIX   n pl. **-TRIXES** or **-TRICES** something within which something else originates or develops

MATRON   n pl. **-S** a married woman of established social position **MATRONAL, MATRONLY** adj

MATSAH   n pl. **-S** matzo

MATT   v **-ED, -ING, -S** to matte

MATTE   v **MATTED, MATTING, MATTES** to produce a dull finish on

MATTED   past tense of mat, matt, and matte

MATTEDLY   adv in a tangled manner

MATTER   v **-ED, -ING, -S** to be of importance

MATTERY   adj producing pus

MATTIN   n pl. **-S** matin

MATTING   n pl. **-S** a woven fabric used as a floor covering

MATTOCK   n pl. **-S** a digging tool

MATTOID   n pl. **-S** a mentally unbalanced person

MATTRASS   n pl. **-ES** matrass

MATTRESS   n pl. **-ES** a large pad filled with resilient material used on or as a bed

MATURATE   v **-RATED, -RATING, -RATES** to mature

MATURE   adj **-TURER, -TUREST** fully developed **MATURELY** adv

MATURE   v **-TURED, -TURING, -TURES** to make or become mature

MATURER   n pl. **-S** one that brings something to maturity

MATURITY   n pl. **-TIES** the state of being mature

MATZA   n pl. **-S** matzo

MATZAH   n pl. **-S** matzo

MATZO   n pl. **-ZOS** or **-ZOT** or **-ZOTH** an unleavened bread

MATZOH *n* pl. **-S** matzo

MATZOON *n* pl. **-S** a food made from milk

MAUD *n* pl. **-S** a Scottish gray and black plaid

MAUDLIN *adj* excessively emotional

MAUGER *prep* maugre

MAUGRE *prep* in spite of

MAUL *v* **-ED, -ING, -S** to injure by beating

MAULER *n* pl. **-S** one that mauls

MAULING *n* pl. **-S** the act of injuring by beating

MAUMET *n* pl. **-S** an idol

MAUMETRY *n* pl. **-RIES** idolatry

MAUN *v* must — MAUN is the only form of this verb; it cannot be conjugated

MAUND *n* pl. **-S** an Asian unit of weight

MAUNDER *v* **-ED, -ING, -S** to talk incoherently

MAUNDY *n* pl. **-DIES** the religious ceremony of washing the feet of the poor

MAUSOLEA *n/pl* large, stately tombs

MAUSY *adj* **MAUSIER, MAUSIEST** mauzy

MAUT *n* pl. **-S** malt

MAUVE *n* pl. **-S** a purple color

MAUZY *adj* **MAUZIER, MAUZIEST** foggy, misty

MAVEN *n* pl. **-S** mavin

MAVERICK *n* pl. **-S** an unbranded range animal

MAVIE *n* pl. **-S** mavis

MAVIN *n* pl. **-S** an expert

MAVIS *n* pl. **-VISES** a songbird

MAW *v* **MAWED, MAWN, MAWING, MAWS** to mow

MAWKISH *adj* offensively sentimental

MAX *v* **-ED, -ING, -ES** to reach the upper limit

MAXI *n* pl. **-S** a long skirt or coat

MAXIBOAT *n* pl. **-S** a large racing yacht

MAXICOAT *n* pl. **-S** a long coat

MAXILLA *n* pl. **-LAS** or **-LAE** the upper jaw or jawbone

MAXIM *n* pl. **-S** a brief statement of a general truth or principle

MAXIMA a pl. of maximum

MAXIMAL *n* pl. **-S** an element of a mathematical set that is followed by no other

MAXIMAND *n* pl. **-S** something that is to be maximized

MAXIMIN *n* pl. **-S** the maximum of a set of minima

MAXIMISE *v* **-MISED, -MISING, -MISES** to maximize

MAXIMITE *n* pl. **-S** a powerful explosive

MAXIMIZE *v* **-MIZED, -MIZING, -MIZES** to make as great as possible

MAXIMUM *n* pl. **-MUMS** or **-MA** the greatest possible amount, quantity, or degree

MAXIXE *n* pl. **-S** a Brazilian dance

MAXWELL *n* pl. **-S** a unit of magnetic flux

MAY *v* **-ED, -ING, -S** to gather flowers in the spring

MAYA *n* pl. **-S** the power to produce illusions, in Hindu philosophy **MAYAN** *adj*

MAYAPPLE *n* pl. **-S** a perennial herb

MAYBE *n* pl. **-S** an uncertainty

MAYBIRD *n* pl. **-S** a bobolink

MAYBUSH *n* pl. **-ES** a flowering shrub

MAYDAY *n* pl. **-DAYS** a radio distress call

MAYEST a present 2d person sing. of may

MAYFLY *n* pl. **-FLIES** a winged insect

MAYHAP *adv* maybe

MAYHEM *n* pl. **-S** the offense of willfully maiming a person

MAYING *n* pl. **-S** the gathering of spring flowers

MAYO *n* pl. **-YOS** mayonnaise

MAYOR *n* pl. **-S** the chief executive official of a city or borough **MAYORAL** *adj*

MAYORESS *n* pl. **-ES** a female mayor

MAYPOLE *n* pl. **-S** a decorated pole used in a spring celebration

MAYPOP *n* pl. **-S** a flowering vine

MAYST a present 2d person sing. of may

MAYVIN *n* pl. **-S** mavin

MAYWEED *n* pl. **-S** a malodorous weed

MAZAEDIA *n/pl* spore-producing organs of certain lichens

MAZARD *n* pl. **-S** the head or face

MAZE *v* **MAZED, MAZING, MAZES** to bewilder **MAZEDLY** *adv*

MAZELIKE *adj* mazy

MAZELTOV *interj* — used to express congratulations

MAZER	*n* pl. **-S** a large drinking bowl
MAZIER	comparative of mazy
MAZIEST	superlative of mazy
MAZILY	*adv* in a mazy manner
MAZINESS	*n* pl. **-ES** the quality of being mazy
MAZING	present participle of maze
MAZOURKA	*n* pl. **-S** mazurka
MAZUMA	*n* pl. **-S** money
MAZURKA	*n* pl. **-S** a Polish dance
MAZY	*adj* **MAZIER, MAZIEST** full of confusing turns and passages
MAZZARD	*n* pl. **-S** a wild cherry
MBAQANGA	*n* pl. **-S** a South African dance music
MBIRA	*n* pl. **-S** an African musical instrument
ME	*n* pl **-S** mi
ME	*pron* the objective case of the pronoun I
MEAD	*n* pl. **-S** an alcoholic beverage
MEADOW	*n* pl. **-S** a tract of grassland **MEADOWY** *adj*
MEAGER	*adj* **MEAGERER, MEAGEREST** deficient in quantity or quality **MEAGERLY** *adv*
MEAGRE	*adj* **MEAGRER, MEAGREST** meager **MEAGRELY** *adv*
MEAL	*n* pl. **-S** the food served and eaten in one sitting
MEALIE	*n* pl. **-S** an ear of corn
MEALIER	comparative of mealy
MEALIEST	superlative of mealy
MEALLESS	*adj* lacking a meal
MEALTIME	*n* pl. **-S** the usual time for a meal
MEALWORM	*n* pl. **-S** the destructive larva of certain beetles
MEALY	*adj* **MEALIER, MEALIEST** soft, dry, and friable
MEALYBUG	*n* pl. **-S** a destructive insect
MEAN	*adj* **MEANER, MEANEST** inferior in grade, quality, or character
MEAN	*v* **MEANT, MEANING, MEANS** to intend
MEANDER	*v* **-ED, -ING, -S** to wander
MEANER	*n* pl. **-S** one that means
MEANIE	*n* pl. **-S** a nasty person
MEANIES	pl. of meany
MEANING	*n* pl. **-S** something that one intends to convey by language
MEANLY	*adv* in a mean manner
MEANNESS	*n* pl. **-ES** the state of being mean
MEANT	past tense of mean
MEANTIME	*n* pl. **-S** the intervening time
MEANY	*n* pl. **MEANIES** meanie
MEASLE	*n* pl. **-S** a tapeworm larva **MEASLED** *adj*
MEASLY	*adj* **-SLIER, -SLIEST** meager
MEASURE	*v* **-SURED, -SURING, -SURES** to ascertain the dimensions, quantity, or capacity of
MEASURER	*n* pl. **-S** one that measures
MEAT	*n* pl. **-S** animal flesh used as food **MEATED** *adj*
MEATAL	*adj* pertaining to a meatus
MEATBALL	*n* pl. **-S** a small ball of chopped meat
MEATHEAD	*n* pl. **-S** a dolt
MEATHOOK	*n* pl. **-S** a hook on which to hang meat
MEATIER	comparative of meaty
MEATIEST	superlative of meaty
MEATILY	*adv* in a meaty manner
MEATLESS	*adj* having no meat
MEATLOAF	*n* pl. **-LOAVES** a baked loaf of ground meat
MEATMAN	*n* pl. **-MEN** a vendor of meat
MEATUS	*n* pl. **-ES** a natural body passage
MEATY	*adj* **MEATIER, MEATIEST** full of meat
MECCA	*n* pl. **-S** a place visited by many people
MECH	*n* pl. **-S** a mechanic
MECHANIC	*n* pl. **-S** a person who works with machines
MECHITZA	*n* pl. **-TZAS** or **-TZOT** a partition separating men and women in a synagogue
MECHOUI	*n* pl. **-S** a meal of meat roasted on a spit
MECONIUM	*n* pl. **-S** the first fecal excretion of a newborn child
MED	*n* pl. **-S** medication
MEDAKA	*n* pl. **-S** a Japanese fish
MEDAL	*v* **-ALED, -ALING, -ALS** or **-ALLED, -ALLING, -ALS** to honor with a medal (a commemorative piece of metal)
MEDALIST	*n* pl. **-S** a person to whom a medal has been awarded
MEDALLIC	*adj* of or pertaining to a medal

MEDALLING a present participle of medal

MEDDLE *v* **-DLED, -DLING, -DLES** to interest oneself in what is not one's concern

MEDDLER *n* pl. **-S** one that meddles

MEDEVAC *v* **-VACED, -VACING, -VACS** or **-VACKED, -VACKING, -VACS** to evacuate the wounded from a battlefield by helicopter

MEDFLY *n* pl. **-FLIES** a Mediterranean fruit fly

MEDIA *n* pl. **-DIAE** the middle layer of a blood or lymph vessel

MEDIA *n* pl. **-S** a channel of communication

MEDIACY *n* pl. **-CIES** the act of mediating

MEDIAD *adv* toward the middle of a body or part

MEDIAE pl. of media

MEDIAL *n* pl. **-S** a sound, syllable, or letter in the middle of a word

MEDIALLY *adv* in a central manner

MEDIAN *n* pl. **-S** a central part

MEDIANLY *adv* medially

MEDIANT *n* pl. **-S** a type of musical tone

MEDIATE *v* **-ATED, -ATING, -ATES** to act between disputing parties in order to bring about a settlement

MEDIATOR *n* pl. **-S** one that mediates

MEDIC *n* pl. **-S** one engaged in medical work

MEDICAID *n* pl. **-S** a type of governmental health program

MEDICAL *n* pl. **-S** a physical examination

MEDICANT *n* pl. **-S** a healing substance

MEDICARE *n* pl. **-S** a type of governmental health program

MEDICATE *v* **-CATED, -CATING, -CATES** to treat with medicine

MEDICIDE *n* pl. **-S** a medically assisted suicide

MEDICINE *v* **-CINED, -CINING, -CINES** to administer medicine (a substance used in the treatment of disease) to

MEDICK *n* pl. **-S** a flowering plant

MEDICO *n* pl. **-COS** a doctor or medical student

MEDIEVAL *n* pl. **-S** a person belonging to the Middle Ages

MEDIGAP *n* pl. **-S** a supplemental health insurance

MEDII pl. of medius

MEDINA *n* pl. **-S** the native quarter of a North African city

MEDIOCRE *adj* neither good nor bad

MEDITATE *v* **-TATED, -TATING, -TATES** to ponder

MEDIUM *n* pl. **-DIUMS** or **-DIA** a surrounding environment in which something functions and thrives

MEDIUS *n* pl. **-DII** the middle finger

MEDIVAC *v* **-VACED, -VACING, -VACS** or **-VACKED, -VACKING, -VACS** medevac

MEDLAR *n* pl. **-S** a Eurasian tree

MEDLEY *n* pl. **-LEYS** a mixture

MEDRESE *n* pl. **-S** madrassa

MEDULLA *n* pl. **-LAS** or **-LAE** the central tissue in the stems of certain plants **MEDULLAR** *adj*

MEDUSA *n* pl. **-SAS** or **-SAE** a jellyfish **MEDUSAL** *adj*

MEDUSAN *n* pl. **-S** medusa

MEDUSOID *n* pl. **-S** medusa

MEED *n* pl. **-S** a deserved reward

MEEK *adj* **MEEKER, MEEKEST** lacking in spirit and courage **MEEKLY** *adv*

MEEKNESS *n* pl. **-ES** the quality of being meek

MEERKAT *n* pl. **-S** an African mongoose

MEET *v* **MET, MEETING, MEETS** to come into the company or presence of

MEETER *n* pl. **-S** one that meets

MEETING *n* pl. **-S** an assembly for a common purpose

MEETLY *adv* suitably

MEETNESS *n* pl. **-ES** suitability

MEG *n* pl. **-S** a megabyte

MEGA *adj* great in size or importance

MEGABAR *n* pl. **-S** a unit of pressure

MEGABIT *n* pl. **-S** a unit of computer information

MEGABUCK *n* pl. **-S** one million dollars

MEGABYTE *n* pl. **-S** 1,048,576 bytes

MEGACITY *n* pl. **-CITIES** a very large city

MEGADEAL *n* pl. **-S** a business deal involving a lot of money

MEGADOSE *n* pl. **-S** an abnormally large dose

MEGADYNE *n* pl. **-S** a unit of force

MEGAFLOP *n* pl. **-S** a measure of computing speed

MEGAHIT *n* pl. **-S** something extremely successful

MEGALITH *n* pl. **-S** a huge stone used in prehistoric monuments

MEGALOPS *n* pl. **-LOPSES** a larval stage of most crabs

MEGAMALL *n* pl. **-S** a very large shopping mall

MEGAPLEX *n* pl. **-ES** a large building having many movie theaters

MEGAPOD *n* pl. **-S** megapode

MEGAPODE *n* pl. **-S** a large-footed bird

MEGARON *n* pl. **-ARA** the great central hall of an ancient Greek house

MEGASS *n* pl. **-ES** a bagasse

MEGASSE *n* pl. **-S** megass

MEGASTAR *n* pl. **-S** an extremely successful performer

MEGATON *n* pl. **-S** a unit of explosive force

MEGAVOLT *n* pl. **-S** a unit of electromotive force

MEGAWATT *n* pl. **-S** a unit of power

MEGILLA *n* pl. **-S** megillah

MEGILLAH *n* pl. **-S** a long, involved story

MEGILP *n* pl. **-S** a substance with which pigments are mixed in painting

MEGILPH *n* pl. **-S** megilp

MEGOHM *n* pl. **-S** a unit of electrical resistance

MEGRIM *n* pl. **-S** a migraine

MEH *adj* not impressive; boring

MEHNDI *n* pl. **-S** the art of painting patterns on the skin with henna

MEIKLE *adj* large

MEINIE *n* pl. **-S** meiny

MEINY *n* pl. **-NIES** a retinue

MEIOSIS *n* pl. **-OSES** a type of cell division **MEIOTIC** *adj*

MEISTER *n* pl. **-S** one who is knowledgeable about something specified

MEL *n* pl. **-S** honey

MELAENA *n* pl. **-S** melena

MELAMED *n* pl. **-LAMDIM** a teacher in a Jewish school

MELAMINE *n* pl. **-S** a chemical compound

MELANGE *n* pl. **-S** a mixture

MELANIAN *adj* pertaining to dark pigmentation

MELANIC *n* pl. **-S** one who is affected with melanism

MELANIN *n* pl. **-S** a dark pigment

MELANISM *n* pl. **-S** abnormally dark pigmentation of the skin

MELANIST *n* pl. **-S** a melanic

MELANITE *n* pl. **-S** a black variety of garnet

MELANIZE *v* **-NIZED, -NIZING, -NIZES** to make dark

MELANOID *n* pl. **-S** a dark pigment

MELANOMA *n* pl. **-MAS** or **-MATA** a darkly pigmented tumor

MELANOUS *adj* having dark skin and hair

MELD *v* **-ED, -ING, -S** to blend

MELDER *n* pl. **-S** the amount of grain ground at one time

MELEE *n* pl. **-S** a confused struggle

MELENA *n* pl. **-S** a condition marked by black tarry stool

MELIC *adj* pertaining to song

MELILITE *n* pl. **-S** a mineral group

MELILOT *n* pl. **-S** a flowering plant

MELINITE *n* pl. **-S** a powerful explosive

MELISMA *n* pl. **-MAS** or **-MATA** melodic embellishment

MELL *v* **-ED, -ING, -S** to mix

MELLIFIC *adj* producing honey

MELLOW *adj* **-LOWER, -LOWEST** soft and full-flavored from ripeness **MELLOWLY** *adv*

MELLOW *v* **-ED, -ING, -S** to make or become mellow

MELODEON *n* pl. **-S** a small accordion

MELODIA *n* pl. **-S** a type of organ stop

MELODIC *adj* pertaining to melody

MELODICA *n* pl. **-S** a harmonica with a small keyboard at one end

MELODIES pl. of melody

MELODION *n* pl. **-S** melodeon

MELODISE *v* **-DISED, -DISING, -DISES** to melodize

MELODIST *n* pl. **-S** a composer of melodies

MELODIZE *v* **-DIZED, -DIZING, -DIZES** to compose a melody

MELODY *n* pl. **-DIES** an agreeable succession of musical sounds

MELOID *n* pl. **-S** a type of beetle

MELON *n* pl. **-S** any of various gourds **MELONY** *adj*

MELT *v* **-ED, -ING, -S** to change from a solid to a liquid state by heat **MELTABLE** *adj*

MELTAGE	*n* pl. **-S** the process of melting	**MENHADEN**	*n* pl. **-S** a marine fish
MELTDOWN	*n* pl. **-S** the melting of the core of a nuclear reactor	**MENHIR**	*n* pl. **-S** a prehistoric monument
		MENIAL	*n* pl. **-S** a domestic servant
MELTER	*n* pl. **-S** one that melts	**MENIALLY**	*adv* in a servile manner
MELTON	*n* pl. **-S** a heavy woolen fabric	**MENINX**	*n* pl. **-NINGES** any of the membranes enclosing the brain and spinal cord
MELTY	*adj* resembling a melted solid		
MEM	*n* pl. **-S** a Hebrew letter		
MEMBER	*n* pl. **-S** a distinct part of a whole **MEMBERED** *adj*	**MENISCUS**	*n* pl. **-CUSES** or **-CI** a crescent-shaped body **MENISCAL** *adj*
MEMBRANE	*n* pl. **-S** a thin, pliable layer of tissue	**MENO**	*adv* less — used as a musical direction
MEME	*n* pl. **-S** an idea or practice that spreads from person to person **MEMETIC** *adj*	**MENOLOGY**	*n* pl. **-GIES** an ecclesiastical calendar
		MENORAH	*n* pl. **-S** a candleholder used in Jewish worship
MEMENTO	*n* pl. **-TOS** or **-TOES** something that serves as a reminder of the past	**MENSA**	*n* pl. **-SAS** or **-SAE** the grinding surface of a tooth
MEMETICS	*n/pl* the study of memes and their effects	**MENSAL**	*adj* pertaining to or used at the table
MEMO	*n* pl. **MEMOS** a note designating something to be remembered	**MENSCH**	*n* pl. **MENSCHES** or **MENSCHEN** an admirable person **MENSCHY** *adj*
MEMOIR	*n* pl. **-S** a biography		
MEMORIAL	*n* pl. **-S** something that serves as a remembrance of a person or event	**MENSE**	*v* **MENSED, MENSING, MENSES** to do honor to
MEMORISE	*v* **-ISED, -ISING, -ISES** to memorize	**MENSEFUL**	*adj* proper
		MENSH	*n* pl. **MENSHES** or **MENSHEN** mensch
MEMORIZE	*v* **-RIZED, -RIZING, -RIZES** to commit to memory		
MEMORY	*n* pl. **-RIES** the mental faculty of retaining and recalling past experience	**MENSTRUA**	*n/pl* solvents
		MENSURAL	*adj* pertaining to measure
		MENSWEAR	*n* pl. **MENSWEAR** clothing for men
MEMSAHIB	*n* pl. **-S** a European woman living in colonial India	**MENTA**	pl. of mentum
MEN	pl. of man	**MENTAL**	*adj* pertaining to the mind **MENTALLY** *adv*
MENACE	*v* **-ACED, -ACING, -ACES** to threaten	**MENTEE**	*n* pl. **-S** one who is being mentored
MENACER	*n* pl. **-S** one that menaces	**MENTHENE**	*n* pl. **-S** a liquid hydrocarbon
MENAD	*n* pl. **-S** maenad	**MENTHOL**	*n* pl. **-S** an alcohol
MENAGE	*n* pl. **-S** a household	**MENTION**	*v* **-ED, -ING, -S** to refer to in a casual manner
MENARCHE	*n* pl. **-S** the first occurrence of menstruation	**MENTO**	*n* pl. **-TOS** a style of Jamaican folk music
MENAZON	*n* pl. **-S** an insecticide		
MEND	*v* **-ED, -ING, -S** to repair **MENDABLE** *adj*	**MENTOR**	*v* **-ED, -ING, -S** to serve as a friend and teacher to
		MENTUM	*n* pl. **-TA** the chin
MENDER	*n* pl. **-S** one that mends	**MENU**	*n* pl. **-S** a list of the dishes available in a restaurant
MENDIGO	*n* pl. **-GOS** a freshwater fish		
MENDING	*n* pl. **-S** an accumulation of articles to be mended	**MENUDO**	*n* pl. **-DOS** a tripe stew with chili peppers
MENFOLK	*n/pl* the men of a family or community	**MEOU**	*v* **-ED, -ING, -S** to meow
MENFOLKS	*n/pl* menfolk	**MEOW**	*v* **-ED, -ING, -S** to make the crying sound of a cat

MEPHITIS *n* pl. **-TISES** an offensive odor **MEPHITIC** *adj*

MERC *n* pl. **-S** or **-ES** a mercenary

MERCADO *n* pl. **-DOS** a market

MERCAPTO *adj* containing a particular chemical group

MERCER *n* pl. **-S** a dealer in textiles

MERCERY *n* pl. **-CERIES** a mercer's shop

MERCH *n* pl. **-ES** merchandise

MERCHANT *v* **-ED, -ING, -S** to buy and sell goods for profit

MERCIES pl. of mercy

MERCIFUL *adj* full of mercy

MERCURY *n* pl. **-RIES** a metallic element **MERCURIC** *adj*

MERCY *n* pl. **-CIES** compassion shown to an offender or enemy

MERE *adj* **MERER, MEREST** being nothing more than **MERELY** *adv*

MERE *n* pl. **-S** a pond or lake

MERENGUE *n* pl. **-S** a ballroom dance

MERGE *v* **MERGED, MERGING, MERGES** to combine

MERGEE *n* pl. **-S** a company acquired by a merger

MERGENCE *n* pl. **-S** the act of merging

MERGER *n* pl. **-S** the union of two or more businesses into a single enterprise

MERGING *n* pl. **-S** the act of combining

MERGUEZ *n* pl. **MERGUEZ** a spicy beef and lamb sausage

MERIDIAN *n* pl. **-S** a circle around the earth passing through both poles

MERINGUE *n* pl. **-S** a topping for pastries

MERINO *n* pl. **-NOS** a fine wool

MERISIS *n* pl. **MERISES** growth

MERISTEM *n* pl. **-S** formative plant tissue

MERISTIC *adj* made up of segments

MERIT *v* **-ED, -ING, -S** to earn

MERK *n* pl. **-S** a former coin of Scotland

MERL *n* pl. **-S** merle

MERLE *n* pl. **-S** a blackbird

MERLIN *n* pl. **-S** a European falcon

MERLON *n* pl. **-S** the solid part of an indented parapet

MERLOT *n* pl. **-S** a dry red wine

MERMAID *n* pl. **-S** a legendary marine creature

MERMAN *n* pl. **-MEN** a legendary marine creature

MERONYM *n* pl. **-S** a term for a part of something that is used to denote the whole of it

MERONYMY *n* pl. **-MIES** the semantic relationship between a part and the whole

MEROPIA *n* pl. **-S** partial blindness **MEROPIC** *adj*

MERRY *adj* **-RIER, -RIEST** cheerful **MERRILY** *adv*

MESA *n* pl. **-S** a land formation having a flat top and steep sides

MESALLY *adv* medially

MESARCH *adj* originating in a mesic habitat

MESCAL *n* pl. **-S** a cactus used as a source of liquor

MESCALIN *n* pl. **-S** mescaline (a hallucinogenic compound)

MESCLUN *n* pl. **-S** a mixture of young tender green herbs

MESDAMES pl. of madame

MESEEMS *v* past tense **MESEEMED,** present 3d person sing. **MESEEMETH** it seems to me — MESEEMS is an impersonal verb and is used only in the 3d person sing.

MESH *v* **-ED, -ING, -ES** to entangle

MESHIER comparative of meshy

MESHIEST superlative of meshy

MESHING *n* pl. **-S** the act of fitting together

MESHUGA *adj* crazy

MESHUGAH *adj* meshuga

MESHUGGA *adj* meshuga

MESHUGGE *adj* meshuga

MESHWORK *n* pl. **-S** a network

MESHY *adj* **MESHIER, MESHIEST** netty

MESIAL *adj* situated in the middle **MESIALLY** *adv*

MESIAN *adj* mesial

MESIC *adj* characterized by a medium supply of moisture

MESMERIC *adj* pertaining to hypnotism

MESNALTY *n* pl. **-TIES** a type of feudal estate

MESNE *n* pl. **-S** a feudal lord holding land from a superior

MESOCARP *n* pl. **-S** the middle layer of a pericarp

MESODERM *n* pl. **-S** the middle germ layer of an embryo

MESOGLEA *n* pl. **-S** a gelatinous material in sponges

MESOMERE *n* pl. **-S** an embryonic segment

MESON *n* pl. **-S** a subatomic particle **MESONIC** *adj*

MESOPHYL *n* pl. **-S** the soft tissue of a leaf

MESOSAUR *n* pl. **-S** an extinct aquatic reptile

MESOSOME *n* pl. **-S** a specialized cellular part

MESOTRON *n* pl. **-S** a meson

MESOZOAN *n* pl. **-S** any of a phylum of wormlike organisms

MESQUIT *n* pl. **-S** mesquite

MESQUITE *n* pl. **-S** a spiny tree or shrub

MESS *v* **-ED, -ING, -ES** to make dirty or untidy

MESSAGE *v* **-SAGED, -SAGING, -SAGES** to send as a message (an oral, written, or signaled communication)

MESSAN *n* pl. **-S** a lapdog

MESSIAH *n* pl. **-S** an expected liberator

MESSIER comparative of messy

MESSIEST superlative of messy

MESSIEURS pl. of monsieur

MESSILY *adv* in a messy manner

MESSMAN *n* pl. **-MEN** a serviceman who works in a dining facility

MESSMATE *n* pl. **-S** a person with whom one eats regularly

MESSUAGE *n* pl. **-S** a dwelling house with its adjacent buildings and land

MESSY *adj* **MESSIER, MESSIEST** dirty or untidy

MESTEE *n* pl. **-S** mustee

MESTESO *n* pl. **-SOS** or **-SOES** mestizo

MESTINO *n* pl. **-NOS** or **-NOES** mestizo

MESTIZA *n* pl. **-S** a female mestizo

MESTIZO *n* pl. **-ZOS** or **-ZOES** a person of mixed ancestry

MET past tense of meet

META *adj* pertaining to positions in a benzene ring separated by one carbon atom

METADATA *n/pl* a set of data that gives information about other data

METAGE *n* pl. **-S** an official measurement of weight or contents

METAL *v* **-ALED, -ALING, -ALS** or **-ALLED, -ALLING, -ALS** to cover with metal (any of various ductile, fusible, and lustrous substances)

METALISE *v* **-ISED, -ISING, -ISES** to metalize

METALIST *n* pl. **-S** one who works with metals

METALIZE *v* **-IZED, -IZING, -IZES** to treat with metal

METALLED a past tense of metal

METALLIC *n* pl. **-S** a fabric or yarn made of or coated with metal

METALLING a present participle of metal

METAMER *n* pl. **-S** a type of chemical compound

METAMERE *n* pl. **-S** a somite

METANOIA *n* pl. **-S** a spiritual conversion

METAPHOR *n* pl. **-S** a type of figure of speech

METATAG *n* pl. **-S** an HTML tag having information about a webpage

METATE *n* pl. **-S** a stone used for grinding grains

METAZOAN *n* pl. **-S** any of a major division of multicellular animals **METAZOAL, METAZOIC** *adj*

METAZOON *n* pl. **-ZOA** a metazoan

METE *v* **METED, METING, METES** to distribute by measure

METEOR *n* pl. **-S** a small celestial body that enters the earth's atmosphere **METEORIC** *adj*

METEPA *n* pl. **-S** a chemical compound

METER *v* **-ED, -ING, -S** to measure by mechanical means

METERAGE *n* pl. **-S** the process of metering

METH *n* pl. **-S** a stimulant drug

METHADON *n* pl. **-S** a narcotic drug

METHANAL *n* pl. **-S** formaldehyde

METHANE *n* pl. **-S** a flammable gas

METHANOL *n* pl. **-S** a toxic alcohol

METHINKS *v* past tense **METHOUGHT** it seems to me — METHINKS is an impersonal verb and is used only in the 3d person sing.

METHOD *n* pl. **-S** a means of procedure

METHODIC *adj* systematic

METHOXY *adj* containing a certain chemical group

METHOXYL *adj* methoxy

METHYL *n* pl. **-S** a univalent radical **METHYLIC** *adj*

METHYLAL *n* pl. **-S** a flammable liquid

METICAL *n* pl. **-CALS** or **-CAIS** a monetary unit of Mozambique

METIER *n* pl. **-S** a vocation

METING present participle of mete

METIS *n* pl. **METIS** a person of mixed ancestry

METISSE *n* pl. **-S** a female metis

METOL *n* pl. **-S** a powder used as a photographic developer

METONYM *n* pl. **-S** a word used in metonymy

METONYMY *n* pl. **-MIES** a type of figure of speech

METOPE *n* pl. **-PES** or **-PAE** a space between two triglyphs

METOPIC *adj* pertaining to the forehead

METOPON *n* pl. **-S** a narcotic drug

METRAZOL *n* pl. **-S** a powder used as a stimulant

METRE *v* **-TRED, -TRING, -TRES** to meter

METRIC *n* pl. **-S** a standard of measurement

METRICAL *adj* pertaining to or composed in a system of arranged and measured rhythm

METRIFY *v* **-FIED, -FYING, -FIES** to compose in metrical form

METRING present participle of metre

METRIST *n* pl. **-S** one who metrifies

METRITIS *n* pl. **-TISES** inflammation of the uterus

METRO *n* pl. **-ROS** a subway

METTLE *n* pl. **-S** quality of character **METTLED** *adj*

METUMP *n* pl. **-S** a tumpline

MEUNIERE *adj* cooked in browned butter

MEW *v* **-ED, -ING, -S** to confine

MEWL *v* **-ED, -ING, -S** to whimper

MEWLER *n* pl. **-S** one that mewls

MEWS *n* pl. **-ES** a street lined with houses that originally were stables

MEZCAL *n* pl. **-S** mescal

MEZE *n* pl. **-S** a Greek or Middle Eastern appetizer

MEZEREON *n* pl. **-S** a flowering shrub

MEZEREUM *n* pl. **-S** mezereon

MEZQUIT *n* pl. **-S** mesquite

MEZQUITE *n* pl. **-S** mesquite

MEZUZA *n* pl. **-S** mezuzah

MEZUZAH *n* pl. **-ZAHS** or **-ZOT** or **-ZOTH** a Judaic scroll

MEZZO *n* pl. **-ZOS** a female voice of a full, deep quality

MHO *n* pl. **MHOS** a unit of electrical conductance

MI *n* pl. **-S** the third tone of the diatonic musical scale

MIAOU *v* **-ED, -ING, -S** to meow

MIAOW *v* **-ED, -ING, -S** to meow

MIASM *n* pl. **-S** miasma

MIASMA *n* pl. **-MAS** or **-MATA** a noxious vapor **MIASMAL, MIASMIC** *adj*

MIAUL *v* **-ED, -ING, -S** to meow

MIB *n* pl. **-S** a type of playing marble

MIC *n* pl. **-S** a microphone

MICA *n* pl. **-S** a mineral

MICAWBER *n* pl. **-S** a person who remains hopeful despite adversity

MICE pl. of mouse

MICELL *n* pl. **-S** micelle

MICELLA *n* pl. **-LAE** micelle

MICELLE *n* pl. **-S** a coherent strand or structure in a fiber **MICELLAR** *adj*

MICHE *v* **MICHED, MICHING, MICHES** to skulk

MICKEY *n* pl. **-EYS** a drugged drink

MICKLE *adj* **-LER, -LEST** large

MICKLE *n* pl. **-S** a large amount

MICKY *n* pl. **MICKIES** mickey

MICRA a pl. of micron

MICRIFY *v* **-FIED, -FYING, -FIES** to make small

MICRO *n* pl. **-CROS** a very small computer

MICROBAR *n* pl. **-S** a unit of atmospheric pressure

MICROBE *n* pl. **-S** a minute life form **MICROBIC** *adj*

MICROBUS *n* pl. **-BUSES** or **-BUSSES** a small bus

MICROCAP *adj* of or pertaining to a company whose retained earnings are very small

MICROCAR *n* pl. **-S** a very small car

MICRODOT *n* pl. **-S** a copy of printed matter reduced to the size of a dot

MICROHM *n* pl. **-S** a unit of electrical resistance

MICROLUX *n* pl. **-LUXES** or **-LUCES** a unit of illumination

MICROMHO *n* pl. **-S** a unit of electrical conductance

MICRON *n* pl. **-CRONS** or **-CRA** a unit of length

MICRURGY *n* pl. **-GIES** the use of minute tools under high magnification

MID *n* pl. **-S** the middle

MIDAIR *n* pl. **-S** a region in the middle of the air

MIDBRAIN *n* pl. **-S** the middle region of the brain

MIDCAP *adj* of or pertaining to a corporation whose retained earnings are between those of a small company and a large corporation

MIDCULT *n* pl. **-S** middle-class culture

MIDDAY *n* pl. **-DAYS** the middle of the day

MIDDEN *n* pl. **-S** a dunghill

MIDDIES pl. of middy

MIDDLE *v* **-DLED, -DLING, -DLES** to place in the middle (the area or point equidistant from extremes or limits)

MIDDLER *n* pl. **-S** a student in an intermediate grade

MIDDLING *n* pl. **-S** a cut of pork

MIDDY *n* pl. **-DIES** a loosely fitting blouse

MIDFIELD *n* pl. **-S** the middle portion of a playing field

MIDGE *n* pl. **-S** a small winged insect

MIDGET *n* pl. **-S** a very small person

MIDGUT *n* pl. **-S** the middle part of the embryonic digestive tract

MIDI *n* pl. **-S** a skirt or coat that extends to the middle of the calf

MIDIRON *n* pl. **-S** a golf club

MIDLAND *n* pl. **-S** the middle part of a country

MIDLEG *n* pl. **-S** the middle of the leg

MIDLIFE *n* pl. **-LIVES** middle age

MIDLIFER *n* pl. **-S** a middle-aged person

MIDLINE *n* pl. **-S** a median line

MIDLIST *n* pl. **-S** a section of a publisher's list of current titles

MIDMONTH *n* pl. **-S** the middle of the month

MIDMOST *n* pl. **-S** a part exactly in the middle

MIDNIGHT *n* pl. **-S** the middle of the night

MIDNOON *n* pl. **-S** midday

MIDPOINT *n* pl. **-S** a point at the middle

MIDRANGE *n* pl. **-S** the middle of a range

MIDRASH *n* pl. **-RASHIM** or **-RASHOTH** or **-RASHOT** an early Jewish interpretation of a biblical text

MIDRIB *n* pl. **-S** the central vein of a leaf

MIDRIFF *n* pl. **-S** the middle part of the body

MIDSHIP *adj* pertaining to the middle of a ship

MIDSHIPS *adv* toward the middle of a ship

MIDSHORE *adj* designating a fishery that is between the inshore and offshore fisheries

MIDSIZE *adj* of intermediate size

MIDSIZED *adj* midsize

MIDSOLE *n* pl. **-S** a middle layer of the sole of a shoe

MIDSPACE *n* pl. **-S** the middle of a space

MIDST *n* pl. **-S** the middle

MIDSTORY *n* pl. **-RIES** the middle of a story

MIDTERM *n* pl. **-S** an examination given in the middle of an academic semester

MIDTOWN *n* pl. **-S** the central part of a city

MIDWATCH *n* pl. **-ES** a watch on a ship between midnight and 4 A.M.

MIDWATER *n* pl. **-S** the middle portion vertically of a body of water

MIDWAY *n* pl. **-WAYS** an avenue at a fair or carnival for concessions and amusements

MIDWEEK *n* pl. **-S** the middle of the week

MIDWIFE *v* **-WIFED, -WIFING, -WIFES** or **-WIVED, -WIVING, -WIVES** to assist a woman in childbirth

MIDYEAR *n* pl. **-S** the middle of the year

MIEN *n* pl. **-S** demeanor

MIFF *v* **-ED, -ING, -S** to annoy

MIFFY *adj* **MIFFIER, MIFFIEST** easily annoyed

MIG *n* pl. **-S** a type of playing marble

MIGAWD *interj* — used to express surprise

MIGG *n* pl. **-S** mig

MIGGLE *n* pl. **-S** a mig

MIGHT *n* pl. **-S** strength

MIGHTY *adj* **MIGHTIER, MIGHTIEST** strong **MIGHTILY** *adv*

MIGNON *n* pl. **-S** a cut of beef

MIGNONNE *adj* daintily small

MIGRAINE *n* pl. **-S** a severe headache

MIGRANT *n* pl. **-S** one that migrates

MIGRATE   v **-GRATED, -GRATING, -GRATES** to move from one region to another

MIGRATOR   n pl. **-S** a migrant

MIHRAB   n pl. **-S** a niche in a mosque

MIJNHEER   n pl. **-S** mynheer

MIKADO   n pl. **-DOS** an emperor of Japan

MIKE   v **MIKED, MIKING, MIKES** to amplify or record by use of a microphone

MIKRON   n pl. **-KRONS** or **-KRA** micron

MIKVA   n pl. **-S** mikvah

MIKVAH   n pl. **-VAHS** or **-VOTH** or **-VOT** or **-VOS** a place for ritual bathing by Orthodox Jews

MIKVEH   n pl. **-S** mikvah

MIL   n pl. **-S** a unit of length

MILADI   n pl. **-S** milady

MILADY   n pl. **-DIES** an English gentlewoman

MILAGE   n pl. **-S** mileage

MILCH   adj giving milk

MILCHIG   adj made of or derived from milk

MILD   v **-ED, -ING, -S** to diminish

MILD   adj **MILDER, MILDEST** not harsh or rough **MILDISH** adj

MILDEN   v **-ED, -ING, -S** to make or become mild

MILDEW   v **-ED, -ING, -S** to affect with mildew (a whitish growth produced by fungi)

MILDEWY   adj affected with or resembling mildew

MILDLY   adv in a mild manner

MILDNESS   n pl. **-ES** the quality of being mild

MILE   n pl. **-S** a unit of distance

MILEAGE   n pl. **-S** total distance expressed in miles

MILEPOST   n pl. **-S** a post indicating distance in miles

MILER   n pl. **-S** one that runs a mile race

MILESIAN   adj pertaining to the native people of Ireland

MILESIMO   n pl. **-MOS** a former monetary unit of Chile

MILFOIL   n pl. **-S** a perennial herb

MILIA   pl. of milium

MILIARIA   n pl. **-S** a skin disease

MILIARY   adj made up of many small projections

MILIEU   n pl. **-LIEUS** or **-LIEUX** environment

MILING   n pl. **-S** the activity of running in a one-mile race

MILITANT   n pl. **-S** a person who is aggressively engaged in a cause

MILITARY   n pl. **-TARIES** armed forces

MILITATE   v **-TATED, -TATING, -TATES** to have influence or effect

MILITIA   n pl. **-S** a citizen army

MILIUM   n pl. **-IA** a small, whitish lump in the skin

MILK   v **-ED, -ING, -S** to draw milk (a whitish, nutritious liquid) from the udder of

MILKER   n pl. **-S** one that milks

MILKFISH   n pl. **-ES** a marine food fish

MILKIER   comparative of milky

MILKIEST   superlative of milky

MILKILY   adv in a milky manner

MILKLESS   adj lacking milk

MILKMAID   n pl. **-S** a woman who milks cows

MILKMAN   n pl. **-MEN** a man who sells or delivers milk

MILKSHED   n pl. **-S** a region supplying milk to a particular community

MILKSOP   n pl. **-S** an effeminate man

MILKWEED   n pl. **-S** a plant that secretes a milky juice

MILKWOOD   n pl. **-S** a tropical tree

MILKWORT   n pl. **-S** a flowering plant

MILKY   adj **MILKIER, MILKIEST** resembling or suggestive of milk

MILL   v **-ED, -ING, -S** to grind by mechanical means **MILLABLE** adj

MILLAGE   n pl. **-S** a type of monetary rate

MILLCAKE   n pl. **-S** a residue from pressed linseed

MILLDAM   n pl. **-S** a dam built to form a millpond

MILLE   n pl. **-S** a thousand

MILLEPED   n pl. **-S** milliped

MILLER   n pl. **-S** one that mills

MILLET   n pl. **-S** a cereal grass

MILLIAMP   n pl. **-S** one thousandth of an ampere

MILLIARD   n pl. **-S** a billion

MILLIARE   n pl. **-S** a unit of area

MILLIARY *n* pl. **-ARIES** an ancient Roman milestone

MILLIBAR *n* pl. **-S** a unit of atmospheric pressure

MILLIEME *n* pl. **-S** unit of value of Egypt and Sudan

MILLIER *n* pl. **-S** a unit of weight

MILLIGAL *n* pl. **-S** a unit of acceleration

MILLILUX *n* pl. **-LUXES** or **-LUCES** a unit of illumination

MILLIME *n* pl. **-S** a coin of Tunisia

MILLIMHO *n* pl. **-MHOS** a unit of electrical conductance

MILLINE *n* pl. **-S** a unit of advertising space

MILLINER *n* pl. **-S** one who makes or sells women's hats

MILLING *n* pl. **-S** a corrugated edge on a coin

MILLIOHM *n* pl. **-S** a unit of electrical resistance

MILLION *n* pl. **-S** a number

MILLIPED *n* pl. **-S** a multi-legged arthropod

MILLIREM *n* pl. **-S** a quantity of ionizing radiation

MILLPOND *n* pl. **-S** a pond for supplying water to run a mill wheel (a type of waterwheel)

MILLRACE *n* pl. **-S** the current of water that drives a mill wheel

MILLRUN *n* pl. **-S** a millrace

MILLWORK *n* pl. **-S** woodwork produced by milling

MILNEB *n* pl. **-S** a fungicide

MILO *n* pl. **-LOS** a cereal grass

MILORD *n* pl. **-S** an English gentleman

MILPA *n* pl. **-S** a field that is cleared from a jungle for farming purposes

MILREIS *n* pl. **MILREIS** a former monetary unit of Portugal

MILT *v* **-ED, -ING, -S** to impregnate with milt (fish sperm)

MILTER *n* pl. **-S** a male fish at breeding time

MILTY *adj* **MILTIER, MILTIEST** full of milt

MIM *adj* primly demure

MIMBAR *n* pl. **-S** minbar

MIME *v* **MIMED, MIMING, MIMES** to mimic

MIMEO *v* **-ED, -ING, -S** to make copies of by use of a mimeograph

MIMER *n* pl. **-S** one that mimes

MIMESIS *n* pl. **-MESISES** or **-MESES** mimicry **MIMETIC** *adj*

MIMETITE *n* pl. **-S** an ore of lead

MIMIC *v* **-ICKED, -ICKING, -ICS** to imitate closely

MIMICAL *adj* of the nature of mimicry

MIMICKER *n* pl. **-S** one that mimics

MIMICKING present participle of mimic

MIMICRY *n* pl. **-RIES** an instance of mimicking

MIMING present participle of mime

MIMOSA *n* pl. **-S** a tropical plant

MIMULUS *n* pl. **-ES** a flowering plant

MINA *n* pl. **-NAS** or **-NAE** an ancient unit of weight and value

MINABLE *adj* capable of being mined

MINACITY *n* pl. **-TIES** the state of being threatening

MINAE a pl. of mina

MINARET *n* pl. **-S** a slender tower attached to a mosque

MINATORY *adj* threatening

MINBAR *n* pl. **-S** a Muslim pulpit

MINCE *v* **MINCED, MINCING, MINCES** to cut into very small pieces

MINCER *n* pl. **-S** one that minces

MINCY *adj* **MINCIER, MINCIEST** affectedly dainty

MIND *v* **-ED, -ING, -S** to heed

MINDEDLY *adv* in the manner of one with a specified kind of mind

MINDER *n* pl. **-S** one that minds

MINDFUL *adj* heedful

MINDLESS *adj* lacking intelligence

MINDSET *n* pl. **-S** a fixed mental attitude

MINE *v* **MINED, MINING, MINES** to dig into for valuable materials

MINEABLE *adj* minable

MINER *n* pl. **-S** one that mines

MINERAL *n* pl. **-S** a naturally occurring inorganic substance having a characteristic set of physical properties

MINGIER comparative of mingy

MINGIEST superlative of mingy

MINGLE *v* **-GLED, -GLING, -GLES** to mix together

MINGLER *n* pl. **-S** one that mingles

MINGY	*adj* **-GIER, -GIEST** mean and stingy **MINGILY** *adv*
MINI	*n* pl. **-S** something distinctively smaller than others of its kind
MINIBAR	*n* pl. **-S** a small refrigerator stocked with beverages
MINIBIKE	*n* pl. **-S** a small motorcycle
MINIBUS	*n* pl. **-BUSES** or **-BUSSES** a small bus
MINICAB	*n* pl. **-S** a small taxicab
MINICAM	*n* pl. **-S** a small portable television camera
MINICAMP	*n* pl. **-S** a short training camp for football players
MINICAR	*n* pl. **-S** a small automobile
MINIDISC	*n* pl. **-S** a miniature compact disc
MINIFY	*v* **-FIED, -FYING, -FIES** to make small or smaller
MINIGOLF	*n* pl. **-S** a game similar to golf played on a small obstacle course
MINIKIN	*n* pl. **-S** a small or dainty creature
MINILAB	*n* pl. **-S** a retail outlet offering rapid on-site film development
MINIM	*n* pl. **-S** a unit of liquid measure
MINIMA	a pl. of minimum
MINIMAL	*n* pl. **-S** an element of a mathematical set that precedes all others
MINIMAX	*n* pl. **-ES** the minimum of a set of maxima
MINIMILL	*n* pl. **-S** a small-scale steel mill
MINIMISE	*v* **-MISED, -MISING, -MISES** to minimize
MINIMIZE	*v* **-MIZED, -MIZING, -MIZES** to make as small as possible
MINIMUM	*n* pl. **-MUMS** or **-MA** the least possible amount, quantity, or degree
MINING	*n* pl. **-S** the process or business of working mines (excavations in the earth)
MINION	*n* pl. **-S** a servile follower
MINIPARK	*n* pl. **-S** a small city park
MINIPILL	*n* pl. **-S** a birth control pill containing no estrogen
MINISH	*v* **-ED, -ING, -ES** to diminish
MINISKI	*n* pl. **-S** a short ski
MINISTER	*v* **-ED, -ING, -S** to give aid or service
MINISTRY	*n* pl. **-TRIES** the act of ministering
MINIUM	*n* pl. **-S** a red pigment
MINIVAN	*n* pl. **-S** a small van
MINIVER	*n* pl. **-S** a white fur
MINK	*n* pl. **-S** a carnivorous mammal
MINKE	*n* pl. **-S** a small whale
MINNEOLA	*n* pl. **-S** a reddish tangelo
MINNOW	*n* pl. **-S** a small fish
MINNY	*n* pl. **-NIES** minnow
MINOR	*v* **-ED, -ING, -S** to pursue a specific subordinate course of study
MINORCA	*n* pl. **-S** any of a breed of large domestic fowls
MINORITY	*n* pl. **-TIES** the smaller number or part
MINSTER	*n* pl. **-S** a large or important church
MINSTREL	*n* pl. **-S** a medieval musician
MINT	*v* **-ED, -ING, -S** to produce by stamping metal, as coins
MINTAGE	*n* pl. **-S** the act of minting
MINTER	*n* pl. **-S** one that mints
MINTY	*adj* **MINTIER, MINTIEST** having the flavor of mint (an aromatic herb)
MINUEND	*n* pl. **-S** a number from which another is to be subtracted
MINUET	*v* **-ED, -ING, -S** to dance a minuet (a slow, stately dance)
MINUS	*n* pl. **-ES** a negative quantity
MINUTE	*adj* **-NUTER, -NUTEST** very small **MINUTELY** *adv*
MINUTE	*v* **-UTED, -UTING, -UTES** to make a brief note of
MINUTIA	*n* pl. **-TIAE** a small detail **MINUTIAL** *adj*
MINX	*n* pl. **-ES** a pert girl **MINXISH** *adj*
MINYAN	*n* pl. **-YANS** or **-YANIM** the minimum number required to be present for the conduct of a Jewish service
MIOSIS	*n* pl. **-OSES** excessive contraction of the pupil of the eye
MIOTIC	*n* pl. **-S** an agent that causes miosis
MIQUELET	*n* pl. **-S** a former Spanish or French soldier
MIR	*n* pl. **MIRS** or **MIRI** a Russian peasant commune
MIRACLE	*n* pl. **-S** an event ascribed to supernatural or divine origin
MIRADOR	*n* pl. **-S** an architectural feature designed to afford an extensive view

MIRAGE   *n* pl. **-S** a type of optical illusion

MIRE   *v* **MIRED, MIRING, MIRES** to cause to stick in swampy ground

MIREPOIX   *n* pl. **MIREPOIX** a sauteed mixture of diced vegetables

MIREX   *n* pl. **-ES** an insecticide

MIRI   a pl. of mir

MIRID   *n* pl. **-S** a variety of leaf bug

MIRIER   comparative of miry

MIRIEST   superlative of miry

MIRIN   *n* pl. **-S** a sweet Japanese cooking wine

MIRINESS   *n* pl. **-ES** the state of being miry

MIRING   present participle of mire

MIRK   *adj* **MIRKER, MIRKEST** murk

MIRK   *n* pl. **-S** murk

MIRKY   *adj* **MIRKIER, MIRKIEST** murky **MIRKILY** *adv*

MIRLITON   *n* pl. **-S** a chayote

MIRROR   *v* **-ED, -ING, -S** to reflect an image of

MIRTH   *n* pl. **-S** spirited gaiety **MIRTHFUL** *adj*

MIRY   *adj* **MIRIER, MIRIEST** swampy

MIRZA   *n* pl. **-S** a Persian title of honor

MISACT   *v* **-ED, -ING, -S** to act badly

MISADAPT   *v* **-ED, -ING, -S** to adapt wrongly

MISADD   *v* **-ED, -ING, -S** to add incorrectly

MISAGENT   *n* pl. **-S** a bad agent

MISAIM   *v* **-ED, -ING, -S** to aim badly

MISALIGN   *v* **-ED, -ING, -S** to align improperly

MISALLOT   *v* **-LOTTED, -LOTTING, -LOTS** to allot wrongly

MISALLY   *v* **-LIED, -LYING, -LIES** to ally badly

MISALTER   *v* **-ED, -ING, -S** to alter wrongly

MISANDRY   *n* pl. **-DRIES** hatred of men

MISAPPLY   *v* **-PLIED, -PLYING, -PLIES** to apply wrongly

MISASSAY   *v* **-ED, -ING, -S** to attempt unsuccessfully

MISATE   past tense of miseat

MISATONE   *v* **-ATONED, -ATONING, -ATONES** to atone wrongly

MISAVER   *v* **-AVERRED, -AVERRING, -AVERS** to speak erroneously

MISAWARD   *v* **-ED, -ING, -S** to award wrongly

MISBEGIN   *v* **-GAN, -GUN, -GINNING, -GINS** to begin wrongly

MISBEGOT   *adj* born out of wedlock

MISBIAS   *v* **-ASED, -ASING, -ASES** or **-ASSED, -ASSING, -ASSES** to bias wrongly

MISBILL   *v* **-ED, -ING, -S** to bill wrongly

MISBIND   *v* **-BOUND, -BINDING, -BINDS** to bind imperfectly

MISBRAND   *v* **-ED, -ING, -S** to brand incorrectly

MISBUILD   *v* **-BUILT, -BUILDING, -BUILDS** to build imperfectly

MISCALL   *v* **-ED, -ING, -S** to call by a wrong name

MISCARRY   *v* **-RIED, -RYING, -RIES** to be unsuccessful

MISCAST   *v* **-CAST, -CASTING, -CASTS** to cast in an unsuitable role

MISCHIEF   *n* pl. **-S** action that causes irritation, harm, or trouble

MISCHOSE   past tense of mischoose (to select improperly)

MISCIBLE   *adj* capable of being mixed

MISCITE   *v* **-CITED, -CITING, -CITES** to misquote

MISCLAIM   *v* **-ED, -ING, -S** to claim wrongfully

MISCLASS   *v* **-ED, -ING, -ES** to put in the wrong class

MISCODE   *v* **-CODED, -CODING, -CODES** to code wrongly

MISCOIN   *v* **-ED, -ING, -S** to coin improperly

MISCOLOR   *v* **-ED, -ING, -S** to color incorrectly

MISCOOK   *v* **-ED, -ING, -S** to cook badly

MISCOPY   *v* **-COPIED, -COPYING, -COPIES** to copy incorrectly

MISCOUNT   *v* **-ED, -ING, -S** to count incorrectly

MISCUE   *v* **-CUED, -CUING** or **-CUEING, -CUES** to make a faulty stroke in billiards

MISCUT   *v* **-CUT, -CUTTING, -CUTS** to cut incorrectly

MISDATE   *v* **-DATED, -DATING, -DATES** to date incorrectly

MISDEAL   *v* **-DEALT, -DEALING, -DEALS** to deal cards incorrectly

MISDEED   *n* pl. **-S** an evil act

MISDEEM   *v* **-ED, -ING, -S** to judge unfavorably

MISDIAL   *v* **-DIALED, -DIALING, -DIALS** or **-DIALLED, -DIALLING, -DIALS** to dial wrongly

MISDO *v* **-DID, -DONE, -DOING, -DOES** to do wrongly

MISDOER *n pl.* **-S** one that misdoes

MISDOING *n pl.* **-S** an instance of doing wrong

MISDONE past participle of misdo

MISDOUBT *v* **-ED, -ING, -S** to doubt

MISDRAW *v* **-DREW, -DRAWN, -DRAWING, -DRAWS** to draw incorrectly

MISDRIVE *v* **-DROVE, -DRIVEN, -DRIVING, -DRIVES** to drive wrongly or improperly

MISE *n pl.* **-S** an agreement or settlement

MISEASE *n pl.* **-S** discomfort

MISEAT *v* **-ATE, -EATEN, -EATING, -EATS** to eat improperly

MISEDIT *v* **-ED, -ING, -S** to edit incorrectly

MISENROL *v* **-ROLLED, -ROLLING, -ROLS** to enroll improperly

MISENTER *v* **-ED, -ING, -S** to enter erroneously

MISENTRY *n pl.* **-TRIES** an erroneous entry

MISER *n pl.* **-S** one who hoards money greedily

MISERERE *n pl.* **-S** a part of a church seat

MISERLY *adj* characteristic of a miser

MISERY *n pl.* **-ERIES** a state of great suffering

MISEVENT *n pl.* **-S** a mishap

MISFAITH *n pl.* **-S** lack of faith; disbelief

MISFEED *v* **-FED, -FEEDING, -FEEDS** to feed wrongly

MISFIELD *v* **-ED, -ING, -S** to field badly

MISFILE *v* **-FILED, -FILING, -FILES** to file in the wrong place

MISFIRE *v* **-FIRED, -FIRING, -FIRES** to fail to fire

MISFIT *v* **-FITTED, -FITTING, -FITS** to fit badly

MISFOCUS *v* **-CUSED, -CUSING, -CUSES** or **-CUSSED, -CUSSING, -CUSSES** to focus badly

MISFORM *v* **-ED, -ING, -S** to misshape

MISFRAME *v* **-FRAMED, -FRAMING, -FRAMES** to frame badly

MISGAUGE *v* **-GAUGED, -GAUGING, -GAUGES** to gauge wrongly or inaccurately

MISGIVE *v* **-GAVE, -GIVEN, -GIVING, -GIVES** to make doubtful or fearful

MISGRADE *v* **-GRADED, -GRADING, -GRADES** to grade incorrectly

MISGRAFT *v* **-ED, -ING, -S** to graft wrongly

MISGROW *v* **-GREW, -GROWN, -GROWING, -GROWS** to grow abnormally

MISGUESS *v* **-ED, -ING, -ES** to guess wrongly

MISGUIDE *v* **-GUIDED, -GUIDING, -GUIDES** to guide wrongly

MISHAP *n pl.* **-S** an unfortunate accident

MISHEAR *v* **-HEARD, -HEARING, -HEARS** to hear incorrectly

MISHIT *v* **-HIT, -HITTING, -HITS** to hit poorly

MISHMASH *n pl.* **-ES** a confused mixture

MISHMOSH *n pl.* **-ES** mishmash

MISHUGAS *n pl.* **-ES** crazy or foolish behavior

MISINFER *v* **-FERRED, -FERRING, -FERS** to infer wrongly

MISINTER *v* **-TERRED, -TERRING, -TERS** to inter improperly

MISJOIN *v* **-ED, -ING, -S** to join improperly

MISJUDGE *v* **-JUDGED, -JUDGING, -JUDGES** to judge wrongly

MISKAL *n pl.* **-S** an Oriental unit of weight

MISKEEP *v* **-KEPT, -KEEPING, -KEEPS** to keep wrongly

MISKEY *v* **-ED, -ING, -S** to key into a machine incorrectly

MISKICK *v* **-ED, -ING, -S** to kick badly

MISKNOW *v* **-KNEW, -KNOWN, -KNOWING, -KNOWS** to fail to understand or recognize

MISLABEL *v* **-BELED, -BELING, -BELS** or **-BELLED, -BELLING, -BELS** to label incorrectly or falsely

MISLABOR *v* **-ED, -ING, -S** to labor badly

MISLAIN past participle of mislie

MISLAY *v* **-LAID, -LAYING, -LAYS** to put in a forgotten place

MISLAYER *n pl.* **-S** one that mislays

MISLEAD *v* **-LED, -LEADING, -LEADS** to lead astray

MISLEARN *v* **-LEARNED** or **-LEARNT, -LEARNING, -LEARNS** to learn wrongly

MISLIE *v* **-LAY, -LAIN, -LYING, -LIES** to lie in a wrong position

MISLIGHT *v* **-LIGHTED** or **-LIT, -LIGHTING, -LIGHTS** to lead astray by its light

MISLIKE *v* **-LIKED, -LIKING, -LIKES** to dislike

MISLIKER   *n* pl. **-S** one that mislikes

MISLIT   a past tense of mislight

MISLIVE   *v* **-LIVED, -LIVING, -LIVES** to live a bad life

MISLODGE   *v* **-LODGED, -LODGING, -LODGES** to lodge in a wrong place

MISLYING   present participle of mislie

MISMAKE   *v* **-MADE, -MAKING, -MAKES** to make incorrectly

MISMARK   *v* **-ED, -ING, -S** to mark wrongly

MISMATCH   *v* **-ED, -ING, -ES** to match badly

MISMATE   *v* **-MATED, -MATING, -MATES** to mate unsuitably

MISMEET   *v* **-MET, -MEETING, -MEETS** to meet under unfortunate circumstances

MISMOVE   *v* **-MOVED, -MOVING, -MOVES** to move wrongly

MISNAME   *v* **-NAMED, -NAMING, -NAMES** to call by a wrong name

MISNOMER   *n* pl. **-S** a name wrongly used

MISO   *n* pl. **-SOS** a type of food paste

MISOGAMY   *n* pl. **-MIES** a hatred of marriage

MISOGYNY   *n* pl. **-NIES** a hatred of women

MISOLOGY   *n* pl. **-GIES** a hatred of debate or reasoning

MISORDER   *v* **-ED, -ING, -S** to order incorrectly

MISPAGE   *v* **-PAGED, -PAGING, -PAGES** to page incorrectly

MISPAINT   *v* **-ED, -ING, -S** to paint wrongly

MISPARSE   *v* **-PARSED, -PARSING, -PARSES** to parse incorrectly

MISPART   *v* **-ED, -ING, -S** to part badly

MISPATCH   *v* **-ED, -ING, -ES** to patch badly

MISPEN   *v* **-PENNED, -PENNING, -PENS** to write incorrectly

MISPLACE   *v* **-PLACED, -PLACING, -PLACES** to put in a wrong place

MISPLAN   *v* **-PLANNED, -PLANNING, -PLANS** to plan badly

MISPLANT   *v* **-ED, -ING, -S** to plant wrongly

MISPLAY   *v* **-ED, -ING, -S** to make a bad play in a game

MISPLEAD   *v* **-PLEADED** or **-PLED, -PLEADING, -PLEADS** to plead wrongly or falsely

MISPOINT   *v* **-ED, -ING, -S** to point improperly

MISPOISE   *v* **-POISED, -POISING, -POISES** to poise incorrectly

MISPRICE   *v* **-PRICED, -PRICING, -PRICES** to price incorrectly

MISPRINT   *v* **-ED, -ING, -S** to print incorrectly

MISPRIZE   *v* **-PRIZED, -PRIZING, -PRIZES** to despise

MISQUOTE   *v* **-QUOTED, -QUOTING, -QUOTES** to quote incorrectly

MISRAISE   *v* **-RAISED, -RAISING, -RAISES** to raise wrongly

MISRATE   *v* **-RATED, -RATING, -RATES** to rate incorrectly

MISREAD   *v* **-READ, -READING, -READS** to read incorrectly

MISREFER   *v* **-FERRED, -FERRING, -FERS** to refer incorrectly

MISRELY   *v* **-LIED, -LYING, -LIES** to rely wrongly

MISROUTE   *v* **-ROUTED, -ROUTING, -ROUTES** to route incorrectly

MISRULE   *v* **-RULED, -RULING, -RULES** to rule unwisely or unjustly

MISS   *v* **-ED, -ING, -ES** to fail to make contact with

MISSABLE   *adj* able to be missed

MISSAL   *n* pl. **-S** a prayer book

MISSAY   *v* **-SAID, -SAYING, -SAYS** to say incorrectly

MISSEAT   *v* **-ED, -ING, -S** to seat wrongly

MISSEL   *n* pl. **-S** a European thrush

MISSEND   *v* **-SENT, -SENDING, -SENDS** to send incorrectly

MISSENSE   *n* pl. **-S** a form of genetic mutation

MISSET   *v* **-SET, -SETTING, -SETS** to set incorrectly

MISSHAPE   *v* **-SHAPED, -SHAPEN, -SHAPING, -SHAPES** to shape badly

MISSHOD   *adj* improperly shod

MISSIES   pl. of missy

MISSILE   *n* pl. **-S** an object or weapon that is thrown or projected

MISSILRY   *n* pl. **-RIES** the science of designing and operating guided missiles

MISSION   *v* **-ED, -ING, -S** to send to perform a specific task

MISSIS   *n* pl. **-SISES** a wife

MISSIVE   *n* pl. **-S** a written communication

MISSORT   *v* **-ED, -ING, -S** to sort badly or improperly

MISSOUND   *v* **-ED, -ING, -S** to sound wrongly

MISSOUT   *n* pl. **-S** a losing throw of dice

MISSPACE   *v* **-SPACED, -SPACING, -SPACES** to space incorrectly

MISSPEAK   *v* **-SPOKE, -SPOKEN, -SPEAKING, -SPEAKS** to speak incorrectly

MISSPELL   *v* **-SPELLED** or **-SPELT, -SPELLING, -SPELLS** to spell incorrectly

MISSPEND   *v* **-SPENT, -SPENDING, -SPENDS** to spend wrongly

MISSPOKE   past tense of misspeak

MISSPOKEN   past participle of misspeak

MISSTAMP   *v* **-ED, -ING, -S** to stamp wrongly

MISSTART   *v* **-ED, -ING, -S** to start off badly

MISSTATE   *v* **-STATED, -STATING, -STATES** to state wrongly

MISSTEER   *v* **-ED, -ING, -S** to steer wrongly

MISSTEP   *v* **-STEPPED, -STEPPING, -STEPS** to step wrongly

MISSTOP   *v* **-STOPPED, -STOPPING, -STOPS** to stop wrongly

MISSTYLE   *v* **-STYLED, -STYLING, -STYLES** to style or call wrongly

MISSUIT   *v* **-ED, -ING, -S** to suit badly

MISSUS   *n* pl. **-ES** missis

MISSY   *n* pl. **MISSIES** a young girl

MIST   *v* **-ED, -ING, -S** to become blurry

MISTAKE   *v* **-TOOK** or **-TEUK, -TAKEN, -TAKING, -TAKES** to interpret wrongly

MISTAKER   *n* pl. **-S** one that mistakes

MISTBOW   *n* pl. **-S** a fogbow

MISTEACH   *v* **-TAUGHT, -TEACHING, -TEACHES** to teach wrongly or badly

MISTEND   *v* **-ED, -ING, -S** to tend to improperly

MISTER   *n* pl. **-S** sir

MISTERM   *v* **-ED, -ING, -S** to call by a wrong name

MISTEUK   a past tense of mistake

MISTHINK   *v* **-THOUGHT, -THINKING, -THINKS** to think wrongly

MISTHROW   *v* **-THREW, -THROWN, -THROWING, -THROWS** to throw errantly

MISTIER   comparative of misty

MISTIEST   superlative of misty

MISTILY   *adv* in a misty manner

MISTIME   *v* **-TIMED, -TIMING, -TIMES** to time wrongly

MISTITLE   *v* **-TLED, -TLING, -TLES** to call by a wrong title

MISTOOK   a past tense of mistake

MISTOUCH   *v* **-ED, -ING, -ES** to touch improperly

MISTRACE   *v* **-TRACED, -TRACING, -TRACES** to trace wrongly

MISTRAIN   *v* **-ED, -ING, -S** to train improperly

MISTRAL   *n* pl. **-S** a cold, dry wind

MISTREAT   *v* **-ED, -ING, -S** to treat badly

MISTRESS   *n* pl. **-ES** a woman in a position of authority

MISTRIAL   *n* pl. **-S** a trial made invalid because of some error in procedure

MISTRUST   *v* **-ED, -ING, -S** to distrust

MISTRUTH   *n* pl. **-S** a lie

MISTRYST   *v* **-ED, -ING, -S** to fail to keep an appointment with

MISTUNE   *v* **-TUNED, -TUNING, -TUNES** to tune incorrectly

MISTUTOR   *v* **-ED, -ING, -S** to instruct or bring up badly

MISTY   *adj* **MISTIER, MISTIEST** blurry

MISTYPE   *v* **-TYPED, -TYPING, -TYPES** to type incorrectly

MISUNION   *n* pl. **-S** a bad union

MISUSAGE   *n* pl. **-S** incorrect use

MISUSE   *v* **-USED, -USING, -USES** to use incorrectly

MISUSER   *n* pl. **-S** one that misuses

MISVALUE   *v* **-UED, -UING, -UES** to value incorrectly

MISWORD   *v* **-ED, -ING, -S** to word wrongly

MISWRITE   *v* **-WROTE** or **-WRIT, -WRITTEN, -WRITING, -WRITES** to write incorrectly

MISYOKE   *v* **-YOKED, -YOKING, -YOKES** to yoke improperly

MITE   *n* pl. **-S** a small arachnid

MITER   *v* **-ED, -ING, -S** to raise to the rank of a bishop

MITERER   *n* pl. **-S** one that miters

MITHER   *n* pl. **-S** mother

MITICIDE   *n* pl. **-S** a substance used to kill mites

MITIER   comparative of mity

MITIEST   superlative of mity

MITIGANT *n* pl. **-S** something that mitigates

MITIGATE *v* **-GATED, -GATING, -GATES** to make less severe

MITIS *n* pl. **-TISES** a type of wrought iron

MITOGEN *n* pl. **-S** a substance that induces mitosis

MITOSIS *n* pl. **-TOSES** a type of cell division **MITOTIC** *adj*

MITRAL *adj* pertaining to a valve of the heart

MITRE *v* **-TRED, -TRING, -TRES** to miter

MITSVAH *n* pl. **-VAHS** or **-VOTH** mitzvah

MITT *n* pl. **-S** a type of baseball glove

MITTEN *n* pl. **-S** a type of covering for the hand **MITTENED** *adj*

MITTIMUS *n* pl. **-ES** a warrant committing a person to prison

MITY *adj* **MITIER, MITIEST** infested with mites

MITZVAH *n* pl. **-VAHS** or **-VOTH** a commandment of Jewish law

MIX *v* **MIXED** or **MIXT, MIXING, MIXES** to put together into one mass **MIXABLE, MIXIBLE** *adj* **MIXEDLY** *adv*

MIXDOWN *n* pl. **-S** the process of combining soundtracks to make a recording

MIXER *n* pl. **-S** one that mixes

MIXOLOGY *n* pl. **-GIES** the art of making mixed drinks

MIXTAPE *n* pl. **-S** a compilation of songs recorded from various sources

MIXTURE *n* pl. **-S** something produced by mixing

MIXUP *n* pl. **-S** a state of confusion

MIZEN *n* pl. **-S** mizzen

MIZUNA *n* pl. **-S** a Japanese mustard

MIZZEN *n* pl. **-S** a type of sail

MIZZLE *v* **-ZLED, -ZLING, -ZLES** to rain in fine droplets

MIZZLY *adj* **-ZLIER, -ZLIEST** characterized by a fine rain

MM *interj* — used to express assent or satisfaction

MMM *interj* mm

MNEMONIC *n* pl. **-S** a device to assist the memory

MO *n* pl. **MOS** a moment

MOA *n* pl. **-S** an extinct flightless bird

MOAN *v* **-ED, -ING, -S** to utter a low, mournful sound

MOANER *n* pl. **-S** one that moans

MOANFUL *adj* moaning

MOAT *v* **-ED, -ING, -S** to surround with a moat (a water-filled trench)

MOATLIKE *adj* suggestive of a moat

MOB *v* **MOBBED, MOBBING, MOBS** to crowd about

MOBBER *n* pl. **-S** one that mobs

MOBBISH *adj* characteristic of a mob (a disorderly crowd of people)

MOBBISM *n* pl. **-S** mobbish conduct

MOBCAP *n* pl. **-S** a woman's cap

MOBILE *n* pl. **-S** a form of sculpture

MOBILISE *v* **-LISED, -LISING, -LISES** to mobilize

MOBILITY *n* pl. **-TIES** the ability to move

MOBILIZE *v* **-LIZED, -LIZING, -LIZES** to put into movement

MOBLED *adj* wrapped in or as if in a hood

MOBLOG *n* pl. **-S** a weblog with data posted from a cell phone

MOBOCRAT *n* pl. **-S** a supporter of mob rule

MOBSTER *n* pl. **-S** a gangster

MOC *n* pl. **-S** a moccasin

MOCCASIN *n* pl. **-S** a type of shoe

MOCHA *n* pl. **-S** a choice, pungent coffee

MOCHI *n* pl. **-S** a Japanese confection made with rice flour and sweetened bean paste

MOCHILA *n* pl. **-S** a leather covering for a saddle

MOCK *v* **-ED, -ING, -S** to ridicule **MOCKABLE** *adj*

MOCKER *n* pl. **-S** one that mocks

MOCKERY *n* pl. **-ERIES** the act of mocking

MOCKTAIL *n* pl. **-S** a cocktail with no alcohol

MOCKUP *n* pl. **-S** a full-sized model

MOD *n* pl. **-S** one who wears boldly stylish clothes

MODAL *n* pl. **-S** a verb used with other verbs to express mood or tense

MODALISM *n* pl. **-S** the doctrine that members of the Trinity are not distinct persons but modes of divine revelation

MODALIST *n* pl. **-S** an adherent of modalism

MODALITY *n* pl. **-TIES** the state of being modal

MODALLY *adv* in a manner pertaining to a mode

MODE *n* pl. **-S** a method of doing or acting

MODEL *v* **-ELED, -ELING, -ELS** or **-ELLED, -ELLING, -ELS** to plan or form after a pattern

MODELER *n* pl. **-S** one that models

MODELING *n* pl. **-S** the treatment of volume in sculpture

MODELIST *n* pl. **-S** one who makes models

MODELLED a past tense of model

MODELLER *n* pl. **-S** modeler

MODELLING a present participle of model

MODEM *v* **-ED, -ING, -S** to transmit by modem (a device for converting signals from one form to another)

MODERATE *v* **-ATED, -ATING, -ATES** to make less extreme

MODERATO *n* pl. **-TOS** a musical passage played at a medium tempo

MODERN *adj* **-ERNER, -ERNEST** pertaining to present or recent time **MODERNLY** *adv*

MODERN *n* pl. **-S** a person of modern times or views

MODERNE *n* pl. **-S** a design style of the 1920s and 1930s

MODEST *adj* **-ESTER, -ESTEST** having a moderate regard for oneself **MODESTLY** *adv*

MODESTY *n* pl. **-TIES** the quality of being modest

MODI pl. of modus

MODICUM *n* pl. **-CUMS** or **-CA** a small amount

MODIFIER *n* pl. **-S** one that modifies

MODIFY *v* **-FIED, -FYING, -FIES** to change in form or character

MODIOLUS *n* pl. **-LI** a bony shaft of the inner ear

MODISH *adj* stylish **MODISHLY** *adv*

MODISTE *n* pl. **-S** a dealer in stylish women's clothing

MODULAR *n* pl. **-S** something built in self-contained units

MODULATE *v* **-LATED, -LATING, -LATES** to adjust to a certain proportion

MODULE *n* pl. **-S** a standard of measurement

MODULO *adv* with respect to a modulus

MODULUS *n* pl. **-LI** a number that produces the same remainder when divided into each of two numbers

MODUS *n* pl. **-DI** a mode

MOFETTE *n* pl. **-S** a noxious emanation from a fissure in the earth

MOFFETTE *n* pl. **-S** mofette

MOG *v* **MOGGED, MOGGING, MOGS** to move away

MOGGIE *n* pl. **-S** moggy

MOGGY *n* pl. **-GIES** a cat

MOGHUL *n* pl. **-S** mogul

MOGUL *n* pl. **-S** an important person

MOGULED *adj* provided with bumps of hard snow

MOHAIR *n* pl. **-S** the long, silky hair of the Angora goat

MOHAWK *n* pl. **-S** a hairstyle marked by a stiff ridge of long hair from front to back

MOHEL *n* pl. **-HELS** or **-HELIM** or **-HALIM** a person who performs Jewish ritual circumcisions

MOHO *n* pl. **MOHOS** a boundary separating the earth's crust and mantle (the region between the crust and the core)

MOHUR *n* pl. **-S** a former gold coin of India

MOI *interj* — used instead of "me?" to feign surprise when accused of something

MOIDORE *n* pl. **-S** a former gold coin of Portugal

MOIETY *n* pl. **-ETIES** a half

MOIL *v* **-ED, -ING, -S** to work hard

MOILER *n* pl. **-S** one that moils

MOIRA *n* pl. **-RAI** fate or destiny, in ancient Greek religion

MOIRE *n* pl. **-S** a fabric having a wavy pattern

MOIST *adj* **MOISTER, MOISTEST** slightly wet

MOISTEN *v* **-ED, -ING, -S** to make or become moist

MOISTFUL *adj* moist

MOISTLY *adv* in a moist manner

MOISTURE *n* pl. **-S** condensed or diffused liquid

MOJARRA *n* pl. **-S** a marine fish

MOJITO *n* pl. **-TOS** a cocktail made of rum, sugar, mint, and lime juice

MOJO *n* pl. **-JOS** or **-JOES** a magic charm

MOKE *n* pl. **-S** a donkey

MOKSHA *n* pl. **-S** the final release of the soul from reincarnations in Hinduism

MOL *n* pl. **-S** mole

MOLA *n* pl. **-S** a marine fish

MOLAL *adj* pertaining to a mole

MOLALITY *n* pl. **-TIES** the number of moles of solute per 1,000 grams of solvent

MOLAR *n* pl. **-S** a grinding tooth

MOLARITY *n* pl. **-TIES** the number of moles of solute per liter of solution

MOLASSES *n* pl. **-LASSESES** a thick syrup

MOLD *v* **-ED, -ING, -S** to work into a particular shape **MOLDABLE** *adj*

MOLDER *v* **-ED, -ING, -S** to turn to dust by natural decay

MOLDIER comparative of moldy

MOLDIEST superlative of moldy

MOLDING *n* pl. **-S** a long, narrow strip used to decorate a surface

MOLDWARP *n* pl. **-S** a burrowing mammal

MOLDY *adj* **MOLDIER, MOLDIEST** musty

MOLE *n* pl. **-S** the quantity of a compound that has a weight equal to the compound's molecular weight

MOLECULE *n* pl. **-S** the smallest physical unit of an element

MOLEHILL *n* pl. **-S** a small mound of earth

MOLESKIN *n* pl. **-S** a cotton fabric

MOLEST *v* **-ED, -ING, -S** to disturb or annoy

MOLESTER *n* pl. **-S** one that molests

MOLIES pl. of moly

MOLINE *adj* having arms forked and curved at the ends — used of a heraldic cross

MOLL *n* pl. **-S** a gangster's girlfriend

MOLLAH *n* pl. **-S** mullah

MOLLIE *n* pl. **-S** a tropical fish

MOLLIES pl. of molly

MOLLIFY *v* **-FIED, -FYING, -FIES** to soothe

MOLLUSC *n* pl. **-S** mollusk

MOLLUSCA *n/pl* skin diseases

MOLLUSK *n* pl. **-S** any of a phylum of soft-bodied invertebrates

MOLLY *n* pl. **-LIES** mollie

MOLOCH *n* pl. **-S** a spiny lizard

MOLT *v* **-ED, -ING, -S** to cast off an outer covering

MOLTEN *adj* made liquid by heat **MOLTENLY** *adv*

MOLTER *n* pl. **-S** one that molts

MOLTO *adv* very — used in musical directions

MOLY *n* pl. **-LIES** a wild garlic

MOLY *n* pl. **MOLYS** molybdenum

MOLYBDIC *adj* pertaining to a certain metallic element

MOM *n* pl. **-S** mother

MOME *n* pl. **-S** a fool

MOMENT *n* pl. **-S** a brief period of time

MOMENTA a pl. of momentum

MOMENTLY *adv* from moment to moment

MOMENTO *n* pl. **-TOS** or **-TOES** memento

MOMENTUM *n* pl. **-TUMS** or **-TA** force of movement

MOMI a pl. of momus

MOMISM *n* pl. **-S** an excessive dependence on mothers

MOMMA *n* pl. **-S** mother

MOMMY *n* pl. **-MIES** mother

MOMSER *n* pl. **-S** a bastard

MOMUS *n* pl. **-MUSES** or **-MI** a carping person

MOMZER *n* pl. **-S** momser

MON *n* pl. **MEN** man

MONACHAL *adj* pertaining to monks

MONACID *n* pl. **-S** monoacid

MONAD *n* pl. **-S** a single-celled organism **MONADAL, MONADIC** *adj*

MONADES pl. of monas

MONADISM *n* pl. **-S** a philosophical doctrine

MONAMINE *n* pl. **-S** an amine containing only one amino group

MONANDRY *n* pl. **-DRIES** the condition of having one husband at a time

MONARCH *n* pl. **-S** an absolute ruler

MONARCHY *n* pl. **-CHIES** rule by a monarch

MONARDA *n* pl. **-S** an aromatic herb

MONAS *n* pl. **MONADES** a monad

MONASTIC *n* pl. **-S** a monk

MONAURAL *adj* pertaining to sound transmission, recording, or reproduction involving a single transmission path

MONAXIAL *adj* having one axis

MONAXON *n* pl. **-S** a straight spicule in sponges

MONAZITE *n* pl. **-S** a mineral

MONDE *n* pl. **-S** the world

MONDO *n* pl. **-DOS** a rapid question and answer technique employed in Zen Buddhism

MONECIAN *adj* having both male and female sex organs in the same individual

MONELLIN *n* pl. **-S** a protein extracted from a West African red berry

MONERAN *n* pl. **-S** a cellular organism that does not have a distinct nucleus

MONETARY *adj* pertaining to money

MONETISE *v* **-TISED, -TISING, -TISES** to monetize

MONETIZE *v* **-TIZED, -TIZING, -TIZES** to coin into money

MONEY *n* pl. **MONEYS** or **MONIES** an official medium of exchange and measure of value

MONEYBAG *n* pl. **-S** a bag for holding money

MONEYED *adj* having much money

MONEYER *n* pl. **-S** one that coins money

MONEYMAN *n* pl. **-MEN** a person who invests large sums of money

MONGEESE a pl. of mongoose

MONGER *v* **-ED, -ING, -S** to peddle

MONGO *n* pl. **-GOS** mungo

MONGOE *n* pl. **-S** mungo

MONGOL *n* pl. **-S** a person affected with a form of mental deficiency

MONGOOSE *n* pl. **-GOOSES** or **-GEESE** a carnivorous mammal

MONGREL *n* pl. **-S** an animal or plant of mixed breed

MONGST *prep* amongst

MONIC *adj* denoting a type of polynomial

MONICKER *n* pl. **-S** moniker

MONIE *adj* many

MONIED *adj* moneyed

MONIES a pl. of money

MONIKER *n* pl. **-S** a name

MONILIA *n* pl. **-IAE** a type of parasitic fungus

MONISH *v* **-ED, -ING, -ES** to warn

MONISM *n* pl. **-S** a philosophical theory

MONIST *n* pl. **-S** an adherent of monism **MONISTIC** *adj*

MONITION *n* pl. **-S** a warning

MONITIVE *adj* giving warning

MONITOR *v* **-ED, -ING, -S** to keep track of

MONITORY *n* pl. **-RIES** a letter of warning

MONK *n* pl. **-S** a man who is a member of a secluded religious order

MONKERY *n* pl. **-ERIES** the mode of life of monks

MONKEY *v* **-ED, -ING, -S** to mimic

MONKFISH *n* pl. **-ES** a marine fish

MONKHOOD *n* pl. **-S** the state of being a monk

MONKISH *adj* pertaining to monks

MONO *n* pl. **MONOS** an infectious disease

MONOACID *n* pl. **-S** a type of acid

MONOBLOC *adj* made in a single casting

MONOCARP *n* pl. **-S** a plant that yields fruit only once before dying

MONOCLE *n* pl. **-S** an eyeglass for one eye **MONOCLED** *adj*

MONOCOT *n* pl. **-S** a type of seed plant

MONOCRAT *n* pl. **-S** an autocrat

MONOCROP *n* pl. **-S** the same crop in the same field year after year

MONOCYTE *n* pl. **-S** a type of white blood cell

MONODIST *n* pl. **-S** one who writes monodies

MONODY *n* pl. **-DIES** an elegy performed by one person **MONODIC** *adj*

MONOECY *n* pl. **-CIES** the condition of being monecian

MONOFIL *n* pl. **-S** a single filament of synthetic fiber

MONOFUEL *n* pl. **-S** a type of rocket propellant

MONOGAMY *n* pl. **-MIES** marriage with one person at a time

MONOGENY *n* pl. **-NIES** asexual reproduction

MONOGERM *adj* being a fruit that produces a single plant

MONOGLOT *n* pl. **-S** a person speaking or writing only one language

MONOGRAM *v* **-GRAMED, -GRAMING, -GRAMS** or **-GRAMMED, -GRAMMING, -GRAMS** to mark with a design of one's initials

MONOGYNY *n* pl. **-NIES** the condition of having one wife at a time

MONOHULL *n* pl. **-S** a vessel with a single hull

MONOKINE *n* pl. **-S** a substance secreted by white blood cells

MONOKINI *n* pl. **-S** the lower half of a bikini

MONOLITH *n* pl. **-S** a large block of stone

MONOLOG *v* **-LOGGED, -LOGGING, -LOGS** to deliver a monolog (a lengthy speech by one person)

MONOLOGY *n* pl. **-GIES** the act of uttering a monolog

MONOMER *n* pl. **-S** a type of chemical compound

MONOMIAL *n* pl. **-S** an algebraic expression consisting of a single term

MONOPOD *n* pl. **-S** a one-legged support for a camera

MONOPODE *n* pl. **-S** a creature having one foot

MONOPODY *n* pl. **-DIES** a measure consisting of a single metrical foot

MONOPOLE *n* pl. **-S** a type of radio antenna

MONOPOLY *n* pl. **-LIES** exclusive control of a commodity or service in a particular market

MONORAIL *n* pl. **-S** a single rail serving as a track for a wheeled vehicle

MONOSKI *n* pl. **-S** a single broad ski for both feet

MONOSOME *n* pl. **-S** an unpaired chromosome

MONOSOMY *n* pl. **-MIES** a condition of having one unpaired chromosome

MONOTINT *n* pl. **-S** a painting done in different shades of one color

MONOTONE *n* pl. **-S** a vocal utterance in one unvaried tone

MONOTONY *n* pl. **-NIES** tedious sameness

MONOTYPE *n* pl. **-S** the only representative of its group

MONOXIDE *n* pl. **-S** a type of oxide

MONS *n* pl. **MONTES** a protuberance of the body

MONSIEUR *n* pl. **MESSIEURS** a French title of courtesy for a man

MONSOON *n* pl. **-S** a seasonal wind

MONSTER *n* pl. **-S** a strange or terrifying creature

MONSTERA *n* pl. **-S** a tropical American plant

MONTAGE *v* **-TAGED, -TAGING, -TAGES** to combine into a composite picture

MONTANE *n* pl. **-S** the lower vegetation belt of a mountain

MONTE *n* pl. **-S** a card game

MONTEITH *n* pl. **-S** a large punch bowl

MONTERO *n* pl. **-ROS** a type of cap

MONTES pl. of mons

MONTH *n* pl. **-S** a period of approximately 30 days

MONTHLY *n* pl. **-LIES** a publication issued once a month

MONTY *n* pl. **-TIES** the full amount expected or possible

MONUMENT *n* pl. **-S** a structure built as a memorial

MONURON *n* pl. **-S** an herbicide

MONY *adj* many

MOO *v* **-ED, -ING, -S** to make the deep, moaning sound of a cow

MOOCH *v* **-ED, -ING, -ES** to obtain without paying

MOOCHER *n* pl. **-S** one that mooches

MOOD *n* pl. **-S** a person's emotional state at a particular moment

MOODY *adj* **MOODIER, MOODIEST** given to changing moods **MOODILY** *adv*

MOOK *n* pl. **-S** a foolish or contemptible person

MOOL *n* pl. **-S** soft soil

MOOLA *n* pl. **-S** moolah

MOOLAH *n* pl. **-S** money

MOOLEY *n* pl. **-EYS** muley

MOON *v* **-ED, -ING, -S** to spend time idly

MOONBEAM *n* pl. **-S** a ray of light from the moon (the earth's natural satellite)

MOONBOW *n* pl. **-S** a rainbow formed by light from the moon

MOONCALF *n* pl. **-CALVES** a foolish person

MOONDOG *n* pl. **-S** a bright spot in the sky formed by moonlight

MOONDUST *n* pl. **-S** dust on the moon

MOONER *n* pl. **-S** one that moons

MOONEYE *n* pl. **-S** a freshwater fish

MOONFISH *n* pl. **-ES** a marine fish

MOONGATE *n* pl. **-S** a circular gateway in a wall

MOONIER comparative of moony

MOONIEST superlative of moony

MOONILY *adv* in a moony manner

MOONISH *adj* fickle

MOONLESS *adj* lacking the light of the moon

MOONLET *n* pl. **-S** a small satellite

MOONLIKE *adj* resembling the moon

MOONLIT *adj* lighted by the moon

MOONPORT *n* pl. **-S** a facility for launching spacecraft to the moon

MOONRISE *n* pl. **-S** the rising of the moon above the horizon

MOONROOF *n* pl. **-S** a glass panel in an automobile roof

MOONSAIL *n* pl. **-S** a light, square sail

MOONSEED *n* pl. **-S** a climbing plant

MOONSET *n* pl. **-S** the setting of the moon below the horizon

MOONSHOT *n* pl. **-S** the launching of a spacecraft to the moon

MOONWALK *v* **-ED, -ING, -S** to walk on the moon

MOONWARD *adv* toward the moon

MOONWORT *n* pl. **-S** a flowering plant

MOONY *adj* **MOONIER, MOONIEST** resembling the moon

MOOR *v* **-ED, -ING, -S** to secure a vessel by means of cables

MOORAGE *n* pl. **-S** the act of mooring

MOORCOCK *n* pl. **-S** the male moorfowl

MOORFOWL *n* pl. **-S** a game bird

MOORHEN *n* pl. **-S** the female moorfowl

MOORIER comparative of moory

MOORIEST superlative of moory

MOORING *n* pl. **-S** a place where a vessel may be moored

MOORISH *adj* marshy

MOORLAND *n* pl. **-S** a tract of marshy land

MOORWORT *n* pl. **-S** a marsh plant

MOORY *adj* **MOORIER, MOORIEST** marshy

MOOSE *n* pl. **MOOSE** a ruminant mammal

MOOT *v* **-ED, -ING, -S** to bring up for discussion

MOOTER *n* pl. **-S** one that moots

MOOTNESS *n* pl. **-ES** the state of being without legal significance

MOP *v* **MOPPED, MOPPING, MOPS** to wipe with a mop (an implement for cleaning floors)

MOPBOARD *n* pl. **-S** a board at the base of a wall

MOPE *v* **MOPED, MOPING, MOPES** to act in a dejected or gloomy manner

MOPED *n* pl. **-S** a type of motorbike

MOPER *n* pl. **-S** one that mopes

MOPERY *n* pl. **-PERIES** an act of dawdling

MOPEY *adj* **MOPIER, MOPIEST** dejected **MOPILY** *adv*

MOPHEAD *n* pl. **-S** a person with thick shaggy hair

MOPIER comparative of mopy

MOPIEST superlative of mopy

MOPINESS *n* pl. **-ES** the state of being mopey

MOPING present participle of mope

MOPINGLY *adv* in a moping manner

MOPISH *adj* given to moping **MOPISHLY** *adv*

MOPOKE *n* pl. **-S** an Australian bird

MOPPED past tense of mop

MOPPER *n* pl. **-S** one that mops

MOPPET *n* pl. **-S** a child

MOPPING present participle of mop

MOPPY *adj* **-PIER, -PIEST** resembling a mop

MOPY *adj* **MOPIER, MOPIEST** mopey

MOQUETTE *n* pl. **-S** a woolen fabric

MOR *n* pl. **-S** a forest humus

MORA *n* pl. **-RAS** or **-RAE** a unit of metrical time in prosody

MORAINE *n* pl. **-S** an accumulation of debris deposited by a glacier **MORAINAL, MORAINIC** *adj*

MORAL *adj* pertaining to principles of right and wrong

MORALE *n* pl. **-S** the state of the spirits of an individual or group

MORALISE *v* **-ISED, -ISING, -ISES** to moralize

MORALISM *n* pl. **-S** the practice of moralizing

MORALIST *n* pl. **-S** a teacher of morality

MORALITY *n* pl. **-TIES** conformity to the rules of right conduct

MORALIZE *v* **-IZED, -IZING, -IZES** to explain in a moral sense

MORALLY *adv* in a moral manner

MORALS *n/pl* rules of conduct with respect to right and wrong

MORASS *n* pl. **-ES** a marsh **MORASSY** *adj*

MORATORY *adj* authorizing delay of payment

MORAY *n* pl. **-RAYS** a tropical eel

MORBID *adj* gruesome **MORBIDLY** *adv*

MORBIFIC *adj* causing disease

MORBILLI *n/pl* a virus disease

MORCEAU *n* pl. **-CEAUX** a short literary or musical composition

MORDANCY *n* pl. **-CIES** a sarcastic quality

MORDANT *v* **-ED, -ING, -S** to treat with a caustic substance

MORDENT *n* pl. **-S** a melodic embellishment

MORE *adj* greater, additional

MOREEN *n* pl. **-S** a heavy fabric

MOREISH *adj* so good that you want to have more

MOREL *n* pl. **-S** an edible mushroom

MORELLE *n* pl. **-S** a flowering plant

MORELLO *n* pl. **-LOS** a variety of sour cherry

MORENESS *n* pl. **-ES** the state of being more

MOREOVER *adv* in addition

MORES *n/pl* the customs of a particular group

MORESQUE *n* pl. **-S** an ancient decorative style

MORGAN *n* pl. **-S** a unit of distance between genes

MORGEN *n* pl. **-S** a Dutch unit of land area

MORGUE *n* pl. **-S** a place where dead bodies are kept for identification

MORIBUND *adj* being about to die

MORION *n* pl. **-S** a type of helmet

MORISH *adj* moreish

MORN *n* pl. **-S** morning

MORNAY *n* pl. **-NAYS** a cheese-flavored white sauce

MORNING *n* pl. **-S** the early part of the day

MOROCCO *n* pl. **-COS** a soft leather

MORON *n* pl. **-S** a mentally deficient person **MORONIC** *adj*

MORONISM *n* pl. **-S** the condition of being a moron

MORONITY *n* pl. **-TIES** moronism

MOROSE *adj* sullen **MOROSELY** *adv*

MOROSITY *n* pl. **-TIES** the state of being morose

MORPH *v* **-ED, -ING, -S** to be transformed

MORPHEME *n* pl. **-S** a linguistic unit

MORPHIA *n* pl. **-S** morphine

MORPHIC *adj* pertaining to form

MORPHIN *n* pl. **-S** morphine

MORPHINE *n* pl. **-S** a narcotic alkaloid

MORPHING *n* pl. **-S** the transformation of one form into another

MORPHO *n* pl. **-PHOS** a tropical butterfly

MORRION *n* pl. **-S** morion

MORRIS *n* pl. **-RISES** an English folk dance

MORRO *n* pl. **-ROS** a rounded elevation

MORROW *n* pl. **-S** the next day

MORSE *adj* designating a code used in telegraphy

MORSEL *v* **-SELED, -SELING, -SELS** or **-SELLED, -SELLING, -SELS** to divide into small pieces

MORT *n* pl. **-S** a note sounded on a hunting horn to announce the killing of an animal

MORTAL *n* pl. **-S** a human being

MORTALLY *adv* fatally

MORTAR *v* **-ED, -ING, -S** to secure with mortar (a type of cement)

MORTARY *adj* containing or resembling mortar

MORTGAGE *v* **-GAGED, -GAGING, -GAGES** to pledge to a creditor as security

MORTICE *v* **-TICED, -TICING, -TICES** to mortise

MORTICER *n* pl. **-S** mortiser

MORTIFY *v* **-FIED, -FYING, -FIES** to humiliate

MORTISE *v* **-TISED, -TISING, -TISES** to join or fasten securely

MORTISER *n* pl. **-S** one that mortises

MORTMAIN *n* pl. **-S** perpetual ownership of land

MORTUARY *n* pl. **-ARIES** a place where dead bodies are kept until burial

MORULA *n* pl. **-LAS** or **-LAE** an embryonic mass of cells **MORULAR** *adj*

MOSAIC *v* **-ICKED, -ICKING, -ICS** to form into a mosaic (a type of inlaid surface decoration)

MOSASAUR *n* pl. **-S** an extinct lizard

MOSCATO *n* pl. **-TOS** a sweet dessert wine

MOSCHATE *adj* musky

MOSELLE *n* pl. **-S** a medium-dry white wine

MOSEY *v* **-ED, -ING, -S** to saunter

MOSH *v* **-ED, -ING, -ES** to engage in frenzied dancing with others at a rock concert

MOSHAV *n* pl. **-SHAVIM** a cooperative settlement of small farms in Israel

MOSHER *n* pl. **-S** one that moshes

MOSHING *n* pl. **-S** frenzied dancing at a rock concert

MOSK *n* pl. **-S** mosque

MOSQUE *n* pl. **-S** a Muslim house of worship

MOSQUITO *n pl.* **-TOS** or **-TOES** a winged insect

MOSS *v* **-ED, -ING, -ES** to cover with moss (a growth of small, leafy-stemmed plants)

MOSSBACK *n pl.* **-S** a large, old fish

MOSSER *n pl.* **-S** one that gathers or works with moss

MOSSLIKE *adj* resembling moss

MOSSO *adv* rapidly — used as a musical direction

MOSSY *adj* **MOSSIER, MOSSIEST** covered with moss

MOST *n pl.* **-S** the greatest amount

MOSTE past tense of mote

MOSTEST *n pl.* **-S** most

MOSTLY *adv* mainly

MOT *n pl.* **-S** a witty saying

MOTE *n pl.* **-S** a small particle

MOTE *v* past tense **MOSTE** may

MOTEL *n pl.* **-S** a roadside hotel

MOTET *n pl.* **-S** a type of choral composition

MOTEY *adj* full of motes

MOTH *n pl.* **-S** a winged insect

MOTHBALL *v* **-ED, -ING, -S** to put into storage

MOTHER *v* **-ED, -ING, -S** to give birth to

MOTHERLY *adj* maternal

MOTHERY *adj* slimy

MOTHLIKE *adj* resembling a moth

MOTHY *adj* **MOTHIER, MOTHIEST** full of moths

MOTIF *n pl.* **-S** a recurring thematic element in an artistic work **MOTIFIC** *adj*

MOTILE *n pl.* **-S** one whose mental imagery consists chiefly of inner feelings of action

MOTILITY *n pl.* **-TIES** the ability to move

MOTION *v* **-ED, -ING, -S** to signal by a bodily movement

MOTIONAL *adj* pertaining to movement

MOTIONER *n pl.* **-S** one that motions

MOTIVATE *v* **-VATED, -VATING, -VATES** to provide with an incentive

MOTIVE *v* **-TIVED, -TIVING, -TIVES** to motivate

MOTIVIC *adj* pertaining to a musical motif

MOTIVITY *n pl.* **-TIES** the ability to move

MOTLEY *adj* **-LEYER, -LEYEST** or **-LIER, -LIEST** composed of diverse elements

MOTLEY *n pl.* **-LEYS** a garment of various colors

MOTMOT *n pl.* **-S** a tropical bird

MOTOR *v* **-ED, -ING, -S** to travel by automobile

MOTORBUS *n pl.* **-BUSES** or **-BUSSES** a bus

MOTORCAR *n pl.* **-S** an automobile

MOTORDOM *n pl.* **-S** the motor vehicle industry

MOTORIC *adj* pertaining to muscular movement

MOTORING *n pl.* **-S** the recreation of traveling by automobile

MOTORISE *v* **-ISED, -ISING, -ISES** to motorize

MOTORIST *n pl.* **-S** one who travels by automobile

MOTORIZE *v* **-IZED, -IZING, -IZES** to equip with motor vehicles

MOTORMAN *n pl.* **-MEN** one who operates an electric streetcar or subway train

MOTORWAY *n pl.* **-WAYS** a type of highway

MOTT *n pl.* **-S** motte

MOTTE *n pl.* **-S** a small growth of trees on a prairie

MOTTLE *v* **-TLED, -TLING, -TLES** to mark with spots or streaks of different colors

MOTTLER *n pl.* **-S** one that mottles

MOTTLING *n pl.* **-S** an irregular arrangement of spots

MOTTO *n pl.* **-TOS** or **-TOES** a short expression of a guiding principle

MOUCH *v* **-ED, -ING, -ES** to mooch

MOUCHOIR *n pl.* **-S** a small handkerchief

MOUE *n pl.* **-S** a pouting grimace

MOUFFLON *n pl.* **-S** mouflon

MOUFLON *n pl.* **-S** a wild sheep

MOUILLE *adj* pronounced with the front of the tongue against the palate

MOUJIK *n pl.* **-S** muzhik

MOULAGE *n pl.* **-S** the making of a cast or mold of a mark for use in a criminal investigation

MOULD *v* **-ED, -ING, -S** to mold

MOULDER *v* **-ED, -ING, -S** to molder

MOULDING *n pl.* **-S** molding

MOULDY *adj* **MOULDIER, MOULDIEST** moldy

MOULIN *n pl.* **-S** a vertical cavity in a glacier

MOULT *v* **-ED, -ING, -S** to molt

MOULTER	*n* pl. **-S** molter
MOUND	*v* **-ED, -ING, -S** to pile
MOUNT	*v* **-ED, -ING, -S** to get up on
MOUNTAIN	*n* pl. **-S** a large, natural elevation of the earth's surface
MOUNTER	*n* pl. **-S** one that mounts
MOUNTING	*n* pl. **-S** something that provides a backing or appropriate setting for something else
MOURN	*v* **-ED, -ING, -S** to feel or express grief or sorrow
MOURNER	*n* pl. **-S** one that mourns
MOURNFUL	*adj* **-FULLER, -FULLEST** expressing grief or sorrow
MOURNING	*n* pl. **-S** an outward sign of grief
MOUSAKA	*n* pl. **-S** moussaka
MOUSE	*n* pl. **MICE** a small rodent
MOUSE	*v* **MOUSED, MOUSING, MOUSES** to catch mice
MOUSEPAD	*n* pl. **-S** a flat pad on which a computer mouse is used
MOUSER	*n* pl. **-S** an animal that catches mice
MOUSEY	*adj* **MOUSIER, MOUSIEST** mousy
MOUSIER	comparative of mousy
MOUSIEST	superlative of mousy
MOUSILY	*adv* in a mousy manner
MOUSING	*n* pl. **-S** a wrapping around the shank end of a hook
MOUSSAKA	*n* pl. **-S** a Middle Eastern dish of meat and eggplant
MOUSSE	*v* **MOUSSED, MOUSSING, MOUSSES** to style with mousse (foamy preparation used in styling hair)
MOUSSEUX	*n* pl. **MOUSSEUX** a sparkling wine
MOUSY	*adj* **MOUSIER, MOUSIEST** resembling a mouse
MOUTH	*v* **-ED, -ING, -S** to put into the mouth
MOUTHER	*n* pl. **-S** a speaker
MOUTHFUL	*n* pl. **-S** as much as the mouth can hold
MOUTHY	*adj* **MOUTHIER, MOUTHIEST** very talkative **MOUTHILY** *adv*
MOUTON	*n* pl. **-S** sheepskin processed to resemble seal or beaver
MOVABLE	*n* pl. **-S** something that can be moved
MOVABLY	*adv* so as to be capable of being moved
MOVANT	*n* pl. **-S** a person who applies to a court for a favorable ruling
MOVE	*v* **MOVED, MOVING, MOVES** to change from one position to another
MOVEABLE	*n* pl. **-S** movable
MOVEABLY	*adv* movably
MOVED	past tense of move
MOVELESS	*adj* incapable of movement
MOVEMENT	*n* pl. **-S** the act of moving
MOVER	*n* pl. **-S** one that moves
MOVIE	*n* pl. **-S** a motion picture
MOVIEDOM	*n* pl. **-S** filmdom
MOVIEOLA	*n* pl. **-S** a device for viewing and editing film
MOVING	present participle of move
MOVINGLY	*adv* so as to affect the emotions
MOVIOLA	*n* pl. **-S** movieola
MOW	*v* **MOWED, MOWN, MOWING, MOWS** to cut down standing herbage
MOWER	*n* pl. **-S** one that mows
MOWING	*n* pl. **-S** the act of cutting down standing herbage
MOXA	*n* pl. **-S** a Chinese plant
MOXIE	*n* pl. **-S** spirit or courage
MOZETTA	*n* pl. **-TAS** or **-TE** mozzetta
MOZO	*n* pl. **-ZOS** a manual laborer
MOZZETTA	*n* pl. **-TAS** or **-TE** a hooded cape worn by bishops
MRIDANGA	*n* pl. **-S** a drum of India
MU	*n* pl. **-S** a Greek letter
MUCH	*n* pl. **-ES** a great amount
MUCHACHA	*n* pl. **-S** a young woman
MUCHACHO	*n* pl. **-CHOS** a young man
MUCHLY	*adv* very much
MUCHNESS	*n* pl. **-ES** the quality of being great
MUCHO	*adj* much, many
MUCID	*adj* musty
MUCIDITY	*n* pl. **-TIES** the state of being mucid
MUCILAGE	*n* pl. **-S** an adhesive substance
MUCIN	*n* pl. **-S** a protein secreted by the mucous membranes **MUCINOID, MUCINOUS** *adj*
MUCK	*v* **-ED, -ING, -S** to fertilize with manure
MUCKER	*n* pl. **-S** a vulgar person

MUCKIER	comparative of mucky
MUCKIEST	superlative of mucky
MUCKILY	*adv* in a mucky manner
MUCKLE	*n* pl. **-S** a large amount
MUCKLUCK	*n* pl. **-S** mukluk
MUCKRAKE	*v* **-RAKED, -RAKING, -RAKES** to search for and expose corruption
MUCKWORM	*n* pl. **-S** a worm found in manure
MUCKY	*adj* **MUCKIER, MUCKIEST** filthy
MUCLUC	*n* pl. **-S** mukluk
MUCOID	*n* pl. **-S** a complex protein **MUCOIDAL** *adj*
MUCOR	*n* pl. **-S** a type of fungus
MUCOSA	*n* pl. **-SAS** or **-SAE** a mucous membrane **MUCOSAL** *adj*
MUCOSE	*adj* mucous
MUCOSITY	*n* pl. **-TIES** the state of being mucous
MUCOUS	*adj* secreting or containing mucus
MUCRO	*n* pl. **-CRONES** or **-CROS** a sharp point at the end of certain plant and animal organs
MUCUS	*n* pl. **-ES** a viscid bodily fluid
MUD	*v* **MUDDED, MUDDING, MUDS** to cover with mud (soft, wet earth)
MUDBANK	*n* pl. **-S** a sloping area of mud alongside a body of water
MUDBUG	*n* pl. **-S** a crayfish
MUDCAP	*v* **-CAPPED, -CAPPING, -CAPS** to cover an explosive with mud before detonating
MUDCAT	*n* pl. **-S** a type of catfish
MUDDER	*n* pl. **-S** a racehorse that runs well on a muddy track
MUDDIED	past tense of muddy
MUDDIER	comparative of muddy
MUDDIES	present 3d person sing. of muddy
MUDDIEST	superlative of muddy
MUDDILY	*adv* in a muddy manner
MUDDING	present participle of mud
MUDDLE	*v* **-DLED, -DLING, -DLES** to mix in a disordered manner
MUDDLER	*n* pl. **-S** one that muddles
MUDDLY	*adj* disordered
MUDDY	*adj* **-DIER, -DIEST** covered or filled with mud
MUDDY	*v* **-DIED, -DYING, -DIES** to make or become muddy

MUDFISH	*n* pl. **-ES** a fish found in mud or muddy water
MUDFLAP	*n* pl. **-S** a flap hung behind a rear wheel of a vehicle to prevent splashing
MUDFLAT	*n* pl. **-S** a level tract alternately covered and left bare by the tide
MUDFLOW	*n* pl. **-S** a moving mass of mud
MUDGUARD	*n* pl. **-S** a fender
MUDHEN	*n* pl. **-S** a bird that lives in marshes
MUDHOLE	*n* pl. **-S** a hole or hollow place full of mud
MUDLARK	*n* pl. **-S** a street urchin
MUDPACK	*n* pl. **-S** cosmetic paste for the face
MUDPIE	*n* pl. **-S** a small mass of mud formed into a pie shape
MUDPUPPY	*n* pl. **-PIES** a large salamander
MUDRA	*n* pl. **-S** a hand gesture in East Indian classical dancing
MUDROCK	*n* pl. **-S** pelite
MUDROOM	*n* pl. **-S** a room for shedding muddy clothing or footwear
MUDSILL	*n* pl. **-S** the lowest supporting timber of a structure
MUDSLIDE	*n* pl. **-S** a mudflow down a slope
MUDSLING	*v* **-SLUNG, -SLINGING, -SLINGS** to use insults and accusations against a rival candidate
MUDSTONE	*n* pl. **-S** a type of rock
MUEDDIN	*n* pl. **-S** muezzin
MUENSTER	*n* pl. **-S** a mild cheese
MUESLI	*n* pl. **-S** a breakfast cereal
MUEZZIN	*n* pl. **-S** a Muslim crier who calls the faithful to prayer
MUFF	*v* **-ED, -ING, -S** to bungle
MUFFIN	*n* pl. **-S** a small, round bread
MUFFLE	*v* **-FLED, -FLING, -FLES** to wrap with something to deaden sound
MUFFLER	*n* pl. **-S** a device for deadening sound
MUFTI	*n* pl. **-S** a judge who interprets Muslim religious law
MUG	*v* **MUGGED, MUGGING, MUGS** to assault with intent to rob
MUGFUL	*n* pl. **-S** as much as a mug can hold
MUGG	*v* **-ED, -ING, -S** to make funny faces
MUGGAR	*n* pl. **-S** mugger
MUGGED	past tense of mug

MUGGEE	n pl. **-S** one who is mugged	**MULLET**	n pl. **-S** an edible fish
MUGGER	n pl. **-S** a large Asian crocodile	**MULLEY**	n pl. **-LEYS** muley
MUGGIER	comparative of muggy	**MULLIGAN**	n pl. **-S** a stew of various meats and vegetables
MUGGIEST	superlative of muggy		
MUGGILY	adv in a muggy manner	**MULLION**	v **-ED, -ING, -S** to provide with vertical dividing strips
MUGGING	n pl. **-S** a street assault or beating		
MUGGINS	n pl. **-ES** a stupid or foolish person	**MULLITE**	n pl. **-S** a mineral
MUGGUR	n pl. **-S** mugger	**MULLOCK**	n pl. **-S** waste earth or rock from a mine **MULLOCKY** adj
MUGGY	adj **-GIER, -GIEST** warm and humid		
		MULTIAGE	adj including people of various ages
MUGHAL	n pl. **-S** mogul		
MUGSHOT	n pl. **-S** a photograph of a person's face for official records	**MULTICAR**	adj owning or involving several cars
		MULTIDAY	adj lasting or usable for many days
MUGWORT	n pl. **-S** a flowering plant	**MULTIFID**	adj divided into many parts
MUGWUMP	n pl. **-S** a political independent	**MULTIJET**	adj having more than two jets
MUHLY	n pl. **MUHLIES** a perennial grass	**MULTIPED**	n pl. **-S** an animal having many feet
MUJIK	n pl. **-S** muzhik		
MUKHTAR	n pl. **-S** the head of the government of a town in Arabic countries	**MULTIPLE**	n pl. **-S** the product of a quantity by an integer
		MULTIPLY	v **-PLIED, -PLYING, -PLIES** to increase in number
MUKLUK	n pl. **-S** a soft boot worn by Inuits		
MUKTUK	n pl. **-S** whale skin used for food	**MULTITON**	adj weighing many tons
MULATTO	n pl. **-TOS** or **-TOES** the offspring of one white and one black parent	**MULTIUSE**	adj having many uses
		MULTIWAY	adj having several paths or routes
MULBERRY	n pl. **-RIES** a tree bearing an edible, berrylike fruit	**MULTURE**	n pl. **-S** a fee paid to a miller for grinding grain
MULCH	v **-ED, -ING, -ES** to provide with a protective covering for the soil	**MUM**	v **MUMMED, MUMMING, MUMS** to act in a disguise
MULCT	v **-ED, -ING, -S** to defraud	**MUMBLE**	v **-BLED, -BLING, -BLES** to speak unclearly
MULE	v **MULED, MULING, MULES** to strike from dies belonging to two different issues, as a coin		
		MUMBLER	n pl. **-S** one that mumbles
		MUMBLING	n pl. **-S** the act of speaking unclearly
MULETA	n pl. **-S** a red cloth used by a matador		
		MUMBLY	adj given to mumbling
MULETEER	n pl. **-S** one who drives mules (hoofed work animals)	**MUMM**	v **-ED, -ING, -S** to mum
		MUMMED	past tense of mum and mumm
MULEY	n pl. **-LEYS** a hornless cow	**MUMMER**	n pl. **-S** one that mums
MULIE	n pl. **-S** a western North American deer	**MUMMERY**	n pl. **-MERIES** a performance by mummers
MULING	present participle of mule		
MULISH	adj stubborn **MULISHLY** adv	**MUMMIED**	past tense of mummy
MULL	v **-ED, -ING, -S** to ponder	**MUMMIES**	present 3d person sing. of mummy
MULLA	n pl. **-S** mullah	**MUMMIFY**	v **-FIED, -FYING, -FIES** to preserve by embalming
MULLAH	n pl. **-S** a Muslim religious leader or teacher		
		MUMMING	n pl. **-S** a performance of a folk play by mummers
MULLEIN	n pl. **-S** a Eurasian herb		
MULLEN	n pl. **-S** mullein	**MUMMY**	v **-MIED, -MYING, -MIES** to mummify
MULLER	n pl. **-S** a grinding implement	**MUMP**	v **-ED, -ING, -S** to beg

MUMPER *n* pl. **-S** one that mumps

MUMPISH *adj* sullen

MUMSY *adj* **MUMSIER, MUMSIEST** maternal

MUMU *n* pl. **-S** muumuu

MUN *n* pl. **-S** man; fellow

MUNCH *v* **-ED, -ING, -ES** to chew with a crackling sound

MUNCHER *n* pl. **-S** one that munches

MUNCHIE *n* pl. **-S** a small amount of food eaten between meals

MUNCHKIN *n* pl. **-S** a small friendly person

MUNCHY *adj* **MUNCHIER, MUNCHIEST** suitable for snacking

MUNDANE *adj* ordinary

MUNDUNGO *n* pl. **-GOS** a foul-smelling tobacco

MUNG *n* pl. **-S** a round green bean

MUNGO *n* pl. **-GOS** or **-GOES** a low-quality wool

MUNGOOSE *n* pl. **-S** mongoose

MUNI *n* pl. **-S** a security issued by a state or local government

MUNIMENT *n* pl. **-S** a means of defense

MUNITION *v* **-ED, -ING, -S** to furnish with war materiel

MUNNION *n* pl. **-S** a muntin

MUNSTER *n* pl. **-S** muenster

MUNTIN *n* pl. **-S** a dividing strip for window panes **MUNTINED** *adj*

MUNTING *n* pl. **-S** muntin

MUNTJAC *n* pl. **-S** a small Asian deer

MUNTJAK *n* pl. **-S** muntjac

MUON *n* pl. **-S** a subatomic particle **MUONIC** *adj*

MUONIUM *n* pl. **-S** an electron and a positive muon bound together

MURA *n* pl. **-S** a Japanese village

MURAENID *n* pl. **-S** a moray

MURAGE *n* pl. **-S** a tax levied for repairing the walls of a town

MURAL *n* pl. **-S** a painting applied directly to a wall or ceiling **MURALED, MURALLED** *adj*

MURALIST *n* pl. **-S** a painter of murals

MURDER *v* **-ED, -ING, -S** to kill unlawfully with premeditated malice

MURDEREE *n* pl. **-S** one that is murdered

MURDERER *n* pl. **-S** one that murders

MURE *v* **MURED, MURING, MURES** to immure

MUREIN *n* pl. **-S** a type of polymer

MUREX *n* pl. **-REXES** or **-RICES** a marine mollusc

MURIATE *n* pl. **-S** chloride

MURIATED *adj* pickled

MURICATE *adj* covered with short, sharp points

MURICES a pl. of murex

MURID *n* pl. **-S** a murine

MURINE *n* pl. **-S** any of a family of small rodents

MURING present participle of mure

MURK *adj* **MURKER, MURKEST** dark **MURKLY** *adv*

MURK *n* pl. **-S** darkness

MURKY *adj* **MURKIER, MURKIEST** dark **MURKILY** *adv*

MURMUR *v* **-ED, -ING, -S** to speak unclearly

MURMURER *n* pl. **-S** one that murmurs

MURPHY *n* pl. **-PHIES** a potato

MURR *n* pl. **-S** murre

MURRA *n* pl. **-S** a substance used to make fine vases and cups in ancient Rome

MURRAIN *n* pl. **-S** a disease of cattle

MURRE *n* pl. **-S** a diving bird

MURRELET *n* pl. **-S** a small diving bird

MURREY *n* pl. **-REYS** a dark purple color

MURRHA *n* pl. **-S** murra **MURRHINE** *adj*

MURRINE *adj* pertaining to murra

MURRY *n* pl. **-RIES** a moray

MURTHER *v* **-ED, -ING, -S** to murder

MUSCA *n* pl. **-CAE** any of a genus of flies

MUSCADEL *n* pl. **-S** muscatel

MUSCADET *n* pl. **-S** a dry white French wine

MUSCAT *n* pl. **-S** a sweet, white grape

MUSCATEL *n* pl. **-S** a wine made from muscat grapes

MUSCID *n* pl. **-S** musca

MUSCLE *v* **-CLED, -CLING, -CLES** to proceed by force

MUSCLY *adj* **-CLIER, -CLIEST** composed of muscle (tissue that produces bodily movement)

MUSCULAR *adj* pertaining to muscle

MUSE   *v* **MUSED, MUSING, MUSES** to ponder

MUSEFUL   *adj* pensive

MUSER   *n* pl. **-S** one that muses

MUSETTE   *n* pl. **-S** a small bagpipe

MUSEUM   *n* pl. **-S** a place where objects of lasting interest or value are cared for and exhibited

MUSH   *v* **-ED, -ING, -ES** to travel over snow with a dog sled

MUSHER   *n* pl. **-S** one that mushes

MUSHING   *n* pl **-S** the act of one that mushes

MUSHRAT   *n* pl. **-S** muskrat

MUSHROOM   *v* **-ED, -ING, -S** to grow or spread rapidly

MUSHY   *adj* **MUSHIER, MUSHIEST** pulpy **MUSHILY** *adv*

MUSIC   *n* pl. **-S** vocal or instrumental sounds organized to produce a unified composition

MUSICAL   *n* pl. **-S** a play in which dialogue is interspersed with songs and dances

MUSICALE   *n* pl. **-S** a program of music performed at a social gathering

MUSICIAN   *n* pl. **-S** one who performs or composes music

MUSICK   *v* **-ED, -ING, -S** to compose music for

MUSING   *n* pl. **-S** contemplation

MUSINGLY   *adv* in a pensive manner

MUSJID   *n* pl. **-S** a mosque

MUSK   *n* pl. **-S** a strongly odorous substance secreted by certain animals

MUSKEG   *n* pl. **-S** a marsh

MUSKET   *n* pl. **-S** a type of firearm

MUSKETRY   *n* pl. **-RIES** the technique of firing small arms

MUSKIE   *n* pl. **-S** a freshwater fish

MUSKIER   comparative of musky

MUSKIEST   superlative of musky

MUSKILY   *adv* in a musky manner

MUSKIT   *n* pl. **-S** mesquite

MUSKOX   *n* pl. **-OXEN** a large bovid of arctic regions

MUSKRAT   *n* pl. **-S** an aquatic rodent

MUSKROOT   *n* pl. **-S** a perennial herb

MUSKY   *adj* **MUSKIER, MUSKIEST** resembling musk

MUSLIN   *n* pl. **-S** a cotton fabric **MUSLINED** *adj*

MUSO   *n* pl. **MUSOS** a musician

MUSPIKE   *n* pl. **-S** a freshwater fish

MUSQUASH   *n* pl. **-ES** a muskrat

MUSS   *v* **-ED, -ING, -ES** to mess

MUSSEL   *n* pl. **-S** a bivalve mollusk

MUSSY   *adj* **MUSSIER, MUSSIEST** messy **MUSSILY** *adv*

MUST   *v* **-ED, -ING, -S** to become musty

MUSTACHE   *n* pl. **-S** a growth of hair on the upper lip

MUSTANG   *n* pl. **-S** a wild horse

MUSTARD   *n* pl. **-S** a pungent seasoning

MUSTARDY   *adj* resembling mustard

MUSTEE   *n* pl. **-S** an octoroon

MUSTELID   *n* pl. **-S** a mammal of the weasel family

MUSTER   *v* **-ED, -ING, -S** to summon or assemble

MUSTH   *n* pl. **-S** a state of frenzy occurring in male elephants

MUSTY   *adj* **MUSTIER, MUSTIEST** having a stale odor **MUSTILY** *adv*

MUT   *n* pl. **-S** mutt

MUTABLE   *adj* capable of change **MUTABLY** *adv*

MUTAGEN   *n* pl. **-S** a substance that causes biological mutation

MUTANT   *n* pl. **-S** something that undergoes mutation

MUTASE   *n* pl. **-S** an enzyme

MUTATE   *v* **-TATED, -TATING, -TATES** to change or cause to change in form

MUTATION   *n* pl. **-S** the act of changing in form **MUTATIVE** *adj*

MUTATOR   *n* pl. **-S** one that causes a change in form

MUTCH   *n* pl. **-ES** a close-fitting cap

MUTCHKIN   *n* pl. **-S** a Scottish unit of liquid measure

MUTE   *adj* **MUTER, MUTEST** characterized by an absence of speech **MUTELY** *adv*

MUTE   *v* **MUTED, MUTING, MUTES** to deaden the sound of **MUTEDLY** *adv*

MUTENESS   *n* pl. **-ES** the state of being mute

MUTER   comparative of mute

MUTEST   superlative of mute

MUTICOUS	*adj* lacking a point
MUTILATE	*v* **-LATED, -LATING, -LATES** to deprive of a limb or other essential part
MUTINE	*v* **-TINED, -TINING, -TINES** to mutiny
MUTINEER	*v* **-ED, -ING, -S** to mutiny
MUTING	present participle of mute
MUTINIED	past tense of mutiny
MUTINIES	present 3d person sing. of mutiny
MUTINING	present participle of mutine
MUTINOUS	*adj* disposed to mutiny
MUTINY	*v* **-NIED, -NYING, -NIES** to revolt against constituted authority
MUTISM	*n* pl. **-S** muteness
MUTON	*n* pl. **-S** a unit of nucleic acid
MUTT	*n* pl. **-S** a mongrel dog
MUTTER	*v* **-ED, -ING, -S** to speak unclearly
MUTTERER	*n* pl. **-S** one that mutters
MUTTON	*n* pl. **-S** the flesh of sheep used as food **MUTTONY** *adj*
MUTUAL	*n* pl. **-S** a mutual fund
MUTUALLY	*adv* in a manner shared in common
MUTUEL	*n* pl. **-S** a system of betting on races
MUTULE	*n* pl. **-S** an ornamental block used in classical Greek architecture **MUTULAR** *adj*
MUUMUU	*n* pl. **-S** a long, loose dress
MUX	*v* **-ED, -ING, -ES** to transmit several messages simultaneously along a single channel
MUZHIK	*n* pl. **-S** a Russian peasant
MUZJIK	*n* pl. **-S** muzhik
MUZZIER	comparative of muzzy
MUZZIEST	superlative of muzzy
MUZZILY	*adv* in a muzzy manner
MUZZLE	*v* **-ZLED, -ZLING, -ZLES** to put a covering over the mouth of to prevent biting or eating
MUZZLER	*n* pl. **-S** one that muzzles
MUZZY	*adj* **-ZIER, -ZIEST** confused
MY	*pron* the possessive form of the pronoun I
MYALGIA	*n* pl. **-S** muscular pain **MYALGIC** *adj*

MYASIS	*n* pl. **MYASES** myiasis
MYC	*n* pl. **-S** a gene that transforms a normal cell into a cancerous cell
MYCELE	*n* pl. **-S** mycelium
MYCELIUM	*n* pl. **-LIA** the vegetative portion of a fungus **MYCELIAL, MYCELIAN, MYCELOID** *adj*
MYCETOMA	*n* pl. **-MAS** or **-MATA** a fungous infection
MYCOLOGY	*n* pl. **-GIES** the branch of botany dealing with fungi
MYCOSIS	*n* pl. **-COSES** a disease caused by a fungus **MYCOTIC** *adj*
MYELIN	*n* pl. **-S** a fatty substance that encases certain nerve fibers **MYELINIC** *adj*
MYELINE	*n* pl. **-S** myelin
MYELITIS	*n* pl. **-LITIDES** inflammation of the bone marrow
MYELOID	*adj* pertaining to bone marrow
MYELOMA	*n* pl. **-MAS** or **-MATA** a tumor of the bone marrow
MYIASIS	*n* pl. **MYIASES** infestation of human tissue by fly maggots
MYLODON	*n* pl. **-S** an extinct giant sloth
MYLONITE	*n* pl. **-S** a type of rock
MYNA	*n* pl. **-S** an Asian bird
MYNAH	*n* pl. **-S** myna
MYNHEER	*n* pl. **-S** a Dutch title of courtesy for a man
MYOBLAST	*n* pl. **-S** a cell capable of giving rise to muscle cells
MYOGENIC	*adj* originating in muscle tissue
MYOGRAPH	*n* pl. **-S** an instrument for recording muscular contractions
MYOID	*adj* resembling muscle
MYOLOGY	*n* pl. **-GIES** the study of muscles **MYOLOGIC** *adj*
MYOMA	*n* pl. **-MAS** or **-MATA** a tumor composed of muscle tissue
MYOMERE	*n* pl. **-S** part of a vertebrate embryo
MYOPATHY	*n* pl. **-THIES** a disorder of muscle tissue
MYOPE	*n* pl. **-S** one who is affected with myopia
MYOPIA	*n* pl. **-S** a visual defect **MYOPIC** *adj*
MYOPY	*n* pl. **-PIES** myopia

MYOSCOPE   *n* pl. **-S** an instrument for observing muscular contractions

MYOSIN   *n* pl. **-S** a protein found in muscle tissue

MYOSIS   *n* pl. **MYOSES** miosis

MYOSITIS   *n* pl. **-TISES** muscular pain from infection

MYOSOTE   *n* pl. **-S** myosotis

MYOSOTIS   *n* pl. **-TISES** a flowering plant

MYOTIC   *n* pl. **-S** miotic

MYOTOME   *n* pl. **-S** a portion of an embryonic somite

MYOTONIA   *n* pl. **-S** temporary muscular rigidity **MYOTONIC** *adj*

MYRIAD   *n* pl. **-S** a very large number

MYRIAPOD   *n* pl. **-S** a multi-legged arthropod

MYRICA   *n* pl. **-S** a medicinal tree bark

MYRIOPOD   *n* pl. **-S** myriapod

MYRMIDON   *n* pl. **-S** or **-ES** a loyal follower

MYRRH   *n* pl. **-S** an aromatic gum resin **MYRRHIC** *adj* **MYRRHY** *adj*

MYRTLE   *n* pl. **-S** an evergreen shrub

MYSELF   *pron* a form of the 1st person sing. pronoun

MYSID   *n* pl. **-S** a small crustacean

MYSOST   *n* pl. **-S** a mild cheese

MYSTAGOG   *n* pl. **-S** a teacher of religious mysteries

MYSTERY   *n* pl. **-TERIES** something that is not or cannot be known, understood, or explained

MYSTIC   *n* pl. **-S** one who professes to have had mystical experiences

MYSTICAL   *adj* spiritually significant or symbolic

MYSTICLY   *adv* in a mystical manner

MYSTIFY   *v* **-FIED, -FYING, -FIES** to perplex

MYSTIQUE   *n* pl. **-S** an aura of mystery or mystical power surrounding a particular person or thing

MYTH   *n* pl. **-S** a type of traditional story

MYTHIC   *adj* mythical

MYTHICAL   *adj* based on or described in a myth

MYTHOS   *n* pl. **-THOI** a myth

MYTHY   *adj* **MYTHIER, MYTHIEST** resembling myth

MYXAMEBA   *n* pl. **-BAS** or **-BAE** a slime mold that resembles an amoeba

MYXEDEMA   *n* pl. **-S** a disease caused by decreased activity of the thyroid gland

MYXOCYTE   *n* pl. **-S** a large cell found in mucous tissue

MYXOID   *adj* containing mucus

MYXOMA   *n* pl. **-MAS** or **-MATA** a tumor composed of mucous tissue

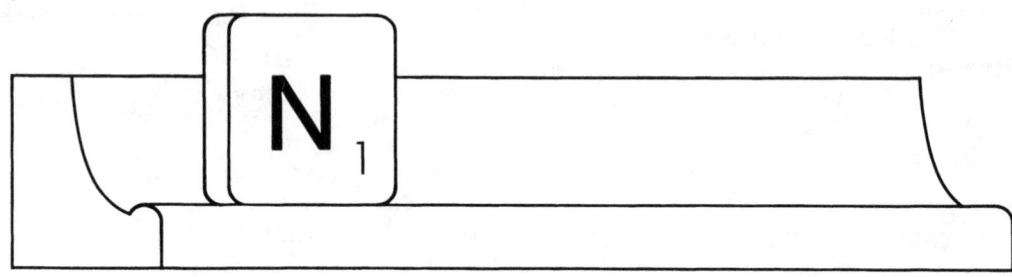

NA	*adv* no; not
NAAN	*n* pl. **-S** nan
NAB	*v* **NABBED, NABBING, NABS** to capture or arrest
NABBER	*n* pl. **-S** one that nabs
NABE	*n* pl. **-S** a neighborhood movie theater
NABIS	*n* pl. **NABIS** a group of French artists
NABOB	*n* pl. **-S** one who becomes rich and prominent **NABOBISH** *adj*
NABOBERY	*n* pl. **-ERIES** the state of being a nabob
NABOBESS	*n* pl. **-ES** a female nabob
NABOBISM	*n* pl. **-S** great wealth and luxury
NACELLE	*n* pl. **-S** a shelter on an aircraft
NACHAS	*n* pl. **NACHAS** pride in another's accomplishments
NACHES	*n* pl. **NACHES** nachas
NACHO	*n* pl. **-CHOS** a tortilla chip topped with cheese and a savory mixture and broiled
NACRE	*n* pl. **-S** the pearly internal layer of certain shells **NACRED, NACREOUS** *adj*
NADA	*n* pl. **-S** nothing
NADIR	*n* pl. **-S** a point on the celestial sphere **NADIRAL** *adj*
NAE	*n* pl. **-S** no
NAETHING	*n* pl. **-S** nothing
NAEVUS	*n* pl. **-VI** nevus **NAEVOID** *adj*
NAFF	*v* **-ED, -ING, -S** to fool around
NAFF	*adj* **NAFFER, NAFFEST** lacking taste or style
NAFFNESS	*n* pl. **-ES** the quality of lacking taste or style
NAG	*v* **NAGGED, NAGGING, NAGS** to find fault incessantly
NAGA	*n* pl. **-S** a half-snake, half-human creature in Hinduism
NAGANA	*n* pl. **-S** a disease of horses in Africa
NAGGER	*n* pl. **-S** one that nags
NAGGING	*n* pl. **-S** the act of finding fault incessantly
NAGGY	*adj* **-GIER, -GIEST** given to nagging
NAGWARE	*n* pl. **-S** software that is at first free but often reminds the user to pay for it
NAH	*adv* no
NAIAD	*n* pl. **-S** or **-ES** a water nymph
NAIF	*n* pl. **-S** a naive person
NAIL	*v* **-ED, -ING, -S** to fasten with a nail (a slender piece of metal)
NAILER	*n* pl. **-S** one that nails
NAILFOLD	*n* pl. **-S** a fold of skin around the fingernail
NAILHEAD	*n* pl. **-S** the top of a nail
NAILLESS	*adj* lacking nails
NAILSET	*n* pl. **-S** a steel rod for driving a nail into something
NAINSOOK	*n* pl. **-S** a cotton fabric
NAIRA	*n* pl. **-S** a monetary unit of Nigeria
NAIRU	*n* pl. **-S** the lowest rate of unemployment at which there is no inflation
NAIVE	*adj* **NAIVER, NAIVEST** lacking sophistication **NAIVELY** *adv*
NAIVE	*n* pl. **-S** a naive person
NAIVETE	*n* pl. **-S** the quality of being naive
NAIVETY	*n* pl. **-TIES** naivete
NAKED	*adj* **-KEDER, -KEDEST** being without clothing or covering **NAKEDLY** *adv*
NAKFA	*n* pl. **-S** a monetary unit of Eritrea
NALA	*n* pl. **-S** nullah

NALED *n* pl. **-S** an insecticide

NALOXONE *n* pl. **-S** a chemical compound

NAM a past tense of nim

NAME *v* **NAMED, NAMING, NAMES** to give a title to **NAMABLE, NAMEABLE** *adj*

NAMELESS *adj* lacking distinction or fame

NAMELY *adv* that is to say

NAMER *n* pl. **-S** one that names

NAMESAKE *n* pl. **-S** one who is named after another

NAMETAG *n* pl. **-S** a tag bearing one's name worn for identification

NAMETAPE *n* pl. **-S** a tape bearing one's name worn for identification

NAMING present participle of name

NAN *n* pl. **-S** a round flat bread

NANA *n* pl. **-S** a grandmother

NANDIN *n* pl. **-S** an evergreen shrub

NANDINA *n* pl. **-S** an Asian shrub

NANISM *n* pl. **-S** abnormal smallness

NANKEEN *n* pl. **-S** a cotton fabric

NANKIN *n* pl. **-S** nankeen

NANNA *n* pl. **-S** nana

NANNIE *n* pl. **-S** nanny

NANNY *v* **-NIED, -NYING, -NIES** to be overprotective toward

NANNYISH *adj* resembling a children's nurse

NANO *n* pl. **-NOS** science that deals with materials on an atomic or molecular scale

NANOBOT *n* pl. **-S** a very small self-propelled machine

NANOGRAM *n* pl. **-S** a unit of mass and weight

NANOTECH *n* pl. **-S** the technology of building electronic devices from individual atoms and molecules

NANOTUBE *n* pl. **-S** a microscopic tube

NANOWATT *n* pl. **-S** a unit of power

NAOS *n* pl. **NAOI** an ancient temple

NAP *v* **NAPPED, NAPPING, NAPS** to sleep briefly

NAPA *n* pl. **-S** a soft leather

NAPALM *v* **-ED, -ING, -S** to assault with a type of incendiary bomb

NAPE *n* pl. **-S** the back of the neck

NAPERY *n* pl. **-PERIES** table linen

NAPHTHA *n* pl. **-S** a volatile liquid

NAPHTHOL *n* pl. **-S** a chemical compound

NAPHTHYL *n* pl. **-S** a radical derived from naphthalene

NAPHTOL *n* pl. **-S** naphthol

NAPIFORM *adj* shaped like a turnip

NAPKIN *n* pl. **-S** a piece of material used to wipe the hands and mouth

NAPLESS *adj* threadbare

NAPOLEON *n* pl. **-S** a type of pastry

NAPPA *n* pl. **-S** napa

NAPPE *n* pl. **-S** a type of rock formation

NAPPED past tense of nap

NAPPER *n* pl. **-S** one that naps

NAPPIE *n* pl. **-S** a diaper

NAPPING present participle of nap

NAPPY *adj* **-PIER, -PIEST** kinky

NAPROXEN *n* pl. **-S** an anti-inflammatory drug

NARC *n* pl. **-S** an undercover drug agent

NARCEIN *n* pl. **-S** narceine

NARCEINE *n* pl. **-S** an opium derivative

NARCISM *n* pl. **-S** excessive love of oneself

NARCISSI *n/pl* bulbous flowering plants

NARCIST *n* pl. **-S** one given to narcism

NARCO *n* pl. **-COS** narc

NARCOMA *n* pl. **-MAS** or **-MATA** a stupor induced by a narcotic

NARCOSE *adj* characterized by stupor

NARCOSIS *n* pl. **-COSES** a drug-induced stupor

NARCOTIC *n* pl. **-S** a drug that dulls the senses

NARD *n* pl. **-S** a fragrant ointment **NARDINE** *adj*

NARDOO *n* pl. **-DOOS** a clover-like plant

NARES pl. of naris

NARGHILE *n* pl. **-S** a hookah

NARGILE *n* pl. **-S** narghile

NARGILEH *n* pl. **-S** narghile

NARIS *n* pl. **NARES** a nostril **NARIAL, NARIC, NARINE** *adj*

NARK *v* **-ED, -ING, -S** to spy or inform

NARKY *adj* **NARKIER, NARKIEST** irritable

NARRATE *v* **-RATED, -RATING, -RATES** to tell a story

NARRATER *n* pl. **-S** narrator

NARRATOR *n* pl. **-S** one that narrates

NARROW *adj* **-ROWER, -ROWEST** of little width **NARROWLY** *adv*

NARROW *v* **-ED, -ING, -S** to make narrow

NARTHEX *n* pl. **-ES** a vestibule in a church

NARWAL *n* pl. **-S** narwhal

NARWHAL *n* pl. **-S** an arctic aquatic mammal

NARWHALE *n* pl. **-S** narwhal

NARY *adj* not one

NASAL *n* pl. **-S** a sound uttered through the nose

NASALISE *v* **-ISED, -ISING, -ISES** to nasalize

NASALISM *n* pl. **-S** nasality

NASALITY *n* pl. **-TIES** the quality or an instance of being produced nasally

NASALIZE *v* **-IZED, -IZING, -IZES** to produce sounds nasally

NASALLY *adv* through the nose

NASCENCE *n* pl. **-S** nascency

NASCENCY *n* pl. **-CIES** birth; origin

NASCENT *adj* coming into existence

NASION *n* pl. **-S** a point in the skull **NASIAL** *adj*

NASTIC *adj* pertaining to an automatic response of plants

NASTY *adj* **-TIER, -TIEST** offensive to the senses **NASTILY** *adv*

NASTY *n* pl. **-TIES** something that is nasty

NATAL *adj* pertaining to one's birth

NATALITY *n* pl. **-TIES** birth rate

NATANT *adj* floating or swimming **NATANTLY** *adv*

NATATION *n* pl. **-S** the act of swimming

NATATORY *adj* pertaining to swimming

NATCH *adv* naturally

NATES *n/pl* the buttocks

NATHLESS *adv* nevertheless

NATION *n* pl. **-S** a politically organized people who share a territory, customs, and history

NATIONAL *n* pl. **-S** a citizen of a nation

NATIVE *n* pl. **-S** an original inhabitant of an area

NATIVELY *adv* in an inborn manner

NATIVISM *n* pl. **-S** a policy of favoring the interests of native inhabitants

NATIVIST *n* pl. **-S** an advocate of nativism

NATIVITY *n* pl. **-TIES** the process of being born

NATRIUM *n* pl. **-S** sodium

NATRON *n* pl. **-S** a chemical compound

NATTER *v* **-ED, -ING, -S** to chatter

NATTERER *n* pl. **-S** one that natters

NATTY *adj* **-TIER, -TIEST** neatly dressed **NATTILY** *adv*

NATURAL *n* pl. **-S** a type of musical note

NATURE *n* pl. **-S** the essential qualities of a person or thing **NATURED** *adj*

NATURISM *n* pl. **-S** nudism

NATURIST *n* pl. **-S** a nudist

NAUGHT *n* pl. **-S** a zero

NAUGHTY *n* pl. **-TIES** one that is naughty

NAUGHTY *adj* **-TIER, -TIEST** disobedient

NAUMACHY *n* pl. **-CHIES** a mock sea battle

NAUPLIUS *n* pl. **-PLII** a form of certain crustaceans **NAUPLIAL** *adj*

NAUSEA *n* pl. **-S** a stomach disturbance

NAUSEANT *n* pl. **-S** an agent that induces nausea

NAUSEATE *v* **-ATED, -ATING, -ATES** to affect with nausea

NAUSEOUS *adj* affected with nausea

NAUTCH *n* pl. **-ES** a dancing exhibition in India

NAUTICAL *adj* pertaining to ships

NAUTILUS *n* pl. **-LUSES** or **-LI** a spiral-shelled mollusk

NAV *n* pl. **-S** navigation

NAVAID *n* pl. **-S** a navigational device

NAVAL *adj* pertaining to ships **NAVALLY** *adv*

NAVAR *n* pl. **-S** a system of air navigation

NAVARIN *n* pl, **-S** lamb stew with vegetables

NAVE *n* pl. **-S** the main part of a church

NAVEL *n* pl. **-S** a depression in the abdomen

NAVETTE *n* pl. **-S** a gem cut in a pointed oval form

NAVICERT *n* pl. **-S** a document permitting a vessel passage through a naval blockade

NAVIES pl. of navy

NAVIGATE *v* **-GATED, -GATING, -GATES** to plan and control the course of

NAVVY *n* pl. **-VIES** a manual laborer

NAVY *n* pl. **-VIES** a nation's warships

NAW *adv* no

NAWAB *n* pl. **-S** a nabob

NAY *n* pl. **NAYS** a negative vote

NAYSAY *v* **-SAID, -SAYING, -SAYS** to oppose or deny

NAYSAYER *n* pl. **-S** one that denies or opposes something

NAZI *n* pl. **-S** a type of fascist

NAZIFY *v* **-FIED, -FYING, -FIES** to cause to be like a nazi

NE *adj* born with the name of

NEAP *n* pl. **-S** a tide of lowest range

NEAR *adj* **NEARER, NEAREST** situated within a short distance **NEARISH** *adj*

NEAR *v* **-ED, -ING, -S** to approach

NEARBY *adj* near

NEARLY *adv* **-LIER, -LIEST** with close approximation

NEARNESS *n* pl. **-ES** the state of being near

NEARSIDE *n* pl. **-S** the left side

NEAT *adj* **NEATER, NEATEST** being in a state of cleanliness and order

NEAT *n* pl. **-S** a bovine

NEATEN *v* **-ED, -ING, -S** to make neat

NEATH *prep* beneath

NEATHERD *n* pl. **-S** a cowherd

NEATLY *adv* in a neat manner

NEATNESS *n* pl. **-ES** the state of being neat

NEATNIK *n* pl. **-S** a compulsively neat person

NEB *n* pl. **-S** the beak of a bird

NEBBISH *n* pl. **-ES** a meek person **NEBBISHY** *adj*

NEBULA *n* pl. **-LAS** or **-LAE** a cloud-like interstellar mass **NEBULAR** *adj*

NEBULE *adj* composed of successive short curves

NEBULISE *v* **-LISED, -LISING, -LISES** to nebulize

NEBULIZE *v* **-LIZED, -LIZING, -LIZES** to reduce to a fine spray

NEBULOSE *adj* nebulous

NEBULOUS *adj* unclear

NEBULY *adj* nebule

NECK *v* **-ED, -ING, -S** to kiss and caress in lovemaking

NECKBAND *n* pl. **-S** a band worn around the neck (the part of the body joining the head to the trunk)

NECKER *n* pl. **-S** one that necks

NECKING *n* pl. **-S** a small molding near the top of a column

NECKLACE *v* **-LACED, -LACING, -LACES** to kill by placing a tire around the neck and setting it on fire

NECKLESS *adj* having no neck

NECKLET *n* pl. **-S** a close-fiting ornament worn around the neck

NECKLIKE *adj* resembling the neck

NECKLINE *n* pl. **-S** the line formed by the neck opening of a garment

NECKTIE *n* pl. **-S** a strip of fabric worn around the neck

NECKWEAR *n* pl. **NECKWEAR** something that is worn around the neck

NECROPSY *v* **-SIED, -SYING, -SIES** to perform an autopsy on

NECROSE *v* **-CROSED, -CROSING, -CROSES** to affect with necrosis

NECROSIS *n* pl. **-CROSES** the death of living tissue **NECROTIC** *adj*

NECTAR *n* pl. **-S** a delicious drink

NECTARY *n* pl. **-TARIES** a plant gland

NEDDY *n* pl. **-DIES** a donkey

NEE *adj* born with the name of

NEED *v* **-ED, -ING, -S** to have an urgent or essential use for

NEEDER *n* pl. **-S** one that needs

NEEDFUL *n* pl. **-S** something that is needed

NEEDIER comparative of needy

NEEDIEST superlative of needy

NEEDILY *adv* in a needy manner

NEEDLE *v* **-DLED, -DLING, -DLES** to sew with a slender, pointed instrument

NEEDLER *n* pl. **-S** one that needles

NEEDLESS *adj* not necessary

NEEDLING *n* pl. **-S** the act of one who needles

NEEDY *adj* **NEEDIER, NEEDIEST** in a state of poverty

NEEM *n* pl. **-S** an East Indian tree

NEEP *n* pl. **-S** a turnip

NEG *n* pl. **-S** a photographic negative

NEGATE *v* **-GATED, -GATING, -GATES** to nullify

NEGATER *n* pl. **-S** one that negates

NEGATION *n* pl. **-S** the act of negating

NEGATIVE *v* **-TIVED, -TIVING, -TIVES** to veto

NEGATON *n* pl. **-S** negatron

NEGATOR *n* pl. **-S** negater

NEGATORY *adj* expressing negation

NEGATRON *n* pl. **-S** an electron

NEGLECT *v* **-ED, -ING, -S** to fail to pay attention to

NEGLIGE *n* pl. **-S** negligee

NEGLIGEE *n* pl. **-S** a woman's dressing gown

NEGROID *n* pl. **-S** member of the black race

NEGRONI *n* pl. **-S** an alcoholic beverage

NEGUS *n* pl. **-ES** an alcoholic beverage

NEIF *n* pl. **-S** nieve

NEIGH *v* **-ED, -ING, -S** to utter the cry of a horse

NEIGHBOR *v* **-ED, -ING, -S** to live close to

NEIST *adj* next

NEITHER *adj* not one or the other

NEKTON *n* pl. **-S** free-swimming marine animals **NEKTONIC** *adj*

NELLIE *n* pl. **-S** an effeminate male

NELLY *n* pl. **-LIES** nellie

NELSON *n* pl. **-S** a wrestling hold

NELUMBO *n* pl. **-BOS** an aquatic herb

NEMA *n* pl. **-S** a nematode

NEMATIC *n* pl. **-S** a liquid crystal in a particular phase

NEMATODE *n* pl. **-S** a kind of worm

NEMESIA *n* pl. **-S** a flowering African plant

NEMESIS *n* pl. **NEMESES** a formidable opponent

NENE *n* pl. **-S** a Hawaiian goose

NEOCON *n* pl. **-S** a neoconservative

NEOLITH *n* pl. **-S** an ancient stone implement

NEOLOGY *n* pl. **-GIES** a new word or phrase **NEOLOGIC** *adj*

NEOMORPH *n* pl. **-S** a type of biological structure

NEOMYCIN *n* pl. **-S** an antibiotic drug

NEON *n* pl. **-S** a gaseous element **NEONED** *adj*

NEONATE *n* pl. **-S** a newborn child **NEONATAL** *adj*

NEOPAGAN *n* pl. **-S** one who practices a modern form of paganism

NEOPHYTE *n* pl. **-S** a novice

NEOPLASM *n* pl. **-S** a tumor

NEOPRENE *n* pl. **-S** a synthetic rubber

NEOTENY *n* pl. **-NIES** attainment of sexual maturity in the larval stage **NEOTENIC** *adj*

NEOTERIC *n* pl. **-S** a modern author

NEOTYPE *n* pl. **-S** a specimen of a species

NEPENTHE *n* pl. **-S** a drug that induces forgetfulness

NEPETA *n* pl. **-S** catnip

NEPHEW *n* pl. **-S** a son of one's brother or sister

NEPHRIC *adj* renal

NEPHRISM *n* pl. **-S** ill health caused by a kidney disease

NEPHRITE *n* pl. **-S** a mineral

NEPHRON *n* pl. **-S** an excretory unit of a kidney

NEPOTISM *n* pl. **-S** favoritism shown to a relative **NEPOTIC** *adj*

NEPOTIST *n* pl. **-S** one who practices nepotism

NERD *n* pl. **-S** a socially inept person **NERDISH** *adj*

NERDY *adj* **NERDIER, NERDIEST** socially inept

NEREID *n* pl. **-S** a sea nymph

NEREIS *n* pl. **-REIDES** a marine worm

NERITIC *adj* pertaining to shallow water

NEROL *n* pl. **-S** a fragrant alcohol

NEROLI *n* pl. **-S** a fragrant oil

NERTS *interj* — used to express defiance

NERTZ *interj* nerts

NERVATE *adj* having veins

NERVE *v* **NERVED, NERVING, NERVES** to give courage to

NERVIER comparative of nervy

NERVIEST superlative of nervy

NERVILY *adv* in a nervy manner

NERVINE *n* pl. **-S** a soothing medicine

NERVING *n* pl. **-S** a type of veterinary operation

NERVOUS *adj* easily excited

NERVULE *n* pl. **-S** nervure

NERVURE *n* pl. **-S** a vascular ridge on a leaf

NERVY *adj* **NERVIER, NERVIEST** impudent

NESCIENT *n* pl. **-S** one who is ignorant

NESS *n* pl. **-ES** a headland

NEST *v* **-ED, -ING, -S** to build a nest (a structure for holding bird eggs)

NESTABLE *adj* capable of being fitted closely within another container

NESTER *n* pl. **-S** one that nests

NESTFUL *n* pl. **-S** as much as a nest can hold

NESTLE *v* **-TLED, -TLING, -TLES** to lie snugly

NESTLER *n* pl. **-S** one that nestles

NESTLIKE *adj* resembling a nest

NESTLING *n* pl. **-S** a young bird

NESTMATE *n* pl. **-S** a bird sharing a nest with another

NESTOR *n* pl. **-S** a wise old man

NET *v* **NETTED, NETTING, NETS** to catch in a net (a type of openwork fabric)

NETBALL *n* pl. **-S** a team game similar to basketball

NETBOOK *n* pl. **-S** a small portable computer

NETFUL *n* pl. **-S** as much as a net can hold

NETHER *adj* situated below

NETIZEN *n* pl. **-S** a frequent user of the Internet

NETLESS *adj* having no net

NETLIKE *adj* resembling a net

NETOP *n* pl. **-S** friend; companion

NETROOTS *n/pl* political activists at the basic level of society who communicate via the Internet

NETSUKE *n* pl. **-S** a button-like fixture on Japanese clothing

NETSURF *v* **-ED, -ING, -S** to browse the Internet for information

NETT *v* **-ED, -ING, -S** to net

NETTABLE *adj* capable of being netted

NETTED past tense of net, nett

NETTER *n* pl. **-S** one that nets

NETTIER comparative of netty

NETTIEST superlative of netty

NETTING *n* pl. **-S** a net

NETTLE *v* **-TLED, -TLING, -TLES** to make angry

NETTLER *n* pl. **-S** one that nettles

NETTLY *adj* **-TLIER, -TLIEST** prickly

NETTY *adj* **-TIER, -TIEST** resembling a net

NETWORK *v* **-ED, -ING, -S** to cover with or as if with crossing lines

NEUK *n* pl. **-S** nook

NEUM *n* pl. **-S** neume

NEUME *n* pl. **-S** a sign used in musical notation **NEUMATIC, NEUMIC** *adj*

NEURAL *adj* pertaining to the nervous system **NEURALLY** *adv*

NEURAXON *n* pl. **-S** a part of a neuron

NEURINE *n* pl. **-S** a ptomaine poison

NEURITIC *n* pl. **-S** one affected with neuritis

NEURITIS *n* pl. **-RITISES** or **-RITIDES** inflammation of a nerve

NEUROID *adj* resembling a nerve

NEUROMA *n* pl. **-MAS** or **-MATA** a type of tumor

NEURON *n* pl. **-S** the basic cellular unit of the nervous system **NEURONAL, NEURONIC** *adj*

NEURONE *n* pl. **-S** neuron

NEUROSIS *n* pl. **-ROSES** a type of emotional disturbance **NEUROSAL** *adj*

NEUROTIC *n* pl. **-S** one affected with a neurosis

NEURULA *n* pl. **-LAS** or **-LAE** a vertebrate embryo **NEURULAR** *adj*

NEUSTON *n* pl. **-S** an aggregate of small aquatic organisms **NEUSTIC** *adj*

NEUTER *v* **-ED, -ING, -S** to castrate

NEUTRAL *n* pl. **-S** one that is impartial

NEUTRINO *n* pl. **-NOS** a subatomic particle

NEUTRON *n* pl. **-S** a subatomic particle

NEVE *n* pl. **-S** a granular snow

NEVER *adv* at no time

NEVUS *n* pl. **-VI** a birthmark **NEVOID** *adj*

NEW *adj* **NEWER, NEWEST** existing only a short time

NEW *n* pl. **-S** something that is new

NEWB *n* pl. **-S** a newbie

NEWBIE *n* pl. **-S** a newcomer

NEWBORN *n* pl. **-S** a recently born infant

NEWCOMER *n* pl. **-S** one that has recently arrived

NEWEL *n* pl. **-S** a staircase support

NEWFOUND *adj* newly found

NEWIE *n* pl. **-S** something new

NEWISH *adj* somewhat new

NEWLY *adv* recently

NEWLYWED *n* pl. **-S** a person recently married

NEWMOWN *adj* recently mown

NEWNESS *n* pl. **-ES** the state of being new

NEWS *n/pl* a report of recent events

NEWSBEAT *n* pl. **-S** a news source that a reporter is assigned to cover

NEWSBOY *n* pl. **-BOYS** a boy who delivers or sells newspapers

NEWSCAST *n* pl. **-S** a news broadcast

NEWSDESK *n* pl. **-S** the department that receives late-breaking news

NEWSFEED *n* pl. **-S** a service that provides news articles for distribution

NEWSGIRL *n* pl. **-S** a girl who delivers or sells newspapers

NEWSHAWK *n* pl. **-S** a newspaper reporter

NEWSIE *n* pl. **-S** newsy

NEWSIER comparative of newsy

NEWSIES pl. of newsy

NEWSIEST superlative of newsy

NEWSLESS *adj* having no news

NEWSMAN *n* pl. **-MEN** a news reporter

NEWSPEAK *n* pl. **-S** a deliberately ambiguous language

NEWSREEL *n* pl. **-S** a short movie presenting current events

NEWSROOM *n* pl. **-S** a room where the news is gathered

NEWSWIRE *n* pl. **-S** a news agency that transmits news copy to subscribers

NEWSY *adj* **NEWSIER, NEWSIEST** full of news

NEWSY *n* pl. **NEWSIES** a newsboy

NEWT *n* pl. **-S** a small salamander

NEWTON *n* pl. **-S** a unit of force

NEWWAVER *n* pl. **-S** a member of a new-wave movement

NEXT *n* pl. **-S** the one that comes immediately after

NEXTDOOR *adj* located in the next building or room

NEXUS *n* pl. **-ES** a connection or link

NGULTRUM *n* pl. **-S** a monetary unit of Bhutan

NGWEE *n* pl. **NGWEE** a monetary unit of Zambia

NIACIN *n* pl. **-S** a B vitamin

NIAGARA *n* pl. **-S** an outpouring or deluge

NIB *v* **NIBBED, NIBBING, NIBS** to provide with a penpoint

NIBBLE *v* **-BLED, -BLING, -BLES** to eat with small bites

NIBBLER *n* pl. **-S** one that nibbles

NIBBLY *n* pl. **-BLIES** a small food item

NIBLET *n* pl. **-S** a small piece of food

NIBLICK *n* pl. **-S** a golf club

NIBLIKE *adj* resembling a penpoint

NICAD *n* pl. **-S** nickel cadmium

NICE *adj* **NICER, NICEST** pleasing to the senses **NICELY** *adv*

NICENESS *n* pl. **-ES** the quality of being nice

NICETY *n* pl. **-TIES** a fine point or distinction

NICHE *v* **NICHED, NICHING, NICHES** to place in a receding space or hollow

NICK *v* **-ED, -ING, -S** to make a shallow cut in

NICKEL *v* **-ELED, -ELING, -ELS** or **-ELLED, -ELLING, -ELS** to plate with nickel (a metallic element)

NICKELIC *adj* pertaining to or containing nickel

NICKER *v* **-ED, -ING, -S** to neigh

NICKLE *v* **-LED, -LING, -LES** to nickel

NICKNACK *n* pl. **-S** a trinket

NICKNAME *v* **-NAMED, -NAMING, -NAMES** to give an alternate name to

NICOISE *adj* served with black olives, tomatoes, olive oil, and often anchovies

NICOL *n* pl. **-S** a type of prism

NICOTIN *n* pl. **-S** nicotine

NICOTINE *n* pl. **-S** a poisonous alkaloid in tobacco

NICTATE *v* **-TATED, -TATING, -TATES** to wink

NIDAL *adj* pertaining to a nidus

NIDATE *v* **-DATED, -DATING, -DATES** to become implanted in the uterus

NIDATION *n* pl. **-S** the act of nidating

NIDE *v* **NIDED, NIDING, NIDES** to nest

NIDERING *n* pl. **-S** a coward

NIDGET *n* pl. **-S** an idiot

NIDI a pl. of nidus

NIDIFY *v* **-FIED, -FYING, -FIES** to nest

NIDING present participle of nide

NIDUS *n* pl. **NIDUSES** or **NIDI** a nest or breeding place

NIECE *n* pl. **-S** a daughter of one's brother or sister

NIELLIST *n* pl. **-S** one that niellos

NIELLO *n* pl. **-LOS** or **-LI** a black metallic substance

NIELLO   *v* **-ED, -ING, -S** to decorate with niello

NIENTE   *adv* softly fading away — used as a musical direction

NIEVE   *n* pl. **-S** the fist or hand

NIFF   *v* **-ED, -ING, -S** to stink

NIFFER   *v* **-ED, -ING, -S** to barter

NIFFY   *adj* **NIFFIER, NIFFIEST** stinky

NIFTY   *adj* **-TIER, -TIEST** stylish; pleasing **NIFTILY** *adv*

NIFTY   *n* pl. **-TIES** something that is nifty

NIGELLA   *n* pl. **-S** an annual herb

NIGGARD   *v* **-ED, -ING, -S** to act stingily

NIGGLE   *v* **-GLED, -GLING, -GLES** to worry over petty details

NIGGLER   *n* pl. **-S** one that niggles

NIGGLING   *n* pl. **-S** petty or meticulous work

NIGGLY   *adj* **-GLIER, -GLIEST** petty

NIGH   *adj* **NIGHER, NIGHEST** near

NIGH   *v* **-ED, -ING, -S** to approach

NIGHNESS   *n* pl. **-ES** the state of being nigh

NIGHT   *n* pl. **-S** the period from sunset to sunrise

NIGHTCAP   *n* pl. **-S** a cap worn to bed

NIGHTIE   *n* pl. **-S** a nightgown

NIGHTJAR   *n* pl. **-S** a nocturnal bird

NIGHTLY   *adv* every night; at night

NIGHTY   *n* pl. **NIGHTIES** nightie

NIGRIFY   *v* **-FIED, -FYING, -FIES** to make black

NIGROSIN   *n* pl. **-S** a type of dye

NIHIL   *n* pl. **-S** nothing

NIHILISM   *n* pl. **-S** a doctrine that denies traditional values

NIHILIST   *n* pl. **-S** an adherent of nihilism

NIHILITY   *n* pl. **-TIES** the state of being nothing

NIKAH   *n* pl. **-S** a Muslim marriage ceremony

NIL   *n* pl. **-S** nothing

NILGAI   *n* pl. **-S** a large antelope

NILGAU   *n* pl. **-S** nilgai

NILGHAI   *n* pl. **-S** nilgai

NILGHAU   *n* pl. **-S** nilgai

NILL   *v* **-ED, -ING, -S** to be unwilling

NIM   *v* **NIMMED** or **NAM, NIMMING, NIMS** to steal

NIMBLE   *adj* **-BLER, -BLEST** agile **NIMBLY** *adv*

NIMBUS   *n* pl. **-BUSES** or **-BI** a luminous cloud **NIMBUSED** *adj*

NIMIETY   *n* pl. **-ETIES** excess **NIMIOUS** *adj*

NIMMED   past tense of nim

NIMMING   present participle of nim

NIMROD   *n* pl. **-S** a hunter

NINE   *n* pl. **-S** a number

NINEBARK   *n* pl. **-S** a flowering shrub

NINEFOLD   *adj* nine times as great

NINEPIN   *n* pl. **-S** a wooden pin used in a bowling game

NINER   *n* pl. **-S** a student in the ninth grade

NINETEEN   *n* pl. **-S** a number

NINETY   *n* pl. **-TIES** a number

NINJA   *n* pl. **-S** a feudal Japanese warrior

NINJUTSU   *n* pl. **-S** the traditional Japanese method of spying

NINNY   *n* pl. **-NIES** a fool **NINNYISH** *adj*

NINON   *n* pl. **-S** a sheer fabric

NINTH   *n* pl. **-S** one of nine equal parts

NINTHLY   *adv* in the ninth place

NIOBATE   *n* pl. **-S** a chemical salt

NIOBITE   *n* pl. **-S** the mineral columbite

NIOBIUM   *n* pl. **-S** a metallic element **NIOBIC, NIOBOUS** *adj*

NIP   *v* **NIPPED, NIPPING, NIPS** to pinch

NIPA   *n* pl. **-S** a palm tree

NIPPER   *n* pl. **-S** one that nips

NIPPIER   comparative of nippy

NIPPIEST   superlative of nippy

NIPPILY   *adv* in a nippy manner

NIPPING   present participle of nip

NIPPLE   *n* pl. **-S** a protuberance on the breast **NIPPLED** *adj*

NIPPY   *adj* **-PIER, -PIEST** sharp or biting

NIQAAB   *n* pl. **-S** niqab

NIQAB   *n* pl. **-S** a veil worn by some Muslim women

NIRVANA   *n* pl. **-S** a blessed state in Buddhism **NIRVANIC** *adj*

NISEI   *n* pl. **-S** one born in America of immigrant Japanese parents

NISI   *adj* not yet final

NISUS   *n* pl. **NISUS** an effort

NIT	*n* pl. **-S** the egg of a parasitic insect
NITE	*n* pl. **-S** night
NITER	*n* pl. **-S** a chemical salt
NITERIE	*n* pl. **-S** nitery
NITERY	*n* pl. **-ERIES** a nightclub
NITID	*adj* bright
NITINOL	*n* pl. **-S** an alloy of nickel and titanium
NITON	*n* pl. **-S** radon
NITPICK	*v* **-ED, -ING, -S** to fuss over petty details
NITPICKY	*adj* **-PICKIER, -PICKIEST** tending to nitpick
NITRATE	*v* **-TRATED, -TRATING, -TRATES** to treat with nitric acid
NITRATOR	*n* pl. **-S** one that nitrates
NITRE	*n* pl. **-S** niter
NITRIC	*adj* containing nitrogen
NITRID	*n* pl. **-S** nitride
NITRIDE	*v* **-TRIDED, -TRIDING, -TRIDES** to convert into a nitride (a compound of nitrogen)
NITRIFY	*v* **-FIED, -FYING, -FIES** to combine with nitrogen
NITRIL	*n* pl. **-S** nitrile
NITRILE	*n* pl. **-S** a chemical compound
NITRITE	*n* pl. **-S** a salt of nitrous acid
NITRO	*n* pl. **-TROS** a nitrated product
NITROGEN	*n* pl. **-S** a gaseous element
NITROLIC	*adj* pertaining to a class of acids
NITROSO	*adj* containing nitrosyl
NITROSYL	*n* pl. **-S** a univalent radical
NITROUS	*adj* containing nitrogen
NITTY	*adj* **-TIER, -TIEST** full of nits
NITWIT	*n* pl. **-S** a stupid person
NIVAL	*adj* pertaining to snow
NIVEOUS	*adj* resembling snow
NIX	*n* pl. **NIXES** or **NIXE** a water sprite
NIX	*v* **-ED, -ING, -ES** to veto
NIXIE	*n* pl. **-S** a female water sprite
NIXY	*n* pl. **NIXIES** an undeliverable piece of mail
NIZAM	*n* pl. **-S** a former sovereign of India
NIZAMATE	*n* pl. **-S** the territory of a nizam
NO	*n* pl. **NOS** or **NOES** a negative reply
NOB	*n* pl. **-S** a wealthy person
NOBBIER	comparative of nobby
NOBBIEST	superlative of nobby
NOBBILY	*adv* in a nobby manner
NOBBLE	*v* **-BLED, -BLING, -BLES** to disable a racehorse
NOBBLER	*n* pl. **-S** one that nobbles
NOBBY	*adj* **-BIER, -BIEST** elegant
NOBELIUM	*n* pl. **-S** a radioactive element
NOBILITY	*n* pl. **-TIES** the social class composed of nobles
NOBLE	*adj* **-BLER, -BLEST** possessing qualities of excellence
NOBLE	*n* pl. **-S** a person of high birth, rank, or title
NOBLEMAN	*n* pl. **-MEN** a noble
NOBLER	comparative of noble
NOBLESSE	*n* pl. **-S** the nobility
NOBLEST	superlative of noble
NOBLY	*adv* in a noble manner
NOBODY	*n* pl. **-BODIES** an unimportant person
NOCEBO	*n* pl. **-BOS** a harmless substance that induces harmful effects in patients having negative expectations
NOCENT	*adj* harmful
NOCK	*v* **-ED, -ING, -S** to notch a bow or arrow
NOCTUID	*n* pl. **-S** a night-flying moth **NOCTUOID** *adj*
NOCTULE	*n* pl. **-S** a large bat
NOCTURN	*n* pl. **-S** a religious service
NOCTURNE	*n* pl. **-S** a musical composition
NOCUOUS	*adj* harmful
NOD	*v* **NODDED, NODDING, NODS** to briefly lower the head forward
NODAL	*adj* of the nature of a node **NODALLY** *adv*
NODALITY	*n* pl. **-TIES** the state of being nodal
NODDED	past tense of nod
NODDER	*n* pl. **-S** one that nods
NODDIES	pl. of noddy
NODDING	present participle of nod
NODDLE	*v* **-DLED, -DLING, -DLES** to nod frequently
NODDY	*n* pl. **-DIES** a fool
NODE	*n* pl. **-S** a swollen enlargement

NODI	pl. of nodus
NODICAL	*adj* pertaining to an astronomical point
NODOSE	*adj* having nodes
NODOSITY	*n* pl. **-TIES** the state of being nodose
NODOUS	*adj* nodose
NODULE	*n* pl. **-S** a small node **NODULAR, NODULOSE, NODULOUS** *adj*
NODUS	*n* pl. **-DI** a difficulty
NOEL	*n* pl. **-S** a Christmas carol
NOES	a pl. of no
NOESIS	*n* pl. **-SISES** the process of reason
NOETIC	*adj* pertaining to reason
NOG	*v* **NOGGED, NOGGING, NOGS** to fill in a space in a wall with bricks
NOGG	*n* pl. **-S** a strong ale
NOGGIN	*n* pl. **-S** a small cup
NOGGING	*n* pl. **-S** a type of masonry
NOH	*n* pl. **NOH** the classical drama of Japan
NOHOW	*adv* in no manner
NOIL	*n* pl. **-S** a kind of short fiber **NOILY** *adj*
NOIR	*n* pl. **-S** a bleak type of crime fiction **NOIRISH** *adj*
NOISE	*v* **NOISED, NOISING, NOISES** to spread as a rumor or report
NOISETTE	*n* pl. **-S** a small round piece of meat
NOISOME	*adj* disgusting; harmful
NOISY	*adj* **NOISIER, NOISIEST** making loud sounds **NOISILY** *adv*
NOLO	*n* pl. **-LOS** a type of legal plea
NOM	*n* pl. **-S** a name
NOMA	*n* pl. **-S** a severe inflammation of the mouth
NOMAD	*n* pl. **-S** a wanderer **NOMADIC** *adj*
NOMADISM	*n* pl. **-S** the mode of life of a nomad
NOMARCH	*n* pl. **-S** the head of a nome
NOMARCHY	*n* pl. **-ARCHIES** a nome
NOMBLES	*n/pl* numbles
NOMBRIL	*n* pl. **-S** a point on a heraldic shield
NOME	*n* pl. **-S** a province of modern Greece
NOMEN	*n* pl. **-MINA** the second name of an ancient Roman
NOMINAL	*n* pl. **-S** a word used as a noun

NOMINATE	*v* **-NATED, -NATING, -NATES** to name as a candidate
NOMINEE	*n* pl. **-S** one that is nominated
NOMISM	*n* pl. **-S** strict adherence to moral law **NOMISTIC** *adj*
NOMOGRAM	*n* pl. **-S** a type of graph
NOMOLOGY	*n* pl. **-GIES** the science of law
NOMOS	*n* pl. **NOMOI** law
NONA	*n* pl. **-S** a virus disease
NONACID	*n* pl. **-S** a substance that is not an acid
NONACTOR	*n* pl. **-S** a person who is not an actor
NONADULT	*n* pl. **-S** a person who is not an adult
NONAGE	*n* pl. **-S** a period of immaturity
NONAGON	*n* pl. **-S** a nine-sided polygon
NONANE	*n* pl. **-S** a colorless liquid hydrocarbon
NONART	*n* pl. **-S** something that is not art
NONARY	*n* pl. **-ARIES** a group of nine
NONBANK	*n* pl. **-S** a business that is not a bank
NONBASIC	*adj* not basic
NONBEING	*n* pl. **-S** lack of being
NONBLACK	*n* pl. **-S** one that is not black
NONBODY	*n* pl. **-BODIES** a person's nonphysical nature
NONBOOK	*n* pl. **-S** a book of little literary merit
NONBRAND	*adj* lacking a brand name
NONCASH	*adj* other than cash
NONCE	*n* pl. **-S** the present occasion
NONCLASS	*n* pl. **-ES** a lack of class
NONCLING	*adj* not clinging
NONCOLA	*n* pl. **-S** a beverage that is not a cola
NONCOLOR	*n* pl. **-S** a lack of color
NONCOM	*n* pl. **-S** a noncommissioned officer
NONCORE	*adj* not being in or relating to a central part
NONCOUNT	*adj* not capable of being counted
NONCRIME	*n* pl. **-S** something that is not a crime
NONDAIRY	*adj* having no milk products
NONDANCE	*n* pl. **-S** an unrhythmic dance
NONDRIP	*adj* that does not drip
NONDRUG	*adj* not involving drugs

NONE *n* pl. **-S** one of seven canonical daily periods for prayer and devotion

NONEGO *n* pl. **-GOS** all that is not part of the ego

NONELECT *adj* not chosen

NONELITE *adj* not belonging to an elite group

NONEMPTY *adj* not empty

NONENTRY *n* pl. **-TRIES** the fact of not entering

NONEQUAL *n* pl. **-S** one that is not equal

NONESUCH *n* pl. **-ES** a person or thing without an equal

NONET *n* pl. **-S** a composition for nine instruments or voices

NONEVENT *n* pl. **-S** an expected event that does not occur

NONFACT *n* pl. **-S** a statement not based on fact

NONFAN *n* pl. **-S** a person who is not a fan (an enthusiast)

NONFARM *adj* not pertaining to the farm

NONFAT *adj* having no fat solids

NONFATAL *adj* not fatal

NONFATTY *adj* not fatty

NONFINAL *adj* not being the last

NONFLUID *n* pl. **-S** a substance that is not a fluid

NONFOCAL *adj* not focal

NONFOOD *adj* pertaining to something other than food

NONFUEL *adj* not used as a fuel

NONGAME *adj* not hunted for food, sport, or fur

NONGAY *n* pl. **-S** a person who is not a homosexual

NONGLARE *n* pl **-S** a lack of glare (harsh brilliant light)

NONGREEN *adj* not green

NONGUEST *n* pl. **-S** one who is not a guest

NONGUILT *n* pl. **-S** the absence of guilt

NONHARDY *adj* not hardy

NONHEME *adj* not containing iron that is bound like that of heme

NONHERO *n* pl. **-ROES** an antihero

NONHOME *adj* not taking place in the home

NONHUMAN *n* pl. **-S** one that is not a human

NONIDEAL *adj* not ideal

NONIMAGE *n* pl. **-S** one having no celebrity status

NONINERT *adj* not inactive

NONIONIC *adj* not ionic

NONIRON *adj* not needing to be ironed

NONISSUE *n* pl. **-S** a topic that is not controversial

NONJUROR *n* pl. **-S** one who refuses to take a required oath

NONJURY *n* pl. **-RIES** a case not involving a jury

NONLABOR *adj* not pertaining to labor

NONLEAFY *adj* not having leaves

NONLEGAL *adj* not legal

NONLEVEL *adj* not flat or even

NONLIFE *n* pl. **-LIVES** the absence of life

NONLOCAL *n* pl. **-S** one that is not local

NONLOYAL *adj* not loyal

NONLYRIC *adj* not lyrical

NONMAJOR *n* pl. **-S** a student who is not majoring in a specified subject

NONMAN *n* pl. **-MEN** a being that is not a man

NONMEAT *adj* not containing meat

NONMETAL *n* pl. **-S** an element that lacks metallic properties

NONMETRO *adj* not metropolitan

NONMODAL *adj* not modal

NONMONEY *adj* not involving money

NONMORAL *adj* not pertaining to morals

NONMUSIC *n* pl. **-S** inferior music

NONNASAL *adj* not involving the nose

NONNAVAL *adj* not naval

NONNEWS *adj* not being news

NONNOBLE *adj* not noble

NONNOVEL *n* pl. **-S** a literary work that is not a novel

NONOBESE *adj* not obese

NONOHMIC *adj* not measured in ohms

NONOILY *adj* not oily

NONORAL *adj* not involving the mouth

NONOWNER *n* pl. **-S** one who is not the owner

NONPAGAN *n* pl. **-S** one who is not a pagan

NONPAID *adj* not paid

NONPAPAL *adj* not papal

NONPAR *adj* being a stock that has no face value

NONPARTY   *n* pl. **-TIES** one not belonging to a party

NONPAST   *n* pl. **-S** a verb form that lacks an inflection for a past tense

NONPEAK   *adj* being a time when something is not at its highest level

NONPLAY   *n* pl. **-PLAYS** a theatrical work that is not a play

NONPLUS   *v* **-PLUSED, -PLUSING, -PLUSES** or **-PLUSSED, -PLUSSING, -PLUSSES** to baffle

NONPOINT   *adj* not occurring at a definite single site

NONPOLAR   *adj* not polar

NONPOOR   *adj* not being poor

NONPRINT   *adj* not involving printed material

NONPROS   *v* **-PROSSED, -PROSSING, -PROSSES** to enter a judgment against a plaintiff who fails to prosecute

NONQUOTA   *adj* not included in or subject to a quota

NONRATED   *adj* not rated

NONRIGID   *adj* not rigid

NONRIVAL   *n* pl. **-S** an unimportant rival

NONROYAL   *adj* not royal

NONRURAL   *adj* not rural

NONSELF   *n* pl. **-SELVES** foreign material in a body

NONSENSE   *n* pl. **-S** behavior or language that is meaningless or absurd

NONSKED   *n* pl. **-S** an airline without scheduled flying times

NONSKID   *adj* designed to inhibit skidding

NONSKIER   *n* pl. **-S** one that does not ski

NONSLIP   *adj* designed to prevent slipping

NONSOLAR   *adj* not solar

NONSOLID   *n* pl. **-S** a substance that is not a solid

NONSTICK   *adj* allowing of easy removal of cooked food particles

NONSTOP   *n* pl. **-S** a flight without a stop en route

NONSTORY   *n* pl. **-RIES** an insignificant news story

NONSTYLE   *n* pl. **-S** a style that is not identifiable

NONSUCH   *n* pl. **-ES** nonesuch

NONSUGAR   *n* pl. **-S** a substance that is not a sugar

NONSUIT   *v* **-ED, -ING, -S** to dismiss the lawsuit of

NONTAX   *n* pl. **-ES** a tax of little consequence

NONTIDAL   *adj* not tidal

NONTITLE   *adj* pertaining to an athletic contest in which a title is not at stake

NONTONAL   *adj* lacking tonality

NONTONIC   *adj* not based on the first tone of a scale

NONTOXIC   *adj* not toxic

NONTRUMP   *adj* not having a trump

NONTRUTH   *n* pl. **-S** something that is not true

NONUNION   *n* pl. **-S** failure of a broken bone to heal

NONUPLE   *n* pl. **-S** a number nine times as great as another

NONURBAN   *adj* not urban

NONUSE   *n* pl. **-S** failure to use

NONUSER   *n* pl. **-S** one that is not a user

NONUSING   *adj* not using

NONVALID   *adj* not valid

NONVIRAL   *adj* not viral

NONVITAL   *adj* not vital

NONVOCAL   *n* pl. **-S** one that does not involve the voice

NONVOTER   *n* pl. **-S** one that does not vote

NONWAGE   *adj* not including or involving wages (money paid for work or services)

NONWAR   *n* pl. **-S** a war that is not officially declared

NONWHITE   *n* pl. **-S** a person who is not of the white race

NONWOODY   *adj* not woody

NONWOOL   *adj* not made of wool

NONWORD   *n* pl. **-S** a word that has no meaning

NONWORK   *adj* not involving work

NONWOVEN   *n* pl. **-S** a fabric not made by weaving

NONYL   *n* pl. **-S** an alkyl radical

NONZERO   *adj* having a value other than zero

NOO   *adv* now

NOODGE   *v* **NOODGED, NOODGING, NOODGES** to nag

NOODLE   *v* **-DLED, -DLING, -DLES** to play idly on a musical instrument

NOODLING *n* pl. **-S** the action of idly playing a musical instrument

NOOGIE *n* pl. **-S** a playful rubbing of one's knuckles on another's head

NOOK *n* pl. **-S** a corner, as in a room **NOOKLIKE** *adj*

NOON *n* pl. **-S** midday

NOONDAY *n* pl. **-DAYS** noon

NOONER *n* pl. **-S** an event that occurs during the middle of the day

NOONING *n* pl. **-S** a meal eaten at noon

NOONTIDE *n* pl. **-S** noon

NOONTIME *n* pl. **-S** noon

NOOSE *v* **NOOSED, NOOSING, NOOSES** to secure with a type of loop

NOOSER *n* pl. **-S** one that nooses

NOPAL *n* pl. **-S** or **-ES** a cactus of Mexico and Central America

NOPALITO *n* pl. **-TOS** the stem of the nopal used as food

NOPE *adv* no

NOPLACE *adv* not in or at any place

NOR *conj* and not

NORDIC *adj* pertaining to cross-country ski racing and ski jumping

NORI *n* pl. **-S** dried seaweed pressed into sheets

NORIA *n* pl. **-S** a type of waterwheel

NORITE *n* pl. **-S** a granular rock **NORITIC** *adj*

NORLAND *n* pl. **-S** a region in the north

NORM *n* pl. **-S** a standard regarded as typical for a specific group

NORMAL *n* pl. **-S** the usual or expected state or form

NORMALCY *n* pl. **-CIES** conformity with the norm

NORMALLY *adv* as a rule; usually

NORMANDE *adj* prepared with foods associated with Normandy

NORMED *adj* having a norm

NORMLESS *adj* having no norm

NORTENA *n* pl. **-S** a style of folk music of northern Mexico and Texas

NORTENO *n* pl. **-NOS** an inhabitant of northern Mexico

NORTH *n* pl. **-S** a point of the compass

NORTHER *n* pl. **-S** a wind or storm from the north

NORTHERN *n* pl. **-S** a person living in the north

NORTHING *n* pl. **-S** movement toward the north

NOSE *v* **NOSED, NOSING, NOSES** to sniff with the nose (the organ of smell)

NOSEBAG *n* pl. **-S** a feedbag

NOSEBAND *n* pl. **-S** a part of a horse's bridle

NOSEDIVE *v* **-DIVED** or **-DOVE, -DIVING, -DIVES** to go into a sudden steep drop

NOSEGAY *n* pl. **-GAYS** a bouquet

NOSELESS *adj* having no nose

NOSELIKE *adj* resembling a nose

NOSEY *adj* **NOSIER, NOSIEST** nosy

NOSH *v* **-ED, -ING, -ES** to eat snacks between meals

NOSHER *n* pl. **-S** one that noshes

NOSIER comparative of nosy

NOSIEST superlative of nosy

NOSILY *adv* in a nosy manner

NOSINESS *n* pl. **-ES** the quality of being nosy

NOSING *n* pl. **-S** a projecting edge

NOSOLOGY *n* pl. **-GIES** a classification of diseases

NOSTOC *n* pl. **-S** a freshwater alga

NOSTRIL *n* pl. **-S** an external opening of the nose

NOSTRUM *n* pl. **-S** a medicine of one's own invention

NOSY *adj* **NOSIER, NOSIEST** unduly curious

NOT *adv* in no way

NOTA pl. of notum

NOTABLE *n* pl. **-S** a person of distinction

NOTABLY *adv* in a distinguished manner

NOTAL *adj* pertaining to a notum

NOTARIAL *adj* pertaining to a notary

NOTARISE *v* **-RISED, -RISING, -RISES** to notarize

NOTARIZE *v* **-RIZED, -RIZING, -RIZES** to certify through a notary

NOTARY *n* pl. **-RIES** a public officer who certifies documents

NOTATE *v* **-TATED, -TATING, -TATES** to put into notation

NOTATION *n* pl. **-S** a system of symbols

NOTATOR *n* pl. **-S** one that notates

NOTCH *v* **-ED, -ING, -ES** to make an angular cut in

NOTCHER *n* pl. **-S** one that notches

NOTCHY   *adj* **NOTCHIER, NOTCHIEST** having angular cuts

NOTE   *v* **NOTED, NOTING, NOTES** to write down

NOTEBOOK   *n* pl. **-S** a book in which to write

NOTECARD   *n* pl. **-S** a card used for sending short messages

NOTECASE   *n* pl. **-S** a billfold

NOTED   past tense of note

NOTEDLY   *adv* in a famous manner

NOTELESS   *adj* undistinguished

NOTELET   *n* pl. **-S** a small sheet of paper for an informal letter

NOTEPAD   *n* pl. **-S** a number of sheets of paper glued together at one end

NOTER   *n* pl. **-S** one that notes

NOTHER   *adj* different

NOTHING   *n* pl. **-S** the absence of all quantity or magnitude

NOTICE   *v* **-TICED, -TICING, -TICES** to become aware of

NOTICER   *n* pl. **-S** one that notices

NOTIFIER   *n* pl. **-S** one that notifies

NOTIFY   *v* **-FIED, -FYING, -FIES** to inform

NOTING   present participle of note

NOTION   *n* pl. **-S** a general idea **NOTIONAL** *adj*

NOTORNIS   *n* pl. **NOTORNIS** a flightless bird

NOTTURNO   *n* pl. **-NI** a nocturne

NOTUM   *n* pl. **-TA** a part of the thorax of an insect

NOUGAT   *n* pl. **-S** a chewy candy

NOUGHT   *n* pl. **-S** naught

NOUMENON   *n* pl. **-MENA** an object of intellectual intuition **NOUMENAL** *adj*

NOUN   *n* pl. **-S** a word used to denote the name of something **NOUNAL, NOUNLESS** *adj* **NOUNALLY** *adv*

NOURISH   *v* **-ED, -ING, -ES** to sustain with food

NOUS   *n* pl. **-ES** mind, reason, or intellect

NOUVEAU   *adj* newly arrived or developed

NOUVELLE   *n* pl. **-S** a style of French cooking

NOVA   *n* pl. **-VAS** or **-VAE** a type of star **NOVALIKE** *adj*

NOVATE   *v* **-VATED, -VATING, -VATES** to replace an old contract with a new one

NOVATION   *n* pl. **-S** the substitution of a new legal obligation for an old one

NOVEL   *n* pl. **-S** a fictional prose narrative

NOVELISE   *v* **-ISED, -ISING, -ISES** to novelize

NOVELIST   *n* pl. **-S** a writer of novels

NOVELIZE   *v* **-IZED, -IZING, -IZES** to put into the form of a novel

NOVELLA   *n* pl. **-LAS** or **-LE** a short novel

NOVELLY   *adv* in a new or unusual manner

NOVELTY   *n* pl. **-TIES** something new or unusual

NOVENA   *n* pl. **-NAS** or **-NAE** a religious devotion lasting nine days

NOVERCAL   *adj* pertaining to a stepmother

NOVICE   *n* pl. **-S** a person new to any field or activity

NOW   *n* pl. **-S** the present time

NOWADAYS   *adv* in these times

NOWAY   *adv* in no way

NOWAYS   *adv* noway

NOWHERE   *n* pl. **-S** a nonexistent place

NOWISE   *adv* not at all

NOWNESS   *n* pl. **-ES** the state of existing at the present time

NOWT   *n* pl. **-S** naught

NOXIOUS   *adj* harmful to health

NOYADE   *n* pl. **-S** an execution by drowning

NOYAU   *n* pl. **-YAUX** a liqueur made of brandy and fruit kernels

NOZZLE   *n* pl. **-S** a projecting spout

NTH   *adj* pertaining to an indefinitely large ordinal number

NU   *n* pl. **-S** a Greek letter

NUANCE   *v* **NUANCED, NUANCING, NUANCES** to give a subtle shade of meaning to

NUB   *n* pl. **-S** a protuberance or knob

NUBBIER   comparative of nubby

NUBBIEST   superlative of nubby

NUBBIN   *n* pl. **-S** an undeveloped fruit

NUBBLE   *n* pl. **-S** a small nub

NUBBLY   *adj* **-BLIER, -BLIEST** having nubbles

NUBBY   *adj* **-BIER, -BIEST** having nubs

NUBIA   *n* pl. **-S** a woman's scarf

NUBILE   *adj* suitable for marriage

NUBILITY   *n* pl. **-TIES** the quality of being nubile

NUBILOSE	*adj* nubilous
NUBILOUS	*adj* cloudy
NUBUCK	*n* pl. **-S** soft sueded leather
NUCELLUS	*n* pl. **-LI** the essential part of a plant ovule **NUCELLAR** *adj*
NUCHA	*n* pl. **-CHAE** the nape of the neck
NUCHAL	*n* pl. **-S** an anatomical part lying in the region of the nape
NUCLEAL	*adj* nuclear
NUCLEAR	*adj* pertaining to a nucleus
NUCLEASE	*n* pl. **-S** an enzyme
NUCLEATE	*v* **-ATED, -ATING, -ATES** to form into a nucleus
NUCLEI	a pl. of nucleus
NUCLEIN	*n* pl. **-S** a protein found in nuclei
NUCLEOID	*n* pl. **-S** the DNA-containing area of certain cells
NUCLEOLE	*n* pl. **-S** a part of a nucleus
NUCLEOLI	*n/pl* nucleoles
NUCLEON	*n* pl. **-S** a subatomic particle
NUCLEUS	*n* pl. **-CLEUSES** or **-CLEI** an essential part of a cell
NUCLIDE	*n* pl. **-S** a species of atom **NUCLIDIC** *adj*
NUDE	*adj* **NUDER, NUDEST** being without clothing or covering **NUDELY** *adv*
NUDE	*n* pl. **-S** a nude figure
NUDENESS	*n* pl. **-ES** nudity
NUDGE	*v* **NUDGED, NUDGING, NUDGES** to push gently
NUDGER	*n* pl. **-S** one that nudges
NUDICAUL	*adj* having leafless stems
NUDIE	*n* pl. **-S** a movie featuring nude performers
NUDISM	*n* pl. **-S** the practice of going nude
NUDIST	*n* pl. **-S** an advocate of nudism
NUDITY	*n* pl. **-TIES** the state of being nude
NUDNICK	*n* pl. **-S** nudnik
NUDNIK	*n* pl. **-S** an annoying person
NUDZH	*v* **-ED, -ING, -ES** to noodge
NUFF	*n* pl. **-S** enough
NUG	*n* pl. **-S** a chunk of wood sawn from a log
NUGATORY	*adj* having no power
NUGGET	*n* pl. **-S** a mass of solid matter **NUGGETY** *adj*
NUISANCE	*n* pl. **-S** a source of annoyance
NUKE	*v* **NUKED, NUKING, NUKES** to attack with nuclear weapons
NULL	*v* **-ED, -ING, -S** to reduce to nothing
NULLAH	*n* pl. **-S** a ravine
NULLIFY	*v* **-FIED, -FYING, -FIES** to make useless or ineffective
NULLITY	*n* pl. **-TIES** something of no legal force
NUMB	*adj* **NUMBER, NUMBEST** lacking sensation
NUMB	*v* **-ED, -ING, -S** to make numb
NUMBAT	*n* pl. **-S** a small Australian mammal
NUMBER	*v* **-ED, -ING, -S** to count
NUMBERER	*n* pl. **-S** one that numbers
NUMBFISH	*n* pl. **-ES** a fish capable of emitting electric shocks
NUMBLES	*n/pl* animal entrails
NUMBLY	*adv* in a numb manner
NUMBNESS	*n* pl. **-ES** the state of being numb
NUMCHUCK	*n* pl. **-S** nunchaku
NUMDAH	*n* pl. **-S** an embroidered rug of India
NUMEN	*n* pl. **-MINA** a deity
NUMERACY	*n* pl. **-CIES** the ability to understand basic mathematics
NUMERAL	*n* pl. **-S** a symbol that expresses a number
NUMERARY	*adj* pertaining to numbers
NUMERATE	*v* **-ATED, -ATING, -ATES** to count
NUMERIC	*n* pl. **-S** a numeral
NUMEROUS	*adj* many
NUMINA	pl. of numen
NUMINOUS	*adj* supernatural
NUMMARY	*adj* pertaining to coins
NUMMULAR	*adj* shaped like a coin
NUMMY	*adj* **NUMMIER, NUMMIEST** delicious
NUMNAH	*n* pl. **-S** a pad placed under a saddle
NUMSKULL	*n* pl. **-S** a dunce
NUN	*n* pl. **-S** a woman belonging to a religious order
NUNATAK	*n* pl. **-S** a mountain peak completely surrounded by glacial ice
NUNCHAKU	*n* pl. **-S** a Japanese weapon
NUNCHUK	*n* pl. **-S** nunchaku

NUNCIO   *n* pl. **-CIOS** an ambassador from the pope

NUNCLE   *n* pl. **-S** an uncle

NUNLIKE   *adj* resembling a nun

NUNNERY   *n* pl. **-NERIES** a religious house for nuns

NUNNISH   *adj* of, pertaining to, or characteristic of a nun

NUPTIAL   *n* pl. **-S** a wedding

NURD   *n* pl. **-S** nerd

NURL   *v* **-ED, -ING, -S** to knurl

NURSE   *v* **NURSED, NURSING, NURSES** to care for the sick or infirm

NURSER   *n* pl. **-S** a baby's bottle

NURSERY   *n* pl. **-ERIES** a room for young children

NURSING   *n* pl. **-S** the profession of one who nurses

NURSLING   *n* pl. **-S** an infant

NURTURAL   *adj* pertaining to the process of nurturing

NURTURE   *v* **-TURED, -TURING, -TURES** to nourish

NURTURER   *n* pl. **-S** one that nurtures

NUT   *v* **NUTTED, NUTTING, NUTS** to gather nuts (hard-shelled dry fruits)

NUTANT   *adj* drooping

NUTATE   *v* **-TATED, -TATING, -TATES** to exhibit nutation

NUTATION   *n* pl. **-S** an oscillatory movement of the axis of a rotating body

NUTBAR   *n* pl. **-S** a bar made from chopped nuts

NUTBROWN   *adj* of a dark brown

NUTCASE   *n* pl. **-S** a crazy person

NUTGALL   *n* pl. **-S** a gallnut

NUTGRASS   *n* pl. **-ES** a perennial herb

NUTHATCH   *n* pl. **-ES** a small bird

NUTHOUSE   *n* pl. **-S** an insane asylum

NUTLET   *n* pl. **-S** a small nut

NUTLIKE   *adj* resembling a nut

NUTMEAT   *n* pl. **-S** the edible kernel of a nut

NUTMEG   *n* pl. **-S** an aromatic seed used as a spice **NUTMEGGY** *adj*

NUTPICK   *n* pl. **-S** a device for extracting the kernels from nuts

NUTRIA   *n* pl. **-S** the coypu

NUTRIENT   *n* pl. **-S** a nourishing substance

NUTSEDGE   *n* pl. **-S** nutgrass

NUTSHELL   *n* pl. **-S** the shell of a nut

NUTSY   *adj* **NUTSIER, NUTSIEST** crazy

NUTTED   past tense of nut

NUTTER   *n* pl. **-S** one that gathers nuts

NUTTING   *n* pl. **-S** the act of gathering nuts

NUTTY   *adj* **-TIER, -TIEST** silly; crazy **NUTTILY** *adv*

NUTWOOD   *n* pl. **-S** a nut-bearing tree

NUZZLE   *v* **-ZLED, -ZLING, -ZLES** to push with the nose

NUZZLER   *n* pl. **-S** one that nuzzles

NYAH   *interj* — used to express contempt for another

NYALA   *n* pl. **-S** an antelope

NYLGHAI   *n* pl. **-S** nilgai

NYLGHAU   *n* pl. **-S** nilgai

NYLON   *n* pl. **-S** a synthetic material **NYLONED** *adj*

NYMPH   *n* pl. **-S** a female spirit **NYMPHAL, NYMPHEAN** *adj*

NYMPH   *v* **-ED, -ING, -S** to fish using a fly (a hook with silk or feathers) that looks like a larva

NYMPHA   *n* pl. **-PHAE** a fold of the vulva

NYMPHET   *n* pl. **-S** a young nymph

NYMPHO   *n* pl. **-PHOS** a woman obsessed by sexual desire

NYSTATIN   *n* pl. **-S** an antibiotic

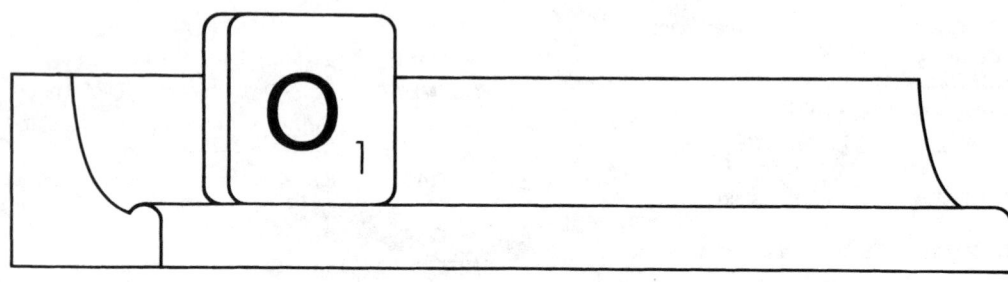

OAF	*n* pl. **OAFS** or **OAVES** a clumsy, stupid person **OAFISH** *adj* **OAFISHLY** *adv*
OAK	*n* pl. **-S** a hardwood tree or shrub **OAKEN, OAKLIKE** *adj*
OAKED	*adj* matured in an oak container
OAKINESS	*n* pl. **-ES** the quality or state of being oaky
OAKMOSS	*n* pl. **-ES** a lichen that grows on oak trees
OAKUM	*n* pl. **-S** loosely twisted hemp fiber
OAKY	*adj* **OAKIER, OAKIEST** tasting of oak sap
OAR	*v* **-ED, -ING, -S** to propel with oars (long, broad-bladed poles)
OARFISH	*n* pl. **-ES** a marine fish
OARLESS	*adj* having no oars
OARLIKE	*adj* resembling an oar
OARLOCK	*n* pl. **-S** a device for holding an oar in place
OARSMAN	*n* pl. **-MEN** a person who rows a boat
OASIS	*n* pl. **OASES** a green area in a desert region
OAST	*n* pl. **-S** a type of kiln
OAT	*n* pl. **-S** a cereal grass
OATCAKE	*n* pl. **-S** a cake made of oatmeal
OATEN	*adj* pertaining to oats
OATER	*n* pl. **-S** a cowboy movie
OATH	*n* pl. **-S** a formal declaration or promise to fulfill a pledge
OATLIKE	*adj* resembling oats
OATMEAL	*n* pl. **-S** meal made from oats
OATY	*adj* **OATIER, OATIEST** tasting or smelling of oats
OAVES	a pl. of oaf
OBA	*n* pl. **-S** a hereditary chief in Benin and Nigeria
OBCONIC	*adj* conical with the apex below
OBDURACY	*n* pl. **-CIES** the quality or an instance of being obdurate
OBDURATE	*adj* stubborn
OBE	*n* pl. **-S** obeah
OBEAH	*n* pl. **-S** a form of sorcery of African origin
OBEAHISM	*n* pl. **-S** the use of obeah
OBEDIENT	*adj* obeying or willing to obey
OBEISANT	*adj* showing reverence or respect
OBELI	pl. of obelus
OBELIA	*n* pl. **-S** a marine hydroid
OBELISE	*v* **-LISED, -LISING, -LISES** to obelize
OBELISK	*n* pl. **-S** a four-sided shaft of stone with a pyramidal top
OBELISM	*n* pl. **-S** the act of obelizing
OBELIZE	*v* **-LIZED, -LIZING, -LIZES** to mark with an obelus
OBELUS	*n* pl. **-LI** a symbol used in ancient manuscripts to indicate a doubtful passage
OBENTO	*n* pl. **-TOS** a Japanese meal packed in a box
OBESE	*adj* very fat **OBESELY** *adv*
OBESITY	*n* pl. **-TIES** the state or condition of being obese
OBEY	*v* **-ED, -ING, -S** to follow the commands or guidance of **OBEYABLE** *adj*
OBEYER	*n* pl. **-S** one that obeys
OBI	*n* pl. **-S** obeah
OBIA	*n* pl. **-S** obeah
OBIISM	*n* pl. **-S** obeahism
OBIT	*n* pl. **-S** an obituary
OBITUARY	*n* pl. **-ARIES** a published notice of a death
OBJECT	*v* **-ED, -ING, -S** to argue in opposition
OBJECTOR	*n* pl. **-S** one that objects

OBJET | *n* pl. **-S** an article of artistic value

OBLAST | *n* pl. **-LASTS** or **-LASTI** an administrative division of Russia

OBLATE | *n* pl. **-S** a layman residing in a monastery

OBLATELY | *adv* elliptically

OBLATION | *n* pl. **-S** the act of making a religious offering **OBLATORY** *adj*

OBLIGATE | *v* **-GATED, -GATING, -GATES** to oblige

OBLIGATO | *n* pl. **-TOS** or **-TI** an important musical part

OBLIGE | *v* **OBLIGED, OBLIGING, OBLIGES** to put in one's debt by a favor or service

OBLIGEE | *n* pl. **-S** one that is obliged

OBLIGER | *n* pl. **-S** one that obliges

OBLIGING | present participle of oblige

OBLIGOR | *n* pl. **-S** one who places himself under a legal obligation

OBLIQUE | *v* **OBLIQUED, OBLIQUING, OBLIQUES** to slant

OBLIVION | *n* pl. **-S** the state of being forgotten; the act of forgetting

OBLONG | *n* pl. **-S** something that is oblong (elongated)

OBLONGLY | *adv* in an oblong manner

OBLOQUY | *n* pl. **-QUIES** abusive language

OBOE | *n* pl. **-S** a woodwind instrument

OBOIST | *n* pl. **-S** one who plays the oboe

OBOL | *n* pl. **-S** a coin of ancient Greece

OBOLE | *n* pl. **-S** a coin of medieval France

OBOLUS | *n* pl. **-LI** an obol

OBOVATE | *adj* ovate with the narrow end at the base

OBOVOID | *adj* ovoid with the narrow end at the base

OBSCENE | *adj* **-SCENER, -SCENEST** indecent

OBSCURE | *adj* **-SCURER, -SCUREST** dark or indistinct

OBSCURE | *v* **-SCURED, -SCURING, -SCURES** to make obscure

OBSEQUY | *n* pl. **-QUIES** a funeral rite

OBSERVE | *v* **-SERVED, -SERVING, -SERVES** to look attentively

OBSERVER | *n* pl. **-S** one that observes

OBSESS | *v* **-ED, -ING, -ES** to dominate the thoughts of

OBSESSOR | *n* pl. **-S** something that obsesses

OBSIDIAN | *n* pl. **-S** a volcanic glass

OBSOLETE | *v* **-LETED, -LETING, -LETES** to make out-of-date

OBSTACLE | *n* pl. **-S** something that obstructs

OBSTRUCT | *v* **-ED, -ING, -S** to get in the way of

OBTAIN | *v* **-ED, -ING, -S** to gain possession of

OBTAINER | *n* pl. **-S** one that obtains

OBTECT | *adj* covered by a hardened secretion

OBTECTED | *adj* obtect

OBTEST | *v* **-ED, -ING, -S** to beseech

OBTRUDE | *v* **-TRUDED, -TRUDING, -TRUDES** to thrust forward

OBTRUDER | *n* pl. **-S** one that obtrudes

OBTUND | *v* **-ED, -ING, -S** to deaden

OBTURATE | *v* **-RATED, -RATING, -RATES** to close or stop up

OBTUSE | *adj* **-TUSER, -TUSEST** dull **OBTUSELY** *adv*

OBTUSITY | *n* pl. **-TIES** the state of being obtuse

OBVERSE | *n* pl. **-S** the side of a coin bearing the main design

OBVERT | *v* **-ED, -ING, -S** to turn so as to show a different surface

OBVIATE | *v* **-ATED, -ATING, -ATES** to prevent or eliminate by effective measures **OBVIABLE** *adj*

OBVIATOR | *n* pl. **-S** one that obviates

OBVIOUS | *adj* easily perceived or understood

OBVOLUTE | *adj* rolled or turned in

OCA | *n* pl. **-S** a South American herb

OCARINA | *n* pl. **-S** a wind instrument

OCCASION | *v* **-ED, -ING, -S** to cause

OCCIDENT | *n* pl. **-S** the west

OCCIPUT | *n* pl. **-PUTS** or **-PITA** the back part of the skull

OCCLUDE | *v* **-CLUDED, -CLUDING, -CLUDES** to close or stop up

OCCLUSAL | *adj* pertaining to the biting surface of a tooth

OCCULT | *v* **-ED, -ING, -S** to conceal

OCCULTER | *n* pl. **-S** one that occults

OCCULTLY | *adv* secretly

OCCUPANT | *n* pl. **-S** a resident

OCCUPIER | *n* pl. **-S** one who occupies

OCCUPY | *v* **-PIED, -PYING, -PIES** to engage the attention or energies of

OCCUR   *v* **-CURRED, -CURRING, -CURS** to take place

OCEAN   *n* pl. **-S** the vast body of salt water that covers most of the earth's surface **OCEANIC** *adj*

OCEANAUT   *n* pl. **-S** an aquanaut

OCELLAR   *adj* pertaining to an ocellus

OCELLATE   *adj* having ocelli

OCELLUS   *n* pl. **-LI** a minute simple eye

OCELOT   *n* pl. **-S** an American wildcat **OCELOID** *adj*

OCH   *interj* — used to express surprise or regret

OCHE   *n* pl. **-S** a line behind which players stand when throwing darts

OCHER   *v* **-ED, -ING, -S** to color with ocher (a red or yellow iron ore used as a pigment)

OCHERISH   *adj* resembling ocher

OCHEROID   *adj* ocherous

OCHEROUS   *adj* containing or resembling ocher

OCHERY   *adj* ocherous

OCHONE   *interj* — used to express grief

OCHRE   *v* **OCHRED, OCHRING, OCHRES** to ocher

OCHREA   *n* pl. **-REAE** or **-REAS** ocrea

OCHREOUS   *adj* ocherous

OCHRING   present participle of ochre

OCHROID   *adj* ocherous

OCHROUS   *adj* ocherous

OCHRY   *adj* ochery

OCICAT   *n* pl. **-S** a domestic cat having a short spotted coat

OCKER   *n* pl. **-S** a boorish person

OCOTILLO   *n* pl. **-LOS** a Mexican shrub

OCREA   *n* pl. **-REAE** or **-REAS** a sheathing plant part

OCREATE   *adj* having ocreae

OCTAD   *n* pl. **-S** a group of eight **OCTADIC** *adj*

OCTAGON   *n* pl. **-S** an eight-sided polygon

OCTAL   *adj* pertaining to a number system with a base of eight

OCTAN   *n* pl. **-S** a fever recurring every eighth day

OCTANE   *n* pl. **-S** a liquid hydrocarbon

OCTANGLE   *n* pl. **-S** an octagon

OCTANOL   *n* pl. **-S** an alcohol

OCTANT   *n* pl. **-S** an eighth of a circle **OCTANTAL** *adj*

OCTARCHY   *n* pl. **-TARCHIES** a government by eight persons

OCTAVE   *n* pl. **-S** a type of musical interval **OCTAVAL** *adj*

OCTAVO   *n* pl. **-VOS** a page size

OCTET   *n* pl. **-S** a group of eight

OCTETTE   *n* pl. **-S** octet

OCTONARY   *n* pl. **-NARIES** a stanza of eight lines

OCTOPOD   *n* pl. **-S** any of an order of eight-armed mollusks

OCTOPOID   *adj* resembling an octopus

OCTOPUS   *n* pl. **-PUSES** or **-PI** or **-PODES** a nocturnal octopod

OCTOROON   *n* pl. **-S** a person of one-eighth black ancestry

OCTROI   *n* pl. **-S** a tax on certain articles brought into a city

OCTUPLE   *v* **-PLED, -PLING, -PLES** to multiply by eight

OCTUPLET   *n* pl. **-S** a group of eight related items

OCTUPLEX   *adj* being eight times as great

OCTUPLING   present participle of octuple

OCTUPLY   *adv* to eight times the degree

OCTYL   *n* pl. **-S** a univalent radical

OCULAR   *n* pl. **-S** an eyepiece

OCULARLY   *adv* by means of the eyes or sight

OCULIST   *n* pl. **-S** a physician who treats diseases of the eye

OCULUS   *n* pl. **-LI** a circular window

OD   *n* pl. **-S** a hypothetical force of natural power

ODA   *n* pl. **-S** a room in a harem

ODAH   *n* pl. **-S** oda

ODALISK   *n* pl. **-S** a female slave in a harem

ODD   *adj* **ODDER, ODDEST** unusual

ODD   *n* pl. **-S** one that is odd

ODDBALL   *n* pl. **-S** an eccentric person

ODDISH   *adj* somewhat odd

ODDITY   *n* pl. **-TIES** one that is odd

ODDLY   *adv* in an odd manner

ODDMENT   *n* pl. **-S** a remnant

ODDNESS   *n* pl. **-ES** the state of being odd

ODE   *n* pl. **-S** a lyric poem

ODEON   *n* pl. **-S** odeum

ODEUM *n* pl. **ODEUMS** or **ODEA** a theater or concert hall

ODIC *adj* pertaining to an ode

ODIOUS *adj* deserving or causing hatred **ODIOUSLY** *adv*

ODIST *n* pl. **-S** one who writes odes

ODIUM *n* pl. **-S** hatred

ODOGRAPH *n* pl. **-S** an odometer

ODOMETER *n* pl. **-S** a device for measuring distance traveled

ODOMETRY *n* pl. **-TRIES** the process of using an odometer

ODONATA *n/pl* insects of an order of predacious insects

ODONATE *n* pl. **-S** any of an order of predacious insects

ODONTOID *n* pl. **-S** a toothlike vertebral projection

ODOR *n* pl. **-S** the property of a substance that affects the sense of smell **ODORED, ODORFUL** *adj*

ODORANT *n* pl. **-S** an odorous substance

ODORIZE *v* **-IZED, -IZING, -IZES** to make odorous

ODORIZER *n* pl. **-S** one that odorizes

ODORLESS *adj* having no odor

ODOROUS *adj* having an odor

ODOUR *n* pl. **-S** odor **ODOURFUL** *adj*

ODYL *n* pl. **-S** an od

ODYLE *n* pl. **-S** odyl

ODYSSEY *n* pl. **-SEYS** a long, wandering journey **ODYSSEAN** *adj*

OE *n* pl. **-S** a whirlwind off the Faeroe islands

OECOLOGY *n* pl. **-GIES** ecology

OEDEMA *n* pl. **-MAS** or **-MATA** edema

OEDIPAL *adj* pertaining to the libidinal feelings in a child toward the parent of the opposite sex

OEDIPEAN *adj* oedipal

OEILLADE *n* pl. **-S** an amorous look

OENOLOGY *n* pl. **-GIES** the study of wines

OENOMEL *n* pl. **-S** an ancient Greek beverage of wine and honey

OERSTED *n* pl. **-S** a unit of magnetic intensity

OESTRIN *n* pl. **-S** estrin

OESTRIOL *n* pl. **-S** estriol

OESTRONE *n* pl. **-S** estrone

OESTROUS *adj* estrous

OESTRUAL *adj* estrual

OESTRUM *n* pl. **-S** estrum

OESTRUS *n* pl. **-ES** estrus

OEUVRE *n* pl. **-S** a work of art

OF *prep* coming from

OFF *v* **-ED, -ING, -S** to go away

OFFAL *n* pl. **-S** waste material

OFFBEAT *n* pl. **-S** an unaccented beat in a musical measure

OFFCAST *n* pl. **-S** a castoff

OFFCUT *n* pl. **-S** something that is cut off

OFFENCE *n* pl. **-S** offense

OFFEND *v* **-ED, -ING, -S** to commit an offense

OFFENDER *n* pl. **-S** one that offends

OFFENSE *n* pl. **-S** a violation of a moral or social code

OFFER *v* **-ED, -ING, -S** to present for acceptance or rejection

OFFEREE *n* pl. **-S** one to whom an offer is made

OFFERER *n* pl. **-S** one that offers

OFFERING *n* pl. **-S** a contribution

OFFEROR *n* pl. **-S** offerer

OFFHAND *adv* without preparation

OFFICE *n* pl. **-S** a position of authority

OFFICER *v* **-ED, -ING, -S** to furnish with officers (persons holding positions of authority)

OFFICIAL *n* pl. **-S** one that holds a position of authority

OFFING *n* pl. **-S** the near future

OFFISH *adj* aloof **OFFISHLY** *adv*

OFFKEY *adj* pitched higher or lower than the correct musical tone

OFFLINE *adj* not connected to a computer network

OFFLOAD *v* **-ED, -ING, -S** to unload

OFFPRINT *v* **-ED, -ING, -S** to reprint an excerpt

OFFRAMP *n* pl. **-S** a road leading off an expressway

OFFSET *v* **-SET, -SETTING, -SETS** to compensate for

OFFSHOOT *n* pl. **-S** a lateral shoot from a main stem

OFFSHORE *n* pl. **-S** an area of submerged land out from the shore

OFFSIDE *n* pl. **-S** an improper football play

OFFSTAGE *n* pl. **-S** a part of a stage not visible to the audience

OFFTRACK *adj* away from a racetrack

OFT *adv* **OFTER, OFTEST** often

OFTEN *adv* **-ENER, -ENEST** frequently

OFTTIMES *adv* often

OGAM *n* pl. **-S** ogham

OGDOAD *n* pl. **-S** a group of eight

OGEE *n* pl. **-S** an S-shaped molding **OGEED** *adj*

OGHAM *n* pl. **-S** an Old Irish alphabet **OGHAMIC** *adj*

OGHAMIST *n* pl. **-S** one who writes in ogham

OGIVE *n* pl. **-S** a pointed arch **OGIVAL** *adj*

OGLE *v* **OGLED, OGLING, OGLES** to stare at

OGLER *n* pl. **-S** one that ogles

OGRE *n* pl. **-S** a monster

OGREISH *adj* resembling an ogre

OGREISM *n* pl. **-S** the state of being ogreish

OGRESS *n* pl. **-ES** a female ogre

OGRISH *adj* ogreish **OGRISHLY** *adv*

OGRISM *n* pl. **-S** ogreism

OH *v* **-ED, -ING, -S** to exclaim in surprise, pain, or desire

OHIA *n* pl. **-S** lehua

OHM *n* pl. **-S** a unit of electrical resistance **OHMIC** *adj*

OHMAGE *n* pl. **-S** electrical resistance expressed in ohms

OHMMETER *n* pl. **-S** an instrument for measuring ohmage

OHO *interj* — used to express surprise or exultation

OI *interj* oy

OIDIUM *n* pl. **OIDIA** a type of fungus **OIDIOID** *adj*

OIK *n* pl. **-S** a very rude or stupid person

OIL *v* **-ED, -ING, -S** to supply with oil (a greasy liquid used for lubrication, fuel, or illumination)

OILBIRD *n* pl. **-S** a tropical bird

OILCAMP *n* pl. **-S** a living area for workers at an oil well

OILCAN *n* pl. **-S** a can for applying lubricating oil

OILCLOTH *n* pl. **-S** a waterproof fabric

OILCUP *n* pl. **-S** a closed cup for supplying lubricant

OILER *n* pl. **-S** one that oils

OILFIELD *n* pl. **-S** an area that yields petroleum

OILHOLE *n* pl. **-S** a hole through which lubricating oil is injected

OILIER comparative of oily

OILIEST superlative of oily

OILILY *adv* in an oily manner

OILINESS *n* pl. **-ES** the state of being oily

OILMAN *n* pl. **-MEN** one who owns or operates oil wells

OILPAPER *n* pl. **-S** a water-resistant paper

OILPROOF *adj* impervious to oil

OILSEED *n* pl. **-S** a seed from which oil is pressed out

OILSKIN *n* pl. **-S** a waterproof fabric

OILSTONE *n* pl. **-S** a stone for sharpening tools

OILTIGHT *adj* being so tight as to prevent the passage of oil

OILWAY *n* pl. **-WAYS** a channel for the passage of oil

OILY *adj* **OILIER, OILIEST** covered or soaked with oil

OINK *v* **-ED, -ING, -S** to utter the natural grunt of a hog

OINOLOGY *n* pl. **-GIES** oenology

OINOMEL *n* pl. **-S** oenomel

OINTMENT *n* pl. **-S** a viscous preparation applied to the skin as a medicine or cosmetic

OITICICA *n* pl. **-S** a South American tree

OKA *n* pl. **-S** a Turkish unit of weight

OKAPI *n* pl. **-S** an African ruminant mammal

OKAY *v* **-ED, -ING, -S** to approve

OKE *n* pl. **-S** oka

OKEH *n* pl. **-S** approval

OKEYDOKE *adj* perfectly all right

OKRA *n* pl. **-S** a tall annual herb

OLD *adj* **OLDER, OLDEST** or **ELDER, ELDEST** living or existing for a relatively long time

OLD *n* pl. **-S** an individual of a specified age

OLDE *adj* old

OLDEN *adj* pertaining to a bygone era

OLDIE *n* pl. **-S** a popular song of an earlier day

OLDISH *adj* somewhat old

OLDNESS *n* pl. **-ES** the state of being old

OLDSQUAW *n* pl. **-S** a sea duck

OLDSTER *n* pl. **-S** an old person

OLDSTYLE *n* pl. **-S** a style of printing type

OLDWIFE *n* pl. **-WIVES** a marine fish

OLDY *n* pl. **OLDIES** oldie

OLE *n* pl. **-S** a shout of approval

OLEA pl. of oleum

OLEANDER *n* pl. **-S** a flowering shrub

OLEASTER *n* pl. **-S** a flowering shrub

OLEATE *n* pl. **-S** a chemical salt

OLEFIN *n* pl. **-S** an alkene **OLEFINIC** *adj*

OLEFINE *n* pl. **-S** olefin

OLEIC *adj* pertaining to oil

OLEIN *n* pl. **-S** the liquid portion of a fat

OLEINE *n* pl. **-S** olein

OLEO *n* pl. **OLEOS** margarine

OLESTRA *n* pl. **-S** a noncaloric fat substitute

OLEUM *n* pl. **-S** a corrosive liquid

OLEUM *n* pl. **OLEA** oil

OLIBANUM *n* pl. **-S** a fragrant resin

OLICOOK *n* pl. **-S** a doughnut

OLIGARCH *n* pl. **-S** a ruler in a government by the few

OLIGOMER *n* pl. **-S** a type of polymer

OLIGURIA *n* pl. **-S** reduced excretion of urine **OLIGURIC** *adj*

OLINGO *n* pl. **-GOS** a small mammal of Central and South America

OLIO *n* pl. **OLIOS** a miscellaneous collection

OLIVARY *adj* shaped like an olive

OLIVE *n* pl. **-S** the small oval fruit of a Mediterranean tree

OLIVINE *n* pl. **-S** a mineral **OLIVINIC** *adj*

OLLA *n* pl. **-S** a wide-mouthed pot or jar

OLLIE *v* **OLLIED, OLLIEING, OLLIES** to perform a maneuver in skateboarding or snowboarding

OLOGIST *n* pl. **-S** an expert in a particular ology

OLOGY *n* pl. **-GIES** a branch of knowledge

OLOROSO *n* pl. **-SOS** a dark sherry

OLYMPIAD *n* pl. **-S** a celebration of the Olympic Games

OM *n* pl. **-S** a mantra used in contemplation of ultimate reality

OMA *n* pl. **-S** grandmother

OMADHAUN *n* pl. **-S** a foolish person

OMASUM *n* pl. **-SA** the third stomach of a ruminant

OMBER *n* pl. **-S** ombre

OMBRE *n* pl. **-S** a card game

OMEGA *n* pl. **-S** a Greek letter

OMELET *n* pl. **-S** a dish of beaten eggs cooked and folded around a filling

OMELETTE *n* pl. **-S** omelet

OMEN *v* **-ED, -ING, -S** to be an omen (a prophetic sign) of

OMENTUM *n* pl. **-TUMS** or **-TA** a fold in an abdominal membrane **OMENTAL** *adj*

OMER *n* pl. **-S** a Hebrew unit of dry measure

OMERTA *n* pl. **-S** a code of silence about criminal activity

OMICRON *n* pl. **-S** a Greek letter

OMIKRON *n* pl. **-S** omicron

OMINOUS *adj* portending evil

OMISSION *n* pl. **-S** something left undone

OMISSIVE *adj* marked by omission

OMIT *v* **OMITTED, OMITTING, OMITS** to leave out

OMITTER *n* pl. **-S** one that omits

OMNIARCH *n* pl. **-S** an almighty ruler

OMNIBUS *n* pl. **-BUSES** or **-BUSSES** a bus

OMNIFIC *adj* unlimited in creative power

OMNIFORM *adj* of all forms

OMNIMODE *adj* of all modes

OMNIVORA *n/pl* omnivores

OMNIVORE *n* pl. **-S** an animal that eats all kinds of food

OMOPHAGY *n* pl. **-GIES** the eating of raw flesh

OMPHALOS *n* pl. **-LOI** or **-LI** a central point

ON *n* pl. **-S** the side of the wicket where a batsman stands in cricket

ONAGER *n* pl. **-GERS** or **-GRI** a wild ass of central Asia

ONANISM *n* pl. **-S** coitus deliberately interrupted to prevent insemination

ONANIST *n* pl. **-S** one who practices onanism

ONBOARD *adj* carried aboard a vehicle

ONCE *adv* one single time

ONCET *adv* once

ONCIDIUM *n* pl. **-S** a tropical orchid

ONCOGENE *n* pl. **-S** a gene that causes a cell to become cancerous

ONCOLOGY *n* pl. **-GIES** the science of tumors

ONCOMING *n* pl. **-S** an approach

ONDOGRAM *n* pl. **-S** a graph of electric wave forms

ONE *n* pl. **-S** a number

ONEFOLD *adj* constituting a single, undivided whole

ONEIRIC *adj* pertaining to dreams

ONENESS *n* pl. **-ES** unity

ONEROUS *adj* burdensome or oppressive

ONERY *adj* **-ERIER, -ERIEST** ornery

ONESELF *pron* a person's self

ONETIME *adj* former

ONGOING *adj* continuing without interruption

ONION *n* pl. **-S** the edible bulb of a cultivated herb **ONIONY** *adj*

ONIUM *adj* characterized by a complex cation

ONLAY *n* pl. **-S** something laid over something else

ONLIEST *adj* only

ONLINE *adj* connected to a computer network

ONLOAD *v* **-ED, -ING, -S** to load a vehicle or container

ONLOOKER *n* pl. **-S** a spectator

ONLY *adv* with nothing or no one else

ONO *n* pl. **ONOS** a large mackerel

ONOMAST *n* pl. **-S** a person who studies proper names

ONRUSH *n* pl. **-ES** a forward rush or flow

ONSCREEN *adj* shown on a movie, television, or display screen

ONSET *n* pl. **-S** a beginning

ONSHORE *adv* toward the shore

ONSIDE *adj* not offside

ONSTAGE *adj* being on a part of the stage visible to the audience

ONSTREAM *adv* in or into production

ONTIC *adj* having real being or existence

ONTO *prep* to a position upon

ONTOGENY *n* pl. **-NIES** the development of an individual organism

ONTOLOGY *n* pl. **-GIES** the branch of philosophy that deals with being

ONUS *n* pl. **-ES** a burden or responsibility

ONWARD *adv* toward a point ahead or in front

ONWARDS *adv* onward

ONYX *n* pl. **-ES** a variety of quartz

OOCYST *n* pl. **-S** a zygote

OOCYTE *n* pl. **-S** an egg before maturation

OODLES *n* pl. **OODLES** a large amount

OODLINS *n* pl. **OODLINS** oodles

OOF *interj* — used to express discomfort

OOGAMETE *n* pl. **-S** a female gamete of certain protozoa

OOGAMOUS *adj* having structurally dissimilar gametes

OOGAMY *n* pl. **-MIES** the state of being oogamous

OOGENY *n* pl. **-NIES** the development of ova

OOGONIUM *n* pl. **-NIUMS** or **-NIA** a female sexual organ in certain algae and fungi **OOGONIAL** *adj*

OOH *v* **-ED, -ING, -S** to exclaim in amazement, joy, or surprise

OOLACHAN *n* pl. **-S** eulachon

OOLICHAN *n* pl. **-S** eulachon

OOLITE *n* pl. **-S** a variety of limestone **OOLITIC** *adj*

OOLITH *n* pl. **-S** oolite

OOLOGIST *n* pl. **-S** an expert in oology

OOLOGY *n* pl. **-GIES** the study of birds' eggs **OOLOGIC** *adj*

OOLONG *n* pl. **-S** a dark Chinese tea

OOMIAC *n* pl. **-S** umiak

OOMIACK *n* pl. **-S** umiak

OOMIAK *n* pl. **-S** umiak

OOMPAH *v* **-ED, -ING, -S** to play a repeated rhythmic bass accompaniment

OOMPH *n* pl. **-S** spirited vigor

OOPHYTE *n* pl. **-S** a stage of development in certain plants **OOPHYTIC** *adj*

OOPS *interj* — used to express mild apology, surprise, or dismay

OORALI *n* pl. **-S** curare

OORIE *adj* ourie

OOSPERM *n* pl. **-S** a fertilized egg

OOSPHERE *n* pl. **-S** an unfertilized egg within an oogonium

OOSPORE *n* pl. **-S** a fertilized egg within an oogonium **OOSPORIC** *adj*

OOT *n* pl. **-S** out

OOTHECA *n* pl. **-CAE** an egg case of certain insects **OOTHECAL** *adj*

OOTID *n* pl. **-S** one of the four sections into which a mature ovum divides

OOZE *v* **OOZED, OOZING, OOZES** to flow or leak out slowly

OOZINESS *n* pl. **-ES** the state of being oozy

OOZY *adj* **OOZIER, OOZIEST** containing or resembling soft mud or slime **OOZILY** *adv*

OP *n* pl. **-S** a style of abstract art

OPA *n* pl. **-S** grandfather

OPACIFY *v* **-FIED, -FYING, -FIES** to make opaque

OPACITY *n* pl. **-TIES** something that is opaque

OPAH *n* pl. **-S** a marine fish

OPAL *n* pl. **-S** a mineral

OPALESCE *v* **-ESCED, -ESCING, -ESCES** to emit an iridescent shimmer of colors

OPALINE *n* pl. **-S** an opaque white glass

OPAQUE *adj* **OPAQUER, OPAQUEST** impervious to light **OPAQUELY** *adv*

OPAQUE *v* **OPAQUED, OPAQUING, OPAQUES** to make opaque

OPE *v* **OPED, OPING, OPES** to open

OPEN *adj* **OPENER, OPENEST** affording unobstructed access, passage, or view

OPEN *v* **-ED, -ING, -S** to cause to become open **OPENABLE** *adj*

OPENCAST *adj* worked from a surface open to the air

OPENER *n* pl. **-S** one that opens

OPENING *n* pl. **-S** a vacant or unobstructed space

OPENLY *adv* in an open manner

OPENNESS *n* pl. **-ES** the state of being open

OPENWORK *n* pl. **-S** ornamental or structural work containing numerous openings

OPERA *n* pl. **-S** a form of musical drama

OPERABLE *adj* usable **OPERABLY** *adv*

OPERAND *n* pl. **-S** a quantity on which a mathematical operation is performed

OPERANT *n* pl. **-S** one that operates

OPERATE *v* **-ATED, -ATING, -ATES** to perform a function

OPERATIC *n* pl. **-S** the technique of staging operas

OPERATOR *n* pl. **-S** a symbol that represents a mathematical function

OPERCELE *n* pl. **-S** opercule

OPERCULA *n/pl* opercules

OPERCULE *n* pl. **-S** an anatomical part that serves as a lid or cover

OPERETTA *n* pl. **-S** a light musical drama with spoken dialogue

OPERON *n* pl. **-S** a type of gene cluster

OPEROSE *adj* involving great labor

OPHIDIAN *n* pl. **-S** a snake

OPHITE *n* pl. **-S** a green mottled igneous rock **OPHITIC** *adj*

OPIATE *v* **-ATED, -ATING, -ATES** to treat with opium

OPINE *v* **OPINED, OPINING, OPINES** to hold or state as an opinion

OPING present participle of ope

OPINION *n* pl. **-S** a conclusion or judgment one holds to be true

OPIOID *n* pl. **-S** a peptide that acts like opium

OPIUM *n* pl. **-S** an addictive narcotic

OPIUMISM *n* pl. **-S** opium addiction

OPOPANAX *n* pl. **-ES** a strong-smelling gum resin

OPOSSUM *n* pl. **-S** an arboreal mammal

OPPIDAN *n* pl. **-S** a townsman

OPPILATE *v* **-LATED, -LATING, -LATES** to obstruct **OPPILANT** *adj*

OPPONENS *n* pl. **OPPONENS** a muscle of the thumb

OPPONENT *n* pl. **-S** one that opposes another

OPPOSE *v* **-POSED, -POSING, -POSES** to be in contention or conflict with

OPPOSER *n* pl. **-S** one that opposes

OPPOSITE *n* pl. **-S** one that is radically different from another in some related way

OPPRESS *v* **-ED, -ING, -ES** to burden by abuse of power or authority

OPPUGN *v* **-ED, -ING, -S** to assail with argument

OPPUGNER	*n* pl. **-S** one that oppugns
OPSIMATH	*n* pl. **-S** a person who learns only late in life
OPSIN	*n* pl. **-S** a type of protein
OPSONIC	*adj* pertaining to opsonin
OPSONIFY	*v* **-FIED, -FYING, -FIES** to opsonize
OPSONIN	*n* pl. **-S** an antibody of blood serum
OPSONISE	*v* **-NISED, -NISING, -NISES** opsonize
OPSONIZE	*v* **-NIZED, -NIZING, -NIZES** to form opsonins in
OPT	*v* **-ED, -ING, -S** to choose
OPTATIVE	*n* pl. **-S** a mood of verbs that expresses a wish or desire
OPTIC	*n* pl. **-S** an eye
OPTICAL	*adj* pertaining to sight
OPTICIAN	*n* pl. **-S** one who makes or deals in optical goods
OPTICIST	*n* pl. **-S** one engaged in the study of light and vision
OPTIMA	a pl. of optimum
OPTIMAL	*adj* most desirable
OPTIME	*n* pl. **-S** an honor student in mathematics at Cambridge University
OPTIMISE	*v* **-MISED, -MISING, -MISES** to optimize
OPTIMISM	*n* pl. **-S** a disposition to look on the favorable side of things
OPTIMIST	*n* pl. **-S** one who exhibits optimism
OPTIMIZE	*v* **-MIZED, -MIZING, -MIZES** to make as perfect, useful, or effective as possible
OPTIMUM	*n* pl. **-MUMS** or **-MA** the most favorable condition for obtaining a given result
OPTION	*v* **-ED, -ING, -S** to grant an option (a right to buy or sell something at a specified price within a specified time) on
OPTIONAL	*n* pl. **-S** an elective course of study
OPTIONEE	*n* pl. **-S** one who holds a legal option
OPTRONIC	*adj* pertaining to the science concerned with electronics and light
OPULENCE	*n* pl. **-S** wealth
OPULENCY	*n* pl. **-CIES** opulence
OPULENT	*adj* wealthy
OPUNTIA	*n* pl. **-S** an American cactus
OPUS	*n* pl. **OPUSES** or **OPERA** a literary or musical work
OPUSCULA	*n/pl* opuscules
OPUSCULE	*n* pl. **-S** a minor work
OQUASSA	*n* pl. **-S** a small lake trout
OR	*n* pl. **-S** the heraldic color gold
ORA	pl. of os
ORACH	*n* pl. **-ES** a cultivated plant
ORACHE	*n* pl. **-S** orach
ORACLE	*n* pl. **-S** a person through whom a deity is believed to speak **ORACULAR** *adj*
ORACY	*n* pl. **-CIES** skill in oral expression and comprehension
ORAD	*adv* toward the mouth
ORAL	*n* pl. **-S** an examination requiring spoken answers
ORALISM	*n* pl. **-S** the use of oral methods of teaching the deaf
ORALIST	*n* pl. **-S** an advocate of oralism
ORALITY	*n* pl. **-TIES** the state of being produced orally
ORALLY	*adv* through the mouth
ORANG	*n* pl. **-S** a large ape
ORANGE	*n* pl. **-S** a citrus fruit
ORANGERY	*n* pl. **-RIES** a place where orange trees are cultivated
ORANGEY	*adj* **-ANGIER, -ANGIEST** orangy
ORANGISH	*adj* of a somewhat orange color
ORANGY	*adj* **-ANGIER, -ANGIEST** resembling or suggestive of an orange
ORATE	*v* **ORATED, ORATING, ORATES** to speak formally
ORATION	*n* pl. **-S** a formal speech
ORATOR	*n* pl. **-S** one that orates
ORATORIO	*n* pl. **-RIOS** a type of musical composition
ORATORY	*n* pl. **-RIES** the art of public speaking
ORATRESS	*n* pl. **-ES** oratrix
ORATRIX	*n* pl. **-TRICES** a female orator
ORATURE	*n* pl. **-S** oral forms of literature, such as folklore
ORB	*v* **-ED, -ING, -S** to form into a circle or sphere
ORBIER	comparative of orby
ORBIEST	superlative of orby

ORBIT *v* **-ED, -ING, -S** to move or revolve around

ORBITAL *n* pl. **-S** a subdivision of a nuclear shell

ORBITER *n* pl. **-S** one that orbits

ORBLESS *adj* lacking an orb

ORBY *adj* **ORBIER, ORBIEST** resembling a circle or sphere

ORC *n* pl. **-S** a marine mammal

ORCA *n* pl. **-S** orc

ORCEIN *n* pl. **-S** a reddish brown dye

ORCHARD *n* pl. **-S** an area for the cultivation of fruit trees

ORCHID *n* pl. **-S** a flowering plant

ORCHIL *n* pl. **-S** a purple dye

ORCHILLA *n* pl. **-S** orchil

ORCHIS *n* pl. **-CHISES** an orchid

ORCHITIS *n* pl. **-TISES** inflammation of the testicle **ORCHITIC** *adj*

ORCIN *n* pl. **-S** orcinol

ORCINOL *n* pl. **-S** a chemical compound

ORDAIN *v* **-ED, -ING, -S** to invest with holy authority

ORDAINER *n* pl. **-S** one that ordains

ORDEAL *n* pl. **-S** a severely difficult or painful experience

ORDER *v* **-ED, -ING, -S** to give a command or instruction to

ORDERER *n* pl. **-S** one that orders

ORDERLY *n* pl. **-LIES** a male attendant

ORDINAL *n* pl. **-S** a number designating position in a series

ORDINAND *n* pl. **-S** a person about to be ordained

ORDINARY *adj* **-NARIER, -NARIEST** of a kind to be expected in the normal order of events

ORDINARY *n* pl. **-NARIES** something that is ordinary

ORDINATE *n* pl. **-S** a particular geometric coordinate

ORDNANCE *n* pl. **-S** artillery; a cannon

ORDO *n* pl. **-DOS** or **-DINES** a calendar of religious directions

ORDURE *n* pl. **-S** manure **ORDUROUS** *adj*

ORE *n* pl. **-S** a mineral or rock containing a valuable metal

OREAD *n* pl. **-S** a mountain nymph in Greek mythology

OREBODY *n* pl. **-BODIES** a mass of ore in a mine

ORECTIC *adj* pertaining to appetites or desires

ORECTIVE *adj* orectic

OREGANO *n* pl. **-NOS** an aromatic herb used as a seasoning

OREIDE *n* pl. **-S** oroide

OREODONT *n* pl. **-S** an extinct sheep-sized mammal

ORFRAY *n* pl. **-FRAYS** orphrey

ORG *n* pl. **-S** an organization

ORGAN *n* pl. **-S** a differentiated part of an organism performing a specific function

ORGANA a pl. of organon and organum

ORGANDIE *n* pl. **-S** organdy

ORGANDY *n* pl. **-DIES** a cotton fabric

ORGANIC *n* pl. **-S** a substance of animal or vegetable origin

ORGANISE *v* **-NISED, -NISING, -NISES** to organize

ORGANISM *n* pl. **-S** any form of animal or plant life

ORGANIST *n* pl. **-S** one who plays the organ (a keyboard musical instrument)

ORGANIZE *v* **-NIZED, -NIZING, -NIZES** to form into an orderly whole

ORGANON *n* pl. **-GANONS** or **-GANA** a system of rules for scientific investigation

ORGANUM *n* pl. **-GANUMS** or **-GANA** organon

ORGANZA *n* pl. **-S** a sheer fabric

ORGASM *v* **-ED, -ING, -S** to experience an orgasm (the climax of sexual excitement) **ORGASMIC, ORGASTIC** *adj*

ORGEAT *n* pl. **-S** an almond-flavored syrup

ORGIAC *adj* of the nature of an orgy

ORGIAST *n* pl. **-S** one who participates in an orgy

ORGIC *adj* orgiac

ORGONE *n* pl. **-S** a postulated energy pervading the universe

ORGULOUS *adj* proud

ORGY *n* pl. **-GIES** a party marked by unrestrained sexual indulgence

ORIBATID *n* pl. **-S** any of a family of eyeless mites

ORIBI *n* pl. **-S** an African antelope

ORICHALC *n* pl. **-S** a yellow metal

ORIEL *n* pl. **-S** a type of projecting window

ORIENT *v* **-ED, -ING, -S** to adjust in relation to something else

ORIENTAL *n* pl. **-S** an inhabitant of an eastern country

ORIENTER *n* pl. **-S** one who helps another to adjust to surroundings

ORIFICE *n* pl. **-S** a mouth or mouthlike opening

ORIGAMI *n* pl. **-S** the Japanese art of paper folding

ORIGAN *n* pl. **-S** marjoram

ORIGANUM *n* pl. **-S** an aromatic herb

ORIGIN *n* pl. **-S** a coming into being

ORIGINAL *n* pl. **-S** the first form of something

ORINASAL *n* pl. **-S** a sound pronounced through both the mouth and nose

ORIOLE *n* pl. **-S** an American songbird

ORISHA *n* pl. **-S** a Yoruba deity

ORISON *n* pl. **-S** a prayer

ORLE *n* pl. **-S** a heraldic border

ORLOP *n* pl. **-S** the lowest deck of a ship

ORMER *n* pl. **-S** an abalone

ORMOLU *n* pl. **-S** an alloy used to imitate gold

ORNAMENT *v* **-ED, -ING, -S** to decorate

ORNATE *adj* elaborately or excessively ornamented **ORNATELY** *adv*

ORNERY *adj* **-NERIER, -NERIEST** stubborn and mean-spirited

ORNIS *n* pl. **ORNITHES** avifauna

ORNITHIC *adj* pertaining to birds

OROGEN *n* pl. **-S** a belt of the earth's crust involved in orogeny

OROGENY *n* pl. **-NIES** the process of mountain formation **OROGENIC** *adj*

OROIDE *n* pl. **-S** an alloy used to imitate gold

OROLOGY *n* pl. **-GIES** the study of mountains

OROMETER *n* pl. **-S** a type of barometer

OROTUND *adj* full and clear in sound

ORPHAN *v* **-ED, -ING, -S** to deprive of both parents

ORPHIC *adj* mystical

ORPHICAL *adj* orphic

ORPHISM *n* pl. **-S** a style of art

ORPHREY *n* pl. **-PHREYS** an ornamental band or border

ORPIMENT *n* pl. **-S** a yellow dye

ORPIN *n* pl. **-S** orpine

ORPINE *n* pl. **-S** a perennial herb

ORRA *adj* occasional

ORRERY *n* pl. **-RERIES** a mechanical model of the solar system

ORRICE *n* pl. **-S** orris

ORRIS *n* pl. **-RISES** a flowering plant

ORT *n* pl. **-S** a scrap of food

ORTHICON *n* pl. **-S** a type of television camera tube

ORTHO *adj* pertaining to reproduction in a photograph of the full range of colors in nature

ORTHODOX *n* pl. **-ES** one holding traditional beliefs

ORTHOEPY *n* pl. **-EPIES** the study of correct pronunciation

ORTHOSIS *n* pl. **-THOSES** an orthotic

ORTHOTIC *n* pl. **-S** a brace for weak joints or muscles

ORTOLAN *n* pl. **-S** a European bird

ORYX *n* pl. **-ES** an African antelope

ORZO *n* pl. **-ZOS** rice-shaped pasta

OS *n* pl. **ORA** an orifice

OS *n* pl. **OSAR** an esker

OS *n* pl. **OSSA** a bone

OSCAR *n* pl. **-S** a South American fish

OSCINE *n* pl. **-S** any of a family of songbirds **OSCININE** *adj*

OSCITANT *adj* yawning

OSCULA pl. of osculum

OSCULANT *adj* adhering closely

OSCULAR *adj* pertaining to the mouth

OSCULATE *v* **-LATED, -LATING, -LATES** to kiss

OSCULE *n* pl. **-S** osculum

OSCULUM *n* pl. **-LA** an opening in a sponge

OSE *n* pl. **-S** an esker

OSETRA *n* pl. **-S** a golden or brownish caviar

OSIER *n* pl. **-S** a European tree **OSIERED** *adj*

OSMATIC *adj* depending mainly on the sense of smell

OSMICS *n/pl* the study of the sense of smell

OSMIUM *n* pl. **-S** a metallic element **OSMIC, OSMIOUS** *adj*

OSMOL *n* pl. **-S** a unit of osmotic pressure **OSMOLAL** *adj*

OSMOLAR *adj* osmotic

OSMOLE *n* pl. **-S** osmol

OSMOSE *v* **-MOSED, -MOSING, -MOSES** to undergo osmosis

OSMOSIS *n* pl. **-MOSES** a form of diffusion of a fluid through a membrane

OSMOTIC *adj* pertaining to osmosis

OSMOUS *adj* containing osmium

OSMUND *n* pl. **-S** any of a genus of large ferns

OSMUNDA *n* pl. **-S** osmund

OSNABURG *n* pl. **-S** a cotton fabric

OSPREY *n* pl. **-PREYS** an American hawk

OSSA pl. of os

OSSATURE *n* pl. **-S** a framework

OSSEIN *n* pl. **-S** a protein substance in bone

OSSEOUS *adj* resembling bone

OSSETRA *n* pl. **-S** osetra

OSSIA *conj* or else — used as a musical direction

OSSICLE *n* pl. **-S** a small bone

OSSIFIC *adj* pertaining to the formation of bone

OSSIFIER *n* pl. **-S** one that ossifies

OSSIFY *v* **-FIED, -FYING, -FIES** to convert into bone

OSSOBUCO *n* pl. **-COS** a dish of veal shanks braised with vegetables and white wine

OSSUARY *n* pl. **-ARIES** a receptacle for the bones of the dead

OSTEAL *adj* osseous

OSTEITIS *n* pl. **-ITIDES** inflammation of bone **OSTEITIC** *adj*

OSTEOID *n* pl. **-S** uncalcified bone matrix

OSTEOMA *n* pl. **-MAS** or **-MATA** a tumor of bone tissue

OSTEOSIS *n* pl. **-OSISES** or **-OSES** the formation of bone

OSTIA pl. of ostium

OSTIARY *n* pl. **-ARIES** a doorkeeper at a church

OSTINATO *n* pl. **-TOS** or **-TI** a constantly recurring musical phrase

OSTIOLE *n* pl. **-S** a small bodily opening **OSTIOLAR** *adj*

OSTIUM *n* pl. **OSTIA** an opening in a bodily organ

OSTLER *n* pl. **-S** hostler

OSTMARK *n* pl. **-S** a former East German monetary unit

OSTOMATE *n* pl. **-S** one who has had an ostomy

OSTOMY *n* pl. **-MIES** a type of surgical operation

OSTOSIS *n* pl. **-TOSISES** or **-TOSES** the formation of bone

OSTRACOD *n* pl. **-S** a minute freshwater crustacean

OSTRACON *n* pl. **-CA** a fragment containing an inscription

OSTRAKON *n* pl. **-KA** ostracon

OSTRICH *n* pl. **-ES** a large, flightless bird

OTAKU *n/pl* young people in Japan who are highly skilled in computer technology

OTALGIA *n* pl. **-S** pain in the ear **OTALGIC** *adj*

OTALGY *n* pl. **-GIES** otalgia

OTHER *n* pl. **-S** one that remains of two or more

OTIC *adj* pertaining to the ear

OTIOSE *adj* lazy **OTIOSELY** *adv*

OTIOSITY *n* pl. **-TIES** the state of being otiose

OTITIS *n* pl. **OTITISES** or **OTITIDES** inflammation of the ear **OTITIC** *adj*

OTOCYST *n* pl. **-S** an organ of balance in many invertebrates

OTOLITH *n* pl. **-S** a hard mass that forms in the inner ear

OTOLOGY *n* pl. **-GIES** the science of the ear **OTOLOGIC** *adj*

OTOSCOPE *n* pl. **-S** an instrument for examining the ear

OTOSCOPY *n* pl. **-PIES** the use of an otoscope

OTOTOXIC *adj* adversely affecting hearing or balance

OTTAR *n* pl. **-S** attar

OTTAVA *n* pl. **-S** an octave

OTTER *n* pl. **-S** a carnivorous mammal

OTTO *n* pl. **-TOS** attar

OTTOMAN *n* pl. **-S** a type of sofa

OUABAIN *n* pl. **-S** a cardiac stimulant

OUCH   *v* **-ED, -ING, -ES** to ornament with ouches (settings for precious stones)

OUD   *n* pl. **-S** a stringed instrument of northern Africa

OUGHT   *v* **-ED, -ING, -S** to owe

OUGIYA   *n* pl. **-S** ouguiya

OUGUIYA   *n* pl. **-S** a monetary unit of Mauritania

OUISTITI   *n* pl. **-S** a South American monkey

OUNCE   *n* pl. **-S** a unit of weight

OUPH   *n* pl. **-S** ouphe

OUPHE   *n* pl. **-S** an elf

OUR   *pron* a possessive form of the pronoun we

OURANG   *n* pl. **-S** orang

OURARI   *n* pl. **-S** curare

OUREBI   *n* pl. **-S** oribi

OURIE   *adj* shivering with cold

OURS   *pron* a possessive form of the pronoun we

OURSELF   *pron* myself — used in formal or regal contexts

OUSEL   *n* pl. **-S** ouzel

OUST   *v* **-ED, -ING, -S** to expel or remove from a position or place

OUSTER   *n* pl. **-S** the act of ousting

OUT   *v* **-ED, -ING, -S** to be revealed

OUTACT   *v* **-ED, -ING, -S** to surpass in acting

OUTADD   *v* **-ED, -ING, -S** to surpass in adding

OUTAGE   *n* pl. **-S** a failure or interruption in use or functioning

OUTARGUE   *v* **-GUED, -GUING, -GUES** to get the better of by arguing

OUTASK   *v* **-ED, -ING, -S** to surpass in asking

OUTATE   past tense of outeat

OUTBACK   *n* pl. **-S** isolated rural country

OUTBAKE   *v* **-BAKED, -BAKING, -BAKES** to surpass in baking

OUTBARK   *v* **-ED, -ING, -S** to surpass in barking

OUTBAWL   *v* **-ED, -ING, -S** to surpass in bawling

OUTBEAM   *v* **-ED, -ING, -S** to surpass in beaming

OUTBEG   *v* **-BEGGED, -BEGGING, -BEGS** to surpass in begging

OUTBID   *v* **-BID, -BIDDEN, -BIDDING, -BIDS** to bid higher than

OUTBITCH   *v* **-ED, -ING, -ES** to surpass in bitching

OUTBLAZE   *v* **-BLAZED, -BLAZING, -BLAZES** to surpass in brilliance of light

OUTBLEAT   *v* **-ED, -ING, -S** to surpass in bleating

OUTBLESS   *v* **-ED, -ING, -ES** to surpass in blessing

OUTBLOOM   *v* **-ED, -ING, -S** to surpass in blooming

OUTBLUFF   *v* **-ED, -ING, -S** to surpass in bluffing

OUTBLUSH   *v* **-ED, -ING, -ES** to surpass in blushing

OUTBOARD   *n* pl. **-S** a type of motor

OUTBOAST   *v* **-ED, -ING, -S** to surpass in boasting

OUTBOUGHT   past tense of outbuy

OUTBOUND   *adj* outward bound

OUTBOX   *v* **-ED, -ING, -ES** to surpass in boxing

OUTBRAG   *v* **-BRAGGED, -BRAGGING, -BRAGS** to surpass in bragging

OUTBRAVE   *v* **-BRAVED, -BRAVING, -BRAVES** to surpass in courage

OUTBRAWL   *v* **-ED, -ING, -S** to surpass in brawling

OUTBREAK   *n* pl. **-S** a sudden eruption

OUTBREED   *v* **-BRED, -BREEDING, -BREEDS** to interbreed relatively unrelated stocks

OUTBRIBE   *v* **-BRIBED, -BRIBING, -BRIBES** to surpass in bribing

OUTBUILD   *v* **-BUILT, -BUILDING, -BUILDS** to surpass in building

OUTBULGE   *v* **-BULGED, -BULGING, -BULGES** to surpass in size

OUTBULK   *v* **-ED, -ING, -S** to surpass in bulking

OUTBULLY   *v* **-LIED, -LYING, -LIES** to surpass in bullying

OUTBURN   *v* **-BURNED** or **-BURNT, -BURNING, -BURNS** to burn longer than

OUTBURST   *n* pl. **-S** a sudden and violent outpouring

OUTBUY   *v* **-BOUGHT, -BUYING, -BUYS** to surpass in buying

OUTBY   *adv* outdoors

OUTBYE   *adv* outby

OUTCALL *n* pl. **-S** a house call by a professional person

OUTCAPER *v* **-ED, -ING, -S** to surpass in capering

OUTCAST *n* pl. **-S** one that is cast out

OUTCASTE *v* **-CASTED, -CASTEING, -CASTES** to expel from one's caste

OUTCATCH *v* **-CAUGHT, -CATCHING, -CATCHES** to surpass in catching

OUTCAVIL *v* **-ILED, -ILING, -ILS** or **-ILLED, -ILLING, -ILS** to surpass in caviling

OUTCHARM *v* **-ED, -ING, -S** to surpass in charming

OUTCHEAT *v* **-ED, -ING, -S** to surpass in cheating

OUTCHIDE *v* **-CHIDED** or **-CHID, -CHIDDEN, -CHIDING, -CHIDES** to surpass in chiding

OUTCITY *n* pl. **-TIES** a city on the outskirts of a larger city

OUTCLASS *v* **-ED, -ING, -ES** to surpass so decisively as to appear of a higher class

OUTCLIMB *v* **-CLIMBED** or **-CLOMB, -CLIMBING, -CLIMBS** to surpass in climbing

OUTCOACH *v* **-ED, -ING, -ES** to surpass in coaching

OUTCOME *n* pl. **-S** a result

OUTCOOK *v* **-ED, -ING, -S** to surpass in cooking

OUTCOUNT *v* **-ED, -ING, -S** to surpass in counting

OUTCRAWL *v* **-ED, -ING, -S** to surpass in crawling

OUTCRIED past tense of outcry

OUTCRIES present 3d person sing. of outcry

OUTCROP *v* **-CROPPED, -CROPPING, -CROPS** to protrude above the soil

OUTCROSS *v* **-ED, -ING, -ES** to cross with a relatively unrelated individual

OUTCROW *v* **-ED, -ING, -S** to surpass in crowing

OUTCROWD *v* **-ED, -ING, -S** to cause to be too crowded

OUTCRY *v* **-CRIED, -CRYING, -CRIES** to cry louder than

OUTCURSE *v* **-CURSED, -CURSING, -CURSES** to surpass in cursing

OUTCURVE *n* pl. **-S** a type of pitch in baseball

OUTDANCE *v* **-DANCED, -DANCING, -DANCES** to surpass in dancing

OUTDARE *v* **-DARED, -DARING, -DARES** to surpass in daring

OUTDATE *v* **-DATED, -DATING, -DATES** to make out-of-date

OUTDO *v* **-DID, -DONE, -DOING, -DOES** to exceed in performance

OUTDODGE *v* **-DODGED, -DODGING, -DODGES** to surpass in dodging

OUTDOER *n* pl. **-S** one that outdoes

OUTDOOR *adj* pertaining to the open air

OUTDOORS *adv* in the open air

OUTDRAG *v* **-DRAGGED, -DRAGGING, -DRAGS** to surpass in drag racing

OUTDRANK past tense of outdrink

OUTDRAW *v* **-DREW, -DRAWN, -DRAWING, -DRAWS** to attract a larger audience than

OUTDREAM *v* **-DREAMED** or **-DREAMT, -DREAMING, -DREAMS** to surpass in dreaming

OUTDRESS *v* **-ED, -ING, -ES** to surpass in dressing

OUTDRINK *v* **-DRANK, -DRUNK, -DRINKING, -DRINKS** to surpass in drinking

OUTDRIVE *v* **-DROVE, -DRIVEN, -DRIVING, -DRIVES** to drive a golf ball farther than

OUTDROP *v* **-DROPPED, -DROPPING, -DROPS** to surpass in dropping

OUTDUEL *v* **-DUELED, -DUELING, -DUELS** or **-DUELLED, -DUELLING, -DUELS** to surpass in dueling

OUTEARN *v* **-ED, -ING, -S** to surpass in earning

OUTEAT *v* **-ATE, -EATEN, -EATING, -EATS** to surpass in eating

OUTECHO *v* **-ED, -ING, -ES** to surpass in echoing

OUTER *n* pl. **-S** a part of a target

OUTFABLE *v* **-BLED, -BLING, -BLES** to surpass in fabling

OUTFACE *v* **-FACED, -FACING, -FACES** to confront unflinchingly

OUTFALL *n* pl. **-S** the outlet of a body of water

OUTFAST *v* **-ED, -ING, -S** to surpass in fasting

OUTFAWN *v* **-ED, -ING, -S** to surpass in fawning

OUTFEAST *v* **-ED, -ING, -S** to surpass in feasting

OUTFEEL *v* **-FELT, -FEELING, -FEELS** to surpass in feeling

OUTFENCE *v* **-FENCED, -FENCING, -FENCES** to surpass in fencing

OUTFIELD *n* pl. **-S** a part of a baseball field

OUTFIGHT *v* **-FOUGHT, -FIGHTING, -FIGHTS** to defeat

OUTFIND *v* **-FOUND, -FINDING, -FINDS** to surpass in finding

OUTFIRE *v* **-FIRED, -FIRING, -FIRES** to surpass in firing

OUTFISH *v* **-ED, -ING, -ES** to surpass in fishing

OUTFIT *v* **-FITTED, -FITTING, -FITS** to equip

OUTFLANK *v* **-ED, -ING, -S** to gain a tactical advantage over

OUTFLOAT *v* **-ED, -ING, -S** to float longer than

OUTFLOW *v* **-ED, -ING, -S** to flow out

OUTFLY *v* **-FLEW, -FLOWN, -FLYING, -FLIES** to surpass in speed of flight

OUTFOOL *v* **-ED, -ING, -S** to surpass in fooling

OUTFOOT *v* **-ED, -ING, -S** to surpass in speed

OUTFOUGHT past tense of outfight

OUTFOUND past tense of outfind

OUTFOX *v* **-ED, -ING, -ES** to outwit

OUTFROWN *v* **-ED, -ING, -S** to frown more than

OUTGAIN *v* **-ED, -ING, -S** to gain more than

OUTGAS *v* **-GASSED, -GASSING, -GASSES** or **-GASES** to remove gas from

OUTGAZE *v* **-GAZED, -GAZING, -GAZES** to surpass in gazing

OUTGIVE *v* **-GAVE, -GIVEN, -GIVING, -GIVES** to give more than

OUTGLARE *v* **-GLARED, -GLARING, -GLARES** to surpass in glaring

OUTGLEAM *v* **-ED, -ING, -S** to surpass in gleaming

OUTGLOW *v* **-ED, -ING, -S** to surpass in glowing

OUTGNAW *v* **-GNAWED, -GNAWN, -GNAWING, -GNAWS** to surpass in gnawing

OUTGO *v* **-WENT, -GONE, -GOING, -GOES** to go beyond

OUTGOING *n* pl. **-S** a departure

OUTGREW past tense of outgrow

OUTGRIN *v* **-GRINNED, -GRINNING, -GRINS** to surpass in grinning

OUTGROSS *v* **-ED, -ING, -ES** to surpass in gross earnings

OUTGROUP *n* pl. **-S** a group of people outside one's own group

OUTGROW *v* **-GREW, -GROWN, -GROWING, -GROWS** to grow too large for

OUTGUESS *v* **-ED, -ING, -ES** to anticipate the actions of

OUTGUIDE *v* **-GUIDED, -GUIDING, -GUIDES** to surpass in guiding

OUTGUN *v* **-GUNNED, -GUNNING, -GUNS** to surpass in firepower

OUTGUSH *v* **-ED, -ING, -ES** to surpass in gushing

OUTHAUL *n* pl. **-S** a rope for extending a sail along a spar

OUTHEAR *v* **-HEARD, -HEARING, -HEARS** to surpass in hearing

OUTHIT *v* **-HIT, -HITTING, -HITS** to get more hits than

OUTHOMER *v* **-ED, -ING, -S** to surpass in hitting home runs

OUTHOUSE *n* pl. **-S** a toilet housed in a small structure

OUTHOWL *v* **-ED, -ING, -S** to surpass in howling

OUTHUMOR *v* **-ED, -ING, -S** to surpass in humoring

OUTHUNT *v* **-ED, -ING, -S** to surpass in hunting

OUTING *n* pl. **-S** a short pleasure trip

OUTJINX *v* **-ED, -ING, -ES** to surpass in jinxing

OUTJUMP *v* **-ED, -ING, -S** to surpass in jumping

OUTJUT *v* **-JUTTED, -JUTTING, -JUTS** to stick out

OUTKEEP *v* **-KEPT, -KEEPING, -KEEPS** to surpass in keeping

OUTKICK *v* **-ED, -ING, -S** to surpass in kicking

OUTKILL *v* **-ED, -ING, -S** to surpass in killing

OUTKISS *v* **-ED, -ING, -ES** to surpass in kissing

OUTLAID past tense of outlay

OUTLAIN past participle of outlie

OUTLAND *n* pl. **-S** a foreign land

OUTLAST *v* **-ED, -ING, -S** to last longer than

OUTLAUGH *v* **-ED, -ING, -S** to surpass in laughing

OUTLAW *v* **-ED, -ING, -S** to prohibit

OUTLAWRY *n* pl. **-RIES** habitual defiance of the law

OUTLAY *v* **-LAID, -LAYING, -LAYS** to pay out

OUTLEAD *v* **-LED, -LEADING, -LEADS** to surpass in leading

OUTLEAP *v* **-LEAPED** or **-LEAPT, -LEAPING, -LEAPS** to surpass in leaping

OUTLEARN *v* **-LEARNED** or **-LEARNT, -LEARNING, -LEARNS** to surpass in learning

OUTLET *n* pl. **-S** a passage for escape or discharge

OUTLIE *v* **-LAY, -LAIN, -LYING, -LIES** to lie beyond

OUTLIER *n* pl. **-S** an outlying area or portion

OUTLINE *v* **-LINED, -LINING, -LINES** to indicate the main features or different parts of

OUTLINER *n* pl. **-S** one that outlines

OUTLIVE *v* **-LIVED, -LIVING, -LIVES** to live longer than

OUTLIVER *n* pl. **-S** one that outlives

OUTLOOK *n* pl. **-S** a point of view

OUTLOVE *v* **-LOVED, -LOVING, -LOVES** to surpass in loving

OUTLYING present participle of outlie

OUTMAN *v* **-MANNED, -MANNING, -MANS** to surpass in manpower

OUTMARCH *v* **-ED, -ING, -ES** to surpass in marching

OUTMATCH *v* **-ED, -ING, -ES** to outdo

OUTMODE *v* **-MODED, -MODING, -MODES** to outdate

OUTMOST *adj* farthest out

OUTMOVE *v* **-MOVED, -MOVING, -MOVES** to move faster or farther than

OUTPACE *v* **-PACED, -PACING, -PACES** to surpass in speed

OUTPAINT *v* **-ED, -ING, -S** to surpass in painting

OUTPASS *v* **-ED, -ING, -ES** to excel in passing a football

OUTPITCH *v* **-ED, -ING, -ES** to surpass in pitching

OUTPITY *v* **-PITIED, -PITYING, -PITIES** to surpass in pitying

OUTPLACE *v* **-PLACED, -PLACING, -PLACES** to discontinue the employment of

OUTPLAN *v* **-PLANNED, -PLANNING, -PLANS** to surpass in planning

OUTPLAY *v* **-ED, -ING, -S** to excel or defeat in a game

OUTPLOD *v* **-PLODDED, -PLODDING, -PLODS** to surpass in plodding

OUTPLOT *v* **-PLOTTED, -PLOTTING, -PLOTS** to surpass in plotting

OUTPOINT *v* **-ED, -ING, -S** to score more points than

OUTPOLL *v* **-ED, -ING, -S** to get more votes than

OUTPORT *n* pl. **-S** a port of export or departure

OUTPOST *n* pl. **-S** a body of troops stationed at a distance from the main body

OUTPOUR *v* **-ED, -ING, -S** to pour out

OUTPOWER *v* **-ED, -ING, -S** to surpass in power

OUTPRAY *v* **-ED, -ING, -S** to surpass in praying

OUTPREEN *v* **-ED, -ING, -S** to surpass in preening

OUTPRESS *v* **-ED, -ING, -ES** to surpass in pressing

OUTPRICE *v* **-PRICED, -PRICING, -PRICES** to surpass in pricing

OUTPSYCH *v* **-ED, -ING, -S** to defeat by psychological means

OUTPULL *v* **-ED, -ING, -S** to attract a larger audience or following than

OUTPUNCH *v* **-ED, -ING, -ES** to surpass in punching

OUTPUPIL *n* **-S** a pupil who lives off campus

OUTPUSH *v* **-ED, -ING, -ES** to surpass in pushing

OUTPUT *v* **-PUTTED, -PUTTING, -PUTS** to produce

OUTQUOTE *v* **-QUOTED, -QUOTING, -QUOTES** to surpass in quoting

OUTRACE *v* **-RACED, -RACING, -RACES** to run faster or farther than

OUTRAGE *v* **-RAGED, -RAGING, -RAGES** to arouse anger or resentment in

OUTRAISE *v* **-RAISED, -RAISING, -RAISES** to surpass in raising

OUTRAN past tense of outrun

OUTRANCE *n* pl. **-S** the last extremity

OUTRANG past tense of outring

OUTRANGE *v* **-RANGED, -RANGING, -RANGES** to surpass in range

OUTRANK *v* **-ED, -ING, -S** to rank higher than

OUTRATE *v* **-RATED, -RATING, -RATES** to surpass in a rating

OUTRAVE   *v* **-RAVED, -RAVING, -RAVES** to surpass in raving

OUTRE   *adj* deviating from what is usual or proper

OUTREACH   *v* **-ED, -ING, -ES** to reach beyond

OUTREAD   *v* **-READ, -READING, -READS** to surpass in reading

OUTRIDE   *v* **-RODE, -RIDDEN, -RIDING, -RIDES** to ride faster or better than

OUTRIDER   *n* pl. **-S** a mounted attendant who rides before or beside a carriage

OUTRIG   *v* **-RIGGED, -RIGGING, -RIGS** to equip (a boat) with outriggers (projections having floats)

OUTRIGHT   *adj* being without limit or reservation

OUTRING   *v* **-RANG, -RUNG, -RINGING, -RINGS** to ring louder than

OUTRIVAL   *v* **-VALED, -VALING, -VALS** or **-VALLED, -VALLING, -VALS** to outdo in a competition or rivalry

OUTRO   *n* pl. **-S** a concluding passage of a piece of music

OUTROAR   *v* **-ED, -ING, -S** to roar louder than

OUTROCK   *v* **-ED, -ING, -S** to surpass in rocking

OUTRODE   past tense of outride

OUTROLL   *v* **-ED, -ING, -S** to roll out

OUTROOT   *v* **-ED, -ING, -S** to pull up by the roots

OUTROW   *v* **-ED, -ING, -S** to surpass in rowing

OUTRUN   *v* **-RAN, -RUNNING, -RUNS** to run faster than

OUTRUNG   past participle of outring

OUTRUSH   *v* **-ED, -ING, -ES** to surpass in rushing

OUTSAID   past tense of outsay

OUTSAIL   *v* **-ED, -ING, -S** to sail faster than

OUTSANG   past tense of outsing

OUTSAT   past tense of outsit

OUTSAVOR   *v* **-ED, -ING, -S** to surpass in a distinctive taste or smell

OUTSAW   past tense of outsee

OUTSAY   *v* **-SAID, -SAYING, -SAYS** to surpass in saying

OUTSCOLD   *v* **-ED, -ING, -S** to surpass in scolding

OUTSCOOP   *v* **-ED, -ING, -S** to surpass in scooping

OUTSCORE   *v* **-SCORED, -SCORING, -SCORES** to score more points than

OUTSCORN   *v* **-ED, -ING, -S** to surpass in scorning

OUTSEE   *v* **-SAW, -SEEN, -SEEING, -SEES** to see beyond

OUTSELL   *v* **-SOLD, -SELLING, -SELLS** to sell more than

OUTSERT   *n* pl. **-S** a folded sheet placed around a folded section of printed matter

OUTSERVE   *v* **-SERVED, -SERVING, -SERVES** to surpass in serving

OUTSET   *n* pl. **-S** a beginning

OUTSHAME   *v* **-SHAMED, -SHAMING, -SHAMES** to surpass in shaming

OUTSHINE   *v* **-SHONE** or **-SHINED, -SHINING, -SHINES** to shine brighter than

OUTSHOOT   *v* **-SHOT, -SHOOTING, -SHOOTS** to shoot better than

OUTSHOUT   *v* **-ED, -ING, -S** to shout louder than

OUTSIDE   *n* pl. **-S** the outer side, surface, or part

OUTSIDER   *n* pl. **-S** one that does not belong to a particular group

OUTSIGHT   *n* pl. **-S** the power of perceiving external things

OUTSIN   *v* **-SINNED, -SINNING, -SINS** to surpass in sinning

OUTSING   *v* **-SANG, -SUNG, -SINGING, -SINGS** to surpass in singing

OUTSIT   *v* **-SAT, -SITTING, -SITS** to remain sitting or in session longer than

OUTSIZE   *n* pl. **-S** an unusual size **OUTSIZED** *adj*

OUTSKATE   *v* **-SKATED, -SKATING, -SKATES** to surpass in skating

OUTSKIRT   *n* pl. **-S** an outlying area

OUTSLEEP   *v* **-SLEPT, -SLEEPING, -SLEEPS** to sleep later than

OUTSLICK   *v* **-ED, -ING, -S** to get the better of by trickery or cunning

OUTSMART   *v* **-ED, -ING, -S** to outwit

OUTSMELL   *v* **-SMELLED** or **-SMELT, -SMELLING, -SMELLS** to surpass in smelling

OUTSMILE   *v* **-SMILED, -SMILING, -SMILES** to surpass in smiling

OUTSMOKE   *v* **-SMOKED, -SMOKING, -SMOKES** to surpass in smoking

OUTSNORE *v* **-SNORED, -SNORING, -SNORES** to surpass in snoring

OUTSOAR *v* **-ED, -ING, -S** to soar beyond

OUTSOLD past tense of outsell

OUTSOLE *n* pl. **-S** the outer sole of a boot or shoe

OUTSPAN *v* **-SPANNED, -SPANNING, -SPANS** to unharness a draft animal

OUTSPEAK *v* **-SPOKE, -SPOKEN, -SPEAKING, -SPEAKS** to outdo in speaking

OUTSPEED *v* **-SPED** or **-SPEEDED, -SPEEDING, -SPEEDS** to go faster than

OUTSPELL *v* **-SPELLED** or **-SPELT, -SPELLING, -SPELLS** to surpass in spelling

OUTSPEND *v* **-SPENT, -SPENDING, -SPENDS** to exceed the limits of in spending

OUTSPOKE past tense of outspeak

OUTSPOKEN past participle of outspeak

OUTSTAND *v* **-STOOD, -STANDING, -STANDS** to endure beyond

OUTSTARE *v* **-STARED, -STARING, -STARES** to outface

OUTSTART *v* **-ED, -ING, -S** to get ahead of at the start

OUTSTATE *v* **-STATED, -STATING, -STATES** to surpass in stating

OUTSTAY *v* **-ED, -ING, -S** to surpass in staying power

OUTSTEER *v* **-ED, -ING, -S** to surpass in steering

OUTSTEP *v* **-STEPPED, -STEPPING, -STEPS** to step beyond

OUTSTOOD past tense of outstand

OUTSTRIP *v* **-STRIPPED, -STRIPPING, -STRIPS** to go faster or farther than

OUTSTUDY *v* **-STUDIED, -STUDYING, -STUDIES** to surpass in studying

OUTSTUNT *v* **-ED, -ING, -S** to surpass in stunting

OUTSULK *v* **-ED, -ING, -S** to surpass in sulking

OUTSUNG past participle of outsing

OUTSWEAR *v* **-SWORE** or **-SWARE, -SWORN, -SWEARING, -SWEARS** to surpass in swearing

OUTSWEEP *v* **-SWEPT, -SWEEPING, -SWEEPS** to surpass in sweeping

OUTSWIM *v* **-SWAM, -SWUM, -SWIMMING, -SWIMS** to swim faster or farther than

OUTSWING *v* **-SWUNG, -SWINGING, -SWINGS** to surpass in swinging

OUTTAKE *n* pl. **-S** a passage outwards

OUTTALK *v* **-ED, -ING, -S** to surpass in talking

OUTTASK *v* **-ED, -ING, -S** to surpass in tasking

OUTTELL *v* **-TOLD, -TELLING, -TELLS** to say openly

OUTTHANK *v* **-ED, -ING, -S** to surpass in thanking

OUTTHINK *v* **-THOUGHT, -THINKING, -THINKS** to get the better of by thinking

OUTTHROB *v* **-THROBBED, -THROBBING, -THROBS** to surpass in throbbing

OUTTHROW *v* **-THREW, -THROWN, -THROWING, -THROWS** to throw farther or more accurately than

OUTTOLD past tense of outtell

OUTTOWER *v* **-ED, -ING, -S** to tower above

OUTTRADE *v* **-TRADED, -TRADING, -TRADES** to get the better of in a trade

OUTTRICK *v* **-ED, -ING, -S** to get the better of by trickery

OUTTROT *v* **-TROTTED, -TROTTING, -TROTS** to surpass in trotting

OUTTRUMP *v* **-ED, -ING, -S** to outplay

OUTTURN *n* pl. **-S** a quantity produced

OUTVALUE *v* **-UED, -UING, -UES** to be worth more than

OUTVAUNT *v* **-ED, -ING, -S** to surpass in vaunting

OUTVIE *v* **-VIED, -VYING, -VIES** to surpass in a competition

OUTVOICE *v* **-VOICED, -VOICING, -VOICES** to surpass in loudness of voice

OUTVOTE *v* **-VOTED, -VOTING, -VOTES** to defeat by a majority of votes

OUTWAIT *v* **-ED, -ING, -S** to exceed in patience

OUTWALK *v* **-ED, -ING, -S** to surpass in walking

OUTWAR *v* **-WARRED, -WARRING, -WARS** to surpass in warring

OUTWARD *adv* toward the outside

OUTWARDS *adv* outward

OUTWASH *n* pl. **-ES** detritus washed from a glacier

OUTWASTE *v* **-WASTED, -WASTING, -WASTES** to surpass in wasting

OUTWATCH *v* **-ED, -ING, -ES** to watch longer than

OUTWEAR *v* **-WORE, -WORN, -WEARING, -WEARS** to last longer than

OUTWEARY *v* **-RIED, -RYING, -RIES** to surpass in wearying

OUTWEEP *v* **-WEPT, -WEEPING, -WEEPS** to weep more than

OUTWEIGH *v* **-ED, -ING, -S** to weigh more than

OUTWENT past tense of outgo

OUTWHIRL *v* **-ED, -ING, -S** to surpass in whirling

OUTWILE *v* **-WILED, -WILING, -WILES** to surpass in wiling

OUTWILL *v* **-ED, -ING, -S** to surpass in willpower

OUTWIND *v* **-ED, -ING, -S** to cause to be out of breath

OUTWISH *v* **-ED, -ING, -ES** to surpass in wishing

OUTWIT *v* **-WITTED, -WITTING, -WITS** to get the better of by superior cleverness

OUTWITH *prep* beyond the limits of

OUTWORE past tense of outwear

OUTWORK *v* **-WORKED** or **-WROUGHT, -WORKING, -WORKS** to work faster or better than

OUTWORN past participle of outwear

OUTWRITE *v* **-WROTE** or **-WRIT, -WRITTEN, -WRITING, -WRITES** to write better than

OUTYELL *v* **-ED, -ING, -S** to yell louder than

OUTYELP *v* **-ED, -ING, -S** to surpass in yelping

OUTYIELD *v* **-ED, -ING, -S** to surpass in yield

OUZEL *n* pl. **-S** a European bird

OUZO *n* pl. **-ZOS** a Greek liqueur

OVA pl. of ovum

OVAL *n* pl. **-S** an oval (egg-shaped) figure or object

OVALITY *n* pl. **-TIES** ovalness

OVALLY *adv* in the shape of an oval

OVALNESS *n* pl. **-ES** the state of being oval

OVARIAL *adj* ovarian

OVARIAN *adj* pertaining to an ovary

OVARIES pl. of ovary

OVARIOLE *n* pl. **-S** one of the tubes of which the ovaries of most insects are composed

OVARITIS *n* pl. **-RITIDES** inflammation of an ovary

OVARY *n* pl. **-RIES** a female reproductive gland

OVATE *adj* egg-shaped **OVATELY** *adv*

OVATION *n* pl. **-S** an expression or demonstration of popular acclaim

OVEN *n* pl. **-S** an enclosed compartment in which substances are heated **OVENLIKE** *adj*

OVENBIRD *n* pl. **-S** an American songbird

OVENWARE *n* pl. **-S** heat-resistant dishes for baking and serving food

OVER *v* **-ED, -ING, -S** to leap above and to the other side of

OVERABLE *adj* excessively able

OVERACT *v* **-ED, -ING, -S** to act with exaggeration

OVERAGE *n* pl. **-S** an amount in excess

OVERAGED *adj* too old to be useful

OVERALL *n* pl. **-S** a loose outer garment

OVERAPT *adj* excessively apt

OVERARCH *v* **-ED, -ING, -ES** to form an arch over

OVERARM *v* **-ED, -ING, -S** to supply with an excess of weaponry

OVERATE past tense of overeat

OVERAWE *v* **-AWED, -AWING, -AWES** to subdue by inspiring awe

OVERBAKE *v* **-BAKED, -BAKING, -BAKES** to bake too long

OVERBEAR *v* **-BORE, -BORNE** or **-BORN, -BEARING, -BEARS** to bring down by superior weight or force

OVERBEAT *v* **-BEAT, -BEATEN, -BEATING, -BEATS** to beat too much

OVERBED *adj* spanning a bed

OVERBET *v* **-BET** or **-BETTED, -BETTING, -BETS** to bet too much

OVERBID *v* **-BID, -BID** or **-BIDDEN, -BIDDING, -BIDS** to bid higher than

OVERBIG *adj* too big

OVERBILL *v* **-ED, -ING, -S** to bill too much

OVERBITE *n* pl. **-S** a faulty closure of the teeth

OVERBLOW *v* **-BLEW, -BLOWN, -BLOWING, -BLOWS** to give excessive importance to

OVERBOIL v -ED, -ING, -S to boil too long

OVERBOLD adj excessively bold or forward

OVERBOOK v -ED, -ING, -S to issue reservations in excess of the space available

OVERBOOT n pl. -S a boot worn over a shoe or another boot

OVERBORE past tense of overbear

OVERBORN a past participle of overbear

OVERBORNE a past participle of overbear

OVERBOUGHT past tense of overbuy

OVERBRED adj bred too finely or to excess

OVERBURN v -BURNED or -BURNT, -BURNING, -BURNS to burn too long

OVERBUSY adj too busy

OVERBUY v -BOUGHT, -BUYING, -BUYS to buy in quantities exceeding need or demand

OVERCALL v -ED, -ING, -S to overbid

OVERCAME past tense of overcome

OVERCAST v -CAST or -CASTED, -CASTING, -CASTS to become cloudy or dark

OVERCOAT n pl. -S a warm coat worn over indoor clothing

OVERCOLD adj too cold

OVERCOME v -CAME, -COMING, -COMES to get the better of

OVERCOOK v -ED, -ING, -S to cook too long

OVERCOOL v -ED, -ING, -S to make too cool

OVERCOY adj too coy

OVERCRAM v -CRAMMED, -CRAMMING, -CRAMS to stuff or cram to excess

OVERCROP v -CROPPED, -CROPPING, -CROPS to exhaust the fertility of by cultivating to excess

OVERCURE v -CURED, -CURING, -CURES to cure too long

OVERCUT v -CUT, -CUTTING, -CUTS to cut too much

OVERDARE v -DARED, -DARING, -DARES to become too daring

OVERDEAR adj too dear; too costly

OVERDECK v -ED, -ING, -S to adorn extravagantly

OVERDO v -DID, -DONE, -DOING, -DOES to do to excess

OVERDOER n pl. -S one that overdoes

OVERDOG n pl. -S one that is dominant or victorious

OVERDOSE v -DOSED, -DOSING, -DOSES to give an excessive dose to

OVERDRAW v -DREW, -DRAWN, -DRAWING, -DRAWS to draw checks on in excess of the balance

OVERDRY v -DRIED, -DRYING, -DRIES to dry too much

OVERDUB v -DUBBED, -DUBBING, -DUBS to add sound to an existing recording

OVERDUE adj not paid when due

OVERDYE v -DYED, -DYEING, -DYES to dye with too much color

OVERDYER n pl. -S one that overdyes

OVEREASY adj too easy

OVEREAT v -ATE, -EATEN, -EATING, -EATS to eat to excess

OVEREDIT v -ED, -ING, -S to edit more than necessary

OVERFAR adj too great in distance, extent, or degree

OVERFAST adj too fast

OVERFAT adj too fat

OVERFEAR v -ED, -ING, -S to fear too much

OVERFEED v -FED, -FEEDING, -FEEDS to feed too much

OVERFILL v -ED, -ING, -S to fill to overflowing

OVERFINE adj excessively fine or particular

OVERFISH v -ED, -ING, -ES to deplete the supply of fish in an area by fishing to excess

OVERFIT adj fitted to excess

OVERFLOW v -FLOWED, -FLOWN, -FLOWING, -FLOWS to flow over the top of

OVERFLY v -FLEW, -FLOWN, -FLYING, -FLIES to fly over

OVERFOND adj too fond or affectionate

OVERFOUL adj too foul

OVERFREE adj too free

OVERFULL adj too full

OVERFUND v -ED, -ING, -S to fund more than required

OVERGILD v -GILDED or -GILT, -GILDING, -GILDS to gild over

OVERGIRD v -GIRDED or -GIRT, -GIRDING, -GIRDS to gird to excess

OVERGLAD adj too glad

OVERGOAD v -ED, -ING, -S to goad too much

OVERGROW v -GREW, -GROWN, -GROWING, -GROWS to grow over

OVERHAND *v* **-ED, -ING, -S** to sew with short, vertical stitches

OVERHANG *v* **-HUNG, -HANGING, -HANGS** to hang or project over

OVERHARD *adj* too hard

OVERHATE *v* **-HATED, -HATING, -HATES** to hate to excess

OVERHAUL *v* **-ED, -ING, -S** to examine carefully for needed repairs

OVERHEAD *n pl.* **-S** the general cost of running a business

OVERHEAP *v* **-ED, -ING, -S** to heap up or accumulate to excess

OVERHEAR *v* **-HEARD, -HEARING, -HEARS** to hear without the speaker's knowledge or intention

OVERHEAT *v* **-ED, -ING, -S** to heat to excess

OVERHIGH *adj* too high

OVERHOLD *v* **-HELD, -HOLDING, -HOLDS** to rate too highly

OVERHOLY *adj* too holy

OVERHOPE *v* **-HOPED, -HOPING, -HOPES** to hope exceedingly

OVERHOT *adj* too hot

OVERHUNG past tense of overhang

OVERHUNT *v* **-ED, -ING, -S** to deplete the supply of game in an area by hunting to excess

OVERHYPE *v* **-HYPED, -HYPING, -HYPES** to hype to excess

OVERIDLE *adj* too idle

OVERJOY *v* **-ED, -ING, -S** to fill with great joy

OVERJUST *adj* too just

OVERKEEN *adj* too keen

OVERKILL *v* **-ED, -ING, -S** to destroy with more nuclear force than required

OVERKIND *adj* too kind

OVERLADE *v* **-LADED, -LADEN, -LADING, -LADES** to load with too great a burden

OVERLAID past tense of overlay

OVERLAIN past participle of overlie

OVERLAND *n pl.* **-S** a train or stagecoach that travels over land

OVERLAP *v* **-LAPPED, -LAPPING, -LAPS** to extend over and cover a part of

OVERLATE *adj* too late

OVERLAX *adj* too lax

OVERLAY *v* **-LAID, -LAYING, -LAYS** to lay over

OVERLEAF *adv* on the other side of the page

OVERLEAP *v* **-LEAPED** or **-LEAPT, -LEAPING, -LEAPS** to leap over

OVERLEND *v* **-LENT, -LENDING, -LENDS** to lend too much

OVERLET *v* **-LET, -LETTING, -LETS** to let to excess

OVERLEWD *adj* too lewd

OVERLIE *v* **-LAY, -LAIN, -LYING, -LIES** to lie over

OVERLIT a past tense of overlight

OVERLIVE *v* **-LIVED, -LIVING, -LIVES** to outlive

OVERLOAD *v* **-ED, -ING, -S** to load to excess

OVERLONG *adj* too long

OVERLOOK *v* **-ED, -ING, -S** to fail to notice

OVERLORD *v* **-ED, -ING, -S** to rule tyrannically

OVERLOUD *adj* too loud

OVERLOVE *v* **-LOVED, -LOVING, -LOVES** to love to excess

OVERLUSH *adj* excessively lush

OVERLY *adv* to an excessive degree

OVERLYING present participle of overlie

OVERMAN *n pl.* **-MEN** a foreman

OVERMAN *v* **-MANNED, -MANNING, -MANS** to provide with more men than are needed

OVERMANY *adj* too many

OVERMEEK *adj* excessively meek

OVERMELT *v* **-ED, -ING, -S** to melt too much

OVERMEN pl. of overman

OVERMILD *adj* too mild

OVERMILK *v* **-ED, -ING, -S** to milk to excess

OVERMINE *v* **-MINED, -MINING, -MINES** to mine to excess

OVERMIX *v* **-ED, -ING, -ES** to mix too much

OVERMUCH *n pl.* **-ES** an excess

OVERNEAR *adj* too near

OVERNEAT *adj* too neat

OVERNEW *adj* too new

OVERNICE *adj* excessively nice

OVERPACK *v* **-ED, -ING, -S** to pack to excess

OVERPASS *v* **-PASSED** or **-PAST, -PASSING, -PASSES** to pass over

OVERPAY *v* **-PAID, -PAYING, -PAYS** to pay too much

OVERPERT *adj* too pert

OVERPLAN *v* **-PLANNED, -PLANNING, -PLANS** to plan to excess

OVERPLAY *v* **-ED, -ING, -S** to exaggerate

OVERPLOT *v* **-PLOTTED, -PLOTTING, -PLOTS** to devise an overly complex plot for

OVERPLUS *n* pl. **-ES** a surplus

OVERPLY *v* **-PLIED, -PLYING, -PLIES** to ply to excess; overwork

OVERPUMP *v* **-ED, -ING, -S** to pump to excess

OVERRAN past tense of overrun

OVERRANK *adj* too luxuriant in growth

OVERRASH *adj* too rash

OVERRATE *v* **-RATED, -RATING, -RATES** to rate too highly

OVERRICH *adj* too rich

OVERRIDE *v* **-RODE, -RIDDEN, -RIDING, -RIDES** to ride over

OVERRIFE *adj* too rife

OVERRIPE *adj* too ripe

OVERRUDE *adj* excessively rude

OVERRUFF *v* **-ED, -ING, -S** to trump with a higher trump card than has already been played

OVERRULE *v* **-RULED, -RULING, -RULES** to disallow the arguments of

OVERRUN *v* **-RAN, -RUNNING, -RUNS** to spread or swarm over

OVERSAD *adj* excessively sad

OVERSALE *n* pl. **-S** the act of overselling

OVERSALT *v* **-ED, -ING, -S** to salt to excess

OVERSAVE *v* **-SAVED, -SAVING, -SAVES** to save too much

OVERSEA *adv* overseas

OVERSEAS *adv* beyond or across the sea

OVERSEE *v* **-SAW, -SEEN, -SEEING, -SEES** to watch over and direct

OVERSEED *v* **-ED, -ING, -S** to seed to excess

OVERSEER *n* pl. **-S** one that oversees

OVERSELL *v* **-SOLD, -SELLING, -SELLS** to sell more of than can be delivered

OVERSET *v* **-SET, -SETTING, -SETS** to turn or tip over

OVERSEW *v* **-SEWED, -SEWN, -SEWING, -SEWS** to overhand

OVERSHOE *n* pl. **-S** a protective outer shoe

OVERSHOT *n* pl. **-S** a type of fabric weave

OVERSICK *adj* too sick

OVERSIDE *n* pl. **-S** the other side of a phonograph record

OVERSIZE *n* pl. **-S** an unusually large size

OVERSLIP *v* **-SLIPPED** or **-SLIPT, -SLIPPING, -SLIPS** to leave out

OVERSLOW *adj* too slow

OVERSOAK *v* **-ED, -ING, -S** to soak too much

OVERSOFT *adj* too soft

OVERSOLD past tense of oversell

OVERSOON *adv* too soon

OVERSOUL *n* pl. **-S** a supreme reality or mind in transcendentalism

OVERSPIN *n* pl. **-S** a forward spin imparted to a ball

OVERSTAY *v* **-ED, -ING, -S** to stay beyond the limits or duration of

OVERSTEP *v* **-STEPPED, -STEPPING, -STEPS** to go beyond

OVERSTIR *v* **-STIRRED, -STIRRING, -STIRS** to stir too much

OVERSUDS *v* **-ED, -ING, -ES** to form an excessive amount of suds

OVERSUP *v* **-SUPPED, -SUPPING, -SUPS** to sup to excess

OVERSURE *adj* too sure

OVERT *adj* open to view

OVERTAKE *v* **-TOOK, -TAKEN, -TAKING, -TAKES** to catch up with

OVERTALK *v* **-ED, -ING, -S** to talk to excess

OVERTAME *adj* too tame

OVERTART *adj* too tart

OVERTASK *v* **-ED, -ING, -S** to task too severely

OVERTAX *v* **-ED, -ING, -ES** to tax too heavily

OVERTHIN *adj* too thin

OVERTIME *v* **-TIMED, -TIMING, -TIMES** to exceed the desired timing for

OVERTIP *v* **-TIPPED, -TIPPING, -TIPS** to tip more than what is customary

OVERTIRE *v* **-TIRED, -TIRING, -TIRES** to tire excessively

OVERTLY *adv* in an overt manner

OVERTOIL *v* **-ED, -ING, -S** to wear out or exhaust by excessive toil

OVERTONE *n* pl. **-S** a higher partial tone

OVERTOOK past tense of overtake

OVERTOP *v* **-TOPPED, -TOPPING, -TOPS** to rise above the top of

OVERTRIM *v* **-TRIMMED, -TRIMMING, -TRIMS** to trim too much

OVERTURE _v_ **-TURED, -TURING, -TURES** to propose

OVERTURN _v_ **-ED, -ING, -S** to turn over

OVERURGE _v_ **-URGED, -URGING, -URGES** to urge too much

OVERUSE _v_ **-USED, -USING, -USES** to use too much

OVERVIEW _n_ pl. **-S** a summary

OVERVOTE _v_ **-VOTED, -VOTING, -VOTES** to defeat by a majority of votes

OVERWARM _v_ **-ED, -ING, -S** to warm too much

OVERWARY _adj_ too wary

OVERWEAK _adj_ too weak

OVERWEAR _v_ **-WORE, -WORN, -WEARING, -WEARS** to wear out

OVERWEEN _v_ **-ED, -ING, -S** to be arrogant

OVERWET _v_ **-WETTED, -WETTING, -WETS** to wet too much

OVERWIDE _adj_ too wide

OVERWILY _adj_ too wily

OVERWIND _v_ **-WOUND, -WINDING, -WINDS** to wind too much, as a watch

OVERWISE _adj_ too wise

OVERWORD _n_ pl. **-S** a word or phrase repeated at intervals in a song

OVERWORE past tense of overwear

OVERWORK _v_ **-WORKED** or **-WROUGHT, -WORKING, -WORKS** to cause to work too hard

OVERWORN past participle of overwear

OVERWOUND past tense of overwind

OVERZEAL _n_ pl. **-S** excess of zeal

OVIBOS _n_ pl. **OVIBOS** a wild ox

OVICIDE _n_ pl. **-S** an agent that kills eggs **OVICIDAL** _adj_

OVIDUCT _n_ pl. **-S** a tube through which ova travel from an ovary **OVIDUCAL** _adj_

OVIFORM _adj_ shaped like an egg

OVINE _n_ pl. **-S** a sheep or a closely related animal

OVIPARA _n/pl_ egg-laying animals

OVIPOSIT _v_ **-ED, -ING, -S** to lay eggs

OVISAC _n_ pl. **-S** a sac containing an ovum or ova

OVOID _n_ pl. **-S** an egg-shaped body

OVOIDAL _n_ pl. **-S** an ovoid

OVOLO _n_ pl. **-LOS** or **-LI** a convex molding

OVONIC _n_ pl. **-S** an electronic device

OVULATE _v_ **-LATED, -LATING, -LATES** to produce ova

OVULE _n_ pl. **-S** a rudimentary seed **OVULAR, OVULARY** _adj_

OVUM _n_ pl. **OVA** the female reproductive cell of animals

OW _interj_ — used to express sudden pain

OWE _v_ **OWED, OWING, OWES** to be under obligation to pay or repay

OWL _n_ pl. **-S** a nocturnal bird

OWLERY _n_ pl. **-ERIES** a place that owls inhabit

OWLET _n_ pl. **-S** a young owl

OWLISH _adj_ resembling an owl **OWLISHLY** _adv_

OWLLIKE _adj_ owlish

OWLY _adj_ **OWLIER, OWLIEST** owlish

OWN _v_ **-ED, -ING, -S** to have as a belonging **OWNABLE** _adj_

OWNER _n_ pl. **-S** one that owns

OWSE _n_ pl. **OWSEN** ox

OWT _n_ pl. **-S** anything

OX _n_ pl. **-ES** a clumsy person

OX _n_ pl. **OXEN** a hoofed mammal

OXALATE _v_ **-LATED, -LATING, -LATES** to treat with an oxalate (a chemical salt)

OXALIS _n_ pl. **-ALISES** a flowering plant **OXALIC** _adj_

OXAZEPAM _n_ pl. **-S** a tranquilizing drug

OXAZINE _n_ pl. **-S** a chemical compound

OXAZOLE _n_ pl. **-S** a liquid chemical compound

OXBLOOD _n_ pl. **-S** a deep red color

OXBOW _n_ pl. **-S** a U-shaped piece of wood in an ox yoke

OXCART _n_ pl. **-S** an ox-drawn cart

OXEN pl. of ox

OXER _n_ pl. **-S** a fence for keeping in cattle

OXEYE _n_ pl. **-S** a flowering plant

OXFORD _n_ pl. **-S** a type of shoe

OXHEART _n_ pl. **-S** a variety of sweet cherry

OXHERD _n_ pl. **-S** one who tends oxen

OXHIDE _n_ pl. **-S** leather made from the skin of an ox

OXIC _adj_ denoting a process in which oxygen in involved

OXID	*n* pl. **-S** oxide
OXIDABLE	*adj* capable of being oxidized
OXIDANT	*n* pl. **-S** an oxidizing agent
OXIDASE	*n* pl. **-S** an oxidizing enzyme **OXIDASIC** *adj*
OXIDATE	*v* **-DATED, -DATING, -DATES** to oxidize
OXIDE	*n* pl. **-S** a binary compound of oxygen with another element or radical **OXIDIC** *adj*
OXIDISE	*v* **-DISED, -DISING, -DISES** to oxidize
OXIDISER	*n* pl. **-S** oxidizer
OXIDIZE	*v* **-DIZED, -DIZING, -DIZES** to combine with oxygen
OXIDIZER	*n* pl. **-S** an oxidant
OXIM	*n* pl. **-S** oxime
OXIME	*n* pl. **-S** a chemical compound
OXIMETER	*n* pl. **-S** an instrument for measuring the amount of oxygen in the blood
OXIMETRY	*n* pl. **-TRIES** the use of an oximeter
OXLIKE	*adj* resembling an ox
OXLIP	*n* pl. **-S** a flowering plant
OXO	*adj* containing oxygen
OXPECKER	*n* pl. **-S** an African bird
OXTAIL	*n* pl. **-S** the tail of an ox
OXTER	*n* pl. **-S** the armpit
OXTONGUE	*n* pl. **-S** a European herb
OXY	*adj* containing oxygen
OXYACID	*n* pl. **-S** an acid that contains oxygen
OXYGEN	*n* pl. **-S** a gaseous element **OXYGENIC** *adj*
OXYMORON	*n* pl. **-MORONS** or **-MORA** a combination of contradictory or incongruous words
OXYPHIL	*n* pl. **-S** oxyphile
OXYPHILE	*n* pl. **-S** an organism that thrives in a relatively acid environment
OXYSALT	*n* pl. **-S** a salt of an oxyacid
OXYSOME	*n* pl. **-S** a structural unit of cellular cristae
OXYTOCIC	*n* pl. **-S** a drug that hastens the process of childbirth
OXYTOCIN	*n* pl. **-S** a pituitary hormone
OXYTONE	*n* pl. **-S** a word having heavy stress on the last syllable
OXYTROPE	*n* pl. **-S** a flowering plant
OY	*interj* — used to express dismay or pain
OYER	*n* pl. **-S** a type of legal writ
OYES	*n* pl. **OYESSES** oyez
OYEZ	*n* pl. **OYEZES** a cry used to introduce the opening of a court of law
OYSTER	*v* **-ED, -ING, -S** to gather oysters (edible mollusks)
OYSTERER	*n* pl. **-S** one that gathers or sells oysters
OZONATE	*v* **-ATED, -ATING, -ATES** to treat or combine with ozone
OZONE	*n* pl. **-S** a form of oxygen **OZONIC** *adj*
OZONIDE	*n* pl. **-S** a compound of ozone
OZONISE	*v* **-ISED, -ISING, -ISES** to ozonize
OZONIZE	*v* **-IZED, -IZING, -IZES** to convert into ozone
OZONIZER	*n* pl. **-S** a device for converting oxygen into ozone
OZONOUS	*adj* pertaining to ozone

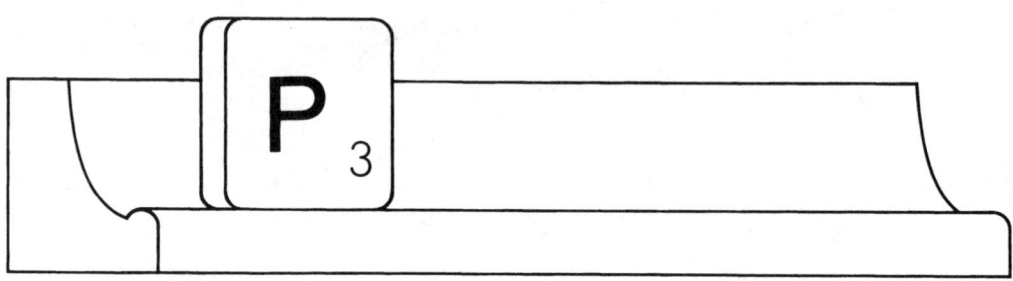

PA	*n* pl. **-S** a father
PAAN	*n* pl. **-S** a betel leaf folded round pieces of betel nut and spices
PABLUM	*n* pl. **-S** insipid writing or speech
PABULUM	*n* pl. **-S** food **PABULAR** *adj*
PAC	*n* pl. **-S** a shoe like a moccasin
PACA	*n* pl. **-S** a large rodent
PACE	*v* **PACED, PACING, PACES** to walk with a regular step
PACER	*n* pl. **-S** a horse whose gait is a pace
PACEY	*adj* **PACIER, PACIEST** keeping a fast pace (rate of speed)
PACHA	*n* pl. **-S** pasha
PACHADOM	*n* pl. **-S** pashadom
PACHALIC	*n* pl. **-S** pashalik
PACHINKO	*n* pl. **-KOS** a Japanese pinball game
PACHISI	*n* pl. **-S** a board game of India
PACHOULI	*n* pl. **-S** an East Indian herb
PACHUCO	*n* pl. **-COS** a flashy Mexican-American youth
PACIER	comparative of pacey and pacy
PACIEST	superlative of pacey and pacy
PACIFIC	*adj* peaceful
PACIFIED	past tense of pacify
PACIFIER	*n* pl. **-S** one that pacifies
PACIFISM	*n* pl. **-S** opposition to war or violence
PACIFIST	*n* pl. **-S** an advocate of pacifism
PACIFY	*v* **-FIED, -FYING, -FIES** to make peaceful
PACING	*n* pl. **-S** the speed at which an event takes place
PACK	*v* **-ED, -ING, -S** to put into a receptacle for transportation or storage **PACKABLE** *adj*
PACKAGE	*v* **-AGED, -AGING, -AGES** to make into a package (a wrapped or boxed object)
PACKAGER	*n* pl. **-S** one that packages
PACKER	*n* pl. **-S** one that packs
PACKET	*v* **-ED, -ING, -S** to make into a small package
PACKING	*n* pl. **-S** material used to pack
PACKLY	*adv* intimately
PACKMAN	*n* pl. **-MEN** a peddler
PACKNESS	*n* pl. **-ES** intimacy
PACKSACK	*n* pl. **-S** a carrying bag to be worn on the back
PACKWAX	*n* pl. **-ES** paxwax
PACT	*n* pl. **-S** an agreement
PACTION	*n* pl. **-S** a pact
PACY	*adj* **PACIER, PACIEST** pacey
PACZKI	*n* pl. **-S** a round doughnut with a filling
PAD	*v* **PADDED, PADDING, PADS** to line or stuff with soft material
PADAUK	*n* pl. **-S** a tropical tree
PADDER	*n* pl. **-S** one that pads
PADDIES	pl. of paddy
PADDING	*n* pl. **-S** material with which to pad
PADDLE	*v* **-DLED, -DLING, -DLES** to propel with a broad-bladed implement
PADDLER	*n* pl. **-S** one that paddles
PADDLING	*n* pl. **-S** the act of one who paddles
PADDOCK	*v* **-ED, -ING, -S** to confine in an enclosure for horses
PADDY	*n* pl. **-DIES** a rice field
PADI	*n* pl. **-S** paddy
PADISHAH	*n* pl. **-S** a sovereign
PADLE	*n* pl. **-S** a hoe
PADLOCK	*v* **-ED, -ING, -S** to secure with a type of lock

PADNAG *n* pl. **-S** a horse that moves along at an easy pace

PADOUK *n* pl. **-S** padauk

PADRE *n* pl. **-DRES** or **-DRI** a Christian clergyman

PADRONA *n* pl. **-S** a female boss or employer

PADRONE *n* pl. **-NES** or **-NI** a master or boss

PADSHAH *n* pl. **-S** padishah

PADUASOY *n* pl. **-SOYS** a strong silk fabric

PAEAN *n* pl. **-S** a song of joy

PAEANISM *n* pl. **-S** the chanting of a paean

PAELLA *n* pl. **-S** a saffron-flavored stew

PAEON *n* pl. **-S** a metrical foot of four syllables **PAEONIC** *adj*

PAESAN *n* pl. **-S** paesano

PAESANO *n* pl. **-NOS** or **-NI** a fellow countryman

PAGAN *n* pl. **-S** a follower of a polytheistic religion

PAGANDOM *n* pl. **-S** the realm of pagans

PAGANISE *v* **-ISED, -ISING, -ISES** to paganize

PAGANISH *adj* resembling a pagan

PAGANISM *n* pl. **-S** an irreligious attitude

PAGANIST *n* pl. **-S** a pagan

PAGANIZE *v* **-IZED, -IZING, -IZES** to make irreligious

PAGE *v* **PAGED, PAGING, PAGES** to summon by calling out the name of

PAGEANT *n* pl. **-S** an elaborate public spectacle

PAGEBOY *n* pl. **-BOYS** a woman's hairstyle

PAGEFUL *n* pl. **-S** as much as a page can hold

PAGER *n* pl. **-S** a beeper

PAGINAL *adj* pertaining to the pages of a book

PAGINATE *v* **-NATED, -NATING, -NATES** to number the pages of

PAGING *n* pl. **-S** a transfer of computer pages

PAGOD *n* pl. **-S** pagoda

PAGODA *n* pl. **-S** a Far Eastern temple

PAGURIAN *n* pl. **-S** a hermit crab

PAGURID *n* pl. **-S** pagurian

PAH *interj* — used as an exclamation of disgust

PAHLAVI *n* pl. **-S** a former coin of Iran

PAHOEHOE *n* pl. **-S** smooth solidified lava

PAID a past tense of pay

PAIK *v* **-ED, -ING, -S** to beat or strike

PAIL *n* pl. **-S** a watertight cylindrical container

PAILFUL *n* pl. **PAILFULS** or **PAILSFUL** as much as a pail can hold

PAILLARD *n* pl. **-S** a slice of meat pounded thin and grilled

PAIN *v* **-ED, -ING, -S** to cause pain (suffering or distress)

PAINCH *n* pl. **-ES** paunch

PAINFUL *adj* **-FULLER, -FULLEST** causing pain

PAINLESS *adj* not causing pain

PAINT *v* **-ED, -ING, -S** to make a representation of with paints (coloring substances)

PAINTBOX *n* pl. **-ES** a box holding dry paints

PAINTER *n* pl. **-S** one that paints

PAINTING *n* pl. **-S** a picture made with paints

PAINTY *adj* **PAINTIER, PAINTIEST** covered with paint

PAIR *v* **-ED, -ING, -S** to arrange in sets of two

PAIRING *n* pl. **-S** a matching of two opponents in a tournament

PAIRWISE *adv* in sets of two

PAISA *n* pl. **PAISAS** or **PAISE** a coin of Pakistan

PAISAN *n* pl. **-S** paisano

PAISANA *n* pl. **-S** a female compatriot

PAISANO *n* pl. **-NOS** a fellow countryman

PAISE a pl. of paisa

PAISLEY *n* pl. **-LEYS** a patterned wool fabric

PAJAMA *n* pl. **-S** a garment for sleeping or lounging

PAJAMAED *adj* wearing pajamas

PAK *n* pl. **-S** pack

PAKEHA *n* pl. **-S** a person who is not of Maori descent

PAKORA *n* pl. **-S** a small spicy cake of fried batter with vegetables or meat

PAL *v* **PALLED, PALLING, PALS** to associate as friends

PALABRA *n* pl. **-S** a word

PALACE *n* pl. **-S** a royal residence **PALACED** *adj*

PALADIN *n* pl. **-S** a knightly champion

PALAIS *n* pl. **PALAIS** a palace

PALAPA *n* pl. **-S** an open-sided dwelling with a roof of palm leaves

PALATAL *n* pl. **-S** a bone of the palate

PALATE *n* pl. **-S** the roof of the mouth

PALATIAL *adj* resembling a palace

PALATINE *n* pl. **-S** a high officer of an empire

PALAVER *v* **-ED, -ING, -S** to chatter

PALAZZO *n* pl. **-ZI** an impressive building

PALAZZOS *n/pl* wide-legged pants for women

PALE *adj* **PALER, PALEST** lacking intensity of color

PALE *v* **PALED, PALING, PALES** to make or become pale

PALEA *n* pl. **-LEAE** a small bract **PALEAL** *adj*

PALEATE *adj* covered with scales

PALEFACE *n* pl. **-S** a white person

PALELY *adv* in a pale manner

PALENESS *n* pl. **-ES** the quality of being pale

PALEOCON *n* pl. **-S** an extremely right-wing conservative

PALEOSOL *n* pl. **-S** a layer of ancient soil

PALER comparative of pale

PALEST superlative of pale

PALESTRA *n* pl. **-TRAS** or **-TRAE** a school for athletics in ancient Greece

PALET *n* pl. **-S** a palea

PALETOT *n* pl. **-S** a loose overcoat

PALETTE *n* pl. **-S** a board on which an artist mixes colors

PALEWAYS *adv* palewise

PALEWISE *adv* vertically

PALFREY *n* pl. **-FREYS** a riding horse

PALI *n* pl. **-S** a cliff in Hawaii

PALIER comparative of paly

PALIEST superlative of paly

PALIKAR *n* pl. **-S** a Greek soldier

PALIMONY *n* pl. **-NIES** an allowance paid to one member of an unmarried couple who have separated

PALING *n* pl. **-S** a picket fence

PALINODE *n* pl. **-S** a formal retraction

PALISADE *v* **-SADED, -SADING, -SADES** to fortify with a heavy fence

PALISH *adj* somewhat pale

PALL *v* **-ED, -ING, -S** to become insipid

PALLADIA *n/pl* safeguards

PALLADIC *adj* pertaining to the metallic element palladium

PALLED past tense of pal

PALLET *v* **-ED, -ING, -S** to place on platforms for storage or moving

PALLETTE *n* pl. **-S** a piece of armor protecting the armpit

PALLIA a pl. of pallium

PALLIAL *adj* pertaining to a part of the brain

PALLIATE *v* **-ATED, -ATING, -ATES** to conceal the seriousness of

PALLID *adj* **PALLIDER, PALLIDEST** pale **PALLIDLY** *adv*

PALLIER comparative of pally

PALLIEST superlative of pally

PALLING present participle of pal or pall

PALLIUM *n* pl. **-LIUMS** or **-LIA** a cloak worn in ancient Rome

PALLOR *n* pl. **-S** paleness

PALLY *adj* **-LIER, -LIEST** marked by close friendship

PALM *v* **-ED, -ING, -S** to touch with the palm (inner surface) of the hand

PALMAR *adj* pertaining to the palm

PALMARY *adj* worthy of praise

PALMATE *adj* resembling an open hand

PALMATED *adj* palmate

PALMBALL *n* pl. **-S** a baseball pitched from the palm and thumb

PALMER *n* pl. **-S** a religious pilgrim

PALMETTE *n* pl. **-S** a type of ornament

PALMETTO *n* pl. **-TOS** or **-TOES** a tropical tree

PALMFUL *n* pl. **-S** as much as a palm can hold

PALMIER *n* pl. **-S** a pastry shaped like a palm leaf

PALMIEST superlative of palmy

PALMIST *n* pl. **-S** a fortune-teller

PALMITIN *n* pl. **-S** a chemical compound

PALMLIKE *adj* resembling a palm tree

PALMTOP *n* pl. **-S** a small computer that fits in the palm of the hand

PALMY *adj* **PALMIER, PALMIEST** marked by prosperity

PALMYRA *n* pl. **-S** a tropical tree

PALOMINO *n* pl. **-NOS** a horse with a golden coat and white mane

PALOOKA *n* pl. **-S** an inferior boxer

PALP *v* **-ED, -ING, -S** to touch

PALPABLE	*adj* capable of being felt **PALPABLY** *adv*
PALPAL	*adj* pertaining to a palpus
PALPATE	*v* **-PATED, -PATING, -PATES** to examine by touch
PALPATOR	*n* pl. **-S** one that palpates
PALPEBRA	*n* pl. **-BRAS** or **-BRAE** an eyelid
PALPUS	*n* pl. **-PI** a sensory organ of an arthropod
PALSA	*n* pl. **-S** a landform of subarctic regions
PALSHIP	*n* pl. **-S** the relation existing between close friends
PALSY	*v* **-SIED, -SYING, -SIES** to paralyze
PALSY	*adj* **-SIER, -SIEST** friendly in a way that is not proper or sincere
PALTER	*v* **-ED, -ING, -S** to talk or act insincerely
PALTERER	*n* pl. **-S** one that palters
PALTRY	*adj* **-TRIER, -TRIEST** petty **PALTRILY** *adv*
PALUDAL	*adj* pertaining to a marsh
PALUDISM	*n* pl. **-S** malaria
PALY	*adj* **PALIER, PALIEST** somewhat pale
PAM	*n* pl. **-S** the jack of clubs in certain card games
PAMPA	*n* pl. **-S** a grassland of South America
PAMPEAN	*n* pl. **-S** a native of the pampas
PAMPER	*v* **-ED, -ING, -S** to treat with extreme or excessive indulgence
PAMPERER	*n* pl. **-S** one that pampers
PAMPERO	*n* pl. **-ROS** a cold, dry wind
PAMPHLET	*n* pl. **-S** a printed work with a paper cover
PAN	*v* **PANNED, PANNING, PANS** to criticize harshly
PANACEA	*n* pl. **-S** a remedy for all diseases or ills **PANACEAN** *adj*
PANACHE	*n* pl. **-S** an ornamental tuft of feathers
PANADA	*n* pl. **-S** a thick sauce
PANAMA	*n* pl. **-S** a lightweight hat
PANATELA	*n* pl. **-S** a long, slender cigar
PANBROIL	*v* **-ED, -ING, -S** to fry in a pan with little or no fat
PANCAKE	*v* **-CAKED, -CAKING, -CAKES** to land an airplane in a certain manner

PANCETTA	*n* pl. **-S** unsmoked Italian bacon
PANCHAX	*n* pl. **-ES** a tropical fish
PANCREAS	*n* pl. **-ES** a large gland
PANDA	*n* pl. **-S** an herbivorous mammal
PANDAN	*n* pl. **-S** pandanus
PANDANUS	*n* pl. **-NUSES** or **-NI** a tropical plant
PANDECT	*n* pl. **-S** a complete body of laws
PANDEMIC	*n* pl. **-S** a widespread disease
PANDER	*v* **-ED, -ING, -S** to provide gratification for others' desires
PANDERER	*n* pl. **-S** one that panders
PANDIED	past tense of pandy
PANDIES	present 3d person sing. of pandy
PANDIT	*n* pl. **-S** a wise or learned man in India
PANDOOR	*n* pl. **-S** pandour
PANDORA	*n* pl. **-S** bandore
PANDORE	*n* pl. **-S** bandore
PANDOUR	*n* pl. **-S** a marauding soldier
PANDOWDY	*n* pl. **-DIES** an apple dessert
PANDURA	*n* pl. **-S** bandore
PANDY	*v* **-DIED, -DYING, -DIES** to punish by striking the hand
PANE	*n* pl. **-S** a sheet of glass for a window **PANED** *adj*
PANEER	*n* pl. **-S** a milk curd cheese
PANEL	*v* **-ELED, -ELING, -ELS** or **-ELLED, -ELLING, -ELS** to decorate with thin sheets of material
PANELESS	*adj* lacking panes
PANELING	*n* pl. **-S** material with which to panel
PANELIST	*n* pl. **-S** a member of a discussion or advisory group
PANELLED	a past tense of panel
PANELLING	a present participle of panel
PANETELA	*n* pl. **-S** panatela
PANFISH	*v* **-ED, -ING, -ES** to fish for any small fish that can be fried whole
PANFORTE	*n* pl. **-S** a hard spicy cake
PANFRY	*v* **-FRIED, -FRYING, -FRIES** to fry in a frying pan
PANFUL	*n* pl. **-S** as much as a pan will hold
PANG	*v* **-ED, -ING, -S** to cause to have spasms of pain
PANGA	*n* pl. **-S** a large knife

PANGEN *n* pl. **-S** a hypothetical heredity-controlling particle of protoplasm

PANGENE *n* pl. **-S** pangen

PANGOLIN *n* pl. **-S** a toothless mammal

PANGRAM *n* pl. **-S** a sentence that includes all the letters of the alphabet

PANHUMAN *adj* pertaining to all humanity

PANIC *v* **-ICKED, -ICKING, -ICS** to be overwhelmed by fear

PANICKY *adj* **-ICKIER, -ICKIEST** tending to panic

PANICLE *n* pl. **-S** a loosely branched flower cluster **PANICLED** *adj*

PANICUM *n* pl. **-S** a grass

PANIER *n* pl. **-S** pannier

PANINO *n* pl. **PANINI** or **PANINIS** a sandwich made with a small bread roll

PANLIKE *adj* resembling a pan (a container used for cooking)

PANMIXIA *n* pl. **-S** random mating within a breeding population

PANMIXIS *n* pl. **-MIXES** panmixia

PANNE *n* pl. **-S** a lustrous velvet

PANNED past tense of pan

PANNER *n* pl. **-S** one that pans

PANNIER *n* pl. **-S** a large basket

PANNIKIN *n* pl. **-S** a small saucepan

PANNING present participle of pan

PANNIST *n* pl. **-S** a person who plays a steel drum

PANOCHA *n* pl. **-S** a coarse Mexican sugar

PANOCHE *n* pl. **-S** panocha

PANOPLY *n* pl. **-PLIES** a suit of armor

PANOPTIC *adj* including everything visible in one view

PANORAMA *n* pl. **-S** a complete view

PANPIPE *n* pl. **-S** a musical instrument

PANSOPHY *n* pl. **-PHIES** universal knowledge

PANSY *n* pl. **-SIES** a flowering plant

PANT *v* **-ED, -ING, -S** to breathe quickly and with difficulty

PANTALET *n* pl. **-S** long underpants trimmed with ruffles

PANTHEON *n* pl. **-S** a temple dedicated to all the gods

PANTHER *n* pl. **-S** a leopard

PANTIE *n* pl. **-S** a woman's or child's undergarment

PANTIES pl. of panty

PANTILE *n* pl. **-S** a roofing tile **PANTILED** *adj*

PANTO *n* pl. **-TOS** a pantomime

PANTOFLE *n* pl. **-S** a slipper

PANTOUM *n* pl. **-S** a verse form

PANTRY *n* pl. **-TRIES** a closet or room for storing kitchen utensils

PANTSUIT *n* pl. **-S** a type of woman's suit

PANTY *n* pl. **PANTIES** pantie

PANZER *n* pl. **-S** an armored combat vehicle

PAP *n* pl. **-S** a soft food for infants

PAPA *n* pl. **-S** a father

PAPACY *n* pl. **-CIES** the office of the pope

PAPADAM *n* pl. **-S** papadum

PAPADOM *n* pl. **-S** papadum

PAPADUM *n* pl. **-S** a thin, crisp bread of India

PAPAIN *n* pl. **-S** an enzyme

PAPAL *adj* pertaining to the pope **PAPALLY** *adv*

PAPALIST *n* pl. **-S** an advocate of papal supremacy

PAPAW *n* pl. **-S** a fleshy fruit

PAPAYA *n* pl. **-S** a melon-like fruit **PAPAYAN** *adj*

PAPER *v* **-ED, -ING, -S** to cover or wrap with paper (a thin sheet of material made of cellulose pulp)

PAPERBOY *n* pl. **-BOYS** a newsboy

PAPERER *n* pl. **-S** one that papers

PAPERY *adj* resembling paper

PAPHIAN *n* pl. **-S** a prostitute

PAPILLA *n* pl. **-LAE** a nipple-like projection **PAPILLAR** *adj*

PAPILLON *n* pl. **-S** a small dog having large ears

PAPOOSE *n* pl. **-S** a Native American baby

PAPPADAM *n* pl. **-S** papadum

PAPPADUM *n* pl. **-S** papadum

PAPPI a pl. of pappus

PAPPIER comparative of pappy

PAPPIES pl. of pappy

PAPPOOSE *n* pl. **-S** papoose

PAPPUS *n* pl. **-PI** a tuft of bristles on the achene of certain plants **PAPPOSE, PAPPOUS** *adj*

PAPPY *adj* **-PIER, -PIEST** resembling pap

PAPPY   *n* pl. **-PIES** a father

PAPRICA   *n* pl. **-S** paprika

PAPRIKA   *n* pl. **-S** a seasoning made from red peppers

PAPULA   *n* pl. **-LAE** or **-LAS** papule

PAPULE   *n* pl. **-S** a pimple **PAPULAR, PAPULOSE, PAPULOUS** *adj*

PAPYRUS   *n* pl. **-RUSES** or **-RI** a tall aquatic plant **PAPYRAL, PAPYRIAN, PAPYRINE** *adj*

PAR   *v* **PARRED, PARRING, PARS** to shoot in a standard number of strokes in golf

PARA   *n* pl. **PARAS** or **PARAE** a woman's status regarding the bearing of offspring

PARABLE   *n* pl. **-S** a simple story conveying a moral or religious lesson

PARABOLA   *n* pl. **-LAS** or **-LAE** a conic section

PARACHOR   *n* pl. **-S** a mathematical constant that relates molecular volume to surface tension

PARADE   *v* **-RADED, -RADING, -RADES** to march in a public procession

PARADER   *n* pl. **-S** one that parades

PARADIGM   *n* pl. **-S** a pattern or example

PARADISE   *n* pl. **-S** a place of extreme beauty or delight

PARADOR   *n* pl. **-DORS** or **-DORES** an inn in Spain

PARADOS   *n* pl. **-ES** a protective embankment

PARADOX   *n* pl. **-ES** a statement seemingly contradictory or absurd yet perhaps true

PARADROP   *v* **-DROPPED, -DROPPING, -DROPS** to deliver by parachute

PARAFFIN   *v* **-ED, -ING, -S** to coat with a waxy substance

PARAFOIL   *n* pl. **-S** a fabric device that resembles a parachute

PARAFORM   *n* pl. **-S** a substance used as an antiseptic

PARAGOGE   *n* pl. **-S** the addition of a sound or sounds at the end of a word

PARAGON   *v* **-ED, -ING, -S** to compare with

PARAKEET   *n* pl. **-S** a small parrot

PARAKITE   *n* pl. **-S** a parachute kite for towing a person through the air by a motorboat

PARALLAX   *n* pl. **-ES** an apparent optical displacement of an object

PARALLEL   *v* **-LELED, -LELING, -LELS** or **-LELLED, -LELLING, -LELS** to be similar or analogous to

PARALYSE   *v* **-LYSED, -LYSING, -LYSES** to paralyze

PARALYZE   *v* **-LYZED, -LYZING, -LYZES** to render incapable of movement

PARAMENT   *n* pl. **-MENTS** or **-MENTA** an ornamental vestment

PARAMO   *n* pl. **-MOS** a plateau region of South America

PARAMOUR   *n* pl. **-S** an illicit lover

PARANG   *n* pl. **-S** a heavy knife

PARANOEA   *n* pl. **-S** paranoia

PARANOIA   *n* pl. **-S** a mental disorder

PARANOIC   *n* pl. **-S** a paranoid

PARANOID   *n* pl. **-S** one affected with paranoia

PARAPET   *n* pl. **-S** a protective wall

PARAPH   *n* pl. **-S** a flourish at the end of a signature

PARAQUAT   *n* pl. **-S** a weed killer

PARAQUET   *n* pl. **-S** parakeet

PARASAIL   *v* **-ED, -ING, -S** to soar while harnessed to a parachute towed by a car or boat

PARASANG   *n* pl. **-S** a Persian unit of distance

PARASHAH   *n* pl. **-SHAHS** or **-SHOTH** or **-SHOT** a portion of the Torah read on the Sabbath

PARASITE   *n* pl. **-S** an organism that lives and feeds on or in another organism

PARASOL   *n* pl. **-S** a small, light umbrella

PARATHA   *n* pl. **-S** a piece of unleavened bread fried on a griddle

PARAVANE   *n* pl. **-S** an underwater device used to cut cables

PARAWING   *n* pl. **-S** a winglike parachute

PARAZOAN   *n* pl. **-S** any of a major division of multicellular animals

PARBAKE   *v* **-BAKED, -BAKING, -BAKES** to bake partially

PARBOIL   *v* **-ED, -ING, -S** to cook partially by boiling for a short time

PARCEL   *v* **-CELED, -CELING, -CELS** or **-CELLED, -CELLING, -CELS** to divide into parts or shares

PARCENER   *n* pl. **-S** a joint heir

PARCH   *v* **-ED, -ING, -ES** to make very dry

PARCHESI   *n* pl. **-S** pachisi

PARCHISI   *n* pl. **-S** pachisi

PARCLOSE *n* pl. **-S** a screen dividing areas in a church

PARD *n* pl. **-S** a leopard

PARDAH *n* pl. **-S** purdah

PARDEE *interj* pardi

PARDI *interj* — used as a mild oath

PARDIE *interj* pardi

PARDINE *adj* pertaining to a leopard

PARDNER *n* pl. **-S** chum; friend

PARDON *v* **-ED, -ING, -S** to release from liability for an offense

PARDONER *n* pl. **-S** one that pardons

PARDY *interj* pardi

PARE *v* **PARED, PARING, PARES** to cut off the outer covering of

PARECISM *n* pl. **-S** the state of having the male and female sexual organs beside or near each other

PAREIRA *n* pl. **-S** a medicinal plant root

PAREN *n* pl. **-S** a parenthesis

PARENT *v* **-ED, -ING, -S** to exercise the functions of a parent (a father or mother)

PARENTAL *adj* pertaining to a parent

PAREO *n* pl. **-REOS** pareu

PARER *n* pl. **-S** one that pares

PARERGON *n* pl. **-GA** a composition derived from a larger work

PARESIS *n* pl. **-RESES** partial loss of the ability to move

PARETIC *n* pl. **-S** one affected with paresis

PAREU *n* pl. **-S** a Polynesian garment

PAREVE *adj* parve

PARFAIT *n* pl. **-S** a frozen dessert

PARFLESH *n* pl. **-ES** a rawhide soaked in lye to remove the hair and dried

PARFOCAL *adj* having lenses with the corresponding focal points in the same plane

PARGE *v* **PARGED, PARGING, PARGES** to parget

PARGET *v* **-GETED, -GETING, -GETS** or **-GETTED, -GETTING, -GETS** to cover with plaster

PARGING *n* pl. **-S** a thin coat of mortar or plaster for sealing masonry

PARGO *n* pl. **-GOS** a food fish

PARHELIA *n/pl* bright circular spots appearing on a solar halo

PARHELIC *adj* pertaining to parhelia

PARIAH *n* pl. **-S** a social outcast

PARIAN *n* pl. **-S** a hard, white porcelain

PARIES *n* pl. **PARIETES** the wall of an organ

PARIETAL *n* pl. **-S** a bone of the skull

PARING *n* pl. **-S** something pared off

PARIS *n* pl. **-ISES** a European herb

PARISH *n* pl. **-ES** an ecclesiastical district

PARITY *n* pl. **-TIES** equality

PARK *v* **-ED, -ING, -S** to leave a vehicle in a location for a time

PARKA *n* pl. **-S** a hooded garment

PARKADE *n* pl. **-S** a multilevel structure for parking vehicles

PARKER *n* pl. **-S** one that parks

PARKETTE *n* pl. **-S** a small public park

PARKIER comparative of parky

PARKIEST superlative of parky

PARKIN *n* pl. **-S** a kind of bread made with molasses and oatmeal

PARKING *n* pl. **-S** an area in which vehicles may be left

PARKLAND *n* pl. **-S** a grassland region with isolated or grouped trees

PARKLIKE *adj* resembling an outdoor recreational area

PARKOUR *n* pl. **-S** the sport of traversing environmental obstacles by running, climbing, or leaping

PARKWAY *n* pl. **-WAYS** a wide highway

PARKY *adj* **PARKIER, PARKIEST** chilly

PARLANCE *n* pl. **-S** a manner of speaking

PARLANDO *adj* sung in a manner suggestive of speech

PARLANTE *adj* parlando

PARLAY *v* **-ED, -ING, -S** to bet an original wager and its winnings on a subsequent event

PARLE *v* **PARLED, PARLING, PARLES** to parley

PARLEY *v* **-LEYED, -LEYING, -LEYS** to discuss terms with an enemy

PARLEYER *n* pl. **-S** one that parleys

PARLOR *n* pl. **-S** a room for the entertainment of visitors

PARLOUR *n* pl. **-S** parlor

PARLOUS *adj* dangerous

PARMESAN *n* pl. **-S** a hard, dry Italian cheese

PARODIC *adj* comically imitative

PARODIST *n* pl. **-S** one who parodies

PARODOS *n* pl. **-DOI** an ode sung in ancient Greek drama

PARODY *v* **-DIED, -DYING, -DIES** to imitate a serious literary work for comic effect

PAROL *n* pl. **-S** an utterance

PAROLE *v* **-ROLED, -ROLING, -ROLES** to release from prison before completion of the imposed sentence

PAROLEE *n* pl. **-S** one who is paroled

PARONYM *n* pl. **-S** a word having the same root as another

PARONYMY *n* pl. **-MIES** the state of being a paronym

PAROQUET *n* pl. **-S** parakeet

PAROSMIA *n* pl. **-S** a distortion of the sense of smell

PAROTIC *adj* situated near the ear

PAROTID *n* pl. **-S** a salivary gland

PAROTOID *n* pl. **-S** a gland of certain toads and frogs

PAROUS *adj* having produced offspring

PAROXYSM *n* pl. **-S** a sudden fit or attack

PARQUET *v* **-ED, -ING, -S** to furnish with a floor of inlaid design

PARR *n* pl. **-S** a young salmon

PARRAL *n* pl. **-S** parrel

PARRED past tense of par

PARREL *n* pl. **-S** a sliding loop of rope or chain used on a ship

PARRIDGE *n* pl. **-S** porridge

PARRIED past tense of parry

PARRIER *n* pl. **-S** one that parries

PARRIES present 3d person sing. of parry

PARRING present participle of par

PARRITCH *n* pl. **-ES** porridge

PARROKET *n* pl. **-S** parakeet

PARROT *v* **-ED, -ING, -S** to repeat or imitate without thought or understanding

PARROTER *n* pl. **-S** one that parrots

PARROTY *adj* resembling a parrot (a hook-billed tropical bird)

PARRY *v* **-RIED, -RYING, -RIES** to ward off a blow

PARSE *v* **PARSED, PARSING, PARSES** to describe and analyze grammatically **PARSABLE** *adj*

PARSEC *n* pl. **-S** a unit of astronomical distance

PARSER *n* pl. **-S** one that parses

PARSLEY *n* pl. **-LEYS** a cultivated herb **PARSLEYED, PARSLIED** *adj*

PARSNIP *n* pl. **-S** a European herb

PARSON *n* pl. **-S** a clergyman **PARSONIC** *adj*

PART *v* **-ED, -ING, -S** to divide or break into separate pieces

PARTAKE *v* **-TOOK, -TAKEN, -TAKING, -TAKES** to participate

PARTAKER *n* pl. **-S** one that partakes

PARTAN *n* pl. **-S** an edible crab

PARTER *n* pl. **-S** one that parts

PARTERRE *n* pl. **-S** a section of a theater

PARTIAL *n* pl. **-S** a simple component of a complex tone

PARTIBLE *adj* divisible

PARTICLE *n* pl. **-S** a very small piece or part

PARTIED past tense of party

PARTIER *n* pl. **-S** partyer

PARTIES present 3d person sing. of party

PARTING *n* pl. **-S** a division or separation

PARTISAN *n* pl. **-S** a firm supporter of a person, party, or cause

PARTITA *n* pl. **-S** a set of related instrumental pieces

PARTITE *adj* divided into parts

PARTIZAN *n* pl. **-S** partisan

PARTLET *n* pl. **-S** a woman's garment

PARTLY *adv* in some measure or degree

PARTNER *v* **-ED, -ING, -S** to associate with in some activity of common interest

PARTON *n* pl. **-S** a hypothetical atomic particle

PARTOOK past tense of partake

PARTWAY *adv* to some extent

PARTY *v* **-TIED, -TYING, -TIES** to attend a social gathering

PARTYER *n* pl. **-S** one that parties

PARTYING *n* pl. **-S** participation in a party

PARURA *n* pl. **-S** parure

PARURE *n* pl. **-S** a set of matched jewelry

PARVE *adj* made without milk or meat

PARVENU *n* pl. **-S** one who has suddenly risen above his class

PARVENUE *n* pl. **-S** a woman who is a parvenu

PARVIS *n pl.* **-VISES** an enclosed area in front of a church

PARVISE *n pl.* **-S** parvis

PARVO *n pl.* **-VOS** a contagious disease of dogs

PARVOLIN *n pl.* **-S** an oily liquid obtained from fish

PASCAL *n pl.* **-S** a unit of pressure

PASCHAL *n pl.* **-S** a candle used in certain religious ceremonies

PASE *n pl.* **-S** a movement of a matador's cape

PASEO *n pl.* **-SEOS** a leisurely stroll

PASH *v* **-ED, -ING, -ES** to strike violently

PASHA *n pl.* **-S** a former Turkish high official

PASHADOM *n pl.* **-S** the rank of a pasha

PASHALIC *n pl.* **-S** pashalik

PASHALIK *n pl.* **-S** the territory of a pasha

PASHKA *n pl.* **-S** paskha

PASHM *n pl.* **-S** the inner fur of some Tibetan animals

PASHMINA *n pl.* **-S** wool obtained from Himalayan goats

PASKA *n pl.* **-S** paskha

PASKHA *n pl.* **-S** a Russian dessert eaten at Easter

PASQUIL *n pl.* **-S** a satire or lampoon

PASS *v* **-ED, -ING, -ES** to go by

PASSABLE *adj* fairly good or acceptable **PASSABLY** *adv*

PASSADE *n pl.* **-S** a turn of a horse backward or forward on the same ground

PASSADO *n pl.* **-DOS** or **-DOES** a forward thrust in fencing

PASSAGE *v* **-SAGED, -SAGING, -SAGES** to make a voyage

PASSANT *adj* walking with the farther forepaw raised — used of a heraldic animal

PASSBAND *n pl.* **-S** a frequency band that permits transmission with maximum efficiency

PASSBOOK *n pl.* **-S** a bankbook

PASSE *adj* outmoded

PASSEE *adj* passe

PASSEL *n pl.* **-S** a large quantity or number

PASSER *n pl.* **-S** one that passes

PASSERBY *n pl.* **PASSERSBY** one who passes by

PASSIBLE *adj* capable of feeling or suffering

PASSIM *adv* here and there

PASSING *n pl.* **-S** a death

PASSION *n pl.* **-S** an intense emotion

PASSIVE *n pl.* **-S** a verb form

PASSKEY *n pl.* **-KEYS** a key that opens several different locks

PASSLESS *adj* incapable of being traveled over or through

PASSOVER *n pl.* **-S** the lamb eaten at the feast of a Jewish holiday

PASSPORT *n pl.* **-S** a document allowing travel from one country to another

PASSUS *n pl.* **-ES** a section of a story or poem

PASSWORD *n pl.* **-S** a secret word that must be spoken to gain admission

PAST *n pl.* **-S** time gone by

PASTA *n pl.* **-S** a food made of dough

PASTE *v* **PASTED, PASTING, PASTES** to fasten with a sticky mixture

PASTEL *n pl.* **-S** a soft, delicate hue

PASTER *n pl.* **-S** one that pastes

PASTERN *n pl.* **-S** a part of a horse's foot

PASTEUP *n pl.* **-S** a finished copy to be photographed for making a printing plate

PASTICCI *n/pl* pastiches

PASTICHE *n pl.* **-S** an artistic work made of fragments from various sources

PASTIE *n pl.* **-S** pasty

PASTIER comparative of pasty

PASTIES pl. of pasty

PASTIEST superlative of pasty

PASTIL *n pl.* **-S** pastille

PASTILLE *n pl.* **-S** a lozenge

PASTILY *adv* in a manner that is pasty

PASTIME *n pl.* **-S** a recreational activity

PASTINA *n pl.* **-S** a type of macaroni

PASTING *n pl.* **-S** a beating

PASTIS *n pl.* **-TISES** a French liqueur

PASTITSO *n pl.* **-TSOS** a Greek dish of ground meat, pasta, white sauce, and cheese

PASTLESS *adj* having no past

PASTNESS *n pl.* **-ES** the state of being past or gone by

PASTOR *v* **-ED, -ING, -S** to serve as the spiritual overseer of

PASTORAL *n* pl. **-S** a literary or artistic work that depicts country life

PASTORLY *adj* befitting a pastor (a spiritual overseer)

PASTRAMI *n* pl. **-S** a highly seasoned smoked beef

PASTROMI *n* pl. **-S** pastrami

PASTRY *n* pl. **-TRIES** a sweet baked food

PASTURAL *adj* pertaining to a pasture

PASTURE *v* **-TURED, -TURING, -TURES** to put in a pasture (a grazing area)

PASTURER *n* pl. **-S** one that pastures livestock

PASTY *adj* **PASTIER, PASTIEST** pale and unhealthy in appearance

PASTY *n* pl. **PASTIES** a meat pie

PAT *v* **PATTED, PATTING, PATS** to touch lightly

PAT *adj* **PATTER, PATTEST** known thoroughly

PATACA *n* pl. **-S** a monetary unit of Macao

PATAGIAL *adj* pertaining to a patagium

PATAGIUM *n* pl. **-GIA** a wing membrane of a bat

PATAMAR *n* pl. **-S** a sailing vessel

PATCH *v* **-ED, -ING, -ES** to mend or cover a hole or weak spot in

PATCHER *n* pl. **-S** one that patches

PATCHY *adj* **PATCHIER, PATCHIEST** uneven in quality **PATCHILY** *adv*

PATE *n* pl. **-S** the top of the head **PATED** *adj*

PATELLA *n* pl. **-LAS** or **-LAE** the flat movable bone at the front of the knee **PATELLAR** *adj*

PATEN *n* pl. **-S** a plate

PATENCY *n* pl. **-CIES** the state of being obvious

PATENT *v* **-ED, -ING, -S** to obtain a patent (a government grant protecting the rights of an inventor) on

PATENTEE *n* pl. **-S** one that holds a patent

PATENTLY *adv* obviously

PATENTOR *n* pl. **-S** one that grants a patent

PATER *n* pl. **-S** a father

PATERNAL *adj* pertaining to a father

PATH *n* pl. **-S** a trodden way or track

PATHETIC *adj* arousing pity

PATHLESS *adj* having no path

PATHNAME *n* pl. **-S** a description of where a file is to be found

PATHOGEN *n* pl. **-S** any disease-producing organism

PATHOS *n* pl. **-ES** a quality that arouses feelings of pity or compassion

PATHWAY *n* pl. **-WAYS** a path

PATIENCE *n* pl. **-S** the quality of being patient

PATIENT *adj* **-TIENTER, -TIENTEST** able to endure disagreeable circumstances without complaint

PATIENT *n* pl. **-S** one who is under medical treatment

PATIN *n* pl. **-S** paten

PATINA *n* pl. **-NAS** or **-NAE** a green film that forms on bronze **PATINAED** *adj*

PATINATE *v* **-NATED, -NATING, -NATES** to give a patina to

PATINE *v* **-TINED, -TINING, -TINES** to cover with a patina

PATINIZE *v* **-NIZED, -NIZING, -NIZES** to patinate

PATIO *n* pl. **-TIOS** an outdoor paved area adjoining a house

PATLY *adv* suitably

PATNESS *n* pl. **-ES** suitability

PATOIS *n* pl. **PATOIS** a dialect

PATONCE *adj* having the arms broaden from the center and end in three-pointed lobes — used of a heraldic cross

PATOOT *n* pl. **-S** patootie

PATOOTIE *n* pl. **-S** the buttocks

PATRIATE *v* **-ATED, -ATING, -ATES** to transfer (power of legislation) to an autonomous country

PATRIOT *n* pl. **-S** one who loves his country

PATROL *v* **-TROLLED, -TROLLING, -TROLS** to pass through an area for the purposes of observation or security

PATRON *n* pl. **-S** a regular customer **PATRONAL, PATRONLY** *adj*

PATROON *n* pl. **-S** a landowner granted manorial rights under old Dutch law

PATSY *n* pl. **-SIES** a person who is easily fooled

PATTAMAR *n* pl. **-S** patamar

PATTED past tense of pat

PATTEE *adj* paty

PATTEN *n* pl. **-S** a shoe having a thick wooden sole **PATTENED** *adj*

PATTER *v* **-ED, -ING, -S** to talk glibly or rapidly

PATTERER *n* pl. **-S** one that patters

PATTERN *v* **-ED, -ING, -S** to make according to a prescribed design

PATTEST superlative of pat

PATTIE *n* pl. **-S** patty

PATTING present participle of pat

PATTY *n* pl. **-TIES** a small, flat cake of chopped food

PATTYPAN *n* pl. **-S** a pan in which patties are baked

PATULENT *adj* patulous

PATULOUS *adj* spreading; open

PATY *adj* formee

PATZER *n* pl. **-S** an inept chess player

PAUA *n* pl. **-S** a large New Zealand shellfish

PAUCITY *n* pl. **-TIES** smallness of number or quantity

PAUGHTY *adj* arrogant

PAULDRON *n* pl. **-S** a piece of armor for the shoulder

PAULIN *n* pl. **-S** a sheet of waterproof material

PAUNCH *n* pl. **-ES** the belly or abdomen **PAUNCHED** *adj*

PAUNCHY *adj* **PAUNCHIER, PAUNCHIEST** having a protruding belly

PAUPER *v* **-ED, -ING, -S** to reduce to poverty

PAURAQUE *n* pl. **-S** a long-tailed nocturnal bird

PAUROPOD *n* pl. **-S** any of a class of minute many-legged animals

PAUSAL *adj* pertaining to a break or rest in speaking or writing

PAUSE *v* **PAUSED, PAUSING, PAUSES** to stop temporarily

PAUSER *n* pl. **-S** one that pauses

PAVAN *n* pl. **-S** a slow, stately dance

PAVANE *n* pl. **-S** pavan

PAVE *v* **PAVED, PAVING, PAVES** to cover with material that forms a firm, level surface

PAVEED *adj* set close together to conceal a metal base

PAVEMENT *n* pl. **-S** a paved surface

PAVER *n* pl. **-S** one that paves

PAVID *adj* timid

PAVILION *v* **-ED, -ING, -S** to cover with a large tent

PAVILLON *n* pl. **-S** the bell of a wind instrument

PAVIN *n* pl. **-S** pavan

PAVING *n* pl. **-S** pavement

PAVIOR *n* pl. **-S** a paver

PAVIOUR *n* pl. **-S** a paver

PAVIS *n* pl. **-ISES** a large medieval shield

PAVISE *n* pl. **-S** pavis

PAVISER *n* pl. **-S** a soldier carrying a pavis

PAVISSE *n* pl. **-S** pavis

PAVLOVA *n* pl. **-S** a meringue dessert

PAVONINE *adj* resembling a peacock

PAW *v* **-ED, -ING, -S** to strike or scrape with a beating motion

PAWER *n* pl. **-S** one that paws

PAWKY *adj* **PAWKIER, PAWKIEST** sly **PAWKILY** *adv*

PAWL *n* pl. **-S** a hinged mechanical part

PAWN *v* **-ED, -ING, -S** to give as security for something borrowed **PAWNABLE** *adj*

PAWNAGE *n* pl. **-S** an act of pawning

PAWNEE *n* pl. **-S** one to whom something is pawned

PAWNER *n* pl. **-S** one that pawns something

PAWNOR *n* pl. **-S** pawner

PAWNSHOP *n* pl. **-S** a place where things are pawned

PAWPAW *n* pl. **-S** papaw

PAX *n* pl. **-ES** a ceremonial embrace given to signify Christian love and unity

PAXWAX *n* pl. **-ES** the nuchal ligament of a quadruped

PAY *v* **PAID** or **PAYED, PAYING, PAYS** to give money or something of value in exchange for goods or services

PAYABLE *adj* profitable **PAYABLY** *adv*

PAYABLES *n/pl* accounts payable

PAYBACK *n* pl. **-S** a return on an investment equal to the original capital outlay

PAYCHECK *n* pl. **-S** a check in payment of wages or salary

PAYDAY *n* pl. **-DAYS** the day on which wages are paid

PAYDOWN *n* pl. **-S** the reduction of debt through repayment

PAYEE   *n* pl. **-S** one to whom money is paid

PAYER   *n* pl. **-S** one that pays

PAYESS   *n/pl* uncut sideburns worn by some Jews

PAYGRADE   *n* pl. **-S** the grade of military personnel according to a base pay scale

PAYLOAD   *n* pl. **-S** the part of a cargo producing income

PAYMENT   *n* pl. **-S** something that is paid

PAYNIM   *n* pl. **-S** a pagan

PAYOFF   *n* pl. **-S** the act of distributing gains

PAYOLA   *n* pl. **-S** a secret payment for favors

PAYOR   *n* pl. **-S** payer

PAYOUT   *n* pl. **-S** money that is paid out

PAYROLL   *n* pl. **-S** a list of employees entitled to payment

PAYSLIP   *n* pl. **-S** a brief record of an employee's wages indicating deductions

PAYWALL   *n* pl. **-S** a system that prevents access to a website without a paid subscription

PAZAZZ   *n* pl. **-ES** pizazz

PE   *n* pl. **-S** a Hebrew letter

PEA   *n* pl. **-S** the edible seed of an annual herb

PEABERRY   *n* pl. **-RIES** a coffee berry having a single round seed

PEABRAIN   *n* pl. **-S** a stupid person

PEACE   *v* **PEACED, PEACING, PEACES** to be or become silent

PEACEFUL   *adj* **-FULLER, -FULLEST** undisturbed; calm

PEACENIK   *n* pl. **-S** one who demonstrates against a war

PEACH   *v* **-ED, -ING, -ES** to inform against someone

PEACHER   *n* pl. **-S** one that peaches

PEACHICK   *n* pl. **-S** a young peafowl

PEACHY   *adj* **PEACHIER, PEACHIEST** dandy

PEACING   present participle of peace

PEACOAT   *n* pl. **-S** a heavy woolen jacket

PEACOCK   *v* **-ED, -ING, -S** to strut vainly

PEACOCKY   *adj* **-COCKIER, -COCKIEST** flamboyant, showy

PEAFOWL   *n* pl. **-S** a large pheasant

PEAG   *n* pl. **-S** wampum

PEAGE   *n* pl. **-S** peag

PEAHEN   *n* pl. **-S** a female peafowl

PEAK   *v* **-ED, -ING, -S** to reach a maximum

PEAKIER   comparative of peaky

PEAKIEST   superlative of peaky

PEAKISH   *adj* somewhat sickly

PEAKLESS   *adj* having no peak (a pointed top)

PEAKLIKE   *adj* resembling a peak

PEAKY   *adj* **PEAKIER, PEAKIEST** sickly

PEAL   *v* **-ED, -ING, -S** to ring out

PEALIKE   *adj* resembling a pea

PEAN   *n* pl. **-S** paean

PEANUT   *n* pl. **-S** the nutlike seed or pod of an annual vine

PEANUTTY   *n* **-NUTTIER, -NUTTIEST** having the taste of peanuts

PEAR   *n* pl. **-S** a fleshy fruit

PEARL   *v* **-ED, -ING, -S** to adorn with pearls (smooth, rounded masses formed in certain mollusks)

PEARLASH   *n* pl. **-ES** an alkaline compound

PEARLER   *n* pl. **-S** one that dives for pearls

PEARLIES   *n/pl* teeth

PEARLITE   *n* pl. **-S** a cast-iron alloy

PEARLY   *adj* **PEARLIER, PEARLIEST** resembling a pearl

PEARMAIN   *n* pl. **-S** a variety of apple

PEART   *adj* **PEARTER, PEARTEST** lively **PEARTLY** *adv*

PEARWOOD   *n* pl. **-S** the wood of the pear tree

PEASANT   *n* pl. **-S** a person of inferior social rank **PEASANTY** *adj*

PEASCOD   *n* pl. **-S** peasecod

PEASE   *n* pl. **PEASES** or **PEASEN** a pea

PEASECOD   *n* pl. **-S** a pea pod

PEAT   *n* pl. **-S** a substance composed of partially decayed vegetable matter

PEATLAND   *n* pl. **-S** land consisting mostly of peat

PEATY   *adj* **PEATIER, PEATIEST** resembling or containing peat

PEAVEY   *n* pl. **-VEYS** a lever used to move logs

PEAVY   *n* pl. **-VIES** peavey

PEBBLE   *v* **-BLED, -BLING, -BLES** to cover with pebbles (small, rounded stones)

PEBBLY *adj* **-BLIER, -BLIEST** resembling pebbles

PEC *n* pl. **-S** a chest muscle

PECAN *n* pl. **-S** a nut-bearing tree

PECCABLE *adj* liable to sin

PECCANCY *n* pl. **-CIES** the state of being peccant

PECCANT *adj* sinful

PECCARY *n* pl. **-RIES** a piglike hoofed mammal

PECCAVI *n* pl. **-S** a confession of sin

PECH *v* **-ED, -ING, -S** to pant

PECHAN *n* pl. **-S** the stomach

PECK *v* **-ED, -ING, -S** to strike with the beak or something pointed

PECKER *n* pl. **-S** one that pecks

PECKISH *adj* irritable

PECKY *adj* **PECKIER, PECKIEST** marked by decay caused by fungi

PECORINO *n* pl. **-NOS** or **-NI** a hard cheese made from sheep's milk

PECTASE *n* pl. **-S** an enzyme

PECTATE *n* pl. **-S** a chemical salt

PECTEN *n* pl. **-TENS** or **-TINES** a comblike anatomical part

PECTIN *n* pl. **-S** a carbohydrate derivative **PECTIC** *adj*

PECTIZE *v* **-TIZED, -TIZING, -TIZES** to change into a jelly

PECTORAL *n* pl. **-S** something worn on the breast

PECULATE *v* **-LATED, -LATING, -LATES** to embezzle

PECULIAR *n* pl. **-S** something belonging exclusively to a person

PECULIUM *n* pl. **-LIA** private property

PED *n* pl. **-S** a natural soil aggregate

PEDAGOG *n* pl. **-S** a teacher

PEDAGOGY *n* pl. **-GIES** the work of a teacher

PEDAL *v* **-ALED, -ALING, -ALS** or **-ALLED, -ALLING, -ALS** to operate by means of foot levers

PEDALER *n* pl. **-S** one that pedals

PEDALFER *n* pl. **-S** a type of soil

PEDALIER *n* pl. **-S** the pedal keyboard of an organ

PEDALLER *n* pl. **-S** pedaler

PEDALO *n* pl. **-LOS** a paddleboat powered by pedals

PEDANT *n* pl. **-S** one who flaunts his knowledge **PEDANTIC** *adj*

PEDANTRY *n* pl. **-RIES** ostentatious display of knowledge

PEDATE *adj* resembling a foot **PEDATELY** *adv*

PEDDLE *v* **-DLED, -DLING, -DLES** to travel about selling wares

PEDDLER *n* pl. **-S** one that peddles

PEDDLERY *n* pl. **-RIES** the trade of a peddler

PEDERAST *n* pl. **-S** a man who engages in sexual activities with boys

PEDES pl. of pes

PEDESTAL *v* **-TALED, -TALING, -TALS** or **-TALLED, -TALLING, -TALS** to provide with an architectural support or base

PEDICAB *n* pl. **-S** a passenger vehicle that is pedaled

PEDICEL *n* pl. **-S** a slender basal part of an organism

PEDICLE *n* pl. **-S** pedicel **PEDICLED** *adj*

PEDICURE *v* **-CURED, -CURING, -CURES** to administer a cosmetic treatment to the feet and toenails

PEDIFORM *adj* shaped like a foot

PEDIGREE *n* pl. **-S** a line of ancestors

PEDIMENT *n* pl. **-S** a triangular architectural part

PEDIPALP *n* pl. **-S** an appendage of an arachnid

PEDLAR *n* pl. **-S** peddler

PEDLARY *n* pl. **-LARIES** peddlery

PEDLER *n* pl. **-S** peddler

PEDLERY *n* pl. **-LERIES** peddlery

PEDOCAL *n* pl. **-S** a type of soil

PEDOLOGY *n* pl. **-GIES** the scientific study of the behavior and development of children

PEDRO *n* pl. **-DROS** a card game

PEDUNCLE *n* pl. **-S** a flower stalk

PEDWAY *n* pl. **-WAYS** a walkway for pedestrians only

PEE *n* pl. **-S** the letter P

PEEBEEN *n* pl. **-S** a large hardwood evergreen tree

PEEK *v* **-ED, -ING, -S** to look furtively or quickly

PEEKABOO *n* pl. **-BOOS** a children's game

PEEKAPOO _n_ pl. **-POOS** a dog that is a cross between a Pekingese and a poodle

PEEL _v_ **-ED, -ING, -S** to strip off an outer covering of **PEELABLE** _adj_

PEELER _n_ pl. **-S** one that peels

PEELING _n_ pl. **-S** a piece or strip that has been peeled off

PEEN _v_ **-ED, -ING, -S** to beat with the non-flat end of a hammerhead

PEENING _n_ pl. **-S** the action of treating sheet metal with metal shot in order to shape it

PEEP _v_ **-ED, -ING, -S** to utter a short, shrill cry

PEEPBO _n_ pl. **-BOS** the game of peekaboo

PEEPER _n_ pl. **-S** one that peeps

PEEPHOLE _n_ pl. **-S** a small opening through which one may look

PEEPSHOW _n_ pl. **-S** an exhibition viewed through a small opening

PEEPUL _n_ pl. **-S** pipal

PEER _v_ **-ED, -ING, -S** to look narrowly or searchingly

PEERAGE _n_ pl. **-S** the rank of a nobleman

PEERESS _n_ pl. **-ES** a noblewoman

PEERIE _n_ pl. **-S** peery

PEERLESS _adj_ having no equal

PEERY _n_ pl. **PEERIES** a child's toy

PEESWEEP _n_ pl. **-S** a lapwing

PEETWEET _n_ pl. **-S** a wading bird

PEEVE _v_ **PEEVED, PEEVING, PEEVES** to annoy

PEEVISH _adj_ irritable

PEEWEE _n_ pl. **-S** an unusually small person or thing

PEEWIT _n_ pl. **-S** pewit

PEG _v_ **PEGGED, PEGGING, PEGS** to fasten with a peg (a wooden pin)

PEGBOARD _n_ pl. **-S** a board with holes for pegs

PEGBOX _n_ pl. **-ES** a part of a stringed instrument

PEGLESS _adj_ lacking a peg

PEGLIKE _adj_ resembling a peg

PEGTOP _n_ pl. **-S** a spinning top having a peg wound with string

PEH _n_ pl. **-S** pe

PEIGNOIR _n_ pl. **-S** a woman's gown

PEIN _v_ **-ED, -ING, -S** to peen

PEISE _v_ **PEISED, PEISING, PEISES** to weigh

PEKAN _n_ pl. **-S** a carnivorous mammal

PEKE _n_ pl. **-S** a small, long-haired dog

PEKEPOO _n_ pl. **-POOS** peekapoo

PEKIN _n_ pl. **-S** a silk fabric

PEKOE _n_ pl. **-S** a black tea

PELAGE _n_ pl. **-S** the coat or covering of a mammal **PELAGIAL** _adj_

PELAGIC _n_ pl. **-S** an inhabitant of the ocean

PELAU _n_ pl. **-S** a dish made with meat, rice, and pigeon peas

PELE _n_ pl. **-S** a medieval fortified tower

PELERINE _n_ pl. **-S** a woman's cape

PELF _n_ pl. **-S** money or wealth

PELHAM _n_ pl. **-S** a type of a horse's mouthpiece

PELICAN _n_ pl. **-S** a large, web-footed bird

PELISSE _n_ pl. **-S** a long outer garment

PELITE _n_ pl. **-S** a rock composed of fine fragments **PELITIC** _adj_

PELLAGRA _n_ pl. **-S** a niacin-deficiency disease

PELLET _v_ **-ED, -ING, -S** to strike with pellets (small rounded masses)

PELLETAL _adj_ resembling a pellet

PELLICLE _n_ pl. **-S** a thin skin or film

PELLMELL _n_ pl. **-S** a jumbled mass

PELLUCID _adj_ transparent

PELMET _n_ pl. **-S** a decorative cornice

PELON _adj_ hairless

PELORIA _n_ pl. **-S** abnormal regularity of a flower form **PELORIAN, PELORIC** _adj_

PELORUS _n_ pl. **-ES** a navigational instrument

PELOTA _n_ pl. **-S** a court game of Spanish origin

PELOTON _n_ pl. **-S** the main body of riders in a bicycle race

PELT _v_ **-ED, -ING, -S** to strike repeatedly with blows or missiles

PELTAST _n_ pl. **-S** a soldier of ancient Greece

PELTATE _adj_ shaped like a shield

PELTER _v_ **-ED, -ING, -S** to pelt

PELTLESS _adj_ lacking a pelt (the skin of an animal)

PELTRY _n_ pl. **-RIES** an animal skin

PELVIC _n_ pl. **-S** a bone of the pelvis

PELVIS *n* pl. **-VISES** or **-VES** a part of the skeleton

PEMBINA *n* pl. **-S** a variety of cranberry

PEMICAN *n* pl. **-S** pemmican

PEMMICAN *n* pl. **-S** a food prepared by Native Americans

PEMOLINE *n* pl. **-S** a drug used as a stimulant

PEMPHIX *n* pl. **-ES** a skin disease

PEN *v* **PENNED, PENNING, PENS** to write with a pen (an instrument for writing with fluid ink)

PENAL *adj* pertaining to punishment

PENALISE *v* **-ISED, -ISING, -ISES** to penalize

PENALITY *n* pl. **-TIES** liability to punishment

PENALIZE *v* **-IZED, -IZING, -IZES** to subject to a penalty

PENALLY *adv* in a penal manner

PENALTY *n* pl. **-TIES** a punishment imposed for violation of a law, rule, or agreement

PENANCE *v* **-ANCED, -ANCING, -ANCES** to impose a type of punishment upon

PENANG *n* pl. **-S** a cotton fabric

PENATES *n/pl* the Roman gods of the household

PENCE a pl. of penny

PENCEL *n* pl. **-S** a small flag

PENCHANT *n* pl. **-S** a strong liking for something

PENCIL *v* **-CILED, -CILING, -CILS** or **-CILLED, -CILLING, -CILS** to produce by using a pencil (a writing and drawing implement)

PENCILER *n* pl. **-S** one that pencils

PEND *v* **-ED, -ING, -S** to remain undecided or unsettled

PENDANT *n* pl. **-S** a hanging ornament

PENDENCY *n* pl. **-CIES** a pending state

PENDENT *n* pl. **-S** pendant

PENDULUM *n* pl. **-S** a type of free swinging body **PENDULAR** *adj*

PENES a pl. of penis

PENGO *n* pl. **-GOS** a former monetary unit of Hungary

PENGUIN *n* pl. **-S** a flightless, aquatic bird

PENICIL *n* pl. **-S** a small tuft of hairs

PENIS *n* pl. **-NISES** or **-NES** the male organ of copulation **PENIAL, PENILE** *adj*

PENITENT *n* pl. **-S** a person who repents his sins

PENKNIFE *n* pl. **-KNIVES** a small pocketknife

PENLIGHT *n* pl. **-S** a small flashlight

PENLITE *n* pl. **-S** penlight

PENMAN *n* pl. **-MEN** an author

PENNA *n* pl. **-NAE** any of the feathers that determine a bird's shape

PENNAME *n* pl. **-S** a name used by an author instead of his real name

PENNANT *n* pl. **-S** a long, narrow flag

PENNATE *adj* having wings or feathers

PENNATED *adj* pennate

PENNE *n* pl. **-S** short tubular pasta

PENNED past tense of pen

PENNER *n* pl. **-S** one that pens

PENNI *n* pl. **-NIS** or **-NIA** a formerly used Finnish coin

PENNIES a pl. of penny

PENNINE *n* pl. **-S** a mineral

PENNING present participle of pen

PENNON *n* pl. **-S** a pennant **PENNONED** *adj*

PENNY *n* pl. **PENNIES** or **PENCE** a coin of the United Kingdom

PENOCHE *n* pl. **-S** penuche

PENOLOGY *n* pl. **-GIES** the science of the punishment of crime

PENONCEL *n* pl. **-S** a small pennon

PENPOINT *n* pl. **-S** the point of a pen

PENSEE *n* pl. **-S** a thought

PENSIL *n* pl. **-S** pencel

PENSILE *adj* hanging loosely

PENSION *v* **-ED, -ING, -S** to grant a retirement allowance to

PENSIONE *n* pl. **-ONES** or **-ONI** a boarding house

PENSIVE *adj* engaged in deep thought

PENSTER *n* pl. **-S** a writer

PENSTOCK *n* pl. **-S** a conduit for conveying water to a waterwheel

PENT *adj* confined

PENTACLE *n* pl. **-S** a five-pointed star

PENTAD *n* pl. **-S** a group of five

PENTAGON *n* pl. **-S** a five-sided polygon

PENTANE *n* pl. **-S** a volatile liquid

PENTANOL *n* pl. **-S** an alcohol

PENTARCH *n* pl. **-S** one of five joint rulers

PENTENE	*n* pl. **-S** a liquid hydrocarbon
PENTODE	*n* pl. **-S** a type of electron tube
PENTOMIC	*adj* made up of five battle groups
PENTOSAN	*n* pl. **-S** a complex carbohydrate
PENTOSE	*n* pl. **-S** a sugar having five carbon atoms per molecule
PENTYL	*n* pl. **-S** amyl
PENUCHE	*n* pl. **-S** a fudge-like candy
PENUCHI	*n* pl. **-S** penuche
PENUCHLE	*n* pl. **-S** pinochle
PENUCKLE	*n* pl. **-S** pinochle
PENULT	*n* pl. **-S** the next to last syllable in a word
PENUMBRA	*n* pl. **-BRAS** or **-BRAE** a partial shadow
PENURY	*n* pl. **-RIES** extreme poverty
PEON	*n* pl. **-S** or **-ES** an unskilled laborer
PEONAGE	*n* pl. **-S** the condition of being a peon
PEONISM	*n* pl. **-S** peonage
PEONY	*n* pl. **-NIES** a flowering plant
PEOPLE	*v* **-PLED, -PLING, -PLES** to furnish with inhabitants
PEOPLER	*n* pl. **-S** one that peoples
PEP	*v* **PEPPED, PEPPING, PEPS** to fill with energy
PEPERONI	*n* pl. **-S** a highly seasoned sausage
PEPINO	*n* pl. **-NOS** a bushy perennial plant with edible fruit
PEPITA	*n* pl. **-S** the edible dried seed of a pumpkin or squash
PEPLOS	*n* pl. **-ES** a garment worn by women in ancient Greece
PEPLUM	*n* pl. **-LUMS** or **-LA** a short section attached to the waistline of a garment **PEPLUMED** *adj*
PEPLUS	*n* pl. **-ES** peplos
PEPO	*n* pl. **-POS** a fruit having a fleshy interior and a hard rind
PEPONIDA	*n* pl. **-S** pepo
PEPONIUM	*n* pl. **-S** pepo
PEPPED	past tense of pep
PEPPER	*v* **-ED, -ING, -S** to season with pepper (a pungent condiment)
PEPPERER	*n* pl. **-S** one that peppers
PEPPERY	*adj* resembling pepper
PEPPING	present participle of pep

PEPPY	*adj* **-PIER, -PIEST** full of energy **PEPPILY** *adv*
PEPSIN	*n* pl. **-S** a digestive enzyme of the stomach
PEPSINE	*n* pl. **-S** pepsin
PEPTALK	*v* **-ED, -ING, -S** to inspire enthusiasm in by an intense, emotional talk
PEPTIC	*n* pl. **-S** a substance that promotes digestion
PEPTID	*n* pl. **-S** peptide
PEPTIDE	*n* pl. **-S** a combination of amino acids **PEPTIDIC** *adj*
PEPTIZE	*v* **-TIZED, -TIZING, -TIZES** to increase the colloidal dispersion of
PEPTIZER	*n* pl. **-S** one that peptizes
PEPTONE	*n* pl. **-S** a protein compound **PEPTONIC** *adj*
PER	*prep* for each
PERACID	*n* pl. **-S** a type of acid
PERC	*n* pl. **-S** a chemical used in dry cleaning
PERCALE	*n* pl. **-S** a cotton fabric
PERCEIVE	*v* **-CEIVED, -CEIVING, -CEIVES** to become aware of through the senses
PERCENT	*n* pl. **-S** one part in a hundred
PERCEPT	*n* pl. **-S** something that is perceived
PERCH	*v* **-ED, -ING, -ES** to sit or rest on an elevated place
PERCHER	*n* pl. **-S** one that perches
PERCID	*n* pl. **-S** a freshwater fish of the perch family
PERCOID	*n* pl. **-S** any of a large suborder of spiny-finned fishes
PERCUSS	*v* **-ED, -ING, -ES** to strike with force
PERDIE	*interj* pardi
PERDU	*n* pl. **-S** a soldier sent on a dangerous mission
PERDUE	*n* pl. **-S** perdu
PERDURE	*v* **-DURED, -DURING, -DURES** to continue to exist
PERDY	*interj* pardi
PERE	*n* pl. **-S** father
PEREGRIN	*n* pl. **-S** a swift falcon much used in falconry
PEREION	*n* pl. **-REIONS** or **-REIA** the thorax of some crustaceans
PEREON	*n* pl. **-REONS** or **-REA** pereion

PEREOPOD *n* pl. **-S** an appendage of the pereion

PERFECT *adj* **-FECTER, -FECTEST** lacking fault or defect; of an extreme kind

PERFECT *v* **-ED, -ING, -S** to make perfect

PERFECTA *n* pl. **-S** a system of betting

PERFECTO *n* pl. **-TOS** a medium-sized cigar

PERFIDY *n* pl. **-DIES** deliberate breach of faith or trust

PERFORCE *adv* of necessity

PERFORM *v* **-ED, -ING, -S** to begin and carry through to completion

PERFUME *v* **-FUMED, -FUMING, -FUMES** to fill with a fragrant odor

PERFUMER *n* pl. **-S** one that perfumes

PERFUMY *adj* scented

PERFUSE *v* **-FUSED, -FUSING, -FUSES** to spread over or through something

PERGOLA *n* pl. **-S** a shaded shelter or passageway

PERHAPS *n* pl. **-ES** something open to doubt or conjecture

PERI *n* pl. **-S** a supernatural being of Persian mythology

PERIANTH *n* pl. **-S** an outer covering of a flower

PERIAPT *n* pl. **-S** an amulet

PERIBLEM *n* pl. **-S** a region of plant tissue

PERICARP *n* pl. **-S** the wall of a ripened plant ovary or fruit

PERICOPE *n* pl. **-PES** or **-PAE** a selection from a book

PERIDERM *n* pl. **-S** an outer layer of plant tissue

PERIDIUM *n* pl. **-DIA** the covering of the spore-bearing organ in many fungi **PERIDIAL** *adj*

PERIDOT *n* pl. **-S** a mineral

PERIGEE *n* pl. **-S** the point in the orbit of a celestial body which is nearest to the earth **PERIGEAL, PERIGEAN** *adj*

PERIGON *n* pl. **-S** an angle equal to 360 degrees

PERIGYNY *n* pl. **-NIES** the state of being situated on a cuplike organ surrounding the pistil

PERIL *v* **-ILED, -ILING, -ILS** or **-ILLED, -ILLING, -ILS** to imperil

PERILLA *n* pl. **-S** an Asian herb

PERILOUS *adj* dangerous

PERILUNE *n* pl. **-S** the point in the orbit of a celestial body which is nearest to the moon

PERINEUM *n* pl. **-NEA** a region of the body at the lower end of the trunk **PERINEAL** *adj*

PERIOD *n* pl. **-S** a portion of time

PERIODIC *adj* recurring at regular intervals

PERIODID *n* pl. **-S** an iodide

PERIOTIC *adj* surrounding the ear

PERIPETY *n* pl. **-TIES** a sudden change in a course of events

PERIPTER *n* pl. **-S** a structure with a row of columns around all sides

PERIQUE *n* pl. **-S** a dark tobacco

PERISARC *n* pl. **-S** a protective covering of certain hydrozoans

PERISH *v* **-ED, -ING, -ES** to die

PERISHER *n* pl. **-S** an annoying person

PERITUS *n* pl. **-TI** an expert theologian

PERIWIG *n* pl. **-S** a wig

PERJURE *v* **-JURED, -JURING, -JURES** to make a perjurer of

PERJURER *n* pl. **-S** one guilty of perjury

PERJURY *n* pl. **-RIES** the willful giving of false testimony under oath in a judicial proceeding

PERK *v* **-ED, -ING, -S** to prepare (coffee) in a percolator

PERKISH *adj* somewhat perky

PERKY *adj* **PERKIER, PERKIEST** jaunty **PERKILY** *adv*

PERLITE *n* pl. **-S** a volcanic glass **PERLITIC** *adj*

PERM *v* **-ED, -ING, -S** to give hair a permanent wave

PERMEANT *adj* that permeates

PERMEASE *n* pl. **-S** a catalyzing agent

PERMEATE *v* **-ATED, -ATING, -ATES** to spread through

PERMIT *v* **-MITTED, -MITTING, -MITS** to allow

PERMUTE *v* **-MUTED, -MUTING, -MUTES** to change the order of

PERNIO *n* pl. **-NIONES** an inflammation on the hands or feet caused by exposure to cold

PEROGI *n* pl. **-ES** pierogi

PEROGIE *n* pl. **-S** pierogi

PEROGY *n* pl. **-OGIES** pierogi

PERONEAL *adj* pertaining to the fibula

PERORAL *adj* occurring through the mouth

PERORATE *v* **-RATED, -RATING, -RATES** to make a lengthy speech

PEROXID *n* pl. **-S** peroxide

PEROXIDE *v* **-IDED, -IDING, -IDES** to treat with peroxide (a bleaching agent)

PEROXY *adj* containing the bivalent group O_2

PERP *n* pl. **-S** a person who commits a crime

PERPEND *v* **-ED, -ING, -S** to ponder

PERPENT *n* pl. **-S** a large building stone

PERPLEX *v* **-ED, -ING, -ES** to make mentally uncertain

PERRON *n* pl. **-S** an outdoor stairway

PERRY *n* pl. **-RIES** a beverage of pear juice often fermented

PERSALT *n* pl. **-S** a chemical salt

PERSE *n* pl. **-S** a blue color

PERSIST *v* **-ED, -ING, -S** to continue resolutely in some activity

PERSON *n* pl. **-S** a human being

PERSONA *n* pl. **-NAE** a character in a literary work

PERSONA *n* pl. **-S** the public role that a person assumes

PERSONAL *n* pl. **-S** a brief, private notice in a newspaper

PERSPIRE *v* **-SPIRED, -SPIRING, -SPIRES** to give off moisture through the pores of the skin **PERSPIRY** *adj*

PERSUADE *v* **-SUADED, -SUADING, -SUADES** to cause to do something by means of argument, reasoning, or entreaty

PERT *adj* **PERTER, PERTEST** impudent **PERTLY** *adv*

PERTAIN *v* **-ED, -ING, -S** to have reference or relation

PERTNESS *n* pl. **-ES** the quality of being pert

PERTURB *v* **-ED, -ING, -S** to disturb greatly

PERUKE *n* pl. **-S** a wig **PERUKED** *adj*

PERUSAL *n* pl. **-S** the act of perusing

PERUSE *v* **-RUSED, -RUSING, -RUSES** to read

PERUSER *n* pl. **-S** one that peruses

PERV *n* pl. **-S** one who is sexually perverted

PERVADE *v* **-VADED, -VADING, -VADES** to spread through every part of

PERVADER *n* pl. **-S** one that pervades

PERVERSE *adj* willfully deviating from desired or expected conduct

PERVERT *v* **-ED, -ING, -S** to turn away from the right course of action

PERVIOUS *adj* capable of being penetrated

PERVO *n* pl. **-VOS** a perv

PERVY *adj* **PERVIER, PERVIEST** sexually perverted

PES *n* pl. **PEDES** a foot or footlike part

PESADE *n* pl. **-S** the position of a horse when rearing

PESETA *n* pl. **-S** a former monetary unit of Spain

PESEWA *n* pl. **-S** a monetary unit of Ghana

PESKY *adj* **-KIER, -KIEST** annoying **PESKILY** *adv*

PESO *n* pl. **-SOS** a monetary unit of various Spanish-speaking countries

PESSARY *n* pl. **-RIES** a contraceptive device worn in the vagina

PEST *n* pl. **-S** an annoying person or thing

PESTER *v* **-ED, -ING, -S** to bother

PESTERER *n* pl. **-S** one that pesters

PESTHOLE *n* pl. **-S** a place liable to epidemic disease

PESTLE *v* **-TLED, -TLING, -TLES** to crush with a club-shaped hand tool

PESTO *n* pl. **-TOS** a sauce of basil, garlic, and olive oil

PESTY *adj* **PESTIER, PESTIEST** annoying

PET *v* **PETTED, PETTING, PETS** to caress with the hand

PETABYTE *n* pl. **-S** one quadrillion bytes

PETAL *n* pl. **-S** a leaflike part of a corolla **PETALED, PETALLED** *adj*

PETALINE *adj* resembling a petal

PETALODY *n* pl. **-DIES** the metamorphosis of various floral organs into petals

PETALOID *adj* resembling a petal

PETALOUS *adj* having petals

PETANQUE *n* pl. **-S** a French form of lawn bowling

PETARD *n* pl. **-S** an explosive device

PETASOS *n* pl. **-ES** petasus

PETASUS *n* pl. **-ES** a broad-brimmed hat worn in ancient Greece

PETCOCK *n* pl. **-S** a small valve or faucet

PETECHIA *n pl.* **-CHIAE** a small hemorrhagic spot on a body surface

PETER *v* **-ED, -ING, -S** to diminish gradually

PETIOLAR *adj* pertaining to a petiole

PETIOLE *n pl.* **-S** the stalk of a leaf **PETIOLED** *adj*

PETIT *adj* small; minor

PETITE *n pl.* **-S** a clothing size for short women

PETITION *v* **-ED, -ING, -S** to make a formal request

PETNAP *v* **-NAPPED, -NAPPING, -NAPS** to steal a pet for profit

PETNAPER *n pl.* **-S** one who steals a pet

PETRALE *n pl.* **-S** a food fish

PETREL *n pl.* **-S** a small seabird

PETRIFY *v* **-FIED, -FYING, -FIES** to convert into stone

PETROL *n pl.* **-S** gasoline

PETROLIC *adj* derived from petroleum

PETRONEL *n pl.* **-S** a portable firearm

PETROSAL *n pl.* **-S** a part of the temporal bone

PETROUS *adj* resembling stone in hardness

PETSAI *n pl.* **-S** Chinese cabbage

PETTABLE *adj* capable of being petted

PETTED past tense of pet

PETTEDLY *adv* peevishly

PETTER *n pl.* **-S** one that pets

PETTI *pl.* of petto

PETTIER comparative of petty

PETTIEST superlative of petty

PETTIFOG *v* **-FOGGED, -FOGGING, -FOGS** to quibble

PETTILY *adv* in a petty manner

PETTING *n pl.* **-S** amorous caressing and kissing

PETTISH *adj* peevish

PETTLE *v* **-TLED, -TLING, -TLES** to caress

PETTO *n pl.* **-TI** the breast

PETTY *adj* **-TIER, -TIEST** insignificant

PETULANT *adj* peevish

PETUNIA *n pl.* **-S** a tropical herb

PETUNTSE *n pl.* **-S** a mineral

PETUNTZE *n pl.* **-S** petuntse

PEW *n pl.* **-S** a bench in church

PEWEE *n pl.* **-S** a small bird

PEWIT *n pl.* **-S** the lapwing

PEWTER *n pl.* **-S** a tin alloy **PEWTERY** *adj*

PEWTERER *n pl.* **-S** one that makes articles of pewter

PEYOTE *n pl.* **-S** a cactus

PEYOTISM *n pl.* **-S** the Native American ritual in which peyote is used

PEYOTL *n pl.* **-S** peyote

PEYTRAL *n pl.* **-S** a piece of armor for the breast of a horse

PEYTREL *n pl.* **-S** peytral

PFENNIG *n pl.* **-NIGS** or **-NIGE** a formerly used bronze coin of Germany

PFFT *interj* — used to express a sudden ending

PFUI *interj* phooey

PHAETON *n pl.* **-S** a light carriage

PHAGE *n pl.* **-S** an organism that destroys bacteria

PHALANGE *n pl.* **-S** any bone of a finger or toe

PHALANX *n pl.* **-ES** a formation of infantry in ancient Greece

PHALLI a *pl.* of phallus

PHALLIC *adj* pertaining to a phallus

PHALLISM *n pl.* **-S** worship of the phallus as symbolic of nature's creative power

PHALLIST *n pl.* **-S** one who practices phallism

PHALLUS *n pl.* **-LUSES** or **-LI** the penis

PHANTASM *n pl.* **-S** a creation of the imagination

PHANTAST *n pl.* **-S** fantast

PHANTASY *v* **-SIED, -SYING, -SIES** to fantasy

PHANTOM *n pl.* **-S** something existing in appearance only

PHARAOH *n pl.* **-S** a ruler of ancient Egypt

PHARISEE *n pl.* **-S** a hypocritically self-righteous person

PHARMA *n pl.* **-S** a pharmaceutical company

PHARMACY *n pl.* **-CIES** a drugstore

PHARMER *n pl.* **-S** one who participates in pharming

PHARMING *n pl.* **-S** the production of pharmaceuticals from genetically altered plants or animals

PHAROS *n pl.* **-ES** a lighthouse or beacon to guide seamen

PHARYNX *n pl.* **-YNXES** or **-YNGES** a section of the digestive tract

PHASE	v **PHASED, PHASING, PHASES** to plan or carry out by phases (distinct stages of development) **PHASEAL, PHASIC** adj	**PHISH**	v **-ED, -ING, -ES** to engage in phishing
PHASEOUT	n pl. **-S** a gradual stopping of operations	**PHISHER**	n pl. **-S** one that phishes
		PHISHING	n pl. **-S** the practice of using email illegally to induce people to reveal personal information
PHASER	n pl. **-S** a type of science-fiction weapon	**PHIZ**	n pl. **-ES** a face or facial expression
PHASIS	n pl. **PHASES** a phase	**PHIZZ**	n pl. **-ES** phiz
PHASMID	n pl. **-S** a tropical insect	**PHLEGM**	n pl. **-S** a thick mucus secreted in the air passages
PHAT	adj **PHATTER, PHATTEST** excellent	**PHLEGMY**	adj **PHLEGMIER, PHLEGMIEST** resembling phlegm
PHATIC	adj sharing feelings rather than ideas	**PHLOEM**	n pl. **-S** a complex plant tissue
PHEASANT	n pl. **-S** a large, long-tailed bird	**PHLOX**	n pl. **-ES** a flowering plant
PHELLEM	n pl. **-S** a layer of plant cells	**PHO**	n pl. **PHOS** a Vietnamese soup of rice noodles and vegetables
PHELONIA	n/pl liturgical vestments	**PHOBIA**	n pl. **-S** an obsessive or irrational fear
PHENATE	n pl. **-S** a salt of carbolic acid		
PHENAZIN	n pl. **-S** a chemical compound	**PHOBIC**	n pl. **-S** one affected with a phobia
PHENETIC	adj pertaining to a type of classificatory system	**PHOCINE**	adj pertaining to seals
		PHOEBE	n pl. **-S** a small bird
PHENETOL	n pl. **-S** a volatile liquid	**PHOEBUS**	n pl. **-ES** the sun
PHENIX	n pl. **-ES** phoenix	**PHOENIX**	n pl. **-ES** a mythical bird
PHENOL	n pl. **-S** a caustic compound	**PHON**	n pl. **-S** a unit of loudness
PHENOLIC	n pl. **-S** a synthetic resin	**PHONAL**	adj pertaining to speech sounds
PHENOM	n pl. **-S** a person of extraordinary ability or promise	**PHONATE**	v **-NATED, -NATING, -NATES** to produce speech sounds
PHENOXY	adj containing a radical derived from phenol	**PHONE**	v **PHONED, PHONING, PHONES** to telephone
PHENYL	n pl. **-S** a univalent chemical radical **PHENYLIC** adj	**PHONEME**	n pl. **-S** a unit of speech **PHONEMIC** adj
PHERESIS	n pl. **-RESES** withdrawal of blood from a donor, removing some components, and returning the remaining blood to the donor	**PHONER**	n pl. **-S** one who calls someone on the telephone
		PHONETIC	adj pertaining to speech sounds
PHEW	interj — used to express relief, fatigue, or disgust	**PHONEY**	adj **-NIER, -NIEST** phony
		PHONEY	v **-ED, -ING, -S** to phony
PHI	n pl. **-S** a Greek letter	**PHONIC**	adj pertaining to the nature of sound
PHIAL	n pl. **-S** a vial		
PHILABEG	n pl. **-S** filibeg	**PHONICS**	n/pl the science of sound
PHILIBEG	n pl. **-S** filibeg	**PHONIED**	past tense of phony
PHILOMEL	n pl. **-S** a songbird	**PHONIER**	comparative of phoney and phony
PHILTER	v **-ED, -ING, -S** to put under the spell of a love potion	**PHONIES**	present 3d person sing. of phony
		PHONIEST	superlative of phoney and phony
PHILTRE	v **-TRED, -TRING, -TRES** to philter	**PHONILY**	adv in a phony manner
PHILTRUM	n pl. **-TRA** the indentation between the upper lip and the nose	**PHONING**	present participle of phone
		PHONO	n pl. **-NOS** a record player
PHIMOSIS	n pl. **-MOSES** the abnormal constriction of the opening of the prepuce **PHIMOTIC** adj	**PHONON**	n pl. **-S** a quantum of vibrational energy

PHONY   *adj* **-NIER, -NIEST** not genuine or real

PHONY   *v* **-NIED, -NYING, -NIES** to alter so as to make appear genuine

PHOOEY   *interj* — used as an exclamation of disgust or contempt

PHORATE   *n* pl. **-S** an insecticide

PHORESY   *n* pl. **-SIES** a symbiotic relationship between some arthropods and fishes **PHORETIC** *adj*

PHORONID   *n* pl. **-S** a wormlike marine animal

PHOSGENE   *n* pl. **-S** a poisonous gas

PHOSPHID   *n* pl. **-S** a chemical compound

PHOSPHIN   *n* pl. **-S** a poisonous gas

PHOSPHOR   *n* pl. **-S** a substance that will emit light when exposed to radiation

PHOT   *n* pl. **-S** a unit of illumination

PHOTIC   *adj* pertaining to light

PHOTICS   *n/pl* the science of light

PHOTINO   *n* pl. **-NOS** a hypothetical elementary particle

PHOTO   *v* **-ED, -ING, -S** to photograph

PHOTOG   *n* pl. **-S** one who takes photographs

PHOTOMAP   *v* **-MAPPED, -MAPPING, -MAPS** to map by means of aerial photography

PHOTON   *n* pl. **-S** an elementary particle **PHOTONIC** *adj*

PHOTOPIA   *n* pl. **-S** vision in bright light **PHOTOPIC** *adj*

PHOTOSET   *v* **-SET, -SETTING, -SETS** to prepare for printing by photographic means

PHPHT   *interj* pht

PHRASAL   *adj* pertaining to a group of two or more associated words

PHRASE   *v* **PHRASED, PHRASING, PHRASES** to express in words

PHRASING   *n* pl. **-S** manner or style of verbal expression

PHRATRY   *n* pl. **-TRIES** a tribal unit among primitive peoples **PHRATRAL, PHRATRIC** *adj*

PHREAK   *v* **-ED, -ING, -S** to gain illegal access to a long-distance telephone service to avoid tolls

PHREAKER   *n* pl. **-S** one that phreaks

PHREATIC   *adj* pertaining to underground waters

PHRENIC   *adj* pertaining to the mind

PHRENSY   *v* **-SIED, -SYING, -SIES** to frenzy

PHT   *interj* — used as an expression of mild anger or annoyance

PHTHALIC   *adj* pertaining to a certain acid

PHTHALIN   *n* pl. **-S** a chemical compound

PHTHISIC   *n* pl. **-S** phthisis

PHTHISIS   *n* pl. **PHTHISES** a disease of the lungs

PHUT   *n* pl. **-S** a dull, abrupt sound

PHYLA   pl. of phylon and phylum

PHYLAE   pl. of phyle

PHYLAR   *adj* pertaining to a phylum

PHYLAXIS   *n* pl. **-AXISES** an inhibiting of infection by the body

PHYLE   *n* pl. **-LAE** a political subdivision in ancient Greece **PHYLIC** *adj*

PHYLESIS   *n* pl. **-LESISES** or **-LESES** the course of evolutionary development **PHYLETIC** *adj*

PHYLLARY   *n* pl. **-RIES** a bract of certain plants

PHYLLITE   *n* pl. **-S** a foliated rock

PHYLLO   *n* pl. **-LOS** very thin pastry dough

PHYLLODE   *n* pl. **-S** a flattened petiole that serves as a leaf

PHYLLOID   *n* pl. **-S** a leaflike plant part

PHYLLOME   *n* pl. **-S** a leaf of a plant

PHYLON   *n* pl. **-LA** a genetically related group

PHYLUM   *n* pl. **-LA** a taxonomic division

PHYSALIS   *n* pl. **-LISES** a plant bearing edible yellow fruit

PHYSED   *n* pl. **-S** physical education

PHYSES   pl. of physis

PHYSIC   *v* **-ICKED, -ICKING, -ICS** to treat with medicine

PHYSICAL   *n* pl. **-S** a medical examination of the body

PHYSIO   *n* pl. **PHYSIOS** a physiotherapist

PHYSIQUE   *n* pl. **-S** the form or structure of the body

PHYSIS   *n* pl. **PHYSES** the principle of growth or change in nature

PHYTANE   *n* pl. **-S** a chemical compound

PHYTIN   *n* pl. **-S** a calcium-magnesium salt

PHYTOID   *adj* resembling a plant

PHYTOL   *n* pl. **-S** an alcohol

PHYTON   *n* pl. **-S** a structural unit of a plant **PHYTONIC** *adj*

PI _n_ pl. **-S** a Greek letter

PI _v_ **PIED, PIEING** or **PIING, PIES** to jumble or disorder

PIA _n_ pl. **-S** a membrane of the brain

PIACULAR _adj_ atoning

PIAFFE _v_ **PIAFFED, PIAFFING, PIAFFES** to perform a piaffer

PIAFFER _n_ pl. **-S** a movement in horsemanship

PIAL _adj_ pertaining to a pia

PIAN _n_ pl. **-S** a tropical disease **PIANIC** _adj_

PIANI _n/pl_ music passages to be played softly

PIANISM _n_ pl. **-S** performance on the piano

PIANIST _n_ pl. **-S** one who plays the piano

PIANO _n_ pl. **-NOS** a musical instrument

PIANOLA _n_ pl. **-S** a type of player piano

PIASABA _n_ pl. **-s** piassava

PIASAVA _n_ pl. **-S** piassava

PIASSABA _n_ pl. **-S** piassava

PIASSAVA _n_ pl. **-S** a coarse, stiff fiber

PIASTER _n_ pl. **-S** a monetary unit of several Arab countries

PIASTRE _n_ pl. **-S** piaster

PIAZZA _n_ pl. **-ZAS** or **-ZE** a public square in an Italian town

PIBAL _n_ pl. **-S** a small balloon for determining the direction and speed of the wind

PIBROCH _n_ pl. **-S** a musical piece played on the bagpipe

PIC _n_ pl. **-S** a photograph

PICA _n_ pl. **-S** a craving for unnatural food **PICAL** _adj_

PICACHO _n_ pl. **-CHOS** an isolated peak of a hill

PICADOR _n_ pl. **-S** or **-ES** a horseman in a bullfight

PICANTE _adj_ prepared with a spicy sauce

PICARA _n_ pl. **-S** a female picaro

PICARO _n_ pl. **-ROS** a vagabond

PICAROON _v_ **-ED, -ING, -S** to act as a pirate

PICAYUNE _n_ pl. **-S** a former Spanish-American coin

PICCATA _n_ pl. **-S** a dish of veal cutlets with a sauce of lemon, white wine, and butter

PICCOLO _n_ pl. **-LOS** a small flute

PICE _n_ pl. **PICE** a former coin of India and Pakistan

PICEOUS _adj_ glossy-black in color

PICIFORM _adj_ pertaining to an order of birds

PICK _v_ **-ED, -ING, -S** to select **PICKABLE** _adj_

PICKADIL _n_ pl. **-S** a type of collar

PICKAX _v_ **-ED, -ING, -ES** to use a pickax (a tool for breaking hard surfaces)

PICKAXE _v_ **-AXED, -AXING, -AXES** to pickax

PICKEER _v_ **-ED, -ING, -S** to skirmish in advance of an army

PICKER _n_ pl. **-S** one that picks

PICKEREL _n_ pl. **-S** a freshwater fish

PICKET _v_ **-ED, -ING, -S** to stand outside of some location, as a business, to publicize one's grievances against it

PICKETER _n_ pl. **-S** one who pickets

PICKIER comparative of picky

PICKIEST superlative of picky

PICKING _n_ pl. **-S** the act of one that picks

PICKLE _v_ **-LED, -LING, -LES** to preserve or flavor in a solution of brine or vinegar

PICKLER _n_ pl. **-S** a vegetable or fruit suitable for pickling

PICKLOCK _n_ pl. **-S** a tool for opening locks

PICKOFF _n_ pl. **-S** a play in baseball

PICKUP _n_ pl. **-S** a small truck

PICKWICK _n_ pl. **-S** a device for raising wicks in oil lamps

PICKY _adj_ **PICKIER, PICKIEST** fussy

PICLORAM _n_ pl. **-S** an herbicide

PICNIC _v_ **-NICKED, -NICKING, -NICS** to go on a picnic (an outdoor excursion with food)

PICNICKY _adj_ pertaining to a picnic

PICOGRAM _n_ pl. **-S** one trillionth of a gram

PICOLIN _n_ pl. **-S** picoline

PICOLINE _n_ pl. **-S** a chemical compound

PICOMOLE _n_ pl. **-S** one trillionth of a mole

PICOT _v_ **-ED, -ING, -S** to edge with ornamental loops

PICOTEE _n_ pl. **-S** a variety of carnation

PICOWAVE _v_ **-WAVED, -WAVING, -WAVES** to irradiate (food) with gamma rays

PICQUET _n_ pl. **-S** piquet

PICRATE	*n* pl. **-S** a chemical salt **PICRATED** *adj*	**PIEZO**	*adj* pertaining to a type of electricity
PICRIC	*adj* having a very bitter taste	**PIFFLE**	*v* **-FLED, -FLING, -FLES** to babble
PICRITE	*n* pl. **-S** an igneous rock **PICRITIC** *adj*	**PIFFLER**	*n* pl. **-S** one that babbles
PICTURE	*v* **-TURED, -TURING, -TURES** to make a visual representation of	**PIG**	*v* **PIGGED, PIGGING, PIGS** to bear pigs (cloven-hoofed mammals)
PICUL	*n* pl. **-S** an Asian unit of weight	**PIGBOAT**	*n* pl. **-S** a submarine
PIDDLE	*v* **-DLED, -DLING, -DLES** to waste time	**PIGEON**	*n* pl. **-S** a short-legged bird
PIDDLER	*n* pl. **-S** one that piddles	**PIGEONRY**	*n* pl. **-RIES** a place for keeping pigeons
PIDDLY	*adj* insignificant	**PIGFISH**	*n* pl. **-ES** a marine fish
PIDDOCK	*n* pl. **-S** a bivalve mollusk	**PIGGED**	past tense of pig
PIDGIN	*n* pl. **-S** a mixed language	**PIGGERY**	*n* pl. **-GERIES** a pigpen
PIE	*v* **PIED, PIEING, PIES** to pi	**PIGGIE**	*n* pl. **-S** piggy
PIEBALD	*n* pl. **-S** a spotted animal	**PIGGIER**	comparative of piggy
PIECE	*v* **PIECED, PIECING, PIECES** to join into a whole	**PIGGIES**	pl. of piggy
PIECER	*n* pl. **-S** one that pieces	**PIGGIEST**	superlative of piggy
PIECING	*n* pl. **-S** material to be sewn together	**PIGGIN**	*n* pl. **-S** a small wooden pail
PIECRUST	*n* pl. **-S** the crust of a pie	**PIGGING**	present participle of pig
PIED	past tense of pie	**PIGGISH**	*adj* greedy or dirty
PIEDFORT	*n* pl. **-S** piefort	**PIGGY**	*adj* **-GIER, -GIEST** piggish
PIEDMONT	*n* pl. **-S** an area lying at the foot of a mountain	**PIGGY**	*n* pl. **-GIES** a small pig
PIEFORT	*n* pl. **-S** an unusually thick coin	**PIGLET**	*n* pl. **-S** a small pig
PIEHOLE	*n* pl. **-S** a mouth	**PIGLIKE**	*adj* resembling a pig
PIEING	*n* pl. **-S** the act of throwing a pie at a public figure	**PIGMENT**	*v* **-ED, -ING, -S** to add a coloring matter to
PIEPLANT	*n* pl. **-S** a rhubarb	**PIGMY**	*n* pl. **-MIES** pygmy
PIER	*n* pl. **-S** a structure extending from land out over water	**PIGNOLI**	*n* pl. **-S** pignolia
PIERCE	*v* **PIERCED, PIERCING, PIERCES** to cut or pass into or through	**PIGNOLIA**	*n* pl. **-S** the edible seed of nut pines
PIERCER	*n* pl. **-S** one that pierces	**PIGNUS**	*n* pl. **-NORA** property held as security for a debt
PIERCING	*n* pl. **-S** a piece of jewelry attached to pierced flesh	**PIGNUT**	*n* pl. **-S** a hickory nut
PIEROGI	*n* pl. **-ES** a small dumpling with a filling	**PIGOUT**	*n* pl. **-S** an instance of eating to excess
PIERROT	*n* pl. **-S** a clown	**PIGPEN**	*n* pl. **-S** a place where pigs are kept
PIETA	*n* pl. **-S** a representation of the Virgin Mary mourning over the body of Christ	**PIGSKIN**	*n* pl. **-S** the skin of a pig
PIETIES	pl. of piety	**PIGSNEY**	*n* pl. **-NEYS** a darling
PIETISM	*n* pl. **-S** piety	**PIGSTICK**	*v* **-ED, -ING, -S** to hunt for wild boar
PIETIST	*n* pl. **-S** a pious person	**PIGSTY**	*n* pl. **-STIES** a pigpen
PIETY	*n* pl. **-TIES** the quality or state of being pious	**PIGTAIL**	*n* pl. **-S** a tight braid of hair
		PIGWEED	*n* pl. **-S** a weedy plant
		PIING	a present participle of pi
		PIKA	*n* pl. **-S** a small mammal

PIKAKE _n_ pl. **-S** an East Indian vine

PIKE _v_ **PIKED, PIKING, PIKES** to pierce with a pike (a long spear)

PIKEMAN _n_ pl. **-MEN** a soldier armed with a pike

PIKER _n_ pl. **-S** a stingy person

PIKI _n_ pl. **-S** thin blue cornmeal bread

PIKING present participle of pike

PILAF _n_ pl. **-S** a dish made of seasoned rice and often meat

PILAFF _n_ pl. **-S** pilaf

PILAR _adj_ pertaining to hair

PILASTER _n_ pl. **-S** a rectangular column

PILAU _n_ pl. **-S** pilaf

PILAW _n_ pl. **-S** pilaf

PILCHARD _n_ pl. **-S** a small marine fish

PILE _v_ **PILED, PILING, PILES** to lay one upon the other

PILEA pl. of pileum

PILEATE _adj_ having a pileus

PILEATED _adj_ pileate

PILED past tense of pile

PILEI pl. of pileus

PILELESS _adj_ not having a raised surface of yarn

PILEOUS _adj_ pilose

PILEUM _n_ pl. **-LEA** the top of a bird's head

PILEUP _n_ pl. **-S** a collision involving several motor vehicles

PILEUS _n_ pl. **-LEI** the umbrella-shaped portion of a mushroom

PILEWORT _n_ pl. **-S** a medicinal plant

PILFER _v_ **-ED, -ING, -S** to steal

PILFERER _n_ pl. **-S** one that pilfers

PILGRIM _v_ **-ED, -ING, -S** to travel to a holy place for religious reasons

PILI _n_ pl. **-S** a Philippine tree

PILIFORM _adj_ resembling a hair

PILING _n_ pl. **-S** a structure of building supports

PILL _v_ **-ED, -ING, -S** to dose with pills (small, rounded masses of medicine)

PILLAGE _v_ **-LAGED, -LAGING, -LAGES** to plunder

PILLAGER _n_ pl. **-S** one that pillages

PILLAR _v_ **-ED, -ING, -S** to provide with vertical building supports

PILLBOX _n_ pl. **-ES** a small box for pills

PILLBUG _n_ pl. **-S** a wood louse that can roll up into a ball

PILLION _n_ pl. **-S** a pad or cushion for an extra rider on a horse or motorcycle

PILLOCK _n_ pl. **-S** a stupid person

PILLORY _v_ **-RIED, -RYING, -RIES** to expose to public ridicule or abuse

PILLOW _v_ **-ED, -ING, -S** to rest on a pillow (a cushion for the head)

PILLOWY _adj_ **-LOWIER, -LOWIEST** resembling a pillow

PILOSE _adj_ covered with hair

PILOSITY _n_ pl. **-TIES** the state of being pilose

PILOT _v_ **-ED, -ING, -S** to control the course of

PILOTAGE _n_ pl. **-S** the act of piloting

PILOTING _n_ pl. **-S** a branch of navigation

PILOUS _adj_ pilose

PILSENER _n_ pl. **-S** pilsner

PILSNER _n_ pl. **-S** a light beer

PILULE _n_ pl. **-S** a small pill **PILULAR** _adj_

PILUS _n_ pl. **-LI** a hair or hairlike structure

PILY _adj_ divided into a number of wedge-shaped heraldic designs

PIMA _n_ pl. **-S** a strong, high-grade cotton

PIMENTO _n_ pl. **-TOS** pimiento

PIMIENTO _n_ pl. **-TOS** a sweet pepper

PIMP _v_ **-ED, -ING, -S** to solicit clients for a prostitute

PIMPING _n_ pl. **-S** the practice of soliciting clients for a prostitute

PIMPLE _n_ pl. **-S** an inflamed swelling of the skin **PIMPLED** _adj_

PIMPLY _adj_ **-PLIER, -PLIEST** covered with pimples

PIN _v_ **PINNED, PINNING, PINS** to fasten with a pin (a slender, pointed piece of metal)

PINA _n_ pl. **-S** a pineapple

PINAFORE _n_ pl. **-S** a child's apron

PINANG _n_ pl. **-S** a palm tree

PINASTER _n_ pl. **-S** a pine tree

PINATA _n_ pl. **-S** a pottery jar used in a Mexican game

PINBALL _v_ **-ED, -ING, -S** to move abruptly from one place to another

PINBONE _n_ pl. **-S** the hipbone

PINCER   *n* pl. **-S** one of the two pivoted parts of a grasping tool

PINCH   *v* **-ED, -ING, -ES** to squeeze between two edges or surfaces

PINCHBUG   *n* pl. **-S** a large beetle

PINCHECK   *n* pl. **-S** a fabric design

PINCHER   *n* pl. **-S** one that pinches

PINCURL   *n* pl. **-S** a curl held in place with a hairpin

PINDER   *n* pl. **-S** an official who formerly impounded stray animals

PINDLING   *adj* puny or sickly

PINE   *v* **PINED, PINING, PINES** to yearn intensely

PINEAL   *n* pl. **-S** a gland in the brain

PINECONE   *n* pl. **-S** a cone-shaped fruit of a pine tree

PINED   past tense of pine

PINELAND   *n* pl. **-S** land forested with pine

PINELIKE   *adj* resembling a pine (an evergreen tree)

PINENE   *n* pl. **-S** the main constituent of turpentine

PINERY   *n* pl. **-ERIES** an area where pineapples are grown

PINESAP   *n* pl. **-S** a fragrant herb

PINETUM   *n* pl. **-TA** a plantation of pine trees

PINEWOOD   *n* pl. **-S** the wood of a pine tree

PINEY   *adj* **PINIER, PINIEST** piny

PINFISH   *n* pl. **-ES** a small marine fish

PINFOLD   *v* **-ED, -ING, -S** to confine in an enclosure for stray animals

PING   *v* **-ED, -ING, -S** to produce a brief, high-pitched sound

PINGER   *n* pl. **-S** a device for producing pulses of sound

PINGO   *n* pl. **-GOS** or **-GOES** a low mound of earth formed by expansion of underlying frost

PINGRASS   *n* pl. **-ES** a European weed

PINGUID   *adj* greasy

PINHEAD   *n* pl. **-S** the head of a pin

PINHOLE   *n* pl. **-S** a small hole made by a pin

PINIER   comparative of piney and piny

PINIEST   superlative of piney and piny

PINING   present participle of pine

PINION   *v* **-ED, -ING, -S** to remove or bind the wing feathers of to prevent flight

PINITE   *n* pl. **-S** a mineral

PINITOL   *n* pl. **-S** an alcohol

PINK   *adj* **PINKER, PINKEST** of a pale reddish hue

PINK   *v* **-ED, -ING, -S** to cut a saw-toothed edge on cloth

PINKEN   *v* **-ED, -ING, -S** to become pink

PINKER   *n* pl. **-S** one that pinks

PINKEY   *n* pl. **-EYS** a ship with a narrow overhanging stern

PINKEYE   *n* pl. **-S** an inflammation of the eye

PINKIE   *n* pl. **-S** the little finger

PINKING   *n* pl. **-S** a method of cutting or decorating

PINKISH   *adj* somewhat pink

PINKLY   *adv* with a pink hue

PINKNESS   *n* pl. **-ES** the state of being pink

PINKO   *n* pl. **PINKOS** or **PINKOES** a person who holds somewhat radical political views

PINKROOT   *n* pl. **-S** a medicinal plant root

PINKY   *adj* **-KIER, -KIEST** pinkish

PINLESS   *adj* lacking pins

PINNA   *n* pl. **-NAS** or **-NAE** a feather, wing, or winglike part

PINNACE   *n* pl. **-S** a small sailing ship

PINNACLE   *v* **-CLED, -CLING, -CLES** to place on a summit

PINNAL   *adj* pertaining to a pinna

PINNATE   *adj* resembling a feather

PINNATED   *adj* pinnate

PINNED   past tense of pin

PINNER   *n* pl. **-S** one that pins

PINNIES   pl. of pinny

PINNING   present participle of pin

PINNIPED   *n* pl. **-S** a mammal with limbs modified into flippers

PINNULA   *n* pl. **-LAE** pinnule **PINNULAR** *adj*

PINNULE   *n* pl. **-S** a pinnate part or organ

PINNY   *n* pl. **-NIES** a pinafore

PINOCHLE   *n* pl. **-S** a card game

PINOCLE   *n* pl. **-S** pinochle

PINOLE   *n* pl. **-S** a finely ground flour

PINON   *n* pl. **-S** or **-ES** a pine tree

PINOT   *n* pl. **-S** a red or white grape

PINOTAGE   *n* pl. **-S** a variety of red wine grape

PINPOINT   *v* **-ED, -ING, -S** to locate precisely

PINPRICK   *v* **-ED, -ING, -S** to puncture with a pin

PINSCHER   *n* pl. **-S** a large, short-haired dog

PINSPOT   *n* pl. **-S** a small powerful spotlight

PINT   *n* pl. **-S** a liquid and dry measure of capacity

PINTA   *n* pl. **-S** a skin disease

PINTADA   *n* pl. **-S** pintado

PINTADO   *n* pl. **-DOS** or **-DOES** a large food fish

PINTAIL   *n* pl. **-S** a river duck

PINTANO   *n* pl. **-NOS** a tropical fish

PINTLE   *n* pl. **-S** a pin on which something turns

PINTO   *n* pl. **-TOS** or **-TOES** a spotted horse

PINTSIZE   *adj* small

PINTUCK   *n* pl. **-S** a very narrow fold of fabric

PINUP   *n* pl. **-S** a picture that may be pinned up on a wall

PINWALE   *n* pl. **-S** a type of fabric

PINWEED   *n* pl. **-S** a perennial herb

PINWHEEL   *v* **-ED, -ING, -S** to revolve at the end of a stick

PINWORK   *n* pl. **-S** a type of embroidery

PINWORM   *n* pl. **-S** a parasitic worm

PINY   *adj* **PINIER, PINIEST** suggestive of or covered with pine trees

PINYIN   *n* pl. **-S** a system for romanizing Chinese ideograms

PINYON   *n* pl. **-S** pinon

PIOLET   *n* pl. **-S** an ice ax

PION   *n* pl. **-S** a subatomic particle **PIONIC** *adj*

PIONEER   *v* **-ED, -ING, -S** to take part in the beginnings of

PIOSITY   *n* pl. **-TIES** an excessive show of piety

PIOUS   *adj* marked by religious reverence **PIOUSLY** *adv*

PIP   *v* **PIPPED, PIPPING, PIPS** to break through the shell of an egg

PIPA   *n* pl. **-S** a four-stringed Chinese lute

PIPAGE   *n* pl. **-S** a system of pipes

PIPAL   *n* pl. **-S** a fig tree of India

PIPE   *v* **PIPED, PIPING, PIPES** to convey by means of a pipe (a hollow cylinder)

PIPEAGE   *n* pl. **-S** pipage

PIPECLAY   *v* **-ED, -ING, -S** to whiten leather with fine white clay

PIPEFISH   *n* pl. **-ES** a slender fish

PIPEFUL   *n* pl. **-S** a quantity sufficient to fill a tobacco pipe

PIPELESS   *adj* having no pipe

PIPELIKE   *adj* resembling a pipe

PIPELINE   *v* **-LINED, -LINING, -LINES** to convey by a line of pipe

PIPER   *n* pl. **-S** one that plays on a tubular musical instrument

PIPERINE   *n* pl. **-S** a chemical compound

PIPESTEM   *n* pl. **-S** the stem of a tobacco pipe

PIPET   *v* **-PETTED, -PETTING, -PETS** to pipette

PIPETTE   *v* **-PETTED, -PETTING, -PETTES** to measure liquid with a calibrated tube

PIPEWORK   *n* pl. **-S** pipes collectively

PIPIER   comparative of pipy

PIPIEST   superlative of pipy

PIPINESS   *n* pl. **-ES** the quality of being pipy

PIPING   *n* pl. **-S** a system of pipes

PIPINGLY   *adv* shrilly

PIPIT   *n* pl. **-S** a songbird

PIPKIN   *n* pl. **-S** a small pot

PIPLESS   *adj* having no small seeds

PIPPED   past tense of pip

PIPPIN   *n* pl. **-S** any of several varieties of apple

PIPPING   present participle of pip

PIPY   *adj* **PIPIER, PIPIEST** shrill

PIQUANCE   *n* pl. **-S** piquancy

PIQUANCY   *n* pl. **-CIES** the quality of being piquant

PIQUANT   *adj* agreeably sharp in taste

PIQUE   *v* **PIQUED, PIQUING, PIQUES** to arouse anger or resentment in

PIQUET   *n* pl. **-S** a card game

PIRACY   *n* pl. **-CIES** robbery on the high seas

PIRAGUA   *n* pl. **-S** a dugout canoe

PIRANA   *n* pl. **-S** piranha

PIRANHA   *n* pl. **-S** a voracious fish

PIRARUCU   *n* pl. **-S** a large food fish

PIRATE   *v* **-RATED, -RATING, -RATES** to commit piracy

PIRATIC   *adj* pertaining to piracy

PIRAYA	*n* pl. **-S** piranha
PIRIFORM	*adj* pyriform
PIRN	*n* pl. **-S** a spinning-wheel bobbin
PIROG	*n* pl. **-ROGEN** or **-ROGHI** or **-ROGI** a large Russian pastry
PIROGI	*n* pl. **-ES** pierogi
PIROGUE	*n* pl. **-S** piragua
PIROQUE	*n* pl. **-S** piragua
PIROZHOK	*n* pl. **-ROZHKI** or **-ROSHKI** or **-ROJKI** a small Russian pastry
PISCARY	*n* pl. **-RIES** a place for fishing
PISCATOR	*n* pl. **-S** a fisherman
PISCINA	*n* pl. **-NAS** or **-NAE** a basin used in certain church ceremonies **PISCINAL** *adj*
PISCINE	*adj* pertaining to fish
PISCO	*n* pl. **-COS** a Peruvian brandy
PISH	*v* **-ED, -ING, -ES** to express contempt
PISHER	*n* pl. **-S** a young or inexperienced person
PISHOGE	*n* pl. **-S** pishogue
PISHOGUE	*n* pl. **-S** an evil spell
PISIFORM	*n* pl. **-S** a small bone of the wrist
PISMIRE	*n* pl. **-S** an ant
PISO	*n* pl. **-SOS** the Philippine peso
PISOLITE	*n* pl. **-S** a limestone
PISOLITH	*n* pl. **-S** a small rounded concretion of limestone
PISSOIR	*n* pl. **-S** a public urinal
PISTACHE	*n* pl. **-S** a shade of green
PISTE	*n* pl. **-S** a downhill ski trail
PISTIL	*n* pl. **-S** the seed-bearing organ of flowering plants
PISTOL	*v* **-TOLED, -TOLING, -TOLS** or **-TOLLED, -TOLLING, -TOLS** to shoot with a small firearm
PISTOLE	*n* pl. **-S** a formerly used European gold coin
PISTON	*n* pl. **-S** a part of an engine
PISTOU	*n* pl. **-S** a sauce made of olive oil, garlic, basil, and often cheese
PIT	*v* **PITTED, PITTING, PITS** to mark with cavities or depressions
PITA	*n* pl. **-S** a strong fiber
PITAHAYA	*n* pl. **-S** a cactus of southwestern U.S. and Mexico
PITAPAT	*v* **-PATTED, -PATTING, -PATS** to make a repeated tapping sound
PITAYA	*n* pl. **-S** pitahaya
PITCH	*v* **-ED, -ING, -ES** to throw
PITCHER	*n* pl. **-S** a container for holding and pouring liquids
PITCHIER	comparative of pitchy
PITCHIEST	superlative of pitchy
PITCHILY	*adv* in a very dark manner
PITCHMAN	*n* pl. **-MEN** a salesman of small wares
PITCHOUT	*n* pl. **-S** a type of pitch in baseball
PITCHY	*adj* **PITCHIER, PITCHIEST** tarry
PITEOUS	*adj* pitiful
PITFALL	*n* pl. **-S** a hidden danger or difficulty
PITH	*v* **-ED, -ING, -S** to sever the spinal cord of
PITHEAD	*n* pl. **-S** a mine entrance
PITHLESS	*adj* lacking force
PITHOS	*n* pl. **PITHOI** a large ancient storage jar
PITHY	*adj* **PITHIER, PITHIEST** concise **PITHILY** *adv*
PITIABLE	*adj* pitiful **PITIABLY** *adv*
PITIED	past tense of pity
PITIER	*n* pl. **-S** one that pities
PITIES	present 3d person sing. of pity
PITIFUL	*adj* **-FULLER, -FULLEST** arousing pity
PITILESS	*adj* having no pity
PITMAN	*n* pl. **-MEN** a mine worker
PITMAN	*n* pl. **-S** a connecting rod
PITON	*n* pl. **-S** a metal spike used in mountain climbing
PITOT	*n* pl. **-S** a tube used to measure the pressure of a fluid stream
PITSAW	*n* pl. **-S** a large saw for cutting logs
PITTA	*n* pl. **-S** a perching bird of Asia, Australia, and Africa
PITTANCE	*n* pl. **-S** a small allowance of money
PITTED	past tense of pit
PITTING	*n* pl. **-S** an arrangement of cavities or depressions
PITY	*v* **PITIED, PITYING, PITIES** to feel pity (sorrow aroused by another's misfortune)
PIU	*adv* more — used as a musical direction

PIVOT   *v* **-ED, -ING, -S** to turn on a shaft or rod

PIVOTAL   *adj* critically important

PIVOTMAN   *n* pl. **-MEN** a center on a basketball team

PIX   *n* pl. **-ES** pyx

PIXEL   *n* pl. **-S** a basic unit of a video image

PIXELATE   *v* **-LATED, -LATING, -LATES** to divide an image into pixels for display in a digital format

PIXIE   *n* pl. **-S** pixy **PIXIEISH** *adj*

PIXILATE   *v* **-LATED, -LATING, -LATES** pixelate

PIXINESS   *n* pl. **-ES** the state of being playfully mischievous

PIXY   *n* pl. **PIXIES** a playfully mischievous fairy or elf **PIXYISH** *adj*

PIZAZZ   *n* pl. **-ES** the quality of being exciting or attractive

PIZAZZY   *adj* having pizazz

PIZZA   *n* pl. **-S** an Italian open pie

PIZZAZ   *n* pl. **-ES** pizazz

PIZZELLE   *n* pl. **-S** a thin, crisp Italian cookie

PIZZERIA   *n* pl. **-S** a place where pizzas are made and sold

PIZZLE   *n* pl. **-S** the penis of an animal

PLACABLE   *adj* capable of being placated **PLACABLY** *adv*

PLACARD   *v* **-ED, -ING, -S** to publicize by means of posters

PLACATE   *v* **-CATED, -CATING, -CATES** to soothe or mollify

PLACATER   *n* pl. **-S** one that placates

PLACE   *v* **PLACED, PLACING, PLACES** to set in a particular position

PLACEBO   *n* pl. **-BOS** or **-BOES** a substance containing no medication that is given for its psychological effect

PLACEMAN   *n* pl. **-MEN** a political appointee to a public office

PLACEMAT   *n* pl. **-S** a table mat (a piece of material for protecting a surface) on which a place setting is laid

PLACENTA   *n* pl. **-TAS** or **-TAE** a vascular organ in most mammals

PLACER   *n* pl. **-S** one that places

PLACET   *n* pl. **-S** a vote of assent

PLACID   *adj* calm or peaceful **PLACIDLY** *adv*

PLACING   *n* pl. **-S** the state of being ranked in a race

PLACK   *n* pl. **-S** a former coin of Scotland

PLACKET   *n* pl. **-S** a slit in a garment

PLACOID   *n* pl. **-S** a fish having platelike scales

PLAFOND   *n* pl. **-S** an elaborately decorated ceiling

PLAGAL   *adj* designating a medieval musical mode

PLAGE   *n* pl. **-S** a bright region on the sun

PLAGIARY   *n* pl. **-RIES** the act of passing off another's work as one's own

PLAGUE   *v* **PLAGUED, PLAGUING, PLAGUES** to harass or torment

PLAGUER   *n* pl. **-S** one that plagues

PLAGUEY   *adj* plaguy

PLAGUY   *adj* troublesome **PLAGUILY** *adv*

PLAICE   *n* pl. **-S** a European flatfish

PLAID   *n* pl. **-S** a woolen scarf of a checkered pattern **PLAIDED** *adj*

PLAIN   *adj* **PLAINER, PLAINEST** evident **PLAINLY** *adv*

PLAIN   *v* **-ED, -ING, -S** to complain

PLAINT   *n* pl. **-S** a complaint

PLAISTER   *v* **-ED, -ING, -S** to plaster

PLAIT   *v* **-ED, -ING, -S** to braid

PLAITER   *n* pl. **-S** one that plaits

PLAITING   *n* pl. **-S** something that is plaited

PLAN   *v* **PLANNED, PLANNING, PLANS** to formulate a plan (a method for achieving an end)

PLANAR   *adj* flat

PLANARIA   *n* pl. **-S** an aquatic flatworm

PLANATE   *adj* having a flat surface

PLANCH   *n* pl. **-ES** a plank

PLANCHE   *n* pl. **-S** planch

PLANCHET   *n* pl. **-S** a flat piece of metal for stamping into a coin

PLANE   *v* **PLANED, PLANING, PLANES** to make smooth or even

PLANER   *n* pl. **-S** one that planes

PLANET   *n* pl. **-S** a celestial body

PLANFORM   *n* pl. **-S** the contour of an object as viewed from above

PLANGENT   *adj* resounding loudly

PLANING   present participle of plane

PLANISH   *v* **-ED, -ING, -ES** to toughen and smooth by hammering lightly

PLANK *v* **-ED, -ING, -S** to cover with planks (long, flat pieces of lumber)

PLANKING *n pl.* **-S** covering made of planks

PLANKTER *n pl.* **-S** any organism that is an element of plankton

PLANKTON *n pl.* **-S** the minute animal and plant life of a body of water **PLANKTIC** *adj*

PLANLESS *adj* having no plan

PLANNED past tense of plan

PLANNER *n pl.* **-S** one that plans

PLANNING *n pl.* **-S** the establishment of goals or policies

PLANOSOL *n pl.* **-S** a type of soil

PLANT *v* **-ED, -ING, -S** to place in the ground for growing

PLANTAIN *n pl.* **-S** a short-stemmed herb

PLANTAR *adj* pertaining to the sole of the foot

PLANTER *n pl.* **-S** one that plants

PLANTING *n pl.* **-S** an area where plants are grown

PLANTLET *n pl.* **-S** a small plant

PLANULA *n pl.* **-LAE** the free-swimming larva of certain organisms **PLANULAR** *adj*

PLAQUE *n pl.* **-S** an ornamental plate or disk

PLASH *v* **-ED, -ING, -ES** to weave together

PLASHER *n pl.* **-S** one that plashes

PLASHY *adj* **PLASHIER, PLASHIEST** marshy

PLASM *n pl.* **-S** plasma

PLASMA *n pl.* **-S** the liquid part of blood **PLASMIC** *adj*

PLASMID *n pl.* **-S** a hereditary structure of a cell

PLASMIN *n pl.* **-S** an enzyme

PLASMOID *n pl.* **-S** a type of high energy particle

PLASMON *n pl.* **-S** a determinant of inheritance believed to exist in cells

PLASTER *v* **-ED, -ING, -S** to cover with plaster (a mixture of lime, sand, and water)

PLASTERY *adj* resembling plaster

PLASTIC *n pl.* **-S** any of a group of synthetic or natural moldable materials

PLASTID *n pl.* **-S** a structure in plant cells

PLASTRON *n pl.* **-S** a part of the shell of a turtle **PLASTRAL** *adj*

PLASTRUM *n pl.* **-S** plastron

PLAT *v* **PLATTED, PLATTING, PLATS** to plait

PLATAN *n pl.* **-S** a large tree

PLATANE *n pl.* **-S** platan

PLATE *v* **PLATED, PLATING, PLATES** to coat with a thin layer of metal

PLATEAU *n pl.* **-TEAUS** or **-TEAUX** a level stretch of elevated land

PLATEAU *v* **-ED, -ING, -S** to reach a period or condition of stability

PLATEFUL *n pl.* **PLATEFULS** or **PLATESFUL** the quantity that fills a plate (a shallow dish)

PLATELET *n pl.* **-S** a small, flattened body

PLATEN *n pl.* **-S** the roller of a typewriter

PLATER *n pl.* **-S** one that plates

PLATESFUL a pl. of plateful

PLATFORM *n pl.* **-S** a raised floor or flat surface

PLATIER comparative of platy

PLATIES a pl. of platy

PLATIEST superlative of platy

PLATINA *n pl.* **-S** platinum

PLATING *n pl.* **-S** a thin layer of metal

PLATINIC *adj* pertaining to platinum

PLATINUM *n pl.* **-S** a metallic element

PLATONIC *adj* purely spiritual and free from sensual desire

PLATOON *v* **-ED, -ING, -S** to alternate with another player at the same position

PLATTED past tense of plat

PLATTER *n pl.* **-S** a large, shallow dish

PLATTING present participle of plat

PLATY *adj* **PLATIER, PLATIEST** split into thin, flat pieces

PLATY *n pl.* **PLATYS** or **PLATIES** a small tropical fish

PLATYPUS *n pl.* **-PUSES** or **-PI** an aquatic mammal

PLAUDIT *n pl.* **-S** an expression of praise

PLAUSIVE *adj* expressing praise

PLAY *v* **-ED, -ING, -S** to engage in amusement or sport **PLAYABLE** *adj*

PLAYA *n pl.* **-S** the bottom of a desert basin

PLAYACT *v* **-ED, -ING, -S** to take part in a theatrical performance

PLAYBACK *n* pl. **-S** the act of replaying a newly made recording

PLAYBILL *n* pl. **-S** a program for a theatrical performance

PLAYBOOK *n* pl. **-S** a book containing one or more literary works for the stage

PLAYBOY *n* pl. **-BOYS** a man devoted to pleasurable activities

PLAYDATE *n* pl. **-S** the scheduled date for showing a theatrical production

PLAYDAY *n* pl. **-DAYS** a holiday

PLAYDOWN *n* pl. **-S** a playoff

PLAYER *n* pl. **-S** one that plays

PLAYFUL *adj* frolicsome

PLAYGIRL *n* pl. **-S** a woman devoted to pleasurable activities

PLAYGOER *n* pl. **-S** one who attends the theater

PLAYLAND *n* pl. **-S** a recreational area

PLAYLESS *adj* lacking playfulness

PLAYLET *n* pl. **-S** a short theatrical performance

PLAYLIKE *adj* resembling a theatrical performance

PLAYLIST *v* **-ED, -ING, -S** to place on a list of recordings to be played on the air

PLAYMATE *n* pl. **-S** a companion in play

PLAYOFF *n* pl. **-S** a series of games played to determine a championship

PLAYPEN *n* pl. **-S** an enclosure in which a young child may play

PLAYROOM *n* pl. **-S** a recreation room

PLAYSET *n* pl. **-S** an outdoor apparatus having equipment for children's activities

PLAYSUIT *n* pl. **-S** a sports outfit for women and children

PLAYTIME *n* pl. **-S** a time for play or amusement

PLAYWEAR *n* pl. **PLAYWEAR** clothing worn for leisure activities

PLAZA *n* pl. **-S** a public square

PLEA *n* pl. **-S** an entreaty

PLEACH *v* **-ED, -ING, -ES** to weave together

PLEAD *v* **PLEADED** or **PLED, PLEADING, PLEADS** to ask for earnestly

PLEADER *n* pl. **-S** one that pleads

PLEADING *n* pl. **-S** an allegation in a legal action

PLEASANT *adj* **-ANTER, -ANTEST** pleasing

PLEASE *v* **PLEASED, PLEASING, PLEASES** to give enjoyment or satisfaction to

PLEASER *n* pl. **-S** one that pleases

PLEASURE *v* **-SURED, -SURING, -SURES** to please

PLEAT *v* **-ED, -ING, -S** to fold in an even manner

PLEATER *n* pl. **-S** one that pleats

PLEATHER *n* pl. **-S** a plastic fabric made to look like leather

PLEATING *n* pl. **-S** an arrangement of pleats (small folds) in a garment

PLEB *n* pl. **-S** a commoner

PLEBE *n* pl. **-S** a freshman at a military or naval academy

PLEBEIAN *n* pl. **-S** a commoner

PLECTRON *n* pl. **-TRONS** or **-TRA** plectrum

PLECTRUM *n* pl. **-TRUMS** or **-TRA** an implement used to pluck the strings of a stringed instrument

PLED a past tense of plead

PLEDGE *v* **PLEDGED, PLEDGING, PLEDGES** to give as security for something borrowed

PLEDGEE *n* pl. **-S** one to whom something is pledged

PLEDGEOR *n* pl. **-S** pledger

PLEDGER *n* pl. **-S** one that pledges something

PLEDGET *n* pl. **-S** a pad of absorbent cotton

PLEDGING present participle of pledge

PLEDGOR *n* pl. **-S** pledger

PLEIAD *n* pl. **-S** or **-ES** a group of seven illustrious persons

PLENA a pl. of plenum

PLENARY *n* pl. **-RIES** a session attended by all members

PLENCH *n* pl. **-ES** a tool serving as pliers and a wrench

PLENISH *v* **-ED, -ING, -ES** to fill up

PLENISM *n* pl. **-S** the doctrine that space is fully occupied by matter

PLENIST *n* pl. **-S** an advocate of plenism

PLENTY *n* pl. **-TIES** a sufficient or abundant amount

PLENUM *n* pl. **-NUMS** or **-NA** space considered as fully occupied by matter

PLEON _n_ pl. **-S** the abdomen of a crustacean **PLEONAL, PLEONIC** _adj_

PLEONASM _n_ pl. **-S** the use of needless words

PLEOPOD _n_ pl. **-S** an appendage of crustaceans

PLEROMA _n_ pl. **-S** the fullness of the divine powers

PLESSOR _n_ pl. **-S** plexor

PLETHORA _n_ pl. **-S** an excess

PLEURA _n_ pl. **-RAS** or **-RAE** a membrane that envelops the lungs **PLEURAL** _adj_

PLEURISY _n_ pl. **-SIES** inflammation of the pleura

PLEURON _n_ pl. **-RA** a part of a thoracic segment of an insect

PLEUSTON _n_ pl. **-S** aquatic vegetation

PLEW _n_ pl. **-S** a beaver skin

PLEX _n_ pl. **-ES** a multiplex

PLEXAL _adj_ pertaining to a plexus

PLEXOR _n_ pl. **-S** a small, hammer-like medical instrument

PLEXUS _n_ pl. **-ES** an interlacing of parts

PLIABLE _adj_ easily bent **PLIABLY** _adv_

PLIANCY _n_ pl. **-CIES** the quality of being pliant

PLIANT _adj_ easily bent **PLIANTLY** _adv_

PLICA _n_ pl. **-CAE** or **-CAS** a fold of skin **PLICAL** _adj_

PLICATE _adj_ pleated

PLICATED _adj_ plicate

PLIE _n_ pl. **-S** a movement in ballet

PLIED past tense of ply

PLIER _n_ pl. **-S** one that plies

PLIES present 3d person sing. of ply

PLIGHT _v_ **-ED, -ING, -S** to promise or bind by a solemn pledge

PLIGHTER _n_ pl. **-S** one that plights

PLIMSOL _n_ pl. **-S** plimsoll

PLIMSOLE _n_ pl. **-S** plimsoll

PLIMSOLL _n_ pl. **-S** a rubber-soled cloth shoe

PLINK _v_ **-ED, -ING, -S** to shoot at random targets

PLINKER _n_ pl. **-S** one that plinks

PLINKY _adj_ **PLINKIER, PLINKIEST** having or making short, sharp metallic sounds

PLINTH _n_ pl. **-S** a stone or slab upon which a column or pedestal rests

PLIOFILM _n_ pl. **-S** a transparent sheet of chlorinated rubber used in packaging

PLIOTRON _n_ pl. **-S** a type of vacuum tube

PLISKIE _n_ pl. **-S** a practical joke

PLISKY _n_ pl. **-KIES** pliskie

PLISSE _n_ pl. **-S** a puckered texture of cloth

PLOD _v_ **PLODDED, PLODDING, PLODS** to walk heavily

PLODDER _n_ pl. **-S** one that plods

PLOIDY _n_ pl. **-DIES** the extent of repetition of the basic number of chromosomes

PLONK _v_ **-ED, -ING, -S** to plunk

PLONKER _n_ pl. **-S** a stupid person

PLOP _v_ **PLOPPED, PLOPPING, PLOPS** to drop or fall heavily

PLOSION _n_ pl. **-S** a release of breath after the articulation of certain consonants

PLOSIVE _n_ pl. **-S** a sound produced by plosion

PLOT _v_ **PLOTTED, PLOTTING, PLOTS** to plan secretly

PLOTLESS _adj_ planless

PLOTLINE _n_ pl. **-S** the main story of a book

PLOTTAGE _n_ pl. **-S** an area of land

PLOTTED past tense of plot

PLOTTER _n_ pl. **-S** one that plots

PLOTTING present participle of plot

PLOTTY _adj_ **-TIER, -TIEST** full of intrigue, as a novel

PLOTTY _n_ pl. **-TIES** a hot, spiced beverage

PLOTZ _v_ **-ED, -ING, -ES** to be overwhelmed by an emotion

PLOUGH _v_ **-ED, -ING, -S** to plow

PLOUGHER _n_ pl. **-S** one that ploughs

PLOVER _n_ pl. **-S** a shore bird

PLOW _v_ **-ED, -ING, -S** to turn up land with a plow (a farm implement) **PLOWABLE** _adj_

PLOWBACK _n_ pl. **-S** a reinvestment of profits in a business

PLOWBOY _n_ pl. **-BOYS** a boy who leads a plow team

PLOWER _n_ pl. **-S** one that plows

PLOWHEAD _n_ pl. **-S** the clevis of a plow

PLOWLAND _n_ pl. **-S** land suitable for cultivation

PLOWMAN *n pl.* **-MEN** a man who plows

PLOY *v* **-ED, -ING, -S** to move from a line into a column

PLOYE *n pl.* **-S** a buckwheat pancake

PLUCK *v* **-ED, -ING, -S** to pull out or off

PLUCKER *n pl.* **-S** one that plucks

PLUCKY *adj* **PLUCKIER, PLUCKIEST** brave and spirited **PLUCKILY** *adv*

PLUG *v* **PLUGGED, PLUGGING, PLUGS** to seal or close with a plug (a piece of material used to fill a hole)

PLUGGER *n pl.* **-S** one that plugs

PLUGHOLE *n pl.* **-S** a drain that can be stopped with a plug

PLUGLESS *adj* having no plug

PLUGOLA *n pl.* **-S** free incidental advertising on radio or television

PLUGUGLY *n pl.* **-LIES** a hoodlum

PLUM *n pl.* **-S** a fleshy fruit

PLUM *adj* **PLUMMER, PLUMMEST** highly desirable

PLUMAGE *n pl.* **-S** the feathers of a bird **PLUMAGED** *adj*

PLUMATE *adj* resembling a feather

PLUMB *v* **-ED, -ING, -S** to determine the depth of

PLUMBAGO *n pl.* **-GOS** graphite

PLUMBER *n pl.* **-S** one who installs and repairs plumbing

PLUMBERY *n pl.* **-ERIES** the work of a plumber

PLUMBIC *adj* containing lead

PLUMBING *n pl.* **-S** the pipe system of a building

PLUMBISM *n pl.* **-S** lead poisoning

PLUMBOUS *adj* containing lead

PLUMBUM *n pl.* **-S** lead

PLUME *v* **PLUMED, PLUMING, PLUMES** to cover with feathers

PLUMELET *n pl.* **-S** a small feather

PLUMERIA *n pl.* **-S** a flowering shrub

PLUMERY *n pl.* **-ERIES** the feathers of a bird

PLUMIER comparative of plumy

PLUMIEST superlative of plumy

PLUMING present participle of plume

PLUMIPED *n pl.* **-S** a bird having feathered feet

PLUMLIKE *adj* resembling a plum

PLUMMET *v* **-ED, -ING, -S** to drop straight down

PLUMMY *adj* **-MIER, -MIEST** full of plums

PLUMOSE *adj* having feathers

PLUMP *adj* **PLUMPER, PLUMPEST** well-rounded and full in form

PLUMP *v* **-ED, -ING, -S** to make plump

PLUMPEN *v* **-ED, -ING, -S** to plump

PLUMPER *n pl.* **-S** a heavy fall

PLUMPISH *adj* somewhat plump

PLUMPLY *adv* in a plump way

PLUMPY *adj* **PLUMPIER, PLUMPIEST** plumpish

PLUMULE *n pl.* **-S** the primary bud of a plant embryo **PLUMULAR** *adj*

PLUMY *adj* **PLUMIER, PLUMIEST** covered with feathers

PLUNDER *v* **-ED, -ING, -S** to rob of goods by force

PLUNGE *v* **PLUNGED, PLUNGING, PLUNGES** to throw or thrust suddenly or forcibly into something

PLUNGER *n pl.* **-S** one that plunges

PLUNK *v* **-ED, -ING, -S** to fall or drop heavily

PLUNKER *n pl.* **-S** one that plunks

PLUNKY *adj* **PLUNKIER, PLUNKIEST** marked by a quick, hollow, metallic sound

PLUOT *n pl.* **-S** a hybrid fruit of plum and apricot

PLURAL *n pl.* **-S** a word that expresses more than one

PLURALLY *adv* in a manner or form that expresses more than one

PLUS *n pl.* **PLUSES** or **PLUSSES** an additional quantity

PLUSH *adj* **PLUSHER, PLUSHEST** luxurious **PLUSHLY** *adv*

PLUSH *n pl.* **-ES** a fabric with a long pile

PLUSHED *adj* showily luxurious

PLUSHY *adj* **PLUSHIER, PLUSHIEST** luxurious **PLUSHILY** *adv*

PLUSSAGE *n pl.* **-S** an amount over and above another

PLUSSES a pl. of plus

PLUTEUS *n pl.* **-TEI** the larva of a sea urchin

PLUTON *n pl.* **-S** a formation of igneous rock **PLUTONIC** *adj*

PLUVIAL *n pl.* **-S** a prolonged period of wet climate

PLUVIAN *adj* characterized by much rain

PLUVIOSE	*adj* pluvious	**PODITE**	*n* pl. **-S** a limb segment of an arthropod **PODITIC** *adj*
PLUVIOUS	*adj* pertaining to rain		
PLY	*v* **PLIED, PLYING, PLIES** to supply with or offer repeatedly **PLYINGLY** *adv*	**PODIUM**	*n* pl. **-DIUMS** or **-DIA** a small platform
		PODLIKE	*adj* resembling a pod (a seed vessel)
PLYER	*n* pl. **-S** plier		
PLYWOOD	*n* pl. **-S** a building material	**PODOCARP**	*adj* designating a family of evergreen trees
PNEUMA	*n* pl. **-S** the soul or spirit		
PO	*n* pl. **POS** a chamber pot	**PODOMERE**	*n* pl. **-S** a podite
POACEOUS	*adj* pertaining to plants of the grass family	**PODSOL**	*n* pl. **-S** podzol **PODSOLIC** *adj*
		PODUNK	*n* pl. **-S** a small, unimportant town
POACH	*v* **-ED, -ING, -ES** to trespass for the purpose of taking game or fish	**PODZOL**	*n* pl. **-S** an infertile soil **PODZOLIC** *adj*
POACHER	*n* pl. **-S** one that poaches	**POECHORE**	*n* pl. **-S** a semiarid region
POACHY	*adj* **POACHIER, POACHIEST** swampy	**POEM**	*n* pl. **-S** a composition in verse
		POESY	*n* pl. **-ESIES** poetry
POBLANO	*n* pl. **-NOS** a mild, dark-green chili pepper	**POET**	*n* pl. **-S** one who writes poems
		POETESS	*n* pl. **-ES** a female poet
POBOY	*n* pl. **-BOYS** a large sandwich on a long split roll	**POETIC**	*adj* pertaining to poetry
		POETICAL	*adj* poetic
POCHARD	*n* pl. **-S** a sea duck	**POETICS**	*n/pl* poetic theory or practice
POCK	*v* **-ED, -ING, -S** to mark with pocks (pustules caused by an eruptive disease)	**POETISE**	*v* **-ISED, -ISING, -ISES** to poetize
		POETISER	*n* pl. **-S** poetizer
POCKET	*v* **-ED, -ING, -S** to place in a pouch sewed into a garment	**POETIZE**	*v* **-IZED, -IZING, -IZES** to write poetry
POCKETER	*n* pl. **-S** one that pockets	**POETIZER**	*n* pl. **-S** one that poetizes
POCKMARK	*v* **-ED, -ING, -S** to mark with scars caused by an eruptive disease	**POETLESS**	*adj* lacking a poet
		POETLIKE	*adj* resembling a poet
POCKY	*adj* **POCKIER, POCKIEST** covered with pocks **POCKILY** *adv*	**POETRY**	*n* pl. **-RIES** literary work in metrical form
POCO	*adv* a little — used as a musical direction	**POGEY**	*n* pl. **-GEYS** any form of government relief
POCOSEN	*n* pl. **-S** pocosin	**POGIES**	pl. of pogy
POCOSIN	*n* pl. **-S** an upland swamp	**POGO**	*v* **-GOED, -GOING, -GOES** or **-GOS** to jump up and down as if on a pogo stick
POCOSON	*n* pl. **-S** pocosin		
POD	*v* **PODDED, PODDING, PODS** to produce seed vessels	**POGONIA**	*n* pl. **-S** a small orchid
		POGONIP	*n* pl. **-S** a dense fog of suspended ice particles
PODAGRA	*n* pl. **-S** gout in the foot **PODAGRAL, PODAGRIC** *adj*		
PODCAST	*v* **-CAST** or **-CASTED, -CASTING, -CASTS** to make a program available in digital format for download over the Internet	**POGROM**	*v* **-ED, -ING, -S** to massacre systematically
		POGY	*n* pl. **-GIES** a marine fish
		POH	*interj* — used to express disgust
PODESTA	*n* pl. **-S** an Italian magistrate	**POI**	*n* pl. **-S** a Hawaiian food
PODGY	*adj* **PODGIER, PODGIEST** pudgy **PODGILY** *adv*	**POIGNANT**	*adj* emotionally distressing
PODIA	a pl. of podium	**POILU**	*n* pl. **-S** a French soldier
PODIATRY	*n* pl. **-TRIES** the study and treatment of the human foot	**POIND**	*v* **-ED, -ING, -S** to seize and sell the property of to satisfy a debt

POINT	*v* **-ED, -ING, -S** to indicate direction with the finger	**POLEAXE**	*v* **-AXED, -AXING, -AXES** to poleax
POINTE	*n* pl. **-S** a ballet position	**POLECAT**	*n* pl. **-S** a carnivorous mammal
POINTER	*n* pl. **-S** one that points	**POLED**	past tense of pole
POINTING	*n* pl. **-S** cement or mortar filling the joints of brickwork	**POLEIS**	pl. of polis
POINTMAN	*n* pl. **-MEN** a certain player in hockey	**POLELESS**	*adj* having no pole
		POLEMIC	*n* pl. **-S** a controversial argument
POINTY	*adj* **POINTIER, POINTIEST** coming to a sharp, tapering end	**POLEMIST**	*n* pl. **-S** one who engages in polemics
POISE	*v* **POISED, POISING, POISES** to hold in a state of equilibrium	**POLEMIZE**	*v* **-MIZED, -MIZING, -MIZES** to engage in polemics
POISER	*n* pl. **-S** one that poises	**POLENTA**	*n* pl. **-S** a thick mush of cornmeal
POISHA	*n* pl. **POISHA** the paisa of Bangladesh	**POLER**	*n* pl. **-S** one that poles
		POLESTAR	*n* pl. **-S** a guiding principle
POISON	*v* **-ED, -ING, -S** to administer a harmful substance to	**POLEWARD**	*adv* in the direction of either extremity of the earth's axis
POISONER	*n* pl. **-S** one that poisons	**POLEYN**	*n* pl. **-S** a protective piece of leather for the knee
POITREL	*n* pl. **-S** peytral		
POKE	*v* **POKED, POKING, POKES** to push or prod **POKABLE** *adj*	**POLICE**	*v* **-LICED, -LICING, -LICES** to make clean or orderly
POKER	*n* pl. **-S** one that pokes	**POLICER**	*n* pl. **-S** one that polices
POKEROOT	*n* pl. **-S** pokeweed	**POLICIER**	*n* pl. **-S** a film featuring police investigating crimes
POKEWEED	*n* pl. **-S** a perennial herb		
POKEY	*n* pl. **-KEYS** poky	**POLICY**	*n* pl. **-CIES** an action or a procedure considered with reference to prudence or expediency
POKIER	comparative of poky		
POKIES	pl. of poky		
POKIEST	superlative of poky	**POLING**	present participle of pole
POKILY	*adv* in a poky manner	**POLIO**	*n* pl. **-LIOS** an infectious virus disease
POKINESS	*n* pl. **-ES** the state of being poky		
POKING	present participle of poke	**POLIS**	*n* pl. **-LEIS** an ancient Greek city-state
POKY	*adj* **POKIER, POKIEST** slow		
POKY	*n* pl. **POKIES** a jail	**POLISH**	*v* **-ED, -ING, -ES** to make smooth and lustrous by rubbing
POL	*n* pl. **-S** a politician		
POLAR	*n* pl. **-S** a straight line related to a point	**POLISHER**	*n* pl. **-S** one that polishes
		POLITE	*adj* **-LITER, -LITEST** showing consideration for others **POLITELY** *adv*
POLARISE	*v* **-ISED, -ISING, -ISES** to polarize		
POLARITY	*n* pl. **-TIES** the possession of two opposite qualities	**POLITIC**	*adj* shrewd
		POLITICK	*v* **-ED, -ING, -S** to engage in politics
POLARIZE	*v* **-IZED, -IZING, -IZES** to give polarity to		
		POLITICO	*n* pl. **-COS** or **-COES** one who politicks
POLARON	*n* pl. **-S** a type of electron		
POLDER	*n* pl. **-S** a tract of low land reclaimed from a body of water	**POLITICS**	*n/pl* the art or science of government
POLE	*v* **POLED, POLING, POLES** to propel with a pole (a long, thin piece of wood or metal)	**POLITY**	*n* pl. **-TIES** a form or system of government
POLEAX	*v* **-ED, -ING, -ES** to strike with an axlike weapon	**POLKA**	*v* **-ED, -ING, -S** to perform a lively dance

POLL *v* **-ED, -ING, -S** to question for the purpose of surveying public opinion

POLLACK *n* pl. **-S** a marine food fish

POLLARD *v* **-ED, -ING, -S** to cut the top branches of a tree back to the trunk

POLLEE *n* pl. **-S** one who is polled

POLLEN *v* **-ED, -ING, -S** to convey pollen (the fertilizing element in a seed plant) to

POLLER *n* pl. **-S** one that polls

POLLEX *n* pl. **-LICES** the innermost digit of the forelimb **POLLICAL** *adj*

POLLING *n* pl. **-S** the registering or casting of votes

POLLINIA *n/pl* masses of pollen grains

POLLINIC *adj* pertaining to pollen

POLLIST *n* pl. **-S** a poller

POLLIWOG *n* pl. **-S** a tadpole

POLLOCK *n* pl. **-S** pollack

POLLSTER *n* pl. **-S** a poller

POLLUTE *v* **-LUTED, -LUTING, -LUTES** to make unclean or impure

POLLUTER *n* pl. **-S** one that pollutes

POLLYWOG *n* pl. **-S** polliwog

POLO *n* pl. **-LOS** a game played on horseback

POLOIST *n* pl. **-S** a polo player

POLONIUM *n* pl. **-S** a radioactive element

POLTROON *n* pl. **-S** a base coward

POLY *n* pl. **POLYS** a type of white blood cell

POLY *n* pl. **POLIES** a garment made of polyester

POLYADIC *adj* involving three or more quantities or individuals

POLYBAG *v* **-BAGGED, -BAGGING, -BAGS** to place something in a polyethylene bag

POLYBRID *n* pl. **-S** a type of hybrid plant

POLYCOT *n* pl. **-S** a type of plant

POLYDRUG *adj* pertaining to the use of several drugs together

POLYENE *n* pl. **-S** a chemical compound **POLYENIC** *adj*

POLYGALA *n* pl. **-S** a flowering plant

POLYGAMY *n* pl. **-MIES** the condition of having more than one spouse at the same time

POLYGENE *n* pl. **-S** a type of gene

POLYGLOT *n* pl. **-S** one that speaks or writes several languages

POLYGON *n* pl. **-S** a closed plane figure bounded by straight lines

POLYGONY *n* pl. **-NIES** an herb

POLYGYNE *adj* having more than one egg-laying queen in an insect colony

POLYGYNY *n* pl. **-NIES** the condition of having more than one wife at the same time

POLYMATH *n* pl. **-S** a person of great and varied learning

POLYMER *n* pl. **-S** a complex chemical compound

POLYNYA *n* pl. **-YAS** or **-YI** an area of open water surrounded by sea ice

POLYOL *n* pl. **-S** an alcohol containing three or more hydroxyl groups

POLYOMA *n* pl. **-S** a type of virus

POLYP *n* pl. **-S** an invertebrate

POLYPARY *n* pl. **-ARIES** the common supporting structure of a polyp colony

POLYPED *n* pl. **-S** something having many legs

POLYPI a pl. of polypus

POLYPIDE *n* pl. **-S** a polyp

POLYPNEA *n* pl. **-S** rapid breathing

POLYPOD *n* pl. **-S** a many-footed organism

POLYPODY *n* pl. **-DIES** a fern

POLYPOID *adj* resembling a polyp

POLYPORE *n* pl. **-S** a type of fungus

POLYPOUS *adj* pertaining to a polyp

POLYPUS *n* pl. **-PUSES** or **-PI** a growth protruding from the mucous lining of an organ

POLYSEMY *n* pl. **-MIES** diversity of meanings

POLYSOME *n* pl. **-S** a cluster of protein particles

POLYTENE *adj* having chromosomes of a certain type

POLYTENY *n* pl. **-NIES** the state of being polytene

POLYTYPE *n* pl. **-S** a crystal structure

POLYURIA *n* pl. **-S** excessive urination **POLYURIC** *adj*

POLYZOAN *n* pl. **-S** a bryozoan

POLYZOIC *adj* composed of many zooids

POM *n* pl. **-S** a Pomeranian dog

POMACE	*n* pl. **-S** the pulpy residue of crushed fruits
POMADE	*v* **-MADED, -MADING, -MADES** to apply a perfumed hair dressing to
POMANDER	*n* pl. **-S** a mixture of aromatic substances
POMATUM	*n* pl. **-S** a perfumed hair dressing
POMBE	*n* pl. **-S** an African drink made from grain and fruit
POME	*n* pl. **-S** a fleshy fruit with a core
POMELO	*n* pl. **-LOS** a grapefruit
POMFRET	*n* pl. **-S** a marine fish
POMMEE	*adj* having arms with knoblike ends — used of a heraldic cross
POMMEL	*v* **-MELED, -MELING, -MELS** or **-MELLED, -MELLING, -MELS** to strike with the fists
POMO	*n* pl. **-MOS** the postmodern movement
POMOLOGY	*n* pl. **-GIES** the study of fruits
POMP	*n* pl. **-S** stately or splendid display
POMPANO	*n* pl. **-NOS** a marine food fish
POMPOM	*n* pl. **-S** an antiaircraft cannon
POMPON	*n* pl. **-S** an ornamental tuft or ball
POMPOUS	*adj* marked by exaggerated self-importance
PONCE	*v* **PONCED, PONCING, PONCES** to pimp
PONCHO	*n* pl. **-CHOS** a type of cloak **PONCHOED** *adj*
POND	*v* **-ED, -ING, -S** to collect into a pond (a small body of water)
PONDER	*v* **-ED, -ING, -S** to consider something deeply and thoroughly
PONDERER	*n* pl. **-S** one that ponders
PONDWEED	*n* pl. **-S** an aquatic plant
PONE	*n* pl. **-S** a corn bread
PONENT	*adj* affirmative
PONG	*v* **-ED, -ING, -S** to stink
PONGAL	*n* pl. **-S** a dish of cooked rice in Tamil-speaking India
PONGEE	*n* pl. **-S** a type of silk
PONGID	*n* pl. **-S** an anthropoid ape
PONGO	*n* pl. **-GOS** an anthropoid ape
PONGY	*adj* **PONGIER, PONGIEST** stinky
PONIARD	*v* **-ED, -ING, -S** to stab with a dagger
PONIED	past tense of pony
PONIES	present 3d person sing. of pony

PONS	*n* pl. **PONTES** a band of nerve fibers in the brain
PONTIFEX	*n* pl. **-FICES** an ancient Roman priest
PONTIFF	*n* pl. **-S** a pope or bishop
PONTIFIC	*adj* pertaining to a pope or bishop
PONTIFICES	pl. of pontifex
PONTIL	*n* pl. **-S** a punty
PONTINE	*adj* pertaining to bridges
PONTON	*n* pl. **-S** pontoon
PONTOON	*n* pl. **-S** a flat-bottomed boat
PONY	*v* **-NIED, -NYING, -NIES** to prepare lessons with the aid of a literal translation
PONYTAIL	*n* pl. **-S** a hairstyle
PONZU	*n* pl. **-S** a tangy sauce used chiefly on seafood
POO	*v* **-ED, -ING, -S** to defecate
POOBAH	*n* pl. **-S** an influential person
POOCH	*v* **-ED, -ING, -ES** to bulge
POOD	*n* pl. **-S** a Russian unit of weight
POODLE	*n* pl. **-S** a heavy-coated dog
POOF	*interj* — used to indicate an instantaneous occurrence
POOH	*v* **-ED, -ING, -S** to express contempt for
POOJA	*n* pl. **-S** puja
POOKA	*n* pl. **-S** a hobgoblin in Irish myths
POOL	*v* **-ED, -ING, -S** to combine in a common fund
POOLER	*n* pl. **-S** one that pools
POOLHALL	*n* pl. **-S** a poolroom
POOLROOM	*n* pl. **-S** an establishment for the playing of billiards
POOLSIDE	*n* pl. **-S** the area surrounding a swimming pool
POON	*n* pl. **-S** an East Indian tree
POOP	*v* **-ED, -ING, -S** to tire out
POOPY	*adj* **POOPIER, POOPIEST** stupid or ineffectual
POOR	*adj* **POORER, POOREST** lacking the means of support
POORI	*n* pl. **-S** a light, flat wheat cake
POORISH	*adj* somewhat poor
POORLY	*adv* in a poor manner
POORNESS	*n* pl. **-ES** the state of being poor
POORTITH	*n* pl. **-S** poverty

POORWILL *n* pl. **-S** a small North American bird

POP *v* **POPPED, POPPING, POPS** to make a sharp, explosive sound

POPCORN *n* pl. **-S** a variety of corn

POPE *n* pl. **-S** the head of the Roman Catholic Church **POPELESS, POPELIKE** *adj*

POPEDOM *n* pl. **-S** the office of a pope

POPEYED *adj* having bulging eyes

POPGUN *n* pl. **-S** a toy gun

POPINJAY *n* pl. **-JAYS** a vain person

POPLAR *n* pl. **-S** a fast-growing tree

POPLIN *n* pl. **-S** a durable fabric

POPLITEI *n/pl* muscles at the back of knees

POPLITIC *adj* pertaining to the part of the leg behind the knee

POPOUT *n* pl. **-S** a type of out in baseball

POPOVER *n* pl. **-S** a very light egg muffin

POPPA *n* pl. **-S** papa

POPPADOM *n* pl. **-S** papadum

POPPADUM *n* pl. **-S** papadum

POPPED past tense of pop

POPPER *n* pl. **-S** one that pops

POPPET *n* pl. **-S** a mechanical valve

POPPIED *adj* covered with poppies

POPPIES pl. of poppy

POPPING present participle of pop

POPPLE *v* **-PLED, -PLING, -PLES** to move in a bubbling or rippling manner

POPPLY *adj* **-PLIER, -PLIEST** choppy

POPPY *n* pl. **-PIES** a flowering plant

POPPY *adj* **-PIER, -PIEST** having the characteristics of pop music

POPSIE *n* pl. **-S** popsy

POPSTER *n* pl. **-S** a pop musician

POPSY *n* pl. **-SIES** a girlfriend

POPULACE *n* pl. **-S** the common people

POPULAR *adj* liked by many people

POPULATE *v* **-LATED, -LATING, -LATES** to inhabit

POPULISM *n* pl. **-S** populists' doctrines

POPULIST *n* pl. **-S** a member of a party which represents the common people

POPULOUS *adj* containing many inhabitants

PORCH *n* pl. **-ES** a covered structure at the entrance to a building **PORCHED** *adj*

PORCINE *adj* pertaining to swine

PORCINI *n* pl. **-S** an edible mushroom

PORCINO *n* pl. **-NI** porcini

PORE *v* **PORED, PORING, PORES** to gaze intently

PORGY *n* pl. **-GIES** a marine food fish

PORIN *n* pl. **-S** any of a class of proteins through which molecules can diffuse

PORISM *n* pl. **-S** a type of mathematical proposition

PORK *v* **-ED, -ING, -S** to eat ravenously

PORKER *n* pl. **-S** a pig

PORKIER comparative of porky

PORKIES pl. of porky

PORKIEST superlative of porky

PORKPIE *n* pl. **-S** a man's hat

PORKWOOD *n* pl. **-S** a tropical tree

PORKY *adj* **PORKIER, PORKIEST** resembling pork

PORKY *n* pl. **-KIES** a porcupine

PORN *n* pl. **-S** pornography

PORNO *n* pl. **-NOS** pornography

PORNY *adj* **PORNIER, PORNIEST** pornographic

POROSE *adj* porous

POROSITY *n* pl. **-TIES** the state of being porous

POROUS *adj* having minute openings **POROUSLY** *adv*

PORPHYRY *n* pl. **-RIES** an igneous rock

PORPOISE *v* **-POISED, -POISING, -POISES** to move forward with rising and falling motions

PORRECT *adj* extended forward

PORRIDGE *n* pl. **-S** a soft food **PORRIDGY** *adj*

PORT *v* **-ED, -ING, -S** to shift to the left side

PORTABLE *n* pl. **-S** something that can be carried

PORTABLY *adv* so as to be capable of being carried

PORTAGE *v* **-TAGED, -TAGING, -TAGES** to transport from one navigable waterway to another

PORTAL *n* pl. **-S** a door, gate, or entrance **PORTALED** *adj*

PORTANCE *n* pl. **-S** demeanor

PORTAPAK *n* pl. **-S** a portable combined video recorder and camera

PORTEND *v* **-ED, -ING, -S** to serve as an omen of

PORTENT *n* pl. **-S** an omen

PORTER *v* **-ED, -ING, -S** to carry luggage for pay

PORTHOLE *n* pl. **-S** a small window in a ship's side

PORTICO *n* pl. **-COS** or **-COES** a type of porch

PORTIERE *n* pl. **-S** a curtain for a doorway

PORTION *v* **-ED, -ING, -S** to divide into shares for distribution

PORTLESS *adj* having no place for ships to load or unload

PORTLY *adj* **-LIER, -LIEST** rather heavy or fat

PORTOLAN *n* pl. **-S** a book of sailing directions

PORTRAIT *n* pl. **-S** a likeness of a person

PORTRAY *v* **-ED, -ING, -S** to represent pictorially

PORTRESS *n* pl. **-ES** a female doorkeeper

PORTSIDE *adv* on the left side of a ship facing forward

POS pl. of po

POSADA *n* pl. **-S** an inn

POSE *v* **POSED, POSING, POSES** to assume a fixed position **POSABLE, POSEABLE** *adj*

POSER *n* pl. **-S** one that poses

POSEUR *n* pl. **-S** an affected or insincere person

POSEY *adj* **POSIER, POSIEST** pretentious

POSH *adj* **POSHER, POSHEST** stylish or elegant **POSHLY** *adv*

POSHNESS *n* pl. **-ES** the quality of being posh

POSIES pl. of posy

POSING present participle of pose

POSINGLY *adv* in a posing manner

POSIT *v* **-ED, -ING, -S** to place

POSITION *v* **-ED, -ING, -S** to put in a particular location

POSITIVE *adj* **-TIVER, -TIVEST** certain

POSITIVE *n* pl. **-S** a quantity greater than zero

POSITRON *n* pl. **-S** a subatomic particle

POSOLE *n* pl. **-S** a thick soup made of pork, corn, garlic, and chili

POSOLOGY *n* pl. **-GIES** a branch of medicine that deals with drug dosages

POSSE *n* pl. **-S** a body of men summoned to aid a peace officer

POSSESS *v* **-ED, -ING, -ES** to have as property

POSSET *n* pl. **-S** a hot, spiced drink

POSSIBLE *adj* **-BLER, -BLEST** capable of happening or proving true **POSSIBLY** *adv*

POSSIBLE *n* pl. **-S** a possibility

POSSUM *n* pl. **-S** opossum

POST *v* **-ED, -ING, -S** to affix in a public place

POSTAGE *n* pl. **-S** the charge for mailing an item

POSTAL *n* pl. **-S** a postcard

POSTALLY *adv* in a manner pertaining to the mails

POSTANAL *adj* situated behind the anus

POSTBAG *n* pl. **-S** a mailbag

POSTBASE *adj* following a base word

POSTBOX *n* pl. **-ES** a mailbox

POSTBOY *n* pl. **-BOYS** a boy who carries mail

POSTBURN *adj* following a burn

POSTCARD *n* pl. **-S** a card for use in the mail

POSTCAVA *n* pl. **-VAE** a vein in higher vertebrates

POSTCODE *n* pl. **-S** a code of numbers and letters used in a mailing address

POSTCOUP *adj* following a coup

POSTDATE *v* **-DATED, -DATING, -DATES** to give a date later than the actual date to

POSTDIVE *adj* following a dive

POSTDOC *n* pl. **-S** one engaged in postdoctoral study

POSTDRUG *adj* following the taking of a drug

POSTEEN *n* pl. **-S** an Afghan outer garment

POSTER *v* **-ED, -ING, -S** to affix public notices on

POSTERN *n* pl. **-S** a rear door or gate

POSTFACE *n* pl. **-S** a brief note placed at the end of a publication

POSTFIRE *adj* following a fire

POSTFIX *v* **-ED, -ING, -ES** to affix at the end of something

POSTFORM *v* **-ED, -ING, -S** to shape subsequently

POSTGAME *adj* following a game

POSTGRAD *n* pl. **-S** a student continuing formal education after graduation

POSTHEAT *n* pl. **-S** heat applied to a metal after welding

POSTHOLE *n* pl. **-S** a hole for a fence post

POSTICHE *n* pl. **-S** an imitation

POSTIE *n* pl. **-TIES** a letter carrier

POSTIN *n* pl. **-S** posteen

POSTING *n* pl. **-S** the act of transferring to a ledger

POSTIQUE *n* pl. **-S** postiche

POSTLUDE *n* pl. **-S** a closing musical piece

POSTMAN *n* pl. **-MEN** a mailman

POSTMARK *v* **-ED, -ING, -S** to stamp mail with an official mark

POSTOP *n* pl. **-S** a patient after undergoing a surgical operation

POSTORAL *adj* situated behind the mouth

POSTPAID *adv* with the postage prepaid

POSTPONE *v* **-PONED, -PONING, -PONES** to put off to a future time

POSTPOSE *v* **-POSED, -POSING, -POSES** to place (a word or phrase) after a grammatically related word

POSTPUNK *adj* pertaining to music coming after punk rock

POSTRACE *adj* following a race

POSTRIOT *adj* following a riot

POSTSHOW *adj* following a show

POSTSYNC *v* **-ED, -ING, -S** to add sound to a film after a scene has been photographed

POSTTAX *adj* remaining after taxes

POSTTEEN *n* pl. **-S** a person older than 19 years

POSTTEST *n* pl. **-S** a test given after an instructional program

POSTURAL *adj* pertaining to the position of the body

POSTURE *v* **-TURED, -TURING, -TURES** to assume a particular position

POSTURER *n* pl. **-S** one that postures

POSTWAR *adj* occurring or existing after a war

POSY *n* pl. **-SIES** a flower or bouquet

POT *v* **POTTED, POTTING, POTS** to put in a pot (a round, fairly deep container)

POTABLE *n* pl. **-S** a liquid suitable for drinking

POTAGE *n* pl. **-S** a thick soup

POTAMIC *adj* pertaining to rivers

POTASH *n* pl. **-ES** an alkaline compound

POTASSIC *adj* pertaining to potassium (a metallic element)

POTATION *n* pl. **-S** the act of drinking

POTATO *n* pl. **-TOES** the edible tuber of a cultivated plant

POTATORY *adj* pertaining to drinking

POTBELLY *n* pl. **-LIES** a protruding abdominal region

POTBOIL *v* **-ED, -ING, -S** to produce inferior literary or artistic work

POTBOUND *adj* having grown too large for its container

POTBOY *n* pl. **-BOYS** a boy who serves customers in a tavern

POTEEN *n* pl. **-S** Irish whiskey that is distilled unlawfully

POTENCE *n* pl. **-S** potency

POTENCY *n* pl. **-CIES** the quality of being potent

POTENT *adj* powerful **POTENTLY** *adv*

POTFUL *n* pl. **-S** as much as a pot can hold

POTHEAD *n* pl. **-S** one who smokes marijuana

POTHEEN *n* pl. **-S** poteen

POTHER *v* **-ED, -ING, -S** to trouble

POTHERB *n* pl. **-S** any herb used as a food or seasoning

POTHOLE *n* pl. **-S** a deep hole in a road **POTHOLED** *adj*

POTHOLER *n* pl. **-S** one who explores deep underground holes or caves

POTHOOK *n* pl. **-S** a hook for lifting or hanging pots

POTHOS *n* pl. **POTHOS** a climbing plant with glossy variegated leaves

POTHOUSE *n* pl. **-S** a tavern

POTICHE *n* pl. **-S** a type of vase

POTION *n* pl. **-S** a magical or medicinal drink

POTLACH *n* pl. **-ES** a ceremonial feast

POTLACHE *n* pl. **-S** potlach

POTLATCH *v* **-ED, -ING, -ES** to hold a ceremonial feast for

POTLIKE *adj* resembling a pot

POTLINE *n* pl. **-S** a row of electrolytic cells

POTLUCK *n* pl. **-S** food which is incidentally available

POTMAN *n* pl. **-MEN** a man who serves customers in a tavern

POTPIE *n* pl. **-S** a deep-dish pie containing meat and vegetables

POTSHARD *n* pl. **-S** potsherd

POTSHERD *n* pl. **-S** a fragment of broken pottery

POTSHOT *v* **-SHOT, -SHOTTING, -SHOTS** to shoot randomly at

POTSIE *n* pl. **-S** potsy

POTSTONE *n* pl. **-S** a variety of steatite

POTSY *n* pl. **-SIES** a children's game

POTTAGE *n* pl. **-S** a thick soup

POTTED past tense of pot

POTTEEN *n* pl. **-S** poteen

POTTER *v* **-ED, -ING, -S** to putter

POTTERER *n* pl. **-S** one that potters

POTTERY *n* pl. **-TERIES** ware molded from clay and hardened by heat

POTTIER comparative of potty

POTTIES pl. of potty

POTTIEST superlative of potty

POTTING present participle of pot

POTTLE *n* pl. **-S** a drinking vessel

POTTO *n* pl. **-TOS** a lemur of tropical Africa

POTTY *adj* **-TIER, -TIEST** of little importance

POTTY *n* pl. **-TIES** a small toilet seat

POTZER *n* pl. **-S** patzer

POUCH *v* **-ED, -ING, -ES** to put in a pouch (a small, flexible receptacle)

POUCHY *adj* **POUCHIER, POUCHIEST** resembling a pouch

POUF *n* pl. **-S** a loose roll of hair **POUFED, POUFFY** *adj*

POUFF *n* pl. **-S** pouf **POUFFED** *adj*

POUFFE *n* pl. **-S** pouf

POULARD *n* pl. **-S** a spayed hen

POULARDE *n* pl. **-S** poulard

POULT *n* pl. **-S** a young domestic fowl

POULTER *n* pl. **-S** one that deals in poultry

POULTICE *v* **-TICED, -TICING, -TICES** to apply a healing substance to

POULTRY *n* pl. **-TRIES** domestic fowls kept for eggs or meat

POUNCE *v* **POUNCED, POUNCING, POUNCES** to make a sudden assault or approach

POUNCER *n* pl. **-S** one that pounces

POUND *v* **-ED, -ING, -S** to strike heavily and repeatedly

POUNDAGE *n* pl. **-S** the act of impounding

POUNDAL *n* pl. **-S** a unit of force

POUNDER *n* pl. **-S** one that pounds

POUR *v* **-ED, -ING, -S** to cause to flow **POURABLE** *adj*

POURER *n* pl. **-S** one that pours

POUSSIE *n* pl. **-S** pussy

POUT *v* **-ED, -ING, -S** to protrude the lips in ill humor

POUTER *n* pl. **-S** one that pouts

POUTFUL *adj* pouty

POUTINE *n* pl. **-S** a dish of french fries and cheese curds topped with gravy

POUTY *adj* **POUTIER, POUTIEST** tending to pout

POVERTY *n* pl. **-TIES** the state of being poor

POW *n* pl. **-S** an explosive sound

POWDER *v* **-ED, -ING, -S** to reduce to powder (matter in a finely divided state)

POWDERER *n* pl. **-S** one that powders

POWDERY *adj* resembling powder

POWER *v* **-ED, -ING, -S** to provide with means of propulsion

POWERFUL *adj* possessing great force

POWTER *n* pl. **-S** a domestic pigeon

POWWOW *v* **-ED, -ING, -S** to hold a conference

POX *v* **-ED, -ING, -ES** to infect with a pox (a disease marked by skin eruptions)

POXVIRUS *n* pl. **-ES** a type of virus

POXY *adj* **POXIER, POXIEST** afflicted with a pox

POYOU *n* pl. **-S** an armadillo of Argentina

POZOLE *n* pl. **-S** posole

POZZOLAN *n* pl. **-S** a finely divided material used to make cement

PRAAM *n* pl. **-S** pram

PRACTIC *adj* practical

PRACTICE *v* **-TICED, -TICING, -TICES** to perform often so as to acquire skill

PRACTISE *v* **-TISED, -TISING, -TISES** to practice

PRAECIPE *n* pl. **-S** a legal writ

PRAEDIAL *adj* pertaining to land

PRAEFECT *n* pl. **-S** prefect

PRAELECT *v* -ED, -ING, -S to prelect

PRAETOR *n* pl. -S an ancient Roman magistrate

PRAHU *n* pl. -S prau

PRAIRIE *n* pl. -S a tract of grassland

PRAISE *v* **PRAISED, PRAISING, PRAISES** to express approval or admiration of

PRAISER *n* pl. -S one that praises

PRAJNA *n* pl. -S ultimate knowledge in Buddhism and Hinduism

PRALINE *n* pl. -S a confection made of nuts cooked in sugar

PRAM *n* pl. -S a flat-bottomed boat

PRANA *n* pl. -S breath as a life-giving force in Hinduism

PRANCE *v* **PRANCED, PRANCING, PRANCES** to spring forward on the hind legs

PRANCER *n* pl. -S one that prances

PRANDIAL *adj* pertaining to a meal

PRANG *v* -ED, -ING, -S to cause to crash

PRANK *v* -ED, -ING, -S to adorn gaudily

PRANKISH *adj* mischievous

PRAO *n* pl. **PRAOS** prau

PRASE *n* pl. -S a mineral

PRAT *n* pl. -S the buttocks

PRATE *v* **PRATED, PRATING, PRATES** to chatter

PRATER *n* pl. -S one that prates

PRATFALL *n* pl. -S a fall on the buttocks

PRATIE *n* pl. -S a potato

PRATIQUE *n* pl. -S clearance given a ship by the health authority of a port

PRATTLE *v* -TLED, -TLING, -TLES to babble

PRATTLER *n* pl. -S one that prattles

PRAU *n* pl. -S a swift Malaysian sailing vessel

PRAWN *v* -ED, -ING, -S to fish for prawns (edible shellfish)

PRAWNER *n* pl. -S one that prawns

PRAXIS *n* pl. **PRAXISES** or **PRAXES** practical use of a theory

PRAY *v* -ED, -ING, -S to address prayers to

PRAYER *n* pl. -S a devout petition to a deity

PREACH *v* -ED, -ING, -ES to advocate or recommend urgently

PREACHER *n* pl. -S one that preaches

PREACHY *adj* **PREACHIER, PREACHIEST** tending to preach

PREACT *v* -ED, -ING, -S to act beforehand

PREADAPT *v* -ED, -ING, -S to adapt beforehand

PREADMIT *v* -MITTED, -MITTING, -MITS to admit beforehand

PREADOPT *v* -ED, -ING, -S to adopt beforehand

PREADULT *n* pl. -S a person not yet an adult

PREAGED *adj* previously aged

PREALLOT *v* -LOTTED, -LOTTING, -LOTS to allot beforehand

PREALTER *v* -ED, -ING, -S to alter beforehand

PREAMBLE *n* pl. -S an introductory statement

PREAMP *n* pl. -S an amplifier

PREANAL *adj* situated in front of the anus

PREAPPLY *v* -PLIED, -PLYING, -PLIES to apply beforehand

PREARM *v* -ED, -ING, -S to arm beforehand

PREAUDIT *n* pl. -S an audit made prior to a final settlement of a transaction

PREAVER *v* -VERRED, -VERRING, -VERS to aver or assert beforehand

PREAXIAL *adj* situated in front of an axis

PREBAKE *v* -BAKED, -BAKING, -BAKES to bake beforehand

PREBASAL *adj* situated in front of a base

PREBEND *n* pl. -S a clergyman's stipend

PREBID *v* -BADE, -BIDDEN, -BIDDING, -BIDS to bid beforehand

PREBILL *v* -ED, -ING, -S to bill beforehand

PREBIND *v* -BOUND, -BINDING, -BINDS to bind beforehand

PREBIRTH *n* pl. -S the period preceding a child's birth

PREBLESS *v* -ED, -ING, -ES to bless beforehand

PREBOARD *v* -ED, -ING, -S to board before the regular time

PREBOIL *v* -ED, -ING, -S to boil beforehand

PREBOOK *v* -ED, -ING, -S to book beforehand

PREBOOM *adj* preceding a sudden expansion of business

PREBOUND past tense of prebind

PREBUILD *v* -BUILT, -BUILDING, -BUILDS to build beforehand

PREBUY *v* -BOUGHT, -BUYING, -BUYS to buy beforehand

PRECAST *v* **-CAST, -CASTING, -CASTS** to cast before placing into position

PRECAVA *n* pl. **-VAE** a vein in higher vertebrates **PRECAVAL** *adj*

PRECEDE *v* **-CEDED, -CEDING, -CEDES** to go before

PRECENT *v* **-ED, -ING, -S** to lead a church choir in singing

PRECEPT *n* pl. **-S** a rule of conduct

PRECESS *v* **-ED, -ING, -ES** to rotate with a complex motion

PRECHECK *v* **-ED, -ING, -S** to check beforehand

PRECHILL *v* **-ED, -ING, -S** to chill beforehand

PRECHOSE past tense of prechoose (to choose beforehand)

PRECIEUX *adj* excessively refined

PRECINCT *n* pl. **-S** a subdivision of a city or town

PRECIOUS *n* pl. **-ES** a darling

PRECIP *n* pl. **-S** precipitation

PRECIPE *n* pl. **-S** praecipe

PRECIS *v* **-ED, -ING, -ES** to make a concise summary of

PRECISE *adj* **-CISER, -CISEST** sharply and clearly defined or stated

PRECITED *adj* previously cited

PRECLEAN *v* **-ED, -ING, -S** to clean beforehand

PRECLEAR *v* **-ED, -ING, -S** to clear beforehand

PRECLUDE *v* **-CLUDED, -CLUDING, -CLUDES** to make impossible by previous action

PRECODE *v* **-CODED, -CODING, -CODES** to code beforehand

PRECOOK *v* **-ED, -ING, -S** to cook beforehand

PRECOOL *v* **-ED, -ING, -S** to cool beforehand

PRECOUP *adj* preceding a coup

PRECRASH *adj* preceding a crash

PRECURE *v* **-CURED, -CURING, -CURES** to cure beforehand

PRECUT *v* **-CUT, -CUTTING, -CUTS** to cut beforehand

PREDATE *v* **-DATED, -DATING, -DATES** to date before the actual or a specified time

PREDATOR *n* pl. **-S** one that plunders

PREDAWN *n* pl. **-S** the time just before dawn

PREDEATH *n* pl. **-S** the period preceding a person's death

PREDELLA *n* pl. **-S** the base of an altarpiece

PREDIAL *adj* praedial

PREDICT *v* **-ED, -ING, -S** to tell of or about in advance

PREDIVE *adj* preceding a dive

PREDRAFT *adj* preceding a draft (a system for selecting players for professional teams)

PREDRILL *v* **-ED, -ING, -S** to drill beforehand

PREDRY *v* **-DRIED, -DRYING, -DRIES** to dry beforehand

PREDUSK *n* pl. **-S** the time just before dusk

PREE *v* **PREED, PREEING, PREES** to test by tasting

PREEDIT *v* **-ED, -ING, -S** to edit beforehand

PREELECT *v* **-ED, -ING, -S** to elect or choose beforehand

PREEMIE *n* pl. **-S** an infant born prematurely

PREEMPT *v* **-ED, -ING, -S** to acquire by prior right

PREEN *v* **-ED, -ING, -S** to smooth or clean with the beak or tongue

PREENACT *v* **-ED, -ING, -S** to enact beforehand

PREENER *n* pl. **-S** one that preens

PREERECT *v* **-ED, -ING, -S** to erect beforehand

PREEXIST *v* **-ED, -ING, -S** to exist before

PREFAB *v* **-FABBED, -FABBING, -FABS** to construct beforehand

PREFACE *v* **-ACED, -ACING, -ACES** to provide with an introductory statement

PREFACER *n* pl. **-S** one that prefaces

PREFADE *v* **-FADED, -FADING, -FADES** to fade beforehand

PREFECT *n* pl. **-S** an ancient Roman official

PREFER *v* **-FERRED, -FERRING, -FERS** to hold in higher regard or esteem

PREFIGHT *adj* preceding a fight

PREFILE *v* **-FILED, -FILING, -FILES** to file beforehand

PREFIRE *v* **-FIRED, -FIRING, -FIRES** to fire beforehand

PREFIX *v* **-ED, -ING, -ES** to add as a prefix (a form affixed to the beginning of a root word)

PREFIXAL *adj* pertaining to or being a prefix

PREFLAME *adj* preceding a flame

PREFOCUS *v* **-CUSED, -CUSING, -CUSES** or **-CUSSED, -CUSSING, -CUSSES** to focus beforehand

PREFORM *v* **-ED, -ING, -S** to form beforehand

PREFRANK *v* **-ED, -ING, -S** to frank beforehand

PREFUND *v* **-ED, -ING, -S** to fund beforehand

PREGAME *n* pl. **-S** the period preceding a game

PREGGERS *adj* pregnant

PREGNANT *adj* carrying a developing fetus in the uterus

PREGUIDE *v* **-GUIDED, -GUIDING, -GUIDES** to guide beforehand

PREHEAT *v* **-ED, -ING, -S** to heat beforehand

PREHUMAN *n* pl. **-S** a prototype of man

PREJUDGE *v* **-JUDGED, -JUDGING, -JUDGES** to judge beforehand

PRELACY *n* pl. **-CIES** the office of a prelate

PRELATE *n* pl. **-S** a high-ranking clergyman **PRELATIC** *adj*

PRELAW *adj* preceding the professional study of law

PRELECT *v* **-ED, -ING, -S** to lecture

PRELEGAL *adj* occurring before the commencement of studies in law

PRELIFE *n* pl. **-LIVES** a life conceived as lived before one's earthly life

PRELIM *n* pl. **-S** a preliminary match

PRELIMIT *v* **-ED, -ING, -S** to limit beforehand

PRELOAD *v* **-ED, -ING, -S** to load beforehand

PRELUDE *v* **-LUDED, -LUDING, -LUDES** to play a musical introduction

PRELUDER *n* pl. **-S** one that preludes

PRELUNCH *adj* preceding lunch

PREMADE *adj* made beforehand

PREMAN *n* pl. **-MEN** a hypothetical ancestor of man

PREMEAL *adj* preceding a meal

PREMED *n* pl. **-S** a student preparing for the study of medicine

PREMEDIC *n* pl. **-S** a premed

PREMEET *adj* preceding a meet

PREMEN pl. of preman

PREMIE *n* pl. **-S** preemie

PREMIER *n* pl. **-S** a prime minister

PREMIERE *v* **-MIERED, -MIERING, -MIERES** to present publicly for the first time

PREMISE *v* **-MISED, -MISING, -MISES** to state in advance

PREMISS *n* pl. **-ES** a proposition in logic

PREMIUM *n* pl. **-S** an additional payment

PREMIX *v* **-MIXED** or **-MIXT, -MIXING, -MIXES** to mix before use

PREMOLAR *n* pl. **-S** a tooth

PREMOLD *v* **-ED, -ING, -S** to mold beforehand

PREMOLT *adj* preceding a molt

PREMORAL *adj* preceding the development of a moral code

PREMORSE *adj* ending abruptly, as if bitten off

PREMOTOR *adj* pertaining to a part of the frontal lobe of the brain

PREMUNE *adj* resistant to a disease

PRENAME *n* pl. **-S** a forename

PRENATAL *adj* prior to birth

PRENOMEN *n* pl. **-MENS** or **-MINA** the first name of an ancient Roman

PRENOON *adj* preceding noon

PRENTICE *v* **-TICED, -TICING, -TICES** to place with an employer for instruction in a trade

PRENUP *n* pl. **-S** an agreement made by a couple before they marry

PREOP *n* pl. **-S** a patient being prepared for surgery

PREORAL *adj* situated in front of the mouth

PREORDER *v* **-ED, -ING, -S** to order beforehand

PREOWNED *adj* owned beforehand by someone else

PREP *v* **PREPPED, PREPPING, PREPS** to attend a preparatory school

PREPACK *v* **-ED, -ING, -S** to package before retail distribution

PREPAID past tense of prepay

PREPARE *v* **-PARED, -PARING, -PARES** to put in proper condition or readiness

PREPARER *n* pl. **-S** one that prepares

PREPASTE *v* **-PASTED, -PASTING, -PASTES** to paste beforehand

PREPAVE *v* **-PAVED, -PAVING, -PAVES** to pave beforehand

PREPAY *v* **-PAID, -PAYING, -PAYS** to pay in advance

PREPENSE *adj* planned in advance

PREPILL *adj* preceding the development of a contraceptive pill

PREPLACE *v* **-PLACED, -PLACING, -PLACES** to place beforehand

PREPLAN v **-PLANNED, -PLANNING, -PLANS** to plan in advance

PREPLANT adj occurring before planting

PREPOSE v **-POSED, -POSING, -POSES** to place something in front of another

PREPPED past tense of prep

PREPPIE n pl. **-S** one who preps

PREPPING present participle of prep

PREPPY adj **-PIER, -PIEST** associated with the style and behavior of preparatory school students **PREPPILY** adv

PREPREG n pl. **-S** reinforcing material already impregnated with a synthetic resin

PREPRESS adj pertaining to the preparation of copy for printing

PREPRICE v **-PRICED, -PRICING, -PRICES** to price beforehand

PREPRINT v **-ED, -ING, -S** to print in advance

PREPUBIS n pl. **-PUBES** a bone situated in front of the pubic bones

PREPUCE n pl. **-S** a fold of skin covering the penis

PREPUNCH v **-ED, -ING, -ES** to punch in advance

PREPUPA n pl. **-PAS** or **-PAE** a stage preceding the pupa

PREPUPAL adj preceding the pupal stage

PREQUEL n pl. **-S** a book whose story precedes that of an earlier work

PRERACE adj preceding a race

PRERADIO adj preceding the development of radio

PRERENAL adj situated in front of the kidney

PRERINSE v **-RINSED, -RINSING, -RINSES** to rinse beforehand

PRERIOT adj preceding a riot

PREROCK adj preceding the development of rock music

PRESA n pl. **-SE** a musical symbol

PRESAGE v **-SAGED, -SAGING, -SAGES** to foretell

PRESAGER n pl. **-S** one that presages

PRESALE n pl. **-S** a sale in advance

PRESCIND v **-ED, -ING, -S** to consider separately

PRESCORE v **-SCORED, -SCORING, -SCORES** to record the sound of before filming

PRESE pl. of presa

PRESELL v **-SOLD, -SELLING, -SELLS** to promote a product not yet being sold to the public

PRESENCE n pl. **-S** close proximity

PRESENT v **-ED, -ING, -S** to bring into the presence of someone

PRESERVE v **-SERVED, -SERVING, -SERVES** to keep free from harm or danger

PRESET v **-SET, -SETTING, -SETS** to set beforehand

PRESHAPE v **-SHAPED, -SHAPING, -SHAPES** to shape beforehand

PRESHIP v **-SHIPPED, -SHIPPING, -SHIPS** to ship beforehand

PRESHOW v **-SHOWED, -SHOWN, -SHOWING, -SHOWS** to show beforehand

PRESIDE v **-SIDED, -SIDING, -SIDES** to occupy the position of authority

PRESIDER n pl. **-S** one that presides

PRESIDIA n/pl Soviet executive committees

PRESIDIO n pl. **-DIOS** a Spanish fort

PRESIFT v **-ED, -ING, -S** to sift beforehand

PRESLEEP adj preceding sleep

PRESLICE v **-SLICED, -SLICING, -SLICES** to slice beforehand

PRESOAK v **-ED, -ING, -S** to soak beforehand

PRESOLD past tense of presell

PRESOLVE v **-SOLVED, -SOLVING, -SOLVES** to solve beforehand

PRESONG adj preceding a song

PRESORT v **-ED, -ING, -S** to sort beforehand

PRESPLIT adj preceding a split

PRESS v **-ED, -ING, -ES** to act upon with steady force

PRESSER n pl. **-S** one that presses

PRESSING n pl. **-S** an instance of stamping with a press

PRESSMAN n pl. **-MEN** a printing press operator

PRESSOR n pl. **-S** a substance that raises blood pressure

PRESSRUN n pl. **-S** a continuous operation of a printing press

PRESSURE v **-SURED, -SURING, -SURES** to apply force to

PREST n pl. **-S** a loan

PRESTAMP v **-ED, -ING, -S** to stamp beforehand

PRESTER n pl. **-S** a priest

PRESTIGE _n_ pl. **-S** distinction or reputation in the eyes of people

PRESTO _n_ pl. **-TOS** a musical passage played in rapid tempo

PRESTORE _v_ **-STORED, -STORING, -STORES** to store beforehand

PRESUME _v_ **-SUMED, -SUMING, -SUMES** to take for granted

PRESUMER _n_ pl. **-S** one that presumes

PRETAPE _v_ **-TAPED, -TAPING, -TAPES** to tape beforehand

PRETASTE _v_ **-TASTED, -TASTING, -TASTES** to taste beforehand

PRETAX _adj_ existing before provision for taxes

PRETEEN _n_ pl. **-S** a child under the age of thirteen

PRETELL _v_ **-TOLD, -TELLING, -TELLS** to tell beforehand

PRETENCE _n_ pl. **-S** pretense

PRETEND _v_ **-ED, -ING, -S** to assume or display a false appearance of

PRETENSE _n_ pl. **-S** the act of pretending

PRETERIT _n_ pl. **-S** a past tense in grammar

PRETERM _n_ pl. **-S** a child born prematurely

PRETEST _v_ **-ED, -ING, -S** to give a preliminary test to

PRETEXT _v_ **-ED, -ING, -S** to allege as an excuse

PRETOLD past tense of pretell

PRETOR _n_ pl. **-S** praetor

PRETRAIN _v_ **-ED, -ING, -S** to train beforehand

PRETREAT _v_ **-ED, -ING, -S** to treat beforehand

PRETRIAL _n_ pl. **-S** a proceeding that precedes a trial

PRETRIM _v_ **-TRIMMED, -TRIMMING, -TRIMS** to trim beforehand

PRETTIFY _v_ **-FIED, -FYING, -FIES** to make pretty

PRETTY _adj_ **-TIER, -TIEST** pleasing to the eye **PRETTILY** _adv_

PRETTY _v_ **-TIED, -TYING, -TIES** to make pretty

PRETYPE _v_ **-TYPED, -TYPING, -TYPES** to type beforehand

PRETZEL _v_ **-ZELLED, -ZELLING, -ZELS** to twist, bend, or contort

PREUNION _n_ pl. **-S** a union beforehand

PREUNITE _v_ **-UNITED, -UNITING, -UNITES** to unite beforehand

PREVAIL _v_ **-ED, -ING, -S** to triumph

PREVALUE _v_ **-UED, -UING, -UES** to value beforehand

PREVENT _v_ **-ED, -ING, -S** to keep from happening

PREVERB _n_ pl. **-S** a prefix or particle preceding the root of a verb

PREVIEW _v_ **-ED, -ING, -S** to view or exhibit in advance

PREVIOUS _adj_ coming or occurring before in time or order

PREVISE _v_ **-VISED, -VISING, -VISES** to foresee

PREVISIT _v_ **-ED, -ING, -S** to visit beforehand

PREVISOR _n_ pl. **-S** one that previses

PREVUE _v_ **-VUED, -VUING, -VUES** to preview

PREWAR _adj_ occurring or existing before a war

PREWARM _v_ **-ED, -ING, -S** to warm beforehand

PREWARN _v_ **-ED, -ING, -S** to warn in advance

PREWASH _v_ **-ED, -ING, -ES** to wash beforehand

PREWEIGH _v_ **-ED, -ING, -S** to weigh beforehand

PREWIRE _v_ **-WIRED, -WIRING, -WIRES** to wire beforehand

PREWORK _v_ **-ED, -ING, -S** to work beforehand

PREWORN _adj_ previously worn by someone

PREWRAP _v_ **-WRAPPED, -WRAPPING, -WRAPS** to wrap beforehand

PREX _n_ pl. **-ES** prexy

PREXY _n_ pl. **PREXIES** a president

PREY _v_ **-ED, -ING, -S** to seize and devour animals for food

PREYER _n_ pl. **-S** one that preys

PREZ _n_ pl. **-ES** a president

PREZZIE _n_ pl. **-S** a gift

PRIAPEAN _adj_ priapic

PRIAPI a pl. of priapus

PRIAPIC _adj_ phallic

PRIAPISM _n_ pl. **-S** a persistent erection of the penis

PRIAPUS _n_ pl. **-PUSES** or **-PI** a representation of the phallus

PRICE _v_ **PRICED, PRICING, PRICES** to set a value on

PRICER _n_ pl. **-S** one that prices

PRICEY _adj_ **PRICIER, PRICIEST** expensive

PRICIER comparative of pricy

PRICIEST	superlative of pricy
PRICILY	*adv* in a pricey manner
PRICING	present participle of price
PRICK	*v* **-ED, -ING, -S** to puncture slightly
PRICKER	*n* pl. **-S** one that pricks
PRICKET	*n* pl. **-S** a spike for holding a candle upright
PRICKIER	comparative of pricky
PRICKIEST	superlative of pricky
PRICKING	*n* pl. **-S** a prickly feeling
PRICKLE	*v* **-LED, -LING, -LES** to prick
PRICKLY	*adj* **-LIER, -LIEST** having many sharp points
PRICKY	*adj* **PRICKIER, PRICKIEST** prickly
PRICY	*adj* **PRICIER, PRICIEST** pricey **PRICILY** *adv*
PRIDE	*v* **PRIDED, PRIDING, PRIDES** to feel pride (a feeling of self-esteem)
PRIDEFUL	*adj* full of pride
PRIED	past tense of pry
PRIEDIEU	*n* pl. **-DIEUS** or **-DIEUX** a piece of furniture for kneeling on during prayer
PRIER	*n* pl. **-S** one that pries
PRIES	present 3d person sing. of pry
PRIEST	*v* **-ED, -ING, -S** to ordain as a priest (one authorized to perform religious rites)
PRIESTLY	*adj* **-LIER, -LIEST** characteristic of or befitting a priest
PRIG	*v* **PRIGGED, PRIGGING, PRIGS** to steal
PRIGGERY	*n* pl. **-GERIES** priggism
PRIGGISH	*adj* marked by priggism
PRIGGISM	*n* pl. **-S** prim adherence to convention
PRILL	*v* **-ED, -ING, -S** to convert into pellets
PRIM	*adj* **PRIMMER, PRIMMEST** formally precise or proper
PRIM	*v* **PRIMMED, PRIMMING, PRIMS** to give a prim expression to
PRIMA	*n* pl. **-S** primo
PRIMACY	*n* pl. **-CIES** the state of being first
PRIMAGE	*n* pl. **-S** an amount paid as an addition to freight charges
PRIMAL	*adj* being at the beginning or foundation **PRIMALLY** *adv*
PRIMARY	*n* pl. **-RIES** a preliminary election

PRIMATAL	*n* pl. **-S** a primate
PRIMATE	*n* pl. **-S** any of an advanced order of mammals
PRIME	*v* **PRIMED, PRIMING, PRIMES** to make ready
PRIMELY	*adv* excellently
PRIMER	*n* pl. **-S** a book that covers the basics of a subject
PRIMERO	*n* pl. **-ROS** a card game
PRIMEVAL	*adj* pertaining to the earliest ages
PRIMI	a pl. of primo
PRIMINE	*n* pl. **-S** the outer covering of an ovule
PRIMING	*n* pl. **-S** the act of one that primes
PRIMLY	*adv* in a prim manner
PRIMMED	past tense of prim
PRIMMER	comparative of prim
PRIMMEST	superlative of prim
PRIMMING	present participle of prim
PRIMNESS	*n* pl. **-ES** the state of being prim
PRIMO	*n* pl. **-MOS** or **-MI** the main part in a musical piece
PRIMP	*v* **-ED, -ING, -S** to dress or adorn carefully
PRIMROSE	*n* pl. **-S** a perennial herb
PRIMSIE	*adj* prim
PRIMULA	*n* pl. **-S** primrose
PRIMUS	*n* pl. **-ES** the head bishop of Scotland
PRINCE	*n* pl. **-S** a non-reigning male member of a royal family
PRINCELY	*adj* **-LIER, -LIEST** of or befitting a prince
PRINCESS	*n* pl. **-ES** a non-reigning female member of a royal family
PRINCIPE	*n* pl. **-PI** a prince
PRINCOCK	*n* pl. **-S** a coxcomb
PRINCOX	*n* pl. **-ES** princock
PRINK	*v* **-ED, -ING, -S** to dress or adorn in a showy manner
PRINKER	*n* pl. **-S** one that prinks
PRINT	*v* **-ED, -ING, -S** to produce by pressed type on a surface
PRINTER	*n* pl. **-S** one that prints
PRINTERY	*n* pl. **-ERIES** a place where printing is done
PRINTING	*n* pl. **-S** a reproduction from a printing surface

PRINTOUT *n* pl. **-S** the printed output of a computer

PRION *n* pl. **-S** a protein particle

PRIOR *n* pl. **-S** an officer in a monastery

PRIORATE *n* pl. **-S** the office of a prior

PRIORESS *n* pl. **-ES** a nun corresponding in rank to a prior

PRIORITY *n* pl. **-TIES** precedence established by importance

PRIORLY *adv* previously

PRIORY *n* pl. **-RIES** a religious house

PRISE *v* **PRISED, PRISING, PRISES** to raise or force with a lever

PRISERE *n* pl. **-S** a succession of vegetational stages

PRISM *n* pl. **-S** a solid which disperses light into a spectrum

PRISMOID *n* pl. **-S** a geometric solid

PRISON *v* **-ED, -ING, -S** to imprison

PRISONER *n* pl. **-S** one that is imprisoned

PRISS *v* **-ED, -ING, -ES** to act in a prissy manner

PRISSY *adj* **-SIER, -SIEST** excessively or affectedly proper **PRISSILY** *adv*

PRISSY *n* pl. **-SIES** one who is prissy

PRISTANE *n* pl. **-S** a chemical compound

PRISTINE *adj* pertaining to the earliest time or state

PRITHEE *interj* — used to express a wish or request

PRIVACY *n* pl. **-CIES** the state of being private

PRIVATE *adj* **-VATER, -VATEST** not for public use or knowledge

PRIVATE *n* pl. **-S** a soldier of lower rank

PRIVET *n* pl. **-S** an ornamental shrub

PRIVITY *n* pl. **-TIES** private knowledge

PRIVY *adj* **PRIVIER, PRIVIEST** private **PRIVILY** *adv*

PRIVY *n* pl. **PRIVIES** an outhouse

PRIZE *v* **PRIZED, PRIZING, PRIZES** to value highly

PRIZER *n* pl. **-S** one who vies for a reward

PRO *n* pl. **PROS** an argument or vote in favor of something

PROA *n* pl. **-S** prau

PROB *n* pl. **-S** a problem

PROBABLE *n* pl. **-S** something likely to occur or prove true

PROBABLY *adv* without much doubt

PROBAND *n* pl. **-S** one whose reactions or responses are studied

PROBANG *n* pl. **-S** a surgical rod

PROBATE *v* **-BATED, -BATING, -BATES** to establish the validity of

PROBE *v* **PROBED, PROBING, PROBES** to investigate or examine thoroughly

PROBER *n* pl. **-S** one that probes

PROBIT *n* pl. **-S** a unit of statistical probability

PROBITY *n* pl. **-TIES** complete and confirmed integrity

PROBLEM *n* pl. **-S** a perplexing question or situation

PROCAINE *n* pl. **-S** a compound used as a local anesthetic

PROCARP *n* pl. **-S** a female sexual organ in certain algae

PROCEED *v* **-ED, -ING, -S** to go forward or onward

PROCESS *v* **-ED, -ING, -ES** to treat or prepare by a special method

PROCHAIN *adj* prochein

PROCHEIN *adj* nearest in time, relation, or degree

PROCLAIM *v* **-ED, -ING, -S** to make known publicly or officially

PROCTOR *v* **-ED, -ING, -S** to supervise

PROCURAL *n* pl. **-S** the act of procuring

PROCURE *v* **-CURED, -CURING, -CURES** to obtain by effort

PROCURER *n* pl. **-S** one that procures

PROD *v* **PRODDED, PRODDING, PRODS** to jab with something pointed

PRODDER *n* pl. **-S** one that prods

PRODIGAL *n* pl. **-S** one who spends lavishly and foolishly

PRODIGY *n* pl. **-GIES** a child having exceptional talent or ability

PRODROME *n* pl. **-DROMES** or **-DROMATA** a sign of impending disease

PRODRUG *n* pl. **-S** an inactive chemical substance that becomes an active drug in the body

PRODUCE *v* **-DUCED, -DUCING, -DUCES** to bring into existence

PRODUCER *n* pl. **-S** one that produces

PRODUCT *n* pl. **-S** something produced by labor or effort

PROEM *n* pl. **-S** an introductory statement **PROEMIAL** *adj*

PROETTE *n* pl. **-S** a female professional athlete

PROF *n* pl. **-S** a professor

PROFANE *v* **-FANED, -FANING, -FANES** to treat with irreverence or abuse

PROFANER *n* pl. **-S** one that profanes

PROFESS *v* **-ED, -ING, -ES** to affirm openly

PROFFER *v* **-ED, -ING, -S** to present for acceptance

PROFILE *v* **-FILED, -FILING, -FILES** to draw an outline of

PROFILER *n* pl. **-S** one that profiles

PROFIT *v* **-ED, -ING, -S** to gain an advantage or benefit

PROFITER *n* pl. **-S** one that profits

PROFORMA *adj* provided in advance of shipment and showing description and quantity

PROFOUND *adj* **-FOUNDER, -FOUNDEST** intellectually deep and penetrating

PROFOUND *n* pl. **-S** something that is very deep

PROFUSE *adj* pouring forth generously

PROG *v* **PROGGED, PROGGING, PROGS** to prowl about for food or plunder

PROGENY *n* pl. **-NIES** a descendant or offspring

PROGERIA *n* pl. **-S** premature aging

PROGGER *n* pl. **-S** one that progs

PROGGING present participle of prog

PROGNOSE *v* **-NOSED, -NOSING, -NOSES** to forecast the probable course of a disease

PROGRADE *adj* pertaining to the orbital motion of a body

PROGRAM *v* **-GRAMED, -GRAMING, -GRAMS** or **-GRAMMED, -GRAMMING, -GRAMS** to arrange in a plan of proceedings

PROGRESS *v* **-ED, -ING, -ES** to move forward or onward

PROGUN *adj* favoring the right to own guns without restrictions

PROHIBIT *v* **-ED, -ING, -S** to forbid by authority

PROJECT *v* **-ED, -ING, -S** to extend outward

PROJET *n* pl. **-S** a plan or outline

PROLABOR *adj* favoring organized labor

PROLAMIN *n* pl. **-S** a simple protein

PROLAN *n* pl. **-S** a sex hormone

PROLAPSE *v* **-LAPSED, -LAPSING, -LAPSES** to fall or slip out of place

PROLATE *adj* extended lengthwise

PROLE *n* pl. **-S** a member of the working class

PROLEG *n* pl. **-S** an abdominal leg of certain insect larvae

PROLIFIC *adj* producing abundantly

PROLINE *n* pl. **-S** an amino acid

PROLIX *adj* tediously long and wordy **PROLIXLY** *adv*

PROLOG *v* **-ED, -ING, -S** to prologue

PROLOGUE *v* **-LOGUED, -LOGUING, -LOGUES** to preface

PROLONG *v* **-ED, -ING, -S** to lengthen in duration

PROLONGE *n* pl. **-S** a rope used for pulling a gun carriage

PROM *n* pl. **-S** a formal dance

PROMINE *n* pl. **-S** a substance that promotes growth

PROMISE *v* **-ISED, -ISING, -ISES** to make a declaration of assurance

PROMISEE *n* pl. **-S** one who is promised something

PROMISER *n* pl. **-S** promisor

PROMISOR *n* pl. **-S** one that promises

PROMO *v* **-ED, -ING, -S** to promote

PROMOTE *v* **-MOTED, -MOTING, -MOTES** to contribute to the progress of

PROMOTER *n* pl. **-S** one that promotes

PROMOTOR *n* pl. **-S** a chemical additive that increases the activity of a catalyst

PROMPT *adj* **PROMPTER, PROMPTEST** quick to act or respond

PROMPT *v* **-ED, -ING, -S** to induce to action

PROMPTER *n* pl. **-S** one that prompts

PROMPTLY *adv* in a prompt manner

PROMULGE *v* **-MULGED, -MULGING, -MULGES** to proclaim

PRONATE *v* **-NATED, -NATING, -NATES** to turn the palm downward or backward

PRONATOR *n* pl. **-S** or **-ES** a forearm or forelimb muscle

PRONE *adj* lying with the front or face downward **PRONELY** *adv*

PRONG *v* **-ED, -ING, -S** to pierce with a pointed projection

PRONOTUM *n* pl. **-NOTA** a hard outer plate of an insect

PRONOUN *n* pl. **-S** a word that may be used in place of a noun

PRONTO *adv* quickly

PROOF *v* **-ED, -ING, -S** to examine for errors

PROOFER *n* pl. **-S** one that proofs

PROP *v* **PROPPED, PROPPING, PROPS** to keep from falling

PROPANE *n* pl. **-S** a flammable gas

PROPANOL *n* pl. **-S** a liquid alcohol used as a solvent

PROPEL *v* **-PELLED, -PELLING, -PELS** to cause to move forward or onward

PROPEND *v* **-ED, -ING, -S** to have a tendency toward

PROPENE *n* pl. **-S** a flammable gas

PROPENOL *n* pl. **-S** a flammable liquid

PROPENSE *adj* tending toward

PROPENYL *adj* pertaining to a certain chemical group

PROPER *adj* **-ERER, -EREST** suitable **PROPERLY** *adv*

PROPER *n* pl. **-S** a portion of the Mass

PROPERTY *n* pl. **-TIES** something owned

PROPHAGE *n* pl. **-S** a form of virus

PROPHASE *n* pl. **-S** the first stage in mitosis

PROPHECY *n* pl. **-CIES** a prediction

PROPHESY *v* **-SIED, -SYING, -SIES** to predict

PROPHET *n* pl. **-S** one who predicts

PROPINE *v* **-PINED, -PINING, -PINES** to offer as a gift

PROPJET *n* pl. **-S** a type of airplane

PROPMAN *n* pl. **-MEN** a man in charge of stage properties

PROPOLIS *n* pl. **-LISES** a resinous substance used as a cement by bees

PROPONE *v* **-PONED, -PONING, -PONES** to propose

PROPOSAL *n* pl. **-S** something that is proposed

PROPOSE *v* **-POSED, -POSING, -POSES** to put forward for consideration or acceptance

PROPOSER *n* pl. **-S** one that proposes

PROPOUND *v* **-ED, -ING, -S** to propose

PROPPED past tense of prop

PROPPING present participle of prop

PROPRIUM *n* pl. **-PRIA** an attribute belonging inseparably to every member of a species

PROPYL *n* pl. **-S** a univalent radical **PROPYLIC** *adj*

PROPYLON *n* pl. **-LA** an entrance to a temple

PROPYNE *n* pl. **-S** a gaseous methyl acetylene

PRORATE *v* **-RATED, -RATING, -RATES** to divide proportionately

PROROGUE *v* **-ROGUED, -ROGUING, -ROGUES** to discontinue a session of

PROSAIC *adj* pertaining to prose

PROSAISM *n* pl. **-S** a prosaic style

PROSAIST *n* pl. **-S** a writer of prose

PROSE *v* **PROSED, PROSING, PROSES** to write prose (writing without metrical structure)

PROSECCO *n* pl. **-COS** an Italian sparkling wine

PROSECT *v* **-ED, -ING, -S** to dissect

PROSER *n* pl. **-S** a prosaist

PROSIER comparative of prosy

PROSIEST superlative of prosy

PROSIFY *v* **-FIED, -FYING, -FIES** to turn into prose

PROSILY *adv* in a prosy manner

PROSING present participle of prose

PROSIT *interj* — used as a drinking toast

PROSO *n* pl. **-SOS** millet

PROSODY *n* pl. **-DIES** the study of poetical forms **PROSODIC** *adj*

PROSOMA *n* pl. **-MAS** or **-MATA** the anterior region of the body of some invertebrates **PROSOMAL** *adj*

PROSPECT *v* **-ED, -ING, -S** to explore for mineral deposits

PROSPER *v* **-ED, -ING, -S** to be successful or fortunate

PROSS *n* pl. **-ES** a prostitute

PROSSIE *n* pl. **-S** a prostitute

PROST *interj* prosit

PROSTATE *n* pl. **-S** a gland in male mammals

PROSTIE *n* pl. **-S** a prostitute

PROSTYLE *n* pl. **-S** a building having a row of columns across the front only

PROSUMER *n* pl. **-S** one who buys electronic products that are in quality between consumer and professional grades

PROSY *adj* **PROSIER, PROSIEST** prosaic

PROTAMIN *n* pl. **-S** a simple protein

PROTASIS *n* pl. **-ASES** the introductory part of a classical drama **PROTATIC** *adj*

PROTEA *n* pl. **-S** an evergreen shrub

PROTEAN *n* pl. **-S** a type of protein

PROTEASE *n* pl. **-S** an enzyme

PROTECT *v* **-ED, -ING, -S** to keep from harm, attack, or injury

PROTEGE *n* pl. **-S** one whose career is promoted by an influential person

PROTEGEE *n* pl. **-S** a female protege

PROTEI pl. of proteus

PROTEID *n* pl. **-S** protein

PROTEIDE *n* pl. **-S** proteid

PROTEIN *n* pl. **-S** a nitrogenous organic compound

PROTEND *v* **-ED, -ING, -S** to extend

PROTEOME *n* pl. **-S** the complement of proteins expressed by a genome

PROTEOSE *n* pl. **-S** a water-soluble protein

PROTEST *v* **-ED, -ING, -S** to express strong objection

PROTEUS *n* pl. **-ES** one that readily changes his appearance or principles

PROTEUS *n* pl. **-TEI** any of a genus of aerobic bacteria

PROTIST *n* pl. **-S** any of a group of unicellular organisms

PROTIUM *n* pl. **-S** an isotope of hydrogen

PROTOCOL *v* **-COLED, -COLING, -COLS** or **-COLLED, -COLLING, -COLS** to form a preliminary draft of an official document

PROTON *n* pl. **-S** a subatomic particle **PROTONIC** *adj*

PROTOPOD *n* pl. **-S** a part of a crustacean appendage

PROTOXID *n* pl. **-S** an oxide

PROTOZOA *n/pl* unicellular microscopic organisms

PROTRACT *v* **-ED, -ING, -S** to prolong

PROTRADE *adj* favoring international trade

PROTRUDE *v* **-TRUDED, -TRUDING, -TRUDES** to extend beyond the main portion

PROTURAN *n* pl. **-S** any of an order of white, wingless insects

PROTYL *n* pl. **-S** protyle

PROTYLE *n* pl. **-S** a hypothetical substance from which all the elements are supposedly derived

PROUD *adj* **PROUDER, PROUDEST** having or displaying pride **PROUDLY** *adv*

PROUDFUL *adj* prideful

PROUNION *adj* favoring labor unions

PROVE *v* **PROVED, PROVEN, PROVING, PROVES** to establish the truth or validity of **PROVABLE** *adj* **PROVABLY** *adv*

PROVENLY *adv* without doubt

PROVER *n* pl. **-S** one that proves

PROVERB *v* **-ED, -ING, -S** to make a byword of

PROVIDE *v* **-VIDED, -VIDING, -VIDES** to supply

PROVIDER *n* pl. **-S** one that provides

PROVINCE *n* pl. **-S** an administrative division of a country

PROVING present participle of prove

PROVIRUS *n* pl. **-ES** a form of virus **PROVIRAL** *adj*

PROVISO *n* pl. **-SOS** or **-SOES** a clause in a document introducing a condition or restriction

PROVOKE *v* **-VOKED, -VOKING, -VOKES** to incite to anger or resentment

PROVOKER *n* pl. **-S** one that provokes

PROVOST *n* pl. **-S** a high-ranking university official

PROW *adj* **PROWER, PROWEST** brave

PROW *n* pl. **-S** the forward part of a ship

PROWAR *adj* favoring war

PROWESS *n* pl. **-ES** exceptional ability

PROWL *v* **-ED, -ING, -S** to move about stealthily

PROWLER *n* pl. **-S** one that prowls

PROXEMIC *adj* pertaining to a branch of environmental study

PROXIMAL *adj* located near the point of origin

PROXIMO *adj* of or occurring in the following month

PROXY *n* pl. **PROXIES** a person authorized to act for another

PRUDE *n* pl. **-S** a prudish person

PRUDENCE *n* pl. **-S** the quality of being prudent

PRUDENT

PRUDENT *adj* having, showing, or exercising good judgment

PRUDERY *n* pl. **-ERIES** excessive regard for propriety, modesty, or morality

PRUDISH *adj* marked by prudery

PRUINOSE *adj* having a powdery covering

PRUNE *v* **PRUNED, PRUNING, PRUNES** to cut off branches or parts from **PRUNABLE** *adj*

PRUNELLA *n* pl. **-S** a strong woolen fabric

PRUNELLE *n* pl. **-S** a plum-flavored liqueur

PRUNELLO *n* pl. **-LOS** prunella

PRUNER *n* pl. **-S** one that prunes

PRUNEY *adj* **PRUNIER, PRUNIEST** resembling a prune

PRUNING present participle of prune

PRUNUS *n* pl. **-ES** a flowering tree

PRURIENT *adj* having lustful thoughts or desires

PRURIGO *n* pl. **-GOS** a skin disease

PRURITUS *n* pl. **-ES** intense itching **PRURITIC** *adj*

PRUSSIC *adj* pertaining to a type of acid

PRUTA *n* pl. **PRUTOT** prutah

PRUTAH *n* pl. **PRUTOTH** a former monetary unit of Israel

PRY *v* **PRIED, PRYING, PRIES** to inquire impertinently into private matters **PRYINGLY** *adv*

PRYER *n* pl. **-S** prier

PRYTHEE *interj* prithee

PSALM *v* **-ED, -ING, -S** to praise in psalms (sacred songs)

PSALMIC *adj* of or pertaining to a psalm

PSALMIST *n* pl. **-S** a writer of psalms

PSALMODY *n* pl. **-DIES** the use of psalms in worship

PSALTER *n* pl. **-S** a book of psalms

PSALTERY *n* pl. **-TERIES** an ancient stringed musical instrument

PSALTRY *n* pl. **-TRIES** psaltery

PSAMMITE *n* pl. **-S** a fine-grained rock

PSAMMON *n* pl. **-S** a group of microorganisms living in waterlogged sands

PSCHENT *n* pl. **-S** a crown worn by ancient Egyptian kings

PSEPHITE *n* pl. **-S** a rock composed of small pebbles

PSEUD *n* pl. **-S** a person pretending to be an intellectual

PSEUDO *n* pl. **PSEUDOS** a pseud

PSHAW *v* **-ED, -ING, -S** to utter an expression of disapproval

PSI *n* pl. **-S** a Greek letter

PSILOCIN *n* pl. **-S** a hallucinogenic drug

PSILOSIS *n* pl. **-LOSES** a tropical disease **PSILOTIC** *adj*

PSIONIC *adj* pertaining to the practical use of psychic powers

PSOAS *n* pl. **PSOAI** or **PSOAE** a muscle of the loin **PSOATIC** *adj*

PSOCID *n* pl. **-S** a minute winged insect

PSORALEA *n* pl. **-S** a plant of the bean family

PSORALEN *n* pl. **-S** a drug used to treat psoriasis

PSST *interj* — used to attract someone's attention

PST *interj* psst

PSYCH *v* **-ED, -ING, -S** to put into the proper frame of mind

PSYCHE *n* pl. **-S** the mental structure of a person

PSYCHIC *n* pl. **-S** one sensitive to extrasensory phenomena

PSYCHISM *n* pl. **-S** a belief that there is a fluid that animates all living beings

PSYCHO *n* pl. **-CHOS** a mentally unstable person

PSYLLA *n* pl. **-S** any of various plant lice

PSYLLID *n* pl. **-S** psylla

PSYLLIUM *n* pl. **-S** the seed of a fleawort

PSYOPS *n/pl* noncombative military operations to influence the enemy's state of mind

PSYWAR *n* pl. **-S** psychological warfare

PTERIN *n* pl. **-S** a chemical compound

PTEROPOD *n* pl. **-S** a type of mollusk

PTERYGIA *n/pl* fleshy growths over the cornea

PTERYLA *n* pl. **-LAE** a feathered area on the skin of a bird

PTISAN *n* pl. **-S** a tea of herbs or barley

PTOMAIN *n* pl. **-S** ptomaine

PTOMAINE *n* pl. **-S** a compound produced by the decomposition of protein

PTOOEY *interj* ptui

PTOSIS *n* pl. **PTOSES** a drooping of the upper eyelid **PTOTIC** *adj*

PTUI *interj* — used to express the sound of spitting

PTYALIN *n* pl. **-S** a salivary enzyme

PTYALISM *n* pl. **-S** an excessive flow of saliva

PUB *n* pl. **-S** a tavern

PUBBING *n* pl. **-S** the practice of drinking in pubs

PUBERTY *n* pl. **-TIES** a period of sexual maturation **PUBERAL, PUBERTAL** *adj*

PUBIC *adj* pertaining to the pubes or pubis

PUBIS *n* pl. **PUBES** the forward portion of either of the hipbones

PUBLIC *n* pl. **-S** the community or the people as a whole

PUBLICAN *n* pl. **-S** one who owns or manages a pub

PUBLICLY *adv* by the public

PUBLISH *v* **-ED, -ING, -ES** to print and issue to the public

PUCCOON *n* pl. **-S** an herb that yields a red dye

PUCE *n* pl. **-S** a dark red color

PUCK *n* pl. **-S** a rubber disk used in ice hockey

PUCKA *adj* pukka

PUCKER *v* **-ED, -ING, -S** to gather into small wrinkles or folds

PUCKERER *n* pl. **-S** one that puckers

PUCKERY *adj* **-ERIER, -ERIEST** having a tendency to pucker

PUCKISH *adj* impish

PUCKSTER *n* pl. **-S** a hockey player

PUD *n* pl. **-S** pudding

PUDDING *n* pl. **-S** a thick, soft dessert

PUDDINGY *adj* resembling a pudding

PUDDLE *v* **-DLED, -DLING, -DLES** to strew with puddles (small pools of water)

PUDDLER *n* pl. **-S** one who subjects iron to puddling

PUDDLING *n* pl. **-S** the process of converting pig iron to wrought iron

PUDDLY *adj* **-DLIER, -DLIEST** full of puddles

PUDENCY *n* pl. **-CIES** modesty

PUDENDUM *n* pl. **-DA** the external genital organs of a woman **PUDENDAL** *adj*

PUDEUR *n* pl. **-S** a sense of shame or embarrassment

PUDGE *n* pl. **-S** fat on a body

PUDGY *adj* **PUDGIER, PUDGIEST** short and fat **PUDGILY** *adv*

PUDIBUND *adj* prudish

PUDIC *adj* pertaining to the pudendum

PUDU *n* pl. **-S** a small deer of South America

PUEBLO *n* pl. **-LOS** a communal dwelling of certain Indian tribes

PUERILE *adj* childish

PUERPERA *n* pl. **-PERAE** a woman who has recently given birth to a child

PUFF *v* **-ED, -ING, -S** to blow in short gusts

PUFFBACK *n* pl. **-S** a small African bird

PUFFBALL *n* pl. **-S** any of various globular fungi

PUFFBIRD *n* pl. **-S** a stocky tropical American bird

PUFFER *n* pl. **-S** one that puffs

PUFFERY *n* pl. **-ERIES** excessive public praise

PUFFIN *n* pl. **-S** a sea bird

PUFFY *adj* **-FIER, -FIEST** swollen **PUFFILY** *adv*

PUG *v* **PUGGED, PUGGING, PUGS** to fill in with clay or mortar

PUGAREE *n* pl. **-S** pugree

PUGGAREE *n* pl. **-S** pugree

PUGGIER comparative of puggy

PUGGIEST superlative of puggy

PUGGING *n* pl. **-S** the act of preparing clay for making bricks or pottery

PUGGISH *adj* somewhat stubby

PUGGREE *n* pl. **-S** pugree

PUGGRY *n* pl. **-GRIES** pugree

PUGGY *adj* **-GIER, -GIEST** puggish

PUGH *interj* — used to express disgust

PUGILISM *n* pl. **-S** the art or practice of fighting with the fists

PUGILIST *n* pl. **-S** one who fights with his fists

PUGMARK *n* pl. **-S** a footprint

PUGREE *n* pl. **-S** a cloth band wrapped around a hat

PUISNE *n* pl. **-S** one of lesser rank

PUISSANT *adj* powerful

PUJA *n* pl. **-S** a Hindu prayer ritual

PUJAH *n* pl. **-S** puja

PUKE *v* **PUKED, PUKING, PUKES** to vomit

PUKEY *adj* **PUKIER, PUKIEST** resembling or suggestive of vomit

PUKKA	*adj* genuine	**PULPOUS**	*adj* pulpy
PUKKAH	*adj* pukka	**PULPWOOD**	*n* pl. **-S** soft wood used in making paper
PUL	*n* pl. **PULS** or **PULI** a coin of Afghanistan	**PULPY**	*adj* **PULPIER, PULPIEST** resembling pulp
PULA	*n* pl. **-S** a monetary unit of Botswana	**PULQUE**	*n* pl. **-S** a fermented Mexican beverage
PULAO	*n* pl. **-LAOS** pilaf	**PULSANT**	*adj* pulsating
PULE	*v* **PULED, PULING, PULES** to whine	**PULSAR**	*n* pl. **-S** a celestial source of radio waves
PULER	*n* pl. **-S** one that pules	**PULSATE**	*v* **-SATED, -SATING, -SATES** to expand and contract rhythmically
PULI	*n* pl. **-LIS** or **-LIK** a long-haired sheepdog	**PULSATOR**	*n* pl. **-S** something that pulsates
PULICENE	*adj* pertaining to fleas	**PULSE**	*v* **PULSED, PULSING, PULSES** to pulsate
PULICIDE	*n* pl. **-S** an agent used for destroying fleas	**PULSEJET**	*n* pl. **-S** a type of engine
PULING	*n* pl. **-S** a plaintive cry	**PULSER**	*n* pl. **-S** a device that causes pulsations
PULINGLY	*adv* in a whining manner	**PULSING**	present participle of pulse
PULK	*n* pl. **-S** a small sled	**PULSION**	*n* pl. **-S** propulsion
PULKA	*n* pl. **-S** pulk	**PULSOJET**	*n* pl. **-S** pulsejet
PULL	*v* **-ED, -ING, -S** to exert force in order to cause motion toward the force	**PULTRUDE**	*v* **-TRUDED, -TRUDING, -TRUDES** to make a plastic object by drawing resin-coated glass fibers through a die
PULLBACK	*n* pl. **-S** a restraint or drawback		
PULLER	*n* pl. **-S** one that pulls	**PULVILLI**	*n/pl* pads between the claws of an insect's foot
PULLET	*n* pl. **-S** a young hen		
PULLEY	*v* **-LEYED, -LEYING, -LEYS** to hoist with a pulley (a device used for lifting weight)	**PULVINUS**	*n* pl. **-NI** a swelling at the base of a leaf **PULVINAR** *adj*
PULLMAN	*n* pl. **-S** a railroad sleeping car	**PUMA**	*n* pl. **-S** a cougar
PULLOUT	*n* pl. **-S** a withdrawal	**PUMELO**	*n* pl. **-LOS** pomelo
PULLOVER	*n* pl. **-S** a garment that is put on by being drawn over the head	**PUMICE**	*v* **-ICED, -ICING, -ICES** to polish with a porous volcanic rock
PULLUP	*n* pl. **-S** the act of raising oneself while hanging by the hands	**PUMICER**	*n* pl. **-S** one that pumices
PULMONIC	*adj* pertaining to the lungs	**PUMICITE**	*n* pl. **-S** a porous volcanic rock
PULMOTOR	*n* pl. **-S** a respiratory device	**PUMMEL**	*v* **-MELED, -MELING, -MELS** or **-MELLED, -MELLING, -MELS** to pommel
PULP	*v* **-ED, -ING, -S** to reduce to pulp (a soft, moist mass of matter)		
PULPAL	*adj* pertaining to pulp **PULPALLY** *adv*	**PUMMELO**	*n* pl. **-LOS** a shaddock
PULPER	*n* pl. **-S** one that pulps	**PUMP**	*v* **-ED, -ING, -S** to cause to flow by means of a pump (a device for moving fluids) **PUMPABLE** *adj*
PULPIER	comparative of pulpy		
PULPIEST	superlative of pulpy	**PUMPER**	*n* pl. **-S** one that pumps
PULPILY	*adv* in a pulpy manner	**PUMPJACK**	*n* pl. **-S** a pumping apparatus at an oil well
PULPING	*n* pl. **-S** the process of reducing to pulp	**PUMPKIN**	*n* pl. **-S** a large, edible fruit
PULPIT	*n* pl. **-S** a platform in a church **PULPITAL** *adj*	**PUMPLESS**	*adj* lacking a pump
		PUMPLIKE	*adj* resembling a pump
PULPLESS	*adj* having no pulp	**PUN**	*v* **PUNNED, PUNNING, PUNS** to make a pun (a play on words)

PUNA   *n* pl. **-S** a cold, arid plateau

PUNCH   *v* **-ED, -ING, -ES** to perforate with a type of tool

PUNCHEON   *n* pl. **-S** a vertical supporting timber

PUNCHER   *n* pl. **-S** one that punches

PUNCHOUT   *n* pl. **-S** a fist fight

PUNCHY   *adj* **PUNCHIER, PUNCHIEST** dazed **PUNCHILY** *adv*

PUNCTATE   *adj* covered with dots

PUNCTUAL   *adj* being on time

PUNCTUM   *n* pl. **-TA** the opening of a tear duct

PUNCTURE   *v* **-TURED, -TURING, -TURES** to pierce with a pointed object

PUNDIT   *n* pl. **-S** a Hindu scholar **PUNDITIC** *adj*

PUNDITRY   *n* pl. **-RIES** the learning of pundits

PUNG   *n* pl. **-S** a box-shaped sleigh

PUNGENCY   *n* pl. **-CIES** the state of being pungent

PUNGENT   *adj* sharply affecting the organs of taste or smell

PUNGLE   *v* **-GLED, -GLING, -GLES** to contribute

PUNIER   comparative of puny

PUNIEST   superlative of puny

PUNILY   *adv* in a puny manner

PUNINESS   *n* pl. **-ES** the state of being puny

PUNISH   *v* **-ED, -ING, -ES** to impose a penalty on in requital for wrongdoing

PUNISHER   *n* pl. **-S** one that punishes

PUNITION   *n* pl. **-S** the act of punishing; punishment

PUNITIVE   *adj* inflicting punishment

PUNITORY   *adj* punitive

PUNJI   *n* pl. **-S** a sharp bamboo stake placed and concealed so as to impale an enemy

PUNK   *adj* **PUNKER, PUNKEST** of inferior quality

PUNK   *n* pl. **-S** dry, decayed wood used as tinder

PUNKA   *n* pl. **-S** a ceiling fan used in India

PUNKAH   *n* pl. **-S** punka

PUNKER   *n* pl. **-S** a punk rock musician

PUNKETTE   *n* pl. **-S** a female punk rocker

PUNKEY   *n* pl. **-KEYS** punkie

PUNKIE   *n* pl. **-S** a biting gnat

PUNKIN   *n* pl. **-S** pumpkin

PUNKISH   *adj* pertaining to a style inspired by punk rock

PUNKY   *adj* **PUNKIER, PUNKIEST** resembling punk

PUNNED   past tense of pun

PUNNER   *n* pl. **-S** a punster

PUNNET   *n* pl. **-S** a small basket

PUNNING   *n* pl. **-S** the act of making a pun

PUNNY   *adj* **-NIER, -NIEST** being or involving a pun

PUNSTER   *n* pl. **-S** one who is given to punning

PUNT   *v* **-ED, -ING, -S** to propel through water with a pole

PUNTER   *n* pl. **-S** one that punts

PUNTO   *n* pl. **-TOS** a hit or thrust in fencing

PUNTY   *n* pl. **-TIES** an iron rod used in glassmaking

PUNY   *adj* **PUNIER, PUNIEST** of inferior size, strength, or significance

PUP   *v* **PUPPED, PUPPING, PUPS** to give birth to puppies

PUPA   *n* pl. **-PAS** or **-PAE** an intermediate stage of a metamorphic insect **PUPAL** *adj*

PUPARIUM   *n* pl. **-IA** a pupal shell **PUPARIAL** *adj*

PUPATE   *v* **-PATED, -PATING, -PATES** to pass through the pupal stage

PUPATION   *n* pl. **-S** the act of pupating

PUPFISH   *n* pl. **-ES** a small, freshwater fish

PUPIL   *n* pl. **-S** a student under the close supervision of a teacher

PUPILAGE   *n* pl. **-S** the state of being a pupil

PUPILAR   *adj* pertaining to a part of the eye

PUPILARY   *adj* pupilar

PUPPED   past tense of pup

PUPPET   *n* pl. **-S** a small figure, as of a person or animal, manipulated by the hand

PUPPETRY   *n* pl. **-RIES** the art of making or manipulating puppets

PUPPING   present participle of pup

PUPPY   *n* pl. **-PIES** a young dog **PUPPYISH** *adj*

PUPPYDOM   *n* pl. **-S** the world of puppies

PUPU   *n* pl. **-S** a dish of Asian foods served as an appetizer

PUR   v **PURRED, PURRING, PURS** to purr

PURANA   n pl. **-S** a Hindu scripture **PURANIC** adj

PURBLIND   adj partially blind

PURCHASE   v **-CHASED, -CHASING, -CHASES** to acquire by the payment of money

PURDA   n pl. **-S** purdah

PURDAH   n pl. **-S** a curtain used in India to seclude women

PURE   adj **PURER, PUREST** free from anything different, inferior, or contaminating

PUREBRED   n pl. **-S** an animal of unmixed stock

PUREE   v **-REED, -REEING, -REES** to reduce to a thick pulp by cooking and sieving

PURELY   adv in a pure manner

PURENESS   n pl. **-ES** the quality of being pure

PURER   comparative of pure

PUREST   superlative of pure

PURFLE   v **-FLED, -FLING, -FLES** to decorate the border of

PURFLER   n pl. **-S** one that purfles

PURFLING   n pl. **-S** an ornamental border

PURGE   v **PURGED, PURGING, PURGES** to purify

PURGER   n pl. **-S** one that purges

PURGING   n pl. **-S** the act of purifying

PURI   n pl. **-S** poori

PURIFIER   n pl. **-S** one that purifies

PURIFY   v **-FIED, -FYING, -FIES** to free from impurities

PURIN   n pl. **-S** purine

PURINE   n pl. **-S** a chemical compound

PURISM   n pl. **-S** strict adherence to traditional correctness

PURIST   n pl. **-S** one who practices purism **PURISTIC** adj

PURITAN   n pl. **-S** a rigorously moral or religious person

PURITY   n pl. **-TIES** the quality of being pure

PURL   v **-ED, -ING, -S** to knit with a particular stitch

PURLIEU   n pl. **-LIEUS** or **-LIEUX** an outlying or neighboring area

PURLIN   n pl. **-S** a horizontal supporting timber

PURLINE   n pl. **-S** purlin

PURLING   n pl. **-S** an inversion of stitches in knitting

PURLOIN   v **-ED, -ING, -S** to steal

PURPLE   adj **-PLER, -PLEST** of a color intermediate between red and blue

PURPLE   v **-PLED, -PLING, -PLES** to make purple

PURPLISH   adj somewhat purple

PURPLY   adj purplish

PURPORT   v **-ED, -ING, -S** to profess or claim

PURPOSE   v **-POSED, -POSING, -POSES** to resolve to perform or accomplish

PURPURA   n pl. **-S** a disease characterized by purple spots on the skin

PURPURE   n pl. **-S** the heraldic color purple

PURPURIC   adj pertaining to purpura

PURPURIN   n pl. **-S** a reddish dye

PURR   v **-ED, -ING, -S** to utter a low, vibrant sound

PURRED   past tense of pur

PURRING   present participle of pur

PURSE   v **PURSED, PURSING, PURSES** to pucker

PURSER   n pl. **-S** an officer in charge of a ship's accounts

PURSIER   comparative of pursy

PURSIEST   superlative of pursy

PURSILY   adv in a pursy manner

PURSING   present participle of purse

PURSLANE   n pl. **-S** a common garden herb

PURSUANT   adv in accordance

PURSUE   v **-SUED, -SUING, -SUES** to follow in order to overtake or capture

PURSUER   n pl. **-S** one that pursues

PURSUIT   n pl. **-S** the act of pursuing

PURSY   adj **PURSIER, PURSIEST** short of breath

PURTY   adj **-TIER, -TIEST** pretty

PURULENT   adj secreting pus

PURVEY   v **-ED, -ING, -S** to supply

PURVEYOR   n pl. **-S** one that purveys

PURVIEW   n pl. **-S** the extent of operation, authority, or concern

PUS   n pl. **-ES** a viscous fluid formed in infected tissue

PUSH   v **-ED, -ING, -ES** to exert force in order to cause motion away from the force

PUSHBACK	n pl. **-S** a negative or unfavorable response	**PUTOUT**	n pl. **-S** an act of causing an out in baseball
PUSHBALL	n pl. **-S** a type of ball game	**PUTREFY**	v **-FIED, -FYING, -FIES** to make or become putrid
PUSHCART	n pl. **-S** a light cart pushed by hand	**PUTRID**	adj being in a decomposed, foul-smelling state **PUTRIDLY** adv
PUSHDOWN	n pl. **-S** a store of computer data	**PUTSCH**	n pl. **-ES** a suddenly executed attempt to overthrow a government
PUSHER	n pl. **-S** one that pushes		
PUSHFUL	adj pushy	**PUTT**	v **-ED, -ING, -S** to hit with a light stroke in golf
PUSHIER	comparative of pushy		
PUSHIEST	superlative of pushy	**PUTTEE**	n pl. **-S** a strip of cloth wound around the leg
PUSHILY	adv in a pushy manner		
PUSHOVER	n pl. **-S** an easily defeated person or team	**PUTTER**	v **-ED, -ING, -S** to occupy oneself in a leisurely or ineffective manner
PUSHPIN	n pl. **-S** a large-headed pin	**PUTTERER**	n pl. **-S** one that putters
PUSHROD	n pl. **-S** a rod for operating the valves in an engine	**PUTTI**	pl. of putto
		PUTTIE	n pl. **-S** puttee
PUSHUP	n pl. **-S** a type of exercise	**PUTTIED**	past tense of putty
PUSHY	adj **PUSHIER, PUSHIEST** offensively aggressive	**PUTTIER**	n pl. **-S** one that putties
		PUTTING	present participle of put
PUSLEY	n pl. **-LEYS** pussley	**PUTTO**	n pl. **-TI** an infant boy in art
PUSLIKE	adj resembling pus	**PUTTY**	v **-TIED, -TYING, -TIES** to fill with a type of cement
PUSS	n pl. **-ES** a cat		
PUSSIER	comparative of pussy	**PUTZ**	v **-ED, -ING, -ES** to waste time
PUSSIES	pl. of pussy	**PUZZLE**	v **-ZLED, -ZLING, -ZLES** to cause uncertainty and indecision in
PUSSIEST	superlative of pussy		
PUSSLEY	n pl. **-LEYS** purslane	**PUZZLER**	n pl. **-S** something that puzzles
PUSSLIKE	adj catlike	**PYA**	n pl. **-S** a copper coin of Myanmar (Burma)
PUSSLY	n pl. **-LIES** pussley		
PUSSY	adj **-SIER, -SIEST** full of pus	**PYAEMIA**	n pl. **-S** pyemia **PYAEMIC** adj
PUSSY	n pl. **PUSSIES** a cat	**PYCNIDIA**	n/pl spore-bearing organs of certain fungi
PUSSYCAT	n pl. **-S** a cat		
PUSTULE	n pl. **-S** a small elevation of the skin containing pus **PUSTULAR, PUSTULED** adj	**PYCNOSIS**	n pl. **-NOSES** pyknosis
		PYCNOTIC	adj pyknotic
		PYE	n pl. **-S** a book of ecclesiastical rules in the pre-Reformation English church
PUT	v **PUT, PUTTING, PUTS** to place in a particular position		
PUTAMEN	n pl. **-MINA** or **-MENS** the hard covering of the kernel of certain fruits	**PYELITIS**	n pl. **-TISES** inflammation of the pelvis or the kidney **PYELITIC** adj
		PYEMIA	n pl. **-S** the presence of pus in the blood **PYEMIC** adj
PUTATIVE	adj generally regarded as such		
PUTDOWN	n pl. **-S** a disparaging or snubbing remark	**PYGIDIUM**	n pl. **-IA** the posterior region of certain invertebrates **PYGIDIAL** adj
PUTLOCK	n pl. **-S** putlog	**PYGMY**	n pl. **-MIES** a small person **PYGMAEAN, PYGMEAN, PYGMOID, PYGMYISH** adj
PUTLOG	n pl. **-S** a horizontal supporting timber		
		PYGMYISM	n pl. **-S** a stunted or dwarfish condition
PUTOFF	n pl. **-S** an excuse		
PUTON	n pl. **-S** a hoax or deception	**PYIC**	adj pertaining to pus

PYIN *n* pl. **-S** a protein compound contained in pus

PYJAMA *n* pl. **-S** pajama

PYKNIC *n* pl. **-S** a person having a broad, stocky build

PYKNOSIS *n* pl. **-NOSES** a shrinking and thickening of a cell nucleus

PYKNOTIC *adj* exhibiting pyknosis

PYLON *n* pl. **-S** a tall structure marking an entrance or approach

PYLORUS *n* pl. **-RUSES** or **-RI** the opening between the stomach and the duodenum **PYLORIC** *adj*

PYODERMA *n* pl. **-S** a pus-causing skin disease

PYOGENIC *adj* producing pus

PYOID *adj* puslike

PYORRHEA *n* pl. **-S** a discharge of pus

PYOSIS *n* pl. **-OSES** the formation of pus

PYRALID *n* pl. **-S** a long-legged moth

PYRAMID *v* **-ED, -ING, -S** to raise or increase by adding amounts gradually

PYRAN *n* pl. **-S** a chemical compound **PYRANOID** *adj*

PYRANOSE *n* pl. **-S** a simple sugar

PYRE *n* pl. **-S** a pile of combustible material

PYRENE *n* pl. **-S** a putamen

PYRENOID *n* pl. **-S** a protein body of certain lower organisms

PYRETIC *adj* pertaining to fever

PYREXIA *n* pl. **-S** fever **PYREXIAL, PYREXIC** *adj*

PYRIC *adj* pertaining to burning

PYRIDINE *n* pl. **-S** a flammable liquid **PYRIDIC** *adj*

PYRIFORM *adj* pear-shaped

PYRITE *n* pl. **-S** a metallic sulfide **PYRITIC, PYRITOUS** *adj*

PYRITISE *v* **-ISED, -ISING, -ISES** to pyritize

PYRITIZE *v* **-IZED, -IZING, -IZES** to convert into pyrite

PYRO *n* pl. **-ROS** a person who has a compulsion to set fires

PYROGEN *n* pl. **-S** a substance that produces fever

PYROGY *n* pl. **-OGIES** pierogi

PYROHY *n* pl. **-OHIES** pierogi

PYROLA *n* pl. **-S** a perennial herb

PYROLIZE *v* **-LIZED, -LIZING, -LIZES** to pyrolyze

PYROLOGY *n* pl. **-GIES** the scientific examination of materials by heat

PYROLYSE *v* **-LYSED, -LYSING, -LYSES** to pyrolyze

PYROLYZE *v* **-LYZED, -LYZING, -LYZES** to affect compounds by the application of heat

PYRONE *n* pl. **-S** a chemical compound

PYRONINE *n* pl. **-S** a dye

PYROPE *n* pl. **-S** a variety of garnet

PYROSIS *n* pl. **-SISES** heartburn

PYROSTAT *n* pl. **-S** a thermostat

PYROXENE *n* pl. **-S** any of a group of minerals common in igneous rocks

PYRRHIC *n* pl. **-S** a type of metrical foot

PYRROL *n* pl. **-S** pyrrole

PYRROLE *n* pl. **-S** a chemical compound **PYRROLIC** *adj*

PYRUVATE *n* pl. **-S** a chemical salt

PYSANKA *n* pl. **PYSANKY** a hand-painted Ukrainian Easter egg

PYTHON *n* pl. **-S** a large snake **PYTHONIC** *adj*

PYURIA *n* pl. **-S** the presence of pus in the urine

PYX *n* pl. **-ES** a container in which the eucharistic bread is kept

PYXIDIUM *n* pl. **-DIA** a type of seed vessel

PYXIE *n* pl. **-S** an evergreen shrub

PYXIS *n* pl. **PYXIDES** a pyxidium

PZAZZ *n* pl. **-ES** pizazz

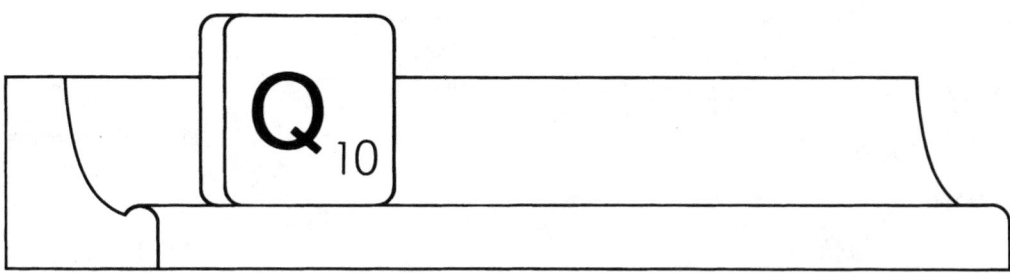

QABALA	*n* pl. **-S** cabala
QABALAH	*n* pl. **-S** cabala
QADI	*n* pl. **-S** cadi
QAID	*n* pl. **-S** caid
QAJAQ	*n* pl. **-S** kayak
QAMUTIK	*n* pl. **-S** komatik
QANAT	*n* pl. **-S** a system of underground tunnels and wells in the Middle East
QAT	*n* pl. **-S** kat
QAWWALI	*n* pl. **-S** a style of Muslim music
QI	*n* pl. **-S** the vital force that in Chinese thought is inherent in all things
QIBLA	*n* pl. **-S** kiblah
QIGONG	*n* pl. **-S** a Chinese system of physical exercises
QINDAR	*n* pl. **-DARS** or **-DARKA** qintar
QINTAR	*n* pl. **-S** a monetary unit of Albania
QIVIUT	*n* pl. **-S** the wool of a musk ox
QOPH	*n* pl. **-S** koph
QUA	*adv* in the capacity of
QUAALUDE	*n* pl. **-S** a sedative drug
QUACK	*v* **-ED, -ING, -S** to utter the characteristic cry of a duck
QUACKERY	*n* pl. **-ERIES** fraudulent practice
QUACKISH	*adj* fraudulent
QUACKISM	*n* pl. **-S** quackery
QUACKY	*adj* **QUACKIER, QUACKIEST** resembling the cry of a duck
QUAD	*v* **QUADDED, QUADDING, QUADS** to space out by means of quadrats
QUADPLEX	*n* pl. **-ES** a building having four units
QUADRANS	*n* pl. **-RANTES** an ancient Roman coin
QUADRANT	*n* pl. **-S** a quarter section of a circle
QUADRAT	*n* pl. **-S** a piece of type metal used for filling spaces
QUADRATE	*v* **-RATED, -RATING, -RATES** to correspond or agree
QUADRATI	*n/pl* rectangular muscles
QUADRIC	*n* pl. **-S** a type of geometric surface
QUADRIGA	*n* pl. **-GAE** a chariot drawn by four horses
QUADROON	*n* pl. **-S** a person of one-quarter black ancestry
QUAERE	*n* pl. **-S** a question
QUAESTOR	*n* pl. **-S** an ancient Roman magistrate
QUAFF	*v* **-ED, -ING, -S** to drink deeply
QUAFFER	*n* pl. **-S** one that quaffs
QUAG	*n* pl. **-S** a quagmire
QUAGGA	*n* pl. **-S** an extinct mammal that resembles a zebra
QUAGGY	*adj* **-GIER, -GIEST** marshy
QUAGMIRE	*n* pl. **-S** an area of marshy ground
QUAGMIRY	*adj* **-MIRIER, -MIRIEST** marshy
QUAHAUG	*n* pl. **-S** quahog
QUAHOG	*n* pl. **-S** an edible clam
QUAI	*n* pl. **-S** quay
QUAICH	*n* pl. **-S** or **-ES** a small drinking vessel
QUAIGH	*n* pl. **-S** quaich
QUAIL	*v* **-ED, -ING, -S** to cower
QUAINT	*adj* **QUAINTER, QUAINTEST** pleasingly old-fashioned or unfamiliar **QUAINTLY** *adv*
QUAKE	*v* **QUAKED, QUAKING, QUAKES** to shake or vibrate
QUAKER	*n* pl. **-S** one that quakes
QUAKY	*adj* **QUAKIER, QUAKIEST** tending to quake **QUAKILY** *adv*

QUALE *n pl.* **-LIA** a property considered apart from things having the property

QUALIFY *v* **-FIED, -FYING, -FIES** to make suitable or capable

QUALITY *n pl.* **-TIES** a characteristic or attribute

QUALM *n pl.* **-S** a feeling of doubt or misgiving

QUALMISH *adj* having qualms

QUALMY *adj* **QUALMIER, QUALMIEST** qualmish

QUAMASH *n pl.* **-ES** camass

QUANDANG *n pl.* **-S** quandong

QUANDARY *n pl.* **-RIES** a dilemma

QUANDONG *n pl.* **-S** an Australian tree

QUANGO *n pl.* **-GOS** a public administrative board

QUANT *v* **-ED, -ING, -S** to propel through water with a pole

QUANTA *pl.* of quantum

QUANTAL *adj* pertaining to a quantum

QUANTIC *n pl.* **-S** a type of mathematical function

QUANTIFY *v* **-FIED, -FYING, -FIES** to determine the quantity of

QUANTILE *n pl.* **-S** any of the values of a random variable that divides a frequency distribution

QUANTISE *v* **-TISED, -TISING, -TISES** to quantize

QUANTITY *n pl.* **-TIES** a specified or indefinite amount or number

QUANTIZE *v* **-TIZED, -TIZING, -TIZES** to limit the possible values of to a discrete set

QUANTONG *n pl.* **-S** quandong

QUANTUM *n pl.* **-TA** a fundamental unit of energy

QUARE *adj* queer

QUARK *n pl.* **-S** a hypothetical atomic particle

QUARREL *v* **-RELED, -RELING, -RELS** or **-RELLED, -RELLING, -RELS** to engage in an angry dispute

QUARRIER *n pl.* **-S** one that quarries

QUARRY *v* **-RIED, -RYING, -RIES** to dig stone from an excavation

QUART *n pl.* **-S** a liquid measure of capacity

QUARTAN *n pl.* **-S** a recurrent malarial fever

QUARTE *n pl.* **-S** a fencing thrust

QUARTER *v* **-ED, -ING, -S** to divide into four equal parts

QUARTERN *n pl.* **-S** one-fourth of something

QUARTET *n pl.* **-S** a group of four

QUARTIC *n pl.* **-S** a type of mathematical function

QUARTIER *n pl.* **-S** a district in a French city

QUARTILE *n pl.* **-S** a portion of a frequency distribution

QUARTO *n pl.* **-TOS** the size of a piece of paper cut four from a sheet

QUARTZ *n pl.* **-ES** a mineral

QUASAR *n pl.* **-S** a distant celestial object emitting strong radio waves

QUASH *v* **-ED, -ING, -ES** to suppress completely

QUASHER *n pl.* **-S** one that quashes

QUASI *adj* similar but not exactly the same

QUASS *n pl.* **-ES** kvass

QUASSIA *n pl.* **-S** a tropical tree

QUASSIN *n pl.* **-S** a medicinal compound obtained from the wood of a quassia

QUATE *adj* quiet

QUATORZE *n pl.* **-S** a set of four cards of the same denomination scoring fourteen points

QUATRAIN *n pl.* **-S** a stanza of four lines

QUATRE *n pl.* **-S** the four at cards or dice

QUAVER *v* **-ED, -ING, -S** to quiver

QUAVERER *n pl.* **-S** one that quavers

QUAVERY *adj* quivery

QUAY *n pl.* **QUAYS** a wharf **QUAYLIKE** *adj*

QUAYAGE *n pl.* **-S** a charge for the use of a quay

QUAYSIDE *n pl.* **-S** the area adjacent to a quay

QUBIT *n pl.* **-S** a quantum bit

QUBYTE *n pl.* **-S** a sequence of eight quantum bits

QUEAN *n pl.* **-S** a harlot

QUEASY *adj* **-SIER, -SIEST** easily nauseated **QUEASILY** *adv*

QUEAZY *adj* **-ZIER, -ZIEST** queasy

QUEEN *v* **-ED, -ING, -S** to make a queen (a female monarch) of

QUEENCUP *n pl.* **-S** a flowering plant

QUEENDOM *n pl.* **-S** the area ruled by a queen

QUEENLY *adj* **-LIER, -LIEST** of or befitting a queen

QUEENY *adj* **QUEENIER, QUEENIEST** showily effeminate

QUEER	*adj* **QUEERER, QUEEREST** deviating from the expected or normal
QUEER	*v* **-ED, -ING, -S** to spoil the effect or success of
QUEERISH	*adj* somewhat queer
QUEERLY	*adv* in a queer manner
QUELEA	*n* pl. **-S** an African weaverbird
QUELL	*v* **-ED, -ING, -S** to suppress
QUELLER	*n* pl. **-S** one that quells
QUENCH	*v* **-ED, -ING, -ES** to put out or extinguish
QUENCHER	*n* pl. **-S** one that quenches
QUENELLE	*n* pl. **-S** a type of dumpling
QUERCINE	*adj* pertaining to oaks
QUERIDA	*n* pl. **-S** a female sweetheart
QUERIED	past tense of query
QUERIER	*n* pl. **-S** a querist
QUERIES	present 3d person sing. of query
QUERIST	*n* pl. **-S** one who queries
QUERN	*n* pl. **-S** a hand-turned grain mill
QUERY	*v* **-RIED, -RYING, -RIES** to question
QUEST	*v* **-ED, -ING, -S** to make a search
QUESTER	*n* pl. **-S** one that quests
QUESTION	*v* **-ED, -ING, -S** to put a question (an inquiry) to
QUESTOR	*n* pl. **-S** quaestor
QUETZAL	*n* pl. **-S** or **-ES** a tropical bird
QUEUE	*v* **QUEUED, QUEUING** or **QUEUEING, QUEUES** to line up
QUEUER	*n* pl. **-S** one that queues
QUEY	*n* pl. **QUEYS** a young cow
QUEZAL	*n* pl. **-S** or **-ES** quetzal
QUIBBLE	*v* **-BLED, -BLING, -BLES** to argue over trivialities
QUIBBLER	*n* pl. **-S** one that quibbles
QUICHE	*n* pl. **-S** a custard-filled pastry
QUICK	*adj* **QUICKER, QUICKEST** acting or capable of acting with speed
QUICK	*n* pl. **-S** a sensitive area of flesh
QUICKEN	*v* **-ED, -ING, -S** to speed up
QUICKIE	*n* pl. **-S** something done quickly
QUICKLY	*adv* in a quick manner
QUICKSET	*n* pl. **-S** a plant suitable for hedges
QUID	*n* pl. **-S** a portion of something to be chewed
QUIDDITY	*n* pl. **-TIES** the true nature of a thing
QUIDNUNC	*n* pl. **-S** a nosy person
QUIET	*adj* **-ETER, -ETEST** making little or no noise
QUIET	*v* **-ED, -ING, -S** to cause to be quiet
QUIETEN	*v* **-ED, -ING, -S** to quiet
QUIETER	*n* pl. **-S** one that quiets
QUIETISM	*n* pl. **-S** a form of religious mysticism
QUIETIST	*n* pl. **-S** an advocate of quietism
QUIETLY	*adv* in a quiet manner
QUIETUDE	*n* pl. **-S** a state of tranquillity
QUIETUS	*n* pl. **-ES** a final settlement
QUIFF	*n* pl. **-S** a lock of hair at the front of the head **QUIFFED** *adj*
QUILL	*v* **-ED, -ING, -S** to press small ridges in
QUILLAI	*n* pl. **-S** an evergreen tree
QUILLAIA	*n* pl. **-S** a quillai
QUILLAJA	*n* pl. **-S** a quillai
QUILLET	*n* pl. **-S** a trivial distinction
QUILLING	*n* pl. **-S** material that is quilled
QUILLOW	*n* pl. **-S** a quilt formed into a pillow
QUILT	*v* **-ED, -ING, -S** to stitch together with padding in between
QUILTER	*n* pl. **-S** one that quilts
QUILTING	*n* pl. **-S** material that is used for making quilts
QUIN	*n* pl. **-S** a quintuplet
QUINARY	*n* pl. **-RIES** a group of five
QUINATE	*adj* arranged in groups of five
QUINCE	*n* pl. **-S** an apple-like fruit
QUINCUNX	*n* pl. **-ES** an arrangement of five objects
QUINELA	*n* pl. **-S** quinella
QUINELLA	*n* pl. **-S** a type of bet in horse racing
QUINIC	*adj* pertaining to quinine
QUINIELA	*n* pl. **-S** quinella
QUININ	*n* pl. **-S** quinine
QUININA	*n* pl. **-S** quinine
QUININE	*n* pl. **-S** a medicinal alkaloid
QUINNAT	*n* pl. **-S** a food fish
QUINOA	*n* pl. **-S** a weedy plant
QUINOID	*n* pl. **-S** a chemical compound
QUINOL	*n* pl. **-S** a chemical compound
QUINOLIN	*n* pl. **-S** a chemical compound
QUINONE	*n* pl. **-S** a chemical compound

QUINSY	*n* pl. **-SIES** an inflammation of the tonsils **QUINSIED** *adj*
QUINT	*n* pl. **-S** a group of five
QUINTA	*n* pl. **-S** a country estate in Portugal or Latin America
QUINTAIN	*n* pl. **-S** an object used as a target in a medieval sport
QUINTAL	*n* pl. **-S** a unit of weight
QUINTAN	*n* pl. **-S** a recurrent fever
QUINTAR	*n* pl. **-S** qintar
QUINTE	*n* pl. **-S** a position in fencing
QUINTET	*n* pl. **-S** a group of five
QUINTIC	*n* pl. **-S** a type of mathematical function
QUINTILE	*n* pl. **-S** a portion of a frequency distribution
QUINTIN	*n* pl. **-S** a fine linen
QUINZHEE	*n* pl. **-S** a shelter made by hollowing out a pile of snow
QUINZIE	*n* pl. **-S** quinzhee
QUIP	*v* **QUIPPED, QUIPPING, QUIPS** to make witty remarks
QUIPPER	*n* pl. **-S** one that quips
QUIPPISH	*adj* witty
QUIPPU	*n* pl. **-S** quipu
QUIPPY	*adj* **-PIER, -PIEST** witty
QUIPSTER	*n* pl. **-S** one that quips
QUIPU	*n* pl. **-S** an ancient calculating device
QUIRE	*v* **QUIRED, QUIRING, QUIRES** to arrange sheets of paper in sets of twenty-four
QUIRK	*v* **-ED, -ING, -S** to twist
QUIRKISH	*adj* quirky
QUIRKY	*adj* **QUIRKIER, QUIRKIEST** peculiar **QUIRKILY** *adv*
QUIRT	*v* **-ED, -ING, -S** to strike with a riding whip
QUISLING	*n* pl. **-S** a traitor who aids the invaders of his country
QUIT	*v* **QUITTED, QUITTING, QUITS** to end one's engagement in or occupation with
QUITCH	*n* pl. **-ES** a perennial grass
QUITE	*adv* to the fullest extent
QUITRENT	*n* pl. **-S** a fixed rent due from a socage tenant
QUITTED	past tense of quit
QUITTER	*n* pl. **-S** one that quits
QUITTING	present participle of quit
QUITTOR	*n* pl. **-S** an inflammation of an animal's hoof
QUIVER	*v* **-ED, -ING, -S** to shake with a slight but rapid motion
QUIVERER	*n* pl. **-S** one that quivers
QUIVERY	*adj* marked by quivering
QUIXOTE	*n* pl. **-S** a quixotic person
QUIXOTIC	*adj* extremely idealistic
QUIXOTRY	*n* pl. **-TRIES** quixotic action or thought
QUIZ	*v* **QUIZZED, QUIZZING, QUIZZES** to test the knowledge of by asking questions
QUIZZER	*n* pl. **-S** one that quizzes
QULLIQ	*n* pl. **-S** kudlik
QUOD	*n* pl. **-S** a prison
QUOHOG	*n* pl. **-S** quahog
QUOIN	*v* **-ED, -ING, -S** to secure with a type of wedge
QUOINING	*n* pl. **-S** the materials (as stones or bricks) used to form an external corner of a building
QUOIT	*v* **-ED, -ING, -S** to play a throwing game similar to ringtoss
QUOKKA	*n* pl. **-S** a short-tailed wallaby
QUOLL	*n* pl. **-S** a small spotted marsupial
QUOMODO	*n* pl. **-DOS** a means or manner
QUONDAM	*adj* that once was
QUORUM	*n* pl. **-S** a particularly chosen group
QUOTA	*n* pl. **-S** a proportional part or share
QUOTE	*v* **QUOTED, QUOTING, QUOTES** to repeat the words of **QUOTABLE** *adj* **QUOTABLY** *adv*
QUOTER	*n* pl. **-S** one that quotes
QUOTH	*v* said — QUOTH is the only accepted form of this verb; it cannot be conjugated
QUOTHA	*interj* — used to express surprise or sarcasm
QUOTIENT	*n* pl. **-S** the number resulting from the division of one number by another
QUOTING	present participle of quote
QURSH	*n* pl. **-ES** a monetary unit of Saudi Arabia
QURUSH	*n* pl. **-ES** qursh
QWERTY	*n* pl. **-TYS** a standard keyboard

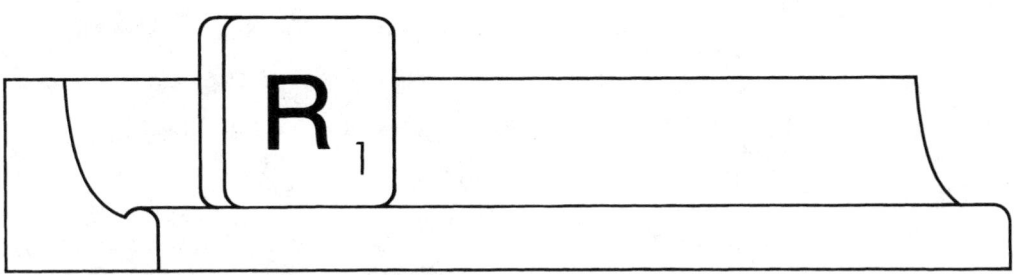

RABASKA *n* pl. **-S** a large canoe

RABAT *n* pl. **-S** a dickey attached to a clerical collar

RABATO *n* pl. **-TOS** a wide, lace-edged collar

RABBET *v* **-ED, -ING, -S** to cut a groove in

RABBI *n* pl. **-S** or **-ES** a Jewish spiritual leader

RABBIN *n* pl. **-S** rabbi

RABBINIC *adj* pertaining to rabbis

RABBIT *v* **-ED, -ING, -S** to hunt rabbits (rodent-like mammals)

RABBITER *n* pl. **-S** one that rabbits

RABBITRY *n* pl. **-RIES** a place where rabbits are kept

RABBITY *adj* resembling a rabbit

RABBLE *v* **-BLED, -BLING, -BLES** to mob

RABBLER *n* pl. **-S** an iron bar used in puddling

RABBONI *n* pl. **-S** master; teacher — used as a Jewish title of respect

RABIC *adj* pertaining to rabies

RABID *adj* affected with rabies **RABIDLY** *adv*

RABIDITY *n* pl. **-TIES** the state of being rabid

RABIES *n* pl. **RABIES** an infectious virus disease **RABIETIC** *adj*

RACCOON *n* pl. **-S** a carnivorous mammal

RACE *v* **RACED, RACING, RACES** to compete in a contest of speed

RACEGOER *n* pl. **-S** one who regularly goes to horse races

RACEMATE *n* pl. **-S** a chemical salt

RACEME *n* pl. **-S** a mode of arrangement of flowers along an axis **RACEMED** *adj*

RACEMIC *adj* pertaining to a racemate

RACEMISM *n* pl. **-S** the state of being racemic

RACEMIZE *v* **-MIZED, -MIZING, -MIZES** to convert into a racemic compound

RACEMOID *adj* pertaining to a raceme

RACEMOSE *adj* having the form of a raceme

RACEMOUS *adj* racemose

RACER *n* pl. **-S** one that races

RACEWALK *v* **-ED, -ING, -S** to walk for speed while maintaining foot contact with the ground and keeping the supporting leg straight

RACEWAY *n* pl. **-WAYS** a channel for conducting water

RACHET *v* **-ED, -ING, -S** ratchet

RACHILLA *n* pl. **-LAE** the central stalk of a grass spikelet

RACHIS *n* pl. **-CHISES** or **-CHIDES** the spinal column **RACHIAL** *adj*

RACHITIS *n* pl. **-TIDES** rickets **RACHITIC** *adj*

RACIAL *adj* pertaining to an ethnic group **RACIALLY** *adv*

RACIER comparative of racy

RACIEST superlative of racy

RACILY *adv* in a racy manner

RACINESS *n* pl. **-ES** the quality of being racy

RACING *n* pl. **-S** the sport of engaging in contests of speed

RACINO *n* pl. **-NOS** a racetrack at which slot machines are available

RACISM *n* pl. **-S** a doctrine of racial superiority

RACIST *n* pl. **-S** an advocate of racism

RACK *v* **-ED, -ING, -S** to place in a type of framework

RACKER *n* pl. **-S** one that racks

RACKET *v* **-ED, -ING, -S** to make a loud noise

RACKETY *adj* **-ETIER, -ETIEST** noisy

RACKFUL *n* pl. **-S** as much as a rack can hold

RACKLE *adj* impetuous; rash

RACKWORK *n* pl. **-S** a type of mechanism

RACLETTE *n* pl. **-S** a cheese dish

RACON *n* pl. **-S** a type of radar transmitter

RACOON *n* pl. **-S** raccoon

RACQUET *n* pl. **-S** a lightweight implement used in various ball games

RACY *adj* **RACIER, RACIEST** bordering on impropriety or indecency

RAD *v* **RADDED, RADDING, RADS** to fear

RAD *adj* **RADDER, RADDEST** very appealing or good

RADAR *n* pl. **-S** an electronic locating device

RADDLE *v* **-DLED, -DLING, -DLES** to weave together

RADIABLE *adj* capable of radiating

RADIAL *n* pl. **-S** a part diverging from a center

RADIALE *n* pl. **-LIA** a bone of the carpus

RADIALLY *adv* in a diverging manner

RADIAN *n* pl. **-S** a unit of angular measure

RADIANCE *n* pl. **-S** brightness

RADIANCY *n* pl. **-CIES** radiance

RADIANT *n* pl. **-S** a point from which rays are emitted

RADIATE *v* **-ATED, -ATING, -ATES** to emit rays

RADIATOR *n* pl. **-S** a heating device

RADICAL *n* pl. **-S** a group of atoms that acts as a unit in chemical compounds

RADICAND *n* pl. **-S** a quantity in mathematics

RADICATE *v* **-CATED, -CATING, -CATES** to cause to take root

RADICEL *n* pl. **-S** a rootlet

RADICES a pl. of radix

RADICLE *n* pl. **-S** a part of a plant embryo

RADII a pl. of radius

RADIO *v* **-ED, -ING, -S** or **-ES** to transmit by radio (an apparatus for wireless communication)

RADIOMAN *n* pl. **-MEN** a radio operator or technician

RADISH *n* pl. **-ES** a pungent, edible root

RADIUM *n* pl. **-S** a radioactive element

RADIUS *n* pl. **-DIUSES** or **-DII** a straight line from the center of a circle to the circumference

RADIUS *v* **-ED, -ING, -ES** to give a rounded form to

RADIX *n* pl. **-DIXES** or **-DICES** the root of a plant

RADOME *n* pl. **-S** a domelike device used to shelter a radar antenna

RADON *n* pl. **-S** a radioactive element

RADULA *n* pl. **-LAS** or **-LAE** a tonguelike organ of mollusks **RADULAR** *adj*

RADWASTE *n* pl. **-S** radioactive waste

RAFF *n* pl. **-S** riffraff

RAFFIA *n* pl. **-S** a palm tree

RAFFISH *adj* tawdry

RAFFLE *v* **-FLED, -FLING, -FLES** to dispose of by a form of lottery

RAFFLER *n* pl. **-S** one that raffles

RAFT *v* **-ED, -ING, -S** to transport on a raft (a type of buoyant structure)

RAFTER *n* pl. **-S** a supporting beam

RAFTERED *adj* furnished with rafters

RAFTING *n* pl. **-S** the sport of traveling down a river on a raft

RAFTSMAN *n* pl. **-MEN** one who manages a raft

RAG *v* **RAGGED, RAGGING, RAGS** to scold

RAGA *n* pl. **-S** a Hindu musical form

RAGBAG *n* pl. **-S** a bag for storing scraps of cloth

RAGE *v* **RAGED, RAGING, RAGES** to act or speak with violent anger

RAGEE *n* pl. **-S** ragi

RAGEFUL *adj* full of violent anger

RAGER *n* pl. **-S** one that rages

RAGG *n* pl. **-S** a wool fiber

RAGGA *n* pl. **-S** music that combines reggae and hip hop

RAGGED *adj* **-GEDER, -GEDEST** tattered **RAGGEDLY** *adv*

RAGGEDY *adj* **-GEDIER, -GEDIEST** somewhat ragged

RAGGEE *n* pl. **-S** ragi

RAGGIES pl. of raggy

RAGGING *n* pl. **-S** the technique of decorating a wall by applying paint with a rag

RAGGLE *n* pl. **-S** a groove cut in masonry

RAGGY *n* pl. **-GIES** ragi

RAGI *n* pl. **-S** an East Indian cereal grass

RAGING	present participle of rage
RAGINGLY	*adv* in a furious manner
RAGLAN	*n* pl. **-S** a type of overcoat
RAGMAN	*n* pl. **-MEN** one who gathers and sells scraps of cloth
RAGOUT	*v* **-ED, -ING, -S** to make into a highly seasoned stew
RAGTAG	*n* pl. **-S** riffraff
RAGTAIL	*adj* ragged, shabby
RAGTIME	*n* pl. **-S** a style of American dance music
RAGTOP	*n* pl. **-S** a convertible automobile
RAGWEED	*n* pl. **-S** a weedy herb
RAGWORM	*n* pl. **-S** an aquatic worm
RAGWORT	*n* pl. **-S** a flowering plant
RAH	*interj* — used to cheer on a team or player
RAI	*n* pl. **-S** a style of popular Algerian music
RAIA	*n* pl. **-S** rayah
RAID	*v* **-ED, -ING, -S** to make a sudden assault on
RAIDER	*n* pl. **-S** one that raids
RAIL	*v* **-ED, -ING, -S** to scold in abusive or insolent language
RAILBED	*n* pl. **-S** a layer of stone or gravel on which a railroad is laid
RAILBIRD	*n* pl. **-S** a racing enthusiast
RAILBUS	*n* pl. **-BUSES** or **-BUSSES** a passenger car equipped for operation on rails
RAILCAR	*n* pl. **-S** a railroad car
RAILCARD	*n* pl. **-S** a card that allows buying railroad tickets at a lower price
RAILER	*n* pl. **-S** one that rails
RAILHEAD	*n* pl. **-S** the end of a railroad line
RAILING	*n* pl. **-S** a fence-like barrier
RAILLERY	*n* pl. **-LERIES** good-natured teasing
RAILMAN	*n* pl. **-MEN** a railroad employee
RAILROAD	*v* **-ED, -ING, -S** to transport by railroad (a type of road on which locomotives are run)
RAILWAY	*n* pl. **-WAYS** a railroad
RAIMENT	*n* pl. **-S** clothing
RAIN	*v* **-ED, -ING, -S** to fall like rain (drops of water condensed from clouds)
RAINBAND	*n* pl. **-S** a dark band in the solar spectrum
RAINBIRD	*n* pl. **-S** a type of bird
RAINBOW	*n* pl. **-S** an arc of spectral colors formed in the sky
RAINCOAT	*n* pl. **-S** a waterproof coat
RAINDROP	*n* pl. **-S** a drop of rain
RAINFALL	*n* pl. **-S** a fall of rain
RAINIER	comparative of rainy
RAINIEST	superlative of rainy
RAINILY	*adv* in a rainy manner
RAINLESS	*adj* having no rain
RAINOUT	*n* pl. **-S** atomic fallout occurring in precipitation
RAINSUIT	*n* pl. **-S** a waterproof jacket and pants
RAINWASH	*v* **-ED, -ING, -ES** to wash material downhill by rain
RAINWEAR	*n* pl. **RAINWEAR** waterproof clothing
RAINY	*adj* **RAINIER, RAINIEST** marked by rain
RAISE	*v* **RAISED, RAISING, RAISES** to move to a higher position **RAISABLE** *adj*
RAISER	*n* pl. **-S** one that raises
RAISIN	*n* pl. **-S** a dried grape **RAISINY** *adj*
RAISING	*n* pl. **-S** an elevation
RAISONNE	*adj* arranged systematically
RAITA	*n* pl. **-S** an Indian salad made with yogurt and chopped vegetables or fruits
RAJ	*n* pl. **-ES** dominion; sovereignty
RAJA	*n* pl. **-S** rajah
RAJAH	*n* pl. **-S** a king or prince in India
RAKE	*v* **RAKED, RAKING, RAKES** to gather with a toothed implement
RAKEE	*n* pl. **-S** raki
RAKEHELL	*n* pl. **-S** a man lacking in moral restraint
RAKEOFF	*n* pl. **-S** a share of profits
RAKER	*n* pl. **-S** one that rakes
RAKI	*n* pl. **-S** a Turkish liqueur
RAKING	present participle of rake
RAKISH	*adj* dapper **RAKISHLY** *adv*
RAKU	*n* pl. **-S** a form of Japanese glazed pottery
RALE	*n* pl. **-S** an abnormal respiratory sound
RALLIER	*n* pl. **-S** one that rallies

RALLINE	*adj* pertaining to a family of marsh birds
RALLY	*v* **-LIED, -LYING, -LIES** to call together for a common purpose
RALLYE	*n* pl. **-S** a type of automobile race
RALLYING	*n* pl. **-S** the sport of driving in rallyes
RALLYIST	*n* pl. **-S** a participant in a rallye
RALPH	*v* **-ED, -ING, -S** to vomit
RAM	*v* **RAMMED, RAMMING, RAMS** to strike with great force
RAMADA	*n* pl. **-S** a roofed, open-sided shelter
RAMAL	*adj* pertaining to a ramus
RAMATE	*adj* having branches
RAMBLA	*n* pl. **-S** a dry ravine
RAMBLE	*v* **-BLED, -BLING, -BLES** to wander
RAMBLER	*n* pl. **-S** one that rambles
RAMBUTAN	*n* pl. **-S** the edible fruit of a Malayan tree
RAMEE	*n* pl. **-S** ramie
RAMEKIN	*n* pl. **-S** a cheese dish
RAMEN	*n* pl. **RAMEN** Japanese noodles in a broth with bits of meat and vegetables
RAMENTUM	*n* pl. **-TA** a scale formed on the surface of leaves
RAMEQUIN	*n* pl. **-S** ramekin
RAMET	*n* pl. **-S** an independent member of a clone
RAMI	pl. of ramus
RAMIE	*n* pl. **-S** an Asian shrub
RAMIFORM	*adj* shaped like a branch
RAMIFY	*v* **-FIED, -FYING, -FIES** to divide into branches
RAMILIE	*n* pl. **-S** ramillie
RAMILLIE	*n* pl. **-S** a type of wig
RAMIN	*n* pl. **-S** a Malaysian tree
RAMJET	*n* pl. **-S** a type of engine
RAMMED	past tense of ram
RAMMER	*n* pl. **-S** one that rams
RAMMIER	comparative of rammy
RAMMIEST	superlative of rammy
RAMMING	present participle of ram
RAMMISH	*adj* resembling a ram (a male sheep)
RAMMY	*adj* **-MIER, -MIEST** rammish
RAMONA	*n* pl. **-S** a plant of the mint family
RAMOSE	*adj* having many branches **RAMOSELY** *adv*
RAMOSITY	*n* pl. **-TIES** the state of being ramose
RAMOUS	*adj* ramose
RAMP	*v* **-ED, -ING, -S** to rise or stand on the hind legs
RAMPAGE	*v* **-PAGED, -PAGING, -PAGES** to move about wildly or violently
RAMPAGER	*n* pl. **-S** one that rampages
RAMPANCY	*n* pl. **-CIES** the state of being rampant
RAMPANT	*adj* unrestrained
RAMPART	*v* **-ED, -ING, -S** to furnish with a fortifying embankment
RAMPIKE	*n* pl. **-S** a standing dead tree
RAMPION	*n* pl. **-S** a European plant
RAMPOLE	*n* pl. **-S** rampike
RAMROD	*v* **-RODDED, -RODDING, -RODS** to supervise
RAMSHORN	*n* pl. **-S** a snail used as an aquarium scavenger
RAMSON	*n* pl. **-S** a broad-leaved garlic
RAMTIL	*n* pl. **-S** a tropical plant
RAMTILLA	*n* pl. **-S** ramtil
RAMULOSE	*adj* having many small branches
RAMULOUS	*adj* ramulose
RAMUS	*n* pl. **-MI** a branch-like part of a structure
RAN	past tense of run and rin
RANCE	*n* pl. **-S** a variety of marble
RANCH	*v* **-ED, -ING, -ES** to work on a ranch (an establishment for raising livestock)
RANCHER	*n* pl. **-S** one that owns or works on a ranch
RANCHERA	*n* pl. **-S** a type of Mexican country music
RANCHERO	*n* pl. **-ROS** a rancher
RANCHING	*n* pl. **-S** the work of running a ranch
RANCHMAN	*n* pl. **-MEN** a rancher
RANCHO	*n* pl. **-CHOS** a ranch
RANCID	*adj* having an unpleasant odor or taste **RANCIDLY** *adv*
RANCOR	*n* pl. **-S** bitter and vindictive enmity **RANCORED** *adj*
RANCOUR	*n* pl. **-S** rancor

RAND *n* pl. **-S** a strip of leather at the heel of a shoe

RANDAN *n* pl. **-S** a boat rowed by three persons

RANDIER comparative of randy

RANDIES pl. of randy

RANDOM *n* pl. **-S** a haphazard course

RANDOMLY *adv* in a haphazard manner

RANDY *adj* **-DIER, -DIEST** lustful

RANDY *n* pl. **RANDIES** a rude person

RANEE *n* pl. **-S** rani

RANG *n* pl. **-S** a row of long lots along a road

RANGE *v* **RANGED, RANGING, RANGES** to place in a particular order

RANGER *n* pl. **-S** an officer supervising the care of a forest

RANGY *adj* **RANGIER, RANGIEST** tall and slender

RANI *n* pl. **-S** the wife of a rajah

RANID *n* pl. **-S** any of a large family of frogs

RANK *adj* **RANKER, RANKEST** strong and disagreeable in odor or taste

RANK *v* **-ED, -ING, -S** to determine the relative position of

RANKER *n* pl. **-S** an enlisted soldier

RANKING *n* pl. **-S** a listing of ranked individuals

RANKISH *adj* somewhat rank

RANKLE *v* **-KLED, -KLING, -KLES** to cause irritation or resentment in

RANKLESS *adj* having no ranks

RANKLY *adv* in a rank manner

RANKNESS *n* pl. **-ES** the state of being rank

RANPIKE *n* pl. **-S** rampike

RANSACK *v* **-ED, -ING, -S** to search thoroughly

RANSOM *v* **-ED, -ING, -S** to obtain the release of by paying a demanded price

RANSOMER *n* pl. **-S** one that ransoms

RANT *v* **-ED, -ING, -S** to speak in a loud or vehement manner

RANTER *n* pl. **-S** one that rants

RANTINGS *n/pl* loud and angry comments

RANULA *n* pl. **-S** a cyst formed under the tongue **RANULAR** *adj*

RAP *v* **RAPPED, RAPPING, RAPS** to strike sharply

RAPACITY *n* pl. **-TIES** the quality of being ravenous

RAPE *v* **RAPED, RAPING, RAPES** to force to submit to sexual intercourse

RAPER *n* pl. **-S** a rapist

RAPESEED *n* pl. **-S** the seed of a European herb

RAPHE *n* pl. **RAPHES** or **RAPHAE** a seamlike ridge between two halves of an organ or part

RAPHIA *n* pl. **-S** raffia

RAPHIDE *n* pl. **-S** a needle-shaped crystal occurring in plant cells

RAPHIS *n* pl. **-PHIDES** raphide

RAPID *adj* **-IDER, -IDEST** fast-moving **RAPIDLY** *adv*

RAPID *n* pl. **-S** a fast-moving part of a river

RAPIDITY *n* pl. **-TIES** swiftness

RAPIER *n* pl. **-S** a long, slender sword **RAPIERED** *adj*

RAPINE *n* pl. **-S** the taking of property by force

RAPING present participle of rape

RAPINI *n/pl* rappini

RAPIST *n* pl. **-S** one who rapes

RAPPAREE *n* pl. **-S** a plunderer

RAPPED past tense of rap

RAPPEE *n* pl. **-S** a strong snuff

RAPPEL *v* **-PELED, -PELING, -PELS** or **-PELLED, -PELLING, -PELS** to descend from a steep height by means of a rope

RAPPEN *n* pl. **RAPPEN** a monetary unit of Switzerland

RAPPER *n* pl. **-S** one that raps

RAPPING present participle of rap

RAPPINI *n/pl* immature turnip plants

RAPPORT *n* pl. **-S** a harmonious relationship

RAPT *adj* deeply engrossed **RAPTLY** *adv*

RAPTNESS *n* pl. **-ES** the state of being rapt

RAPTOR *n* pl. **-S** a bird of prey

RAPTURE *v* **-TURED, -TURING, -TURES** to fill with great joy

RARE *adj* **RARER, RAREST** occurring infrequently

RARE *v* **RARED, RARING, RARES** to be enthusiastic

RAREBIT   *n* pl. **-S** a cheese dish

RAREFIER   *n* pl. **-S** one that rarefies

RAREFY   *v* **-EFIED, -EFYING, -EFIES** to make less dense

RARELY   *adv* not often

RARENESS   *n* pl. **-ES** the quality of being rare

RARER   comparative of rare

RARERIPE   *n* pl. **-S** a fruit that ripens early

RAREST   superlative of rare

RARIFY   *v* **-FIED, -FYING, -FIES** to rarefy

RARING   *adj* full of enthusiasm

RARITY   *n* pl. **-TIES** rareness

RAS   *n* pl. **-ES** an Ethiopian prince

RASBORA   *n* pl. **-S** a tropical fish

RASCAL   *n* pl. **-S** an unscrupulous or dishonest person

RASCALLY   *adj* characteristic of a rascal

RASE   *v* **RASED, RASING, RASES** to raze

RASER   *n* pl. **-S** one that rases

RASH   *adj* **RASHER, RASHEST** acting without due caution or forethought

RASH   *n* pl. **-ES** a skin eruption **RASHLIKE** *adj*

RASHER   *n* pl. **-S** a thin slice of meat

RASHLY   *adv* in a rash manner

RASHNESS   *n* pl. **-ES** the state of being rash

RASING   present participle of rase

RASORIAL   *adj* habitually scratching the ground for food

RASP   *v* **-ED, -ING, -S** to rub with something rough

RASPER   *n* pl. **-S** one that rasps

RASPING   *n* pl. **-S** a tiny piece of wood removed with a coarse file

RASPISH   *adj* irritable

RASPY   *adj* **RASPIER, RASPIEST** rough

RASSLE   *v* **-SLED, -SLING, -SLES** to wrestle

RASSLER   *n* pl. **-S** a wrestler

RASTER   *n* pl. **-S** the area reproducing images on the picture tube of a television set

RASURE   *n* pl. **-S** erasure

RAT   *v* **RATTED, RATTING, RATS** to hunt rats (long-tailed rodents)

RATABLE   *adj* capable of being rated **RATABLY** *adv*

RATABLES   *n/pl* taxable properties

RATAFEE   *n* pl. **-S** ratafia

RATAFIA   *n* pl. **-S** an almond-flavored liqueur

RATAL   *n* pl. **-S** an amount on which rates are assessed

RATAN   *n* pl. **-S** rattan

RATANY   *n* pl. **-NIES** rhatany

RATAPLAN   *v* **-PLANNED, -PLANNING, -PLANS** to make a rapidly repeating sound

RATATAT   *n* pl. **-S** a quick, sharp rapping sound

RATBAG   *n* pl. **-S** an eccentric or disagreeable person

RATCH   *n* pl. **-ES** a mechanism that allows motion in one direction only

RATCHET   *v* **-ED, -ING, -S** to increase or decrease by small amounts

RATE   *v* **RATED, RATING, RATES** to estimate the value of

RATEABLE   *adj* ratable **RATEABLY** *adv*

RATEL   *n* pl. **-S** a carnivorous mammal

RATER   *n* pl. **-S** one that rates

RATFINK   *n* pl. **-S** a contemptible person

RATFISH   *n* pl. **-ES** a marine fish

RATH   *adj* rathe

RATHE   *adj* appearing or ripening early

RATHER   *adv* preferably

RATHOLE   *n* pl. **-S** a hole made by a rat

RATICIDE   *n* pl. **-S** a substance for killing rats

RATIFIER   *n* pl. **-S** one that ratifies

RATIFY   *v* **-FIED, -FYING, -FIES** to approve and sanction formally

RATINE   *n* pl. **-S** a heavy fabric woven loosely

RATING   *n* pl. **-S** relative estimate or evaluation

RATIO   *n* pl. **-TIOS** a proportional relationship

RATION   *v* **-ED, -ING, -S** to distribute in fixed portions

RATIONAL   *n* pl. **-S** a number that can be expressed as a quotient of integers

RATITE   *n* pl. **-S** a flightless bird

RATLIKE   *adj* resembling a rat

RATLIN   *n* pl. **-S** ratline

RATLINE   *n* pl. **-S** one of the ropes forming the steps of a ship's rope ladder

RATO   *n* pl. **-TOS** a rocket-assisted airplane takeoff

RATOON   *v* **-ED, -ING, -S** to sprout from a root planted the previous year

RATOONER   *n* pl. **-S** a plant that ratoons

RATSBANE   *n* pl. **-S** rat poison

RATTAIL   *n* pl. **-S** a marine fish

RATTAN   *n* pl. **-S** a palm tree

RATTED   past tense of rat

RATTEEN   *n* pl. **-S** a coarse woolen fabric

RATTEN   *v* **-ED, -ING, -S** to harass

RATTENER   *n* pl. **-S** one that rattens

RATTER   *n* pl. **-S** an animal used for catching rats

RATTIER   comparative of ratty

RATTIEST   superlative of ratty

RATTILY   *adv* in a manner suggestive of rats

RATTING   present participle of rat

RATTISH   *adj* ratlike

RATTLE   *v* **-TLED, -TLING, -TLES** to make a quick succession of short, sharp sounds

RATTLER   *n* pl. **-S** one that rattles

RATTLING   *n* pl. **-S** ratline

RATTLY   *adj* **-TLIER, -TLIEST** tending to rattle

RATTON   *n* pl. **-S** a rat

RATTOON   *v* **-ED, -ING, -S** to ratoon

RATTRAP   *n* pl. **-S** a trap for catching rats

RATTY   *adj* **-TIER, -TIEST** infested with rats

RAUCITY   *n* pl. **-TIES** the state of being raucous

RAUCOUS   *adj* loud and unruly

RAUNCH   *n* pl. **-ES** vulgarity

RAUNCHY   *adj* **-CHIER, -CHIEST** slovenly

RAVAGE   *v* **-AGED, -AGING, -AGES** to destroy

RAVAGER   *n* pl. **-S** one that ravages

RAVE   *v* **RAVED, RAVING, RAVES** to speak irrationally or incoherently

RAVEL   *v* **-ELED, -ELING, -ELS** or **-ELLED, -ELLING, -ELS** to separate the threads of

RAVELER   *n* pl. **-S** one that ravels

RAVELIN   *n* pl. **-S** a type of fortification

RAVELING   *n* pl. **-S** a loose thread

RAVELLED   a past tense of ravel

RAVELLER   *n* pl. **-S** raveler

RAVELLING   a present participle of ravel

RAVELLY   *adj* tangled

RAVEN   *v* **-ED, -ING, -S** to eat in a ravenous manner

RAVENER   *n* pl. **-S** one that ravens

RAVENING   *n* pl. **-S** rapacity

RAVENOUS   *adj* extremely hungry

RAVER   *n* pl. **-S** one that raves

RAVEY   *adj* **RAVIER, RAVIEST** characteristic of a rave (an all-night dance party with fast electronic music)

RAVIGOTE   *n* pl. **-S** a spiced vinegar sauce

RAVIN   *v* **-ED, -ING, -S** to raven

RAVINE   *n* pl. **-S** a narrow, steep-sided valley

RAVING   *n* pl. **-S** irrational, incoherent speech

RAVINGLY   *adv* in a delirious manner

RAVIOLI   *n* pl. **-S** an Italian pasta dish

RAVISH   *v* **-ED, -ING, -ES** to seize and carry off by force

RAVISHER   *n* pl. **-S** one that ravishes

RAW   *adj* **RAWER, RAWEST** uncooked

RAW   *n* pl. **-S** a sore or irritated spot

RAWBONED   *adj* having little flesh

RAWHIDE   *v* **-HIDED, -HIDING, -HIDES** to beat with a type of whip

RAWIN   *n* pl. **-S** a wind measurement made by tracking a balloon with radar

RAWISH   *adj* somewhat raw

RAWLY   *adv* in a raw manner

RAWNESS   *n* pl. **-ES** the state of being raw

RAX   *v* **-ED, -ING, -ES** to stretch out

RAY   *v* **-ED, -ING, -S** to emit rays (narrow beams of light)

RAYA   *n* pl. **-S** rayah

RAYAH   *n* pl. **-S** a non-Muslim inhabitant of Turkey

RAYGRASS   *n* pl. **-ES** ryegrass

RAYLESS   *adj* having no rays

RAYLIKE   *adj* resembling a narrow beam of light

RAYON   *n* pl. **-S** a synthetic fiber

RAZE   *v* **RAZED, RAZING, RAZES** to tear down or demolish

RAZEE   *v* **-ZEED, -ZEEING, -ZEES** to make lower by removing the upper deck, as a ship

RAZER   *n* pl. **-S** one that razes

RAZOR	*v* **-ED, -ING, -S** to shave or cut with a sharp-edged instrument	**READY**	*adj* **READIER, READIEST** prepared
RAZZ	*v* **-ED, -ING, -ES** to deride	**READY**	*v* **READIED, READYING, READIES** to make ready
RAZZIA	*n* pl. **-S** a hostile raid by Moors	**REAGENT**	*n* pl. **-S** a substance used in a chemical reaction to ascertain the nature or composition of another
RAZZLE	*n* pl. **-S** a flamboyant colorful display		
RE	*n* pl. **-S** the second tone of the diatonic musical scale	**REAGIN**	*n* pl. **-S** a type of antibody **REAGINIC** *adj*
REACH	*v* **-ED, -ING, -ES** to stretch out or put forth	**REAL**	*adj* **REALER, REALEST** having actual existence
REACHER	*n* pl. **-S** one that reaches	**REAL**	*n* pl. **-S** or **-ES** a former monetary unit of Spain
REACT	*v* **-ED, -ING, -S** to respond to a stimulus	**REAL**	*n* pl. **REIS** a monetary unit of Brazil
REACTANT	*n* pl. **-S** one that reacts	**REALGAR**	*n* pl. **-S** a mineral
REACTION	*n* pl. **-S** the act of reacting	**REALIA**	*n/pl* objects used by a teacher to illustrate everyday living
REACTIVE	*adj* tending to react		
REACTOR	*n* pl. **-S** one that reacts	**REALISE**	*v* **-ISED, -ISING, -ISES** to realize
READ	*v* **READ, READING, READS** to look at so as to take in the meaning of, as something written or printed **READABLE** *adj* **READABLY** *adv*	**REALISER**	*n* pl. **-S** one that realises
		REALISM	*n* pl. **-S** concern with fact or reality
		REALIST	*n* pl. **-S** one who is concerned with fact or reality
READER	*n* pl. **-S** one that reads	**REALITY**	*n* pl. **-TIES** something that is real
READERLY	*adj* typical of a reader	**REALIZE**	*v* **-IZED, -IZING, -IZES** to understand completely
READIED	past tense of ready		
READIER	comparative of ready	**REALIZER**	*n* pl. **-S** one that realizes
READIES	present 3d person sing. of ready	**REALLY**	*adv* actually
READIEST	superlative of ready	**REALM**	*n* pl. **-S** a kingdom
READILY	*adv* in a ready manner	**REALNESS**	*n* pl. **-ES** the state of being real
READING	*n* pl. **-S** material that is read	**REALTY**	*n* pl. **-TIES** property in buildings and land
READOUT	*n* pl. **-S** a presentation of computer data	**REAM**	*v* **-ED, -ING, -S** to enlarge with a reamer

Following is a list of self-explanatory verbs containing the prefix RE- (again):

REABSORB	*v* **-ED, -ING, -S**	**READOPT**	*v* **-ED, -ING, -S**	**REARM**	*v* **-ED, -ING, -S**
REACCEDE	*v* **-CEDED, -CEDING, -CEDES**	**READORN**	*v* **-ED, -ING, -S**	**REAROUSE**	*v* **-AROUSED, -AROUSING, -AROUSES**
		REAFFIRM	*v* **-ED, -ING, -S**		
		REAFFIX	*v* **-ED, -ING, -ES**		
REACCENT	*v* **-ED, -ING, -S**	**REALIGN**	*v* **-ED, -ING, -S**	**REARREST**	*v* **-ED, -ING, -S**
REACCEPT	*v* **-ED, -ING, -S**	**REALLOT**	*v* **-LOTTED, -LOTTING, -LOTS**	**REASCEND**	*v* **-ED, -ING, -S**
REACCUSE	*v* **-CUSED, -CUSING, -CUSES**			**REASSAIL**	*v* **-ED, -ING, -S**
		REALTER	*v* **-ED, -ING, -S**	**REASSERT**	*v* **-ED, -ING, -S**
		REANNEX	*v* **-ED, -ING, -ES**	**REASSESS**	*v* **-ED, -ING, -ES**
READAPT	*v* **-ED, -ING, -S**	**REANOINT**	*v* **-ED, -ING, -S**	**REASSIGN**	*v* **-ED, -ING, -S**
READD	*v* **-ED, -ING, -S**	**REAPPEAR**	*v* **-ED, -ING, -S**	**REASSORT**	*v* **-ED, -ING, -S**
READDICT	*v* **-ED, -ING, -S**	**REAPPLY**	*v* **-PLIED, -PLYING, -PLIES**	**REASSUME**	*v* **-SUMED, -SUMING, -SUMES**
READJUST	*v* **-ED, -ING, -S**				
READMIT	*v* **-MITTED, -MITTING, -MITS**	**REARGUE**	*v* **-GUED, -GUING, -GUES**		

REAMER	*n* pl. **-S** a tool used to enlarge holes	**REBATO**	*n* pl. **-TOS** rabato
		REBBE	*n* pl. **-S** a rabbi
REAP	*v* **-ED, -ING, -S** to cut for harvest **REAPABLE** *adj*	**REBEC**	*n* pl. **-S** an ancient stringed instrument
REAPER	*n* pl. **-S** one that reaps	**REBECK**	*n* pl. **-S** rebec
REAPHOOK	*n* pl. **-S** an implement used in reaping	**REBEL**	*v* **-BELLED, -BELLING, -BELS** to oppose the established government of one's land
REAR	*v* **-ED, -ING, -S** to lift upright		
REARER	*n* pl. **-S** one that rears	**REBELDOM**	*n* pl. **-S** an area controlled by rebels
REARING	*n* pl. **-S** the act of an animal standing on its rear limbs	**REBIRTH**	*n* pl. **-S** a new or second birth
REARMICE	*n/pl* reremice	**REBOANT**	*adj* resounding loudly
REARMOST	*adj* coming or situated last	**REBOP**	*n* pl. **-S** a type of music
REARWARD	*n* pl. **-S** the rearmost division of an army	**REBORN**	*adj* born again
		REBOUND	*v* **-ED, -ING, -S** to spring back
REASCENT	*n* pl. **-S** a new or second ascent	**REBOZO**	*n* pl. **-ZOS** a long scarf
REASON	*v* **-ED, -ING, -S** to derive inferences or conclusions from known or presumed facts	**REBRANCH**	*v* **-ED, -ING, -ES** to form secondary branches
		REBRAND	*v* **-ED, -ING, -S** to change the corporate image of a company
REASONER	*n* pl. **-S** one that reasons		
REATA	*n* pl. **-S** riata	**REBUFF**	*v* **-ED, -ING, -S** to reject or refuse curtly
REAVE	*v* **REAVED** or **REFT, REAVING, REAVES** to plunder	**REBUKE**	*v* **-BUKED, -BUKING, -BUKES** to criticize sharply
REAVER	*n* pl. **-S** one that reaves		
REB	*n* pl. **-S** a Confederate soldier	**REBUKER**	*n* pl. **-S** one that rebukes
REBAR	*n* pl. **-S** a steel rod for use in reinforced concrete	**REBURIAL**	*n* pl. **-S** a second burial
		REBUS	*n* pl. **-ES** a type of puzzle
REBASE	*v* **-BASED, -BASING, -BASES** to set a new foundation for something	**REBUT**	*v* **-BUTTED, -BUTTING, -BUTS** to refute
REBATE	*v* **-BATED, -BATING, -BATES** to deduct or return from a payment or bill	**REBUTTAL**	*n* pl. **-S** argument or proof that rebuts
		REBUTTER	*n* pl. **-S** one that rebuts
REBATER	*n* pl. **-S** one that rebates	**REBUTTING**	present participle of rebut

---

List of self-explanatory verbs containing the prefix RE- (continued):

REASSURE	*v* **-SURED, -SURING, -SURES**	**REBID**	*v* **-BID, -BIDDEN, -BIDDING, -BIDS**	**REBORE**	*v* **-BORED, -BORING, -BORES**
		REBILL	*v* **-ED, -ING, -S**		
REATTACH	*v* **-ED, -ING, -ES**	**REBIND**	*v* **-BOUND, -BINDING, -BINDS**	**REBOTTLE**	*v* **-TLED, -TLING, -TLES**
REATTACK	*v* **-ED, -ING, -S**				
REATTAIN	*v* **-ED, -ING, -S**			**REBOUGHT**	past tense of rebuy
REAVAIL	*v* **-ED, -ING, -S**	**REBLEND**	*v* **-BLENDED** or **-BLENT, -BLENDING, -BLENDS**		
REAVOW	*v* **-ED, -ING, -S**			**REBOUND**	past tense of rebind
REAWAKE	*v* **-AWAKED** or **-AWOKE, -AWOKEN, -AWAKING, -AWAKES**	**REBLOOM**	*v* **-ED, -ING, -S**		
		REBOARD	*v* **-ED, -ING, -S**	**REBREED**	*v* **-BRED, -BREEDING, -BREEDS**
		REBODY	*v* **-BODIED, -BODYING, -BODIES**		
REAWAKEN	*v* **-ED, -ING, -S**			**REBUILD**	*v* **-BUILT** or **-BUILDED, -BUILDING, -BUILDS**
REBAIT	*v* **-ED, -ING, -S**	**REBOIL**	*v* **-ED, -ING, -S**		
REBEGIN	*v* **-GAN, -GUN, -GINNING, -GINS**	**REBOOK**	*v* **-ED, -ING, -S**		
		REBOOT	*v* **-ED, -ING, -S**		

REC	*n* pl. **-S** recreation	**RECIT**	*n* pl. **-S** the part of a story in which the events are related without enhancement
RECALL	*v* **-ED, -ING, -S** to call back		
RECALLER	*n* pl. **-S** one that recalls	**RECITAL**	*n* pl. **-S** a detailed account
RECAMIER	*n* pl. **-S** a backless couch	**RECITE**	*v* **-CITED, -CITING, -CITES** to declaim or say from memory
RECANT	*v* **-ED, -ING, -S** to make a formal retraction or disavowal of	**RECITER**	*n* pl. **-S** one that recites
RECANTER	*n* pl. **-S** one that recants	**RECK**	*v* **-ED, -ING, -S** to be concerned about
RECAP	*v* **-CAPPED, -CAPPING, -CAPS** to review by a brief summary	**RECKLESS**	*adj* foolishly heedless of danger
RECCE	*v* **RECCED, RECCEING, RECCES** to reconnoiter	**RECKON**	*v* **-ED, -ING, -S** to count or compute
RECEDE	*v* **-CEDED, -CEDING, -CEDES** to move back or away	**RECKONER**	*n* pl. **-S** one that reckons
		RECLAIM	*v* **-ED, -ING, -S** to make suitable for cultivation or habitation
RECEIPT	*v* **-ED, -ING, -S** to mark as having been paid	**RECLAME**	*n* pl. **-S** publicity
RECEIVE	*v* **-CEIVED, -CEIVING, -CEIVES** to come into possession of	**RECLINE**	*v* **-CLINED, -CLINING, -CLINES** to lean or lie back
RECEIVER	*n* pl. **-S** one that receives	**RECLINER**	*n* pl. **-S** one that reclines
RECENCY	*n* pl. **-CIES** the state of being recent	**RECLUSE**	*n* pl. **-S** one who lives in solitude and seclusion
RECENT	*adj* **-CENTER, -CENTEST** of or pertaining to a time not long past **RECENTLY** *adv*	**RECOIL**	*v* **-ED, -ING, -S** to draw back in fear or disgust
		RECOILER	*n* pl. **-S** one that recoils
RECEPT	*n* pl. **-S** a type of mental image	**RECON**	*v* **-CONNED, -CONNING, -CONS** to reconnoiter
RECEPTOR	*n* pl. **-S** a nerve ending specialized to receive stimuli	**RECONVEY**	*v* **-ED, -ING, -S** to convey back to a previous position
RECESS	*v* **-ED, -ING, -ES** to place in a receding space or hollow	**RECORD**	*v* **-ED, -ING, -S** to set down for preservation
RECHEAT	*n* pl. **-S** a hunting call	**RECORDER**	*n* pl. **-S** one that records
RECIPE	*n* pl. **-S** a set of instructions for making something	**RECOUNT**	*v* **-ED, -ING, -S** to relate in detail
		RECOUP	*v* **-ED, -ING, -S** to get back the equivalent of
RECISION	*n* pl. **-S** a cancellation		

List of self-explanatory verbs containing the prefix RE- (continued):

REBURY	*v* **-BURIED, -BURYING, -BURIES**	**RECHANGE**	*v* **-CHANGED, -CHANGING, -CHANGES**	**RECLASP**	*v* **-ED, -ING, -S**
				RECLEAN	*v* **-ED, -ING, -S**
				RECLOTHE	*v* **-CLOTHED** or
REBUTTON	*v* **-ED, -ING, -S**	**RECHARGE**	*v* **-CHARGED, -CHARGING, -CHARGES**		**-CLAD, -CLOTHING, -CLOTHES**
REBUY	*v* **-BOUGHT, -BUYING, -BUYS**				
		RECHART	*v* **-ED, -ING, -S**	**RECOAL**	*v* **-ED, -ING, -S**
RECANE	*v* **-CANED, -CANING, -CANES**	**RECHECK**	*v* **-ED, -ING, -S**	**RECOAT**	*v* **-ED, -ING, -S**
		RECHEW	*v* **-ED, -ING, -S**	**RECOCK**	*v* **-ED, -ING, -S**
		RECHOOSE	*v* **-CHOSE, -CHOSEN, -CHOOSING, -CHOOSES**	**RECODE**	*v* **-CODED, -CODING, -CODES**
RECARPET	*v* **-ED, -ING, -S**				
RECARRY	*v* **-RIED, -RYING, -RIES**			**RECODIFY**	*v* **-FIED, -FYING, -FIES**
RECAST	*v* **-CAST, -CASTING, -CASTS**	**RECIRCLE**	*v* **-CLED, -CLING, -CLES**		
		RECLAD	*v* **-CLADDED, -CLADDING, -CLADS**	**RECOIN**	*v* **-ED, -ING, -S**
				RECOLOR	*v* **-ED, -ING, -S**
RECEMENT	*v* **-ED, -ING, -S**			**RECOLOUR**	*v* **-ED, -ING, -S**
RECENSOR	*v* **-ED, -ING, -S**			**RECOMB**	*v* **-ED, -ING, -S**

RECOUPE	*adj* divided twice
RECOURSE	*n* pl. **-S** a turning or applying to someone or something for aid
RECOVER	*v* **-ED, -ING, -S** to obtain again after losing
RECOVERY	*n* pl. **-ERIES** an economic upturn
RECREANT	*n* pl. **-S** a coward
RECREATE	*v* **-ATED, -ATING, -ATES** to refresh mentally or physically
RECRUIT	*v* **-ED, -ING, -S** to engage for military service
RECTA	a pl. of rectum
RECTAL	*adj* pertaining to the rectum **RECTALLY** *adv*
RECTI	pl. of rectus
RECTIFY	*v* **-FIED, -FYING, -FIES** to correct
RECTO	*n* pl. **-TOS** a right-hand page of a book
RECTOR	*n* pl. **-S** a clergyman in charge of a parish
RECTORY	*n* pl. **-RIES** a rector's dwelling
RECTRIX	*n* pl. **-TRICES** a feather of a bird's tail
RECTUM	*n* pl. **-TUMS** or **-TA** the terminal portion of the large intestine
RECTUS	*n* pl. **-TI** a straight muscle
RECUR	*v* **-CURRED, -CURRING, -CURS** to happen again
RECURVE	*v* **-CURVED, -CURVING, -CURVES** to curve backward or downward
RECUSAL	*n* pl. **-S** the act of recusing
RECUSANT	*n* pl. **-S** one who refuses to accept established authority
RECUSE	*v* **-CUSED, -CUSING, -CUSES** to disqualify or challenge as judge in a particular case
RECYCLE	*v* **-CLED, -CLING, -CLES** to process in order to extract useful materials
RECYCLER	*n* pl. **-S** one that recycles
RED	*adj* **REDDER, REDDEST** of the color of blood
RED	*v* **REDDED, REDDING, REDS** to redd
REDACT	*v* **-ED, -ING, -S** to prepare for publication
REDACTOR	*n* pl. **-S** one that redacts
REDAN	*n* pl. **-S** a type of fortification
REDARGUE	*v* **-GUED, -GUING, -GUES** to disprove
REDBAIT	*v* **-ED, -ING, -S** to denounce as Communist
REDBAY	*n* pl. **-BAYS** a small tree
REDBIRD	*n* pl. **-S** a bird with red plumage
REDBONE	*n* pl. **-S** a hunting dog
REDBRICK	*n* pl. **-S** a modern British university
REDBUD	*n* pl. **-S** a small tree
REDBUG	*n* pl. **-S** a chigger
REDCAP	*n* pl. **-S** a porter
REDCOAT	*n* pl. **-S** a British soldier during the American Revolution
REDD	*v* **-ED, -ING, -S** to put in order
REDDED	past tense of red and redd
REDDEN	*v* **-ED, -ING, -S** to make or become red
REDDER	*n* pl. **-S** one that redds

List of self-explanatory verbs containing the prefix RE- (continued):

RECOMMIT	*v* **-MITTED, -MITTING, -MITS**	**REDAMAGE**	*v* **-AGED, -AGING, -AGES**	**REDIAL**	*v* **-DIALED, -DIALING, -DIALS** or **-DIALLED, -DIALLING, -DIALS**
RECONFER	*v* **-FERRED, -FERRING, -FERS**	**REDATE**	*v* **-DATED, -DATING, -DATES**		
RECOOK	*v* **-ED, -ING, -S**	**REDECIDE**	*v* **-CIDED, -CIDING, -CIDES**		
RECOPY	*v* **-COPIED, -COPYING, -COPIES**			**REDID**	past tense of redo
		REDEFEAT	*v* **-ED, -ING, -S**	**REDIGEST**	*v* **-ED, -ING, -S**
		REDEFECT	*v* **-ED, -ING, -S**	**REDIP**	*v* **-DIPPED** or **-DIPT, -DIPPING, -DIPS**
RECORK	*v* **-ED, -ING, -S**	**REDEFINE**	*v* **-FINED, -FINING, -FINES**		
RECOUPLE	*v* **-PLED, -PLING, -PLES**			**REDIVIDE**	*v* **-VIDED, -VIDING, -VIDES**
RECRATE	*v* **-CRATED, -CRATING, -CRATES**	**REDEFY**	*v* **-FIED, -FYING, -FIES**	**REDO**	*v* **-DID, -DONE, -DOING, -DOES**
		REDEMAND	*v* **-ED, -ING, -S**		
RECROSS	*v* **-ED, -ING, -ES**	**REDENY**	*v* **-NIED, -NYING, -NIES**	**REDOCK**	*v* **-ED, -ING, -S**
RECROWN	*v* **-ED, -ING, -S**			**REDON**	*v* **-DONNED, -DONNING, -DONS**
RECUT	*v* **-CUT, -CUTTING, -CUTS**	**REDEPLOY**	*v* **-ED, -ING, -S**		
		REDESIGN	*v* **-ED, -ING, -S**		

REDDEST	superlative of red
REDDIER	comparative of reddy
REDDIEST	superlative of reddy
REDDING	present participle of red and redd
REDDISH	*adj* somewhat red
REDDLE	*v* **-DLED, -DLING, -DLES** to ruddle
REDDY	*adj* **REDDIER, REDDIEST** reddish
REDE	*v* **REDED, REDING, REDES** to advise
REDEAR	*n* pl. **-S** a common sunfish
REDEEM	*v* **-ED, -ING, -S** to buy back
REDEEMER	*n* pl. **-S** one that redeems
REDEYE	*n* pl. **-S** a railroad danger signal
REDFIN	*n* pl. **-S** a freshwater fish
REDFISH	*n* pl. **-ES** an edible rockfish
REDHEAD	*n* pl. **-S** a person with red hair
REDHORSE	*n* pl. **-S** a freshwater fish
REDIA	*n* pl. **-DIAS** or **-DIAE** the larva of certain flatworms **REDIAL** *adj*
REDING	present participle of rede
REDIRECT	*v* **-ED, -ING, -S** to change the course or direction of
REDLEG	*n* pl. **-S** a bird with red legs
REDLINE	*v* **-LINED, -LINING, -LINES** to withhold loans or insurance from certain neighborhoods
REDLINER	*n* pl. **-S** one that redlines
REDLY	*adv* with red color
REDNESS	*n* pl. **-ES** the state of being red
REDO	*n* pl. **-DOS** something that is done again
REDOLENT	*adj* fragrant
REDOUBLE	*v* **-BLED, -BLING, -BLES** to double
REDOUBT	*n* pl. **-S** an enclosed fortification
REDOUND	*v* **-ED, -ING, -S** to have an effect
REDOUT	*n* pl. **-S** a condition in which blood is driven to the head
REDOWA	*n* pl. **-S** a lively dance
REDOX	*n* pl. **-ES** a type of chemical reaction
REDPOLL	*n* pl. **-S** a small finch
REDRAFT	*v* **-ED, -ING, -S** to make a revised copy of
REDRAWER	*n* pl. **-S** one that redraws
REDRESS	*v* **-ED, -ING, -ES** to set right
REDROOT	*n* pl. **-S** a perennial herb
REDSHANK	*n* pl. **-S** a shore bird
REDSHIFT	*n* pl. **-S** a displacement of the spectrum of a celestial body toward the longer wavelengths
REDSHIRT	*v* **-ED, -ING, -S** to keep a college athlete out of varsity play in order to extend his eligibility
REDSKIN	*n* pl. **-S** a variety of peanut
REDSTART	*n* pl. **-S** a small songbird
REDTAIL	*n* pl. **-S** a type of hawk
REDTOP	*n* pl. **-S** a type of grass
REDUCE	*v* **-DUCED, -DUCING, -DUCES** to diminish
REDUCER	*n* pl. **-S** one that reduces
REDUCTOR	*n* pl. **-S** an apparatus for the reduction of metallic ions in solution

List of self-explanatory verbs containing the prefix RE- (continued):

REDRAW	*v* **-DREW, -DRAWN, -DRAWING, -DRAWS**	**REDYE**	*v* **-DYED, -DYEING, -DYES**	**REENACT**	*v* **-ED, -ING, -S**
		REEARN	*v* **-ED, -ING, -S**	**REENDOW**	*v* **-ED, -ING, -S**
		REECHO	*v* **-ED, -ING, -ES**	**REENGAGE**	*v* **-GAGED, -GAGING, -GAGES**
REDREAM	*v* **-DREAMED** or **-DREAMT, -DREAMING, -DREAMS**	**REEDIT**	*v* **-ED, -ING, -S**		
		REEJECT	*v* **-ED, -ING, -S**	**REENJOY**	*v* **-ED, -ING, -S**
		REELECT	*v* **-ED, -ING, -S**	**REENLIST**	*v* **-ED, -ING, -S**
		REEMBARK	*v* **-ED, -ING, -S**	**REENROLL**	*v* **-ED, -ING, -S**
REDRILL	*v* **-ED, -ING, -S**	**REEMBODY**	*v* **-BODIED, -BODYING, -BODIES**	**REENTER**	*v* **-ED, -ING, -S**
REDRIVE	*v* **-DROVE, -DRIVEN, -DRIVING, -DRIVES**			**REEQUIP**	*v* **-EQUIPPED, -EQUIPPING, -EQUIPS**
		REEMERGE	*v* **-EMERGED, -EMERGING, -EMERGES**	**REERECT**	*v* **-ED, -ING, -S**
REDRY	*v* **-DRIED, -DRYING, -DRIES**			**REEVOKE**	*v* **-EVOKED, -EVOKING, -EVOKES**
		REEMIT	*v* **-EMITTED, -EMITTING, -EMITS**		
REDUB	*v* **-DUBBED, -DUBBING, -DUBS**			**REEXPEL**	*v* **-PELLED, -PELLING, -PELS**
		REEMPLOY	*v* **-ED, -ING, -S**		

REDUVIID	*n* pl. **-S** a bloodsucking insect
REDUX	*adj* brought back
REDWARE	*n* pl. **-S** an edible seaweed
REDWATER	*n* pl. **-S** a blood disease of cattle
REDWING	*n* pl. **-S** a European thrush
REDWOOD	*n* pl. **-S** a very tall evergreen tree
REE	*n* pl. **-S** the female Eurasian sandpiper
REEBOK	*n* pl. **-S** rhebok
REECHY	*adj* **REECHIER, REECHIEST** foul, rancid
REED	*v* **-ED, -ING, -S** to fasten with reeds (the stalks of tall grasses)
REEDBIRD	*n* pl. **-S** the bobolink
REEDBUCK	*n* pl. **-S** an African antelope
REEDIER	comparative of reedy
REEDIEST	superlative of reedy
REEDIFY	*v* **-FIED, -FYING, -FIES** to rebuild
REEDILY	*adv* with a thin, piping sound
REEDING	*n* pl. **-S** a convex molding
REEDLIKE	*adj* resembling a reed
REEDLING	*n* pl. **-S** a marsh bird
REEDMAN	*n* pl. **-MEN** one who plays a reed instrument
REEDY	*adj* **REEDIER, REEDIEST** abounding in reeds
REEF	*v* **-ED, -ING, -S** to reduce the area of a sail **REEFABLE** *adj*
REEFER	*n* pl. **-S** one that reefs
REEFY	*adj* **REEFIER, REEFIEST** abounding in ridges of rock
REEK	*v* **-ED, -ING, -S** to give off a strong, unpleasant odor
REEKER	*n* pl. **-S** one that reeks
REEKY	*adj* **REEKIER, REEKIEST** reeking
REEL	*v* **-ED, -ING, -S** to wind on a type of rotary device **REELABLE** *adj*
REELER	*n* pl. **-S** one that reels
REELING	*n* pl. **-S** sustained noise
REENTRY	*n* pl. **-TRIES** a new or second entry
REEST	*v* **-ED, -ING, -S** to balk
REEVE	*v* **REEVED** or **ROVE, ROVEN, REEVING, REEVES** to fasten by passing through or around something
REF	*v* **REFFED, REFFING, REFS** to referee
REFACE	*v* **-FACED, -FACING, -FACES** to repair the outer surface of
REFECT	*v* **-ED, -ING, -S** to refresh with food and drink
REFEL	*v* **-FELLED, -FELLING, -FELS** to reject
REFER	*v* **-FERRED, -FERRING, -FERS** to direct to a source for help or information
REFEREE	*v* **-EED, -EEING, -EES** to supervise the play in certain sports
REFERENT	*n* pl. **-S** something referred to
REFERRAL	*n* pl. **-S** one that is referred
REFERRED	past tense of refer
REFERRER	*n* pl. **-S** one that refers
REFERRING	present participle of refer
REFFED	past tense of ref

List of self-explanatory verbs containing the prefix RE- (continued):

REEXPORT	*v* **-ED, -ING, -S**	**REFENCE**	*v* **-FENCED, -FENCING, -FENCES**	**REFLEW**	past tense of refly
REEXPOSE	*v* **-POSED, -POSING, -POSES**	**REFIGHT**	*v* **-FOUGHT, -FIGHTING, -FIGHTS**	**REFLIES**	present 3d person sing. of refly
REFALL	*v* **-FELL, -FALLEN, -FALLING, -FALLS**	**REFIGURE**	*v* **-URED, -URING, -URES**	**REFLOAT**	*v* **-ED, -ING, -S**
				REFLOOD	*v* **-ED, -ING, -S**
				REFLOW	*v* **-ED, -ING, -S**
		REFILE	*v* **-FILED, -FILING, -FILES**	**REFLOWER**	*v* **-ED, -ING, -S**
REFASTEN	*v* **-ED, -ING, -S**	**REFILL**	*v* **-ED, -ING, -S**	**REFLY**	*v* **-FLEW, -FLOWN, -FLYING, -FLIES**
REFEED	*v* **-FED, -FEEDING, -FEEDS**	**REFILM**	*v* **-ED, -ING, -S**		
		REFILTER	*v* **-ED, -ING, -S**	**REFOCUS**	*v* **-CUSED, -CUSING, -CUSES** or **-CUSSED, -CUSSING, -CUSSES**
		REFIND	*v* **-FOUND, -FINDING, -FINDS**		
REFEEL	*v* **-FELT, -FEELING, -FEELS**	**REFIRE**	*v* **-FIRED, -FIRING, -FIRES**		
REFELL	past tense of refall	**REFIX**	*v* **-ED, -ING, -ES**	**REFOLD**	*v* **-ED, -ING, -S**

REFFING	*n* pl. **-S** the work of a referee
REFINE	*v* **-FINED, -FINING, -FINES** to free from impurities
REFINER	*n* pl. **-S** one that refines
REFINERY	*n* pl. **-ERIES** a place where crude material is refined
REFINING	*n* pl. **-S** the process of removing impurities from something
REFINISH	*v* **-ED, -ING, -ES** to give a new surface to
REFIT	*v* **-FITTED, -FITTING, -FITS** to prepare and equip for additional use
REFLAG	*v* **-FLAGGED, -FLAGGING, -FLAGS** to give a new registered nationality to (a ship)
REFLATE	*v* **-FLATED, -FLATING, -FLATES** to inflate again
REFLECT	*v* **-ED, -ING, -S** to turn or throw back from a surface
REFLET	*n* pl. **-S** special brilliance of surface
REFLEX	*v* **-ED, -ING, -ES** to bend back
REFLEXLY	*adv* in a reflexed manner
REFLUENT	*adj* flowing back
REFLUX	*v* **-ED, -ING, -ES** to cause to flow back
REFOREST	*v* **-ED, -ING, -S** to replant with trees
REFORM	*v* **-ED, -ING, -S** to change to a better state
REFORMER	*n* pl. **-S** one that reforms
REFRACT	*v* **-ED, -ING, -S** to deflect in a particular manner, as a ray of light
REFRAIN	*v* **-ED, -ING, -S** to keep oneself back
REFRESH	*v* **-ED, -ING, -ES** to restore the well-being and vigor of
REFT	a past tense of reave
REFUGE	*v* **-UGED, -UGING, -UGES** to give or take shelter
REFUGEE	*n* pl. **-S** one who flees for safety
REFUGIUM	*n* pl. **-GIA** a stable area during a period of continental climactic change
REFUND	*v* **-ED, -ING, -S** to give back
REFUNDER	*n* pl. **-S** one that refunds
REFUSAL	*n* pl. **-S** the act of refusing
REFUSE	*v* **-FUSED, -FUSING, -FUSES** to express oneself as unwilling to accept, do, or comply with
REFUSER	*n* pl. **-S** one that refuses
REFUSNIK	*n* pl. **-S** a Soviet citizen who was refused permission to emigrate
REFUTAL	*n* pl. **-S** the act of refuting
REFUTE	*v* **-FUTED, -FUTING, -FUTES** to prove to be false or erroneous
REFUTER	*n* pl. **-S** one that refutes
REG	*n* pl. **-S** a regulation
REGAINER	*n* pl. **-S** one that regains
REGAL	*adj* of or befitting a king
REGALE	*v* **-GALED, -GALING, -GALES** to delight
REGALER	*n* pl. **-S** one that regales
REGALIA	*n/pl* the rights and privileges of a king
REGALITY	*n* pl. **-TIES** regal authority

List of self-explanatory verbs containing the prefix RE- (continued):

REFORGE	*v* **-FORGED, -FORGING, -FORGES**	**REFUEL**	*v* **-ELED, -ELING, -ELS** or **-ELLED, -ELLING, -ELS**	**REGLOSS**	*v* **-ED, -ING, -ES**
				REGLOW	*v* **-ED, -ING, -S**
REFORMAT	*v* **-MATTED, -MATTING, -MATS**	**REGAIN**	*v* **-ED, -ING, -S**	**REGLUE**	*v* **-GLUED, -GLUING, -GLUES**
		REGATHER	*v* **-ED, -ING, -S**		
REFOUGHT	past tense of refight	**REGAUGE**	*v* **-GAUGED, -GAUGING, -GAUGES**	**REGRADE**	*v* **-GRADED, -GRADING, -GRADES**
REFOUND	*v* **-ED, -ING, -S**				
REFRAME	*v* **-FRAMED, -FRAMING, -FRAMES**	**REGEAR**	*v* **-ED, -ING, -S**	**REGRAFT**	*v* **-ED, -ING, -S**
		REGILD	*v* **-GILDED** or **-GILT, -GILDING, -GILDS**	**REGRANT**	*v* **-ED, -ING, -S**
				REGREEN	*v* **-ED, -ING, -S**
REFREEZE	*v* **-FROZE, -FROZEN, -FREEZING, -FREEZES**	**REGIVE**	*v* **-GAVE, -GIVEN, -GIVING, -GIVES**	**REGREW**	past tense of regrow
				REGRIND	*v* **-GROUND, -GRINDING, -GRINDS**
REFRONT	*v* **-ED, -ING, -S**	**REGLAZE**	*v* **-GLAZED, -GLAZING, -GLAZES**		
REFRY	*v* **-FRIED, -FRYING, -FRIES**			**REGROOM**	*v* **-ED, -ING, -S**

REGALLY	*adv* in a regal manner	**REGLET**	*n* pl. **-S** a flat, narrow molding
REGARD	*v* **-ED, -ING, -S** to look upon with a particular feeling	**REGMA**	*n* pl. **-MATA** a type of fruit
		REGNA	pl. of regnum
REGATTA	*n* pl. **-S** a boat race	**REGNAL**	*adj* pertaining to a king or his reign
REGELATE	*v* **-LATED, -LATING, -LATES** to refreeze ice by reducing the pressure	**REGNANCY**	*n* pl. **-CIES** the state of being regnant
		REGNANT	*adj* reigning
REGENCY	*n* pl. **-CIES** the office of a regent	**REGNUM**	*n* pl. **-NA** dominion
REGENT	*n* pl. **-S** one who rules in the place of a sovereign **REGENTAL** *adj*	**REGOLITH**	*n* pl. **-S** a layer of loose rock
		REGORGE	*v* **-GORGED, -GORGING, -GORGES** to vomit
REGES	pl. of rex		
REGGAE	*n* pl. **-S** a form of popular Jamaican music	**REGOSOL**	*n* pl. **-S** a type of soil
		REGRATE	*v* **-GRATED, -GRATING, -GRATES** to buy up in order to sell for a higher price in the same area
REGICIDE	*n* pl. **-S** the killing of a king		
REGIE	*n* pl. **-S** a government regulatory body in Quebec		
		REGREET	*v* **-ED, -ING, -S** to greet in return
REGIFT	*v* **-ED, -ING, -S** to give a gift one has received to someone else	**REGRESS**	*v* **-ED, -ING, -ES** to go back
		REGRET	*v* **-GRETTED, -GRETTING, -GRETS** to look back upon with sorrow or remorse
REGIFTER	*n* pl. **-S** one that regifts		
REGIME	*n* pl. **-S** a system of government		
REGIMEN	*n* pl. **-S** a systematic plan	**REGROWTH**	*n* pl. **-S** a new or second growth
REGIMENT	*v* **-ED, -ING, -S** to form into military units	**REGULAR**	*n* pl. **-S** a habitual customer
		REGULATE	*v* **-LATED, -LATING, -LATES** to control according to rule
REGINA	*n* pl. **-NAS** or **-NAE** queen **REGINAL** *adj*		
		REGULUS	*n* pl. **-LUSES** or **-LI** a mass that forms beneath the slag in a furnace **REGULINE** *adj*
REGION	*n* pl. **-S** an administrative area or division		
REGIONAL	*n* pl. **-S** something that serves as a region	**REHAB**	*v* **-HABBED, -HABBING, -HABS** to restore to a good condition
REGISTER	*v* **-ED, -ING, -S** to record officially	**REHABBER**	*n* pl. **-S** one that rehabs
REGISTRY	*n* pl. **-TRIES** the act of registering	**REHEARSE**	*v* **-HEARSED, -HEARSING, -HEARSES** to practice in preparation for a public appearance
REGIUS	*adj* holding a professorship founded by the sovereign		

List of self-explanatory verbs containing the prefix RE- (continued):

REGROOVE	*v* **-GROOVED, -GROOVING, -GROOVES**	**REHASH**	*v* **-ED, -ING, -ES**	**REIMAGE**	*v* **-AGED, -AGING, -AGES**
		REHEAR	*v* **-HEARD, -HEARING, -HEARS**	**REIMPORT**	*v* **-ED, -ING, -S**
REGROUND	past tense of regrind			**REIMPOSE**	*v* **-POSED, -POSING, -POSES**
		REHEAT	*v* **-ED, -ING, -S**		
REGROUP	*v* **-ED, -ING, -S**	**REHEEL**	*v* **-ED, -ING, -S**		
REGROW	*v* **-GREW, -GROWN, -GROWING, -GROWS**	**REHEM**	*v* **-HEMMED, -HEMMING, -HEMS**	**REINCITE**	*v* **-CITED, -CITING, -CITES**
				REINCUR	*v* **-CURRED, -CURRING, -CURS**
		REHINGE	*v* **-HINGED, -HINGING, -HINGES**		
REHAMMER	*v* **-ED, -ING, -S**			**REINDEX**	*v* **-ED, -ING, -ES**
REHANDLE	*v* **-DLED, -DLING, -DLES**	**REHIRE**	*v* **-HIRED, -HIRING, -HIRES**	**REINDICT**	*v* **-ED, -ING, -S**
				REINDUCE	*v* **-DUCED, -DUCING, -DUCES**
REHANG	*v* **-HUNG** or **-HANGED, -HANGING, -HANGS**	**REHUNG**	a past tense of rehang		
		REIGNITE	*v* **-NITED, -NITING, -NITES**	**REINDUCT**	*v* **-ED, -ING, -S**
REHARDEN	*v* **-ED, -ING, -S**			**REINFECT**	*v* **-ED, -ING, -S**

REHEATER	*n* pl. **-S** one that reheats	**REJECTER**	*n* pl. **-S** one that rejects
REHOBOAM	*n* pl. **-S** a wine bottle	**REJECTOR**	*n* pl. **-S** rejecter
REHOUSE	*v* **-HOUSED, -HOUSING, -HOUSES** to establish in a new housing unit	**REJIG**	*v* **-JIGGED, -JIGGING, -JIGS** to rejigger
REI	*n* pl. **-S** an erroneous English form for a former Portuguese coin	**REJIGGER**	*v* **-ED, -ING, -S** to alter
		REJOICE	*v* **-JOICED, -JOICING, -JOICES** to feel joyful
REIF	*n* pl. **-S** robbery	**REJOICER**	*n* pl. **-S** one that rejoices
REIFIER	*n* pl. **-S** one that reifies	**RELAPSE**	*v* **-LAPSED, -LAPSING, -LAPSES** to fall or slip back into a former state
REIFY	*v* **-IFIED, -IFYING, -IFIES** to regard as real or concrete		
REIGN	*v* **-ED, -ING, -S** to exercise sovereign power	**RELAPSER**	*n* pl. **-S** one that relapses
REIKI	*n* pl. **-S** a healing technique involving touching with the hands	**RELATE**	*v* **-LATED, -LATING, -LATES** to give an account of
REIN	*v* **-ED, -ING, -S** to restrain	**RELATER**	*n* pl. **-S** one that relates
REINDEER	*n* pl. **-S** a large deer	**RELATION**	*n* pl. **-S** a significant association between two or more things
REINJURY	*n* pl. **-RIES** a second injury		
REINLESS	*adj* unrestrained	**RELATIVE**	*n* pl. **-S** one who is connected with another by blood or marriage
REINSMAN	*n* pl. **-MEN** a skilled rider of horses	**RELATOR**	*n* pl. **-S** relater
REIS	pl. of real	**RELAX**	*v* **-ED, -ING, -ES** to make less tense or rigid
REISHI	*n* pl. **-S** a mushroom having a shiny cap		
REISSUER	*n* pl. **-S** one that reissues	**RELAXANT**	*n* pl. **-S** a drug that relieves muscular tension
REITBOK	*n* pl. **-S** the reedbuck	**RELAXER**	*n* pl. **-S** one that relaxes
REIVE	*v* **REIVED, REIVING, REIVES** to plunder	**RELAXIN**	*n* pl. **-S** a female hormone
		RELAY	*v* **-ED, -ING, -S** to send along by using fresh sets to replace tired ones
REIVER	*n* pl. **-S** one that reives		
REIVING	*n* pl. **-S** an act or instance of plundering		
REJECT	*v* **-ED, -ING, -S** to refuse to accept, consider, or make use of	**RELEASE**	*v* **-LEASED, -LEASING, -LEASES** to set free
		RELEASEE	*n* pl. **-S** one that is released
REJECTEE	*n* pl. **-S** one that is rejected	**RELEASER**	*n* pl. **-S** one that releases

---

List of self-explanatory verbs containing the prefix RE- (continued):

REINFORM	*v* **-ED, -ING, -S**	**REINVITE**	*v* **-VITED, -VITING, -VITES**	**REKNIT**	*v* **-KNITTED, -KNITTING, -KNITS**
REINFUSE	*v* **-FUSED, -FUSING, -FUSES**	**REINVOKE**	*v* **-VOKED, -VOKING, -VOKES**	**REKNOT**	*v* **-KNOTTED, -KNOTTING, -KNOTS**
REINJECT	*v* **-ED, -ING, -S**				
REINJURE	*v* **-JURED, -JURING, -JURES**	**REISSUE**	*v* **-SUED, -SUING, -SUES**	**RELABEL**	*v* **-BELED, -BELING, -BELS**
REINK	*v* **-ED, -ING, -S**	**REJACKET**	*v* **-ED, -ING, -S**		or **-BELLED,**
REINSERT	*v* **-ED, -ING, -S**	**REJOIN**	*v* **-ED, -ING, -S**		**-BELLING,**
REINSURE	*v* **-SURED, -SURING, -SURES**	**REJUDGE**	*v* **-JUDGED, -JUDGING, -JUDGES**		**-BELS**
				RELACE	*v* **-LACED, -LACING, -LACES**
REINTER	*v* **-TERRED, -TERRING, -TERS**	**REJUGGLE**	*v* **-GLED, -GLING, -GLES**	**RELAND**	*v* **-ED, -ING, -S**
REINVADE	*v* **-VADED, -VADING, -VADES**	**REKEY**	*v* **-ED, -ING, -S**	**RELAUNCH**	*v* **-ED, -ING, -ES**
REINVENT	*v* **-ED, -ING, -S**	**REKINDLE**	*v* **-DLED, -DLING, -DLES**	**RELAY**	*v* **-LAID, -LAYING, -LAYS**
REINVEST	*v* **-ED, -ING, -S**				

RELEASOR	*n* pl. **-S** releaser	**RELIVE**	*v* **-LIVED, -LIVING, -LIVES** to experience again
RELEGATE	*v* **-GATED, -GATING, -GATES** to assign	**RELLENO**	*n* pl. **-S** a Mexican dish of a stuffed and fried green chile
RELENT	*v* **-ED, -ING, -S** to become less severe	**RELOADER**	*n* pl. **-S** one that reloads
RELEVANT	*adj* pertaining to the matter at hand	**RELOCATE**	*v* **-CATED, -CATING, -CATES** to establish in a new place
RELEVE	*n* pl. **-S** a raising onto the toe in ballet	**RELUCENT**	*adj* reflecting light
RELIABLE	*n* pl. **-S** one that can be relied on	**RELUCT**	*v* **-ED, -ING, -S** to show opposition
RELIABLY	*adv* in a manner that can be relied on	**RELUME**	*v* **-LUMED, -LUMING, -LUMES** to light again
RELIANCE	*n* pl. **-S** confident or trustful dependence	**RELUMINE**	*v* **-MINED, -MINING, -MINES** to relume
RELIANT	*adj* showing reliance	**RELY**	*v* **-LIED, -LYING, -LIES** to place trust or confidence
RELIC	*n* pl. **-S** a surviving memorial of something past	**REM**	*n* pl. **-S** a quantity of ionizing radiation
RELICT	*n* pl. **-S** an organism surviving in a changed environment	**REMAILER**	*n* pl. **-S** an Internet service that forwards email anonymously
RELIED	past tense of rely	**REMAIN**	*v* **-ED, -ING, -S** to continue in the same state
RELIEF	*n* pl. **-S** aid in the form of money or necessities	**REMAKER**	*n* pl. **-S** one that remakes
RELIER	*n* pl. **-S** one that relies	**REMAN**	*v* **-MANNED, -MANNING, -MANS** to furnish with a fresh supply of men
RELIES	present 3d person sing. of rely		
RELIEVE	*v* **-LIEVED, -LIEVING, -LIEVES** to lessen or free from pain or discomfort	**REMAND**	*v* **-ED, -ING, -S** to send back
		REMANENT	*adj* remaining
RELIEVER	*n* pl. **-S** one that relieves	**REMANNED**	past tense of reman
RELIEVO	*n* pl. **-VOS** the projection of figures or forms from a flat background	**REMANNING**	present participle of reman
		REMARK	*v* **-ED, -ING, -S** to say or write briefly or casually
RELIGION	*n* pl. **-S** the worship of a god or the supernatural	**REMARKER**	*n* pl. **-S** one that remarks
RELIQUE	*n* pl. **-S** relic	**REMARQUE**	*n* pl. **-S** a mark made in the margin of an engraved plate
RELISH	*v* **-ED, -ING, -ES** to enjoy		

List of self-explanatory verbs containing the prefix RE- (continued):

RELEARN	*v* **-LEARNED** or **-LEARNT, -LEARNING, -LEARNS**	**RELIT**	a past tense of relight	**REMATE**	*v* **-MATED, -MATING, -MATES**
		RELOAD	*v* **-ED, -ING, -S**	**REMEET**	*v* **-MET, -MEETING, -MEETS**
RELEND	*v* **-LENT, -LENDING, -LENDS**	**RELOAN**	*v* **-ED, -ING, -S**		
		RELOCK	*v* **-ED, -ING, -S**	**REMELT**	*v* **-ED, -ING, -S**
		RELOOK	*v* **-ED, -ING, -S**	**REMEND**	*v* **-ED, -ING, -S**
RELET	*v* **-LET, -LETTING, -LETS**	**REMAIL**	*v* **-ED, -ING, -S**	**REMERGE**	*v* **-MERGED, -MERGING, -MERGES**
		REMAKE	*v* **-MADE, -MAKING, -MAKES**		
RELETTER	*v* **-ED, -ING, -S**			**REMET**	past tense of remeet
RELIGHT	*v* **-LIGHTED** or **-LIT, -LIGHTING, -LIGHTS**	**REMAP**	*v* **-MAPPED, -MAPPING, -MAPS**	**REMIX**	*v* **-MIXED** or **-MIXT, -MIXING, -MIXES**
		REMARKET	*v* **-ED, -ING, -S**		
RELINE	*v* **-LINED, -LINING, -LINES**	**REMARRY**	*v* **-RIED, -RYING, -RIES**	**REMODIFY**	*v* **-FIED, -FYING, -FIES**
RELINK	*v* **-ED, -ING, -S**	**REMASTER**	*v* **-ED, -ING, -S**		
RELIST	*v* **-ED, -ING, -S**	**REMATCH**	*v* **-ED, -ING, -ES**	**REMOLD**	*v* **-ED, -ING, -S**

REMEDIAL *adj* intended to correct something

REMEDY *v* **-DIED, -DYING, -DIES** to relieve or cure

REMEMBER *v* **-ED, -ING, -S** to bring to mind again

REMEX *n* pl. **REMIGES** a flight feather of a bird's wing **REMIGIAL** *adj*

REMIND *v* **-ED, -ING, -S** to cause to remember

REMINDER *n* pl. **-S** one that reminds

REMINT *v* **-ED, -ING, -S** to melt down and make into new coin

REMISE *v* **-MISED, -MISING, -MISES** to give up a claim to

REMISS *adj* careless **REMISSLY** *adv*

REMIT *v* **-MITTED, -MITTING, -MITS** to send money in payment

REMITTAL *n* pl. **-S** the act of remitting

REMITTER *n* pl. **-S** one that remits

REMITTOR *n* pl. **-S** remitter

REMIXER *n* pl. **-S** one that remixes (as a recording)

REMNANT *n* pl. **-S** something remaining

REMODEL *v* **-ELED, -ELING, -ELS** or **-ELLED, -ELLING, -ELS** to make over

REMOLADE *n* pl. **-S** a piquant sauce

REMORA *n* pl. **-S** a type of marine fish **REMORID** *adj*

REMORSE *n* pl. **-S** deep anguish caused by a sense of guilt

REMOTE *adj* **-MOTER, -MOTEST** situated far away **REMOTELY** *adv*

REMOTE *n* pl. **-S** a broadcast originating outside a studio

REMOTION *n* pl. **-S** the act of removing

REMOVAL *n* pl. **-S** the act of removing

REMOVE *v* **-MOVED, -MOVING, -MOVES** to take or move away

REMOVER *n* pl. **-S** one that removes

REMUDA *n* pl. **-S** a herd of horses

RENAL *adj* pertaining to the kidneys

RENATURE *v* **-TURED, -TURING, -TURES** to restore natural qualities

REND *v* **RENT** or **RENDED, RENDING, RENDS** to tear apart forcibly

RENDER *v* **-ED, -ING, -S** to cause to be or become

RENDERER *n* pl. **-S** one that renders

RENDIBLE *adj* capable of being rent

RENDZINA *n* pl. **-S** a type of soil

RENEGADE *v* **-GADED, -GADING, -GADES** to become a traitor

RENEGADO *n* pl. **-DOS** or **-DOES** a traitor

RENEGE *v* **-NEGED, -NEGING, -NEGES** to fail to carry out a promise or commitment

RENEGER *n* pl. **-S** one that reneges

RENEGUE *v* **-NEGUED, -NEGUING, -NEGUES** to renege

RENEW *v* **-ED, -ING, -S** to make new or as if new again

RENEWAL *n* pl. **-S** the act of renewing

RENEWER *n* pl. **-S** one that renews

RENIFORM *adj* kidney-shaped

List of self-explanatory verbs containing the prefix RE- (continued):

REMOULD	*v* **-ED, -ING, -S**	**REOIL**	*v* **-ED, -ING, -S**	**REPARK**	*v* **-ED, -ING, -S**
REMOUNT	*v* **-ED, -ING, -S**	**REOPEN**	*v* **-ED, -ING, -S**	**REPASS**	*v* **-ED, -ING, -ES**
RENAIL	*v* **-ED, -ING, -S**	**REOPPOSE**	*v* **-POSED,**	**REPATCH**	*v* **-ED, -ING, -ES**
RENAME	*v* **-NAMED,**		**-POSING,**	**REPAVE**	*v* **-PAVED,**
	-NAMING,		**-POSES**		**-PAVING,**
	-NAMES	**REORDAIN**	*v* **-ED, -ING, -S**		**-PAVES**
RENEST	*v* **-ED, -ING, -S**	**REORDER**	*v* **-ED, -ING, -S**	**REPEG**	*v* **-PEGGED,**
RENOTIFY	*v* **-FIED, -FYING,**	**REORIENT**	*v* **-ED, -ING, -S**		**-PEGGING,**
	-FIES	**REOUTFIT**	*v* **-FITTED,**		**-PEGS**
RENUMBER	*v* **-ED, -ING, -S**		**-FITTING, -FITS**	**REPEOPLE**	*v* **-PLED, -PLING,**
REOBJECT	*v* **-ED, -ING, -S**	**REPACIFY**	*v* **-FIED, -FYING,**		**-PLES**
REOBTAIN	*v* **-ED, -ING, -S**		**-FIES**	**REPERK**	*v* **-ED, -ING, -S**
REOCCUPY	*v* **-PIED, -PYING,**	**REPACK**	*v* **-ED, -ING, -S**	**REPHRASE**	*v* **-PHRASED,**
	-PIES	**REPAINT**	*v* **-ED, -ING, -S**		**-PHRASING,**
REOCCUR	*v* **-CURRED,**	**REPANEL**	*v* **-ELED, -ELING,**		**-PHRASES**
	-CURRING,		**-ELS** or **-ELLED,**	**REPIN**	*v* **-PINNED,**
	-CURS		**-ELLING, -ELS**		**-PINNING,**
REOFFEND	*v* **-ED, -ING, -S**	**REPAPER**	*v* **-ED, -ING, -S**		**-PINS**

RENIG	v **-NIGGED, -NIGGING, -NIGS** to renege	**REP**	v **REPPED, REPPING, REPS** to represent
RENIN	n pl. **-S** an enzyme	**REPAID**	past tense of repay
RENITENT	adj resisting physical pressure	**REPAIR**	v **-ED, -ING, -S** to restore to good condition
RENMINBI	n pl. **RENMINBI** currency in the People's Republic of China	**REPAIRER**	n pl. **-S** one that repairs
RENNASE	n pl. **-S** rennin	**REPAND**	adj having a wavy margin **REPANDLY** adv
RENNET	n pl. **-S** a lining membrane in the stomach of certain young animals	**REPARTEE**	n pl. **-S** a quick, witty reply
RENNIN	n pl. **-S** an enzyme	**REPAST**	v **-ED, -ING, -S** to eat or feast
RENO	n pl. **RENOS** a renovated house	**REPAY**	v **-PAID, -PAYING, -PAYS** to pay back
RENOGRAM	n pl. **-S** a photographic depiction of the course of renal excretion	**REPEAL**	v **-ED, -ING, -S** to revoke
RENOUNCE	v **-NOUNCED, -NOUNCING, -NOUNCES** to disown	**REPEALER**	n pl. **-S** one that repeals
		REPEAT	v **-ED, -ING, -S** to say or do again
RENOVATE	v **-VATED, -VATING, -VATES** to make like new	**REPEATER**	n pl. **-S** one that repeats
RENOWN	v **-ED, -ING, -S** to make famous	**REPEL**	v **-PELLED, -PELLING, -PELS** to drive back
RENT	v **-ED, -ING, -S** to obtain temporary use of in return for compensation **RENTABLE** adj	**REPELLER**	n pl. **-S** one that repels
		REPENT	v **-ED, -ING, -S** to feel remorse or self-reproach for a past action
RENTAL	n pl. **-S** an amount paid or collected as rent	**REPENTER**	n pl. **-S** one that repents
RENTE	n pl. **-S** annual income under French law	**REPETEND**	n pl. **-S** a phrase or sound that is repeated
RENTER	n pl. **-S** one that rents	**REPINE**	v **-PINED, -PINING, -PINES** to express discontent
RENTIER	n pl. **-S** one that receives a fixed income	**REPINER**	n pl. **-S** one that repines
RENVOI	n pl. **-S** the expulsion by a government of an alien	**REPLACE**	v **-PLACED, -PLACING, -PLACES** to take the place of
REOFFER	v **-ED, -ING, -S** to offer for public sale	**REPLACER**	n pl. **-S** one that replaces
		REPLETE	n pl. **-S** a worker ant that serves as a living storehouse for liquid food
REORG	v **-ED, -ING, -S** to reorganize		
REOVIRUS	n pl. **-ES** a type of virus	**REPLEVIN**	v **-ED, -ING, -S** to replevy

---

List of self-explanatory verbs containing the prefix RE- (continued):

REPLAN	v **-PLANNED, -PLANNING, -PLANS**	**REPLOW**	v **-ED, -ING, -S**	**REPROBE**	v **-PROBED, -PROBING, -PROBES**
REPLANT	v **-ED, -ING, -S**	**REPLUMB**	v **-ED, -ING, -S**		
REPLATE	v **-PLATED, -PLATING, -PLATES**	**REPLUNGE**	v **-PLUNGED, -PLUNGING, -PLUNGES**	**REPUMP**	v **-ED, -ING, -S**
				REPURIFY	v **-FIED, -FYING, -FIES**
REPLAY	v **-ED, -ING, -S**	**REPOINT**	v **-ED, -ING, -S**	**REPURSUE**	v **-SUED, -SUING, -SUES**
REPLEAD	v **-PLEADED** or **-PLED, -PLEADING, -PLEADS**	**REPOLISH**	v **-ED, -ING, -ES**	**RERACK**	v **-ED, -ING, -S**
		REPOLL	v **-ED, -ING, -S**	**RERAISE**	v **-RAISED, -RAISING, -RAISES**
		REPOT	v **-POTTED, -POTTING, -POTS**		
REPLEDGE	v **-PLEDGED, -PLEDGING, -PLEDGES**	**REPOUR**	v **-ED, -ING, -S**	**REREAD**	v **-READ, -READING, -READS**
		REPOWER	v **-ED, -ING, -S**		
REPLOT	v **-PLOTTED, -PLOTTING, -PLOTS**	**REPRICE**	v **-PRICED, -PRICING, -PRICES**	**RERECORD**	v **-ED, -ING, -S**
				REREMIND	v **-ED, -ING, -S**
		REPRINT	v **-ED, -ING, -S**	**RERENT**	v **-ED, -ING, -S**

REPLEVY	*v* **-PLEVIED, -PLEVYING, -PLEVIES** to regain possession of by legal action
REPLICA	*n* pl. **-S** a close copy or reproduction
REPLICON	*n* pl. **-S** a section of nucleic acid that replicates as a unit
REPLIER	*n* pl. **-S** one that replies
REPLY	*v* **-PLIED, -PLYING, -PLIES** to answer
REPO	*n* pl. **-POS** something repossessed
REPORT	*v* **-ED, -ING, -S** to give an account of
REPORTER	*n* pl. **-S** one that reports
REPOSAL	*n* pl. **-S** the act of reposing
REPOSE	*v* **-POSED, -POSING, -POSES** to lie at rest
REPOSER	*n* pl. **-S** one that reposes
REPOSIT	*v* **-ED, -ING, -S** to put away
REPOUSSE	*n* pl. **-S** a raised design hammered in metal
REPP	*n* pl. **-S** a cross-ribbed fabric
REPPED	*adj* resembling repp
REPRESS	*v* **-ED, -ING, -ES** to keep under control
REPRIEVE	*v* **-PRIEVED, -PRIEVING, -PRIEVES** to postpone the punishment of
REPRISAL	*n* pl. **-S** an act of retaliation
REPRISE	*v* **-PRISED, -PRISING, -PRISES** to take back by force
REPRO	*n* pl. **-PROS** a trial sheet of printed material suitable for photographic reproduction
REPROACH	*v* **-ED, -ING, -ES** to find fault with
REPROOF	*n* pl. **-S** criticism for a fault
REPROVAL	*n* pl. **-S** reproof
REPROVE	*v* **-PROVED, -PROVING, -PROVES** to rebuke
REPROVER	*n* pl. **-S** one that reproves
REPTANT	*adj* creeping or crawling
REPTILE	*n* pl. **-S** any of a class of cold-blooded, air-breathing vertebrates
REPTILIA	*n/pl* buildings for housing reptiles
REPUBLIC	*n* pl. **-S** a constitutional form of government
REPUGN	*v* **-ED, -ING, -S** to oppose
REPULSE	*v* **-PULSED, -PULSING, -PULSES** to drive back
REPULSER	*n* pl. **-S** one that repulses
REPUTE	*v* **-PUTED, -PUTING, -PUTES** to consider to be as specified
REQUEST	*v* **-ED, -ING, -S** to express a desire for
REQUIEM	*n* pl. **-S** a musical composition for the dead
REQUIN	*n* pl. **-S** a voracious shark
REQUINTO	*n* pl. **-TOS** a small guitar
REQUIRE	*v* **-QUIRED, -QUIRING, -QUIRES** to have need of
REQUIRER	*n* pl. **-S** one that requires
REQUITAL	*n* pl. **-S** something given in return, compensation, or retaliation
REQUITE	*v* **-QUITED, -QUITING, -QUITES** to make equivalent return for
REQUITER	*n* pl. **-S** one that requites
RERAN	past tense of rerun

List of self-explanatory verbs containing the prefix RE- (continued):

REREPEAT	*v* **-ED, -ING, -S**	**RESALUTE**	*v* **-LUTED, -LUTING, -LUTES**	**RESECURE**	*v* **-CURED, -CURING, -CURES**
REREVIEW	*v* **-ED, -ING, -S**				
RERIG	*v* **-RIGGED, -RIGGING, -RIGS**	**RESAMPLE**	*v* **-PLED, -PLING, -PLES**	**RESEE**	*v* **-SAW, -SEEN, -SEEING, -SEES**
		RESAT	past tense of resit		
RERISE	*v* **-ROSE, -RISEN, -RISING, -RISES**	**RESAW**	*v* **-SAWED, -SAWN, -SAWING, -SAWS**	**RESEED**	*v* **-ED, -ING, -S**
				RESEEK	*v* **-SOUGHT, -SEEKING, -SEEKS**
REROLL	*v* **-ED, -ING, -S**	**RESAY**	*v* **-SAID, -SAYING, -SAYS**		
REROOF	*v* **-ED, -ING, -S**				
REROSE	past tense of rerise	**RESCHOOL**	*v* **-ED, -ING, -S**	**RESEEN**	past participle of resee
		RESCORE	*v* **-SCORED, -SCORING, -SCORES**		
REROUTE	*v* **-ROUTED, -ROUTING, -ROUTES**			**RESEIZE**	*v* **-SEIZED, -SEIZING, -SEIZES**
		RESCREEN	*v* **-ED, -ING, -S**		
RESADDLE	*v* **-DLED, -DLING, -DLES**	**RESCULPT**	*v* **-ED, -ING, -S**	**RESELECT**	*v* **-ED, -ING, -S**
		RESEAL	*v* **-ED, -ING, -S**	**RESELL**	*v* **-SOLD, -SELLING, -SELLS**
RESAID	past tense of resay	**RESEASON**	*v* **-ED, -ING, -S**		
RESAIL	*v* **-ED, -ING, -S**	**RESEAT**	*v* **-ED, -ING, -S**		

REREDOS	*n* pl. **-ES** an ornamental screen behind an altar	**RESERVER**	*n* pl. **-S** one that reserves
REREMICE	*n/pl* bats (flying mammals)	**RESES**	pl. of res
REREWARD	*n* pl. **-S** rearward	**RESETTER**	*n* pl. **-S** one that resets
REROLLER	*n* pl. **-S** one that rerolls	**RESH**	*n* pl. **-ES** a Hebrew letter
RERUN	*v* **-RAN, -RUNNING, -RUNS** to present a repetition of a recorded performance	**RESHAPER**	*n* pl. **-S** one that reshapes something
		RESID	*n* pl. **-S** a type of fuel oil
RES	*n* pl. **RESES** a university or college residence	**RESIDE**	*v* **-SIDED, -SIDING, -SIDES** to dwell permanently or continuously
RESALE	*n* pl. **-S** the act of selling again	**RESIDENT**	*n* pl. **-S** one who resides
RESCALE	*v* **-SCALED, -SCALING, -SCALES** to plan on a new scale	**RESIDER**	*n* pl. **-S** a resident
		RESIDUAL	*n* pl. **-S** something left over
RESCIND	*v* **-ED, -ING, -S** to annul	**RESIDUE**	*n* pl. **-S** something remaining after the removal of a part
RESCRIPT	*n* pl. **-S** something rewritten		
RESCUE	*v* **-CUED, -CUING, -CUES** to free from danger	**RESIDUUM**	*n* pl. **-SIDUUMS** or **-SIDUA** residue
		RESIGN	*v* **-ED, -ING, -S** to give up one's office or position
RESCUEE	*n* pl. **-S** one that is rescued		
RESCUER	*n* pl. **-S** one that rescues	**RESIGNER**	*n* pl. **-S** one that resigns
RESEARCH	*v* **-ED, -ING, -ES** to investigate thoroughly	**RESILE**	*v* **-SILED, -SILING, -SILES** to spring back
RESEAU	*n* pl. **-SEAUS** or **-SEAUX** a filter screen for making color films	**RESILIN**	*n* pl. **-S** an elastic substance in the cuticles of many insects
RESECT	*v* **-ED, -ING, -S** to excise part of an organ or structure surgically	**RESIN**	*v* **-ED, -ING, -S** to treat with resin (a viscous substance obtained from certain plants)
RESEDA	*n* pl. **-S** a flowering plant		
RESELLER	*n* pl. **-S** one that resells	**RESINATE**	*v* **-ATED, -ATING, -ATES** to resin
RESEMBLE	*v* **-BLED, -BLING, -BLES** to be similar to	**RESINIFY**	*v* **-FIED, -FYING, -FIES** to convert into resin
RESENT	*v* **-ED, -ING, -S** to feel or express annoyance or ill will at	**RESINOID**	*n* pl. **-S** a resinous substance
		RESINOUS	*adj* resembling resin
RESERVE	*v* **-SERVED, -SERVING, -SERVES** to keep back for future use	**RESINY**	*adj* resinous
		RESIST	*v* **-ED, -ING, -S** to strive against

List of self-explanatory verbs containing the prefix RE- (continued):

RESEND	*v* **-SENT, -SENDING, -SENDS**	**RESHINE**	*v* **-SHINED** or **-SHONE, -SHINING, -SHINES**	**RESHOW**	*v* **-SHOWED, -SHOWN, -SHOWING, -SHOWS**
RESET	*v* **-SET, -SETTING, -SETS**			**RESHOWER**	*v* **-ED, -ING, -S**
RESETTLE	*v* **-TLED, -TLING, -TLES**	**RESHIP**	*v* **-SHIPPED, -SHIPPING, -SHIPS**	**RESIFT**	*v* **-ED, -ING, -S**
				RESIGHT	*v* **-ED, -ING, -S**
RESEW	*v* **-SEWED, -SEWN, -SEWING, -SEWS**	**RESHOE**	*v* **-SHOD** or **-SHOED, -SHOEING, -SHOES**	**RESILVER**	*v* **-ED, -ING, -S**
				RESIT	*v* **-SAT, -SITTING, -SITS**
RESHAPE	*v* **-SHAPED, -SHAPING, -SHAPES**	**RESHONE**	a past tense of reshine	**RESITE**	*v* **-SITED, -SITING, -SITES**
RESHAVE	*v* **-SHAVED, -SHAVEN, -SHAVING, -SHAVES**	**RESHOOT**	*v* **-SHOT, -SHOOTING, -SHOOTS**	**RESIZE**	*v* **-SIZED, -SIZING, -SIZES**
				RESKETCH	*v* **-ED, -ING, -ES**
				RESLATE	*v* **-SLATED, -SLATING, -SLATES**

RESISTER	*n* pl. **-S** one that resists	**RESPOND**	*v* **-ED, -ING, -S** to say or act in return
RESISTOR	*n* pl. **-S** a device in an electric circuit	**RESPONSA**	*n/pl* written rabbinic decisions
RESKIN	*v* **-SKINNED, -SKINNING, -SKINS** to replace the outermost layer of an aircraft or motor vehicle	**RESPONSE**	*n* pl. **-S** a reply or reaction
		REST	*v* **-ED, -ING, -S** to refresh oneself by ceasing work or activity
RESOJET	*n* pl. **-S** a pulsejet	**RESTER**	*n* pl. **-S** one that rests
RESOLUTE	*adj* **-LUTER, -LUTEST** characterized by firmness or determination	**RESTFUL**	*adj* **-FULLER, -FULLEST** tranquil
		RESTIVE	*adj* difficult to control
RESOLUTE	*n* pl. **-S** one who is resolute	**RESTLESS**	*adj* unable or disinclined to remain at rest
RESOLVE	*v* **-SOLVED, -SOLVING, -SOLVES** to make a firm decision about	**RESTORAL**	*n* pl. **-S** the act of restoring
RESOLVER	*n* pl. **-S** one that resolves	**RESTORE**	*v* **-STORED, -STORING, -STORES** to bring back to a former or original condition
RESONANT	*n* pl. **-S** a resounding sound		
RESONATE	*v* **-NATED, -NATING, -NATES** to resound	**RESTORER**	*n* pl. **-S** one that restores
RESORB	*v* **-ED, -ING, -S** to absorb again	**RESTRAIN**	*v* **-ED, -ING, -S** to hold back from action
RESORCIN	*n* pl. **-S** a chemical compound	**RESTRICT**	*v* **-ED, -ING, -S** to keep within certain boundaries
RESORT	*v* **-ED, -ING, -S** to go frequently or habitually	**RESTROOM**	*n* pl. **-S** a room furnished with toilets and sinks
RESORTER	*n* pl. **-S** one that resorts	**RESULT**	*v* **-ED, -ING, -S** to occur as a consequence
RESOUND	*v* **-ED, -ING, -S** to make a loud, long, or echoing sound	**RESUME**	*v* **-SUMED, -SUMING, -SUMES** to take up again after interruption
RESOURCE	*v* **-SOURCED, -SOURCING, -SOURCES** to provide with supplies	**RESUMER**	*n* pl. **-S** one that resumes
		RESUPINE	*adj* lying on the back
RESPECT	*v* **-ED, -ING, -S** to have a high regard for	**RESURGE**	*v* **-SURGED, -SURGING, -SURGES** to rise again
RESPIRE	*v* **-SPIRED, -SPIRING, -SPIRES** to breathe	**RET**	*v* **RETTED, RETTING, RETS** to soak in order to loosen the fiber from the woody tissue
RESPITE	*v* **-SPITED, -SPITING, -SPITES** to relieve temporarily		

List of self-explanatory verbs containing the prefix RE- (continued):

RESMELT	*v* **-ED, -ING, -S**	**RESPACE**	*v* **-SPACED, -SPACING, -SPACES**	**RESPLIT**	*v* **-SPLIT, -SPLITTING, -SPLITS**
RESMOOTH	*v* **-ED, -ING, -S**				
RESOAK	*v* **-ED, -ING, -S**				
RESOD	*v* **-SODDED, -SODDING, -SODS**	**RESPADE**	*v* **-SPADED, -SPADING, -SPADES**	**RESPOKE**	past tense of respeak
				RESPOKEN	past participle of respeak
RESOFTEN	*v* **-ED, -ING, -S**	**RESPEAK**	*v* **-SPOKE, -SPOKEN, -SPEAKING, -SPEAKS**		
RESOLD	past tense of resell			**RESPOOL**	*v* **-ED, -ING, -S**
RESOLDER	*v* **-ED, -ING, -S**			**RESPOT**	*v* **-SPOTTED, -SPOTTING, -SPOTS**
RESOLE	*v* **-SOLED, -SOLING, -SOLES**	**RESPELL**	*v* **-SPELLED** or **-SPELT, -SPELLING, -SPELLS**		
RESOUGHT	past tense of reseek			**RESPRANG**	a past tense of respring
RESOW	*v* **-SOWED, -SOWN, -SOWING, -SOWS**	**RESPLICE**	*v* **-SPLICED, -SPLICING, -SPLICES**	**RESPRAY**	*v* **-ED, -ING, -S**
				RESPREAD	*v* **-SPREAD, -SPREADING, -SPREADS**

RETABLE	*n* pl. **-S** a raised shelf above an altar	**RETIFORM**	*adj* arranged like a net
RETABLO	*n* pl. **-BLOS** a retable	**RETINA**	*n* pl. **-NAS** or **-NAE** a membrane of the eye
RETAIL	*v* **-ED, -ING, -S** to sell in small quantities	**RETINAL**	*n* pl. **-S** retinene
RETAILER	*n* pl. **-S** one that retails	**RETINE**	*n* pl. **-S** a substance in cells that retards growth and cell division
RETAIN	*v* **-ED, -ING, -S** to keep possession of	**RETINENE**	*n* pl. **-S** a pigment in the retina
RETAINER	*n* pl. **-S** one that retains	**RETINITE**	*n* pl. **-S** a fossil resin
RETAKE	*v* **-TOOK, -TAKEN, -TAKING, -TAKES** to take back	**RETINOID**	*n* pl. **-S** a compound analogous to vitamin A
RETAKER	*n* pl. **-S** one that retakes	**RETINOL**	*n* pl. **-S** a liquid hydrocarbon
RETARD	*v* **-ED, -ING, -S** to slow the progress of	**RETINUE**	*n* pl. **-S** a group of attendants **RETINUED** *adj*
RETARDER	*n* pl. **-S** one that retards	**RETINULA**	*n* pl. **-LAS** or **-LAE** a neural receptor of an arthropod's eye
RETCH	*v* **-ED, -ING, -ES** to make an effort to vomit	**RETIRANT**	*n* pl. **-S** a retiree
RETCHING	*n* pl. **-S** an effort to vomit	**RETIRE**	*v* **-TIRED, -TIRING, -TIRES** to go away or withdraw
RETE	*n* pl. **-TIA** an anatomical mesh or network	**RETIREE**	*n* pl. **-S** one who has retired from his vocation
RETELLER	*n* pl. **-S** one who tells something again	**RETIRER**	*n* pl. **-S** one that retires
RETEM	*n* pl. **-S** a desert shrub	**RETIRING**	*adj* shy
RETENE	*n* pl. **-S** a chemical compound	**RETOOK**	past tense of retake
RETIAL	*adj* pertaining to a rete	**RETOOL**	*v* **-ED, -ING, -S** to reequip with tools
RETIARII	*n/pl* ancient Roman gladiators	**RETORT**	*v* **-ED, -ING, -S** to answer back sharply
RETIARY	*adj* resembling a net	**RETORTER**	*n* pl. **-S** one that retorts
RETICENT	*adj* tending to be silent	**RETOUCH**	*v* **-ED, -ING, -ES** to add new details or touches to
RETICLE	*n* pl. **-S** a network of lines in the eyepiece of an optical instrument	**RETRACE**	*v* **-TRACED, -TRACING, -TRACES** to go back over
RETICULA	*n/pl* netlike structures	**RETRACER**	*n* pl. **-S** one that retraces
RETICULE	*n* pl. **-S** a woman's handbag		

List of self-explanatory verbs containing the prefix RE- (continued):

RESPRING	*v* **-SPRANG** or **-SPRUNG, -SPRINGING, -SPRINGS**	**RESTOCK**	*v* **-ED, -ING, -S**	**RESTRUNG**	past tense of restring
		RESTOKE	*v* **-STOKED, -STOKING, -STOKES**	**RESTUDY**	*v* **-STUDIED, -STUDYING, -STUDIES**
RESPROUT	*v* **-ED, -ING, -S**				
RESTABLE	*v* **-BLED, -BLING, -BLES**	**RESTRESS**	*v* **-ED, -ING, -ES**	**RESTUFF**	*v* **-ED, -ING, -S**
		RESTRIKE	*v* **-STRUCK, -STRICKEN, -STRIKING, -STRIKES**	**RESTYLE**	*v* **-STYLED, -STYLING, -STYLES**
RESTACK	*v* **-ED, -ING, -S**				
RESTAFF	*v* **-ED, -ING, -S**				
RESTAGE	*v* **-STAGED, -STAGING, -STAGES**	**RESTRING**	*v* **-STRUNG, -STRINGING, -STRINGS**	**RESUBMIT**	*v* **-MITTED, -MITTING, -MITS**
				RESUMMON	*v* **-ED, -ING, -S**
RESTAMP	*v* **-ED, -ING, -S**	**RESTRIVE**	*v* **-STROVE, -STRIVEN, -STRIVING, -STRIVES**	**RESUPPLY**	*v* **-PLIED, -PLYING, -PLIES**
RESTART	*v* **-ED, -ING, -S**				
RESTATE	*v* **-STATED, -STATING, -STATES**			**RESURVEY**	*v* **-ED, -ING, -S**
		RESTRUCK	past tense of restrike	**RETACK**	*v* **-ED, -ING, -S**
RESTITCH	*v* **-ED, -ING, -ES**			**RETACKLE**	*v* **-LED, -LING, -LES**

RETRACT	*v* **-ED, -ING, -S** to take back
RETRAL	*adj* situated toward the back **RETRALLY** *adv*
RETREAD	*v* **-TROD** or **-TREADED, -TRODDEN, -TREADING, -TREADS** to furnish with a new tread
RETREAT	*v* **-ED, -ING, -S** to go back or backward
RETRENCH	*v* **-ED, -ING, -ES** to curtail
RETRIAL	*n* pl. **-S** a second trial
RETRIEVE	*v* **-TRIEVED, -TRIEVING, -TRIEVES** to get back
RETRO	*n* pl. **-ROS** a rocket on a spacecraft that produces thrust in a direction opposite to the line of flight
RETROACT	*v* **-ED, -ING, -S** to act in return
RETROD	a past tense of retread
RETROFIT	*v* **-FITTED, -FITTING, -FITS** to furnish with new parts not originally available
RETRONYM	*n* pl. **-S** a term coined to distinguish the original referent from a later development
RETRORSE	*adj* bent backward
RETSINA	*n* pl. **-S** a resin-flavored Greek wine
RETTED	past tense of ret
RETTING	present participle of ret
RETURN	*v* **-ED, -ING, -S** to come or go back
RETURNEE	*n* pl. **-S** one that has returned
RETURNER	*n* pl. **-S** one that returns
RETUSE	*adj* having a rounded apex with a shallow notch — used of leaves
REUNION	*n* pl. **-S** a reuniting of persons after separation
REUNITER	*n* pl. **-S** one that reunites
REUPTAKE	*n* pl. **-S** the reabsorption of a chemical into the cell that released it
REUSABLE	*n* pl. **-S** something that can be reused
REV	*v* **REVVED, REVVING, REVS** to increase the speed of
REVAMP	*v* **-ED, -ING, -S** to make over
REVAMPER	*n* pl. **-S** one that revamps
REVANCHE	*n* pl. **-S** a political policy designed to regain lost territory
REVEAL	*v* **-ED, -ING, -S** to make known
REVEALER	*n* pl. **-S** one that reveals
REVEHENT	*adj* carrying back
REVEILLE	*n* pl. **-S** a morning bugle call
REVEL	*v* **-ELED, -ELING, -ELS** or **-ELLED, -ELLING, -ELS** to engage in revelry
REVELER	*n* pl. **-S** one that revels
REVELLER	*n* pl. **-S** reveler
REVELRY	*n* pl. **-RIES** noisy merrymaking
REVENANT	*n* pl. **-S** one that returns
REVENGE	*v* **-VENGED, -VENGING, -VENGES** to inflict injury in return for
REVENGER	*n* pl. **-S** one that revenges
REVENUE	*n* pl. **-S** the income of a government **REVENUAL, REVENUED** *adj*
REVENUER	*n* pl. **-S** a revenue officer

List of self-explanatory verbs containing the prefix RE- (continued):

RETAG	*v* **-TAGGED, -TAGGING, -TAGS**	**RETEAR**	*v* **-TORE, -TORN, -TEARING, -TEARS**	**RETINT**	*v* **-ED, -ING, -S**
				RETITLE	*v* **-TLED, -TLING, -TLES**
RETAILOR	*v* **-ED, -ING, -S**	**RETELL**	*v* **-TOLD, -TELLING, -TELLS**	**RETOLD**	past tense of retell
RETALLY	*v* **-LIED, -LYING, -LIES**			**RETORE**	past tense of retear
RETAPE	*v* **-TAPED, -TAPING, -TAPES**	**RETEMPER**	*v* **-ED, -ING, -S**	**RETORN**	past participle of retear
		RETEST	*v* **-ED, -ING, -S**		
RETARGET	*v* **-ED, -ING, -S**	**RETHINK**	*v* **-THOUGHT, -THINKING, -THINKS**	**RETOTAL**	*v* **-TALED, -TALING, -TALS** or **-TALLED, -TALLING, -TALS**
RETASTE	*v* **-TASTED, -TASTING, -TASTES**	**RETHREAD**	*v* **-ED, -ING, -S**		
		RETIE	*v* **-TIED, -TYING** or **-TIEING, -TIES**	**RETRACK**	*v* **-ED, -ING, -S**
RETAX	*v* **-ED, -ING, -ES**	**RETILE**	*v* **-TILED, -TILING, -TILES**	**RETRAIN**	*v* **-ED, -ING, -S**
RETEACH	*v* **-TAUGHT, -TEACHING, -TEACHES**	**RETIME**	*v* **-TIMED, -TIMING, -TIMES**	**RETRIM**	*v* **-TRIMMED, -TRIMMING, -TRIMS**
RETEAM	*v* **-ED, -ING, -S**				

REVERB	v **-ED, -ING, -S** to continue in a series of echoes	**REVISE**	v **-VISED, -VISING, -VISES** to make a new or improved version of
REVERE	v **-VERED, -VERING, -VERES** to regard with great respect	**REVISER**	n pl. **-S** one that revises
		REVISION	n pl. **-S** a revised version
REVEREND	n pl. **-S** a clergyman	**REVISOR**	n pl. **-S** reviser
REVERENT	adj deeply respectful	**REVISORY**	adj pertaining to revision
REVERER	n pl. **-S** one that reveres	**REVIVAL**	n pl. **-S** renewed attention to or interest in something
REVERIE	n pl. **-S** a daydream		
REVERIES	pl. of revery	**REVIVE**	v **-VIVED, -VIVING, -VIVES** to bring back to life or consciousness
REVERING	present participle of revere		
REVERS	n pl. **REVERS** a part of a garment turned back to show the inside	**REVIVER**	n pl. **-S** one that revives
		REVIVIFY	v **-FIED, -FYING, -FIES** to give new life to
REVERSAL	n pl. **-S** the act of reversing		
REVERSE	v **-VERSED, -VERSING, -VERSES** to turn or move in the opposite direction	**REVOKE**	v **-VOKED, -VOKING, -VOKES** to annul by taking back
		REVOKER	n pl. **-S** one that revokes
REVERSER	n pl. **-S** one that reverses	**REVOLT**	v **-ED, -ING, -S** to rise up against authority
REVERSO	n pl. **-VERSOS** verso		
REVERT	v **-ED, -ING, -S** to return to a former state	**REVOLTER**	n pl. **-S** one that revolts
		REVOLUTE	adj rolled backward or downward
REVERTER	n pl. **-S** one that reverts	**REVOLVE**	v **-VOLVED, -VOLVING, -VOLVES** to turn about an axis
REVERY	n pl. **-ERIES** reverie		
REVET	v **-VETTED, -VETTING, -VETS** to face with masonry	**REVOLVER**	n pl. **-S** a type of handgun
		REVUE	n pl. **-S** a type of musical show
REVIEWAL	n pl. **-S** the act of reviewing	**REVUIST**	n pl. **-S** a writer of revues
REVIEWER	n pl. **-S** one that reviews	**REVULSED**	adj affected with revulsion
REVILE	v **-VILED, -VILING, -VILES** to denounce with abusive language	**REVVED**	past tense of rev
		REVVING	present participle of rev
REVILER	n pl. **-S** one that reviles	**REWARD**	v **-ED, -ING, -S** to give recompense to for worthy behavior
REVILING	n pl. **-S** the act of denouncing with abusive language		
		REWARDER	n pl. **-S** one that rewards
REVISAL	n pl. **-S** a revision	**REWINDER**	n pl. **-S** one that rewinds

---

List of self-explanatory verbs containing the prefix RE- (continued):

RETRY	v **-TRIED, -TRYING, -TRIES**	**REVALUE**	v **-UED, -UING, -UES**	**REWAN**	a past tense of rewin
RETUNE	v **-TUNED, -TUNING, -TUNES**	**REVERIFY**	v **-FIED, -FYING, -FIES**	**REWARM**	v **-ED, -ING, -S**
				REWASH	v **-ED, -ING, -ES**
RETWIST	v **-ED, -ING, -S**	**REVEST**	v **-ED, -ING, -S**	**REWAX**	v **-ED, -ING, -ES**
RETYING	present participle of retie	**REVIEW**	v **-ED, -ING, -S**	**REWEAR**	v **-WORE, -WORN, -WEARING, -WEARS**
		REVISIT	v **-ED, -ING, -S**		
RETYPE	v **-TYPED, -TYPING, -TYPES**	**REVOICE**	v **-VOICED, -VOICING, -VOICES**	**REWEAVE**	v **-WOVE** or **-WEAVED, -WOVEN, -WEAVING, -WEAVES**
REUNIFY	v **-FIED, -FYING, -FIES**				
		REVOTE	v **-VOTED, -VOTING, -VOTES**		
REUNITE	v **-UNITED, -UNITING, -UNITES**	**REWAKE**	v **-WAKED** or **-WOKE, -WOKEN, -WAKING, -WAKES**	**REWED**	v **-WEDDED, -WEDDING, -WEDS**
REUSE	v **-USED, -USING, -USES**			**REWEIGH**	v **-ED, -ING, -S**
REUTTER	v **-ED, -ING, -S**	**REWAKEN**	v **-ED, -ING, -S**	**REWELD**	v **-ED, -ING, -S**

REWORD	v **-ED, -ING, -S** to state again in other words		**RHEOPHIL**	adj living in flowing water
REWRITER	n pl. **-S** one that rewrites		**RHEOSTAT**	n pl. **-S** a resistor used to control electric current
REX	n pl. **-ES** an animal with a single wavy layer of hair		**RHESUS**	n pl. **-ES** an Asian monkey
REX	n pl. **REGES** king		**RHETOR**	n pl. **-S** a teacher of rhetoric
REYNARD	n pl. **-S** a fox		**RHETORIC**	n pl. **-S** the study of effective speech and writing
REZ	n pl. **REZES** or **REZZES** an area of land set aside for Native Americans		**RHEUM**	n pl. **-S** a watery discharge from the eyes or nose **RHEUMIC** adj
REZERO	v **-ED, -ING, -ES** or **-S** to reset (a gauge) back to zero		**RHEUMY**	adj **RHEUMIER, RHEUMIEST** marked by rheum
RHABDOM	n pl. **-S** a rodlike structure in the retinula		**RHINAL**	adj pertaining to the nose
RHABDOME	n pl. **-S** rhabdom		**RHINITIS**	n pl. **RHINITIDES** inflammation of the mucous membranes of the nose
RHACHIS	n pl. **-CHISES** or **-CHIDES** rachis		**RHINO**	n pl. **-NOS** a rhinoceros
RHAMNOSE	n pl. **-S** a sugar found in plants		**RHIZOBIA**	n/pl rod-shaped bacteria
RHAMNUS	n pl. **-ES** a thorny tree or shrub		**RHIZOID**	n pl. **-S** a rootlike structure
RHAPHE	n pl. **-PHES** or **-PHAE** raphe		**RHIZOMA**	n pl. **-MATA** rhizome
RHAPSODE	n pl. **-S** a reciter of epic poetry in ancient Greece		**RHIZOME**	n pl. **-S** a rootlike, underground stem **RHIZOMIC** adj
RHAPSODY	n pl. **-DIES** an exalted expression of feeling		**RHIZOPOD**	n pl. **-S** any of a class of protozoans
RHATANY	n pl. **-NIES** a South American shrub		**RHIZOPUS**	n pl. **-PUSES** or **-PI** any of a genus of mold fungi
RHEA	n pl. **-S** a flightless bird		**RHO**	n pl. **RHOS** a Greek letter
RHEBOK	n pl. **-S** a large antelope		**RHODAMIN**	n pl. **-S** a red dye
RHEMATIC	adj pertaining to a verb		**RHODIUM**	n pl. **-S** a metallic element **RHODIC** adj
RHEME	n pl. **-S** a statement of fact or opinion		**RHODORA**	n pl. **-S** a flowering shrub
RHENIUM	n pl. **-S** a metallic element		**RHOMB**	n pl. **-S** a rhombus
RHEOBASE	n pl. **-S** the smallest amount of electricity required to stimulate a nerve		**RHOMBIC**	adj having the shape of a rhombus
			RHOMBOID	n pl. **-S** a type of geometric figure
RHEOLOGY	n pl. **-GIES** the study of matter in the fluid state		**RHOMBUS**	n pl. **-BUSES** or **-BI** a type of geometric figure

---

List of self-explanatory verbs containing the prefix RE- (continued):

REWET	v **-WETTED, -WETTING, -WETS**	**REWON**	a past tense of rewin	**REWRAP**	v **-WRAPPED** or **-WRAPT, -WRAPPING, -WRAPS**
REWIDEN	v **-ED, -ING, -S**	**REWORE**	past tense of rewear		
REWIN	v **-WON** or **-WAN, -WINNING, -WINS**	**REWORK**	v **-WORKED** or **-WROUGHT, -WORKING, -WORKS**	**REWRITE**	v **-WROTE, -WRITTEN, -WRITING, -WRITES**
REWIND	v **-WOUND** or **-WINDED, -WINDING, -WINDS**	**REWORN**	past participle of rewear		
REWIRE	v **-WIRED, -WIRING, -WIRES**	**REWOUND**	a past tense of rewind	**REWROUGHT**	a past tense of rework
REWOKE	a past tense of rewake	**REWOVE**	a past tense of reweave	**REZONE**	v **-ZONED, -ZONING, -ZONES**
REWOKEN	past participle of rewake	**REWOVEN**	past participle of reweave		

RHONCHUS *n pl.* **-CHI** a rattling respiratory sound **RHONCHAL** *adj*

RHOTIC *adj* pertaining to a dialect of English in which the letter r at the end of a syllable is pronounced

RHUBARB *n pl.* **-S** a perennial herb

RHUMB *n pl.* **-S** a point of the mariner's compass

RHUMBA *v* **-ED, -ING, -S** to rumba

RHUS *n pl.* **-ES** any of a genus of shrubs and trees

RHYME *v* **RHYMED, RHYMING, RHYMES** to compose verse with corresponding terminal sounds

RHYMER *n pl.* **-S** one that rhymes

RHYOLITE *n pl.* **-S** a volcanic rock

RHYTHM *n pl.* **-S** movement or procedure with uniform recurrence of strong and weak elements

RHYTHMIC *n pl.* **-S** the science of rhythm

RHYTON *n pl.* **-TONS** or **-TA** an ancient Greek drinking horn

RIA *n pl.* **-S** a long, narrow inlet

RIAL *n pl.* **-S** a monetary unit of Iran

RIALTO *n pl.* **-TOS** a marketplace

RIANT *adj* cheerful **RIANTLY** *adv*

RIATA *n pl.* **-S** a lasso

RIB *v* **RIBBED, RIBBING, RIBS** to poke fun at

RIBALD *n pl.* **-S** one who uses crude language

RIBALD *adj* **RIBALDER, RIBALDEST** characterized by crude language

RIBALDLY *adv* crudely

RIBALDRY *n pl.* **-RIES** crude language

RIBAND *n pl.* **-S** a ribbon

RIBBAND *n pl.* **-S** a long, narrow strip used in shipbuilding

RIBBED past tense of rib

RIBBER *n pl.* **-S** one that ribs

RIBBIE *n pl.* **-S** a run batted in

RIBBIER comparative of ribby

RIBBIEST superlative of ribby

RIBBING *n pl.* **-S** the act of one that ribs

RIBBIT *n pl.* **-S** the sound made by a frog

RIBBON *v* **-ED, -ING, -S** to decorate with ribbons (narrow strips of fine fabric)

RIBBONY *adj* resembling ribbon

RIBBY *adj* **-BIER, -BIEST** marked by prominent ribs (curved bony rods in the body)

RIBES *n pl.* **RIBES** a flowering shrub

RIBEYE *n pl.* **-S** a cut of beef

RIBGRASS *n pl.* **-ES** a weedy plant

RIBIER *n pl.* **-S** a large, black grape

RIBLESS *adj* having no ribs

RIBLET *n pl.* **-S** the rib end in a breast of lamb or veal

RIBLIKE *adj* resembling a rib

RIBOSE *n pl.* **-S** a pentose sugar

RIBOSOME *n pl.* **-S** a particle composed of protein and ribonucleic acid

RIBOZYME *n pl.* **-S** a molecule of RNA that functions as an enzyme

RIBULOSE *n pl.* **-S** a type of sugar

RIBWORT *n pl.* **-S** ribgrass

RICE *v* **RICED, RICING, RICES** to press through a ricer

RICEBIRD *n pl.* **-S** the bobolink

RICER *n pl.* **-S** a kitchen utensil consisting of a container perforated with small holes

RICERCAR *n pl.* **-S** an instrumental composition

RICH *adj* **RICHER, RICHEST** having wealth

RICHEN *v* **-ED, -ING, -S** to make rich

RICHES *n/pl* wealth

RICHLY *adv* in a rich manner

RICHNESS *n pl.* **-ES** the state of being rich

RICHWEED *n pl.* **-S** a flowering plant

RICIN *n pl.* **-S** a poisonous protein

RICING present participle of rice

RICINUS *n pl.* **-ES** a large-leaved plant

RICK *v* **-ED, -ING, -S** to pile hay in stacks

RICKETS *n/pl* a disease resulting from vitamin D deficiency

RICKETY *adj* **-ETIER, -ETIEST** likely to fall or collapse

RICKEY *n pl.* **-EYS** an alcoholic beverage containing lime juice, sugar, and soda water

RICKRACK *n pl.* **-S** a flat braid used as a trimming

RICKSHA *n pl.* **-S** rickshaw

RICKSHAW *n pl.* **-S** a small, two-wheeled passenger vehicle

RICOCHET	v **-CHETED, -CHETING, -CHETS** or **-CHETTED, -CHETTING, -CHETS** to rebound from a surface
RICOTTA	n pl. **-S** an Italian cheese
RICRAC	n pl. **-S** rickrack
RICTUS	n pl. **-ES** the expanse of the open mouth **RICTAL** adj
RID	v **RID** or **RIDDED, RIDDING, RIDS** to free from something objectionable
RIDABLE	adj capable of being ridden
RIDDANCE	n pl. **-S** deliverance
RIDDEN	past participle of ride
RIDDER	n pl. **-S** one that rids
RIDDING	present participle of rid
RIDDLE	v **-DLED, -DLING, -DLES** to pierce with many holes
RIDDLER	n pl. **-S** one that riddles
RIDE	v **RODE, RIDDEN, RIDING, RIDES** to sit on, control, and be conveyed by an animal or machine
RIDEABLE	adj ridable
RIDENT	adj laughing
RIDER	n pl. **-S** one that rides
RIDGE	v **RIDGED, RIDGING, RIDGES** to form into ridges (long, narrow elevations)
RIDGEL	n pl. **-S** a ridgling
RIDGETOP	n pl. **-S** the crest of a ridge
RIDGEWAY	n pl. **-WAYS** a road or track along a ridge
RIDGIER	comparative of ridgy
RIDGIEST	superlative of ridgy
RIDGIL	n pl. **-S** a ridgling
RIDGING	present participle of ridge
RIDGLING	n pl. **-S** a male animal with undescended testicles
RIDGY	adj **RIDGIER, RIDGIEST** having ridges
RIDICULE	v **-CULED, -CULING, -CULES** to make fun of
RIDING	n pl. **-S** the act of one that rides
RIDLEY	n pl. **-LEYS** a sea turtle
RIDOTTO	n pl. **-TOS** a public musical entertainment in 18th century England
RIEL	n pl. **-S** a monetary unit of Cambodia
RIESLING	n pl. **-S** a white Rhine wine
RIEVER	n pl. **-S** reaver
RIF	v **RIFFED, RIFFING, RIFS** to dismiss from employment
RIFAMPIN	n pl. **-S** an antibiotic
RIFE	adj **RIFER, RIFEST** abundant **RIFELY** adv
RIFENESS	n pl. **-ES** the state of being rife
RIFF	v **-ED, -ING, -S** to riffle
RIFFAGE	n pl. **-S** a series of musical phrases
RIFFED	past tense of rif
RIFFING	present participle of rif
RIFFLE	v **-FLED, -FLING, -FLES** to flip through hastily
RIFFLER	n pl. **-S** a filing and scraping tool
RIFFRAFF	n pl. **-S** the disreputable element of society
RIFLE	v **-FLED, -FLING, -FLES** to search through and rob
RIFLEMAN	n pl. **-MEN** a soldier armed with a rifle (a type of firearm)
RIFLER	n pl. **-S** one that rifles
RIFLERY	n pl. **-RIES** the practice of shooting at targets with a rifle
RIFLING	n pl. **-S** the system of grooves in a gun barrel
RIFLIP	n pl. **-S** a fragment of DNA
RIFT	v **-ED, -ING, -S** to form rifts (clefts)
RIFTLESS	adj having no rift
RIG	v **RIGGED, RIGGING, RIGS** to put in proper condition for use
RIGADOON	n pl. **-S** a lively dance
RIGATONI	n pl. **-S** a tubular pasta
RIGAUDON	n pl. **-S** rigadoon
RIGGED	past tense of rig
RIGGER	n pl. **-S** one that rigs
RIGGING	n pl. **-S** the system of lines, chains, and tackle used aboard a ship
RIGHT	adj **RIGHTER, RIGHTEST** being in accordance with what is good, proper, or just
RIGHT	v **-ED, -ING, -S** to put in proper order or condition
RIGHTER	n pl. **-S** one that rights
RIGHTFUL	adj just or proper
RIGHTIER	comparative of righty
RIGHTIES	pl. of righty
RIGHTIEST	superlative of righty
RIGHTISH	adj somewhat right
RIGHTISM	n pl. **-S** a conservative political philosophy

RIGHTIST — *n* pl. **-S** an advocate of rightism

RIGHTLY — *adv* in a right manner

RIGHTO — *interj* — used to express cheerful consent

RIGHTY — *n* pl. **RIGHTIES** a right-handed person

RIGHTY — *adj* **RIGHTIER, RIGHTIEST** politically conservative

RIGID — *adj* **RIGIDER, RIGIDEST** not flexible; strict, harsh

RIGIDIFY — *v* **-FIED, -FYING, -FIES** to make rigid

RIGIDITY — *n* pl. **-TIES** the state of being rigid

RIGIDLY — *adv* in a rigid manner

RIGOR — *n* pl. **-S** strictness or severity

RIGORISM — *n* pl. **-S** strictness or severity in conduct or attitude

RIGORIST — *n* pl. **-S** one that professes rigorism

RIGOROUS — *adj* characterized by rigor

RIGOUR — *n* pl. **-S** rigor

RIKISHA — *n* pl. **-S** rickshaw

RIKISHI — *n* pl. **RIKISHI** a sumo wrestler

RIKSHAW — *n* pl. **-S** rickshaw

RILE — *v* **RILED, RILING, RILES** to anger

RILEY — *adj* angry

RILIEVO — *n* pl. **-VI** relievo

RILL — *v* **-ED, -ING, -S** to flow like a rill (a small brook)

RILLE — *n* pl. **-S** a valley on the moon's surface

RILLET — *n* pl. **-S** a small rill

RIM — *v* **RIMMED, RIMMING, RIMS** to provide with a rim (an outer edge)

RIME — *v* **RIMED, RIMING, RIMES** to rhyme

RIMER — *n* pl. **-S** one that rimes

RIMESTER — *n* pl. **-S** a rimer

RIMFIRE — *n* pl. **-S** a cartridge having the primer set in the rim of the shell

RIMIER — comparative of rimy

RIMIEST — superlative of rimy

RIMINESS — *n* pl. **-ES** the condition of being rimy

RIMING — present participle of rime

RIMLAND — *n* pl. **-S** an outlying area

RIMLESS — *adj* having no rim

RIMMED — past tense of rim

RIMMER — *n* pl. **-S** a reamer

RIMMING — present participle of rim

RIMOSE — *adj* marked by cracks **RIMOSELY** *adv*

RIMOSITY — *n* pl. **-TIES** the state of being rimose

RIMOUS — *adj* rimose

RIMPLE — *v* **-PLED, -PLING, -PLES** to wrinkle

RIMROCK — *n* pl. **-S** a type of rock formation

RIMSHOT — *n* pl. **-S** a sound made by a drumstick striking the rim and head of a drum

RIMY — *adj* **RIMIER, RIMIEST** frosty

RIN — *v* **RAN, RINNING, RINS** to run or melt

RIND — *n* pl. **-S** a thick and firm outer covering **RINDED, RINDY** *adj*

RIND — *v* **-ED, -ING, -S** to strip the bark from

RINDLESS — *adj* lacking a rind

RING — *v* **-ED, -ING, -S** to form a ring (a circular band) around

RING — *v* **RANG, RUNG, RINGING, RINGS** to give forth a clear, resonant sound

RINGBARK — *v* **-ED, -ING, -S** to make an encircling cut through the bark of

RINGBOLT — *n* pl. **-S** a type of eyebolt

RINGBONE — *n* pl. **-S** a bony growth on a horse's foot

RINGDOVE — *n* pl. **-S** a European pigeon

RINGENT — *adj* having open liplike parts

RINGER — *n* pl. **-S** one that rings

RINGETTE — *n* pl. **-S** a team sport for women played on ice using a rubber ring

RINGGIT — *n* pl. **-S** a monetary unit of Malaysia

RINGHALS — *n* pl. **-ES** a venomous snake

RINGLESS — *adj* being without a ring

RINGLET — *n* pl. **-S** a curly lock of hair

RINGLETY — *adj* resembling or suggestive of a ringlet

RINGLIKE — *adj* resembling a ring

RINGNECK — *n* pl. **-S** a bird having a ring of color around the neck

RINGSIDE — *n* pl. **-S** the area just outside a boxing or wrestling ring (a square enclosure)

RINGSTER — *n* pl. **-S** one of a group of people united for political or economic reasons

RINGTAIL — *n* pl. **-S** an animal having a tail with ringlike markings

RINGTAW *n* pl. **-S** a game of marbles

RINGTONE *n* pl. **-S** a sound made by a cell phone when receiving a call

RINGTOSS *n* pl. **-ES** a game in which the object is to toss a ring onto an upright stick

RINGWORK *n* pl. **-S** a fortified circular trench around a castle

RINGWORM *n* pl. **-S** a skin disease

RINK *n* pl. **-S** a surface of ice for skating

RINKHALS *n* pl. **-ES** ringhals

RINKSIDE *n* pl **-S** the area adjacent to a rink

RINNING present participle of rin

RINSE *v* **RINSED, RINSING, RINSES** to cleanse with clear water **RINSABLE, RINSIBLE** *adj*

RINSER *n* pl. **-S** one that rinses

RINSING *n* pl. **-S** the act of one that rinses

RIOJA *n* pl. **-S** a dry red Spanish wine

RIOT *v* **-ED, -ING, -S** to take part in a violent public disturbance

RIOTER *n* pl. **-S** one that riots

RIOTING *n* pl. **-S** a violent public disturbance

RIOTOUS *adj* characterized by rioting

RIP *v* **RIPPED, RIPPING, RIPS** to tear or cut apart roughly

RIPARIAN *adj* pertaining to the bank of a river

RIPCORD *n* pl. **-S** a cord pulled to release a parachute

RIPE *adj* **RIPER, RIPEST** fully developed **RIPELY** *adv*

RIPE *v* **RIPED, RIPING, RIPES** to cleanse

RIPEN *v* **-ED, -ING, -S** to become ripe

RIPENER *n* pl. **-S** one that ripens

RIPENESS *n* pl. **-ES** the state of being ripe

RIPER comparative of ripe

RIPEST superlative of ripe

RIPIENO *n* pl. **-NOS** or **-NI** tutti

RIPING present participle of ripe

RIPOFF *n* pl. **-S** an instance of stealing

RIPOST *v* **-ED, -ING, -S** to riposte

RIPOSTE *v* **-POSTED, -POSTING, -POSTES** to make a return thrust in fencing

RIPPABLE *adj* capable of being ripped

RIPPED past tense of rip

RIPPER *n* pl. **-S** one that rips

RIPPING *adj* excellent

RIPPLE *v* **-PLED, -PLING, -PLES** to form ripples (small waves)

RIPPLER *n* pl. **-S** a toothed tool for cleaning flax fiber

RIPPLET *n* pl. **-S** a small ripple

RIPPLING present participle of ripple

RIPPLY *adj* **-PLIER, -PLIEST** marked by ripples

RIPRAP *v* **-RAPPED, -RAPPING, -RAPS** to strengthen with a foundation of broken stones

RIPSAW *v* **-SAWED, -SAWN, -SAWING, -SAWS** to saw wood by cutting with the grain

RIPSTOP *n* pl. **-S** a fabric woven so that small tears do not spread

RIPTIDE *n* pl. **-S** a tide that opposes other tides

RISE *v* **ROSE, RISEN, RISING, RISES** to move upward

RISER *n* pl. **-S** one that rises

RISHI *n* pl. **-S** a Hindu sage

RISIBLE *adj* inclined to laugh **RISIBLY** *adv*

RISIBLES *n/pl* a sense of the ridiculous

RISING *n* pl. **-S** the act of one that rises

RISK *v* **-ED, -ING, -S** to expose to a risk (a chance of injury or loss)

RISKER *n* pl. **-S** one that risks

RISKLESS *adj* free of risk

RISKY *adj* **RISKIER, RISKIEST** dangerous **RISKILY** *adv*

RISOTTO *n* pl. **-TOS** a rice dish

RISQUE *adj* bordering on impropriety or indecency

RISSOLE *n* pl. **-S** a small roll filled with meat or fish

RISTRA *n* pl. **-S** a string on which foodstuffs are tied for storage

RISUS *n* pl. **-ES** a grin or laugh

RITARD *n* pl. **-S** a musical passage with a gradual slackening in tempo

RITE *n* pl. **-S** a ceremonial act or procedure

RITTER *n* pl. **-S** a knight

RITUAL *n* pl. **-S** a system of rites

RITUALLY *adv* ceremonially

RITZ *n* pl. **-ES** pretentious display

RITZY *adj* **RITZIER, RITZIEST** elegant **RITZILY** *adv*

RIVAGE *n* pl. **-S** a coast, shore, or bank

RIVAL   *v* **-VALED, -VALING, -VALS** or **-VALLED, -VALLING, -VALS** to strive to equal or surpass

RIVALRY   *n* pl. **-RIES** competition

RIVE   *v* **RIVED, RIVEN, RIVING, RIVES** to tear apart

RIVER   *n* pl. **-S** a large, natural stream of water

RIVERBED   *n* pl. **-S** the area covered or once covered by a river

RIVERINE   *adj* pertaining to a river

RIVERMAN   *n* pl. **-MEN** a man who works on a river

RIVET   *v* **-ETED, -ETING, -ETS** or **-ETTED, -ETTING, -ETS** to fasten with a type of metal bolt

RIVETER   *n* pl. **-S** one that rivets

RIVIERA   *n* pl. **-S** a coastal resort area

RIVIERE   *n* pl. **-S** a necklace of precious stones

RIVING   present participle of rive

RIVULET   *n* pl. **-S** a small stream

RIVULOSE   *adj* having narrow, winding lines

RIVULUS   *n* pl. **-ES** a small tropical American fish

RIYAL   *n* pl. **-S** a monetary unit of Saudi Arabia

ROACH   *v* **-ED, -ING, -ES** to cause to arch

ROAD   *n* pl. **-S** an open way for public passage

ROADBED   *n* pl. **-S** the foundation for a railroad track

ROADEO   *n* pl. **-EOS** a competition for truck drivers

ROADIE   *n* pl. **-S** a person who works for traveling entertainers

ROADKILL   *n* pl. **-S** an animal that has been killed on a road

ROADLESS   *adj* having no roads

ROADSHOW   *n* pl. **-S** a theatrical show on tour

ROADSIDE   *n* pl. **-S** the area along the side of a road

ROADSTER   *n* pl. **-S** a light, open automobile

ROADWAY   *n* pl. **-WAYS** a road

ROADWORK   *n* pl. **-S** outdoor running as a form of physical conditioning

ROAM   *v* **-ED, -ING, -S** to move about without purpose or plan

ROAMER   *n* pl. **-S** one that roams

ROAMING   *n* pl. **-S** the use of a cell phone outside its local area

ROAN   *n* pl. **-S** an animal having a coat sprinkled with white or gray

ROAR   *v* **-ED, -ING, -S** to utter a loud, deep sound

ROARER   *n* pl. **-S** one that roars

ROARING   *n* pl. **-S** a loud, deep sound

ROAST   *v* **-ED, -ING, -S** to cook with dry heat

ROASTER   *n* pl. **-S** one that roasts

ROASTING   *n* pl. **-S** a severe criticism

ROB   *v* **ROBBED, ROBBING, ROBS** to take property from illegally

ROBALO   *n* pl. **-LOS** a marine food fish

ROBAND   *n* pl. **-S** a piece of yarn used to fasten a sail

ROBATA   *n* pl. **-S** a grill used for Japanese cooking

ROBBER   *n* pl. **-S** one that robs

ROBBERY   *n* pl. **-BERIES** the act of one who robs

ROBBIN   *n* pl. **-S** a roband

ROBBING   present participle of rob

ROBE   *v* **ROBED, ROBING, ROBES** to cover with a robe (a long, loose outer garment)

ROBIN   *n* pl. **-S** a songbird

ROBINIA   *n* pl. **-S** a North American tree or shrub

ROBLE   *n* pl. **-S** an oak tree

ROBOCALL   *n* pl. **-S** a telephone call from an automated source that delivers a prerecorded message to a large number of people

ROBORANT   *n* pl. **-S** an invigorating drug

ROBOT   *n* pl. **-S** a humanlike machine that performs various functions **ROBOTIC** *adj*

ROBOTICS   *n/pl* a field of interest concerned with robots

ROBOTISE   *v* **-ISED, -ISING, -ISES** to robotize

ROBOTISM   *n* pl. **-S** the state of being a robot

ROBOTIZE   *v* **-IZED, -IZING, -IZES** to make automatic

ROBOTRY   *n* pl. **-RIES** the science of robots

ROBUST   *adj* **-BUSTER, -BUSTEST** strong and healthy **ROBUSTLY** *adv*

ROBUSTA   *n* pl. **-S** a coffee grown in Africa

ROC   *n* pl. **-S** a legendary bird of prey

ROCAILLE   *n* pl. **-S** rococo

ROCHET   *n* pl. **-S** a linen vestment

ROCK   v -**ED**, -**ING**, -**S** to move back and forth **ROCKABLE** adj

ROCKABY   n pl. -**BIES** a song used to lull a child to sleep

ROCKABYE   n pl. -**S** rockaby

ROCKAWAY   n pl. -**WAYS** a light carriage

ROCKER   n pl. -**S** a rocking chair

ROCKERY   n pl. -**ERIES** a rock garden

ROCKET   v -**ED**, -**ING**, -**S** to convey by means of a rocket (a device propelled by the reaction of escaping gases)

ROCKETER   n pl. -**S** one that designs or launches rockets

ROCKETRY   n pl. -**RIES** the science of rockets

ROCKFALL   n pl. -**S** a mass of fallen rocks

ROCKFISH   n pl. -**ES** a fish living around rocks

ROCKIER   comparative of rocky

ROCKIEST   superlative of rocky

ROCKILY   adv in a rocky manner

ROCKLESS   adj having no rocks

ROCKLIKE   adj resembling a rock (a large mass of stone)

ROCKLING   n pl. -**S** a marine fish

ROCKOON   n pl. -**S** a small rocket

ROCKROSE   n pl. -**S** a flowering plant

ROCKWEED   n pl. -**S** a brown seaweed

ROCKWOOL   n pl. -**S** mineral wool used for insulation

ROCKWORK   n pl. -**S** a natural mass of rocks

ROCKY   adj **ROCKIER, ROCKIEST** unsteady

ROCOCO   n pl. -**COS** a style of architecture and decoration

ROD   v **RODDED, RODDING, RODS** to provide with a rod (a straight, slender piece of material)

RODE   n pl. -**S** a cable attached to the anchor of a small boat

RODENT   n pl. -**S** a gnawing mammal

RODEO   v -**ED**, -**ING**, -**S** to perform cowboy skills in a contest

RODLESS   adj having no rod

RODLIKE   adj resembling a rod

RODMAN   n pl. -**MEN** a surveyor's assistant

RODNEY   n pl. -**NEYS** a small fishing boat

RODSMAN   n pl. -**MEN** rodman

ROE   n pl. -**S** the mass of eggs within a female fish

ROEBUCK   n pl. -**S** the male of a small Eurasian deer

ROENTGEN   n pl. -**S** a unit of radiation dosage

ROGATION   n pl. -**S** the proposal of a law in ancient Rome

ROGATORY   adj requesting information

ROGER   v -**ED**, -**ING**, -**S** to indicate that a message has been received

ROGUE   v **ROGUED, ROGUEING** or **ROGUING, ROGUES** to defraud

ROGUERY   n pl. -**ERIES** roguish conduct

ROGUISH   adj dishonest

ROIL   v -**ED**, -**ING**, -**S** to make muddy

ROILY   adj **ROILIER, ROILIEST** muddy

ROISTER   v -**ED**, -**ING**, -**S** to revel

ROLAMITE   n pl. -**S** a nearly frictionless mechanical device

ROLE   n pl. -**S** a part played by an actor

ROLF   v -**ED**, -**ING**, -**S** to practice a type of massage

ROLFER   n pl. -**S** one that rolfs

ROLL   v -**ED**, -**ING**, -**S** to move along by repeatedly turning over **ROLLABLE** adj

ROLLAWAY   n pl. -**WAYS** a piece of furniture that can be rolled away when not in use

ROLLBACK   n pl. -**S** a return to a lower level of prices or wages

ROLLER   n pl. -**S** a rotating cylinder

ROLLICK   v -**ED**, -**ING**, -**S** to frolic

ROLLICKY   adj given to rollicking

ROLLIE   n pl. -**S** a hand-rolled cigarette

ROLLING   n pl. -**S** the act of one that rolls

ROLLMOP   n pl. -**S** a fillet of herring

ROLLOUT   n pl. -**S** a type of play in football

ROLLOVER   n pl. -**S** a motor vehicle accident in which the vehicle overturns

ROLLTOP   adj having a flexible, sliding cover

ROLLUP   n pl. -**S** something that is rolled into the shape of a tube

ROLLWAY   n pl. -**WAYS** an incline for rolling logs

ROM   n pl. -**S** a Gypsy man or boy

ROMAINE   n pl. -**S** a variety of lettuce

ROMAJI   n pl. -**S** a system of transliterating Japanese into the Latin alphabet

ROMAN   n pl. -**S** a metrical narrative of medieval France

ROMANCE   *v* **-MANCED, -MANCING, -MANCES** to woo

ROMANCER   *n* pl. **-S** one that romances

ROMANISE   *v* **-ISED, -ISING, -ISES** to romanize

ROMANIZE   *v* **-IZED, -IZING, -IZES** to write in the Roman alphabet

ROMANO   *n* pl. **-NOS** an Italian cheese

ROMANTIC   *n* pl. **-S** a fanciful person

ROMAUNT   *n* pl. **-S** a long, medieval tale

ROMEO   *n* pl. **-MEOS** a male lover

ROMP   *v* **-ED, -ING, -S** to play boisterously

ROMPER   *n* pl. **-S** one that romps

ROMPISH   *adj* inclined to romp

RONDE   *n* pl. **-S** a dance in which the dancers move in a circle

RONDEAU   *n* pl. **-DEAUX** a short poem of fixed form

RONDEL   *n* pl. **-S** a rondeau of 14 lines

RONDELET   *n* pl. **-S** a rondeau of 5 or 7 lines

RONDELLE   *n* pl. **-S** rondel

RONDO   *n* pl. **-DOS** a type of musical composition

RONDURE   *n* pl. **-S** a circle or sphere

RONIN   *n* pl. **-S** a wandering samurai

RONION   *n* pl. **-S** a mangy animal or person

RONNEL   *n* pl. **-S** an insecticide

RONTGEN   *n* pl. **-S** roentgen

RONYON   *n* pl. **-S** ronion

ROO   *n* pl. **ROOS** a kangaroo

ROOD   *n* pl. **-S** a crucifix

ROOF   *v* **-ED, -ING, -S** to provide with a roof (the external upper covering of a building)

ROOFER   *n* pl. **-S** one that builds or repairs roofs

ROOFIE   *n* pl. **-S** a tablet of a powerful sedative

ROOFING   *n* pl. **-S** material for a roof

ROOFLESS   *adj* having no roof

ROOFLIKE   *adj* resembling a roof

ROOFLINE   *n* pl. **-S** the profile of a roof

ROOFTOP   *n* pl. **-S** a roof

ROOFTREE   *n* pl. **-S** a horizontal timber in a roof

ROOIBOS   *n* pl. **-ES** a South African evergreen shrub

ROOK   *v* **-ED, -ING, -S** to swindle

ROOKERY   *n* pl. **-ERIES** a colony of rooks (European crows)

ROOKIE   *n* pl. **-S** a novice

ROOKY   *adj* **ROOKIER, ROOKIEST** abounding in rooks

ROOM   *v* **-ED, -ING, -S** to occupy a room (a walled space within a building)

ROOMER   *n* pl. **-S** a lodger

ROOMETTE   *n* pl. **-S** a small room

ROOMFUL   *n* pl. **ROOMFULS** or **ROOMSFUL** as much as a room can hold

ROOMIE   *n* pl. **-S** a roommate

ROOMMATE   *n* pl. **-S** one with whom a room is shared

ROOMY   *adj* **ROOMIER, ROOMIEST** spacious **ROOMILY** *adv*

ROORBACH   *n* pl. **-S** roorback

ROORBACK   *n* pl. **-S** a false story used for political advantage

ROOSE   *v* **ROOSED, ROOSING, ROOSES** to praise

ROOSER   *n* pl. **-S** one that rooses

ROOST   *v* **-ED, -ING, -S** to settle down for rest or sleep

ROOSTER   *n* pl. **-S** a male chicken

ROOT   *v* **-ED, -ING, -S** to put forth a root (an underground portion of a plant)

ROOTAGE   *n* pl. **-S** a system of roots

ROOTBALL   *n* pl. **-S** the mass of a plant's roots and surrounding soil

ROOTCAP   *n* pl. **-S** the loose mass of cells that covers the tip of some roots

ROOTER   *n* pl. **-S** one that gives encouragement or support

ROOTHOLD   *n* pl. **-S** the embedding of a plant to soil through the growing of roots

ROOTIER   comparative of rooty

ROOTIEST   superlative of rooty

ROOTLE   *v* **-TLED, -TLING, -TLES** to dig in the ground as with the snout

ROOTLESS   *adj* having no roots

ROOTLET   *n* pl. **-S** a small root

ROOTLIKE   *adj* resembling a root

ROOTSY   *adj* **ROOTSIER, ROOTSIEST** showing traditional musical origins

ROOTWORM   *n* pl. **-S** a beetle whose larvae feed on the roots of crop plants

ROOTY   *adj* **ROOTIER, ROOTIEST** full of roots

ROPE   *v* **ROPED, ROPING, ROPES** to bind with a rope (a thick line of twisted fibers) **ROPABLE** *adj*

ROPELIKE	*adj* resembling a rope	**ROSEOLA**	*n* pl. **-S** a rose-colored skin rash **ROSEOLAR** *adj*
ROPER	*n* pl. **-S** one that ropes	**ROSEROOT**	*n* pl. **-S** a perennial herb
ROPERY	*n* pl. **-ERIES** a place where ropes are made	**ROSERY**	*n* pl. **-ERIES** a place where roses are grown
ROPEWALK	*n* pl. **-S** a long path where ropes are made	**ROSESLUG**	*n* pl. **-S** a larval sawfly that eats rose leaves
ROPEWAY	*n* pl. **-WAYS** an aerial cable used to transport freight	**ROSET**	*n* pl. **-S** resin
ROPEY	*adj* **ROPIER, ROPIEST** ropy	**ROSETTE**	*n* pl. **-S** an ornament resembling a rose **ROSETTED** *adj*
ROPIER	comparative of ropy	**ROSEWOOD**	*n* pl. **-S** a tropical tree
ROPIEST	superlative of ropy	**ROSHI**	*n* pl. **-S** the spiritual leader of a group of Zen Buddhists
ROPILY	*adv* in a ropy manner	**ROSIER**	comparative of rosy
ROPINESS	*n* pl. **-ES** the quality of being ropy	**ROSIEST**	superlative of rosy
ROPING	*n* pl. **-S** the act of binding with a rope	**ROSILY**	*adv* in a rosy manner
ROPY	*adj* **ROPIER, ROPIEST** resembling a rope or ropes	**ROSIN**	*v* **-ED, -ING, -S** to treat with rosin (a brittle resin)
ROQUE	*n* pl. **-S** a form of croquet	**ROSINESS**	*n* pl. **-ES** the state of being rosy
ROQUET	*v* **-ED, -ING, -S** to cause one's own ball to hit another in croquet	**ROSING**	present participle of rose
ROQUETTE	*n* pl. **-S** an arugula	**ROSINOL**	*n* pl. **-S** rosin oil
RORQUAL	*n* pl. **-S** a large whale	**ROSINOUS**	*adj* resembling rosin
ROSACE	*n* pl. **-S** an ornamentation resembling a rose	**ROSINY**	*adj* rosinous
ROSACEA	*n* pl. **-S** a chronic inflammation of parts of the face	**ROSOLIO**	*n* pl. **-LIOS** a liqueur made from raisins and brandy
ROSARIAN	*n* pl. **-S** a cultivator of roses	**ROSTELLA**	*n/pl* small, beaklike structures
ROSARIUM	*n* pl. **-IUMS** or **-IA** a rose garden	**ROSTER**	*v* **-ED, -ING, -S** to place in a list of names
ROSARY	*n* pl. **-RIES** a series of prayers in the Roman Catholic Church	**ROSTI**	*n* pl. **-S** a Swiss dish of fried grated potatoes topped with cheese
ROSCOE	*n* pl. **-S** a pistol	**ROSTRA**	a pl. of rostrum
ROSE	*v* **ROSED, ROSING, ROSES** to make the color of a rose (a reddish flower)	**ROSTRAL**	*adj* pertaining to a rostrum
		ROSTRATE	*adj* having a rostrum
ROSEATE	*adj* rose-colored	**ROSTRUM**	*n* pl. **-TRUMS** or **-TRA** a beaklike process or part
ROSEBAY	*n* pl. **-BAYS** an evergreen shrub	**ROSULATE**	*adj* arranged in the form of a rosette
ROSEBOWL	*n* pl. **-S** a bowl for displaying cut roses		
ROSEBUD	*n* pl. **-S** the bud of a rose	**ROSY**	*adj* **ROSIER, ROSIEST** rose-colored
ROSEBUSH	*n* pl. **-ES** a shrub that bears roses	**ROT**	*v* **ROTTED, ROTTING, ROTS** to decompose
ROSED	past tense of rose	**ROTA**	*n* pl. **-S** a roster
ROSEFISH	*n* pl. **-ES** a marine food fish	**ROTARY**	*n* pl. **-RIES** a rotating part or device
ROSEHIP	*n* pl. **-S** the aggregate fruit of the rose plant	**ROTATE**	*v* **-TATED, -TATING, -TATES** to turn about an axis
ROSELIKE	*adj* resembling a rose		
ROSELLA	*n* pl. **-S** an Australian parakeet	**ROTATION**	*n* pl. **-S** the act or an instance of rotating **ROTATIVE** *adj*
ROSELLE	*n* pl. **-S** a tropical plant		
ROSEMARY	*n* pl. **-MARIES** an evergreen shrub	**ROTATOR**	*n* pl. **-ES** or **-S** one that rotates

ROTATORY *adj* pertaining to rotation

ROTCH *n* pl. **-ES** rotche

ROTCHE *n* pl. **-S** a seabird

ROTE *n* pl. **-S** mechanical routine

ROTENONE *n* pl. **-S** an insecticide

ROTGUT *n* pl. **-S** inferior liquor

ROTI *n* pl. **-S** an unleavened bread

ROTIFER *n* pl. **-S** a microscopic aquatic organism

ROTIFORM *adj* shaped like a wheel

ROTINI *n* pl. **-S** pasta in small spirals

ROTL *n* pl. **ROTLS** or **ARTAL** a unit of weight in Muslim countries

ROTO *n* pl. **-TOS** a type of printing process

ROTOR *n* pl. **-S** a rotating part of a machine

ROTOTILL *v* **-ED, -ING, -S** to till soil with a type of farming implement

ROTTE *n* pl. **-S** a medieval stringed instrument

ROTTED past tense of rot

ROTTEN *adj* **-TENER, -TENEST** being in a state of decay **ROTTENLY** *adv*

ROTTER *n* pl. **-S** a scoundrel

ROTTING present participle of rot

ROTUND *adj* **ROTUNDER, ROTUNDEST** marked by roundness **ROTUNDLY** *adv*

ROTUNDA *n* pl. **-S** a round building

ROTURIER *n* pl. **-S** a commoner

ROUBLE *n* pl. **-S** ruble

ROUCHE *n* pl. **-S** ruche

ROUE *n* pl. **-S** a lecherous man

ROUEN *n* pl. **-S** any of a breed of domestic ducks

ROUGE *v* **ROUGED, ROUGING, ROUGES** to color with a red cosmetic

ROUGH *adj* **ROUGHER, ROUGHEST** having an uneven surface

ROUGH *v* **-ED, -ING, -S** to make rough

ROUGHAGE *n* pl. **-S** coarse, bulky food

ROUGHDRY *v* **-DRIED, -DRYING, -DRIES** to dry without ironing, as washed clothes

ROUGHEN *v* **-ED, -ING, -S** to make rough

ROUGHER *n* pl. **-S** one that roughs

ROUGHHEW *v* **-HEWED, -HEWN, -HEWING, -HEWS** to shape roughly

ROUGHING *n* pl. **-S** an excessive use of force in hockey

ROUGHISH *adj* somewhat rough

ROUGHLEG *n* pl. **-S** a large hawk

ROUGHLY *adv* in a rough manner

ROUGHOUT *n* pl. **-S** an unfinished roughly shaped artifact

ROUGHY *n* pl. **ROUGHIES** a small fish having rough scales

ROUGING present participle of rouge

ROUILLE *n* pl. **-S** a peppery garlic sauce

ROULADE *n* pl. **-S** a musical embellishment

ROULEAU *n* pl. **-LEAUS** or **-LEAUX** a roll of coins wrapped in paper

ROULETTE *v* **-LETTED, -LETTING, -LETTES** to make tiny slits in

ROUND *adj* **ROUNDER, ROUNDEST** shaped like a sphere

ROUND *v* **-ED, -ING, -S** to make round

ROUNDEL *n* pl. **-S** a round figure or object

ROUNDER *n* pl. **-S** a tool for rounding

ROUNDISH *adj* somewhat round

ROUNDLET *n* pl. **-S** a small circle

ROUNDLY *adv* in a round manner

ROUNDUP *n* pl. **-S** the driving together of cattle scattered over a range

ROUP *v* **-ED, -ING, -S** to auction

ROUPET *adj* roupy

ROUPY *adj* **ROUPIER, ROUPIEST** hoarse **ROUPILY** *adv*

ROUSE *v* **ROUSED, ROUSING, ROUSES** to bring out of a state of sleep or inactivity **ROUSABLE** *adj*

ROUSER *n* pl. **-S** one that rouses

ROUSSEAU *n* pl. **-S** fried pemmican

ROUST *v* **-ED, -ING, -S** to arouse and drive out

ROUSTER *n* pl. **-S** a wharf laborer and deckhand

ROUT *v* **-ED, -ING, -S** to defeat overwhelmingly

ROUTE *v* **ROUTED, ROUTING** or **ROUTEING, ROUTES** to send on a particular course

ROUTEMAN *n* pl. **-MEN** one who conducts business on a customary course

ROUTER *n* pl. **-S** a scooping tool

ROUTEWAY *n* pl. **-WAYS** an established course of travel

ROUTH *n* pl. **-S** an abundance

ROUTINE	*n* pl. **-S** a regular course of procedure
ROUTING	present participle of route
ROUX	*n* pl. **ROUX** a mixture of butter and flour
ROVE	*v* **ROVED, ROVING, ROVES** to roam
ROVEN	a past participle of reeve
ROVER	*n* pl. **-S** one that roves
ROVING	*n* pl. **-S** a roll of textile fibers
ROVINGLY	*adv* in a roving manner
ROW	*v* **-ED, -ING, -S** to propel by means of oars **ROWABLE** *adj*
ROWAN	*n* pl. **-S** a Eurasian tree
ROWBOAT	*n* pl. **-S** a small boat designed to be rowed
ROWDY	*adj* **-DIER, -DIEST** disorderly in behavior **ROWDILY** *adv*
ROWDY	*n* pl. **-DIES** a rowdy person
ROWDYISH	*adj* tending to be rowdy
ROWDYISM	*n* pl. **-S** disorderly behavior
ROWEL	*v* **-ELED, -ELING, -ELS** or **-ELLED, -ELLING, -ELS** to prick with a spiked wheel in order to urge forward
ROWEN	*n* pl. **-S** a second growth of grass
ROWER	*n* pl. **-S** one that rows
ROWING	*n* pl. **-S** the sport of racing in light, long, and narrow rowboats
ROWLOCK	*n* pl. **-S** an oarlock
ROWTH	*n* pl. **-S** routh
ROYAL	*n* pl. **-S** a size of printing paper
ROYALISM	*n* pl. **-S** support of a monarch or monarchy
ROYALIST	*n* pl. **-S** a supporter of a monarch or monarchy
ROYALLY	*adv* in a kingly manner
ROYALTY	*n* pl. **-TIES** the status or power of a monarch
ROYSTER	*v* **-ED, -ING, -S** to roister
ROZZER	*n* pl. **-S** a policeman
RUANA	*n* pl. **-S** a woolen poncho
RUB	*v* **RUBBED, RUBBING, RUBS** to move along the surface of a body with pressure
RUBABOO	*n* pl. **-BOOS** a type of soup
RUBACE	*n* pl. **-S** rubasse
RUBAIYAT	*n* pl. **RUBAIYAT** four-lined stanzas in Persian poetry
RUBASSE	*n* pl. **-S** a variety of quartz
RUBATO	*n* pl. **-TOS** or **-TI** a fluctuation of speed within a musical phrase
RUBBABOO	*n* pl. **-BOOS** rubaboo
RUBBED	past tense of rub
RUBBER	*v* **-ED, -ING, -S** to stretch one's neck in looking at something
RUBBERY	*adj* **-BERIER, -BERIEST** resembling rubber (an elastic substance)
RUBBIES	pl. of rubby
RUBBING	*n* pl. **-S** an image produced by rubbing
RUBBISH	*n* pl. **-ES** worthless, unwanted matter **RUBBISHY** *adj*
RUBBISH	*v* **-ED, -ING, -ES** to reject as worthless
RUBBLE	*v* **-BLED, -BLING, -BLES** to reduce to rubble (broken pieces)
RUBBLY	*adj* **-BLIER, -BLIEST** abounding in rubble
RUBBOARD	*n* pl. **-S** a corrugated rectangular board used as a percussion instrument
RUBBY	*n* pl. **-BIES** an alcoholic given to drinking rubbing alcohol
RUBBYDUB	*n* pl. **-S** a rubby
RUBDOWN	*n* pl. **-S** a brisk rubbing of the body
RUBE	*n* pl. **-S** a rustic
RUBEL	*n* pl. **RUBELS** or **RUBLI** a monetary unit of Belarus
RUBELLA	*n* pl. **-S** a virus disease
RUBEOLA	*n* pl. **-S** a virus disease **RUBEOLAR** *adj*
RUBICUND	*adj* ruddy
RUBIDIUM	*n* pl. **-S** a metallic element **RUBIDIC** *adj*
RUBIED	past tense of ruby
RUBIER	comparative of ruby
RUBIES	present 3d person sing. of ruby
RUBIEST	superlative of ruby
RUBIGO	*n* pl. **-GOS** red iron oxide
RUBIOUS	*adj* ruby-colored
RUBLE	*n* pl. **-S** a monetary unit of Russia
RUBOFF	*n* pl. **-S** a deep impression made by close contact
RUBOUT	*n* pl. **-S** an instance of obliterating something

RUBRIC *n* pl. **-S** a part of a manuscript or book that appears in red **RUBRICAL** *adj*

RUBUS *n* pl. **RUBUS** a plant of the rose family

RUBY *adj* **-BIER, -BIEST** of a deep-red color

RUBY *v* **-BIED, -BYING, -BIES** to tint with the color of a ruby (a deep-red precious stone)

RUBYLIKE *adj* resembling a ruby

RUCHE *n* pl. **-S** a pleated strip of fine fabric

RUCHED *adj* trimmed with a ruche

RUCHING *n* pl. **-S** a ruche

RUCK *v* **-ED, -ING, -S** to wrinkle or crease

RUCKLE *v* **-LED, -LING, -LES** to ruck

RUCKSACK *n* pl. **-S** a knapsack

RUCKUS *n* pl. **-ES** a noisy disturbance

RUCOLA *n* pl. **-S** arugula

RUCTION *n* pl. **-S** a ruckus

RUCTIOUS *adj* quarrelsome

RUDD *n* pl. **-S** a freshwater fish

RUDDER *n* pl. **-S** a vertical blade used to direct the course of a vessel

RUDDIED past tense of ruddy

RUDDIER comparative of ruddy

RUDDIES present 3d person sing. of ruddy

RUDDIEST superlative of ruddy

RUDDILY *adv* in a ruddy manner

RUDDLE *v* **-DLED, -DLING, -DLES** to color with a red dye

RUDDOCK *n* pl. **-S** a European bird

RUDDY *adj* **-DIER, -DIEST** having a healthy, reddish color

RUDDY *v* **-DIED, -DYING, -DIES** to make ruddy

RUDE *adj* **RUDER, RUDEST** discourteous or impolite **RUDELY** *adv*

RUDENESS *n* pl. **-ES** the quality of being rude

RUDERAL *n* pl. **-S** a plant growing in poor land

RUDERY *n* pl. **-ERIES** a rude act

RUDESBY *n* pl. **-BIES** a rude person

RUDEST superlative of rude

RUDIMENT *n* pl. **-S** a basic principle or element

RUDIST *n* pl. **-S** a cone-shaped extinct mollusk

RUDISTID *n* pl. **-S** a rudist

RUE *v* **RUED, RUING** or **RUEING, RUES** to feel sorrow or remorse for

RUEFUL *adj* feeling sorrow or remorse **RUEFULLY** *adv*

RUER *n* pl. **-S** one that rues

RUFF *v* **-ED, -ING, -S** to trump

RUFFE *n* pl. **-S** a freshwater fish

RUFFIAN *n* pl. **-S** a tough, lawless person

RUFFLE *v* **-FLED, -FLING, -FLES** to destroy the smoothness of

RUFFLER *n* pl. **-S** one that ruffles

RUFFLIKE *adj* resembling a ruff (a pleated collar)

RUFFLING present participle of ruffle

RUFFLY *adj* **-FLIER, -FLIEST** not smooth

RUFIYAA *n* pl. **RUFIYAA** a monetary unit of the Maldives

RUFOUS *n* pl. **-ES** a reddish-brown color

RUG *v* **RUGGED, RUGGING, RUGS** to tear roughly

RUGA *n* pl. **-GAE** an anatomical fold or wrinkle **RUGAL, RUGATE** *adj*

RUGALACH *n* pl. **RUGALACH** rugelach

RUGBY *n* pl. **-BIES** a form of football

RUGELACH *n* pl. **-S** a cookie of cream-cheese dough spread with a filling and rolled up

RUGGED *adj* **-GEDER, -GEDEST** having an uneven surface **RUGGEDLY** *adv*

RUGGER *n* pl. **-S** rugby

RUGGING present participle of rug

RUGLIKE *adj* resembling a rug (a thick fabric used as a floor covering)

RUGOLA *n* pl. **-S** arugula

RUGOSA *n* pl. **-S** a flowering plant

RUGOSE *adj* full of wrinkles **RUGOSELY** *adv*

RUGOSITY *n* pl. **-TIES** the state of being rugose

RUGOUS *adj* rugose

RUGRAT *n* pl. **-S** a young child

RUGULOSE *adj* having small wrinkles

RUIN *v* **-ED, -ING, -S** to destroy **RUINABLE** *adj*

RUINATE *v* **-ATED, -ATING, -ATES** to ruin

RUINER *n* pl. **-S** one that ruins

RUING present participle of rue

RUINOUS	*adj* destructive
RUKH	*n* pl. **-S** a roc
RULE	*v* **RULED, RULING, RULES** to exercise control over **RULABLE** *adj*
RULELESS	*adj* not restrained or regulated by law
RULER	*n* pl. **-S** one that rules
RULING	*n* pl. **-S** an authoritative decision
RULY	*adj* **RULIER, RULIEST** orderly
RUM	*adj* **RUMMER, RUMMEST** odd
RUM	*n* pl. **-S** an alcoholic liquor
RUMAKI	*n* pl. **-S** chicken liver wrapped together with water chestnuts in a bacon slice
RUMBA	*v* **-ED, -ING, -S** to perform a ballroom dance
RUMBLE	*v* **-BLED, -BLING, -BLES** to make a deep, thunderous sound
RUMBLER	*n* pl. **-S** one that rumbles
RUMBLING	*n* pl. **-S** a thunderous sound
RUMBLY	*adj* tending to rumble
RUMDUM	*n* pl. **-S** an alcoholic
RUMEN	*n* pl. **-MENS** or **-MINA** a part of the stomach of a ruminant **RUMINAL** *adj*
RUMINANT	*n* pl. **-S** a hoofed, even-toed mammal
RUMINATE	*v* **-NATED, -NATING, -NATES** to chew again
RUMLY	*adv* in an odd or peculiar way
RUMMAGE	*v* **-MAGED, -MAGING, -MAGES** to search thoroughly through
RUMMAGER	*n* pl. **-S** one that rummages
RUMMER	*n* pl. **-S** a large drinking glass
RUMMEST	superlative of rum
RUMMY	*adj* **-MIER, -MIEST** odd
RUMMY	*n* pl. **-MIES** a card game
RUMNESS	*n* pl. **-ES** the quality or state of being odd or peculiar
RUMOR	*v* **-ED, -ING, -S** to spread by hearsay
RUMOUR	*v* **-ED, -ING, -S** to rumor
RUMP	*n* pl. **-S** the lower and back part of the trunk **RUMPLESS** *adj*
RUMPLE	*v* **-PLED, -PLING, -PLES** to wrinkle
RUMPLY	*adj* **-PLIER, -PLIEST** rumpled
RUMPOT	*n* pl. **-S** an alcoholic
RUMPUS	*n* pl. **-ES** a noisy disturbance
RUN	*v* **RAN, RUNNING, RUNS** to move by rapid steps
RUNABOUT	*n* pl. **-S** a small, open auto
RUNAGATE	*n* pl. **-S** a deserter
RUNAWAY	*n* pl. **-AWAYS** one that runs away
RUNBACK	*n* pl. **-S** a type of run in football
RUNDLE	*n* pl. **-S** a rung
RUNDLET	*n* pl. **-S** a small barrel
RUNDOWN	*n* pl. **-S** a summary
RUNE	*n* pl. **-S** a letter of an ancient alphabet **RUNELIKE** *adj*
RUNG	*n* pl. **-S** a crosspiece forming a step of a ladder **RUNGED** *adj* **RUNGLESS** *adj*
RUNIC	*adj* pertaining to a rune
RUNKLE	*v* **-KLED, -KLING, -KLES** to wrinkle
RUNLESS	*adj* scoring no runs in baseball
RUNLET	*n* pl. **-S** a small stream
RUNNABLE	*adj* capable of being run
RUNNEL	*n* pl. **-S** a small stream
RUNNER	*n* pl. **-S** one that runs
RUNNING	*n* pl. **-S** a race
RUNNY	*adj* **-NIER, -NIEST** tending to drip
RUNOFF	*n* pl. **-S** rainfall that is not absorbed by the soil
RUNOUT	*n* pl. **-S** the end of a film strip
RUNOVER	*n* pl. **-S** matter for publication that exceeds the allotted space
RUNROUND	*n* pl. **-S** evasive action
RUNT	*n* pl. **-S** a small person or animal **RUNTISH** *adj*
RUNTY	*adj* **RUNTIER, RUNTIEST** small
RUNWAY	*n* pl. **-WAYS** a landing and takeoff strip for aircraft
RUPEE	*n* pl. **-S** a monetary unit of India
RUPIAH	*n* pl. **-S** a monetary unit of Indonesia
RUPTURE	*v* **-TURED, -TURING, -TURES** to burst
RURAL	*adj* pertaining to the country
RURALISE	*v* **-ISED, -ISING, -ISES** to ruralize
RURALISM	*n* pl. **-S** the state of being rural
RURALIST	*n* pl. **-S** one who lives in the country
RURALITE	*n* pl. **-S** a ruralist
RURALITY	*n* pl. **-TIES** the state of being rural

RURALIZE *v* **-IZED, -IZING, -IZES** to make rural

RURALLY *adv* in a rural manner

RURBAN *adj* partially rural and urban

RUSE *n* pl. **-S** a deception

RUSH *v* **-ED, -ING, -ES** to move swiftly

RUSHEE *n* pl. **-S** a college student seeking admission to a fraternity or sorority

RUSHER *n* pl. **-S** one that rushes

RUSHIER comparative of rushy

RUSHIEST superlative of rushy

RUSHING *n* pl. **-S** yardage gained in football by running plays

RUSHLIKE *adj* resembling a rush (a grasslike marsh plant)

RUSHY *adj* **RUSHIER, RUSHIEST** abounding in rushes

RUSINE *adj* pertaining to a genus of deer

RUSK *n* pl. **-S** a sweetened biscuit

RUSSET *v* **-ED, -ING, -S** to make or become reddish or yellowish brown in color

RUSSETY *adj* of a reddish or yellowish brown color

RUSSIFY *v* **-FIED, -FYING, -FIES** to make Russian

RUSSULA *n* pl. **-S** a woodland fungus

RUST *v* **-ED, -ING, -S** to form rust (a reddish coating that forms on iron) **RUSTABLE** *adj*

RUSTIC *n* pl. **-S** one who lives in the country

RUSTICAL *n* pl. **-S** a rustic

RUSTICLY *adv* in a rural manner

RUSTIER comparative of rusty

RUSTIEST superlative of rusty

RUSTILY *adv* in a rusty manner

RUSTLE *v* **-TLED, -TLING, -TLES** to make a succession of slight, soft sounds

RUSTLER *n* pl. **-S** one that rustles

RUSTLESS *adj* free from rust

RUSTY *adj* **RUSTIER, RUSTIEST** covered with rust

RUT *v* **RUTTED, RUTTING, RUTS** to make ruts (grooves) in

RUTABAGA *n* pl. **-S** a plant having a thick, edible root

RUTH *n* pl. **-S** compassion

RUTHENIC *adj* pertaining to a rare, metallic element

RUTHFUL *adj* full of compassion

RUTHLESS *adj* having no compassion

RUTILANT *adj* having a reddish glow

RUTILE *n* pl. **-S** a mineral

RUTIN *n* pl. **-S** a chemical compound

RUTTED past tense of rut

RUTTIER comparative of rutty

RUTTIEST superlative of rutty

RUTTILY *adv* in a rutty manner

RUTTING present participle of rut

RUTTISH *adj* lustful

RUTTY *adj* **-TIER, -TIEST** marked by ruts

RYA *n* pl. **-S** a Scandinavian handwoven rug

RYE *n* pl. **-S** a cereal grass

RYEGRASS *n* pl. **-ES** a European grass

RYKE *v* **RYKED, RYKING, RYKES** to reach

RYND *n* pl. **-S** an iron support

RYOKAN *n* pl. **-S** a Japanese inn

RYOT *n* pl. **-S** a tenant farmer in India

RYU *n* pl. **-S** a school of Japanese martial arts

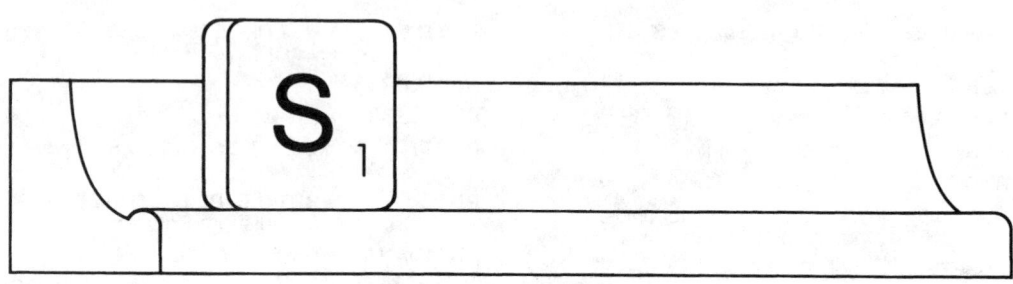

SAB   *v* **SABBED, SABBING, SABS** to sob

SABAL   *n* pl. **-S** a palmetto

SABATON   *n* pl. **-S** a piece of armor for the foot

SABAYON   *n* pl. **-S** a sauce of whipped egg yolks, sugar, and wine

SABBAT   *n* pl. **-S** an assembly of demons and witches

SABBATH   *n* pl. **-S** sabbat

SABBATIC   *n* pl. **-S** a year of release from normal teaching duties

SABBED   past tense of sab

SABBING   present participle of sab

SABE   *v* **SABED, SABEING, SABES** to savvy

SABER   *v* **-ED, -ING, -S** to strike with a saber (a type of sword)

SABICU   *n* pl. **-S** a Caribbean tree

SABIN   *n* pl. **-S** a unit of sound absorption

SABINE   *n* pl. **-S** savin

SABIR   *n* pl. **-S** a French-based pidgin language

SABKHA   *n* pl. **-S** a coastal, flat, periodically flooded area in northern Africa

SABLE   *n* pl. **-S** a carnivorous mammal

SABOT   *n* pl. **-S** a wooden shoe **SABOTED** *adj*

SABOTAGE   *v* **-TAGED, -TAGING, -TAGES** to destroy maliciously

SABOTEUR   *n* pl. **-S** one who sabotages

SABRA   *n* pl. **-S** a native Israeli

SABRE   *v* **-BRED, -BRING, -BRES** to saber

SABULOSE   *adj* sabulous

SABULOUS   *adj* sandy

SAC   *n* pl. **-S** a pouch-shaped structure in an animal or plant

SACATON   *n* pl. **-S** a perennial grass

SACBUT   *n* pl. **-S** sackbut

SACCADE   *n* pl. **-S** a rapid, jerky movement of the eye **SACCADIC** *adj*

SACCATE   *adj* having a sac

SACCULAR   *adj* resembling a sac

SACCULE   *n* pl. **-S** a small sac

SACCULUS   *n* pl. **-LI** saccule

SACHEM   *n* pl. **-S** a Native American chief **SACHEMIC** *adj*

SACHET   *n* pl. **-S** a small bag containing perfumed powder **SACHETED** *adj*

SACK   *v* **-ED, -ING, -S** to put into a sack (a large bag) **SACKABLE** *adj*

SACKBUT   *n* pl. **-S** a medieval trombone

SACKER   *n* pl. **-S** one that sacks

SACKFUL   *n* pl. **SACKFULS** or **SACKSFUL** as much as a sack can hold

SACKING   *n* pl. **-S** material for making sacks

SACKLIKE   *adj* resembling a sack

SACLIKE   *adj* resembling a sac

SACQUE   *n* pl. **-S** a loose-fitting dress

SACRA   pl. of sacrum

SACRAL   *n* pl. **-S** a vertebra or nerve situated near the sacrum

SACRARIA   *n/pl* ancient Roman shrines

SACRED   *adj* **SACREDER, SACREDEST** holy **SACREDLY** *adv*

SACRING   *n* pl. **-S** the consecration of bread and wine of the Eucharist

SACRIST   *n* pl. **-S** a person in charge of a sacristy

SACRISTY   *n* pl. **-TIES** a room in which sacred vessels and vestments are kept

SACRUM   *n* pl. **-CRUMS** or **-CRA** a bone of the pelvis

SAD   *adj* **SADDER, SADDEST** unhappy

SADDEN   *v* **-ED, -ING, -S** to make sad

SADDHU   *n* pl. **-S** sadhu

SADDISH	*adj* somewhat sad
SADDLE	*v* **-DLED, -DLING, -DLES** to put a saddle (a leather seat for a rider) on
SADDLER	*n* pl. **-S** one that makes, repairs, or sells saddles
SADDLERY	*n* pl. **-DLERIES** the shop of a saddler
SADE	*n* pl. **-S** a Hebrew letter
SADHE	*n* pl. **-S** sade
SADHU	*n* pl. **-S** a Hindu holy man
SADI	*n* pl. **-S** sade
SADIRON	*n* pl. **-S** a heavy flatiron
SADISM	*n* pl. **-S** a tendency to take delight in inflicting pain
SADIST	*n* pl. **-S** one marked by sadism **SADISTIC** *adj*
SADLY	*adv* in a sad manner
SADNESS	*n* pl. **-ES** the state of being sad
SAE	*adv* so
SAFARI	*v* **-ED, -ING, -S** to go on a hunting expedition
SAFE	*adj* **SAFER, SAFEST** free from danger **SAFELY** *adv*
SAFE	*n* pl. **-S** a metal receptacle for storing valuables
SAFENESS	*n* pl. **-ES** the quality of being safe
SAFETY	*v* **-TIED, -TYING, -TIES** to protect against failure, breakage, or accident
SAFFRON	*n* pl. **-S** a flowering plant
SAFFRONY	*adj* resembling saffron
SAFRANIN	*n* pl. **-S** a red dye
SAFROL	*n* pl. **-S** safrole
SAFROLE	*n* pl. **-S** a poisonous liquid
SAG	*v* **SAGGED, SAGGING, SAGS** to bend or sink downward from weight or pressure
SAGA	*n* pl. **-S** a medieval Scandinavian narrative
SAGACITY	*n* pl. **-TIES** wisdom
SAGAMAN	*n* pl. **-MEN** a writer of sagas
SAGAMORE	*n* pl. **-S** an Algonquian Indian chief
SAGANASH	*n* pl. **-ES** a white man — an Algonquian Indian term
SAGBUT	*n* pl. **-S** sackbut
SAGE	*adj* **SAGER, SAGEST** wise **SAGELY** *adv*
SAGE	*n* pl. **-S** an aromatic herb used as seasoning
SAGEHOOD	*n* pl. **-S** the state of being wise
SAGENESS	*n* pl. **-ES** wisdom
SAGGAR	*v* **-ED, -ING, -S** to bake in a saggar (a protective clay casing)
SAGGARD	*n* pl. **-S** a saggar
SAGGED	past tense of sag
SAGGER	*v* **-ED, -ING, -S** to saggar
SAGGING	present participle of sag
SAGGY	*adj* **-GIER, -GIEST** characterized by sagging
SAGIER	comparative of sagy
SAGIEST	superlative of sagy
SAGITTAL	*adj* resembling an arrow or arrowhead
SAGO	*n* pl. **-GOS** a tropical tree
SAGUARO	*n* pl. **-ROS** a tall cactus
SAGUM	*n* pl. **-GA** a cloak worn by ancient Roman soldiers
SAGY	*adj* **SAGIER, SAGIEST** flavored with sage
SAHIB	*n* pl. **-S** sir; master — used as a term of respect in colonial India
SAHIWAL	*n* pl. **-S** any of a breed of humped dairy cattle
SAHUARO	*n* pl. **-ROS** saguaro
SAICE	*n* pl. **-S** syce
SAID	*n* pl. **-S** sayyid
SAIGA	*n* pl. **-S** a small antelope
SAIL	*v* **-ED, -ING, -S** to move across the surface of water by the action of wind **SAILABLE** *adj*
SAILBOAT	*n* pl. **-S** a boat that sails
SAILER	*n* pl. **-S** a vessel that sails
SAILFISH	*n* pl. **-ES** a large marine fish
SAILING	*n* pl. **-S** the act of one that sails
SAILLESS	*adj* lacking a sail
SAILOR	*n* pl. **-S** a member of a ship's crew **SAILORLY** *adj*
SAILPAST	*n* pl. **-S** the sailing of ships past a place
SAIMIN	*n* pl. **-S** a Hawaiian noodle soup
SAIN	*v* **-ED, -ING, -S** to make the sign of the cross on
SAINFOIN	*n* pl. **-S** a perennial herb
SAINT	*v* **-ED, -ING, -S** to declare to be a saint (a person of exceptional holiness)
SAINTDOM	*n* pl. **-S** the state of being a saint

SAINTLY *adj* **-LIER, -LIEST** of or befitting a saint

SAITH a present 3d person sing. of say

SAITHE *n* pl. **SAITHE** a marine food fish

SAIYID *n* pl. **-S** sayyid

SAJOU *n* pl. **-S** a capuchin

SAKE *n* pl. **-S** benefit, interest, or advantage

SAKER *n* pl. **-S** a Eurasian falcon

SAKI *n* pl. **-S** a Japanese liquor

SAKTI *n* pl. **-S** the wife of a god in Hinduism

SAL *n* pl. **-S** salt

SALAAM *v* **-ED, -ING, -S** to greet with a low bow

SALABLE *adj* capable of being or fit to be sold **SALABLY** *adv*

SALACITY *n* pl. **-TIES** lewdness

SALAD *n* pl. **-S** a dish of green, raw vegetables

SALADANG *n* pl. **-S** a wild ox

SALAL *n* pl. **-S** a small shrub

SALAMI *n* pl. **-S** a seasoned sausage

SALARIAT *n* pl. **-S** the class of salaried persons

SALARY *v* **-RIED, -RYING, -RIES** to pay a periodic, fixed compensation to

SALAT *n* pl. **-S** the ritual prayer of Muslims

SALCHOW *n* pl. **-S** a figure-skating jump

SALE *n* pl. **-S** the act or an instance of selling

SALEABLE *adj* salable **SALEABLY** *adv*

SALEP *n* pl. **-S** a starchy meal ground from the roots of certain orchids

SALEROOM *n* pl. **-S** a room in which goods are displayed for sale

SALESMAN *n* pl. **-MEN** a man who sells merchandise

SALIC *adj* pertaining to a group of igneous rocks

SALICIN *n* pl. **-S** a chemical compound

SALICINE *n* pl. **-S** salicin

SALIENCE *n* pl. **-S** a projecting feature or detail

SALIENCY *n* pl. **-CIES** salience

SALIENT *n* pl. **-S** the part of a fortification projecting closest to the enemy

SALIFY *v* **-FIED, -FYING, -FIES** to combine with a salt

SALINA *n* pl. **-S** a pond, marsh, or lake containing salt water

SALINE *n* pl. **-S** a salt solution

SALINITY *n* pl. **-TIES** a concentration of salt

SALINIZE *v* **-NIZED, -NIZING, -NIZES** to treat with salt

SALIVA *n* pl. **-S** a fluid secreted by the glands of the mouth **SALIVARY** *adj*

SALIVATE *v* **-VATED, -VATING, -VATES** to secrete saliva

SALL *v* shall — SALL is the only form of this verb; it cannot be conjugated

SALLET *n* pl. **-S** a light medieval helmet

SALLIED past tense of sally

SALLIER *n* pl. **-S** one that sallies

SALLIES present 3d person sing. of sally

SALLOW *adj* **-LOWER, -LOWEST** of a sickly yellowish color **SALLOWLY** *adv*

SALLOW *v* **-ED, -ING, -S** to make sallow

SALLOWY *adj* abounding in willow trees

SALLY *v* **-LIED, -LYING, -LIES** to rush out suddenly

SALMI *n* pl. **-S** a dish of roasted game birds

SALMON *n* pl. **-S** a food fish

SALMONID *n* pl. **-S** a fish of the salmon family

SALMONY *adj* resembling salmon

SALOL *n* pl. **-S** a chemical compound

SALON *n* pl. **-S** a large room in which guests are received

SALOON *n* pl. **-S** a tavern

SALOOP *n* pl. **-S** a hot drink made from an infusion of aromatic herbs

SALP *n* pl. **-S** salpa

SALPA *n* pl. **-PAS** or **-PAE** a free-swimming tunicate

SALPIAN *n* pl. **-S** salpa

SALPICON *n* pl. **-S** a mixture of chopped foods in a sauce used as stuffings

SALPID *n* pl. **-S** salpa

SALPINX *n* pl. **-PINGES** an anatomical tube

SALSA *n* pl. **-S** a spicy sauce of tomatoes, onions, and peppers

SALSIFY *n* pl. **-FIES** a European herb

SALSILLA *n* pl. **-S** a tropical plant

SALT *adj* **SALTER, SALTEST** salty

SALT   v **-ED, -ING, -S** to treat with salt (a crystalline compound used as a seasoning and preservative)

SALTANT   adj jumping or dancing

SALTBOX   n pl. **-ES** a type of house

SALTBUSH   n pl. **-ES** a salt-tolerant plant

SALTER   n pl. **-S** one that salts

SALTERN   n pl. **-S** a place where salt is produced

SALTERY   n pl. **-ERIES** a factory where fish is salted for storage

SALTIE   n pl. **-S** a deep-sea vessel sailing the Great Lakes

SALTIER   n pl. **-S** saltire

SALTIEST   superlative of salty

SALTILY   adv in a salty manner

SALTINE   n pl. **-S** a salted cracker

SALTING   n pl. **-S** land regularly flooded by tides

SALTIRE   n pl. **-S** a heraldic design

SALTISH   adj somewhat salty

SALTLESS   adj having no salt

SALTLIKE   adj resembling salt

SALTNESS   n pl. **-ES** the state of being salty

SALTPAN   n pl. **-S** a large pan for making salt by evaporation

SALTWORK   n pl. **-S** a saltern

SALTWORT   n pl. **-S** a seaside herb

SALTY   adj **SALTIER, SALTIEST** tasting of or containing salt

SALUKI   n pl. **-S** a tall, slender dog

SALUT   interj — used to express friendship before a drink

SALUTARY   adj producing a beneficial effect

SALUTE   v **-LUTED, -LUTING, -LUTES** to greet with a sign of welcome or respect

SALUTER   n pl. **-S** one that salutes

SALVABLE   adj capable of being saved **SALVABLY** adv

SALVAGE   v **-VAGED, -VAGING, -VAGES** to save from loss or destruction

SALVAGEE   n pl. **-S** one in whose favor salvage has been effected

SALVAGER   n pl. **-S** one that salvages

SALVE   v **SALVED, SALVING, SALVES** to soothe

SALVER   n pl. **-S** a tray or serving platter

SALVIA   n pl. **-S** a flowering plant

SALVIFIC   adj having the power to save

SALVING   present participle of salve

SALVO   v **-ED, -ING, -S** or **-ES** to discharge firearms simultaneously

SALVOR   n pl. **-S** a salvager

SALWAR   n pl. **-S** shalwar

SAMADHI   n pl. **-S** a state of concentration in yoga

SAMARA   n pl. **-S** a dry, one-seeded fruit

SAMARIUM   n pl. **-S** a metallic element

SAMBA   v **-ED, -ING, -S** to perform a Brazilian dance

SAMBAL   n pl. **-S** a spicy condiment

SAMBAR   n pl. **-S** a large Asian deer

SAMBHAR   n pl. **-S** sambar

SAMBHUR   n pl. **-S** sambar

SAMBO   n pl. **-BOS** or **-BOES** a Latin American of mixed black and Indian ancestry

SAMBUCA   n pl. **-S** an ancient stringed instrument

SAMBUKE   n pl. **-S** sambuca

SAMBUR   n pl. **-S** sambar

SAME   adj resembling in every relevant respect

SAMECH   n pl. **-S** samek

SAMEK   n pl. **-S** a Hebrew letter

SAMEKH   n pl. **-S** samek

SAMENESS   n pl. **-ES** lack of change or variety

SAMEY   adj **SAMIER, SAMIEST** lacking variety

SAMFU   n pl. **-S** a casual Chinese outfit of jacket and pants

SAMIEL   n pl. **-S** the simoom

SAMISEN   n pl. **-S** a Japanese stringed instrument

SAMITE   n pl. **-S** a silk fabric

SAMIZDAT   n pl. **-S** a system in the Soviet Union for printing and distributing unauthorized literature

SAMLET   n pl. **-S** a young salmon

SAMOSA   n pl. **-S** a filled pastry turnover

SAMOVAR   n pl. **-S** a metal urn for heating water

SAMP   n pl. **-S** coarsely ground corn

SAMPAN   n pl. **-S** a flat-bottomed Chinese skiff

SAMPHIRE   n pl. **-S** a European herb

SAMPLE *v* **-PLED, -PLING, -PLES** to test a representative portion of a whole

SAMPLER *n* pl. **-S** one that samples

SAMPLING *n* pl. **-S** a small part selected for analysis

SAMSARA *n* pl. **-S** the cycle of birth, death, and rebirth in Buddhism **SAMSARIC** *adj*

SAMSHU *n* pl. **-S** a Chinese liquor

SAMSKARA *n* pl. **-S** a Hindu purification ceremony

SAMURAI *n* pl. **-S** a Japanese warrior

SAN *n* pl. **-S** a sanatorium

SANATIVE *adj* having the power to cure or heal

SANCTA a pl. of sanctum

SANCTIFY *v* **-FIED, -FYING, -FIES** to make holy

SANCTION *v* **-ED, -ING, -S** to authorize

SANCTITY *n* pl. **-TIES** holiness

SANCTUM *n* pl. **-TUMS** or **-TA** a sacred place

SAND *v* **-ED, -ING, -S** to smooth by rubbing with an abrasive **SANDABLE** *adj*

SANDAL *v* **-DALED, -DALING, -DALS** or **-DALLED, -DALLING, -DALS** to provide with sandals (light, open shoes)

SANDARAC *n* pl. **-S** an aromatic resin

SANDBAG *v* **-BAGGED, -BAGGING, -BAGS** to surround with bags of sand (loose granular rock material)

SANDBANK *n* pl. **-S** a large mass of sand

SANDBAR *n* pl. **-S** a ridge of sand formed in a river or sea

SANDBOX *n* pl. **-ES** a box containing sand for children to play in

SANDBUR *n* pl. **-S** an annual herb

SANDBURR *n* pl. **-S** sandbur

SANDDAB *n* pl. **-S** a small flatfish

SANDER *n* pl. **-S** one that sands

SANDFISH *n* pl. **-ES** a marine fish

SANDFLY *n* pl. **-FLIES** a biting fly

SANDHI *n* pl. **-S** a process of phonetic modification

SANDHILL *n* pl. **-S** a hill of sand

SANDHOG *n* pl. **-S** a worker who digs or works in sand

SANDIER comparative of sandy

SANDIEST superlative of sandy

SANDLESS *adj* lacking sand

SANDLIKE *adj* resembling sand

SANDLING *n* pl. **-S** a marine fish

SANDLOT *n* pl. **-S** a vacant lot

SANDMAN *n* pl. **-MEN** a mythical person who makes children sleepy by sprinkling sand in their eyes

SANDPEEP *n* pl. **-S** a wading bird

SANDPILE *n* pl. **-S** a pile of sand

SANDPIT *n* pl. **-S** a pit dug in sandy soil

SANDSHOE *n* pl. **-S** a lightweight sneaker

SANDSOAP *n* pl. **-S** a type of soap

SANDSPIT *n* pl. **-S** a small point of land created by sand dunes

SANDSPUR *n* pl. **-S** a sandbur

SANDWICH *v* **-ED, -ING, -ES** to place between two layers or objects

SANDWORM *n* pl. **-S** a sand-dwelling worm

SANDWORT *n* pl. **-S** a flowering plant

SANDY *adj* **SANDIER, SANDIEST** containing or covered with sand

SANDYISH *adj* somewhat sandy

SANE *adj* **SANER, SANEST** mentally sound **SANELY** *adv*

SANE *v* **SANED, SANING, SANES** to sain

SANENESS *n* pl. **-ES** sanity

SANG past tense of sing

SANGA *n* pl. **-S** sangar

SANGAR *n* pl. **-S** a temporary fortification for two or three men

SANGAREE *n* pl. **-S** an alcoholic beverage

SANGER *n* pl. **-S** sangar

SANGH *n* pl. **-S** an association promoting unity between the different groups in Hinduism

SANGHA *n* pl. **-S** a Buddhist religious community

SANGRAIL *n* pl. **-S** the legendary cup used by Christ at the Last Supper

SANGREAL *n* pl. **-S** sangrail

SANGRIA *n* pl. **-S** an alcoholic beverage

SANGUINE *n* pl. **-S** a red color

SANICLE *n* pl. **-S** a medicinal herb

SANIDINE *n* pl. **-S** a glassy variety of feldspar

SANIES *n* pl. **SANIES** a fluid discharged from wounds **SANIOUS** *adj*

SANING present participle of sane

SANITARY n pl. **-TARIES** a public urinal

SANITATE v **-TATED, -TATING, -TATES** to sanitize

SANITISE v **-TISED, -TISING, -TISES** to sanitize

SANITIZE v **-TIZED, -TIZING, -TIZES** to guard against infection or disease by cleaning or sterilizing

SANITY n pl. **-TIES** the state of being sane

SANJAK n pl. **-S** an administrative district of Turkey

SANK past tense of sink

SANNOP n pl. **-S** sannup

SANNUP n pl. **-S** a married male Native American

SANNYASI n pl. **-S** a Hindu monk

SANS prep without

SANSAR n pl. **-S** sarsar

SANSEI n pl. **-S** a grandchild of Japanese immigrants to the United States

SANSERIF n pl. **-S** a typeface without serifs

SANTALIC adj pertaining to sandalwood

SANTALOL n pl. **-S** sandalwood oil

SANTERA n pl. **-S** a priestess of santeria

SANTERIA n pl. **-S** a religion of the Caribbean region

SANTERO n pl. **-ROS** a priest of santeria

SANTIM n pl. **-TIMS** or **-TIMI** or **-TIMU** a formerly used coin of Latvia

SANTIR n pl. **-S** a Persian dulcimer

SANTO n pl. **-TOS** a wooden image of a saint

SANTOL n pl. **-S** a tropical tree

SANTONIN n pl. **-S** a chemical compound

SANTOOR n pl. **-S** santir

SANTOUR n pl. **-S** santir

SANTUR n pl. **-S** santir

SANYASI n pl. **-S** sannyasi

SAP v **SAPPED, SAPPING, SAPS** to deplete or weaken gradually

SAPAJOU n pl. **-S** a capuchin

SAPELE n pl. **-S** a large tropical African tree

SAPHEAD n pl. **-S** a foolish, stupid, or gullible person

SAPHENA n pl. **-NAS** or **-NAE** a vein of the leg

SAPID adj pleasant to the taste

SAPIDITY n pl. **-TIES** the state of being sapid

SAPIENCE n pl. **-S** wisdom

SAPIENCY n pl. **-CIES** sapience

SAPIENS adj pertaining to recent man

SAPIENT n pl. **-S** a wise person

SAPLESS adj lacking vitality

SAPLING n pl. **-S** a young tree

SAPONIFY v **-FIED, -FYING, -FIES** to convert into soap

SAPONIN n pl. **-S** a soapy substance obtained from plants

SAPONINE n pl. **-S** saponin

SAPONITE n pl. **-S** a mineral found in veins and cavities of rocks

SAPOR n pl. **-S** flavor **SAPOROUS** adj

SAPOTA n pl. **-S** an evergreen tree

SAPOTE n pl. **-S** a tropical American tree

SAPOUR n pl. **-S** sapor

SAPPED past tense of sap

SAPPER n pl. **-S** a military engineer

SAPPHIC n pl. **-S** a type of verse form

SAPPHIRE n pl. **-S** a blue gem

SAPPHISM n pl. **-S** lesbianism

SAPPHIST n pl. **-S** a lesbian

SAPPING n pl. **-S** the removal of the foundation of a building so as to weaken it

SAPPY adj **-PIER, -PIEST** silly **SAPPILY** adv

SAPREMIA n pl. **-S** a form of blood poisoning **SAPREMIC** adj

SAPROBE n pl. **-S** an organism that derives its nourishment from decaying organic matter **SAPROBIC** adj

SAPROPEL n pl. **-S** mud consisting chiefly of decaying organic matter

SAPSAGO n pl. **-GOS** a hard green cheese

SAPWOOD n pl. **-S** the newly formed outer wood of a tree

SARABAND n pl. **-S** a stately Spanish dance

SARAN n pl. **-S** a thermoplastic resin

SARANGI n pl. **-S** a stringed instrument of India

SARAPE n pl. **-S** serape

SARCASM n pl. **-S** a sharply mocking or contemptuous remark

SARCENET n pl. **-S** a silk fabric

SARCINA n pl. **-NAS** or **-NAE** a spherical bacterium

SARCOID n pl. **-S** a disease of horses

SARCOMA *n pl.* **-MAS** or **-MATA** a type of tumor

SARCOUS *adj* composed of flesh or muscle

SARD *n pl.* **-S** a variety of quartz

SARDANA *n pl.* **-S** a Spanish folk dance

SARDAR *n pl.* **-S** sirdar

SARDINE *v* **-DINED, -DINING, -DINES** to pack tightly

SARDIUS *n pl.* **-ES** sard

SARDONIC *adj* mocking

SARDONYX *n pl.* **-ES** a variety of quartz

SAREE *n pl.* **-S** sari

SARGASSO *n pl.* **-GASSOS** or **-GASSOES** or **-GASSA** a brownish seaweed

SARGE *n pl.* **-S** sergeant

SARGO *n pl.* **-GOS** a silvery marine fish

SARI *n pl.* **-S** an outer garment worn by Hindu women

SARIN *n pl.* **-S** a toxic gas

SARK *n pl.* **-S** a shirt

SARKY *adj* **SARKIER, SARKIEST** sarcastic **SARKILY** *adv*

SARMENT *n pl.* **-S** a type of plant stem

SARMENTA *n/pl* sarments

SARNIE *n pl.* **-S** a sandwich

SAROD *n pl.* **-S** a stringed instrument of India

SARODE *n pl.* **-S** sarod

SARODIST *n pl.* **-S** one who plays the sarod

SARONG *n pl.* **-S** an outer garment worn in the Pacific islands

SAROS *n pl.* **-ES** the eclipse cycle of the sun and moon

SARSAR *n pl.* **-S** a cold, whistling wind

SARSEN *n pl.* **-S** a large sandstone block

SARSENET *n pl.* **-S** sarcenet

SARSNET *n pl.* **-S** sarcenet

SARTOR *n pl.* **-S** a tailor

SARTORII *n/pl* flat, narrow thigh muscles

SASANQUA *n pl.* **-S** a Japanese camellia

SASH *v* **-ED, -ING, -ES** to furnish with a frame in which glass is set

SASHAY *v* **-ED, -ING, -S** to flounce

SASHIMI *n pl.* **-S** a Japanese dish of sliced raw fish

SASHLESS *adj* lacking a sash (a long band worn around the waist)

SASIN *n pl.* **-S** an antelope of India

SASS *v* **-ED, -ING, -ES** to talk impudently to

SASSABY *n pl.* **-BIES** an African antelope

SASSIER comparative of sassy

SASSIES pl. of sassy

SASSIEST superlative of sassy

SASSILY *adv* in a sassy manner

SASSWOOD *n pl.* **-S** an African tree

SASSY *adj* **SASSIER, SASSIEST** impudent

SASSY *n pl.* **-SIES** sasswood

SASTRUGA *n pl.* **-GI** a ridge of snow formed by the wind in polar regions

SAT past tense of sit

SATANG *n pl.* **-S** a monetary unit of Thailand

SATANIC *adj* extremely evil

SATANISM *n pl.* **-S** worship of the powers of evil

SATANIST *n pl.* **-S** one who practices satanism

SATARA *n pl.* **-S** a woolen fabric

SATAY *n pl.* **-TAYS** marinated meat that is skewered and broiled and dipped in peanut sauce

SATCHEL *n pl.* **-S** a small carrying bag

SATCOM *n pl.* **-S** satellite communications

SATE *v* **SATED, SATING, SATES** to satiate

SATEEN *n pl.* **-S** a cotton fabric

SATEM *adj* pertaining to a group of Indo-European languages

SATI *n pl.* **-S** suttee

SATIABLE *adj* capable of being satiated **SATIABLY** *adv*

SATIATE *v* **-ATED, -ATING, -ATES** to satisfy to or beyond capacity

SATIETY *n pl.* **-ETIES** the state of being satiated

SATIN *v* **-ED, -ING, -S** to give a glossy surface to

SATINET *n pl.* **-S** a thin satin

SATING present participle of sate

SATINPOD *n pl.* **-S** a flowering plant

SATINY *adj* resembling satin

SATIRE *n pl.* **-S** the use of derisive wit to attack folly or wickedness **SATIRIC** *adj*

SATIRISE *v* **-RISED, -RISING, -RISES** to satirize

SATIRIST *n* pl. **-S** one who satirizes

SATIRIZE *v* **-RIZED, -RIZING, -RIZES** to subject to satire

SATISFY *v* **-FIED, -FYING, -FIES** to provide fully with what is desired, expected, or needed

SATORI *n* pl. **-S** the illumination of spirit sought by Zen Buddhists

SATRAP *n* pl. **-S** a governor of a province in ancient Persia

SATRAPY *n* pl. **-PIES** the territory of a satrap

SATSANG *n* pl. **-S** a sacred gathering in Hinduism

SATSUMA *n* pl. **-S** a variety of orange

SATURANT *n* pl. **-S** a substance used to saturate

SATURATE *v* **-RATED, -RATING, -RATES** to fill completely with something that permeates

SATYR *n* pl. **-S** a woodland deity of Greek mythology **SATYRIC** *adj*

SATYRID *n* pl. **-S** a brownish butterfly

SAU *n* pl. **SAU** xu

SAUCE *v* **SAUCED, SAUCING, SAUCES** to season with sauce (a flavorful liquid dressing)

SAUCEBOX *n* pl. **-ES** a saucy person

SAUCEPAN *n* pl. **-S** a deep cooking pan with a handle

SAUCEPOT *n* pl. **-S** a deep cooking pot with two handles

SAUCER *n* pl. **-S** a small, shallow dish

SAUCH *n* pl. **-S** saugh

SAUCIER *n* pl. **-S** a chef who specializes in sauces

SAUCING present participle of sauce

SAUCY *adj* **SAUCIER, SAUCIEST** impudent **SAUCILY** *adv*

SAUGER *n* pl. **-S** a freshwater fish

SAUGH *n* pl. **-S** a willow tree **SAUGHY** *adj*

SAUL *n* pl. **-S** soul

SAULT *n* pl. **-S** a waterfall

SAUNA *v* **-ED, -ING, -S** to take a dry heat bath

SAUNTER *v* **-ED, -ING, -S** to walk in a leisurely manner

SAUREL *n* pl. **-S** a marine fish

SAURIAN *n* pl. **-S** any of a suborder of reptiles

SAUROPOD *n* pl. **-S** any of a suborder of large dinosaurs

SAURY *n* pl. **-RIES** a marine fish

SAUSAGE *n* pl. **-S** finely chopped and seasoned meat stuffed into a casing

SAUTE *v* **-TEED** or **-TED, -TEING, -TES** to fry in a small amount of fat

SAUTERNE *n* pl. **-S** a sweet white wine

SAUTOIR *n* pl. **-S** a saltire

SAUTOIRE *n* pl. **-S** sautoir

SAVABLE *adj* capable of being saved

SAVAGE *adj* **-AGER, -AGEST** fierce **SAVAGELY** *adv*

SAVAGE *v* **-AGED, -AGING, -AGES** to attack or treat brutally

SAVAGERY *n* pl. **-RIES** the quality of being savage

SAVAGISM *n* pl. **-S** savagery

SAVANNA *n* pl. **-S** a flat, treeless grassland

SAVANNAH *n* pl. **-S** savanna

SAVANT *n* pl. **-S** a man of profound learning

SAVARIN *n* pl. **-S** a yeast cake baked in a ring mold

SAVATE *n* pl. **-S** a pugilistic sport

SAVE *v* **SAVED, SAVING, SAVES** to rescue from danger, injury, or loss **SAVEABLE** *adj*

SAVELOY *n* pl. **-LOYS** a highly seasoned sausage

SAVER *n* pl. **-S** one that saves

SAVIN *n* pl. **-S** an evergreen shrub

SAVINE *n* pl. **-S** savin

SAVING *n* pl. **-S** the act or an instance of saving

SAVINGLY *adv* in a thrifty manner

SAVIOR *n* pl. **-S** one that saves

SAVIOUR *n* pl. **-S** savior

SAVOR *v* **-ED, -ING, -S** to taste or smell with pleasure

SAVORER *n* pl. **-S** one that savors

SAVOROUS *adj* savory

SAVORY *adj* **-VORIER, -VORIEST** pleasant to the taste or smell **SAVORILY** *adv*

SAVORY *n* pl. **-VORIES** a savory dish served before or after a meal

SAVOUR *v* **-ED, -ING, -S** to savor

SAVOURER *n* pl. **-S** savorer

SAVOURY *adj* **-VOURIER, -VOURIEST** savory

SAVOURY *n* pl. **-VOURIES** a savory

SAVOY	*n pl.* **-VOYS** a variety of cabbage
SAVVY	*adj* **-VIER, -VIEST** shrewd
SAVVY	*v* **-VIED, -VYING, -VIES** to understand **SAVVILY** *adv*
SAW	*v* **SAWED, SAWN, SAWING, SAWS** to cut or divide with a saw (a type of cutting tool)
SAWBILL	*n pl.* **-S** a tropical bird
SAWBONES	*n pl.* **-BONESES** a surgeon
SAWBUCK	*n pl.* **-S** a sawhorse
SAWDUST	*n pl.* **-S** small particles of wood produced in sawing **SAWDUSTY** *adj*
SAWER	*n pl.* **-S** one that saws
SAWFISH	*n pl.* **-ES** a marine fish
SAWFLY	*n pl.* **-FLIES** a winged insect
SAWGRASS	*n pl.* **-ES** a sedge with spiny-edged leaves
SAWHORSE	*n pl.* **-S** a rack used to support a piece of wood being sawed
SAWLIKE	*adj* resembling a saw
SAWLOG	*n pl.* **-S** a log large enough to saw into boards
SAWMILL	*n pl.* **-S** a place where logs are sawed
SAWN	a past participle of saw
SAWNEY	*n pl.* **-NEYS** a foolish person
SAWTOOTH	*n pl.* **-TEETH** a cutting edge on a saw
SAWYER	*n pl.* **-S** one that saws wood for a living
SAX	*n pl.* **-ES** a saxophone
SAXATILE	*adj* living or growing among rocks
SAXHORN	*n pl.* **-S** a brass wind instrument
SAXIST	*n pl.* **-S** a saxophone player
SAXMAN	*n pl.* **-MEN** a saxophone player
SAXONY	*n pl.* **-NIES** a woolen fabric
SAXTUBA	*n pl.* **-S** a bass saxhorn
SAY	*v* **SAID, SAYING,** present sing. 2d person **SAY** or **SAYEST** or **SAYST,** 3d person **SAYS** or **SAITH** to utter **SAYABLE** *adj*
SAYED	*n pl.* **-S** sayyid
SAYER	*n pl.* **-S** one that says
SAYID	*n pl.* **-S** sayyid
SAYING	*n pl.* **-S** a maxim
SAYONARA	*n pl.* **-S** goodby
SAYST	a present 2d person sing. of say
SAYYID	*n pl.* **-S** lord; sir — used as a title of respect for a Muslim dignitary
SCAB	*v* **SCABBED, SCABBING, SCABS** to become covered with a scab (a crust that forms over a healing wound)
SCABBARD	*v* **-ED, -ING, -S** to put into a sheath, as a sword
SCABBLE	*v* **-BLED, -BLING, -BLES** to shape roughly
SCABBY	*adj* **-BIER, -BIEST** covered with scabs **SCABBILY** *adv*
SCABIES	*n pl.* **SCABIES** a skin disease
SCABIOSA	*n pl.* **-S** scabious
SCABIOUS	*n pl.* **-ES** a flowering plant
SCABLAND	*n pl.* **-S** rocky land with little soil cover
SCABLIKE	*adj* resembling a scab
SCABROUS	*adj* roughened with small projections
SCAD	*n pl.* **-S** a marine fish
SCAFFOLD	*v* **-ED, -ING, -S** to provide with a scaffold (a temporary platform for workmen)
SCAG	*n pl.* **-S** heroin
SCALABLE	*adj* capable of being scaled **SCALABLY** *adv*
SCALADE	*n pl.* **-S** an act of scaling the walls of a fortification
SCALADO	*n pl.* **-DOS** scalade
SCALAGE	*n pl.* **-S** a percentage deduction to compensate for shrinkage
SCALAR	*n pl.* **-S** a mathematical quantity possessing only magnitude
SCALARE	*n pl.* **-S** a tropical fish
SCALAWAG	*n pl.* **-S** a rascal
SCALD	*v* **-ED, -ING, -S** to burn with hot liquid or steam
SCALDIC	*adj* skaldic
SCALE	*v* **SCALED, SCALING, SCALES** to climb up or over
SCALENE	*n pl.* **-S** a triangle having no two sides equal
SCALENUS	*n pl.* **-NI** a muscle of the neck
SCALEPAN	*n pl.* **-S** a pan on a weighing scale
SCALER	*n pl.* **-S** one that scales
SCALEUP	*n pl.* **-S** an increase based on a fixed ratio
SCALIER	comparative of scaly
SCALIEST	superlative of scaly

SCALING *n* pl. **-S** the formation of scales on the skin

SCALL *n* pl. **-S** a scaly eruption of the skin

SCALLION *n* pl. **-S** an onion-like plant

SCALLOP *v* **-ED, -ING, -S** to bake in a sauce topped with bread crumbs

SCALP *v* **-ED, -ING, -S** to remove an upper part from

SCALPEL *n* pl. **-S** a small surgical knife

SCALPER *n* pl. **-S** one that scalps

SCALY *adj* **SCALIER, SCALIEST** peeling off in flakes

SCAM *v* **SCAMMED, SCAMMING, SCAMS** to cheat or swindle

SCAMMER *n* pl. **-S** one that scams

SCAMMONY *n* pl. **-NIES** a climbing plant

SCAMP *v* **-ED, -ING, -S** to perform in a hasty or careless manner

SCAMPER *v* **-ED, -ING, -S** to run playfully about

SCAMPI *n* pl. **SCAMPI** or **SCAMPIES** large shrimp used in Italian cooking

SCAMPISH *adj* rascally

SCAMSTER *n* pl. **-S** one that scams

SCAN *v* **SCANNED, SCANNING, SCANS** to examine closely

SCANDAL *v* **-DALED, -DALING, -DALS** or **-DALLED, -DALLING, -DALS** to defame

SCANDENT *adj* climbing, as a plant

SCANDIA *n* pl. **-S** an oxide of scandium

SCANDIUM *n* pl. **-S** a metallic element **SCANDIC** *adj*

SCANNED past tense of scan

SCANNER *n* pl. **-S** one that scans

SCANNING *n* pl. **-S** close examination

SCANSION *n* pl. **-S** the analysis of verse into metrical feet and rhythm patterns

SCANT *adj* **SCANTER, SCANTEST** meager

SCANT *v* **-ED, -ING, -S** to provide with a meager portion

SCANTIES *n/pl* brief panties for women

SCANTLY *adv* in a scant manner

SCANTY *adj* **SCANTIER, SCANTIEST** meager **SCANTILY** *adv*

SCAPE *v* **SCAPED, SCAPING, SCAPES** to escape

SCAPHOID *n* pl. **-S** a bone of the wrist

SCAPOSE *adj* bearing a leafless stalk

SCAPULA *n* pl. **-LAS** or **-LAE** a bone of the shoulder

SCAPULAR *n* pl. **-S** a sleeveless outer garment worn by monks

SCAR *v* **SCARRED, SCARRING, SCARS** to form a scar (a mark left by the healing of injured tissue)

SCARAB *n* pl. **-S** a large, black beetle

SCARCE *adj* **SCARCER, SCARCEST** infrequently seen or found

SCARCELY *adv* by a narrow margin

SCARCITY *n* pl. **-TIES** the quality of being scarce

SCARE *v* **SCARED, SCARING, SCARES** to frighten

SCARED *adj* **SCAREDER, SCAREDEST** afraid

SCARER *n* pl. **-S** one that scares

SCAREY *adj* **SCARIER, SCARIEST** scary

SCARF *n* pl. **SCARFS** or **SCARVES** a piece of cloth worn for warmth or protection

SCARF *v* **-ED, -ING, -S** to cover with a scarf

SCARFER *n* pl. **-S** one that eats or drinks voraciously

SCARFPIN *n* pl. **-S** a tiepin

SCARIER comparative of scarey and scary

SCARIEST superlative of scarey and scary

SCARIFY *v* **-FIED, -FYING, -FIES** to make superficial cuts in

SCARILY *adv* in a scary manner

SCARING present participle of scare

SCARIOSE *adj* scarious

SCARIOUS *adj* thin, dry, and membranous

SCARLESS *adj* having no scars

SCARLET *n* pl. **-S** a red color

SCARP *v* **-ED, -ING, -S** to cut or make into a steep slope

SCARPER *v* **-ED, -ING, -S** to flee

SCARPH *v* **-ED, -ING, -S** to unite by means of a type of joint

SCARRED past tense of scar

SCARRING present participle of scar

SCARRY *adj* **-RIER, -RIEST** marked with scars

SCART *v* **-ED, -ING, -S** to scratch

SCARVED *adj* wearing a scarf

SCARVES a pl. of scarf

SCARY	*adj* **SCARIER, SCARIEST** frightening
SCAT	*v* **SCATTED, SCATTING, SCATS** to leave hastily
SCATBACK	*n* pl. **-S** a type of player in football
SCATHE	*v* **SCATHED, SCATHING, SCATHES** to criticize severely
SCATT	*n* pl. **-S** a tax
SCATTED	past tense of scat
SCATTER	*v* **-ED, -ING, -S** to go or send in various directions
SCATTING	present participle of scat
SCATTY	*adj* **-TIER, -TIEST** crazy **SCATTILY** *adv*
SCAUP	*n* pl. **-S** a sea duck
SCAUPER	*n* pl. **-S** an engraving tool
SCAUR	*n* pl. **-S** a protruding, isolated rock
SCAVENGE	*v* **-ENGED, -ENGING, -ENGES** to search through rubbish for usable items
SCENA	*n* pl. **-S** an elaborate composition for a single voice
SCENARIO	*n* pl. **-IOS** a summary of the plot of a dramatic work
SCEND	*v* **-ED, -ING, -S** to rise upward, as a ship on a wave
SCENE	*n* pl. **-S** the place where some action or event occurs
SCENERY	*n* pl. **-ERIES** a picturesque landscape or view
SCENIC	*n* pl. **-S** a depiction of natural scenery
SCENICAL	*adj* pertaining to scenery
SCENT	*v* **-ED, -ING, -S** to fill with an odor
SCEPTER	*v* **-ED, -ING, -S** to invest with royal authority
SCEPTIC	*n* pl. **-S** skeptic
SCEPTRAL	*adj* pertaining to royal authority
SCEPTRE	*v* **-TRED, -TRING, -TRES** to scepter
SCHAPPE	*n* pl. **-S** a silk fabric
SCHAV	*n* pl. **-S** a chilled soup
SCHEDULE	*v* **-ULED, -ULING, -ULES** to assign to a certain date or time
SCHEMA	*n* pl. **-MAS** or **-MATA** a generalized diagram or plan
SCHEME	*v* **SCHEMED, SCHEMING, SCHEMES** to plan or plot
SCHEMER	*n* pl. **-S** one that schemes
SCHEMING	*n* pl. **-S** the act of planning or plotting
SCHERZO	*n* pl. **-ZOS** or **-ZI** a lively musical movement
SCHILLER	*n* pl. **-S** a brownish luster occurring on certain minerals
SCHISM	*n* pl. **-S** a division into opposing parties
SCHIST	*n* pl. **-S** a rock that readily splits into parallel layers
SCHIZIER	comparative of schizy
SCHIZIEST	superlative of schizy
SCHIZO	*n* pl. **SCHIZOS** a schizoid
SCHIZOID	*n* pl. **-S** a person affected with a type of psychotic disorder
SCHIZONT	*n* pl. **-S** an organism that reproduces by a form of asexual reproduction
SCHIZY	*adj* **SCHIZIER, SCHIZIEST** affected with schizophrenia
SCHIZZY	*adj* **SCHIZZIER, SCHIZZIEST** schizy
SCHLEP	*v* **SCHLEPPED, SCHLEPPING, SCHLEPS** to lug or drag
SCHLEPP	*v* **-ED, -ING, -S** to schlep
SCHLEPPY	*adj* **-PIER, -PIEST** shabby, run-down
SCHLIERE	*n* pl. **-REN** a small streak in an igneous rock
SCHLOCK	*n* pl. **-S** inferior merchandise
SCHLOCKY	*adj* **SCHLOCKIER, SCHLOCKIEST** of inferior quality
SCHLUB	*n* pl. **-S** a stupid or unattractive person
SCHLUMP	*v* **-ED, -ING, -S** to go about lazily or sloppily dressed
SCHLUMPY	*adj* **SCHLUMPIER, SCHLUMPIEST** unattractive, slovenly
SCHMALTZ	*n* pl. **-ES** excessive sentimentality
SCHMALZ	*n* pl. **-ES** schmaltz
SCHMALZY	*adj* **SCHMALZIER, SCHMALZIEST** characterized by schmaltz
SCHMATTE	*n* pl. **-S** a ragged garment
SCHMEAR	*v* **-ED, -ING, -S** to schmeer
SCHMEER	*v* **-ED, -ING, -S** to bribe
SCHMELZE	*n* pl. **-S** a type of decorative glass
SCHMO	*n* pl. **SCHMOES** or **SCHMOS** a stupid person
SCHMOE	*n* pl. **-S** schmo

SCHMOOS	*v* **-ED, -ING, -ES** to schmooze
SCHMOOSE	*v* **SCHMOOSED, SCHMOOSING, SCHMOOSES** to schmooze
SCHMOOZE	*v* **SCHMOOZED, SCHMOOZING, SCHMOOZES** to gossip
SCHMOOZY	*adj* **SCHMOOZIER, SCHMOOZIEST** given to schmoozing
SCHMUCK	*v* **-ED, -ING, -S** to hit or flatten
SCHMUCKY	*adj* **SCHMUCKIER, SCHMUCKIEST** foolish, contemptible
SCHMUTZ	*n* pl. **-ES** dirt, grime
SCHNAPPS	*n* pl. **SCHNAPPS** a strong liquor
SCHNAPS	*n* pl. **SCHNAPS** schnapps
SCHNECKE	*n* pl. **-KEN** a sweet roll
SCHNOOK	*n* pl. **-S** an easily deceived person
SCHNOZ	*n* pl. **-ES** the nose
SCHNOZZ	*n* pl. **-ES** schnoz
SCHOLAR	*n* pl. **-S** a learned person
SCHOLIUM	*n* pl. **-LIUMS** or **-LIA** an explanatory marginal note
SCHOOL	*v* **-ED, -ING, -S** to educate in an institution of learning
SCHOONER	*n* pl. **-S** a sailing vessel
SCHORL	*n* pl. **-S** a mineral
SCHRIK	*n* pl. **-S** sudden fright
SCHROD	*n* pl. **-S** scrod
SCHTICK	*n* pl. **-S** shtick
SCHTIK	*n* pl. **-S** shtick
SCHTUM	*adj* silent
SCHUIT	*n* pl. **-S** a Dutch sailing vessel
SCHUL	*n* pl. **SCHULS** or **SCHULN** shul
SCHUSS	*v* **-ED, -ING, -ES** to make a fast, straight run in skiing
SCHUSSER	*n* pl. **-S** one that schusses
SCHVITZ	*v* **-ED, -ING, -ES** to shvitz
SCHWA	*n* pl. **-S** a type of vowel sound
SCIAENID	*n* pl. **-S** a carnivorous fish
SCIATIC	*n* pl. **-S** a nerve, vein, or artery situated near the hip
SCIATICA	*n* pl. **-S** a painful disorder of the hip and adjoining areas
SCIENCE	*n* pl. **-S** a department of systematized knowledge
SCILICET	*adv* namely
SCILLA	*n* pl. **-S** a flowering plant
SCIMETAR	*n* pl. **-S** scimitar
SCIMITAR	*n* pl. **-S** a curved sword used by Arabs and Turks
SCIMITER	*n* pl. **-S** scimitar
SCINCOID	*n* pl. **-S** one of a family of smooth, short-limbed lizards
SCIOLISM	*n* pl. **-S** superficial knowledge
SCIOLIST	*n* pl. **-S** one whose knowledge is superficial
SCION	*n* pl. **-S** a child or descendant
SCIROCCO	*n* pl. **-COS** sirocco
SCIRRHUS	*n* pl. **-RHUSES** or **-RHI** a hard tumor
SCISSILE	*adj* capable of being cut or split easily
SCISSION	*n* pl. **-S** the act of cutting or splitting
SCISSOR	*v* **-ED, -ING, -S** to cut with a two-bladed cutting implement
SCISSURE	*n* pl. **-S** a lengthwise cut
SCIURID	*n* pl. **-S** a sciurine
SCIURINE	*n* pl. **-S** a rodent of the squirrel family
SCIUROID	*adj* resembling a squirrel
SCLAFF	*v* **-ED, -ING, -S** to strike the ground with the club before hitting the ball in golf
SCLAFFER	*n* pl. **-S** one that sclaffs
SCLERA	*n* pl. **-RAS** or **-RAE** the white, fibrous outer coat of the eyeball **SCLERAL** *adj*
SCLEREID	*n* pl. **-S** a type of plant cell
SCLERITE	*n* pl. **-S** one of the hard plates forming the outer covering of an arthropod
SCLEROID	*adj* sclerous
SCLEROMA	*n* pl. **-MAS** or **-MATA** a hardened patch of cellular tissue
SCLEROSE	*v* **-ROSED, -ROSING, -ROSES** to become hard, as tissue
SCLEROUS	*adj* hardened
SCOFF	*v* **-ED, -ING, -S** to express rude doubt or derision
SCOFFER	*n* pl. **-S** one that scoffs
SCOFFLAW	*n* pl. **-S** a habitual law violator
SCOLD	*v* **-ED, -ING, -S** to rebuke harshly
SCOLDER	*n* pl. **-S** one that scolds
SCOLDING	*n* pl. **-S** a harsh reproof
SCOLEX	*n* pl. **-LECES** or **-LICES** the knoblike head of a tapeworm

SCOLIOMA *n* pl. **-S** abnormal curvature of the spine

SCOLLOP *v* **-ED, -ING, -S** to scallop

SCOMBRID *n* pl. **-S** a fish of the mackerel family

SCONCE *v* **SCONCED, SCONCING, SCONCES** to fine

SCONE *n* pl. **-S** a flat, round cake

SCOOCH *v* **-ED, -ING, -ES** to slide with short movements

SCOOP *v* **-ED, -ING, -S** to take up with a scoop (a spoon-shaped utensil)

SCOOPER *n* pl. **-S** one that scoops

SCOOPFUL *n* pl. **SCOOPFULS** or **SCOOPSFUL** as much as a scoop will hold

SCOOT *v* **-ED, -ING, -S** to go quickly

SCOOTCH *v* **-ED, -ING, -ES** to scooch

SCOOTER *v* **-ED, -ING, -S** to ride a two-wheeled vehicle

SCOP *n* pl. **-S** an Old English poet

SCOPA *n* pl. **-PAE** a small tuft of hair on the body of an insect

SCOPE *v* **SCOPED, SCOPING, SCOPES** to look at in order to evaluate

SCOPULA *n* pl. **-LAS** or **-LAE** a dense tuft of hairs

SCORCH *v* **-ED, -ING, -ES** to burn slightly so as to alter the color or taste

SCORCHER *n* pl. **-S** one that scorches

SCORE *v* **SCORED, SCORING, SCORES** to make a point in a game or contest

SCOREPAD *n* pl. **-S** a pad on which scored points are recorded

SCORER *n* pl. **-S** one that scores

SCORIA *n* pl. **-RIAE** the refuse of a smelted metal or ore

SCORIFY *v* **-FIED, -FYING, -FIES** to reduce to scoria

SCORING *n* pl. **-S** the act of scoring in a game

SCORN *v* **-ED, -ING, -S** to treat or regard with contempt

SCORNER *n* pl. **-S** one that scorns

SCORNFUL *adj* feeling or expressing contempt

SCORPION *n* pl. **-S** a stinging arachnid

SCOT *n* pl. **-S** a tax

SCOTCH *v* **-ED, -ING, -ES** to put a definite end to

SCOTER *n* pl. **-S** a sea duck

SCOTIA *n* pl. **-S** a concave molding

SCOTOMA *n* pl. **-MAS** or **-MATA** a blind spot in the field of vision

SCOTOPIA *n* pl. **-S** vision in dim light **SCOTOPIC** *adj*

SCOTTIE *n* pl. **-S** a short-legged terrier

SCOUR *v* **-ED, -ING, -S** to cleanse or polish by hard rubbing

SCOURER *n* pl. **-S** one that scours

SCOURGE *v* **SCOURGED, SCOURGING, SCOURGES** to punish severely

SCOURGER *n* pl. **-S** one that scourges

SCOURING *n* pl. **-S** material removed by scouring

SCOUSE *n* pl. **-S** a type of meat stew

SCOUT *v* **-ED, -ING, -S** to observe for the purpose of obtaining information

SCOUTER *n* pl. **-S** one that scouts

SCOUTH *n* pl. **-S** plenty

SCOUTHER *v* **-ED, -ING, -S** to scorch

SCOUTING *n* pl. **-S** the act of one that scouts

SCOW *v* **-ED, -ING, -S** to transport by scow (a flat-bottomed boat)

SCOWDER *v* **-ED, -ING, -S** to scouther

SCOWL *v* **-ED, -ING, -S** to frown angrily

SCOWLER *n* pl. **-S** one that scowls

SCRABBLE *v* **-BLED, -BLING, -BLES** to claw or grope about frantically

SCRABBLY *adj* **-BLIER, -BLIEST** raspy

SCRAG *v* **SCRAGGED, SCRAGGING, SCRAGS** to wring the neck of

SCRAGGLY *adj* **-GLIER, -GLIEST** uneven

SCRAGGY *adj* **-GIER, -GIEST** scrawny

SCRAICH *v* **-ED, -ING, -S** to utter a shrill cry

SCRAIGH *v* **-ED, -ING, -S** to scraich

SCRAM *v* **SCRAMMED, SCRAMMING, SCRAMS** to leave quickly

SCRAMBLE *v* **-BLED, -BLING, -BLES** to move or climb hurriedly

SCRAMJET *n* pl. **-S** a type of aircraft engine

SCRAN *n* pl. **-S** food

SCRANNEL *n* pl. **-S** a thin person

SCRAP *v* **SCRAPPED, SCRAPPING, SCRAPS** to discard

SCRAPE *v* **SCRAPED, SCRAPING, SCRAPES** to rub so as to remove an outer layer

SCRAPER *n* pl. **-S** one that scrapes

SCRAPIE *n* pl. **-S** a disease of sheep

SCRAPING *n* pl. **-S** something scraped off

SCRAPPED past tense of scrap

SCRAPPER *n* pl. **-S** a fighter

SCRAPPING present participle of scrap

SCRAPPLE *n* pl. **-S** a seasoned mixture of ground meat and cornmeal

SCRAPPY *adj* **-PIER, -PIEST** marked by fighting spirit

SCRATCH *v* **-ED, -ING, -ES** to make a thin, shallow cut or mark on

SCRATCHY *adj* **SCRATCHIER, SCRATCHIEST** made by scratching

SCRAVEL *v* **-ED, -ING, -S** to move quickly, scramble

SCRAWB *v* **-ED, -ING, -S** to scrob

SCRAWL *v* **-ED, -ING, -S** to write hastily or illegibly

SCRAWLER *n* pl. **-S** one that scrawls

SCRAWLY *adj* **SCRAWLIER, SCRAWLIEST** written hastily or illegibly

SCRAWNY *adj* **-NIER, -NIEST** extremely thin

SCREAK *v* **-ED, -ING, -S** to screech

SCREAKY *adj* screechy

SCREAM *v* **-ED, -ING, -S** to utter a prolonged, piercing cry

SCREAMER *n* pl. **-S** one that screams

SCREE *n* pl. **-S** a mass of rocks at the foot of a slope

SCREECH *v* **-ED, -ING, -ES** to utter a harsh, shrill cry

SCREECHY *adj* **SCREECHIER, SCREECHIEST** screeching

SCREED *v* **-ED, -ING, -S** to shred

SCREEN *v* **-ED, -ING, -S** to provide with a screen (a device designed to divide, conceal, or protect)

SCREENER *n* pl. **-S** one that screens

SCREW *v* **-ED, -ING, -S** to attach with a screw (a type of metal fastener)

SCREWER *n* pl. **-S** one that screws

SCREWUP *n* pl. **-S** an instance of bungling

SCREWY *adj* **SCREWIER, SCREWIEST** crazy

SCRIBAL *adj* pertaining to a public clerk or secretary

SCRIBBLE *v* **-BLED, -BLING, -BLES** to write hastily or carelessly

SCRIBBLY *adj* consisting of scribbles (careless writings)

SCRIBE *v* **SCRIBED, SCRIBING, SCRIBES** to mark with a scriber

SCRIBER *n* pl. **-S** a pointed instrument used for marking off material to be cut

SCRIED past tense of scry

SCRIES present 3d person sing. of scry

SCRIEVE *v* **SCRIEVED, SCRIEVING, SCRIEVES** to move along swiftly and smoothly

SCRIM *n* pl. **-S** a cotton fabric

SCRIMP *v* **-ED, -ING, -S** to be very or overly thrifty

SCRIMPER *n* pl. **-S** one that scrimps

SCRIMPIT *adj* meager

SCRIMPY *adj* **SCRIMPIER, SCRIMPIEST** meager

SCRIP *n* pl. **-S** a small piece of paper

SCRIPT *v* **-ED, -ING, -S** to prepare a written text for, as a play or motion picture

SCRIPTER *n* pl. **-S** one that scripts

SCRITCH *n* pl. **-ES** a quiet scraping sound

SCRIVE *v* **SCRIVED, SCRIVING, SCRIVES** to engrave

SCROB *v* **SCROBBED, SCROBBING, SCROBS** to scrape with or as with claws

SCROD *n* pl. **-S** a young cod

SCROFULA *n* pl. **-S** a disease of the lymph glands

SCROGGY *adj* **-GIER, -GIEST** of stunted growth

SCROLL *v* **-ED, -ING, -S** to move text across a display screen

SCROLLER *n* pl. **-S** a computer game in which the background scrolls past

SCROOCH *v* **-ED, -ING, -ES** to crouch

SCROOGE *n* pl. **-S** a miserly person

SCROOP *v* **-ED, -ING, -S** to make a harsh, grating sound

SCROOTCH *v* **-ED, -ING, -ES** to scrooch

SCROTUM *n* pl. **-TUMS** or **-TA** the pouch of skin that contains the testes **SCROTAL** *adj*

SCROUGE *v* **SCROUGED, SCROUGING, SCROUGES** to crowd

SCROUNGE *v* **SCROUNGED, SCROUNGING, SCROUNGES** to gather by foraging

SCROUNGY *adj* **SCROUNGIER, SCROUNGIEST** dirty

SCRUB   v **SCRUBBED, SCRUBBING, SCRUBS** to rub hard in order to clean

SCRUBBER   n pl. **-S** one that scrubs

SCRUBBY   adj **-BIER, -BIEST** inferior in size or quality

SCRUFF   v **-ED, -ING, -S** to make scruffy

SCRUFFY   adj **-FIER, -FIEST** shabby

SCRUM   v **SCRUMMED, SCRUMMING, SCRUMS** to engage in a scrummage (a formation around the ball in rugby)

SCRUMMY   adj **-MIER, -MIEST** delicious

SCRUMPLE   v **-PLED, -PLING, -PLES** to crumple, wrinkle

SCRUMPY   n pl. **-PIES** rough cider

SCRUNCH   v **-ED, -ING, -ES** to crush

SCRUNCHY   n pl. **SCRUNCHIES** an elastic band for fastening the hair

SCRUPLE   v **-PLED, -PLING, -PLES** to hesitate because of ethical considerations

SCRUTINY   n pl. **-NIES** a close examination

SCRY   v **SCRIED, SCRYING, SCRIES** to foretell the future by using a crystal ball

SCRYER   n pl. **-S** one that scries

SCUBA   v **-ED, -ING, -S** to swim underwater using a breathing device with compressed air

SCUD   v **SCUDDED, SCUDDING, SCUDS** to run or move swiftly

SCUDO   n pl. **-DI** a former Italian coin

SCUFF   v **-ED, -ING, -S** to walk without lifting the feet

SCUFFER   n pl. **-S** one that scuffs

SCUFFLE   v **-FLED, -FLING, -FLES** to struggle in a rough, confused manner

SCUFFLER   n pl. **-S** one that scuffles

SCULCH   n pl. **-ES** clean trash

SCULK   v **-ED, -ING, -S** to skulk

SCULKER   n pl. **-S** skulker

SCULL   v **-ED, -ING, -S** to propel with a type of oar

SCULLER   n pl. **-S** one that sculls

SCULLERY   n pl. **-LERIES** a room in which kitchen utensils are cleaned and stored

SCULLION   n pl. **-S** a kitchen servant who does menial work

SCULP   v **-ED, -ING, -S** to sculpt

SCULPIN   n pl. **-S** a freshwater fish

SCULPT   v **-ED, -ING, -S** to form an image or representation of from solid material

SCULPTOR   n pl. **-S** one that sculpts

SCULTCH   n pl. **-ES** sculch

SCUM   v **SCUMMED, SCUMMING, SCUMS** to remove the scum (impure or extraneous matter) from

SCUMBAG   n pl. **-S** a dirtbag

SCUMBALL   n pl. **-S** a dirtbag

SCUMBLE   v **-BLED, -BLING, -BLES** to soften the outlines or colors of by rubbing lightly

SCUMLESS   adj having no scum

SCUMLIKE   adj resembling scum

SCUMMED   past tense of scum

SCUMMER   n pl. **-S** one that scums

SCUMMING   present participle of scum

SCUMMY   adj **-MIER, -MIEST** covered with scum **SCUMMILY** adv

SCUNGILE   n pl. **-GILI** a conch used as food

SCUNNER   v **-ED, -ING, -S** to feel loathing or disgust

SCUP   n pl. **-S** a marine food fish

SCUPPAUG   n pl. **-S** scup

SCUPPER   v **-ED, -ING, -S** to ambush

SCURF   n pl. **-S** scaly or shredded dry skin

SCURFY   adj **SCURFIER, SCURFIEST** covered with scurf

SCURRIL   adj scurrile

SCURRILE   adj expressed in coarse and abusive language

SCURRY   v **-RIED, -RYING, -RIES** to move hurriedly

SCURVY   adj **-VIER, -VIEST** base or contemptible **SCURVILY** adv

SCURVY   n pl. **-VIES** a disease resulting from vitamin C deficiency

SCUT   n pl. **-S** a short tail, as of a rabbit

SCUTA   pl. of scutum

SCUTAGE   n pl. **-S** a tax exacted by a feudal lord in lieu of military service

SCUTATE   adj shaped like a shield

SCUTCH   v **-ED, -ING, -ES** to separate the woody fiber from by beating

SCUTCHER   n pl. **-S** one that scutches

SCUTE   n pl. **-S** a horny plate or scale

SCUTELLA *n/pl* small, scutate organs or parts

SCUTTER *v* **-ED, -ING, -S** to scurry

SCUTTLE *v* **-TLED, -TLING, -TLES** to scurry

SCUTUM *n* pl. **-TA** scute

SCUTWORK *n* pl. **-S** tedious or menial work

SCUZZ *n* pl. **-ES** a dirty or contemptible person

SCUZZBAG *n* pl. **-S** a dirty or contemptible person

SCUZZY *adj* **-ZIER, -ZIEST** dirty or shabby

SCYPHATE *adj* shaped like a cup

SCYPHUS *n* pl. **-PHI** a Greek cup with two handles

SCYTHE *v* **SCYTHED, SCYTHING, SCYTHES** to cut with a scythe (a single-bladed cutting implement)

SEA *n* pl. **-S** the ocean

SEABAG *n* pl. **-S** a bag used by a sailor

SEABEACH *n* pl. **-ES** a beach lying along the sea

SEABED *n* pl. **-S** a seafloor

SEABIRD *n* pl. **-S** a bird frequenting the ocean or seacoast

SEABOARD *n* pl. **-S** the seacoast

SEABOOT *n* pl. **-S** a waterproof boot

SEABORNE *adj* carried on or over the sea

SEACOAST *n* pl. **-S** land bordering on the sea

SEACOCK *n* pl. **-S** a valve in a ship's hull

SEACRAFT *n* pl. **-S** skill in sea navigation

SEADOG *n* pl. **-S** a fogbow

SEADROME *n* pl. **-S** an airport in the sea

SEAFARER *n* pl. **-S** a sailor

SEAFLOOR *n* pl. **-S** the bottom of a sea

SEAFOAM *n* pl. **-S** foam formed on the sea

SEAFOOD *n* pl. **-S** edible fish or shellfish from the sea

SEAFOWL *n* pl. **-S** a seabird

SEAFRONT *n* pl. **-S** an area along the edge of the sea

SEAGIRT *adj* surrounded by the sea

SEAGOING *adj* designed for use on the sea

SEAGRASS *n* pl. **-ES** a grasslike plant living in or close to the sea

SEAGULL *n* pl. **-S** a gull frequenting the sea

SEAHORSE *n* pl. **-S** a fish of the pipefish family

SEAKALE *n* pl. **-S** a coastal plant with edible shoots

SEAL *v* **-ED, -ING, -S** to close or make secure against access, leakage, or passage **SEALABLE** *adj*

SEALANT *n* pl. **-S** a sealing agent

SEALER *n* pl. **-S** one that seals

SEALERY *n* pl. **-ERIES** the occupation of hunting seals

SEALIFT *v* **-ED, -ING, -S** to transport (military personnel and equipment) by ship

SEALING *n* pl. **-S** the act of securing something against leakage, access, or passage

SEALLIKE *adj* resembling a seal (an aquatic mammal)

SEALSKIN *n* pl. **-S** the skin of a seal

SEAM *v* **-ED, -ING, -S** to join with a seam (a line formed by sewing two pieces of fabric together)

SEAMAN *n* pl. **-MEN** a sailor **SEAMANLY** *adj*

SEAMARK *n* pl. **-S** a landmark serving as a navigational guide to mariners

SEAMER *n* pl. **-S** one that seams

SEAMIER comparative of seamy

SEAMIEST superlative of seamy

SEAMLESS *adj* having no seam

SEAMLIKE *adj* resembling a seam

SEAMOUNT *n* pl. **-S** an undersea mountain

SEAMSTER *n* pl. **-S** a person whose occupation is sewing

SEAMY *adj* **SEAMIER, SEAMIEST** unpleasant

SEANCE *n* pl. **-S** a meeting of persons seeking spiritualistic messages

SEAPIECE *n* pl. **-S** a seascape

SEAPLANE *n* pl. **-S** an airplane designed to take off from or land on the water

SEAPORT *n* pl. **-S** a harbor or town accessible to seagoing ships

SEAQUAKE *n* pl. **-S** an undersea earthquake

SEAR *adj* **SEARER, SEAREST** sere

SEAR *v* **-ED, -ING, -S** to burn the surface of

SEARCH *v* **-ED, -ING, -ES** to look through or over carefully in order to find something

SEARCHER *n* pl. **-S** one that searches

SEAROBIN *n* pl. **-S** a marine fish

SEASCAPE *n* pl. **-S** a picture of the sea

SEASCOUT *n* pl. **-S** a boy scout trained in water activities

SEASHELL *n* pl. **-S** the shell of a marine mollusk

SEASHORE *n* pl. **-S** land bordering on the sea

SEASICK *adj* affected with nausea caused by the motion of a vessel at sea

SEASIDE *n* pl. **-S** the seashore

SEASON *v* **-ED, -ING, -S** to heighten or improve the flavor of by adding savory ingredients

SEASONAL *n* pl. **-S** an employee or product associated with a time of the year

SEASONER *n* pl. **-S** one that seasons

SEAT *v* **-ED, -ING, -S** to place on a seat (something on which one sits)

SEATBACK *n* pl. **-S** the back of a seat

SEATBELT *n* pl. **-S** an arrangement of straps to keep a person steady in a seat

SEATER *n* pl. **-S** one that seats

SEATING *n* pl. **-S** material for covering seats

SEATLESS *adj* having no seat

SEATMATE *n* pl. **-S** one with whom one shares a seat

SEATRAIN *n* pl. **-S** a ship equipped to carry railroad cars

SEATROUT *n* pl. **-S** a marine fish

SEATWORK *n* pl. **-S** work done at one's seat

SEAWALL *n* pl. **-S** a wall to protect a shoreline from erosion

SEAWAN *n* pl. **-S** wampum

SEAWANT *n* pl. **-S** seawan

SEAWARD *n* pl. **-S** the direction toward the open sea

SEAWARE *n* pl. **-S** seaweed used as fertilizer

SEAWATER *n* pl. **-S** water from the sea

SEAWAY *n* pl. **-WAYS** the headway made by a ship

SEAWEED *n* pl. **-S** a plant growing in the sea **SEAWEEDY** *adj*

SEBACIC *adj* derived from a certain acid

SEBASIC *adj* sebacic

SEBUM *n* pl. **-S** a fatty matter secreted by certain glands of the skin

SEC *n* pl. **-S** secant

SECALOSE *n* pl. **-S** a complex carbohydrate

SECANT *n* pl. **-S** a trigonometric function of an angle

SECANTLY *adv* in an intersecting manner

SECATEUR *n* pl. **-S** a pruning tool

SECCO *n* pl. **-COS** the art of painting on dry plaster

SECEDE *v* **-CEDED, -CEDING, -CEDES** to withdraw formally from an alliance or association

SECEDER *n* pl. **-S** one that secedes

SECERN *v* **-ED, -ING, -S** to discern as separate

SECLUDE *v* **-CLUDED, -CLUDING, -CLUDES** to remove or set apart from others

SECOND *v* **-ED, -ING, -S** to give support or encouragement to

SECONDE *n* pl. **-S** a position in fencing

SECONDEE *n* pl. **-S** a worker who is transferred to another job temporarily

SECONDER *n* pl. **-S** one that seconds

SECONDLY *adv* in the next place after the first

SECONDO *n* pl. **-DI** the lower part in a piano duet

SECPAR *n* pl. **-S** a parsec

SECRECY *n* pl. **-CIES** the condition of being secret

SECRET *adj* **-CRETER, -CRETEST** kept from knowledge or view

SECRET *n* pl. **-S** something kept from the knowledge of others

SECRETE *v* **-CRETED, -CRETING, -CRETES** to generate and separate out from cells or bodily fluids

SECRETIN *n* pl. **-S** a hormone

SECRETLY *adv* in a secret manner

SECRETOR *n* pl. **-S** one that secretes

SECT *n* pl. **-S** a group of people united by common beliefs or interests

SECTARY *n* pl. **-RIES** a member of a sect

SECTILE *adj* capable of being cut smoothly

SECTION *v* **-ED, -ING, -S** to divide into sections (distinct parts)

SECTOR *v* **-ED, -ING, -S** to divide into sectors (sections)

SECTORAL *adj* of or pertaining to a sector

SECULAR *n* pl. **-S** a layman

SECUND *adj* having the parts or organs arranged on one side only **SECUNDLY** *adv*

SECUNDUM *adv* according to

SECURE *adj* **-CURER, -CUREST** free from danger **SECURELY** *adv*

SECURE *v* **-CURED, -CURING, -CURES** to make firm or tight

SECURER   *n* pl. **-S** one that secures something

SECURING   present participle of secure

SECURITY   *n* pl. **-TIES** the state of being secure

SEDAN   *n* pl. **-S** a type of automobile

SEDARIM   a pl. of seder

SEDATE   *adj* **-DATER, -DATEST** calm **SEDATELY** *adv*

SEDATE   *v* **-DATED, -DATING, -DATES** to administer a sedative to

SEDATION   *n* pl. **-S** the reduction of stress or excitement by the use of sedatives

SEDATIVE   *n* pl. **-S** a drug that induces a calm state

SEDER   *n* pl. **-DERS** or **-DARIM** a Jewish ceremonial dinner

SEDERUNT   *n* pl. **-S** a prolonged sitting

SEDGE   *n* pl. **-S** a marsh plant

SEDGY   *adj* **SEDGIER, SEDGIEST** abounding in sedge

SEDILE   *n* pl. **-LIA** one of the seats in a church for the use of the officiating clergy

SEDILIUM   *n* pl. **-LIA** sedile

SEDIMENT   *v* **-ED, -ING, -S** to settle to the bottom of a liquid

SEDITION   *n* pl. **-S** incitement of rebellion against a government

SEDUCE   *v* **-DUCED, -DUCING, -DUCES** to lead astray **SEDUCIVE** *adj*

SEDUCER   *n* pl. **-S** one that seduces

SEDULITY   *n* pl. **-TIES** the state of being sedulous

SEDULOUS   *adj* diligent

SEDUM   *n* pl. **-S** a flowering plant

SEE   *v* **SAW, SEEN, SEEING, SEES** to perceive with the eyes **SEEABLE** *adj*

SEECATCH   *n* pl. **-CATCHIE** an adult male fur seal

SEED   *v* **-ED, -ING, -S** to plant seeds (propagative plant structures) in

SEEDBED   *n* pl. **-S** land prepared for seeding

SEEDCAKE   *n* pl. **-S** a sweet cake containing aromatic seeds

SEEDCASE   *n* pl. **-S** a pericarp

SEEDER   *n* pl. **-S** one that seeds

SEEDIER   comparative of seedy

SEEDIEST   superlative of seedy

SEEDILY   *adv* in a seedy manner

SEEDLESS   *adj* having no seeds

SEEDLIKE   *adj* resembling a seed

SEEDLING   *n* pl. **-S** a young plant

SEEDMAN   *n* pl. **-MEN** seedsman

SEEDPOD   *n* pl. **-S** a type of seed vessel

SEEDSMAN   *n* pl. **-MEN** a dealer in seeds

SEEDTIME   *n* pl. **-S** the season for sowing seeds

SEEDY   *adj* **SEEDIER, SEEDIEST** containing seeds; inferior in condition or quality

SEEING   *n* pl. **-S** the act of one that sees

SEEK   *v* **SOUGHT, SEEKING, SEEKS** to go in search of

SEEKER   *n* pl. **-S** one that seeks

SEEL   *v* **-ED, -ING, -S** to stitch closed the eyes of, as a falcon during training

SEELY   *adj* frail

SEEM   *v* **-ED, -ING, -S** to give the impression of being

SEEMER   *n* pl. **-S** one that seems

SEEMING   *n* pl. **-S** outward appearance

SEEMLY   *adj* **-LIER, -LIEST** of pleasing appearance

SEEN   past participle of see

SEEP   *v* **-ED, -ING, -S** to pass slowly through small openings

SEEPAGE   *n* pl. **-S** the quantity of fluid that has seeped

SEEPY   *adj* **SEEPIER, SEEPIEST** soaked or oozing with water

SEER   *n* pl. **-S** a prophet

SEERESS   *n* pl. **-ES** a female seer

SEESAW   *v* **-ED, -ING, -S** to move up and down or back and forth

SEETHE   *v* **SEETHED, SEETHING, SEETHES** to surge or foam as if boiling

SEG   *n* pl. **-S** one who advocates racial segregation

SEGETAL   *adj* growing in fields of grain

SEGGAR   *n* pl. **-S** a saggar

SEGMENT   *v* **-ED, -ING, -S** to divide into sections

SEGNO   *n* pl. **-GNOS** or **-GNI** a musical sign

SEGO   *n* pl. **-GOS** a perennial herb

SEGUE *v* **-GUED, -GUEING, -GUES** to proceed without pause from one musical theme to another

SEI *n* pl. **-S** a rorqual

SEICENTO *n* pl. **-TOS** the seventeenth century

SEICHE *n* pl. **-S** an oscillation of the surface of a lake or landlocked sea

SEIDEL *n* pl. **-S** a large beer glass

SEIF *n* pl. **-S** a long, narrow sand dune

SEIGNEUR *n* pl. **-S** seignior

SEIGNIOR *n* pl. **-S** a feudal lord

SEIGNORY *n* pl. **-GNORIES** the power of a seignior

SEINE *v* **SEINED, SEINING, SEINES** to catch fish with a large, vertically hanging net

SEINER *n* pl. **-S** one that seines

SEINING *n* pl. **-S** the act of catching fish with a seine

SEISE *v* **SEISED, SEISING, SEISES** to seize **SEISABLE** *adj*

SEISER *n* pl. **-S** seizer

SEISIN *n* pl. **-S** seizin

SEISING *n* pl. **-S** seizing

SEISM *n* pl. **-S** an earthquake **SEISMAL, SEISMIC** *adj*

SEISMISM *n* pl. **-S** the natural activity involved in earthquakes

SEISOR *n* pl. **-S** seizor

SEISURE *n* pl. **-S** seizure

SEITAN *n* pl. **-S** a food made from wheat gluten

SEIZA *n* pl. **-S** a kneeling position in Japanese martial arts

SEIZE *v* **SEIZED, SEIZING, SEIZES** to take hold of suddenly and forcibly **SEIZABLE** *adj*

SEIZER *n* pl. **-S** one that seizes

SEIZIN *n* pl. **-S** legal possession of land

SEIZING *n* pl. **-S** the act of one that seizes

SEIZOR *n* pl. **-S** one that takes seizin

SEIZURE *n* pl. **-S** the act of seizing

SEJANT *adj* represented in a sitting position — used of a heraldic animal

SEJEANT *adj* sejant

SEL *n* pl. **-S** self

SELADANG *n* pl. **-S** saladang

SELAH *n* pl. **-S** a word of unknown meaning often marking the end of a verse in the Psalms

SELAMLIK *n* pl. **-S** the portion of a Turkish house reserved for men

SELCOUTH *adj* unusual

SELDOM *adj* infrequent **SELDOMLY** *adv*

SELECT *v* **-ED, -ING, -S** to choose

SELECTEE *n* pl. **-S** one that is selected

SELECTLY *adv* by selection

SELECTOR *n* pl. **-S** one that selects

SELENATE *n* pl. **-S** a chemical salt

SELENIC *adj* pertaining to selenium

SELENIDE *n* pl. **-S** a compound of selenium

SELENITE *n* pl. **-S** a variety of gypsum

SELENIUM *n* pl. **-S** a nonmetallic element **SELENOUS** *adj*

SELF *n* pl. **SELVES** the total, essential, or particular being of one person

SELF *v* **-ED, -ING, -S** to inbreed

SELFDOM *n* pl. **-S** selfhood

SELFHEAL *n* pl. **-S** a perennial herb

SELFHOOD *n* pl. **-S** the state of being an individual person

SELFIE *n* pl. **-S** an image of oneself taken by oneself using a phone camera

SELFISH *adj* concerned chiefly or only with oneself

SELFLESS *adj* unselfish

SELFNESS *n* pl. **-ES** selfhood

SELFSAME *adj* identical

SELFWARD *adv* toward oneself

SELKIE *n* pl. **-S** a creature in Scottish and Irish folklore

SELL *v* **SOLD, SELLING, SELLS** to give up to another for money or other valuable consideration **SELLABLE** *adj*

SELLE *n* pl. **-S** a saddle

SELLER *n* pl. **-S** one that sells

SELLOFF *n* pl. **-S** the sale of a large number of stocks, bonds, or commodities

SELLOUT *n* pl. **-S** a performance for which all seats have been sold

SELSYN *n* pl. **-S** a type of remote-control device

SELTZER *n* pl. **-S** carbonated mineral water

SELVA *n* pl. **-S** a tropical rain forest

SELVAGE *n* pl. **-S** the edge of a woven fabric finished to prevent raveling **SELVAGED** *adj*

SELVEDGE *n* pl. **-S** selvage

SELVES pl. of self

SEMANTIC *adj* pertaining to meaning

SEMATIC *adj* serving as a warning

SEME *n* pl. **-S** a semee pattern

SEMEE *adj* covered all over with small heraldic figures

SEMEME *n* pl. **-S** the meaning of a morpheme **SEMEMIC** *adj*

SEMEN *n* pl. **-MENS** or **-MINA** a fluid produced in the male reproductive organs

SEMESTER *n* pl. **-S** a period constituting half of an academic year

SEMI *n* pl. **-S** a freight trailer

SEMIARID *adj* characterized by light rainfall

SEMIBALD *adj* partly bald

SEMIBOLD *adj* printed in a typeface with strokes not as thick as boldface

SEMICOMA *n* pl. **-S** a coma from which a person can be aroused

SEMIDEAF *adj* partly deaf

SEMIDOME *n* pl. **-S** a half dome

SEMIDRY *adj* moderately dry

SEMIFIT *adj* conforming somewhat to the lines of the body

SEMIGALA *adj* somewhat gala

SEMIHARD *adj* moderately hard

SEMIHIGH *adj* moderately high

SEMIHOBO *n* pl. **-BOS** or **-BOES** a person having some of the characteristics of a hobo

SEMILLON *n* pl. **-S** a white grape grown in France

SEMILOG *adj* having one scale logarithmic and the other arithmetic

SEMIMAT *adj* having a slight luster

SEMIMATT *adj* semimat

SEMIMILD *adj* moderately mild

SEMIMUTE *adj* having partially lost the faculty of speech

SEMINA a pl. of semen

SEMINAL *adj* pertaining to semen

SEMINAR *n* pl. **-S** an advanced study group at a college or university

SEMINARY *n* pl. **-NARIES** a school for the training of priests, ministers, or rabbis

SEMINOMA *n* pl. **-MAS** or **-MATA** a malignant tumor of the testis

SEMINUDE *adj* partly nude

SEMIOPEN *adj* partly open

SEMIOSIS *n* pl. **-OSES** a process in which something functions as a sign to an organism

SEMIOTIC *n* pl. **-S** a general theory of signs and symbolism

SEMIOVAL *adj* somewhat oval

SEMIPRO *n* pl. **-PROS** one who is engaged in some field or sport for pay on a part-time basis

SEMIRAW *adj* somewhat raw

SEMIS *n* pl. **-MISES** a coin of ancient Rome

SEMISOFT *adj* moderately soft

SEMITIST *n* pl. **-S** one who favors Jewish interests

SEMITONE *n* pl. **-S** a type of musical tone

SEMIWILD *adj* somewhat wild

SEMOLINA *n* pl. **-S** a granular product of wheat used for pasta

SEMPLE *adj* of humble birth

SEMPLICE *adj* simple — used as a musical direction

SEMPRE *adv* in the same manner throughout — used as a musical direction

SEN *n* pl. **SEN** a monetary unit of Japan

SENARIUS *n* pl. **-NARII** a Greek or Latin verse consisting of six metrical feet

SENARY *adj* pertaining to the number six

SENATE *n* pl. **-S** an assembly having high deliberative and legislative functions

SENATOR *n* pl. **-S** a member of a senate

SEND *v* **-ED, -ING, -S** to scend

SEND *v* **SENT, SENDING, SENDS** to cause to go **SENDABLE** *adj*

SENDAL *n* pl. **-S** a silk fabric

SENDER *n* pl. **-S** one that sends

SENDOFF *n* pl. **-S** a farewell celebration

SENDUP *n* pl. **-S** a parody

SENE *n* pl. **-S** a monetary unit of Samoa

SENECA *n* pl. **-S** senega

SENECIO *n* pl. **-CIOS** a flowering plant

SENEGA *n* pl. **-S** a medicinal plant root

SENESCE *v* **-ESCED, -ESCING, -ESCES** to grow old

SENGI *n* pl. **SENGI** a former monetary unit of Zaire

SENHOR *n* pl. **-S** or **-ES** a Portuguese or Brazilian gentleman

SENHORA *n* pl. **-S** a married Portuguese or Brazilian woman

SENILE *n* pl. **-S** one who exhibits senility

SENILELY *adv* in a senile manner

SENILITY *n* pl. **-TIES** mental and physical infirmity due to old age

SENIOR *n* pl. **-S** a person who is older than another

SENITI *n* pl. **SENITI** a monetary unit of Tonga

SENNA *n* pl. **-S** a medicinal plant

SENNET *n* pl. **-S** a call sounded on a trumpet signaling the entrance or exit of actors

SENNIGHT *n* pl. **-S** a week

SENNIT *n* pl. **-S** braided straw used in making hats

SENOPIA *n* pl. **-S** an improvement of near vision

SENOR *n* pl. **-S** or **-ES** a Spanish gentleman

SENORA *n* pl. **-S** a married Spanish woman

SENORITA *n* pl. **-S** an unmarried Spanish girl or woman

SENRYU *n* pl. **SENRYU** a Japanese poem

SENSA pl. of sensum

SENSATE *v* **-SATED, -SATING, -SATES** to sense

SENSE *v* **SENSED, SENSING, SENSES** to perceive by the senses (any of certain agencies through which an individual receives impressions of the external world)

SENSEFUL *adj* sensible

SENSEI *n* pl. **-S** a teacher of Japanese martial arts

SENSIBLE *adj* **-BLER, -BLEST** having or showing good judgment **SENSIBLY** *adv*

SENSIBLE *n* pl. **-S** something that can be sensed

SENSILLA *n* pl. **-LAE** a simple sense organ

SENSING present participle of sense

SENSOR *n* pl. **-S** a device that receives and responds to a stimulus

SENSORIA *n/pl* the parts of the brain concerned with the reception and interpretation of sensory stimuli

SENSORY *adj* pertaining to the senses or sensation

SENSUAL *adj* pertaining to the physical senses

SENSUM *n* pl. **-SA** an object of perception or sensation

SENSUOUS *adj* pertaining to or derived from the senses

SENT *n* pl. **SENTI** a monetary unit of Estonia

SENTE *n* pl. **LICENTE** or **LISENTE** a monetary unit of Lesotho

SENTENCE *v* **-TENCED, -TENCING, -TENCES** to declare judicially the extent of punishment to be imposed

SENTI *n* pl. **SENTI** a former monetary unit of Tanzania

SENTIENT *n* pl. **-S** a person or thing capable of sensation

SENTIMO *n* pl. **-MOS** a monetary unit of the Philippines

SENTINEL *v* **-NELED, -NELING, -NELS** or **-NELLED, -NELLING, -NELS** to stand guard

SENTRY *n* pl. **-TRIES** one who stands guard

SEPAL *n* pl. **-S** one of the individual leaves of a calyx **SEPALED, SEPALINE, SEPALLED, SEPALOID, SEPALOUS** *adj*

SEPARATE *v* **-RATED, -RATING, -RATES** to set or keep apart

SEPIA *n* pl. **-S** a brown pigment **SEPIC** *adj*

SEPOY *n* pl. **-POYS** a native of India serving in the British army

SEPPUKU *n* pl. **-S** a Japanese form of suicide

SEPS *n* pl. **-ES** an African lizard

SEPSIS *n* pl. **SEPSES** bacterial invasion of the body

SEPT *n* pl. **-S** a clan

SEPTA pl. of septum

SEPTAGE *n* pl. **-S** the waste in a septic tank

SEPTAL *adj* pertaining to a septum

SEPTARIA *n/pl* limestone nodules

SEPTATE *adj* having a septum

SEPTET *n* pl. **-S** a group of seven

SEPTETTE *n* pl. **-S** septet

SEPTIC *n* pl. **-S** an agent producing sepsis **SEPTICAL** *adj*

SEPTIMAL *adj* based on the number seven

SEPTIME *n* pl. **-S** a position in fencing

SEPTORIA *n* pl. **-S** a type of fungus

SEPTUM *n* pl. **-TUMS** or **-TA** a dividing membrane or partition

SEPTUPLE *v* **-PLED, -PLING, -PLES** to make seven times as great

SEQUEL *n* pl. **-S** something that follows and serves as a continuation

SEQUELA *n* pl. **-QUELAE** an abnormal condition resulting from a preceding disease

SEQUENCE *v* **-QUENCED, -QUENCING, -QUENCES** to arrange in consecutive order

SEQUENCY *n* pl. **-CIES** the following of one thing after another

SEQUENT *n* pl. **-S** something that follows

SEQUIN *v* **-ED, -ING, -S** to affix sequins (shiny ornamental discs) to

SEQUITUR *n* pl. **-S** the conclusion of an inference

SEQUOIA *n* pl. **-S** a large evergreen tree

SER *n* pl. **-S** a unit of weight of India

SERA a pl. of serum

SERAC *n* pl. **-S** a large mass of ice broken off of a glacier

SERAGLIO *n* pl. **-GLIOS** a harem

SERAI *n* pl. **-S** a Turkish palace

SERAIL *n* pl. **-S** a seraglio

SERAL *adj* pertaining to a series of ecological changes

SERAPE *n* pl. **-S** a colorful woolen shawl

SERAPH *n* pl. **-APHS** or **-APHIM** or **-APHIN** a winged celestial being **SERAPHIC** *adj*

SERAPHIM *n* pl. **-S** seraph

SERDAB *n* pl. **-S** a chamber within an ancient Egyptian tomb

SERE *adj* **SERER, SEREST** withered; dry

SERE *v* **SERED, SERING, SERES** to sear

SERE *n* pl. **-S** a natural series of plant or animal communities

SEREIN *n* pl. **-S** a fine rain falling from an apparently clear sky

SERENADE *v* **-NADED, -NADING, -NADES** to perform an honorific evening song for

SERENATA *n* pl. **-TAS** or **-TE** a dramatic cantata

SERENE *adj* **SERENER, SERENEST** calm; tranquil **SERENELY** *adv*

SERENE *n* pl. **-S** a serene condition or expanse

SERENITY *n* pl. **-TIES** the state of being serene

SERER comparative of sere

SEREST superlative of sere

SERF *n* pl. **-S** a feudal slave

SERFAGE *n* pl. **-S** serfdom

SERFDOM *n* pl. **-S** the state of being a serf

SERFHOOD *n* pl. **-S** serfdom

SERFISH *adj* characteristic of a serf

SERFLIKE *adj* serfish

SERGE *v* **SERGED, SERGING, SERGES** to finish (a cut edge of a seam) with overcast stitches

SERGEANT *n* pl. **-S** a noncommissioned military officer

SERGER *n* pl. **-S** a machine for serging

SERGING *n* pl. **-S** a process of finishing the raw edges of a fabric

SERIAL *n* pl. **-S** a literary or dramatic work presented in successive installments

SERIALLY *adv* in the manner or form of a serial

SERIATE *v* **-ATED, -ATING, -ATES** to put into a series

SERIATIM *adv* serially

SERICIN *n* pl. **-S** a kind of protein

SERIEMA *n* pl. **-S** a Brazilian bird

SERIES *n* pl. **SERIES** an arrangement of one after another

SERIF *n* pl. **-S** a fine line used to finish off the main stroke of a letter **SERIFED, SERIFFED** *adj*

SERIN *n* pl. **-S** a European finch

SERINE *n* pl. **-S** an amino acid

SERING present participle of sere

SERINGA *n* pl. **-S** a Brazilian tree

SERIOUS *adj* thoughtful or subdued in appearance or manner

SERJEANT *n* pl. **-S** sergeant

SERMON *n* pl. **-S** a religious discourse **SERMONIC** *adj*

SEROLOGY *n* pl. **-GIES** the science of serums

SEROSA *n* pl. **-SAS** or **-SAE** a thin membrane lining certain bodily cavities **SEROSAL** *adj*

SEROSITY *n* pl. **-TIES** the quality or state of being serous

SEROTINE *n* pl. **-S** a European bat

SEROTINY *n pl.* **-NIES** the condition of having late or gradual seed dispersal

SEROTYPE *v* **-TYPED, -TYPING, -TYPES** to classify (microorganisms) according to a characteristic set of antigens

SEROUS *adj* of or resembling serum

SEROVAR *n pl.* **-S** a group of microorganisms having a characteristic set of antigens

SEROW *n pl.* **-S** an Asian antelope

SERPENT *n pl.* **-S** a snake

SERPIGO *n pl.* **-GOS** or **-GOES** or **-GINES** a spreading skin eruption

SERRANID *n pl.* **-S** a marine fish

SERRANO *n pl.* **-NOS** a small hot pepper

SERRATE *v* **-RATED, -RATING, -RATES** to furnish with toothlike projections

SERRY *v* **-RIED, -RYING, -RIES** to crowd together

SERUM *n pl.* **-RUMS** or **-RA** the watery portion of whole blood **SERUMAL** *adj*

SERVABLE *adj* capable of serving or being served

SERVAL *n pl.* **-S** an African wildcat

SERVANT *n pl.* **-S** one that serves others

SERVE *v* **SERVED, SERVING, SERVES** to work for

SERVER *n pl.* **-S** one that serves another

SERVERY *n pl.* **-ERIES** a counter or room from which meals are served

SERVICE *v* **-VICED, -VICING, -VICES** to repair

SERVICER *n pl.* **-S** one that services

SERVILE *adj* slavishly submissive

SERVING *n pl.* **-S** a portion of food

SERVITOR *n pl.* **-S** a male servant

SERVO *n pl.* **-VOS** an automatic device used to control another mechanism

SESAME *n pl.* **-S** an East Indian plant

SESAMOID *n pl.* **-S** a nodular mass of bone or cartilage

SESH *n pl.* **-ES** a session

SESSILE *adj* permanently attached

SESSION *n pl.* **-S** a meeting of a legislative or judicial body for the transaction of business

SESSPOOL *n pl.* **-S** cesspool

SESTERCE *n pl.* **-S** a coin of ancient Rome

SESTET *n pl.* **-S** a stanza of six lines

SESTINA *n pl.* **-S** a type of verse form

SESTINE *n pl.* **-S** sestina

SET *v* **SET, SETTING, SETS** to put in a particular position

SETA *n pl.* **-TAE** a coarse, stiff hair **SETAL** *adj*

SETBACK *n pl.* **-S** a defeat

SETENANT *n pl.* **-S** a postage stamp that differs in design from others in the same sheet

SETIFORM *adj* having the form of a seta

SETLINE *n pl.* **-S** a strong fishing line

SETOFF *n pl.* **-S** something that offsets something else

SETON *n pl.* **-S** a type of surgical thread

SETOSE *adj* covered with setae

SETOUS *adj* setose

SETOUT *n pl.* **-S** a display

SETSCREW *n pl.* **-S** a type of screw

SETT *n pl.* **-S** the burrow of a badger

SETTEE *n pl.* **-S** a long seat with a high back

SETTER *n pl.* **-S** one that sets

SETTING *n pl.* **-S** the scenery used in a dramatic production

SETTLE *v* **-TLED, -TLING, -TLES** to place in a desired state or order

SETTLER *n pl.* **-S** one that settles

SETTLING *n pl.* **-S** sediment

SETTLOR *n pl.* **-S** one that makes a legal settlement

SETULOSE *adj* covered with seta

SETULOUS *adj* setulose

SETUP *n pl.* **-S** the way something is arranged

SEV *n pl.* **-S** an Indian food of deep-fried strands of flour

SEVEN *n pl.* **-S** a number

SEVENTH *n pl.* **-S** one of seven equal parts

SEVENTY *n pl.* **-TIES** a number

SEVER *v* **-ED, -ING, -S** to divide or cut into parts

SEVERAL *n pl.* **-S** a few persons or things

SEVERE *adj* **-VERER, -VEREST** unsparing in the treatment of others **SEVERELY** *adv*

SEVERITY *n pl.* **-TIES** the quality or state of being severe

SEVERY *n* pl. **-ERIES** a compartment in a vaulted ceiling

SEVICHE *n* pl. **-S** a dish of raw fish

SEVRUGA *n* pl. **-S** caviar from the Caspian Sea

SEW *v* **SEWED, SEWN, SEWING, SEWS** to mend or fasten with a needle and thread **SEWABLE** *adj*

SEWAGE *n* pl. **-S** the waste matter carried off by sewers

SEWAN *n* pl. **-S** seawan

SEWAR *n* pl. **-S** a medieval servant

SEWER *v* **-ED, -ING, -S** to clean or maintain sewers (underground conduits for waste)

SEWERAGE *n* pl. **-S** sewage

SEWING *n* pl. **-S** material that has been or is to be sewed

SEWN a past participle of sew

SEX *v* **-ED, -ING, -ES** to determine the sex (the property by which organisms are classified according to reproductive functions) of

SEXER *n* pl. **-S** one that sexes

SEXIER comparative of sexy

SEXIEST superlative of sexy

SEXILY *adv* in a sexy manner

SEXINESS *n* pl. **-ES** the quality or state of being sexy

SEXISM *n* pl. **-S** prejudice or discrimination against women

SEXIST *n* pl. **-S** one that practices sexism

SEXLESS *adj* lacking sexual characteristics

SEXOLOGY *n* pl. **-GIES** the study of human sexual behavior

SEXPERT *n* pl. **-S** an expert in sexual matters

SEXPOT *n* pl. **-S** a sexually attractive woman

SEXT *n* pl. **-S** one of seven canonical daily periods for prayer and devotion

SEXTAIN *n* pl. **-S** a stanza of six lines

SEXTAN *n* pl. **-S** a recurrent malarial fever

SEXTANT *n* pl. **-S** an instrument for measuring angular distances

SEXTARII *n/pl* ancient Roman units of liquid measure

SEXTET *n* pl. **-S** a group of six

SEXTETTE *n* pl. **-S** sextet

SEXTILE *n* pl. **-S** the position of two celestial bodies when they are sixty degrees apart

SEXTING *n* pl. **-S** the sending of sexually explicit messages or images by cell phone

SEXTO *n* pl. **-TOS** sixmo

SEXTON *n* pl. **-S** a maintenance worker of a church

SEXTUPLE *v* **-PLED, -PLING, -PLES** to make six times as great

SEXTUPLY *adv* to six times as much or as many

SEXUAL *adj* pertaining to sex **SEXUALLY** *adv*

SEXY *adj* **SEXIER, SEXIEST** arousing sexual desire

SFERICS *n/pl* an electronic detector of storms

SFORZATO *n* pl. **-TOS** the playing of a tone or chord with sudden force

SFUMATO *n* pl. **-TOS** a technique used in painting

SH *interj* — used to urge silence

SHA *interj* — used to urge silence

SHABBY *adj* **-BIER, -BIEST** ragged **SHABBILY** *adv*

SHACK *v* **-ED, -ING, -S** to live or dwell

SHACKLE *v* **-LED, -LING, -LES** to confine with metal fastenings placed around the wrists or ankles

SHACKLER *n* pl. **-S** one that shackles

SHACKO *n* pl. **-KOS** or **-KOES** shako

SHACKY *adj* **SHACKIER, SHACKIEST** dilapidated

SHAD *n* pl. **-S** a food fish

SHADBLOW *n* pl. **-S** a shadbush

SHADBUSH *n* pl. **-ES** a flowering tree or shrub

SHADCHAN *n* pl. **-CHANS** or **-CHANIM** a Jewish marriage broker

SHADDOCK *n* pl. **-S** a citrus fruit

SHADDUP *interj* — used to silence someone

SHADE *v* **SHADED, SHADING, SHADES** to screen from light or heat

SHADER *n* pl. **-S** one that shades

SHADFLY *n* pl. **-FLIES** a winged insect

SHADIER comparative of shady

SHADIEST superlative of shady

SHADILY *adv* in a shady manner

SHADING *n* pl. **-S** protection against light or heat

SHADKHAN *n* pl. **-KHANS** or **-KHANIM** shadchan

SHADOOF *n* pl. **-S** a device used in Egypt for raising water for irrigation

SHADOW *v* **-ED, -ING, -S** to make dark or gloomy

SHADOWER *n* pl. **-S** one that shadows

SHADOWY *adj* **-OWIER, -OWIEST** dark

SHADRACH *n* pl. **-S** a mass of unfused material in the hearth of a blast furnace

SHADUF *n* pl. **-S** shadoof

SHADY *adj* **SHADIER, SHADIEST** shaded

SHAFT *v* **-ED, -ING, -S** to push or propel with a pole

SHAFTING *n* pl. **-S** a system of rods for transmitting motion or power

SHAG *v* **SHAGGED, SHAGGING, SHAGS** to make shaggy

SHAGBARK *n* pl. **-S** a hardwood tree

SHAGGY *adj* **-GIER, -GIEST** covered with long, coarse hair **SHAGGILY** *adv*

SHAGREEN *n* pl. **-S** the rough skin of certain sharks

SHAH *n* pl. **-S** an Iranian ruler

SHAHADA *n* pl. **-S** the Muslim profession of faith

SHAHADAH *n* pl. **-S** shahada

SHAHDOM *n* pl. **-S** the territory ruled by a shah

SHAHEED *n* pl. **-S** shahid

SHAHID *n* pl. **-S** a Muslim martyr

SHAIKH *n* pl. **-S** sheik

SHAIRD *n* pl. **-S** shard

SHAIRN *n* pl. **-S** sharn

SHAITAN *n* pl. **-S** an evil spirit

SHAKE *v* **SHOOK, SHAKEN, SHAKING, SHAKES** to move to and fro with short, rapid movements **SHAKABLE** *adj*

SHAKEOUT *n* pl. **-S** a minor economic recession

SHAKER *n* pl. **-S** one that shakes

SHAKEUP *n* pl. **-S** a total reorganization

SHAKIER comparative of shaky

SHAKIEST superlative of shaky

SHAKILY *adv* in a shaky manner

SHAKING present participle of shake

SHAKO *n* pl. **-KOS** or **-KOES** a type of military hat

SHAKY *adj* **SHAKIER, SHAKIEST** shaking

SHALE *n* pl. **-S** a fissile rock

SHALED *adj* having a shell or husk

SHALEY *adj* **SHALIER, SHALIEST** shaly

SHALIER comparative of shaly

SHALIEST superlative of shaly

SHALL *v* present sing. 2d person **SHALL** or **SHALT**, past sing. 2d person **SHOULD** or **SHOULDST** or **SHOULDEST** — used as an auxiliary to express futurity, inevitability, or command

SHALLOON *n* pl. **-S** a woolen fabric

SHALLOP *n* pl. **-S** a small, open boat

SHALLOT *n* pl. **-S** a plant resembling an onion

SHALLOW *adj* **-LOWER, -LOWEST** having little depth

SHALLOW *v* **-ED, -ING, -S** to make shallow

SHALOM *n* pl. **-S** a word used as a Jewish greeting or farewell

SHALT a present 2d person sing. of shall

SHALWAR *n* pl. **-S** a pair of loose trousers worn by some women of India

SHALY *adj* **SHALIER, SHALIEST** resembling shale

SHAM *v* **SHAMMED, SHAMMING, SHAMS** to feign

SHAMABLE *adj* capable of being shamed **SHAMABLY** *adv*

SHAMAL *n* pl. **-S** a hot, dry wind

SHAMAN *n* pl. **-S** a medicine man among certain Native Americans **SHAMANIC** *adj*

SHAMAS *n* pl. **-MOSIM** shammes

SHAMBA *n* pl. **-S** a farm in East Africa

SHAMBLE *v* **-BLED, -BLING, -BLES** to walk awkwardly

SHAME *v* **SHAMED, SHAMING, SHAMES** to cause to feel a painful sense of guilt or degradation

SHAMEFUL *adj* disgraceful

SHAMES *n* pl. **-MOSIM** shammes

SHAMIANA *n* pl. **-S** a large tent in India

SHAMISEN *n* pl. **-S** samisen

SHAMMAS *n* pl. **-MASIM** shammes

SHAMMASH *n* pl. **-MASHIM** shammes

SHAMMED past tense of sham

SHAMMER	*n* pl. **-S** one that shams
SHAMMES	*n* pl. **-MOSIM** a minor official of a synagogue
SHAMMIED	past tense of shammy
SHAMMIES	present 3d person sing. of shammy
SHAMMING	present participle of sham
SHAMMOS	*n* pl. **-MOSIM** shammes
SHAMMOSIM	pl. of shammes
SHAMMY	*v* **-MIED, -MYING, -MIES** to chamois
SHAMOIS	*n* pl. **SHAMOIS** chamois
SHAMOS	*n* pl. **-MOSIM** shammes
SHAMOSIM	pl. of shames
SHAMOY	*v* **-ED, -ING, -S** to chamois
SHAMPOO	*v* **-ED, -ING, -S** to cleanse with a special preparation
SHAMROCK	*n* pl. **-S** a three-leaved plant
SHAMUS	*n* pl. **-ES** a private detective
SHANDY	*n* pl. **-DIES** an alcoholic drink
SHANGHAI	*v* **-ED, -ING, -S** to kidnap for service aboard a ship
SHANK	*v* **-ED, -ING, -S** to hit sharply to the right, as a golf ball
SHANNY	*n* pl. **-NIES** a marine fish
SHANTEY	*n* pl. **-TEYS** chantey
SHANTI	*n* pl. **-S** peace
SHANTIES	pl. of shanty
SHANTIH	*n* pl. **-S** shanti
SHANTUNG	*n* pl. **-S** a silk fabric
SHANTY	*n* pl. **-TIES** a small, crudely built dwelling
SHAPE	*v* **SHAPED, SHAPEN, SHAPING, SHAPES** to give shape (outward form) to **SHAPABLE** *adj*
SHAPELY	*adj* **-LIER, -LIEST** having a pleasing shape
SHAPER	*n* pl. **-S** one that shapes
SHAPEUP	*n* pl. **-S** a system of hiring a work crew
SHAPING	present participle of shape
SHARD	*n* pl. **-S** a fragment of broken pottery
SHARE	*v* **SHARED, SHARING, SHARES** to have, get, or use in common with another or others **SHARABLE** *adj*
SHARER	*n* pl. **-S** one that shares
SHARIA	*n* pl. **-S** Islamic law based on the Koran
SHARIAH	*n* pl. **-S** sharia
SHARIAT	*n* pl. **-S** sharia
SHARIF	*n* pl. **-S** sherif
SHARING	present participle of share
SHARK	*v* **-ED, -ING, -S** to live by trickery
SHARKER	*n* pl. **-S** one that sharks
SHARKISH	*adj* behaving like a shark (a predatory fish)
SHARN	*n* pl. **-S** cow dung **SHARNY** *adj*
SHARP	*adj* **SHARPER, SHARPEST** suitable for or capable of cutting or piercing
SHARP	*v* **-ED, -ING, -S** to raise in pitch, as a musical tone
SHARPEN	*v* **-ED, -ING, -S** to make sharp
SHARPER	*n* pl. **-S** a swindler
SHARPIE	*n* pl. **-S** a very alert person
SHARPISH	*adj* somewhat sharp
SHARPLY	*adv* in a sharp manner
SHARPY	*n* pl. **SHARPIES** sharpie
SHASHLIK	*n* pl. **-S** kabob
SHASLIK	*n* pl. **-S** shashlik
SHASTA	*n* pl. **-S** a flowering plant
SHATOOSH	*n* pl. **-ES** a fabric made from the wool of the chiru
SHATTER	*v* **-ED, -ING, -S** to break into pieces
SHAUGH	*n* pl. **-S** a thicket
SHAUL	*v* **-ED, -ING, -S** to shoal
SHAVE	*v* **SHAVED, SHAVEN, SHAVING, SHAVES** to sever the hair close to the roots **SHAVABLE** *adj*
SHAVER	*n* pl. **-S** one that shaves
SHAVIE	*n* pl. **-S** a trick or prank
SHAVING	*n* pl. **-S** something shaved off
SHAW	*v* **SHAWED, SHAWN, SHAWING, SHAWS** to show
SHAWARMA	*n* pl. **-S** a sandwich of lamb or chicken, vegetables, and often tahini wrapped in pita bread
SHAWL	*v* **-ED, -ING, -S** to wrap in a shawl (a piece of cloth worn as a covering)
SHAWM	*n* pl. **-S** an early woodwind instrument
SHAY	*n* pl. **SHAYS** a chaise
SHAYKH	*n* pl. **-S** sheik

SHAZAM   *interj* — used to signify a magical occurrence

SHE   *n* pl. **-S** a female person

SHEA   *n* pl. **-S** an African tree

SHEAF   *v* **-ED, -ING, -S** to sheave

SHEAL   *n* pl. **-S** shealing

SHEALING   *n* pl. **-S** a shepherd's hut

SHEAR   *v* **SHEARED** or **SHORE, SHORN, SHEARING, SHEARS** to cut the hair or wool from

SHEARER   *n* pl. **-S** one that shears

SHEARING   *n* pl. **-S** an instance of cutting hair or wool

SHEATH   *v* **-ED, -ING, -S** to sheathe

SHEATHE   *v* **SHEATHED, SHEATHING, SHEATHES** to put into a protective case

SHEATHER   *n* pl. **-S** one that sheathes

SHEAVE   *v* **SHEAVED, SHEAVING, SHEAVES** to gather into a bundle

SHEBANG   *n* pl. **-S** a situation, organization, or matter

SHEBEAN   *n* pl. **-S** shebeen

SHEBEEN   *n* pl. **-S** a place where liquor is sold illegally

SHED   *v* **SHEDDED, SHEDDING, SHEDS** to house in a shed (a small, low structure)

SHEDABLE   *adj* capable of being cast off

SHEDDER   *n* pl. **-S** one that casts off something

SHEDLIKE   *adj* resembling a shed

SHEEN   *v* **-ED, -ING, -S** to shine

SHEENFUL   *adj* shining

SHEENY   *adj* **SHEENIER, SHEENIEST** shining

SHEEP   *n* pl. **SHEEP** a ruminant mammal

SHEEPCOT   *n* pl. **-S** an enclosure for sheep

SHEEPDOG   *n* pl. **-S** a dog trained to guard and herd sheep

SHEEPISH   *adj* embarrassed

SHEEPMAN   *n* pl. **-MEN** a person who raises sheep

SHEER   *adj* **SHEERER, SHEEREST** of very thin texture **SHEERLY** *adv*

SHEER   *v* **-ED, -ING, -S** to swerve

SHEESH   *interj* — used to express mild annoyance

SHEET   *v* **-ED, -ING, -S** to cover with a sheet (a thin, rectangular piece of material)

SHEETER   *n* pl. **-S** one that sheets

SHEETFED   *adj* pertaining to a type of printing press

SHEETING   *n* pl. **-S** material in the form of sheets

SHEEVE   *n* pl. **-S** a grooved pulley wheel

SHEHNAI   *n* pl. **-S** a double-reed wind instrument of India

SHEIK   *n* pl. **-S** an Arab chief

SHEIKDOM   *n* pl. **-S** the area ruled by a sheik

SHEIKH   *n* pl. **-S** sheik

SHEILA   *n* pl. **-S** a young woman

SHEITAN   *n* pl. **-S** shaitan

SHEITEL   *n* pl. **-S** a wig worn by a married Jewish woman

SHEKEL   *n* pl. **SHEKELS** or **SHEKELIM** or **SHEKALIM** an ancient unit of weight and money

SHELDUCK   *n* pl. **-S** a European duck

SHELF   *n* pl. **SHELVES** a flat rigid structure used to support articles

SHELFFUL   *n* pl. **-S** as much as a shelf can hold

SHELL   *v* **-ED, -ING, -S** to divest of a shell (a hard outer covering)

SHELLAC   *v* **-LACKED, -LACKING, -LACS** to cover with a thin varnish

SHELLACK   *v* **-ED, -ING, -S** to shellac

SHELLER   *n* pl. **-S** one that shells

SHELLY   *adj* **SHELLIER, SHELLIEST** abounding in seashells

SHELTA   *n* pl. **-S** an esoteric jargon of Gaelic

SHELTER   *v* **-ED, -ING, -S** to provide cover or protection for

SHELTIE   *n* pl. **-S** a small, shaggy pony

SHELTY   *n* pl. **-TIES** sheltie

SHELVE   *v* **SHELVED, SHELVING, SHELVES** to place on a shelf

SHELVER   *n* pl. **-S** one that shelves

SHELVES   pl. of shelf

SHELVING   *n* pl. **-S** material for shelves

SHELVY   *adj* **SHELVIER, SHELVIEST** inclining gradually

SHEN *n pl.* **SHEN** the spiritual element of a person's psyche

SHENAI *n pl.* **-S** shehnai

SHEND *v* **SHENT, SHENDING, SHENDS** to disgrace

SHEOL *n pl.* **-S** hell

SHEPHERD *v* **-ED, -ING, -S** to watch over carefully

SHEQEL *n pl.* **SHEQELS** or **SHEQALIM** shekel

SHERBERT *n pl.* **-S** sherbet

SHERBET *n pl.* **-S** a frozen fruit-flavored mixture

SHERD *n pl.* **-S** shard

SHEREEF *n pl.* **-S** sherif

SHERIF *n pl.* **-S** an Arab ruler

SHERIFF *n pl.* **-S** a law-enforcement officer of a county

SHERLOCK *n pl.* **-S** a detective

SHERO *n pl.* **-ROES** a woman regarded as a hero

SHEROOT *n pl.* **-S** cheroot

SHERPA *n pl.* **-S** a soft fabric for linings

SHERRIED *adj* cooked or flavored with sherry

SHERRIS *n pl.* **-RISES** sherry

SHERRY *n pl.* **-RIES** a type of wine

SHERWANI *n pl.* **-S** a knee-length coat worn by some men of India

SHETLAND *n pl.* **-S** a wool yarn

SHEUCH *n pl.* **-S** sheugh

SHEUGH *n pl.* **-S** a ditch

SHEW *v* **SHEWED, SHEWN, SHEWING, SHEWS** to show

SHEWER *n pl.* **-S** one that shews

SHH *interj* sh

SHHH *interj* sh

SHIATSU *n pl.* **-S** a massage using finger pressure

SHIATZU *n pl.* **-S** shiatsu

SHIBAH *n pl.* **-S** shiva

SHICKER *n pl.* **-S** a drunkard

SHIED past tense of shy

SHIEL *n pl.* **-S** shieling

SHIELD *v* **-ED, -ING, -S** to provide with a protective cover or shelter

SHIELDER *n pl.* **-S** one that shields

SHIELING *n pl.* **-S** shealing

SHIER *n pl.* **-S** a horse having a tendency to shy

SHIES present 3d person sing. of shy

SHIEST a superlative of shy

SHIFT *v* **-ED, -ING, -S** to move from one position to another

SHIFTER *n pl.* **-S** one that shifts

SHIFTING *n pl.* **-S** the act of moving from one place to another

SHIFTY *adj* **SHIFTIER, SHIFTIEST** tricky **SHIFTILY** *adv*

SHIGELLA *n pl.* **-LAS** or **-LAE** any of a genus of aerobic bacteria

SHIITAKE *n pl.* **-S** a dark Oriental mushroom

SHIKAR *v* **-KARRED, -KARRING, -KARS** to hunt

SHIKARA *n pl.* **-S** a light, flat-bottomed boat in Kashmir

SHIKAREE *n pl.* **-S** a big game hunter

SHIKARI *n pl.* **-S** shikaree

SHIKKER *n pl.* **-S** shicker

SHIKRA *n pl.* **-S** a small sparrow hawk

SHILINGI *n pl.* **SHILINGI** a monetary unit of Tanzania

SHILL *v* **-ED, -ING, -S** to act as a decoy

SHILLALA *n pl.* **-S** a short, thick club

SHILLING *n pl.* **-S** a former monetary unit of Great Britain

SHILPIT *adj* sickly

SHILY *adv* in a shy manner

SHIM *v* **SHIMMED, SHIMMING, SHIMS** to fill out or level by inserting a thin wedge

SHIMMER *v* **-ED, -ING, -S** to glimmer

SHIMMERY *adj* shimmering

SHIMMY *v* **-MIED, -MYING, -MIES** to vibrate or wobble

SHIN *v* **SHINNED, SHINNING, SHINS** to climb by gripping and pulling alternately with the hands and legs

SHINBONE *n pl.* **-S** the tibia

SHINDIG *n pl.* **-S** an elaborate dance or party

SHINDY *n pl.* **-DYS** or **-DIES** a shindig

SHINE *v* **SHONE** or **SHINED, SHINING, SHINES** to emit light

SHINER *n pl.* **-S** one that shines

SHINGLE *v* **-GLED, -GLING, -GLES** to cover with shingles (thin, oblong pieces of building material)

SHINGLER *n* pl. **-S** one that shingles

SHINGLY *adj* covered with small, loose stones

SHINIER comparative of shiny

SHINIEST superlative of shiny

SHINILY *adv* in a shiny manner

SHINING *adj* emitting or reflecting light

SHINLEAF *n* pl. **-LEAFS** or **-LEAVES** a perennial herb

SHINNED past of shin

SHINNERY *n* pl. **-NERIES** a dense growth of small trees

SHINNEY *v* **-ED, -ING, -S** to play a form of hockey

SHINNING present participle of shin

SHINNY *v* **-NIED, -NYING, -NIES** to shin

SHINTY *n* pl. **-TIES** a Scottish game similar to field hockey

SHINY *adj* **SHINIER, SHINIEST** filled with light

SHIP *v* **SHIPPED, SHIPPING, SHIPS** to transport by ship (a vessel suitable for navigation in deep water)

SHIPLAP *n* pl. **-S** an overlapping joint used in carpentry

SHIPLESS *adj* lacking a ship

SHIPLOAD *n* pl. **-S** as much as a ship can carry

SHIPMAN *n* pl. **-MEN** a sailor

SHIPMATE *n* pl. **-S** a fellow sailor

SHIPMENT *n* pl. **-S** something that is shipped

SHIPPED past tense of ship

SHIPPEN *n* pl. **-S** a cowshed

SHIPPER *n* pl. **-S** one that ships

SHIPPING *n* pl. **-S** the business of one that ships

SHIPPON *n* pl. **-S** shippen

SHIPSIDE *n* pl. **-S** the area alongside a ship

SHIPTIME *n* pl. **-S** the annual arrival of a supply ship

SHIPWAY *n* pl. **-WAYS** a canal deep enough to serve ships

SHIPWORM *n* pl. **-S** a wormlike mollusk

SHIPYARD *n* pl. **-S** a place where ships are built or repaired

SHIRAZ *n* pl. **-ES** a type of wine

SHIRE *n* pl. **-S** a territorial division of Great Britain

SHIRK *v* **-ED, -ING, -S** to avoid work or duty

SHIRKER *n* pl. **-S** one that shirks

SHIRR *v* **-ED, -ING, -S** to draw into three or more parallel rows, as cloth

SHIRRING *n* pl. **-S** a shirred arrangement of cloth

SHIRT *n* pl. **-S** a garment for the upper part of the body **SHIRTED** *adj*

SHIRTING *n* pl. **-S** fabric used for making shirts

SHIRTY *adj* **SHIRTIER, SHIRTIEST** angry **SHIRTILY** *adv*

SHIST *n* pl. **-S** schist

SHITAKE *n* pl. **-S** shiitake

SHITTAH *n* pl. **-S** a hardwood tree

SHITTIM *n* pl. **-S** the wood of the shittah

SHIUR *n* pl. **SHIURIM** a Talmudic study session

SHIV *n* pl. **-S** a knife

SHIVA *n* pl. **-S** a period of mourning

SHIVAH *n* pl. **-S** shiva

SHIVAREE *v* **-REED, -REEING, -REES** to chivaree

SHIVE *n* pl. **-S** a thin fragment

SHIVER *v* **-ED, -ING, -S** to tremble with fear or cold

SHIVERER *n* pl. **-S** one that shivers

SHIVERY *adj* shivering

SHIVITI *n* pl. **-S** a plaque with a Hebrew verse

SHLEMIEL *n* pl. **-S** an unlucky bungler

SHLEP *v* **SHLEPPED, SHLEPPING, SHLEPS** to schlep

SHLEPP *v* **-ED, -ING, -S** to schlep

SHLEPPER *n* pl. **-S** one that schleps

SHLEPPY *adj* **-PIER, -PIEST** schleppy

SHLOCK *n* pl. **-S** schlock

SHLOCKY *adj* **SHLOCKIER, SHLOCKIEST** schlocky

SHLUB *n* pl. **-S** schlub

SHLUMP *v* **-ED, -ING, -S** to schlump

SHLUMPY *adj* slovenly

SHMALTZ *n* pl. **-ES** schmaltz

SHMALTZY *adj* **SHMALTZIER, SHMALTZIEST** schmalzy

SHMATTE *n* pl. **-S** schmatte

SHMEAR *v* **-ED, -ING, -S** to schmeer

SHMEER   *v* **-ED, -ING, -S** to schmeer

SHMO   *n* pl. **SHMOES** schmo

SHMOE   *n* pl. **-S** schmo

SHMOOZE   *v* **SHMOOZED, SHMOOZING, SHMOOZES** to schmooze

SHMOOZER   *n* pl. **-S** one that shmoozes

SHMOOZY   *adj* **SHMOOZIER, SHMOOZIEST** schmoozy

SHMUCK   *n* pl. **-S** schmuck

SHMUCKY   *adj* **SHMUCKIER, SHMUCKIEST** schmucky

SHNAPPS   *n* pl. **SHNAPPS** schnapps

SHNAPS   *n* pl. **SHNAPS** schnapps

SHNOOK   *n* pl. **-S** schnook

SHNORRER   *n* pl. **-S** one who takes advantage of the generosity of others

SHOAL   *adj* **SHOALER, SHOALEST** shallow

SHOAL   *v* **-ED, -ING, -S** to become shallow

SHOALY   *adj* **SHOALIER, SHOALIEST** full of shallow areas

SHOAT   *n* pl. **-S** a young hog

SHOCHET   *n* pl. **-CHETIM** a person who slaughters animals and fowl according to Jewish law

SHOCHU   *n* pl. **-S** a Japanese liquor

SHOCK   *v* **-ED, -ING, -S** to strike with great surprise, horror, or disgust

SHOCKER   *n* pl. **-S** one that shocks

SHOD   a past tense of shoe

SHODDEN   a past participle of shoe

SHODDY   *adj* **-DIER, -DIEST** of inferior quality **SHODDILY** *adv*

SHODDY   *n* pl. **-DIES** a low-quality wool

SHOE   *n* pl. **SHOES** or **SHOON** a covering for the foot

SHOE   *v* **SHOD** or **SHOED, SHODDEN, SHOEING, SHOES** to provide with shoes

SHOEBILL   *n* pl. **-S** a wading bird

SHOEBOX   *n* pl. **-ES** an oblong box for holding a pair of shoes

SHOEHORN   *v* **-ED, -ING, -S** to force into a small space

SHOELACE   *n* pl. **-S** a lace for fastening a shoe

SHOELESS   *adj* having no shoe

SHOEPAC   *n* pl. **-S** a waterproof boot

SHOEPACK   *n* pl. **-S** shoepac

SHOER   *n* pl. **-S** one that shoes horses

SHOETREE   *n* pl. **-S** a device shaped like a foot that is inserted into a shoe to preserve its shape

SHOFAR   *n* pl. **SHOFARS** or **SHOFROTH** a ram's-horn trumpet blown in certain Jewish rituals

SHOG   *v* **SHOGGED, SHOGGING, SHOGS** to move along

SHOGI   *n* pl. **-S** a Japanese game like chess

SHOGUN   *n* pl. **-S** a former military leader of Japan **SHOGUNAL** *adj*

SHOJI   *n* pl. **-S** a paper screen used as a partition or door in a Japanese house

SHOJO   *n* pl. **SHOJO** manga intended primarily for girls

SHOLOM   *n* pl. **-S** shalom

SHONE   a past tense of shine

SHOO   *v* **-ED, -ING, -S** to drive away

SHOOFLY   *n* pl. **-FLIES** a child's rocker

SHOOK   *n* pl. **-S** a set of parts for assembling a barrel or packing

SHOOL   *v* **-ED, -ING, -S** to shovel

SHOON   a pl. of shoe

SHOOSH   *v* **-ED, -ING, -ES** to move with a rushing sound

SHOOT   *v* **SHOT, SHOOTING, SHOOTS** to hit, wound, or kill with a missile discharged from a weapon

SHOOTER   *n* pl. **-S** one that shoots

SHOOTING   *n* pl. **-S** the act of one that shoots

SHOOTIST   *n* pl. **-S** one that is skilled at shooting

SHOOTOUT   *n* pl. **-S** a battle fought with handguns or rifles

SHOP   *v* **SHOPPED, SHOPPING, SHOPS** to examine goods with intent to buy

SHOPBOY   *n* pl. **-BOYS** a salesclerk

SHOPGIRL   *n* pl. **-S** a salesgirl

SHOPHAR   *n* pl. **-PHARS** or **-PHROTH** shofar

SHOPLESS   *adj* having no stores

SHOPLIFT   *v* **-ED, -ING, -S** to steal goods from a store

SHOPMAN   *n* pl. **-MEN** one who owns or operates a small store

SHOPPE   *n* pl. **-S** a small store

SHOPPED   past tense of shop

SHOPPER   *n* pl. **-S** one that shops

SHOPPING   *n* pl. **-S** the act of one that shops

SHOPPY	*adj* **SHOPPIER, SHOPPIEST** conducive to shopping
SHOPTALK	*n* pl. **-S** conversation concerning one's business or occupation
SHOPWORN	*adj* worn out from being on display in a store
SHORAN	*n* pl. **-S** a type of navigational system
SHORE	*v* **SHORED, SHORING, SHORES** to prop with a supporting timber
SHORING	*n* pl. **-S** a system of supporting timbers
SHORL	*n* pl. **-S** schorl
SHORN	a past participle of shear
SHORT	*adj* **SHORTER, SHORTEST** having little length
SHORT	*v* **-ED, -ING, -S** to cause a type of electrical malfunction in
SHORTAGE	*n* pl. **-S** an insufficient supply or amount
SHORTCUT	*v* **-CUT, -CUTTING, -CUTS** to take a shorter or quicker way
SHORTEN	*v* **-ED, -ING, -S** to make or become shorter
SHORTIA	*n* pl. **-S** a perennial herb
SHORTIE	*n* pl. **-S** shorty
SHORTIES	pl. of shorty
SHORTISH	*adj* somewhat short
SHORTLY	*adv* in a short time
SHORTY	*n* pl. **SHORTIES** one that is short
SHOT	*v* **SHOTTED, SHOTTING, SHOTS** to load with shot (small lead or steel pellets)
SHOTE	*n* pl. **-S** shoat
SHOTGUN	*v* **-GUNNED, -GUNNING, -GUNS** to shoot with a type of gun
SHOTHOLE	*n* pl. **-S** a hole drilled in rock to hold explosives
SHOTT	*n* pl. **-S** chott
SHOTTED	past tense of shot
SHOTTEN	*adj* having spawned — used of a fish
SHOTTING	present participle of shot
SHOULD	past tense of shall
SHOULDER	*v* **-ED, -ING, -S** to assume the burden or responsibility of
SHOULDEST	a 2d person sing. past tense of shall
SHOULDST	a 2d person sing. past tense of shall
SHOUT	*v* **-ED, -ING, -S** to utter loudly
SHOUTER	*n* pl. **-S** one that shouts
SHOUTY	*adj* **SHOUTIER, SHOUTIEST** given to or characterized by shouting
SHOVE	*v* **SHOVED, SHOVING, SHOVES** to push roughly
SHOVEL	*v* **-ELED, -ELING, -ELS** or **-ELLED, -ELLING, -ELS** to take up with a shovel (a digging implement)
SHOVELER	*n* pl. **-S** one that shovels
SHOVER	*n* pl. **-S** one that shoves
SHOVING	present participle of shove
SHOW	*v* **SHOWED, SHOWN, SHOWING, SHOWS** to cause or permit to be seen **SHOWABLE** *adj*
SHOWBIZ	*n* pl. **-BIZZES** show business
SHOWBOAT	*v* **-ED, -ING, -S** to show off
SHOWCASE	*v* **-CASED, -CASING, -CASES** to exhibit
SHOWDOWN	*n* pl. **-S** an event that forces the conclusion of an issue
SHOWER	*v* **-ED, -ING, -S** to bathe in a spray of water
SHOWERER	*n* pl. **-S** one that showers
SHOWERY	*adj* abounding with brief periods of rain
SHOWGIRL	*n* pl. **-S** a chorus girl
SHOWGOER	*n* pl. **-S** one that attends a show
SHOWIER	comparative of showy
SHOWIEST	superlative of showy
SHOWILY	*adv* in a showy manner
SHOWING	*n* pl. **-S** an exhibition or display
SHOWMAN	*n* pl. **-MEN** a theatrical producer
SHOWN	past participle of show
SHOWOFF	*n* pl. **-S** one given to pretentious display
SHOWRING	*n* pl. **-S** a ring where animals are displayed
SHOWROOM	*n* pl. **-S** a room used for the display of merchandise
SHOWTIME	*n* pl. **-S** the time at which an entertainment is to start
SHOWY	*adj* **SHOWIER, SHOWIEST** making a great or brilliant display
SHOYU	*n* pl. **-S** soy sauce
SHRANK	past tense of shrink
SHRAPNEL	*n* pl. **-S** fragments from an exploding bomb, mine, or shell

SHRED — *v* **SHREDDED, SHREDDING, SHREDS** to tear into small strips

SHREDDER — *n pl.* **-S** one that shreds

SHREW — *v* **-ED, -ING, -S** to curse

SHREWD — *adj* **SHREWDER, SHREWDEST** having keen insight **SHREWDLY** *adv*

SHREWDIE — *n pl.* **-S** a shrewd person

SHREWISH — *adj* ill-tempered

SHRI — *n pl.* **-S** sri

SHRIEK — *v* **-ED, -ING, -S** to utter a shrill cry

SHRIEKER — *n pl.* **-S** one that shrieks

SHRIEKY — *adj* **SHRIEKIER, SHRIEKIEST** shrill

SHRIEVAL — *adj* pertaining to a sheriff

SHRIEVE — *v* **SHRIEVED, SHRIEVING, SHRIEVES** to shrive

SHRIFT — *n pl.* **-S** the act of shriving

SHRIKE — *n pl.* **-S** a predatory bird

SHRILL — *adj* **SHRILLER, SHRILLEST** having a high-pitched and piercing quality **SHRILLY** *adv*

SHRILL — *v* **-ED, -ING, -S** to utter a shrill sound

SHRIMP — *v* **-ED, -ING, -S** to catch shrimps (small marine decapods)

SHRIMPER — *n pl.* **-S** a shrimp fisher

SHRIMPY — *adj* **SHRIMPIER, SHRIMPIEST** abounding in shrimp

SHRINE — *v* **SHRINED, SHRINING, SHRINES** to place in a shrine (a receptacle for sacred relics)

SHRINK — *v* **SHRANK, SHRUNK** or **SHRUNKEN, SHRINKING, SHRINKS** to contract or draw back

SHRINKER — *n pl.* **-S** one that shrinks

SHRIVE — *v* **SHROVE** or **SHRIVED, SHRIVEN, SHRIVING, SHRIVES** to hear the confession of and grant absolution to

SHRIVEL — *v* **-ELED, -ELING, -ELS** or **-ELLED, -ELLING, -ELS** to contract into wrinkles

SHRIVER — *n pl.* **-S** one that shrives

SHROFF — *v* **-ED, -ING, -S** to test the genuineness of, as a coin

SHROOM — *n pl.* **-S** a mushroom (a type of fungus)

SHROOMER — *n pl.* **-S** one who enjoys eating mushrooms

SHROUD — *v* **-ED, -ING, -S** to wrap in burial clothing

SHROVE — a past tense of shrive

SHRUB — *n pl.* **-S** a low, woody plant

SHRUBBY — *adj* **-BIER, -BIEST** covered with shrubs

SHRUG — *v* **SHRUGGED, SHRUGGING, SHRUGS** to raise and contract the shoulders

SHRUNK — a past tense of shrink

SHRUNKEN — a past participle of shrink

SHTETEL — *n pl.* **SHTETELS** or **SHTETLACH** a Jewish village

SHTETL — *n pl.* **SHTETLS** or **SHTETLACH** shtetel

SHTICK — *n pl.* **-S** an entertainment routine

SHTICKY — *adj* **SHTICKIER, SHTICKIEST** resembling a shtick

SHTIK — *n pl.* **-S** shtick

SHTUM — *adj* schtum

SHUCK — *v* **-ED, -ING, -S** to remove the husk or shell from

SHUCKER — *n pl.* **-S** one that shucks

SHUCKING — *n pl.* **-S** the act of one that shucks

SHUDDER — *v* **-ED, -ING, -S** to tremble

SHUDDERY — *adj* shuddering

SHUFFLE — *v* **-FLED, -FLING, -FLES** to walk without lifting the feet

SHUFFLER — *n pl.* **-S** one that shuffles

SHUL — *n pl.* **SHULS** or **SHULN** a synagogue

SHUMAI — *n/pl* Japanese dumplings

SHUN — *v* **SHUNNED, SHUNNING, SHUNS** to avoid

SHUNNER — *n pl.* **-S** one that shuns

SHUNPIKE — *v* **-PIKED, -PIKING, -PIKES** to travel on side roads to avoid expressways

SHUNT — *v* **-ED, -ING, -S** to turn aside

SHUNTER — *n pl.* **-S** one that shunts

SHURA — *n pl.* **-S** an advisory council

SHUSH — *v* **-ED, -ING, -ES** to silence

SHUSHER — *n pl.* **-S** one that shushes

SHUT — *v* **SHUT, SHUTTING, SHUTS** to close

SHUTDOWN — *n pl.* **-S** a temporary closing of an industrial plant

SHUTE — *v* **SHUTED, SHUTING, SHUTES** to chute

SHUTEYE — *n pl.* **-S** sleep

SHUTOFF	*n* pl. **-S** a device that shuts something off
SHUTOUT	*n* pl. **-S** a game in which one team fails to score
SHUTTER	*v* **-ED, -ING, -S** to provide with shutters (hinged window covers)
SHUTTING	present participle of shut
SHUTTLE	*v* **-TLED, -TLING, -TLES** to move or travel back and forth
SHUTTLER	*n* pl. **-S** one that shuttles
SHVITZ	*v* **-ED, -ING, -ES** to sweat
SHWA	*n* pl. **-S** schwa
SHWANPAN	*n* pl. **-S** swanpan
SHY	*adj* **SHIER, SHIEST** or **SHYER, SHYEST** timid
SHY	*v* **SHIED, SHYING, SHIES** to move suddenly back or aside, as in fear
SHYER	*n* pl. **-S** shier
SHYLOCK	*v* **-ED, -ING, -S** to lend money at high interest rates
SHYLY	*adv* in a shy manner
SHYNESS	*n* pl. **-ES** the state of being shy
SHYSTER	*n* pl. **-S** an unscrupulous lawyer or politician
SI	*n* pl. **-S** ti
SIAL	*n* pl. **-S** a type of rock formation **SIALIC** *adj*
SIALID	*n* pl. **-S** an alderfly
SIALIDAN	*n* pl. **-S** sialid
SIALOID	*adj* resembling saliva
SIAMANG	*n* pl. **-S** a large, black gibbon
SIAMESE	*n* pl. **-S** a water pipe with a connection for two hoses
SIB	*n* pl. **-S** a sibling
SIBB	*n* pl. **-S** sib
SIBILANT	*n* pl. **-S** a speech sound produced by the fricative passage of breath through a narrow orifice
SIBILATE	*v* **-LATED, -LATING, -LATES** to hiss
SIBLING	*n* pl. **-S** one having the same parents as another
SIBSHIP	*n* pl. **-S** a group of children having the same parents
SIBYL	*n* pl. **-S** a female prophet **SIBYLIC, SIBYLLIC** *adj*
SIC	*v* **SICCED, SICCING, SICS** to urge to attack
SICCAN	*adj* such
SICE	*n* pl. **-S** syce

SICK	*adj* **SICKER, SICKEST** affected with disease or ill health
SICK	*v* **-ED, -ING, -S** to sic
SICKBAY	*n* pl. **-BAYS** a ship's hospital
SICKBED	*n* pl. **-S** a sick person's bed
SICKEE	*n* pl. **-S** sickie
SICKEN	*v* **-ED, -ING, -S** to make sick
SICKENER	*n* pl. **-S** one that sickens
SICKERLY	*adv* securely
SICKIE	*n* pl. **-S** an emotionally sick person
SICKISH	*adj* somewhat sick
SICKLE	*v* **-LED, -LING, -LES** to cut with an agricultural implement having a single blade
SICKLY	*adj* **-LIER, -LIEST** appearing as if sick **SICKLILY** *adv*
SICKLY	*v* **-LIED, -LYING, -LIES** to make sickly
SICKNESS	*n* pl. **-ES** the state of being sick
SICKO	*n* pl. **SICKOS** sickie
SICKOUT	*n* pl. **-S** an organized absence of workers claiming to be sick
SICKROOM	*n* pl. **-S** a room occupied by a sick person
SIDALCEA	*n* pl. **-S** a North American herb
SIDDHA	*n* pl. **-S** one who has attained perfection in Hinduism
SIDDHI	*n* pl. **-S** the perfection attained by a siddha
SIDDUR	*n* pl. **-DURS** or **-DURIM** a Jewish prayer book
SIDE	*v* **SIDED, SIDING, SIDES** to agree with or support
SIDEARM	*v* **-ED, -ING, -S** to pitch a ball at or below shoulder level
SIDEBAND	*n* pl. **-S** a band of radio frequencies
SIDEBAR	*n* pl. **-S** a short news story accompanying a major story
SIDEBURN	*n* **-S** either of two strips of hair grown by a man down each side of the face
SIDECAR	*n* pl. **-S** a passenger car attached to a motorcycle
SIDED	past tense of side
SIDEHILL	*n* pl. **-S** a hillside
SIDEKICK	*n* pl. **-S** a close friend
SIDELESS	*adj* having no sides
SIDELINE	*v* **-LINED, -LINING, -LINES** to put out of action

SIDELING *adj* sloping

SIDELOCK *n* pl. **-S** a long lock of hair falling from the side of the head

SIDELONG *adj* directed to one side

SIDEMAN *n* pl. **-MEN** a member of a jazz band

SIDEMEAT *n* pl. **-S** meat cut from the side of the pig

SIDEREAL *adj* pertaining to the stars

SIDERITE *n* pl. **-S** a mineral

SIDEROAD *n* pl. **-S** a rural road

SIDESHOW *n* pl. **-S** a small show offered in addition to a main attraction

SIDESLIP *v* **-SLIPPED, -SLIPPING, -SLIPS** to slip to one side

SIDESMAN *n* pl. **-MEN** a lay assistant at an Anglican church

SIDESPIN *n* pl. **-S** a type of spin imparted to a ball

SIDESTEP *v* **-STEPPED, -STEPPING, -STEPS** to step to one side

SIDEWALK *n* pl. **-S** a paved walk for pedestrians

SIDEWALL *n* pl. **-S** a side surface of a tire

SIDEWARD *adv* toward one side

SIDEWAY *adv* sideways

SIDEWAYS *adv* toward or from one side

SIDEWISE *adv* sideways

SIDH *n* pl. **SIDHE** a hill inhabited by supernatural beings in Irish folklore

SIDING *n* pl. **-S** material used for surfacing a frame building

SIDLE *v* **-DLED, -DLING, -DLES** to move sideways

SIDLER *n* pl. **-S** one that sidles

SIEGE *v* **SIEGED, SIEGING, SIEGES** to attempt to capture or gain

SIEMENS *n* pl. **SIEMENS** a unit of electrical conductance

SIENITE *n* pl. **-S** syenite

SIENNA *n* pl. **-S** a brown pigment

SIEROZEM *n* pl. **-S** a type of soil

SIERRA *n* pl. **-S** a mountain range **SIERRAN** *adj*

SIESTA *n* pl. **-S** an afternoon nap or rest

SIEUR *n* pl. **-S** an old French title of respect for a man

SIEVE *v* **SIEVED, SIEVING, SIEVES** to pass through a sieve (a utensil for separating the coarse parts from the fine parts of loose matter)

SIEVERT *n* pl. **-S** a unit of ionizing radiation

SIFAKA *n* pl. **-S** a lemur of Madagascar

SIFFLEUR *n* pl. **-S** an animal that makes a whistling noise

SIFT *v* **-ED, -ING, -S** to sieve

SIFTER *n* pl. **-S** one that sifts

SIFTING *n* pl. **-S** the work of a sifter

SIG *n* pl. **-S** a short personalized message at the end of an email

SIGANID *n* pl. **-S** any of a family of fishes

SIGH *v* **-ED, -ING, -S** to let out a sigh (a deep, audible breath)

SIGHER *n* pl. **-S** one that sighs

SIGHLESS *adj* uttering no sigh

SIGHLIKE *adj* resembling a sigh

SIGHT *v* **-ED, -ING, -S** to observe or notice

SIGHTER *n* pl. **-S** one that sights

SIGHTING *n* pl. **-S** an observation

SIGHTLY *adj* **-LIER, -LIEST** pleasing to look at

SIGHTSEE *v* **-SAW, -SEEN, -SEEING, -SEES** to visit and view places of interest

SIGIL *n* pl. **-S** an official seal

SIGLOS *n* pl. **-LOI** an ancient Persian coin

SIGLUM *n* pl. **SIGLA** an abbreviation to indicate the source of an edited text

SIGMA *n* pl. **-S** a Greek letter **SIGMATE** *adj*

SIGMOID *n* pl. **-S** an S-shaped curve in a bodily part

SIGN *v* **-ED, -ING, -S** to write one's name on

SIGNA *v* write on the label — no other form of this imperative verb is used

SIGNAGE *n* pl. **-S** a system of signs in a community

SIGNAL *v* **-NALED, -NALING, -NALS** or **-NALLED, -NALLING, -NALS** to notify by a means of communication

SIGNALER *n* pl. **-S** one that signals

SIGNALLY *adv* notably

SIGNEE *n* pl. **-S** a signer of a document

SIGNER *n* pl. **-S** one that signs

SIGNET	*v* **-ED, -ING, -S** to mark with an official seal
SIGNIFY	*v* **-FIED, -FYING, -FIES** to make known
SIGNING	*n* pl. **-S** the act of writing one's signature on a document or in a book
SIGNIOR	*n* pl. **-GNIORS** or **-GNIORI** signor
SIGNIORY	*n* pl. **-GNIORIES** signory
SIGNOR	*n* pl. **-GNORS** or **-GNORI** an Italian title of courtesy for a man
SIGNORA	*n* pl. **-GNORAS** or **-GNORE** an Italian title of courtesy for a married woman
SIGNORE	*n* pl. **-GNORI** signor
SIGNORY	*n* pl. **-GNORIES** seigniory
SIGNPOST	*v* **-ED, -ING, -S** to provide with signposts (posts bearing signs)
SIKA	*n* pl. **-S** a small deer native to Asia
SIKE	*n* pl. **-S** syke
SIKER	*adj* secure
SIKSIK	*n* pl. **-S** the Arctic ground squirrel
SILAGE	*n* pl. **-S** fodder that has been preserved in a silo
SILANE	*n* pl. **-S** a chemical compound
SILD	*n* pl. **-S** a young herring
SILENCE	*v* **-LENCED, -LENCING, -LENCES** to make silent
SILENCER	*n* pl. **-S** one that silences
SILENI	pl. of silenus
SILENT	*adj* **-LENTER, -LENTEST** making no sound or noise **SILENTLY** *adv*
SILENTS	*n/pl* silent movies
SILENUS	*n* pl. **-NI** a woodland deity of Greek mythology
SILESIA	*n* pl. **-S** a cotton fabric
SILEX	*n* pl. **-ES** silica
SILICA	*n* pl. **-S** a form of silicon
SILICATE	*n* pl. **-S** a chemical salt
SILICIC	*adj* pertaining to silicon
SILICIDE	*n* pl. **-S** a silicon compound
SILICIFY	*v* **-FIED, -FYING, -FIES** to convert into silica
SILICIUM	*n* pl. **-S** silicon
SILICLE	*n* pl. **-S** a short, flat silique
SILICON	*n* pl. **-S** a nonmetallic element
SILICONE	*n* pl. **-S** a silicon compound
SILICULA	*n* pl. **-LAE** a silicle
SILIQUA	*n* pl. **-QUAE** silique
SILIQUE	*n* pl. **-LIQUES** a type of seed capsule
SILK	*v* **-ED, -ING, -S** to cover with silk (a soft, lustrous fabric)
SILKEN	*adj* made of silk
SILKIE	*n* pl. **-S** selkie
SILKIER	comparative of silky
SILKIES	pl. of silky
SILKIEST	superlative of silky
SILKILY	*adv* in a silky manner
SILKLIKE	*adj* resembling silk
SILKWEED	*n* pl. **-S** milkweed
SILKWORM	*n* pl. **-S** a caterpillar that spins a cocoon of silk fibers
SILKY	*adj* **SILKIER, SILKIEST** resembling silk
SILKY	*n* pl. **SILKIES** a glossy-coated terrier
SILL	*n* pl. **-S** the horizontal piece at the base of a window
SILLABUB	*n* pl. **-S** an alcoholic dessert
SILLER	*n* pl. **-S** silver
SILLIBUB	*n* pl. **-S** sillabub
SILLY	*adj* **-LIER, -LIEST** showing a lack of good sense **SILLILY** *adv*
SILLY	*n* pl. **-LIES** a silly person
SILO	*v* **-ED, -ING, -S** to store in a silo (a tall, cylindrical structure)
SILOXANE	*n* pl. **-S** a chemical compound
SILT	*v* **-ED, -ING, -S** to fill with silt (a sedimentary material)
SILTY	*adj* **SILTIER, SILTIEST** full of silt
SILURID	*n* pl. **-S** any of a family of catfishes
SILUROID	*n* pl. **-S** a silurid
SILVA	*n* pl. **-VAS** or **-VAE** sylva
SILVAN	*n* pl. **-S** sylvan
SILVER	*v* **-ED, -ING, -S** to cover with silver (a metallic element)
SILVERER	*n* pl. **-S** one that silvers
SILVERIER	comparative of silvery
SILVERIEST	superlative of silvery
SILVERLY	*adv* with a silvery appearance
SILVERN	*adj* silvery
SILVERTIP	*n* pl. **-S** a grizzly bear with white-tipped hairs
SILVERY	*adj* **-VERIER, -VERIEST** resembling silver

SILVEX — *n* pl. **-ES** an herbicide

SILVICAL — *adj* pertaining to silvics

SILVICS — *n/pl* the study of forest trees

SIM — *n* pl. **-S** simulation

SIMA — *n* pl. **-S** an igneous rock

SIMAR — *n* pl. **-S** a woman's light jacket or robe

SIMARUBA — *n* pl. **-S** a tropical tree

SIMAZINE — *n* pl. **-S** an herbicide

SIMCHA — *n* pl. **-S** a Jewish private party

SIMIAN — *n* pl. **-S** an ape or monkey

SIMILAR — *adj* being like but not completely identical to

SIMILE — *n* pl. **-S** a figure of speech

SIMIOID — *adj* simious

SIMIOUS — *adj* pertaining to simians

SIMITAR — *n* pl. **-S** scimitar

SIMLIN — *n* pl. **-S** cymling

SIMMER — *v* **-ED, -ING, -S** to cook below or just at the boiling point

SIMNEL — *n* pl. **-S** a crisp bread

SIMOLEON — *n* pl. **-S** a dollar

SIMONIAC — *n* pl. **-S** one who practices simony

SIMONIES — pl. of simony

SIMONIST — *n* pl. **-S** a simoniac

SIMONIZE — *v* **-NIZED, -NIZING, -NIZES** to polish with wax

SIMONY — *n* pl. **-NIES** the buying or selling of a church office

SIMOOM — *n* pl. **-S** a hot, dry desert wind

SIMOON — *n* pl. **-S** simoom

SIMP — *n* pl. **-S** a foolish person

SIMPER — *v* **-ED, -ING, -S** to smile in a silly manner

SIMPERER — *n* pl. **-S** one that simpers

SIMPLE — *adj* **SIMPLER, SIMPLEST** not complex or complicated

SIMPLE — *n* pl. **-S** something that is simple

SIMPLEX — *n* pl. **-PLEXES** or **-PLICES** or **-PLICIA** a simple word

SIMPLIFY — *v* **-FIED, -FYING, -FIES** to make simple

SIMPLISM — *n* pl. **-S** the tendency to oversimplify an issue or problem

SIMPLIST — *n* pl. **-S** a person given to simplism

SIMPLY — *adv* in a simple manner

SIMULANT — *n* pl. **-S** one that simulates

SIMULAR — *n* pl. **-S** a simulant

SIMULATE — *v* **-LATED, -LATING, -LATES** to take on the appearance of

SIN — *v* **SINNED, SINNING, SINS** to commit a sin (an offense against religious or moral law)

SINAPISM — *n* pl. **-S** a pasty mixture applied to an irritated part of the body

SINCE — *adv* from then until now

SINCERE — *adj* **-CERER, -CEREST** free from hypocrisy or falseness

SINCIPUT — *n* pl. **-CIPUTS** or **-CIPITA** the forehead

SINE — *n* pl. **-S** a trigonometric function of an angle

SINECURE — *n* pl. **-S** an office or position requiring little or no work

SINEW — *v* **-ED, -ING, -S** to strengthen

SINEWY — *adj* lean and muscular

SINFONIA — *n* pl. **-NIAS** or **-NIE** a symphony

SINFUL — *adj* marked by sin **SINFULLY** *adv*

SING — *v* **SANG, SUNG, SINGING, SINGS** to utter with musical inflections of the voice **SINGABLE** *adj*

SINGE — *v* **SINGED, SINGEING, SINGES** to burn slightly

SINGER — *n* pl. **-S** one that sings

SINGING — *n* pl. **-S** the act or sound of one that sings

SINGLE — *v* **-GLED, -GLING, -GLES** to select from a group

SINGLET — *n* pl. **-S** a man's undershirt or jersey

SINGLY — *adv* without the company of others

SINGSONG — *n* pl. **-S** monotonous cadence in speaking or reading

SINGULAR — *n* pl. **-S** a word form that denotes one person or thing

SINH — *n* pl. **-S** a hyperbolic function of an angle

SINICIZE — *v* **-CIZED, -CIZING, -CIZES** to modify by Chinese influence

SINISTER — *adj* threatening or portending evil

SINK — *v* **SANK, SUNK** or **SUNKEN, SINKING, SINKS** to move to a lower level **SINKABLE** *adj*

SINKAGE — *n* pl. **-S** the act, process, or degree of sinking

SINKER — *n* pl. **-S** one that sinks

SINKFUL — *n* pl. **-S** as much as a sink can hold

SINKHOLE *n* pl. **-S** a natural depression in a land surface

SINLESS *adj* free from sin

SINNED past tense of sin

SINNER *n* pl. **-S** one that sins

SINNET *n* pl. **-S** sennet

SINNING present participle of sin

SINOLOGY *n* pl. **-GIES** the study of the Chinese

SINOPIA *n* pl. **-PIAS** or **-PIE** a red pigment

SINSYNE *adv* since

SINTER *v* **-ED, -ING, -S** to make cohesive by the combined action of heat and pressure

SINUATE *v* **-ATED, -ATING, -ATES** to curve in and out

SINUOUS *adj* characterized by curves, bends, or turns

SINUS *n* pl. **-ES** a cranial cavity

SINUSOID *n* pl. **-S** a mathematical curve

SIP *v* **SIPPED, SIPPING, SIPS** to drink in small quantities

SIPE *v* **SIPED, SIPING, SIPES** to seep

SIPHON *v* **-ED, -ING, -S** to draw off through a siphon (a type of tube)

SIPHONAL *adj* of or pertaining to a siphon

SIPHONIC *adj* siphonal

SIPING present participle of sipe

SIPPABLE *adj* capable of being sipped

SIPPED past tense of sip

SIPPER *n* pl. **-S** one that sips

SIPPET *n* pl. **-S** a small piece of bread soaked in gravy

SIPPING present participle of sip

SIR *n* pl. **-S** a respectful form of address used to a man

SIRDAR *n* pl. **-S** a person of rank in India

SIRE *v* **SIRED, SIRING, SIRES** to beget

SIREE *n* pl. **-S** sirree

SIREN *n* pl. **-S** a device that produces a penetrating warning sound

SIRENIAN *n* pl. **-S** any of an order of aquatic mammals

SIRING present participle of sire

SIRLOIN *n* pl. **-S** a cut of beef

SIROCCO *n* pl. **-COS** a hot, dry wind

SIRRA *n* pl. **-S** sirrah

SIRRAH *n* pl. **-S** a form of address used to inferiors

SIRREE *n* pl. **-S** sir

SIRUP *v* **-ED, -ING, -S** to syrup

SIRUPY *adj* **-UPIER, -UPIEST** syrupy

SIRVENTE *n* pl. **-S** a satirical medieval song or poem

SIS *n* pl. **SISES** or **SISSES** sister

SISAL *n* pl. **-S** a strong fiber used for rope

SISKIN *n* pl. **-S** a Eurasian finch

SISSY *adj* **SISSIER, SISSIEST** sissyish

SISSY *n* pl. **-SIES** an effeminate man or boy

SISSYISH *adj* resembling a sissy

SISTER *v* **-ED, -ING, -S** to treat like a sister (a female sibling)

SISTERLY *adj* of or resembling a sister

SISTROID *adj* included between the convex sides of two intersecting curves

SISTRUM *n* pl. **-TRUMS** or **-TRA** an ancient Egyptian percussion instrument

SIT *v* **SAT, SAT** or **SITTEN, SITTING, SITS** to rest on the buttocks

SITAR *n* pl. **-S** a lute of India

SITARIST *n* pl. **-S** one who plays the sitar

SITCOM *n* pl. **-S** a television comedy series with continuing characters

SITE *v* **SITED, SITING, SITES** to place in position for operation

SITH *adv* since

SITHENCE *adv* since

SITHENS *adv* since

SITING present participle of site

SITOLOGY *n* pl. **-GIES** the science of nutrition and diet

SITREP *n* pl. **-S** a report on the current military situation

SITTEN a past participle of sit

SITTER *n* pl. **-S** one that sits

SITTING *n* pl. **-S** a meeting or session

SITUATE *v* **-ATED, -ATING, -ATES** to place in a certain position

SITUP *n* pl. **-S** an exercise in which one moves from a lying to a sitting position

SITUS *n* pl. **-TUSES** a position or location

SITZMARK *n* pl. **-S** a mark left in the snow by a skier who has fallen backward

SIVER *n* pl. **-S** a sewer

SIX   *n* pl. **-ES** a number

SIXER   *n* pl. **-S** the leader of a group of six Brownies or Cubs

SIXFOLD   *adj* being six times as great as

SIXMO   *n* pl. **-MOS** a paper size

SIXPENCE   *n* pl. **-S** a formerly used British coin worth six pennies

SIXPENNY   *adj* worth sixpence

SIXTE   *n* pl. **-S** a fencing parry

SIXTEEN   *n* pl. **-S** a number

SIXTH   *n* pl. **-S** one of six equal parts

SIXTHLY   *adv* in the sixth place

SIXTIETH   *n* pl. **-S** one of sixty equal parts

SIXTY   *n* pl. **-TIES** a number

SIXTYISH   *adj* being about sixty years old

SIZABLE   *adj* of considerable size **SIZABLY** *adv*

SIZAR   *n* pl. **-S** a British student who receives financial assistance from his college

SIZE   *v* **SIZED, SIZING, SIZES** to arrange according to size (physical proportions)

SIZEABLE   *adj* sizable **SIZEABLY** *adv*

SIZER   *n* pl. **-S** sizar

SIZINESS   *n* pl. **-ES** the quality or state of being sizy

SIZING   *n* pl. **-S** a substance used as a glaze or filler for porous materials

SIZY   *adj* **SIZIER, SIZIEST** viscid

SIZZLE   *v* **-ZLED, -ZLING, -ZLES** to burn or fry with a hissing sound

SIZZLER   *n* pl. **-S** a very hot day

SJAMBOK   *v* **-ED, -ING, -S** to strike with a whip used in South Africa

SKA   *n* pl. **-S** a popular music of Jamaica

SKAG   *n* pl. **-S** heroin

SKALD   *n* pl. **-S** an ancient Scandinavian poet **SKALDIC** *adj*

SKANK   *v* **-ED, -ING, -S** to dance in a loose-limbed manner

SKANKER   *n* pl. **-S** one that skanks

SKANKY   *adj* **SKANKIER, SKANKIEST** filthy or sleazy

SKAT   *n* pl. **-S** a card game

SKATE   *v* **SKATED, SKATING, SKATES** to glide over ice or the ground on skates (shoes fitted with runners or wheels)

SKATER   *n* pl. **-S** one that skates

SKATING   *n* pl. **-S** the sport of gliding on skates

SKATOL   *n* pl. **-S** skatole

SKATOLE   *n* pl. **-S** a chemical compound

SKEAN   *n* pl. **-S** a type of dagger

SKEANE   *n* pl. **-S** a length of yarn wound in a loose coil

SKED   *v* **SKEDDED, SKEDDING, SKEDS** to schedule

SKEE   *v* **SKEED, SKEEING, SKEES** to ski

SKEEN   *n* pl. **-S** skean

SKEET   *n* pl. **-S** the sport of shooting at clay pigeons hurled in the air by spring traps

SKEETER   *n* pl. **-S** a skeet shooter

SKEEVY   *adj* **SKEEVIER, SKEEVIEST** repulsive, disgusting

SKEG   *n* pl. **-S** a timber that connects the keel and sternpost of a ship

SKEIGH   *adj* proud

SKEIN   *v* **-ED, -ING, -S** to wind into long, loose coils

SKELETON   *n* pl. **-S** the supporting or protective framework of a human or animal body **SKELETAL** *adj*

SKELL   *n* pl. **-S** a homeless person

SKELLUM   *n* pl. **-S** a rascal

SKELM   *n* pl. **-S** skellum

SKELP   *v* **SKELPED** or **SKELPIT, SKELPING, SKELPS** to slap

SKELTER   *v* **-ED, -ING, -S** to scurry

SKENE   *n* pl. **-S** skean

SKEP   *n* pl. **-S** a beehive

SKEPSIS   *n* pl. **-SISES** the attitude or outlook of a skeptic

SKEPTIC   *n* pl. **-S** a person who doubts generally accepted ideas

SKERRY   *n* pl. **-RIES** a small, rocky island

SKETCH   *v* **-ED, -ING, -ES** to make a rough, hasty drawing of

SKETCHER   *n* pl. **-S** one that sketches

SKETCHY   *adj* **SKETCHIER, SKETCHIEST** lacking in completeness or clearness

SKEW   *v* **-ED, -ING, -S** to turn aside

SKEWBACK   *n* pl. **-S** a sloping surface against which the end of an arch rests

SKEWBALD *n* pl. **-S** a horse having patches of brown and white

SKEWER *v* **-ED, -ING, -S** to pierce with a long pin, as meat

SKEWNESS *n* pl. **-ES** lack of symmetry

SKI *v* **-ED, -ING, -S** to travel on skis (long, narrow strips of wood or metal)

SKIABLE *adj* capable of being skied over

SKIAGRAM *n* pl. **-S** a picture made up of shadows or outlines

SKIBOB *v* **-BOBBED, -BOBBING, -BOBS** to ride a bike-like vehicle with skis instead of wheels

SKID *v* **SKIDDED, SKIDDING, SKIDS** to slide sideways as a result of a loss of traction

SKIDDER *n* pl. **-S** one that skids

SKIDDING *n* pl. **-S** the work of hauling logs from a cutting area

SKIDDOO *v* **-ED, -ING, -S** to go away

SKIDDY *adj* **-DIER, -DIEST** likely to cause skidding

SKIDOO *v* **-ED, -ING, -S** to skiddoo

SKIDOOER *n* pl. **-S** one that rides on a snowmobile

SKIDPAD *n* pl. **-S** a road surface on which drivers can practice controlling skidding

SKIDWAY *n* pl. **-WAYS** a platform on which logs are piled for loading or sawing

SKIED past tense of ski and sky

SKIER *n* pl. **-S** one that skis

SKIES present 3d person sing. of sky

SKIEY *adj* skyey

SKIFF *n* pl. **-S** a small, open boat

SKIFFLE *v* **-FLED, -FLING, -FLES** to play a particular style of music

SKIING *n* pl. **-S** the sport of traveling on skis

SKIJORER *n* pl. **-S** a skier who is drawn over snow by dogs, a horse, or vehicle

SKILFUL *adj* skillful

SKILFULL *adj* skillful

SKILL *n* pl. **-S** the ability to do something well **SKILLED** *adj*

SKILLESS *adj* having no skill

SKILLET *n* pl. **-S** a frying pan

SKILLFUL *adj* having skill

SKILLING *n* pl. **-S** a former coin of Scandinavian countries

SKIM *v* **SKIMMED, SKIMMING, SKIMS** to remove floating matter from the surface of

SKIMMER *n* pl. **-S** one that skims

SKIMMIA *n* pl. **-S** an evergreen shrub

SKIMMING *n* pl. **-S** something that is skimmed from a liquid

SKIMP *v* **-ED, -ING, -S** to scrimp

SKIMPY *adj* **SKIMPIER, SKIMPIEST** scanty **SKIMPILY** *adv*

SKIN *v* **SKINNED, SKINNING, SKINS** to strip or deprive of skin (the membranous tissue covering the body of an animal)

SKINFUL *n* pl. **-S** as much as a skin container can hold

SKINHEAD *n* pl. **-S** one whose hair is cut very short

SKINK *v* **-ED, -ING, -S** to pour out or serve, as liquor

SKINKER *n* pl. **-S** one that skinks

SKINLESS *adj* having no skin

SKINLIKE *adj* resembling skin

SKINNED past tense of skin

SKINNER *n* pl. **-S** one that skins

SKINNING present participle of skin

SKINNY *adj* **-NIER, -NIEST** very thin

SKINNY *n* pl. **-NIES** one that is skinny

SKINT *adj* having no money

SKIORING *n* pl. **-S** a form of skiing

SKIP *v* **SKIPPED, SKIPPING, SKIPS** to move with light springing steps

SKIPJACK *n* pl. **-S** a marine fish

SKIPLANE *n* pl. **-S** an airplane designed to take off from or land on snow

SKIPPED past tense of skip

SKIPPER *v* **-ED, -ING, -S** to act as master or captain of

SKIPPET *n* pl. **-S** a small box for protecting an official seal

SKIPPING present participle of skip

SKIRL *v* **-ED, -ING, -S** to produce a shrill sound

SKIRMISH *v* **-ED, -ING, -ES** to engage in a minor battle

SKIRR *v* **-ED, -ING, -S** to move rapidly

SKIRRET *n* pl. **-S** an Asian herb

SKIRT	*v* **-ED, -ING, -S** to go or pass around
SKIRTER	*n* pl. **-S** one that skirts
SKIRTING	*n* pl. **-S** a board at the base of a wall
SKIT	*n* pl. **-S** a short dramatic scene
SKITE	*v* **SKITED, SKITING, SKITES** to move away quickly
SKITTER	*v* **-ED, -ING, -S** to move lightly or rapidly along a surface
SKITTERY	*adj* **-TERIER, -TERIEST** skittish
SKITTISH	*adj* easily frightened
SKITTLE	*n* pl. **-S** a wooden pin used in a bowling game
SKIVE	*v* **SKIVED, SKIVING, SKIVES** to pare
SKIVER	*n* pl. **-S** one that skives
SKIVVY	*v* **-VIED, -VYING, -VIES** to work as a female servant
SKIWEAR	*n* pl. **SKIWEAR** clothing suitable for wear while skiing
SKLENT	*v* **-ED, -ING, -S** to slant
SKOAL	*v* **-ED, -ING, -S** to drink to the health of
SKOL	*v* **-ED, -ING, -S** to skoal
SKOOKUM	*n* pl. **-S** an evil spirit
SKORT	*n* pl. **-S** a pair of shorts that resembles a skirt
SKOSH	*n* pl. **-ES** a small amount
SKREEGH	*v* **-ED, -ING, -S** to screech
SKREIGH	*v* **-ED, -ING, -S** to screech
SKRY	*v* **SKRIED, SKRYING, SKRIES** to scry
SKUA	*n* pl. **-S** a predatory seabird
SKULK	*v* **-ED, -ING, -S** to move about stealthily
SKULKER	*n* pl. **-S** one that skulks
SKULL	*v* **-ED, -ING, -S** to hit on the head
SKULLCAP	*n* pl. **-S** a close-fitting cap
SKUNK	*v* **-ED, -ING, -S** to defeat overwhelmingly
SKUNKY	*adj* **SKUNKIER, SKUNKIEST** having a smell suggestive of a skunk (a mammal that can spray a foul-smelling liquid)
SKY	*v* **SKIED** or **SKYED, SKYING, SKIES** to hit or throw toward the sky (the upper atmosphere)
SKYBOARD	*n* pl. **-S** a board with foot bindings that is used for skysurfing
SKYBORNE	*adj* airborne
SKYBOX	*n* pl. **-ES** an enclosure of seats situated high in a stadium
SKYCAP	*n* pl. **-S** a porter at an airport
SKYDIVE	*v* **-DIVED** or **-DOVE, -DIVING, -DIVES** to parachute from an airplane for sport
SKYDIVER	*n* pl. **-S** one that skydives
SKYEY	*adj* resembling the sky
SKYGLOW	*n* pl. **-S** a glow in the night sky resulting from urban lights
SKYHOOK	*n* pl. **-S** a hook conceived as being suspended from the sky
SKYJACK	*v* **-ED, -ING, -S** to hijack an airplane
SKYLARK	*v* **-ED, -ING, -S** to frolic
SKYLESS	*adj* having the sky obscured by clouds
SKYLIGHT	*n* pl. **-S** a window in a roof or ceiling
SKYLIKE	*adj* resembling the sky
SKYLINE	*n* pl. **-S** the horizon
SKYLIT	*adj* having a skylight
SKYMAN	*n* pl. **-MEN** an aviator
SKYPHOS	*n* pl. **-PHOI** a drinking vessel used in ancient Greece
SKYSAIL	*n* pl. **-S** a type of sail
SKYSCAPE	*n* pl. **-S** a view of the sky
SKYSURF	*v* **-ED, -ING, -S** to perform maneuvers during free fall while riding on a skyboard
SKYWALK	*n* pl. **-S** an elevated walkway between two buildings
SKYWARD	*adv* toward the sky
SKYWARDS	*adv* skyward
SKYWATCH	*v* **-ED, -ING, -ES** to observe the sky for heavenly bodies or aircraft
SKYWAY	*n* pl. **-WAYS** an elevated highway
SKYWRITE	*v* **-WROTE, -WRITTEN, -WRITING, -WRITES** to write in the sky by releasing a visible vapor from an airplane
SLAB	*v* **SLABBED, SLABBING, SLABS** to remove slabs (broad, flat pieces) from a log
SLABBER	*v* **-ED, -ING, -S** to slobber
SLABBERY	*adj* slobbery
SLABBING	*n* pl. **-S** the act of removing slabs from a log
SLABBY	*adj* **-BIER, -BIEST** covered or paved with slabs

SLABLIKE	*adj* resembling a slab
SLACK	*adj* **SLACKER, SLACKEST** not tight or taut
SLACK	*v* **-ED, -ING, -S** to slacken
SLACKEN	*v* **-ED, -ING, -S** to make less tight or taut
SLACKER	*n* pl. **-S** a shirker
SLACKLY	*adv* in a slack manner
SLAG	*v* **SLAGGED, SLAGGING, SLAGS** to convert into slag (the fused residue of a smelted ore)
SLAGGING	*n* pl. **-S** the process of converting ore into slag
SLAGGY	*adj* **-GIER, -GIEST** resembling slag
SLAHAL	*n* pl. **-S** lahal
SLAIN	past participle of slay
SLAINTE	*interj* — used to toast one's health
SLAKE	*v* **SLAKED, SLAKING, SLAKES** to quench **SLAKABLE** *adj*
SLAKER	*n* pl. **-S** one that slakes
SLALOM	*v* **-ED, -ING, -S** to ski in a zigzag course
SLALOMER	*n* pl. **-S** one that sloloms
SLAM	*v* **SLAMMED, SLAMMING, SLAMS** to shut forcibly and noisily
SLAMMER	*n* pl. **-S** a jail
SLAMMING	*n* pl. **-S** the practice of switching a person's telephone service from one company to another without permission
SLANDER	*v* **-ED, -ING, -S** to defame
SLANG	*v* **-ED, -ING, -S** to use slang (extremely informal or vulgar language)
SLANGY	*adj* **SLANGIER, SLANGIEST** being or containing slang **SLANGILY** *adv*
SLANK	a past tense of slink
SLANT	*v* **-ED, -ING, -S** to deviate from the horizontal or vertical
SLANTY	*adj* **SLANTIER, SLANTIEST** deviating from the horizontal or vertical **SLANTLY** *adv*
SLAP	*v* **SLAPPED, SLAPPING, SLAPS** to strike with the open hand
SLAPDASH	*n* pl. **-ES** careless work
SLAPJACK	*n* pl. **-S** a pancake
SLAPPER	*n* pl. **-S** one that slaps
SLAPPING	present participle of slap
SLAPSHOT	*n* pl. **-S** a type of shot in hockey
SLASH	*v* **-ED, -ING, -ES** to cut with violent sweeping strokes
SLASHER	*n* pl. **-S** one that slashes
SLASHING	*n* pl. **-S** the act of one that slashes
SLAT	*v* **SLATTED, SLATTING, SLATS** to provide with slats (narrow strips of wood or metal)
SLATCH	*n* pl. **-ES** a calm between breaking waves
SLATE	*v* **SLATED, SLATING, SLATES** to cover with slate (a roofing material)
SLATER	*n* pl. **-S** one that slates
SLATEY	*adj* **SLATIER, SLATIEST** slaty
SLATHER	*v* **-ED, -ING, -S** to spread thickly
SLATIER	comparative of slaty
SLATIEST	superlative of slaty
SLATING	*n* pl. **-S** the act of one that slates
SLATTED	past tense of slat
SLATTERN	*n* pl. **-S** a slovenly woman
SLATTING	*n* pl. **-S** material for making slats
SLATY	*adj* **SLATIER, SLATIEST** resembling slate
SLAVE	*v* **SLAVED, SLAVING, SLAVES** to work like a slave (one who is owned by another)
SLAVER	*v* **-ED, -ING, -S** to drool
SLAVERER	*n* pl. **-S** one that slavers
SLAVERY	*n* pl. **-ERIES** ownership of one person by another
SLAVEY	*n* pl. **-EYS** a female servant
SLAVING	present participle of slave
SLAVISH	*adj* pertaining to or characteristic of a slave
SLAW	*n* pl. **-S** coleslaw
SLAY	*v* **SLEW** or **SLAYED, SLAIN, SLAYING, SLAYS** to kill violently **SLAYABLE** *adj*
SLAYER	*n* pl. **-S** one that slays
SLAYING	*n* pl. **-S** the act or an instance of killing
SLEAVE	*v* **SLEAVED, SLEAVING, SLEAVES** to separate into filaments
SLEAZE	*v* **SLEAZED, SLEAZING, SLEAZES** to behave in a sleazy manner
SLEAZO	*n* pl. **SLEAZOS** a sleazoid
SLEAZOID	*n* pl. **-S** a person of low morals or character

SLEAZY   *adj* **SLEAZIER, SLEAZIEST** of low quality or character **SLEAZILY** *adv*

SLED   *v* **SLEDDED, SLEDDING, SLEDS** to convey on a sled (a vehicle for carrying people or loads over snow or ice)

SLEDDER   *n* pl. **-S** one that sleds

SLEDDING   *n* pl. **-S** the act of one that sleds

SLEDGE   *v* **SLEDGED, SLEDGING, SLEDGES** to convey on a type of sled

SLEEK   *adj* **SLEEKER, SLEEKEST** smooth and glossy

SLEEK   *v* **-ED, -ING, -S** to make sleek

SLEEKEN   *v* **-ED, -ING, -S** to sleek

SLEEKER   *n* pl. **-S** one that sleeks

SLEEKIT   *adj* sleek

SLEEKLY   *adv* in a sleek manner

SLEEKY   *adj* **SLEEKIER, SLEEKIEST** sleek

SLEEP   *v* **SLEPT, SLEEPING, SLEEPS** to be in a natural, periodic state of rest

SLEEPER   *n* pl. **-S** one that sleeps

SLEEPING   *n* pl. **-S** the act of one that sleeps

SLEEPY   *adj* **SLEEPIER, SLEEPIEST** ready or inclined to sleep **SLEEPILY** *adv*

SLEET   *v* **-ED, -ING, -S** to shower sleet (frozen rain)

SLEETY   *adj* **SLEETIER, SLEETIEST** resembling sleet

SLEEVE   *v* **SLEEVED, SLEEVING, SLEEVES** to furnish with a sleeve (the part of a garment covering the arm)

SLEEVEEN   *n* pl. **-S** a mischievous person

SLEEVING   *n* pl. **-S** tubular insulation for electric cables

SLEIGH   *v* **-ED, -ING, -S** to ride in a sled

SLEIGHER   *n* pl. **-S** one that sleighs

SLEIGHT   *n* pl. **-S** deftness

SLENDER   *adj* **-DERER, -DEREST** thin

SLEPT   past tense of sleep

SLEUTH   *v* **-ED, -ING, -S** to act as a detective

SLEW   *v* **-ED, -ING, -S** to slue

SLICE   *v* **SLICED, SLICING, SLICES** to cut into thin, flat pieces

SLICER   *n* pl. **-S** one that slices

SLICK   *adj* **SLICKER, SLICKEST** smooth and slippery

SLICK   *v* **-ED, -ING, -S** to make slick

SLICKEN   *v* **-ED, -ING, -S** to make slick

SLICKER   *n* pl. **-S** an oilskin raincoat

SLICKLY   *adv* in a slick manner

SLIDE   *v* **SLID, SLIDDEN, SLIDING, SLIDES** to move smoothly along a surface **SLIDABLE** *adj*

SLIDER   *n* pl. **-S** one that slides

SLIDEWAY   *n* pl. **-WAYS** a route along which something slides

SLIER   a comparative of sly

SLIEST   a superlative of sly

SLIEVE   *n* pl. **-S** a mountain

SLIGHT   *adj* **SLIGHTER, SLIGHTEST** small in size or amount **SLIGHTLY** *adv*

SLIGHT   *v* **-ED, -ING, -S** to treat with disregard

SLIGHTER   *n* pl. **-S** one that slights

SLILY   *adv* in a sly manner

SLIM   *adj* **SLIMMER, SLIMMEST** slender

SLIM   *v* **SLIMMED, SLIMMING, SLIMS** to make slim

SLIME   *v* **SLIMED, SLIMING, SLIMES** to cover with slime (viscous mud)

SLIMIER   comparative of slimy

SLIMIEST   superlative of slimy

SLIMILY   *adv* in a slimy manner

SLIMING   present participle of slime

SLIMLINE   *adj* slender in design or build

SLIMLY   *adv* in a slim manner

SLIMMED   past tense of slim

SLIMMER   *n* pl. **-S** a dieter

SLIMMEST   superlative of slim

SLIMMING   *n* pl. **-S** the reducing of one's weight

SLIMNESS   *n* pl. **-ES** the state of being slim

SLIMPSY   *adj* **-SIER, -SIEST** slimsy

SLIMSY   *adj* **-SIER, -SIEST** flimsy

SLIMY   *adj* **SLIMIER, SLIMIEST** resembling slime

SLING   *v* **SLUNG, SLINGING, SLINGS** to throw with a sudden motion

SLINGER   *n* pl. **-S** one that slings

SLINK   *v* **SLUNK** or **SLANK** or **SLINKED, SLINKING, SLINKS** to move stealthily

SLINKY   *adj* **SLINKIER, SLINKIEST** stealthy **SLINKILY** *adv*

SLIP | *v* **SLIPPED** or **SLIPT, SLIPPING, SLIPS** to slide suddenly and accidentally
SLIPCASE | *n* pl. **-S** a protective box for a book
SLIPE | *v* **SLIPED, SLIPING, SLIPES** to peel
SLIPFORM | *v* **-ED, -ING, -S** to construct with the use of a mold in which concrete is placed to set
SLIPKNOT | *n* pl. **-S** a type of knot
SLIPLESS | *adj* free from errors
SLIPOUT | *n* pl. **-S** an insert in a newspaper
SLIPOVER | *n* pl. **-S** a pullover
SLIPPAGE | *n* pl. **-S** a falling off from a standard or level
SLIPPED | a past tense of slip
SLIPPER | *n* pl. **-S** a light, low shoe
SLIPPERY | *adj* **-PERIER, -PERIEST** causing or tending to cause slipping
SLIPPING | present participle of slip
SLIPPY | *adj* **-PIER, -PIEST** slippery **SLIPPILY** *adv*
SLIPSHOD | *adj* carelessly done or made
SLIPSLOP | *n* pl. **-S** watery food
SLIPSOLE | *n* pl. **-S** a thin insole
SLIPT | a past tense of slip
SLIPUP | *n* pl. **-S** a mistake
SLIPWARE | *n* pl. **-S** a type of pottery
SLIPWAY | *n* pl. **-WAYS** an area sloping toward the water in a shipyard
SLIT | *v* **SLITTED, SLITTING, SLITS** to make a slit (a long, narrow cut) in
SLITHER | *v* **-ED, -ING, -S** to slide from side to side
SLITHERY | *adj* slippery
SLITLESS | *adj* having no slits
SLITLIKE | *adj* resembling a slit
SLITTED | past tense of slit
SLITTER | *n* pl. **-S** one that slits
SLITTING | present participle of slit
SLITTY | *adj* **-TIER, -TIEST** being long and narrow
SLIVER | *v* **-ED, -ING, -S** to cut into long, thin pieces
SLIVERER | *n* pl. **-S** one that slivers
SLIVOVIC | *n* pl. **-ES** a plum brandy
SLOB | *n* pl. **-S** a slovenly or boorish person
SLOBBER | *v* **-ED, -ING, -S** to drool

SLOBBERY | *adj* slobbering
SLOBBISH | *adj* resembling a slob
SLOBBY | *adj* **SLOBBIER, SLOBBIEST** characteristic of a slob
SLOE | *n* pl. **-S** a plumlike fruit
SLOG | *v* **SLOGGED, SLOGGING, SLOGS** to plod
SLOGAN | *n* pl. **-S** a motto adopted by a group **SLOGANED** *adj*
SLOGGER | *n* pl. **-S** one that slogs
SLOID | *n* pl. **-S** sloyd
SLOJD | *n* pl. **-S** sloyd
SLOMO | *n* pl. **-MOS** slow motion
SLOOP | *n* pl. **-S** a type of sailing vessel
SLOP | *v* **SLOPPED, SLOPPING, SLOPS** to spill or splash
SLOPE | *v* **SLOPED, SLOPING, SLOPES** to slant
SLOPER | *n* pl. **-S** one that slopes
SLOPPY | *adj* **-PIER, -PIEST** messy **SLOPPILY** *adv*
SLOPWORK | *n* pl. **-S** the manufacture of cheap clothing
SLOSH | *v* **-ED, -ING, -ES** to move with a splashing motion
SLOSHY | *adj* **SLOSHIER, SLOSHIEST** slushy
SLOT | *v* **SLOTTED, SLOTTING, SLOTS** to cut a long, narrow opening in
SLOTBACK | *n* pl. **-S** a type of football player
SLOTH | *n* pl. **-S** a slow-moving arboreal mammal
SLOTHFUL | *adj* sluggish
SLOTTED | past tense of slot
SLOTTER | *n* pl. **-S** a machine for slotting
SLOTTING | present participle of slot
SLOUCH | *v* **-ED, -ING, -ES** to sit, stand, or move with a drooping posture
SLOUCHER | *n* pl. **-S** one that slouches
SLOUCHY | *adj* **SLOUCHIER, SLOUCHIEST** slouching
SLOUGH | *v* **-ED, -ING, -S** to cast off
SLOUGHY | *adj* **SLOUGHIER, SLOUGHIEST** miry
SLOVEN | *n* pl. **-S** a slovenly person
SLOVENLY | *adj* **-LIER, -LIEST** habitually untidy or unclean
SLOW | *adj* **SLOWER, SLOWEST** moving with little speed

SLOW *v* **-ED, -ING, -S** to lessen the speed of

SLOWDOWN *n* pl. **-S** a lessening of pace

SLOWISH *adj* somewhat slow

SLOWLY *adv* in a slow manner

SLOWNESS *n* pl. **-ES** the state of being slow

SLOWPOKE *n* pl. **-S** a slow individual

SLOWWORM *n* pl. **-S** a European lizard having no legs

SLOYD *n* pl. **-S** a Swedish system of manual training

SLUB *v* **SLUBBED, SLUBBING, SLUBS** to draw out and twist slightly

SLUBBER *v* **-ED, -ING, -S** to stain or dirty

SLUBBING *n* pl. **-S** a slightly twisted roll of textile fibers

SLUDGE *v* **SLUDGED, SLUDGING, SLUDGES** to form sludge (a muddy mass or sediment)

SLUDGY *adj* **SLUDGIER, SLUDGIEST** covered with sludge

SLUE *v* **SLUED, SLUING, SLUES** to cause to move sideways

SLUFF *v* **-ED, -ING, -S** to discard a card or cards

SLUG *v* **SLUGGED, SLUGGING, SLUGS** to strike heavily

SLUGABED *n* pl. **-S** one inclined to stay in bed out of laziness

SLUGFEST *n* pl. **-S** a vigorous fight

SLUGGARD *n* pl. **-S** a habitually lazy person

SLUGGED past tense of slug

SLUGGER *n* pl. **-S** one that slugs

SLUGGING present participle of slug

SLUGGISH *adj* displaying little movement or activity

SLUICE *v* **SLUICED, SLUICING, SLUICES** to wash with a sudden flow of water

SLUICY *adj* falling in streams

SLUING present participle of slue

SLUM *v* **SLUMMED, SLUMMING, SLUMS** to visit slums (squalid urban areas)

SLUMBER *v* **-ED, -ING, -S** to sleep

SLUMBERY *adj* sleepy

SLUMGUM *n* pl. **-S** the residue remaining after honey is extracted from a honeycomb

SLUMISM *n* pl. **-S** the prevalence of slums

SLUMLORD *n* pl. **-S** a landlord of slum property

SLUMMED past tense of slum

SLUMMER *n* pl. **-S** one that slums

SLUMMING present participle of slum

SLUMMY *adj* **-MIER, -MIEST** resembling a slum

SLUMP *v* **-ED, -ING, -S** to fall or sink suddenly

SLUMPY *adj* **SLUMPIER, SLUMPIEST** characterized by a fall in value or amount

SLUNG past tense of sling

SLUNK a past tense of slink

SLUR *v* **SLURRED, SLURRING, SLURS** to pass over lightly or carelessly

SLURB *n* pl. **-S** a poorly planned suburban area **SLURBAN** *adj*

SLURP *v* **-ED, -ING, -S** to eat or drink noisily

SLURPY *adj* **SLURPIER, SLURPIEST** characterized by the sucking sound made when slurping

SLURRY *v* **-RIED, -RYING, -RIES** to convert into a type of watery mixture

SLURVE *n* pl. **-S** a type of pitch in baseball

SLUSH *v* **-ED, -ING, -ES** to splash with slush (partly melted snow)

SLUSHY *n* pl. **SLUSHIES** a confection consisting of flavored slushy ice

SLUSHY *adj* **SLUSHIER, SLUSHIEST** resembling slush **SLUSHILY** *adv*

SLUT *n* pl. **-S** a slovenly woman **SLUTTISH** *adj*

SLUTTY *adj* **SLUTTIER, SLUTTIEST** characteristic of a slut

SLY *adj* **SLIER, SLIEST** or **SLYER, SLYEST** crafty **SLYLY** *adv*

SLYBOOTS *n* pl. **SLYBOOTS** a sly person

SLYNESS *n* pl. **-ES** the quality or state of being sly

SLYPE *n* pl. **-S** a narrow passage in an English cathedral

SMACK *v* **-ED, -ING, -S** to strike sharply

SMACKER *n* pl. **-S** one that smacks

SMALL *adj* **SMALLER, SMALLEST** of limited size or quantity

SMALL *n* pl. **-S** a small part

SMALLAGE *n* pl. **-S** a wild celery

SMALLISH *adj* somewhat small

SMALLPOX *n* pl. **-ES** a virus disease

SMALT *n* pl. **-S** a blue pigment

SMALTI a pl. of smalto

SMALTINE *n* pl. **-S** smaltite

SMALTITE *n* pl. **-S** a mineral

SMALTO *n* pl. **-TOS** or **-TI** colored glass used in mosaics

SMARAGD *n* pl. **-S** an emerald

SMARAGDE *n* pl. **-S** smaragd

SMARM *v* **-ED, -ING, -S** to use excessive flattery to obtain favors

SMARMY *adj* **SMARMIER, SMARMIEST** marked by excessive flattery **SMARMILY** *adv*

SMART *adj* **SMARTER, SMARTEST** characterized by mental acuity **SMARTISH** *adj*

SMART *v* **-ED, -ING, -S** to cause a sharp, stinging pain

SMARTASS *n* pl. **-ES** a smarty

SMARTEN *v* **-ED, -ING, -S** to improve in appearance

SMARTIE *n* pl. **-S** smarty

SMARTLY *adv* in a smart manner

SMARTY *n* pl. **SMARTIES** an obnoxiously conceited person

SMASH *v* **-ED, -ING, -ES** to shatter violently

SMASHER *n* pl. **-S** one that smashes

SMASHUP *n* pl. **-S** a collision of motor vehicles

SMATTER *v* **-ED, -ING, -S** to speak with little knowledge

SMAZE *n* pl. **-S** an atmospheric mixture of smoke and haze

SMEAR *v* **-ED, -ING, -S** to spread with a sticky, greasy, or dirty substance

SMEARER *n* pl. **-S** one that smears

SMEARY *adj* **SMEARIER, SMEARIEST** smeared

SMECTIC *adj* pertaining to a phase of a liquid crystal

SMECTITE *n* pl. **-S** a clayey mineral

SMEDDUM *n* pl. **-S** ground malt powder

SMEEK *v* **-ED, -ING, -S** to smoke

SMEGMA *n* pl. **-S** sebum

SMELL *v* **SMELLED** or **SMELT, SMELLING, SMELLS** to perceive by means of the olfactory nerves

SMELLER *n* pl. **-S** one that smells

SMELLY *adj* **SMELLIER, SMELLIEST** having an unpleasant odor

SMELT *v* **-ED, -ING, -S** to melt or fuse, as ores

SMELTER *n* pl. **-S** one that smelts

SMELTERY *n* pl. **-ERIES** a place for smelting

SMELTING *n* pl. **-S** the process of melting ores to obtain metal

SMERK *v* **-ED, -ING, -S** to smirk

SMEW *n* pl. **-S** a Eurasian duck

SMIDGE *n* pl. **-S** a smidgen

SMIDGEN *n* pl. **-S** a very small amount

SMIDGEON *n* pl. **-S** smidgen

SMIDGIN *n* pl. **-S** smidgen

SMILAX *n* pl. **-ES** a twining plant

SMILE *v* **SMILED, SMILING, SMILES** to upturn the corners of the mouth in pleasure

SMILER *n* pl. **-S** one that smiles

SMILEY *n* pl. **SMILEYS** or **SMILIES** a representation of a smiling face

SMILEY *adj* **SMILIER, SMILIEST** displaying a smile

SMIRCH *v* **-ED, -ING, -ES** to soil

SMIRK *v* **-ED, -ING, -S** to smile in an affected or smug manner

SMIRKER *n* pl. **-S** one that smirks

SMIRKY *adj* **SMIRKIER, SMIRKIEST** smirking **SMIRKILY** *adv*

SMITE *v* **SMOTE, SMIT** or **SMITTEN, SMITING, SMITES** to strike heavily

SMITER *n* pl. **-S** one that smites

SMITH *n* pl. **-S** a worker in metals

SMITHERS *n/pl* small fragments

SMITHERY *n* pl. **-ERIES** the trade of a smith

SMITHING *n* pl. **-S** the work of a smith

SMITHY *n* pl. **SMITHIES** the workshop of a smith

SMITING present participle of smite

SMITTEN a past participle of smite

SMOCK *v* **-ED, -ING, -S** to furnish with a smock (a loose outer garment)

SMOCKING *n* pl. **-S** a type of embroidery

SMOG *n* pl. **-S** an atmospheric mixture of smoke and fog **SMOGLESS** *adj*

SMOGGY *adj* **-GIER, -GIEST** filled with smog

SMOKE *v* **SMOKED, SMOKING, SMOKES** to emit smoke (the gaseous product of burning materials) **SMOKABLE** *adj*

SMOKEBOX *n pl.* **-ES** a chamber for producing and containing smoke

SMOKEPOT *n pl.* **-S** a container for giving off smoke

SMOKER *n pl.* **-S** one that smokes

SMOKEY *adj* **SMOKIER, SMOKIEST** smoky

SMOKEY *n pl.* **SMOKEYS** or **SMOKIES** a police officer who patrols highways

SMOKIE *n pl.* **-S** a sausage or hot dog

SMOKING *n pl.* **-S** the inhaling and exhaling of the smoke of tobacco or a drug

SMOKY *adj* **SMOKIER, SMOKIEST** filled with smoke **SMOKILY** *adv*

SMOLDER *v* **-ED, -ING, -S** to burn with no flame

SMOLT *n pl.* **-S** a young salmon

SMOOCH *v* **-ED, -ING, -ES** to kiss

SMOOCHER *n pl.* **-S** one that smooches

SMOOCHY *adj* **SMOOCHIER, SMOOCHIEST** suitable for smooching

SMOOSH *v* **-ED, -ING, -ES** to squash

SMOOTH *adj* **SMOOTHER, SMOOTHEST** having a surface that is free from irregularities

SMOOTH *v* **-ED, -ING, -S** or **-ES** to make smooth

SMOOTHE *v* **SMOOTHED, SMOOTHING, SMOOTHES** to smooth

SMOOTHEN *v* **-ED, -ING, -S** to smooth

SMOOTHER *n pl.* **-S** one that smooths

SMOOTHIE *n pl.* **-S** a person with polished manners

SMOOTHLY *adv* in a smooth manner

SMOOTHY *n pl.* **SMOOTHIES** smoothie

SMORG *n pl.* **-S** a smorgasbord

SMOTE past tense of smite

SMOTHER *v* **-ED, -ING, -S** to prevent from breathing

SMOTHERY *adj* tending to smother

SMOULDER *v* **-ED, -ING, -S** to smolder

SMRITI *n pl.* **-S** a text of Hindu religious teachings

SMUDGE *v* **SMUDGED, SMUDGING, SMUDGES** to smear or dirty

SMUDGING *n pl.* **-S** the act of smearing

SMUDGY *adj* **SMUDGIER, SMUDGIEST** smudged **SMUDGILY** *adv*

SMUG *adj* **SMUGGER, SMUGGEST** highly self-satisfied

SMUGGLE *v* **-GLED, -GLING, -GLES** to import or export illicitly

SMUGGLER *n pl.* **-S** one that smuggles

SMUGLY *adv* in a smug manner

SMUGNESS *n pl.* **-ES** the quality or state of being smug

SMUSH *v* **-ED, -ING, -ES** to smoosh

SMUT *v* **SMUTTED, SMUTTING, SMUTS** to soil

SMUTCH *v* **-ED, -ING, -ES** to smudge

SMUTCHY *adj* **SMUTCHIER, SMUTCHIEST** smudgy

SMUTTY *adj* **-TIER, -TIEST** obscene **SMUTTILY** *adv*

SNACK *v* **-ED, -ING, -S** to eat a light meal

SNACKER *n pl.* **-S** one that snacks

SNACKY *adj* **SNACKIER, SNACKIEST** suitable as a light meal

SNAFFLE *v* **-FLED, -FLING, -FLES** to obtain by devious means

SNAFU *v* **-ED, -ING, -S** to bring into a state of confusion

SNAG *v* **SNAGGED, SNAGGING, SNAGS** to catch on a snag (a jagged protuberance)

SNAGGER *n pl.* **-S** a person who uses illegal fishing methods

SNAGGLE *n pl.* **-S** a tangled or knotted mass

SNAGGY *adj* **-GIER, -GIEST** full of snags

SNAGLIKE *adj* resembling a snag

SNAIL *v* **-ED, -ING, -S** to move slowly

SNAKE *v* **SNAKED, SNAKING, SNAKES** to move like a snake (a limbless reptile)

SNAKEBIT *adj* unlucky

SNAKEPIT *n pl.* **-S** a psychiatric hospital

SNAKEY *adj* **SNAKIER, SNAKIEST** snaky

SNAKING present participle of snake

SNAKISH *adj* resembling a snake

SNAKY *adj* **SNAKIER, SNAKIEST** resembling a snake **SNAKILY** *adv*

SNAP *v* **SNAPPED, SNAPPING, SNAPS** to make a sharp cracking sound

SNAPBACK *n pl.* **-S** a sudden rebound or recovery

SNAPLESS *adj* lacking a snap (a type of fastening device)

SNAPPER *n pl.* **-S** one that snaps

SNAPPIER comparative of snappy

SNAPPIEST superlative of snappy

SNAPPILY	*adv* in a snappy manner
SNAPPING	present participle of snap
SNAPPISH	*adj* tending to speak in an impatient or irritable manner
SNAPPY	*adj* **-PIER, -PIEST** snappish
SNAPSHOT	*v* **-SHOTTED, -SHOTTING, -SHOTS** to photograph informally and quickly
SNAPWEED	*n* pl. **-S** a flowering plant
SNARE	*v* **SNARED, SNARING, SNARES** to trap
SNARER	*n* pl. **-S** one that snares
SNARF	*v* **-ED, -ING, -S** to eat or drink greedily
SNARFLE	*v* **-FLED, -FLING, -FLES** to snarf
SNARING	present participle of snare
SNARK	*n* pl. **-S** an imaginary animal
SNARKY	*adj* **SNARKIER, SNARKIEST** snappish **SNARKILY** *adv*
SNARL	*v* **-ED, -ING, -S** to growl viciously
SNARLER	*n* pl. **-S** one that snarls
SNARLY	*adj* **SNARLIER, SNARLIEST** tangled
SNASH	*n* pl. **-ES** abusive language
SNATCH	*v* **-ED, -ING, -ES** to seize suddenly
SNATCHER	*n* pl. **-S** one that snatches
SNATCHY	*adj* **SNATCHIER, SNATCHIEST** occurring irregularly
SNATH	*n* pl. **-S** the handle of a scythe
SNATHE	*n* pl. **-S** snath
SNAW	*v* **-ED, -ING, -S** to snow
SNAZZY	*adj* **-ZIER, -ZIEST** very stylish **SNAZZILY** *adv*
SNEAK	*v* **SNEAKED** or **SNUCK, SNEAKING, SNEAKS** to move stealthily
SNEAKBOX	*n* pl. **-ES** a small boat masked with brush and weeds that is used for wildfowl hunting
SNEAKER	*n* pl. **-S** one that sneaks
SNEAKY	*adj* **SNEAKIER, SNEAKIEST** deceitful **SNEAKILY** *adv*
SNEAP	*v* **-ED, -ING, -S** to chide
SNECK	*n* pl. **-S** a latch
SNED	*v* **SNEDDED, SNEDDING, SNEDS** to prune
SNEER	*v* **-ED, -ING, -S** to curl the lip in contempt
SNEERER	*n* pl. **-S** one that sneers
SNEERFUL	*adj* given to sneering
SNEERY	*adj* **SNEERIER, SNEERIEST** marked by sneering
SNEESH	*n* pl. **-ES** snuff
SNEEZE	*v* **SNEEZED, SNEEZING, SNEEZES** to make a sudden, involuntary expiration of breath
SNEEZER	*n* pl. **-S** one that sneezes
SNEEZY	*adj* **SNEEZIER, SNEEZIEST** tending to sneeze
SNELL	*adj* **SNELLER, SNELLEST** keen
SNELL	*v* **-ED, -ING, -S** to attach a short line to a fishhook
SNIB	*v* **SNIBBED, SNIBBING, SNIBS** to latch
SNICK	*v* **-ED, -ING, -S** to nick
SNICKER	*v* **-ED, -ING, -S** to utter a partly stifled laugh
SNICKERY	*adj* tending to snicker
SNIDE	*adj* **SNIDER, SNIDEST** maliciously derogatory **SNIDELY** *adv*
SNIFF	*v* **-ED, -ING, -S** to inhale audibly through the nose
SNIFFER	*n* pl. **-S** one that sniffs
SNIFFIER	comparative of sniffy
SNIFFIEST	superlative of sniffy
SNIFFILY	*adv* in a sniffy manner
SNIFFISH	*adj* haughty
SNIFFLE	*v* **-FLED, -FLING, -FLES** to sniff repeatedly
SNIFFLER	*n* pl. **-S** one that sniffles
SNIFFLY	*adj* **-FLIER, -FLIEST** that sniffles
SNIFFY	*adj* **-FIER, -FIEST** sniffish
SNIFTER	*n* pl. **-S** a pear-shaped liquor glass
SNIGGER	*v* **-ED, -ING, -S** to snicker
SNIGGLE	*v* **-GLED, -GLING, -GLES** to fish for eels
SNIGGLER	*n* pl. **-S** one that sniggles
SNIGLET	*n* pl. **-S** a word coined for something not having a name
SNIP	*v* **SNIPPED, SNIPPING, SNIPS** to cut with a short, quick stroke
SNIPE	*v* **SNIPED, SNIPING, SNIPES** to shoot at individuals from a concealed place
SNIPER	*n* pl. **-S** one that snipes
SNIPING	*n* pl. **-S** the act of one that snipes
SNIPPED	past tense of snip
SNIPPER	*n* pl. **-S** one that snips

SNIPPET *n* pl. **-S** a small piece snipped off

SNIPPETY *adj* **-PETIER, -PETIEST** snippy

SNIPPING *n* pl. **-S** a piece of something that has been snipped off

SNIPPY *adj* **-PIER, -PIEST** snappish **SNIPPILY** *adv*

SNIT *n* pl. **-S** a state of agitation

SNITCH *v* **-ED, -ING, -ES** to tattle

SNITCHER *n* pl. **-S** one that snitches

SNITTY *adj* **-TIER, -TIEST** disagreeably ill-tempered

SNIVEL *v* **-ELED, -ELING, -ELS** or **-ELLED, -ELLING, -ELS** to cry or whine with sniffling

SNIVELER *n* pl. **-S** one that snivels

SNIVELLY *adj* tending to whine with sniffling

SNOB *n* pl. **-S** one who tends to avoid or rebuff those regarded as inferior

SNOBBERY *n* pl. **-BERIES** snobbish behavior

SNOBBIER comparative of snobby

SNOBBIEST superlative of snobby

SNOBBILY *adv* in a snobby manner

SNOBBISH *adj* characteristic of a snob

SNOBBISM *n* pl. **-S** snobbery

SNOBBY *adj* **-BIER, -BIEST** snobbish

SNOCOACH *n* pl. **-ES** a bus-like vehicle with large tires or tracks for traveling on snow

SNOG *v* **SNOGGED, SNOGGING, SNOGS** to kiss

SNOGGER *n* pl. **-S** one that snogs

SNOOD *v* **-ED, -ING, -S** to secure with a snood (a net or fabric cap for the hair)

SNOOK *v* **-ED, -ING, -S** to sniff

SNOOKER *v* **-ED, -ING, -S** to trick

SNOOL *v* **-ED, -ING, -S** to yield meekly

SNOOP *v* **-ED, -ING, -S** to pry about

SNOOPER *n* pl. **-S** one who snoops

SNOOPY *adj* **SNOOPIER, SNOOPIEST** given to snooping **SNOOPILY** *adv*

SNOOSE *n* pl. **-S** chewing tobacco

SNOOT *v* **-ED, -ING, -S** to treat with disdain

SNOOTFUL *n* pl. **-S** enough alcoholic liquor to make one drunk

SNOOTY *adj* **SNOOTIER, SNOOTIEST** snobbish **SNOOTILY** *adv*

SNOOZE *v* **SNOOZED, SNOOZING, SNOOZES** to sleep lightly

SNOOZER *n* pl. **-S** one that snoozes

SNOOZLE *v* **-ZLED, -ZLING, -ZLES** to nuzzle

SNOOZY *adj* **SNOOZIER, SNOOZIEST** drowsy

SNORE *v* **SNORED, SNORING, SNORES** to breathe loudly while sleeping

SNORER *n* pl. **-S** one that snores

SNORING *n* pl. **-S** the act of breathing loudly while sleeping

SNORKEL *v* **-ED, -ING, -S** to swim underwater with a type of breathing device

SNORT *v* **-ED, -ING, -S** to exhale noisily through the nostrils

SNORTER *n* pl. **-S** one that snorts

SNOT *n* pl. **-S** nasal mucus

SNOTTY *adj* **-TIER, -TIEST** arrogant **SNOTTILY** *adv*

SNOUT *v* **-ED, -ING, -S** to provide with a nozzle

SNOUTISH *adj* snouty

SNOUTY *adj* **SNOUTIER, SNOUTIEST** resembling a long, projecting nose

SNOW *v* **-ED, -ING, -S** to fall as snow (precipitation in the form of ice crystals)

SNOWBALL *v* **-ED, -ING, -S** to increase at a rapidly accelerating rate

SNOWBANK *n* pl. **-S** a mound of snow

SNOWBELL *n* pl. **-S** a flowering shrub

SNOWBELT *n* pl. **-S** a region that receives an appreciable amount of snow each year

SNOWBIRD *n* pl. **-S** a small bird

SNOWBUSH *n* pl. **-ES** a flowering shrub

SNOWCAP *n* pl. **-S** a covering of snow

SNOWCAT *n* pl. **-S** a tracklaying vehicle for travel on snow

SNOWDROP *n* pl. **-S** a European herb

SNOWFALL *n* pl. **-S** a fall of snow

SNOWFLEA *n* pl. **-S** a wingless insect appearing on snow in the spring

SNOWIER comparative of snowy

SNOWIEST superlative of snowy

SNOWILY *adv* in a snowy manner

SNOWLAND *n* pl. **-S** an area marked by a great amount of snow

SNOWLESS *adj* having no snow

SNOWLIKE *adj* resembling snow

SNOWMAN *n* pl. **-MEN** a figure of a person that is made of snow

SNOWMELT *n* pl. **-S** water produced by the melting of snow

SNOWMOLD *n* pl. **-S** a fungus disease of grasses near the edge of melting snow

SNOWPACK *n* pl. **-S** an accumulation of packed snow

SNOWPLOW *v* **-ED, -ING, -S** to execute a type of skiing maneuver

SNOWSHED *n* pl. **-S** a structure built to provide protection against snow

SNOWSHOE *v* **-SHOED, -SHOEING, -SHOES** to walk on snowshoes (oval frames that allow a person to walk on deep snow)

SNOWSUIT *n* pl. **-S** a child's garment for winter wear

SNOWY *adj* **SNOWIER, SNOWIEST** abounding in snow

SNUB *v* **SNUBBED, SNUBBING, SNUBS** to treat with contempt or neglect

SNUBBER *n* pl. **-S** one that snubs

SNUBBY *adj* **-BIER, -BIEST** blunt

SNUBNESS *n* pl. **-ES** bluntness

SNUCK a past tense of sneak

SNUFF *v* **-ED, -ING, -S** to use or inhale snuff (powdered tobacco)

SNUFFBOX *n* pl. **-ES** a box for holding snuff

SNUFFER *n* pl. **-S** one that snuffs

SNUFFIER comparative of snuffy

SNUFFIEST superlative of snuffy

SNUFFILY *adv* in a snuffy manner

SNUFFLE *v* **-FLED, -FLING, -FLES** to sniffle

SNUFFLER *n* pl. **-S** one that snuffles

SNUFFLY *adj* **-FLIER, -FLIEST** tending to snuffle

SNUFFY *adj* **SNUFFIER, SNUFFIEST** dingy

SNUG *adj* **SNUGGER, SNUGGEST** warmly comfortable

SNUG *v* **SNUGGED, SNUGGING, SNUGS** to make snug

SNUGGERY *n* pl. **-GERIES** a snug place

SNUGGEST superlative of snug

SNUGGIES *n/pl* women's long underwear

SNUGGING present participle of snug

SNUGGLE *v* **-GLED, -GLING, -GLES** to lie or press closely

SNUGGLY *adj* **SNUGGLIER, SNUGGLIEST** warm and cozy

SNUGLY *adv* in a snug manner

SNUGNESS *n* pl. **-ES** the quality or state of being snug

SNYE *n* pl. **-S** a side channel in a river or creek

SO *n* pl. **SOS** sol

SOAK *v* **-ED, -ING, -S** to wet something thoroughly

SOAKAGE *n* pl. **-S** the act of soaking

SOAKER *n* pl. **-S** one that soaks

SOAKING *n* pl. **-S** the act of wetting something thoroughly

SOAP *v* **-ED, -ING, -S** to treat with soap (a cleansing agent)

SOAPBARK *n* pl. **-S** a tropical tree

SOAPBOX *v* **-ED, -ING, -ES** to deliver an informal impassioned speech on the street

SOAPER *n* pl. **-S** a serial melodrama on radio or television

SOAPFISH *n* pl. **-ES** a tropical fish that produces toxic mucus

SOAPIER comparative of soapy

SOAPIEST superlative of soapy

SOAPILY *adv* in a soapy manner

SOAPLESS *adj* having no soap

SOAPLIKE *adj* resembling soap

SOAPSUDS *n/pl* suds (soapy water)

SOAPWORT *n* pl. **-S** a perennial herb

SOAPY *adj* **SOAPIER, SOAPIEST** containing or resembling soap

SOAR *v* **-ED, -ING, -S** to fly at a great height

SOARER *n* pl. **-S** one that soars

SOARING *n* pl. **-S** the sport of flying in a heavier-than-air craft without power

SOAVE *n* pl. **-S** an Italian wine

SOB *v* **SOBBED, SOBBING, SOBS** to cry with a convulsive catching of the breath

SOBA *n* pl. **-S** a Japanese noodle made from buckwheat flour

SOBBER *n* pl. **-S** one that sobs

SOBEIT *conj* provided that

SOBER *adj* **SOBERER, SOBEREST** having control of one's faculties

SOBER *v* **-ED, -ING, -S** to make sober

SOBERIZE *v* **-IZED, -IZING, -IZES** to sober

SOBERLY *adv* in a sober manner

SOBFUL *adj* given to sobbing

SOBRIETY *n pl.* **-ETIES** the quality or state of being sober

SOC *n pl.* **-ES** a sociology course

SOCA *n pl.* **-S** a blend of soul and calypso music

SOCAGE *n pl.* **-S** a form of feudal land tenure

SOCAGER *n pl.* **-S** a tenant by socage

SOCCAGE *n pl.* **-S** socage

SOCCER *n pl.* **-S** a type of ball game

SOCIABLE *n pl.* **-S** a social

SOCIABLY *adv* in a friendly manner

SOCIAL *n pl.* **-S** a friendly gathering

SOCIALLY *adv* with respect to society

SOCIETY *n pl.* **-ETIES** an organized group of persons **SOCIETAL** *adj*

SOCK *n pl.* **SOCKS** or **SOX** a knitted or woven covering for the foot

SOCK *v* **-ED, -ING, -S** to strike forcefully

SOCKET *v* **-ED, -ING, -S** to furnish with a socket (an opening for receiving something)

SOCKETTE *n pl.* **-S** a very short sock

SOCKEYE *n pl.* **-S** a food fish

SOCKLESS *adj* having no socks

SOCKMAN *n pl.* **-MEN** socman

SOCKO *adj* strikingly impressive

SOCLE *n pl.* **-S** a block used as a base for a column or pedestal

SOCMAN *n pl.* **-MEN** a socager

SOD *v* **SODDED, SODDING, SODS** to cover with sod (turf)

SODA *n pl.* **-S** a type of chemical compound **SODALESS** *adj*

SODALIST *n pl.* **-S** a member of a sodality

SODALITE *n pl.* **-S** a mineral

SODALITY *n pl.* **-TIES** a society

SODAMIDE *n pl.* **-S** a chemical compound

SODDED past tense of sod

SODDEN *v* **-ED, -ING, -S** to make soggy

SODDENLY *adv* in a soggy manner

SODDIE *n pl.* **-S** a soddy

SODDING present participle of sod

SODDY *n pl.* **-DIES** a house built of sod

SODIUM *n pl.* **-S** a metallic element **SODIC** *adj*

SODOM *n pl.* **-S** a place notorious for vice and corruption

SODOMISE *v* **-ISED, -ISING, -ISES** to sodomize

SODOMIST *n pl.* **-S** a sodomite

SODOMITE *n pl.* **-S** one who practices sodomy

SODOMIZE *v* **-IZED, -IZING, -IZES** to engage in sodomy with

SODOMY *n pl.* **-OMIES** unnatural copulation

SOEVER *adv* at all

SOFA *n pl.* **-S** a long, upholstered seat

SOFABED *n pl.* **-S** a sofa that can be made into a bed

SOFAR *n pl.* **-S** a system for locating underwater explosions

SOFFIT *n pl.* **-S** the underside of an architectural structure

SOFT *adj* **SOFTER, SOFTEST** yielding readily to pressure

SOFT *n pl.* **-S** a soft object or part

SOFTA *n pl.* **-S** a Muslim theological student

SOFTBACK *n pl.* **-S** a book bound in a flexible paper cover

SOFTBALL *n pl.* **-S** a type of ball

SOFTCORE *adj* less than explicit in depicting sex acts

SOFTEN *v* **-ED, -ING, -S** to make soft

SOFTENER *n pl.* **-S** one that softens

SOFTHEAD *n pl.* **-S** a foolish person

SOFTIE *n pl.* **-S** softy

SOFTIES pl. of softy

SOFTISH *adj* somewhat soft

SOFTLY *adv* in a soft manner

SOFTNESS *n pl.* **-ES** the quality or state of being soft

SOFTWARE *n pl.* **-S** written or printed data used in computer operations

SOFTWOOD *n pl.* **-S** the soft wood of various trees

SOFTY *n pl.* **SOFTIES** a sentimental person

SOGGED *adj* soggy

SOGGY *adj* **-GIER, -GIEST** heavy with moisture **SOGGILY** *adv*

SOH *n pl.* **-S** sol

SOIGNE *adj* carefully done

SOIGNEE *adj* soigne

SOIL *v* **-ED, -ING, -S** to make dirty

SOILAGE *n pl.* **-S** green crops for feeding animals

SOILLESS *adj* carried on without soil (finely divided rock mixed with organic matter)

SOILURE *n* pl. **-S** a stain or smudge

SOIREE *n* pl. **-S** an evening party

SOJA *n* pl. **-S** the soybean

SOJOURN *v* **-ED, -ING, -S** to stay temporarily

SOJU *n* pl. **-S** Korean vodka distilled from rice or sweet potato

SOKE *n* pl. **-S** a feudal right to administer justice within a certain territory

SOKEMAN *n* pl. **-MEN** socman

SOKOL *n* pl. **-S** an international group promoting physical fitness

SOL *n* pl. **-S** the fifth tone of the diatonic musical scale

SOLA *n* pl. **-S** a swamp plant of India

SOLACE *v* **-LACED, -LACING, -LACES** to console

SOLACER *n* pl. **-S** one that solaces

SOLAN *n* pl. **-S** a gannet

SOLAND *n* pl. **-S** solan

SOLANDER *n* pl. **-S** a protective box for library materials

SOLANIN *n* pl. **-S** solanine

SOLANINE *n* pl. **-S** a poisonous alkaloid

SOLANO *n* pl. **-NOS** a strong, hot wind

SOLANUM *n* pl. **-S** any of a genus of herbs and shrubs

SOLAR *n* pl. **-S** a solarium

SOLARIA a pl. of solarium

SOLARISE *v* **-ISED, -ISING, -ISES** to solarize

SOLARISM *n* pl. **-S** an interpretation of folk tales as concepts of the nature of the sun

SOLARIUM *n* pl. **-IUMS** or **-IA** a room exposed to the sun

SOLARIZE *v* **-IZED, -IZING, -IZES** to expose to sunlight

SOLATE *v* **-ATED, -ATING, -ATES** to change to a fluid colloidal system

SOLATION *n* pl. **-S** the act of solating

SOLATIUM *n* pl. **-TIA** a compensation given for damage to the feelings

SOLD past tense of sell

SOLDAN *n* pl. **-S** a Muslim ruler

SOLDER *v* **-ED, -ING, -S** to join closely together

SOLDERER *n* pl. **-S** one that solders

SOLDIER *v* **-ED, -ING, -S** to perform military service

SOLDIERY *n* pl. **-DIERIES** the military profession

SOLDO *n* pl. **-DI** a former coin of Italy

SOLE *v* **SOLED, SOLING, SOLES** to furnish with a sole (the bottom surface of a shoe or boot)

SOLECISE *v* **-CISED, -CISING, -CISES** to solecize

SOLECISM *n* pl. **-S** an ungrammatical combination of words in a sentence

SOLECIST *n* pl. **-S** one who solecizes

SOLECIZE *v* **-CIZED, -CIZING, -CIZES** to use solecisms

SOLED past tense of sole

SOLEI a pl. of soleus

SOLELESS *adj* having no sole

SOLELY *adv* singly

SOLEMN *adj* **-EMNER, -EMNEST** serious **SOLEMNLY** *adv*

SOLENESS *n* pl. **-ES** the state of being the only one

SOLENOID *n* pl. **-S** a type of electric coil

SOLERA *n* pl. **-S** a Spanish method of producing wine

SOLERET *n* pl. **-S** solleret

SOLEUS *n* pl. **-LEUSES** or **-LEI** a muscle in the calf of the leg

SOLFEGE *n* pl. **-S** a type of singing exercise

SOLFEGGI *n/pl* solfeges

SOLGEL *adj* involving some changes in the state of a colloidal system

SOLI a pl. of solo

SOLICIT *v* **-ED, -ING, -S** to ask for earnestly

SOLID *adj* **-IDER, -IDEST** having definite shape and volume

SOLID *n* pl. **-S** a solid substance

SOLIDAGO *n* pl. **-GOS** a flowering plant

SOLIDARY *adj* united

SOLIDI pl. of solidus

SOLIDIFY *v* **-FIED, -FYING, -FIES** to make solid

SOLIDITY *n* pl. **-TIES** the quality or state of being solid

SOLIDLY *adv* in a solid manner

SOLIDUS *n* pl. **-DI** a coin of ancient Rome

SOLING present participle of sole

SOLION *n* pl. **-S** an electronic detecting and amplifying device

SOLIQUID *n* pl. **-S** a fluid colloidal system

SOLITARY *n* pl. **-TARIES** one who lives alone

SOLITON *n* pl. **-S** a solitary wave in physics

SOLITUDE *n* pl. **-S** the state of being alone

SOLLERET *n* pl. **-S** a sabaton

SOLO *n* pl. **-LOS** or **-LI** a musical composition for a single voice or instrument

SOLO *v* **-ED, -ING, -S** or **-ES** to perform alone

SOLOIST *n* pl. **-S** one that performs a solo

SOLON *n* pl. **-S** a wise lawgiver

SOLONETS *n* pl. **-ES** solonetz

SOLONETZ *n* pl. **-ES** a type of soil

SOLSTICE *n* pl. **-S** the time of the year when the sun is at its greatest distance from the celestial equator

SOLUBLE *n* pl. **-S** something that is soluble (capable of being dissolved)

SOLUBLY *adv* in a soluble manner

SOLUM *n* pl. **-LUMS** or **-LA** a soil layer

SOLUNAR *adj* listing the rising and setting times of the sun and moon

SOLUS *adj* alone

SOLUTE *n* pl. **-S** a dissolved substance

SOLUTION *n* pl. **-S** a homogeneous liquid mixture

SOLVABLE *adj* capable of being solved

SOLVATE *v* **-VATED, -VATING, -VATES** to convert into a type of ion

SOLVE *v* **SOLVED, SOLVING, SOLVES** to find the answer or explanation for

SOLVENCY *n* pl. **-CIES** the ability to pay all debts

SOLVENT *n* pl. **-S** a substance capable of dissolving others

SOLVER *n* pl. **-S** one that solves

SOLVING present participle of solve

SOM *n* pl. **SOMS** a monetary unit of Kyrgyzstan

SOMA *n* pl. **-MAS** or **-MATA** the body of an organism **SOMATIC** *adj*

SOMAN *n* pl. **-S** a toxic chemical warfare agent

SOMBER *adj* **SOMBERER, SOMBEREST** gloomy **SOMBERLY** *adv*

SOMBRE *adj* **SOMBRER, SOMBREST** somber **SOMBRELY** *adv*

SOMBRERO *n* pl. **-ROS** a broad-brimmed hat

SOMBROUS *adj* somber

SOME *adj* being an unspecified number or part

SOMEBODY *n* pl. **-BODIES** an important person

SOMEDAY *adv* at some future time

SOMEDEAL *adv* to some degree

SOMEHOW *adv* by some means

SOMEONE *n* pl. **-S** a somebody

SOMERSET *v* **-SETED, -SETING, -SETS** or **-SETTED, -SETTING, -SETS** to roll the body in a complete circle, head over heels

SOMETIME *adv* at some future time

SOMEWAY *adv* somehow

SOMEWAYS *adv* someway

SOMEWHAT *n* pl. **-S** an unspecified number or part

SOMEWHEN *adv* sometime

SOMEWISE *adv* somehow

SOMITE *n* pl. **-S** a longitudinal segment of the body of some animals **SOMITAL, SOMITIC** *adj*

SOMONI *n* pl. **-S** a monetary unit of Tajikistan

SON *n* pl. **-S** a male child

SONANCE *n* pl. **-S** sound

SONANT *n* pl. **-S** a sound uttered with vibration of the vocal cords **SONANTAL, SONANTIC** *adj*

SONAR *n* pl. **-S** an underwater locating device

SONARMAN *n* pl. **-MEN** a person who operates sonar equipment

SONATA *n* pl. **-S** a type of musical composition

SONATINA *n* pl. **-TINAS** or **-TINE** a short sonata

SONDE *n* pl. **-S** a device for observing atmospheric phenomena

SONDER *n* pl. **-S** a class of small yachts

SONE *n* pl. **-S** a unit of loudness

SONG *n* pl. **-S** a musical composition written or adapted for singing

SONGBIRD *n* pl. **-S** a bird that utters a musical call

SONGBOOK *n* pl. **-S** a book of songs

SONGFEST *n* pl. **-S** an informal gathering for group singing

SONGFUL *adj* melodious

SONGLESS   *adj* incapable of singing

SONGLIKE   *adj* resembling a song

SONGSTER   *n* pl. **-S** a singer

SONHOOD   *n* pl. **-S** the state of being a son

SONIC   *adj* pertaining to sound

SONICATE   *v* **-CATED, -CATING, -CATES** to disrupt with sound waves

SONICS   *n/pl* the science dealing with the practical applications of sound

SONLESS   *adj* having no son

SONLIKE   *adj* resembling a son

SONLY   *adj* pertaining to a son

SONNET   *v* **-NETED, -NETING, -NETS** or **-NETTED, -NETTING, -NETS** to compose a sonnet (a type of poem)

SONNY   *n* pl. **-NIES** a small boy

SONOBUOY   *n* pl. **-BUOYS** a buoy that detects and transmits underwater sounds

SONOGRAM   *n* pl. **-S** an image produced by ultrasound

SONORANT   *n* pl. **-S** a type of voiced sound

SONORITY   *n* pl. **-TIES** the quality or state of being sonorous

SONOROUS   *adj* characterized by a full and loud sound

SONOVOX   *n* pl. **-ES** a sound effects device

SONSHIP   *n* pl. **-S** the state of being a son

SONSIE   *adj* **-SIER, -SIEST** sonsy

SONSY   *adj* **-SIER, -SIEST** comely

SOOCHONG   *n* pl. **-S** souchong

SOOEY   *interj* — used in calling pigs

SOOK   *n* pl. **-S** souk

SOON   *adv* **SOONER, SOONEST** in the near future **SOONISH** *adj*

SOONER   *n* pl. **-S** one who settles on government land before it is officially opened for settlement

SOOT   *v* **-ED, -ING, -S** to cover with soot (a black substance produced by combustion)

SOOTH   *adj* **SOOTHER, SOOTHEST** true

SOOTH   *n* pl. **-S** truth

SOOTHE   *v* **SOOTHED, SOOTHING, SOOTHES** to restore to a quiet or normal state

SOOTHER   *n* pl. **-S** one that soothes

SOOTHLY   *adv* in truth

SOOTHSAY   *v* **-SAID, -SAYING, -SAYS** to predict

SOOTY   *adj* **SOOTIER, SOOTIEST** covered with soot **SOOTILY** *adv*

SOP   *v* **SOPPED, SOPPING, SOPS** to dip or soak in a liquid

SOPH   *n* pl. **-S** a sophomore

SOPHIES   pl. of sophy

SOPHISM   *n* pl. **-S** a plausible but fallacious argument

SOPHIST   *n* pl. **-S** one that uses sophisms

SOPHY   *n* pl. **-PHIES** a ruler of Persia

SOPITE   *v* **-PITED, -PITING, -PITES** to put to sleep

SOPOR   *n* pl. **-S** an abnormally deep sleep

SOPPED   past tense of sop

SOPPING   *adj* very wet

SOPPY   *adj* **-PIER, -PIEST** very wet **SOPPILY** *adv*

SOPRANO   *n* pl. **-NOS** or **-NI** the highest singing voice

SORA   *n* pl. **-S** a marsh bird

SORB   *v* **-ED, -ING, -S** to take up and hold by absorption or adsorption **SORBABLE** *adj*

SORBATE   *n* pl. **-S** a sorbed substance

SORBENT   *n* pl. **-S** a substance that sorbs

SORBET   *n* pl. **-S** sherbet

SORBIC   *adj* pertaining to a type of fruit

SORBITAN   *n* pl. **-S** a chemical compound

SORBITOL   *n* pl. **-S** a chemical compound

SORBOSE   *n* pl. **-S** a type of sugar

SORCERER   *n* pl. **-S** one who practices sorcery

SORCERY   *n* pl. **-CERIES** alleged use of supernatural powers

SORD   *n* pl. **-S** a flight of mallards

SORDID   *adj* filthy **SORDIDLY** *adv*

SORDINE   *n* pl. **-S** a device used to muffle the tone of a musical instrument

SORDINO   *n* pl. **-NI** sordine

SORDOR   *n* pl. **-S** a sordid state

SORE   *v* **SORED, SORING, SORES** to mutilate the feet of (a horse) so as to force a particular gait

SORE   *adj* **SORER, SOREST** painfully sensitive to the touch

SOREHEAD   *n* pl. **-S** a person who is easily angered or offended

SOREL   *n* pl. **-S** sorrel

SORELY   *adv* in a sore manner

SORENESS *n* pl. **-ES** the quality or state of being sore

SORER comparative of sore

SOREST superlative of sore

SORGHO *n* pl. **-GHOS** sorgo

SORGHUM *n* pl. **-S** a cereal grass

SORGO *n* pl. **-GOS** a variety of sorghum

SORI pl. of sorus

SORICINE *adj* belonging to the shrew family of mammals

SORING *n* pl. **-S** the practice of making a horse's front feet sore to force high stepping

SORITES *n* pl. **SORITES** a type of argument used in logic **SORITIC** *adj*

SORN *v* **-ED, -ING, -S** to force oneself on others for food and lodging

SORNER *n* pl. **-S** one that sorns

SOROCHE *n* pl. **-S** mountain sickness

SORORAL *adj* sisterly

SORORATE *n* pl. **-S** the marriage of a man usually with his deceased wife's sister

SORORITY *n* pl. **-TIES** a social club for women

SOROSIS *n* pl. **-ROSISES** or **-ROSES** a women's club or society

SORPTION *n* pl. **-S** the act or process of sorbing **SORPTIVE** *adj*

SORREL *n* pl. **-S** a reddish brown color

SORRIER comparative of sorry

SORRIEST superlative of sorry

SORRILY *adv* in a sorry manner

SORROW *v* **-ED, -ING, -S** to grieve

SORROWER *n* pl. **-S** one that sorrows

SORRY *adj* **-RIER, -RIEST** feeling grief or penitence

SORT *v* **-ED, -ING, -S** to arrange according to kind, class, or size **SORTABLE** *adj* **SORTABLY** *adv*

SORTAL *n* pl. **-S** a term that classifies an entity as being of a particular kind

SORTER *n* pl. **-S** one that sorts

SORTES *n/pl* divination by chance selection of a passage in an authoritative text

SORTIE *v* **-TIED, -TIEING, -TIES** to attack suddenly from a defensive position

SORTING *n* pl. **-S** the separating of items into groups

SORUS *n* pl. **-RI** a cluster of plant reproductive bodies

SOT *n* pl. **-S** a habitual drunkard

SOTH *n* pl. **-S** sooth

SOTOL *n* pl. **-S** a flowering plant

SOTTED *adj* besotted **SOTTEDLY** *adv*

SOTTISH *adj* resembling a sot

SOU *n* pl. **-S** a formerly used French coin

SOUARI *n* pl. **-S** a tropical tree

SOUBISE *n* pl. **-S** a sauce of onions and butter

SOUCAR *n* pl. **-S** a Hindu banker

SOUCHONG *n* pl. **-S** a Chinese tea

SOUDAN *n* pl. **-S** soldan

SOUFFLE *n* pl. **-S** a light, baked dish

SOUFFLED *adj* made puffy by beating and baking

SOUGH *v* **-ED, -ING, -S** to make a moaning or sighing sound

SOUGHT past tense of seek

SOUK *n* pl. **-S** a marketplace in northern Africa and the Middle East

SOUKOUS *n* pl. **-ES** a dance music in the Democratic Republic of the Congo

SOUL *n* pl. **-S** the spiritual aspect of human beings **SOULED, SOULLESS, SOULLIKE** *adj*

SOULFUL *adj* full of emotion

SOULMATE *n* pl. **-S** a person with whom one is perfectly suited

SOULSTER *n* pl. **-S** a singer of soul music

SOUND *adj* **SOUNDER, SOUNDEST** being in good health or condition

SOUND *v* **-ED, -ING, -S** to make a sound (something that stimulates the auditory receptors)

SOUNDBOX *n* pl. **-ES** a resonant cavity in a musical instrument

SOUNDER *n* pl. **-S** one that sounds

SOUNDING *n* pl. **-S** a sampling of opinions

SOUNDLY *adv* in a sound manner

SOUNDMAN *n* pl. **-MEN** a person who controls the quality of sound being recorded

SOUP *v* **-ED, -ING, -S** to increase the power or efficiency of

SOUPCON *n* pl. **-S** a minute amount

SOUPLESS *adj* having no soup (a liquid food often having solid ingredients)

SOUPLIKE	*adj* resembling soup	**SOVRANTY**	*n* pl. **-TIES** a monarchy
SOUPY	*adj* **SOUPIER, SOUPIEST** foggy **SOUPILY** *adv*	**SOW**	*v* **SOWED, SOWN, SOWING, SOWS** to scatter over land for growth, as seed **SOWABLE** *adj*
SOUR	*adj* **SOURER, SOUREST** sharp or biting to the taste	**SOWANS**	*n* pl. **SOWANS** sowens
SOUR	*v* **-ED, -ING, -S** to make or become sour	**SOWAR**	*n* pl. **-S** a mounted native soldier in India
SOURBALL	*n* pl. **-S** a sour candy	**SOWBACK**	*n* pl. **-S** a low ridge of sand
SOURCE	*v* **SOURCED, SOURCING, SOURCES** to obtain from a point of origin	**SOWBELLY**	*n* pl. **-LIES** pork cured in salt
		SOWBREAD	*n* pl. **-S** a flowering plant
SOURCING	*n* pl. **-S** the act of obtaining something from a point of origin	**SOWBUG**	*n* pl. **-S** a wood louse
		SOWCAR	*n* pl. **-S** soucar
SOURDINE	*n* pl. **-S** sordine	**SOWENS**	*n* pl. **SOWENS** porridge made from oat husks
SOURGUM	*n* pl. **-S** a softwood tree of eastern North America		
		SOWER	*n* pl. **-S** one that sows
SOURISH	*adj* somewhat sour	**SOWING**	*n* pl. **-S** the act of scattering seeds
SOURLY	*adv* in a sour manner	**SOWN**	past participle of sow
SOURNESS	*n* pl. **-ES** the quality or state of being sour	**SOX**	a pl. of sock
		SOY	*n* pl. **SOYS** the soybean
SOURPUSS	*n* pl. **-ES** a grouchy person	**SOYA**	*n* pl. **-S** soy
SOURSOP	*n* pl. **-S** a tropical tree	**SOYBEAN**	*n* pl. **-S** the seed of a cultivated Asian herb
SOURWOOD	*n* pl. **-S** a flowering tree		
SOUSE	*v* **SOUSED, SOUSING, SOUSES** to immerse something in a liquid	**SOYMEAL**	*n* pl. **-S** the residue from the extraction of oil from soybean seeds
SOUSER	*n* pl. **-S** a drunkard		
SOUSLIK	*n* pl. **-S** suslik	**SOYMILK**	*n* pl. **-S** a milk substitute made from soybeans
SOUTACHE	*n* pl. **-S** a flat, narrow braid		
SOUTANE	*n* pl. **-S** a cassock	**SOYUZ**	*n* pl. **-ES** a manned spacecraft of the former Soviet Union
SOUTER	*n* pl. **-S** a shoemaker		
SOUTH	*v* **-ED, -ING, -S** to move toward the south (a cardinal point of the compass)	**SOZIN**	*n* pl. **-S** a type of protein
		SOZINE	*n* pl. **-S** sozin
		SOZZLED	*adj* drunk
SOUTHER	*n* pl. **-S** a wind or storm from the south	**SPA**	*n* pl. **-S** a mineral spring
		SPACE	*v* **SPACED, SPACING, SPACES** to set some distance apart
SOUTHERN	*n* pl. **-S** a person living in the south		
SOUTHING	*n* pl. **-S** movement toward the south	**SPACELAB**	*n* pl. **-S** a spacecraft equipped with a laboratory
		SPACEMAN	*n* pl. **-MEN** an astronaut
SOUTHPAW	*n* pl. **-S** a left-handed person	**SPACER**	*n* pl. **-S** one that spaces
SOUTHRON	*n* pl. **-S** a southern	**SPACEY**	*adj* **SPACIER, SPACIEST** weird in behavior
SOUVENIR	*n* pl. **-S** a memento		
SOUVLAKI	*n* pl. **-S** a Greek shish kebab	**SPACIAL**	*adj* spatial
SOVIET	*n* pl. **-S** a legislative body in a Communist country	**SPACING**	*n* pl. **-S** the distance between any two objects
SOVKHOZ	*n* pl. **-KHOZES** or **-KHOZY** a state-owned farm in the former Soviet Union		
		SPACIOUS	*adj* vast or ample in extent
		SPACKLE	*v* **-LED, -LING, -LES** to fill cracks or holes in a surface with paste
SOVRAN	*n* pl. **-S** a monarch		
SOVRANLY	*adv* supremely	**SPACY**	*adj* **SPACIER, SPACIEST** spacey

SPADE   *v* **SPADED, SPADING, SPADES** to take up with a spade (a digging implement)

SPADEFUL   *n* pl. **-S** as much as a spade can hold

SPADER   *n* pl. **-S** one that spades

SPADICES   pl. of spadix

SPADILLE   *n* pl. **-S** the highest trump in certain card games

SPADING   present participle of spade

SPADIX   *n* pl. **-DIXES** or **-DICES** a flower cluster

SPADO   *n* pl. **-DONES** a castrated man or animal

SPAE   *v* **SPAED, SPAEING, SPAES** to foretell

SPAEING   *n* pl. **-S** the act of foretelling

SPAETZLE   *n* pl. **-S** a tiny dumpling

SPAGYRIC   *n* pl. **-S** a person skilled in alchemy

SPAHEE   *n* pl. **-S** spahi

SPAHI   *n* pl. **-S** a Turkish cavalryman

SPAIL   *n* pl. **-S** spale

SPAIT   *n* pl. **-S** spate

SPAKE   a past tense of speak

SPALDEEN   *n* pl. **-S** a small hollow rubber ball

SPALE   *n* pl. **-S** a splinter or chip

SPALL   *v* **-ED, -ING, -S** to break up into fragments

SPALLER   *n* pl. **-S** one that spalls

SPALLING   *n* pl. **-S** a chip of stone or ore

SPALPEEN   *n* pl. **-S** a rascal

SPALTED   *adj* denoting wood having irregular lines resulting from fungal decay

SPAM   *v* **SPAMMED, SPAMMING, SPAMS** to send unsolicited e-mail to a large number of addresses

SPAMBOT   *n* pl. **-S** a computer program that sends out unsolicited e-mail

SPAMMER   *n* pl. **-S** one that spams

SPAMMING   *n* pl. **-S** the practice of sending out unsolicited email

SPAN   *v* **SPANNED, SPANNING, SPANS** to extend over or across

SPANCEL   *v* **-CELED, -CELING, -CELS** or **-CELLED, -CELLING, -CELS** to bind or fetter with a rope

SPANDEX   *n* pl. **-ES** a synthetic elastic fiber **SPANDEXED** *adj*

SPANDREL   *n* pl. **-S** a space between two adjoining arches

SPANDRIL   *n* pl. **-S** spandrel

SPANG   *adv* directly

SPANGLE   *v* **-GLED, -GLING, -GLES** to adorn with spangles (bits of sparkling metal)

SPANGLY   *adj* **-GLIER, -GLIEST** covered with spangles

SPANIEL   *n* pl. **-S** a dog with silky hair

SPANK   *v* **-ED, -ING, -S** to slap on the buttocks

SPANKER   *n* pl. **-S** one that spanks

SPANKING   *n* pl. **-S** the act of one that spanks

SPANLESS   *adj* having no extent

SPANNED   past tense of span

SPANNER   *n* pl. **-S** one that spans

SPANNING   present participle of span

SPANWORM   *n* pl. **-S** an inchworm

SPAR   *v* **SPARRED, SPARRING, SPARS** to provide with spars (stout poles used to support rigging)

SPARABLE   *n* pl. **-S** a type of nail

SPARE   *adj* **SPARER, SPAREST** meager **SPARELY** *adv*

SPARE   *v* **SPARED, SPARING, SPARES** to refrain from punishing, harming, or destroying

SPARER   *n* pl. **-S** one that spares

SPARERIB   *n* pl. **-S** a cut of pork

SPARGE   *v* **SPARGED, SPARGING, SPARGES** to sprinkle

SPARGER   *n* pl. **-S** one that sparges

SPARID   *n* pl. **-S** any of a family of marine fishes

SPARING   present participle of spare

SPARK   *v* **-ED, -ING, -S** to give off sparks (small fiery particles)

SPARKER   *n* pl. **-S** something that sparks

SPARKIER   comparative of sparky

SPARKIEST   superlative of sparky

SPARKILY   *adv* in a lively manner

SPARKISH   *adj* jaunty

SPARKLE   *v* **-KLED, -KLING, -KLES** to give off or reflect flashes of light

SPARKLER   *n* pl. **-S** something that sparkles

SPARKLET   *n* pl. **-S** a small spark

SPARKLY   *adj* **-KLIER, -KLIEST** tending to sparkle

SPARKY   *adj* **SPARKIER, SPARKIEST** lively

SPARLIKE   *adj* resembling a spar

SPARLING _n_ pl. **-S** a young herring

SPAROID _n_ pl. **-S** a sparid

SPARRED past tense of spar

SPARRING present participle of spar

SPARROW _n_ pl. **-S** a small bird

SPARRY _adj_ **-RIER, -RIEST** resembling spar (a lustrous mineral)

SPARSE _adj_ **SPARSER, SPARSEST** thinly distributed **SPARSELY** _adv_

SPARSITY _n_ pl. **-TIES** the quality or state of being sparse

SPARTAN _adj_ avoiding luxury and comfort

SPARTINA _n_ pl. **-S** a salt-marsh grass of coastal regions

SPASM _v_ **-ED, -ING, -S** to undergo an involuntary muscular contraction

SPASTIC _n_ pl. **-S** one suffering from a paralysis with muscle spasms

SPAT _v_ **SPATTED, SPATTING, SPATS** to strike lightly

SPATE _n_ pl. **-S** a freshet

SPATHE _n_ pl. **-S** a leaflike organ of certain plants **SPATHAL, SPATHED, SPATHOSE** _adj_

SPATHIC _adj_ sparry

SPATIAL _adj_ of or pertaining to space

SPATTED past tense of spat

SPATTER _v_ **-ED, -ING, -S** to scatter in drops

SPATTING present participle of spat

SPATULA _n_ pl. **-S** a mixing implement **SPATULAR** _adj_

SPATZLE _n_ pl. **-S** spaetzle

SPAVIE _n_ pl. **-S** spavin **SPAVIET** _adj_

SPAVIN _n_ pl. **-S** a disease of horses **SPAVINED** _adj_

SPAWN _v_ **-ED, -ING, -S** to deposit eggs

SPAWNER _n_ pl. **-S** one that spawns

SPAY _v_ **-ED, -ING, -S** to remove the ovaries of

SPEAK _v_ **SPOKE** or **SPAKE, SPOKEN, SPEAKING, SPEAKS** to utter words

SPEAKER _n_ pl. **-S** one that speaks

SPEAKING _n_ pl. **-S** a speech or discourse

SPEAN _v_ **-ED, -ING, -S** to wean

SPEAR _v_ **-ED, -ING, -S** to pierce with a spear (a long, pointed weapon)

SPEARER _n_ pl. **-S** one that spears

SPEARGUN _n_ pl. **-S** a gun that shoots a spear

SPEARING _n_ pl. **-S** the act of piercing with a spear

SPEARMAN _n_ pl. **-MEN** a person armed with a spear

SPEC _v_ **SPECCED, SPECCING, SPECS** to write specifications for

SPECIAL _adj_ **-CIALER, -CIALEST** of a distinct kind or character

SPECIAL _n_ pl. **-S** a special person or thing

SPECIATE _v_ **-ATED, -ATING, -ATES** to undergo a type of evolutionary process

SPECIE _n_ pl. **-S** coined money

SPECIFIC _n_ pl. **-S** a remedy intended for a particular disease

SPECIFY _v_ **-FIED, -FYING, -FIES** to state in detail

SPECIMEN _n_ pl. **-S** a part or individual representative of a group or whole

SPECIOUS _adj_ having a false look of truth or authenticity

SPECK _v_ **-ED, -ING, -S** to mark with small spots

SPECKLE _v_ **-LED, -LING, -LES** to speck

SPECKY _adj_ **SPECKIER, SPECKIEST** marked with small spots

SPECTATE _v_ **-TATED, -TATING, -TATES** to attend and view

SPECTER _n_ pl. **-S** a visible disembodied spirit

SPECTRA a pl. of spectrum

SPECTRAL _adj_ resembling a specter

SPECTRE _n_ pl. **-S** specter

SPECTRUM _n_ pl. **-TRUMS** or **-TRA** an array of the components of a light wave

SPECULUM _n_ pl. **-LUMS** or **-LA** a medical instrument **SPECULAR** _adj_

SPEECH _n_ pl. **-ES** the faculty or act of speaking

SPEED _v_ **SPED** or **SPEEDED, SPEEDING, SPEEDS** to move swiftly

SPEEDER _n_ pl. **-S** one that speeds

SPEEDIER comparative of speedy

SPEEDIEST superlative of speedy

SPEEDILY _adv_ in a speedy manner

SPEEDING _n_ pl. **-S** the act of driving faster than the law allows

SPEEDO _n_ pl. **SPEEDOS** a speedometer

SPEEDUP _n_ pl. **-S** an acceleration of production without an increase in pay

SPEEDWAY	*n* pl. **-WAYS** a road designed for rapid travel
SPEEDY	*adj* **SPEEDIER, SPEEDIEST** swift
SPEEL	*v* **-ED, -ING, -S** to climb
SPEER	*v* **-ED, -ING, -S** to inquire
SPEERING	*n* pl. **-S** inquiry
SPEIL	*v* **-ED, -ING, -S** to speel
SPEIR	*v* **-ED, -ING, -S** to speer
SPEISE	*n* pl. **-S** speiss
SPEISS	*n* pl. **-ES** a metallic mixture obtained in smelting certain ores
SPELAEAN	*adj* spelean
SPELEAN	*adj* living in caves
SPELL	*v* **SPELLED** or **SPELT, SPELLING, SPELLS** to name or write the letters of in order
SPELLER	*n* pl. **-S** one that spells words
SPELLING	*n* pl. **-S** a sequence of letters composing a word
SPELT	*n* pl. **-S** a variety of wheat
SPELTER	*n* pl. **-S** zinc in the form of ingots
SPELTZ	*n* pl. **-ES** spelt
SPELUNK	*v* **-ED, -ING, -S** to explore caves
SPENCE	*n* pl. **-S** a pantry
SPENCER	*n* pl. **-S** a trysail
SPEND	*v* **SPENT, SPENDING, SPENDS** to pay out
SPENDER	*n* pl. **-S** one that spends
SPENDY	*adj* **SPENDIER, SPENDIEST** expensive
SPENSE	*n* pl. **-S** spence
SPENT	past tense of spend
SPERM	*n* pl. **-S** a male gamete **SPERMIC** *adj*
SPERMARY	*n* pl. **-RIES** an organ in which sperms are formed
SPERMINE	*n* pl. **-S** a chemical compound
SPERMOUS	*adj* resembling or made up of sperms
SPEW	*v* **-ED, -ING, -S** to vomit
SPEWER	*n* pl. **-S** one that spews
SPHAGNUM	*n* pl. **-S** a grayish moss
SPHENE	*n* pl. **-S** a mineral
SPHENIC	*adj* shaped like a wedge
SPHENOID	*n* pl. **-S** a bone of the skull
SPHERAL	*adj* of, pertaining to, or having the form of a sphere
SPHERE	*v* **SPHERED, SPHERING, SPHERES** to form into a sphere (a type of geometric solid)
SPHERIC	*adj* spheral
SPHERICS	*n/pl* the geometry of figures on the surface of a sphere
SPHERIER	comparative of sphery
SPHERIEST	superlative of sphery
SPHERING	present participle of sphere
SPHEROID	*n* pl. **-S** a type of geometric solid
SPHERULE	*n* pl. **-S** a small sphere
SPHERY	*adj* **SPHERIER, SPHERIEST** resembling a sphere
SPHINGES	a pl. of sphinx
SPHINGID	*n* pl. **-S** the hawkmoth
SPHINX	*n* pl. **SPHINXES** or **SPHINGES** a monster in Egyptian mythology
SPHYGMUS	*n* pl. **-ES** the pulse **SPHYGMIC** *adj*
SPHYNX	*n* pl. **-ES** a cat of a breed of hairless cats
SPICA	*n* pl. **-CAS** or **-CAE** an ear of grain **SPICATE, SPICATED** *adj*
SPICCATO	*n* pl. **-TOS** a method of playing a stringed instrument
SPICE	*v* **SPICED, SPICING, SPICES** to season with a spice (an aromatic vegetable substance)
SPICER	*n* pl. **-S** one that spices
SPICERY	*n* pl. **-ERIES** a spicy quality
SPICEY	*adj* **SPICIER, SPICIEST** spicy
SPICIER	comparative of spicy
SPICIEST	superlative of spicy
SPICILY	*adv* in a spicy manner
SPICING	present participle of spice
SPICULA	*n* pl. **-LAE** spicule **SPICULAR** *adj*
SPICULE	*n* pl. **-S** a needlelike structure
SPICULUM	*n* pl. **-LA** spicule
SPICY	*adj* **SPICIER, SPICIEST** containing spices
SPIDER	*v* **-ED, -ING, -S** to move in a scuttling manner
SPIDERY	*adj* **-DERIER, -DERIEST** resembling a spider (a type of arachnid)
SPIED	past tense of spy
SPIEGEL	*n* pl. **-S** a type of cast iron
SPIEL	*v* **-ED, -ING, -S** to talk at length
SPIELER	*n* pl. **-S** one that spiels
SPIER	*v* **-ED, -ING, -S** to speer

SPIES	present 3d person sing. of spy
SPIFF	*v* **-ED, -ING, -S** to make spiffy
SPIFFING	*adj* spiffy
SPIFFY	*v* **-FIED, -FYING, -FIES** to make stylish
SPIFFY	*adj* **-FIER, -FIEST** stylish **SPIFFILY** *adv*
SPIGOT	*n* pl. **-S** a faucet
SPIKE	*v* **SPIKED, SPIKING, SPIKES** to fasten with a spike (a long, thick nail)
SPIKELET	*n* pl. **-S** a type of flower cluster
SPIKER	*n* pl. **-S** one that spikes
SPIKEY	*adj* **SPIKIER, SPIKIEST** spiky
SPIKING	present participle of spike
SPIKY	*adj* **SPIKIER, SPIKIEST** resembling a spike **SPIKILY** *adv*
SPILE	*v* **SPILED, SPILING, SPILES** to stop up with a wooden plug
SPILIKIN	*n* pl. **-S** a strip of wood used in a game
SPILING	*n* pl. **-S** a piling
SPILITE	*n* pl. **-S** a form of basalt **SPILITIC** *adj*
SPILL	*v* **SPILLED** or **SPILT, SPILLING, SPILLS** to cause to run out of a container
SPILLAGE	*n* pl. **-S** something that is spilled
SPILLER	*n* pl. **-S** one that spills
SPILLWAY	*n* pl. **-WAYS** a channel for surplus water in a reservoir
SPILT	a past tense of spill
SPILTH	*n* pl. **-S** spillage
SPIN	*v* **SPUN, SPINNING, SPINS** to draw out and twist into threads
SPINACH	*n* pl. **-ES** a cultivated herb **SPINACHY** *adj*
SPINAGE	*n* pl. **-S** spinach
SPINAL	*n* pl. **-S** an injection of an anesthetic into the spinal cord
SPINALLY	*adv* with respect to the spine
SPINATE	*adj* bearing thorns
SPINDLE	*v* **-DLED, -DLING, -DLES** to impale on a slender rod
SPINDLER	*n* pl. **-S** one that spindles
SPINDLY	*adj* **-DLIER, -DLIEST** long and slender
SPINE	*n* pl. **-S** the vertebral column **SPINED** *adj*
SPINEL	*n* pl. **-S** a mineral
SPINELLE	*n* pl. **-S** spinel
SPINET	*n* pl. **-S** a small piano
SPINIER	comparative of spiny
SPINIEST	superlative of spiny
SPINIFEX	*n* pl. **-ES** an Australian grass
SPINLESS	*adj* having no rotation
SPINNER	*n* pl. **-S** one that spins
SPINNERY	*n* pl. **-NERIES** a spinning mill
SPINNEY	*n* pl. **-NEYS** a thicket
SPINNING	*n* pl. **-S** the act of one that spins
SPINNY	*n* pl. **-NIES** spinney
SPINNY	*adj* **SPINNIER, SPINNIEST** crazy, foolish
SPINOFF	*n* pl. **-S** a new application or incidental result
SPINOR	*n* pl. **-S** a type of mathematical vector
SPINOSE	*adj* spiny
SPINOUS	*adj* spiny
SPINOUT	*n* pl. **-S** a rotational skid by an automobile
SPINSTER	*n* pl. **-S** an unmarried woman who is past the usual age for marrying
SPINTO	*n* pl. **-TOS** a singing voice that is lyric and dramatic
SPINULA	*n* pl. **-LAE** spinule
SPINULE	*n* pl. **-S** a small thorn
SPINY	*adj* **SPINIER, SPINIEST** bearing or covered with thorns
SPIRACLE	*n* pl. **-S** an orifice through which breathing occurs
SPIRAEA	*n* pl. **-S** spirea
SPIRAL	*v* **-RALED, -RALING, -RALS** or **-RALLED, -RALLING, -RALS** to move like a spiral (a type of plane curve)
SPIRALLY	*adv* in a spiral manner
SPIRANT	*n* pl. **-S** a speech sound produced by the forcing of breath through a narrow passage
SPIRE	*v* **SPIRED, SPIRING, SPIRES** to rise in a tapering manner
SPIREA	*n* pl. **-S** a flowering shrub
SPIREM	*n* pl. **-S** spireme
SPIREME	*n* pl. **-S** a filament forming part of a cell nucleus during mitosis
SPIRIER	comparative of spiry
SPIRIEST	superlative of spiry

SPIRILLA   *n/pl* spirally twisted, aerobic bacteria

SPIRING   present participle of spire

SPIRIT   *v* **-ED, -ING, -S** to carry off secretly

SPIRITUS   *n* pl. **SPIRITUS** spirit

SPIROID   *adj* resembling a spiral

SPIRT   *v* **-ED, -ING, -S** to spurt

SPIRULA   *n* pl. **-LAS** or **-LAE** a spiral-shelled mollusk

SPIRY   *adj* **SPIRIER, SPIRIEST** tall, slender, and tapering

SPIT   *v* **SPITTED, SPITTING, SPITS** to impale on a spit (a pointed rod on which meat is turned)

SPITAL   *n* pl. **-S** a hospital

SPITBALL   *n* pl. **-S** a type of pitch in baseball

SPITE   *v* **SPITED, SPITING, SPITES** to treat with malice

SPITEFUL   *adj* **-FULLER, -FULLEST** malicious

SPITFIRE   *n* pl. **-S** a quick-tempered person

SPITTED   past tense of spit

SPITTER   *n* pl. **-S** a spitball

SPITTING   present participle of spit

SPITTLE   *n* pl. **-S** saliva **SPITTLY** *adj*

SPITTOON   *n* pl. **-S** a receptacle for saliva

SPITTY   *adj* **-TIER, -TIEST** marked with saliva

SPITZ   *n* pl. **-ES** a dog having a heavy coat

SPIV   *n* pl. **-S** an unscrupulous petty criminal **SPIVVISH** *adj*

SPIVVY   *adj* **SPIVVIER, SPIVVIEST** resembling a spiv in dress or conduct

SPLAKE   *n* pl. **-S** a freshwater fish

SPLASH   *v* **-ED, -ING, -ES** to scatter a liquid about

SPLASHER   *n* pl. **-S** one that splashes

SPLASHY   *adj* **SPLASHIER, SPLASHIEST** showy

SPLAT   *v* **SPLATTED, SPLATTING, SPLATS** to flatten on impact

SPLATTER   *v* **-ED, -ING, -S** to spatter

SPLAY   *v* **-ED, -ING, -S** to spread out

SPLEEN   *n* pl. **-S** a ductless organ of the body

SPLEENY   *adj* **SPLEENIER, SPLEENIEST** peevish

SPLENDID   *adj* **-DIDER, -DIDEST** magnificent

SPLENDOR   *n* pl. **-S** magnificence

SPLENIAL   *adj* pertaining to the splenius

SPLENIC   *adj* pertaining to the spleen

SPLENIUM   *n* pl. **-NIA** or **-NIUMS** a surgical bandage

SPLENIUS   *n* pl. **-NII** a muscle of the neck

SPLENT   *n* pl. **-S** a splint

SPLICE   *v* **SPLICED, SPLICING, SPLICES** to join at the ends

SPLICER   *n* pl. **-S** one that splices

SPLIFF   *n* pl. **-S** a marijuana cigarette

SPLINE   *v* **SPLINED, SPLINING, SPLINES** to provide with a spline (a key that connects two rotating mechanical parts)

SPLINT   *v* **-ED, -ING, -S** to brace with a splint (a thin piece of wood)

SPLINTER   *v* **-ED, -ING, -S** to split into sharp, slender pieces

SPLIT   *v* **SPLIT, SPLITTING, SPLITS** to separate lengthwise

SPLITTER   *n* pl. **-S** one that splits

SPLODGE   *v* **SPLODGED, SPLODGING, SPLODGES** to splotch

SPLODGY   *adj* **SPLODGIER, SPLODGIEST** splotchy

SPLORE   *n* pl. **-S** a carousal

SPLOSH   *v* **-ED, -ING, -ES** to splash

SPLOTCH   *v* **-ED, -ING, -ES** to mark with large, irregular spots

SPLOTCHY   *adj* **SPLOTCHIER, SPLOTCHIEST** splotched

SPLURGE   *v* **SPLURGED, SPLURGING, SPLURGES** to spend money lavishly

SPLURGER   *n* pl. **-S** one that splurges

SPLURGY   *adj* **SPLURGIER, SPLURGIEST** tending to splurge

SPLURT   *v* **-ED, -ING, -S** to gush forth in a stream or jet

SPLUTTER   *v* **-ED, -ING, -S** to speak rapidly and confusedly

SPODE   *n* pl. **-S** a fine china

SPODOSOL   *n* pl. **-S** an acidic forest soil

SPOIL   *v* **SPOILED** or **SPOILT, SPOILING, SPOILS** to impair the value or quality of

SPOILAGE   *n* pl. **-S** something that is spoiled or wasted

SPOILER   *n* pl. **-S** one that spoils

SPOKE   v **SPOKED, SPOKING, SPOKES** to provide with spokes (rods that support the rim of a wheel)

SPOKEN   past participle of speak

SPOLIATE   v **-ATED, -ATING, -ATES** to plunder

SPONDAIC   n pl. **-S** a spondee

SPONDEE   n pl. **-S** a type of metrical foot

SPONGE   v **SPONGED, SPONGING** or **SPONGEING, SPONGES** to wipe with a sponge (a mass of absorbent material)

SPONGER   n pl. **-S** one that sponges

SPONGIER   comparative of spongy

SPONGIEST   superlative of spongy

SPONGILY   adv in a spongy manner

SPONGIN   n pl. **-S** a fibrous material

SPONGING   present participle of sponge

SPONGY   adj **SPONGIER, SPONGIEST** resembling a sponge

SPONSAL   adj pertaining to marriage

SPONSION   n pl. **-S** the act of sponsoring

SPONSON   n pl. **-S** a projection from the side of a ship

SPONSOR   v **-ED, -ING, -S** to make oneself responsible for

SPONTOON   n pl. **-S** a spear-like weapon

SPOOF   v **-ED, -ING, -S** to ridicule in fun

SPOOFER   n pl. **-S** one that spoofs

SPOOFERY   n pl. **-ERIES** good-natured ridicule

SPOOFY   adj humorously satiric

SPOOK   v **-ED, -ING, -S** to scare

SPOOKERY   n pl. **-ERIES** something spooky

SPOOKISH   adj spooky

SPOOKY   adj **SPOOKIER, SPOOKIEST** scary **SPOOKILY** adv

SPOOL   v **-ED, -ING, -S** to wind on a small cylinder

SPOOLER   n pl. **-S** one that spools

SPOOLING   n pl. **-S** the temporary storage of data for later output

SPOON   v **-ED, -ING, -S** to take up with a spoon (a type of eating utensil)

SPOONER   n pl. **-S** one that behaves in an amorous way

SPOONEY   adj **SPOONIER, SPOONIEST** spoony

SPOONEY   n pl. **-EYS** a spoony

SPOONFUL   n pl. **SPOONFULS** or **SPOONSFUL** as much as a spoon can hold

SPOONSFUL   a pl. of spoonful

SPOONY   adj **SPOONIER, SPOONIEST** overly sentimental **SPOONILY** adv

SPOONY   n pl. **SPOONIES** a spoony person

SPOOR   v **-ED, -ING, -S** to track an animal

SPOORER   n pl. **-S** one that spoors

SPORADIC   adj occurring at irregular intervals

SPORAL   adj of, pertaining to, or resembling a spore

SPORE   v **SPORED, SPORING, SPORES** to produce spores (asexual, usually single-celled reproductive bodies)

SPOROID   adj resembling a spore

SPOROZOA   n/pl parasitic one-celled animals

SPORRAN   n pl. **-S** a large purse worn by Scottish Highlanders

SPORT   v **-ED, -ING, -S** to frolic

SPORTER   n pl. **-S** one that sports

SPORTFUL   adj sportive

SPORTIF   n pl. **-S** a person who is active or interested in physical competitions

SPORTIVE   adj playful

SPORTY   adj **SPORTIER, SPORTIEST** showy **SPORTILY** adv

SPORULE   n pl. **-S** a small spore **SPORULAR** adj

SPOT   v **SPOTTED, SPOTTING, SPOTS** to mark with spots (small, roundish discolorations)

SPOTLESS   adj perfectly clean

SPOTLIT   a past tense of spotlight

SPOTTER   n pl. **-S** one that spots

SPOTTING   n pl. **-S** the practice of watching for examples of something

SPOTTY   adj **-TIER, -TIEST** marked with spots **SPOTTILY** adv

SPOUSAL   n pl. **-S** marriage

SPOUSE   v **SPOUSED, SPOUSING, SPOUSES** to marry

SPOUT   v **-ED, -ING, -S** to eject in a rapid stream

SPOUTER   n pl. **-S** one that spouts

SPOUTING   n pl. **-S** a channel for draining off water from a roof

SPRADDLE   v **-DLED, -DLING, -DLES** to straddle

SPRAG *n* pl. **-S** a device used to prevent a vehicle from rolling backward

SPRAIN *v* **-ED, -ING, -S** to weaken by a sudden and violent twisting or wrenching

SPRANG *n* pl. **-S** a weaving technique to form an openwork mesh

SPRAT *n* pl. **-S** a small herring

SPRATTLE *v* **-TLED, -TLING, -TLES** to struggle

SPRAWL *v* **-ED, -ING, -S** to stretch out ungracefully

SPRAWLER *n* pl. **-S** one that sprawls

SPRAWLY *adj* **SPRAWLIER, SPRAWLIEST** tending to sprawl

SPRAY *v* **-ED, -ING, -S** to disperse in fine particles

SPRAYER *n* pl. **-S** one that sprays

SPREAD *v* **SPREAD, SPREADING, SPREADS** to open or expand over a larger area

SPREADER *n* pl. **-S** one that spreads

SPREE *n* pl. **-S** an unrestrained indulgence in an activity

SPRENT *adj* sprinkled over

SPRIER a comparative of spry

SPRIEST a superlative of spry

SPRIG *v* **SPRIGGED, SPRIGGING, SPRIGS** to fasten with small, thin nails

SPRIGGER *n* pl. **-S** one that sprigs

SPRIGGY *adj* **-GIER, -GIEST** having small branches

SPRIGHT *n* pl. **-S** sprite

SPRING *v* **SPRANG** or **SPRUNG, SPRINGING, SPRINGS** to move upward suddenly and swiftly

SPRINGAL *n* pl. **-S** a young man

SPRINGE *v* **SPRINGED, SPRINGEING, SPRINGES** to catch with a type of snare

SPRINGER *n* pl. **-S** one that springs

SPRINGY *adj* **SPRINGIER, SPRINGIEST** resilient

SPRINKLE *v* **-KLED, -KLING, -KLES** to scatter drops or particles on

SPRINT *v* **-ED, -ING, -S** to run at top speed

SPRINTER *n* pl. **-S** one that sprints

SPRIT *n* pl. **-S** a ship's spar

SPRITE *n* pl. **-S** an elf or fairy

SPRITELY *adj* **-LIER, -LIEST** full of energy

SPRITZ *v* **-ED, -ING, -ES** to spray

SPRITZER *n* pl. **-S** a beverage of white wine and soda water

SPRITZY *adj* **SPRITZIER, SPRITZIEST** emitting a spray

SPROCKET *n* pl. **-S** a toothlike projection that engages with the links of a chain

SPROG *n* pl. **-S** a small child

SPROGLET *n* pl. **-S** a sprog

SPROUT *v* **-ED, -ING, -S** to begin to grow

SPRUCE *adj* **SPRUCER, SPRUCEST** neat and trim in appearance **SPRUCELY** *adv*

SPRUCE *v* **SPRUCED, SPRUCING, SPRUCES** to make spruce

SPRUCY *adj* **SPRUCIER, SPRUCIEST** spruce

SPRUE *n* pl. **-S** a tropical disease

SPRUG *n* pl. **-S** a sparrow

SPRUNG a past tense of spring

SPRY *adj* **SPRYER, SPRYEST** or **SPRIER, SPRIEST** nimble **SPRYLY** *adv*

SPRYNESS *n* pl. **-ES** the quality or state of being spry

SPUD *v* **SPUDDED, SPUDDING, SPUDS** to remove with a spade-like tool

SPUDDER *n* pl. **-S** a tool for removing bark from trees

SPUDGEL *n* pl. **-S** a bucket attached to a long pole

SPUE *v* **SPUED, SPUING, SPUES** to spew

SPUMANTE *n* pl. **-S** an Italian sparkling wine

SPUME *v* **SPUMED, SPUMING, SPUMES** to foam

SPUMIER comparative of spumy

SPUMIEST superlative of spumy

SPUMING present participle of spume

SPUMONE *n* pl. **-S** an Italian ice cream

SPUMONI *n* pl. **-S** spumone

SPUMOUS *adj* spumy

SPUMY *adj* **SPUMIER, SPUMIEST** foamy

SPUN past tense of spin

SPUNK *v* **-ED, -ING, -S** to begin to burn

SPUNKIE *n* pl. **-S** a light caused by the combustion of marsh gas

SPUNKY *adj* **SPUNKIER, SPUNKIEST** plucky **SPUNKILY** *adv*

SPUR   v **SPURRED, SPURRING, SPURS** to urge on with a spur (a horseman's goad)

SPURGALL   v **-ED, -ING, -S** to injure with a spur

SPURGE   n pl. **-S** a tropical plant

SPURIOUS   adj not genuine

SPURLESS   adj lacking a spur

SPURN   v **-ED, -ING, -S** to reject with contempt

SPURNER   n pl. **-S** one that spurns

SPURRED   past tense of spur

SPURRER   n pl. **-S** one that spurs

SPURREY   n pl. **-REYS** spurry

SPURRIER   n pl. **-S** one that makes spurs

SPURRING   present participle of spur

SPURRY   n pl. **-RIES** a European weed

SPURT   v **-ED, -ING, -S** to gush forth

SPURTER   n pl. **-S** one that spurts

SPURTLE   n pl. **-S** a stick for stirring porridge

SPUTNIK   n pl. **-S** a Soviet artificial earth satellite

SPUTTER   v **-ED, -ING, -S** to eject particles in short bursts

SPUTTERY   adj ejecting in short bursts

SPUTUM   n pl. **-TA** saliva

SPY   v **SPIED, SPYING, SPIES** to watch secretly

SPYGLASS   n pl. **-ES** a small telescope

SPYWARE   n pl. **-S** computer software by which personal information is covertly sent to another computer

SQUAB   n pl. **-S** a young pigeon

SQUABBLE   v **-BLED, -BLING, -BLES** to quarrel

SQUABBY   adj **-BIER, -BIEST** short and fat

SQUAD   v **SQUADDED, SQUADDING, SQUADS** to form into squads (small organized groups)

SQUADDIE   n pl. **-S** a military recruit

SQUADDY   n pl. **-DIES** squaddie

SQUADRON   v **-ED, -ING, -S** to arrange in squadrons (units of military organization)

SQUALENE   n pl. **-S** a chemical compound

SQUALID   adj **-IDER, -IDEST** marked by filthiness caused by neglect or poverty

SQUALL   v **-ED, -ING, -S** to cry or scream loudly

SQUALLER   n pl. **-S** one that squalls

SQUALLY   adj **SQUALLIER, SQUALLIEST** gusty

SQUALOR   n pl. **-S** the quality or state of being squalid

SQUAMA   n pl. **-MAE** a scale **SQUAMOSE, SQUAMOUS** adj

SQUAMATE   n pl. **-S** any of an order of reptiles

SQUANDER   v **-ED, -ING, -S** to spend wastefully

SQUARE   adj **SQUARER, SQUAREST** having four equal sides and four right angles; rigidly conventional

SQUARE   v **SQUARED, SQUARING, SQUARES** to make square

SQUARELY   adv in a straightforward and honest manner

SQUARER   n pl. **-S** one that squares

SQUAREST   superlative of square

SQUARING   present participle of square

SQUARISH   adj somewhat square

SQUARK   n pl. **-S** the hypothetical boson analogue of a quark

SQUASH   v **-ED, -ING, -ES** to press into a pulp or flat mass

SQUASHER   n pl. **-S** one that squashes

SQUASHY   adj **SQUASHIER, SQUASHIEST** soft and moist

SQUAT   adj **SQUATTER, SQUATTEST** short and thick **SQUATLY** adv

SQUAT   v **SQUATTED, SQUATTING, SQUATS** to bend one's knees and sit on one's heels

SQUATTER   v **-ED, -ING, -S** to move through water

SQUATTY   adj **-TIER, -TIEST** squat

SQUAWK   v **-ED, -ING, -S** to utter a loud, harsh cry

SQUAWKER   n pl. **-S** one that squawks

SQUEAK   v **-ED, -ING, -S** to make a sharp, high-pitched sound

SQUEAKER   n pl. **-S** one that squeaks

SQUEAKY   adj **SQUEAKIER, SQUEAKIEST** tending to squeak

SQUEAL   v **-ED, -ING, -S** to utter a sharp, shrill cry

SQUEALER   n pl. **-S** one that squeals

SQUEEGEE   v **-GEED, -GEEING, -GEES** to wipe with a squeegee (an implement for removing water from a surface)

SQUEEZE *v* **SQUEEZED, SQUEEZING, SQUEEZES** to press hard upon

SQUEEZER *n* pl. **-S** one that squeezes

SQUEG *v* **SQUEGGED, SQUEGGING, SQUEGS** to oscillate in an irregular manner

SQUELCH *v* **-ED, -ING, -ES** to squash

SQUELCHY *adj* **SQUELCHIER, SQUELCHIEST** squashy

SQUIB *v* **SQUIBBED, SQUIBBING, SQUIBS** to lampoon

SQUIBBER *n* pl. **-S** an infield grounder that becomes a base hit

SQUID *v* **SQUIDDED, SQUIDDING, SQUIDS** to fish for squid (ten-armed marine mollusks)

SQUIDGY *adj* **SQUIDGIER, SQUIDGIEST** squashy, soggy

SQUIFFED *adj* drunk

SQUIFFY *adj* **-FIER, -FIEST** squiffed

SQUIGGLE *v* **-GLED, -GLING, -GLES** to wriggle

SQUIGGLY *adj* **-GLIER, -GLIEST** wriggly

SQUILGEE *v* **-GEED, -GEEING, -GEES** to squeegee

SQUILL *n* pl. **-S** a Eurasian herb

SQUILLA *n* pl. **-LAS** or **-LAE** a burrowing crustacean

SQUINCH *v* **-ED, -ING, -ES** to squint

SQUINNY *adj* **-NIER, -NIEST** squinty

SQUINNY *v* **-NIED, -NYING, -NIES** to squint

SQUINT *adj* **SQUINTER, SQUINTEST** cross-eyed

SQUINT *v* **-ED, -ING, -S** to look with the eyes partly closed

SQUINTER *n* pl. **-S** one that squints

SQUINTY *adj* **SQUINTIER, SQUINTIEST** marked by squinting

SQUIRE *v* **SQUIRED, SQUIRING, SQUIRES** to serve as a squire (an escort)

SQUIREEN *n* pl. **-S** an owner of a small estate

SQUIRELY *adj* of or befitting a squire

SQUIRISH *adj* of, resembling, or befitting a squire

SQUIRL *n* pl. **-S** an ornamental curve in handwriting

SQUIRM *v* **-ED, -ING, -S** to wriggle

SQUIRMER *n* pl. **-S** one that squirms

SQUIRMY *adj* **SQUIRMIER, SQUIRMIEST** wriggly

SQUIRREL *v* **-RELED, -RELING, -RELS** or **-RELLED, -RELLING, -RELS** to store up for future use

SQUIRT *v* **-ED, -ING, -S** to eject in a thin, swift stream

SQUIRTER *n* pl. **-S** one that squirts

SQUISH *v* **-ED, -ING, -ES** to squash

SQUISHY *adj* **SQUISHIER, SQUISHIEST** squashy

SQUITTERS *n/pl* diarrhea

SQUOOSH *v* **-ED, -ING, -ES** to squash

SQUOOSHY *adj* **SQUOOSHIER, SQUOOSHIEST** squashy

SQUUSH *v* **-ED, -ING, -ES** to squash

SRADDHA *n* pl. **-S** sradha

SRADHA *n* pl. **-S** a Hindu ceremonial offering

SRI *n* pl. **-S** mister; sir — used as a Hindu title of respect

STAB *v* **STABBED, STABBING, STABS** to pierce with a pointed weapon

STABBER *n* pl. **-S** one that stabs

STABBING *n* pl. **-S** the act of piercing someone with a pointed weapon

STABILE *n* pl. **-S** a stationary abstract sculpture

STABLE *adj* **-BLER, -BLEST** resistant to sudden change or position or condition

STABLE *v* **-BLED, -BLING, -BLES** to put in a stable (a shelter for domestic animals)

STABLER *n* pl. **-S** one that keeps a stable

STABLING *n* pl. **-S** accommodation for animals in a stable

STABLISH *v* **-ED, -ING, -ES** to establish

STABLY *adv* in a stable manner

STACCATO *n* pl. **-TOS** or **-TI** a musical passage marked by the short, clear-cut playing of tones

STACK *v* **-ED, -ING, -S** to pile

STACKER *n* pl. **-S** one that stacks

STACKUP *n* pl. **-S** an arrangement of circling airplanes over an airport waiting to land

STACTE *n* pl. **-S** a spice used by the ancient Jews in making incense

STADDLE *n* pl. **-S** a platform on which hay is stacked

STADE *n* pl. **-S** an ancient Greek unit of length

STADIA *n pl.* **-S** a method of surveying distances

STADIUM *n pl.* **-S** a structure in which athletic events are held

STAFF *v* **-ED, -ING, -S** to provide with a staff (a body of assistants)

STAFFER *n pl.* **-S** a member of a staff

STAFFING *n pl.* **-S** the providing with a staff

STAG *v* **STAGGED, STAGGING, STAGS** to attend a social function without a female companion

STAGE *v* **STAGED, STAGING, STAGES** to produce for public view

STAGEFUL *n pl.* **-S** as much or as many as a stage can hold

STAGER *n pl.* **-S** an experienced person

STAGETTE *n pl.* **-S** an all-female party for a woman about to be married

STAGEY *adj* **STAGIER, STAGIEST** stagy

STAGGARD *n pl.* **-S** a full-grown male red deer

STAGGART *n pl.* **-S** staggard

STAGGED past tense of stag

STAGGER *v* **-ED, -ING, -S** to walk or stand unsteadily

STAGGERY *adj* unsteady

STAGGIE *n pl.* **-S** a colt

STAGGING present participle of stag

STAGGY *adj* **-GIER, -GIEST** having the appearance of a mature male

STAGHORN *n pl.* **-S** a stag's horn used for a knife handle

STAGIER comparative of stagey and stagy

STAGIEST superlative of stagey and stagy

STAGILY *adv* in a stagy manner

STAGING *n pl.* **-S** a temporary platform

STAGNANT *adj* not moving or flowing

STAGNATE *v* **-NATED, -NATING, -NATES** to become stagnant

STAGY *adj* **STAGIER, STAGIEST** having a theatrical quality

STAID *adj* **STAIDER, STAIDEST** sober and sedate **STAIDLY** *adv*

STAIG *n pl.* **-S** a colt

STAIN *v* **-ED, -ING, -S** to discolor or dirty

STAINER *n pl.* **-S** one that stains

STAIR *n pl.* **-S** a rest for the foot used in going from one level to another

STAIRWAY *n pl.* **-WAYS** a flight of stairs

STAITHE *n pl.* **-S** a wharf equipped for transferring coal from railroad cars into ships

STAKE *v* **STAKED, STAKING, STAKES** to fasten with a stake (a pointed piece of wood or metal)

STAKEOUT *n pl.* **-S** a surveillance of an area especially by the police

STAKER *n pl.* **-S** one that marks off an area with stakes

STALAG *n pl.* **-S** a German prisoner-of-war camp

STALE *adj* **STALER, STALEST** not fresh **STALELY** *adv*

STALE *v* **STALED, STALING, STALES** to become stale

STALK *v* **-ED, -ING, -S** to pursue stealthily

STALKER *n pl.* **-S** one that stalks

STALKING *n pl.* **-S** the act of one that stalks

STALKY *adj* **STALKIER, STALKIEST** long and slender **STALKILY** *adv*

STALL *v* **-ED, -ING, -S** to stop the progress of

STALLION *n pl.* **-S** an uncastrated male horse

STALWART *n pl.* **-S** an unwavering partisan

STAMEN *n pl.* **-S** the pollen-bearing organ of flowering plants **STAMENED** *adj*

STAMINA *n pl.* **-S** endurance **STAMINAL** *adj*

STAMMEL *n pl.* **-S** a red color

STAMMER *v* **-ED, -ING, -S** to speak with involuntary breaks and pauses

STAMP *v* **-ED, -ING, -S** to bring the foot down heavily

STAMPEDE *v* **-PEDED, -PEDING, -PEDES** to cause to run away in headlong panic

STAMPER *n pl.* **-S** one that stamps

STANCE *n pl.* **-S** a manner of standing

STANCH *adj* **STANCHER, STANCHEST** staunch

STANCH *v* **-ED, -ING, -ES** to stop the flow of blood from

STANCHER *n pl.* **-S** one that stanches

STANCHLY *adv* in a stanch manner

STAND *v* **STOOD, STANDING, STANDS** to assume or maintain an upright position

STANDARD *n pl.* **-S** an established measure of comparison

STANDBY *n pl.* **-BYS** one that can be relied on

STANDEE   *n* pl. **-S** one who stands because of the lack of seats

STANDER   *n* pl. **-S** one that stands

STANDING   *n* pl. **-S** a position or condition in society

STANDISH   *n* pl. **-ES** a receptacle for pens and ink

STANDOFF   *n* pl. **-S** a tie or draw, as in a game

STANDOUT   *n* pl. **-S** one that shows marked superiority

STANDPAT   *adj* resisting or opposing change

STANDUP   *n* pl. **-S** a comic monologue by a performer alone on a stage

STANE   *v* **STANED, STANING, STANES** to stone

STANG   *v* **-ED, -ING, -S** to sting

STANHOPE   *n* pl. **-S** a light, open carriage

STANINE   *n* pl. **-S** one of the nine classes into which a set of scores are divided

STANING   present participle of stane

STANK   *n* pl. **-S** a pond

STANNARY   *n* pl. **-RIES** a tin-mining region

STANNIC   *adj* pertaining to tin

STANNITE   *n* pl. **-S** an ore of tin

STANNOUS   *adj* pertaining to tin

STANNUM   *n* pl. **-S** tin

STANOL   *n* pl. **-S** a fully saturated phytosterol

STANZA   *n* pl. **-S** a division of a poem **STANZAED, STANZAIC** *adj*

STAPEDES   pl. of stapes

STAPELIA   *n* pl. **-S** an African plant

STAPES   *n* pl. **-PEDES** a bone of the middle ear

STAPH   *n* pl. **-S** any of various spherical bacteria

STAPLE   *v* **-PLED, -PLING, -PLES** to fasten by means of a U-shaped metal loop

STAPLER   *n* pl. **-S** a stapling device

STAR   *v* **STARRED, STARRING, STARS** to shine as a star (a natural luminous body visible in the sky)

STARCH   *v* **-ED, -ING, -ES** to treat with starch (a solid carbohydrate)

STARCHER   *n* pl. **-S** one that starches

STARCHY   *adj* **STARCHIER, STARCHIEST** containing starch

STARDOM   *n* pl. **-S** the status of a preeminent performer

STARDUST   *n* pl. **-S** a romantic quality

STARE   *v* **STARED, STARING, STARES** to gaze fixedly

STARER   *n* pl. **-S** one that stares

STARETS   *n* pl. **STARTSY** a spiritual adviser in the Eastern Orthodox Church

STARFISH   *n* pl. **-ES** a star-shaped marine animal

STARGAZE   *v* **-GAZED, -GAZING, -GAZES** to gaze at the stars

STARING   present participle of stare

STARK   *adj* **STARKER, STARKEST** harsh in appearance **STARKLY** *adv*

STARKERS   *adj* naked

STARLESS   *adj* having no stars

STARLET   *n* pl. **-S** a small star

STARLIKE   *adj* resembling a star

STARLING   *n* pl. **-S** a European bird

STARLIT   *adj* lighted by the stars

STARNOSE   *n* pl. **-S** a burrowing mammal

STARRED   past tense of star

STARRING   present participle of star

STARRY   *adj* **-RIER, -RIEST** abounding with stars **STARRILY** *adv*

STARSHIP   *n* pl. **-S** a spaceship for interstellar travel

START   *v* **-ED, -ING, -S** to set out

STARTER   *n* pl. **-S** one that starts

STARTLE   *v* **-TLED, -TLING, -TLES** to frighten or surprise suddenly

STARTLER   *n* pl. **-S** one that startles

STARTSY   pl. of starets

STARTUP   *n* pl. **-S** the act of starting something

STARVE   *v* **STARVED, STARVING, STARVES** to die from lack of food

STARVER   *n* pl. **-S** one that starves

STARWORT   *n* pl. **-S** a flowering plant

STASES   pl. of stasis

STASH   *v* **-ED, -ING, -ES** to store in a secret place

STASIMON   *n* pl. **-MA** a choral ode in ancient Greek drama

STASIS   *n* pl. **STASES** a stoppage of the normal flow of bodily fluids

STAT   *n* pl. **-S** a statistic

STATABLE   *adj* capable of being stated

STATAL   *adj* pertaining to a national government

STATANT   *adj* standing with all feet on the ground — used of a heraldic animal

STATE   *v* **STATED, STATING, STATES** to set forth in words

STATEDLY   *adv* regularly

STATELET   *n* pl. **-S** a small state (a political community)

STATELY   *adj* **-LIER, -LIEST** dignified

STATER   *n* pl. **-S** one that states

STATIC   *n* pl. **-S** random noise produced in a radio or television receiver **STATICAL** *adj*

STATICE   *n* pl. **-S** a flowering plant

STATICKY   *adj* marked by static

STATIN   *n* pl. **-S** any of a class of drugs that reduce serum cholesterol levels

STATING   present participle of state

STATION   *v* **-ED, -ING, -S** to assign to a position

STATISM   *n* pl. **-S** a theory of government

STATIST   *n* pl. **-S** an adherent of statism

STATIVE   *n* pl. **-S** a verb that expresses a condition

STATOR   *n* pl. **-S** the part of a machine about which the rotor revolves

STATUARY   *n* pl. **-ARIES** a group of statues

STATUE   *n* pl. **-S** a three-dimensional work of art **STATUED** *adj*

STATURE   *n* pl. **-S** the natural height of a human or animal body **STATURED** *adj*

STATUS   *n* pl. **-ES** relative position

STATUSY   *adj* conferring prestige

STATUTE   *n* pl. **-S** a law enacted by the legislative branch of a government

STAUMREL   *n* pl. **-S** a dolt

STAUNCH   *adj* **STAUNCHER, STAUNCHEST** firm and dependable

STAUNCH   *v* **-ED, -ING, -ES** to stanch

STAVE   *v* **STAVED** or **STOVE, STAVING, STAVES** to drive or thrust away

STAW   a past tense of steal

STAY   *v* **STAYED** or **STAID, STAYING, STAYS** to continue in a place or condition

STAYER   *n* pl. **-S** one that stays

STAYSAIL   *n* pl. **-S** a type of sail

STEAD   *v* **-ED, -ING, -S** to be of advantage to

STEADIED   past tense of steady

STEADIER   *n* pl. **-S** one that steadies

STEADING   *n* pl. **-S** a small farm

STEADY   *adj* **STEADIER, STEADIEST** firm in position **STEADILY** *adv*

STEADY   *v* **STEADIED, STEADYING, STEADIES** to make steady

STEAK   *n* pl. **-S** a slice of meat

STEAL   *v* **STOLE** or **STAW, STOLEN, STEALING, STEALS** to take without right or permission

STEALAGE   *n* pl. **-S** theft

STEALER   *n* pl. **-S** one that steals

STEALING   *n* pl. **-S** the act of one that steals

STEALTH   *n* pl. **-S** stealthy procedure

STEALTHY   *adj* **STEALTHIER, STEALTHIEST** intended to escape observation

STEAM   *v* **-ED, -ING, -S** to expose to steam (water in the form of vapor)

STEAMER   *v* **-ED, -ING, -S** to travel by steamship

STEAMIE   *n* pl. **-S** a steamed hot dog

STEAMY   *adj* **STEAMIER, STEAMIEST** marked by steam **STEAMILY** *adv*

STEAPSIN   *n* pl. **-S** an enzyme

STEARATE   *n* pl. **-S** a chemical salt

STEARIN   *n* pl. **-S** the solid portion of a fat **STEARIC** *adj*

STEARINE   *n* pl. **-S** stearin

STEATITE   *n* pl. **-S** a variety of talc

STEDFAST   *adj* staunch

STEED   *n* pl. **-S** a horse

STEEK   *v* **-ED, -ING, -S** to shut

STEEL   *v* **-ED, -ING, -S** to cover with steel (a tough iron alloy)

STEELIE   *n* pl. **-S** a steel playing marble

STEELY   *adj* **STEELIER, STEELIEST** resembling steel

STEENBOK   *n* pl. **-S** an African antelope

STEEP   *adj* **STEEPER, STEEPEST** inclined sharply

STEEP   *v* **-ED, -ING, -S** to soak in a liquid

STEEPEN   *v* **-ED, -ING, -S** to make steep

STEEPER   *n* pl. **-S** one that steeps

STEEPISH   *adj* somewhat steep

STEEPLE   *n* pl. **-S** a tapering structure on a church tower

STEEPLE — v **-PLED, -PLING, -PLES** to place the fingers or hands in the form of a steeple

STEEPLY — adv in a steep manner

STEER — v **-ED, -ING, -S** to direct the course of

STEERAGE — n pl. **-S** the act of steering

STEERER — n pl. **-S** one that steers

STEERING — n pl. **-S** the act of directing the course of a vehicle or vessel

STEEVE — v **STEEVED, STEEVING, STEEVES** to stow in the hold of a ship

STEEVING — n pl. **-S** the angular elevation of a bowsprit from a ship's keel

STEGODON — n pl. **-S** an extinct elephant-like mammal

STEIN — n pl. **-S** a beer mug

STEINBOK — n pl. **-S** steenbok

STELA — n pl. **-LAE** or **-LAI** an inscribed slab used as a monument **STELAR, STELENE** adj

STELE — n pl. **-S** the central portion of vascular tissue in a plant stem **STELIC** adj

STELLA — n pl. **-S** a formerly used coin of the United States

STELLAR — adj pertaining to the stars

STELLATE — adj shaped like a star

STELLIFY — v **-FIED, -FYING, -FIES** to convert into a star

STEM — v **STEMMED, STEMMING, STEMS** to remove stems (ascending axes of a plant) from

STEMLESS — adj having no stem

STEMLIKE — adj resembling a stem

STEMMA — n pl. **-MAS** or **-MATA** a scroll recording the genealogy of a family in ancient Rome

STEMMED — past tense of stem

STEMMER — n pl. **-S** one that removes stems

STEMMERY — n pl. **-MERIES** a place where tobacco leaves are stripped

STEMMING — present participle of stem

STEMMY — adj **-MIER, -MIEST** abounding in stems

STEMSON — n pl. **-S** a supporting timber of a ship

STEMWARE — n pl. **-S** a type of glassware

STENCH — n pl. **-ES** a foul odor

STENCHY — adj **STENCHIER, STENCHIEST** having a stench

STENCIL — v **-CILED, -CILING, -CILS** or **-CILLED, -CILLING, -CILS** to mark by means of a perforated sheet of material

STENGAH — n pl. **-S** a mixed drink

STENO — n pl. **STENOS** a stenographer

STENOKY — n pl. **-KIES** the ability of an organism to live only under a narrow range of conditions

STENOSED — adj affected with stenosis

STENOSIS — n pl. **-NOSES** a narrowing of a bodily passage **STENOTIC** adj

STENT — n pl. **-S** a tubular device inserted into a blood vessel

STENTOR — n pl. **-S** a person having a very loud voice

STEP — v **STEPPED, STEPPING, STEPS** to move by lifting the foot and setting it down in another place

STEPDAD — n pl. **-S** a stepfather

STEPDAME — n pl. **-S** a stepmother

STEPLESS — adj lacking steps (structures for passing from one level to the next)

STEPLIKE — adj resembling a stair

STEPMOM — n pl. **-S** a stepmother

STEPPE — n pl. **-S** a vast treeless plain

STEPPED — past tense of step

STEPPER — n pl. **-S** one that steps

STEPPING — present participle of step

STEPSON — n pl. **-S** a son of one's spouse by a former marriage

STEPWISE — adj marked by a gradual progression

STERANE — n pl. **-S** a chemical compound

STERE — n pl. **-S** a unit of volume

STEREO — v **-ED, -ING, -S** to make a type of printing plate

STERIC — adj pertaining to the spatial relationships of atoms in a molecule

STERICAL — adj steric

STERIGMA — n pl. **-MAS** or **-MATA** a spore-bearing stalk of certain fungi

STERILE — adj incapable of producing offspring

STERLET — n pl. **-S** a small sturgeon

STERLING — n pl. **-S** British money

STERN — adj **STERNER, STERNEST** unyielding

STERN   *n* pl. **-S** the rear part of a ship **STERNED** *adj*

STERNA   a pl. of sternum

STERNAL   *adj* pertaining to the sternum

STERNITE   *n* pl. **-S** a somitic sclerite

STERNLY   *adv* in a stern manner

STERNSON   *n* pl. **-S** a reinforcing post of a ship

STERNUM   *n* pl. **-NUMS** or **-NA** a long, flat supporting bone of most vertebrates

STERNWAY   *n* pl. **-WAYS** the backward movement of a vessel

STEROID   *n* pl. **-S** a type of chemical compound

STEROL   *n* pl. **-S** a type of solid alcohol

STERTOR   *n* pl. **-S** a deep snoring sound

STET   *v* **STETTED, STETTING, STETS** to cancel a previously made printing correction

STEVIA   *n* pl. **-S** a South American herb with sweet-tasting leaves

STEW   *v* **-ED, -ING, -S** to cook by boiling slowly **STEWABLE** *adj*

STEWARD   *v* **-ED, -ING, -S** to manage

STEWBUM   *n* pl. **-S** a drunken bum (a vagrant)

STEWPAN   *n* pl. **-S** a pan used for stewing

STEWPOT   *n* pl. **-S** a large pot for stewing

STEWY   *adj* having the characteristics of a stew (food cooked by stewing)

STEY   *adj* steep

STHENIA   *n* pl. **-S** excessive energy **STHENIC** *adj*

STIBIAL   *adj* pertaining to stibium

STIBINE   *n* pl. **-S** a poisonous gas

STIBIUM   *n* pl. **-S** antimony

STIBNITE   *n* pl. **-S** an ore of antimony

STICH   *n* pl. **-S** a line of poetry **STICHIC** *adj*

STICK   *v* **-ED, -ING, -S** to support with slender pieces of wood

STICK   *v* **STUCK, STICKING, STICKS** to pierce with a pointed object

STICKER   *n* pl. **-S** an adhesive label **STICKERED** *adj*

STICKFUL   *n* pl. **-S** an amount of set type

STICKIE   *n* pl. **-S** sticky

STICKIER   comparative of sticky

STICKIES   pl. of sticky

STICKIEST   superlative of sticky

STICKILY   *adv* in a sticky manner

STICKIT   *adj* unsuccessful

STICKLE   *v* **-LED, -LING, -LES** to argue stubbornly

STICKLER   *n* pl. **-S** one that stickles

STICKMAN   *n* pl. **-MEN** one who supervises the play at a dice table

STICKOUT   *n* pl. **-S** one that is conspicuous

STICKPIN   *n* pl. **-S** a decorative tiepin

STICKUM   *n* pl. **-S** a substance that causes adhesion

STICKUP   *n* pl. **-S** a robbery at gunpoint

STICKY   *n* pl. **STICKIES** a slip of notepaper having an adhesive strip on the back

STICKY   *adj* **STICKIER, STICKIEST** tending to adhere

STICTION   *n* pl. **-S** the force required to begin to move a body that is in contact with another body

STIED   a past tense of sty

STIES   present 3d person sing. of sty

STIFF   *adj* **STIFFER, STIFFEST** difficult to bend or stretch

STIFF   *v* **-ED, -ING, -S** to cheat someone by not paying

STIFFEN   *v* **-ED, -ING, -S** to make stiff

STIFFISH   *adj* somewhat stiff

STIFFLY   *adv* in a stiff manner

STIFLE   *v* **-FLED, -FLING, -FLES** to smother

STIFLER   *n* pl. **-S** one that stifles

STIGMA   *n* pl. **-MAS** or **-MATA** a mark of disgrace **STIGMAL** *adj*

STILBENE   *n* pl. **-S** a chemical compound

STILBITE   *n* pl. **-S** a mineral

STILE   *n* pl. **-S** a series of steps for passing over a fence or wall

STILETTO   *v* **-ED, -ING, -S** or **-ES** to stab with a stiletto (a short dagger)

STILL   *adj* **STILLER, STILLEST** free from sound or motion

STILL   *v* **-ED, -ING, -S** to make still

STILLAGE   *n* pl. **-S** a low platform on which to keep goods off the floor

STILLMAN   *n* pl. **-MEN** one who operates a distillery

STILLSON   *n* pl. **-S** a large wrench (a tool for gripping and turning)

STILLY   *adj* **STILLIER, STILLIEST** still

STILT	*v* **-ED, -ING, -S** to raise on stilts (long, slender poles)	**STIRPS**	*n* pl. **STIRPES** a family or branch of a family
STIME	*n* pl. **-S** a glimpse	**STIRRED**	past tense of stir
STIMULUS	*n* pl. **-LI** something that causes a response	**STIRRER**	*n* pl. **-S** one that stirs
		STIRRING	*n* pl. **-S** a beginning of motion
STIMY	*v* **-MIED, -MYING, -MIES** to stymie	**STIRRUP**	*n* pl. **-S** a support for the foot of a horseman
STING	*v* **STUNG, STINGING, STINGS** to prick painfully	**STITCH**	*v* **-ED, -ING, -ES** to join by making in-and-out movements with a threaded needle
STINGE	*n* pl. **-S** a mean or stingy person		
STINGER	*n* pl. **-S** one that stings	**STITCHER**	*n* pl. **-S** one that stitches
STINGIER	comparative of stingy	**STITHY**	*v* **STITHIED, STITHYING, STITHIES** to forge on an anvil
STINGIEST	superlative of stingy		
STINGILY	*adv* in a stingy manner	**STIVER**	*n* pl. **-S** a formerly used Dutch coin
STINGO	*n* pl. **-GOS** a strong ale or beer	**STOA**	*n* pl. **STOAE** or **STOAI** or **STOAS** an ancient Greek covered walkway
STINGRAY	*n* pl. **-RAYS** a flat-bodied marine fish		
		STOAT	*n* pl. **-S** a weasel with a black-tipped tail
STINGY	*adj* **-GIER, -GIEST** unwilling to spend or give	**STOB**	*v* **STOBBED, STOBBING, STOBS** to stab
STINK	*v* **STANK** or **STUNK, STINKING, STINKS** to emit a foul odor		
		STOCCADO	*n* pl. **-DOS** a thrust with a rapier
STINKARD	*n* pl. **-S** a despicable person	**STOCCATA**	*n* pl. **-S** stoccado
STINKBUG	*n* pl. **-S** an insect that emits a foul odor	**STOCK**	*v* **-ED, -ING, -S** to keep for future sale or use
STINKER	*n* pl. **-S** one that stinks	**STOCKADE**	*v* **-ADED, -ADING, -ADES** to build a type of protective fence around
STINKO	*adj* drunk		
STINKPOT	*n* pl. **-S** a jar containing foul-smelling combustibles formerly used in warfare	**STOCKAGE**	*n* pl. **-S** the amount of supplies on hand
		STOCKCAR	*n* pl. **-S** a boxcar for carrying livestock
STINKY	*adj* **STINKIER, STINKIEST** emitting a foul odor	**STOCKER**	*n* pl. **-S** a young animal suitable for being fattened for market
STINT	*v* **-ED, -ING, -S** to limit		
STINTER	*n* pl. **-S** one that stints	**STOCKIER**	comparative of stocky
STIPE	*n* pl. **-S** a slender supporting part of a plant **STIPED** *adj*	**STOCKIEST**	superlative of stocky
		STOCKILY	*adv* in a stocky manner
STIPEL	*n* pl. **-S** a small stipule	**STOCKING**	*n* pl. **-S** a knitted or woven covering for the foot and leg
STIPEND	*n* pl. **-S** a fixed sum of money paid periodically		
STIPES	*n* pl. **STIPITES** a stipe	**STOCKISH**	*adj* stupid
STIPPLE	*v* **-PLED, -PLING, -PLES** to draw, paint, or engrave by means of dots or short touches	**STOCKIST**	*n* pl. **-S** one who stocks goods
		STOCKMAN	*n* pl. **-MEN** one who owns or raises livestock
STIPPLER	*n* pl. **-S** one that stipples	**STOCKPOT**	*n* pl. **-S** a pot in which broth is prepared
STIPULE	*n* pl. **-S** an appendage at the base of a leaf in certain plants **STIPULAR, STIPULED** *adj*		
		STOCKY	*adj* **STOCKIER, STOCKIEST** having a short, thick body
STIR	*v* **STIRRED, STIRRING, STIRS** to pass an implement through in circular motions	**STODGE**	*v* **STODGED, STODGING, STODGES** to stuff full with food
		STODGY	*adj* **STODGIER, STODGIEST** boring **STODGILY** *adv*
STIRK	*n* pl. **-S** a young cow		
STIRP	*n* pl. **-S** lineage	**STOGEY**	*n* pl. **-GEYS** stogy

STOGIE   *n* pl. **-S** stogy

STOGY   *n* pl. **-GIES** a long, slender cigar

STOIC   *n* pl. **-S** one who is indifferent to pleasure or pain **STOICAL** *adj*

STOICISM   *n* pl. **-S** indifference to pleasure or pain

STOKE   *v* **STOKED, STOKING, STOKES** to supply a furnace with fuel

STOKER   *n* pl. **-S** one that stokes

STOKESIA   *n* pl. **-S** a perennial herb

STOLE   *n* pl. **-S** a long wide scarf **STOLED** *adj*

STOLEN   past participle of steal

STOLID   *adj* **-IDER, -IDEST** showing little or no emotion **STOLIDLY** *adv*

STOLLEN   *n* pl. **-S** a sweet bread

STOLON   *n* pl. **-S** a type of plant stem **STOLONIC** *adj*

STOLPORT   *n* pl. **-S** an airport for aircraft needing comparatively short runways

STOMA   *n* pl. **-MAS** or **-MATA** a minute opening in the epidermis of a plant organ

STOMACH   *v* **-ED, -ING, -S** to tolerate

STOMACHY   *adj* paunchy

STOMAL   *adj* stomatal

STOMATA   a pl. of stoma

STOMATAL   *adj* pertaining to a stoma

STOMATE   *n* pl. **-S** a stoma

STOMATIC   *adj* pertaining to the mouth

STOMODEA   *n/pl* embryonic oral cavities

STOMP   *v* **-ED, -ING, -S** to tread heavily

STOMPER   *n* pl. **-S** one that stomps

STOMPY   *adj* **STOMPIER, STOMPIEST** conducive to stomping the feet

STONE   *v* **STONED, STONING, STONES** to pelt with stones (pieces of concreted earthy or mineral matter) **STONABLE** *adj*

STONECUT   *n* pl. **-S** a print made from an image engraved on a stone

STONEFLY   *n* pl. **-FLIES** a winged insect

STONER   *n* pl. **-S** one that stones

STONEY   *adj* **STONIER, STONIEST** stony

STONIER   comparative of stony

STONIEST   superlative of stony

STONILY   *adv* in a stony manner

STONING   present participle of stone

STONISH   *v* **-ED, -ING, -ES** to astonish

STONK   *v* **-ED, -ING, -S** to bombard with artillery fire

STONKER   *n* pl. **-S** something very large or impressive of its kind

STONKING   *adj* remarkable, exciting

STONY   *adj* **STONIER, STONIEST** abounding in stones

STOOD   past tense of stand

STOOGE   *v* **STOOGED, STOOGING, STOOGES** to act as a comedian's straight man

STOOK   *v* **-ED, -ING, -S** to stack (as bundles of grain) upright in a field for drying

STOOKER   *n* pl. **-S** one that stooks

STOOKING   *n* pl. **-S** the work of a stooker

STOOL   *v* **-ED, -ING, -S** to defecate

STOOLIE   *n* pl. **-S** an informer

STOOP   *v* **-ED, -ING, -S** to bend the body forward and down

STOOPER   *n* pl. **-S** one who stoops

STOP   *v* **STOPPED** or **STOPT, STOPPING, STOPS** to discontinue the progress or motion of

STOPBAND   *n* pl. **-S** a band of frequencies limited by a filter

STOPBANK   *n* pl. **-S** an embankment along a river

STOPCOCK   *n* pl. **-S** a type of faucet

STOPE   *v* **STOPED, STOPING, STOPES** to excavate in layers, as ore

STOPER   *n* pl. **-S** one that stopes

STOPGAP   *n* pl. **-S** a temporary substitute

STOPING   *n* pl. **-S** the process of excavating in layers

STOPOFF   *n* pl. **-S** a stopover

STOPOVER   *n* pl. **-S** a brief stop in the course of a journey

STOPPAGE   *n* pl. **-S** the act of stopping

STOPPED   a past tense of stop

STOPPER   *v* **-ED, -ING, -S** to plug

STOPPING   present participle of stop

STOPPLE   *v* **-PLED, -PLING, -PLES** to stopper

STOPT   a past tense of stop

STOPWORD   *n* pl. **-S** a frequently used word that is not searchable by search engines

STORABLE	*n* pl. **-S** something that can be stored
STORAGE	*n* pl. **-S** a place for storing
STORAX	*n* pl. **-ES** a fragrant resin
STORE	*v* **STORED, STORING, STORES** to put away for future use
STOREMAN	*n* pl. **-MEN** a man who looks after stored goods
STORER	*n* pl. **-S** one that stores
STOREY	*n* pl. **-REYS** a horizontal division of a building **STOREYED** *adj*
STORIED	past tense of story
STORIES	present 3d person sing. of story
STORING	present participle of store
STORK	*n* pl. **-S** a wading bird
STORM	*v* **-ED, -ING, -S** to blow violently
STORMY	*adj* **STORMIER, STORMIEST** storming **STORMILY** *adv*
STORY	*v* **-RIED, -RYING, -RIES** to relate as a story (an account of an event or series of events)
STOSS	*adj* facing the direction from which a glacier moves
STOT	*v* **STOTTED, STOTTING, STOTS** to bound with a stiff-legged gait
STOTIN	*n* pl. **-TINS** or **-TINOV** a former monetary unit of Slovenia
STOTINKA	*n* pl. **-KI** a monetary unit of Bulgaria
STOTT	*v* **-ED, -ING, -S** to stot
STOUND	*v* **-ED, -ING, -S** to ache
STOUP	*n* pl. **-S** a basin for holy water
STOUR	*n* pl. **-S** dust
STOURE	*n* pl. **-S** stour
STOURIE	*adj* stoury
STOURY	*adj* dusty
STOUT	*adj* **STOUTER, STOUTEST** fat
STOUT	*n* pl. **-S** a strong, dark ale
STOUTEN	*v* **-ED, -ING, -S** to make stout
STOUTISH	*adj* somewhat stout
STOUTLY	*adv* in a stout manner
STOVE	*v* **STOVED, STOVING, STOVES** to heat something in a heating apparatus
STOVER	*n* pl. **-S** coarse food for cattle
STOVETOP	*n* pl. **-S** the upper surface of a cooking apparatus
STOW	*v* **-ED, -ING, -S** to pack **STOWABLE** *adj*
STOWAGE	*n* pl. **-S** goods in storage
STOWAWAY	*n* pl. **-AWAYS** one who hides aboard a conveyance to obtain free passage
STOWP	*n* pl. **-S** stoup
STRADDLE	*v* **-DLED, -DLING, -DLES** to sit, stand, or walk with the legs wide apart
STRAFE	*v* **STRAFED, STRAFING, STRAFES** to attack with machine-gun fire from an airplane
STRAFER	*n* pl. **-S** one that strafes
STRAGGLE	*v* **-GLED, -GLING, -GLES** to stray
STRAGGLY	*adj* **-GLIER, -GLIEST** irregularly spread out
STRAIGHT	*adj* **STRAIGHTER, STRAIGHTEST** extending uniformly in one direction without bends or irregularities
STRAIGHT	*v* **-ED, -ING, -S** to make straight
STRAIN	*v* **-ED, -ING, -S** to exert to the utmost
STRAINER	*n* pl. **-S** a utensil used to separate liquids from solids
STRAIT	*adj* **STRAITER, STRAITEST** narrow **STRAITLY** *adv*
STRAIT	*n* pl. **-S** a narrow waterway connecting two larger bodies of water
STRAITEN	*v* **-ED, -ING, -S** to make strait
STRAKE	*n* pl. **-S** a line of planking extending along a ship's hull **STRAKED** *adj*
STRAMASH	*n* pl. **-ES** an uproar
STRAMONY	*n* pl. **-NIES** a poisonous weed
STRAND	*v* **-ED, -ING, -S** to leave in an unfavorable situation
STRANDER	*n* pl. **-S** a machine that twists fibers into rope
STRANG	*adj* strong
STRANGE	*n* pl. **-S** a fundamental quark
STRANGE	*adj* **STRANGER, STRANGEST** unusual or unfamiliar
STRANGER	*v* **-ED, -ING, -S** to estrange
STRANGLE	*v* **-GLED, -GLING, -GLES** to choke to death
STRAP	*v* **STRAPPED, STRAPPING, STRAPS** to fasten with a strap (a narrow strip of flexible material)
STRAPPER	*n* pl. **-S** one that straps
STRAPPY	*adj* **STRAPPIER, STRAPPIEST** having straps

STRASS   *n* pl. **-ES** a brilliant glass used in making imitation gems

STRATA   *n* pl. **-S** a dish of alternating layers of food

STRATAL   *adj* pertaining to a stratum

STRATEGY   *n* pl. **-GIES** a plan for obtaining a specific goal

STRATH   *n* pl. **-S** a wide river valley

STRATI   pl. of stratus

STRATIFY   *v* **-FIED, -FYING, -FIES** to form or arrange in layers

STRATOUS   *adj* stratal

STRATUM   *n* pl. **-TUMS** or **-TA** a layer of material

STRATUS   *n* pl. **-TI** or **-TUSES** a type of cloud

STRAVAGE   *v* **-VAGED, -VAGING, -VAGES** to stroll

STRAVAIG   *v* **-ED, -ING, -S** to stravage

STRAW   *v* **-ED, -ING, -S** to cover with straw (stalks of threshed grain)

STRAWHAT   *adj* pertaining to a summer theater situated in a resort area

STRAWY   *adj* **STRAWIER, STRAWIEST** resembling straw

STRAY   *v* **-ED, -ING, -S** to wander from the proper area or course

STRAYER   *n* pl. **-S** one that strays

STREAK   *v* **-ED, -ING, -S** to cover with streaks (long, narrow marks)

STREAKER   *n* pl. **-S** one that streaks

STREAKY   *adj* **STREAKIER, STREAKIEST** covered with streaks

STREAM   *v* **-ED, -ING, -S** to flow in a steady current

STREAMER   *n* pl. **-S** a long, narrow flag

STREAMY   *adj* **STREAMIER, STREAMIEST** streaming

STREEK   *v* **-ED, -ING, -S** to stretch

STREEKER   *n* pl. **-S** one that streeks

STREEL   *v* **-ED, -ING, -S** to saunter

STREET   *n* pl. **-S** a public thoroughfare **STREETED** *adj*

STRENGTH   *n* pl. **-S** capacity for exertion or endurance

STREP   *n* pl. **-S** any of various spherical or oval bacteria

STRESS   *v* **-ED, -ING, -ES** to place emphasis on

STRESSOR   *n* pl. **-S** a type of stimulus

STRETCH   *v* **-ED, -ING, -ES** to draw out or open to full length

STRETCHY   *adj* **STRETCHIER, STRETCHIEST** having a tendency to stretch

STRETTA   *n* pl. **-TAS** or **-TE** stretto

STRETTO   *n* pl. **-TOS** or **-TI** a concluding musical passage played at a faster tempo

STREUSEL   *n* pl. **-S** a topping for coffee cakes

STREW   *v* **STREWED, STREWN, STREWING, STREWS** to scatter about

STREWER   *n* pl. **-S** one that strews

STRIA   *n* pl. **STRIAE** a thin groove, stripe, or streak

STRIATE   *v* **-ATED, -ATING, -ATES** to mark with striae

STRIATUM   *n* pl. **-TA** a mass of nervous tissue within the brain **STRIATAL** *adj*

STRICK   *n* pl. **-S** a bunch of flax fibers

STRICKEN   *adj* strongly affected or afflicted

STRICKLE   *v* **-LED, -LING, -LES** to shape or smooth with a strickle (an instrument for leveling off grain)

STRICT   *adj* **STRICTER, STRICTEST** kept within narrow and specific limits **STRICTLY** *adv*

STRIDE   *v* **STRODE, STRIDDEN, STRIDING, STRIDES** to walk with long steps

STRIDENT   *adj* shrill

STRIDER   *n* pl. **-S** one that strides

STRIDING   present participle of stride

STRIDOR   *n* pl. **-S** a strident sound

STRIFE   *n* pl. **-S** bitter conflict or dissension

STRIGIL   *n* pl. **-S** a scraping instrument

STRIGOSE   *adj* covered with short, stiff hairs

STRIKE   *v* **STRUCK** or **STROOK, STRICKEN** or **STRUCKEN, STRIKING, STRIKES** to hit forcibly

STRIKER   *n* pl. **-S** one that strikes

STRIKING   *n* pl. **-S** the act of hitting something forcibly

STRINE   *n* pl. **-S** English as spoken in Australia

STRING   *v* **STRUNG** or **STRINGED, STRINGING, STRINGS** to provide with strings (slender cords)

STRINGER   *n* pl. **-S** one that strings

STRINGY   *adj* **STRINGIER, STRINGIEST** resembling a string or strings

STRIP	*v* **STRIPPED** or **STRIPT**, **STRIPPING**, **STRIPS** to remove the outer covering from
STRIPE	*v* **STRIPED**, **STRIPING**, **STRIPES** to mark with stripes (long, distinct bands)
STRIPER	*n* pl. **-S** a food and game fish
STRIPEY	*adj* **STRIPIER**, **STRIPIEST** stripy
STRIPIER	comparative of stripy
STRIPIEST	superlative of stripy
STRIPING	*n* pl. **-S** the stripes marked or painted on something
STRIPPED	a past tense of strip
STRIPPER	*n* pl. **-S** one that strips
STRIPPING	present participle of strip
STRIPT	a past tense of strip
STRIPY	*adj* **STRIPIER**, **STRIPIEST** marked with stripes
STRIVE	*v* **STROVE** or **STRIVED**, **STRIVEN**, **STRIVING**, **STRIVES** to exert much effort or energy
STRIVER	*n* pl. **-S** one that strives
STROBE	*v* **STROBED**, **STROBING**, **STROBES** to produce brief, high-intensity flashes of light
STROBIC	*adj* spinning
STROBIL	*n* pl. **-S** strobile
STROBILA	*n* pl. **-LAE** the entire body of a tapeworm
STROBILE	*n* pl. **-S** the conical, multiple fruit of certain trees
STROBILI	*n/pl* strobiles
STROBING	*n* pl. **-S** the process of producing high-intensity flashes of light
STRODE	a past tense of stride
STROKE	*v* **STROKED**, **STROKING**, **STROKES** to rub gently
STROKER	*n* pl. **-S** one that strokes
STROLL	*v* **-ED**, **-ING**, **-S** to walk in a leisurely manner
STROLLER	*n* pl. **-S** one that strolls
STROMA	*n* pl. **-MATA** the substance that forms the framework of an organ or cell **STROMAL** *adj*
STRONG	*adj* **STRONGER**, **STRONGEST** having great strength **STRONGLY** *adv*
STRONGYL	*n* pl. **-S** a parasitic worm
STRONTIA	*n* pl. **-S** a chemical compound **STRONTIC** *adj*
STROOK	a past tense of strike
STROP	*v* **STROPPED**, **STROPPING**, **STROPS** to sharpen on a strip of leather
STROPHE	*n* pl. **-S** a part of an ancient Greek choral ode **STROPHIC** *adj*
STROPPER	*n* pl. **-S** one that strops
STROPPY	*adj* **-PIER**, **-PIEST** unruly
STROUD	*n* pl. **-S** a coarse woolen blanket
STROVE	a past tense of strive
STROW	*v* **STROWED**, **STROWN**, **STROWING**, **STROWS** to strew
STROY	*v* **-ED**, **-ING**, **-S** to destroy
STROYER	*n* pl. **-S** one that stroys
STRUCK	a past tense of strike
STRUCKEN	a past participle of strike
STRUDEL	*n* pl. **-S** a type of pastry
STRUGGLE	*v* **-GLED**, **-GLING**, **-GLES** to make strenuous efforts against opposition
STRUM	*v* **STRUMMED**, **STRUMMING**, **STRUMS** to play a stringed instrument by running the fingers lightly across the strings
STRUMA	*n* pl. **-MAS** or **-MAE** scrofula
STRUMMER	*n* pl. **-S** one that strums
STRUMMING	present participle of strum
STRUMOSE	*adj* having a struma
STRUMOUS	*adj* having or pertaining to a struma
STRUMPET	*n* pl. **-S** a prostitute
STRUNG	a past tense of string
STRUNT	*v* **-ED**, **-ING**, **-S** to strut
STRUT	*v* **STRUTTED**, **STRUTTING**, **STRUTS** to walk with a pompous air
STRUTTER	*n* pl. **-S** one that struts
STUB	*v* **STUBBED**, **STUBBING**, **STUBS** to strike accidentally against a projecting object
STUBBIER	comparative of stubby
STUBBIEST	superlative of stubby
STUBBILY	*adv* in a stubby manner
STUBBING	present participle of stub
STUBBLE	*n* pl. **-S** a short, rough growth of beard **STUBBLED** *adj*
STUBBLY	*adj* **-BLIER**, **-BLIEST** covered with stubble
STUBBORN	*adj* **-BORNER**, **-BORNEST** unyielding

STUBBY	*adj* **-BIER, -BIEST** short and thick **STUBBILY** *adv*
STUBBY	*n* pl. **-BIES** a short squat bottle of beer
STUCCO	*v* **-ED, -ING, -ES** or **-S** to coat with a type of plaster
STUCCOER	*n* pl. **-S** one that stuccoes
STUCK	past tense of stick
STUD	*v* **STUDDED, STUDDING, STUDS** to set thickly with small projections
STUDBOOK	*n* pl. **-S** a record of the pedigree of purebred animals
STUDDIE	*n* pl. **-S** an anvil
STUDDING	*n* pl. **-S** the framework of a wall
STUDENT	*n* pl. **-S** a person formally engaged in learning
STUDFISH	*n* pl. **-ES** a freshwater fish
STUDIED	past tense of study
STUDIER	*n* pl. **-S** one that studies
STUDIES	present 3d person sing. of study
STUDIO	*n* pl. **-DIOS** an artist's workroom
STUDIOUS	*adj* given to study
STUDLY	*adj* **-LIER, -LIEST** muscular and attractive
STUDWORK	*n* pl. **-S** studding
STUDY	*v* **STUDIED, STUDYING, STUDIES** to apply the mind to the acquisition of knowledge
STUFF	*v* **-ED, -ING, -S** to fill or pack tightly
STUFFER	*n* pl. **-S** one that stuffs
STUFFING	*n* pl. **-S** material with which something is stuffed
STUFFY	*adj* **STUFFIER, STUFFIEST** poorly ventilated **STUFFILY** *adv*
STUIVER	*n* pl. **-S** stiver
STULL	*n* pl. **-S** a supporting timber in a mine
STULTIFY	*v* **-FIED, -FYING, -FIES** to cause to appear absurd
STUM	*v* **STUMMED, STUMMING, STUMS** to increase the fermentation of by adding grape juice
STUMBLE	*v* **-BLED, -BLING, -BLES** to miss one's step in walking or running
STUMBLER	*n* pl. **-S** one that stumbles
STUMP	*v* **-ED, -ING, -S** to baffle
STUMPAGE	*n* pl. **-S** uncut marketable timber
STUMPER	*n* pl. **-S** a baffling question
STUMPY	*adj* **STUMPIER, STUMPIEST** short and thick **STUMPILY** *adv*
STUN	*v* **STUNNED, STUNNING, STUNS** to render senseless or incapable of action
STUNG	past tense of sting
STUNK	a past tense of stink
STUNNER	*n* pl. **-S** one that stuns
STUNSAIL	*n* pl. **-S** a type of sail
STUNT	*v* **-ED, -ING, -S** to hinder the normal growth of
STUNTMAN	*n* pl. **-MEN** a person who substitutes for an actor in scenes involving dangerous activities
STUPA	*n* pl. **-S** a Buddhist shrine
STUPE	*n* pl. **-S** a medicated cloth to be applied to a wound
STUPEFY	*v* **-FIED, -FYING, -FIES** to dull the senses of
STUPID	*adj* **-PIDER, -PIDEST** mentally slow **STUPIDLY** *adv*
STUPID	*n* pl. **-S** a stupid person
STUPOR	*n* pl. **-S** a state of reduced sensibility
STURDY	*adj* **-DIER, -DIEST** strong and durable **STURDILY** *adv*
STURDY	*n* pl. **-DIES** a disease of sheep **STURDIED** *adj*
STURGEON	*n* pl. **-S** an edible fish
STURT	*n* pl. **-S** contention
STUTTER	*v* **-ED, -ING, -S** to speak with spasmodic repetition
STY	*v* **STIED** or **STYED, STYING, STIES** to keep in a pigpen
STYE	*n* pl. **-S** an inflamed swelling of the eyelid
STYGIAN	*adj* gloomy
STYLAR	*adj* pertaining to a stylus
STYLATE	*adj* bearing a stylet
STYLE	*v* **STYLED, STYLING, STYLES** to name
STYLER	*n* pl. **-S** one that styles
STYLET	*n* pl. **-S** a small, stiff organ or appendage of certain animals
STYLI	a pl. of stylus
STYLING	*n* pl. **-S** the way in which something is styled
STYLISE	*v* **-ISED, -ISING, -ISES** to stylize
STYLISER	*n* pl. **-S** one that stylises
STYLISH	*adj* fashionable

STYLIST   *n* pl. **-S** one who is a master of a literary or rhetorical style

STYLITE   *n* pl. **-S** an early Christian ascetic **STYLITIC** *adj*

STYLIZE   *v* **-IZED, -IZING, -IZES** to make conventional

STYLIZER   *n* pl. **-S** one that stylizes

STYLOID   *n* pl. **-S** a slender projection of bone

STYLOPID   *n* pl. **-S** a stylops

STYLOPS   *n* pl. **STYLOPS** an insect that is a parasite of other insects

STYLUS   *n* pl. **-LUSES** or **-LI** a pointed instrument for writing, marking, or engraving

STYMIE   *v* **-MIED, -MIEING, -MIES** to thwart

STYMY   *v* **-MIED, -MYING, -MIES** to stymie

STYPSIS   *n* pl. **-SISES** the use of a styptic

STYPTIC   *n* pl. **-S** a substance used to check bleeding

STYRAX   *n* pl. **-ES** storax

STYRENE   *n* pl. **-S** a liquid hydrocarbon

SUABLE   *adj* capable of being sued **SUABLY** *adv*

SUASION   *n* pl. **-S** persuasion **SUASIVE, SUASORY** *adj*

SUAVE   *adj* **SUAVER, SUAVEST** smoothly affable and polite **SUAVELY** *adv*

SUAVITY   *n* pl. **-TIES** the state of being suave

SUB   *v* **SUBBED, SUBBING, SUBS** to act as a substitute

SUBA   *n* pl. **-S** subah

SUBABBOT   *n* pl. **-S** a subordinate abbot

SUBACID   *adj* slightly sour

SUBACRID   *adj* somewhat acrid

SUBACUTE   *adj* somewhat acute

SUBADAR   *n* pl. **-S** subahdar

SUBADULT   *n* pl. **-S** an individual approaching adulthood

SUBAGENT   *n* pl. **-S** a subordinate agent

SUBAH   *n* pl. **-S** a province of India

SUBAHDAR   *n* pl. **-S** a governor of a subah

SUBALAR   *adj* situated under the wings

SUBAREA   *n* pl. **-S** a subdivision of an area

SUBARID   *adj* somewhat arid

SUBATOM   *n* pl. **-S** a component of an atom

SUBAURAL   *adj* scarcely hearable

SUBAXIAL   *adj* somewhat axial

SUBBASE   *n* pl. **-S** the lowest part of a base

SUBBASIN   *n* pl. **-S** a section of an area drained by a river

SUBBASS   *n* pl. **-ES** a pedal stop producing the lowest tones of an organ

SUBBED   past tense of sub

SUBBING   *n* pl. **-S** a thin coating on the support of a photographic film

SUBBLOCK   *n* pl. **-S** a subdivision of a block

SUBBREED   *n* pl. **-S** a distinguishable strain within a breed

SUBCASTE   *n* pl. **-S** a subdivision of a caste

SUBCAUSE   *n* pl. **-S** a subordinate cause

SUBCELL   *n* pl. **-S** a subdivision of a cell

SUBCHIEF   *n* pl. **-S** a subordinate chief

SUBCLAIM   *n* pl. **-S** a subordinate claim

SUBCLAN   *n* pl. **-S** a subdivision of a clan

SUBCLASS   *v* **-ED, -ING, -ES** to place in a subdivision of a class

SUBCLERK   *n* pl. **-S** a subordinate clerk

SUBCODE   *n* pl. **-S** a subdivision of a code

SUBCOOL   *v* **-ED, -ING, -S** to cool below the freezing point without solidification

SUBCULT   *n* pl. **-S** a subdivision of a cult

SUBCUTIS   *n* pl. **-CUTISES** or **-CUTES** the deeper part of the dermis

SUBDEAN   *n* pl. **-S** a subordinate dean

SUBDEB   *n* pl. **-S** a girl the year before she becomes a debutante

SUBDEPOT   *n* pl. **-S** a military depot that operates under the jurisdiction of another depot

SUBDUAL   *n* pl. **-S** the act of subduing

SUBDUCE   *v* **-DUCED, -DUCING, -DUCES** to take away

SUBDUCT   *v* **-ED, -ING, -S** to subduce

SUBDUE   *v* **-DUED, -DUING, -DUES** to bring under control

SUBDUER   *n* pl. **-S** one that subdues

SUBDURAL   *adj* situated under the dura mater

SUBDWARF   *n* pl. **-S** a small star of relatively low luminosity

SUBECHO   *n* pl. **-ECHOES** an inferior echo

SUBEDIT   *v* **-ED, -ING, -S** to act as the assistant editor of

SUBENTRY   *n* pl. **-TRIES** an entry made under a more general entry

SUBEPOCH   *n* pl. **-S** a subdivision of an epoch

SUBER   *n* pl. **-S** phellem

SUBERECT *adj* nearly erect

SUBERIC *adj* pertaining to cork

SUBERIN *n* pl. **-S** a substance found in cork cells

SUBERISE *v* **-ISED, -ISING, -ISES** to suberize

SUBERIZE *v* **-IZED, -IZING, -IZES** to convert into cork tissue

SUBEROSE *adj* corky

SUBEROUS *adj* suberose

SUBFIELD *n* pl. **-S** a subset of a mathematical field that is itself a field

SUBFILE *n* pl. **-S** a subdivision of a file

SUBFIX *n* pl. **-ES** a distinguishing symbol or letter written below another character

SUBFLOOR *n* pl. **-S** a rough floor laid as a base for a finished floor

SUBFLUID *adj* somewhat fluid

SUBFRAME *n* pl. **-S** a frame for the attachment of a finish frame

SUBFUSC *n* pl. **-S** dark dull clothing

SUBGENRE *n* pl. **-S** a subdivision of a genre

SUBGENUS *n* pl. **-GENUSES** or **-GENERA** a subdivision of a genus

SUBGOAL *n* pl. **-S** a subordinate goal

SUBGRADE *n* pl. **-S** a surface on which a pavement is placed

SUBGRAPH *n* pl. **-S** a graph contained within a larger graph

SUBGROUP *v* **-ED, -ING, -S** to divide into smaller groups

SUBGUM *n* pl. **-S** a Chinese dish of mixed vegetables

SUBHEAD *n* pl. **-S** the heading of a subdivision

SUBHUMAN *n* pl. **-S** one that is less than human

SUBHUMID *adj* somewhat humid

SUBIDEA *n* pl. **-S** an inferior idea

SUBINDEX *n* pl. **-DEXES** or **-DICES** a subfix

SUBITEM *n* pl. **-S** an item that forms a subdivision of a larger topic

SUBITO *adv* quickly — used as a musical direction

SUBJECT *v* **-ED, -ING, -S** to cause to experience

SUBJOIN *v* **-ED, -ING, -S** to add at the end

SUBLATE *v* **-LATED, -LATING, -LATES** to cancel

SUBLEASE *v* **-LEASED, -LEASING, -LEASES** to sublet

SUBLET *v* **-LET, -LETTING, -LETS** to rent leased property to another

SUBLEVEL *n* pl. **-S** a lower level

SUBLIME *adj* **-LIMER, -LIMEST** of elevated or noble quality

SUBLIME *v* **-LIMED, -LIMING, -LIMES** to make sublime

SUBLIMER *n* pl. **-S** one that sublimes

SUBLIMEST superlative of sublime

SUBLIMIT *n* pl. **-S** a limit within a limit

SUBLINE *n* pl. **-S** an inbred line within a strain

SUBLOT *n* pl. **-S** a subdivision of a lot

SUBLUNAR *adj* pertaining to the earth

SUBMENU *n* pl. **-S** a secondary list of options for a computer

SUBMERGE *v* **-MERGED, -MERGING, -MERGES** to place below the surface of a liquid

SUBMERSE *v* **-MERSED, -MERSING, -MERSES** to submerge

SUBMISS *adj* inclined to submit

SUBMIT *v* **-MITTED, -MITTING, -MITS** to yield to the power of another

SUBNASAL *adj* situated under the nose

SUBNET *n* pl. **-S** a system of interconnections within a communications system

SUBNICHE *n* pl. **-S** a subdivision of a habitat

SUBNODAL *adj* situated under a node

SUBOCEAN *adj* existing below the floor of the ocean

SUBOPTIC *adj* situated under the eyes

SUBORAL *adj* situated under the mouth

SUBORDER *n* pl. **-S** a category of related families within an order

SUBORN *v* **-ED, -ING, -S** to induce to commit perjury

SUBORNER *n* pl. **-S** one that suborns

SUBOVAL *adj* nearly oval

SUBOVATE *adj* nearly ovate

SUBOXIDE *n* pl. **-S** an oxide containing relatively little oxygen

SUBPANEL *n* pl. **-S** a subdivision of a panel

SUBPAR *adj* below par

SUBPART *n* pl. **-S** a subdivision of a part

SUBPENA *v* **-ED, -ING, -S** to subpoena

SUBPHASE *n* pl. **-S** a subdivision of a phase

SUBPHYLA *n/pl* divisions within a phylum

SUBPLOT *n* pl. **-S** a secondary literary plot

SUBPOENA *v* **-ED, -ING, -S** to summon with a type of judicial writ

SUBPOLAR *adj* situated just outside the polar circles

SUBPRIME *adj* denoting a loan that is at a higher interest rate than a prime rate

SUBPUBIC *adj* situated under the pubis

SUBRACE *n* pl. **-S** a subdivision of a race

SUBRENT *n* pl. **-S** rent from a subtenant

SUBRING *n* pl. **-S** a subset of a mathematical ring that is itself a ring

SUBRULE *n* pl. **-S** a subordinate rule

SUBSALE *n* pl. **-S** a resale of purchased goods

SUBSCALE *n* pl. **-S** a subdivision of a scale

SUBSEA *adj* situated below the surface of the sea

SUBSECT *n* pl. **-S** a sect directly derived from another

SUBSENSE *n* pl. **-S** a subdivision of a sense

SUBSERE *n* pl. **-S** a type of ecological succession

SUBSERVE *v* **-SERVED, -SERVING, -SERVES** to serve to promote

SUBSET *n* pl. **-S** a mathematical set contained within a larger set

SUBSHAFT *n* pl. **-S** a shaft that is beneath another shaft

SUBSHELL *n* pl. **-S** one of the orbitals making up an electron shell of an atom

SUBSHRUB *n* pl. **-S** a low shrub

SUBSIDE *v* **-SIDED, -SIDING, -SIDES** to sink to a lower or normal level

SUBSIDER *n* pl. **-S** one that subsides

SUBSIDY *n* pl. **-DIES** a grant or contribution of money

SUBSIST *v* **-ED, -ING, -S** to continue to exist

SUBSITE *n* pl. **-S** a subdivision of a site

SUBSKILL *n* pl. **-S** a subordinate skill

SUBSOIL *v* **-ED, -ING, -S** to plow so as to turn up the subsoil (the layer of earth beneath the surface soil)

SUBSOLAR *adj* situated directly beneath the sun

SUBSONIC *adj* moving at a speed less than that of sound

SUBSPACE *n* pl. **-S** a subset of a mathematical space

SUBSTAGE *n* pl. **-S** a part of a microscope for supporting accessories

SUBSTATE *n* pl. **-S** a subdivision of a state

SUBSUME *v* **-SUMED, -SUMING, -SUMES** to include within a larger group

SUBTASK *n* pl. **-S** a subordinate task

SUBTAXON *n* pl. **-TAXONS** or **-TAXA** a subdivision of a taxon

SUBTEEN *n* pl. **-S** a person approaching the teenage years

SUBTEND *v* **-ED, -ING, -S** to extend under or opposite to

SUBTEST *n* pl. **-S** a subdivision of a test

SUBTEXT *n* pl. **-S** written or printed matter under a more general text

SUBTHEME *n* pl. **-S** a subordinate theme

SUBTILE *adj* **-TILER, -TILEST** subtle

SUBTILIN *n* pl. **-S** an antibiotic

SUBTILTY *n* pl. **-TIES** subtlety

SUBTITLE *v* **-TLED, -TLING, -TLES** to give a secondary title to

SUBTLE *adj* **-TLER, -TLEST** so slight as to be difficult to detect **SUBTLY** *adv*

SUBTLETY *n* pl. **-TIES** the state of being subtle

SUBTONE *n* pl. **-S** a low or subdued tone

SUBTONIC *n* pl. **-S** a type of musical tone

SUBTOPIA *n* pl. **-S** the suburbs of a city

SUBTOPIC *n* pl. **-S** a secondary topic

SUBTOTAL *v* **-TALED, -TALING, -TALS** or **-TALLED, -TALLING, -TALS** to total a portion of

SUBTRACT *v* **-ED, -ING, -S** to take away

SUBTRADE *n* pl. **-S** a specialist hired by a general contractor

SUBTREND *n* pl. **-S** a subordinate trend

SUBTRIBE *n* pl. **-S** a subdivision of a tribe

SUBTUNIC *n* pl. **-S** a tunic worn under another tunic

SUBTYPE *n* pl. **-S** a type that is subordinate to or included in another type

SUBULATE *adj* slender and tapering to a point

SUBUNIT *n* pl. **-S** a unit that is a part of a larger unit

SUBURB *n* pl. **-S** a residential area adjacent to a city **SUBURBED** *adj*

SUBURBAN *n* pl. **-S** one who lives in a suburb

SUBURBIA *n* pl. **-S** the suburbs of a city

SUBVENE *v* **-VENED, -VENING, -VENES** to arrive or occur as a support or relief

SUBVERT *v* **-ED, -ING, -S** to destroy completely

SUBVICAR *n* pl. **-S** a subordinate vicar

SUBVIRAL *adj* pertaining to a part of a virus

SUBVIRUS *n* pl. **-ES** a viral protein smaller than a virus

SUBVOCAL *adj* mentally formulated as words

SUBWAY *v* **-ED, -ING, -S** to travel by an underground railroad

SUBWORLD *n* pl. **-S** a subdivision of a sphere of interest or activity

SUBZERO *adj* registering less than zero

SUBZONE *n* pl. **-S** a subdivision of a zone

SUCCAH *n* pl. **-CAHS** or **-COTH** sukkah

SUCCEED *v* **-ED, -ING, -S** to accomplish something desired or intended

SUCCESS *n* pl. **-ES** the attainment of something desired or intended

SUCCINCT *adj* **-CINCTER, -CINCTEST** clearly expressed in few words

SUCCINIC *adj* pertaining to amber

SUCCINYL *n* pl. **-S** a univalent radical

SUCCOR *v* **-ED, -ING, -S** to go to the aid of

SUCCORER *n* pl. **-S** one that succors

SUCCORY *n* pl. **-RIES** chicory

SUCCOTH a pl. of succah

SUCCOUR *v* **-ED, -ING, -S** to succor

SUCCUBA *n* pl. **-BAS** or **-BAE** a succubus

SUCCUBUS *n* pl. **-BUSES** or **-BI** a female demon

SUCCUMB *v* **-ED, -ING, -S** to yield to superior force

SUCCUSS *v* **-ED, -ING, -ES** to shake violently

SUCH *adj* of that kind

SUCHLIKE *n* pl **-S** a thing of such a kind

SUCHNESS *n* pl. **-ES** essential or characteristic quality

SUCK *v* **-ED, -ING, -S** to draw in by establishing a partial vacuum

SUCKER *v* **-ED, -ING, -S** to strip of lower shoots or branches

SUCKFISH *n* pl. **-ES** a remora

SUCKLE *v* **-LED, -LING, -LES** to give milk to from the breast

SUCKLER *n* pl. **-S** one that suckles

SUCKLESS *adj* having no juice

SUCKLING *n* pl. **-S** an unweaned mammal

SUCKY *adj* **SUCKIER, SUCKIEST** extremely objectionable

SUCRASE *n* pl. **-S** an enzyme

SUCRE *n* pl. **-S** a former monetary unit of Ecuador

SUCROSE *n* pl. **-S** a type of sugar

SUCTION *v* **-ED, -ING, -S** to remove by the process of sucking

SUDARIUM *n* pl. **-IA** a cloth for wiping the face

SUDARY *n* pl. **-RIES** sudarium

SUDATION *n* pl. **-S** excessive sweating

SUDATORY *n* pl. **-RIES** a hot-air bath for inducing sweating

SUDD *n* pl. **-S** a floating mass of vegetation

SUDDEN *adj* happening quickly and without warning **SUDDENLY** *adv*

SUDDEN *n* pl. **-S** a sudden occurrence

SUDOKU *n* pl. **-S** a puzzle involving the numbers 1 through 9

SUDOR *n* pl. **-S** sweat **SUDORAL** *adj*

SUDS *v* **-ED, -ING, -ES** to wash in soapy water

SUDSER *n* pl. **-S** a soap opera

SUDSLESS *adj* having no suds

SUDSY *adj* **SUDSIER, SUDSIEST** foamy

SUE *v* **SUED, SUING, SUES** to institute legal proceedings against

SUEDE *v* **SUEDED, SUEDING, SUEDES** to finish leather with a soft, napped surface

SUER *n* pl. **-S** one that sues

SUET *n* pl. **-S** the hard, fatty tissue around the kidneys of cattle and sheep **SUETY** *adj*

SUETE *n* pl. **-S** a southeasterly wind in areas of Cape Breton Island

SUFFARI *n* pl. **-S** a safari

SUFFER *v* **-ED, -ING, -S** to feel pain or distress

SUFFERER *n* pl. **-S** one that suffers

SUFFICE *v* **-FICED, -FICING, -FICES** to be adequate

SUFFICER *n* pl. **-S** one that suffices

SUFFIX *v* **-ED, -ING, -ES** to add as a suffix (a form affixed to the end of a root word)

SUFFIXAL *adj* pertaining to or being a suffix

SUFFLATE *v* **-FLATED, -FLATING, -FLATES** to inflate

SUFFRAGE *n* pl. **-S** the right to vote

SUFFUSE *v* **-FUSED, -FUSING, -FUSES** to spread through or over

SUGAR *v* **-ED, -ING, -S** to cover with sugar (a sweet carbohydrate)

SUGARER *n* pl. **-S** one that makes sugar

SUGARING *n* pl. **-S** the process of boiling down maple sap into syrup

SUGARY *adj* **-ARIER, -ARIEST** containing or resembling sugar

SUGGEST *v* **-ED, -ING, -S** to bring or put forward for consideration

SUGH *v* **-ED, -ING, -S** to sough

SUICIDAL *adj* self-destructive

SUICIDE *v* **-CIDED, -CIDING, -CIDES** to kill oneself intentionally

SUING present participle of sue

SUINT *n* pl. **-S** a natural grease found in the wool of sheep

SUIT *v* **-ED, -ING, -S** to be appropriate to

SUITABLE *adj* appropriate **SUITABLY** *adv*

SUITCASE *n* pl. **-S** a flat, rectangular piece of luggage

SUITE *n* pl. **-S** a series of things forming a unit

SUITER *n* pl. **-S** a suitcase holding a specified number of suits (sets of garments)

SUITING *n* pl. **-S** fabric for making suits

SUITLIKE *adj* resembling a suit (a set of garments)

SUITOR *n* pl. **-S** one that is courting a woman

SUK *n* pl. **-S** souk

SUKH *n* pl. **-S** a souk

SUKIYAKI *n* pl. **-S** a Japanese dish

SUKKAH *n* pl. **-KAHS** or **-KOTH** or **-KOT** a temporary shelter in which meals are eaten during a Jewish festival

SULCATE *adj* having long, narrow furrows

SULCATED *adj* sulcate

SULCUS *n* pl. **-CI** a narrow furrow **SULCAL** *adj*

SULDAN *n* pl. **-S** soldan

SULFA *n* pl. **-S** a bacteria-inhibiting drug

SULFATE *v* **-FATED, -FATING, -FATES** to treat with sulfuric acid

SULFID *n* pl. **-S** sulfide

SULFIDE *n* pl. **-S** a sulfur compound

SULFINYL *n* pl. **-S** a bivalent radical

SULFITE *n* pl. **-S** a chemical salt **SULFITIC** *adj*

SULFO *adj* sulfonic

SULFONE *n* pl. **-S** a sulfur compound

SULFONIC *adj* containing a certain univalent radical

SULFONYL *n* pl. **-S** a bivalent radical

SULFUR *v* **-ED, -ING, -S** to treat with sulfur (a nonmetallic element)

SULFURET *v* **-RETED, -RETING, -RETS** or **-RETTED, -RETTING, -RETS** to treat with sulfur

SULFURIC *adj* pertaining to sulfur

SULFURY *adj* resembling sulfur

SULFURYL *n* pl. **-S** sulfonyl

SULK *v* **-ED, -ING, -S** to be sulky

SULKER *n* pl. **-S** one that sulks

SULKY *adj* **SULKIER, SULKIEST** sullenly aloof or withdrawn **SULKILY** *adv*

SULKY *n* pl. **SULKIES** a light horse-drawn vehicle

SULLAGE *n* pl. **-S** sewage

SULLEN *adj* **-LENER, -LENEST** showing a brooding ill humor or resentment **SULLENLY** *adv*

SULLY *v* **-LIED, -LYING, -LIES** to soil

SULPHA *n* pl. **-S** sulfa

SULPHATE *v* **-PHATED, -PHATING, -PHATES** to sulfate

SULPHID *n* pl. **-S** sulfide

SULPHIDE *n* pl. **-S** sulfide

SULPHITE *n* pl. **-S** sulfite

SULPHONE *n* pl. **-S** sulfone

SULPHUR *v* **-ED, -ING, -S** to sulfur

SULPHURY *adj* sulfury

SULTAN *n* pl. **-S** the ruler of a Muslim country **SULTANIC** *adj*

SULTANA *n* pl. **-S** a sultan's wife

SULTRY *adj* **-TRIER, -TRIEST** very hot and humid **SULTRILY** *adv*

SULU *n* pl. **-S** a Melanesian skirt

SUM *v* **SUMMED, SUMMING, SUMS** to add into one total

SUM *n* pl. **SUMY** a monetary unit of Uzbekistan

SUMAC *n* pl. **-S** a flowering tree or shrub

SUMACH *n* pl. **-S** sumac

SUMI *n* pl. **-S** a type of black Japanese ink

SUMLESS *adj* too large for calculation

SUMMA *n* pl. **-MAS** or **-MAE** a comprehensive work on a topic

SUMMABLE *adj* capable of being summed

SUMMAND *n* pl. **-S** an addend

SUMMARY *n* pl. **-RIES** a short restatement

SUMMATE *v* **-MATED, -MATING, -MATES** to sum

SUMMED past tense of sum

SUMMER *v* **-ED, -ING, -S** to pass the summer (the warmest season of the year)

SUMMERLY *adj* summery

SUMMERY *adj* **-MERIER, -MERIEST** characteristic of summer

SUMMING present participle of sum

SUMMIT *v* **-ED, -ING, -S** to participate in a highest-level conference

SUMMITAL *adj* pertaining to the highest point

SUMMITRY *n* pl. **-RIES** the use of conferences between chiefs of state for international negotiation

SUMMON *v* **-ED, -ING, -S** to order to appear

SUMMONER *n* pl. **-S** one that summons

SUMMONS *v* **-ED, -ING, -ES** to summon with a court order

SUMO *n* pl. **-MOS** a Japanese form of wrestling

SUMOIST *n* pl. **-S** a sumo wrestler

SUMP *n* pl. **-S** a low area serving as a drain or receptacle for liquids

SUMPTER *n* pl. **-S** a pack animal

SUMPWEED *n* pl. **-S** a marsh plant

SUN *v* **SUNNED, SUNNING, SUNS** to expose to the sun (the star around which the earth revolves)

SUNBACK *adj* cut low to expose the back to sunlight

SUNBAKED *adj* baked by the sun

SUNBATH *n* pl. **-S** an exposure to sunlight

SUNBATHE *v* **-BATHED, -BATHING, -BATHES** to take a sunbath

SUNBEAM *n* pl. **-S** a beam of sunlight **SUNBEAMY** *adj*

SUNBED *n* pl. **-S** a device for acquiring tan skin artificially

SUNBELT *n* pl. **-S** the southern and southwestern states of the U.S.

SUNBIRD *n* pl. **-S** a tropical bird

SUNBLOCK *n* pl. **-S** a preparation to protect the skin from the sun's rays

SUNBOW *n* pl. **-S** an arc of spectral colors formed by the sun shining through a mist

SUNBURN *v* **-BURNED** or **-BURNT, -BURNING, -BURNS** to burn or discolor from exposure to the sun

SUNBURST *n* pl. **-S** a burst of sunlight

SUNCARE *n* pl. **-S** protection of the skin from damage by the sun

SUNCHOKE *n* pl. **-S** a type of sunflower

SUNDAE *n* pl. **-S** a dish of ice cream served with a topping

SUNDECK *n* pl. **-S** a deck that is exposed to the sun

SUNDER *v* **-ED, -ING, -S** to break apart

SUNDERER *n* pl. **-S** one that sunders

SUNDEW *n* pl. **-S** a marsh plant

SUNDIAL *n* pl. **-S** a type of time-telling device

SUNDOG *n* pl. **-S** a small rainbow

SUNDOWN *v* **-ED, -ING, -S** to experience nighttime confusion

SUNDRESS *n* pl. **-ES** a dress with an abbreviated bodice

SUNDRIES *n/pl* miscellaneous items

SUNDROPS *n* pl. **SUNDROPS** a flowering plant

SUNDRY *adj* miscellaneous **SUNDRILY** *adv*

SUNFAST *adj* resistant to fading by the sun

SUNFISH *n* pl. **-ES** a marine fish

SUNG past participle of sing

SUNGLASS *n* pl. **-ES** a lens for concentrating the sun's rays in order to produce heat

SUNGLOW *n* pl. **-S** a glow in the sky caused by the sun

SUNK a past participle of sink

SUNKEN a past participle of sink

SUNKER *n* pl. **-S** a ridge of rock near the surface of the sea

SUNKET *n* pl. **-S** a tidbit

SUNLAMP *n* pl. **-S** a lamp that radiates ultraviolet rays

SUNLAND *n* pl. **-S** an area marked by a great amount of sunshine

SUNLESS *adj* having no sunlight

SUNLIGHT *n* pl. **-S** the light of the sun

SUNLIKE *adj* resembling the sun

SUNLIT	*adj* lighted by the sun
SUNN	*n* pl. **-S** an East Indian shrub
SUNNA	*n* pl. **-S** the body of traditional Muslim law
SUNNAH	*n* pl. **-S** sunna
SUNNED	past tense of sun
SUNNING	present participle of sun
SUNNY	*adj* **-NIER, -NIEST** filled with sunlight **SUNNILY** *adv*
SUNPORCH	*n* pl. **-ES** a porch that admits much sunlight
SUNPROOF	*adj* resistant to damage by sunlight
SUNRAY	*n* pl. **-RAYS** a ray of sunlight
SUNRISE	*n* pl. **-S** the ascent of the sun above the horizon in the morning
SUNROOF	*n* pl. **-S** an automobile roof having an openable panel
SUNROOM	*n* pl. **-S** a room built to admit a great amount of sunlight
SUNSCALD	*n* pl. **-S** an injury of woody plants caused by the sun
SUNSET	*n* pl. **-S** the descent of the sun below the horizon in the evening
SUNSHADE	*n* pl. **-S** something used as a protection from the sun
SUNSHINE	*n* pl. **-S** the light of the sun **SUNSHINY** *adj*
SUNSPOT	*n* pl. **-S** a dark spot on the surface of the sun
SUNSTAR	*n* pl. **-S** a type of starfish
SUNSTONE	*n* pl. **-S** a variety of quartz
SUNSUIT	*n* pl. **-S** a type of playsuit
SUNTAN	*v* **-TANNED, -TANNING, -TANS** to become tan
SUNTRAP	*n* pl. **-S** a pleasantly sunny sheltered place
SUNUP	*n* pl. **-S** sunrise
SUNWARD	*adv* toward the sun
SUNWARDS	*adv* sunward
SUNWISE	*adv* from left to right
SUP	*v* **SUPPED, SUPPING, SUPS** to eat supper
SUPE	*n* pl. **-S** an actor without a speaking part
SUPER	*v* **-ED, -ING, -S** to reinforce with a thin cotton mesh, as a book
SUPERADD	*v* **-ED, -ING, -S** to add further
SUPERB	*adj* **-PERBER, -PERBEST** of excellent quality **SUPERBLY** *adv*
SUPERBAD	*adj* exceedingly bad
SUPERBUG	*n* pl. **-S** a strain of bacteria that is resistant to all antibiotics
SUPERCAR	*n* pl. **-S** a superior car
SUPERCOP	*n* pl. **-S** a superior police officer
SUPEREGO	*n* pl. **-EGOS** a part of the psyche
SUPERFAN	*n* pl. **-S** an exceedingly devoted enthusiast
SUPERFIX	*n* pl. **-ES** a recurrent pattern of stress in speech
SUPERFLY	*adj* showily pretentious
SUPERHIT	*n* pl. **-S** something exceedingly successful
SUPERHOT	*adj* exceedingly hot
SUPERIOR	*n* pl. **-S** one of higher rank, quality, or authority than another
SUPERJET	*n* pl. **-S** a type of jet airplane
SUPERLIE	*v* **-LAY, -LAIN, -LYING, -LIES** to lie above
SUPERMAN	*n* pl. **-MEN** a hypothetical superior man
SUPERMOM	*n* pl. **-S** a superior mom
SUPERNAL	*adj* pertaining to the sky
SUPERPRO	*n* pl. **-PROS** a superior professional
SUPERSEX	*n* pl. **-ES** a type of sterile organism
SUPERSPY	*n* pl. **-SPIES** a superior spy
SUPERTAX	*n* pl. **-ES** an additional tax
SUPINATE	*v* **-NATED, -NATING, -NATES** to turn so that the palm is facing upward
SUPINE	*n* pl. **-S** a Latin verbal noun
SUPINELY	*adv* in an inactive manner
SUPPED	past tense of sup
SUPPER	*n* pl. **-S** an evening meal
SUPPING	present participle of sup
SUPPLANT	*v* **-ED, -ING, -S** to take the place of
SUPPLE	*adj* **-PLER, -PLEST** pliant **SUPPLELY** *adv*
SUPPLE	*v* **-PLED, -PLING, -PLES** to make supple
SUPPLIER	*n* pl. **-S** one that supplies
SUPPLY	*v* **-PLIED, -PLYING, -PLIES** to furnish with what is needed
SUPPORT	*v* **-ED, -ING, -S** to hold up or add strength to
SUPPOSAL	*n* pl. **-S** something supposed
SUPPOSE	*v* **-POSED, -POSING, -POSES** to assume to be true
SUPPOSER	*n* pl. **-S** one that supposes

SUPPRESS   *v* **-ED, -ING, -ES** to put an end to forcibly

SUPRA   *adv* above

SUPREME   *n* pl. **-S** a smooth white sauce made with chicken stock

SUPREME   *adj* **-PREMER, -PREMEST** highest in power or authority

SUPREMO   *n* pl. **-MOS** one who is highest in authority

SUQ   *n* pl. **-S** souk

SURA   *n* pl. **-S** a chapter of the Koran

SURAH   *n* pl. **-S** a silk fabric

SURAL   *adj* pertaining to the calf of the leg

SURBASE   *n* pl. **-S** a molding or border above the base of a structure **SURBASED** *adj*

SURCEASE   *v* **-CEASED, -CEASING, -CEASES** to cease

SURCOAT   *n* pl. **-S** an outer coat or cloak

SURD   *n* pl. **-S** a voiceless speech sound

SURE   *adj* **SURER, SUREST** free from doubt

SUREFIRE   *adj* sure to meet expectations

SURELY   *adv* certainly

SURENESS   *n* pl. **-ES** the state of being sure

SURER   comparative of sure

SUREST   superlative of sure

SURETY   *n* pl. **-TIES** sureness

SURF   *v* **-ED, -ING, -S** to ride breaking waves on a long, narrow board **SURFABLE** *adj*

SURFACE   *v* **-FACED, -FACING, -FACES** to apply an outer layer to

SURFACER   *n* pl. **-S** one that surfaces

SURFBIRD   *n* pl. **-S** a shore bird

SURFBOAT   *n* pl. **-S** a strong rowboat

SURFEIT   *v* **-ED, -ING, -S** to supply to excess

SURFER   *n* pl. **-S** one that surfs

SURFFISH   *n* pl. **-ES** a marine fish

SURFIER   comparative of surfy

SURFIEST   superlative of surfy

SURFING   *n* pl. **-S** the act or sport of riding the surf (breaking waves)

SURFLIKE   *adj* resembling breaking waves

SURFMAN   *n* pl. **-MEN** one who is skilled in handling a boat in surf

SURFSIDE   *adj* situated near the seashore

SURFY   *adj* **SURFIER, SURFIEST** abounding in breaking waves

SURGE   *v* **SURGED, SURGING, SURGES** to move in a swelling manner

SURGEON   *n* pl. **-S** one who practices surgery

SURGER   *n* pl. **-S** one that surges

SURGERY   *n* pl. **-GERIES** the treatment of medical problems by operation

SURGICAL   *adj* pertaining to surgery

SURGING   present participle of surge

SURGY   *adj* surging

SURICATE   *n* pl. **-S** a burrowing mammal

SURIMI   *n* pl. **-S** an inexpensive fish product

SURLY   *adj* **-LIER, -LIEST** sullenly rude **SURLILY** *adv*

SURMISE   *v* **-MISED, -MISING, -MISES** to infer with little evidence

SURMISER   *n* pl. **-S** one that surmises

SURMOUNT   *v* **-ED, -ING, -S** to get over or across

SURNAME   *v* **-NAMED, -NAMING, -NAMES** to give a family name to

SURNAMER   *n* pl. **-S** one that surnames

SURPASS   *v* **-ED, -ING, -ES** to go beyond

SURPLICE   *n* pl. **-S** a loose-fitting vestment

SURPLUS   *v* **-PLUSED, -PLUSING, -PLUSES** or **-PLUSSED, -PLUSSING, -PLUSSES** to treat as being in excess of what is needed

SURPRINT   *v* **-ED, -ING, -S** to print over something already printed

SURPRISE   *v* **-PRISED, -PRISING, -PRISES** to come upon unexpectedly

SURPRIZE   *v* **-PRIZED, -PRIZING, -PRIZES** to surprise

SURRA   *n* pl. **-S** a disease of domestic animals

SURREAL   *adj* having dreamlike qualities

SURREY   *n* pl. **-REYS** a light carriage

SURROUND   *v* **-ED, -ING, -S** to extend completely around

SURROYAL   *n* pl. **-S** the topmost prong of a stag's antler

SURTAX   *v* **-ED, -ING, -ES** to assess with an extra tax

SURTITLE   *n* pl. **-S** a translation of a foreign-language dialogue displayed above a screen or stage

SURTOUT   *n* pl. **-S** a close-fitting overcoat

SURVEIL   *v* **-VEILLED, -VEILLING, -VEILS** to watch closely

SURVEY	*v* **-ED, -ING, -S** to determine the boundaries, area, or elevations of by measuring angles and distances	**SWACKED**	*adj* drunk
SURVEYOR	*n* pl. **-S** one that surveys land	**SWADDLE**	*v* **-DLED, -DLING, -DLES** to wrap in bandages
SURVIVAL	*n* pl. **-S** a living or continuing longer than another person or thing	**SWAG**	*v* **SWAGGED, SWAGGING, SWAGS** to sway
SURVIVE	*v* **-VIVED, -VIVING, -VIVES** to remain in existence	**SWAGE**	*v* **SWAGED, SWAGING, SWAGES** to shape with a hammering tool
SURVIVER	*n* pl. **-S** survivor	**SWAGER**	*n* pl. **-S** one that swages
SURVIVOR	*n* pl. **-S** one that survives	**SWAGGER**	*v* **-ED, -ING, -S** to walk with a pompous air
SUS	*v* **-ED, -ING, -ES** to suss	**SWAGGIE**	*n* pl. **-S** a swagman
SUSHI	*n* pl. **-S** a dish of cold rice cakes topped with strips of raw fish	**SWAGGING**	present participle of swag
		SWAGING	present participle of swage
SUSLIK	*n* pl. **-S** a Eurasian rodent	**SWAGMAN**	*n* pl. **-MEN** a hobo
SUSPECT	*v* **-ED, -ING, -S** to think guilty on slight evidence	**SWAIL**	*n* pl. **-S** swale
		SWAIN	*n* pl. **-S** a country boy **SWAINISH** *adj*
SUSPEND	*v* **-ED, -ING, -S** to cause to stop for a period	**SWALE**	*n* pl. **-S** a tract of low, marshy ground
SUSPENSE	*n* pl. **-S** a state of mental uncertainty or excitement	**SWALLOW**	*v* **-ED, -ING, -S** to take through the mouth and esophagus into the stomach
SUSPIRE	*v* **-PIRED, -PIRING, -PIRES** to sigh		
SUSS	*v* **-ED, -ING, -ES** to figure out or check out	**SWAM**	past tense of swim
		SWAMI	*n* pl. **-S** a Hindu religious teacher
SUSTAIN	*v* **-ED, -ING, -S** to maintain by providing with food and drink	**SWAMIES**	pl. of swamy
		SWAMP	*v* **-ED, -ING, -S** to inundate
SUSURRUS	*n* pl. **-ES** a soft rustling sound	**SWAMPER**	*n* pl. **-S** one that lives in a swampy area
SUTLER	*n* pl. **-S** one that peddles goods to soldiers		
		SWAMPISH	*adj* swampy
SUTRA	*n* pl. **-S** a Hindu aphorism	**SWAMPY**	*adj* **SWAMPIER, SWAMPIEST** marshy
SUTTA	*n* pl. **-S** sutra		
SUTTEE	*n* pl. **-S** a Hindu widow cremated on her husband's funeral pyre to show her devotion to him	**SWAMY**	*n* pl. **-MIES** swami
		SWAN	*v* **SWANNED, SWANNING, SWANS** to swear
SUTURAL	*adj* pertaining to the line of junction between two bones	**SWANG**	a past tense of swing
		SWANHERD	*n* pl. **-S** one who tends swans (large aquatic birds)
SUTURE	*v* **-TURED, -TURING, -TURES** to unite by sewing		
		SWANK	*adj* **SWANKER, SWANKEST** imposingly elegant
SUZERAIN	*n* pl. **-S** a feudal lord		
SVARAJ	*n* pl. **-ES** swaraj	**SWANK**	*v* **-ED, -ING, -S** to swagger
SVEDBERG	*n* pl. **-S** a unit of time	**SWANKY**	*adj* **SWANKIER, SWANKIEST** swank **SWANKILY** *adv*
SVELTE	*adj* **SVELTER, SVELTEST** gracefully slender **SVELTELY** *adv*		
		SWANLIKE	*adj* resembling a swan
SWAB	*v* **SWABBED, SWABBING, SWABS** to clean with a large mop	**SWANNED**	past tense of swan
		SWANNERY	*n* pl. **-NERIES** a place where swans are raised
SWABBER	*n* pl. **-S** one that swabs		
SWABBIE	*n* pl. **-S** a sailor	**SWANNING**	present participle of swan
SWABBING	present participle of swab	**SWANNY**	*v* to declare — used only in the 1st person sing.
SWABBY	*n* pl. **-BIES** swabbie		

SWANPAN *n pl.* **-S** a Chinese abacus

SWANSKIN *n pl.* **-S** the skin of a swan

SWAP *v* **SWAPPED, SWAPPING, SWAPS** to trade

SWAPFILE *n pl.* **-S** a computer file with space for transferred programs

SWAPPER *n pl.* **-S** one that swaps

SWARAJ *n pl.* **-ES** self-government in British India

SWARD *v* **-ED, -ING, -S** to cover with turf

SWARE a past tense of swear

SWARF *n pl.* **-S** material removed by a cutting tool

SWARM *v* **-ED, -ING, -S** to move in a large group

SWARMER *n pl.* **-S** one that swarms

SWARMING *n pl.* **-S** the surrounding of a victim by a group of attackers

SWART *adj* swarthy

SWARTH *n pl.* **-S** turf

SWARTHY *adj* **-THIER, -THIEST** having a dark complexion

SWARTY *adj* swarthy

SWASH *v* **-ED, -ING, -ES** to swagger

SWASHER *n pl.* **-S** one that swashes

SWASTICA *n pl.* **-S** swastika

SWASTIKA *n pl.* **-S** a geometrical figure used as a symbol or ornament

SWAT *v* **SWATTED, SWATTING, SWATS** to hit sharply

SWATCH *n pl.* **-ES** a sample piece of cloth

SWATH *n pl.* **-S** a row of cut grass or grain

SWATHE *v* **SWATHED, SWATHING, SWATHES** to wrap in bandages

SWATHER *n pl.* **-S** one that swathes

SWATTED past tense of swat

SWATTER *n pl.* **-S** one that swats

SWATTING present participle of swat

SWAY *v* **-ED, -ING, -S** to move slowly back and forth **SWAYABLE** *adj*

SWAYBACK *n pl.* **-S** an abnormal sagging of the back

SWAYER *n pl.* **-S** one that sways

SWAYFUL *adj* capable of influencing

SWEAR *v* **SWORE** or **SWARE, SWORN, SWEARING, SWEARS** to utter a solemn oath

SWEARER *n pl.* **-S** one that swears

SWEARING *n pl.* **-S** the act of uttering a solemn oath

SWEAT *v* **-ED, -ING, -S** to perspire

SWEATBOX *n pl.* **-ES** a small enclosure in which one is made to sweat

SWEATER *n pl.* **-S** a knitted outer garment **SWEATERED** *adj*

SWEATY *adj* **SWEATIER, SWEATIEST** covered with perspiration **SWEATILY** *adv*

SWEDE *n pl.* **-S** a rutabaga

SWEENEY *n pl.* **-NEYS** sweeny

SWEENY *n pl.* **-NIES** atrophy of the shoulder muscles in horses

SWEEP *v* **SWEPT, SWEEPING, SWEEPS** to clear or clean with a brush or broom

SWEEPER *n pl.* **-S** one that sweeps

SWEEPING *n pl.* **-S** the act of one that sweeps

SWEEPY *adj* **SWEEPIER, SWEEPIEST** of wide range or scope

SWEER *adj* lazy

SWEET *adj* **SWEETER, SWEETEST** pleasing to the taste

SWEET *n pl.* **-S** something that is sweet

SWEETEN *v* **-ED, -ING, -S** to make sweet

SWEETIE *n pl.* **-S** darling

SWEETING *n pl.* **-S** a sweet apple

SWEETISH *adj* somewhat sweet

SWEETLIP *n pl.* **-S** a fish having a protruding mouth

SWEETLY *adv* in a sweet manner

SWEETSOP *n pl.* **-S** a tropical tree

SWELL *adj* **SWELLER, SWELLEST** stylish

SWELL *v* **SWELLED, SWOLLEN, SWELLING, SWELLS** to increase in size or volume

SWELLING *n pl.* **-S** something that is swollen

SWELTER *v* **-ED, -ING, -S** to suffer from oppressive heat

SWELTRY *adj* **-TRIER, -TRIEST** oppressively hot

SWEPT past tense of sweep

SWERVE *v* **SWERVED, SWERVING, SWERVES** to turn aside suddenly from a straight course

SWERVER *n pl.* **-S** one that swerves

SWEVEN *n pl.* **-S** a dream or vision

SWIDDEN *n* pl. **-S** an agricultural plot produced by burning off the vegetative cover

SWIFT *adj* **SWIFTER, SWIFTEST** moving with a great rate of motion

SWIFT *n* pl. **-S** a fast-flying bird

SWIFTER *n* pl. **-S** a rope on a ship

SWIFTIE *n* pl. **-S** a person who acts or thinks quickly

SWIFTLET *n* pl. **-S** a cave-dwelling swift

SWIFTLY *adv* in a swift manner

SWIG *v* **SWIGGED, SWIGGING, SWIGS** to drink deeply or rapidly

SWIGGER *n* pl. **-S** one that swigs

SWILE *n* pl. **-S** a seal (a marine mammal)

SWILER *n* pl. **-S** one that hunts seals

SWILING *n* pl. **-S** the activity of hunting seals

SWILL *v* **-ED, -ING, -S** to swig

SWILLER *n* pl. **-S** one that swills

SWIM *v* **SWAM, SWUM, SWIMMING, SWIMS** to propel oneself in water by natural means

SWIMMER *n* pl. **-S** one that swims

SWIMMING *n* pl. **-S** the act of one that swims

SWIMMY *adj* **-MIER, -MIEST** dizzy **SWIMMILY** *adv*

SWIMSUIT *n* pl. **-S** a bathing suit

SWIMWEAR *n* pl. **SWIMWEAR** clothing suitable for swimming

SWINDLE *v* **-DLED, -DLING, -DLES** to take money or property from by fraudulent means

SWINDLER *n* pl. **-S** one that swindles

SWINE *n* pl. **-S** a contemptible person

SWINEPOX *n* pl. **-ES** a disease of swine

SWING *v* **SWUNG** or **SWANG, SWINGING, SWINGS** to move freely back and forth

SWINGBY *n* pl. **-BYS** a mission in which a spacecraft uses a planet's gravitational pull for making course changes

SWINGE *v* **SWINGED, SWINGEING, SWINGES** to flog

SWINGER *n* pl. **-S** one that swings

SWINGIER comparative of swingy

SWINGIEST superlative of swingy

SWINGING *adj* **SWINGINGEST** lively and hip

SWINGING *n* pl. **-S** the practice of swapping sex partners

SWINGLE *v* **-GLED, -GLING, -GLES** to scutch

SWINGMAN *n* pl. **-MEN** a basketball player who can play guard or forward

SWINGY *adj* **SWINGIER, SWINGIEST** marked by swinging

SWINISH *adj* resembling or befitting a pig

SWINK *v* **-ED, -ING, -S** to toil

SWINNEY *n* pl. **-NEYS** sweeny

SWIPE *v* **SWIPED, SWIPING, SWIPES** to strike with a sweeping blow

SWIPER *n* pl. **-S** one that swipes

SWIPES *n/pl* spoiled beer

SWIPLE *n* pl. **-S** a part of a threshing device

SWIPPLE *n* pl. **-S** swiple

SWIRL *v* **-ED, -ING, -S** to move with a whirling motion

SWIRLY *adj* **SWIRLIER, SWIRLIEST** swirling

SWISH *v* **-ED, -ING, -ES** to move with a prolonged hissing sound

SWISH *adj* **SWISHER, SWISHEST** 1. smart, fashionable 2. effeminate

SWISHER *n* pl. **-S** one that swishes

SWISHY *adj* **SWISHIER, SWISHIEST** swishing; effeminate

SWISS *n* pl. **-ES** a cotton fabric

SWITCH *v* **-ED, -ING, -ES** to beat with a flexible rod

SWITCHEL *n* pl. **-S** a drink made with water, molasses, and vinegar and often ginger

SWITCHER *n* pl. **-S** one that switches

SWITH *adv* quickly

SWITHE *adv* swith

SWITHER *v* **-ED, -ING, -S** to doubt

SWITHLY *adv* swith

SWIVE *v* **SWIVED, SWIVING, SWIVES** to copulate with

SWIVEL *v* **-ELED, -ELING, -ELS** or **-ELLED, -ELLING, -ELS** to turn on a pivoted support

SWIVET *n* pl. **-S** a state of nervous excitement

SWIZZLE *v* **-ZLED, -ZLING, -ZLES** to drink excessively

SWIZZLER *n* pl. **-S** one that swizzles

SWOB *v* **SWOBBED, SWOBBING, SWOBS** to swab

SWOBBER *n* pl. **-S** swabber

SWOLLEN past participle of swell

SWOON	*v* **-ED, -ING, -S** to faint
SWOONER	*n* pl. **-S** one that swoons
SWOONY	*adj* **SWOONIER, SWOONIEST** languid, dazed
SWOOP	*v* **-ED, -ING, -S** to make a sudden descent
SWOOPER	*n* pl. **-S** one that swoops
SWOOPY	*adj* **SWOOPIER, SWOOPIEST** having sweeping lines or features
SWOOSH	*v* **-ED, -ING, -ES** to move with a rustling sound
SWOP	*v* **SWOPPED, SWOPPING, SWOPS** to swap
SWOPPER	*n* pl. **-S** swapper
SWORD	*n* pl. **-S** a weapon having a long blade for cutting or thrusting
SWORDMAN	*n* pl. **-MEN** one skilled in the use of a sword
SWORE	a past tense of swear
SWORN	past participle of swear
SWOT	*v* **SWOTTED, SWOTTING, SWOTS** to swat
SWOTTER	*n* pl. **-S** one that swots
SWOUN	*v* **-ED, -ING, -S** to swoon
SWOUND	*v* **-ED, -ING, -S** to swoon
SWUM	past participle of swim
SWUNG	a past tense of swing
SYBARITE	*n* pl. **-S** a person devoted to pleasure and luxury
SYBO	*n* pl. **-BOES** the cibol
SYCAMINE	*n* pl. **-S** the mulberry tree
SYCAMORE	*n* pl. **-S** a North American tree
SYCE	*n* pl. **-S** a male servant in India
SYCEE	*n* pl. **-S** fine uncoined silver formerly used in China as money
SYCOMORE	*n* pl. **-S** sycamore
SYCON	*n* pl. **-S** a type of sponge **SYCONOID** *adj*
SYCONIUM	*n* pl. **-NIA** a fleshy multiple fruit
SYCOSIS	*n* pl. **-COSES** an inflammatory disease of the hair follicles
SYENITE	*n* pl. **-S** an igneous rock **SYENITIC** *adj*
SYKE	*n* pl. **-S** a small stream
SYLI	*n* pl. **-S** a former monetary unit of Guinea
SYLLABI	a pl. of syllabus
SYLLABIC	*n* pl. **-S** a speech sound of high sonority

SYLLABLE	*v* **-BLED, -BLING, -BLES** to pronounce syllables (units of spoken language)
SYLLABUB	*n* pl. **-S** sillabub
SYLLABUS	*n* pl. **-BUSES** or **-BI** an outline of a course of study
SYLPH	*n* pl. **-S** a slender, graceful girl or woman **SYLPHIC, SYLPHISH, SYLPHY** *adj*
SYLPHID	*n* pl. **-S** a young sylph
SYLVA	*n* pl. **-VAS** or **-VAE** the forest trees of an area
SYLVAN	*n* pl. **-S** one that lives in a forest
SYLVATIC	*adj* pertaining to a forest
SYLVIN	*n* pl. **-S** sylvite
SYLVINE	*n* pl. **-S** sylvite
SYLVITE	*n* pl. **-S** an ore of potassium
SYMBION	*n* pl. **-S** symbiont
SYMBIONT	*n* pl. **-S** an organism living in close association with another
SYMBIOT	*n* pl. **-S** symbiont
SYMBIOTE	*n* pl. **-S** symbiont
SYMBOL	*v* **-BOLED, -BOLING, -BOLS** or **-BOLLED, -BOLLING, -BOLS** to serve as a symbol (a representation) of
SYMBOLIC	*adj* pertaining to a symbol
SYMMETRY	*n* pl. **-TRIES** an exact correspondence between the opposite halves of a figure
SYMPATHY	*n* pl. **-THIES** a feeling of compassion for another's suffering
SYMPATRY	*n* pl. **-RIES** the state of occupying the same area without loss of identity from interbreeding
SYMPHONY	*n* pl. **-NIES** an orchestral composition
SYMPODIA	*n/pl* plant stems made up of a series of superposed branches
SYMPOSIA	*n/pl* conferences for the purpose of discussion
SYMPTOM	*n* pl. **-S** an indication of something
SYN	*adv* syne
SYNAGOG	*n* pl. **-S** a building for Jewish worship
SYNANON	*n* pl. **-S** a method of group therapy for drug addicts
SYNAPSE	*v* **-APSED, -APSING, -APSES** to come together in synapsis
SYNAPSID	*n* pl. **-S** one of a group of extinct reptiles

SYNAPSIS *n* pl. **-APSES** the point at which a nervous impulse passes from one neuron to another **SYNAPTIC** *adj*

SYNC *v* **-ED, -ING, -S** to cause to operate in unison

SYNCARP *n* pl. **-S** a fleshy multiple fruit

SYNCARPY *n* pl. **-PIES** the state of being a syncarp

SYNCH *v* **-ED, -ING, -S** to sync

SYNCHRO *n* pl. **-CHROS** a selsyn

SYNCLINE *n* pl. **-S** a type of rock formation

SYNCOM *n* pl. **-S** a type of communications satellite

SYNCOPE *n* pl. **-S** the contraction of a word by omitting one or more sounds from the middle **SYNCOPAL, SYNCOPIC** *adj*

SYNCYTIA *n/pl* masses of protoplasm resulting from cell fusion

SYNDESIS *n* pl. **-DESISES** or **-DESES** synapsis

SYNDET *n* pl. **-S** a synthetic detergent

SYNDETIC *adj* serving to connect

SYNDIC *n* pl. **-S** a business agent **SYNDICAL** *adj*

SYNDROME *n* pl. **-S** a group of symptoms that characterize a particular disorder

SYNE *adv* since

SYNECTIC *adj* pertaining to a system of problem solving

SYNERGIA *n* pl. **-S** synergy

SYNERGID *n* pl. **-S** a cell found in the embryo sac of a seed plant

SYNERGY *n* pl. **-GIES** combined action **SYNERGIC** *adj*

SYNESIS *n* pl. **-SISES** a type of grammatical construction

SYNFUEL *n* pl. **-S** a fuel derived from fossil fuels

SYNGAMY *n* pl. **-MIES** the union of two gametes **SYNGAMIC** *adj*

SYNGAS *n* pl. **-GASES** or **-GASSES** a mixture of carbon monoxide and hydrogen used in chemical synthesis

SYNGENIC *adj* relating to or being genetically identical individuals with respect to reaction to antigens

SYNKARYA *n/pl* cell nuclei formed by the fusion of two preexisting nuclei

SYNOD *n* pl. **-S** a church council **SYNODAL, SYNODIC** *adj*

SYNONYM *n* pl. **-S** a word having the same meaning as another

SYNONYME *n* pl. **-S** synonym

SYNONYMY *n* pl. **-MIES** equivalence of meaning

SYNOPSIS *n* pl. **-OPSES** a summary **SYNOPTIC** *adj*

SYNOVIA *n* pl. **-S** a lubricating fluid secreted by certain membranes **SYNOVIAL** *adj*

SYNTAGM *n* pl. **-S** syntagma

SYNTAGMA *n* pl. **-MAS** or **-MATA** a syntactic element

SYNTAX *n* pl. **-ES** the way in which words are put together to form phrases and sentences

SYNTH *n* pl. **-S** a synthesizer

SYNTHASE *n* pl. **-S** an enzyme that acts as a catalyst in linking two molecules

SYNTHPOP *n* pl. **-S** popular music played with synthesizers

SYNTONE *n* pl. **-S** a person having a syntonic temperament

SYNTONIC *adj* having a temperament responsive to a given social environment

SYNTONY *n* pl. **-NIES** the tuning of transmitters and receivers with each other

SYNTYPE *n* pl. **-S** each of a set of type specimens on which the name of a new species is based

SYNURA *n* pl. **-RAE** any of a genus of protozoa

SYPH *n* pl. **-S** syphilis

SYPHER *v* **-ED, -ING, -S** to overlap so as to make an even surface, as beveled plank edges

SYPHILIS *n* pl. **-LISES** a venereal disease

SYPHON *v* **-ED, -ING, -S** to siphon

SYPHONAL *adj* siphonal

SYPHONIC *adj* siphonic

SYREN *n* pl. **-S** siren

SYRETTE *n* pl. **-S** a small tube fitted with a hypodermic needle containing a single dose of medication

SYRINGA *n* pl. **-S** an ornamental shrub

SYRINGE *v* **-RINGED, -RINGING, -RINGES** to cleanse or treat with injected fluid

SYRINX *n* pl. **-INXES** or **-INGES** the vocal organ of a bird

SYRPHIAN   *n* pl. **-S** syrphid

SYRPHID   *n* pl. **-S** a winged insect

SYRUP   *v* **-ED, -ING, -S** to sweeten with a thick sweet liquid

SYRUPY   *adj* **-UPIER, -UPIEST** resembling a thick, sticky, sweet liquid

SYSADMIN   *n* pl. **-S** a system administrator

SYSOP   *n* pl. **-S** the administrator of a computer bulletin board

SYSTEM   *n* pl. **-S** a group of interacting elements forming a unified whole

SYSTEMIC   *n* pl. **-S** a type of pesticide

SYSTOLE   *n* pl. **-S** the normal rhythmic contraction of the heart **SYSTOLIC** *adj*

SYZYGY   *n* pl. **-GIES** the configuration of the earth, moon, and sun lying in a straight line **SYZYGAL, SYZYGIAL** *adj*

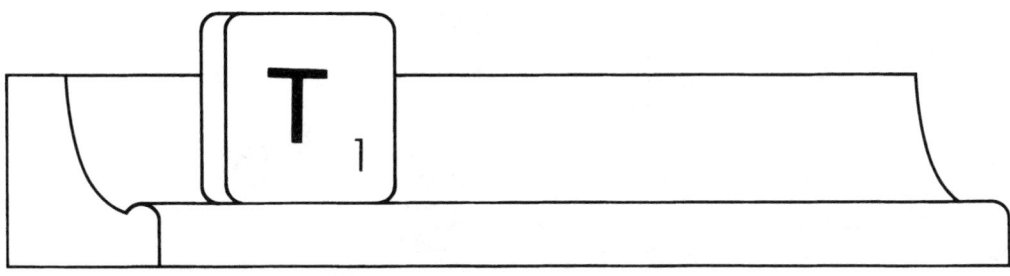

TA	*n* pl. **-S** an expression of gratitude
TAB	*v* **TABBED, TABBING, TABS** to name or designate
TABANID	*n* pl. **-S** a bloodsucking insect
TABARD	*n* pl. **-S** a sleeveless outer garment **TABARDED** *adj*
TABARET	*n* pl. **-S** a silk fabric
TABBED	past tense of tab
TABBING	*n* pl. **-S** the use of the tab key on a keyboard
TABBIS	*n* pl. **-BISES** a silk fabric
TABBY	*v* **-BIED, -BYING, -BIES** to give a wavy appearance to
TABER	*v* **-ED, -ING, -S** to tabor
TABES	*n* pl. **TABES** a syphilitic disease
TABETIC	*n* pl. **-S** one affected with tabes
TABID	*adj* affected with tabes
TABLA	*n* pl. **-S** a small drum
TABLE	*v* **-BLED, -BLING, -BLES** to place on a table (a piece of furniture having a flat upper surface)
TABLEAU	*n* pl. **-LEAUS** or **-LEAUX** a picture
TABLEFUL	*n* pl. **TABLEFULS** or **TABLESFUL** as much as a table can hold
TABLET	*v* **-LETED, -LETING, -LETS** or **-LETTED, -LETTING, -LETS** to inscribe on a small, flat surface
TABLETOP	*n* pl. **-S** the top of a table
TABLING	*n* pl. **-S** the setting of data or information in tables (columns)
TABLOID	*n* pl. **-S** a small newspaper
TABOO	*v* **-ED, -ING, -S** to exclude from use, approach, or mention
TABOOLEY	*n* pl. **-LEYS** tabouli
TABOR	*v* **-ED, -ING, -S** to beat on a small drum
TABORER	*n* pl. **-S** one that tabors
TABORET	*n* pl. **-S** a small drum
TABORIN	*n* pl. **-S** taborine
TABORINE	*n* pl. **-S** a taboret
TABOULEH	*n* pl. **-S** tabouli
TABOULI	*n* pl. **-S** a Lebanese salad containing bulgur wheat, tomatoes, parsley, onions, and mint
TABOUR	*v* **-ED, -ING, -S** to tabor
TABOURER	*n* pl. **-S** taborer
TABOURET	*n* pl. **-S** taboret
TABU	*v* **-ED, -ING, -S** to taboo
TABULAR	*adj* of or pertaining to a list
TABULATE	*v* **-LATED, -LATING, -LATES** to arrange in a list
TABULI	*n* pl. **-S** tabouli
TABUN	*n* pl. **-S** a chemical compound
TACAN	*n* pl. **-S** a navigational system for aircraft
TACE	*n* pl. **-S** a tasset
TACET	*v* be silent — used as a musical direction
TACH	*n* pl. **-S** a device for indicating speed of rotation
TACHE	*n* pl. **-S** a clasp or buckle
TACHINID	*n* pl. **-S** a grayish fly
TACHISM	*n* pl. **-S** action painting
TACHISME	*n* pl. **-S** tachism
TACHIST	*n* pl. **-S** an action painter
TACHISTE	*n* pl. **-S** tachist
TACHYON	*n* pl. **-S** a theoretical subatomic particle
TACIT	*adj* unspoken **TACITLY** *adv*
TACITURN	*adj* habitually silent
TACK	*v* **-ED, -ING, -S** to fasten with tacks (short, sharp-pointed nails)
TACKER	*n* pl. **-S** one that tacks
TACKET	*n* pl. **-S** a hobnail
TACKEY	*adj* **TACKIER, TACKIEST** tacky

TACKIER	comparative of tacky
TACKIEST	superlative of tacky
TACKIFY	*v* **-FIED, -FYING, -FIES** to make tacky
TACKILY	*adv* in a tacky manner
TACKLE	*v* **-LED, -LING, -LES** to seize and throw to the ground
TACKLER	*n* pl. **-S** one that tackles
TACKLESS	*adj* having no tacks
TACKLING	*n* pl. **-S** equipment
TACKY	*adj* **TACKIER, TACKIEST** adhesive
TACNODE	*n* pl. **-S** a point of contact between two curves
TACO	*n* pl. **-COS** a tortilla folded around a filling
TACONITE	*n* pl. **-S** a low-grade iron ore
TACRINE	*n* pl. **-S** a drug for treating Alzheimer's disease
TACT	*n* pl. **-S** skill in dealing with delicate situations
TACTFUL	*adj* having tact
TACTIC	*n* pl. **-S** a maneuver for gaining an objective **TACTICAL** *adj*
TACTILE	*adj* pertaining to the sense of touch
TACTION	*n* pl. **-S** the act of touching
TACTLESS	*adj* lacking tact
TACTUAL	*adj* tactile
TAD	*n* pl. **-S** a small boy
TADPOLE	*n* pl. **-S** the aquatic larva of an amphibian
TAE	*prep* to
TAEL	*n* pl. **-S** a Chinese unit of weight
TAENIA	*n* pl. **-NIAS** or **-NIAE** a tapeworm **TAENIOID** *adj*
TAENITE	*n* pl. **-S** a nickel-iron alloy in meteorites
TAFFAREL	*n* pl. **-S** taffrail
TAFFEREL	*n* pl. **-S** taffrail
TAFFETA	*n* pl. **-S** a lustrous fabric
TAFFIA	*n* pl. **-S** tafia
TAFFRAIL	*n* pl. **-S** a rail around the stern of a ship
TAFFY	*n* pl. **-FIES** a chewy candy
TAFIA	*n* pl. **-S** an inferior rum
TAG	*v* **TAGGED, TAGGING, TAGS** to provide with a tag (an identifying marker)
TAGALONG	*n* pl. **-S** one that follows another
TAGBOARD	*n* pl. **-S** a material for making shipping tags
TAGETES	*n* pl. **TAGETES** a flowering plant
TAGGANT	*n* pl. **-S** a substance added to a product to indicate its source of manufacture
TAGGED	past tense of tag
TAGGER	*n* pl. **-S** one that tags
TAGGING	present participle of tag
TAGINE	*n* pl. **-S** tajine
TAGLIKE	*adj* resembling a tag
TAGLINE	*n* pl. **-S** the final line of a play or joke that makes the point
TAGMEME	*n* pl. **-S** the smallest unit of meaningful grammatical relation
TAGMEMIC	*adj* pertaining to a grammar in which a tagmeme is the basic unit
TAGRAG	*n* pl. **-S** riffraff
TAHINA	*n* pl. **-S** tahini
TAHINI	*n* pl. **-S** a paste of sesame seeds
TAHR	*n* pl. **-S** a goatlike mammal
TAHSIL	*n* pl. **-S** a district in India
TAIGA	*n* pl. **-S** a subarctic evergreen forest
TAIGLACH	*n* pl. **TAIGLACH** teiglach
TAIKO	*n* pl. **-KOS** a barrel-shaped Japanese drum
TAIL	*v* **-ED, -ING, -S** to provide with a tail (a hindmost part)
TAILBACK	*n* pl. **-S** a member of the backfield in some football formations
TAILBONE	*n* pl. **-S** the coccyx
TAILCOAT	*n* pl. **-S** a man's coat
TAILER	*n* pl. **-S** one that secretly follows another
TAILFAN	*n* pl. **-S** a fanlike swimming organ at the rear of some crustaceans
TAILFIN	*n* pl. **-S** a fin at the posterior end of a fish
TAILGATE	*v* **-GATED, -GATING, -GATES** to drive dangerously close behind another vehicle
TAILHOOK	*n* pl. **-S** a hook lowered from the tail of an aircraft to engage a braking cable
TAILING	*n* pl. **-S** the part of a projecting stone or brick that is inserted into a wall
TAILLAMP	*n* pl. **-S** a light at the rear of a vehicle
TAILLE	*n* pl. **-S** a former French tax

TAILLESS	*adj* having no tail
TAILLEUR	*n* pl. **-S** a woman's tailored suit
TAILLIKE	*adj* resembling a tail
TAILOR	*v* **-ED, -ING, -S** to fit with clothes
TAILPIPE	*n* pl. **-S** an exhaust pipe
TAILRACE	*n* pl. **-S** a part of a millrace
TAILSKID	*n* pl. **-S** a support on which the tail of an airplane rests
TAILSPIN	*v* **-SPINNED** or **-SPUN, -SPINNING, -SPINS** to spin headlong down toward earth
TAILWIND	*n* pl. **-S** a wind coming from behind a moving vehicle
TAIN	*n* pl. **-S** a thin plate
TAINT	*v* **-ED, -ING, -S** to touch or affect slightly with something bad
TAIPAN	*n* pl. **-S** a venomous snake
TAJ	*n* pl. **-ES** a tall, conical cap worn in Muslim countries
TAJINE	*n* pl. **-S** an earthenware Moroccan cooking pot
TAKA	*n* pl. **-S** a monetary unit of Bangladesh
TAKAHE	*n* pl. **-S** a flightless bird
TAKE	*v* **TOOK, TAKEN, TAKING, TAKES** to get possession of **TAKABLE, TAKEABLE** *adj*
TAKEAWAY	*n* pl. **-AWAYS** prepared food to be taken away from its place of sale
TAKEDOWN	*n* pl. **-S** an article that can be taken apart easily
TAKEOFF	*n* pl. **-S** the act of rising in flight
TAKEOUT	*n* pl. **-S** the act of removing
TAKEOVER	*n* pl. **-S** the act of assuming control
TAKER	*n* pl. **-S** one that takes
TAKEUP	*n* pl. **-S** the act of taking something up
TAKIN	*n* pl. **-S** a goatlike mammal
TAKING	*n* pl. **-S** a seizure
TAKINGLY	*adv* in an attractive manner
TALA	*n* pl. **-S** a traditional rhythmic pattern of music in India
TALAPOIN	*n* pl. **-S** a small African monkey
TALAR	*n* pl. **-S** a long cloak
TALARIA	*n/pl* winged sandals worn by various figures of classical mythology
TALBOT	*n* pl. **-S** a large dog of an extinct breed

TALC	*v* **TALCKED, TALCKING, TALCS** or **TALCED, TALCING, TALCS** to treat with talc (a soft mineral with a soapy texture) **TALCKY, TALCOSE, TALCOUS, TALCY** *adj*
TALCUM	*v* **-ED, -ING, -S** to treat with a powder made from talc
TALE	*n* pl. **-S** a story
TALEGGIO	*n* pl. **-GIOS** a soft creamy cheese
TALENT	*n* pl. **-S** a special natural ability **TALENTED** *adj*
TALER	*n* pl. **-S** a formerly used German coin
TALESMAN	*n* pl. **-MEN** a person summoned to fill a vacancy on a jury
TALI	pl. of talus
TALION	*n* pl. **-S** a retaliation for a crime
TALIPED	*n* pl. **-S** a person afflicted with clubfoot
TALIPES	*n* pl. **TALIPES** clubfoot
TALIPOT	*n* pl. **-S** a tall palm tree
TALISMAN	*n* pl. **-S** an object believed to possess magical powers
TALK	*v* **-ED, -ING, -S** to communicate by speaking
TALKABLE	*adj* able to be talked about
TALKBACK	*n* pl. **-S** a one-way communications link between a control booth and a recording studio
TALKER	*n* pl. **-S** one that talks
TALKFEST	*n* pl. **-S** a gabfest
TALKIE	*n* pl. **-S** a moving picture with synchronized sound
TALKING	*n* pl. **-S** conversation
TALKY	*adj* **TALKIER, TALKIEST** tending to talk a great deal
TALL	*n* pl. **-S** a garment size for tall persons
TALL	*adj* **TALLER, TALLEST** having great height
TALLAGE	*v* **-LAGED, -LAGING, -LAGES** to tax
TALLBOY	*n* pl. **-BOYS** a highboy
TALLIED	past tense of tally
TALLIER	*n* pl. **-S** one that tallies
TALLIES	present 3d person sing. of tally
TALLIS	*n* pl. **-LISES** or **-LISIM** tallith
TALLISH	*adj* somewhat tall
TALLIT	*n* pl. **-LITS** or **-LITIM** tallith

TALLITH *n pl.* **-LITHS** or **-LITHIM** a Jewish prayer shawl

TALLNESS *n pl.* **-ES** the state of being tall

TALLOL *n pl.* **-S** a resinous liquid

TALLOW *v* **-ED, -ING, -S** to smear with tallow (a mixture of animal fats)

TALLOWY *adj* resembling tallow

TALLY *v* **-LIED, -LYING, -LIES** to count

TALLYHO *v* **-HOED, -HOING, -HOS** or **-HOES** to make an encouraging shout to hunting hounds

TALLYMAN *n pl.* **-MEN** a person who tallies

TALMUDIC *adj* pertaining to the body of Jewish civil and religious law

TALON *n pl.* **-S** a claw of a bird of prey **TALONED** *adj*

TALOOKA *n pl.* **-S** taluk

TALUK *n pl.* **-S** an estate in India

TALUKA *n pl.* **-S** taluk

TALUS *n pl.* **-ES** a slope formed by an accumulation of rock debris

TALUS *n pl.* **-LI** a bone of the foot

TAM *n pl.* **-S** a tight-fitting Scottish cap

TAMABLE *adj* capable of being tamed

TAMAL *n pl.* **-S** tamale

TAMALE *n pl.* **-S** a Mexican dish

TAMANDU *n pl.* **-S** tamandua

TAMANDUA *n pl.* **-S** an arboreal anteater

TAMARACK *n pl.* **-S** a timber tree

TAMARAO *n pl.* **-RAOS** tamarau

TAMARAU *n pl.* **-S** a small buffalo of the Philippines

TAMARI *n pl.* **-S** a Japanese soy sauce

TAMARIN *n pl.* **-S** a South American monkey

TAMARIND *n pl.* **-S** a tropical tree

TAMARISK *n pl.* **-S** an evergreen shrub

TAMASHA *n pl.* **-S** a public entertainment in India

TAMBAC *n pl.* **-S** tombac

TAMBAK *n pl.* **-S** tombac

TAMBALA *n pl.* **TAMBALAS** or **MATAMBALA** a monetary unit of Malawi

TAMBOUR *v* **-ED, -ING, -S** to embroider on a round wooden frame

TAMBOURA *n pl.* **-S** tambura

TAMBUR *n pl.* **-S** tambura

TAMBURA *n pl.* **-S** a stringed instrument

TAME *adj* **TAMER, TAMEST** gentle or docile

TAME *v* **TAMED, TAMING, TAMES** to make tame

TAMEABLE *adj* tamable

TAMEIN *n pl.* **-S** a garment worn by Burmese women

TAMELESS *adj* not capable of being tamed

TAMELY *adv* in a tame manner

TAMENESS *n pl.* **-ES** the state of being tame

TAMER *n pl.* **-S** one that tames

TAMEST superlative of tame

TAMING present participle of tame

TAMIS *n pl.* **-ISES** a strainer made of cloth mesh

TAMMIE *n pl.* **-S** tammy

TAMMY *n pl.* **-MIES** a fabric of mixed fibers

TAMP *v* **-ED, -ING, -S** to pack down by tapping

TAMPALA *n pl.* **-S** an annual herb

TAMPAN *n pl.* **-S** a biting insect

TAMPER *v* **-ED, -ING, -S** to interfere in a harmful manner

TAMPERER *n pl.* **-S** one that tampers

TAMPING *n pl.* **-S** the act of packing down by tapping

TAMPION *n pl.* **-S** a plug for the muzzle of a cannon

TAMPON *v* **-ED, -ING, -S** to plug with a cotton pad

TAN *adj* **TANNER, TANNEST** brown from the sun's rays

TAN *v* **TANNED, TANNING, TANS** to convert hide into leather by soaking in chemicals

TANAGER *n pl.* **-S** a brightly colored bird

TANBARK *n pl.* **-S** a tree bark used as a source of tannin

TANDEM *n pl.* **-S** a bicycle built for two

TANDOOR *n pl.* **-DOORS** or **-DOORI** a clay oven

TANDOORI *n pl.* **-S** food cooked in a tandoor

TANG *v* **-ED, -ING, -S** to provide with a pungent flavor

TANGA *n pl.* **TANGA** a former monetary unit of Tajikistan

TANGELO *n pl.* **-LOS** a citrus fruit

TANGENCE *n pl.* **-S** tangency

TANGENCY *n pl.* **-CIES** the state of being in immediate physical contact

TANGENT *n* pl. **-S** a straight line in contact with a curve at one point

TANGIBLE *n* pl. **-S** something palpable

TANGIBLY *adv* palpably

TANGIER comparative of tangy

TANGIEST superlative of tangy

TANGLE *v* **-GLED, -GLING, -GLES** to bring together in intricate confusion

TANGLER *n* pl. **-S** one that tangles

TANGLY *adj* **-GLIER, -GLIEST** tangled

TANGO *v* **-GOED, -GOING, -GOS** or **-GOES** to perform a Latin American dance

TANGRAM *n* pl. **-S** a Chinese puzzle

TANGY *adj* **TANGIER, TANGIEST** pungent

TANIST *n* pl. **-S** the heir apparent to a Celtic chief

TANISTRY *n* pl. **-RIES** the system of electing a tanist

TANK *v* **-ED, -ING, -S** to store in a tank (a container usually for liquids)

TANKA *n* pl. **-S** a Japanese verse form

TANKAGE *n* pl. **-S** the capacity of a tank

TANKARD *n* pl. **-S** a tall drinking vessel

TANKER *n* pl. **-S** a ship designed to transport liquids

TANKFUL *n* pl. **-S** the amount a tank can hold

TANKINI *n* pl. **-S** a woman's swimsuit consisting of bikini briefs and a tank top

TANKLESS *adj* having no tank

TANKLIKE *adj* resembling a tank

TANKSHIP *n* pl. **-S** a tanker

TANNABLE *adj* capable of being tanned

TANNAGE *n* pl. **-S** the process of tanning

TANNATE *n* pl. **-S** a chemical salt

TANNED past tense of tan

TANNER *n* pl. **-S** one that tans

TANNERY *n* pl. **-NERIES** a place where hides are tanned

TANNEST superlative of tan

TANNIC *adj* pertaining to tannin

TANNIN *n* pl. **-S** a chemical compound used in tanning

TANNING *n* pl. **-S** the process of converting hides into leather

TANNISH *adj* somewhat tan

TANREC *n* pl. **-S** tenrec

TANSY *n* pl. **-SIES** a perennial herb

TANTALUM *n* pl. **-S** a metallic element **TANTALIC** *adj*

TANTALUS *n* pl. **-ES** a case for wine bottles

TANTARA *n* pl. **-S** the sound of a trumpet or horn

TANTIVY *n* pl. **-TIVIES** a hunting cry

TANTO *n* pl. **-TOS** a short Japanese sword

TANTRA *n* pl. **-S** one of a class of Hindu religious writings **TANTRIC** *adj*

TANTRISM *n* pl. **-S** a school of Buddhism incorporating Hindu and pagan elements

TANTRIST *n* pl. **-S** an adherent of tantrism

TANTRUM *n* pl. **-S** a fit of rage

TANUKI *n* pl. **-S** a raccoon dog

TANYARD *n* pl. **-S** the section of a tannery containing the vats

TAO *n* pl. **-S** the path of virtuous conduct according to a Chinese philosophy

TAP *v* **TAPPED, TAPPING, TAPS** to strike gently

TAPA *n* pl. **-S** a cloth made from tree bark

TAPADERA *n* pl. **-S** a part of a saddle

TAPADERO *n* pl. **-ROS** tapadera

TAPALO *n* pl. **-LOS** a scarf worn in Latin American countries

TAPE *v* **TAPED, TAPING, TAPES** to fasten with tape (a long, narrow strip or band) **TAPEABLE** *adj*

TAPELESS *adj* being without tape

TAPELIKE *adj* resembling tape

TAPELINE *n* pl. **-S** a tape for measuring distances

TAPENADE *n* pl. **-S** a spread made with black olives, capers, and anchovies

TAPER *v* **-ED, -ING, -S** to become gradually narrower toward one end

TAPERER *n* pl. **-S** one that carries a candle in a religious procession

TAPESTRY *v* **-TRIED, -TRYING, -TRIES** to decorate with woven wall hangings

TAPETUM *n* pl. **-TA** a layer of cells in some plants **TAPETAL** *adj*

TAPEWORM *n* pl. **-S** a parasitic worm

TAPHOLE *n* pl. **-S** a hole in a blast furnace

TAPHOUSE *n* pl. **-S** a tavern

TAPING *n* pl. **-S** the act or an instance of recording something on magnetic tape

TAPIOCA *n* pl. **-S** a starchy food

TAPIR *n* pl. **-S** a hoofed mammal

TAPIS *n* pl. **-PISES** material used for wall hangings and floor coverings

TAPLESS *adj* lacking a tap (a device to stop the flow of liquid or gas)

TAPPABLE *adj* capable of being tapped

TAPPED past tense of tap

TAPPER *n* pl. **-S** one that taps

TAPPET *n* pl. **-S** a sliding rod that causes another part of a mechanism to move

TAPPING *n* pl. **-S** the process or means by which something is tapped

TAPROOM *n* pl. **-S** a barroom

TAPROOT *n* pl. **-S** the main root of a plant

TAPSTER *n* pl. **-S** one that dispenses liquor in a barroom

TAQUERIA *n* pl. **-S** a restaurant specializing in tacos and burritos

TAR *v* **TARRED, TARRING, TARS** to cover with tar (a black viscous liquid)

TARABISH *n* pl. **-ES** a type of card game

TARAMA *n* pl. **-S** a Greek paste of fish roe, garlic, lemon juice, and olive oil

TARANTAS *n* pl. **-ES** a Russian carriage

TARBOOSH *n* pl. **-ES** a cap worn by Muslim men

TARBUSH *n* pl. **-ES** tarboosh

TARDIER comparative of tardy

TARDIES pl. of tardy

TARDIVE *adj* having symptoms that develop slowly

TARDO *adj* slow — used as a musical direction

TARDY *adj* **TARDIER, TARDIEST** late **TARDILY** *adv*

TARDY *n* pl. **-DIES** an instance of being late

TARDYON *n* pl. **-S** a subatomic particle that travels slower than the speed of light

TARE *v* **TARED, TARING, TARES** to determine the weight of a container holding goods

TARGA *n* pl. **-S** a type of convertible sports car

TARGE *n* pl. **-S** a small, round shield

TARGET *v* **-ED, -ING, -S** to make a goal of

TARIFF *v* **-ED, -ING, -S** to tax imported or exported goods

TARING present participle of tare

TARLATAN *n* pl. **-S** a cotton fabric

TARLETAN *n* pl. **-S** tarlatan

TARMAC *v* **-MACKED, -MACKING, -MACS** to cause (an aircraft) to sit on a taxiway

TARN *n* pl. **-S** a small mountain lake

TARNAL *adj* damned **TARNALLY** *adv*

TARNISH *v* **-ED, -ING, -ES** to dull the luster of

TARO *n* pl. **-ROS** a tropical plant

TAROC *n* pl. **-S** tarok

TAROK *n* pl. **-S** a card game

TAROT *n* pl. **-S** any of a set of playing cards used for fortune-telling

TARP *n* pl. **-S** a protective canvas covering

TARPAN *n* pl. **-S** an Asian wild horse

TARPAPER *n* pl. **-S** a heavy paper coated with tar

TARPON *n* pl. **-S** a marine game fish

TARRAGON *n* pl. **-S** a perennial herb

TARRE *v* **TARRED, TARRING, TARRES** to urge to action

TARRED past tense of tar

TARRIER *n* pl. **-S** one that tarries

TARRING present participle of tar and tarre

TARRY *adj* **-RIER, -RIEST** resembling tar

TARRY *v* **-RIED, -RYING, -RIES** to delay or be slow in acting or doing

TARSAL *n* pl. **-S** a bone of the foot

TARSI pl. of tarsus

TARSIA *n* pl. **-S** intarsia

TARSIER *n* pl. **-S** a nocturnal primate

TARSUS *n* pl. **TARSI** a part of the foot

TART *adj* **TARTER, TARTEST** having a sharp, sour taste

TART *v* **-ED, -ING, -S** to dress up

TARTAN *n* pl. **-S** a patterned woolen fabric

TARTANA *n* pl. **-S** a Mediterranean sailing vessel

TARTAR *n* pl. **-S** a crust on the teeth **TARTARIC** *adj*

TARTARE *adj* served raw

TARTIER comparative of tarty

TARTIEST superlative of tarty

TARTISH *adj* somewhat tart

TARTLET *n* pl. **-S** a small pie

TARTLY *adv* in a tart manner

TARTNESS *n* pl. **-ES** the state of being tart

TARTRATE *n* pl. **-S** a chemical salt

TARTUFE *n* pl. **-S** tartuffe

TARTUFFE *n* pl. **-S** a hypocrite

TARTUFO *n* pl. **-FI** or **-FOS** a white truffle

TARTY *adj* **TARTIER, TARTIEST** suggestive of a prostitute **TARTILY** *adv*

TARWEED *n* pl. **-S** a flowering plant

TARZAN *n* pl. **-S** a person of superior strength and agility

TASE *v* **TASED, TASING, TASES** to stun with a gun that fires electrified darts

TASK *v* **-ED, -ING, -S** to assign a job to

TASKBAR *n* pl. **-S** a row of graphical controls on a computer screen

TASKWORK *n* pl. **-S** hard work

TASS *n* pl. **-ES** a drinking cup

TASSE *n* pl. **-S** tasset

TASSEL *v* **-SELED, -SELING, -SELS** or **-SELLED, -SELLING, -SELS** to adorn with dangling ornaments

TASSET *n* pl. **-S** a piece of plate armor for the upper thigh

TASSIE *n* pl. **-S** tass

TASSO *n* pl. **-SOS** spicy cured pork

TASTE *v* **TASTED, TASTING, TASTES** to perceive the flavor of by taking into the mouth **TASTABLE** *adj*

TASTEFUL *adj* tasty

TASTER *n* pl. **-S** one that tastes

TASTING *n* pl. **-S** a gathering for sampling wines or foods

TASTY *adj* **TASTIER, TASTIEST** pleasant to the taste **TASTILY** *adv*

TAT *v* **TATTED, TATTING, TATS** to make tatting

TATAMI *n* pl. **-S** straw matting used as a floor covering

TATAR *n* pl. **-S** a ferocious person

TATE *n* pl. **-S** a tuft of hair

TATER *n* pl. **-S** a potato

TATHATA *n* pl. **-S** the ultimate nature of all things in Buddhism

TATOUAY *n* pl. **-AYS** a South American armadillo

TATSOI *n* pl. **-S** an Asian mustard

TATTED past tense of tat

TATTER *v* **-ED, -ING, -S** to become torn and worn

TATTIE *n* pl. **-S** a potato

TATTIER comparative of tatty

TATTIEST superlative of tatty

TATTILY *adv* in a tatty manner

TATTING *n* pl. **-S** delicate handmade lace

TATTLE *v* **-TLED, -TLING, -TLES** to reveal the activities of another

TATTLER *n* pl. **-S** one that tattles

TATTOO *v* **-ED, -ING, -S** to mark the skin with indelible pigments

TATTOOER *n* pl. **-S** one that tattoos

TATTY *adj* **-TIER, -TIEST** shabby

TAU *n* pl. **-S** a Greek letter

TAUGHT past tense of teach

TAUNT *v* **-ED, -ING, -S** to challenge or reproach sarcastically

TAUNTER *n* pl. **-S** one that taunts

TAUON *n* pl. **-S** an unstable lepton

TAUPE *n* pl. **-S** a dark gray color

TAURINE *n* pl. **-S** a chemical compound

TAUT *adj* **TAUTER, TAUTEST** fully stretched, so as not to be slack

TAUT *v* **-ED, -ING, -S** to tangle

TAUTAUG *n* pl. **-S** tautog

TAUTEN *v* **-ED, -ING, -S** to make taut

TAUTLY *adv* in a taut manner

TAUTNESS *n* pl. **-ES** the state of being taut

TAUTOG *n* pl. **-S** a marine fish

TAUTOMER *n* pl. **-S** a type of chemical compound

TAUTONYM *n* pl. **-S** a type of taxonomic designation

TAV *n* pl. **-S** a Hebrew letter

TAVERN *n* pl. **-S** a place where liquor is sold to be drunk on the premises

TAVERNA *n* pl. **-S** a cafe in Greece

TAVERNER *n* pl. **-S** one that runs a tavern

TAW *v* **-ED, -ING, -S** to convert into white leather by the application of minerals

TAWDRY *adj* **-DRIER, -DRIEST** gaudy **TAWDRILY** *adv*

TAWDRY *n* pl. **-DRIES** gaudy finery

TAWER *n* pl. **-S** one that taws

TAWIE   *adj* docile

TAWNEY   *n* pl. **-NEYS** tawny

TAWNY   *adj* **-NIER, -NIEST** light brown **TAWNILY** *adv*

TAWNY   *n* pl. **-NIES** a light brown color

TAWPIE   *n* pl. **-S** a foolish young person

TAWSE   *v* **TAWSED, TAWSING, TAWSES** to flog

TAX   *v* **-ED, -ING, -ES** to place a tax (a charge imposed by authority for public purposes) on

TAXA   a pl. of taxon

TAXABLE   *adj* subject to tax **TAXABLY** *adv*

TAXABLE   *n* pl. **-S** a taxable item

TAXATION   *n* pl. **-S** the process of taxing

TAXEME   *n* pl. **-S** a minimum grammatical feature of selection **TAXEMIC** *adj*

TAXER   *n* pl. **-S** one that taxes

TAXI   *v* **TAXIED, TAXIING** or **TAXYING, TAXIS** or **TAXIES** to travel in a taxicab

TAXICAB   *n* pl. **-S** an automobile for hire

TAXIMAN   *n* pl. **-MEN** the operator of a taxicab

TAXINGLY   *adv* in an onerous manner

TAXITE   *n* pl. **-S** a volcanic rock **TAXITIC** *adj*

TAXIWAY   *n* pl. **-WAYS** a paved strip at an airport

TAXLESS   *adj* free from taxation

TAXMAN   *n* pl. **-MEN** one who collects taxes

TAXOL   *n* pl. **-S** a medicinal substance from a yew tree

TAXON   *n* pl. **TAXONS** or **TAXA** a unit of scientific classification

TAXONOMY   *n* pl. **-MIES** the study of scientific classification

TAXPAID   *adj* paid for by taxes

TAXPAYER   *n* pl. **-S** one that pays taxes

TAXUS   *n* pl. **TAXUS** an evergreen tree or shrub

TAXWISE   *adj* pertaining to taxes

TAXYING   a present participle of taxi

TAYBERRY   *n* pl. **-RIES** a dark red fruit that is a cross between a blackberry and a raspberry

TAYRA   *n* pl. **-S** a large mammal of Central and South America

TAZZA   *n* pl. **-ZAS** or **-ZE** an ornamental bowl

TE   *n* pl. **-S** ti

TEA   *n* pl. **-S** a beverage made by infusing dried leaves in boiling water

TEABERRY   *n* pl. **-RIES** a North American shrub

TEABOARD   *n* pl. **-S** a tray for serving tea

TEABOWL   *n* pl. **-S** a teacup having no handle

TEABOX   *n* pl. **-ES** a box for tea leaves

TEACAKE   *n* pl. **-S** a small cake served with tea

TEACART   *n* pl. **-S** a wheeled table used in serving tea

TEACH   *v* **TAUGHT, TEACHING, TEACHES** to impart knowledge or skill to

TEACHER   *n* pl. **-S** one that teaches

TEACHING   *n* pl. **-S** a doctrine

TEACUP   *n* pl. **-S** a cup in which tea is served

TEAHOUSE   *n* pl. **-S** a public establishment serving tea

TEAK   *n* pl. **-S** an East Indian tree

TEAKWOOD   *n* pl. **-S** the wood of the teak

TEAL   *n* pl. **-S** a river duck

TEALIKE   *adj* resembling tea

TEAM   *v* **-ED, -ING, -S** to form a team (a group of persons associated in a joint action)

TEAMAKER   *n* pl. **-S** one that makes tea

TEAMMATE   *n* pl. **-S** a member of the same team

TEAMSTER   *n* pl. **-S** a truck driver

TEAMWORK   *n* pl. **-S** cooperative effort to achieve a common goal

TEAPOT   *n* pl. **-S** a vessel used in making and serving tea

TEAPOY   *n* pl. **-POYS** a small table used in serving tea

TEAR   *v* **-ED, -ING, -S** to emit tears (drops of saline liquid secreted by a gland of the eye)

TEAR   *v* **TORE, TORN, TEARING, TEARS** to pull apart or into pieces **TEARABLE** *adj*

TEARAWAY   *n* pl. **-AWAYS** a rebellious person

TEARDOWN   *n* pl. **-S** the process of disassembling

TEARDROP   *n* pl. **-S** a tear

TEARER   *n* pl. **-S** one that tears or rips

TEARFUL   *adj* full of tears

TEARGAS _v_ **-GASSED, -GASSING, -GASES** or **-GASSES** to subject to a gas that irritates the eyes

TEARIER comparative of teary

TEARIEST superlative of teary

TEARILY _adv_ in a teary manner

TEARLESS _adj_ being without tears

TEARLIKE _adj_ resembling a tear

TEAROOM _n_ pl. **-S** a restaurant serving tea

TEARY _adj_ **TEARIER, TEARIEST** tearful

TEASE _v_ **TEASED, TEASING, TEASES** to make fun of **TEASABLE** _adj_

TEASEL _v_ **-SELED, -SELING, -SELS** or **-SELLED, -SELLING, -SELS** to raise a soft surface on fabric with a bristly flower head

TEASELER _n_ pl. **-S** one that teasels

TEASER _n_ pl. **-S** one that teases

TEASHOP _n_ pl. **-S** a tearoom

TEASING present participle of tease

TEASPOON _n_ pl. **-S** a small spoon

TEAT _n_ pl. **-S** a mammary gland **TEATED** _adj_

TEATIME _n_ pl. **-S** the customary time for tea

TEAWARE _n_ pl. **-S** a tea service

TEAZEL _v_ **-ZELED, -ZELING, -ZELS** or **-ZELLED, -ZELLING, -ZELS** to teasel

TEAZLE _v_ **-ZLED, -ZLING, -ZLES** to teasel

TEC _n_ pl. **-S** tech

TECH _n_ pl. **-S** a technician

TECHED _adj_ crazy

TECHIE _n_ pl. **-S** a technician

TECHNIC _n_ pl. **-S** technique

TECHNO _n_ pl. **-NOS** a style of disco music

TECHNOID _n_ pl. **-S** a technician

TECHY _adj_ **TECHIER, TECHIEST** tetchy **TECHILY** _adv_

TECTA a pl. of tectum

TECTAL _adj_ pertaining to a tectum

TECTITE _n_ pl. **-S** tektite

TECTONIC _adj_ pertaining to construction

TECTRIX _n_ pl. **-TRICES** a small feather of a bird's wing

TECTUM _n_ pl. **-TUMS** or **-TA** a rooflike structure

TED _v_ **TEDDED, TEDDING, TEDS** to spread for drying

TEDDER _v_ **-ED, -ING, -S** to ted (hay) with a machine

TEDDY _n_ pl. **-DIES** a woman's undergarment

TEDIOUS _adj_ causing weariness

TEDIUM _n_ pl. **-S** the state of being tedious

TEE _v_ **TEED, TEEING, TEES** to place a golf ball on a small peg

TEEL _n_ pl. **-S** sesame

TEEM _v_ **-ED, -ING, -S** to be full to overflowing

TEEMER _n_ pl. **-S** one that teems

TEEN _n_ pl. **-S** a teenager

TEENAGE _adj_ pertaining to teenagers

TEENAGED _adj_ teenage

TEENAGER _n_ pl. **-S** a person between the ages of thirteen and nineteen

TEENDOM _n_ pl. **-S** teenagers collectively

TEENER _n_ pl. **-S** a teenager

TEENFUL _adj_ filled with grief

TEENSY _adj_ **-SIER, -SIEST** tiny

TEENTSY _adj_ **-SIER, -SIEST** tiny

TEENY _adj_ **-NIER, -NIEST** tiny

TEENYBOP _adj_ pertaining to a young teenager

TEEPEE _n_ pl. **-S** tepee

TEETER _v_ **-ED, -ING, -S** to move unsteadily

TEETH pl. of tooth

TEETHE _v_ **TEETHED, TEETHING, TEETHES** to cut teeth

TEETHER _n_ pl. **-S** an object for a baby to bite on during teething

TEETHING _n_ pl. **-S** the first growth of teeth

TEETOTAL _v_ **-TALED, -TALING, -TALS** or **-TALLED, -TALLING, -TALS** to abstain completely from alcoholic beverages

TEETOTUM _n_ pl. **-S** a spinning toy

TEEVEE _n_ pl **-S** a television set

TEFF _n_ pl. **-S** a cereal grass

TEFILLIN _n/pl_ the phylacteries worn by Jews

TEG _n_ pl. **-S** tegg

TEGG _n_ pl. **-S** a sheep in its second year

TEGMEN _n_ pl. **-MINA** a covering

TEGMENTA _n/pl_ anatomical coverings

TEGMINAL _adj_ pertaining to a tegmen

TEGU _n_ pl. **-S** a large lizard of South America

TEGUA _n_ pl. **-S** a type of moccasin

TEGULA *n* pl. **-LAE** a flat roof tile used in ancient Rome

TEGULAR *adj* resembling a tile

TEGUMEN *n* pl. **-MINA** tegmen

TEGUMENT *n* pl. **-S** a covering

TEIGLACH *n* pl. **TEIGLACH** a confection consisting of balls of dough boiled in honey

TEIID *n* pl. **-S** a tropical American lizard

TEIN *n* pl. **-S** a monetary unit of Kazakhstan

TEIND *n* pl. **-S** a tithe

TEKKIE *n* pl. **-S** techie

TEKTITE *n* pl. **-S** a glassy body believed to be of meteoritic origin **TEKTITIC** *adj*

TEL *n* pl. **-S** an ancient mound in the Middle East

TELA *n* pl. **-LAE** an anatomical tissue

TELAMON *n* pl. **-ES** a male figure used as a supporting column

TELCO *n* pl. **-COS** a telecommunications company

TELE *n* pl. **-S** a television set

TELECAST *v* **-ED, -ING, -S** to broadcast by television

TELECINE *n* pl. **-S** the broadcasting of a movie on television

TELECOM *n* pl. **-S** telecommunication

TELECOMM *n* pl. **-S** telecommunication

TELEDU *n* pl. **-S** a carnivorous mammal

TELEFAX *v* **-ED, -ING, -ES** to transmit graphic material over telephone lines

TELEFILM *n* pl. **-S** a motion picture made for television

TELEGA *n* pl. **-S** a Russian wagon

TELEGONY *n* pl. **-NIES** the supposed influence of a previous sire on the offspring of later matings of the mother with other males

TELEGRAM *v* **-GRAMMED, -GRAMMING, -GRAMS** to send a message by telegraph

TELEMAN *n* pl. **-MEN** a naval officer

TELEMARK *v* **-ED, -ING, -S** to perform a type of turn in skiing

TELEOST *n* pl. **-S** a bony fish

TELEPATH *n* pl. **-S** one who can communicate with another by some means other than the senses

TELEPLAY *n* pl. **-PLAYS** a play written for television

TELEPORT *v* **-ED, -ING, -S** to transport by a process that involves no physical means

TELERAN *n* pl. **-S** a system of air navigation

TELESHOP *v* **-SHOPPED, -SHOPPING, -SHOPS** to shop by interactive telecommunications systems

TELESIS *n* pl. **TELESES** planned progress

TELESTIC *n* pl. **-S** a type of acrostic

TELETEXT *n* pl. **-S** a communications system in which printed matter is telecast to subscribers

TELETHON *n* pl. **-S** a fund-raising television program

TELETYPE *v* **-TYPED, -TYPING, -TYPES** to send by teletypewriter

TELEVIEW *v* **-ED, -ING, -S** to observe by means of television

TELEVISE *v* **-VISED, -VISING, -VISES** to broadcast by television (an electronic system of transmitting images and sound)

TELEWORK *v* **-ED, -ING, -S** to work at home using an electronic linkup with a central office

TELEX *v* **-ED, -ING, -ES** to send a message by a type of telegraphic system

TELFER *v* **-ED, -ING, -S** to telpher

TELFORD *n* pl. **-S** a road made of stones

TELIAL *adj* pertaining to a telium

TELIC *adj* directed toward a goal

TELICITY *n* pl. **-TIES** the quality of being telic

TELIUM *n* pl. **-LIA** a sorus on the host plant of a rust fungus

TELL *v* **TOLD, TELLING, TELLS** to give a detailed account of **TELLABLE** *adj*

TELLER *n* pl. **-S** one that tells

TELLIES a pl. of telly

TELLTALE *n* pl. **-S** a tattler

TELLURIC *adj* pertaining to the earth

TELLY *n* pl. **-LYS** or **-LIES** a television set

TELNET *v* **-NETTED, -NETTING, -NETS** or **-NETED, -NETING, -NETS** to access an account over the Internet using an appropriate procedure

TELOME *n* pl. **-S** a structural unit of a vascular plant **TELOMIC** *adj*

TELOMERE   *n* pl. **-S** the natural end of a chromosome

TELOS   *n* pl. **TELOI** an ultimate end

TELPHER   *v* **-ED, -ING, -S** to transport by a system of aerial cable cars

TELSON   *n* pl. **-S** the terminal segment of an arthropod **TELSONIC** *adj*

TEMBLOR   *n* pl. **-S** or **-ES** an earthquake

TEMERITY   *n* pl. **-TIES** foolish boldness

TEMP   *v* **-ED, -ING, -S** to work as a temporary employee

TEMPEH   *n* pl. **-S** an Asian food

TEMPER   *v* **-ED, -ING, -S** to moderate by adding a counterbalancing agent

TEMPERA   *n* pl. **-S** a technique of painting

TEMPERER   *n* pl. **-S** one that tempers

TEMPEST   *v* **-ED, -ING, -S** to agitate violently

TEMPI   a pl. of tempo

TEMPLAR   *n* pl. **-S** a lawyer or student of law in London

TEMPLATE   *n* pl. **-S** a pattern used as a guide in making something

TEMPLE   *n* pl. **-S** a house of worship **TEMPLED** *adj*

TEMPLET   *n* pl. **-S** template

TEMPO   *n* pl. **-POS** or **-PI** the rate of speed of a musical piece

TEMPORAL   *n* pl. **-S** a bone of the skull

TEMPT   *v* **-ED, -ING, -S** to entice to commit an unwise or immoral act

TEMPTER   *n* pl. **-S** one that tempts

TEMPURA   *n* pl. **-S** a Japanese dish

TEN   *n* pl. **-S** a number

TENABLE   *adj* capable of being held **TENABLY** *adv*

TENACE   *n* pl. **-S** a combination of two high cards in some card games

TENACITY   *n* pl. **-TIES** perseverance or persistence

TENACULA   *n/pl* hooked surgical instruments

TENAIL   *n* pl. **-S** tenaille

TENAILLE   *n* pl. **-S** an outer defense

TENANCY   *n* pl. **-CIES** the temporary occupancy of something that belongs to another

TENANT   *v* **-ED, -ING, -S** to inhabit

TENANTRY   *n* pl. **-RIES** tenancy

TENCH   *n* pl. **-ES** a freshwater fish

TEND   *v* **-ED, -ING, -S** to be disposed or inclined

TENDANCE   *n* pl. **-S** watchful care

TENDENCE   *n* pl. **-S** tendance

TENDENCY   *n* pl. **-CIES** an inclination to act or think in a particular way

TENDER   *adj* **-DERER, -DEREST** soft or delicate

TENDER   *v* **-ED, -ING, -S** to present for acceptance

TENDERER   *n* pl. **-S** one that tenders

TENDERLY   *adv* in a tender manner

TENDON   *n* pl. **-S** a band of tough, fibrous tissue

TENDRIL   *n* pl. **-S** a leafless organ of climbing plants

TENDU   *n* pl. **-S** an Asian ebony tree

TENEBRAE   *n/pl* a religious service

TENEMENT   *n* pl. **-S** an apartment house

TENESI   *n* pl. **TENESI** a monetary unit of Turkmenistan

TENESMUS   *n* pl. **-ES** an urgent but ineffectual effort to defecate or urinate **TENESMIC** *adj*

TENET   *n* pl. **-S** a principle, belief, or doctrine held to be true

TENFOLD   *n* pl. **-S** an amount ten times as great as a given unit

TENGE   *n* pl. **-S** a monetary unit of Kazakhstan

TENIA   *n* pl. **-NIAS** or **-NIAE** a tapeworm

TENIASIS   *n* pl. **TENIASES** infestation with tapeworms

TENNE   *n* pl. **-S** an orange-brown color

TENNE   *n* pl. **TENNESI** a monetary unit of Turkmenistan

TENNER   *n* pl. **-S** a ten-dollar bill

TENNIES   *n/pl* low-cut sneakers

TENNIS   *n* pl. **-NISES** an outdoor ball game

TENNIST   *n* pl. **-S** a tennis player

TENNO   *n* pl. **-NOS** the emperor of Japan considered as a divinity

TENNY   *n* pl. **-NIES** tenne

TENON   *v* **-ED, -ING, -S** to unite by means of a tenon (a projection on the end of a piece of wood)

TENONER   *n* pl. **-S** one that tenons

TENOR   *n* pl. **-S** a high male singing voice

TENORINO   *n* pl. **-NI** a high tenor

TENORIST *n* pl. **-S** one who sings tenor or plays a tenor instrument

TENORITE *n* pl. **-S** a mineral

TENORMAN *n* pl. **-MEN** a person who plays tenor saxophone

TENOTOMY *n* pl. **-MIES** the surgical division of a tendon

TENOUR *n* pl. **-S** tenor

TENPENCE *n* pl. **-S** the sum of ten pennies

TENPENNY *adj* worth tenpence

TENPIN *n* pl. **-S** a bowling pin

TENREC *n* pl. **-S** a mammal that feeds on insects

TENSE *adj* **TENSER, TENSEST** taut **TENSELY** *adv*

TENSE *v* **TENSED, TENSING, TENSES** to make tense

TENSIBLE *adj* capable of being stretched **TENSIBLY** *adv*

TENSILE *adj* tensible

TENSION *v* **-ED, -ING, -S** to make tense

TENSITY *n* pl. **-TIES** the state of being tense

TENSIVE *adj* causing tensity

TENSOR *n* pl. **-S** a muscle that stretches a body part

TENT *v* **-ED, -ING, -S** to live in a tent (a type of portable shelter)

TENTACLE *n* pl. **-S** an elongated, flexible appendage of some animals

TENTAGE *n* pl. **-S** a supply of tents

TENTER *v* **-ED, -ING, -S** to stretch on a type of frame

TENTH *n* pl. **-S** one of ten equal parts

TENTHLY *adv* in the tenth place

TENTIE *adj* **TENTIER, TENTIEST** tenty

TENTIER comparative of tenty

TENTIEST superlative of tenty

TENTLESS *adj* having no tent

TENTLIKE *adj* resembling a tent

TENTORIA *n/pl* the internal skeletons of the heads of insects

TENTPOLE *n* pl. **-S** a big-budget movie whose high earnings are intended to offset the cost of less profitable ones

TENTY *adj* **TENTIER, TENTIEST** watchful

TENUIS *n* pl. **-UES** a voiceless phonetic stop

TENUITY *n* pl. **-ITIES** lack of substance or strength

TENUOUS *adj* having little substance or strength

TENURE *v* **-URED, -URING, -URES** to grant tenure (the status of holding one's position on a permanent basis) to

TENURIAL *adj* of or pertaining to tenure

TENUTO *n* pl. **-TOS** or **-TI** a musical note or chord held longer than its normal duration

TEOCALLI *n* pl. **-S** an Aztec temple

TEOPAN *n* pl. **-S** a teocalli

TEOSINTE *n* pl. **-S** an annual grass

TEPA *n* pl. **-S** a chemical compound

TEPACHE *n* pl. **-S** a Mexican drink made with pineapple, brown sugar, and water

TEPAL *n* pl. **-S** a division of a perianth

TEPEE *n* pl. **-S** a conical tent of some Native Americans

TEPEFY *v* **-FIED, -FYING, -FIES** to make tepid

TEPHRA *n* pl. **-S** solid material ejected from a volcano

TEPHRITE *n* pl. **-S** a volcanic rock

TEPID *adj* moderately warm **TEPIDLY** *adv*

TEPIDITY *n* pl. **-TIES** the state of being tepid

TEPOY *n* pl. **-POYS** teapoy

TEQUILA *n* pl. **-S** a Mexican liquor

TERABYTE *n* pl. **-S** one trillion bytes

TERAFLOP *n* pl. **-S** a measure of computing speed

TERAI *n* pl. **-S** a sun hat with a wide brim

TERAOHM *n* pl. **-S** one trillion ohms

TERAPH *n* pl. **-APHIM** an image of a Semitic household god

TERATISM *n* pl. **-S** a malformed fetus **TERATOID** *adj*

TERATOMA *n* pl. **-MAS** or **-MATA** a type of tumor

TERAWATT *n* pl. **-S** one trillion watts

TERBIA *n* pl. **-S** an oxide of terbium

TERBIUM *n* pl. **-S** a metallic element **TERBIC** *adj*

TERCE *n* pl. **-S** tierce

TERCEL *n* pl. **-S** a male falcon

TERCELET *n* pl. **-S** tercel

TERCET *n* pl. **-S** a group of three lines of verse

TEREBENE *n* pl. **-S** a mixture of terpenes

TEREBIC *adj* pertaining to an acid derived from oil of turpentine

TEREDO *n* pl. **-DOS** or **-DINES** a bivalve mollusk

TEREFAH *adj* tref

TERES *n* pl. **TERETES** either of two muscles helping to rotate the arm

TERETE *adj* cylindrical and slightly tapering

TERGAL *adj* pertaining to a tergum

TERGITE *n* pl. **-S** a tergum

TERGUM *n* pl. **-GA** a back part of a segment of an arthropod

TERIYAKI *n* pl. **-S** a Japanese food

TERM *v* **-ED, -ING, -S** to give a name to

TERMER *n* pl. **-S** a prisoner serving a specified sentence

TERMINAL *n* pl. **-S** an end or extremity

TERMINER *n* pl. **-S** a type of court in some states

TERMINUS *n* pl. **-NUSES** or **-NI** a terminal

TERMITE *n* pl. **-S** an insect resembling an ant **TERMITIC** *adj*

TERMLESS *adj* having no limits

TERMLY *adv* periodically

TERMOR *n* pl. **-S** one that holds land for a certain number of years

TERMTIME *n* pl. **-S** the time when a school or court is in session

TERN *n* pl. **-S** a seabird

TERNARY *n* pl. **-RIES** a group of three

TERNATE *adj* arranged in groups of three

TERNE *n* pl. **-S** an alloy of lead and tin

TERNION *n* pl. **-S** a group of three

TERPENE *n* pl. **-S** a chemical compound **TERPENIC** *adj*

TERPINOL *n* pl. **-S** a fragrant liquid

TERRA *n* pl. **-RAE** earth; land

TERRACE *v* **-RACED, -RACING, -RACES** to provide with a terrace (a raised embankment)

TERRAIN *n* pl. **-S** a tract of land

TERRANE *n* pl. **-S** a rock formation

TERRAPIN *n* pl. **-S** a North American tortoise

TERRARIA *n/pl* glass enclosures for plants or small animals

TERRAS *n* pl. **-ES** trass

TERRASSE *n* pl. **TERRASSE** a paved area outside a French cafe

TERRAZZO *n* pl. **-ZOS** a mosaic flooring

TERREEN *n* pl. **-S** terrine

TERRELLA *n* pl. **-S** a spherical magnet

TERRENE *n* pl. **-S** a land area

TERRET *n* pl. **-S** a metal ring on a harness

TERRIBLE *adj* very bad **TERRIBLY** *adv*

TERRIER *n* pl. **-S** a small, active dog

TERRIES pl. of terry

TERRIFIC *adj* very good; fine

TERRIFY *v* **-FIED, -FYING, -FIES** to fill with terror

TERRINE *n* pl. **-S** an earthenware jar

TERRIT *n* pl. **-S** terret

TERROIR *n* pl. **-S** the combination of factors that gives wine grapes their distinctive character

TERROR *n* pl. **-S** intense fear

TERRY *n* pl. **-RIES** an absorbent fabric

TERSE *adj* **TERSER, TERSEST** succinct **TERSELY** *adv*

TERTIAL *n* pl. **-S** a flight feather of a bird's wing

TERTIAN *n* pl. **-S** a recurrent fever

TERTIARY *n* pl. **-ARIES** a tertial

TERZETTO *n* pl. **-TOS** or **-TI** a vocal or instrumental trio

TESLA *n* pl. **-S** a unit of magnetic induction

TESSERA *n* pl. **-SERAE** a small square used in mosaic work **TESSERAL** *adj*

TEST *v* **-ED, -ING, -S** to evaluate by an examination **TESTABLE** *adj*

TESTA *n* pl. **-TAE** the hard outer coating of a seed

TESTACY *n* pl. **-CIES** the state of having left a will at death

TESTATE *n* pl. **-S** a testator

TESTATOR *n* pl. **-S** one that makes a will

TESTEE *n* pl. **-S** one that is tested

TESTER *n* pl. **-S** one that tests

TESTES pl. of testis

TESTICLE *n* pl. **-S** a testis

TESTIER comparative of testy

TESTIEST superlative of testy

TESTIFY *v* **-FIED, -FYING, -FIES** to make a declaration of truth under oath

TESTILY *adv* in a testy manner

TESTING *n* pl. **-S** the act of evaluating one by an examination

TESTIS *n* pl. **TESTES** a male reproductive gland

TESTON *n* pl. **-S** a former French coin

TESTOON *n* pl. **-S** teston

TESTUDO *n* pl. **-DOS** or **-DINES** a portable screen used as a shield by the ancient Romans

TESTY *adj* **TESTIER, TESTIEST** irritable

TET *n* pl. **-S** teth

TETANAL *adj* pertaining to tetanus

TETANIC *n* pl. **-S** a drug capable of causing convulsions

TETANIES pl. of tetany

TETANISE *v* **-NISED, -NISING, -NISES** to tetanize

TETANIZE *v* **-NIZED, -NIZING, -NIZES** to affect with convulsions

TETANUS *n* pl. **-ES** an infectious disease **TETANOID** *adj*

TETANY *n* pl. **-NIES** a condition marked by painful muscular spasms

TETCHED *adj* crazy

TETCHY *adj* **TETCHIER, TETCHIEST** irritable **TETCHILY** *adv*

TETH *n* pl. **-S** a Hebrew letter

TETHER *v* **-ED, -ING, -S** to fasten to a fixed object with a rope

TETOTUM *n* pl. **-S** teetotum

TETRA *n* pl. **-S** a tropical fish

TETRACID *n* pl. **-S** a type of acid

TETRAD *n* pl. **-S** a group of four **TETRADIC** *adj*

TETRAGON *n* pl. **-S** a four-sided polygon

TETRAMER *n* pl. **-S** a type of polymer

TETRAPOD *n* pl. **-S** a four-footed animal

TETRARCH *n* pl. **-S** one of four joint rulers

TETRI *n* pl. **-S** a monetary unit of the Republic of Georgia

TETRODE *n* pl. **-S** a type of electron tube

TETROSE *n* pl. **-S** a sugar whose molecules contain four carbon atoms

TETROXID *n* pl. **-S** a type of oxide

TETRYL *n* pl. **-S** a chemical compound

TETTER *n* pl. **-S** a skin disease

TEUCH *adj* teugh

TEUGH *adj* tough **TEUGHLY** *adv*

TEVATRON *n* pl. **-S** a particle accelerator

TEW *v* **-ED, -ING, -S** to work hard

TEXAS *n* pl. **-ES** the uppermost structure on a steamboat

TEXT *v* **-ED, -ING, -S** to send a message from one cell phone to another

TEXTBOOK *n* pl. **-S** a book used in the study of a subject

TEXTER *n* pl. **-S** one that texts

TEXTILE *n* pl. **-S** a woven fabric

TEXTLESS *adj* having no text

TEXTUAL *adj* pertaining to a text

TEXTUARY *n* pl. **-ARIES** a specialist in the study of the Scriptures

TEXTURAL *adj* pertaining to the surface characteristics of something

TEXTURE *v* **-TURED, -TURING, -TURES** to make by weaving

THACK *v* **-ED, -ING, -S** to thatch

THAE *adj* these; those

THAIRM *n* pl. **-S** tharm

THALAMUS *n* pl. **-MI** a part of the brain **THALAMIC** *adj*

THALER *n* pl. **-S** taler

THALI *n* pl. **-S** a platter on which food is served in India

THALLIUM *n* pl. **-S** a metallic element **THALLIC, THALLOUS** *adj*

THALLUS *n* pl. **-LUSES** or **-LI** a plant body without true root, stem, or leaf **THALLOID** *adj*

THALWEG *n* pl. **-S** the line defining the lowest points along the length of a riverbed

THAN *conj* — used to introduce the second element of a comparison

THANAGE *n* pl. **-S** the land held by a thane

THANATOS *n* pl. **-ES** an instinctual desire for death

THANE *n* pl. **-S** a man holding land by military service in Anglo-Saxon England

THANEDOM *n* pl. **-S** the domain of a thane

THANK *v* **-ED, -ING, -S** to express gratitude to

THANKER *n* pl. **-S** one that thanks

THANKFUL *adj* **-FULLER, -FULLEST** feeling gratitude

THARM *n* pl. **-S** the belly

THAT *pron* pl. **THOSE** the one indicated

THATAWAY *adv* in that direction

THATCH *v* **-ED, -ING, -ES** to cover with thatch (plant stalks or foliage)

THATCHER   n pl. **-S** one that thatches

THATCHY   adj **THATCHIER, THATCHIEST** resembling thatch

THAW   v **-ED, -ING, -S** to melt

THAWER   n pl. **-S** one that thaws

THAWING   n pl. **-S** the melting of a frozen substance

THAWLESS   adj never thawing

THE   definite article — used to specify or make particular

THEARCHY   n pl. **-CHIES** rule by a god

THEATER   n pl. **-S** a building for dramatic presentations **THEATRIC** adj

THEATRE   n pl. **-S** theater

THEBAINE   n pl. **-S** a poisonous alkaloid

THEBE   n pl. **-S** a monetary unit of Botswana

THECA   n pl. **-CAE** a protective anatomical covering **THECAL, THECATE** adj

THEE   pron the objective case of the pronoun thou

THEELIN   n pl. **-S** estrone

THEELOL   n pl. **-S** estriol

THEFT   n pl. **-S** the act of stealing

THEGN   n pl. **-S** thane **THEGNLY** adj

THEIN   n pl. **-S** theine

THEINE   n pl. **-S** caffeine

THEIR   adj belonging to them

THEIRS   pron a possessive form of the pronoun they

THEISM   n pl. **-S** belief in the existence of a god

THEIST   n pl. **-S** one who believes in the existence of a god **THEISTIC** adj

THELITIS   n pl. **-TISES** inflammation of the nipple

THEM   pron the objective case of the pronoun they

THEMATIC   n pl. **-S** a stamp collected according to its subject

THEME   v **THEMED, THEMING, THEMES** to plan something according to a central subject

THEMSELF   pron a person of unspecified sex

THEN   n pl. **-S** that time

THENAGE   n pl. **-S** thanage

THENAL   adj pertaining to the palm of the hand

THENAR   n pl. **-S** the palm of the hand

THENCE   adv from that place

THEOCRAT   n pl. **-S** a person who rules as a representative of a god

THEODICY   n pl. **-CIES** a defense of God's goodness in respect to the existence of evil

THEOGONY   n pl. **-NIES** an account of the origin of the gods

THEOLOG   n pl. **-S** a student of theology

THEOLOGY   n pl. **-GIES** the study of religion

THEONOMY   n pl. **-MIES** rule by a god

THEORBO   n pl. **-BOS** a stringed musical instrument

THEOREM   n pl. **-S** a proposition that is demonstrably true or is assumed to be so

THEORIES   pl. of theory

THEORISE   v **-RISED, -RISING, -RISES** to theorize

THEORIST   n pl. **-S** one that theorizes

THEORIZE   v **-RIZED, -RIZING, -RIZES** to form theories

THEORY   n pl. **-RIES** a group of propositions used to explain a class of phenomena

THERAPY   n pl. **-PIES** the treatment of illness or disability

THERE   n pl. **-S** that place

THEREAT   adv at that place or time

THEREBY   adv by that means

THEREFOR   adv for that

THEREIN   adv in that place

THEREMIN   n pl. **-S** a musical instrument

THEREOF   adv of that

THEREON   adv on that

THEREOUT   adv out of that

THERETO   adv to that

THERIAC   n pl. **-S** molasses

THERIACA   n pl. **-S** theriac

THERIAN   n pl. **-S** any of a subclass of mammals

THERM   n pl. **-S** a unit of quantity of heat

THERMAE   n/pl hot springs

THERMAL   n pl. **-S** a rising mass of warm air

THERME   n pl. **-S** therm

THERMEL   n pl. **-S** a device for temperature measurement

THERMIC   adj pertaining to heat

THERMION *n* pl. **-S** an ion emitted by a heated body

THERMITE *n* pl. **-S** a metallic mixture that produces intense heat when ignited

THERMOS *n* pl. **-ES** a container used to keep liquids either hot or cold

THEROID *adj* resembling a beast

THEROPOD *n* pl. **-S** a carnivorous dinosaur

THESAURI *n/pl* dictionaries of synonyms and antonyms

THESE pl. of this

THESIS *n* pl. **THESES** a proposition put forward for discussion

THESP *n* pl. **-S** an actor

THESPIAN *n* pl. **-S** an actor or actress

THETA *n* pl. **-S** a Greek letter

THETIC *adj* arbitrary

THETICAL *adj* thetic

THEURGY *n* pl. **-GIES** divine intervention in human affairs **THEURGIC** *adj*

THEW *n* pl. **-S** a well-developed muscle

THEWLESS *adj* weak

THEWY *adj* **THEWIER, THEWIEST** brawny

THEY *pron* the 3d person pl. pronoun in the nominative case

THIAMIN *n* pl. **-S** thiamine

THIAMINE *n* pl. **-S** a B vitamin

THIAZIDE *n* pl. **-S** a drug used to treat high blood pressure

THIAZIN *n* pl. **-S** thiazine

THIAZINE *n* pl. **-S** a chemical compound

THIAZOL *n* pl. **-S** thiazole

THIAZOLE *n* pl. **-S** a chemical compound

THICK *adj* **THICKER, THICKEST** having relatively great extent from one surface to its opposite

THICK *n* pl. **-S** the thickest part

THICKEN *v* **-ED, -ING, -S** to make thick

THICKET *n* pl. **-S** a dense growth of shrubs or small trees **THICKETY** *adj*

THICKISH *adj* somewhat thick

THICKLY *adv* in a thick manner

THICKSET *n* pl. **-S** a thicket

THIEF *n* pl. **THIEVES** one that steals

THIEVE *v* **THIEVED, THIEVING, THIEVES** to steal

THIEVERY *n* pl. **-ERIES** the act or practice of stealing

THIEVISH *adj* given to stealing

THIGH *n* pl. **-S** a part of the leg **THIGHED** *adj*

THILL *n* pl. **-S** a shaft of a vehicle

THIMBLE *n* pl. **-S** a cap used to protect the fingertip during sewing

THIN *adj* **THINNER, THINNEST** having relatively little density or thickness

THIN *v* **THINNED, THINNING, THINS** to make thin

THINCLAD *n* pl. **-S** a runner on a track team

THINDOWN *n* pl. **-S** a lessening in the number of atomic particles and cosmic rays passing through the earth's atmosphere

THINE *pron* a possessive form of the pronoun thou

THING *n* pl. **-S** an inanimate object

THINGY *n* pl. **THINGIES** something whose name is unknown or forgotten

THINK *v* **THOUGHT, THINKING, THINKS** to formulate in the mind

THINKER *n* pl. **-S** one that thinks

THINKING *n* pl. **-S** an opinion or judgment

THINLY *adv* in a thin manner

THINNED past tense of thin

THINNER *n* pl. **-S** one that thins

THINNESS *n* pl. **-ES** the quality or state of being thin

THINNEST superlative of thin

THINNING present participle of thin

THINNISH *adj* somewhat thin

THIO *adj* containing sulfur

THIOL *n* pl. **-S** a sulfur compound **THIOLIC** *adj*

THIONATE *n* pl. **-S** a chemical salt

THIONIC *adj* pertaining to sulfur

THIONIN *n* pl. **-S** a violet dye

THIONINE *n* pl. **-S** thionin

THIONYL *n* pl. **-S** sulfinyl

THIOPHEN *n* pl. **-S** a chemical compound

THIOTEPA *n* pl. **-S** a chemical compound

THIOUREA *n* pl. **-S** a chemical compound

THIR *pron* these

THIRAM *n* pl. **-S** a chemical compound

THIRD *n* pl. **-S** one of three equal parts

THIRDLY *adv* in the third place

THIRL *v* **-ED, -ING, -S** to thrill

THIRLAGE *n* pl. **-S** an obligation requiring feudal tenants to grind grain at a certain mill

THIRST *v* **-ED, -ING, -S** to feel a desire or need to drink

THIRSTER *n* pl. **-S** one that thirsts

THIRSTY *adj* **THIRSTIER, THIRSTIEST** feeling a desire or need to drink

THIRTEEN *n* pl. **-S** a number

THIRTY *n* pl. **-TIES** a number

THIS *pron* pl. **THESE** the person or thing just mentioned

THISAWAY *adv* this way

THISTLE *n* pl. **-S** a prickly plant

THISTLY *adj* **-TLIER, -TLIEST** prickly

THITHER *adv* in that direction

THO *conj* though

THOLE *v* **THOLED, THOLING, THOLES** to endure

THOLEPIN *n* pl. **-S** a pin that serves as an oarlock

THOLOS *n* pl. **-LOI** a circular, underground tomb

THONG *v* **-ED, -ING, -S** to flog with a whip

THONGY *adj* **THONGIER, THONGIEST** resembling an item of clothing made from a narrow strip of fabric

THORAX *n* pl. **-RAXES** or **-RACES** the part of the body between the neck and the abdomen **THORACAL, THORACIC** *adj*

THORIA *n* pl. **-S** an oxide of thorium

THORIC *adj* pertaining to thorium

THORITE *n* pl. **-S** a thorium ore

THORIUM *n* pl. **-S** a metallic element

THORN *v* **-ED, -ING, -S** to prick with a thorn (a sharp, rigid projection on a plant)

THORNY *adj* **THORNIER, THORNIEST** full of thorns **THORNILY** *adv*

THORO *adj* thorough

THORON *n* pl. **-S** a radioactive isotope of radon

THOROUGH *adj* **THOROUGHER, THOROUGHEST** complete in all respects

THORP *n* pl. **-S** a small village

THORPE *n* pl. **-S** thorp

THOSE pl. of that

THOU *v* **-ED, -ING, -S** to address as "thou" (the 2d person sing. pronoun in the nominative case)

THOUGH *conj* despite the fact that

THOUGHT *n* pl. **-S** a product of thinking

THOUSAND *n* pl. **-S** a number

THOWLESS *adj* listless

THRALDOM *n* pl. **-S** servitude

THRALL *v* **-ED, -ING, -S** to enslave

THRASH *v* **-ED, -ING, -ES** to beat

THRASHER *n* pl. **-S** one that thrashes

THRASHY *adj* **THRASHIER, THRASHIEST** characteristic of a style of fast, loud, punk-rock music

THRAVE *n* pl. **-S** a unit of measure for grain

THRAW *v* **-ED, -ING, -S** to twist

THRAWART *adj* stubborn

THRAWN *adj* twisted **THRAWNLY** *adv*

THREAD *v* **-ED, -ING, -S** to pass a thread (a very slender cord) through

THREADER *n* pl. **-S** one that threads

THREADY *adj* **THREADIER, THREADIEST** resembling a thread

THREAP *v* **-ED, -ING, -S** to dispute

THREAPER *n* pl. **-S** one that threaps

THREAT *v* **-ED, -ING, -S** to threaten

THREATEN *v* **-ED, -ING, -S** to be a source of danger to

THREE *n* pl. **-S** a number

THREEP *v* **-ED, -ING, -S** to threap

THRENODE *n* pl. **-S** a threnody

THRENODY *n* pl. **-DIES** a song of lamentation

THRESH *v* **-ED, -ING, -ES** to separate the grain or seeds from a plant mechanically

THRESHER *n* pl. **-S** one that threshes

THREW past tense of throw

THRICE *adv* three times

THRIFT *n* pl. **-S** care and wisdom in the management of one's resources

THRIFTY *adj* **THRIFTIER, THRIFTIEST** displaying thrift

THRILL *v* **-ED, -ING, -S** to excite greatly

THRILLER *n* pl. **-S** one that thrills

THRIP *n* pl. **-S** a British coin

THRIVE *v* **THROVE** or **THRIVED, THRIVEN, THRIVING, THRIVES** to grow vigorously

THRIVER *n* pl. **-S** one that thrives

THRO *prep* through

THROAT *v* **-ED, -ING, -S** to utter in a hoarse voice

THROATY *adj* **THROATIER, THROATIEST** hoarse

THROB *v* **THROBBED, THROBBING, THROBS** to pulsate

THROBBER *n* pl. **-S** one that throbs

THROE *n* pl. **-S** a violent spasm of pain

THROMBIN *n* pl. **-S** an enzyme

THROMBUS *n* pl. **-BI** a clot occluding a blood vessel

THRONE *v* **THRONED, THRONING, THRONES** to place on a throne (a royal chair)

THRONG *v* **-ED, -ING, -S** to crowd into

THROSTLE *n* pl. **-S** a songbird

THROTTLE *v* **-TLED, -TLING, -TLES** to strangle

THROUGH *prep* by way of

THROVE a past tense of thrive

THROW *v* **THREW, THROWN, THROWING, THROWS** to propel through the air with a movement of the arm

THROWER *n* pl. **-S** one that throws

THRU *prep* through

THRUM *v* **THRUMMED, THRUMMING, THRUMS** to play a stringed instrument idly or monotonously

THRUMMER *n* pl. **-S** one that thrums

THRUMMY *adj* **-MIER, -MIEST** shaggy

THRUPUT *n* pl. **-S** the amount of raw material processed within a given time

THRUSH *n* pl. **-ES** a songbird

THRUST *v* **-ED, -ING, -S** to push forcibly

THRUSTER *n* pl. **-S** one that thrusts

THRUSTOR *n* pl. **-S** thruster

THRUWAY *n* pl. **-WAYS** an express highway

THUD *v* **THUDDED, THUDDING, THUDS** to make a dull, heavy sound

THUG *n* pl. **-S** a brutal ruffian or assassin

THUGGEE *n* pl. **-S** thuggery in India

THUGGERY *n* pl. **-GERIES** thuggish behavior

THUGGISH *adj* characteristic of a thug

THUJA *n* pl. **-S** an evergreen tree or shrub

THULIA *n* pl. **-S** an oxide of thulium

THULIUM *n* pl. **-S** a metallic element

THUMB *v* **-ED, -ING, -S** to leaf through with the thumb (the short, thick digit of the human hand)

THUMBKIN *n* pl. **-S** a screw that is turned by the thumb and fingers

THUMBNUT *n* pl. **-S** a nut that is turned by the thumb and fingers

THUMP *v* **-ED, -ING, -S** to strike so as to make a dull, heavy sound

THUMPER *n* pl. **-S** one that thumps

THUNDER *v* **-ED, -ING, -S** to produce a loud, resounding sound

THUNDERY *adj* accompanied with thunder

THUNK *v* **-ED, -ING, -S** to make a sudden, muffled sound

THURIBLE *n* pl. **-S** a censer

THURIFER *n* pl. **-S** one who carries a thurible in a religious ceremony

THURL *n* pl. **-S** the hip joint in cattle

THUS *adv* in this manner

THUSLY *adv* thus

THUYA *n* pl. **-S** thuja

THWACK *v* **-ED, -ING, -S** to strike with something flat

THWACKER *n* pl. **-S** one that thwacks

THWART *v* **-ED, -ING, -S** to prevent the accomplishment of

THWARTER *n* pl. **-S** one that thwarts

THWARTLY *adv* athwart

THY *adj* belonging to thou

THYME *n* pl. **-S** an aromatic herb

THYMEY *adj* **THYMIER, THYMIEST** thymy

THYMI a pl. of thymus

THYMIC *adj* pertaining to thyme

THYMIER comparative of thymey and thymy

THYMIEST superlative of thymey and thymy

THYMINE *n* pl. **-S** a chemical compound

THYMOL *n* pl. **-S** a chemical compound

THYMOMA *n* pl. **-MAS** or **-MATA** a tumor arising from thymus tissue

THYMOSIN *n* pl. **-S** a hormone secreted by the thymus

THYMUS *n* pl. **-MUSES** or **-MI** a glandular structure in the body

THYMY *adj* **THYMIER, THYMIEST** abounding in thyme

THYREOID *adj* pertaining to the thyroid

THYROID *n* pl. **-S** an endocrine gland

THYROXIN   *n* pl. **-S** an amino acid

THYRSE   *n* pl. **-S** thyrsus

THYRSUS   *n* pl. **-SI** a type of flower cluster **THYRSOID** *adj*

THYSELF   *pron* yourself

TI   *n* pl. **-S** the seventh tone of the diatonic musical scale

TIAN   *n* pl. **-S** a large oval cooking pot

TIARA   *n* pl. **-S** a jeweled headpiece worn by women **TIARAED** *adj*

TIBIA   *n* pl. **-IAS** or **-IAE** a bone of the leg **TIBIAL** *adj*

TIBIALIS   *n* pl. **TIBIALES** a muscle in the calf of the leg

TIC   *v* **TICCED, TICCING, TICS** to have an involuntary muscular contraction

TICAL   *n* pl. **-S** a former Thai unit of weight

TICK   *v* **-ED, -ING, -S** to make a recurrent clicking sound

TICKER   *n* pl. **-S** one that ticks

TICKET   *v* **-ED, -ING, -S** to attach a tag to

TICKING   *n* pl. **-S** a strong cotton fabric

TICKLACE   *n* pl. **-S** a type of small seabird

TICKLE   *v* **-LED, -LING, -LES** to touch lightly so as to produce a tingling sensation

TICKLER   *n* pl. **-S** one that tickles

TICKLISH   *adj* sensitive to tickling

TICKLY   *adj* **-LIER, -LIEST** ticklish

TICKSEED   *n* pl. **-S** a flowering plant

TICKTACK   *v* **-ED, -ING, -S** to ticktock

TICKTOCK   *v* **-ED, -ING, -S** to make the ticking sound of a clock

TICTAC   *v* **-TACKED, -TACKING, -TACS** to ticktock

TICTOC   *v* **-TOCKED, -TOCKING, -TOCS** to ticktock

TIDAL   *adj* pertaining to the tides **TIDALLY** *adv*

TIDBIT   *n* pl. **-S** a choice bit of food

TIDDLER   *n* pl. **-S** a small fish

TIDDLY   *adj* **-DLIER, -DLIEST** slightly drunk

TIDE   *v* **TIDED, TIDING, TIDES** to flow like the tide (the rise and fall of the ocean's waters)

TIDELAND   *n* pl. **-S** land alternately covered and uncovered by the tide

TIDELESS   *adj* lacking a tide

TIDELIKE   *adj* resembling a tide

TIDELINE   *n* pl. **-S** a line on a shore marking the highest point of the tide

TIDEMARK   *n* pl. **-S** a mark showing the highest or lowest point of a tide

TIDERIP   *n* pl. **-S** a riptide

TIDEWAY   *n* pl. **-WAYS** a tidal channel

TIDIED   past tense of tidy

TIDIER   *n* pl. **-S** one that tidies

TIDIES   present 3d person sing. of tidy

TIDIEST   superlative of tidy

TIDILY   *adv* in a tidy manner

TIDINESS   *n* pl. **-ES** the state of being tidy

TIDING   *n* pl. **-S** a piece of news

TIDY   *adj* **-DIER, -DIEST** neat and orderly

TIDY   *v* **-DIED, -DYING, -DIES** to make tidy

TIDYTIPS   *n* pl. **TIDYTIPS** an annual herb

TIE   *v* **TIED, TYING** or **TIEING, TIES** to fasten with a cord or rope

TIEBACK   *n* pl. **-S** a loop for holding a curtain back to one side

TIEBREAK   *n* pl. **-S** a contest to select a winner from among contestants with a tied score

TIECLASP   *n* pl. **-S** a clasp for securing a necktie

TIED   past tense of tie

TIEING   a present participle of tie

TIELESS   *adj* having no necktie

TIEPIN   *n* pl. **-S** a pin for securing a necktie

TIER   *v* **-ED, -ING, -S** to arrange in tiers (rows placed one above another)

TIERCE   *n* pl. **-S** one of seven canonical daily periods for prayer and devotion

TIERCED   *adj* divided into three equal parts

TIERCEL   *n* pl. **-S** tercel

TIFF   *v* **-ED, -ING, -S** to have a petty quarrel

TIFFANY   *n* pl. **-NIES** a thin, mesh fabric

TIFFIN   *v* **-ED, -ING, -S** to lunch

TIGER   *n* pl. **-S** a large feline mammal

TIGEREYE   *n* pl. **-S** a gemstone

TIGERISH   *adj* resembling a tiger

TIGHT   *adj* **TIGHTER, TIGHTEST** firmly or closely fixed in place **TIGHTLY** *adv*

TIGHTEN   *v* **-ED, -ING, -S** to make tight

TIGHTS   *n/pl* a close-fitting garment

TIGHTWAD *n* pl. **-S** a miser

TIGLON *n* pl. **-S** the offspring of a male tiger and a female lion

TIGNON *n* pl. **-S** a piece of cloth worn as a headdress in Louisiana

TIGON *n* pl. **-S** tiglon

TIGRESS *n* pl. **-ES** a female tiger

TIGRISH *adj* tigerish

TIKE *n* pl. **-S** tyke

TIKI *n* pl. **-S** a wood or stone image of a Polynesian god

TIKKA *n* pl. **-S** an Indian dish of meat cooked on a skewer

TIL *n* pl. **-S** the sesame plant

TILAK *n* pl. **-S** a mark worn on the forehead by Hindus

TILAPIA *n* pl. **-S** an African fish

TILBURY *n* pl. **-BURIES** a carriage having two wheels

TILDE *n* pl. **-S** a mark placed over a letter to indicate its sound

TILE *v* **TILED, TILING, TILES** to cover with tiles (thin slabs of baked clay)

TILEFISH *n* pl. **-ES** a marine food fish

TILELIKE *adj* resembling a tile

TILER *n* pl. **-S** one that tiles

TILING *n* pl. **-S** a surface of tiles

TILL *v* **-ED, -ING, -S** to prepare land for crops by plowing **TILLABLE** *adj*

TILLAGE *n* pl. **-S** cultivated land

TILLER *v* **-ED, -ING, -S** to put forth stems from a root

TILLITE *n* pl. **-S** rock made up of consolidated clay, sand, gravel, and boulders

TILT *v* **-ED, -ING, -S** to cause to slant **TILTABLE** *adj*

TILTER *n* pl. **-S** one that tilts

TILTH *n* pl. **-S** tillage

TILTYARD *n* pl. **-S** an area for jousting contests

TIMARAU *n* pl. **-S** tamarau

TIMBAL *n* pl. **-S** a large drum

TIMBALE *n* pl. **-S** a pastry shell shaped like a drum

TIMBER *v* **-ED, -ING, -S** to furnish with timber (wood used as a building material) **TIMBERY** *adj*

TIMBRE *n* pl. **-S** the quality given to a sound by its overtones **TIMBRAL** *adj*

TIMBREL *n* pl. **-S** a percussion instrument

TIME *v* **TIMED, TIMING, TIMES** to determine the speed or duration of

TIMECARD *n* pl. **-S** a card for recording an employee's times of arrival and departure

TIMELESS *adj* having no beginning or end

TIMELINE *n* pl. **-S** a schedule of events

TIMELY *adj* **-LIER, -LIEST** occurring at the right moment

TIMEOUS *adj* timely

TIMEOUT *n* pl. **-S** a brief suspension of activity

TIMER *n* pl. **-S** one that times

TIMEWORK *n* pl. **-S** work paid for by the hour or by the day

TIMEWORN *adj* showing the effects of long use or wear

TIMID *adj* **-IDER, -IDEST** lacking courage or self-confidence **TIMIDLY** *adv*

TIMIDITY *n* pl. **-TIES** the quality of being timid

TIMING *n* pl. **-S** the selection of the proper moment for doing something

TIMOLOL *n* pl. **-S** a drug used to treat glaucoma

TIMOROUS *adj* fearful

TIMOTHY *n* pl. **-THIES** a European grass

TIMPANO *n* pl. **-NI** a kettledrum

TIMPANUM *n* pl. **-NUMS** or **-NA** tympanum

TIN *v* **TINNED, TINNING, TINS** to coat with tin (a metallic element)

TINAMOU *n* pl. **-S** a South American game bird

TINCAL *n* pl. **-S** crude borax

TINCT *v* **-ED, -ING, -S** to tinge

TINCTURE *v* **-TURED, -TURING, -TURES** to tinge

TINDER *n* pl. **-S** readily combustible material **TINDERY** *adj*

TINE *v* **TINED, TINING, TINES** to lose

TINEA *n* pl. **-S** a fungous skin disease **TINEAL** *adj*

TINEID *n* pl. **-S** one of a family of moths

TINFOIL *n* pl. **-S** a thin metal sheeting

TINFUL *n* pl. **-S** as much as a tin container can hold

TING   *v* **-ED, -ING, -S** to emit a high-pitched metallic sound

TINGE   *v* **TINGED, TINGEING** or **TINGING, TINGES** to apply a trace of color to

TINGLE   *v* **-GLED, -GLING, -GLES** to cause a prickly, stinging sensation

TINGLER   *n* pl. **-S** one that tingles

TINGLY   *adj* **-GLIER, -GLIEST** tingling

TINHORN   *n* pl. **-S** a showily pretentious person

TINIER   comparative of tiny

TINIEST   superlative of tiny

TINILY   *adv* in a tiny manner

TININESS   *n* pl. **-ES** the quality of being tiny

TINING   present participle of tine

TINKER   *v* **-ED, -ING, -S** to repair in an unskilled or experimental manner

TINKERER   *n* pl. **-S** one that tinkers

TINKLE   *v* **-KLED, -KLING, -KLES** to make slight, sharp, metallic sounds

TINKLER   *n* pl. **-S** one that tinkles

TINKLING   *n* pl. **-S** the sound made by something that tinkles

TINKLY   *adj* **-KLIER, -KLIEST** producing a tinkling sound

TINLIKE   *adj* resembling tin

TINMAN   *n* pl. **-MEN** a tinsmith

TINNED   past tense of tin

TINNER   *n* pl. **-S** a tin miner

TINNIER   comparative of tinny

TINNIEST   superlative of tinny

TINNILY   *adv* in a tinny manner

TINNING   present participle of tin

TINNITUS   *n* pl. **-ES** a ringing sound in the ears

TINNY   *adj* **-NIER, -NIEST** of or resembling tin

TINPLATE   *v* **-PLATED, -PLATING, -PLATES** to coat an object with tin

TINPOT   *adj* of little importance

TINSEL   *v* **-SELED, -SELING, -SELS** or **-SELLED, -SELLING, -SELS** to give a showy or gaudy appearance to

TINSELLY   *adj* cheaply gaudy

TINSELY   *adj* tinsely

TINSMITH   *n* pl. **-S** one who works with tin

TINSNIPS   *n/pl* a tool for cutting sheet metal

TINSTONE   *n* pl. **-S** a tin ore

TINT   *v* **-ED, -ING, -S** to color slightly or delicately

TINTER   *n* pl. **-S** one that tints

TINTING   *n* pl. **-S** the process of one that tints

TINTLESS   *adj* lacking color

TINTYPE   *n* pl. **-S** a kind of photograph

TINWARE   *n* pl. **-S** articles made of tinplate

TINWORK   *n* pl. **-S** something made of tin

TINY   *adj* **TINIER, TINIEST** very small

TIP   *v* **TIPPED, TIPPING, TIPS** to tilt

TIPCART   *n* pl. **-S** a type of cart

TIPCAT   *n* pl. **-S** a game resembling baseball

TIPI   *n* pl. **-S** tepee

TIPLESS   *adj* having no point or extremity

TIPOFF   *n* pl. **-S** a hint or warning

TIPPABLE   *adj* capable of being tipped

TIPPED   past tense of tip

TIPPER   *n* pl. **-S** one that tips

TIPPET   *n* pl. **-S** a covering for the shoulders

TIPPIER   comparative of tippy

TIPPIEST   superlative of tippy

TIPPING   present participle of tip

TIPPLE   *v* **-PLED, -PLING, -PLES** to drink alcoholic beverages

TIPPLER   *n* pl. **-S** one that tipples

TIPPY   *adj* **-PIER, -PIEST** unsteady

TIPPYTOE   *v* **-TOED, -TOEING, -TOES** to tiptoe

TIPSHEET   *n* pl. **-S** a publication with tips for betting on races or investing in stocks

TIPSIER   comparative of tipsy

TIPSIEST   superlative of tipsy

TIPSILY   *adv* in a tipsy manner

TIPSTAFF   *n* pl. **-STAFFS** or **-STAVES** an attendant in a court of law

TIPSTER   *n* pl. **-S** one that sells information to gamblers

TIPSTOCK   *n* pl. **-S** a part of a gun

TIPSY   *adj* **-SIER, -SIEST** slightly drunk

TIPTOE   *v* **-TOED, -TOEING, -TOES** to walk on the tips of one's toes

TIPTOP   *n* pl. **-S** the highest point

TIRADE   *n* pl. **-S** a long, vehement speech

TIRAMISU — *n* pl. **-S** a dessert made with ladyfingers, mascarpone, chocolate, and espresso

TIRE — *v* **TIRED, TIRING, TIRES** to grow tired

TIRED — *adj* **TIREDER, TIREDEST** sapped of strength **TIREDLY** *adv*

TIRELESS — *adj* seemingly incapable of tiring

TIRESOME — *adj* tedious

TIRING — present participle of tire

TIRL — *v* **-ED, -ING, -S** to make a vibrating sound

TIRO — *n* pl. **-ROS** tyro

TIRRIVEE — *n* pl. **-S** a tantrum

TISANE — *n* pl. **-S** a ptisan

TISSUAL — *adj* pertaining to tissue

TISSUE — *v* **-SUED, -SUING, -SUES** to weave into tissue (a fine sheer fabric)

TISSUEY — *adj* resembling tissue

TISSULAR — *adj* affecting an organism's tissue (structural material)

TIT — *n* pl. **-S** a small bird

TITAN — *n* pl. **-S** a person of great size

TITANATE — *n* pl. **-S** a chemical salt

TITANESS — *n* pl. **-ES** a female titan

TITANIA — *n* pl. **-S** a mineral

TITANIC — *adj* of great size

TITANISM — *n* pl. **-S** revolt against social conventions

TITANITE — *n* pl. **-S** a mineral

TITANIUM — *n* pl. **-S** a metallic element

TITANOUS — *adj* pertaining to titanium

TITBIT — *n* pl. **-S** tidbit

TITCH — *n* pl. **-ES** a small amount

TITCHIE — *adj* **TITCHIER, TITCHIEST** titchy

TITCHY — *adj* **TITCHIER, TITCHIEST** very small

TITER — *n* pl. **-S** the strength of a chemical solution

TITFER — *n* pl. **-S** a hat

TITHABLE — *adj* subject to the payment of tithes

TITHE — *v* **TITHED, TITHING, TITHES** to pay a tithe (a small tax)

TITHER — *n* pl. **-S** one that tithes

TITHING — *n* pl. **-S** the act of levying tithes

TITHONIA — *n* pl. **-S** a tall herb

TITI — *n* pl. **-S** an evergreen shrub or tree

TITIAN — *n* pl. **-S** a reddish brown color

TITIVATE — *v* **-VATED, -VATING, -VATES** to dress smartly

TITLARK — *n* pl. **-S** a songbird

TITLE — *v* **-TLED, -TLING, -TLES** to furnish with a title (a distinctive appellation)

TITLIST — *n* pl. **-S** a sports champion

TITMAN — *n* pl. **-MEN** the smallest of a litter of pigs

TITMOUSE — *n* pl. **-MICE** a small bird

TITRABLE — *adj* capable of being titrated

TITRANT — *n* pl. **-S** the reagent used in titration

TITRATE — *v* **-TRATED, -TRATING, -TRATES** to determine the strength of a solution by adding a reagent until a desired reaction occurs

TITRATOR — *n* pl. **-S** one that titrates

TITRE — *n* pl. **-S** titer

TITTER — *v* **-ED, -ING, -S** to utter a restrained, nervous laugh

TITTERER — *n* pl. **-S** one that titters

TITTIE — *n* pl. **-S** a sister

TITTLE — *n* pl. **-S** a very small mark in writing or printing

TITTUP — *v* **-TUPED, -TUPING, -TUPS** or **-TUPPED, -TUPPING, -TUPS** to move in a lively manner

TITTUPPY — *adj* shaky; unsteady

TITTY — *n* pl. **-TIES** a teat

TITUBANT — *adj* marked by wavering

TITULAR — *n* pl. **-S** one who holds a title

TITULARY — *n* pl. **-LARIES** a titular

TIVY — *adv* with great speed

TIX — *n/pl* tickets

TIYIN — *n* pl. **-S** a monetary unit of Kyrgyzstan

TIYN — *n* pl. **-S** a monetary unit of Kazakhstan

TIZ — *n* pl. **-ES** tizzy

TIZZ — *n* pl. **-ES** tizzy

TIZZY — *n* pl. **-ZIES** a state of nervous confusion

TMESIS — *n* pl. **TMESES** the separation of the parts of a compound word by an intervening word or words

TO — *prep* in the direction of

TOAD — *n* pl. **-S** a tailless, jumping amphibian

TOADFISH — *n* pl. **-ES** a marine fish

TOADFLAX	*n* pl. **-ES** a perennial herb	**TOEHOLD**	*n* pl. **-S** a space that supports the toes in climbing
TOADIED	past tense of toady	**TOEING**	present participle of toe
TOADIES	present 3d person sing. of toady	**TOELESS**	*adj* having no toes
TOADISH	*adj* resembling a toad	**TOELIKE**	*adj* resembling a toe
TOADLESS	*adj* having no toads	**TOENAIL**	*v* **-ED, -ING, -S** to fasten with obliquely driven nails
TOADLET	*n* pl. **-S** a small toad		
TOADLIKE	*adj* resembling a toad	**TOEPIECE**	*n* pl. **-S** a piece of a shoe designed to cover the toes
TOADY	*v* **TOADIED, TOADYING, TOADIES** to engage in servile flattering	**TOEPLATE**	*n* pl. **-S** a metal tab attached to the tip of a shoe
TOADYISH	*adj* characteristic of one that toadies	**TOERAG**	*n* pl. **-S** a contemptible person
TOADYISM	*n* pl. **-S** toadyish behavior	**TOESHOE**	*n* pl. **-S** a dance slipper without a heel
TOAST	*v* **-ED, -ING, -S** to brown by exposure to heat	**TOFF**	*n* pl. **-S** a dandy
		TOFFEE	*n* pl. **-S** a chewy candy
TOASTER	*n* pl. **-S** a device for toasting	**TOFFY**	*n* pl. **-FIES** toffee
TOASTING	*n* pl. **-S** the adding of rhythmic speech to reggae music	**TOFT**	*n* pl. **-S** a hillock
		TOFU	*n* pl. **-S** a soft food product made from soybean milk
TOASTY	*adj* **TOASTIER, TOASTIEST** comfortably warm	**TOG**	*v* **TOGGED, TOGGING, TOGS** to clothe
TOBACCO	*n* pl. **-COS** or **-COES** an annual herb cultivated for its leaves	**TOGA**	*n* pl. **-GAS** or **-GAE** an outer garment worn in ancient Rome **TOGAED** *adj*
TOBOGGAN	*v* **-ED, -ING, -S** to ride on a long, narrow sled		
		TOGATE	*adj* pertaining to ancient Rome
TOBY	*n* pl. **-BIES** a type of drinking mug	**TOGATED**	*adj* wearing a toga
TOCCATA	*n* pl. **-TAS** or **-TE** a musical composition usually for an organ	**TOGETHER**	*adv* into a union or relationship
		TOGGED	past tense of tog
TOCHER	*v* **-ED, -ING, -S** to give a dowry to	**TOGGERY**	*n* pl. **-GERIES** clothing
TOCK	*n* pl. **-S** a short, hollow sound	**TOGGING**	present participle of tog
TOCO	*n* pl. **-COS** a South American toucan	**TOGGLE**	*v* **-GLED, -GLING, -GLES** to fasten with a type of pin or short rod
TOCOLOGY	*n* pl. **-GIES** the branch of medicine dealing with childbirth	**TOGGLER**	*n* pl. **-S** one that toggles
		TOGUE	*n* pl. **-S** a freshwater fish
TOCSIN	*n* pl. **-S** an alarm sounded on a bell	**TOIL**	*v* **-ED, -ING, -S** to work strenuously
TOD	*n* pl. **-S** a British unit of weight	**TOILE**	*n* pl. **-S** a sheer linen fabric
TODAY	*n* pl. **-DAYS** the present day	**TOILER**	*n* pl. **-S** one that toils
TODDLE	*v* **-DLED, -DLING, -DLES** to walk unsteadily	**TOILET**	*v* **-ED, -ING, -S** to dress and groom oneself
TODDLER	*n* pl. **-S** one that toddles	**TOILETRY**	*n* pl. **-TRIES** an article used in dressing and grooming oneself
TODDY	*n* pl. **-DIES** an alcoholic beverage		
TODY	*n* pl. **-DIES** a West Indian bird	**TOILETTE**	*n* pl. **-S** the act of dressing and grooming oneself
TOE	*v* **TOED, TOEING, TOES** to touch with the toe (one of the terminal members of the foot)		
		TOILFUL	*adj* toilsome
		TOILSOME	*adj* demanding much exertion
TOEA	*n* pl. **-S** a monetary unit of Papua New Guinea	**TOILWORN**	*adj* worn by toil
		TOIT	*v* **-ED, -ING, -S** to saunter
TOECAP	*n* pl. **-S** a covering for the tip of a shoe or boot	**TOKAMAK**	*n* pl. **-S** a doughnut-shaped nuclear reactor
TOECLIP	*n* pl. **-S** a device that holds the front of a cyclist's shoe to the pedal		

TOKAY	*n* pl. **-KAYS** a Malaysian gecko
TOKE	*v* **TOKED, TOKING, TOKES** to take a puff on a marijuana cigarette
TOKEN	*v* **-ED, -ING, -S** to serve as a sign of
TOKENISM	*n* pl. **-S** the policy of making only a superficial effort
TOKER	*n* pl. **-S** one that tokes
TOKING	present participle of toke
TOKOLOGY	*n* pl. **-GIES** tocology
TOKOMAK	*n* pl. **-S** tokamak
TOKONOMA	*n* pl. **-S** a small alcove in a Japanese house
TOLA	*n* pl. **-S** a unit of weight used in India
TOLAN	*n* pl. **-S** a chemical compound
TOLANE	*n* pl. **-S** tolan
TOLAR	*n* pl. **-LARS** or **-LARJEV** a former monetary unit of Slovenia
TOLBOOTH	*n* pl. **-S** a prison
TOLD	past tense of tell
TOLE	*v* **TOLED, TOLING, TOLES** to allure
TOLEDO	*n* pl. **-DOS** a finely tempered sword
TOLERANT	*adj* inclined to tolerate
TOLERATE	*v* **-ATED, -ATING, -ATES** to allow without active opposition
TOLEWARE	*n* pl. **-S** objects made of elaborately decorated sheet metal
TOLIDIN	*n* pl. **-S** tolidine
TOLIDINE	*n* pl. **-S** a chemical compound
TOLING	present participle of tole
TOLL	*v* **-ED, -ING, -S** to collect or impose a toll (a fixed charge for a service or privilege)
TOLLAGE	*n* pl. **-S** a toll
TOLLBAR	*n* pl. **-S** a tollgate
TOLLER	*n* pl. **-S** a collector of tolls
TOLLGATE	*v* **-GATED, -GATING, -GATES** to block a business deal pending payment of a bribe
TOLLING	*n* pl. **-S** the collecting of tolls
TOLLMAN	*n* pl. **-MEN** a toller
TOLLWAY	*n* pl. **-WAYS** a road on which tolls are collected
TOLT	*n* pl. **-S** an isolated hill
TOLU	*n* pl. **-S** a fragrant resin
TOLUATE	*n* pl. **-S** a chemical salt

TOLUENE	*n* pl. **-S** a flammable liquid
TOLUIC	*adj* pertaining to any of four isomeric acids derived from toluene
TOLUID	*n* pl. **-S** toluide
TOLUIDE	*n* pl. **-S** an amide
TOLUIDIN	*n* pl. **-S** an amine
TOLUOL	*n* pl. **-S** toluene
TOLUOLE	*n* pl. **-S** toluol
TOLUYL	*n* pl. **-S** a univalent chemical radical
TOLYL	*n* pl. **-S** a univalent chemical radical
TOM	*n* pl. **-S** the male of various animals
TOMAHAWK	*v* **-ED, -ING, -S** to strike with a light ax
TOMALLEY	*n* pl. **-LEYS** the liver of a lobster
TOMAN	*n* pl. **-S** a formerly used coin of Iran
TOMATO	*n* pl. **-TOES** the fleshy, edible fruit of a perennial plant **TOMATOEY** *adj*
TOMB	*v* **-ED, -ING, -S** to place in a tomb (a burial vault or chamber)
TOMBAC	*n* pl. **-S** an alloy of copper and zinc
TOMBACK	*n* pl. **-S** tombac
TOMBAK	*n* pl. **-S** tombac
TOMBAL	*adj* pertaining to a tomb
TOMBLESS	*adj* having no tomb
TOMBLIKE	*adj* resembling a tomb
TOMBOLA	*n* pl. **-S** a gambling game that is a type of lottery
TOMBOLO	*n* pl. **-LOS** a sandbar connecting an island to the mainland
TOMBOY	*n* pl. **-BOYS** a girl who prefers boyish activities
TOMCAT	*v* **-CATTED, -CATTING, -CATS** to engage in sexually promiscuous behavior — used of a male
TOMCOD	*n* pl. **-S** a marine fish
TOME	*n* pl. **-S** a large book
TOMENTUM	*n* pl. **-TA** a network of small blood vessels
TOMFOOL	*n* pl. **-S** a foolish person
TOMMY	*n* pl. **-MIES** a loaf of bread
TOMMYCOD	*n* pl. **-S** tomcod
TOMMYROT	*n* pl. **-S** nonsense
TOMOGRAM	*n* pl. **-S** a photograph made with X-rays
TOMORROW	*n* pl. **-S** the day following today

TOMPION	*n* pl. **-S** tampion
TOMTIT	*n* pl. **-S** any of various small active birds
TON	*n* pl. **-S** a unit of weight
TONAL	*adj* pertaining to tone **TONALLY** *adv*
TONALITY	*n* pl. **-TIES** a system of tones
TONDO	*n* pl. **-DOS** or **-DI** a circular painting
TONE	*v* **TONED, TONING, TONES** to give a particular tone (a sound of definite pitch and vibration) to
TONEARM	*n* pl. **-S** the pivoted part of a record player that holds the needle
TONELESS	*adj* lacking in tone
TONEME	*n* pl. **-S** a tonal unit of speech **TONEMIC** *adj*
TONER	*n* pl. **-S** one that tones
TONETICS	*n/pl* the phonetic study of tone in language **TONETIC** *adj*
TONETTE	*n* pl. **-S** a simple flute
TONEY	*adj* **TONIER, TONIEST** tony
TONG	*v* **-ED, -ING, -S** to lift with a type of grasping device
TONGA	*n* pl. **-S** a light cart used in India
TONGER	*n* pl. **-S** one that tongs
TONGMAN	*n* pl. **-MEN** a member of a Chinese secret society
TONGUE	*v* **TONGUED, TONGUING, TONGUES** to touch with the tongue (an organ of the mouth)
TONGUING	*n* pl. **-S** the use of the tongue in articulating notes on a wind instrument
TONIC	*n* pl. **-S** something that invigorates or refreshes
TONICITY	*n* pl. **-TIES** normal, healthy bodily condition
TONIER	comparative of toney and tony
TONIEST	superlative of toney and tony
TONIFY	*v* **-FIED, -FYING, -FIES** to give tone to
TONIGHT	*n* pl. **-S** the present night
TONING	present participle of tone
TONISH	*adj* stylish **TONISHLY** *adv*
TONLET	*n* pl. **-S** a skirt of plate armor
TONNAGE	*n* pl. **-S** total weight in tons
TONNE	*n* pl. **-S** a unit of weight

TONNEAU	*n* pl. **-NEAUS** or **-NEAUX** the rear seating compartment of an automobile
TONNER	*n* pl. **-S** an object having a specified tonnage
TONNISH	*adj* tonish
TONSIL	*n* pl. **-S** a lymphoid organ **TONSILAR** *adj*
TONSURE	*v* **-SURED, -SURING, -SURES** to shave the head of
TONTINE	*n* pl. **-S** a form of collective life insurance
TONUS	*n* pl. **-ES** a normal state of tension in muscle tissue
TONY	*adj* **TONIER, TONIEST** stylish
TOO	*adv* in addition
TOODLE	*v* **-DLED, -DLING, -DLES** to tootle
TOOK	past tense of take
TOOL	*v* **-ED, -ING, -S** to form or finish with a tool (an implement used in manual work)
TOOLBAR	*n* pl. **-S** a row of icons on a computer screen that activate functions
TOOLBOX	*n* pl. **-ES** a box for tools
TOOLER	*n* pl. **-S** one that tools
TOOLHEAD	*n* pl. **-S** a part of a machine
TOOLING	*n* pl. **-S** ornamentation done with tools
TOOLLESS	*adj* having no tools
TOOLPUSH	*n* pl. **-ES** a worker who directs the drilling on an oil rig
TOOLROOM	*n* pl. **-S** a room where tools are stored
TOOLSET	*n* pl. **-S** a set of tools
TOOLSHED	*n* pl. **-S** a building where tools are stored
TOOM	*adj* empty
TOON	*n* pl. **-S** an East Indian tree
TOONIE	*n* pl. **-S** a Canadian two-dollar coin
TOOT	*v* **-ED, -ING, -S** to sound a horn or whistle in short blasts
TOOTER	*n* pl. **-S** one that toots
TOOTH	*n* pl. **TEETH** one of the hard structures attached in a row to each jaw
TOOTH	*v* **-ED, -ING, -S** to furnish with toothlike projections
TOOTHY	*adj* **TOOTHIER, TOOTHIEST** having or showing prominent teeth **TOOTHILY** *adv*

TOOTLE   *v* **-TLED, -TLING, -TLES** to toot softly or repeatedly

TOOTLER   *n* pl. **-S** one that tootles

TOOTS   *n* pl. **-ES** a woman or girl — usually used as a form of address

TOOTSIE   *n* pl. **-S** tootsy

TOOTSY   *n* pl. **-SIES** a foot

TOP   *v* **TOPPED, TOPPING, TOPS** to cut off the top (the highest part, point, or surface) of

TOPAZ   *n* pl. **-ES** a mineral **TOPAZINE** *adj*

TOPCOAT   *n* pl. **-S** a lightweight overcoat

TOPCROSS   *n* pl. **-ES** a cross between a purebred male and inferior female stock

TOPE   *v* **TOPED, TOPING, TOPES** to drink liquor to excess

TOPEE   *n* pl. **-S** topi

TOPER   *n* pl. **-S** one that topes

TOPFUL   *adj* topfull

TOPFULL   *adj* full to the top

TOPH   *n* pl. **-S** tufa

TOPHE   *n* pl. **-S** tufa

TOPHUS   *n* pl. **-PHI** a deposit of urates in the tissue around a joint

TOPI   *n* pl. **-S** a sun helmet

TOPIARY   *n* pl. **-ARIES** the art of trimming shrubs into shapes

TOPIC   *n* pl. **-S** a subject of discourse

TOPICAL   *n* pl. **-S** a postage stamp in a collection with designs relating to the same subject

TOPING   present participle of tope

TOPKICK   *n* pl. **-S** a first sergeant

TOPKNOT   *n* pl. **-S** an ornament for the hair

TOPLESS   *adj* having no top

TOPLINE   *n* pl. **-S** the outline of the top of an animal's body

TOPLOFTY   *adj* **-LOFTIER, -LOFTIEST** haughty

TOPMAST   *n* pl. **-S** a mast of a ship

TOPMOST   *adj* highest

TOPNOTCH   *adj* excellent

TOPO   *adj* topographic

TOPOI   pl. of topos

TOPOLOGY   *n* pl. **-GIES** a branch of mathematics

TOPONYM   *n* pl. **-S** the name of a place

TOPONYMY   *n* pl. **-MIES** the study of toponyms

TOPOS   *n* pl. **-POI** a stock rhetorical theme

TOPOTYPE   *n* pl. **-S** a specimen selected from a locality typical of a species

TOPPED   past tense of top

TOPPER   *n* pl. **-S** one that tops

TOPPING   *n* pl. **-S** something that forms a top

TOPPLE   *v* **-PLED, -PLING, -PLES** to fall forward

TOPSAIL   *n* pl. **-S** a sail of a ship

TOPSIDE   *n* pl. **-S** the upper portion of a ship

TOPSIDER   *n* pl. **-S** one who is at the highest level of authority

TOPSOIL   *v* **-ED, -ING, -S** to remove the surface layer of soil from

TOPSPIN   *n* pl. **-S** a forward spin imparted to a ball

TOPSTONE   *n* pl. **-S** the stone at the top of a structure

TOPWATER   *adj* floating on or near the top of the water

TOPWORK   *v* **-ED, -ING, -S** to graft scions of another variety of plant on the main branches of

TOQUE   *n* pl. **-S** a close-fitting woman's hat

TOQUET   *n* pl. **-S** toque

TOQUILLA   *n* pl. **-S** a palmlike plant of South America

TOR   *n* pl. **-S** a high, craggy hill

TORA   *n* pl. **-S** torah

TORAH   *n* pl. **-RAHS** or **-ROTH** or **-ROT** a law or precept

TORC   *n* pl. **-S** a metal collar or necklace

TORCH   *v* **-ED, -ING, -ES** to set on fire

TORCHERE   *n* pl. **-S** a type of electric lamp

TORCHIER   *n* pl. **-S** torchere

TORCHLIT   *adj* lighted by torches (poles with a burning end)

TORCHON   *n* pl. **-S** a coarse lace

TORCHY   *adj* **TORCHIER, TORCHIEST** characteristic of a torch song

TORE   *n* pl. **-S** a torus

TOREADOR   *n* pl. **-S** a bullfighter

TORERO   *n* pl. **-ROS** a bullfighter

TOREUTIC   *adj* pertaining to a type of metalwork

TORI   pl. of torus

TORIC   *n* pl. **-S** a lens designed to correct astigmatism

TORIES   pl. of tory

TORII   *n* pl. **TORII** the gateway of a Japanese temple

TORMENT   *v* **-ED, -ING, -S** to inflict with great bodily or mental suffering

TORN   past participle of tear

TORNADO   *n* pl. **-DOS** or **-DOES** a violent windstorm **TORNADIC** *adj*

TORNILLO   *n* pl. **-LOS** a flowering shrub

TORO   *n* pl. **-ROS** a bull

TOROID   *n* pl. **-S** a type of geometric surface **TOROIDAL** *adj*

TOROSE   *adj* cylindrical and swollen at intervals

TOROSITY   *n* pl. **-TIES** the quality or state of being torose

TOROT   a pl. of torah

TOROTH   a pl. of torah

TOROUS   *adj* torose

TORPEDO   *v* **-ED, -ING, -ES** or **-S** to damage or sink with an underwater missile

TORPEFY   *v* **-FIED, -FYING, -FIES** to make sluggish

TORPID   *n* pl. **-S** a racing boat

TORPIDLY   *adv* in a sluggish manner

TORPOR   *n* pl. **-S** mental or physical inactivity

TORQUATE   *adj* having a torques

TORQUE   *v* **TORQUED, TORQUING, TORQUES** to cause to twist

TORQUER   *n* pl. **-S** one that torques

TORQUES   *n* pl. **-QUESES** a band of feathers, hair, or coloration around the neck

TORQUEY   *adj* **-QUIER, -QUIEST** providing force to cause rotation

TORR   *n* pl. **-S** a unit of pressure

TORREFY   *v* **-FIED, -FYING, -FIES** to subject to intense heat

TORRENT   *n* pl. **-S** a rapid stream of water

TORRID   *adj* **-RIDER, -RIDEST** extremely hot **TORRIDLY** *adv*

TORRIFY   *v* **-FIED, -FYING, -FIES** to torrefy

TORSADE   *n* pl. **-S** a twisted cord

TORSE   *n* pl. **-S** a wreath of twisted silks

TORSI   a pl. of torso

TORSION   *n* pl. **-S** the act of twisting

TORSK   *n* pl. **-S** a marine food fish

TORSO   *n* pl. **-SOS** or **-SI** the trunk of the human body

TORT   *n* pl. **-S** a civil wrong

TORTA   *n* pl **-S** an elaborate dessert

TORTE   *n* pl. **TORTES** or **TORTEN** a rich cake

TORTELLI   *n/pl* pieces of pasta stuffed with cheese, meat, or vegetables

TORTILE   *adj* twisted; coiled

TORTILLA   *n* pl. **-S** a round, flat cake of unleavened cornmeal

TORTIOUS   *adj* of the nature of a tort

TORTOISE   *n* pl. **-S** any of an order of reptiles having the body enclosed in a bony shell

TORTONI   *n* pl. **-S** a type of ice cream

TORTRIX   *n* pl. **-TRIXES** or **-TRICES** a small moth

TORTUOUS   *adj* marked by repeated turns or bends

TORTURE   *v* **-TURED, -TURING, -TURES** to subject to severe physical pain

TORTURER   *n* pl. **-S** one that tortures

TORULA   *n* pl. **-LAS** or **-LAE** a type of fungus

TORUS   *n* pl. **-RI** or **-RUSES** a large convex molding

TORY   *n* pl. **-RIES** a political conservative

TOSA   *n* pl. **-S** a dog of a breed of mastiff

TOSH   *n* pl. **-ES** nonsense

TOSS   *v* **TOSSED** or **TOST, TOSSING, TOSSES** to throw lightly

TOSSER   *n* pl. **-S** one that tosses

TOSSPOT   *n* pl. **-S** a drunkard

TOSSUP   *n* pl. **-S** an even choice or chance

TOST   a past tense of toss

TOSTADA   *n* pl. **-S** a tortilla fried in deep fat

TOSTADO   *n* pl. **-DOS** tostada

TOSTONE   *n* pl. **-S** a Mexican dish of fried plantains

TOT   *v* **TOTTED, TOTTING, TOTS** to total

TOTABLE   *adj* capable of being toted

TOTAL   *v* **-TALED, -TALING, -TALS** or **-TALLED, -TALLING, -TALS** to ascertain the entire amount of

TOTALISE   *v* **-ISED, -ISING, -ISES** to totalize

TOTALISM   *n* pl. **-S** centralized control by an autocratic authority

TOTALIST   *n* pl. **-S** one who tends to regard things as a unified whole

TOTALITY   *n* pl. **-TIES** the quality or state of being complete

TOTALIZE	*v* **-IZED, -IZING, -IZES** to make complete	**TOURER**	*n* pl. **-S** a large, open automobile
TOTALLED	a past tense of total	**TOURING**	*n* pl. **-S** cross-country skiing for pleasure
TOTALLING	a present participle of total	**TOURISM**	*n* pl. **-S** the practice of touring for pleasure
TOTALLY	*adv* completely		
TOTE	*v* **TOTED, TOTING, TOTES** to carry by hand **TOTEABLE** *adj*	**TOURIST**	*n* pl. **-S** one who tours for pleasure **TOURISTY** *adj*
TOTEM	*n* pl. **-S** a natural object serving as the emblem of a family or clan **TOTEMIC** *adj*	**TOURISTA**	*n* pl. **-S** turista
		TOURNEY	*v* **-ED, -ING, -S** to compete in a tournament
TOTEMISM	*n* pl. **-S** a system of tribal division according to totems	**TOUSE**	*v* **TOUSED, TOUSING, TOUSES** to tousle
TOTEMIST	*n* pl. **-S** a specialist in totemism	**TOUSLE**	*v* **-SLED, -SLING, -SLES** to dishevel
TOTEMITE	*n* pl. **-S** a totemist		
TOTER	*n* pl. **-S** one that totes	**TOUT**	*v* **-ED, -ING, -S** to solicit brazenly
TOTHER	*pron* the other	**TOUTER**	*n* pl. **-S** one that touts
TOTING	present participle of tote	**TOUTON**	*n* pl. **-S** a deep-fried round of bread dough
TOTTED	past tense of tot		
TOTTER	*v* **-ED, -ING, -S** to walk unsteadily	**TOUZLE**	*v* **-ZLED, -ZLING, -ZLES** to tousle
TOTTERER	*n* pl. **-S** one that totters	**TOVARICH**	*n* pl. **-ES** comrade
TOTTERY	*adj* shaky	**TOVARISH**	*n* pl. **-ES** tovarich
TOTTING	present participle of tot	**TOW**	*v* **-ED, -ING, -S** to pull by means of a rope or chain **TOWABLE** *adj*
TOUCAN	*n* pl. **-S** a tropical bird		
TOUCH	*v* **-ED, -ING, -ES** to be in or come into contact with	**TOWAGE**	*n* pl. **-S** the price paid for towing
		TOWARD	*prep* in the direction of
TOUCHE	*interj* — used to acknowledge a hit in fencing	**TOWARDLY**	*adj* favorable
		TOWARDS	*prep* toward
TOUCHER	*n* pl. **-S** one that touches	**TOWAWAY**	*n* pl. **-AWAYS** the act of towing away a vehicle
TOUCHPAD	*n* pl. **-S** a keypad sensitized to finger movement or pressure		
		TOWBOAT	*n* pl. **-S** a tugboat
TOUCHUP	*n* pl. **-S** an act of finishing by adding minor improvements	**TOWEL**	*v* **-ELED, -ELING, -ELS** or **-ELLED, -ELLING, -ELS** to wipe with a towel (an absorbent cloth)
TOUCHY	*adj* **TOUCHIER, TOUCHIEST** overly sensitive **TOUCHILY** *adv*		
		TOWELING	*n* pl. **-S** material used for towels
TOUGH	*adj* **TOUGHER, TOUGHEST** strong and resilient	**TOWER**	*v* **-ED, -ING, -S** to rise to a great height
TOUGH	*v* **-ED, -ING, -S** to endure hardship	**TOWERY**	*adj* **-ERIER, -ERIEST** very tall
TOUGHEN	*v* **-ED, -ING, -S** to make tough	**TOWHEAD**	*n* pl. **-S** a head of light blond hair
TOUGHIE	*n* pl. **-S** a tough person	**TOWHEE**	*n* pl. **-S** a common finch
TOUGHISH	*adj* somewhat tough	**TOWIE**	*n* pl. **-S** a form of contract bridge for three players
TOUGHLY	*adv* in a tough manner		
TOUGHY	*n* pl. **TOUGHIES** toughie	**TOWLINE**	*n* pl. **-S** a line used in towing
TOUPEE	*n* pl. **-S** a wig worn to cover a bald spot	**TOWMOND**	*n* pl. **-S** a year
		TOWMONT	*n* pl. **-S** towmond
TOUPIE	*n* pl. **-S** a round boneless smoked ham	**TOWN**	*n* pl. **-S** a center of population smaller than a city
TOUR	*v* **-ED, -ING, -S** to travel from place to place	**TOWNEE**	*n* pl. **-S** a townsman
TOURACO	*n* pl. **-COS** an African bird	**TOWNFOLK**	*n/pl* the inhabitants of a town

TOWNHOME *n* pl. **-S** one of a series of contiguous houses of two or three stories

TOWNIE *n* pl. **-S** a nonstudent who lives in a college town

TOWNIES pl. of towny

TOWNISH *adj* characteristic of a town

TOWNLESS *adj* having no towns

TOWNLET *n* pl. **-S** a small town

TOWNSHIP *n* pl. **-S** an administrative division of a county

TOWNSITE *n* pl. **-S** the site of a town

TOWNSMAN *n* pl. **-MEN** a resident of a town

TOWNWARD *adv* toward the town

TOWNWEAR *n* pl. **TOWNWEAR** apparel that is suitable for wear in the city

TOWNY *n* pl. **TOWNIES** townie

TOWPATH *n* pl. **-S** a path along a river that is used by animals towing boats

TOWPLANE *n* pl. **-S** an airplane that tows gliders

TOWROPE *n* pl. **-S** a rope used in towing

TOWSACK *n* pl. **-S** a sack made of a coarse fabric

TOWY *adj* resembling coarse hemp or flax fiber

TOXAEMIA *n* pl. **-S** toxemia **TOXAEMIC** *adj*

TOXEMIA *n* pl. **-S** the condition of having toxins in the blood **TOXEMIC** *adj*

TOXIC *n* pl. **-S** a poisonous substance

TOXICAL *adj* toxic

TOXICANT *n* pl. **-S** a poisonous substance

TOXICITY *n* pl. **-TIES** the quality of being poisonous

TOXIN *n* pl. **-S** a poisonous substance

TOXINE *n* pl. **-S** toxin

TOXOID *n* pl. **-S** a type of toxin

TOY *v* **-ED**, **-ING**, **-S** to amuse oneself as if with a toy (a child's plaything)

TOYER *n* pl. **-S** one that toys

TOYISH *adj* frivolous

TOYLAND *n* pl. **-S** the toy industry

TOYLESS *adj* having no toy

TOYLIKE *adj* resembling a toy

TOYO *n* pl. **-YOS** a smooth straw used in making hats

TOYON *n* pl. **-S** an ornamental evergreen shrub

TOYSHOP *n* pl. **-S** a shop where toys are sold

TOYTOWN *n* pl. **-S** a small model of a town

TRABEATE *adj* constructed with horizontal beams

TRACE *v* **TRACED**, **TRACING**, **TRACES** to follow the course of

TRACER *n* pl. **-S** one that traces

TRACERY *n* pl. **-ERIES** ornamental work of interlaced lines

TRACHEA *n* pl. **-CHEAS** or **-CHEAE** the passage for conveying air to the lungs **TRACHEAL** *adj*

TRACHEID *n* pl. **-S** a long, tubular plant cell

TRACHLE *v* **-LED**, **-LING**, **-LES** to draggle

TRACHOMA *n* pl. **-S** a disease of the eye

TRACHYTE *n* pl. **-S** a light-colored igneous rock

TRACING *n* pl. **-S** something that is traced

TRACK *v* **-ED**, **-ING**, **-S** to follow the marks left by an animal, a person, or a vehicle

TRACKAGE *n* pl. **-S** the track system of a railroad

TRACKBED *n* pl. **-S** a roadbed for a railroad

TRACKER *n* pl. **-S** one that tracks

TRACKING *n* pl. **-S** the placement of students within a curriculum

TRACKMAN *n* pl. **-MEN** a railroad worker

TRACKPAD *n* pl. **-S** a touchpad

TRACKWAY *n* pl. **-WAYS** a trodden path

TRACT *n* pl. **-S** an expanse of land

TRACTATE *n* pl. **-S** a treatise

TRACTILE *adj* capable of being drawn out in length

TRACTION *n* pl. **-S** the act of pulling or drawing over a surface **TRACTIVE** *adj*

TRACTOR *n* pl. **-S** a motor vehicle used in farming

TRACTRIX *n* pl. **-TRICES** a mathematical curve

TRAD *adj* traditional

TRADE *v* **TRADED**, **TRADING**, **TRADES** to give in exchange for another commodity **TRADABLE** *adj*

TRADEOFF *n* pl. **-S** a giving up of one thing in return for another

TRADER *n* pl. **-S** one that trades

TRADING *n* pl. **-S** the action of exchanging commodities

TRADITOR *n* pl. **-ES** a traitor among the early Christians

TRADUCE *v* **-DUCED, -DUCING, -DUCES** to defame

TRADUCER *n* pl. **-S** one that traduces

TRAFFIC *v* **-FICKED, -FICKING, -FICS** to engage in buying and selling

TRAGEDY *n* pl. **-DIES** a disastrous event

TRAGI pl. of tragus

TRAGIC *n* pl. **-S** the element of a drama that produces tragedy

TRAGICAL *adj* of the nature of a tragedy

TRAGOPAN *n* pl. **-S** an Asian pheasant

TRAGUS *n* pl. **-GI** a part of the external opening of the ear

TRAIK *v* **-ED, -ING, -S** to trudge

TRAIL *v* **-ED, -ING, -S** to drag along a surface

TRAILER *v* **-ED, -ING, -S** to transport by means of a trailer (a vehicle drawn by another)

TRAIN *v* **-ED, -ING, -S** to instruct systematically

TRAINEE *n* pl. **-S** a person receiving training

TRAINER *n* pl. **-S** one that trains

TRAINFUL *n* pl. **-S** as much as a railroad train can hold

TRAINING *n* pl. **-S** systematic instruction

TRAINMAN *n* pl. **-MEN** a railroad employee

TRAINWAY *n* pl. **-WAYS** a railway

TRAIPSE *v* **TRAIPSED, TRAIPSING, TRAIPSES** to walk about in an idle or aimless manner

TRAIT *n* pl. **-S** a distinguishing characteristic

TRAITOR *n* pl. **-S** one who betrays another

TRAJECT *v* **-ED, -ING, -S** to transmit

TRAM *v* **TRAMMED, TRAMMING, TRAMS** to convey in a tramcar

TRAMCAR *n* pl. **-S** a streetcar

TRAMEL *v* **-ELED, -ELING, -ELS** or **-ELLED, -ELLING, -ELS** to trammel

TRAMELL *v* **-ED, -ING, -S** to trammel

TRAMLESS *adj* having no tramcar

TRAMLINE *n* pl. **-S** a streetcar line

TRAMMED past tense of tram

TRAMMEL *v* **-MELED, -MELING, -MELS** or **-MELLED, -MELLING, -MELS** to hinder

TRAMMING present participle of tram

TRAMP *v* **-ED, -ING, -S** to walk with a firm, heavy step

TRAMPER *n* pl. **-S** one that tramps

TRAMPISH *adj* resembling a vagabond

TRAMPLE *v* **-PLED, -PLING, -PLES** to tread on heavily

TRAMPLER *n* pl. **-S** one that tramples

TRAMPY *adj* **TRAMPIER, TRAMPIEST** having the characteristics of a vagrant

TRAMROAD *n* pl. **-S** a railway in a mine

TRAMWAY *n* pl. **-WAYS** a tramline

TRANCE *v* **TRANCED, TRANCING, TRANCES** to put into a trance (a semiconscious state)

TRANCHE *n* pl. **-S** a portion

TRANGAM *n* pl. **-S** a gewgaw

TRANK *v* **-ED, -ING, -S** to tranquilize

TRANNIE *n* pl. **-S** tranny

TRANNY *n* pl. **-NIES** a transmission

TRANQ *n* pl. **-S** trank

TRANQUIL *adj* **-QUILER, -QUILEST** or **-QUILLER, -QUILLEST** free from disturbance

TRANS *adj* characterized by the arrangement of different atoms on opposite sides of the molecule

TRANSACT *v* **-ED, -ING, -S** to carry out

TRANSECT *v* **-ED, -ING, -S** to cut across

TRANSEPT *n* pl. **-S** a major transverse part of the body of a church

TRANSFER *v* **-FERRED, -FERRING, -FERS** to convey from one source to another

TRANSFIX *v* **-FIXED** or **-FIXT, -FIXING, -FIXES** to impale

TRANSHIP *v* **-SHIPPED, -SHIPPING, -SHIPS** to transfer from one conveyance to another

TRANSIT *v* **-ED, -ING, -S** to pass across or through

TRANSMIT *v* **-MITTED, -MITTING, -MITS** to send from one place or person to another

TRANSOM *n* pl. **-S** a small window above a door or another window

TRANSUDE *v* **-SUDED, -SUDING, -SUDES** to pass through a membrane

TRAP *v* **TRAPPED** or **TRAPT, TRAPPING, TRAPS** to catch in a trap (a device for capturing and holding animals)

TRAPAN   *v* **-PANNED, -PANNING, -PANS** to trephine

TRAPBALL   *n* pl. **-S** a type of ball game

TRAPDOOR   *n* pl. **-S** a lifting or sliding door covering an opening

TRAPES   *v* **-ED, -ING, -ES** to traipse

TRAPEZE   *n* pl. **-S** a gymnastic apparatus

TRAPEZIA   *n/pl* four-sided polygons having no parallel sides

TRAPEZII   *n/pl* triangular muscles of the back

TRAPLIKE   *adj* resembling a trap

TRAPLINE   *n* pl. **-S** a series of traps

TRAPNEST   *v* **-ED, -ING, -S** to determine the productivity of hens with a type of nest

TRAPPEAN   *adj* pertaining to traprock

TRAPPED   a past tense of trap

TRAPPER   *n* pl. **-S** one that traps

TRAPPING   *n* pl. **-S** a covering for a horse

TRAPPOSE   *adj* trappean

TRAPPOUS   *adj* trappean

TRAPROCK   *n* pl. **-S** an igneous rock

TRAPT   a past tense of trap

TRAPUNTO   *n* pl. **-TOS** a decorative quilted design

TRASH   *v* **-ED, -ING, -ES** to free from trash (worthless or waste matter)

TRASHER   *n* pl. **-S** one that destroys or damages

TRASHMAN   *n* pl. **-MEN** a person who removes trash

TRASHY   *adj* **TRASHIER, TRASHIEST** resembling trash **TRASHILY** *adv*

TRASS   *n* pl. **-ES** a volcanic rock

TRAUCHLE   *v* **-LED, -LING, -LES** to trachle

TRAUMA   *n* pl. **-MAS** or **-MATA** a severe emotional shock

TRAVAIL   *v* **-ED, -ING, -S** to toil

TRAVE   *n* pl. **-S** a frame for confining a horse

TRAVEL   *v* **-ELED, -ELING, -ELS** or **-ELLED, -ELLING, -ELS** to go from one place to another

TRAVELER   *n* pl. **-S** one that travels

TRAVELOG   *n* pl. **-S** a lecture or film on traveling

TRAVERSE   *v* **-VERSED, -VERSING, -VERSES** to pass across or through

TRAVESTY   *v* **-TIED, -TYING, -TIES** to parody

TRAVOIS   *n* pl. **-ES** a type of sled

TRAVOISE   *n* pl. **-S** travois

TRAWL   *v* **-ED, -ING, -S** to fish by dragging a net along the sea bottom

TRAWLER   *n* pl. **-S** a boat used for trawling

TRAWLEY   *n* pl. **-LEYS** a small truck or car for conveying material

TRAWLNET   *n* pl. **-S** the large net used in trawling

TRAY   *n* pl. **TRAYS** a flat, shallow receptacle

TRAYF   *adj* not prepared according to Jewish law

TRAYFUL   *n* pl. **-S** as much as a tray will hold

TREACLE   *n* pl. **-S** molasses

TREACLY   *adj* **-CLIER, -CLIEST** cloyingly sweet and sentimental

TREAD   *v* **TROD** or **TRODE** or **TREADED, TRODDEN, TREADING, TREADS** to walk on, over, or along

TREADER   *n* pl. **-S** one that treads

TREADLE   *v* **-DLED, -DLING, -DLES** to work a foot lever

TREADLER   *n* pl. **-S** one that treadles

TREASON   *n* pl. **-S** violation of allegiance toward one's country

TREASURE   *v* **-SURED, -SURING, -SURES** to value highly

TREASURY   *n* pl. **-SURIES** a place where funds are received, kept, and disbursed

TREAT   *v* **-ED, -ING, -S** to behave in a particular way toward

TREATER   *n* pl. **-S** one that treats

TREATING   *n* pl. **-S** the act of providing someone with something pleasurable

TREATISE   *n* pl. **-S** a formal and systematic written account of a subject

TREATY   *n* pl. **-TIES** a formal agreement between two or more nations

TREBLE   *v* **-BLED, -BLING, -BLES** to triple

TREBLY   *adv* triply

TRECENTO   *n* pl. **-TOS** the fourteenth century

TREDDLE   *v* **-DLED, -DLING, -DLES** to treadle

TREE   *v* **TREED, TREEING, TREES** to drive up a tree (a tall, woody plant)

TREELAWN   *n* pl. **-S** the strip of lawn between the street and the sidewalk

TREELESS   *adj* having no tree

TREELIKE   *adj* resembling a tree

TREELINE *n* pl. **-S** the limit north of which trees do not grow

TREEN *n* pl. **-S** an article made from wood

TREENAIL *n* pl. **-S** a wooden peg used for fastening timbers

TREETOP *n* pl. **-S** the top of a tree

TREF *adj* unfit for use according to Jewish law

TREFAH *adj* tref

TREFOIL *n* pl. **-S** a plant having ternate leaves

TREHALA *n* pl. **-S** a sweet, edible substance forming the pupal case of certain weevils

TREK *v* **TREKKED, TREKKING, TREKS** to make a slow or arduous journey

TREKKER *n* pl. **-S** one that treks

TRELLIS *v* **-ED, -ING, -ES** to provide with a trellis (a frame used as a support for climbing plants)

TREM *n* pl. **-S** an electric guitar lever for producing a tremolo

TREMBLE *v* **-BLED, -BLING, -BLES** to shake involuntarily

TREMBLER *n* pl. **-S** one that trembles

TREMBLOR *n* pl. **-S** an earth tremor

TREMBLY *adj* **-BLIER, -BLIEST** marked by trembling

TREMOLO *n* pl. **-LOS** a vibrating musical effect

TREMOR *v* **-ED, -ING, -S** to undergo a shaking or quivering

TRENAIL *n* pl. **-S** treenail

TRENCH *v* **-ED, -ING, -ES** to dig a long, narrow excavation in the ground

TRENCHER *n* pl. **-S** a wooden platter for serving food

TREND *v* **-ED, -ING, -S** to take a particular course

TRENDIFY *v* **-FIED, -FYING, -FIES** to make something trendy

TRENDOID *n* pl. **-S** a trendy person

TRENDY *adj* **TRENDIER, TRENDIEST** very fashionable **TRENDILY** *adv*

TRENDY *n* pl. **TRENDIES** a trendy person

TREPAN *v* **-PANNED, -PANNING, -PANS** to trephine

TREPANG *n* pl. **-S** a marine animal

TREPHINE *v* **-PHINED, -PHINING, -PHINES** to operate on with a surgical saw

TREPID *adj* timorous

TRESPASS *v* **-ED, -ING, -ES** to enter upon the land of another unlawfully

TRESS *v* **-ED, -ING, -ES** to arrange the hair in long locks

TRESSEL *n* pl. **-S** trestle

TRESSOUR *n* pl. **-S** tressure

TRESSURE *n* pl. **-S** a type of heraldic design

TRESSY *adj* **TRESSIER, TRESSIEST** abounding in tresses

TRESTLE *n* pl. **-S** a framework for supporting a bridge

TRET *n* pl. **-S** an allowance formerly paid to purchasers for waste incurred in transit

TREVALLY *n* pl. **-LIES** or **-LYS** an Australian food fish

TREVET *n* pl. **-S** trivet

TREWS *n/pl* close-fitting tartan trousers

TREY *n* pl. **TREYS** a three in cards, dice, or dominoes

TREYF *adj* trayf

TREYFA *adj* trayf

TRIABLE *adj* subject to judicial examination

TRIAC *n* pl. **-S** an electronic device used to control power

TRIACID *n* pl. **-S** a type of acid

TRIACTOR *n* pl. **-S** a trifecta

TRIAD *n* pl. **-S** a group of three

TRIADIC *n* pl. **-S** a member of a triad

TRIADISM *n* pl. **-S** the quality or state of being a triad

TRIAGE *v* **-AGED, -AGING, -AGES** to practice a system of treating disaster victims

TRIAL **-ALED, -ALING, -ALS** or **-ALLED, -ALLING, -ALS** to test something to assess its performance

TRIALIST *n* pl. **-S** a person who participates in a test of something

TRIANGLE *n* pl. **-S** a polygon having three sides

TRIARCHY *n* pl. **-CHIES** government by three persons

TRIAXIAL *adj* having three axes

TRIAZIN *n* pl. **-S** triazine

TRIAZINE *n* pl. **-S** a chemical compound

TRIAZOLE *n* pl. **-S** a chemical compound

TRIBADE *n* pl. **-S** a lesbian **TRIBADIC** *adj*

TRIBAL *n* pl. **-S** a member of an aboriginal people of India

TRIBALLY	*adv* in a manner characteristic of a tribe	**TRIDENT**	*n* pl. **-S** a spear having three prongs
TRIBASIC	*adj* having three replaceable hydrogen atoms	**TRIDUUM**	*n* pl. **-S** a period of three days of prayer
TRIBE	*n* pl. **-S** a group of people sharing a common ancestry and culture	**TRIED**	past tense of try
TRIBRACH	*n* pl. **-S** a type of metrical foot	**TRIENE**	*n* pl. **-S** a type of chemical compound
TRIBUNAL	*n* pl. **-S** a court of justice	**TRIENNIA**	*n/pl* periods of three years
TRIBUNE	*n* pl. **-S** a defender of the rights of the people	**TRIENS**	*n* pl. **-ENTES** a coin of ancient Rome
TRIBUTE	*n* pl. **-S** something given to show respect, gratitude, or admiration	**TRIER**	*n* pl. **-S** one that tries
		TRIES	present 3d person sing. of try
TRICE	*v* **TRICED, TRICING, TRICES** to haul up with a rope	**TRIETHYL**	*adj* containing three ethyl groups
TRICEP	*n* pl. **-S** a triceps	**TRIFECTA**	*n* pl. **-S** a system of betting
TRICEPS	*n* pl. **-ES** an arm muscle	**TRIFFID**	*n* pl. **-S** a fictional predatory plant
TRICHINA	*n* pl. **-NAS** or **-NAE** a parasitic worm	**TRIFID**	*adj* divided into three parts
TRICHITE	*n* pl. **-S** a minute mineral body found in volcanic rocks	**TRIFLE**	*v* **-FLED, -FLING, -FLES** to waste time
TRICHOID	*adj* hairlike		
TRICHOME	*n* pl. **-S** a hairlike outgrowth	**TRIFLER**	*n* pl. **-S** one that trifles
TRICING	present participle of trice	**TRIFLING**	*n* pl. **-S** a waste of time
TRICITY	*n* pl. **-TIES** an area that comprises three adjoining independent cities	**TRIFOCAL**	*n* pl. **-S** a type of lens
		TRIFOLD	*adj* having three parts
TRICK	*v* **-ED, -ING, -S** to deceive	**TRIFORIA**	*n/pl* galleries in a church
TRICKER	*n* pl. **-S** one that tricks	**TRIFORM**	*adj* having three forms
TRICKERY	*n* pl. **-ERIES** deception	**TRIG**	*adj* **TRIGGER, TRIGGEST** neat
TRICKIE	*adj* **TRICKIER, TRICKIEST** tricky	**TRIG**	*v* **TRIGGED, TRIGGING, TRIGS** to make trig
TRICKIER	comparative of tricky		
TRICKIEST	superlative of tricky	**TRIGAMY**	*n* pl. **-MIES** the crime of being married to three people at once
TRICKILY	*adv* in a tricky manner		
TRICKISH	*adj* tricky	**TRIGGER**	*v* **-ED, -ING, -S** to actuate
TRICKLE	*v* **-LED, -LING, -LES** to flow or fall in drops	**TRIGLY**	*adv* in a trig manner
		TRIGLYPH	*n* pl. **-S** an architectural ornament
TRICKLY	*adj* **-LIER, -LIEST** marked by trickling	**TRIGNESS**	*n* pl. **-ES** the quality or state of being trig
TRICKSY	*adj* **-SIER, -SIEST** mischievous		
TRICKY	*adj* **TRICKIER, TRICKIEST** characterized by deception	**TRIGO**	*n* pl. **-GOS** wheat
		TRIGON	*n* pl. **-S** an ancient stringed instrument
TRICLAD	*n* pl. **-S** an aquatic flatworm	**TRIGONAL**	*adj* shaped like a triangle
TRICOLOR	*n* pl. **-S** a flag having three colors	**TRIGRAM**	*n* pl. **-S** a cluster of three successive letters
TRICORN	*n* pl. **-S** a hat with the brim turned up on three sides	**TRIGRAPH**	*n* pl. **-S** a group of three letters representing one sound
TRICORNE	*n* pl. **-S** tricorn		
TRICOT	*n* pl. **-S** a knitted fabric	**TRIHEDRA**	*n/pl* figures having three plane surfaces meeting at a point
TRICTRAC	*n* pl. **-S** a form of backgammon	**TRIJET**	*n* pl. **-S** an airplane powered by three jet engines
TRICYCLE	*v* **-CLED, -CLING, -CLES** to ride a vehicle having three wheels		
		TRIKE	*n* pl. **-S** a tricycle

TRILBY *n* pl. **-BIES** a soft felt hat **TRILBIED** *adj*

TRILITH *n* pl. **-S** a prehistoric structure of three large stones

TRILL *v* **-ED, -ING, -S** to sing or play with a vibrating effect

TRILLER *n* pl. **-S** one that trills

TRILLION *n* pl. **-S** a number

TRILLIUM *n* pl. **-S** a flowering plant

TRILOBAL *adj* trilobed

TRILOBED *adj* having three lobes

TRILOGY *n* pl. **-GIES** a group of three related literary works

TRIM *adj* **TRIMMER, TRIMMEST** neat and orderly

TRIM *v* **TRIMMED, TRIMMING, TRIMS** to make trim by cutting

TRIMARAN *n* pl. **-S** a sailing vessel

TRIMER *n* pl. **-S** a type of chemical compound **TRIMERIC** *adj*

TRIMETER *n* pl. **-S** a verse of three metrical feet

TRIMLY *adv* in a trim manner

TRIMMED past tense of trim

TRIMMER *n* pl. **-S** one that trims

TRIMMEST superlative of trim

TRIMMING *n* pl. **-S** something added as a decoration

TRIMNESS *n* pl. **-ES** the state of being trim

TRIMORPH *n* pl. **-S** a substance existing in three forms

TRIMOTOR *n* pl. **-S** an airplane powered by three engines

TRIMPOT *n* pl. **-S** a small instrument for adjusting resistance or voltage

TRINAL *adj* having three parts

TRINARY *adj* consisting of three parts

TRINDLE *v* **-DLED, -DLING, -DLES** to trundle

TRINE *v* **TRINED, TRINING, TRINES** to place in a particular astrological position

TRINITY *n* pl. **-TIES** a group of three

TRINKET *v* **-ED, -ING, -S** to deal secretly

TRINKUMS *n/pl* small ornaments

TRINODAL *adj* having three nodes

TRIO *n* pl. **TRIOS** a group of three

TRIODE *n* pl. **-S** a type of electron tube

TRIOL *n* pl. **-S** a type of chemical compound

TRIOLET *n* pl. **-S** a short poem of fixed form

TRIOSE *n* pl. **-S** a simple sugar

TRIOXID *n* pl. **-S** trioxide

TRIOXIDE *n* pl. **-S** a type of oxide

TRIP *v* **TRIPPED, TRIPPING, TRIPS** to stumble

TRIPACK *n* pl. **-S** a type of film pack

TRIPART *adj* divided into three parts

TRIPE *n* pl. **-S** a part of the stomach of a ruminant that is used as food

TRIPEDAL *adj* having three feet

TRIPHASE *adj* having three phases

TRIPLANE *n* pl. **-S** a type of airplane

TRIPLE *v* **-PLED, -PLING, -PLES** to make three times as great

TRIPLET *n* pl. **-S** a group of three of one kind

TRIPLEX *v* **-ED, -ING, -ES** to provide something in triplicate

TRIPLITE *n* pl. **-S** a mineral

TRIPLOID *n* pl. **-S** a cell having a chromosome number that is three times the basic number

TRIPLY *adv* in a triple degree, manner, or number

TRIPMAN *n* pl. **-MEN** a man hired to work on a trip

TRIPOD *n* pl. **-S** a stand having three legs **TRIPODAL, TRIPODIC** *adj*

TRIPODY *n* pl. **-DIES** a verse of three metrical feet

TRIPOLI *n* pl. **-S** a soft, friable rock

TRIPOS *n* pl. **-ES** a tripod

TRIPPANT *adj* walking — used of a heraldic animal

TRIPPED past tense of trip

TRIPPER *n* pl. **-S** one that trips

TRIPPET *n* pl. **-S** a part of a mechanism designed to strike another part

TRIPPING *n* pl. **-S** the act of one that trips

TRIPPY *adj* **-PIER, -PIEST** suggesting a trip on psychedelic drugs

TRIPTAN *n* pl. **-S** a drug for treating migraine attacks

TRIPTANE *n* pl. **-S** a chemical compound

TRIPTYCA *n* pl. **-S** a triptych

TRIPTYCH *n* pl. **-S** an ancient writing tablet

TRIPWIRE *n* pl. **-S** a low-placed hidden wire that sets off an alarm or a trap

TRIREME *n* pl. **-S** an ancient Greek or Roman warship

TRISCELE *n* pl. **-S** triskele

TRISECT *v* **-ED, -ING, -S** to divide into three equal parts

TRISEME *n* pl. **-S** a type of metrical foot **TRISEMIC** *adj*

TRISHAW *n* pl. **-S** a pedicab

TRISKELE *n* pl. **-S** a figure consisting of three branches radiating from a center

TRISMUS *n* pl. **-ES** lockjaw **TRISMIC** *adj*

TRISOME *n* pl. **-S** an organism having one chromosome in addition to the usual diploid number

TRISOMIC *n* pl. **-S** a trisome

TRISOMY *n* pl. **-MIES** the condition of being a trisome

TRISTATE *adj* pertaining to an area made up of three adjoining states

TRISTE *adj* sad

TRISTEZA *n* pl. **-S** a disease of citrus trees

TRISTFUL *adj* sad

TRISTICH *n* pl. **-S** a stanza of three lines

TRITE *adj* **TRITER, TRITEST** used so often as to be made commonplace **TRITELY** *adv*

TRITHING *n* pl. **-S** an administrative division in England

TRITICUM *n* pl. **-S** a cereal grass

TRITIUM *n* pl. **-S** an isotope of hydrogen

TRITOMA *n* pl. **-S** an African herb

TRITON *n* pl. **-S** a marine mollusk

TRITONE *n* pl. **-S** a musical interval of three whole tones

TRIUMPH *v* **-ED, -ING, -S** to be victorious

TRIUMVIR *n* pl. **-VIRS** or **-VIRI** one of a ruling body of three in ancient Rome

TRIUNE *n* pl. **-S** a trinity

TRIUNITY *n* pl. **-TIES** a trinity

TRIVALVE *n* pl. **-S** a type of shell

TRIVET *n* pl. **-S** a small stand having three legs

TRIVIA *n/pl* insignificant matters

TRIVIAL *adj* insignificant

TRIVIUM *n* pl. **-IA** a group of studies in medieval schools

TROAK *v* **-ED, -ING, -S** to troke

TROCAR *n* pl. **-S** a surgical instrument

TROCHAIC *n* pl. **-S** a trochee

TROCHAL *adj* shaped like a wheel

TROCHAR *n* pl. **-S** trocar

TROCHE *n* pl. **-S** a medicated lozenge

TROCHEE *n* pl. **-S** a type of metrical foot

TROCHIL *n* pl. **TROCHILS** or **TROCHILI** an African bird

TROCHLEA *n* pl. **-LEAS** or **-LEAE** an anatomical structure resembling a pulley

TROCHOID *n* pl. **-S** a type of geometric curve

TROCK *v* **-ED, -ING, -S** to troke

TROD a past tense of tread

TRODDEN past participle of tread

TRODE a past tense of tread

TROFFER *n* pl. **-S** a fixture for fluorescent lighting

TROG *n* pl. **-S** a hooligan

TROGON *n* pl. **-S** a tropical bird

TROIKA *n* pl. **-S** a Russian carriage

TROILISM *n* pl. **-S** sexual relations involving three persons

TROILITE *n* pl. **-S** a mineral

TROILUS *n* pl. **-ES** a large butterfly

TROIS *n* pl. **TROIS** the number three

TROKE *v* **TROKED, TROKING, TROKES** to exchange

TROLAND *n* pl. **-S** a unit of measurement of retinal response to light

TROLL *v* **-ED, -ING, -S** to fish with a slowly trailing line

TROLLER *n* pl. **-S** one that trolls

TROLLEY *v* **-ED, -ING, -S** to convey by streetcar

TROLLING *n* pl. **-S** the act of one that trolls

TROLLISH *adj* resembling a troll (a mythological dwarf)

TROLLOP *n* pl. **-S** a prostitute **TROLLOPY** *adj*

TROLLY *v* **-LIED, -LYING, -LIES** to trolley

TROMBONE *n* pl. **-S** a brass wind instrument

TROMMEL *n* pl. **-S** a screen used for sifting rock, ore, or coal

TROMP *v* **-ED, -ING, -S** to tramp

TROMPE *n* pl. **-S** a device used for supplying air to a furnace

TRONA *n* pl. **-S** a mineral

TRONE	*n* pl. **-S** a weighing device
TROOP	*v* **-ED, -ING, -S** to move or gather in crowds
TROOPER	*n* pl. **-S** a cavalryman
TROOPIAL	*n* pl. **-S** troupial
TROOZ	*n/pl* trews
TROP	*adv* too much
TROPE	*n* pl. **-S** the figurative use of a word
TROPHIC	*adj* pertaining to nutrition
TROPHY	*v* **-PHIED, -PHYING, -PHIES** to honor with a trophy (a symbol of victory)
TROPIC	*n* pl. **-S** either of two circles of the celestial sphere on each side of the equator
TROPICAL	*n* pl **-S** a plant of the region lying between the tropics
TROPIN	*n* pl. **-S** tropine
TROPINE	*n* pl. **-S** a poisonous alkaloid
TROPISM	*n* pl. **-S** the involuntary response of an organism to an external stimulus
TROPONIN	*n* pl. **-S** a protein of muscle
TROPPO	*adj* too much — used in musical directions
TROT	*v* **TROTTED, TROTTING, TROTS** to go at a gait between a walk and a run
TROTH	*v* **-ED, -ING, -S** to betroth
TROTLINE	*n* pl. **-S** a strong fishing line
TROTTER	*n* pl. **-S** a horse that trots
TROTTING	*n* pl. **-S** harness racing
TROTYL	*n* pl. **-S** an explosive
TROU	*n/pl* trousers
TROUBLE	*v* **-BLED, -BLING, -BLES** to distress
TROUBLER	*n* pl. **-S** one that troubles
TROUGH	*n* pl. **-S** a long, narrow receptacle
TROUNCE	*v* **TROUNCED, TROUNCING, TROUNCES** to beat severely
TROUNCER	*n* pl. **-S** one that trounces
TROUPE	*v* **TROUPED, TROUPING, TROUPES** to tour with a theatrical company
TROUPER	*n* pl. **-S** a member of a theatrical company
TROUPIAL	*n* pl. **-S** a tropical bird
TROUSER	*adj* pertaining to trousers
TROUSERS	*n/pl* a garment for the lower part of the body
TROUT	*n* pl. **-S** a freshwater fish
TROUTING	*n* pl. **-S** the activity of fishing for trout
TROUTY	*adj* **TROUTIER, TROUTIEST** abounding in trout
TROUVERE	*n* pl. **-S** a medieval poet
TROUVEUR	*n* pl. **-S** trouvere
TROVE	*n* pl. **-S** a valuable discovery
TROVER	*n* pl. **-S** a type of legal action
TROW	*v* **-ED, -ING, -S** to suppose
TROWEL	*v* **-ELED, -ELING, -ELS** or **-ELLED, -ELLING, -ELS** to smooth with a trowel (a hand tool having a flat blade)
TROWELER	*n* pl. **-S** one that trowels
TROWSERS	*n/pl* trousers
TROWTH	*n* pl. **-S** truth
TROY	*n* pl. **TROYS** a system of weights
TRUANCY	*n* pl. **-CIES** an act of truanting
TRUANT	*v* **-ED, -ING, -S** to stay out of school without permission
TRUANTLY	*adv* in a manner of one who shirks duty
TRUANTRY	*n* pl. **-RIES** truancy
TRUCE	*v* **TRUCED, TRUCING, TRUCES** to suspend hostilities by mutual agreement
TRUCK	*v* **-ED, -ING, -S** to transport by truck (an automotive vehicle designed to carry loads)
TRUCKAGE	*n* pl. **-S** transportation of goods by trucks
TRUCKER	*n* pl. **-S** a truck driver
TRUCKFUL	*n* pl. **-S** as much as a truck can hold
TRUCKING	*n* pl. **-S** truckage
TRUCKLE	*v* **-LED, -LING, -LES** to yield weakly
TRUCKLER	*n* pl. **-S** one that truckles
TRUCKMAN	*n* pl. **-MEN** a trucker
TRUDGE	*v* **TRUDGED, TRUDGING, TRUDGES** to walk tiredly
TRUDGEN	*n* pl. **-S** a swimming stroke
TRUDGEON	*n* pl. **-S** trudgen
TRUDGER	*n* pl. **-S** one that trudges
TRUDGING	present participle of trudge
TRUE	*adj* **TRUER, TRUEST** consistent with fact or reality

TRUE	v **TRUED, TRUING** or **TRUEING, TRUES** to bring to conformity with a standard or requirement
TRUEBLUE	n pl. **-S** a person of unwavering loyalty
TRUEBORN	adj genuinely such by birth
TRUEBRED	adj designating an animal of unmixed stock
TRUED	past tense of true
TRUEING	a present participle of true
TRUELOVE	n pl. **-S** a sweetheart
TRUENESS	n pl. **-ES** the quality or state of being true
TRUER	comparative of true
TRUEST	superlative of true
TRUFFE	n pl. **-S** truffle
TRUFFLE	n pl. **-S** an edible fungus **TRUFFLED** adj
TRUFFLING	n pl. **-S** the activity of hunting for truffles
TRUG	n pl. **-S** a gardener's basket
TRUING	a present participle of true
TRUISM	n pl. **-S** an obvious truth **TRUISTIC** adj
TRULL	n pl. **-S** a prostitute
TRULY	adv in conformity with fact or reality
TRUMEAU	n pl. **-MEAUX** a column supporting part of a doorway
TRUMP	v **-ED, -ING, -S** to outdo
TRUMPERY	n pl. **-ERIES** worthless finery
TRUMPET	v **-ED, -ING, -S** to sound on a trumpet (a brass wind instrument)
TRUNCAL	adj affecting the trunk (the central part) of the body
TRUNCATE	v **-CATED, -CATING, -CATES** to shorten by cutting off a part
TRUNDLE	v **-DLED, -DLING, -DLES** to propel by causing to rotate
TRUNDLER	n pl. **-S** one that trundles
TRUNK	n pl. **-S** the main stem of a tree **TRUNKED** adj
TRUNKFUL	n pl. **-S** as much as a trunk (a storage box) can hold
TRUNKING	n pl. **-S** a system of electrical or telephone lines
TRUNNEL	n pl. **-S** treenail
TRUNNION	n pl. **-S** a pin or pivot on which something can be rotated
TRUSS	v **-ED, -ING, -ES** to secure tightly
TRUSSER	n pl. **-S** one that trusses

TRUSSING	n pl. **-S** the framework of a structure
TRUST	v **-ED, -ING, -S** to place confidence in
TRUSTEE	v **-TEED, -TEEING, -TEES** to commit to the care of an administrator
TRUSTER	n pl. **-S** one that trusts
TRUSTFUL	adj inclined to trust
TRUSTOR	n pl. **-S** one that trustees his property
TRUSTY	adj **TRUSTIER, TRUSTIEST** worthy of trust **TRUSTILY** adv
TRUSTY	n pl. **TRUSTIES** one worthy of trust
TRUTH	n pl. **-S** conformity to fact or reality
TRUTHFUL	adj telling the truth
TRY	v **TRIED, TRYING, TRIES** to attempt
TRYINGLY	adv in a distressing manner
TRYMA	n pl. **-MATA** a type of nut
TRYOUT	n pl. **-S** a test of ability
TRYPSIN	n pl. **-S** an enzyme **TRYPTIC** adj
TRYSAIL	n pl. **-S** a type of sail
TRYST	v **-ED, -ING, -S** to agree to meet
TRYSTE	n pl. **-S** a market
TRYSTER	n pl. **-S** one that trysts
TRYWORKS	n/pl a type of furnace
TSADDIK	n pl. **-DIKIM** zaddik
TSADE	n pl. **-S** sade
TSADI	n pl. **-S** sade
TSAR	n pl. **-S** czar
TSARDOM	n pl. **-S** czardom
TSAREVNA	n pl. **-S** czarevna
TSARINA	n pl. **-S** czarina
TSARISM	n pl. **-S** czarism
TSARIST	n pl. **-S** czarist
TSARITZA	n pl. **-S** czaritza
TSATSKE	n pl. **-S** chachka
TSETSE	n pl. **-S** an African fly
TSIMMES	n pl. **TSIMMES** tzimmes
TSK	v **-ED, -ING, -S** to utter an exclamation of annoyance
TSKTSK	v **-ED, -ING, -S** to tsk
TSOORIS	n pl. **TSOORIS** tsuris
TSORES	n pl. **TSORES** tsuris
TSORIS	n pl. **TSORIS** tsuris
TSORRISS	n pl. **TSORRISS** tsuris

TSOTSI	*n* pl. **-S** a black African urban criminal	**TUBLIKE**	*adj* resembling a tub
TSOURIS	*n* pl. **TSOURIS** tsuris	**TUBULAR**	*n* pl. **-S** a completely enclosed bicycle tire
TSUBA	*n* pl. **-S** a part of a Japanese sword	**TUBULATE**	*v* **-LATED, -LATING, -LATES** to form into a tube
TSUBO	*n* pl. **-BOS** a Japanese unit of area	**TUBULE**	*n* pl. **-S** a small tube
TSUNAMI	*n* pl. **-S** a very large ocean wave **TSUNAMIC** *adj*	**TUBULIN**	*n* pl. **-S** a protein that polymerizes to form tiny tubules
TSURIS	*n* pl. **TSURIS** or **TSURISES** a series of misfortunes	**TUBULOSE**	*adj* tubulous
TUATARA	*n* pl. **-S** a large reptile	**TUBULOUS**	*adj* having the form of a tube
TUATERA	*n* pl. **-S** tuatara	**TUBULURE**	*n* pl. **-S** a short cylindrical opening
TUB	*v* **TUBBED, TUBBING, TUBS** to wash in a tub (a round, open vessel)	**TUCHIS**	*n* pl. **-ES** tuchus
		TUCHUN	*n* pl. **-S** a Chinese military governor
TUBA	*n* pl. **-BAS** or **-BAE** a brass wind instrument	**TUCHUS**	*n* pl. **-ES** the buttocks
TUBAIST	*n* pl. **-S** a tuba player	**TUCK**	*v* **-ED, -ING, -S** to fold under
TUBAL	*adj* pertaining to a tube	**TUCKAHOE**	*n* pl. **-S** the edible root of certain arums
TUBATE	*adj* tubular	**TUCKER**	*v* **-ED, -ING, -S** to weary
TUBBABLE	*adj* suitable for washing in a tub	**TUCKET**	*n* pl. **-S** a trumpet fanfare
TUBBED	past tense of tub	**TUCKING**	*n* pl. **-S** a series of stitched folds in a garment
TUBBER	*n* pl. **-S** one that tubs		
TUBBING	present participle of tub	**TUCKSHOP**	*n* pl. **-S** a confectioner's shop
TUBBY	*adj* **-BIER, -BIEST** short and fat	**TUFA**	*n* pl. **-S** a porous limestone
TUBE	*v* **TUBED, TUBING, TUBES** to provide with a tube (a long, hollow cylinder)	**TUFF**	*n* pl. **-S** a volcanic rock
		TUFFET	*n* pl. **-S** a clump of grass
TUBELESS	*adj* having no tube	**TUFOLI**	*n* pl. **TUFOLI** a large macaroni shell
TUBELIKE	*adj* resembling a tube		
TUBENOSE	*n* pl. **-S** a bird having tubular nostrils	**TUFT**	*v* **-ED, -ING, -S** to form into tufts (clusters of flexible outgrowths attached at the base)
TUBER	*n* pl. **-S** a thick underground stem	**TUFTER**	*n* pl. **-S** one that tufts
TUBERCLE	*n* pl. **-S** a small, rounded swelling	**TUFTING**	*n* pl. **-S** a cluster of tufts used for decoration
TUBEROID	*adj* pertaining to a tuber		
TUBEROSE	*n* pl. **-S** a Mexican herb	**TUFTY**	*adj* **TUFTIER, TUFTIEST** abounding in tufts **TUFTILY** *adv*
TUBEROUS	*adj* pertaining to a tuber		
TUBEWELL	*n* pl. **-S** a water well in which a long steel tube is bored into an underground aquifer	**TUG**	*v* **TUGGED, TUGGING, TUGS** to pull with force
		TUGBOAT	*n* pl. **-S** a boat built for towing
TUBEWORK	*n* pl. **-S** tubing	**TUGGER**	*n* pl. **-S** one that tugs
TUBEWORM	*n* pl. **-S** a marine worm that builds and lives in a tube	**TUGGING**	present participle of tug
		TUGHRIK	*n* pl. **-S** tugrik
TUBFUL	*n* pl. **-S** as much as a tub will hold	**TUGLESS**	*adj* being without a rope or chain with which to pull
TUBIFEX	*n* pl. **-ES** an aquatic worm		
TUBIFORM	*adj* tubular	**TUGRIK**	*n* pl. **-S** a monetary unit of Mongolia
TUBING	*n* pl. **-S** material in the form of a tube	**TUI**	*n* pl. **-S** a bird of New Zealand
TUBIST	*n* pl. **-S** a tubaist	**TUILE**	*n* pl. **TUILE** a thin cookie made with almonds

TUILLE	*n* pl. **-S** a tasset
TUITION	*n* pl. **-S** a fee for instruction
TULADI	*n* pl. **-S** a freshwater fish
TULE	*n* pl. **-S** a tall marsh plant
TULIP	*n* pl. **-S** a flowering plant
TULLE	*n* pl. **-S** a silk material
TULLIBEE	*n* pl. **-S** a freshwater fish
TULSI	*n* pl. **-S** a type of basil
TUM	*n* pl. **-S** a person's stomach (an organ of digestion) or abdomen
TUMBLE	*v* **-BLED, -BLING, -BLES** to fall or roll end over end
TUMBLER	*n* pl. **-S** one that tumbles
TUMBLING	*n* pl. **-S** the sport of gymnastics
TUMBREL	*n* pl. **-S** a type of cart
TUMBRIL	*n* pl. **-S** tumbrel
TUMEFY	*v* **-FIED, -FYING, -FIES** to swell
TUMESCE	*v* **-MESCED, -MESCING, -MESCES** to become swollen
TUMID	*adj* swollen **TUMIDLY** *adv*
TUMIDITY	*n* pl. **-TIES** the quality or state of being tumid
TUMMLER	*n* pl. **-S** an entertainer who encourages audience participation
TUMMY	*n* pl. **-MIES** the stomach
TUMOR	*n* pl. **-S** an abnormal swelling **TUMORAL, TUMOROUS** *adj*
TUMOUR	*n* pl. **-S** tumor
TUMP	*v* **-ED, -ING, -S** to tip over
TUMPLINE	*n* pl. **-S** a strap for supporting a load on the back
TUMULAR	*adj* having the form of a mound
TUMULI	a pl. of tumulus
TUMULOSE	*adj* full of mounds
TUMULOUS	*adj* tumulose
TUMULT	*n* pl. **-S** a great din and commotion
TUMULUS	*n* pl. **-LUSES** or **-LI** a mound over a grave
TUN	*v* **TUNNED, TUNNING, TUNS** to store in a large cask
TUNA	*n* pl. **-S** a marine food fish
TUNABLE	*adj* capable of being tuned **TUNABLY** *adv*
TUNDISH	*n* pl. **-ES** a receptacle for molten metal
TUNDRA	*n* pl. **-S** a level, treeless expanse of arctic land

TUNE	*v* **TUNED, TUNING, TUNES** to put into the proper pitch
TUNEABLE	*adj* tunable **TUNEABLY** *adv*
TUNEFUL	*adj* melodious
TUNELESS	*adj* not tuneful
TUNER	*n* pl. **-S** one that tunes
TUNEUP	*n* pl. **-S** an adjustment to ensure efficient operation
TUNG	*n* pl. **-S** a Chinese tree
TUNGSTEN	*n* pl. **-S** a metallic element **TUNGSTIC** *adj*
TUNIC	*n* pl. **-S** a loose-fitting garment
TUNICA	*n* pl. **-CAE** an enveloping membrane or layer of body tissue
TUNICATE	*n* pl. **-S** a small marine animal
TUNICLE	*n* pl. **-S** a type of vestment
TUNING	*n* pl. **-S** the act of adjusting a musical instrument to a correct pitch
TUNKET	*n* pl. **-S** hell
TUNNAGE	*n* pl. **-S** tonnage
TUNNED	past tense of tun
TUNNEL	*v* **-NELED, -NELING, -NELS** or **-NELLED, -NELLING, -NELS** to dig a tunnel (an underground passageway)
TUNNELER	*n* pl. **-S** one that tunnels
TUNNING	present participle of tun
TUNNY	*n* pl. **-NIES** a tuna
TUP	*v* **TUPPED, TUPPING, TUPS** to copulate with a ewe — used of a ram
TUPELO	*n* pl. **-LOS** a softwood tree
TUPIK	*n* pl. **-S** an Inuit tent
TUPPENCE	*n* pl. **-S** twopence
TUPPENNY	*adj* twopenny
TUPPING	*n* pl. **-S** the act of a ram copulating with a ewe
TUQUE	*n* pl. **-S** a knitted woolen cap
TURACO	*n* pl. **-COS** touraco
TURACOU	*n* pl. **-S** touraco
TURBAN	*n* pl. **-S** a head covering worn by Muslims **TURBANED** *adj*
TURBARY	*n* pl. **-RIES** a place where peat can be dug
TURBETH	*n* pl. **-S** turpeth
TURBID	*adj* thick or opaque with roiled sediment **TURBIDLY** *adv*

TURBINAL *n* pl. **-S** a bone of the nasal passage

TURBINE *n* pl. **-S** a type of engine

TURBIT *n* pl. **-S** a domestic pigeon

TURBITH *n* pl. **-S** turpeth

TURBO *n* pl. **-BOS** a turbine

TURBOCAR *n* pl. **-S** an auto powered by a gas turbine

TURBOFAN *n* pl. **-S** a type of jet engine

TURBOJET *n* pl. **-S** a type of jet engine

TURBOT *n* pl. **-S** a European flatfish

TURDINE *adj* belonging to a large family of singing birds

TUREEN *n* pl. **-S** a large, deep bowl

TURF *n* pl. **TURFS** or **TURVES** a surface layer of earth containing a dense growth of grass

TURF *v* **-ED, -ING, -S** to cover with turf

TURFIER comparative of turfy

TURFIEST superlative of turfy

TURFLESS *adj* having no turf

TURFLIKE *adj* resembling turf

TURFMAN *n* pl. **-MEN** a person who is devoted to horse racing

TURFSKI *n* pl. **-S** a type of ski

TURFY *adj* **TURFIER, TURFIEST** covered with turf

TURGENCY *n* pl. **-CIES** turgor

TURGENT *adj* turgid

TURGID *adj* swollen **TURGIDLY** *adv*

TURGITE *n* pl. **-S** an iron ore

TURGOR *n* pl. **-S** the quality or state of being turgid

TURION *n* pl. **-S** a thick new growth on a plant

TURISTA *n* pl. **-S** intestinal sickness affecting a tourist in a foreign country

TURK *n* pl. **-S** one who eagerly advocates change

TURKEY *n* pl. **-KEYS** a large American bird

TURKOIS *n* pl. **-ES** turquois

TURMERIC *n* pl. **-S** an East Indian herb

TURMOIL *v* **-ED, -ING, -S** to throw into an uproar

TURN *v* **-ED, -ING, -S** to move around a central point **TURNABLE** *adj*

TURNCOAT *n* pl. **-S** a traitor

TURNCOCK *n* pl. **-S** an employee who turns water on or off at the main

TURNDOWN *n* pl. **-S** a rejection

TURNER *n* pl. **-S** one that turns

TURNERY *n* pl. **-ERIES** the process of shaping articles on a lathe

TURNHALL *n* pl. **-S** a building where gymnasts practice

TURNING *n* pl. **-S** a rotation about an axis

TURNIP *n* pl. **-S** an edible plant root **TURNIPY** *adj*

TURNKEY *n* pl. **-KEYS** a person who has charge of a prison's keys

TURNOFF *n* pl. **-S** a road that branches off from a larger one

TURNON *n* pl. **-S** something that arouses interest

TURNOUT *n* pl. **-S** an assemblage of people

TURNOVER *n* pl. **-S** an upset or overthrow

TURNPIKE *n* pl. **-S** a toll road

TURNSOLE *n* pl. **-S** a plant that turns with the sun

TURNSPIT *n* pl. **-S** one that turns a roasting spit

TURNUP *n* pl. **-S** a part of a garment that is turned up

TURPETH *n* pl. **-S** a medicinal plant root

TURPS *n* pl. **TURPS** turpentine

TURQUOIS *n* pl. **-ES** a greenish blue gem

TURR *n* pl. **-S** a murre

TURRET *n* pl. **-S** a small tower **TURRETED** *adj*

TURRICAL *adj* resembling a turret

TURTLE *v* **-TLED, -TLING, -TLES** to catch turtles (tortoises)

TURTLER *n* pl. **-S** one that turtles

TURTLING *n* pl. **-S** the act of one that turtles

TURVES a pl. of turf

TUSCHE *n* pl. **-S** a liquid used in lithography

TUSH *v* **-ED, -ING, -ES** to tusk

TUSHERY *n* pl. **-ERIES** pretentious writing

TUSHIE *n* pl. **-S** the buttocks

TUSHY *n* pl. **TUSHIES** tushie

TUSK *v* **-ED, -ING, -S** to gore with a tusk (a long, pointed tooth extending outside of the mouth)

TUSKER *n* pl. **-S** an animal with tusks

TUSKLESS *adj* having no tusk

TUSKLIKE *adj* resembling a tusk

TUSKY	*adj* **TUSKIER, TUSKIEST** having tusks
TUSSAH	*n* pl. **-S** an Asian silkworm
TUSSAL	*adj* pertaining to a cough
TUSSAR	*n* pl. **-S** tussah
TUSSEH	*n* pl. **-S** tussah
TUSSER	*n* pl. **-S** tussah
TUSSIS	*n* pl. **TUSSISES** or **TUSSES** a cough **TUSSIVE** *adj*
TUSSLE	*v* **-SLED, -SLING, -SLES** to struggle
TUSSOCK	*n* pl. **-S** a clump of grass **TUSSOCKY** *adj*
TUSSOR	*n* pl. **-S** tussah
TUSSORE	*n* pl. **-S** tussah
TUSSUCK	*n* pl. **-S** tussock
TUSSUR	*n* pl. **-S** tussah
TUT	*v* **TUTTED, TUTTING, TUTS** to utter an exclamation of impatience
TUTEE	*n* pl. **-S** one who is being tutored
TUTELAGE	*n* pl. **-S** the act of tutoring
TUTELAR	*n* pl. **-S** a tutelary
TUTELARY	*n* pl. **-LARIES** one who has the power to protect
TUTOR	*v* **-ED, -ING, -S** to instruct privately
TUTORAGE	*n* pl. **-S** tutelage
TUTORESS	*n* pl. **-ES** a female who tutors
TUTORIAL	*n* pl. **-S** a session of tutoring
TUTOYER	*v* **-TOYERED** or **-TOYED, -TOYERING, -TOYERS** to address familiarly
TUTTED	past tense of tut
TUTTI	*n* pl. **-S** a musical passage performed by all the performers
TUTTING	present participle of tut
TUTTY	*n* pl. **-TIES** an impure zinc oxide
TUTU	*n* pl. **-S** a short ballet skirt **TUTUED** *adj*
TUX	*n* pl. **-ES** a tuxedo
TUXEDO	*n* pl. **-DOS** or **-DOES** a man's semiformal dinner coat **TUXEDOED** *adj*
TUYER	*n* pl. **-S** tuyere
TUYERE	*n* pl. **-S** a pipe through which air is forced into a blast furnace
TWA	*n* pl. **-S** two
TWADDLE	*v* **-DLED, -DLING, -DLES** to talk foolishly
TWADDLER	*n* pl. **-S** one that twaddles
TWAE	*n* pl. **-S** two
TWAIN	*n* pl. **-S** a set of two
TWANG	*v* **-ED, -ING, -S** to make a sharp, vibrating sound
TWANGER	*n* pl. **-S** one that twangs
TWANGLE	*v* **-GLED, -GLING, -GLES** to twang
TWANGLER	*n* pl. **-S** one that twangles
TWANGY	*adj* **TWANGIER, TWANGIEST** twanging
TWANKY	*n* pl. **-KIES** a variety of green tea
TWASOME	*n* pl. **-S** twosome
TWATTLE	*v* **-TLED, -TLING, -TLES** to twaddle
TWEAK	*v* **-ED, -ING, -S** to pinch and twist sharply
TWEAKY	*adj* **TWEAKIER, TWEAKIEST** twitchy
TWEE	*adj* **TWEER, TWEEST** affectedly cute or dainty
TWEED	*n* pl. **-S** a coarse woolen fabric
TWEEDLE	*v* **-DLED, -DLING, -DLES** to perform casually on a musical instrument
TWEEDY	*adj* **TWEEDIER, TWEEDIEST** resembling or wearing tweed **TWEEDILY** *adv*
TWEEN	*n* pl. **-S** a child typically between the ages of eight and twelve
TWEENER	*n* pl. **-S** a player having some but not all of the qualifications for two or more positions
TWEENESS	*n* pl. **-ES** the state of being twee
TWEENY	*n* pl. **TWEENIES** a housemaid
TWEEP	*n* pl. **-S** one who uses the Twitter online message service
TWEET	*v* **-ED, -ING, -S** to chirp
TWEETER	*n* pl. **-S** a loudspeaker designed to reproduce high-pitched sounds
TWEEZE	*v* **TWEEZED, TWEEZING, TWEEZES** to pluck with a tweezer
TWEEZER	*n* pl. **-S** a pincerlike tool
TWELFTH	*n* pl. **-S** the number twelve in a series
TWELVE	*n* pl. **-S** a number
TWELVEMO	*n* pl. **-MOS** a page size
TWENTY	*n* pl. **-TIES** a number
TWERP	*n* pl. **-S** a small, impudent person
TWERPY	*adj* **TWERPIER, TWERPIEST** resembling a twerp

TWIBIL	*n* pl. **-S** a battle-ax with two cutting edges	**TWINSET**	*n* pl. **-S** a matching pair of sweaters to be worn together
TWIBILL	*n* pl. **-S** twibil	**TWINSHIP**	*n* pl. **-S** close similarity or association
TWICE	*adv* two times		
TWIDDLE	*v* **-DLED, -DLING, -DLES** to play idly with something	**TWINY**	*adj* **TWINIER, TWINIEST** resembling twine (a strong string)
TWIDDLER	*n* pl. **-S** one that twiddles	**TWIRL**	*v* **-ED, -ING, -S** to rotate rapidly
TWIDDLY	*adj* **-DLIER, -DLIEST** having many turns	**TWIRLER**	*n* pl. **-S** one that twirls
		TWIRLY	*adj* **TWIRLIER, TWIRLIEST** curved
TWIER	*n* pl. **-S** tuyere		
TWIG	*v* **TWIGGED, TWIGGING, TWIGS** to observe	**TWIRP**	*n* pl. **-S** twerp
		TWIST	*v* **-ED, -ING, -S** to combine by winding together
TWIGGEN	*adj* made of twigs (small branches)		
TWIGGY	*adj* **-GIER, -GIEST** twiglike	**TWISTER**	*n* pl. **-S** one that twists
TWIGLESS	*adj* having no twigs	**TWISTING**	*n* pl. **-S** a form of trickery used in selling life insurance
TWIGLIKE	*adj* resembling a twig		
TWILIGHT	*n* pl. **-S** the early evening light	**TWISTOR**	*n* pl. **-S** a complex variable in descriptions of space-time
TWILIT	*adj* lighted by twilight	**TWISTY**	*adj* **TWISTIER, TWISTIEST** full of curves
TWILL	*v* **-ED, -ING, -S** to weave so as to produce a diagonal pattern		
		TWIT	*v* **TWITTED, TWITTING, TWITS** to ridicule
TWILLING	*n* pl. **-S** a twilled fabric		
TWIN	*v* **TWINNED, TWINNING, TWINS** to bring together in close association	**TWITCH**	*v* **-ED, -ING, -ES** to move or pull with a sudden motion
		TWITCHER	*n* pl. **-S** one that twitches
TWINBORN	*adj* born at the same birth	**TWITCHY**	*adj* **TWITCHIER, TWITCHIEST** fidgety
TWINE	*v* **TWINED, TWINING, TWINES** to twist together		
		TWITTED	past tense of twit
TWINER	*n* pl. **-S** one that twines	**TWITTER**	*v* **-ED, -ING, -S** to utter a succession of chirping sounds
TWINGE	*v* **TWINGED, TWINGING** or **TWINGEING, TWINGES** to affect with a sharp pain		
		TWITTERY	*adj* nervously agitated
		TWITTING	present participle of twit
TWINIER	comparative of twiny	**TWITTISH**	*adj* silly, foolish
TWINIEST	superlative of twiny	**TWIXT**	*prep* between
TWINIGHT	*adj* pertaining to a baseball doubleheader that begins in the late afternoon	**TWIZZLE**	*n* pl. **-S** a maneuver in figure skating
		TWO	*n* pl. **TWOS** a number
TWINING	present participle of twine	**TWOFER**	*n* pl. **-S** something sold at the rate of two for the price of one
TWINJET	*n* pl. **-S** an aircraft with two jet engines		
		TWOFOLD	*n* pl. **-S** an amount twice as great as a given unit
TWINK	*n* pl. **-S** a weak or ineffectual person		
TWINKIE	*n* pl. **-S** a twink	**TWONESS**	*n* pl. **-ES** the state of being two
TWINKLE	*v* **-KLED, -KLING, -KLES** to shine with a flickering or sparkling light	**TWOONIE**	*n* pl. **-S** toonie
		TWOPENCE	*n* pl. **-S** a British coin worth two pennies
TWINKLER	*n* pl. **-S** one that twinkles		
TWINKLY	*adj* twinkling	**TWOPENNY**	*adj* worth twopence
TWINKY	*n* pl. **-KIES** a twink	**TWOSOME**	*n* pl. **-S** a group of two
TWINNED	past tense of twin	**TWYER**	*n* pl. **-S** tuyere
TWINNING	*n* pl. **-S** the bearing of two children at the same birth	**TYCHISM**	*n* pl. **-S** the proposition that chance is operative in the universe

TYCOON *n* pl. **-S** a wealthy and powerful business person

TYE *n* pl. **-S** a chain on a ship

TYEE *n* pl. **-S** a food fish

TYER *n* pl. **-S** one that ties

TYIN *n* pl. **TYIN** a monetary unit of Kazakhstan

TYING a present participle of tie

TYIYN *n* pl. **TYIYN** a monetary unit of Kyrgyzstan

TYKE *n* pl. **-S** a small child

TYLOSIN *n* pl. **-S** an antibiotic

TYMBAL *n* pl. **-S** timbal

TYMPAN *n* pl. **-S** a drum

TYMPANA a pl. of tympanum

TYMPANAL *adj* tympanic

TYMPANIC *adj* pertaining to the tympanum

TYMPANO *n* pl. **-NI** timpano

TYMPANUM *n* pl. **-NUMS** or **-NA** the middle ear

TYMPANY *n* pl. **-NIES** a swelling of the abdomen

TYNE *v* **TYNED, TYNING, TYNES** to tine

TYPAL *adj* typical

TYPE *v* **TYPED, TYPING, TYPES** to write with a typewriter **TYPABLE, TYPEABLE** *adj*

TYPEBAR *n* pl. **-S** a part of a typewriter

TYPECASE *n* pl. **-S** a tray for holding printing type

TYPECAST *v* **-CAST, -CASTING, -CASTS** to cast in an acting role befitting one's own nature

TYPED past tense of type

TYPEFACE *n* pl. **-S** the face of printing type

TYPESET *v* **-SET, -SETTING, -SETS** to set in type

TYPEY *adj* **TYPIER, TYPIEST** typy

TYPHOID *n* pl. **-S** an infectious disease

TYPHON *n* pl. **-S** a type of signal horn

TYPHOON *n* pl. **-S** a tropical hurricane **TYPHONIC** *adj*

TYPHOSE *adj* pertaining to typhoid

TYPHUS *n* pl. **-ES** an infectious disease **TYPHOUS** *adj*

TYPIC *adj* typical

TYPICAL *adj* having the nature of a representative specimen

TYPIER comparative of typey and typy

TYPIEST superlative of typey and typy

TYPIFIER *n* pl. **-S** one that typifies

TYPIFY *v* **-FIED, -FYING, -FIES** to serve as a typical example of

TYPING *n* pl. **-S** the activity of writing with a typewriter

TYPIST *n* pl. **-S** one who types

TYPO *n* pl. **-POS** a typographical error

TYPOLOGY *n* pl. **-GIES** the study of classification according to common characteristics

TYPP *n* pl. **-S** a unit of yarn size

TYPY *adj* **TYPIER, TYPIEST** characterized by strict conformance to the characteristics of a group

TYRAMINE *n* pl. **-S** a chemical compound

TYRANNIC *adj* characteristic of a tyrant

TYRANNY *n* pl. **-NIES** the rule of a tyrant

TYRANT *n* pl. **-S** an absolute ruler

TYRE *v* **TYRED, TYRING, TYRES** to furnish with a covering for a wheel

TYRO *n* pl. **-ROS** a beginner **TYRONIC** *adj*

TYROPITA *n* pl. **-S** a pastry made with layers of phyllo and filled with a cheese-egg mixture

TYROSINE *n* pl. **-S** an amino acid

TYTHE *v* **TYTHED, TYTHING, TYTHES** to tithe

TZADDIK *n* pl. **-DIKIM** zaddik

TZAR *n* pl. **-S** czar

TZARDOM *n* pl. **-S** czardom

TZAREVNA *n* pl. **-S** czarevna

TZARINA *n* pl. **-S** czarina

TZARISM *n* pl. **-S** czarism

TZARIST *n* pl. **-S** czarist

TZARITZA *n* pl. **-S** czaritza

TZATZIKI *n* pl. **-S** a dish of yogurt with cucumber, garlic, and sometimes mint

TZEDAKAH *n* pl. **-S** charitable giving as a moral obligation among Jews

TZETZE *n* pl. **-S** tsetse

TZIGANE *n* pl. **-S** a gypsy

TZIMMES *n* pl. **TZIMMES** a vegetable stew

TZITZIS *n/pl* zizith

TZITZIT *n/pl* zizith

TZITZITH *n/pl* zizith

TZURIS *n* pl. **TZURIS** or **TZURISES** tsuris

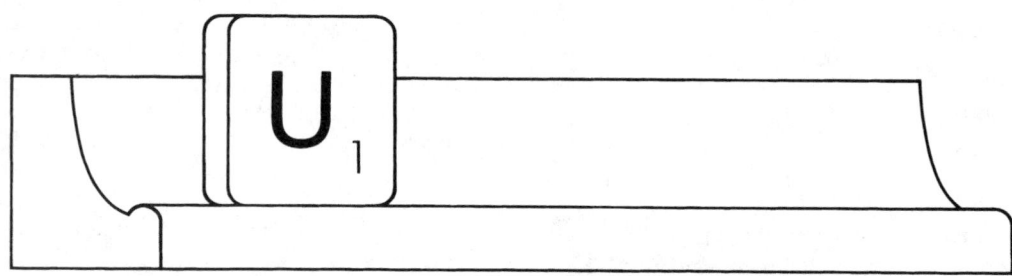

UAKARI	*n* pl. **-S** a South American monkey
UBIETY	*n* pl. **-ETIES** the state of having a definite location
UBIQUE	*adv* everywhere
UBIQUITY	*n* pl. **-TIES** the state of being everywhere at the same time
UDDER	*n* pl. **-S** a mammary gland **UDDERED** *adj*
UDO	*n* pl. **UDOS** a Japanese herb
UDOMETER	*n* pl. **-S** a rain gauge
UDOMETRY	*n* pl. **-TRIES** the measurement of rain
UDON	*n* pl. **-S** a Japanese noodle made with wheat flour
UFOLOGY	*n* pl. **-GIES** the study of unidentified flying objects
UGH	*n* pl. **-S** the sound of a cough or grunt
UGLIER	comparative of ugly
UGLIES	pl. of ugly
UGLIEST	superlative of ugly
UGLIFIER	*n* pl. **-S** one that uglifies
UGLIFY	*v* **-FIED, -FYING, -FIES** to make ugly
UGLINESS	*n* pl. **-ES** the state of being ugly
UGLY	*adj* **-LIER, -LIEST** displeasing to the sight **UGLILY** *adv*
UGLY	*n* pl. **-LIES** one that is ugly
UGSOME	*adj* disgusting
UH	*interj* — used to express hesitation
UHLAN	*n* pl. **-S** one of a body of Prussian cavalry
UINTAITE	*n* pl. **-S** a variety of asphalt
UKASE	*n* pl. **-S** an edict
UKE	*n* pl. **-S** ukelele
UKELELE	*n* pl. **-S** ukulele
UKULELE	*n* pl. **-S** a small guitar-like instrument
ULAMA	*n* pl. **-S** ulema
ULAN	*n* pl. **-S** uhlan
ULCER	*v* **-ED, -ING, -S** to affect with an ulcer (a type of lesion)
ULCERATE	*v* **-ATED, -ATING, -ATES** to ulcer
ULCEROUS	*adj* being or affected with an ulcer
ULEMA	*n* pl. **-S** a Muslim scholar
ULEXITE	*n* pl. **-S** a mineral
ULLAGE	*n* pl. **-S** the amount that a container lacks of being full **ULLAGED** *adj*
ULNA	*n* pl. **-NAS** or **-NAE** a bone of the forearm **ULNAR** *adj*
ULNAD	*adv* toward the ulna
ULPAN	*n* pl. **-PANIM** a school in Israel for teaching Hebrew
ULSTER	*n* pl. **-S** a long, loose overcoat
ULTERIOR	*adj* more remote
ULTIMA	*n* pl. **-S** the last syllable of a word
ULTIMACY	*n* pl. **-CIES** the state of being last or final
ULTIMATA	*n/pl* final proposals
ULTIMATE	*v* **-MATED, -MATING, -MATES** to come to an end
ULTIMO	*adj* of or occurring in the preceding month
ULTISOL	*n* pl. **-S** a reddish-yellow acid soil
ULTRA	*n* pl. **-S** an ultraist
ULTRADRY	*adj* extremely dry
ULTRAHIP	*adj* extremely hip
ULTRAHOT	*adj* extremely hot
ULTRAISM	*n* pl. **-S** advocacy of extreme measures
ULTRAIST	*n* pl. **-S** an advocate of extreme measures
ULTRALOW	*adj* extremely low
ULTRARED	*n* pl. **-S** infrared
ULU	*n* pl. **-S** an Inuit knife
ULULANT	*adj* howling

ULULATE	*v* **-LATED, -LATING, -LATES** to howl	**UMM**	*interj* um
ULVA	*n* pl. **-S** an edible seaweed	**UMMA**	*n* pl. **-S** the whole community of Muslims
UM	*v* **UMMED, UMMING, UMS** to hesitate or pause in speaking	**UMMAH**	*n* pl. **-S** umma
UMAMI	*n* pl. **-S** a taste characteristic of monosodium glutamate	**UMP**	*v* **-ED, -ING, -S** to umpire
		UMPH	*n* pl. **-S** oomph
UMANGITE	*n* pl. **-S** a mineral consisting of copper selenide	**UMPIRAGE**	*n* pl. **-S** the function of an umpire
UMBEL	*n* pl. **-S** a type of flower cluster **UMBELED, UMBELLAR, UMBELLED** *adj*	**UMPIRE**	*v* **-PIRED, -PIRING, -PIRES** to act as umpire (a person appointed to rule on the plays in a game)
UMBELLET	*n* pl. **-S** a small umbel	**UMPTEEN**	*adj* indefinitely numerous
UMBELULE	*n* pl. **-S** a secondary umbel	**UMPTY**	*adj* umpteen
UMBER	*v* **-ED, -ING, -S** to color with a brown pigment	**UMTEENTH**	*adj* being the last in an indefinitely numerous series
UMBILICI	*n/pl* navels	**UN**	*pron* pl. **-S** one
UMBLES	*n/pl* the entrails of a deer	**UNAI**	*n* pl. **-S** unau
UMBO	*n* pl. **-BOS** or **-BONES** the rounded elevation at the center of a shield **UMBONAL, UMBONATE, UMBONIC** *adj*	**UNAKITE**	*n* pl. **-S** an igneous rock
		UNANCHOR	*v* **-ED, -ING, -S** to loosen from an anchor
UMBRA	*n* pl. **-BRAS** or **-BRAE** a dark area **UMBRAL** *adj*	**UNANELED**	*adj* not having received the sacrament of anointing of the sick
UMBRAGE	*n* pl. **-S** resentment	**UNARM**	*v* **-ED, -ING, -S** to disarm
UMBRELLA	*v* **-ED, -ING, -S** to provide with an umbrella (a portable cover for protection from rain or sun)	**UNARY**	*adj* consisting of a single element
		UNAU	*n* pl. **-S** a two-toed sloth
UMBRETTE	*n* pl. **-S** a wading bird	**UNAWARES**	*adv* without warning
UMIAC	*n* pl. **-S** umiak	**UNBALE**	*v* **-BALED, -BALING, -BALES** to loosen from a compressed bundle
UMIACK	*n* pl. **-S** umiak		
UMIAK	*n* pl. **-S** an open Inuit boat	**UNBAN**	*v* **-BANNED, -BANNING, -BANS** to remove a prohibition against
UMIAQ	*n* pl. **-S** umiak		
UMLAUT	*v* **-ED, -ING, -S** to modify a vowel sound by partial assimilation to a succeeding sound	**UNBAR**	*v* **-BARRED, -BARRING, -BARS** to remove a bar from
		UNBATED	*adj* unabated

Following is a list of self-explanatory adjectives and adverbs containing the prefix UN- (not):

UNABATED	*adj*	**UNAIDED**	*adj*	**UNATONED**	*adj*
UNABLE	*adj*	**UNAIMED**	*adj*	**UNAVOWED**	*adj*
UNABUSED	*adj*	**UNAIRED**	*adj*	**UNAWAKE**	*adj*
UNACIDIC	*adj*	**UNAKIN**	*adj*	**UNAWAKED**	*adj*
UNACTED	*adj*	**UNALIKE**	*adj*	**UNAWARE**	*adj*
UNADDED	*adj*	**UNALLIED**	*adj*	**UNAWED**	*adj*
UNADEPT	*adj*	**UNAMAZED**	*adj*	**UNAXED**	*adj*
UNADULT	*adj*	**UNAMUSED**	*adj*	**UNBACKED**	*adj*
UNAFRAID	*adj*	**UNAPT**	*adj*	**UNBAKED**	*adj*
UNAGED	*adj*	**UNAPTLY**	*adv*	**UNBANDED**	*adj*
UNAGEING	*adj*	**UNARCHED**	*adj*	**UNBANNED**	*adj*
UNAGILE	*adj*	**UNARGUED**	*adj*	**UNBARBED**	*adj*
UNAGING	*adj*	**UNARTFUL**	*adj*	**UNBASED**	*adj*
UNAGREED	*adj*	**UNASKED**	*adj*	**UNBASTED**	*adj*

UNBE	*v* **UNBEING** to cease to have being
UNBEAR	*v* **-BEARED, -BEARING, -BEARS** to free from the pressure of a rein
UNBELIEF	*n* pl. **-S** lack of belief
UNBELT	*v* **-ED, -ING, -S** to remove the belt of
UNBEND	*v* **-BENT** or **-BENDED, -BENDING, -BENDS** to make or allow to become straight
UNBID	*adj* unbidden
UNBIDDEN	*adj* not invited
UNBIND	*v* **-BOUND, -BINDING, -BINDS** to free from bindings
UNBLIND	*v* **-ED, -ING, -S** to free from blindness or illusion
UNBLOCK	*v* **-ED, -ING, -S** to free from being blocked
UNBODIED	*adj* having no body
UNBOLT	*v* **-ED, -ING, -S** to open by withdrawing a bolt (a metal bar)
UNBONNET	*v* **-ED, -ING, -S** to uncover the head
UNBOSOM	*v* **-ED, -ING, -S** to reveal
UNBOTTLE	*v* **-TLED, -TLING, -TLES** to release from or as if from a bottle
UNBOUND	past tense of unbind
UNBOX	*v* **-ED, -ING, -ES** to remove from a box
UNBRACE	*v* **-BRACED, -BRACING, -BRACES** to free from braces
UNBRAID	*v* **-ED, -ING, -S** to separate the strands of
UNBRAKE	*v* **-BRAKED, -BRAKING, -BRAKES** to release a brake
UNBREECH	*v* **-ED, -ING, -ES** to remove the breeches of
UNBRIDLE	*v* **-DLED, -DLING, -DLES** to set loose
UNBUCKLE	*v* **-LED, -LING, -LES** to loosen a buckle
UNBUILD	*v* **-BUILT, -BUILDING, -BUILDS** to demolish
UNBUNDLE	*v* **-DLED, -DLING, -DLES** to price separately
UNBURDEN	*v* **-ED, -ING, -S** to free from a burden
UNBURY	*v* **-BURIED, -BURYING, -BURIES** to remove from the ground after burial
UNBUTTON	*v* **-ED, -ING, -S** to unfasten the buttons of
UNCAGE	*v* **-CAGED, -CAGING, -CAGES** to release from a cage
UNCAKE	*v* **-CAKED, -CAKING, -CAKES** to break up a cake (a block of compacted matter)
UNCANNY	*adj* **-NIER, -NIEST** strange and inexplicable
UNCAP	*v* **-CAPPED, -CAPPING, -CAPS** to remove the cap from
UNCARED	*adj* not properly taken care of
UNCASE	*v* **-CASED, -CASING, -CASES** to remove from a case
UNCHAIN	*v* **-ED, -ING, -S** to free by removing a chain
UNCHAIR	*v* **-ED, -ING, -S** to remove from a chairmanship
UNCHANCY	*adj* unlucky
UNCHARGE	*v* **-CHARGED, -CHARGING, -CHARGES** to acquit
UNCHOKE	*v* **-CHOKED, -CHOKING, -CHOKES** to free from obstruction

List of self-explanatory adjectives and adverbs containing the prefix UN- (continued):

UNBATHED	*adj*	**UNBOUGHT**	*adj*	**UNCARING**	*adj*
UNBEATEN	*adj*	**UNBOUNCY**	*adj*	**UNCARTED**	*adj*
UNBENIGN	*adj*	**UNBOWED**	*adj*	**UNCARVED**	*adj*
UNBIASED	*adj*	**UNBOWING**	*adj*	**UNCASHED**	*adj*
UNBILLED	*adj*	**UNBRED**	*adj*	**UNCASKED**	*adj*
UNBITTED	*adj*	**UNBRIGHT**	*adj*	**UNCAST**	*adj*
UNBITTEN	*adj*	**UNBROKE**	*adj*	**UNCATCHY**	*adj*
UNBITTER	*adj*	**UNBROKEN**	*adj*	**UNCAUGHT**	*adj*
UNBLAMED	*adj*	**UNBULKY**	*adj*	**UNCAUSED**	*adj*
UNBLEST	*adj*	**UNBURNED**	*adj*	**UNCEDED**	*adj*
UNBLOODY	*adj*	**UNBURNT**	*adj*	**UNCHARY**	*adj*
UNBOBBED	*adj*	**UNBUSTED**	*adj*	**UNCHASTE**	*adj* **-CHASTER, -CHASTEST**
UNBOILED	*adj*	**UNBUSY**	*adj*		
UNBONDED	*adj*	**UNCALLED**	*adj*	**UNCHEWED**	*adj*
UNBONED	*adj*	**UNCANDID**	*adj*	**UNCHIC**	*adj*
UNBOOTED	*adj*	**UNCANNED**	*adj*	**UNCHICLY**	*adv*
UNBORN	*adj*	**UNCARDED**	*adj*	**UNCHOSEN**	*adj*

UNCHURCH	*v* **-ED, -ING, -ES** to expel from a church	**UNCOCK**	*v* **-ED, -ING, -S** to remove from a cocked position
UNCI	pl. of uncus	**UNCOFFIN**	*v* **-ED, -ING, -S** to remove from a coffin
UNCIA	*n* pl. **-CIAE** a coin of ancient Rome	**UNCOIL**	*v* **-ED, -ING, -S** to release from a coiled position
UNCIAL	*n* pl. **-S** a style of writing		
UNCIALLY	*adv* in the uncial style	**UNCORK**	*v* **-ED, -ING, -S** to draw the cork
UNCIFORM	*n* pl. **-S** a bone of the wrist	**UNCOUPLE**	*v* **-PLED, -PLING, -PLES** to disconnect
UNCINAL	*adj* uncinate		
UNCINATE	*adj* bent at the end like a hook	**UNCOVER**	*v* **-ED, -ING, -S** to remove the covering from
UNCINUS	*n* pl. **-NI** an uncinate structure	**UNCRATE**	*v* **-CRATED, -CRATING, -CRATES** to remove from a crate
UNCLAD	a past tense of unclothe		
UNCLAMP	*v* **-ED, -ING, -S** to free from a clamp	**UNCREATE**	*v* **-ATED, -ATING, -ATES** to deprive of existence
UNCLASP	*v* **-ED, -ING, -S** to free from a clasp	**UNCROSS**	*v* **-ED, -ING, -ES** to change from a crossed position
UNCLE	*n* pl. **-S** the brother of one's father or mother	**UNCROWN**	*v* **-ED, -ING, -S** to deprive of a crown
UNCLENCH	*v* **-ED, -ING, -ES** to open from a clenched position	**UNCTION**	*n* pl. **-S** the act of anointing
UNCLINCH	*v* **-ED, -ING, -ES** to unclench	**UNCTUOUS**	*adj* greasy
UNCLIP	*v* **-CLIPPED, -CLIPPING, -CLIPS** to remove a clip (a fastening device) from	**UNCUFF**	*v* **-ED, -ING, -S** to remove handcuffs from
		UNCURB	*v* **-ED, -ING, -S** to remove restraints from
UNCLOAK	*v* **-ED, -ING, -S** to remove a cloak from	**UNCURL**	*v* **-ED, -ING, -S** to straighten the curls of
UNCLOG	*v* **-CLOGGED, -CLOGGING, -CLOGS** to free from a difficulty or obstruction	**UNCUS**	*n* pl. **-CI** a hook-shaped anatomical part
UNCLOSE	*v* **-CLOSED, -CLOSING, -CLOSES** to open	**UNDE**	*adj* wavy
		UNDEAD	*n* pl. **UNDEAD** a vampire
UNCLOTHE	*v* **-CLOTHED** or **-CLAD, -CLOTHING, -CLOTHES** to divest of clothing	**UNDEE**	*adj* unde
		UNDELETE	*v* **-LETED, -LETING, -LETES** to cancel the deletion of
UNCLOUD	*v* **-ED, -ING, -S** to free from clouds		
UNCO	*n* pl. **-COS** a stranger	**UNDER**	*prep* in a lower position than

---

List of self-explanatory adjectives and adverbs containing the prefix UN- (continued):

UNCIVIL	*adj*	**UNCOMMON**	*adj* **-MONER,**	**UNDECKED**	*adj*
UNCLASSY	*adj*		**-MONEST**	**UNDENIED**	*adj*
UNCLAWED	*adj*	**UNCOOKED**	*adj*	**UNDENTED**	*adj*
UNCLEAN	*adj* **-CLEANER,**	**UNCOOL**	*adj*	**UNDEVOUT**	*adj*
	-CLEANEST	**UNCOOLED**	*adj*	**UNDIMMED**	*adj*
UNCLEAR	*adj* **-CLEARER,**	**UNCOUTH**	*adj*	**UNDOABLE**	*adj*
	-CLEAREST	**UNCOY**	*adj*	**UNDOCILE**	*adj*
UNCLEFT	*adj*	**UNCRAZY**	*adj*	**UNDOTTED**	*adj*
UNCLOUDY	*adj*	**UNCREWED**	*adj*	**UNDREAMT**	*adj*
UNCLOYED	*adj*	**UNCUFFED**	*adj*	**UNDRIED**	*adj*
UNCOATED	*adj*	**UNCURED**	*adj*	**UNDUBBED**	*adj*
UNCODED	*adj*	**UNCURSED**	*adj*	**UNDULLED**	*adj*
UNCOINED	*adj*	**UNCUT**	*adj*	**UNDYED**	*adj*
UNCOMBED	*adj*	**UNCUTE**	*adj*	**UNEAGER**	*adj*
UNCOMELY	*adj*	**UNDAMPED**	*adj*	**UNEARNED**	*adj*
UNCOMIC	*adj*	**UNDARING**	*adj*	**UNEATEN**	*adj*
		UNDATED	*adj*	**UNEDIBLE**	*adj*

UNDERACT *v* **-ED, -ING, -S** to act subtly and with restraint

UNDERAGE *n* pl. **-S** a shortage

UNDERARM *n* pl. **-S** the armpit

UNDERATE past tense of undereat

UNDERBID *v* **-BID, -BIDDING, -BIDS** to bid lower than

UNDERBUD *v* **-BUDDED, -BUDDING, -BUDS** to bud from beneath

UNDERBUY *v* **-BOUGHT, -BUYING, -BUYS** to buy at a lower price than

UNDERCUT *v* **-CUT, -CUTTING, -CUTS** to cut under

UNDERDO *v* **-DID, -DONE, -DOING, -DOES** to do insufficiently

UNDERDOG *n* pl. **-S** one who is expected to lose

UNDEREAT *v* **-ATE, -EATEN, -EATING, -EATS** to eat an insufficient amount

UNDERFED *adj* fed an insufficient amount

UNDERFUR *n* pl. **-S** the thick, soft fur beneath the outer coat of certain mammals

UNDERGO *v* **-WENT, -GONE, -GOING, -GOES** to be subjected to

UNDERGOD *n* pl. **-S** a lesser god

UNDERJAW *n* pl. **-S** the lower jaw

UNDERLAIN past participle of underlie

UNDERLAP *v* **-LAPPED, -LAPPING, -LAPS** to extend partly under

UNDERLAY *v* **-LAID, -LAYING, -LAYS** to place under

UNDERLET *v* **-LET, -LETTING, -LETS** to lease at less than the usual value

UNDERLIE *v* **-LAY, -LAIN, -LYING, -LIES** to lie under

UNDERLIP *n* pl. **-S** the lower lip

UNDERLIT *adj* lacking adequate light

UNDERMAN *v* **-MANNED, -MANNING, -MANS** to fail to provide with enough workers

UNDERPAD *n* pl. **-S** a layer of soft foam laid under carpeting

UNDERPAY *v* **-PAID, -PAYING, -PAYS** to pay less than is deserved

UNDERPIN *v* **-PINNED, -PINNING, -PINS** to support from below

UNDERRUN *v* **-RAN, -RUNNING, -RUNS** to pass or extend under

UNDERSEA *adv* beneath the surface of the sea

UNDERSET *n* pl. **-S** a current below the surface of the ocean

UNDERSOW *v* **-SOWED, -SOWN, -SOWING, -SOWS** to sow land already seeded with a later-growing crop

UNDERTAX *v* **-ED, -ING, -ES** to tax less than the usual amount

UNDERTOW *n* pl. **-S** the seaward pull of receding waves breaking on a shore

UNDERUSE *v* **-USED, -USING, -USES** to use less than fully

UNDERWAY *adv* in progress

UNDERWENT past tense of undergo

UNDID past tense of undo

UNDIES *n/pl* underwear

UNDINE *n* pl. **-S** a female water spirit

UNDO *v* **-DID, -DONE, -DOING, -DOES** to bring to ruin

UNDO *n* pl. **UNDOS** a computer feature that allows the user to reverse the effect of the last action

---

List of self-explanatory adjectives and adverbs containing the prefix UN- (continued):

UNEDITED	*adj*	**UNFAIRLY**	*adv*	**UNFLEXED**	*adj*
UNENDED	*adj*	**UNFAKED**	*adj*	**UNFLUTED**	*adj*
UNENDING	*adj*	**UNFALLEN**	*adj*	**UNFOILED**	*adj*
UNENVIED	*adj*	**UNFAMOUS**	*adj*	**UNFOND**	*adj*
UNERASED	*adj*	**UNFANCY**	*adj*	**UNFORCED**	*adj*
UNEROTIC	*adj*	**UNFAZED**	*adj*	**UNFORGED**	*adj*
UNERRING	*adj*	**UNFEARED**	*adj*	**UNFORKED**	*adj*
UNEVADED	*adj*	**UNFED**	*adj*	**UNFORMED**	*adj*
UNEVEN	*adj* **-EVENER, -EVENEST**	**UNFELT**	*adj*	**UNFOUGHT**	*adj*
		UNFELTED	*adj*	**UNFOUND**	*adj*
UNEVENLY	*adv*	**UNFILIAL**	*adj*	**UNFRAMED**	*adj*
UNEXOTIC	*adj*	**UNFILLED**	*adj*	**UNFUNDED**	*adj*
UNEXPERT	*adj*	**UNFILMED**	*adj*	**UNFUNNY**	*adj* **-NIER, -NIEST**
UNFADED	*adj*	**UNFIRED**	*adj*	**UNFUSED**	*adj*
UNFADING	*adj*	**UNFISHED**	*adj*	**UNFUSSY**	*adj* **-FUSSIER, -FUSSIEST**
UNFAIR	*adj* **-FAIRER, -FAIREST**	**UNFLASHY**	*adj*		
		UNFLAWED	*adj*	**UNGALLED**	*adj*

UNDOCK v **-ED, -ING, -S** to move away from a dock

UNDOER n pl. **-S** one that undoes

UNDOING n pl. **-S** a cause of ruin

UNDONE past participle of undo

UNDOUBLE v **-BLED, -BLING, -BLES** to unfold

UNDRAPE v **-DRAPED, -DRAPING, -DRAPES** to strip of drapery

UNDRAW v **-DREW, -DRAWN, -DRAWING, -DRAWS** to draw open

UNDRESS v **-DRESSED** or **-DREST, -DRESSING, -DRESSES** to remove one's clothing

UNDRUNK adj not swallowed

UNDUE adj exceeding what is appropriate or normal

UNDULANT adj undulating

UNDULAR adj undulating

UNDULATE v **-LATED, -LATING, -LATES** to move with a wavelike motion

UNDULOUS adj undulating

UNDULY adv in an undue manner

UNDY adj unde

UNDYING adj not subject to death

UNEARTH v **-ED, -ING, -S** to dig up

UNEASE n pl. **-S** mental or physical discomfort

UNEASY adj **-EASIER, -EASIEST** marked by mental or physical discomfort **UNEASILY** adv

UNEQUAL n pl. **-S** one that is not equal to another

UNFAITH n pl. **-S** lack of faith

UNFASTEN v **-ED, -ING, -S** to release from fastenings

UNFENCE v **-FENCED, -FENCING, -FENCES** to remove a fence from

UNFETTER v **-ED, -ING, -S** to free from fetters

UNFIT v **-FITTED, -FITTING, -FITS** to make unsuitable

UNFITLY adv in an unsuitable manner

UNFIX v **-FIXED** or **-FIXT, -FIXING, -FIXES** to unfasten

UNFOLD v **-ED, -ING, -S** to open something that is folded

UNFOLDER n pl. **-S** one that unfolds

UNFORGOT adj not forgotten

UNFREE v **-FREED, -FREEING, -FREES** to deprive of freedom

UNFREEZE v **-FROZE, -FROZEN, -FREEZING, -FREEZES** to cause to thaw

UNFRIEND v **-ED, -ING, -S** to defriend

UNFROCK v **-ED, -ING, -S** to divest of ecclesiastical authority

UNFURL v **-ED, -ING, -S** to unroll

UNGAINLY adj **-LIER, -LIEST** awkward

UNGIRD v **-GIRDED** or **-GIRT, -GIRDING, -GIRDS** to remove a belt from

UNGLOVE v **-GLOVED, -GLOVING, -GLOVES** to uncover by removing a glove

UNGLUE v **-GLUED, -GLUING, -GLUES** to disjoin

UNGODLY adj **-LIER, -LIEST** impious

UNGOT adj ungotten

UNGOTTEN adj not obtained

UNGREEN adj **-GREENER, -GREENEST** harmful to the environment

---

List of self-explanatory adjectives and adverbs containing the prefix UN- (continued):

UNGARBED	adj	**UNHALVED**	adj	**UNHUMAN**	adj
UNGATED	adj	**UNHAPPY**	adj **-PIER, -PIEST**	**UNHUNG**	adj
UNGAZING	adj	**UNHARMED**	adj	**UNHURT**	adj
UNGELDED	adj	**UNHASTY**	adj	**UNIDEAL**	adj
UNGENIAL	adj	**UNHEALED**	adj	**UNIMBUED**	adj
UNGENTLE	adj	**UNHEARD**	adj	**UNIRONED**	adj
UNGENTLY	adv	**UNHEATED**	adj	**UNIRONIC**	adj
UNGIFTED	adj	**UNHEDGED**	adj	**UNISSUED**	adj
UNGIVING	adj	**UNHEEDED**	adj	**UNJADED**	adj
UNGLAZED	adj	**UNHELPED**	adj	**UNJOINED**	adj
UNGOWNED	adj	**UNHEROIC**	adj	**UNJOYFUL**	adj
UNGRACED	adj	**UNHEWN**	adj	**UNJUDGED**	adj
UNGRADED	adj	**UNHIP**	adj **-HIPPER, -HIPPEST**	**UNJUST**	adj
UNGREEDY	adj			**UNJUSTLY**	adv
UNGROUND	adj	**UNHIRED**	adj	**UNKEELED**	adj
UNGUIDED	adj	**UNHOLILY**	adv	**UNKEPT**	adj
UNHAILED	adj	**UNHOLY**	adj **-LIER, -LIEST**		

UNGROUP   *v* **-ED, -ING, -S** to separate from a group

UNGUAL   *adj* pertaining to an unguis

UNGUARD   *v* **-ED, -ING, -S** to leave unprotected

UNGUENT   *n* pl. **-S** an ointment

UNGUENTA   *n/pl* ointments

UNGUIS   *n* pl. **-GUES** a nail, claw, or hoof

UNGULA   *n* pl. **-LAE** an unguis **UNGULAR** *adj*

UNGULATE   *n* pl. **-S** a hoofed mammal

UNGULED   *adj* having hoofs of a color that is different from the body — used of a heraldic animal

UNHAIR   *v* **-ED, -ING, -S** to remove the hair from

UNHAIRER   *n* pl. **-S** one that unhairs

UNHALLOW   *v* **-ED, -ING, -S** to profane

UNHAND   *v* **-ED, -ING, -S** to remove the hand from

UNHANDY   *adj* **-HANDIER, -HANDIEST** difficult to handle

UNHANG   *v* **-HUNG** or **-HANGED, -HANGING, -HANGS** to detach from a hanging support

UNHAPPEN   *v* **-ED, -ING, -S** to become as though never having happened

UNHASP   *v* **-ED, -ING, -S** to unfasten

UNHAT   *v* **-HATTED, -HATTING, -HATS** to remove one's hat

UNHEALTH   *n* pl. **-S** a state of ill health

UNHELM   *v* **-ED, -ING, -S** to remove the helmet of

UNHINGE   *v* **-HINGED, -HINGING, -HINGES** to remove from hinges

UNHITCH   *v* **-ED, -ING, -ES** to free from being hitched

UNHOOD   *v* **-ED, -ING, -S** to remove a hood from

UNHOOK   *v* **-ED, -ING, -S** to remove from a hook

UNHOPED   *adj* not hoped for or expected

UNHORSE   *v* **-HORSED, -HORSING, -HORSES** to cause to fall from a horse

UNHOUSE   *v* **-HOUSED, -HOUSING, -HOUSES** to deprive of a protective shelter

UNHUSK   *v* **-ED, -ING, -S** to remove the husk from

UNI   *n* pl. **-S** 1. a uniform 2. university

UNIALGAL   *adj* pertaining to a single algal cell

UNIAXIAL   *adj* having one axis

UNIBODY   *n* pl. **-BODIES** a single molded unit that forms the bodywork and chassis of a vehicle

UNIBROW   *n* pl. **-S** a single continuous eyebrow formed when hair grows above the bridge of the nose

UNICED   *adj* not covered with icing

UNICOLOR   *adj* of one color

UNICOM   *n* pl. **-S** a radio communications system at some airports

UNICORN   *n* pl. **-S** a mythical horselike creature

UNICUM   *n* pl. **-CA** a unique example or specimen

UNICYCLE   *v* **-CLED, -CLING, -CLES** to ride a one-wheeled vehicle

UNIDEAED   *adj* lacking ideas

List of self-explanatory adjectives and adverbs containing the prefix UN- (continued):

UNKIND	*adj* **-KINDER, -KINDEST**	**UNLISTED**	*adj*	**UNMATTED**	*adj*
UNKINDLY	*adv* **-LIER, -LIEST**	**UNLIT**	*adj*	**UNMEANT**	*adj*
UNKINGLY	*adj*	**UNLIVELY**	*adj*	**UNMELLOW**	*adj*
UNKISSED	*adj*	**UNLOBED**	*adj*	**UNMELTED**	*adj*
UNKOSHER	*adj*	**UNLOVED**	*adj*	**UNMENDED**	*adj*
UNLAWFUL	*adj*	**UNLOVELY**	*adj* **-LIER, -LIEST**	**UNMERRY**	*adj*
UNLEASED	*adj*	**UNLOVING**	*adj*	**UNMET**	*adj*
UNLED	*adj*	**UNLUCKY**	*adj* **-LUCKIER, -LUCKIEST**	**UNMILLED**	*adj*
UNLETHAL	*adj*			**UNMINED**	*adj*
UNLETTED	*adj*	**UNMACHO**	*adj*	**UNMODISH**	*adj*
UNLEVIED	*adj*	**UNMAILED**	*adj*	**UNMOLTEN**	*adj*
UNLICKED	*adj*	**UNMANFUL**	*adj*	**UNMOVED**	*adj*
UNLIKE	*adj*	**UNMANLY**	*adj* **-LIER, -LIEST**	**UNMOVING**	*adj*
UNLIKED	*adj*	**UNMAPPED**	*adj*	**UNMOWN**	*adj*
UNLIKELY	*adj* **-LIER, -LIEST**	**UNMARKED**	*adj*	**UNNAMED**	*adj*
UNLINED	*adj*	**UNMARRED**	*adj*	**UNNEEDED**	*adj*
		UNMATED	*adj*	**UNNOISY**	*adj*

UNIFACE *n* pl. **-S** a coin having a design on only one side

UNIFIC *adj* unifying

UNIFIED past tense of unify

UNIFIER *n* pl. **-S** one that unifies

UNIFIES present 3d person sing. of unify

UNIFILAR *adj* having only one thread, wire, or fiber

UNIFORM *adj* **-FORMER, -FORMEST** unchanging

UNIFORM *v* **-ED, -ING, -S** to make uniform

UNIFY *v* **-FIED, -FYING, -FIES** to make into a coherent whole

UNILOBED *adj* having one lobe

UNIMODAL *adj* having or involving one mode

UNINSTAL *v* **-STALLED, -STALLING, -STALS** to remove a file or an application from a computer

UNION *n* pl. **-S** a number of persons, parties, or political entities united for a common purpose

UNIONISE *v* **-ISED, -ISING, -ISES** to unionize

UNIONISM *n* pl. **-S** the principle of forming a union

UNIONIST *n* pl. **-S** an advocate of unionism

UNIONIZE *v* **-IZED, -IZING, -IZES** to form into a union

UNIPOD *n* pl. **-S** a one-legged support

UNIPOLAR *adj* showing only one kind of polarity

UNIQUE *adj* **UNIQUER, UNIQUEST** existing as the only one of its kind; very unusual **UNIQUELY** *adv*

UNIQUE *n* pl. **-S** something that is unique

UNISEX *n* pl. **-ES** the condition of not being distinguishable as to sex

UNISIZE *adj* made to fit all sizes

UNISON *n* pl. **-S** complete agreement **UNISONAL** *adj*

UNIT *n* pl. **-S** a specific quantity used as a standard of measurement

UNITAGE *n* pl. **-S** amount in units

UNITARD *n* pl. **-S** a leotard that also covers the legs

UNITARY *adj* pertaining to a unit

UNITE *v* **UNITED, UNITING, UNITES** to bring together so as to form a whole **UNITEDLY** *adv*

UNITER *n* pl. **-S** one that unites

UNITIES pl. of unity

UNITIVE *adj* serving to unite

UNITIZE *v* **-IZED, -IZING, -IZES** to divide into units

UNITIZER *n* pl. **-S** one that unitizes

UNITRUST *n* pl. **-S** a type of annuity trust

UNITY *n* pl. **-TIES** the state of being one single entity

UNIVALVE *n* pl. **-S** a mollusk having a single shell

UNIVERSE *n* pl. **-S** the totality of all existing things

UNIVOCAL *n* pl. **-S** a word having only one meaning

UNJAM *v* **-JAMMED, -JAMMING, -JAMS** to undo things tightly crammed together

UNJOINT *v* **-ED, -ING, -S** to separate at a juncture

UNKEMPT *adj* untidy

List of self-explanatory adjectives and adverbs containing the prefix UN- (continued):

UNNOTED	*adj*	**UNPLIANT**	*adj*	**UNPURE**	*adj*
UNOILED	*adj*	**UNPLOWED**	*adj*	**UNPURELY**	*adv*
UNOPEN	*adj*	**UNPOETIC**	*adj*	**UNPURGED**	*adj*
UNOPENED	*adj*	**UNPOISED**	*adj*	**UNQUIET**	*adj* **-ETER,**
UNORNATE	*adj*	**UNPOLITE**	*adj*		**-ETEST**
UNOWNED	*adj*	**UNPOLLED**	*adj*	**UNRAISED**	*adj*
UNPADDED	*adj*	**UNPOSED**	*adj*	**UNRAKED**	*adj*
UNPAID	*adj*	**UNPOSTED**	*adj*	**UNRANKED**	*adj*
UNPAIRED	*adj*	**UNPOTTED**	*adj*	**UNRATED**	*adj*
UNPARTED	*adj*	**UNPRETTY**	*adj*	**UNRAZED**	*adj*
UNPAVED	*adj*	**UNPRICED**	*adj*	**UNREAD**	*adj*
UNPAYING	*adj*	**UNPRIMED**	*adj*	**UNREADY**	*adj* **-READIER,**
UNPEELED	*adj*	**UNPRIZED**	*adj*		**-READIEST**
UNPITIED	*adj*	**UNPROBED**	*adj*	**UNREAL**	*adj*
UNPITTED	*adj*	**UNPROVED**	*adj*	**UNREALLY**	*adv*
UNPLACED	*adj*	**UNPROVEN**	*adj*	**UNRENTED**	*adj*
UNPLAYED	*adj*	**UNPRUNED**	*adj*	**UNREPAID**	*adj*

UNKEND	*adj* unkenned	**UNLIMBER**	*v* **-ED, -ING, -S** to prepare for action
UNKENNED	*adj* not known or recognized	**UNLINK**	*v* **-ED, -ING, -S** to unfasten the links (connecting devices) of
UNKENNEL	*v* **-NELED, -NELING, -NELS** or **-NELLED, -NELLING, -NELS** to release from a kennel	**UNLIVE**	*v* **-LIVED, -LIVING, -LIVES** to live so as to make amends for
UNKENT	*adj* unkenned	**UNLOAD**	*v* **-ED, -ING, -S** to remove the load or cargo from
UNKINK	*v* **-ED, -ING, -S** to remove curls from	**UNLOADER**	*n* pl. **-S** one that unloads
UNKNIT	*v* **-KNITTED, -KNITTING, -KNITS** to unravel	**UNLOCK**	*v* **-ED, -ING, -S** to unfasten the lock of
UNKNOT	*v* **-KNOTTED, -KNOTTING, -KNOTS** to undo a knot in	**UNLOOSE**	*v* **-LOOSED, -LOOSING, -LOOSES** to set free
UNKNOWN	*n* pl. **-S** one that is not known	**UNLOOSEN**	*v* **-ED, -ING, -S** to unloose
UNLACE	*v* **-LACED, -LACING, -LACES** to unfasten the laces of	**UNMAKE**	*v* **-MADE, -MAKING, -MAKES** to destroy
UNLADE	*v* **-LADED, -LADEN, -LADING, -LADES** to unload	**UNMAKER**	*n* pl. **-S** one that unmakes
UNLASH	*v* **-ED, -ING, -ES** to untie the lashing (a type of binding) of	**UNMAN**	*v* **-MANNED, -MANNING, -MANS** to deprive of courage
UNLATCH	*v* **-ED, -ING, -ES** to open by lifting the latch (a fastening device)	**UNMASK**	*v* **-ED, -ING, -S** to remove a mask from
UNLAY	*v* **-LAID, -LAYING, -LAYS** to untwist	**UNMASKER**	*n* pl. **-S** one that unmasks
UNLEAD	*v* **-ED, -ING, -S** to remove the lead from	**UNMEET**	*adj* improper **UNMEETLY** *adv*
		UNMESH	*v* **-ED, -ING, -ES** to disentangle
UNLEADED	*n* pl. **-S** a product containing no lead	**UNMEW**	*v* **-ED, -ING, -S** to set free
UNLEARN	*v* **-LEARNED** or **-LEARNT, -LEARNING, -LEARNS** to put out of one's knowledge or memory	**UNMINGLE**	*v* **-GLED, -GLING, -GLES** to separate things that are mixed
UNLEASH	*v* **-ED, -ING, -ES** to free from a leash	**UNMITER**	*v* **-ED, -ING, -S** to depose from the rank of bishop
UNLESS	*conj* except on the condition that	**UNMITRE**	*v* **-TRED, -TRING, -TRES** to unmiter
UNLET	*adj* not rented	**UNMIX**	*v* **-MIXED** or **-MIXT, -MIXING, -MIXES** to separate from a mixture
UNLEVEL	*v* **-ELED, -ELING, -ELS** or **-ELLED, -ELLING, -ELS** to make uneven	**UNMOLD**	*v* **-ED, -ING, -S** to remove from a mold

---

List of self-explanatory adjectives and adverbs containing the prefix UN- (continued):

UNRESTED	*adj*	**UNSATED**	*adj*	**UNSHADED**	*adj*
UNRHYMED	*adj*	**UNSAVED**	*adj*	**UNSHAKEN**	*adj*
UNRIBBED	*adj*	**UNSAVORY**	*adj*	**UNSHAMED**	*adj*
UNRIDDEN	*adj*	**UNSAWED**	*adj*	**UNSHAPED**	*adj*
UNRIFLED	*adj*	**UNSAWN**	*adj*	**UNSHAPEN**	*adj*
UNRIMED	*adj*	**UNSCALED**	*adj*	**UNSHARED**	*adj*
UNRINSED	*adj*	**UNSEARED**	*adj*	**UNSHARP**	*adj*
UNRISEN	*adj*	**UNSEEDED**	*adj*	**UNSHAVED**	*adj*
UNROPED	*adj*	**UNSEEING**	*adj*	**UNSHAVEN**	*adj*
UNROUGH	*adj*	**UNSEEMLY**	*adj* **-LIER, -LIEST**	**UNSHED**	*adj*
UNRULED	*adj*	**UNSEEN**	*adj*	**UNSHOD**	*adj*
UNRUSHED	*adj*	**UNSEIZED**	*adj*	**UNSHORN**	*adj*
UNRUSTED	*adj*	**UNSENT**	*adj*	**UNSHOWY**	*adj*
UNSAFE	*adj* **-SAFER, -SAFEST**	**UNSERVED**	*adj*	**UNSHRUNK**	*adj*
		UNSEXUAL	*adj*	**UNSHUT**	*adj*
UNSAFELY	*adv*	**UNSEXY**	*adj* **-SEXIER, -SEXIEST**	**UNSIFTED**	*adj*
UNSALTED	*adj*			**UNSIGNED**	*adj*

UNMOOR *v* **-ED, -ING, -S** to release from moorings

UNMORAL *adj* amoral

UNMOULD *v* **-ED, -ING, -S** to unmold

UNMUFFLE *v* **-FLED, -FLING, -FLES** to free from something that muffles

UNMUZZLE *v* **-ZLED, -ZLING, -ZLES** to remove a muzzle from

UNNAIL *v* **-ED, -ING, -S** to remove the nails from

UNNERVE *v* **-NERVED, -NERVING, -NERVES** to deprive of courage

UNOAKED *adj* not matured in an oak container — used of wine

UNPACK *v* **-ED, -ING, -S** to remove the contents of

UNPACKER *n* pl. **-S** one that unpacks

UNPAGED *adj* having no page numbers

UNPEG *v* **-PEGGED, -PEGGING, -PEGS** to remove the pegs from

UNPEN *v* **-PENNED** or **-PENT, -PENNING, -PENS** to release from confinement

UNPEOPLE *v* **-PLED, -PLING, -PLES** to remove people from

UNPERSON *n* pl. **-S** one who is removed completely from recognition

UNPICK *v* **-ED, -ING, -S** to remove the stitches from

UNPILE *v* **-PILED, -PILING, -PILES** to take or disentangle from a pile

UNPIN *v* **-PINNED, -PINNING, -PINS** to remove the pins from

UNPLAIT *v* **-ED, -ING, -S** to undo the plaits of

UNPLUG *v* **-PLUGGED, -PLUGGING, -PLUGS** to take a plug out of

UNPUCKER *v* **-ED, -ING, -S** to remove the wrinkles from

UNPUZZLE *v* **-ZLED, -ZLING, -ZLES** to work out the obscured meaning of

UNQUIET *n* pl. **-S** a state of unrest

UNQUOTE *v* **-QUOTED, -QUOTING, -QUOTES** to close a quotation

UNRAVEL *v* **-ELED, -ELING, -ELS** or **-ELLED, -ELLING, -ELS** to separate the threads of

UNREASON *v* **-ED, -ING, -S** to disrupt the sanity of

UNREEL *v* **-ED, -ING, -S** to unwind from a reel

UNREELER *n* pl. **-S** one that unreels

UNREEVE *v* **-REEVED** or **-ROVE, -ROVEN, -REEVING, -REEVES** to withdraw a rope from an opening

UNRENT *adj* not torn

UNREPAIR *n* pl. **-S** lack of repair

UNREST *n* pl. **-S** a disturbed or uneasy state

UNRETIRE *v* **-TIRED, -TIRING, -TIRES** to return to work after having taken retirement

UNRIDDLE *v* **-DLED, -DLING, -DLES** to solve

UNRIG *v* **-RIGGED, -RIGGING, -RIGS** to divest of rigging

UNRIP *v* **-RIPPED, -RIPPING, -RIPS** to rip open

UNRIPE *adj* **-RIPER, -RIPEST** not ripe
UNRIPELY *adv*

UNRIVET *v* **-ETED, -ETING, -ETS** or **-ETTED, -ETTING, -ETS** to remove rivets (metal bolts) from

UNROBE *v* **-ROBED, -ROBING, -ROBES** to undress

List of self-explanatory adjectives and adverbs containing the prefix UN- (continued):

UNSILENT	*adj*	**UNSOUND**	*adj* **-SOUNDER, -SOUNDEST**	**UNSTUFFY**	*adj*
UNSINFUL	*adj*			**UNSTUNG**	*adj*
UNSIZED	*adj*	**UNSOURED**	*adj*	**UNSUBTLE**	*adj*
UNSLAKED	*adj*	**UNSOWED**	*adj*	**UNSUBTLY**	*adv*
UNSLICED	*adj*	**UNSOWN**	*adj*	**UNSUITED**	*adj*
UNSLICK	*adj*	**UNSPENT**	*adj*	**UNSUNG**	*adj*
UNSMART	*adj*	**UNSPILT**	*adj*	**UNSUNK**	*adj*
UNSMOKED	*adj*	**UNSPLIT**	*adj*	**UNSURE**	*adj*
UNSOAKED	*adj*	**UNSPOILT**	*adj*	**UNSURELY**	*adv*
UNSOBER	*adj*	**UNSPRUNG**	*adj*	**UNSWAYED**	*adj*
UNSOCIAL	*adj*	**UNSPUN**	*adj*	**UNSWEPT**	*adj*
UNSOILED	*adj*	**UNSTABLE**	*adj* **-BLER, -BLEST**	**UNTAGGED**	*adj*
UNSOLD	*adj*			**UNTAKEN**	*adj*
UNSOLID	*adj*	**UNSTABLY**	*adv*	**UNTAME**	*adj*
UNSOLVED	*adj*	**UNSTEADY**	*adj* **-STEADIER, -STEADIEST**	**UNTAMED**	*adj*
UNSORTED	*adj*			**UNTANNED**	*adj*
UNSOUGHT	*adj*	**UNSTONED**	*adj*	**UNTAPPED**	*adj*

UNROLL   *v* **-ED, -ING, -S** to open something that is rolled up

UNROOF   *v* **-ED, -ING, -S** to strip off the roof of

UNROOT   *v* **-ED, -ING, -S** to uproot

UNROPE   *v* **-ROPED, -ROPING, -ROPES** to detach oneself from a rope

UNROUND   *v* **-ED, -ING, -S** to articulate without rounding the lips

UNROVE   a past tense of unreeve

UNROVEN   a past participle of unreeve

UNRULY   *adj* **-LIER, -LIEST** difficult to control

UNSADDLE   *v* **-DLED, -DLING, -DLES** to remove the saddle from

UNSAFETY   *n pl.* **-TIES** lack of safety

UNSAY   *v* **-SAID, -SAYING, -SAYS** to retract something said

UNSCREW   *v* **-ED, -ING, -S** to remove the screws from

UNSEAL   *v* **-ED, -ING, -S** to remove the seal of

UNSEAM   *v* **-ED, -ING, -S** to open the seams of

UNSEAT   *v* **-ED, -ING, -S** to remove from a seat

UNSELL   *v* **-SOLD, -SELLING, -SELLS** to persuade to change an opinion or belief

UNSET   *v* **-SET, -SETTING, -SETS** to unsettle

UNSETTLE   *v* **-TLED, -TLING, -TLES** to make unstable

UNSEW   *v* **-SEWED, -SEWN, -SEWING, -SEWS** to undo the sewing of

UNSEX   *v* **-ED, -ING, -ES** to deprive of sexual power

UNSHELL   *v* **-ED, -ING, -S** to remove the shell from

UNSHIFT   *v* **-ED, -ING, -S** to release the shift key on a typewriter

UNSHIP   *v* **-SHIPPED, -SHIPPING, -SHIPS** to unload from a ship

UNSICKER   *adj* unreliable

UNSIGHT   *v* **-ED, -ING, -S** to prevent from seeing

UNSLING   *v* **-SLUNG, -SLINGING, -SLINGS** to remove from a slung position

UNSNAG   *v* **-SNAGGED, -SNAGGING, -SNAGS** to free of snags

UNSNAP   *v* **-SNAPPED, -SNAPPING, -SNAPS** to undo the snaps of

UNSNARL   *v* **-ED, -ING, -S** to untangle

UNSOLDER   *v* **-ED, -ING, -S** to separate

UNSONCY   *adj* unsonsie

UNSONSIE   *adj* unlucky

UNSONSY   *adj* unsonsie

UNSPEAK   *v* **-SPOKE, -SPOKEN, -SPEAKING, -SPEAKS** to unsay

UNSPHERE   *v* **-SPHERED, -SPHERING, -SPHERES** to remove from a sphere

UNSPOOL   *v* **-ED, -ING, -S** to unwind from a small cylinder

UNSTACK   *v* **-ED, -ING, -S** to remove from a stack

UNSTATE   *v* **-STATED, -STATING, -STATES** to deprive of status

UNSTAYED   *adj* not secured with ropes or wires

UNSTEADY   *v* **-STEADIED, -STEADYING, -STEADIES** to make not firm or stable

UNSTEEL   *v* **-ED, -ING, -S** to make soft

UNSTEP   *v* **-STEPPED, -STEPPING, -STEPS** to remove from a socket

UNSTICK   *v* **-STUCK, -STICKING, -STICKS** to disjoin

UNSTITCH   *v* **-ED, -ING, -ES** to remove the stitches from

---

List of self-explanatory adjectives and adverbs containing the prefix UN- (continued):

UNTASTED	*adj*		**UNTINGED**	*adj*		**UNTRULY**	*adv*
UNTAXED	*adj*		**UNTIPPED**	*adj*		**UNTRUSTY**	*adj*
UNTENDED	*adj*		**UNTIRED**	*adj*		**UNTUFTED**	*adj*
UNTESTED	*adj*		**UNTIRING**	*adj*		**UNTURNED**	*adj*
UNTHAWED	*adj*		**UNTITLED**	*adj*		**UNUNITED**	*adj*
UNTIDILY	*adv*		**UNTOLD**	*adj*		**UNURGED**	*adj*
UNTIDY	*adj* **-DIER, -DIEST**		**UNTORN**	*adj*		**UNUSABLE**	*adj*
			UNTRACED	*adj*		**UNUSED**	*adj*
UNTILLED	*adj*		**UNTRENDY**	*adj*		**UNUSUAL**	*adj*
UNTILTED	*adj*		**UNTRIED**	*adj*		**UNVALUED**	*adj*
UNTIMED	*adj*		**UNTRUE**	*adj* **-TRUER, -TRUEST**		**UNVARIED**	*adj*
UNTIMELY	*adj* **-LIER, -LIEST**					**UNVEINED**	*adj*

UNSTOP *v* **-STOPPED, -STOPPING, -STOPS** to remove a stopper from

UNSTRAP *v* **-STRAPPED, -STRAPPING, -STRAPS** to remove a strap from

UNSTRESS *n* pl. **-ES** a syllable having relatively weak stress

UNSTRING *v* **-STRUNG, -STRINGING, -STRINGS** to remove from a string

UNSTUCK past tense of unstick

UNSWATHE *v* **-SWATHED, -SWATHING, -SWATHES** to unbind

UNSWEAR *v* **-SWORE, -SWORN, -SWEARING, -SWEARS** to retract something sworn

UNTACK *v* **-ED, -ING, -S** to remove a tack from

UNTANGLE *v* **-GLED, -GLING, -GLES** to free from tangles

UNTEACH *v* **-TAUGHT, -TEACHING, -TEACHES** to cause to unlearn something

UNTENTED *adj* not probed or attended to

UNTETHER *v* **-ED, -ING, -S** to free from a tether

UNTHAW *v* **-ED, -ING, -S** to thaw

UNTHINK *v* **-THOUGHT, -THINKING, -THINKS** to dismiss from the mind

UNTHREAD *v* **-ED, -ING, -S** to remove the thread from

UNTHRONE *v* **-THRONED, -THRONING, -THRONES** to remove from a throne

UNTIDY *v* **-DIED, -DYING, -DIES** to make untidy

UNTIE *v* **-TIED, -TYING** or **-TIEING, -TIES** to free from something that ties

UNTIL *prep* up to the time of

UNTO *prep* to

UNTONED *adj* lacking in muscular definition

UNTOWARD *adj* unruly

UNTRACK *v* **-ED, -ING, -S** to cause to escape from a slump

UNTREAD *v* **-TROD** or **-TREADED, -TRODDEN, -TREADING, -TREADS** to tread back

UNTRIM *v* **-TRIMMED, -TRIMMING, -TRIMS** to strip of trimming

UNTRUSS *v* **-ED, -ING, -ES** to free from a truss

UNTRUTH *n* pl. **-S** something that is untrue

UNTUCK *v* **-ED, -ING, -S** to release from being tucked up

UNTUNE *v* **-TUNED, -TUNING, -TUNES** to put out of tune

UNTWINE *v* **-TWINED, -TWINING, -TWINES** to separate the twisted or tangled parts of

UNTWIST *v* **-ED, -ING, -S** to untwine

UNTYING present participle of untie

UNUNBIUM *n* pl. **-S** a synthetic element

UNVEIL *v* **-ED, -ING, -S** to remove a covering from

UNVOICE *v* **-VOICED, -VOICING, -VOICES** to deprive of voice or vocal quality

UNWAGED *adj* not receiving money for work

UNWASHED *n* pl. **-S** an ignorant or underprivileged group

UNWEAVE *v* **-WOVE, -WOVEN, -WEAVING, -WEAVES** to undo something woven

UNWEIGHT *v* **-ED, -ING, -S** to reduce the weight of

UNWIND *v* **-WOUND, -WINDING, -WINDS** to reverse the winding of

UNWINDER *n* pl. **-S** one that unwinds

UNWISDOM *n* pl. **-S** lack of wisdom

UNWISH *v* **-ED, -ING, -ES** to cease to wish for

List of self-explanatory adjectives and adverbs containing the prefix UN- (continued):

UNVERSED	*adj*	**UNWARIEST**	superlative of unwary	**UNWED**	*adj*
UNVESTED	*adj*			**UNWEDDED**	*adj*
UNVEXED	*adj*	**UNWARILY**	*adv*	**UNWEEDED**	*adj*
UNVEXT	*adj*	**UNWARMED**	*adj*	**UNWELDED**	*adj*
UNVIABLE	*adj*	**UNWARNED**	*adj*	**UNWELL**	*adj*
UNVOCAL	*adj*	**UNWARPED**	*adj*	**UNWEPT**	*adj*
UNWALLED	*adj*	**UNWARY**	*adj* **-WARIER, -WARIEST**	**UNWET**	*adj*
UNWANING	*adj*			**UNWETTED**	*adj*
UNWANTED	*adj*	**UNWASTED**	*adj*	**UNWHITE**	*adj*
UNWARIER	comparative of unwary	**UNWAXED**	*adj*	**UNWIELDY**	*adj* **-WIELDIER, -WIELDIEST**
		UNWEANED	*adj*		
		UNWEARY	*adj*		

UNWIT	*v* **-WITTED, -WITTING, -WITS** to make insane
UNWONTED	*adj* unusual
UNWORTHY	*n* pl. **-THIES** an unworthy person
UNWOUND	past tense of unwind
UNWOVE	past tense of unweave
UNWOVEN	past participle of unweave
UNWRAP	*v* **-WRAPPED, -WRAPPING, -WRAPS** to remove the wrapping from
UNYEANED	*adj* unborn
UNYOKE	*v* **-YOKED, -YOKING, -YOKES** to free from a yoke
UNZIP	*v* **-ZIPPED, -ZIPPING, -ZIPS** to open the zipper of
UP	*v* **UPPED, UPPING, UPS** to raise
UPALONG	*n* pl. **-S** a location away from a person or place
UPAS	*n* pl. **-ES** an Asian tree
UPBEAR	*v* **-BORE, -BORNE, -BEARING, -BEARS** to raise aloft
UPBEARER	*n* pl. **-S** one that upbears
UPBEAT	*n* pl. **-S** an unaccented beat in a musical measure
UPBIND	*v* **-BOUND, -BINDING, -BINDS** to bind completely
UPBOIL	*v* **-ED, -ING, -S** to boil up
UPBORE	past tense of upbear
UPBORNE	past participle of upbear
UPBOUND	past tense of upbind
UPBOW	*n* pl. **-S** a type of stroke in playing a bowed instrument
UPBRAID	*v* **-ED, -ING, -S** to reproach severely
UPBUILD	*v* **-BUILT, -BUILDING, -BUILDS** to build up
UPBY	*adv* upbye
UPBYE	*adv* a little farther on
UPCAST	*v* **-CAST, -CASTING, -CASTS** to cast up
UPCHUCK	*v* **-ED, -ING, -S** to vomit
UPCLIMB	*v* **-ED, -ING, -S** to climb up

UPCOAST	*adv* up the coast
UPCOIL	*v* **-ED, -ING, -S** to coil up
UPCOMING	*adj* about to happen or appear
UPCOURT	*adv* in the opposite half of a basketball court
UPCURL	*v* **-ED, -ING, -S** to curl up
UPCURVE	*v* **-CURVED, -CURVING, -CURVES** to curve upward
UPDART	*v* **-ED, -ING, -S** to dart up
UPDATE	*v* **-DATED, -DATING, -DATES** to bring up to date
UPDATER	*n* pl. **-S** one that updates
UPDIVE	*v* **-DIVED** or **-DOVE, -DIVING, -DIVES** to spring upward
UPDO	*n* pl. **-DOS** an upswept hairdo
UPDOMING	*n* pl. **-S** the upward deformation of a rock mass into a dome shape
UPDRAFT	*n* pl. **-S** an upward movement of air
UPDRY	*v* **-DRIED, -DRYING, -DRIES** to dry completely
UPEND	*v* **-ED, -ING, -S** to set or stand on end
UPFIELD	*adv* into the part of the field toward which the offensive team is going
UPFLING	*v* **-FLUNG, -FLINGING, -FLINGS** to fling up
UPFLOW	*v* **-ED, -ING, -S** to flow up
UPFOLD	*v* **-ED, -ING, -S** to fold up
UPFRONT	*adj* honest; candid
UPGATHER	*v* **-ED, -ING, -S** to gather up
UPGAZE	*v* **-GAZED, -GAZING, -GAZES** to gaze up
UPGIRD	*v* **-GIRDED** or **-GIRT, -GIRDING, -GIRDS** to gird completely
UPGOING	*adj* going up
UPGRADE	*v* **-GRADED, -GRADING, -GRADES** to raise to a higher grade or standard
UPGRADER	*n* pl. **-S** one that upgrades
UPGROW	*v* **-GREW, -GROWN, -GROWING, -GROWS** to grow up
UPGROWTH	*n* pl. **-S** the process of growing up
UPHEAP	*v* **-ED, -ING, -S** to heap up

List of self-explanatory adjectives and adverbs containing the prefix UN- (continued):

UNWIFELY	*adj*		**UNWON**	*adj*		**UNWORTHY**	*adj* **-THIER,**
UNWILLED	*adj*		**UNWOODED**	*adj*			**-THIEST**
UNWISE	*adj* **-WISER,**		**UNWOOED**	*adj*		**UNWRUNG**	*adj*
	-WISEST		**UNWORKED**	*adj*		**UNYOUNG**	*adj*
UNWISELY	*adv*		**UNWORN**	*adj*		**UNZONED**	*adj*

UPHEAVAL *n* pl. **-S** the act of upheaving

UPHEAVE *v* **-HEAVED** or **-HOVE, -HEAVING, -HEAVES** to heave up

UPHEAVER *n* pl. **-S** one that upheaves

UPHILL *n* pl. **-S** an upward slope

UPHOARD *v* **-ED, -ING, -S** to hoard up

UPHOLD *v* **-HELD, -HOLDING, -HOLDS** to hold aloft

UPHOLDER *n* pl. **-S** one that upholds

UPHOVE a past tense of upheave

UPHROE *n* pl. **-S** euphroe

UPKEEP *n* pl. **-S** the cost of maintaining something in good condition

UPLAND *n* pl. **-S** the higher land of a region

UPLANDER *n* pl. **-S** an inhabitant of an upland

UPLEAP *v* **-LEAPED** or **-LEAPT, -LEAPING, -LEAPS** to leap up

UPLIFT *v* **-ED, -ING, -S** to lift up

UPLIFTER *n* pl. **-S** one that uplifts

UPLIGHT *v* **-LIGHTED** or **-LIT, -LIGHTING, -LIGHTS** to light to a higher degree

UPLINK *v* **-ED, -ING, -S** to transmit (data) to a spacecraft or satellite

UPLOAD *v* **-ED, -ING, -S** to transfer information from a small computer to a larger computer

UPMARKET *adj* upscale

UPMOST *adj* highest

UPO *prep* upon

UPON *prep* on

UPPED past tense of up

UPPER *n* pl. **-S** the part of a boot or shoe above the sole

UPPERCUT *v* **-CUT, -CUTTING, -CUTS** to strike an upward blow

UPPILE *v* **-PILED, -PILING, -PILES** to pile up

UPPING *n* pl. **-S** the process of marking young swans for identification purposes

UPPISH *adj* uppity **UPPISHLY** *adv*

UPPITY *adj* tending to be snobbish and arrogant

UPPROP *v* **-PROPPED, -PROPPING, -PROPS** to prop up

UPRAISE *v* **-RAISED, -RAISING, -RAISES** to raise up

UPRAISER *n* pl. **-S** one that upraises

UPRATE *v* **-RATED, -RATING, -RATES** to improve the power output of an engine

UPREACH *v* **-ED, -ING, -ES** to reach up

UPREAR *v* **-ED, -ING, -S** to upraise

UPRIGHT *v* **-ED, -ING, -S** to make vertical

UPRISE *v* **-ROSE, -RISEN, -RISING, -RISES** to rise up

UPRISER *n* pl. **-S** one that uprises

UPRISING *n* pl. **-S** a revolt

UPRIVER *n* pl. **-S** an area lying toward the source of a river

UPROAR *n* pl. **-S** a state of noisy excitement and confusion

UPROOT *v* **-ED, -ING, -S** to pull up by the roots

UPROOTAL *n* pl. **-S** the act of uprooting

UPROOTER *n* pl. **-S** one that uproots

UPROSE past tense of uprise

UPROUSE *v* **-ROUSED, -ROUSING, -ROUSES** to rouse up

UPRUSH *v* **-ED, -ING, -ES** to rush up

UPSCALE *v* **-SCALED, -SCALING, -SCALES** to make appealing to affluent consumers

UPSELL *v* **-SOLD, -SELLING, -SELLS** to try to sell a customer something more expensive

UPSEND *v* **-SENT, -SENDING, -SENDS** to send upward

UPSET *v* **-SET, -SETTING, -SETS** to overturn

UPSETTER *n* pl. **-S** one that upsets

UPSHIFT *v* **-ED, -ING, -S** to shift into a higher gear

UPSHOOT *v* **-SHOT, -SHOOTING, -SHOOTS** to shoot upward

UPSHOT *n* pl. **-S** the final result

UPSIDE *n* pl. **-S** a positive aspect

UPSILON *n* pl. **-S** a Greek letter

UPSIZE *v* **-SIZED, -SIZING, -SIZES** to increase in size

UPSKILL *v* **-ED, -ING, -S** to improve the job skills of someone

UPSLOPE *n* pl. **-S** an upward slope

UPSOAR *v* **-ED, -ING, -S** to soar upward

UPSPRING *v* **-SPRANG** or **-SPRUNG, -SPRINGING, -SPRINGS** to spring up

UPSTAGE *v* **-STAGED, -STAGING, -STAGES** to outdo theatrically

UPSTAGER	*n* pl. **-S** one that upstages
UPSTAIR	*adj* pertaining to an upper floor
UPSTAIRS	*adv* up the stairs
UPSTAND	*v* **-STOOD, -STANDING, -STANDS** to stand up on one's feet
UPSTARE	*v* **-STARED, -STARING, -STARES** to stare upward
UPSTART	*v* **-ED, -ING, -S** to spring up suddenly
UPSTATE	*n* pl. **-S** the northern region of a state
UPSTATER	*n* pl. **-S** an inhabitant of an upstate region
UPSTEP	*v* **-STEPPED, -STEPPING, -STEPS** to step up
UPSTIR	*v* **-STIRRED, -STIRRING, -STIRS** to stir up
UPSTOOD	past tense of upstand
UPSTREAM	*adv* toward the source of a stream
UPSTROKE	*n* pl. **-S** an upward stroke
UPSURGE	*v* **-SURGED, -SURGING, -SURGES** to surge up
UPSWEEP	*v* **-SWEPT, -SWEEPING, -SWEEPS** to sweep upward
UPSWELL	*v* **-SWELLED, -SWOLLEN, -SWELLING, -SWELLS** to swell up
UPSWING	*v* **-SWUNG, -SWINGING, -SWINGS** to swing upward
UPTAKE	*n* pl. **-S** an upward ventilating shaft
UPTALK	*n* pl. **-S** a manner of ending a declarative sentence with a rising intonation
UPTEAR	*v* **-TORE, -TORN, -TEARING, -TEARS** to tear out by the roots
UPTEMPO	*n* pl. **-POS** a fast or lively tempo
UPTHROW	*v* **-THREW, -THROWN, -THROWING, -THROWS** to throw upward
UPTHRUST	*v* **-ED, -ING, -S** to thrust up
UPTICK	*n* pl. **-S** an increase or rise
UPTIGHT	*adj* nervous
UPTILT	*v* **-ED, -ING, -S** to tilt upward
UPTIME	*n* pl. **-S** the time during which machinery is functioning
UPTORE	past tense of uptear
UPTORN	past participle of uptear
UPTOSS	*v* **-ED, -ING, -ES** to toss upward
UPTOWN	*n* pl. **-S** the upper part of a city
UPTOWNER	*n* pl. **-S** one that lives uptown

UPTREND	*n* pl. **-S** a tendency upward or toward growth
UPTURN	*v* **-ED, -ING, -S** to turn up or over
UPWAFT	*v* **-ED, -ING, -S** to waft upward
UPWARD	*adv* toward a higher place or position **UPWARDLY** *adv*
UPWARDS	*adv* upward
UPWELL	*v* **-ED, -ING, -S** to well up
UPWIND	*n* pl. **-S** a wind that blows against one's course
URACIL	*n* pl. **-S** a chemical compound
URAEMIA	*n* pl. **-S** uremia **URAEMIC** *adj*
URAEUS	*n* pl. **URAEUSES** or **URAEI** the figure of the sacred serpent on the headdress of ancient Egyptian rulers
URALITE	*n* pl. **-S** a mineral **URALITIC** *adj*
URANIA	*n* pl. **-S** uranium dioxide
URANIC	*adj* pertaining to uranium
URANIDE	*n* pl. **-S** uranium
URANISM	*n* pl. **-S** homosexuality
URANITE	*n* pl. **-S** a mineral **URANITIC** *adj*
URANIUM	*n* pl. **-S** a radioactive element
URANOUS	*adj* pertaining to uranium
URANYL	*n* pl. **-S** a bivalent radical **URANYLIC** *adj*
URARE	*n* pl. **-S** curare
URARI	*n* pl. **-S** curare
URASE	*n* pl. **-S** urease
URATE	*n* pl. **-S** a chemical salt **URATIC** *adj*
URB	*n* pl. **-S** an urban area
URBAN	*adj* pertaining to a city
URBANE	*adj* **-BANER, -BANEST** refined and elegant **URBANELY** *adv*
URBANISE	*v* **-ISED, -ISING, -ISES** to urbanize
URBANISM	*n* pl. **-S** the lifestyle of city dwellers
URBANIST	*n* pl. **-S** a specialist in city planning
URBANITE	*n* pl. **-S** one who lives in a city
URBANITY	*n* pl. **-TIES** the quality of being urbane
URBANIZE	*v* **-IZED, -IZING, -IZES** to cause to take on urban characteristics
URBIA	*n* pl. **-S** cities collectively
URCHIN	*n* pl. **-S** a mischievous boy
URD	*n* pl. **-S** an annual bean grown in India

UREA   *n* pl. **-S** a chemical compound **UREAL** *adj*

UREASE   *n* pl. **-S** an enzyme

UREDIA   pl. of uredium

UREDIAL   *adj* pertaining to a uredium

UREDINIA   *n/pl* uredia

UREDIUM   *n* pl. **-DIA** a spore-producing organ of certain fungi

UREDO   *n* pl. **-DOS** a skin irritation

UREIC   *adj* pertaining to urea

UREIDE   *n* pl. **-S** a chemical compound

UREMIA   *n* pl. **-S** an abnormal condition of the blood **UREMIC** *adj*

URETER   *n* pl. **-S** the duct that conveys urine from the kidney to the bladder **URETERAL, URETERIC** *adj*

URETHAN   *n* pl. **-S** urethane

URETHANE   *n* pl. **-S** a chemical compound

URETHRA   *n* pl. **-THRAS** or **-THRAE** the duct through which urine is discharged from the bladder **URETHRAL** *adj*

URETIC   *adj* pertaining to urine

URGE   *v* **URGED, URGING, URGES** to force forward

URGENCY   *n* pl. **-CIES** the quality of being urgent

URGENT   *adj* requiring immediate attention **URGENTLY** *adv*

URGER   *n* pl. **-S** one that urges

URGING   *n* pl. **-S** an attempt to persuade someone to do something

URGINGLY   *adv* in an urging manner

URIAL   *n* pl. **-S** a wild Asian sheep

URIC   *adj* pertaining to urine

URIDINE   *n* pl. **-S** a chemical compound

URINAL   *n* pl. **-S** a fixture used for urinating

URINARY   *n* pl. **-NARIES** a urinal

URINATE   *v* **-NATED, -NATING, -NATES** to discharge urine

URINATOR   *n* pl. **-S** one that urinates

URINE   *n* pl. **-S** a liquid containing body wastes

URINEMIA   *n* pl. **-S** uremia **URINEMIC** *adj*

URINOSE   *adj* pertaining to urine

URINOUS   *adj* pertaining to urine

URN   *n* pl. **-S** a type of vase **URNLIKE** *adj*

UROBOROS   *n* pl. **-ES** a circular symbol of a snake or dragon swallowing its own tail **UROBORIC** *adj*

UROCHORD   *n* pl. **-S** a rodlike structure in certain lower vertebrates

URODELE   *n* pl. **-S** a type of amphibian

UROGRAM   *n* pl. **-S** an X-ray of part of the urinary tract

UROLITH   *n* pl. **-S** a concretion in the urinary tract

UROLOGY   *n* pl. **-GIES** the branch of medicine dealing with the urinary tract **UROLOGIC** *adj*

UROPOD   *n* pl. **-S** an abdominal limb of an arthropod **UROPODAL** *adj*

UROPYGIA   *n/pl* the humps from which birds' tail feathers grow

UROSCOPY   *n* pl. **-PIES** analysis of the urine as a means of diagnosis

UROSTYLE   *n* pl. **-S** a part of the vertebral column of frogs and toads

URP   *v* **-ED, -ING, -S** to vomit

URSA   *n* pl. **-SAE** a female bear

URSID   *n* pl. **-S** a mammal of the family Ursidae

URSIFORM   *adj* having the form of a bear

URSINE   *adj* pertaining to a bear

URTEXT   *n* pl. **-TEXTS** or **-TEXTE** the original text

URTICANT   *n* pl. **-S** an urticating substance

URTICATE   *v* **-CATED, -CATING, -CATES** to cause itching or stinging

URUS   *n* pl. **-ES** an extinct European ox

URUSHIOL   *n* pl. **-S** a toxic liquid

US   *pron* the objective case of the pronoun we

USABLE   *adj* capable of being used **USABLY** *adv*

USAGE   *n* pl. **-S** a firmly established and generally accepted practice or procedure

USANCE   *n* pl. **-S** usage

USAUNCE   *n* pl. **-S** usance

USE   *v* **USED, USING, USES** to put into service

USEABLE   *adj* usable **USEABLY** *adv*

USEFUL   *adj* serving a purpose **USEFULLY** *adv*

USELESS   *adj* serving no purpose

USER   *n* pl. **-S** one that uses

USERNAME *n* pl. **-S** an identifying sequence of characters used for logging on to a computer system

USHER *v* **-ED, -ING, -S** to conduct to a place

USING present participle of use

USNEA *n* pl. **-S** any of a genus of lichens

USQUABAE *n* pl. **-S** usquebae

USQUE *n* pl. **-S** usquebae

USQUEBAE *n* pl. **-S** whiskey

USTULATE *adj* scorched

USUAL *n* pl. **-S** something that is usual (ordinary)

USUALLY *adv* ordinarily

USUFRUCT *n* pl. **-S** the legal right to use another's property so long as it is not damaged or altered

USURER *n* pl. **-S** one that practices usury

USURIES pl. of usury

USURIOUS *adj* practicing usury

USURP *v* **-ED, -ING, -S** to seize and hold without legal authority

USURPER *n* pl. **-S** one that usurps

USURY *n* pl. **-RIES** the lending of money at an exorbitant interest rate

UT *n* pl. **-S** the musical tone C in the French solmization system now replaced by do

UTA *n* pl. **-S** any of a genus of large lizards

UTE *n* pl. **-S** a utility vehicle

UTENSIL *n* pl. **-S** a useful implement

UTERUS *n* pl. **UTERUSES** or **UTERI** an organ of female mammals **UTERINE** *adj*

UTILE *n* pl. **-S** an African hardwood tree

UTILIDOR *n* pl. **-S** an insulated system of pipes for use in arctic regions

UTILISE *v* **-LISED, -LISING, -LISES** to utilize

UTILISER *n* pl. **-S** utilizer

UTILITY *n* pl. **-TIES** the quality of being useful

UTILIZE *v* **-LIZED, -LIZING, -LIZES** to make use of

UTILIZER *n* pl. **-S** one that utilizes

UTMOST *n* pl. **-S** the greatest degree or amount

UTOPIA *n* pl. **-S** a place of ideal perfection

UTOPIAN *n* pl. **-S** one who believes in the perfectibility of human society

UTOPISM *n* pl. **-S** the body of ideals or principles of a utopian

UTOPIST *n* pl. **-S** a utopian

UTRICLE *n* pl. **-S** a saclike cavity in the inner ear

UTRICULI *n/pl* utricles

UTTER *v* **-ED, -ING, -S** to give audible expression to

UTTERER *n* pl. **-S** one that utters

UTTERLY *adv* totally

UVEA *n* pl. **-S** a layer of the eye **UVEAL** *adj*

UVEITIS *n* pl. **-ITISES** inflammation of the uvea **UVEITIC** *adj*

UVEOUS *adj* pertaining to the uvea

UVULA *n* pl. **-LAS** or **-LAE** the pendent, fleshy portion of the soft palate

UVULAR *n* pl. **-S** a uvularly produced sound

UVULARLY *adv* with the use of the uvula

UVULITIS *n* pl. **-TISES** inflammation of the uvula

UXORIAL *adj* pertaining to a wife

UXORIOUS *adj* excessively submissive or devoted to one's wife

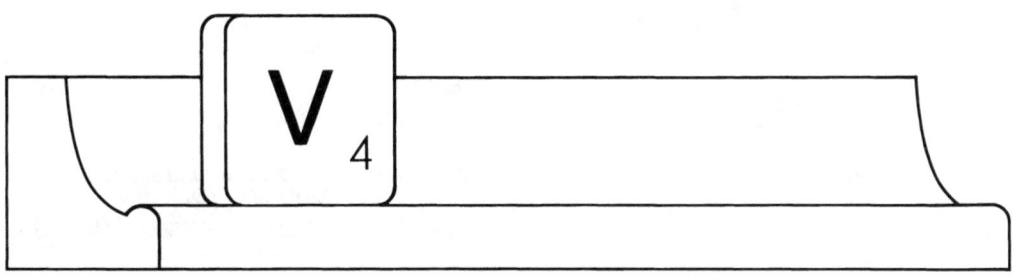

VAC *n* pl. **-S** a vacuum cleaner

VACANCY *n* pl. **-CIES** the quality or state of being vacant

VACANT *adj* empty **VACANTLY** *adv*

VACATE *v* **-CATED, -CATING, -CATES** to make vacant

VACATION *v* **-ED, -ING, -S** to take a vacation (a period of time devoted to rest and relaxation)

VACCINA *n* pl. **-S** vaccinia

VACCINE *n* pl. **-S** a preparation given to produce immunity to a specific disease **VACCINAL** *adj*

VACCINEE *n* pl. **-S** one that is vaccinated

VACCINIA *n* pl. **-S** cowpox

VACUA a pl. of vacuum

VACUITY *n* pl. **-ITIES** an empty space

VACUOLE *n* pl. **-S** a small cavity in organic tissue **VACUOLAR** *adj*

VACUOUS *adj* empty

VACUUM *n* pl. **VACUUMS** or **VACUA** a space entirely devoid of matter

VACUUM *v* **-ED, -ING, -S** to use a device that cleans by suction

VADOSE *adj* located above the permanent groundwater level

VAGABOND *v* **-ED, -ING, -S** to live like a vagabond (a vagrant)

VAGAL *adj* pertaining to the vagus nerve **VAGALLY** *adv*

VAGARY *n* pl. **-RIES** a whim

VAGI pl. of vagus

VAGILE *adj* free to move about

VAGILITY *n* pl. **-TIES** freedom of movement

VAGINA *n* pl. **-NAS** or **-NAE** the passage leading from the uterus to the vulva **VAGINAL** *adj*

VAGINATE *adj* enclosed in a sheath

VAGOTOMY *n* pl. **-MIES** surgical division of the vagus nerve

VAGRANCY *n* pl. **-CIES** the state of being a vagrant

VAGRANT *n* pl. **-S** a wanderer with no apparent means of support

VAGROM *adj* wandering

VAGUE *adj* **VAGUER, VAGUEST** not clearly expressed or understood **VAGUISH** *adj* **VAGUELY** *adv*

VAGUS *n* pl. **-GI** a cranial nerve

VAHINE *n* pl. **-S** wahine

VAIL *v* **-ED, -ING, -S** to lower

VAIN *adj* **VAINER, VAINEST** filled with undue admiration for oneself **VAINLY** *adv*

VAINNESS *n* pl. **-ES** the quality or state of being vain

VAIR *n* pl. **-S** a fur used for lining and trimming medieval garments

VAKEEL *n* pl. **-S** a native lawyer in India

VAKIL *n* pl. **-S** vakeel

VALANCE *v* **-LANCED, -LANCING, -LANCES** to furnish with a short drapery

VALE *n* pl. **-S** a valley

VALENCE *n* pl. **-S** the degree of combining power of an element or radical

VALENCIA *n* pl. **-S** a woven fabric

VALENCY *n* pl. **-CIES** valence

VALERATE *n* pl. **-S** a chemical salt

VALERIAN *n* pl. **-S** a perennial herb **VALERIC** *adj*

VALET *v* **-ED, -ING, -S** to act as a personal servant to

VALGUS *n* pl. **-ES** the position of a joint that is abnormally turned outward **VALGOID** *adj*

VALIANCE *n* pl. **-S** valor

VALIANCY *n* pl. **-CIES** valor

VALIANT   *n* pl. **-S** a courageous person

VALID   *adj* based on evidence that can be supported

VALIDATE   *v* **-DATED, -DATING, -DATES** to give legal force to

VALIDITY   *n* pl. **-TIES** the quality or state of being valid

VALIDLY   *adv* in a valid manner

VALINE   *n* pl. **-S** an amino acid

VALISE   *n* pl. **-S** a small piece of hand luggage

VALKYR   *n* pl. **-S** valkyrie

VALKYRIE   *n* pl. **-S** a maiden in Norse mythology

VALLATE   *adj* bordered by a raised edge

VALLEY   *n* pl. **-LEYS** a depression of the earth's surface **VALLEYED** *adj*

VALLUM   *n* pl. **-S** a defensive wall of earth and stone

VALONIA   *n* pl. **-S** a substance obtained from dried acorn cups and used in tanning and dyeing

VALOR   *n* pl. **-S** courage

VALORISE   *v* **-ISED, -ISING, -ISES** to valorize

VALORIZE   *v* **-IZED, -IZING, -IZES** to establish and maintain the price of by governmental action

VALOROUS   *adj* courageous

VALOUR   *n* pl. **-S** valor

VALSE   *n* pl. **-S** a concert waltz

VALUABLE   *n* pl. **-S** a possession of value

VALUABLY   *adv* with value

VALUATE   *v* **-ATED, -ATING, -ATES** to appraise

VALUATOR   *n* pl. **-S** one that valuates

VALUE   *v* **-UED, -UING, -UES** to estimate the value (the quality that renders a thing useful or desirable) of

VALUER   *n* pl. **-S** one that values

VALUTA   *n* pl. **-S** the agreed or exchange value of a currency

VALVAL   *adj* resembling or pertaining to a valve

VALVAR   *adj* valval

VALVATE   *adj* having valves or parts resembling valves

VALVE   *v* **VALVED, VALVING, VALVES** to provide with a valve (a device for controlling the flow of a liquid or gas)

VALVELET   *n* pl. **-S** a small valve

VALVULA   *n* pl. **-LAE** valvule

VALVULAR   *adj* pertaining to a valve

VALVULE   *n* pl. **-S** a small valve

VAMBRACE   *n* pl. **-S** a piece of armor for the forearm

VAMOOSE   *v* **-MOOSED, -MOOSING, -MOOSES** to leave quickly

VAMOSE   *v* **-MOSED, -MOSING, -MOSES** to vamoose

VAMP   *v* **-ED, -ING, -S** to repair or patch

VAMPER   *n* pl. **-S** one that vamps

VAMPIRE   *n* pl. **-S** a reanimated corpse believed to feed on sleeping persons' blood **VAMPIRIC** *adj*

VAMPISH   *adj* seductive

VAMPLATE   *n* pl. **-S** a circular metal plate on a spear or lance for protecting the hand

VAMPY   *adj* **VAMPIER, VAMPIEST** seductive

VAN   *v* **VANNED, VANNING, VANS** to transport in a van (a type of motor vehicle)

VANADATE   *n* pl. **-S** a chemical salt

VANADIUM   *n* pl. **-S** a metallic element **VANADIC, VANADOUS** *adj*

VANDA   *n* pl. **-S** a tropical orchid

VANDAL   *n* pl. **-S** one who willfully destroys or defaces property **VANDALIC** *adj*

VANDYKE   *n* pl. **-S** a short, pointed beard **VANDYKED** *adj*

VANE   *n* pl. **-S** a device for showing the direction of the wind **VANED** *adj*

VANG   *n* pl. **-S** a rope on a ship

VANGUARD   *n* pl. **-S** the forefront of a movement

VANILLA   *n* pl. **-S** a flavoring extract **VANILLIC** *adj*

VANILLIN   *n* pl. **-S** a chemical compound used in flavoring

VANISH   *v* **-ED, -ING, -ES** to disappear

VANISHER   *n* pl. **-S** one that vanishes

VANITAS   *n* pl. **-ES** a still-life painting having symbols of death or change

VANITORY   *n* pl. **-RIES** a combined dressing table and basin

VANITY   *n* pl. **-TIES** inflated pride in oneself **VANITIED** *adj*

VANLOAD   *n* pl. **-S** the quantity that a van can carry

VANMAN *n* pl. **-MEN** a person who drives a van

VANNED past tense of van

VANNER *n* pl. **-S** a person who owns a van

VANNING present participle of van

VANPOOL *n* pl. **-S** an arrangement whereby several commuters travel in one van

VANQUISH *v* **-ED, -ING, -ES** to defeat in battle

VANTAGE *n* pl. **-S** superiority over a competitor

VANWARD *adv* toward the front

VAPID *adj* insipid **VAPIDLY** *adv*

VAPIDITY *n* pl. **-TIES** the quality or state of being vapid

VAPOR *v* **-ED, -ING, -S** to emit vapor (visible floating moisture)

VAPORER *n* pl. **-S** one that vapors

VAPORING *n* pl. **-S** boastful talk

VAPORISE *v* **-ISED, -ISING, -ISES** to vaporize

VAPORISH *adj* resembling vapor

VAPORIZE *v* **-IZED, -IZING, -IZES** to convert into vapor

VAPOROUS *adj* vaporish

VAPORY *adj* vaporish

VAPOUR *v* **-ED, -ING, -S** to vapor

VAPOURER *n* pl. **-S** vaporer

VAPOURY *adj* vapory

VAQUERO *n* pl. **-ROS** a cowboy

VAR *n* pl. **-S** a unit of reactive power

VARA *n* pl. **-S** a Spanish unit of length

VARACTOR *n* pl. **-S** a capacitor with variable capacitance

VAREC *n* pl. **-S** seaweed

VARENYKY *n/pl* Ukrainian stuffed dumplings

VARIA *n* pl. **-S** a miscellany of literary works

VARIABLE *n* pl. **-S** something that varies

VARIABLY *adv* in a varying manner

VARIANCE *n* pl. **-S** a license to perform an act contrary to the usual rule

VARIANT *n* pl. **-S** a variable

VARIATE *v* **-ATED, -ATING, -ATES** to vary

VARICEAL *adj* pertaining to or involving a varix

VARICES pl. of varix

VARICOSE *adj* abnormally swollen or dilated

VARIED past tense of vary

VARIEDLY *adv* in a varied manner

VARIER *n* pl. **-S** one that varies

VARIES present 3d person sing. of vary

VARIETAL *n* pl. **-S** a wine designated by the variety of grape

VARIETY *n* pl. **-ETIES** something differing from others of the same general kind

VARIFORM *adj* having various forms

VARIOLA *n* pl. **-S** smallpox **VARIOLAR** *adj*

VARIOLE *n* pl. **-S** a foveola

VARIORUM *n* pl. **-S** an edition containing various versions of a text

VARIOUS *adj* of diverse kinds

VARISTOR *n* pl. **-S** a type of electrical resistor

VARIX *n* pl. **VARICES** a varicose vein

VARLET *n* pl. **-S** a knave

VARLETRY *n* pl. **-RIES** a group of common people

VARMENT *n* pl. **-S** varmint

VARMINT *n* pl. **-S** an animal considered to be a pest

VARNA *n* pl. **-S** any of the four main Hindu social classes

VARNISH *v* **-ED, -ING, -ES** to give a glossy appearance to

VARNISHY *adj* glossy

VAROOM *v* **-ED, -ING, -S** to vroom

VARROA *n* pl. **-S** a mite that is a parasite of the honeybee

VARSITY *n* pl. **-TIES** the principal team representing a university, college, or school in any activity

VARUS *n* pl. **-ES** a malformation of a bone or joint

VARVE *n* pl. **-S** a deposit of sedimentary material **VARVED** *adj*

VARY *v* **VARIED, VARYING, VARIES** to become or make different

VAS *n* pl. **VASA** an anatomical duct **VASAL** *adj*

VASCULAR *adj* pertaining to ducts that convey body fluids

VASCULUM *n* pl. **-LUMS** or **-LA** a box used to hold plant specimens

VASE *n* pl. **-S** a rounded, decorative container **VASELIKE** *adj*

VASEFUL *n* pl. **-S** as much as a vase can hold

VASIFORM *adj* having the form of a vase

VASOTOMY *n* pl. **-MIES** a surgical cutting of the vas deferens

VASSAL *n* pl. **-S** a person granted the use of land by a feudal lord in return for homage and allegiance

VAST *adj* **VASTER, VASTEST** of great extent or size

VAST *n* pl. **-S** a vast space

VASTIER comparative of vasty

VASTIEST superlative of vasty

VASTITY *n* pl. **-ITIES** vastness

VASTLY *adv* to a vast extent or degree

VASTNESS *n* pl. **-ES** the quality or state of being vast

VASTY *adj* **VASTIER, VASTIEST** vast

VAT *v* **VATTED, VATTING, VATS** to put into a vat (a large container for holding liquids)

VATFUL *n* pl. **-S** as much as a vat can hold

VATIC *adj* pertaining to a prophet

VATICAL *adj* vatic

VATICIDE *n* pl. **-S** the killing of a prophet

VATTED past tense of vat

VATTING present participle of vat

VATU *n* pl. **-S** a monetary unit of Vanuatu

VAU *n* pl. **-S** vav

VAULT *v* **-ED, -ING, -S** to provide with a vault (an arched ceiling)

VAULTER *n* pl. **-S** one that leaps

VAULTING *n* pl. **-S** the structure forming a vault

VAULTY *adj* **VAULTIER, VAULTIEST** resembling a vault

VAUNT *v* **-ED, -ING, -S** to brag

VAUNTER *n* pl. **-S** one that vaunts

VAUNTFUL *adj* boastful

VAUNTIE *adj* boastful

VAUNTY *adj* vauntie

VAV *n* pl. **-S** a Hebrew letter

VAVASOR *n* pl. **-S** a high-ranking vassal

VAVASORY *n* pl. **-RIES** the estate of a vavasor

VAVASOUR *n* pl. **-S** vavasor

VAVASSOR *n* pl. **-S** vavasor

VAW *n* pl. **-S** vav

VAWARD *n* pl. **-S** the foremost part

VAWNTIE *adj* vaunty

VEAL *v* **-ED, -ING, -S** to kill and prepare a calf for food

VEALER *n* pl. **-S** a calf raised for food

VEALY *adj* **VEALIER, VEALIEST** immature

VECTOR *v* **-ED, -ING, -S** to guide in flight by means of radioed directions

VEDALIA *n* pl. **-S** an Australian ladybug

VEDETTE *n* pl. **-S** a small boat used for scouting

VEE *n* pl. **-S** the letter V

VEEJAY *n* pl. **-JAYS** an announcer on a program of music videos

VEENA *n* pl. **-S** vina

VEEP *n* pl. **-S** a vice president

VEEPEE *n* pl. **-S** veep

VEER *v* **-ED, -ING, -S** to change direction

VEERY *n* pl. **-RIES** a songbird

VEG *v* **VEGGED, VEGGING, VEGES** or **VEGGES** to spend time idly

VEGA *n* pl. **-S** a large plain or valley

VEGAN *n* pl. **-S** one that eats only plant products

VEGANISM *n* pl. **-S** the practice of eating only plant products

VEGETAL *adj* pertaining to plants

VEGETANT *adj* characteristic of plant life

VEGETATE *v* **-TATED, -TATING, -TATES** to grow in the manner of a plant

VEGETE *adj* healthy

VEGETIST *n* pl. **-S** one that eats only plant products

VEGETIVE *adj* growing or capable of growing

VEGGIE *n* pl. **-S** a vegetable

VEGIE *n* pl. **-S** veggie

VEHEMENT *adj* ardent

VEHICLE *n* pl. **-S** a device used as a means of conveyance

VEIL *v* **-ED, -ING, -S** to provide with a veil (a piece of sheer fabric worn over the face)

VEILEDLY *adv* in a disguised manner

VEILER *n* pl. **-S** one that veils

VEILING *n* pl. **-S** a veil

VEILLESS *adj* not veiled

VEILLIKE *adj* resembling a veil

VEIN *v* **-ED, -ING, -S** to fill with veins (tubular blood vessels)

VEINAL *adj* of or pertaining to the veins

VEINER *n* pl. **-S** a tool used in wood carving

VEINIER	comparative of veiny
VEINIEST	superlative of veiny
VEINING	*n* pl. **-S** a network of veins
VEINLESS	*adj* having no veins
VEINLET	*n* pl. **-S** a small vein
VEINLIKE	*adj* resembling a vein
VEINOUS	*adj* having prominent veins
VEINULE	*n* pl. **-S** venule
VEINULET	*n* pl. **-S** venule
VEINY	*adj* **VEINIER, VEINIEST** full of veins
VELA	pl. of velum
VELAMEN	*n* pl. **-MINA** a velum
VELAR	*n* pl. **-S** a kind of speech sound
VELARIUM	*n* pl. **-IA** an awning over an ancient Roman theater
VELARIZE	*v* **-IZED, -IZING, -IZES** to pronounce with the back of the tongue touching the soft palate
VELATE	*adj* having a velum
VELD	*n* pl. **-S** veldt
VELDT	*n* pl. **-S** a grassland of southern Africa
VELIGER	*n* pl. **-S** a larval stage of certain mollusks
VELITES	*n/pl* foot soldiers of ancient Rome
VELLEITY	*n* pl. **-ITIES** a very low degree of desire
VELLUM	*n* pl. **-S** a fine parchment
VELOCE	*adv* rapidly — used as a musical direction
VELOCITY	*n* pl. **-TIES** rapidity of motion
VELOUR	*n* pl. **-S** a fabric resembling velvet
VELOUTE	*n* pl. **-S** a type of sauce
VELUM	*n* pl. **-LA** a thin membranous covering or partition
VELURE	*v* **-LURED, -LURING, -LURES** to smooth with a velvet or silk pad, as a hat
VELVERET	*n* pl. **-S** a fabric resembling velvet
VELVET	*n* pl. **-S** a soft, smooth fabric **VELVETED** *adj*
VELVETY	*adj* **-VETIER, -VETIEST** resembling velvet in texture
VENA	*n* pl. **-NAE** a vein
VENAL	*adj* open to bribery **VENALLY** *adv*
VENALITY	*n* pl. **-TIES** the quality or state of being venal
VENATIC	*adj* pertaining to hunting
VENATION	*n* pl. **-S** an arrangement of veins
VEND	*v* **-ED, -ING, -S** to sell
VENDABLE	*n* pl. **-S** vendible
VENDACE	*n* pl. **-S** a European fish
VENDEE	*n* pl. **-S** a buyer
VENDER	*n* pl. **-S** vendor
VENDETTA	*n* pl. **-S** a feud between two families
VENDEUSE	*n* pl. **-S** a saleswoman
VENDIBLE	*n* pl. **-S** a salable article
VENDIBLY	*adv* salably
VENDOR	*n* pl. **-S** a seller
VENDUE	*n* pl. **-S** a public sale
VENEER	*v* **-ED, -ING, -S** to overlay with thin layers of material
VENEERER	*n* pl. **-S** one that veneers
VENENATE	*v* **-NATED, -NATING, -NATES** to poison
VENENE	*n* pl. **-S** venin
VENENOSE	*adj* poisonous
VENERATE	*v* **-ATED, -ATING, -ATES** to revere
VENEREAL	*adj* involving the genital organs
VENERY	*n* pl. **-ERIES** sexual intercourse
VENETIAN	*n* pl. **-S** a flexible window screen
VENGE	*v* **VENGED, VENGING, VENGES** to avenge
VENGEFUL	*adj* seeking to avenge
VENIAL	*adj* easily excused or forgiven **VENIALLY** *adv*
VENIN	*n* pl. **-S** a toxin found in snake venom
VENINE	*n* pl. **-S** venin
VENIRE	*n* pl. **-S** a type of judicial writ
VENISON	*n* pl. **-S** the edible flesh of a deer
VENOGRAM	*n* pl. **-S** a roentgenogram of a vein
VENOLOGY	*n* pl. **-GIES** the study of veins
VENOM	*v* **-ED, -ING, -S** to inject with venom (a poisonous secretion of certain animals)
VENOMER	*n* pl. **-S** one that venoms
VENOMOUS	*adj* poisonous
VENOSE	*adj* venous
VENOSITY	*n* pl. **-TIES** the quality or state of being venous
VENOUS	*adj* full of veins **VENOUSLY** *adv*
VENT	*v* **-ED, -ING, -S** to provide with a vent (an opening for the escape of gas or liquid)

VENTAGE   *n* pl. **-S** a small opening

VENTAIL   *n* pl. **-S** the adjustable front of a medieval helmet

VENTER   *n* pl. **-S** the abdomen

VENTLESS   *adj* having no vent

VENTRAL   *n* pl. **-S** a fin located on the underside of a fish

VENTURE   *v* **-TURED, -TURING, -TURES** to risk

VENTURER   *n* pl. **-S** one that ventures

VENTURI   *n* pl. **-S** a device for measuring the flow of a fluid

VENUE   *n* pl. **-S** the locale of an event

VENULE   *n* pl. **-S** a small vein **VENULAR, VENULOSE, VENULOUS** *adj*

VERA   *adj* very

VERACITY   *n* pl. **-TIES** conformity to truth

VERANDA   *n* pl. **-S** a type of porch

VERANDAH   *n* pl. **-S** veranda

VERATRIA   *n* pl. **-S** veratrin

VERATRIN   *n* pl. **-S** a poisonous mixture of alkaloids

VERATRUM   *n* pl. **-S** a poisonous herb

VERB   *n* pl. **-S** a word used to express an act, occurrence, or mode of being

VERBAL   *n* pl. **-S** a word derived from a verb

VERBALLY   *adv* in a spoken manner

VERBATIM   *adv* word for word

VERBENA   *n* pl. **-S** a flowering plant

VERBIAGE   *n* pl. **-S** an excess of words

VERBID   *n* pl. **-S** a verbal

VERBIFY   *v* **-FIED, -FYING, -FIES** to use as a verb

VERBILE   *n* pl. **-S** one whose mental imagery consists of words

VERBLESS   *adj* lacking a verb

VERBOSE   *adj* wordy

VERBOTEN   *adj* forbidden

VERDANCY   *n* pl. **-CIES** the quality or state of being verdant

VERDANT   *adj* green with vegetation

VERDERER   *n* pl. **-S** an officer in charge of the royal forests of England

VERDEROR   *n* pl. **-S** verderer

VERDICT   *n* pl. **-S** the decision at the end of a legal proceeding

VERDIN   *n* pl. **-S** a small bird

VERDITER   *n* pl. **-S** a blue or green pigment

VERDURE   *n* pl. **-S** green vegetation **VERDURED** *adj*

VERECUND   *adj* shy

VERGE   *v* **VERGED, VERGING, VERGES** to come near

VERGENCE   *n* pl. **-S** a movement of one eye in relation to the other

VERGER   *n* pl. **-S** a church official

VERGLAS   *n* pl. **-ES** a thin coating of ice on rock

VERIDIC   *adj* truthful

VERIER   comparative of very

VERIEST   superlative of very

VERIFIER   *n* pl. **-S** one that verifies

VERIFY   *v* **-FIED, -FYING, -FIES** to prove to be true

VERILY   *adv* in truth

VERISM   *n* pl. **-S** realism in art or literature **VERISTIC** *adj*

VERISMO   *n* pl. **-MOS** verism

VERIST   *n* pl. **-S** one who practices verism

VERITAS   *n* pl. **-TATES** truth

VERITE   *n* pl. **-S** the technique of filming so as to convey candid realism

VERITY   *n* pl. **-TIES** truth

VERJUICE   *n* pl. **-S** the juice of sour or unripe fruit

VERJUS   *n* pl. **-ES** verjuice

VERMEIL   *n* pl. **-S** a red color

VERMES   pl. of vermis

VERMIAN   *adj* pertaining to worms

VERMIN   *n* pl. **VERMIN** small, common, harmful, or objectionable animals

VERMIS   *n* pl. **-MES** a part of the brain

VERMOULU   *adj* eaten by worms

VERMOUTH   *n* pl. **-S** a liqueur

VERMUTH   *n* pl. **-S** vermouth

VERNACLE   *n* pl. **-S** vernicle

VERNAL   *adj* pertaining to spring **VERNALLY** *adv*

VERNICLE   *n* pl. **-S** veronica

VERNIER   *n* pl. **-S** an auxiliary scale used with a main scale to obtain fine measurements

VERNIX   *n* pl. **-ES** a fatty substance covering the skin of a fetus

VERONAL   *n* pl. **-S** a sedative drug

VERONICA   *n* pl. **-S** a handkerchief bearing the image of Christ's face

VERRUCA	*n* pl. **-CAS** or **-CAE** a wart
VERSAL	*n* pl. **-S** an ornate capital letter used to begin a verse or paragraph
VERSANT	*n* pl. **-S** the slope of a mountain or mountain chain
VERSE	*v* **VERSED, VERSING, VERSES** to versify
VERSELET	*n* pl. **-S** a short group of lines that form a unit in a poem or song
VERSEMAN	*n* pl. **-MEN** one who versifies
VERSER	*n* pl. **-S** a verseman
VERSET	*n* pl. **-S** a versicle
VERSICLE	*n* pl. **-S** a short line of metrical writing
VERSIFY	*v* **-FIED, -FYING, -FIES** to change from prose into metrical form
VERSIN	*n* pl. **-S** versine
VERSINE	*n* pl. **-S** a trigonometric function of an angle
VERSING	present participle of verse
VERSION	*v* **-ED, -ING, -S** to create a new account or description from a particular point of view
VERSO	*n* pl. **-SOS** a left-hand page of a book
VERST	*n* pl. **-S** a Russian measure of distance
VERSTE	*n* pl. **-S** verst
VERSUS	*prep* against
VERT	*n* pl. **-S** the heraldic color green
VERTEBRA	*n* pl. **-BRAS** or **-BRAE** any of the bones or segments forming the spinal column
VERTEX	*n* pl. **-TEXES** or **-TICES** the highest point of something
VERTICAL	*n* pl. **-S** something that is vertical (extending up and down)
VERTICIL	*n* pl. **-S** a circular arrangement, as of flowers or leaves, about a point on an axis
VERTIGO	*n* pl. **-GOES** or **-GOS** or **-GINES** a disordered state in which the individual or his surroundings seem to whirl dizzily
VERTISOL	*n* pl. **-S** a type of clayey soil
VERTU	*n* pl. **-S** virtu
VERVAIN	*n* pl. **-S** a flowering plant
VERVE	*n* pl. **-S** vivacity
VERVET	*n* pl. **-S** an African monkey
VERY	*adj* **VERIER, VERIEST** absolute

VESICA	*n* pl. **-CAE** a bladder **VESICAL** *adj*
VESICANT	*n* pl. **-S** a chemical warfare agent that induces blistering
VESICATE	*v* **-CATED, -CATING, -CATES** to blister
VESICLE	*n* pl. **-S** a small bladder
VESICULA	*n* pl. **-LAE** a vesicle
VESPER	*n* pl. **-S** an evening service, prayer, or song
VESPERAL	*n* pl. **-S** a covering for an altar cloth
VESPIARY	*n* pl. **-ARIES** a nest of wasps
VESPID	*n* pl. **-S** a wasp
VESPINE	*adj* pertaining to wasps
VESSEL	*n* pl. **-S** a craft for traveling on water **VESSELED** *adj*
VEST	*v* **-ED, -ING, -S** to place in the control of
VESTA	*n* pl. **-S** a short friction match
VESTAL	*n* pl. **-S** a chaste woman
VESTALLY	*adv* chastely
VESTEE	*n* pl. **-S** a garment worn under a woman's jacket or blouse
VESTIARY	*n* pl. **-ARIES** a dressing room
VESTIGE	*n* pl. **-S** a visible sign of something that is no longer in existence
VESTIGIA	*n/pl* vestiges
VESTING	*n* pl. **-S** the right of an employee to share in and withdraw from a pension fund without penalty
VESTLESS	*adj* being without a vest
VESTLIKE	*adj* resembling a vest (a short, sleeveless garment)
VESTMENT	*n* pl. **-S** one of the ceremonial garments of the clergy
VESTRY	*n* pl. **-TRIES** a room in which vestments are kept **VESTRAL** *adj*
VESTURAL	*adj* pertaining to clothing
VESTURE	*v* **-TURED, -TURING, -TURES** to clothe
VESUVIAN	*n* pl. **-S** a mineral
VET	*v* **VETTED, VETTING, VETS** to treat animals medically
VETCH	*n* pl. **-ES** a climbing plant
VETERAN	*n* pl. **-S** a former member of the armed forces
VETIVER	*n* pl. **-S** an Asian grass
VETIVERT	*n* pl. **-S** the essential oil of the vetiver
VETO	*v* **-ED, -ING, -ES** to forbid or prevent authoritatively

VETOER *n* pl. **-S** one that vetoes

VETTED past tense of vet

VETTER *n* pl. **-S** one that evaluates something for approval

VETTING present participle of vet

VEX *v* **VEXED** or **VEXT, VEXING, VEXES** to annoy

VEXATION *n* pl. **-S** a cause of trouble

VEXEDLY *adv* in a vexed manner

VEXER *n* pl. **-S** one that vexes

VEXIL *n* pl. **-S** vexillum

VEXILLUM *n* pl. **-LA** the web or vane of a feather **VEXILLAR** *adj*

VEXINGLY *adv* in a vexing manner

VEXT a past tense of vex

VIA *prep* by way of

VIABLE *adj* capable of living **VIABLY** *adv*

VIADUCT *n* pl. **-S** a type of bridge

VIAL *v* **VIALED, VIALING, VIALS** or **VIALLED, VIALLING, VIALS** to put in a vial (a small container for liquids)

VIAND *n* pl. **-S** an article of food

VIATIC *adj* pertaining to traveling

VIATICAL *n* pl. **-S** a type of life insurance arrangement

VIATICUM *n* pl. **-CUMS** or **-CA** an allowance for traveling expenses

VIATOR *n* pl. **-ES** or **-S** a traveler

VIBE *n* pl. **-S** a vibration

VIBIST *n* pl. **-S** one who plays the vibraphone

VIBRANCE *n* pl. **-S** vibrancy

VIBRANCY *n* pl. **-CIES** the quality or state of being vibrant

VIBRANT *n* pl. **-S** a sonant

VIBRATE *v* **-BRATED, -BRATING, -BRATES** to move back and forth rapidly

VIBRATO *n* pl. **-TOS** a tremulous or pulsating musical effect

VIBRATOR *n* pl. **-S** something that vibrates

VIBRIO *n* pl. **-RIOS** any of a genus of bacteria shaped like a comma **VIBRIOID** *adj*

VIBRION *n* pl. **-S** vibrio

VIBRISSA *n* pl. **-SAE** one of the stiff hairs growing about the mouth of certain mammals

VIBRONIC *adj* pertaining to changes in molecular energy states resulting from vibrational energy

VIBURNUM *n* pl. **-S** a flowering shrub

VICAR *n* pl. **-S** a church official

VICARAGE *n* pl. **-S** the office of a vicar

VICARATE *n* pl. **-S** vicarage

VICARIAL *adj* pertaining to a vicar

VICARLY *adj* vicarial

VICE *v* **VICED, VICING, VICES** to vise

VICELESS *adj* having no immoral habits

VICELIKE *adj* viselike

VICENARY *adj* pertaining to the number twenty

VICEROY *n* pl. **-ROYS** one who rules as the representative of a sovereign

VICHY *n* pl. **-CHIES** a type of mineral water

VICINAGE *n* pl. **-S** vicinity

VICINAL *adj* nearby

VICING present participle of vice

VICINITY *n* pl. **-TIES** the region near or about a place

VICIOUS *adj* dangerously aggressive

VICOMTE *n* pl. **-S** a French nobleman

VICTIM *n* pl. **-S** one who suffers from a destructive or injurious action

VICTOR *n* pl. **-S** one who defeats an adversary

VICTORIA *n* pl. **-S** a light carriage

VICTORY *n* pl. **-RIES** a successful outcome in a contest or struggle

VICTRESS *n* pl. **-ES** a female victor

VICTUAL *v* **-UALED, -UALING, -UALS** or **-UALLED, -UALLING, -UALS** to provide with food

VICUGNA *n* pl. **-S** vicuna

VICUNA *n* pl. **-S** a ruminant mammal

VID *n* pl. **-S** a video

VIDALIA *n* pl. **-S** a sweet onion of the southern U.S.

VIDE *v* see — used to direct a reader to another item; VIDE is the only form of this verb; it cannot be conjugated

VIDEO *v* **-ED, -ING, -S** to record visual images on magnetic tape or disc

VIDEOCAM *n* pl. **-S** a camera for recording images and usually sound

VIDEOTEX *n* pl. **-ES** an electronic system for transmitting data to a subscriber's video screen

VIDETTE *n* pl. **-S** vedette

VIDICON *n* pl. **-S** a type of television camera tube

VIDIOT *n* pl. **-S** a habitual, undiscriminating viewer of television

VIDUITY *n* pl. **-ITIES** the quality or state of being a widow

VIE *v* **VIED, VYING, VIES** to strive for superiority

VIELLE *n* pl. **-S** a musical instrument played by turning a handle

VIER *n* pl. **-S** one that vies

VIEW *v* **-ED, -ING, -S** to look at **VIEWABLE** *adj*

VIEWBOOK *n* pl. **-S** a promotional booklet with pictures that is published by a college or university

VIEWDATA *n* pl. **VIEWDATA** a videotex

VIEWER *n* pl. **-S** one that views

VIEWIER comparative of viewy

VIEWIEST superlative of viewy

VIEWING *n* pl. **-S** an act of seeing, watching, or looking

VIEWLESS *adj* having no opinions

VIEWPORT *n* pl. **-S** a framed area on a display screen for viewing information

VIEWSHED *n* pl. **-S** the natural environment visible from a viewing point

VIEWY *adj* **VIEWIER, VIEWIEST** showy

VIFF *v* **-ED, -ING, -S** to change direction abruptly of a vertical take-off aircraft

VIG *n* pl. **-S** a vigorish

VIGA *n* pl. **-S** a ceiling beam in Spanish architecture

VIGIA *n* pl. **-S** a warning on a navigational chart

VIGIL *n* pl. **-S** a period of watchfulness maintained during normal sleeping hours

VIGILANT *adj* watchful

VIGNERON *n* pl. **-S** a winegrower

VIGNETTE *v* **-GNETTED, -GNETTING, -GNETTES** to describe briefly

VIGOR *n* pl. **-S** active strength or force

VIGORISH *n* pl. **-ES** a charge paid to a bookie on a bet

VIGOROSO *adv* with emphasis and spirit — used as a musical direction

VIGOROUS *adj* full of vigor

VIGOUR *n* pl. **-S** vigor

VIHUELA *n* pl. **-S** a type of early Spanish guitar

VIKING *n* pl. **-S** a Scandinavian pirate

VILAYET *n* pl. **-S** an administrative division of Turkey

VILE *adj* **VILER, VILEST** morally despicable or physically repulsive **VILELY** *adv*

VILENESS *n* pl. **-ES** the state of being vile

VILIFIER *n* pl. **-S** one that vilifies

VILIFY *v* **-FIED, -FYING, -FIES** to defame

VILIPEND *v* **-ED, -ING, -S** to vilify

VILL *n* pl. **-S** a village

VILLA *n* pl. **-LAS** or **-LAE** an agricultural estate of ancient Rome

VILLADOM *n* pl. **-S** the world constituted by suburban residences and their occupants

VILLAGE *n* pl. **-S** a small community in a rural area

VILLAGER *n* pl. **-S** one who lives in a village

VILLAGEY *adj* pertaining to or characteristic of a village

VILLAIN *n* pl. **-S** a cruelly malicious person

VILLAINY *n* pl. **-LAINIES** conduct characteristic of a villain

VILLATIC *adj* rural

VILLEIN *n* pl. **-S** a type of serf

VILLUS *n* pl. **-LI** one of the hairlike projections found on certain membranes **VILLOSE, VILLOUS** *adj*

VIM *n* pl. **-S** energy

VIMEN *n* pl. **-MINA** a long, flexible branch of a plant **VIMINAL** *adj*

VIN *n* pl. **-S** French wine

VINA *n* pl. **-S** a stringed instrument of India

VINAL *n* pl. **-S** a synthetic textile fiber

VINASSE *n* pl. **-S** a residue left after the distillation of liquor

VINCA *n* pl. **-S** a flowering plant

VINCIBLE *adj* capable of being conquered **VINCIBLY** *adv*

VINCULUM *n* pl. **-LUMS** or **-LA** a unifying bond **VINCULAR** *adj*

VINDALOO *n* pl. **-LOOS** a curried dish made with meat, garlic, and wine

VINE *v* **VINED, VINING, VINES** to grow like a vine (a climbing plant)

VINEAL *adj* vinous

VINEGAR *n* pl. **-S** a sour liquid used as a condiment or preservative **VINEGARY** *adj*

VINERY *n* pl. **-ERIES** a place in which grapevines are grown

VINEYARD *n* pl. **-S** an area planted with grapevines

VINIC *adj* derived from wine

VINIER comparative of viny

VINIEST superlative of viny

VINIFERA *n* pl. **-S** a European grape

VINIFY *v* **-FIED, -FYING, -FIES** to convert into wine by fermentation

VINING present participle of vine

VINO *n* pl. **-NOS** wine

VINOSITY *n* pl. **-TIES** the character of a wine

VINOUS *adj* pertaining to wine **VINOUSLY** *adv*

VINTAGE *n* pl. **-S** a season's yield of wine from a vineyard

VINTAGER *n* pl. **-S** one that harvests wine grapes

VINTNER *n* pl. **-S** a wine merchant

VINY *adj* **VINIER, VINIEST** covered with vines

VINYL *n* pl. **-S** a type of plastic **VINYLIC** *adj*

VIOL *n* pl. **-S** a stringed instrument

VIOLA *n* pl. **-S** a stringed instrument

VIOLABLE *adj* capable of being violated **VIOLABLY** *adv*

VIOLATE *v* **-LATED, -LATING, -LATES** to break or disregard the terms or requirements of

VIOLATER *n* pl. **-S** violator

VIOLATOR *n* pl. **-S** one that violates

VIOLENCE *n* pl. **-S** violent action

VIOLENT *adj* marked by intense physical force or roughness

VIOLET *n* pl. **-S** a flowering plant

VIOLIN *n* pl. **-S** a stringed instrument

VIOLIST *n* pl. **-S** one who plays the viol or viola

VIOLONE *n* pl. **-S** a stringed instrument

VIOMYCIN *n* pl. **-S** an antibiotic

VIPER *n* pl. **-S** a venomous snake **VIPERINE, VIPERISH, VIPEROUS** *adj*

VIRAEMIA *n* pl. **-S** viremia **VIRAEMIC** *adj*

VIRAGO *n* pl. **-GOS** or **-GOES** a noisy, domineering woman

VIRAL *adj* pertaining to or caused by a virus **VIRALLY** *adv*

VIRELAI *n* pl. **-S** virelay

VIRELAY *n* pl. **-LAYS** a medieval French verse form

VIREMIA *n* pl. **-S** the presence of a virus in the blood **VIREMIC** *adj*

VIREO *n* pl. **-EOS** a small bird

VIRES pl. of vis

VIRGA *n* pl. **-GAS** or **-GAE** wisps of precipitation evaporating before reaching ground

VIRGATE *n* pl. **-S** an early English measure of land area

VIRGER *n* pl. **-S** verger

VIRGIN *n* pl. **-S** a person who has never had sexual intercourse

VIRGINAL *n* pl. **-S** a musical instrument

VIRGULE *n* pl. **-S** a diagonal printing mark used to separate alternatives

VIRICIDE *n* pl. **-S** a substance that destroys viruses

VIRID *adj* verdant

VIRIDIAN *n* pl. **-S** a bluish-green pigment

VIRIDITY *n* pl. **-TIES** verdancy

VIRILE *adj* having masculine vigor **VIRILELY** *adv*

VIRILISE *v* **-ISED, -ISING, -ISES** to virilize

VIRILISM *n* pl. **-S** the development of male secondary sex characteristics in a female

VIRILITY *n* pl. **-TIES** the quality or state of being virile

VIRILIZE *v* **-IZED, -IZING, -IZES** to induce male characteristics in (a female)

VIRION *n* pl. **-S** a virus particle

VIRL *n* pl. **-S** a metal ring or cap put around a shaft to prevent splitting

VIROID *n* pl. **-S** a viruslike plant pathogen

VIROLOGY *n* pl. **-GIES** the study of viruses

VIROSIS *n* pl. **-ROSES** infection with a virus

VIRTU *n* pl. **-S** a love or taste for the fine arts

VIRTUAL *adj* having the effect but not the actual form of what is specified

VIRTUE	*n* pl. **-S** moral excellence	**VISTA**	*n* pl. **-S** a distant view **VISTAED** *adj*
VIRTUOSA	*n* pl. **-SAS** or **-SE** a female virtuoso	**VISUAL**	*n* pl. **-S** something that illustrates by pictures or diagrams
VIRTUOSO	*n* pl. **-SOS** or **-SI** a highly skilled artistic performer	**VISUALLY**	*adv* with regard to sight
VIRTUOUS	*adj* characterized by virtue	**VITA**	*n* pl. **-TAE** a brief, autobiographical sketch
VIRUCIDE	*n* pl. **-S** viricide	**VITAL**	*adj* necessary to life
VIRULENT	*adj* extremely poisonous	**VITALISE**	*v* **-ISED, -ISING, -ISES** to vitalize
VIRUS	*n* pl. **-ES** any of a class of submicroscopic pathogens	**VITALISM**	*n* pl. **-S** a philosophical doctrine
VIRUSOID	*n* pl. **-S** a particle of RNA associated with some plant viruses	**VITALIST**	*n* pl. **-S** an advocate of vitalism
VIS	*n* pl. **VIRES** force or power	**VITALITY**	*n* pl. **-TIES** exuberant physical strength or mental vigor
VISA	*v* **-ED, -ING, -S** to put an official endorsement on, as a passport	**VITALIZE**	*v* **-IZED, -IZING, -IZES** to give life to
VISAGE	*n* pl. **-S** the face or facial expression of a person **VISAGED** *adj*	**VITALLY**	*adv* in a vital manner
		VITALS	*n/pl* vital organs
VISARD	*n* pl. **-S** vizard	**VITAMER**	*n* pl. **-S** a type of chemical compound
VISCACHA	*n* pl. **-S** a burrowing rodent		
VISCERA	pl. of viscus	**VITAMIN**	*n* pl. **-S** any of various organic substances essential to proper nutrition
VISCERAL	*adj* pertaining to the internal organs		
VISCID	*adj* thick and adhesive **VISCIDLY** *adv*	**VITAMINE**	*n* pl. **-S** vitamin
		VITELLIN	*n* pl. **-S** a protein found in egg yolk
VISCOID	*adj* somewhat viscid	**VITELLUS**	*n* pl. **-LUSES** or **-LI** the yolk of an egg
VISCOSE	*n* pl. **-S** a viscous solution		
VISCOUNT	*n* pl. **-S** a British nobleman	**VITESSE**	*n* pl. **-S** speed
VISCOUS	*adj* having relatively high resistance to flow	**VITIATE**	*v* **-ATED, -ATING, -ATES** to impair the value or quality of **VITIABLE** *adj*
VISCUS	*n* pl. **-CERA** an internal organ	**VITIATOR**	*n* pl. **-S** one that vitiates
VISE	*v* **VISED, VISING, VISES** to hold in a vise (a clamping device)	**VITILIGO**	*n* pl. **-GOS** a skin disease
VISE	*v* **VISEED, VISEING, VISES** to visa	**VITRAIN**	*n* pl. **-S** the material in the vitreous layers of banded bituminous coal
VISELIKE	*adj* resembling a vise	**VITREOUS**	*n* pl. **-ES** the jelly that fills the eyeball
VISIBLE	*adj* capable of being seen **VISIBLY** *adv*		
VISION	*v* **-ED, -ING, -S** to imagine	**VITRIC**	*adj* pertaining to glass
VISIONAL	*adj* imaginary	**VITRICS**	*n/pl* the art of making or decorating glass articles
VISIT	*v* **-ED, -ING, -S** to go or come to see someone or something	**VITRIFY**	*v* **-FIED, -FYING, -FIES** to convert into glass
VISITANT	*n* pl. **-S** a visitor	**VITRINE**	*n* pl. **-S** a glass showcase for art objects
VISITER	*n* pl. **-S** visitor		
VISITING	*n* pl. **-S** the act or an instance of visiting someone or something	**VITRIOL**	*v* **-OLED, -OLING, -OLS** or **-OLLED, -OLLING, -OLS** to treat with sulfuric acid
VISITOR	*n* pl. **-S** one that visits	**VITTA**	*n* pl. **-TAE** a streak or band of color **VITTATE** *adj*
VISIVE	*adj* visible		
VISOR	*v* **-ED, -ING, -S** to provide with a visor (a projecting brim)	**VITTLE**	*v* **-TLED, -TLING, -TLES** to victual
		VITULINE	*adj* pertaining to a calf

VIVA   *n* pl. **-S** a shout or cry used to express approval

VIVACE   *n* pl. **-S** a musical passage played in a brisk spirited manner

VIVACITY   *n* pl. **-TIES** the quality or state of being lively

VIVARIUM   *n* pl. **-IUMS** or **-IA** a place for raising and keeping live animals

VIVARY   *n* pl. **-RIES** vivarium

VIVAT   *n* pl. **-S** viva

VIVE   *interj* — used as an exclamation of approval

VIVERRID   *n* pl. **-S** any of a family of small carnivorous mammals

VIVERS   *n/pl* food

VIVID   *adj* **-IDER, -IDEST** strikingly bright or intense **VIVIDLY** *adv*

VIVIFIC   *adj* vivifying

VIVIFIER   *n* pl. **-S** one that vivifies

VIVIFY   *v* **-FIED, -FYING, -FIES** to give life to

VIVIPARA   *n/pl* animals that bring forth living young

VIVISECT   *v* **-ED, -ING, -S** to dissect the living body of

VIXEN   *n* pl. **-S** a shrewish woman **VIXENISH, VIXENLY** *adj*

VIZARD   *n* pl. **-S** a mask **VIZARDED** *adj*

VIZCACHA   *n* pl. **-S** viscacha

VIZIER   *n* pl. **-S** a high official in some Muslim countries

VIZIR   *n* pl. **-S** vizier **VIZIRIAL** *adj*

VIZIRATE   *n* pl. **-S** the office of a vizir

VIZOR   *v* **-ED, -ING, -S** to visor

VIZSLA   *n* pl. **-S** a Hungarian breed of dog

VLEI   *n* pl. **-S** a hollow in South Africa in which water collects

VLOG   *v* **VLOGGED, VLOGGING, VLOGS** to blog video material

VLOGGER   *n* pl. **-S** one that vlogs

VOCAB   *n* pl. **-S** a vocabulary

VOCABLE   *n* pl. **-S** a word

VOCABLY   *adv* in a manner that may be voiced aloud

VOCAL   *n* pl. **-S** a sound produced with the voice

VOCALESE   *n* pl. **-S** a form of jazz singing

VOCALIC   *n* pl. **-S** a vowel sound

VOCALISE   *v* **-ISED, -ISING, -ISES** to vocalize

VOCALISM   *n* pl. **-S** the act of vocalizing

VOCALIST   *n* pl. **-S** a singer

VOCALITY   *n* pl. **-TIES** possession or exercise of vocal powers

VOCALIZE   *v* **-IZED, -IZING, -IZES** to produce with the voice

VOCALLY   *adv* with the voice

VOCATION   *n* pl. **-S** the work in which a person is regularly employed

VOCATIVE   *n* pl. **-S** a grammatical case used in some languages

VOCES   pl. of vox

VOCODER   *n* pl. **-S** an electronic device used in transmitting speech signals

VODCAST   *v* **-CAST** or **-CASTED, -CASTING, -CASTS** to make video files available for download over the Internet

VODKA   *n* pl. **-S** a liquor

VODOU   *n* pl. **-S** vodun

VODOUN   *n* pl. **-S** vodun

VODUN   *n* pl. **-S** a primitive religion of the West Indies

VOE   *n* pl. **-S** a small bay, creek, or inlet

VOG   *n* pl. **-S** air pollution caused by volcanic emissions

VOGIE   *adj* vain

VOGUE   *v* **VOGUED, VOGUING** or **VOGUEING, VOGUES** to imitate poses of fashion models

VOGUEING   *n* pl. **-S** voguing

VOGUER   *n* pl. **-S** one that vogues

VOGUING   *n* pl. **-S** a dance consisting of a series of styled poses

VOGUISH   *adj* fashionable

VOICE   *v* **VOICED, VOICING, VOICES** to express or utter

VOICEFUL   *adj* sonorous

VOICER   *n* pl. **-S** one that voices

VOICING   *n* pl. **-S** the tonal quality of an instrument in an ensemble

VOID   *v* **-ED, -ING, -S** to make void (of no legal force or effect) **VOIDABLE** *adj*

VOIDANCE   *n* pl. **-S** the act or process of voiding

VOIDER   *n* pl. **-S** one that voids

VOIDNESS   *n* pl. **-ES** the quality or state of being void

VOILA   *interj* — used to call attention to something

VOILE   *n* pl. **-S** a sheer fabric

VOLANT   *adj* flying or capable of flying

VOLANTE   *adj* moving with light rapidity — used as a musical direction

VOLAR   *adj* pertaining to flight

VOLATILE   *n* pl. **-S** a winged creature

VOLCANIC   *n* pl. **-S** a rock produced by a volcano

VOLCANO   *n* pl. **-NOS** or **-NOES** an opening in the earth's crust through which molten rock and gases are ejected

VOLE   *v* **VOLED, VOLING, VOLES** to win all the tricks in a card game

VOLERY   *n* pl. **-ERIES** a large birdcage

VOLITANT   *adj* volant

VOLITION   *n* pl. **-S** the power of choosing or determining

VOLITIVE   *adj* pertaining to volition

VOLK   *n* pl. **-S** the Afrikaner people

VOLLEY   *v* **-ED, -ING, -S** to return a tennis ball before it touches the ground

VOLLEYER   *n* pl. **-S** one that volleys

VOLOST   *n* pl. **-S** an administrative district in Russia

VOLPLANE   *v* **-PLANED, -PLANING, -PLANES** to glide in an airplane

VOLT   *v* **-ED, -ING, -S** to make a quick movement in fencing to avoid a thrust

VOLTA   *n* pl. **-TE** a turning

VOLTAGE   *n* pl. **-S** electromotive force expressed in volts

VOLTAISM   *n* pl. **-S** electricity produced by chemical action **VOLTAIC** *adj*

VOLTE   *n* pl. **-S** a fencing movement

VOLTI   *v* turn — used to direct musicians to turn the page

VOLUBLE   *adj* talkative **VOLUBLY** *adv*

VOLUME   *v* **-UMED, -UMING, -UMES** to send or give out in large quantities

VOLUMISE   *v* **-ISED, -ISING, -ISES** to volumize

VOLUMIZE   *v* **-IZED, -IZING, -IZES** to give body to (hair)

VOLUTE   *n* pl. **-S** a spiral architectural ornament **VOLUTED** *adj*

VOLUTIN   *n* pl. **-S** a granular substance that is common in microorganisms

VOLUTION   *n* pl. **-S** a spiral

VOLVA   *n* pl. **-S** a membranous sac that encloses certain immature mushrooms **VOLVATE** *adj*

VOLVOX   *n* pl. **-ES** any of a genus of freshwater protozoa

VOLVULUS   *n* pl. **-LUSES** or **-LI** a twisting of the intestine that causes obstruction

VOMER   *n* pl. **-S** a bone of the skull **VOMERINE** *adj*

VOMICA   *n* pl. **-CAE** a cavity in the body containing pus

VOMIT   *v* **-ED, -ING, -S** to eject the contents of the stomach through the mouth

VOMITER   *n* pl. **-S** one that vomits

VOMITIVE   *n* pl. **-S** an emetic

VOMITO   *n* pl. **-TOS** the black vomit of yellow fever

VOMITORY   *n* pl. **-RIES** an emetic

VOMITOUS   *adj* pertaining to vomiting

VOMITUS   *n* pl. **-ES** vomited matter

VOMITY   *adj* resembling or smelling of vomit

VOODOO   *v* **-ED, -ING, -S** to hex

VORACITY   *n* pl. **-TIES** the quality or state of being ravenous

VORLAGE   *n* pl. **-S** a position in skiing

VORTEX   *n* pl. **-TEXES** or **-TICES** a whirling mass of fluid **VORTICAL** *adj*

VOTABLE   *adj* capable of being voted on

VOTARESS   *n* pl. **-ES** a female votary

VOTARIST   *n* pl. **-S** a votary

VOTARY   *n* pl. **-RIES** a person who is bound by religious vows

VOTE   *v* **VOTED, VOTING, VOTES** to cast a vote (a formal expression of will or opinion)

VOTEABLE   *adj* votable

VOTELESS   *adj* having no vote

VOTER   *n* pl. **-S** one that votes

VOTING   present participle of vote

VOTIVE   *n* pl. **-S** a small squat candle

VOTIVELY   *adv* in a manner expressing devotion or gratitude

VOTRESS   *n* pl. **-ES** votaress

VOUCH   *v* **-ED, -ING, -ES** to give one's personal assurance or guarantee

VOUCHEE   *n* pl. **-S** one for whom another vouches

VOUCHER   *v* **-ED, -ING, -S** to establish the authenticity of

VOUDON   *n* pl. **-S** vodun

VOUDOUN   *n* pl. **-S** vodun

VOUSSOIR   *n* pl. **-S** a wedge-shaped building stone

VOUVRAY   *n* pl. **-VRAYS** a French white wine

VOW   *v* **-ED, -ING, -S** to make a vow (a solemn promise)

VOWEL   *n* pl. **-S** a type of speech sound **VOWELED, VOWELLED** *adj*

VOWELIZE   *v* **-IZED, -IZING, -IZES** to provide with symbols used to indicate vowels

VOWER   *n* pl. **-S** one that vows

VOWLESS   *adj* having made no vow

VOX   *n* pl. **VOCES** voice

VOXEL   *n* pl. **-S** each of an array of elements of volume in graphic simulation

VOYAGE   *v* **-AGED, -AGING, -AGES** to travel

VOYAGER   *n* pl. **-S** one that voyages

VOYAGEUR   *n* pl. **-S** a person employed by a fur company to transport goods between distant stations

VOYAGING   *n* pl. **-S** the action of travelling over or across, especially by sea

VOYEUR   *n* pl. **-S** one who is sexually gratified by looking at sexual objects or acts

VROOM   *v* **-ED, -ING, -S** to run an engine at high speed

VROUW   *n* pl. **-S** a Dutch woman

VROW   *n* pl. **-S** vrouw

VUG   *n* pl. **-S** a small cavity in a rock or lode

VUGG   *n* pl. **-S** vug

VUGGY   *adj* **-GIER, -GIEST** abounding in vugs

VUGH   *n* pl. **-S** vug

VUGULAR   *adj* pertaining to vugs

VULCANIC   *adj* pertaining to a volcano

VULGAR   *adj* **-GARER, -GAREST** crude **VULGARLY** *adv*

VULGAR   *n* pl. **-S** a common person

VULGATE   *n* pl. **-S** the common speech of a people

VULGO   *adv* commonly

VULGUS   *n* pl. **-ES** an exercise in Latin formerly required of pupils in some English public schools

VULN   *v* **-ED, -ING, -S** to wound

VULPINE   *adj* pertaining to a fox

VULTURE   *n* pl. **-S** a bird of prey

VULVA   *n* pl. **-VAS** or **-VAE** the external genital organs of a female **VULVAL, VULVAR, VULVATE** *adj*

VULVITIS   *n* pl. **-TISES** inflammation of the vulva

VUM   *interj* — used to express surprise

VYING   present participle of vie

VYINGLY   *adv* in a vying manner

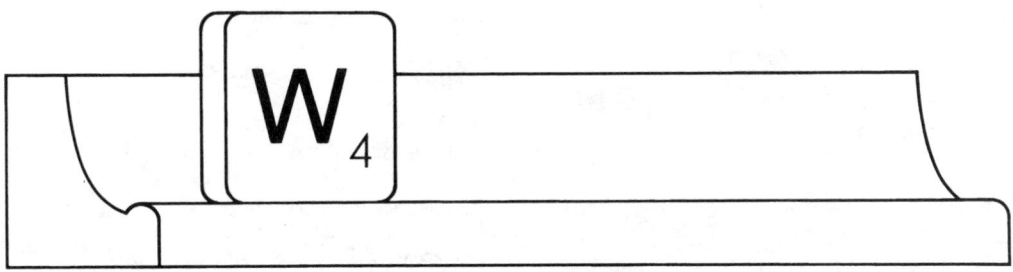

WAAH	*interj* — used to express wailing
WAB	*n* pl. **-S** a web
WABBLE	*v* **-BLED, -BLING, -BLES** to wobble
WABBLER	*n* pl. **-S** one that wabbles
WABBLY	*adj* **-BLIER, -BLIEST** wobbly
WACK	*adj* **WACKER, WACKEST** very bad
WACK	*n* pl. **-S** a wacky person
WACKE	*n* pl. **-S** a type of basaltic rock
WACKED	*adj* whacked
WACKO	*n* pl. **WACKOS** or **WACKOES** a wacky person
WACKY	*adj* **WACKIER, WACKIEST** very irrational **WACKILY** *adv*
WAD	*v* **WADDED, WADDING, WADS** to form into a wad (a small mass of soft material)
WADABLE	*adj* wadeable
WADDER	*n* pl. **-S** one that wads
WADDIE	*n* pl. **-S** a cowboy
WADDIED	past tense of waddy
WADDIES	present 3d person sing. of waddy
WADDING	*n* pl. **-S** a wad
WADDLE	*v* **-DLED, -DLING, -DLES** to walk with short, swaying steps
WADDLER	*n* pl. **-S** one that waddles
WADDLY	*adj* having or being a waddling gait
WADDY	*v* **-DIED, -DYING, -DIES** to strike with a thick club
WADE	*v* **WADED, WADING, WADES** to walk through water
WADEABLE	*adj* capable of being passed through by wading
WADER	*n* pl. **-S** one that wades
WADI	*n* pl. **-S** the bed of a usually dry watercourse
WADIES	pl. of wady
WADING	present participle of wade
WADMAAL	*n* pl. **-S** wadmal
WADMAL	*n* pl. **-S** a thick woolen fabric
WADMEL	*n* pl. **-S** wadmal
WADMOL	*n* pl. **-S** wadmal
WADMOLL	*n* pl. **-S** wadmal
WADSET	*v* **-SET, -SETTING, -SETS** to mortgage
WADY	*n* pl. **-DIES** wadi
WAE	*n* pl. **-S** woe
WAEFUL	*adj* woeful
WAENESS	*n* pl. **-ES** woeness
WAESUCK	*interj* waesucks
WAESUCKS	*interj* — used to express pity
WAFER	*v* **-ED, -ING, -S** to seal with an adhesive disk
WAFERY	*adj* resembling a wafer (a thin, crisp biscuit)
WAFF	*v* **-ED, -ING, -S** to wave
WAFFIE	*n* pl. **-S** a vagabond
WAFFLE	*v* **-FLED, -FLING, -FLES** to talk vaguely or indecisively
WAFFLER	*n* pl. **-S** one that waffles
WAFFLING	*n* pl. **-S** an indecisive statement or position
WAFFLY	*adj* **-FLIER, -FLIEST** indecisive
WAFT	*v* **-ED, -ING, -S** to carry lightly over air or water
WAFTAGE	*n* pl. **-S** the act of wafting
WAFTER	*n* pl. **-S** one that wafts
WAFTURE	*n* pl. **-S** waftage
WAG	*v* **WAGGED, WAGGING, WAGS** to move briskly up and down or to and fro
WAGE	*v* **WAGED, WAGING, WAGES** to engage in or carry on

WAGELESS *adj* unpaid

WAGER *v* **-ED, -ING, -S** to risk on an uncertain outcome

WAGERER *n* pl. **-S** one that wagers

WAGERING *n* pl. **-S** the act of risking something on an uncertain outcome

WAGGED past tense of wag

WAGGER *n* pl. **-S** one that wags

WAGGERY *n* pl. **-GERIES** waggish behavior

WAGGING present participle of wag

WAGGISH *adj* playfully humorous

WAGGLE *v* **-GLED, -GLING, -GLES** to wag

WAGGLY *adj* **-GLIER, -GLIEST** unsteady

WAGGON *v* **-ED, -ING, -S** to wagon

WAGGONER *n* pl. **-S** wagoner

WAGING present participle of wage

WAGON *v* **-ED, -ING, -S** to convey by wagon (a four-wheeled, horse-drawn vehicle)

WAGONAGE *n* pl. **-S** conveyance by wagon

WAGONER *n* pl. **-S** one who drives a wagon

WAGSOME *adj* waggish

WAGTAIL *n* pl. **-S** a songbird

WAHCONDA *n* pl. **-S** wakanda

WAHINE *n* pl. **-S** a Hawaiian woman

WAHOO *n* pl. **-HOOS** a flowering shrub

WAIF *v* **-ED, -ING, -S** to throw away

WAIFISH *adj* waiflike

WAIFLIKE *adj* resembling a waif (a homeless child)

WAIL *v* **-ED, -ING, -S** to utter a long, mournful cry

WAILER *n* pl. **-S** one that wails

WAILFUL *adj* mournful

WAILSOME *adj* wailful

WAIN *n* pl. **-S** a large, open wagon

WAINSCOT *v* **-SCOTED, -SCOTING, -SCOTS** or **-SCOTTED, -SCOTTING, -SCOTS** to line the walls of with wooden paneling

WAIR *v* **-ED, -ING, -S** to spend

WAIST *n* pl. **-S** the part of the body between the ribs and the hips **WAISTED** *adj*

WAISTER *n* pl. **-S** a seaman stationed in the middle section of a ship

WAISTING *n* pl. **-S** a type of dressmaking material

WAIT *v* **-ED, -ING, -S** to stay in expectation of

WAITER *v* **-ED, -ING, -S** to work as a male server in a restaurant

WAITING *n* pl. **-S** the act of one who waits

WAITLIST *v* **-ED, -ING, -S** to put on a list of persons waiting

WAITRESS *v* **-ED, -ING, -ES** to work as a female server in a restaurant

WAITRON *n* pl. **-S** a server in a restaurant

WAIVE *v* **WAIVED, WAIVING, WAIVES** to give up intentionally

WAIVER *n* pl. **-S** the act of waiving something

WAKAME *n* pl. **-S** a brown seaweed native to Asia

WAKANDA *n* pl. **-S** a supernatural force in Sioux beliefs

WAKE *v* **WAKED** or **WOKE, WOKEN, WAKING, WAKES** to rouse from sleep

WAKEFUL *adj* not sleeping or able to sleep

WAKELESS *adj* unbroken — used of sleep

WAKEN *v* **-ED, -ING, -S** to wake

WAKENER *n* pl. **-S** one that wakens

WAKENING *n* pl. **-S** the act of one that wakens

WAKER *n* pl. **-S** one that wakes

WAKERIFE *adj* wakeful

WAKIKI *n* pl. **-S** shell money of the South Sea Islands

WAKING *n* pl. **-S** the state of being awake

WALE *v* **WALED, WALING, WALES** to mark with welts

WALER *n* pl. **-S** an Australian-bred saddle horse

WALI *n* pl. **-S** the governor of a province in an Arab country

WALIES pl. of waly

WALK *v* **-ED, -ING, -S** to advance on foot **WALKABLE** *adj*

WALKAWAY *n* pl. **-AWAYS** an easy victory

WALKER *n* pl. **-S** one that walks

WALKIES *interj* — used to command a dog to prepare for a walk

WALKING *n* pl. **-S** the act of one that walks

WALKOUT *n* pl. **-S** a strike by workers

WALKOVER *n* pl. **-S** a walkaway

WALKUP *n* pl. **-S** an apartment house having no elevator

WALKWAY *n* pl. **-WAYS** a passage for walking

WALKYRIE	*n* pl. **-S** valkyrie
WALL	*v* **-ED, -ING, -S** to provide with a wall (an upright structure built to enclose an area)
WALLA	*n* pl. **-S** wallah
WALLABY	*n* pl. **-BIES** a small kangaroo
WALLAH	*n* pl. **-S** a person engaged in a particular occupation or activity
WALLAROO	*n* pl. **-ROOS** a large kangaroo
WALLET	*n* pl. **-S** a flat folding case
WALLEY	*n* pl. **-LEYS** a type of jump in figure skating
WALLEYE	*n* pl. **-S** an eye having a white cornea **WALLEYED** *adj*
WALLIE	*n* pl. **-S** a valet
WALLIES	pl. of wally
WALLOP	*v* **-ED, -ING, -S** to beat soundly
WALLOPER	*n* pl. **-S** one that wallops
WALLOW	*v* **-ED, -ING, -S** to roll about
WALLOWER	*n* pl. **-S** one that wallows
WALLY	*n* pl. **-LIES** waly
WALNUT	*n* pl. **-S** an edible nut
WALRUS	*n* pl. **-ES** a marine mammal
WALTZ	*v* **-ED, -ING, -ES** to perform a ballroom dance
WALTZER	*n* pl. **-S** one that waltzes
WALY	*n* pl. **WALIES** something visually pleasing
WAMBLE	*v* **-BLED, -BLING, -BLES** to move unsteadily
WAMBLY	*adj* **-BLIER, -BLIEST** unsteady
WAME	*n* pl. **-S** the belly
WAMEFOU	*n* pl. **-S** a bellyful
WAMEFUL	*n* pl. **-S** wamefou
WAMMUS	*n* pl. **-ES** wamus
WAMPISH	*v* **-ED, -ING, -ES** to throw about
WAMPUM	*n* pl. **-S** a form of currency formerly used by Native Americans
WAMPUS	*n* pl. **-ES** wamus
WAMUS	*n* pl. **-ES** a heavy outer jacket
WAN	*adj* **WANNER, WANNEST** unnaturally pale
WAN	*v* **WANNED, WANNING, WANS** to become wan
WAND	*n* pl. **-S** a slender rod
WANDER	*v* **-ED, -ING, -S** to move about with no destination or purpose
WANDERER	*n* pl. **-S** one that wanders
WANDEROO	*n* pl. **-ROOS** an Asian monkey
WANDLE	*adj* supple
WANE	*v* **WANED, WANING, WANES** to decrease in size or extent
WANEY	*adj* **WANIER, WANIEST** wany
WANGAN	*n* pl. **-S** wanigan
WANGLE	*v* **-GLED, -GLING, -GLES** to obtain or accomplish by contrivance
WANGLER	*n* pl. **-S** one that wangles
WANGUN	*n* pl. **-S** wanigan
WANIER	comparative of waney and wany
WANIEST	superlative of waney and wany
WANIGAN	*n* pl. **-S** a supply chest used in a logging camp
WANING	present participle of wane
WANION	*n* pl. **-S** vengeance
WANLY	*adv* in a wan manner
WANNABE	*n* pl. **-S** one who aspires to be like someone else
WANNABEE	*n* **-S** wannabe
WANNED	past tense of wan
WANNER	comparative of wan
WANNESS	*n* pl. **-ES** the quality of being wan
WANNEST	superlative of wan
WANNIGAN	*n* pl. **-S** wanigan
WANNING	present participle of wan
WANT	*v* **-ED, -ING, -S** to have a desire for
WANTAGE	*n* pl. **-S** something that is lacking
WANTER	*n* pl. **-S** one that wants
WANTON	*v* **-ED, -ING, -S** to behave immorally
WANTONER	*n* pl. **-S** one that wantons
WANTONLY	*adv* immorally
WANY	*adj* **WANIER, WANIEST** waning in some parts
WAP	*v* **WAPPED, WAPPING, WAPS** to wrap
WAPITI	*n* pl. **-S** a large deer
WAR	*v* **WARRED, WARRING, WARS** to engage in war (a state of open, armed conflict)
WARBIRD	*n* pl. **-S** a vintage military aircraft
WARBLE	*v* **-BLED, -BLING, -BLES** to sing with melodic embellishments
WARBLER	*n* pl. **-S** one that warbles
WARBLY	*adj* **-BLIER, -BLIEST** voiced in a trilling or quavering manner
WARCRAFT	*n* pl. **-S** the art of war

WARD   *v* **-ED, -ING, -S** to turn aside

WARDEN   *n* pl. **-S** the chief officer of a prison

WARDENRY   *n* pl. **-RIES** the office of a warden

WARDER   *n* pl. **-S** a person who guards something

WARDLESS   *adj* having no ward (part of a lock casing)

WARDRESS   *n* pl. **-ES** a female warden

WARDROBE   *n* pl. **-S** a collection of garments

WARDROBE   *v* **-ROBED, -ROBING, -ROBES** to provide with a collection of garments

WARDROOM   *n* pl. **-S** a dining area for officers on a warship

WARDSHIP   *n* pl. **-S** the state of being under a guardian

WARE   *v* **WARED, WARING, WARES** to beware of

WAREROOM   *n* pl. **-S** a room in which goods are displayed for sale

WAREZ   *n* pl. **WAREZ** illegally copied software

WARFARE   *n* pl. **-S** the act of engaging in war

WARFARIN   *n* pl. **-S** a chemical compound

WARGAME   *v* **-GAMED, -GAMING, -GAMES** to engage in simulated military conflicts

WARGAMER   *n* pl. **-S** one that wargames

WARHEAD   *n* pl. **-S** the front part of a missile containing the explosive

WARHORSE   *n* pl. **-S** a musical or dramatic work that has been performed to excess

WARIER   comparative of wary

WARIEST   superlative of wary

WARILY   *adv* in a wary manner

WARINESS   *n* pl. **-ES** the state of being wary

WARING   present participle of ware

WARISON   *n* pl. **-S** a call to attack

WARK   *v* **-ED, -ING, -S** to endure pain

WARLESS   *adj* free from war

WARLIKE   *adj* disposed to engage in war

WARLOCK   *n* pl. **-S** a sorcerer

WARLORD   *n* pl. **-S** a military leader of a warlike nation

WARM   *adj* **WARMER, WARMEST** moderately hot

WARM   *v* **-ED, -ING, -S** to make warm

WARMAKER   *n* pl. **-S** one that wars

WARMER   *n* pl. **-S** one that warms

WARMING   *n* pl. **-S** the act or an instance of making something warm

WARMISH   *adj* somewhat warm

WARMLY   *adv* in a warm manner

WARMNESS   *n* pl. **-ES** the state of being warm

WARMOUTH   *n* pl. **-S** a freshwater fish

WARMTH   *n* pl. **-S** warmness

WARMUP   *n* pl. **-S** a preparatory exercise or procedure

WARN   *v* **-ED, -ING, -S** to make aware of impending or possible danger

WARNER   *n* pl. **-S** one that warns

WARNING   *n* pl. **-S** something that warns

WARP   *v* **-ED, -ING, -S** to turn or twist out of shape

WARPAGE   *n* pl. **-S** the act of warping

WARPAINT   *n* pl. **-S** paint used to decorate the face and body before battle

WARPATH   *n* pl. **-S** the route taken by attacking Native Americans

WARPER   *n* pl. **-S** one that warps

WARPLANE   *n* pl. **-S** an airplane armed for combat

WARPOWER   *n* pl. **-S** the power to make war

WARPWISE   *adv* in a vertical direction

WARRAGAL   *n* pl. **-S** warrigal

WARRANT   *v* **-ED, -ING, -S** to give authority to

WARRANTY   *v* **-TIED, -TYING, -TIES** to provide a written guarantee for

WARRED   past tense of war

WARREN   *n* pl. **-S** a place where rabbits live and breed

WARRENER   *n* pl. **-S** the keeper of a warren

WARRIGAL   *n* pl. **-S** a dingo

WARRING   present participle of war

WARRIOR   *n* pl. **-S** one engaged or experienced in warfare

WARSAW   *n* pl. **-S** a marine fish

WARSHIP   *n* pl. **-S** a ship armed for combat

WARSLE   *v* **-SLED, -SLING, -SLES** to wrestle

WARSLER   *n* pl. **-S** a wrestler

WARSTLE   *v* **-TLED, -TLING, -TLES** to wrestle

WARSTLER   *n* pl. **-S** a wrestler

WART   *n* pl. **-S** a protuberance on the skin **WARTED** *adj*

WARTHOG   *n* pl. **-S** an African wild hog

WARTIER   comparative of warty

WARTIEST   superlative of warty

WARTIME   *n* pl. **-S** a time of war

WARTLESS   *adj* having no warts

WARTLIKE   *adj* resembling a wart

WARTY   *adj* **WARTIER, WARTIEST** covered with warts

WARWORK   *n* pl. **-S** work done during a war

WARWORN   *adj* showing the effects of war

WARY   *adj* **WARIER, WARIEST** watchful

WAS   1st and 3d person sing. past indicative of be

WASABI   *n* pl. **-S** a pungent herb

WASH   *v* **-ED, -ING, -ES** to cleanse by immersing in or applying a liquid

WASHABLE   *n* pl. **-S** something that can be washed without damage

WASHBAG   *n* pl. **-S** a small bag for carrying toiletries when traveling

WASHBOWL   *n* pl. **-S** a bowl used for washing oneself

WASHDAY   *n* pl. **-DAYS** a day set aside for washing clothes

WASHER   *n* pl. **-S** one that washes

WASHIER   comparative of washy

WASHIEST   superlative of washy

WASHING   *n* pl. **-S** articles washed or to be washed

WASHOUT   *n* pl. **-S** an erosion of earth by the action of water

WASHRAG   *n* pl. **-S** a small cloth used for washing oneself

WASHROOM   *n* pl. **-S** a lavatory

WASHTUB   *n* pl. **-S** a tub used for washing clothes

WASHUP   *n* pl. **-S** the act of washing clean

WASHY   *adj* **WASHIER, WASHIEST** overly diluted

WASP   *n* pl. **-S** a stinging insect **WASPISH, WASPLIKE** *adj*

WASPY   *adj* **WASPIER, WASPIEST** resembling a wasp **WASPILY** *adv*

WASSAIL   *v* **-ED, -ING, -S** to drink to the health of

WAST   *n* pl. **-S** west

WASTABLE   *adj* capable of being wasted

WASTAGE   *n* pl. **-S** something that is wasted

WASTE   *v* **WASTED, WASTING, WASTES** to use thoughtlessly

WASTEFUL   *adj* tending to waste

WASTELOT   *n* pl. **-S** a vacant lot

WASTER   *n* pl. **-S** one that wastes

WASTERIE   *n* pl. **-S** wastry

WASTERY   *n* pl. **-RIES** wastry

WASTEWAY   *n* pl. **-WAYS** a channel for excess water

WASTING   present participle of waste

WASTREL   *n* pl. **-S** one that wastes

WASTRIE   *n* pl. **-S** wastry

WASTRY   *n* pl. **-RIES** reckless extravagance

WAT   *adj* **WATTER, WATTEST** wet

WAT   *n* pl. **-S** a hare

WATAP   *n* pl. **-S** a thread made from the roots of various trees

WATAPE   *n* pl. **-S** watap

WATCH   *v* **-ED, -ING, -ES** to observe carefully

WATCHCRY   *n* pl. **-CRIES** a password

WATCHDOG   *v* **-DOGGED, -DOGGING, -DOGS** to act as a guardian for

WATCHER   *n* pl. **-S** one that watches

WATCHEYE   *n* pl. **-S** a walleye

WATCHFUL   *adj* closely observant or alert

WATCHMAN   *n* pl. **-MEN** a man employed to stand guard

WATCHOUT   *n* pl. **-S** the act of looking out for something

WATER   *v* **-ED, -ING, -S** to sprinkle with water (a transparent, odorless, tasteless liquid)

WATERAGE   *n* pl. **-S** the conveyance of goods by water

WATERBED   *n* pl. **-S** a bed whose mattress is a plastic bag filled with water

WATERBUS   *n* pl. **-BUSES** or **-BUSSES** a large motorboat for carrying passengers

WATERDOG   *n* pl. **-S** a large salamander

WATERER   *n* pl. **-S** one that waters

WATERHEN   *n* pl. **-S** the American coot

WATERIER   comparative of watery

WATERIEST   superlative of watery

WATERILY   *adv* in a watery manner

WATERING   *n* pl. **-S** the act of one that waters

WATERISH   *adj* watery

WATERJET   *n* pl. **-S** a stream of water forced through a small opening

WATERLOG   *v* **-LOGGED, -LOGGING, -LOGS** to soak with water

WATERLOO   *n* pl. **-LOOS** a decisive defeat

WATERMAN	*n* pl. **-MEN** a boatman
WATERSKI	*n* pl. **-S** a ski for skiing on water
WATERWAY	*n* pl. **-WAYS** a navigable body of water
WATERY	*adj* **-TERIER, -TERIEST** containing water
WATT	*n* pl. **-S** a unit of power
WATTAGE	*n* pl. **-S** an amount of power in terms of watts
WATTAPE	*n* pl. **-S** watap
WATTER	comparative of wat
WATTEST	superlative of wat
WATTHOUR	*n* pl. **-S** a unit of energy
WATTLE	*v* **-TLED, -TLING, -TLES** to weave into a network
WATTLESS	*adj* denoting a type of electric current
WAUCHT	*v* **-ED, -ING, -S** to waught
WAUGH	*adj* damp
WAUGHT	*v* **-ED, -ING, -S** to drink deeply
WAUK	*v* **-ED, -ING, -S** to wake
WAUL	*v* **-ED, -ING, -S** to cry like a cat
WAUR	*adj* worse
WAVE	*v* **WAVED, WAVING, WAVES** to move freely back and forth or up and down
WAVEBAND	*n* pl. **-S** a range of radio frequencies
WAVEFORM	*n* pl. **-S** a type of mathematical graph
WAVELESS	*adj* having no waves (moving ridges on the surface of a liquid)
WAVELET	*n* pl. **-S** a small wave
WAVELIKE	*adj* resembling a wave
WAVEOFF	*n* pl. **-S** the act of denying landing permission to an approaching aircraft
WAVER	*v* **-ED, -ING, -S** to move back and forth
WAVERER	*n* pl. **-S** one that wavers
WAVERY	*adj* wavering
WAVEY	*n* pl. **-VEYS** the snow goose
WAVICLE	*n* pl. **-S** a subatomic particle that can act like both a wave and a particle
WAVIER	comparative of wavy
WAVIES	pl. of wavy
WAVIEST	superlative of wavy
WAVILY	*adv* in a wavy manner
WAVINESS	*n* pl. **-ES** the state of being wavy
WAVING	present participle of wave
WAVY	*adj* **WAVIER, WAVIEST** having waves
WAVY	*n* pl. **-VIES** wavey
WAW	*n* pl. **-S** vav
WAWL	*v* **-ED, -ING, -S** to waul
WAX	*v* **-ED, -ING, -ES** to coat with wax (a natural, heat-sensitive substance) **WAXABLE** *adj*
WAXBERRY	*n* pl. **-RIES** a berry with a waxy coating
WAXBILL	*n* pl. **-S** a tropical bird
WAXEN	*adj* covered with wax
WAXER	*n* pl. **-S** one that waxes
WAXIER	comparative of waxy
WAXIEST	superlative of waxy
WAXILY	*adv* in a waxy manner
WAXINESS	*n* pl. **-ES** the quality of being waxy
WAXING	*n* pl. **-S** the act of one that waxes
WAXLIKE	*adj* resembling wax
WAXPLANT	*n* pl. **-S** a tropical plant
WAXWEED	*n* pl. **-S** an annual herb
WAXWING	*n* pl. **-S** a type of passerine bird
WAXWORK	*n* pl. **-S** an effigy made of wax
WAXWORM	*n* pl. **-S** a moth that infests beehives
WAXY	*adj* **WAXIER, WAXIEST** resembling wax
WAY	*n* pl. **WAYS** a method of doing something
WAYANG	*n* pl. **-S** a performance featuring puppets or human dancers
WAYBILL	*n* pl. **-S** a list of goods relative to a shipment
WAYFARER	*n* pl. **-S** a traveler
WAYGOING	*n* pl. **-S** the act of leaving
WAYLAY	*v* **-LAID, -LAYING, -LAYS** to ambush
WAYLAYER	*n* pl. **-S** one that waylays
WAYLESS	*adj* having no road or path
WAYMARK	*n* pl. **-S** an object that serves as a guide for travelers
WAYPOINT	*n* pl. **-S** a point between major points along a route
WAYSIDE	*n* pl. **-S** the side of a road
WAYWARD	*adj* willful
WAYWORN	*adj* fatigued by travel

WE	*pron* 1st person pl. pronoun in the nominative case
WEAK	*adj* **WEAKER, WEAKEST** lacking strength
WEAKEN	*v* **-ED, -ING, -S** to make weak
WEAKENER	*n* pl. **-S** one that weakens
WEAKFISH	*n* pl. **-ES** a marine fish
WEAKISH	*adj* somewhat weak
WEAKLING	*n* pl. **-S** a weak person
WEAKLY	*adj* **-LIER, -LIEST** weak and sickly
WEAKNESS	*n* pl. **-ES** the state of being weak
WEAKON	*n* pl. **-S** a subatomic particle
WEAKSIDE	*n* pl. **-S** the side of a basketball court with fewer players
WEAL	*n* pl. **-S** a welt
WEALD	*n* pl. **-S** a woodland
WEALTH	*n* pl. **-S** a great quantity of valuable material
WEALTHY	*adj* **WEALTHIER, WEALTHIEST** having wealth
WEAN	*v* **-ED, -ING, -S** to withhold mother's milk from and substitute other nourishment
WEANER	*n* pl. **-S** one that weans
WEANLING	*n* pl. **-S** a recently weaned child or animal
WEAPON	*v* **-ED, -ING, -S** to supply with a weapon (an instrument used in combat)
WEAPONRY	*n* pl. **-RIES** an aggregate of weapons
WEAR	*v* **WORE, WORN, WEARING, WEARS** to have on one's person
WEARABLE	*n* pl. **-S** a garment
WEARER	*n* pl. **-S** one that wears something
WEARIED	past tense of weary
WEARIER	comparative of weary
WEARIES	present 3d person sing. of weary
WEARIFUL	*adj* tiresome
WEARISH	*adj* tasteless
WEARY	*adj* **-RIER, -RIEST** tired **WEARILY** *adv*
WEARY	*v* **-RIED, -RYING, -RIES** to make or become weary
WEASAND	*n* pl. **-S** the throat
WEASEL	*v* **-SELED, -SELING, -SELS** or **-SELLED, -SELLING, -SELS** to act evasively
WEASELLY	*adj* resembling a weasel (a small carnivorous mammal)
WEASELY	*adj* weaselly
WEASON	*n* pl. **-S** weasand
WEATHER	*v* **-ED, -ING, -S** to expose to atmospheric conditions
WEAVE	*v* **WOVE** or **WEAVED, WOVEN, WEAVING, WEAVES** to form by interlacing threads
WEAVER	*n* pl. **-S** one that weaves
WEAVING	*n* pl. **-S** the activity of creating woven materials
WEAZAND	*n* pl. **-S** weasand
WEB	*v* **WEBBED, WEBBING, WEBS** to provide with a web (an interlaced fabric or structure)
WEBBING	*n* pl. **-S** a woven strip of fiber
WEBBY	*adj* **-BIER, -BIEST** weblike
WEBCAM	*n* pl. **-S** a camera used for transmitting live images over the World Wide Web
WEBCAST	*v* **-ED, -ING, -S** to transmit sound and images via the World Wide Web
WEBER	*n* pl. **-S** a unit of magnetic flux
WEBFED	*adj* designed to print a continuous roll of paper
WEBFOOT	*n* pl. **-FEET** a foot having the toes joined by a membrane
WEBINAR	*n* pl. **-S** a live interactive educational presentation conducted on a website
WEBISODE	*n* pl. **-S** an episode of a television show that can be viewed on a website
WEBLESS	*adj* having no webs
WEBLIKE	*adj* resembling a web
WEBLOG	*n* pl. **-S** a website that contains an online personal journal
WEBPAGE	*n* pl. **-S** a single document on the World Wide Web
WEBSITE	*n* pl. **-S** a set of interconnected webpages maintained by an individual or organization
WEBSTER	*n* pl. **-S** a weaver
WEBWORK	*n* pl. **-S** a weblike pattern or structure
WEBWORM	*n* pl. **-S** a web-spinning caterpillar
WEBZINE	*n* pl. **-S** a magazine published on the Internet
WECHT	*n* pl. **-S** weight
WED	*v* **WEDDED, WEDDING, WEDS** to marry
WEDDER	*n* pl. **-S** one that weds

WEDDING *n* pl. **-S** a marriage ceremony

WEDEL *v* **-ED, -ING, -S** to perform a wedeln

WEDELN *n* pl. **-S** a skiing technique

WEDGE *v* **WEDGED, WEDGING, WEDGES** to force apart with a wedge (a tapering piece of wood or metal)

WEDGIE *n* pl. **-S** a type of woman's shoe

WEDGY *adj* **WEDGIER, WEDGIEST** resembling a wedge

WEDLOCK *n* pl. **-S** the state of being married

WEE *adj* **WEER, WEEST** very small

WEE *v* **WEED, WEEING, WEES** to urinate

WEED *v* **-ED, -ING, -S** to remove weeds (undesirable plants)

WEEDBED *n* pl. **-S** an area of a body of water having many weeds

WEEDER *n* pl. **-S** one that weeds

WEEDIER comparative of weedy

WEEDIEST superlative of weedy

WEEDILY *adv* in a weedy manner

WEEDLESS *adj* having no weeds

WEEDLIKE *adj* resembling a weed

WEEDLINE *n* pl. **-S** the edge of a weedbed

WEEDY *adj* **WEEDIER, WEEDIEST** resembling a weed

WEEK *n* pl. **-S** a period of seven days

WEEKDAY *n* pl. **-DAYS** any day of the week except Saturday and Sunday

WEEKEND *v* **-ED, -ING, -S** to spend the weekend (the end of the week)

WEEKLONG *adj* continuing for a week

WEEKLY *n* pl. **-LIES** a publication issued once a week

WEEL *adj* well

WEEN *v* **-ED, -ING, -S** to suppose

WEENIE *n* pl. **-S** a wiener

WEENSY *adj* **-SIER, -SIEST** tiny

WEENY *adj* **-NIER, -NIEST** tiny

WEEP *v* **WEPT, WEEPING, WEEPS** to express sorrow by shedding tears

WEEPER *n* pl. **-S** one that weeps

WEEPIE *n* pl. **-S** a very maudlin movie

WEEPING *n* pl. **-S** the act of one that weeps

WEEPY *adj* **WEEPIER, WEEPIEST** tending to weep **WEEPILY** *adv*

WEER comparative of wee

WEEST superlative of wee

WEET *v* **-ED, -ING, -S** to know

WEEVER *n* pl. **-S** a marine fish

WEEVIL *n* pl. **-S** a small beetle **WEEVILED, WEEVILLY, WEEVILY** *adj*

WEEWEE *v* **-WEED, -WEEING, -WEES** to urinate

WEFT *n* pl. **-S** a woven fabric or garment

WEFTWISE *adv* in a horizontal direction

WEIGELA *n* pl. **-S** a flowering shrub

WEIGELIA *n* pl. **-S** weigela

WEIGH *v* **-ED, -ING, -S** to determine the weight of

WEIGHER *n* pl. **-S** one that weighs

WEIGHMAN *n* pl. **-MEN** one whose occupation is weighing goods

WEIGHT *v* **-ED, -ING, -S** to add weight (heaviness) to

WEIGHTER *n* pl. **-S** one that weights

WEIGHTY *adj* **WEIGHTIER, WEIGHTIEST** having great weight

WEINER *n* pl. **-S** wiener

WEIR *n* pl. **-S** a fence placed in a stream to catch fish

WEIRD *v* **-ED, -ING, -S** to cause to experience a strange sensation

WEIRD *adj* **WEIRDER, WEIRDEST** mysteriously strange

WEIRD *n* pl. **-S** destiny

WEIRDIE *n* pl. **-S** a very strange person

WEIRDIES pl. of weirdy

WEIRDLY *adv* in a weird manner

WEIRDO *n* pl. **WEIRDOES** or **WEIRDOS** a weirdie

WEIRDY *n* pl. **WEIRDIES** weirdie

WEKA *n* pl. **-S** a flightless bird

WELCH *v* **-ED, -ING, -ES** to welsh

WELCHER *n* pl. **-S** one that welshes

WELCOME *v* **-COMED, -COMING, -COMES** to greet cordially

WELCOMER *n* pl. **-S** one that welcomes

WELD *v* **-ED, -ING, -S** to join by applying heat **WELDABLE** *adj*

WELDER *n* pl. **-S** one that welds

WELDLESS *adj* having no welded joints

WELDMENT *n* pl. **-S** a unit composed of welded pieces

WELDOR *n* pl. **-S** welder

WELFARE	n pl. **-S** general well-being	**WERGILD**	n pl. **-S** wergeld
WELKIN	n pl. **-S** the sky	**WERT**	a 2d person sing. past tense of be
WELL	v **-ED, -ING, -S** to rise to the surface and flow forth	**WERWOLF**	n pl. **-WOLVES** werewolf
		WESKIT	n pl. **-S** a vest
WELLADAY	n pl. **-DAYS** wellaway	**WESSAND**	n pl. **-S** weasand
WELLAWAY	n pl. **-WAYS** an expression of sorrow	**WEST**	n pl. **-S** a cardinal point of the compass
WELLBORN	adj of good birth or ancestry	**WESTER**	v **-ED, -ING, -S** to move toward the west
WELLCURB	n pl. **-S** the stone ring around a well (a hole dug in the ground to obtain water)	**WESTERLY**	n pl. **-LIES** a wind from the west
		WESTERN	n pl. **-S** one who lives in the west
WELLDOER	n pl. **-S** a doer of good deeds	**WESTING**	n pl. **-S** a shifting west
WELLHEAD	n pl. **-S** the source of a spring or stream	**WESTMOST**	adj farthest west
		WESTWARD	n pl. **-S** a direction toward the west
WELLHOLE	n pl. **-S** the shaft of a well	**WET**	adj **WETTER, WETTEST** covered or saturated with a liquid
WELLIE	n pl. **-S** a Wellington boot		
WELLIES	pl. of welly	**WET**	v **WETTED, WETTING, WETS** to make wet
WELLNESS	n pl. **-ES** the state of being healthy		
WELLSITE	n pl. **-S** a mineral	**WETA**	n pl. **-S** a large wingless insect of New Zealand
WELLY	n pl. **-LIES** wellie		
WELSH	v **-ED, -ING, -ES** to fail to pay a debt	**WETHER**	n pl. **-S** a gelded male sheep
		WETLAND	n pl. **-S** land containing much soil moisture
WELSHER	n pl. **-S** one that welshes		
WELT	v **-ED, -ING, -S** to mark with welts (ridges or lumps raised on the skin)	**WETLY**	adv in a wet manner
		WETNESS	n pl. **-ES** the state of being wet
		WETPROOF	adj waterproof
WELTER	v **-ED, -ING, -S** to roll about	**WETSUIT**	n pl. **-S** a close-fitting rubberlike suit worn in cold water by skin divers
WELTING	n pl. **-S** a cord or strip used to reinforce a seam		
		WETTABLE	adj capable of being wetted
WEN	n pl. **-S** a benign tumor of the skin	**WETTED**	past tense of wet
WENCH	v **-ED, -ING, -ES** to consort with prostitutes	**WETTER**	n pl. **-S** one that wets
		WETTEST	superlative of wet
WENCHER	n pl. **-S** one that wenches	**WETTING**	n pl. **-S** a liquid used in moistening something
WEND	v **-ED, -ING, -S** to proceed along		
WENDIGO	n pl. **-GOS** windigo	**WETTISH**	adj somewhat wet
WENNISH	adj wenny	**WETWARE**	n pl. **-S** the human brain when considered as functionally equivalent to a computer
WENNY	adj **-NIER, -NIEST** resembling a wen		
WENT	past tense of go	**WHA**	pron who
WEPT	past tense of weep	**WHACK**	v **-ED, -ING, -S** to strike sharply
WERE	a pl. and 2d person sing. past indicative, and past subjunctive of be	**WHACKED**	adj 1. intoxicated on alcohol or drugs 2. exhausted
		WHACKER	n pl. **-S** one that whacks
WEREGILD	n pl. **-S** wergeld	**WHACKING**	n pl. **-S** the act or an instance of striking something sharply
WEREWOLF	n pl. **-WOLVES** a person capable of assuming the form of a wolf		
		WHACKO	n pl. **WHACKOS** wacko
WERGELD	n pl. **-S** a price paid for the taking of a man's life in Anglo-Saxon law	**WHACKY**	adj **WHACKIER, WHACKIEST** wacky
WERGELT	n pl. **-S** wergeld		

WHALE   *v* **WHALED, WHALING, WHALES** to engage in the hunting of whales (large marine mammals)

WHALEMAN   *n* pl. **-MEN** a whaler

WHALER   *n* pl. **-S** a person engaged in whaling

WHALING   *n* pl. **-S** the industry of hunting and processing whales

WHAM   *v* **WHAMMED, WHAMMING, WHAMS** to hit with a loud impact

WHAMMO   *interj* — used to indicate a startling event

WHAMMY   *n* pl. **-MIES** a supernatural spell bringing bad luck

WHAMO   *interj* whammo

WHANG   *v* **-ED, -ING, -S** to beat with a whip

WHANGEE   *n* pl. **-S** an Asian grass

WHAP   *v* **WHAPPED, WHAPPING, WHAPS** to whop

WHAPPER   *n* pl. **-S** whopper

WHARF   *v* **-ED, -ING, -S** to moor to a wharf (a docking place for vessels)

WHARFAGE   *n* pl. **-S** the use of a wharf

WHARVE   *n* pl. **-S** a round piece of wood used in spinning thread

WHAT   *n* pl. **-S** the true nature of something

WHATEVER   *adj* being what or who it may be

WHATNESS   *n* pl. **-ES** the true nature of something

WHATNOT   *n* pl. **-S** an ornamental set of shelves

WHATSIS   *n* pl. **-SISES** whatsit

WHATSIT   *n* pl. **-S** something whose name is unknown or forgotten

WHATSO   *pron* what or who it may be

WHAUP   *n* pl. **-S** a European bird

WHEAL   *n* pl. **-S** a welt

WHEAT   *n* pl. **-S** a cereal grass

WHEATEAR   *n* pl. **-S** a small bird of northern regions

WHEATEN   *n* pl. **-S** a pale yellowish color

WHEE   *interj* — used to express delight

WHEEDLE   *v* **-DLED, -DLING, -DLES** to attempt to persuade by flattery

WHEEDLER   *n* pl. **-S** one that wheedles

WHEEL   *v* **-ED, -ING, -S** to convey on wheels (circular frames designed to turn on an axis)

WHEELER   *n* pl. **-S** one that wheels

WHEELIE   *n* pl. **-S** a maneuver made on a wheeled vehicle

WHEELING   *n* pl. **-S** the condition of a road for vehicles

WHEELMAN   *n* pl. **-MEN** a helmsman

WHEEN   *n* pl. **-S** a fairly large amount

WHEEP   *v* **-ED, -ING, -S** to wheeple

WHEEPLE   *v* **-PLED, -PLING, -PLES** to give forth a prolonged whistle

WHEEZE   *v* **WHEEZED, WHEEZING, WHEEZES** to breathe with a whistling sound

WHEEZER   *n* pl. **-S** one that wheezes

WHEEZY   *adj* **WHEEZIER, WHEEZIEST** characterized by wheezing **WHEEZILY** *adv*

WHELK   *n* pl. **-S** a pustule

WHELKY   *adj* **WHELKIER, WHELKIEST** marked with whelks

WHELM   *v* **-ED, -ING, -S** to cover with water

WHELP   *v* **-ED, -ING, -S** to give birth to

WHEN   *n* pl. **-S** the time in which something is done or occurs

WHENAS   *conj* at which time

WHENCE   *conj* from what place

WHENEVER   *conj* at whatever time

WHERE   *n* pl. **-S** the place at or in which something is located or occurs

WHEREAS   *n* pl. **-ES** an introductory statement of a formal document

WHEREAT   *conj* at which

WHEREBY   *conj* by which

WHEREIN   *conj* in which

WHEREOF   *conj* of which

WHEREON   *conj* on which

WHERETO   *conj* to which

WHEREVER   *conj* in or to whatever place

WHERRY   *v* **-RIED, -RYING, -RIES** to transport in a light rowboat

WHERVE   *n* pl. **-S** wharve

WHET   *v* **WHETTED, WHETTING, WHETS** to sharpen by friction

WHETHER   *conj* if it be the case that

WHETTER   *n* pl. **-S** one that whets

WHEW   *n* pl. **-S** a whistling sound

WHEY   *n* pl. **WHEYS** the watery part of milk **WHEYEY, WHEYISH** *adj*

WHEYFACE   *n* pl. **-S** a pale, sallow face

WHEYLIKE   *adj* resembling whey

WHICH	*pron* what particular one or ones
WHICKER	*v* **-ED, -ING, -S** to whinny
WHID	*v* **WHIDDED, WHIDDING, WHIDS** to move rapidly and quietly
WHIDAH	*n* pl. **-S** whydah
WHIFF	*v* **-ED, -ING, -S** to blow or convey with slight gusts of air
WHIFFER	*n* pl. **-S** one that whiffs
WHIFFET	*n* pl. **-S** an insignificant person
WHIFFLE	*v* **-FLED, -FLING, -FLES** to move or think erratically
WHIFFLER	*n* pl. **-S** one that whiffles
WHIFFY	*adj* **WHIFFIER, WHIFFIEST** having an unpleasant smell
WHIG	*n* pl. **-S** one who interprets history as a continuing victory of progress over reactionary forces
WHILE	*v* **WHILED, WHILING, WHILES** to cause to pass pleasantly
WHILOM	*adv* formerly
WHILST	*conj* during the time that
WHIM	*n* pl. **-S** an impulsive idea
WHIMBREL	*n* pl. **-S** a shore bird
WHIMPER	*v* **-ED, -ING, -S** to cry with plaintive, broken sounds
WHIMSEY	*n* pl. **-SEYS** whimsy
WHIMSY	*n* pl. **-SIES** a whim **WHIMSIED** *adj*
WHIN	*n* pl. **-S** furze
WHINCHAT	*n* pl. **-S** a songbird
WHINE	*v* **WHINED, WHINING, WHINES** to utter a plaintive, high-pitched sound
WHINER	*n* pl. **-S** one that whines
WHINEY	*adj* **WHINIER, WHINIEST** whiny
WHINGE	*v* **WHINGED, WHINGEING** or **WHINGING, WHINGES** to whine
WHINGER	*n* pl. **-S** one that whinges
WHINGY	*adj* **WHINGIER, WHINGIEST** tending to whinge
WHINIER	comparative of whiney and whiny
WHINIEST	superlative of whiney and whiny
WHINING	present participle of whine
WHINNY	*adj* **-NIER, -NIEST** abounding in whin
WHINNY	*v* **-NIED, -NYING, -NIES** to neigh in a low or gentle manner
WHINY	*adj* **WHINIER, WHINIEST** tending to whine

WHIP	*v* **WHIPPED** or **WHIPT, WHIPPING, WHIPS** to strike with a whip (an instrument for administering corporal punishment)
WHIPCORD	*n* pl. **-S** a strong, twisted cord
WHIPLASH	*v* **-ED, -ING, -ES** to move like the action of a whip
WHIPLESS	*adj* lacking a whip
WHIPLIKE	*adj* resembling a whip
WHIPPED	a past tense of whip
WHIPPER	*n* pl. **-S** one that whips
WHIPPET	*n* pl. **-S** a small, swift dog
WHIPPING	*n* pl. **-S** material used to whip
WHIPPIT	*n* pl. **-S** a small container of nitrous oxide
WHIPPY	*adj* **-PIER, -PIEST** pertaining to or resembling a whip
WHIPRAY	*n* pl. **-RAYS** a stingray
WHIPSAW	*v* **-SAWED, -SAWN, -SAWING, -SAWS** to cut with a narrow, tapering saw
WHIPT	a past tense of whip
WHIPTAIL	*n* pl. **-S** a lizard having a long, slender tail
WHIPWORM	*n* pl. **-S** a parasitic worm
WHIR	*v* **WHIRRED, WHIRRING, WHIRS** to move with a buzzing sound
WHIRL	*v* **-ED, -ING, -S** to revolve rapidly
WHIRLER	*n* pl. **-S** one that whirls
WHIRLY	*adj* **WHIRLIER, WHIRLIEST** marked by a whirling motion
WHIRLY	*n* pl. **WHIRLIES** a small tornado
WHIRR	*v* **-ED, -ING, -S** to whir
WHIRRED	past tense of whir
WHIRRING	present participle of whir
WHIRRY	*v* **-RIED, -RYING, -RIES** to hurry
WHISH	*v* **-ED, -ING, -ES** to move with a hissing sound
WHISHT	*v* **-ED, -ING, -S** to hush
WHISK	*v* **-ED, -ING, -S** to move briskly
WHISKER	*n* pl. **-S** a hair on a man's face **WHISKERY** *adj*
WHISKEY	*n* pl. **-KEYS** a liquor
WHISKY	*n* pl. **-KIES** whiskey
WHISPER	*v* **-ED, -ING, -S** to speak softly
WHISPERY	*adj* resembling a whisper
WHIST	*v* **-ED, -ING, -S** to hush

WHISTLE	*v* **-TLED, -TLING, -TLES** to make a shrill, clear musical sound
WHISTLER	*n* pl. **-S** one that whistles
WHIT	*n* pl. **-S** a particle
WHITE	*adj* **WHITER, WHITEST** of the color of pure snow
WHITE	*v* **WHITED, WHITING, WHITES** to whiten
WHITECAP	*n* pl. **-S** a wave with a crest of foam
WHITEFLY	*n* pl. **-FLIES** a small whitish insect
WHITELY	*adv* in a white manner
WHITEN	*v* **-ED, -ING, -S** to make white
WHITENER	*n* pl. **-S** one that whitens
WHITEOUT	*n* pl. **-S** an arctic weather condition
WHITER	comparative of white
WHITEST	superlative of white
WHITEY	*adj* whity
WHITHER	*adv* to what place
WHITIER	comparative of whity
WHITIEST	superlative of whity
WHITING	*n* pl. **-S** a marine food fish
WHITISH	*adj* somewhat white
WHITLOW	*n* pl. **-S** an inflammation of the finger or toe
WHITRACK	*n* pl. **-S** a weasel
WHITTER	*n* pl. **-S** a large draft of liquor
WHITTLE	*v* **-TLED, -TLING, -TLES** to cut or shave bits from
WHITTLER	*n* pl. **-S** one that whittles
WHITTRET	*n* pl. **-S** a weasel
WHITY	*adj* **WHITIER, WHITIEST** whitish
WHIZ	*v* **WHIZZED, WHIZZING, WHIZZES** to move with a buzzing or hissing sound
WHIZBANG	*n* pl. **-S** a type of explosive shell
WHIZZ	*v* **-ED, -ING, -ES** to whiz
WHIZZER	*n* pl. **-S** one that whizzes
WHIZZES	present 3d person sing. of whiz
WHIZZING	present participle of whiz
WHIZZY	*adj* **-ZIER, -ZIEST** marvelous in construction or operation
WHO	*pron* what or which person or persons
WHOA	*interj* — used to command an animal to stop
WHODUNIT	*n* pl. **-S** a mystery story
WHOEVER	*pron* whatever person
WHOLE	*n* pl. **-S** all the parts or elements entering into and making up a thing
WHOLISM	*n* pl. **-S** holism
WHOLLY	*adv* totally
WHOM	*pron* the objective case of who
WHOMEVER	*pron* the objective case of whoever
WHOMP	*v* **-ED, -ING, -S** to defeat decisively
WHOMSO	*pron* the objective case of whoso
WHOOF	*v* **-ED, -ING, -S** to make a deep snorting sound
WHOOMP	*n* pl. **-S** a sudden loud sound
WHOOMPH	*n* pl. **-S** whoomp
WHOOP	*v* **-ED, -ING, -S** to utter loud cries
WHOOPEE	*n* pl. **-S** boisterous fun
WHOOPER	*n* pl. **-S** one that whoops
WHOOPIE	*n* pl. **-S** whoopee
WHOOPLA	*n* pl. **-S** a noisy commotion
WHOOSH	*v* **-ED, -ING, -ES** to move with a hissing sound
WHOOSIS	*n* pl. **-SISES** an object or person whose name is not known
WHOP	*v* **WHOPPED, WHOPPING, WHOPS** to strike forcibly
WHOPPER	*n* pl. **-S** something unusually large
WHORE	*v* **WHORED, WHORING, WHORES** to consort with prostitutes
WHOREDOM	*n* pl. **-S** prostitution
WHORESON	*n* pl. **-S** a bastard
WHORING	*n* pl. **-S** the use of the services of a prostitute
WHORISH	*adj* lewd
WHORL	*v* **-ED, -ING, -S** to move in a twisted or convoluted fashion
WHORT	*n* pl. **-S** an edible berry
WHORTLE	*n* pl. **-S** whort
WHOSE	*pron* the possessive case of who
WHOSESO	*pron* possessive of whoso
WHOSEVER	*pron* the possessive case of whoever
WHOSIS	*n* pl. **-SISES** whoosis
WHOSIT	*n* pl. **-S** whoosis
WHOSO	*pron* whoever
WHUMP	*v* **-ED, -ING, -S** to thump
WHUP	*v* **WHUPPED, WHUPPING, WHUPS** to defeat decisively
WHY	*n* pl. **WHYS** the reason or cause of something
WHYDA	*n* pl. **-S** whydah

WHYDAH	*n* pl. **-S** an African bird	**WIELDER**	*n* pl. **-S** one that wields
WICCA	*n* pl. **-S** a form of nature-oriented witchcraft	**WIELDY**	*adj* **WIELDIER, WIELDIEST** easily wielded
WICCAN	*n* pl. **-S** one who practices wicca	**WIENER**	*n* pl. **-S** a frankfurter
WICH	*n* pl. **-ES** wych	**WIENIE**	*n* pl. **-S** a wiener
WICK	*n* pl. **-S** a bundle of loosely twisted fibers in a candle or oil lamp	**WIFE**	*n* pl. **WIVES** a woman married to a man
WICKAPE	*n* pl. **-S** wicopy	**WIFE**	*v* **WIFED, WIFING, WIFES** to wive
WICKED	*adj* **-EDER, -EDEST** evil **WICKEDLY** *adv*	**WIFEDOM**	*n* pl. **-S** the status or function of a wife
WICKER	*n* pl. **-S** a slender, pliant twig or branch	**WIFEHOOD**	*n* pl. **-S** the state of being a wife
WICKET	*n* pl. **-S** a small door or gate	**WIFELESS**	*adj* having no wife
WICKING	*n* pl. **-S** material for wicks	**WIFELIKE**	*adj* wifely
WICKIUP	*n* pl. **-S** a Native American hut	**WIFELY**	*adj* **-LIER, -LIEST** of or befitting a wife
WICKLESS	*adj* having no wick	**WIFEY**	*n* pl. **WIFEYS** a wife
WICKYUP	*n* pl. **-S** wickiup	**WIFING**	present participle of wife
WICOPY	*n* pl. **-PIES** a flowering shrub	**WIFTY**	*adj* **-TIER, -TIEST** ditsy
WIDDER	*n* pl. **-S** a widow	**WIG**	*v* **WIGGED, WIGGING, WIGS** to provide with a wig (an artificial covering of hair for the head)
WIDDIE	*n* pl. **-S** widdy		
WIDDLE	*v* **-DLED, -DLING, -DLES** to wriggle	**WIGAN**	*n* pl. **-S** a stiff fabric
WIDDY	*n* pl. **-DIES** a hangman's noose	**WIGEON**	*n* pl. **-S** widgeon
WIDE	*adj* **WIDER, WIDEST** having great extent from side to side **WIDELY** *adv*	**WIGGED**	past tense of wig
		WIGGER	*n* pl. **-S** an unreliable or eccentric person
WIDE	*n* pl. **-S** a type of bowled ball in cricket	**WIGGERY**	*n* pl. **-GERIES** a wig
WIDEBAND	*adj* operating over a wide band of frequencies	**WIGGIER**	comparative of wiggy
		WIGGIEST	superlative of wiggy
WIDEBODY	*n* pl. **-BODIES** a jet aircraft having a wide fuselage	**WIGGING**	*n* pl. **-S** a scolding
WIDEN	*v* **-ED, -ING, -S** to make wide or wider	**WIGGLE**	*v* **-GLED, -GLING, -GLES** to move with short, quick movements from side to side
WIDENER	*n* pl. **-S** one that widens	**WIGGLER**	*n* pl. **-S** one that wiggles
WIDENESS	*n* pl. **-ES** the state of being wide	**WIGGLY**	*adj* **-GLIER, -GLIEST** tending to wiggle
WIDEOUT	*n* pl. **-S** a receiver in football		
WIDER	comparative of wide	**WIGGY**	*adj* **-GIER, -GIEST** crazy
WIDEST	superlative of wide	**WIGHT**	*n* pl. **-S** a living being
WIDGEON	*n* pl. **-S** a river duck	**WIGLESS**	*adj* having no wig
WIDGET	*n* pl. **-S** a gadget	**WIGLET**	*n* pl. **-S** a small wig
WIDISH	*adj* somewhat wide	**WIGLIKE**	*adj* resembling a wig
WIDOW	*v* **-ED, -ING, -S** to deprive of a husband	**WIGMAKER**	*n* pl. **-S** one that makes wigs
WIDOWER	*n* pl. **-S** a man whose wife has died and who has not remarried	**WIGWAG**	*v* **-WAGGED, -WAGGING, -WAGS** to move back and forth
WIDTH	*n* pl. **-S** extent from side to side	**WIGWAM**	*n* pl. **-S** a Native American dwelling
WIDTHWAY	*adv* from side to side		
WIELD	*v* **-ED, -ING, -S** to handle or use effectively	**WIKI**	*n* pl. **-S** a website that allows any user to add or edit content

WIKIUP   *n* pl. **-S** wickiup

WILCO   *interj* — used to indicate that a message received will be complied with

WILD   *v* **-ED, -ING, -S** to go about in a group attacking others

WILD   *adj* **WILDER, WILDEST** living in a natural state

WILDCARD   *n* pl. **-S** a symbol used in a database search to represent unspecified characters

WILDCAT   *v* **-CATTED, -CATTING, -CATS** to search for oil in an area of doubtful productivity

WILDER   *v* **-ED, -ING, -S** to bewilder

WILDFIRE   *n* pl. **-S** a raging, destructive fire

WILDFOWL   *n* pl. **-S** a wild game bird

WILDING   *n* pl. **-S** a wild plant or animal

WILDISH   *adj* somewhat wild

WILDLAND   *n* pl. **-S** uncultivated land

WILDLIFE   *n* pl. **WILDLIFE** wild animals and vegetation

WILDLING   *n* pl. **-S** a wilding

WILDLY   *adv* in a wild manner

WILDNESS   *n* pl. **-ES** the state of being wild

WILDWOOD   *n* pl. **-S** natural forest land

WILE   *v* **WILED, WILING, WILES** to entice

WILFUL   *adj* willful **WILFULLY** *adv*

WILIER   comparative of wily

WILIEST   superlative of wily

WILILY   *adv* in a wily manner

WILINESS   *n* pl. **-ES** the quality of being wily

WILING   present participle of wile

WILL   *v* **-ED, -ING, -S** to decide upon **WILLABLE** *adj*

WILL   *v* past sing. 2d person **WOULD** or **WOULDEST** or **WOULDST** — used as an auxiliary followed by a simple infinitive to express futurity, inclination, likelihood, or requirement

WILLER   *n* pl. **-S** one that wills

WILLET   *n* pl. **-S** a shore bird

WILLFUL   *adj* bent on having one's own way

WILLIED   past tense of willy

WILLIES   present 3d person sing. of willy

WILLING   *adj* **-INGER, -INGEST** inclined or favorably disposed in mind

WILLIWAU   *n* pl. **-S** williwaw

WILLIWAW   *n* pl. **-S** a violent gust of cold wind

WILLOW   *v* **-ED, -ING, -S** to clean textile fibers with a certain machine

WILLOWER   *n* pl. **-S** one that willows

WILLOWY   *adj* **-LOWIER, -LOWIEST** pliant

WILLY   *v* **-LIED, -LYING, -LIES** to willow

WILLYARD   *adj* willful

WILLYART   *adj* willyard

WILLYWAW   *n* pl. **-S** williwaw

WILT   *v* **-ED, -ING, -S** to become limp

WILY   *adj* **WILIER, WILIEST** crafty

WIMBLE   *v* **-BLED, -BLING, -BLES** to bore with a hand tool

WIMP   *v* **-ED, -ING, -S** to act in a timid manner

WIMPISH   *adj* wimpy

WIMPLE   *v* **-PLED, -PLING, -PLES** to pleat

WIMPY   *adj* **WIMPIER, WIMPIEST** weak, ineffectual

WIN   *v* **WINNED, WINNING, WINS** to winnow

WIN   *v* **WON** or **WAN, WINNING, WINS** to be victorious

WINCE   *v* **WINCED, WINCING, WINCES** to flinch

WINCER   *n* pl. **-S** one that winces

WINCEY   *n* pl. **-CEYS** a type of fabric

WINCH   *v* **-ED, -ING, -ES** to raise with a winch (a hoisting machine)

WINCHER   *n* pl. **-S** one that winches

WINCING   present participle of wince

WIND   *v* **WOUND** or **WINDED, WINDING, WINDS** to pass around an object or fixed center **WINDABLE** *adj*

WINDAGE   *n* pl. **-S** the effect of the wind (air in natural motion) on a projectile

WINDBAG   *n* pl. **-S** a talkative person

WINDBELL   *n* pl. **-S** a light bell that can be sounded by the wind

WINDBURN   *v* **-BURNED** or **-BURNT, -BURNING, -BURNS** to be affected with skin irritation caused by exposure to the wind

WINDER   *n* pl. **-S** one that winds

WINDFALL   *n* pl. **-S** a sudden and unexpected gain

WINDFLAW   *n* pl. **-S** a gust of wind

WINDGALL   *n* pl. **-S** a swelling on a horse's leg

WINDIER   comparative of windy

WINDIEST	superlative of windy
WINDIGO	*n* pl. **-GOS** or **-GOES** an evil demon in Algonquian mythology
WINDILY	*adv* in a windy manner
WINDING	*n* pl. **-S** material wound about an object
WINDLASS	*v* **-ED, -ING, -ES** to raise with a windlass (a hoisting machine)
WINDLE	*v* **-DLED, -DLING, -DLES** to wind
WINDLESS	*adj* being without wind
WINDLING	*n* pl. **-S** a bundle of straw
WINDLOAD	*n* pl. **-S** the force exerted by the wind on a structure
WINDMILL	*v* **-ED, -ING, -S** to rotate solely under the force of a passing airstream
WINDOW	*v* **-ED, -ING, -S** to provide with a window (an opening in a wall to admit light and air)
WINDOWY	*adj* having many windows
WINDPACK	*n* pl. **-S** snow that has been compacted by the wind
WINDPIPE	*n* pl. **-S** the trachea
WINDROW	*v* **-ED, -ING, -S** to arrange as hay or grain in long rows
WINDSAIL	*n* pl. **-S** a funnel of sailcloth used to convey air down into the lower parts of a ship
WINDSLAB	*n* pl. **-S** a crust formed on soft snow by the wind
WINDSOCK	*n* pl. **-S** a device used to indicate wind direction
WINDSURF	*v* **-ED, -ING, -S** to sail on a sailboard
WINDUP	*n* pl. **-S** a conclusion
WINDWARD	*n* pl. **-S** the direction from which the wind blows
WINDWAY	*n* pl. **-WAYS** a passage for air
WINDY	*adj* **WINDIER, WINDIEST** marked by strong wind
WINE	*v* **WINED, WINING, WINES** to provide with wine (the fermented juice of the grape)
WINELESS	*adj* having no wine
WINERY	*n* pl. **-ERIES** an establishment for making wine
WINESAP	*n* pl. **-S** a red apple with somewhat tart flesh
WINESHOP	*n* pl. **-S** a shop where wine is sold
WINESKIN	*n* pl. **-S** a goatskin bag for holding wine
WINESOP	*n* pl. **-S** a food sopped in wine
WINEY	*adj* **WINIER, WINIEST** winy
WING	*v* **-ED, -ING, -S** to travel by means of wings (organs of flight)
WINGBACK	*n* pl. **-S** a certain player in football
WINGBEAT	*n* pl. **-S** one full set of motions of a wing in flying
WINGBOW	*n* pl. **-S** a mark on the wing of a domestic fowl
WINGDING	*n* pl. **-S** a lively party
WINGEDLY	*adv* swiftly
WINGER	*n* pl. **-S** a certain player in soccer
WINGIER	comparative of wingy
WINGIEST	superlative of wingy
WINGLESS	*adj* having no wings
WINGLET	*n* pl. **-S** a small wing
WINGLIKE	*adj* resembling a wing
WINGMAN	*n* pl. **-MEN** a pilot behind the leader of a flying formation
WINGNUT	*n* pl. **-S** a nut with projections for gripping with the thumb and finger
WINGOVER	*n* pl. **-S** a flight maneuver
WINGSPAN	*n* pl. **-S** the distance from the tip of one of a pair of wings to that of the other
WINGTIP	*n* pl. **-S** a type of man's shoe
WINGY	*adj* **WINGIER, WINGIEST** swift
WINIER	comparative of winey and winy
WINIEST	superlative of winey and winy
WINING	present participle of wine
WINISH	*adj* winy
WINK	*v* **-ED, -ING, -S** to close and open one eye quickly
WINKER	*n* pl. **-S** one that winks
WINKLE	*v* **-KLED, -KLING, -KLES** to displace, extract, or evict from a position
WINKLER	*n* pl. **-S** one that winkles
WINLESS	*adj* having no wins
WINNABLE	*adj* able to be won
WINNED	past tense of win (to winnow)
WINNER	*n* pl. **-S** one that wins
WINNING	*n* pl. **-S** money won in a game or competition
WINNOCK	*n* pl. **-S** a window
WINNOW	*v* **-ED, -ING, -S** to free grain from impurities
WINNOWER	*n* pl. **-S** one that winnows

WINO	*n* pl. **WINOS** or **WINOES** one who is habitually drunk on wine
WINSOME	*adj* **-SOMER, -SOMEST** charming
WINTER	*v* **-ED, -ING, -S** to pass the winter (the coldest season of the year)
WINTERER	*n* pl. **-S** one that winters
WINTERLY	*adj* wintry
WINTERY	*adj* **-TERIER, -TERIEST** wintry
WINTLE	*v* **-TLED, -TLING, -TLES** to stagger
WINTRY	*adj* **-TRIER, -TRIEST** characteristic of winter **WINTRILY** *adv*
WINY	*adj* **WINIER, WINIEST** having the taste or qualities of wine
WINZE	*n* pl. **-S** a steeply inclined mine shaft
WIPE	*v* **WIPED, WIPING, WIPES** to rub lightly in order to clean or dry **WIPEABLE** *adj*
WIPEOUT	*n* pl. **-S** a fall from a surfboard
WIPER	*n* pl. **-S** one that wipes
WIRE	*v* **WIRED, WIRING, WIRES** to fasten with wire (a slender rod, strand, or thread of ductile metal) **WIRABLE** *adj*
WIREDRAW	*v* **-DREW, -DRAWN, -DRAWING, -DRAWS** to draw into wire
WIREHAIR	*n* pl. **-S** a dog having a wiry coat
WIRELESS	*v* **-ED, -ING, -ES** to radio
WIRELIKE	*adj* resembling wire
WIRELINE	*n* pl. **-S** a telegraph or telephone wire
WIREMAN	*n* pl. **-MEN** one who makes or works with wire
WIRER	*n* pl. **-S** one that wires
WIRETAP	*v* **-TAPPED, -TAPPING, -TAPS** to intercept messages by means of a concealed monitoring device
WIREWAY	*n* pl. **-WAYS** a tube for protecting electric wires
WIREWORK	*n* pl. **-S** an article made of wire
WIREWORM	*n* pl. **-S** a wirelike worm
WIRIER	comparative of wiry
WIRIEST	superlative of wiry
WIRILY	*adv* in a wiry manner
WIRINESS	*n* pl. **-ES** the quality of being wiry
WIRING	*n* pl. **-S** a system of electric wires
WIRRA	*interj* — used to express sorrow

WIRY	*adj* **WIRIER, WIRIEST** resembling wire
WIS	*v* past tense **WIST** to know — WIS and WIST are the only accepted forms of this verb; it cannot be conjugated further
WISDOM	*n* pl. **-S** the power of true and right discernment
WISE	*adj* **WISER, WISEST** having wisdom
WISE	*v* **WISED, WISING, WISES** to become aware or informed
WISEACRE	*n* pl. **-S** a pretentiously wise person
WISEASS	*n* pl. **-ES** a wiseacre
WISED	past tense of wise
WISEGUY	*n* pl. **-GUYS** a mobster
WISELY	*adv* **-LIER, -LIEST** in a wise manner
WISENESS	*n* pl. **-ES** wisdom
WISENT	*n* pl. **-S** a European bison
WISER	comparative of wise
WISEST	superlative of wise
WISH	*v* **-ED, -ING, -ES** to feel an impulse toward attainment or possession of something
WISHA	*interj* — used to express surprise
WISHBONE	*n* pl. **-S** a forked bone in front of a bird's breastbone
WISHER	*n* pl. **-S** one that wishes
WISHFUL	*adj* desirous
WISHLESS	*adj* not wishful
WISING	present participle of wise
WISP	*v* **-ED, -ING, -S** to twist into a wisp (a small bunch or bundle)
WISPIER	comparative of wispy
WISPIEST	superlative of wispy
WISPILY	*adv* in a wispy manner
WISPISH	*adj* wispy
WISPLIKE	*adj* wispy
WISPY	*adj* **WISPIER, WISPIEST** resembling a wisp
WISS	*v* **-ED, -ING, -ES** to wish
WIST	*v* **-ED, -ING, -S** to know
WISTARIA	*n* pl. **-S** wisteria
WISTERIA	*n* pl. **-S** a flowering shrub
WISTFUL	*adj* yearning
WIT	*n* pl. **-S** intelligence

WIT	*v* **WIST, WITING** or **WITTING,** present sing. 1st person **WOT,** 2d **WOST,** 3d **WOT,** present pl. **WITE** to know
WITAN	*n* pl. **-S** an Anglo-Saxon council to the king
WITCH	*v* **-ED, -ING, -ES** to bewitch
WITCHERY	*n* pl. **-ERIES** sorcery
WITCHING	*n* pl. **-S** sorcery
WITCHY	*adj* **WITCHIER, WITCHIEST** malicious
WITE	*v* **WITED, WITING, WITES** to blame
WITH	*prep* in the company of
WITHAL	*adv* in addition
WITHDRAW	*v* **-DREW, -DRAWN, -DRAWING, -DRAWS** to move back or away
WITHE	*v* **WITHED, WITHING, WITHES** to bind with flexible twigs
WITHER	*v* **-ED, -ING, -S** to dry up and wilt
WITHERER	*n* pl. **-S** one that withers
WITHEROD	*n* pl. **-S** a North American shrub
WITHHOLD	*v* **-HELD, -HOLDING, -HOLDS** to hold back
WITHIER	comparative of withy
WITHIES	pl. of withy
WITHIEST	superlative of withy
WITHIN	*n* pl. **-S** an interior place or area
WITHING	present participle of withe
WITHOUT	*n* pl. **-S** an exterior place or area
WITHY	*adj* **WITHIER, WITHIEST** flexible and tough
WITHY	*n* pl. **WITHIES** a flexible twig
WITING	present participle of wit and wite
WITLESS	*adj* lacking intelligence
WITLING	*n* pl. **-S** one who considers himself witty
WITLOOF	*n* pl. **-S** chicory
WITNESS	*v* **-ED, -ING, -ES** to see or know by personal experience
WITNEY	*n* pl. **-NEYS** a heavy woolen fabric
WITTED	*adj* having intelligence
WITTER	*v* **-ED, -ING, -S** to speak at length on trivial matters
WITTIER	comparative of witty
WITTIEST	superlative of witty
WITTILY	*adv* in a witty manner
WITTING	*n* pl. **-S** knowledge
WITTOL	*n* pl. **-S** a man who tolerates his wife's infidelity
WITTY	*adj* **-TIER, -TIEST** humorously clever
WIVE	*v* **WIVED, WIVING, WIVES** to marry a woman
WIVER	*n* pl. **-S** wivern
WIVERN	*n* pl. **-S** a two-legged dragon
WIVES	pl. of wife
WIVING	present participle of wive
WIZ	*n* pl. **WIZZES** or **WIZES** a very clever or skillful person
WIZARD	*n* pl. **-S** a sorcerer **WIZARDLY** *adj*
WIZARDRY	*n* pl. **-RIES** sorcery
WIZEN	*v* **-ED, -ING, -S** to shrivel
WIZZEN	*n* pl. **-S** weasand
WO	*n* pl. **WOS** woe
WOAD	*n* pl. **-S** a blue dye **WOADED** *adj*
WOADWAX	*n* pl. **-ES** an ornamental shrub
WOALD	*n* pl. **-S** a yellow pigment
WOBBLE	*v* **-BLED, -BLING, -BLES** to move unsteadily
WOBBLER	*n* pl. **-S** one that wobbles
WOBBLY	*adj* **-BLIER, -BLIEST** unsteady
WOBBLY	*n* pl. **-BLIES** a member of the Industrial Workers of the World
WOBEGONE	*adj* affected with woe
WODGE	*n* pl. **-S** a chunk of something
WOE	*n* pl. **-S** tremendous grief
WOEFUL	*adj* **-FULLER, -FULLEST** full of woe **WOEFULLY** *adv*
WOENESS	*n* pl. **-ES** sadness
WOESOME	*adj* woeful
WOFUL	*adj* **-FULLER, -FULLEST** woeful **WOFULLY** *adv*
WOGGLE	*n* pl. **-S** a ring through which a Scout's neckerchief is threaded
WOK	*n* pl. **-S** a cooking utensil
WOKE	a past tense of wake
WOKEN	a past participle of wake
WOLD	*n* pl. **-S** an elevated tract of open land
WOLF	*n* pl. **WOLVES** a carnivorous mammal
WOLF	*v* **-ED, -ING, -S** to devour voraciously
WOLFER	*n* pl. **-S** one who hunts wolves
WOLFFISH	*n* pl. **-ES** a marine fish

WOLFISH *adj* wolflike

WOLFLIKE *adj* resembling a wolf

WOLFRAM *n* pl. **-S** tungsten

WOLFSKIN *n* pl. **-S** the skin of a wolf

WOLVER *n* pl. **-S** wolfer

WOLVES pl. of wolf

WOMAN *n* pl. **WOMEN** an adult human female

WOMAN *v* **-MANED, -MANING, -MANS** or **-MANNED, -MANNING, -MANS** to provide with a staff of women

WOMANISE *v* **-ISED, -ISING, -ISES** to womanize

WOMANISH *adj* characteristic of a woman

WOMANISM *n* pl. **-S** a belief in or respect for women

WOMANIST *n* pl. **-S** a supporter of womanism

WOMANIZE *v* **-IZED, -IZING, -IZES** to make effeminate

WOMANLY *adj* **-LIER, -LIEST** having the qualities of a woman

WOMB *n* pl. **-S** the uterus **WOMBED** *adj*

WOMBAT *n* pl. **-S** a nocturnal mammal

WOMBLIKE *adj* resembling a womb

WOMBY *adj* **WOMBIER, WOMBIEST** hollow

WOMEN pl. of woman

WOMERA *n* pl. **-S** a device used to propel spears

WOMMERA *n* pl. **-S** womera

WOMYN *n/pl* women

WON *v* **WONNED, WONNING, WONS** to dwell

WONDER *v* **-ED, -ING, -S** to have a feeling of curiosity or doubt

WONDERER *n* pl. **-S** one that wonders

WONDROUS *adj* marvelous

WONK *n* pl. **-S** an overly studious student **WONKISH** *adj*

WONKERY *n* pl. **-ERIES** the qualities or activities of a wonk

WONKY *adj* **-KIER, -KIEST** unsteady **WONKILY** *adv*

WONNED past tense of won

WONNER *n* pl. **-S** a prodigy

WONNING present participle of won

WONT *v* **-ED, -ING, -S** to make accustomed to

WONTEDLY *adv* in a usual manner

WONTON *n* pl. **-S** a pork-filled dumpling used in Chinese cooking

WOO *v* **-ED, -ING, -S** to seek the affection of **WOOABLE** *adj*

WOOD *v* **-ED, -ING, -S** to furnish with wood (the hard, fibrous substance beneath the bark of a tree or shrub)

WOODBIN *n* pl. **-S** a bin for holding firewood

WOODBIND *n* pl. **-S** woodbine

WOODBINE *n* pl. **-S** a European shrub

WOODBOX *n* pl. **-ES** a woodbin

WOODCHAT *n* pl. **-S** a European shrike

WOODCOCK *n* pl. **-S** a game bird

WOODCUT *n* pl. **-S** an engraved block of wood

WOODEN *adj* **-ENER, -ENEST** resembling wood in stiffness **WOODENLY** *adv*

WOODFERN *n* pl. **-S** an evergreen fern

WOODHEN *n* pl. **-S** the weka

WOODIE *n* pl. **-S** woody

WOODIER comparative of woody

WOODIES pl. of woody

WOODIEST superlative of woody

WOODLAND *n* pl. **-S** land covered with trees

WOODLARK *n* pl. **-S** a songbird

WOODLESS *adj* having no wood

WOODLICE *n/pl* sowbugs

WOODLORE *n* pl. **-S** knowledge of the forest

WOODLOT *n* pl. **-S** an area restricted to the growing of forest trees

WOODMAN *n* pl. **-MEN** woodsman

WOODMICE *n/pl* field mice

WOODNOTE *n* pl. **-S** a song or call of a forest bird

WOODPILE *n* pl. **-S** a pile of wood

WOODRAT *n* pl. **-S** a North American rat having a well-furred tail and large ears

WOODRUFF *n* pl. **-S** an aromatic herb

WOODRUSH *n* pl. **-ES** a grasslike plant having leaves fringed with long hairs

WOODSHED *v* **-SHEDDED, -SHEDDING, -SHEDS** to practice on a musical instrument

WOODSIA *n* pl. **-S** a small fern

WOODSMAN *n* pl. **-MEN** one who works or lives in the forest

WOODSY *adj* **WOODSIER, WOODSIEST** suggestive of a forest

WOODTONE *n* pl. **-S** a finish that imitates wood

WOODWASP *n* pl. **-S** a large wasplike insect

WOODWAX *n* pl. **-ES** woadwax

WOODWIND *n* pl. **-S** a musical wind instrument

WOODWORK *n* pl. **-S** work made of wood

WOODWORM *n* pl. **-S** a wood-boring worm

WOODY *adj* **WOODIER, WOODIEST** containing or resembling wood

WOODY *n* pl. **WOODIES** a wood-paneled station wagon

WOODYARD *n* pl. **-S** a yard where wood is chopped or stored

WOOER *n* pl. **-S** one that woos

WOOF *v* **-ED, -ING, -S** to utter a gruff barking sound

WOOFER *n* pl. **-S** a loudspeaker designed to reproduce low-pitched sounds

WOOINGLY *adv* attractively

WOOL *n* pl. **-S** the dense, soft hair forming the coat of certain mammals

WOOLED *adj* having wool of a specified kind

WOOLEN *n* pl. **-S** a fabric made of wool

WOOLER *n* pl. **-S** a domestic animal raised for its wool

WOOLFELL *n* pl. **-S** woolskin

WOOLHAT *n* pl. **-S** one who works a small farm

WOOLIE *n* pl. **-S** a woolly

WOOLIER comparative of wooly

WOOLIES pl. of wooly

WOOLIEST superlative of wooly

WOOLLED *adj* wooled

WOOLLEN *n* pl. **-S** woolen

WOOLLIES pl. of woolly

WOOLLIKE *adj* resembling wool

WOOLLY *adj* **-LIER, -LIEST** consisting of or resembling wool **WOOLLILY** *adv*

WOOLLY *n* pl. **-LIES** a garment made of wool

WOOLMAN *n* pl. **-MEN** a dealer in wool

WOOLPACK *n* pl. **-S** a bag for packing a bale of wool

WOOLSACK *n* pl. **-S** a sack of wool

WOOLSHED *n* pl. **-S** a building in which sheep are sheared

WOOLSKIN *n* pl. **-S** a sheepskin with the wool still on it

WOOLWORK *n* pl. **-S** needlework

WOOLY *adj* **WOOLIER, WOOLIEST** woolly

WOOLY *n* pl. **WOOLIES** a woolly

WOOMERA *n* pl. **-S** womera

WOONERF *n* pl. **-S** a road in the Netherlands primarily for pedestrians and cyclists

WOOPIE *n* pl. **-S** a well-off older person

WOOPS *v* **-ED, -ING, -ES** to vomit

WOOPY *n* pl. **-PIES** woopie

WOORALI *n* pl. **-S** curare

WOORARI *n* pl. **-S** curare

WOOSH *v* **-ED, -ING, -ES** to whoosh

WOOZY *adj* **-ZIER, -ZIEST** dazed **WOOZILY** *adv*

WORD *v* **-ED, -ING, -S** to express in words (speech sounds that communicate meaning)

WORDAGE *n* pl. **-S** the number of words used

WORDBOOK *n* pl. **-S** a dictionary

WORDIER comparative of wordy

WORDIEST superlative of wordy

WORDILY *adv* in a wordy manner

WORDING *n* pl. **-S** the act or style of expressing in words

WORDLESS *adj* being without words

WORDPLAY *n* pl. **-PLAYS** a witty exchange of words

WORDY *adj* **WORDIER, WORDIEST** using many or too many words

WORE past tense of wear

WORK *v* **WORKED** or **WROUGHT, WORKING, WORKS** to exert one's powers of body or mind for some purpose

WORKABLE *adj* capable of being done **WORKABLY** *adv*

WORKADAY *adj* everyday

WORKBAG *n* pl. **-S** a bag for holding work instruments and materials

WORKBOAT *n* pl. **-S** a boat used for commercial purposes

WORKBOOK *n* pl. **-S** an exercise book for a student

WORKBOOT *n* pl. **-S** a sturdy leather boot for workers

WORKBOX *n* pl. **-ES** a box for holding work instruments and materials

WORKDAY *n* pl. **-DAYS** a day on which work is done

WORKER *n* pl. **-S** one that works

WORKFARE *n* pl. **-S** a welfare program that requires recipients to perform public-service work

WORKFLOW *n* pl. **-S** the amount of work to and from an office or employee

WORKFOLK *n/pl* manual laborers

WORKHOUR *n* pl. **-S** any of the hours of the day during which work is done

WORKING *n* pl. **-S** a mining excavation

WORKLESS *adj* unemployed

WORKLOAD *n* pl. **-S** the amount of work assigned to an employee

WORKMAN *n* pl. **-MEN** a male worker

WORKMATE *n* pl. **-S** a fellow worker

WORKOUT *n* pl. **-S** a period of physical exercise

WORKROOM *n* pl. **-S** a room in which work is done

WORKSHOP *v* **-SHOPPED, -SHOPPING, -SHOPS** to perform and discuss (a play) before public performance

WORKSITE *n* pl. **-S** an area where work takes place

WORKSONG *n* pl. **-S** a song sung while doing physical work

WORKTOP *n* pl. **-S** a work surface especially in a kitchen

WORKUP *n* pl. **-S** an intensive diagnostic study

WORKWEAR *n* pl. **WORKWEAR** heavy-duty clothes for physical work

WORKWEEK *n* pl. **-S** the number of hours worked in a week

WORLD *n* pl. **-S** the earth and all its inhabitants

WORLDER *n* pl. **-S** one who belongs to a specified class, time, domain, or sphere of activity

WORLDLY *adj* **-LIER, -LIEST** pertaining to the world

WORM *v* **-ED, -ING, -S** to rid of worms (small, limbless invertebrates)

WORMCAST *n* pl. **-S** a mass of earth left on the surface by a burrowing earthworm

WORMER *n* pl. **-S** one that worms

WORMGEAR *n* pl. **-S** a gear wheel driven by a worm (a rotating shaft with threads)

WORMHOLE *n* pl. **-S** a hole made by a burrowing worm

WORMIER comparative of wormy

WORMIEST superlative of wormy

WORMIL *n* pl. **-S** a lump in the skin of an animal's back

WORMISH *adj* wormlike

WORMLIKE *adj* resembling a worm

WORMROOT *n* pl. **-S** pinkroot

WORMSEED *n* pl. **-S** a tropical plant

WORMWOOD *n* pl. **-S** a European herb

WORMY *adj* **WORMIER, WORMIEST** infested with worms

WORN *adj* affected by wear or use

WORNNESS *n* pl. **-ES** the state of being worn

WORRIER *n* pl. **-S** one that worries

WORRIT *v* **-ED, -ING, -S** to worry

WORRY *v* **-RIED, -RYING, -RIES** to feel anxious and uneasy about something

WORSE *n* pl. **-S** something that is worse (bad in a greater degree)

WORSEN *v* **-ED, -ING, -S** to make or become worse

WORSER *adj* worse

WORSET *n* pl. **-S** worsted

WORSHIP *v* **-SHIPED, -SHIPING, -SHIPS** or **-SHIPPED, -SHIPPING, -SHIPS** to honor and love as a divine being

WORST *v* **-ED, -ING, -S** to defeat

WORSTED *n* pl. **-S** a woolen yarn

WORT *n* pl. **-S** a plant, herb, or vegetable

WORTH *v* **-ED, -ING, -S** to befall

WORTHFUL *adj* worthy

WORTHY *adj* **-THIER, -THIEST** having value or merit **WORTHILY** *adv*

WORTHY *n* pl. **-THIES** a worthy person

WOST a present 2d person sing. of wit

WOT *v* **WOTTED, WOTTING, WOTS** to know

WOTCHER *interj* — used as a casual greeting

WOULD past tense of will

WOULDEST a 2d person sing. past tense of will

WOULDST a 2d person sing. past tense of will

WOUND *v* **-ED, -ING, -S** to inflict an injury upon

WOVE a past tense of weave

WOVEN *n* pl. **-S** a woven fabric

WOW *v* **-ED, -ING, -S** to excite to enthusiastic approval

WOWEE *interj* — used to express astonishment or admiration

WOWSER *n* pl. **-S** a puritanical person

WRACK *v* **-ED, -ING, -S** to wreck

WRACKFUL	*adj* destructive
WRAITH	*n* pl. **-S** a ghost
WRANG	*n* pl. **-S** a wrong
WRANGLE	*v* **-GLED, -GLING, -GLES** to argue noisily
WRANGLER	*n* pl. **-S** one that wrangles
WRAP	*v* **WRAPPED** or **WRAPT, WRAPPING, WRAPS** to enclose in something wound or folded about
WRAPPER	*n* pl. **-S** one that wraps
WRAPPING	*n* pl. **-S** the material in which something is wrapped
WRASSE	*n* pl. **-S** a marine fish
WRASSLE	*v* **-SLED, -SLING, -SLES** to wrastle
WRASTLE	*v* **-TLED, -TLING, -TLES** to wrestle
WRATH	*v* **-ED, -ING, -S** to make wrathful
WRATHFUL	*adj* extremely angry
WRATHY	*adj* **WRATHIER, WRATHIEST** wrathful **WRATHILY** *adv*
WREAK	*v* **-ED, -ING, -S** to inflict
WREAKER	*n* pl. **-S** one that wreaks
WREATH	*n* pl. **-S** a band of flowers **WREATHY** *adj*
WREATHE	*v* **WREATHED, WREATHEN, WREATHING, WREATHES** to shape into a wreath
WREATHER	*n* pl. **-S** one that wreathes
WRECK	*v* **-ED, -ING, -S** to cause the ruin of
WRECKAGE	*n* pl. **-S** the act of wrecking
WRECKER	*n* pl. **-S** one that wrecks
WRECKFUL	*adj* destructive
WRECKING	*n* pl. **-S** the occupation of salvaging wrecked objects
WREN	*n* pl. **-S** a small songbird
WRENCH	*v* **-ED, -ING, -ES** to twist suddenly and forcibly
WRENCHER	*n* pl. **-S** one that wrenches
WRENTIT	*n* pl. **-S** a long-tailed North American songbird
WREST	*v* **-ED, -ING, -S** to take away by force
WRESTER	*n* pl. **-S** one that wrests
WRESTLE	*v* **-TLED, -TLING, -TLES** to engage in a type of hand-to-hand contest
WRESTLER	*n* pl. **-S** one that wrestles
WRETCH	*n* pl. **-ES** a wretched person
WRETCHED	*adj* **-EDER, -EDEST** extremely unhappy

WRICK	*v* **-ED, -ING, -S** to wrench
WRIED	past tense of wry
WRIER	a comparative of wry
WRIES	present 3d person sing. of wry
WRIEST	a superlative of wry
WRIGGLE	*v* **-GLED, -GLING, -GLES** to turn or twist in a sinuous manner
WRIGGLER	*n* pl. **-S** one that wriggles
WRIGGLY	*adj* **-GLIER, -GLIEST** wriggling
WRIGHT	*n* pl. **-S** one who constructs or creates
WRING	*v* **WRUNG** or **WRINGED, WRINGING, WRINGS** to twist so as to compress
WRINGER	*n* pl. **-S** one that wrings
WRINKLE	*v* **-KLED, -KLING, -KLES** to make wrinkles (small ridges or furrows) in
WRINKLY	*adj* **-KLIER, -KLIEST** having wrinkles
WRIST	*v* **-ED, -ING, -S** to sweep the puck along the ice before shooting it
WRISTER	*n* pl. **-S** a type of shot in hockey
WRISTLET	*n* pl. **-S** a band worn around the wrist
WRISTY	*adj* **WRISTIER, WRISTIEST** using much wrist action
WRIT	*n* pl. **-S** a written legal order
WRITE	*v* **WROTE, WRITTEN, WRITING, WRITES** to form characters or symbols on a surface with an instrument **WRITABLE** *adj*
WRITEOFF	*n* pl. **-S** an uncollectible debt that is cancelled
WRITER	*n* pl. **-S** one that writes
WRITERLY	*adj* characteristic of a writer
WRITHE	*v* **WRITHED, WRITHING, WRITHES** to squirm or twist in pain
WRITHEN	*adj* twisted
WRITHER	*n* pl. **-S** one that writhes
WRITING	*n* pl. **-S** a written composition
WRITTEN	past participle of write
WRONG	*adj* **WRONGER, WRONGEST** not according to what is right, proper, or correct
WRONG	*v* **-ED, -ING, -S** to treat injuriously or unjustly
WRONGER	*n* pl. **-S** one that wrongs
WRONGFUL	*adj* wrong

WRONGLY	*adv* in a wrong manner
WROTE	past tense of write
WROTH	*adj* very angry
WROTHFUL	*adj* wroth
WROUGHT	a past tense of work
WRUNG	a past tense of wring
WRY	*adj* **WRIER, WRIEST** or **WRYER, WRYEST** contorted **WRYLY** *adv*
WRY	*v* **WRIED, WRYING, WRIES** to contort
WRYNECK	*n* pl. **-S** a European bird
WRYNESS	*n* pl. **-ES** the state of being wry
WUD	*adj* insane
WURST	*n* pl. **-S** sausage
WURTZITE	*n* pl **-S** a mineral
WURZEL	*n* pl. **-S** a variety of beet
WUSHU	*n* pl. **WUSHU** Chinese martial arts

WUSS	*n* pl. **-ES** a wimp (a weak, ineffectual person)
WUSSY	*adj* **WUSSIER, WUSSIEST** wimpy
WUSSY	*n* pl. **-SIES** a wuss
WUTHER	*v* **-ED, -ING, -S** to blow with a dull roaring sound
WYCH	*n* pl. **-ES** a European elm
WYE	*n* pl. **-S** the letter Y
WYLE	*v* **WYLED, WYLING, WYLES** to beguile
WYN	*n* pl. **-S** wynn
WYND	*n* pl. **-S** a narrow street
WYNN	*n* pl. **-S** the rune for W
WYSIWYG	*adj* denoting the text on a display screen that exactly corresponds to its appearance on a printout
WYTE	*v* **WYTED, WYTING, WYTES** to wite
WYVERN	*n* pl. **-S** wivern

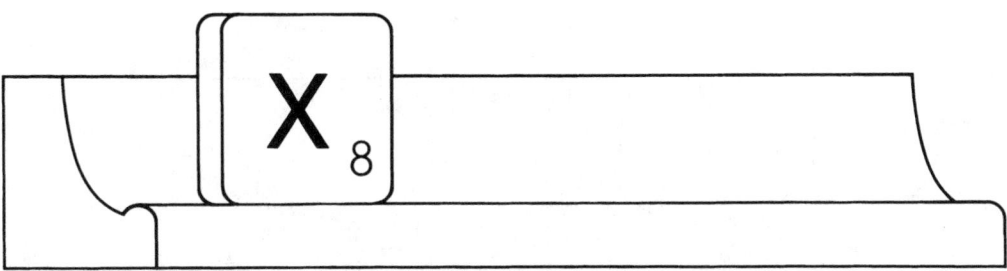

XANTHAN   *n* pl. **-S** a gum produced by bacterial fermentation

XANTHATE   *n* pl. **-S** a chemical salt

XANTHEIN   *n* pl. **-S** the water-soluble part of the coloring matter in yellow flowers

XANTHENE   *n* pl. **-S** a chemical compound

XANTHIC   *adj* tending to have a yellow color

XANTHIN   *n* pl. **-S** a yellow pigment

XANTHINE   *n* pl. **-S** a chemical compound

XANTHOMA   *n* pl. **-MAS** or **-MATA** a skin disease

XANTHONE   *n* pl. **-S** a chemical compound

XANTHOUS   *adj* yellow

XEBEC   *n* pl. **-S** a Mediterranean sailing vessel

XENIA   *n* pl. **-S** the effect of pollen on certain plant structures **XENIAL** *adj*

XENIC   *adj* pertaining to a type of culture medium

XENOGAMY   *n* pl. **-MIES** the transfer of pollen from one plant to another

XENOGENY   *n* pl. **-NIES** the supposed production of offspring totally different from the parent

XENOLITH   *n* pl. **-S** a rock fragment included in another rock

XENON   *n* pl. **-S** a gaseous element

XENOPUS   *n* pl. **-PUSES** a frog native to southern Africa

XENOTIME   *n* pl. **-S** a yellowish-brown mineral

XERARCH   *adj* developing in a dry area

XERIC   *adj* requiring only a small amount of moisture

XEROSERE   *n* pl. **-S** a dry-land sere

XEROSIS   *n* pl. **-ROSES** abnormal dryness of a body part or tissue **XEROTIC** *adj*

XEROX   *v* **-ED, -ING, -ES** to copy on a xerographic copier

XERUS   *n* pl. **-ES** an African ground squirrel

XI   *n* pl. **-S** a Greek letter

XIPHOID   *n* pl. **-S** a part of the sternum

XU   *n* pl. **XU** a monetary unit of Vietnam

XYLAN   *n* pl. **-S** a substance found in cell walls of plants

XYLEM   *n* pl. **-S** a complex plant tissue

XYLENE   *n* pl. **-S** a flammable hydrocarbon

XYLIDIN   *n* pl. **-S** xylidine

XYLIDINE   *n* pl. **-S** a chemical compound

XYLITOL   *n* pl. **-S** an alcohol

XYLOCARP   *n* pl. **-S** a hard, woody fruit

XYLOID   *adj* resembling wood

XYLOL   *n* pl. **-S** xylene

XYLOSE   *n* pl. **-S** a type of sugar

XYLOTOMY   *n* pl. **-MIES** the preparation of sections of wood for microscopic examination

XYLYL   *n* pl. **-S** a univalent radical

XYST   *n* pl. **-S** xystus

XYSTER   *n* pl. **-S** a surgical instrument for scraping bones

XYSTOS   *n* pl. **-TOI** xystus

XYSTUS   *n* pl. **-TI** a roofed area where athletes trained in ancient Greece

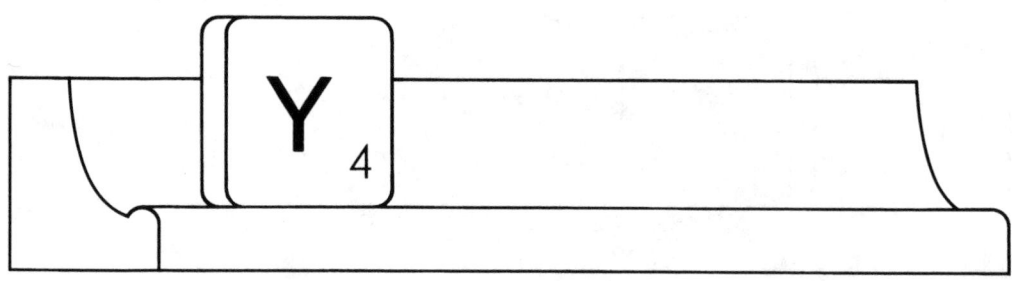

YA	*n* pl. **-S** an Asian pear
YABBER	*v* **-ED, -ING, -S** to jabber
YABBIE	*n* pl. **-S** yabby
YABBY	*n* pl. **-BIES** an Australian crayfish
YACHT	*v* **-ED, -ING, -S** to sail in a yacht (a vessel used for pleasure cruising or racing)
YACHTER	*n* pl. **-S** one who sails a yacht
YACHTIE	*n* pl. **-S** a yachter
YACHTING	*n* pl. **-S** the sport of sailing in yachts
YACHTMAN	*n* pl. **-MEN** a yachter
YACK	*v* **-ED, -ING, -S** to yak
YAFF	*v* **-ED, -ING, -S** to bark
YAFFLE	*n* pl. **-S** the European green woodpecker
YAG	*n* pl. **-S** a synthetic garnet
YAGE	*n* pl. **-S** a tropical vine of the Amazon region
YAGER	*n* pl. **-S** jaeger
YAGI	*n* pl. **-S** a type of shortwave antenna
YAH	*interj* — used as an exclamation of disgust
YAHOO	*n* pl. **-HOOS** a coarse, uncouth person
YAHOOISM	*n* pl. **-S** coarse, uncouth behavior
YAHRZEIT	*n* pl. **-S** an anniversary of the death of a family member observed by Jews
YAIRD	*n* pl. **-S** a garden
YAK	*v* **YAKKED, YAKKING, YAKS** to chatter
YAKITORI	*n* pl. **-S** marinated chicken pieces on skewers
YAKKER	*n* pl. **-S** one that yaks
YAKUZA	*n* pl. **YAKUZA** an alliance of Japanese criminal organizations
YALD	*adj* yauld
YAM	*n* pl. **-S** a plant having an edible root
YAMALKA	*n* pl. **-S** yarmulke
YAMEN	*n* pl. **-S** the residence of a Chinese public official
YAMMER	*v* **-ED, -ING, -S** to whine or complain peevishly
YAMMERER	*n* pl. **-S** one that yammers
YAMULKA	*n* pl. **-S** yarmulke
YAMUN	*n* pl. **-S** yamen
YANG	*n* pl. **-S** the masculine active principle in Chinese cosmology
YANK	*v* **-ED, -ING, -S** to pull suddenly
YANQUI	*n* pl. **-S** a United States citizen
YANTRA	*n* pl. **-S** a geometrical diagram used in meditation
YAP	*v* **YAPPED, YAPPING, YAPS** to bark shrilly
YAPOCK	*n* pl. **-S** an aquatic mammal
YAPOK	*n* pl. **-S** yapock
YAPON	*n* pl. **-S** yaupon
YAPPED	past tense of yap
YAPPER	*n* pl. **-S** one that yaps
YAPPING	present participle of yap
YAPPY	*adj* **-PIER, -PIEST** inclined to yap
YAR	*adj* yare
YARAK	*n* pl. **-S** a fit condition for hunting — used of a hawk
YARD	*v* **-ED, -ING, -S** to put in a yard (a tract of ground adjacent to a building)
YARDAGE	*n* pl. **-S** the use of an enclosure for livestock at a railroad station
YARDARM	*n* pl. **-S** either end of a ship's spar
YARDBIRD	*n* pl. **-S** an army recruit
YARDER	*n* pl. **-S** one having a specified number of yards in length

YARDLAND	*n* pl. **-S** an old English unit of land measure
YARDMAN	*n* pl. **-MEN** a man employed to do outdoor work
YARDWAND	*n* pl. **-S** a measuring stick
YARDWORK	*n* pl. **-S** the work of caring for a lawn
YARE	*adj* **YARER, YAREST** nimble **YARELY** *adv*
YARMELKE	*n* pl. **-S** yarmulke
YARMULKA	*v* pl. **-S** yarmulke
YARMULKE	*n* pl. **-S** a skullcap worn by Jewish males
YARN	*v* **-ED, -ING, -S** to tell a long story
YARNER	*n* pl. **-S** one that yarns
YARROW	*n* pl. **-S** a perennial herb
YASHMAC	*n* pl. **-S** yashmak
YASHMAK	*n* pl. **-S** a veil worn by Muslim women
YASMAK	*n* pl. **-S** yashmak
YATAGAN	*n* pl. **-S** yataghan
YATAGHAN	*n* pl. **-S** a Turkish sword
YATTER	*v* **-ED, -ING, -S** to talk idly
YAUD	*n* pl. **-S** an old mare
YAULD	*adj* vigorous
YAUP	*v* **-ED, -ING, -S** to yawp
YAUPER	*n* pl. **-S** one that yaups
YAUPON	*n* pl. **-S** an evergreen shrub
YAUTIA	*n* pl. **-S** a tropical plant
YAW	*v* **-ED, -ING, -S** to deviate from an intended course
YAWEY	*adj* pertaining to yaws (an infectious disease)
YAWL	*v* **-ED, -ING, -S** to yowl
YAWMETER	*n* pl. **-S** an instrument in an aircraft
YAWN	*v* **-ED, -ING, -S** to open the mouth wide with a deep inhalation of air
YAWNER	*n* pl. **-S** one that yawns
YAWP	*v* **-ED, -ING, -S** to utter a loud, harsh cry
YAWPER	*n* pl. **-S** one that yawps
YAWPING	*n* pl. **-S** a loud, harsh cry
YAY	*n* pl. **YAYS** yea
YCLAD	*adj* clothed
YCLEPED	*adj* yclept
YCLEPT	*adj* called; named
YE	*pron* you

YEA	*n* pl. **-S** an affirmative vote
YEAH	*n* pl. **-S** an affirmative reply
YEALING	*n* pl. **-S** a person of the same age
YEAN	*v* **-ED, -ING, -S** to bear young
YEANLING	*n* pl. **-S** the young of a sheep or goat
YEAR	*n* pl. **-S** a period of time consisting of 365 or 366 days
YEARBOOK	*n* pl. **-S** a book published each year by a graduating class
YEAREND	*n* pl. **-S** the end of a year
YEARLING	*n* pl. **-S** an animal past its first year and not yet two years old
YEARLONG	*adj* lasting through a year
YEARLY	*n* pl. **-LIES** a publication appearing once a year
YEARN	*v* **-ED, -ING, -S** to have a strong or deep desire
YEARNER	*n* pl. **-S** one that yearns
YEARNING	*n* pl. **-S** a strong or deep desire
YEASAYER	*n* pl. **-S** one that affirms something
YEAST	*v* **-ED, -ING, -S** to foam
YEASTY	*adj* **YEASTIER, YEASTIEST** foamy **YEASTILY** *adv*
YECCH	*n* pl. **-S** something disgusting
YECH	*n* pl. **-S** yecch
YECHY	*adj* disgusting
YEELIN	*n* pl. **-S** yealing
YEESH	*interj* — used to express frustration
YEGG	*n* pl. **-S** a burglar
YEGGMAN	*n* pl. **-MEN** a yegg
YEH	*adv* — used to express assent or agreement
YELD	*adj* not giving milk
YELK	*n* pl. **-S** yolk
YELL	*v* **-ED, -ING, -S** to cry out loudly
YELLER	*n* pl. **-S** one that yells
YELLING	*n* pl. **-S** the act or an instance of making a loud cry
YELLOW	*adj* **-LOWER, -LOWEST** of a bright color like that of ripe lemons **YELLOWLY** *adv*
YELLOW	*v* **-ED, -ING, -S** to make or become yellow
YELLOWY	*adj* somewhat yellow
YELP	*v* **-ED, -ING, -S** to utter a sharp, shrill cry
YELPER	*n* pl. **-S** one that yelps

YEN	*v* **YENNED, YENNING, YENS** to yearn
YENTA	*n* pl. **-S** a gossipy woman
YENTE	*n* pl. **-S** yenta
YEOMAN	*n* pl. **-MEN** an independent farmer **YEOMANLY** *adj*
YEOMANRY	*n* pl. **-RIES** the collective body of yeomen
YEOW	*interj* — used to express pain or shock
YEP	*n* pl. **-S** an affirmative reply
YERBA	*n* pl. **-S** a South American beverage resembling tea
YERK	*v* **-ED, -ING, -S** to beat vigorously
YES	*v* **YESSED, YESSING, YESSES** or **YESES** to give an affirmative reply to
YESHIVA	*n* pl. **-VAS** or **-VOT** or **-VOTH** an orthodox Jewish school
YESHIVAH	*n* pl. **-S** yeshiva
YESSIR	*interj* — used to express assent
YESSIREE	*interj* yessir
YESSUM	*interj* — used to express assent to a woman
YESTER	*adj* pertaining to yesterday
YESTERN	*adj* yester
YESTREEN	*n* pl. **-S** the previous evening
YET	*adv* up to now
YETI	*n* pl. **-S** the abominable snowman
YETT	*n* pl. **-S** a gate
YEUK	*v* **-ED, -ING, -S** to itch
YEUKY	*adj* itchy
YEW	*n* pl. **-S** an evergreen tree or shrub
YIELD	*v* **-ED, -ING, -S** to give up
YIELDER	*n* pl. **-S** one that yields
YIKES	*interj* — used to express fear or pain
YILL	*n* pl. **-S** ale
YIN	*n* pl. **-S** the feminine passive principle in Chinese cosmology
YINCE	*adv* once
YIP	*v* **YIPPED, YIPPING, YIPS** to yelp
YIPE	*interj* — used to express fear or surprise
YIPES	*interj* yipe
YIPPEE	*interj* — used to express joy
YIPPIE	*n* pl. **-S** a politically radical hippie
YIPPING	present participle of yip
YIRD	*n* pl. **-S** earth
YIRR	*v* **-ED, -ING, -S** to snarl
YIRTH	*n* pl. **-S** yird
YLEM	*n* pl. **-S** hypothetical matter from which the elements are derived
YO	*interj* — used to call attention or to express affirmation
YOB	*n* pl. **-S** a hooligan
YOBBERY	*n* pl. **-BERIES** the behavior of a yob
YOBBISH	*adj* characteristic of a yob
YOBBO	*n* pl. **-BOS** or **-BOES** a yob
YOBBY	*adj* **-BIER, -BIEST** resembling a yob
YOCK	*v* **-ED, -ING, -S** to laugh boisterously
YOD	*n* pl. **-S** a Hebrew letter
YODEL	*v* **-DELED, -DELING, -DELS** or **-DELLED, -DELLING, -DELS** to sing with a fluctuating voice
YODELER	*n* pl. **-S** one that yodels
YODELLER	*n* pl. **-S** yodeler
YODH	*n* pl. **-S** yod
YODLE	*v* **-DLED, -DLING, -DLES** to yodel
YODLER	*n* pl. **-S** yodeler
YOGA	*n* pl. **-S** a Hindu philosophy involving physical and mental disciplines
YOGEE	*n* pl. **-S** yogi
YOGH	*n* pl. **-S** a Middle English letter
YOGHOURT	*n* pl. **-S** yogurt
YOGHURT	*n* pl. **-S** yogurt
YOGI	*n* pl. **-S** a person who practices yoga
YOGIC	*adj* pertaining to yoga
YOGIN	*n* pl. **-S** yogi
YOGINI	*n* pl. **-S** a female yogi
YOGISM	*n* pl. **-S** the practice or system of yoga
YOGOURT	*n* pl. **-S** yogurt
YOGURT	*n* pl. **-S** a food made from milk
YOHIMBE	*n* pl. **-S** a topical African tree
YOICKS	*interj* — used to encourage hunting hounds
YOK	*n* pl. **-S** a boisterous laugh
YOKE	*v* **YOKED, YOKING, YOKES** to fit with a yoke (a wooden frame for joining together draft animals)
YOKEL	*n* pl. **-S** a naive or gullible rustic

YOKELESS *adj* having no yoke

YOKELISH *adj* resembling a yokel

YOKEMATE *n* pl. **-S** a companion in work

YOKING present participle of yoke

YOKOZUNA *n* pl. **-S** a champion sumo wrestler

YOLK *n* pl. **-S** the yellow portion of an egg **YOLKED** *adj*

YOLKLESS *adj* lacking a yolk

YOLKY *adj* **YOLKIER, YOLKIEST** resembling a yolk

YOM *n* pl. **YOMIM** day

YOMP *v* **-ED, -ING, -S** to march with heavy equipment over difficult terrain

YON *adv* over there

YOND *adv* over there

YONDER *n* pl. **-S** the far distance

YONI *n* pl. **-S** a symbol for the vulva in Hindu religion **YONIC** *adj*

YONKER *n* pl. **-S** younker

YONKS *n/pl* a very long time

YOOF *n* pl. **-S** youth

YORE *n* pl. **-S** time past

YOU *n* pl. **-S** something identified with the person addressed

YOUNG *adj* **YOUNGER, YOUNGEST** being in the early period of life or growth

YOUNG *n* pl. **-S** offspring

YOUNGER *n* pl. **-S** an inferior in age

YOUNGISH *adj* somewhat young

YOUNKER *n* pl. **-S** a young gentleman

YOUPON *n* pl. **-S** yaupon

YOUR *adj* a possessive form of the pronoun you

YOURN *pron* yours

YOURS *pron* a possessive form of the pronoun you

YOURSELF *pron* pl. **-SELVES** a form of the 2d person pronoun

YOUSE *pron* you

YOUTH *n* pl. **-S** a young person

YOUTHEN *v* **-ED, -ING, -S** to make youthful

YOUTHFUL *adj* young

YOW *v* **-ED, -ING, -S** to yowl

YOWE *n* pl. **-S** a ewe

YOWIE *n* pl. **-S** a small ewe

YOWL *v* **-ED, -ING, -S** to utter a loud, long, mournful cry

YOWLER *n* pl. **-S** one that yowls

YPERITE *n* pl. **-S** a poisonous gas

YTTERBIA *n* pl. **-S** a chemical compound **YTTERBIC** *adj*

YTTRIA *n* pl. **-S** a chemical compound

YTTRIUM *n* pl. **-S** a metallic element **YTTRIC** *adj*

YUAN *n* pl. **-S** a monetary unit of China

YUCA *n* pl. **-S** yucca

YUCCA *n* pl. **-S** a tropical plant

YUCCH *interj* — used to express disgust

YUCH *interj* yucch

YUCK *v* **-ED, -ING, -S** to yuk

YUCKY *adj* **YUCKIER, YUCKIEST** disgusting

YUGA *n* pl. **-S** an age of time in Hinduism

YUK *v* **YUKKED, YUKKING, YUKS** to laugh loudly

YUKATA *n* pl. **-S** a light cotton kimono

YUKKY *adj* **YUKKIER, YUKKIEST** yucky

YULAN *n* pl. **-S** a Chinese tree

YULE *n* pl. **-S** Christmas time

YULETIDE *n* pl. **-S** yule

YUM *interj* — used to express pleasurable satisfaction

YUMMY *adj* **-MIER, -MIEST** delicious

YUMMY *n* pl. **-MIES** something delicious

YUP *n* pl. **-S** a yuppie

YUPON *n* pl. **-S** yaupon

YUPPIE *n* pl. **-S** a young professional person working in a city

YUPPIFY *v* **-FIED, -FYING, -FIES** to make appealing to yuppies

YUPPY *n* pl. **-PIES** yuppie

YUPPYDOM *n* pl. **-S** the state of being a yuppie

YURT *n* pl. **YURTS** or **YURTA** a portable tent

YUTZ *n* pl. **-ES** a stupid, foolish, or ineffectual person

YUZU *n* pl. **-S** a sour Japanese citrus fruit

YWIS *adv* iwis

ZA   *n* pl. **-S** a pizza

ZABAIONE   *n* pl. **-S** a dessert resembling custard

ZABAJONE   *n* pl. **-S** zabaione

ZACATON   *n* pl. **-S** a Mexican grass

ZADDICK   *n* pl. **-DIKIM** zaddik

ZADDIK   *n* pl. **-DIKIM** a virtuous person by Jewish religious standards

ZAFFAR   *n* pl. **-S** zaffer

ZAFFER   *n* pl. **-S** a blue ceramic coloring

ZAFFIR   *n* pl. **-S** zaffer

ZAFFRE   *n* pl. **-S** zaffer

ZAFTIG   *adj* full-bosomed

ZAG   *v* **ZAGGED, ZAGGING, ZAGS** to turn sharply

ZAIBATSU   *n* pl. **ZAIBATSU** a powerful family combine in Japan

ZAIDA   *n* pl. **-S** zeda

ZAIDEH   *n* pl. **-S** zeda

ZAIDY   *n* pl. **-DIES** zeda

ZAIKAI   *n* pl. **-S** the business community of Japan

ZAIRE   *n* pl. **-S** a former monetary unit of Zaire

ZAKAT   *n* pl. **-S** payment made annually under Islamic law on certain kinds of property

ZAMARRA   *n* pl. **-S** a sheepskin coat

ZAMARRO   *n* pl. **-ROS** zamarra

ZAMIA   *n* pl. **-S** a tropical plant

ZAMINDAR   *n* pl. **-S** a tax collector in precolonial India

ZANANA   *n* pl. **-S** zenana

ZANDER   *n* pl. **-S** a freshwater fish

ZANINESS   *n* pl. **-ES** the quality or state of being zany

ZANY   *adj* **ZANIER, ZANIEST** ludicrously comical **ZANILY** *adv*

ZANY   *n* pl. **-NIES** a zany person

ZANYISH   *adj* somewhat zany

ZANZA   *n* pl. **-S** an African musical instrument

ZAP   *v* **ZAPPED, ZAPPING, ZAPS** to kill or destroy instantaneously

ZAPATEO   *n* pl. **-TEOS** a Spanish dance

ZAPPER   *n* pl. **-S** a device that zaps

ZAPPY   *adj* **-PIER, -PIEST** zippy

ZAPTIAH   *n* pl. **-S** a Turkish policeman

ZAPTIEH   *n* pl. **-S** zaptiah

ZARATITE   *n* pl. **-S** a chemical compound

ZAREBA   *n* pl. **-S** an improvised stockade

ZAREEBA   *n* pl. **-S** zareba

ZARF   *n* pl. **-S** a metal holder for a coffee cup

ZARIBA   *n* pl. **-S** zareba

ZARZUELA   *n* pl. **-S** a Spanish operetta

ZASTRUGA   *n* pl. **-GI** sastruga

ZAX   *n* pl. **-ES** a tool for cutting roof slates

ZAYIN   *n* pl. **-S** a Hebrew letter

ZAZEN   *n* pl. **-S** meditation in Zen Buddhism

ZEAL   *n* pl. **-S** enthusiastic devotion

ZEALOT   *n* pl. **-S** one who is zealous

ZEALOTRY   *n* pl. **-RIES** excessive zeal

ZEALOUS   *adj* filled with zeal

ZEATIN   *n* pl. **-S** a chemical compound found in maize

ZEBEC   *n* pl. **-S** xebec

ZEBECK   *n* pl. **-S** xebec

ZEBRA   *n* pl. **-S** an African mammal that is related to the horse **ZEBRAIC** *adj*

ZEBRANO   *n* pl. **-BRANOS** a tree having striped wood

ZEBRASS   *n* pl. **-ES** the offspring of a zebra and an ass

ZEBRINE *n* pl. **-S** the offspring of a male horse and a female zebra

ZEBROID *adj* resembling a zebra

ZEBU *n* pl. **-S** an Asian ox

ZECCHIN *n* pl. **-S** zecchino

ZECCHINO *n* pl. **-NOS** or **-NI** a former gold coin of Italy

ZECHIN *n* pl. **-S** zecchino

ZED *n* pl. **-S** the letter Z

ZEDA *n* pl. **-S** grandfather

ZEDOARY *n* pl. **-ARIES** the medicinal root of a tropical plant

ZEE *n* pl. **-S** the letter Z

ZEIN *n* pl. **-S** a simple protein

ZEK *n* pl. **-S** an inmate in a Soviet labor camp

ZELKOVA *n* pl. **-S** a Japanese tree

ZEMINDAR *n* pl. **-S** zamindar

ZEMSTVO *n* pl. **-VOS** or **-VA** an elective council in czarist Russia

ZENAIDA *n* pl. **-S** a wild dove

ZENANA *n* pl. **-S** the section of a house in India reserved for women

ZENDO *n* pl. **-DOS** a place where Zen Buddhists meditate and study

ZENITH *n* pl. **-S** the highest point **ZENITHAL** *adj*

ZEOLITE *n* pl. **-S** a mineral **ZEOLITIC** *adj*

ZEP *n* pl. **-S** a long sandwich

ZEPHYR *n* pl. **-S** a gentle breeze

ZEPPELIN *n* pl. **-S** a long, rigid airship

ZEPPOLE *n* pl. **-POLES** or **-POLI** a deep-fried pastry

ZERK *n* pl. **-S** a grease fitting

ZERO *v* **-ED, -ING, -ES** or **-S** to aim at the exact center of a target

ZEROTH *adj* being numbered zero in a series

ZEST *v* **-ED, -ING, -S** to fill with zest (invigorating excitement)

ZESTER *n* pl. **-S** a utensil for peeling citrus rind

ZESTFUL *adj* full of zest

ZESTLESS *adj* lacking zest

ZESTY *adj* **ZESTIER, ZESTIEST** marked by zest **ZESTILY** *adv*

ZETA *n* pl. **-S** a Greek letter

ZETETIC *adj* proceeding by inquiry

ZEUGMA *n* pl. **-S** the use of a word to modify or govern two or more words, while applying to each in a different sense

ZIBELINE *n* pl. **-S** a soft fabric

ZIBET *n* pl. **-S** an Asian civet

ZIBETH *n* pl. **-S** zibet

ZIG *v* **ZIGGED, ZIGGING, ZIGS** to turn sharply

ZIGGURAT *n* pl. **-S** an ancient Babylonian temple tower

ZIGZAG *v* **-ZAGGED, -ZAGGING, -ZAGS** to proceed on a course marked by sharp turns

ZIGZAGGY *adj* marked by sharp turns

ZIKKURAT *n* pl. **-S** ziggurat

ZIKURAT *n* pl. **-S** ziggurat

ZILCH *n* pl. **-ES** nothing

ZILL *n* pl. **-S** one of a pair of finger cymbals

ZILLAH *n* pl. **-S** an administrative district in India

ZILLION *n* pl. **-S** an indeterminately large number

ZIN *n* pl. **-S** a dry red wine

ZINC *v* **ZINCED, ZINCING, ZINCS** or **ZINCKED, ZINCKING, ZINCS** to coat with zinc (a metallic element)

ZINCATE *n* pl. **-S** a chemical salt

ZINCIC *adj* pertaining to zinc

ZINCIFY *v* **-FIED, -FYING, -FIES** to coat with zinc

ZINCITE *n* pl. **-S** an ore of zinc

ZINCKED a past tense of zinc

ZINCKING a present participle of zinc

ZINCKY *adj* resembling zinc

ZINCO *n* pl. **-COS** a letterpress printing plate made of zinc

ZINCOID *adj* zincic

ZINCOUS *adj* zincic

ZINCY *adj* zincky

ZINE *n* pl. **-S** a magazine

ZINEB *n* pl. **-S** an insecticide

ZING *v* **-ED, -ING, -S** to move with a high-pitched humming sound

ZINGANO *n* pl. **-NI** zingaro

ZINGARA *n* pl. **-RE** a female gypsy

ZINGARO *n* pl. **-RI** a gypsy

ZINGER *n* pl. **-S** a pointed witty retort or remark

ZINGY *adj* **ZINGIER, ZINGIEST** enjoyably exciting

ZINKIFY *v* **-FIED, -FYING, -FIES** to zincify

ZINKY *adj* zincky

ZINNIA *n* pl. **-S** a tropical plant

ZIP *v* **ZIPPED, ZIPPING, ZIPS** to move with speed and vigor

ZIPLESS *adj* lacking vigor or energy

ZIPLOCK *adj* having a groove and ridge that form a tight seal when joined

ZIPOLA *n* pl. **-S** zippo

ZIPPER *v* **-ED, -ING, -S** to fasten with a zipper (a fastener consisting of two rows of interlocking teeth)

ZIPPO *n* pl. **-POS** nothing

ZIPPY *adj* **-PIER, -PIEST** full of energy **ZIPPILY** *adv*

ZIRAM *n* pl. **-S** a chemical salt

ZIRCALOY *n* pl. **-S** a zirconium alloy

ZIRCON *n* pl. **-S** a mineral

ZIRCONIA *n* pl. **-S** a chemical compound

ZIRCONIC *adj* pertaining to the metallic element zirconium

ZIT *n* pl. **-S** a pimple

ZITHER *n* pl. **-S** a stringed instrument

ZITHERN *n* pl. **-S** zither

ZITI *n* pl. **-S** a tubular pasta

ZIZIT *n/pl* zizith

ZIZITH *n/pl* the tassels on the four corners of a Jewish prayer shawl

ZIZZ *n* **-ED, -ING, -ES** to make a buzzing sound

ZIZZLE *v* **-ZLED, -ZLING, -ZLES** to sizzle

ZLOTY *n* pl. **ZLOTE** or **ZLOTIES** or **ZLOTYCH** or **ZLOTYS** a monetary unit of Poland

ZOA a pl. of zoon

ZOARIUM *n* pl. **-IA** a colony of bryozoans **ZOARIAL** *adj*

ZOCALO *n* pl. **-LOS** the public square in a Mexican city or town

ZODIAC *n* pl. **-S** an imaginary belt encircling the celestial sphere **ZODIACAL** *adj*

ZOEA *n* pl. **ZOEAS** or **ZOEAE** a larval form of certain crustaceans **ZOEAL** *adj*

ZOECIUM *n* pl. **-CIA** zooecium

ZOETROPE *n* pl. **-S** an optical toy in which a series of pictures rotates to give the illusion of motion

ZOFTIG *adj* zaftig

ZOIC *adj* pertaining to animals or animal life

ZOISITE *n* pl. **-S** a mineral

ZOMBI *n* pl. **-S** zombie

ZOMBIE *n* pl. **-S** a will-less human capable only of automatic movement

ZOMBIFY *v* **-FIED, -FYING, -FIES** to turn into a zombie

ZOMBIISM *n* pl. **-S** the system of beliefs connected with a West African snake god

ZONA *n* pl. **-NAE** a transparent substance surrounding the ovum of mammals

ZONAL *adj* pertaining to a zone **ZONALLY** *adv*

ZONARY *adj* zonal

ZONATE *adj* arranged in zones

ZONATED *adj* zonate

ZONATION *n* pl. **-S** arrangement in zones

ZONE *v* **ZONED, ZONING, ZONES** to arrange in zones (areas distinguished from other adjacent areas)

ZONELESS *adj* having no zone or belt

ZONER *n* pl. **-S** one that zones

ZONETIME *n* pl. **-S** standard time used at sea

ZONING *n* pl. **-S** the division of a city or land into areas subject to planning restrictions

ZONK *v* **-ED, -ING, -S** to stupefy

ZONULA *n* pl. **-LAS** or **-LAE** zonule

ZONULE *n* pl. **-S** a small zone **ZONULAR** *adj*

ZOO *n* pl. **ZOOS** a place where animals are kept for public exhibition

ZOOCHORE *n* pl. **-S** a plant dispersed by animals

ZOOECIUM *n* pl. **-CIA** a sac secreted and lived in by an aquatic organism

ZOOEY *adj* **ZOOIER, ZOOIEST** resembling a zoo

ZOOGENIC *adj* caused by animals or their activities

ZOOGENY *n* pl. **-NIES** the development or evolution of animals

ZOOGLEA *n* pl. **-GLEAS** or **-GLEAE** a jellylike mass of bacteria **ZOOGLEAL** *adj*

ZOOGLOEA *n* pl. **-GLOEAS** or **-GLOEAE** zooglea

ZOOID *n* pl. **-S** an organic cell or body capable of independent movement **ZOOIDAL** *adj*

ZOOKS *interj* — used as a mild oath

ZOOLATER *n* pl. **-S** one that worships animals

ZOOLATRY *n* pl. **-TRIES** the worship of animals

ZOOLOGY *n* pl. **-GIES** the science that deals with animals **ZOOLOGIC** *adj*

ZOOM *v* **-ED, -ING, -S** to move with a loud humming sound

ZOOMABLE *adj* capable of being viewed at various levels of detail and magnification

ZOOMANIA *n* pl. **-S** an excessive interest in animals

ZOOMETRY *n* pl. **-TRIES** the measurement of animals or animal parts

ZOOMORPH *n* pl. **-S** something in the form of an animal

ZOON *n* pl. **ZOONS** or **ZOA** the whole product of one fertilized egg **ZOONAL** *adj*

ZOON *v* **-ED, -ING, -S** to zoom

ZOONOSIS *n* pl. **-NOSES** a disease that can be transmitted from animals to humans **ZOONOTIC** *adj*

ZOOPHILE *n* pl. **-S** a lover of animals

ZOOPHILY *n* pl. **-LIES** a love of animals

ZOOPHOBE *n* pl. **-S** one who fears or hates animals

ZOOPHYTE *n* pl. **-S** an invertebrate animal

ZOOSPERM *n* pl. **-S** the male fertilizing element of an animal

ZOOSPORE *n* pl. **-S** a type of spore

ZOOTOMY *n* pl. **-MIES** the dissection of animals **ZOOTOMIC** *adj*

ZOOTY *adj* **ZOOTIER, ZOOTIEST** flashy in manner or style

ZORI *n* pl. **-S** a type of sandal

ZORIL *n* pl. **-S** a small African mammal

ZORILLA *n* pl. **-S** zoril

ZORILLE *n* pl. **-S** zoril

ZORILLO *n* pl. **-LOS** zoril

ZOSTER *n* pl. **-S** a virus disease

ZOUAVE *n* pl. **-S** a French infantryman

ZOUK *n* pl. **-S** a dance music of the French West Indies

ZOUNDS *interj* — used as a mild oath

ZOWEE *interj* zowie

ZOWIE *interj* — used to express surprise or pleasure

ZOYSIA *n* pl. **-S** a perennial grass

ZUCCHINI *n* pl. **-S** a vegetable

ZUGZWANG *n* pl. **-S** a situation in chess that forces a disadvantageous move

ZUPPA *n* pl. **-S** a fish soup

ZUZ *n* pl. **ZUZIM** an ancient Hebrew silver coin

ZWIEBACK *n* pl. **-S** a sweetened bread

ZYDECO *n* pl. **-COS** popular music of southern Louisiana

ZYGOID *adj* pertaining to a zygote

ZYGOMA *n* pl. **-MAS** or **-MATA** the cheekbone

ZYGOSIS *n* pl. **-GOSES** the union of two gametes **ZYGOSE** *adj*

ZYGOSITY *n* pl. **-TIES** the makeup of a particular zygote

ZYGOTE *n* pl. **-S** a cell formed by the union of two gametes **ZYGOTIC** *adj*

ZYGOTENE *n* pl. **-S** a stage in meiosis

ZYMASE *n* pl. **-S** an enzyme

ZYME *n* pl. **-S** an enzyme

ZYMOGEN *n* pl. **-S** a substance that develops into an enzyme when suitably activated

ZYMOGENE *n* pl. **-S** zymogen

ZYMOGRAM *n* pl. **-S** a record of separated proteins after electrophoresis

ZYMOLOGY *n* pl. **-GIES** the science of fermentation

ZYMOSAN *n* pl. **-S** an insoluble fraction of yeast cell walls

ZYMOSIS *n* pl. **-MOSES** fermentation **ZYMOTIC** *adj*

ZYMURGY *n* pl. **-GIES** a branch of chemistry dealing with fermentation

ZYZZYVA *n* pl. **-S** a tropical weevil

ZZZ *interj* — used to suggest the sound of snoring

A SELECTION OF USEFUL WORDS FOR PLAYERS

Letter values

A is worth 1	G is worth 2	M is worth 3	S is worth 1	Y is worth 4
B is worth 3	H is worth 4	N is worth 1	T is worth 1	Z is worth 10
C is worth 3	I is worth 1	O is worth 1	U is worth 1	
D is worth 2	J is worth 8	P is worth 3	V is worth 4	
E is worth 1	K is worth 5	Q is worth 10	W is worth 4	
F is worth 4	L is worth 1	R is worth 1	X is worth 8	

Q words not followed by U

BUQSHA	NIQAABS	QAMUTIK	QIGONGS	QWERTYS
BUQSHAS	NIQAB	QAMUTIKS	QINDAR	SHEQEL
BURQA	NIQABS	QANAT	QINDARS	SHEQELS
BURQAS	QABALA	QANATS	QINDARKA	SHEQALIM
CINQ	QABALAS	QAT	QINTAR	SUQ
CINQS	QABALAH	QATS	QINTARS	SUQS
FAQIR	QABALAHS	QAWWALI	QIVIUT	TRANQ
FAQIRS	QADI	QAWWALIS	QIVIUTS	TRANQS
KAMOTIQ	QADIS	QI	QOPH	UMIAQ
KAMOTIQS	QAID	QIS	QOPHS	UMIAQS
MBAQANGA	QAIDS	QIBLA	QULLIQ	
MBAQANGAS	QAJAQ	QIBLAS	QULLIQS	
NIQAAB	QAJAQS	QIGONG	QWERTY	

2- to 7-letter words with no AEIOU vowels

BY	SLY	SCRY	LYNCH	FLYSCH
HM	SPY	SHHH	MYRRH	GHYLLS
MM	STY	SKRY	MYTHS	GLYCYL
MY	SYN	SPRY	MYTHY	GLYPHS
SH	THY	SYNC	NYMPH	GRRRLS
	TRY	SYPH	PHPHT	LYMPHS
BRR	TSK	TSKS	PSYCH	MYRRHS
BYS	WHY	TYPP	PYGMY	MYRRHY
CRY	WRY	TYPY	RYNDS	NYMPHS
CWM	WYN	WHYS	SHYLY	PSYCHS
DRY	ZZZ	WYCH	SLYLY	RHYTHM
FLY		WYND	STYMY	SPHYNX
FRY	BRRR	WYNN	SYLPH	SPRYLY
GRR	BYRL	WYNS	SYNCH	SYLPHS
GYM	CWMS	XYST	SYNCS	SYLPHY
GYP	CYST		SYNTH	SYNCHS
HMM	DRYS	BYRLS	SYPHS	SYNTHS
HYP	GYMS	CRWTH	THYMY	SYZYGY
MMM	GYPS	CRYPT	TRYST	TRYSTS
MYC	HWYL	CYSTS	TYPPS	TSKTSK
NTH	HYMN	DRYLY	WRYLY	XYLYLS
PHT	HYPS	FLYBY	WYNDS	
PLY	LYCH	GHYLL	WYNNS	GLYCYLS
PRY	LYNX	GLYPH	XYLYL	RHYTHMS
PST	MYCS	GRRRL	XYSTS	TSKTSKS
PYX	MYTH	GYPSY		
SHH	PFFT	HWYLS	CRWTHS	
SHY	PSST	HYMNS	CRYPTS	
SKY	RYND	LYMPH	FLYBYS	

2- to 6-letter words containing J, Q, X, or Z

AX	PYX	CAZH	JANE	JUBA
EX	QAT	CHEZ	JAPE	JUBE
JO	QIS	CINQ	JARL	JUCO
OX	QUA	COAX	JARS	JUDO
QI	RAJ	COXA	JATO	JUDY
XI	RAX	COZY	JAUK	JUGA
XU	REX	CRUX	JAUP	JUGS
ZA	REZ	CZAR	JAVA	JUJU
	SAX	DAZE	JAWS	JUKE
ADZ	SEX	DEXY	JAYS	JUKU
AJI	SIX	DITZ	JAZZ	JUMP
AXE	SOX	DJIN	JEAN	JUNK
AZO	SUQ	DOJO	JEED	JUPE
BIZ	TAJ	DOUX	JEEP	JURA
BOX	TAX	DOXY	JEER	JURY
COX	TIX	DOZE	JEES	JUST
COZ	TIZ	DOZY	JEEZ	JUTE
CUZ	TUX	EAUX	JEFE	JUTS
DEX	VEX	EXAM	JEHU	KOJI
FAX	VOX	EXEC	JELL	LAZE
FEZ	WAX	EXED	JEON	LAZY
FIX	WIZ	EXES	JERK	LUTZ
FIZ	XIS	EXIT	JESS	LUXE
FOX	ZAG	EXON	JEST	LYNX
GOX	ZAP	EXPO	JETE	MAXI
HAJ	ZAS	FALX	JETS	MAZE
HEX	ZAX	FAUX	JEUX	MAZY
JAB	ZED	FAZE	JIAO	MEZE
JAG	ZEE	FIXT	JIBB	MINX
JAM	ZEK	FIZZ	JIBE	MIXT
JAR	ZEP	FLAX	JIBS	MOJO
JAW	ZIG	FLEX	JIFF	MOXA
JAY	ZIN	FLUX	JIGS	MOZO
JEE	ZIP	FOXY	JILL	NAZI
JET	ZIT	FOZY	JILT	NEXT
JEU	ZOA	FRIZ	JIMP	NIXE
JIB	ZOO	FUJI	JINK	NIXY
JIG	ZUZ	FUTZ	JINN	ONYX
JIN	ZZZ	FUZE	JINS	OOZE
JOB		FUZZ	JINX	OOZY
JOE	ADZE	GAZE	JIRD	ORYX
JOG	AJAR	GEEZ	JIVE	ORZO
JOT	AJEE	GOJI	JIVY	OUZO
JOW	AJIS	GRIZ	JOBS	OXEN
JOY	APEX	HADJ	JOCK	OXER
JUG	AQUA	HAJI	JOES	OXES
JUN	AXAL	HAJJ	JOEY	OXIC
JUS	AXED	HAZE	JOGS	OXID
JUT	AXEL	HAZY	JOHN	OXIM
KEX	AXES	HOAX	JOIN	OYEZ
LAX	AXIL	IBEX	JOKE	PHIZ
LEX	AXIS	ILEX	JOKY	PIXY
LOX	AXLE	IXIA	JOLE	PLEX
LUX	AXON	IZAR	JOLT	POXY
MAX	AZAN	JABS	JOOK	PREX
MIX	AZON	JACK	JOSH	PREZ
MUX	BAZZ	JADE	JOSS	PUJA
NIX	BIZE	JAGG	JOTA	PUTZ
OXO	BOXY	JAGS	JOTS	QADI
OXY	BOZO	JAIL	JOUK	QAID
PAX	BRUX	JAKE	JOWL	QATS
PIX	BUZZ	JAMB	JOWS	QOPH
POX	CALX	JAMS	JOYS	QUAD

QUAG	ZOOS	BOXER	EQUIP	GLOZE
QUAI	ZORI	BOXES	EXACT	GOJIS
QUAY	ZOUK	BOXLA	EXALT	GONZO
QUEY	ZYME	BOZOS	EXAMS	GOXES
QUID		BRAXY	EXCEL	GRAZE
QUIN	ABUZZ	BRAZA	EXECS	GROSZ
QUIP	ADDAX	BRAZE	EXERT	GYOZA
QUIT	ADMIX	BURQA	EXILE	HADJI
QUIZ	ADOZE	BUXOM	EXINE	HAFIZ
QUOD	ADZED	BUZZY	EXING	HAJES
RAJA	ADZES	CAJON	EXIST	HAJIS
RAZE	AFFIX	CALIX	EXITS	HAJJI
RAZZ	AGAZE	CALYX	EXONS	HAMZA
RITZ	AJIVA	CAPIZ	EXPAT	HAPAX
ROUX	AJUGA	CAREX	EXPEL	HAZAN
SEXT	AMAZE	CIMEX	EXPOS	HAZED
SEXY	ANNEX	CINQS	EXTOL	HAZEL
SIZE	AQUAE	CLOZE	EXTRA	HAZER
SIZY	AQUAS	CODEX	EXUDE	HAZES
SOJA	ARROZ	COLZA	EXULT	HEEZE
SOJU	ATAXY	COMIX	EXURB	HELIX
SUQS	AUXIN	COQUI	FAQIR	HERTZ
TAXA	AXELS	COXAE	FAXED	HEXAD
TAXI	AXIAL	COXED	FAXES	HEXED
TEXT	AXILE	COXES	FAZED	HEXER
TIZZ	AXILS	COZEN	FAZES	HEXES
TZAR	AXING	COZES	FEAZE	HEXYL
VEXT	AXIOM	COZEY	FEDEX	HIJAB
WAXY	AXION	COZIE	FEEZE	HIJRA
WHIZ	AXITE	CRAZE	FEZES	HUZZA
XYST	AXLES	CRAZY	FIQUE	HYRAX
YUTZ	AXMAN	CROZE	FIXED	IMMIX
YUZU	AXMEN	CULEX	FIXER	INBOX
ZAGS	AXONE	CYLIX	FIXES	INDEX
ZANY	AXONS	CZARS	FIXIT	INFIX
ZAPS	AZANS	DAZED	FIZZY	IXIAS
ZARF	AZIDE	DAZES	FJELD	IXNAY
ZEAL	AZINE	DEOXY	FJORD	IXORA
ZEBU	AZLON	DESEX	FLAXY	IXTLE
ZEDA	AZOIC	DETOX	FOREX	IZARD
ZEDS	AZOLE	DEWAX	FOXED	IZARS
ZEES	AZONS	DEXES	FOXES	JABOT
ZEIN	AZOTE	DEXIE	FRITZ	JACAL
ZEKS	AZOTH	DIAZO	FRIZZ	JACKS
ZEPS	AZUKI	DITZY	FROZE	JACKY
ZERK	AZURE	DIXIT	FUJIS	JADED
ZERO	BAIZA	DIZEN	FURZE	JADES
ZEST	BAIZE	DIZZY	FURZY	JAGER
ZETA	BANJO	DJINN	FUZED	JAGGS
ZIGS	BAZAR	DJINS	FUZEE	JAGGY
ZILL	BAZOO	DOJOS	FUZES	JAGRA
ZINC	BEAUX	DOOZY	FUZIL	JAILS
ZINE	BEMIX	DOXIE	FUZZY	JAKES
ZING	BEZEL	DOZED	GALAX	JALAP
ZINS	BEZIL	DOZEN	GANJA	JALOP
ZIPS	BHAJI	DOZER	GAUZE	JAMBE
ZITI	BIJOU	DOZES	GAUZY	JAMBS
ZITS	BIZES	EEJIT	GAZAR	JAMMY
ZIZZ	BLAZE	EJECT	GAZED	JANES
ZOEA	BLITZ	EJIDO	GAZER	JANNY
ZOIC	BONZE	ENJOY	GAZES	JANTY
ZONA	BOOZE	ENZYM	GHAZI	JAPAN
ZONE	BOOZY	EPOXY	GIZMO	JAPED
ZONK	BORAX	EQUAL	GLAZE	JAPER
ZOOM	BORTZ	EQUES	GLAZY	JAPES
ZOON	BOXED	EQUID	GLITZ	JARLS

JATOS	JOLLY	LAZAR	PHIZZ	QUINT
JAUKS	JOLTS	LAZED	PHLOX	QUIPS
JAUNT	JOLTY	LAZES	PIEZO	QUIPU
JAUPS	JOMON	LEXES	PIQUE	QUIRE
JAVAS	JONES	LEXIS	PIXEL	QUIRK
JAWAN	JOOKS	LOXED	PIXES	QUIRT
JAWED	JORAM	LOXES	PIXIE	QUITE
JAZZY	JORUM	LUXES	PIZZA	QUITS
JEANS	JOTAS	MAIZE	PLAZA	QUODS
JEBEL	JOTTY	MAJOR	PLOTZ	QUOIN
JEEPS	JOUAL	MAQUI	PONZU	QUOIT
JEERS	JOUKS	MATZA	POOJA	QUOLL
JEEZE	JOULE	MATZO	POXED	QUOTA
JEFES	JOUST	MAUZY	POXES	QUOTE
JEHAD	JOWAR	MAXED	PREXY	QUOTH
JEHUS	JOWED	MAXES	PRIZE	QURSH
JELLS	JOWLS	MAXIM	PROXY	RADIX
JELLY	JOWLY	MAXIS	PUJAH	RAJAH
JEMMY	JOYED	MAZED	PUJAS	RAJAS
JENNY	JUBAS	MAZER	PUNJI	RAJES
JERID	JUBES	MAZES	PYXES	RAXED
JERKS	JUCOS	MEZES	PYXIE	RAXES
JERKY	JUDAS	MEZZO	PYXIS	RAZED
JERRY	JUDGE	MIREX	PZAZZ	RAZEE
JESSE	JUDOS	MIRZA	QADIS	RAZER
JESTS	JUGAL	MIXED	QAIDS	RAZES
JETES	JUGUM	MIXER	QAJAQ	RAZOR
JETON	JUICE	MIXES	QANAT	REDOX
JETTY	JUICY	MIXUP	QIBLA	REDUX
JEWEL	JUJUS	MIZEN	QOPHS	REFIX
JIBBA	JUKED	MOJOS	QUACK	REJIG
JIBBS	JUKES	MOXAS	QUADS	RELAX
JIBED	JUKUS	MOXIE	QUAFF	REMEX
JIBER	JULEP	MOZOS	QUAGS	REMIX
JIBES	JUMAR	MUJIK	QUAIL	RETAX
JIFFS	JUMBO	MUREX	QUAIS	REWAX
JIFFY	JUMPS	MUXED	QUAKE	REXES
JIGGY	JUMPY	MUXES	QUAKY	REZES
JIHAD	JUNCO	MUZZY	QUALE	RIOJA
JILLS	JUNKS	NAZIS	QUALM	RITZY
JILTS	JUNKY	NERTZ	QUANT	ROQUE
JIMMY	JUNTA	NEXUS	QUARE	SAJOU
JIMPY	JUNTO	NINJA	QUARK	SAXES
JINGO	JUPES	NIQAB	QUART	SCUZZ
JINKS	JUPON	NIXED	QUASH	SEIZA
JINNI	JURAL	NIXES	QUASI	SEIZE
JINNS	JURAT	NIXIE	QUASS	SEXED
JIRDS	JUREL	NIZAM	QUATE	SEXER
JIVED	JUROR	NUDZH	QUAYS	SEXES
JIVER	JUSTS	OBJET	QUBIT	SEXTO
JIVES	JUTES	OOZED	QUEAN	SEXTS
JIVEY	JUTTY	OOZES	QUEEN	SHOJI
JNANA	JUVIE	ORZOS	QUEER	SHOJO
JOCKO	KANJI	OUZEL	QUELL	SILEX
JOCKS	KANZU	OUZOS	QUERN	SIXER
JOCKY	KAZOO	OXBOW	QUERY	SIXES
JOEYS	KEXES	OXERS	QUEST	SIXMO
JOHNS	KLUTZ	OXEYE	QUEUE	SIXTE
JOINS	KOJIS	OXIDE	QUEYS	SIXTH
JOINT	KOPJE	OXIDS	QUICK	SIXTY
JOIST	KUDZU	OXIME	QUIDS	SIZAR
JOKED	KYLIX	OXIMS	QUIET	SIZED
JOKER	LATEX	OXLIP	QUIFF	SIZER
JOKES	LAXER	OXTER	QUILL	SIZES
JOKEY	LAXES	OZONE	QUILT	SLOJD
JOLES	LAXLY	PAXES	QUINS	SMAZE

SOJAS	XENIA	ZOONS	AZURES	BREEZY
SOJUS	XENIC	ZOOTY	AZYGOS	BRONZE
SOYUZ	XENON	ZORIL	BAIZAS	BRONZY
SOZIN	XERIC	ZORIS	BAIZES	BRUXED
SPITZ	XEROX	ZOUKS	BANJAX	BRUXES
SQUAB	XERUS	ZOWEE	BANJOS	BUQSHA
SQUAD	XYLAN	ZOWIE	BANZAI	BURQAS
SQUAT	XYLEM	ZUPPA	BARQUE	BUZUKI
SQUEG	XYLOL	ZUZIM	BASQUE	BUZZED
SQUIB	XYLYL	ZYMES	BAZAAR	BUZZER
SQUID	XYSTI		BAZARS	BUZZES
TAJES	XYSTS	ABJECT	BAZOOS	BYZANT
TAXED	YUZUS	ABJURE	BAZZED	CAIQUE
TAXER	ZAIDA	ABLAZE	BAZZES	CAJOLE
TAXES	ZAIDY	ACAJOU	BEEZER	CALQUE
TAXIS	ZAIRE	ACQUIT	BEGAZE	CALXES
TAXOL	ZAKAT	ADIEUX	BEMIXT	CASQUE
TAXON	ZAMIA	ADJOIN	BENZAL	CAUDEX
TAXUS	ZANZA	ADJURE	BENZIN	CERVIX
TAZZA	ZAPPY	ADJUST	BENZOL	CHAZAN
TAZZE	ZARFS	ADMIXT	BENZYL	CHEQUE
TELEX	ZAXES	ADNEXA	BEZANT	CHINTZ
TEXAS	ZAYIN	ADZING	BEZAZZ	CINQUE
TEXTS	ZAZEN	ADZUKI	BEZELS	CIRQUE
THUJA	ZEALS	AFFLUX	BEZILS	CLAQUE
TIZES	ZEBEC	AGNIZE	BEZOAR	CLAXON
TIZZY	ZEBRA	AJIVAS	BHAJIS	CLIMAX
TOPAZ	ZEBUS	AJOWAN	BIAXAL	CLIQUE
TOQUE	ZEDAS	AJUGAS	BIFLEX	CLIQUY
TOXIC	ZEINS	ALEXIA	BIJOUS	CLOQUE
TOXIN	ZENDO	ALEXIN	BIJOUX	CLOZES
TRANQ	ZERKS	ALKOXY	BISQUE	COAXAL
TROOZ	ZEROS	AMAZED	BIZONE	COAXED
TUQUE	ZESTS	AMAZES	BIZZES	COAXER
TUXES	ZESTY	AMAZON	BLAZED	COAXES
TWIXT	ZETAS	ANNEXE	BLAZER	COCCYX
TZARS	ZIBET	ANOXIA	BLAZES	COJOIN
UMIAQ	ZILCH	APEXES	BLAZON	COLZAS
UNBOX	ZILLS	ASSIZE	BLINTZ	COMMIX
UNFIX	ZINCO	ATAXIA	BLOWZY	CONVEX
UNJAM	ZINCS	ATAXIC	BOLLIX	COQUET
UNMIX	ZINCY	AUSPEX	BOLLOX	COQUIS
UNSEX	ZINEB	AUXINS	BOMBAX	COROZO
UNZIP	ZINES	AXEMAN	BOMBYX	CORTEX
USQUE	ZINGS	AXEMEN	BONZER	CORYZA
VARIX	ZINGY	AXENIC	BONZES	COWPOX
VEXED	ZINKY	AXILLA	BOOJUM	COXING
VEXER	ZIPPO	AXIOMS	BOOZED	COZENS
VEXES	ZIPPY	AXIONS	BOOZER	COZEYS
VEXIL	ZIRAM	AXISES	BOOZES	COZIED
VIXEN	ZITIS	AXITES	BORZOI	COZIER
VIZIR	ZIZIT	AXLIKE	BOSQUE	COZIES
VIZOR	ZLOTY	AXONES	BOXCAR	COZZES
VOXEL	ZOEAE	AXONIC	BOXERS	CRAZED
WALTZ	ZOEAS	AXSEED	BOXFUL	CRAZES
WAREZ	ZOMBI	AZALEA	BOXIER	CROJIK
WAXED	ZONAE	AZIDES	BOXING	CROZER
WAXEN	ZONAL	AZINES	BOXLAS	CROZES
WAXER	ZONED	AZLONS	BRAIZE	CRUXES
WAXES	ZONER	AZOLES	BRAZAS	CUZZES
WHIZZ	ZONES	AZONAL	BRAZED	DAZING
WINZE	ZONKS	AZONIC	BRAZEN	DAZZLE
WIZEN	ZOOEY	AZOTES	BRAZER	DEEJAY
WIZES	ZOOID	AZOTHS	BRAZES	DEFUZE
WOOZY	ZOOKS	AZOTIC	BRAZIL	DEIXIS
XEBEC	ZOOMS	AZUKIS	BREEZE	DEJECT

DELUXE	EXCIDE	FIXITY	GRAZES	JABIRU
DESOXY	EXCISE	FIXURE	GROSZE	JABOTS
DEXIES	EXCITE	FIZGIG	GROSZY	JACALS
DEXTER	EXCUSE	FIZZED	GUZZLE	JACANA
DEXTRO	EXEDRA	FIZZER	GYOZAS	JACKAL
DEZINC	EXEMPT	FIZZES	GYTTJA	JACKED
DIAZIN	EXEQUY	FIZZLE	HADJEE	JACKER
DIAZOS	EXERTS	FJELDS	HADJES	JACKET
DIOXAN	EXEUNT	FJORDS	HADJIS	JADING
DIOXID	EXHALE	FLAXEN	HAJJES	JADISH
DIOXIN	EXHORT	FLAXES	HAJJIS	JAEGER
DIPLEX	EXHUME	FLEXED	HALLUX	JAGERS
DIQUAT	EXILED	FLEXES	HALUTZ	JAGGED
DITZES	EXILER	FLEXOR	HAMZAH	JAGGER
DIXITS	EXILES	FLOOZY	HAMZAS	JAGRAS
DIZENS	EXILIC	FLUXED	HANDAX	JAGUAR
DJEBEL	EXINES	FLUXES	HATBOX	JAILED
DJEMBE	EXISTS	FOOZLE	HAZANS	JAILER
DJIBBA	EXITED	FORNIX	HAZARD	JAILOR
DJINNI	EXODOI	FOXIER	HAZELS	JALAPS
DJINNS	EXODOS	FOXILY	HAZERS	JALOPS
DJINNY	EXODUS	FOXING	HAZIER	JALOPY
DONJON	EXOGEN	FOZIER	HAZILY	JAMBED
DONZEL	EXONYM	FRAZIL	HAZING	JAMBES
DOOZER	EXOTIC	FREEZE	HAZMAT	JAMMED
DOOZIE	EXPAND	FRENZY	HAZZAN	JAMMER
DOXIES	EXPATS	FRIEZE	HEEZED	JANGLE
DOZENS	EXPECT	FRIJOL	HEEZES	JANGLY
DOZERS	EXPELS	FRIZED	HEJIRA	JANNEY
DOZIER	EXPEND	FRIZER	HEXADE	JAPANS
DOZILY	EXPERT	FRIZES	HEXADS	JAPERS
DOZING	EXPIRE	FRIZZY	HEXANE	JAPERY
DUPLEX	EXPIRY	FROUZY	HEXERS	JAPING
EARWAX	EXPORT	FROWZY	HEXING	JARFUL
ECZEMA	EXPOSE	FROZEN	HEXONE	JARGON
EEJITS	EXSECT	FURZES	HEXOSE	JARINA
EFFLUX	EXSERT	FUTZED	HEXYLS	JARRAH
EJECTA	EXTANT	FUTZES	HIJABS	JARRED
EJECTS	EXTEND	FUZEES	HIJACK	JARVEY
EJIDOS	EXTENT	FUZILS	HIJRAH	JASMIN
ELIXIR	EXTERN	FUZING	HIJRAS	JASPER
ENJAMB	EXTOLL	FUZZED	HOAXED	JASSID
ENJOIN	EXTOLS	FUZZES	HOAXER	JAUKED
ENJOYS	EXTORT	GAIJIN	HOAXES	JAUNCE
ENZYME	EXTRAS	GALAXY	HOTBOX	JAUNTS
ENZYMS	EXUDED	GANJAH	HUTZPA	JAUNTY
EPIZOA	EXUDES	GANJAS	HUZZAH	JAUPED
EQUALS	EXULTS	GAUZES	HUZZAS	JAWANS
EQUATE	EXURBS	GAZABO	IBEXES	JAWING
EQUIDS	FAJITA	GAZARS	ICEBOX	JAYGEE
EQUINE	FANJET	GAZEBO	ILEXES	JAYVEE
EQUIPS	FAQIRS	GAZERS	INFLUX	JAZZBO
EQUITY	FAQUIR	GAZING	INJECT	JAZZED
ERSATZ	FAXING	GAZUMP	INJERA	JAZZER
ETHOXY	FAZING	GEEZER	INJURE	JAZZES
EUTAXY	FEAZED	GHAZAL	INJURY	JEBELS
EVZONE	FEAZES	GHAZIS	INKJET	JEEING
EXACTA	FEEZED	GIZMOS	IODIZE	JEEPED
EXACTS	FEEZES	GLAZED	IONIZE	JEERED
EXALTS	FEIJOA	GLAZER	IXODID	JEERER
EXAMEN	FEZZES	GLAZES	IXORAS	JEESLY
EXARCH	FIQUES	GLITZY	IXTLES	JEEZLY
EXCEED	FIXATE	GLOZED	IZARDS	JEHADI
EXCELS	FIXERS	GLOZES	IZZARD	JEHADS
EXCEPT	FIXING	GRAZED	JABBED	JEJUNA
EXCESS	FIXITS	GRAZER	JABBER	JEJUNE

JELLED	JOGGER	JUMPER	MAJLIS	OBJETS
JENNET	JOGGLE	JUNCOS	MAJORS	ONYXES
JERBOA	JOHNNY	JUNGLE	MAMZER	OOZIER
JEREED	JOINED	JUNGLY	MANQUE	OOZING
JERIDS	JOINER	JUNIOR	MAQUIS	OPAQUE
JERKED	JOINTS	JUNKED	MARQUE	ORYXES
JERKER	JOISTS	JUNKER	MASJID	OUTBOX
JERKIN	JOJOBA	JUNKET	MASQUE	OUTFOX
JERRID	JOKERS	JUNKIE	MASTIX	OUTJUT
JERSEY	JOKIER	JUNTAS	MATRIX	OUZELS
JESSED	JOKING	JUNTOS	MATZAH	OXALIS
JESSES	JOLTED	JUPONS	MATZAS	OXBOWS
JESTED	JOLTER	JURANT	MATZOH	OXCART
JESTER	JORAMS	JURATS	MATZOS	OXEYES
JETLAG	JORDAN	JURELS	MATZOT	OXFORD
JETONS	JORUMS	JURIED	MAXIMA	OXHERD
JETSAM	JOSEPH	JURIES	MAXIMS	OXHIDE
JETSOM	JOSHED	JURIST	MAXING	OXIDES
JETTED	JOSHER	JURORS	MAXIXE	OXIMES
JETTON	JOSHES	JUSTED	MAZARD	OXLIKE
JEWELS	JOSSES	JUSTER	MAZERS	OXLIPS
JEZAIL	JOSTLE	JUSTLE	MAZIER	OXTAIL
JIBBAH	JOTTED	JUSTLY	MAZILY	OXTERS
JIBBAS	JOTTER	JUTTED	MAZING	OXYGEN
JIBBED	JOUALS	JUVIES	MAZUMA	OYEZES
JIBBER	JOUKED	KAIZEN	MENINX	OZONES
JIBERS	JOULES	KAMEEZ	MEZCAL	PACZKI
JIBING	JOUNCE	KANJIS	MEZUZA	PAJAMA
JICAMA	JOUNCY	KANZUS	MEZZOS	PANZER
JIGGED	JOURNO	KAZOOS	MINXES	PATZER
JIGGER	JOUSTS	KHAZEN	MIRZAS	PAXWAX
JIGGLE	JOVIAL	KIBITZ	MIXERS	PAZAZZ
JIGGLY	JOWARS	KLAXON	MIXING	PEGBOX
JIGSAW	JOWING	KLUTZY	MIXUPS	PEROXY
JIHADI	JOYFUL	KOLHOZ	MIZENS	PHENIX
JIHADS	JOYING	KOLKOZ	MIZUNA	PHIZES
JILTED	JOYOUS	KOPJES	MIZZEN	PIAZZA
JILTER	JOYPAD	KUDZUS	MIZZLE	PIAZZE
JIMINY	JOYPOP	KUVASZ	MIZZLY	PICKAX
JIMMIE	JUBBAH	KWANZA	MOJITO	PIQUED
JIMPER	JUBHAH	LARYNX	MOJOES	PIQUES
JIMSON	JUBILE	LAXEST	MOMZER	PIQUET
JINGAL	JUDDER	LAXITY	MOSQUE	PIXELS
JINGKO	JUDGED	LAZARS	MOUJIK	PIXIES
JINGLE	JUDGER	LAZIED	MOXIES	PIZAZZ
JINGLY	JUDGES	LAZIER	MUJIKS	PIZZAS
JINKED	JUDIES	LAZIES	MUSJID	PIZZAZ
JINKER	JUDOKA	LAZILY	MUSKOX	PIZZLE
JINNEE	JUGATE	LAZING	MUXING	PLAQUE
JINNIS	JUGFUL	LAZULI	MUZHIK	PLAZAS
JINXED	JUGGED	LEXEME	MUZJIK	PLEXAL
JINXES	JUGGLE	LEXICA	MUZZLE	PLEXES
JITNEY	JUGULA	LIQUID	MYXOID	PLEXOR
JITTER	JUGUMS	LIQUOR	MYXOMA	PLEXUS
JIVERS	JUICED	LIZARD	NAZIFY	PODZOL
JIVIER	JUICER	LOGJAM	NINJAS	POLEAX
JIVING	JUICES	LOQUAT	NIQAAB	POLLEX
JNANAS	JUJUBE	LOXING	NIQABS	PONZUS
JOBBED	JUKING	LUMMOX	NIXIES	POOJAS
JOBBER	JULEPS	LUTZES	NIXING	POTZER
JOBBIE	JUMARS	LUXATE	NIZAMS	POXIER
JOCKEY	JUMBAL	LUXURY	NONTAX	POXING
JOCKOS	JUMBIE	LYNXES	NOYAUX	POZOLE
JOCOSE	JUMBLE	MAGNOX	NOZZLE	PRAJNA
JOCUND	JUMBOS	MAHZOR	NUZZLE	PRAXES
JOGGED	JUMPED	MAIZES	OBJECT	PRAXIS

PREFIX	QUERNS	REZERO	SNEEZE	TOQUET
PREMIX	QUESTS	REZONE	SNEEZY	TORQUE
PRETAX	QUEUED	REZZES	SNOOZE	TOUZLE
PREXES	QUEUER	RIOJAS	SNOOZY	TOXICS
PREZES	QUEUES	RISQUE	SOZINE	TOXINE
PRIZED	QUEZAL	RITZES	SOZINS	TOXINS
PRIZER	QUICHE	ROMAJI	SPADIX	TOXOID
PRIZES	QUICKS	ROQUES	SPELTZ	TRANQS
PROJET	QUIETS	ROQUET	SPHINX	TRIJET
PROLIX	QUIFFS	ROZZER	SPHYNX	TUQUES
PUJAHS	QUILLS	SACQUE	SPRITZ	TUXEDO
PULQUE	QUILTS	SAJOUS	SQUABS	TWEEZE
PUNJIS	QUINCE	SANJAK	SQUADS	TZETZE
PUTZED	QUINIC	SAXIST	SQUALL	TZURIS
PUTZES	QUININ	SAXMAN	SQUAMA	UBIQUE
PUZZLE	QUINOA	SAXMEN	SQUARE	UMIAQS
PYJAMA	QUINOL	SAXONY	SQUARK	UNAXED
PYXIES	QUINSY	SCHIZO	SQUASH	UNFIXT
QABALA	QUINTA	SCHIZY	SQUATS	UNIQUE
QAJAQS	QUINTE	SCHNOZ	SQUAWK	UNISEX
QANATS	QUINTS	SCOLEX	SQUEAK	UNJAMS
QIBLAS	QUIPPU	SCUZZY	SQUEAL	UNJUST
QIGONG	QUIPPY	SEIZAS	SQUEGS	UNMIXT
QINDAR	QUIPUS	SEIZED	SQUIBS	UNSEXY
QINTAR	QUIRED	SEIZER	SQUIDS	UNVEXT
QIVIUT	QUIRES	SEIZES	SQUILL	UNZIPS
QUACKS	QUIRKS	SEIZIN	SQUINT	UPGAZE
QUACKY	QUIRKY	SEIZOR	SQUIRE	UPSIZE
QUAERE	QUIRTS	SEJANT	SQUIRL	URTEXT
QUAFFS	QUITCH	SEQUEL	SQUIRM	USQUES
QUAGGA	QUIVER	SEQUIN	SQUIRT	VEEJAY
QUAGGY	QULLIQ	SEXERS	SQUISH	VERJUS
QUAHOG	QUOHOG	SEXIER	SQUUSH	VERNIX
QUAICH	QUOINS	SEXILY	STANZA	VERTEX
QUAIGH	QUOITS	SEXING	STORAX	VEXERS
QUAILS	QUOKKA	SEXISM	STYRAX	VEXILS
QUAINT	QUOLLS	SEXIST	SUBFIX	VEXING
QUAKED	QUORUM	SEXPOT	SUFFIX	VIXENS
QUAKER	QUOTAS	SEXTAN	SURTAX	VIZARD
QUAKES	QUOTED	SEXTET	SVARAJ	VIZIER
QUALIA	QUOTER	SEXTON	SWARAJ	VIZIRS
QUALMS	QUOTES	SEXTOS	SYNTAX	VIZORS
QUALMY	QUOTHA	SEXUAL	SYRINX	VIZSLA
QUANGO	QURUSH	SHAZAM	SYZYGY	VOLVOX
QUANTA	QWERTY	SHEQEL	TAJINE	VORTEX
QUANTS	RAJAHS	SHIRAZ	TARZAN	VOXELS
QUARKS	RAMJET	SHOJIS	TAXEME	WAXERS
QUARRY	RAXING	SHVITZ	TAXERS	WAXIER
QUARTE	RAZEED	SILVEX	TAXIED	WAXILY
QUARTO	RAZEES	SIXERS	TAXIES	WAXING
QUARTS	RAZERS	SIXMOS	TAXING	WHEEZE
QUARTZ	RAZING	SIXTES	TAXITE	WHEEZY
QUASAR	RAZORS	SIXTHS	TAXMAN	WHIZZY
QUATRE	RAZZED	SIZARS	TAXMEN	WINZES
QUAVER	RAZZES	SIZERS	TAXOLS	WIZARD
QUBITS	RAZZIA	SIZIER	TAXONS	WIZENS
QUBYTE	RAZZLE	SIZING	TAZZAS	WIZZEN
QUEANS	REBOZO	SIZZLE	TEABOX	WIZZES
QUEASY	REFLEX	SKYBOX	TEAZEL	WURZEL
QUEAZY	REFLUX	SLEAZE	TEAZLE	XEBECS
QUEENS	REJECT	SLEAZO	TEXTED	XENIAS
QUEENY	REJIGS	SLEAZY	TEXTER	XENONS
QUEERS	REJOIN	SLOJDS	THORAX	XYLANS
QUELEA	REMIXT	SMAZES	THUJAS	XYLEMS
QUELLS	REQUIN	SMILAX	TIZZES	XYLENE
QUENCH	RESIZE	SNAZZY	TOQUES	XYLOID

XYLOLS	ZAKATS	ZENITH	ZIPOLA	ZONERS
XYLOSE	ZAMIAS	ZEPHYR	ZIPPED	ZONING
XYLYLS	ZANANA	ZEROED	ZIPPER	ZONKED
XYSTER	ZANDER	ZEROES	ZIPPOS	ZONULA
XYSTOI	ZANIER	ZEROTH	ZIRAMS	ZONULE
XYSTOS	ZANIES	ZESTED	ZIRCON	ZOOIDS
XYSTUS	ZANZAS	ZESTER	ZITHER	ZOOIER
YAKUZA	ZAPPED	ZEUGMA	ZIZITH	ZOOMED
YANQUI	ZAPPER	ZIBETH	ZIZZED	ZOONED
YUTZES	ZAREBA	ZIBETS	ZIZZES	ZORILS
ZADDIK	ZARIBA	ZIGGED	ZIZZLE	ZOSTER
ZAFFAR	ZAYINS	ZIGZAG	ZLOTYS	ZOUAVE
ZAFFER	ZAZENS	ZILLAH	ZOARIA	ZOUNDS
ZAFFIR	ZEALOT	ZINCED	ZOCALO	ZOYSIA
ZAFFRE	ZEATIN	ZINCIC	ZODIAC	ZUPPAS
ZAFTIG	ZEBECK	ZINCKY	ZOECIA	ZYDECO
ZAGGED	ZEBECS	ZINCOS	ZOFTIG	ZYGOID
ZAIDAS	ZEBRAS	ZINEBS	ZOMBIE	ZYGOMA
ZAIDEH	ZECHIN	ZINGED	ZOMBIS	ZYGOTE
ZAIKAI	ZENANA	ZINGER	ZONARY	ZYMASE
ZAIRES	ZENDOS	ZINNIA	ZONATE	

North American SCRABBLE Players Association

Making words, building friendships

Established in 2009, the North American SCRABBLE Players Association — NASPA — is a community of tournament, club and avid home players of the SCRABBLE Brand Crossword Game. We foster an atmosphere for people of all skill levels to play their favorite game, improve their abilities and above all, meet people who share a similar love of the game.

To learn more about the world of official competition and our:

WORDS... our members have access to the full *Official Tournament and Club Word List* with every acceptable word of up to 15 letters.

PEOPLE... make lifelong friendships with other players near you and always have someone that you can play your favorite game with.

RULES... learn how to use a game timer, how to challenge a play, and when to call for one of our certified tournament directors for a ruling.

RATINGS... are you a world-championship contender rated above 2,000, or a 500-rated novice? Test your skills and find out.

EVENTS... how serious is your game? Do you want to play weekly at your local club, monthly at one-day tournaments, or compete at multi-day regionals or even the National SCRABBLE Championship?

Please find us at:

Web: http://www.scrabbleplayers.org

Email: info@scrabbleplayers.org

Twitter: @NASPA

Facebook: scrbblplyrs

Mail: NASPA, P.O. Box 12115, Dallas, TX, 75225–0115